The Gramophone
Jazz
Good CD *Guide*

UK ISBN 0 902470 59 0

USA ISBN 0 902470 65 5

Recording companies reserve the right to withdraw any Compact Disc without giving prior notice, and although every effort is made to obtain the latest information for inclusion in this book, no guarantee can be given that all the discs listed are immediately available. Any difficulties should be referred to the issuing company concerned. When ordering, purchasers are advised to quote all the relevant information in addition to the disc numbers. The publishers cannot accept responsibility for the consequences of any error.

Sales and distribution

Book trade

North America

Music Sales Corporation
257 Park Avenue South,
New York, NY 10010, USA.
Telephone (212) 254 2100
Fax (212) 254 2013

UK and Rest of World

Music Sales Limited
Newmarket Road, Bury St Edmunds,
Suffolk IP33 3YB, Great Britain.
Telephone +44 (0)1284 702600
Fax +44 (0)1284 768301

Record trade and private

North America

Music Sales Corporation
257 Park Avenue South,
New York, NY 10010, USA.
Telephone (212) 254 2100
Fax (212) 254 2013

UK and Rest of world

Gramophone Publications Limited
177-179 Kenton Road, Harrow,
Middlesex HA3 0HA, Great Britain.
Telephone +44 (0)181 907 4476
Fax +44 (0)181 907 0073

The Gramophone Jazz *Good* **CD** *Guide*

Published by

**Gramophone Publications Limited,
177-179 Kenton Road, Harrow,
Middlesex HA3 0HA, Great Britain.**

Editor	**Keith Shadwick**
Production	**Dermot Jones**
Design	**Dinah Lone**
Contributors	**Chuck Berg** **Bob Blumenthal** **Francis Davis** **Dave Gelly** **Mark Gilbert** **Simon Hopkins** **Miles Kington** **Art Lange** **Graham Lock** **Barry McRae** **Alun Morgan** **Chris Parker** **Brian Priestley** **Tony Russell** **Keith Shadwick** **Alyn Shipton** **Steve Voce** **Kevin Whitehead**
Editorial Director	**Christopher Pollard**

Cover illustration John Brennan
Printed in England by William Clowes Limited,
Beccles, Suffolk, NR34 9QE.

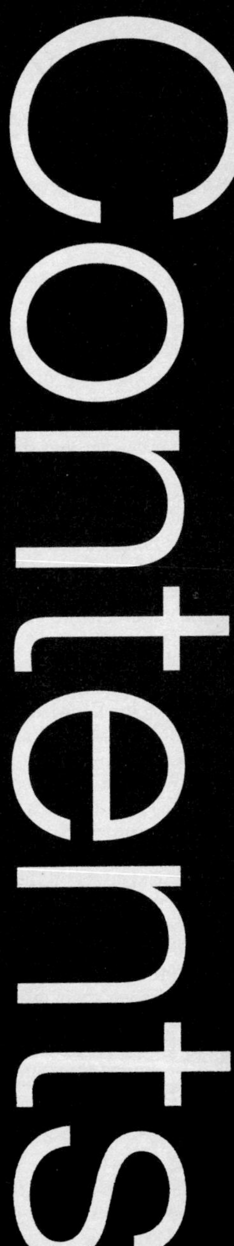
Contents

Introduction

Keith Shadwick Editor

Although the first acknowledged jazz recording was made as late as 1917, over a decade after Enrico Caruso began his spectacular recording career and over two decades after Edison's cylinders began the era of recorded sound, the music itself is not far off its centenary. That makes it a good time to be compiling a reference book such as the one you are holding in your hands, because the perspective gained is inevitably more long-term, the judgement more dispassionate and less amateur the further the music being discussed is from our own times.

Not that this book deals only with music which is at least 50 years old, either in deed or spirit: the jazz of every age and style is to be found discussed on the ensuing pages. The team chosen to make the recommendations is a carefully balanced one, with writers allowed to choose the artists they are interested in writing about, from the Original Dixieland Jazz Band to recent CD débutees such as Danilo Perez and D.D. Jackson. One aspect of the team's composition about which I am particularly pleased is that I have been able to include reviews by some of the best current U.S. writers: this can only be a good thing, bringing a better balance to the book's overall viewpoint. That aside, I am gratified that so many of the authors from both sides of the Atlantic whose writing I personally admire consented to be involved in this project.

Aims of the Guide

The basic premise of this Guide is that the average person interested in jazz doesn't have a kaleidoscopic knowledge of – or even an interest in – every current jazz release worldwide. They have their firm favourites they'd like to follow up on some more; they also have players they are getting interested in and would like some guidance on. That's where the Guide steps in, because in the vast majority of cases we recommend a single title made by that artist as being a good summation of their output. There are cases where the current selection of CDs by a given player is not very strong, so the critic concerned has graded accordingly. In some instances, he has also suggested a currently unavailable album to look out for when it finally makes it onto CD. With players who have had a more widespread effect on the music, the Guide has multiple entries which give an accurate and balanced perspective on each particular career as it is currently reflected on CD. A good example is Duke Ellington, who has 13 entries here. So, too, does Miles Davis. So that the reader gets a multifaceted outlook on these artists, rather than the same point of view -however favourable- no critic writes more than one entry about any given artist. This gives us (to take the Ellington example) the following writers giving their insights and opinions on different Ellington achievements: Chuck Berg, Bob Blumenthal, Francis Davis, Dave Gelly, Miles Kington, Graham Lock, Barry McRae, Alun Morgan, Brian Priestley, Alyn Shipton, Steve Voce and Kevin Whitehead and me. This diversity of opinion can only be a good thing in building up an accurate picture of what is the best currently available on the Duke Ellington front.

A word about scope

In a reference book such as this, one of the most fundamental issues to be grappled with is: where are the lines which, once transgressed, declare us to be in non-jazz territory? All solutions to this question, however they are couched, are finally going to be subjective and based on a private set of criteria. The rule of thumb applied by me to this book is: does it feel like jazz? Does the performer have an interpretation of the material to hand which has roots in the basic tenets of the jazz tradition? A positive reply to these questions has given this book an exceptionally wide scope, applied to each of this century's jazz decades, and allowed a number of perhaps marginal performers to be included (many critics would argue that Glenn Miller, for example, has no place in this Guide). If your eyebrows are raised by any of the names you come across, I can only suggest that you have a close listen to the disc being reviewed, and perhaps the reason for its inclusion will then become clear.

New releases, deletions and title availability

One of the problems which lies outside of our control in the compiling of this book is the availability of titles on an international basis. Many titles, especially those owned by the major multinational companies, are available in some territories and not in others. Thus an album can be released in, say, France, but never released in the UK or the USA. This doesn't necessarily mean that it is completely unavailable in those countries, but that it is available only as an import and therefore invariably it will be harder to find and more expensive when you do find it. The other problem brought about specifically by the larger companies is the one of deletions: while an album can be available in, say, the USA for a number of years after its initial release, it could well be deleted by the domestic UK company (and vice-versa).

When it comes to the smaller independents, the problems are simpler, but no less frustrating: with albums released by these companies, availability is usually sustained for much greater lengths of time, but it is unconscionably difficult to find a copy of the desired title outside of the specialist shops and mail order firms, due to local distribution deals and the reluctance of the larger retailers to carry constant stocks of slower-moving items from small companies.

All of this lies outside of our control, but I can at least affirm that at the time of going to press, every item in this book was currently domestically available either in the USA or in Europe (or, most happily, both). For precisely the availability problems mentioned above, Japanese releases have not been included, unless they have been made available domestically in the USA or Europe. Conversely, if there is an artist missing from this guide (and I am aware of many), the most common (although not only) reason is the simple non-availability of their work on CD, however many LPs or MCs may still be around.

It may strike some readers as unrealistic highmindedness, but I have also ruled out all CDs which are self-evident 'pirate releases': albums or performances stolen from other companies or owners and released in a country with vague or non-existent copyright laws, then exported elsewhere. As the artists and their heirs benefit not one jot from such releases, and have never sanctioned the release of such material, it will not be brought to your attention here. Should you want to buy such discs, then I am sure you will seek them out anyway, without our help.

The reviews

The review section is organised in the simplest way possible - strict artist surname (or, where applicable, group name) A-Z, with an appendix (similarly listed) for Various artists. To deal with the tail rather than the dog first, the Various artists section makes no pretence at covering anything but a tiny proportion of what is available in this category. The reason is simple: most compilations are not aimed at someone with a serious interest in the music, but more at impulse purchasers. The Various artists entries here have been included on the critera that they either allow discussion of artists not covered by a single entry as a leader, or they are a well-conceived and very useful reference-point or introduction to an area or sub-genre in the music which otherwise may not be very well represented.

Acknowledgements

In a book of this nature, the editor invariably relies on the goodwill and co-operation of a great many people. In this imperfect world it has come as a genuinely pleasant surprise that so many people connected with the music and recording industries have been so helpful during the gestation period. There is not room enough to thank everyone, but those below have helped more than their jobs called upon them to:

Record companies/distributors: Steve Sanderson, Kerstan Mackness and Graham Griffith at New Note Distribution; Jo Nagle, Eva Pakula and Jo Pratt at EMI (UK); Laurie Staff and Trevor Manwaring at Harmonia Mundi; Gladys Oghenkaio, Phil Knox-Roberts and Andrea Gibbs at Warners; Trish Coogan, Adam Sieff and Sharon Kelly at Sony/Columbia (UK); Mike Cox at Discovery Imports (UK), Richard Cook, Anne Therese O'Neill, Becky Stevenson and Michael Lang at PolyGram (UK and US); Michael Deacon at BMG; Tony Williams at Spotlite; Philippe Vincent at Ida; Terri Hinte at Fantasy Group; Don Lucoff at DL Media/Blue Note (US); Monique Walker at GRP/Impulse! (US); John Martin at Topic; Samantha Richards at Charly; Gail Clark and John Crosby at Ace; Helen Moore and Jeremy Elliott at Complete Record Co; Sue Brown at Geffen/MCA (UK); John Jack and Hazel at Cadillac; Amjad Ali at Stash; Jennifer Dirkes at Delmark; John Martin at Topic; Francois Zalacain at Sunnyside; Peter Jacobsen at VSOP Records; Ann Cater at Conifer Records; Alistair Robertson at Hep; Joe Fields at Muse; John Steadman at JSP.

Interested and disinterested parties: Sid Whelan and Jay Hoffman (New York), who put in a tremendous sustained effort to help us locate and hear hard-to-obtain albums from far-away companies and were helpful in many other ways besides; Manek Daver, author of the David Stone Martin monographs, for unlooked-for enthusiasm, courtesy and unfailing helpfulness; Peter Fincham at Mole Jazz, London, for his knowledge, resourcefulness and unflappable good humour in many last-minute situations; Steve Voce for his always fair and careful opinions on a whole range of matters, plus his bravery beyond the call of duty on the editorial front; Barry McRae for ingenious solutions to many intractible problems; Alun Morgan and Art Lange for unfailing help and courtesy; Dermot Jones, Ivor Humphreys and Dinah Lone at ***Gramophone*** for sheer perseverence against the odds and inspired guesses; and of course my wife Alison, for her patience, understanding and help during many a long dark night of worry. The first Weird Nightmare is now over: the next one is about to begin...

Using the guide

I have endeavoured to keep the terminology and symbols as simple as possible, so that there are no artificial barriers erected between the reader and the text. Being someone who has extreme difficulty with anything not intended to be interpreted literally in a reference book, I have kept closely to the notion that simple = good, complex = bad. Therefore, in a normal entry, there will be a typical amount of basic information which the reader can expect. The leader, album title, record company and catalogue number, personnel and recording date are invariably given, but I have also included the following: the number of discs (where there is more than one); running time; performance and recording quality rating (from one to ten); a symbol to indicate membership of the Basic Jazz Library (most don't have this, because most aren't essential purchases if you were starting a jazz collection); price guide (budget, mid and full price are the three most common categories used here). I give an example here in elucidation:

John Coltrane

1926-1967

A Love Supreme **Coltrane** (ts); **McCoy Tyner** (p); **Jimmy Garrison** (b); **Elvin Jones** (d).
MCA/Impulse! Ⓜ GRD 155 (33 minutes). Recorded 1964.
✔

⑩ ❼

Thereafter follows the critique. Every entry is initialled, so that the reader can quickly establish just who is giving these pithy opinions.

Considering the dangers of grading anything, from ball bearings to olive oil, a few words about the gradings applied here may not go astray:

⑩ a well-nigh perfect representation of what the artist concerned is on about. In the vast majority of cases, the artist also has something significant to say.
⑨ a highly satisfying and significant album which however not perhaps the best-ever example of the artist in question's work. There may be a drawback in the recording which prevents it from being included in the above category.
⑧ a fine example of the artist's output, and a superior effort all round. Can be purchased with confidence.
⑦ a very good album of its kind, although it is probable that the average album in this category is not particularly ambitious in conception.
⑥ a good album with nothing much wrong with it at all, but probably lacking that extra spark which pushes you to the edge of your seat in excited anticipation as the bars tick by.
⑤ a fair album with good points to it, but with weaknesses or periods of mediocrity within its playing-time.
④ a passingly fair album, but one with obvious problems. It will probably fail to give much satisfaction to the ininitiated. One for the curious or the faithful only.
③ a poor album, incompetently executed and thoughtlessly assembled.
② an unworthy effort which should be avoided
① or less: beware! You could be in for a serious waste of money.

Considering that this is a guide to the best CDs currently available, the incidence of albums under ⑥ is relatively low, and there is nothing here which rates a zero (although there are a handful with a reference to the text below), but the categories are explained for completeness' sake.

There is a mirror grading which applies to recording quality as well, and I think the general comments above can also happily apply to this aspect. At all times, critics have graded the recording quality with a mind to the fact that a great deal of the music was recorded in less than DDD sound in the first place. What we have attempted to do is grade according to the original sound quality and (where applicable) the relative success (or lack of it) of the digital transfers to the new medium.

Recording Dates

A brief explanation of date usage. Where a CD is compiled from music recorded in more than one year, a glance at the form of separation used between the dates quoted will reveal some date information. For example, 1934/38 means that there are performances from those two years on the disc in question. A marking of 1934-38 means that there are performances from those two years, plus other years in between these dates.

The price guide

It is as well to point out at this stage that, although we have attempted accuracy in all aspects of this guide, pricing can vary dramatically from one country to another, and often even within the same country, state or town. Sometimes even the same shop will have two copies of the same album at two different price levels. Our pricing indicators are based on information passed on to us either by the record companies themselves or their official representatives in Britain or America.

Ⓕ Full price
Ⓜ Medium price
Ⓑ Budget price

Appendices

Apart from the review section, this book also includes reference sections designed to help the reader to locate discs in which they become interested. Hence we have a list of labels, main jazz distributors for both the UK and the USA, a list of recommended specialist dealers and a Basic Jazz Library, which is explained below.

Basic jazz library

 There are albums (and before them, shellac discs) in the history of this music which undoubtedly stand as cornerstones in its evolution; some of them because they were the high water marks of a particular artist or epoch of significance, others because they signal the beginning of something new and exciting. To help the user of this Guide build a balanced and comprehensive selection of jazz on CD with the fewest number of titles, I have built into this book a designation: Basic Jazz Library. This library was chosen by the critics who wrote the reviews as they wrote those reviews, and so the titles in the Library chose themselves. Each designated title has a Basic jazz library moniker by it, but for quick reference purposes, I have extrapolated all such entries into a separate list which appears as one of the first appendices. Of course, no two people will agree on what should constitute such a library, but this list reflects the informed opinion of 18 jazz writers.

The Mosaic question

Mosaic is a U.S. mail-order company which, over the past decade or so, has made available some great jazz treasures of the past. However, all their boxed sets are collectors' editions of a range of jazz artists, and only available in limited editions specifically designed only to be available direct from the record company itself. That makes them pretty hard to find in record shops, and when they do find their way there, they are at a very high price, as the retailers have had to pay the normal mail order rate for them, then add something on top to cover their own costs and give themselves some sort of margin.

Given such a complicated situation, it seemed counter-productive to recommend such releases in the general run of the Guide. As mentioned above, the general tenor of the label makes it very much one for serious collectors only, most of whom will already be familiar with their activities. Thus, for example, when it comes to tenorist Ike Quebec, this guide recommends a very fine one-disc Blue Note compilation of his later work, widely available at mid price, rather than either of the two Mosaic boxes which detail at length his Blue Note years. I can only add that if anyone should feel moved to enquire into any of the releases on the Mosaic label, they will not be disappointed by the high levels of research, documentation and remastering which are the standard fare for the company. Anyone wanting further information can write to Mosaic Records at 35 Melrose Place, Stamford, CT 06902 USA.

Abbreviations

acc	accordion
af	alto flute
arr	arranger
as	alto saxophone
b	double bass
bb	brass bass
bcl	bass clarinet
bf	bass flute
bhn	baritone horn
bj	banjo
bmba	bass marimba
bn	bassoon
bs	baritone saxophone
bss	bass saxophone
bt	bass trumpet
btb	bass trombone
c	cornet
cbcl	contrabass clarinet
cbs	contrabass saxophone
cel	celeste
cga	conga
cl	clarinet
cms	c-melody saxophone
comp	composer
cond	conductor
cym	cymbals
d	drums
dir	director
ehn	english horn
el	electric/electronic
elb	electric bass
euph	euphonium
EWI	electronic wind instrument
f	flute
fhn	flügelhorn
frn	french horn
g	guitar
gfs	goofus
gspiel	glockenspiel
gsyn	guitar synthesizer
h	harpsicord
hca	harmonica
hmn	harmonium
hp	harp
jh	jew's harp
kba	kalimba
kbds	keyboards
kz	kazoo
mand	mandolin
mba	marimba
mph	mellophone
ob	oboe
orch	orchestra
org	organ
p	piano
perc	percusion
pic	piccolo
pic t	piccolo trumpet
pkt t	pocket trumpet
prog	programming
rec	recorder
snino s	sopranino saxophone
ss	soprano saxophone
ssph	sousaphone
st	slide trumpet
syn	synthesizer
t	trumpet
tb	trombone
tba	tuba
thn	tenor horn
tim	timpani
ts	tenor saxophone
v	vocal
va	viola
vb	vibraphone
vc	cello
vn	violin
vtb	valve trombone
wbd	washboard
xyl	xylophone

Basic jazz library

Muhal Richard Abrams
The Hearinga Suite
Black Saint 120103-2

Julian 'Cannonball' Adderley
Somethin' Else
Blue Note B21Y-49338

Louis Armstrong
Portrait of the Artist as a Young Man
Columbia/Legacy 57176
The Complete Recordings of Louis Armstrong and The Blues Singers
Affinity AFS1018-6
Hot Fives And Sevens, Volumes 1-4
JSP CD312/3/4/5
Satchmo: A Musical Autobiography
Jazz Unlimited JUCD 2003-05
The California Concerts
MCA/GRP 46132

Art Ensemble Of Chicago
The Art Ensemble 1967-68
Nessa NCD-2500A-E

Albert Ayler
Spiritual Unity
ESP 1002-2
In Greenwich Village
Impulse! MCAD-39123

Mildred Bailey
The Rockin' Chair lady
MCA GRP 16442

Count Basie
Count Basie: The Original American Decca Recordings
MCA/Decca GRD-3-6112
The Essential Count Basie, Volume 1
Columbia 460061-2
The Complete Atomic Mr Basie
Roulette 8 28635 2

Sidney Bechet
The Ledgendary Sidney Bechet
RCA Bluebird ND86590
Jazz Classics, Volumes 1 and 2
Blue Note 789384/85 2

Bix Beiderbecke
Volume 1: Singin' The Blues
Columbia 466309-2

Art Blakey
The History of Art Blakey and the Jazz Messengers
Blue Note CDP7 97190-2
Free For All
Blue Note CDP7 84170-2
Album of the Year
Timeless SJP 155

Carla Bley
Escalator over the Hill
JCOA 839-310-2

Paul Bley
Open, To Love
ECM 1023 (827 751 – 2)

Anthony Braxton
Willisau (Quartet) 1991
hatART4 61001/04

The Brecker Brothers
Collection, Volumes 1 & 2
RCA Novus ND 90442/83076

Peter Brötzmann
Machine Gun
FMP CD 24

Clifford Brown
The Complete Paris Sessions, Volumes 1-3
Vogue 15461/63-2

Bill Bruford
Feels Good To Me
Editions EG/Virgin Japan VJD-28051

Don Byron
Tuskegee Experiments
Elektra Nonesuch 979280-2

Benny Carter
Central City Sketches
MusicMaster CIJD60126X

Oscar 'Papa' Celestin
New Orleans Classics
Azure AZ-CD-12

Don Cherry
Art Deco
A&M CD 5258

Charlie Christian
Solo Flight
Vintage Jazz Classics VJC 1021-2

Cozy Cole
1944,
Classics 819

Nat King Cole
Big Band Cole
Capitol CDP7 96259-2

Ornette Coleman
The Shape of Jazz to Come
Atlantic 781317-2
Free Jazz
Atlantic 781364-2
Virgin Beauty
Columbia Partrait RK 44301

Steve Coleman
The Tao Of Mad Phat
RCA Novus 63160 2

John Coltrane
Blue Train
Blue Note CDP7 46095-2
Giant Steps
Atlantic Jazz 781 337-2
My Favorite Things
Atlantic Jazz 782346-2
Coltrane's Sound
Atlantic Jazz 781419-2
Coltrane Live at Birdland
Impulse! MCAD-33109
A Love Supreme
Impulse! GRD 155

Meditations
Impulse! GRD 39139
Chick Corea
Now He Sings, Now He Sobs
Blue Note CDP7 90055-2
Tadd Dameron
Fontainebleau
Prestige OJCCD 055-2
Miles Davis
Birth Of The Cool
Capitol CDP7 92862-2
Chronicle
Prestige 8PCD 012-2
Round About Midnight
Columbia 460605-2
Miles Ahead
Columbia CK 53225
Porgy And Bess
Columbia 450985 2
Kind of Blue
Columbia 460603-2
Miles Smiles
Columbia 471004 2
A Tribute to Jack Johnson
Columbia CK 47036
Paul Desmond
East Of The Sun
DSCD 840
Two of a Mind
RCA Bluebird ND 90364-2
Eric Dolphy
Memorial Album
Prestige OJCCD-353-2
Out to Lunch
Blue Note CDP7 46524-2
Last Date
EmArcy/Limelight 510 124-2
Charles Earland
Unforgettable
Muse MCD 5455
Billy Eckstine
No Cover, No Minimum
Roulette CDP7 98583-2
Roy Eldridge
After You've Gone
MCA/Decca GRP 16052
Duke Ellington
Early Ellington (1927-1934)
RCA Bluebird ND 86852
Reminiscing in tempo
Columbia/Legacy CK 48654
The Duke's Men-Small Groups Volumes 1 & 2
Columbia CK 46995/48835
Fargo, North Dakota November 7, 1940
Vintage Jazz Classics 1019/20 – 2
The Blanton-Webster Band
RCA Bluebird ND 85659
Black, Brown & Beige
RCA Bluebird 6641-2-RB
The Great Ellington Units
RCA Bluebird ND 86751
Ellington At Newport
Columbia 4723855 2
The Far East Suite-Special Mix
RCA Bluebird 366551 2
Robin Eubanks
Karma
JMT 834 446-2

Bill Evans
At The Village Vanguard
Riverside FCD-60-017
Empathy/A Simple Matter Of Conviction
Verve 837 757-2
Gil Evans
Out Of The Cool
Impulse! MCAD-5653
The Individualism Of Gil Evans
Verve 833 804-2
Art Farmer
Portrait Of Art Farmer
Contemporary OJCCD 166-2
Ella Fitzgerald
The Original American Decca Recordings
MCA/Decca GRP26192
The Best Of the Song Books
Verve 519 804 – 2
At the Opera House
Verve 831 269-2
Ganelin Trio
Poco-A-Poco
Leo CD LR 101
Erroll Garner
Concert By The Sea
Columbia 451042-2
Solitaire
Mercury 518 279-2
Kenny Garrett
Black Hope
Warner Bros. 945017-2
Stan Getz
Stan Getz & J.J. Johnson at the Opera House
Verve 831 272-2
Focus
Verve 821 982-2
Sweet Rain
Verve 815 054-2
Anniversary
EmArcy 838 769-2
Dizzy Gillespie
The Complete RCA Victor Recordings
RCA Bluebird 66528 2
Shaw 'Nuff
Musicraft MVSCD-53
Dizzy Gillespie's Big 4
Pablo OJC 443-2
Egberto Gismonti
Danca Das Cabecas
ECM 1089 (827 750-2)
Globe Unity Orchestra
Rumbling
FMP CD 40
Benny Goodman
The Birth Of Swing
RCA Bluebird ND 90601/3
Henry Grimes
The Call
ESP-Disk 1026-2
Lionel Hampton
1937-38, 1938-39, 1939-40
Classics 524, 534, 562
Flying Home
MCA/Decca Jazz MCAD-42349
Herbie Hancock
Maiden Voyage
Blue Note CDPB21Y 46339-2
Headhunters
Columbia Legacy 471239 2

Bill Hardman
What's Up
SteepleChase SCCD 31254
Bill Harris
Woody Herman Live 1957 Featuring Bill Harris, Volume 1
Status STCD107
Coleman Hawkins
Holywood Stampede
Capitol CDP7 92596-2
Tubby Hayes
For Members Only
Master Mix CDCHE 110
Fletcher Henderson
Louis With Fletcher Henderson
Forte Records Productions F-38001/03
Woody Herman
Keeper Of The Flame
Capitol CDP7 98453-2
Conrad Herwig
New York Hardball
Ken Music/Bellaphon 660 56 002
Andrew Hill
Point Of Departure
Blue Note CDP 84167-2
Earl Hines
Grand Reunion
Verve/Limelight 528 137-2
Plays Duke Ellington
New World 361/62-2
Billie Holiday
The Voice of Jazz
Affinity CD AFS BOX 1019-8
The Quintessential Billie Holiday, Volume 9
Columbia CK 47031
The Complete Original American Decca Recordings
MCA/Decca GRP 26012
Wayne Horvitz
Miracle Mile
Elektra Nonesuch 79278-2
Bobby Hutcherson
Cruisin' The Bird
Landmark LCD 1517-2
Dick Hyman
Music From My Fair Lady
Concord Jazz CCD 4393
Ed Jackson
Wake Up Call
New World CounterCurrents 80451-2
Willis Jackson
Bar Wars
Muse MCD 6011
Keith Jarrett
Belonging
ECM 1050 (829 115-2)
The Köln Concert
ECM 1064/65 (810 06-2)
Bunk Johnson
1944,
American Music AMDC 3
J.J. Johnson
The Eminent Jay Jay Johnson, Volumes 1 and 2
Blue Note CDP7 81505/06-2
Jo Jones
Jo Jones Special
Vanguard 662 132
Quincy Jones
This is How I Feel About Jazz
Impulse GRP11152
Louis Jordan
Five Guys Named Moe
MCA DMCL 1718
Shiela Jordan
Portrait of Shiela
Blue Note CDP7 89002 2
Stan Kenton
Stan Kenton in Hi-Fi
Capitol Jazz CDP7 98451-2
Rahsaan Roland Kirk
Kirk's Work
Prestige PR 72110
We Free Kings
Mercury 826 455-2
Rip,RIg & Panic/Now Please Don't Cry, Beautiful Edith
Emarcy 832 164-2
Lee Konitz
Subconscious-Lee
Prestige OJC186-2
Live At The Half Note
Verve 521 659-2
Steve Lacy
Futurities
hatART 6031/32
Yusef Lateef
The Centaur and the Phoenix
Riverside OJCCD 721
Meade Lux Lewis
1927-1939/1939-1941
Classics 722, 743
McKinney's Cotton Pickers
The Band Don Redman Built
RCA/Bluebird ND 90517
John McLaughlin
Extrapolation
Polydor 841598-2
Inner Mounting Flame
Columbia CK 31067
Marian McPartland
Piano Jazz with Guest Bill Evans
The Jazz Alliance TJA-12005
Wynton Marsalis
Citi Movement
Columbia CK 53324
Helen Merrill
Collaboration
EmArcy 834 205-2
Charles Mingus
Pithecanthropus Erectus
Atlantic Jazz 781456-2
Mingus Ah Um
Columbia 450436-2
Blues & Roots
Atlantic Jazz 781336-2
Charles Mingus Presents Charles Mingus
Candid CD 9005
The Black Saint and The Sinner Lady
Impulse! MCAD-5649
Let My Children Hear Music
Columbia/Legacy CK 48910
The Missourians
Cab Calloway & The Missourians, 1929-30
JSP JSPCD 328

Hank Mobley
Soul Station
CDP7 46528-2
The Modern Jazz Quartet
Odds Against Tomorrow
EMI/UA/Blue Note CDP7 93415-2
Echoes
Pablo CD2312.142
Grachan Moncur III
Some Other Stuff
Blue Note CDP8 32092 2
Thelonious Monk
Complete Blue Note Recordings
Blue Note CDP8 30363 2
The Unique Thelonious Monk
Riverside OJCCD-064-2
Brilliant Corners
Riverside OJCCD-026-2
Monk's Music
Riverside OJCCD-084-2
The Thelonious Monk Orchestra at Town Hall
Riverside OJCCD-206-2
Wes Montgomery
Impressions: The Verve Jazz Sides
Verve 521 690-2
Lee Morgan
The Best of Lee Morgan
Blue Note CDP7 91138-2
Jelly Roll Morton
The Pearls
Bluebird ND 86588
His Complete Victor Recordings
RCA Bluebird ND82361 (2)
Bennie Moton
Kansas City Orchestra 1923-1927/1930-32
Classics 518, 519
Gerry Mulligan
Best of Gerry Mulligan with Chet Baker
Pacific Jazz CDP7 95481-2
David Murray
Hope Scope
Black Saint 120 139-2
Fats Navarro
Nostalgia
Denon/Savoy SV-0123
Oliver Nelson
Blues and The Abstract Truth
Impulse! MCAD 5659
New Orleans Rhythm
N.O.R.K. and Jelly Roll Morton
Milestone MCD 47020-2
Jimmie Noone
New Orleans Jazz Giants 1936-40
JSP JSPCD 336
Red Norvo
Knock On Wood
Affinity CD AFS 1017
King Oliver
King Oliver's Jazz Band 1923
Jazz Archives 157 46-2
Charlie Parker
The Immortal Charlie Parker
Denon/Savoy SV-0102
The Charlie Parker Story
Denon/Savoy SV-0105
Charlie Parker On Dial: The Complete Sessions
Spotlite/Dial SPJ-CD 4-101
Jazz At The Philharmonic, 1946
Verve 513 756-2
The Quintet: Jazz at Massey Hall
Debut OJCCD 044-2
Jaco Pastorius
Jaco Pastorius
Epic CDEPC81453
Art Pepper
Art Pepper Meets The Rhythm Section
Contemporary OJCCD 5338
Art Pepper + Eleven: Modern Jazz Classics
Contemporary OJCCD 341-2
Oscar Peterson
Night Train
Verve 821 724-2
King Pleasure (Clarence Beeks)
King Pleasure Sings/Annie Ross Sings
Prestige OJCCD 217-2
Bud Powell
The Complete Blue Note and Roost Recordings
Blue Note 8 30083 2
The Complete Bud Powell on Verve
Verve 521 669-2
Bobby Previte
Weather Clear, Track Fast
Enja R2 79667
Sammy Price
And His Texas Blusicians 1929-41
Classics 696
Dudu Pukwana
In The Townships
Earthworks/Virgin CDEWV5
Don Pullen
New Beginnings
Blue Note CDP7 91785-2
Freddie Redd
Music From The Connection
Blue Note CDP8 89392 2 1
Don Redman
Don Redman And His Orchestra 1931-33
Classics 543
Django Reinhardt
Chronological Volume 1
JSP CD 341
Swing in Paris, 1939-40
Affinity CD AFS 1003-5
Emily Remier
Transitions
Concord CCD 4236
We insist – Freedom Now Suite
Candid CCD 9002
Sonny Rollins
Saxophone Colossus
Prestige OJCCD 291-2
A Night at the Village Vanguard, Volumes 1 & 2
Blue Note CDP46517/18-2
The Bridge
RCA Bluebird ND 90633
On The Outside
Bluebird ND 82496
Alfie
Impulse! MCAD-39107
Wallace Roney
Obsession
Muse MCD 5423
Jimmy Rushing
The You and Me That Used to Be
RCA Novus 6460-2

George Russell
Ezz-Thetics
Riverside OJCCD-070-2
The Outer View
Riverside OJCCD 616-2
Jazz Reunion
Candid CCD 79020

David Sanborn
Close Up
Reprise 925715-2

Louis Sclavis
Ellington On The Air
Ida 032 CD

John Scofield
Still Warm
Gramavision 18-8508-2

Sonny Sharrock
Ask the Ages
Axiom 848 957-2

Artie Shaw
Begin the Beguine
ND 86274

Woody Shaw
Cassandra Night
Muse MCD 6007

Archie Shepp
Goin' Home
SteepleChase SCCD 31079

Horace Silver
Horace Silver and the Jazz Messengers
Blue Note CDP7 46140-2
Song For My Father
Blue Note CDP7 84185-2

Frank Sinatra
Come Dance With Me!
Capitol CDP7 48470-2

Bessie Smith
1925-33
Hermes HRM 6003

Jimmy Smith
Open House
CDP7 84269-2

Leo Smith
Process Of The Great Ancestry
Chief CD6

Willie Smith
Snooty Fruity
CBS 4663643 2

Willie 'The Lion' Smith
Willie 'The Lion' Smith and His Cubs
CBC 1-012

Eddie South
Eddie South 1923-37
Classics 707

Muggsy Spanier
The 'Ragtime Band' Sessions
RCA Bluebird 366550 2

Spontaneous Music Ensemble
Karyobin
Chronoscope CPE 2001 2

String Trio of New York
Time Never Lies
Stash 544

Maxine Sullivan
Swingin' Sweet
Concord CCD 4351

Sun Ra
The Heliocentric Worlds Of Sun Ra, Volumes 1 and 2
ESP-Disk 1014/17-2

John Surman
Such Winters of Memory
ECM 1254 810 621-2

Ralph Sutton
Last Of The Whorehouse Piano Players (The Original Sessions)
Chiaroscuro CR(D) 206

Buddy Tate
The Ballad Artstry of Buddy Tate
Sackville CD 2-3034

Art Tatum
The Complete Capitol Recordings, Volumes 1 and 2
Capitol CDP7 92866/67-2
The Complete Pablo Solo Masterpieces
Pablo 7 PACD 4404-2

Cecil Taylor
Jumpin' Punkins
Candid CD 9013
Unit Structures
Blue Note CDP 784237-2
Conquistador!
Blue Note CDP 784260 2

Frank Teschemacher
Muggsy, Tesch and The Chicagoans
Village VILCD 001-2

Gary Thomas
By Any Means Necessary
JMT 834 432-2

Ralph Towner
Solstice
ECM 1060 (825 458-2)

Lennie Tristano
Lennie Tristano/The New Tristano
Rhino/Atlantic 271595-2

'Big' Joe Turner
The Boss Of The Blues
Atlantic 781459-2

McCoy Tyner
Manhattan Moods
Blue Note CDP 828423 2

Sarah Vaughan
Sarah Vaughan With Clifford Brown
EmArcy 814 641-2
Swingin' Easy
EmArcy 514 072-2
Crazy and Mixed Up
Pablo PACD 2312 137-2

Joe Venuti
Violin Jazz
Yazoo 1062

Edward Vesala
Ode To The Death of Jazz
ECM 1413 (843 196-2)

Fats Waller
The Joint is Jumpin'
RCA Bluebird ND 86288
The Last Years (1940-43)
RCA Bluebird ND 90411

Dinah Washington
For Those in Love
EmArcy 514 073-2

Ethel Waters
Ethel Waters (1929 -39)
Timeless CBC 1-007

Eric Watson
The Memory of Water
Label Bleu LBLC 6535
Ernie Watts
Unity
JVC JVC-2046-2
Weather Report
I Sing The Body Electric
Columbia 468207 2
Heavy Weather
Columbia 468209 2
Chick Webb
Rhythm Man
Hep HEPCD 1023
Eberhard Weber
The Colours of Chloë
ECM 1042 (833 331-2)
Ben Webster
Soulville
Verve 833551-2
Ben Webster Meets Oscar Peterson
Verve 829 167-2
Dicky Wells
Swingin' in Paris
Charly LeJazz CD 20
Randy Weston
The Spirit Of Our Ancestors
Antilles 511 896-2
Lee Wiley
Night in Manhattan
Columbia SRS 75010
Teddy Wilson
Teddy Wilson and His Orchestra 1939-41
Classics 620
Jimmy Witherspoon
Rockin' With Spoon
Charly CD BM 25
Lester Young
A Lester Young Story
Jazz Archives 157342
Lester-Amadeus!
Phontastic CD 7639
The Complete Lester Young
Mercury 830 920-2
Lester Young Trio
Verve 521 650-2
The President Plays with The Oscar Peterson Trio
Verve 831 670-2
Joe Zawinul
Zawinul
Atlantic 781579-2
John Zorn
Spy vs. Spy
Elektra/Musician 960844-2
Various Artists
A Piano Anthology
MCA/Decca GRP 16392
California Cool Blue
Blue Note CDP7 80707 2
Classic Jazz Piano
RCA Bluebird 6754-2-RB
Music Of George And Ira Gershwin
Blue Note 7 80706
New Thing At Newport
Impulse! GRP 11052
New York Horns, 1924-1928
Hot n' Sweet 151022
Prestige First Sessions, Vol 1
Prestige PCD-24114-2

The reviews

John Abercrombie

1944

Timeless **Abercrombie** (g, elg); **Jan Hammer** (p, org, syn); **Jack DeJohnette** (d). ECM Ⓔ 1047 (829 114-2) (44 minutes). Recorded 1974.

⑥ ❽

Although there have been recent vigorous exceptions, Abercrombie's work over the last decade or so has generally reflected his admiration for the pastel-toned Jim Hall school of guitar playing. However, this untypically energetic début for ECM shows that in the heady seventies even the apparently deferential Abercrombie was not immune to the allure of high octane fusion. Keyboardist Jan Hammer was only six months out of John McLaughlin's Mahavishnu Orchestra, and the influence of that group looms large in much of this music. Hammer's frenetically-paced opener quickly sets the scene, inspiring eight-bar exchanges between his galloping Hammond and Abercrombie's uncommonly aggressive staccato guitar (shades of the type of guitar work to come many years later on Abercrombie's recent **Speak of the Devil**), complete with the overdrive and phase-shift effects typical of McLaughlin's sound at the time.

Other tracks, such as the limpid piano and acoustic guitar duets of *Love Song* and *Remembering*, announce Abercrombie's more meditative inclinations, as well as being redolent of Mahavishnu's quieter moments. There isn't much of the unmodified changes playing that Abercrombie has latterly developed, but the record is seductively atmospheric, dynamically varied, and incidentally shows that the organ trio had places to go after Jimmy Smith. It was recorded in the LP era, so the playing time is average, but there's no lack of breadth in the music. **MG**

Rabih Abou-Khalil

Blue Camel **Abou-Khalil** (oud); **Kenny Wheeler** (t, flh); **Charlie Mariano** (as); **Steve Swallow** (b); **Milton Cardona** (cgas); **Nabil Khaiat** (frame d); **Ramesh Shotham** (s. Indian d, perc). Enja Ⓔ ENJ-7053-2 (61 minutes). Recorded 1992.

⑧ ❽

As Rabih Abou-Khalil himself points out, "the music of the first world is much less foreign to the Third World than vice versa", and **Blue Camel**, its participants coming from India, North and South America, goes some distance towards proving this point. Rabih Abou-Khalil is a virtuoso player, and his eight pieces on this album employ the classical rhythms and modes of his traditional music, yet they are arranged in such a way as to accommodate improvisation from jazz musicians Kenny Wheeler, Charlie Mariano and Steve Swallow, and their interaction with the percussion of Milton Cardona, Nabil Khaiat and Ramesh Shotham. The main problem bedevilling such an accommodation lies in the fact that the pieces rely for their power more on rhythmic than harmonic development, so Kenny Wheeler, for instance, who is virtually peerless in the jazz world for his ability to breeze inventively through changes, has to adapt to an entirely novel approach, and take his cues from the percussion players. It must be said that Charlie Mariano adapts to this process more easily than the Canadian. Likewise Steve Swallow, although the contributions of each player are never less than cogent, but overall, it is difficult to see quite what Abou-Khalil's exhilarating and beautifully contemplative music gains from the presence of jazz musicians within it. All the most satisfying passages on **Blue Camel** feature the rich and resonant oud, improvising at the prompting of percussionists. The experiment must thus be put down as a failure, but a consistently intriguing and occasionally deeply enjoyable one. **CP**

Muhal Richard Abrams

1930

Levels and Degrees of Light **Abrams** (cl, p); **Anthony Braxton** (as); **Maurice McIntyre** (ts); **Leroy Jenkins** (vn); **Charles Clark**, **Leonard Jones** (b); **Gordon Emmanuel** (vb); **Thurman Barker** (d); **Penelope Taylor** (v); **David Moore** (poet). Delmark Ⓔ DD413 (43 minutes). Recorded 1967.

⑧ ❼

Levels and Degrees of Light was the third record from Chicago's AACM organisation, the first under the leadership of their éminence grise, Muhal Richard Abrams. Though it does not have the shock value of Roscoe Mitchell's **Sound** (the initial AACM release), the album is not short on fascination. The title-track is a striking exploration of higher registers, Abrams's clarinet and Penelope Taylor's wordless soprano soaring over a swirl of vibes and cymbals to create a soundworld of crystalline beauty. Although Abrams used the voice again on his later **Rejoicing with the Light** (not yet on CD), this facet of his work has since remained largely undocumented.

The CD's centrepiece is *The Bird Song*, which begins with David Moore declaiming vivid images of apocalypse, moves through a quiet passage of violin, chimes and birdsong, then climaxes with an intense ensemble free-for-all. The closing *My Thoughts are My Future-Now and Forever* is a more conventional sequence of solos, Abrams's fast, skipping piano lines carrying just a hint of his stride and bebop roots.

The disc's variety of forms and unusual timbral palettes set out a radical programme that Abrams's subsequent music has continued to explore. His later records often show greater assurance, but *Levels and Degrees of Light* has a spark of invention that still excites. The CD version removes the heavy artificial reverberation in which the original vinyl release was bathed. **GL**

Blues Forever **Abrams** (p); **Baikida Carroll** (t, flh); **Craig Harris** (tb); **Jimmy Vass** (as, f); **Eugene Ghee** (ts, cl); **Wallace McMillan** (bs, f); **Vincent Chancey** (frh); **Howard Johnson** (tba, bs); **Jean-Paul Bourelly** (g); **Michael Logan** (b); **Andrew Cyrille** (d). Black Saint Ⓔ 0061 (43 minutes). Recorded 1981.

⑥ ❽

As wide-ranging in form and imaginative in content as they are, Abrams's early albums, on Delmark and Arista, give only a partial account of his vast talents. Thoroughly experienced in the jazz tradition prior to the sixties, it was his desire to find new creative outlets that led to his co-founding the AACM (Association for the Advancement of Creative Musicians) in 1965 and serving as its paterfamilias for many years. It was not until the eighties, and a series of successful recordings for Black Saint, that Abrams's vivid, original concepts for larger ensembles were documented. **Blues Forever** revels in the expanded palette at his disposal—for example, *Ancient And Future Reflections* blends growl trombone, muted trumpet, clarinet, tuba, french horn, and paired flutes with chamber music delicacy and an improvisational edge. Meanings emerge from multiple levels of activity. His ability to draw on different styles—from pre-swing to collective improvisation—fluently, without direct quotation, is evident in *Duet For One World* and the intertwining lines of *Quartet To Quartet*. Most notably, the title tune reminds us of the everpresent nature of the blues (in both 'down-home' and more sophisticated fashion), Muhal's Chicago roots and a vision that links past and future. **AL**

The Hearinga Suite **Abrams** (p, syn, cond); **Ron Tooley**, **Jack Walrath**, **Cecil Bridgewater**, **Frank Gordon** (t); **Clifton Anderson**, **Dick Griffin** (tb); **Jack Jeffers**, **Bill Lowe**, (btb); **John Purcell** (f, cl, ts); **Marty Ehrlich** (picc, f, cl, as); **Patience Higgins** (bcl, ts); **Courtnay Wynter** (bn, bcl, ts); **Charles Davis** (bar, ss); **Deidre Murray** (vc); **Fred Hopkins** (b); **Warren Smith** (vb, gspl, perc); **Andrew Cyrille** (d). Black Saint Ⓔ 120103-2 (42 minutes). Recorded 1989

✔ ⑨ ❽

Abrams's writing for medium to larger groups in the eighties had been ambitious but **The Hearinga Suite** of 1989 used a much larger aggregation and posed problems commensurate with the numerical increase. This CD shows that, although Abrams handled the task with some skill, his diversity of approach created some elements of disunity. On the credit side, internal contrapuntal dialogues as well as solos by the likes of Ehrlich, Gordon, Hopkins, Murray and Walrath are ideally cushioned and there is not a jarring moment. But while every title has individual merit, the suite as a whole lacks stylistic consistency. It rightly shuns sequential ambitions but the band's actual identity is often confused in a catalogue of unusual ensemble voicings and cute instrumental devices.

Seesall teams conversational voice-overs with an Ellingtonian ensemble sound. *Oldfotalk* has a Kollektief style lift that never explodes into the threatened Breckerish climax, while the title-track has a Gil Evans-ish lightness of texture. *Aura Of Thought* boasts a simulated string section while Wynter's stately swing-era tenor ushers *Bermix* into tone poem territory. It must qualify as a fine recording project but it does suggest that it is a blueprint for four or five more integrated works. **BMcR**

Blu Blu Blu **Abrams** (p, syn, bells, cond); **Jack Walrath** (t); **Alfred Patterson** (tb); **Mark Taylor** (frh); **Joe Daley** (tba); **John Purcell** (as, f, cl); **Robert De Bellis** (as, cl, bcl); **Eugene Ghee** (ts, cl, bcl); **Patience Higgins** (bs, fl, cl); **Warren Smith** (vb, timp); **David Fiuczynski** (g); **Brad Jones**, **Lindsey Horner** (b); **Thurman Barker** (d); **Joel Brandon** (whistler). Black Saint Ⓔ 120117-2 (77 minutes). Recorded 1990.

⑨ ❽

Abrams's masterpiece is **The Hearinga Suite**, reviewed above. Although lacking **Hearinga**'s thematic unity and lyrical rapture, this compensates with a greater breadth that confirms Abrams's stature as Duke Ellington's and Charles Mingus's greatest living heir. The title-track is an earthy tribute to Muddy Waters sparked by Abrams's sly piano and Fiuczynski's boomeranging guitar (more evocative of B.B. King than Waters, though it hardly matters). Among the other highlights is a stirring reprise of *Bloodline*, a modernistic salute to the big bands originally recorded by Abrams in 1983, on **Rejoicing in the Light**. The slightly quieter, more speculative pieces here convey something of the urgent intellectual activity that one associates with pre-**Pithecanthropus Erectus** Mingus, although Abrams's pieces are generally more angular in design and more successful in interweaving composition and improvisation. The presence of a whistler shouldn't send up a red flag; Brandon is an ex-flautist who adds just the right amount of shrillness to the ensembles, and whose unique gift Abrams exploits to telling advantage on a section of *One for the Whistler* in 5/4. Even so, the standout soloist throughout the programme is trumpeter Walrath, and the standout on this particular piece is Ghee, an unsung tenor saxophonist whose yearning solo is what one tends to remember afterwards. **FD**

George Adams

1942-1992

Adams/Pullen Quartet Live At The Village Vanguard **Adams** (ts); **Pullen** (p); **Cameron Brown** (b); **Dannie Richmond** (d). Soul Note Ⓕ SN1094 CD (56 minutes). Recorded 1983.

⑧ ❻

A pupil of jazz flute pioneer Wayman Carver, Adams's early musical experience was in the r&b field. Through the seventies he worked with Art Blakey, Charles Mingus and Gil Evans, and in 1979 he formed a quartet with Pullen. This became the above line-up when Cameron joined the group in the early eighties, and it was still making public appearances, with a replacement for the late Dannie Richmond, until shortly before Adams's own demise. This CD finds the quartet in prime form and gives the listener a clear picture of Adams's various musical personalities. On *Intentions* and *Diana* he is a staggeringly inventive soloist, strictly from the John Coltrane generation but steeped in high-proof bluesy spirit, totally at home with the turbulent buoyancy provided by the explosive trio at his back. Both his opening cadenza and coda on *Solitude* display a Garneresque detachment from the theme, but the main body of the piece offers for comparison two more facets of his playing. He treats the theme statement to a romantic stroll, maintaining an almost mainstream gait, with the odd irascible aside tossed in our direction. In contrast, his solo takes him into Albert Ayler territory, the statements stark, the passion naked and with thoughtful improvisation kept to a minimum. Adams may have worn different hats, but here they all suit his highly personal musical outfit. **BMcR**

Pepper Adams

1930-1986

The Cool Sound Of Pepper Adams **Adams** (bs); **Bernard McKinney** (euph); **Hank Jones** (p); **George Duvivier** (b); **Elvin Jones** (d). Denon/Savoy Ⓜ SV-0198 (33 minutes). Recorded 1957.

⑧ ❽

Pepper Adams was one of the most fluent, constructive and exciting baritone soloists to emerge in the fifties. Like Serge Chaloff he refused to be snared by the apparent unwieldiness of his chosen instrument and perfected a technique which enabled him to produce multi-noted, long-lined solos with the facility of an alto player. The content of his work was never facile, however, and his blues playing in particular was exceptional in its intensity and depth of feeling. This album is one of the first he made under his own name and, despite its title, is anything but cool. The opening track is a long and superb blues performance followed by another blues, *Seein' Red*, but this time with the altered chords in bars one to four of the chorus. *Like What Is This?* is unsurprisingly based on the chords of *What Is This Thing Called Love?* and the closing *Skippy* is a heavily Parker-influenced bebop tune. McKinney is a good soloist who achieves a sound midway between those of french horn and valve trombone, but the rhythm section is quite outstanding. Elvin Jones, on one of his earliest record dates, already shows the qualities which were to bring him to prominence. The playing time should have been increased by the inclusion of the alternative take of *Seein' Red* which was included on the Savoy LP version of this CD. **AM**

Steve Adams

In Out Side **Adams** (pic, f, ss, as, ts, bs); **Ken Filiano** (b, chimes). 9Winds Ⓕ NWCD 0156 (57 minutes). Recorded 1991/92.

⑥ ❽

It is sometimes damning a project with faint praise to call it interesting, but this time I mean it with no hidden agenda. This is a creative and engaging use of a recording studio's capacity for double-tracking and going back over pieces of work to create multiple layers of conversation between two imaginative instrumentalists. Both men exhibit a fine capacity for humour as well as contemplative stillness or fiery, brazen playing. Adams tends to lead the way, his 'angle' on the music more proactive than Filiano's, who enjoys embellishment and counterpoint and is content to supply it in many forms.

The album is given a great deal of variety through the sheer number of instruments Adams plays, but there is more to the versatility of the music than that: these two have worked at making small definitive statements and know when to stop: an art not all musicians manage to master in their careers. Some of the pieces here are as short as 40 seconds: one track (a walking blues) is five minutes, another (a slowish ballad) just over seven. Nothing outwears its welcome, and as Adams comments in the CD booklet about four so-called *Haiku*s, "The Haiku pieces are something we have always done—pieces that are only one thought long. No rambling or association." Freedom through discipline and hard work, then. Not a bad idea ... **KS**

Julian 'Cannonball' Adderley

1928-1975

Somethin' Else **Adderley** (as), **Miles Davis** (t), **Hank Jones** (p), **Sam Jones** (b), **Art Blakey** (d). Blue Note Ⓜ B21Y-49338 (41 minutes). Recorded 1958.

✔  

Cannonball Adderley still stands as one of jazzdom's most passionate and lyrical saxophone voices. His boppishly swinging style and wailing gospel-inflected tone, one of the few readily recognizable signature sounds in jazz, was appreciated by musicians and the public alike. An exponent of the overlapping hard-bop and soul schools of the sixties, the altoist first gained prominence in 1955 with Oscar Pettiford. In 1957, pressed by financial exigencies when his own group foundered, Adderley joined Miles Davis in what would prove a profitable association for both men. Indeed, in his ensuing two years with the trumpeter, Adderley played a large role in catapulting Davis, and himself, to the jazz world's front ranks, thus paving the way for Adderley's later successes as a leader.

In this deceptively relaxed but often edgy 1958 date, Adderley shares the spotlight with Davis, then his employer. It is a meeting of co-equals where the menu includes such familiar fare as *Autumn Leaves* (using the Ahmad Jamal-penned introduction), *Love for Sale* and *Dancing in the Dark*. And while we hear Davis moving closer to the shrouded intensities of *Kind of Blue* (1959), we also hear the melismatic and bluesy Parker-inflected declamations that would inform so much of Adderley's later work. But though Parker was his touchstone (along with a large dose of Benny Carter), Adderley evolved a singular approach at once sophisticated and primal, and passionately lyrical. The CD version of this classic has an extra track, *Alison's Uncle*. **CB**

In San Francisco **Adderley** (as); **Nat Adderley** (c); **Bobby Timmons** (p); **Sam Jones** (b); **Louis Hayes** (d). Riverside Ⓜ OJCCD 032 (61 minutes). Recorded 1959 .

⑧ ❻

Cannonball Adderley never sounded quite at one with the Miles Davis set-up. His alto soared happily, with a lighter-than-air feel, and that didn't wholly suit the sombre Davis ambience. When Adderley made this record—one of the first he made with a group of his own—he had just emerged from his years with Miles, and his choice of sidemen, including his cornet-playing brother Nat and the funky pianist Bobby Timmons, late of the hard-bop Jazz Messengers, created a sophisticated modern version of a good-time group. At a time in jazz when 'live' club recordings were a rare occurrence, his new company Riverside (Cannonball had just left Mercury) ventured into the Jazz Workshop in San Francisco and came away with this hour's worth of in-person, audience-sparked jazz.

The occasional funky cliché aside, the group generates considerable excitement. Cannonball is in wonderful form and the rhythm section, one of this period's great unsung teams, is spot-on. The album spawned a number of what were to become Adderley staples, but one of the best tracks is *Hi-Fly*, which Adderley announces as being by "the young composer and pianist, Randy Weston". The 11 minutes of *Straight, No Chaser* is a bonus, as the track was not on the original LP. **MK**

Live In Japan **Adderley** (as); **Nat Adderley** (c); **Joe Zawinul** (p); **Victor Gaskin** (b); **Roy McCurdy** (d). Capitol Ⓜ CDP 7 93560 2 (43 minutes). Recorded 1966.

⑧ ❼

When this album was released, Adderley and his group were riding a wave of popularity which saw them on the same level as Getz and Brubeck, and a long way in front of his old boss, Miles Davis. Certainly these three artists were the only ones from the modern jazz mainstream to have top ten hit singles during the 1960s, and it says something about Cannonball's clarity of musical vision that, as with Getz and Brubeck, his approach to music stayed much the same as it had ever been. It also shows what Miles thought of the situation that he used pianist Zawinul (both compositionally and as a sideman) when it came time for him to make the move into crossover territory.

This album was recorded during the group's second tour of Japan (there is a fine Riverside CD, **Nippon Soul**, which documents his 1963 sextet's Tokyo concerts), and catches them playing Zawinul's *Mercy, Mercy, Mercy* before it became a runaway bestseller single. This version of the band had been together for about a year before the tour (Charles Lloyd, who had taken Yusef Lateef's place in the sextet, had left in 1965 to form his soon-to-be-famous quartet); it shows plenty of spirit and a smooth discipline which was not always to be observed towards the end of the decade, when endless repetition of the old hits on the road led to vacillation between self-indulgent solos (especially from brother Nat) and perfunctory tinkerings with their original character (wild tempo fluctuations; shifts in the rhythmic character of, say, *Jive Samba*; re-harmonisation of the gospel-inflected pieces like *Dat Dere*, and so on).

No doubt they had played in front of more obviously enthusiastic audiences than this Tokyo crowd (a recent reissue from 1969, **Country Preacher**, suffers from a little bit *too* much rapport), but the band tended to make its best albums away from the recording studio, and this dynamic set shows them functioning at or near top form on every track. Everything played is to the point and meaningful, and many of the hits are here. It is all, as ever with Adderley's bands, terrific fun. **KS**

Paris Concert 1969 **Adderley** (as); **Nat Adderley** (c, v); **Joe Zawinul** (p); **Victor Gaskin** (b); **Roy McCurdy** (d). Europe 1 Ⓕ 710 381 (61 minutes). Recorded 1969.

⑥ ❻

Recorded in Paris's Salle Pleyel, this was originally broadcast as a radio programme in a series called *For Those Who Love Jazz*, produced by Frank Tenot and Daniel Filipacchi. By 1969 Adderley's quintet was a very popular unit backed up by a string of best-selling LPs on Riverside and Capitol.

In person, the quintet by then tended towards routinism, given to trotting out recorded hits in a somewhat glib fashion. The French audience clearly had fixed ideas about what they wanted to hear and the band's polite version of *Black Orpheus* is given muted applause and some booing; however, the following *Work Song* is very warmly received. A lengthy and turgid excerpt from a work by William Fischer titled *Experience In E* adds little to the overall value of the programme, although the inevitable slide into the then-fashionable soul element (*Walk Tall*, *The Blooz*, with a vocal from Nat sounding like a Jack Sheldon comedy routine, and the final *Mercy, Mercy, Mercy*) is an improvement. There is one unintentionally hilarious touch, supplied by the CD packaging: the opening track is a Zawinul composition clearly announced by Cannonball as *Rumpelstiltskin*, but listed three times as *Rufus Still Skinned*! C'est la vie ... **AM**

Nat Adderley 1931

Work Song **Adderley** (c); **Bobby Timmons** (p); **Wes Montgomery** (g); **Sam Jones, Keter Betts** (vc, b); **Percy Heath** (b); **Louis Hayes** (d). Riverside Ⓜ OJCCD-363-2 (39 minutes). Recorded 1960.

⑧ ❻

Nat Adderley tended to be overshadowed by his elder brother Cannonball in the days when the two co-led a band but this album, although not the first under his own name, did much to establish him in his own right. On cornet, which he seems to have preferred to trumpet, he sounds at times like Miles Davis, especially when muted (as on *Mean To Me*, for example). But he is nevertheless a very individual player with a perky sound on up-tempo tunes and an easy fluidity of conception and execution. He wrote *Work Song* and gives it the definitive treatment here, backed by some good Bobby Timmons piano. On ballads, notably *I've Got A Crush On You*, he is very melodic in his extemporisations, relying on the kind of approach usually associated with Ruby Braff or Bobby Hackett. The personnel listed above is a collective one, as there are a number of switches, particularly in the bass and cello roles, during the course of the nine titles. Wes Montgomery solos effectively, but tends to play a subservient role to the leader. **AM**

Air

Live Air **Henry Threadgill** (as, f, perc); **Fred Hopkins** (b); **Steve McCall** (d). Black Saint Ⓕ price 0034 (40 minutes). Recorded 1976/77.

⑥ ❻

A second generation ensemble from Chicago's Association for the Advancement of Creative Musicians (though drummer Steve McCall was one of the AACM's founding members in 1964), Air first came together in the early seventies to provide arrangements of Scott Joplin rags for a theatrical production. (Their subsequent 1979 recording of Joplin and Jelly Roll Morton tunes, *Air Lore*, is one of their best, but not currently available on CD). Their fine early LPs have yet to be reissued on CD, and **Live Air**, recorded about the time of their third studio LP but not released until 1980, is (despite short playing time and uneven sound quality) at least representative of the group in its heyday. The compositions by Henry Threadgill reflect a few of their many personal influences and stylistic concerns, ranging from Japanese to Latin musics and dynamically interwoven free improvisations. *Eulogy For Charles Clark* (dedicated to an AACM friend and bassist who died tragically young) is an especially evocative piece, beginning and ending with the quiet, sparse, delicate sounds of shakuhachi-like flute, arco bass, and bells, framing a broad alto sax and bass theme played over a funereal drum cadence. *Keep Right On Playing Thru The Mirror Over The Water* is another noteworthy performance, where a melody line that floats, dips, and pivots like a bird in flight gives way to McCall's extended mallet solo; on the return of alto sax and bass the music gradually builds in levels of intensity, culminating in the kind of three-part interaction that defined Air's group improvising. The band's ultimate break-up, after more than a decade of outstanding music, was mourned by many listeners. **AL**

Toshiko Akiyoshi 1929

Remembering Bud-Cleopatra's Dream **Akiyoshi** (p); **George Mraz, Ray Drummond** (b); **Lewis Nash, Al Harewood** (d). Evidence Ⓕ ECD 22034-2 (57 minutes). Recorded 1990.

⑥ ❻

Only two women in the history of jazz have ever made their names as pianist and composer as well as leaders of successful big bands. Carla Bley is the other, but in a sense Akiyoshi had the bigger job because she came from Japan to the US in the fifties (although she spent just nine years in Japan, having been born and raised in Dairen, China), and how on earth she ever managed to persuade her parents that a she had a future as a big band leader in the US one can only guess at. She did her learning in the night clubs of Tokyo (Hampton Hawes met and played with her in those early days, when her allegiance was to Bud Powell) and in a sense this CD represents her return to these early frenetic times and to Powell's memory. Nobody makes a fortune these days issuing tributes to Bud

Powell, so it must be Akiyoshi's own personal act of homage, from a now-mature pupil, to the old master. Powell was never one of the great tune-writers , not even by bop standards, and his lines now sound more dated than Akiyoshi's own playing, but it is a pretty good CD for all that and well worth the detour. **MK**

Carnegie Hall Concert **Akiyoshi** (p, leader); **Mike Ponella**, **John Eckert**, **Greg Gisbert** (t); **Joe Magnarelli**, **Herb Besson**, **Conrad Herwig**, **Larry Farrell** (tb); **Matt Finders** (btb); **Frank Wess** (fl, as), **Jim Snidero** (pic, fl, cl, as, ts) **Lew Tabackin** (fl, ss, ts), **Walt Weiskopf** (fl, cl, ss, ts), **Scott Robinson** (bs, bcl), **Peter Washington** (b), **Terry Clarke** (d). Guest trumpet: **Freddie Hubbard**. Columbia Ⓕ 48805-2 (77 minutes). Recorded 1991.

⑧ ❽

Akiyoshi has been living in the US for over 30 years and for a goodly amount of that time she has been giving vigorous new life to the old pre-avant big-band formulas. The band she co-led with her husband, flautist/saxophonist Lew Tabackin (who is featured on this new album) in the seventies was vital in its own time for keeping the idea alive that an acoustic band which swung did not have to sound like a Quincy Jones or Count Basie re-hash. That band is documented on an RCA Novus reissue which is worth having, but this new album is something special.

There is a wonderful balance inbetween both the compositions and their arrangements in this concert. Impeccably played throughout, they display Akiyoshi's incredible ear for instrumental blends, and this is nowhere more evident than in the Akiyoshi arrangement for the only piece on the album not written by her, Frank Wess's *Your Beauty is a Song of Love*. There are passing reflections of other large group leaders and composers, including Mingus and Ellington, but what comes over most strongly is that Akiyoshi has almost single-handedly wrought something contemporary and worthwhile from the advances made by people such as Gary McFarland, Oliver Nelson and Gil Evans 25 years ago and more. Like these men, Akiyoshi proves repeatedly that formal structures and symmetry in compositions do not preclude imagination and flair. She also does not need to parody other styles to make her points.

By turns absorbing, exciting and evocative, this album should be sought out. Excellent recorded sound, too, considering it's a live date and few people know how to record a big band anymore. **KS**

Manny Albam

1922

Sketches From The Book Of Life Big Bands including **Joe Newman**, **Freddie Hubbard** (t); **J.J. Johnson** (tb); **Phil Woods**, **Frank Wess** (as); **Mike Mainieri** (vb). LRC Ⓜ CDC 9035 (61 minutes). Recorded 1965-66.

⑥ ❻

There are better examples of Albam's work than this, but he is very much an endangered musical species and this is the only collection of his work available on CD. Originally a baritone sax player, Albam began writing for big bands during the last years of the swing era, but the broadness of his canvas meant that his works soon demanded contemporary and non-denominational interpretation. Although he retained elements of swing in his arrangements, he was primarily influenced by his studies of classical music in his magnificent creations of the fifties onwards and some of his pieces, like his *Concerto For Alto Saxophone* written for Phil Woods, are fully developed extended-form compositions.

Although these pieces are shorter, they show the composer's typical precision and individuality—in his works for Kenton and Herman, for instance, he was apt to shape his writing to the character of the bands. Here he mixes his jazz soloists into his orchestra with dazzling (if at times bombastic) results. He has a unique ability to make huge orchestras swing very hard indeed, as evinced by *Zing! Went The Strings Of My Heart* and other interpretations of standards on this album. **SV**

Joe Albany

1924-1988

The Right Combination **Albany** (p); **Warne Marsh** (ts); **Bob Whitlock** (bs); **Ralph Garretson** (d). Riverside Ⓜ OJCCD-1749-2 (43 minutes). Recorded 1957.

⑧ ❻

Albany was one of the more shadowy figures of the post-war jazz years, a man with a great 'inside' reputation as Charlie Parker's favourite pianist but whose appearance on record was limited to just four sides with Lester Young and two with Georgie Auld. Although he made several trio and solo albums, principally in Europe, during the seventies and eighties, none of them has the magic of *The* **Right Combination**. Never intended for issue, it emanates from a rehearsal in Garretson's apartment and has the boxiness of an amateur recording, although at no time is the playing of Marsh or Albany indistinct. There are many occasions when Albany overcomes the mechanical qualities of his instrument by producing single-note lines which slither across the chords like a saxophone. Warne Marsh, one of the greatest pure improvisers jazz has ever heard, responds with solos of remarkable invention. Their version of *Body and Soul* is a stunning example of empathy while Clifford Brown's intriguing tune *Daahoud* provides a challenge to which Joe and Warne respond admirably. Gary Hobish's remastering has given the instruments greater clarity than was present on the LP, making this CD of even greater value. **AM**

Howard Alden

1963

The Howard Alden Trio Plus Special Guests Ren Peplowski & Warren Vaché **Alden** (g); **Vaché** (c); **Peplowski** (cl, ts); **Lynn Seaton** (b); **Mel Lewis** (d); Concord Ⓕ CCD-4378 (49 minutes). Recorded 1989.

⑧ ❽

Alden is that rarity of rarities - a young musician whose basic affinities lie with pre-bop styles, yet who is not averse to bop and post-bop material; a latter-day Dick Wellstood of the guitar. He has recorded in various formats, including a quintet co-led with trombonist Dan Barrett, a two-guitar combo with George Van Eps and his own trio. This album is looser than the sets with Barrett, yet allows Alden to show his comping sensitivity by adding either Vaché or Peplowski on most of the 11 tracks. Tune choices are typically astute - a pair each from Ellington and Reinhardt; some Bird, Monk, Waller and Van Eps; and a few choice warhorses, rarely of the overplayed variety. The guitarist has picked two horn soloists with an intimate, deferential approach to the classic material, and paired them with a rhythm section that lets enough of its more abstract inclinations out to provide the necessary jolt. Through it all, Alden remains relaxed and engaged, avoiding both easy choices and grandstanding, and blurring distinctions between the mouldy and the modern. **BB**

Monty Alexander

1944

Caribbean Circle **Alexander** (p, narr); **Jon Faddis**, **E. Dankworth** (a.k.a. Wynton Marsalis) (t); **Slide Hampton** (tb, arr); **Dave Glasser** (as); **Frank Foster** (ts); **Ira Coleman**, **Anthony Jackson** (b), **Herlin Riley**, **Othello Molineaux**, **Steve Ferrone**, **Robert Thomas Jr**, **Marjorie Wylie** (d, perc). Chesky Ⓕ JD80 (58 minutes). Recorded 1992.

⑥ ❽

Born Bernard Montgomery Alexander in Kingston, Jamaica on D-Day, Monty has been a consistently impressive pianist with many records to his credit on the Pacific Jazz, MPS, Pablo and Concord labels. His eclectic style puts him in the same general category as Oscar Peterson, with the difference that he has always made references to his Caribbean origins. He has sometimes employed talented musicians from his native Jamaica, such as guitarist Ernest Ranglin. This Chesky release comprises a dozen tracks of variable quality, three of which present Alexander as narrator, affecting a West Indian patois which sounds considerably less authentic than the music. Despite the list of names, most of the tracks are played by an orthodox trio and it is here that the disc comes to life. Few other pianists can better Alexander when it comes to producing driving, accurately played keyboard excitement as he does here on *Three Little Birds*, for example. His tribute to Miles Davis, *Oh Why?*, is also memorable, but surprisingly one of the most impressive tracks is *When The Saints Go Marching In*, which contains a brazen-toned and strutting trumpet solo from Dankworth. **AM**

Lorez Alexandria

1929

The Great/More of the Great **Alexandria** (v); with various groups including **Bud Shank** (f); **Paul Horn** (as, f); **Ray Crawford** (g); **Wynton Kelly** (p); **Al McKibbon** (b); **Jimmy Cobb** (d). Impulse! Ⓜ MCAD33116 (69 minutes). Recorded 1964-65.

⑥ ❻

There are no definitive versions among these 20 songs, but no disasters either. At the time when these two albums were recorded Lorez Alexandria had a growing reputation as the hipsters's vocalist, largely as a result of her excellent taste in material and accompanists. Essentially, she comes across as a very good cabaret artiste, a bit on the breathless side at times and with a tendency to overdo the meaningful pauses, but musical rather than theatrical (more Lena Horne than Eartha Kitt, if you take my meaning).

She certainly did not shy away from challenges. Among the songs here are *Angel Eyes*, *No More*, *My One And Only Love* and *But Beautiful*, each a little minefield in its way and efficiently negotiated. **DG**

Hasaan Ibn Ali

The Max Roach Trio Featuring the Legendary Hasaan **Ali** (p); **Art Davis** (b); **Max Roach** (d). Atlantic Jazz Ⓜ 782273-2 (41 minutes). Recorded 1964.

⑦ ❺

Hasaan falls into that select group of unfortunates (other fully paid-up members include Elmo Hope, Herbie Nichols, Von Freeman and Cal Massey) who have both an outside dose of talent and an original musical vision, and spend their professional careers suffering for it. This is the only record he has ever made, and it is his date in all but name (clearly, Atlantic records didn't think that his name alone on the cover would be enough to get sales out of double figures, and they were probably right). All credit then to Roach who, alone among his peers, went past just talking to his friends about this Philadelphia legend and organised a record date for him.

The big drawback on this session is a chronically sick piano: somebody must have spent days getting it to sound so bad. That Hasaan overcomes this obstacle sufficiently to deliver his special pianistic brew (all seven tracks are Hasaan originals) and make the listener concentrate through the instrument's shortcomings speaks volumes for his talent and his perseverence. A self-professed fan of Elmo Hope (a musician Hasaan sees as giving the lead to both Monk and Powell in the forties), he displays a similar angularity, rhythmic asymmetry and combination of the traditional and the revolutionary. There is little of the be-bop pianistic vocabulary in Hasaan's playing: like Monk, Nichols and the young Cecil Taylor, he has a very heavy touch and a decidedly firm, measured rhythmic pulse. His music can be equally as dissonant, surprising and intriguing as any of the above players.

Roach and Davis provide detailed and greatly sympathetic support to Hasaan, giving him the attention and commitment he deserves. This is an album for the specialist listener, but it rewards close and careful study. **KS**

Geri Allen

1933

Maroons Allen (p); **Marcus Belgrave** (t); **Wallace Roney** (t); **Anthony Cox** (b); **Dwayne Dolphin** (b); **Pheeroan akLaff** (d); **Tanni Tabal** (d, perc). Blue Note Ⓕ CDP7 99493-2 (72 minutes). Recorded 1992.

⑦ ❽

Allen has established herself as a stalwart of the M-Base movement and made considerable impact with her trio including bassist Charlie Haden and drummer Paul Motian. This CD is more ambitious in its line-up but rates with the best of the trio dates. Much has been made of the diminuendo side of her playing, but like most of her output this release displays a constant strength, whether she is driving in a hard-bop manner on *Laila's House*, drilling Monk-like disciplines into *For John Malachi* or providing the quiet dignity in *Prayer For Peace*. On two titles she maintains complete control in a quintet with two bassists and two drummer and throughout matches the emotional intensity of her two trumpeters. Roney still paints with Milesian brushstrokes but he is the better of two good horn men, on *Prayer For Peace* in particular giving evidence that he enjoys the cushion of his leader's reflective piano. Allen's writing is another plus in her music, moving from straight-ahead mainstream bop through the South Side Chicago of *Feed The Fire 111* to the almost formally orchestral quartet, *Maroons*. **BMcR**

Henry 'Red' Allen

1908-1967

Henry Allen and his New York Orchestra 1929-30 Volumes 1 and 2 Allen (t, v); **Otis Johnson** (t); **J.C. Higginbotham**, **Jimmy Archey** (tb); **Albert Nicholas**, **Charlie Holmes**, **Teddy Hill**, **Thornton Blue**, **Greely Walton** (reeds); **Luis Russell** (p); **Will Johnson** (bj, g, v); **Pops Foster** (b), **Emest Hill** (bb); **Paul Barbarin** (d, vb); **Victoria Spivey**, **Sweet Peas** (Addie Spivey), **The Four Wanderers**, **Dick Robertson**, **Vic Dickenson** (v). JSP Ⓕ JSPCD332/33 (two discs, oas:138 minutes). Recorded 1929-30.

⑧ ❿

Often unjustly overlooked as a transitional figure in the history of jazz trumpet, Allen worked briefly with hometown heroes King Oliver and Jelly Roll Morton, but his main sideman associations were with the early swing outfits of Fletcher Henderson and Mills Blue Rhythm Band, plus the Luis Russell group whose members contribute to these first recordings under his own name. Naturally impressed by the then-current work of Armstrong (for whom Russell worked at this period and again later), Allen lacked Satchmo's power but capitalized on his freely rhythmic fantasias. Red's unique rubbery tone sounded equally appropriate playing obliquely-phrased lead parts or backing the Spivey sisters, who sing separately on several tracks of each volume.

Common to all except a few items is the excellent New Orleans bass-and-drums team of Foster and Barbarin (incidentally, the excellent remastering makes it clear that Foster plays bowed bass rather than tuba on *Telephoning The Blues*). JSP's disposition of the alternate takes between these two different chronological programmes requires both of them to be recommended. If a choice has to be made, the guest vocals by Robertson and Vic Dickenson on Volume Two pale beside Allen's own singing on the Volume One-only *Patrol Wagon Blues*. **BP**

Original 1933-41 Recordings Allen (t, v); with various personnel, including: **Dickie Wells**, **J.C. Higginbotham** (tb); **Buster Bailey**, **Cecil Scott**, **Edmond Hall** (cl); **Hilton Jefferson**, **Tab Smith** (as); **Chu Berry**, **Joe Garland** (ts); **Horace Henderson**, **Fletcher Henderson**, **Edgar Hayes**, **Clyde Hart**, **Billy Kyle**, **Ken Kersey** (p); **Danny Barker** (g); **John Kirby** (b); **Paul Barbarin**, **Kaiser Marshall**, **Cozy Cole** (d). Tax Ⓕ S32 (70 minutes). Recorded 1933-41.

⑦ ❻

By the time these recordings were made, Red Allen was an established and (as far it was possible under the all-embracing influence of the seminal Louis Armstrong) original stylist, both as a vocalist and trumpeter. Even the most cursory listen will establish key identifying traits such as Allen's wonderfully throwaway sense of time over a metric pulse, is his love of large intervallic leaps and contrasting low-down gutbucket slurs and growls. In this last sense, if not in others, he continues the King Oliver tradition, rather than Armstrong's; he was an inspired distorter of the trumpet's open tone, as well as someone who could play with commanding authority and astonishing technical ease. His natural sound was lighter and rather thinner than Armstrong's.

This Tax disc covers a period when Allen led the sections of a number of bands, those of Fletcher Henderson, Lucky Millinder and Luis Russell included, and also occasionally led his own studio groups. The transfers are clean and true, the track selection serviceable and one gets a good helping of both Allen the vocalist and Allen the trumpeter. He is often in the company of top-drawer talent, with the rhythm sections in particular contributing some serious swinging. **KS**

World on a String **Allen** (t, v); **J.C. Higginbotham** (tb); **Buster Bailey** (cl); **Coleman Hawkins** (ts); **Monty Napoleon** (p); **Everett Barksdale** (g); **Lloyd Trotman** (b); **Cozy Cole** (d). RCA Bluebird Ⓜ ND82497 (61 minutes). Recorded 1957.

⑨ ❽

This Allen-Hawkins reunion - they had last worked together in 1933 - is brimful of zest and fun. Like Hawkins, Allen continued to develop as a player, so much so that a 1965 *down beat* profile acclaimed him "the most avant-garde trumpeter in New York". He did not play free jazz, but his mastery of the horn was so complete he attained the kind of freedom that can make even traditional forms sound freshly-minted.

Hawkins apart, the other players on these dates were regular Allen associates. They all perform well but it is invariably Allen's solos that catch the ear. The *down beat* article listed a few examples from his astonishing range of trumpet effects: "bends, smears, half-valve effects, rips, glissandos, flutter-tonguing", yet he is rarely more than a step or two from the melody line. His ballad feature here, *I Cover the Waterfront*, is rated "one of the most magnificent extended trumpet solos of that or any period" by Gunther Schuller (in *The Swing Era*). The trumpeter sounds nearly as good on several other tracks, notably *I've Got the World on a String*, where Hawkins too is at his majestic best. The final bonus is that Allen sings on four tracks, his light-toned, personal phrasing a delight on the blues *Let Me Miss You, Baby* and a declamatory *St. James Infirmary*. **GL**

Mose Allison 1927

Back Country Suite **Allison** (p, v); **Taylor La Fargue** (b); **Frank Isola** (d). Prestige Ⓜ OJCCD-075-2 (35 minutes). Recorded 1957.

⑦ ❽

Born in Mississippi and weaned on the boogie and blues music of the area, Allison came to be-bop via swing-era piano stylists such as Nat King Cole. In the mid-fifties he worked in New York as a sideman with the likes of Zoot Sims and Stan Getz, but since that time has performed mainly as a cabaret artist with his own trio. This CD highlights the range of moods that he puts into his piano work. The longer pieces take on a special character, with *I Thought About You* treated as straight ahead bebop, *Blueberry Hill* featured as only Thelonious Monk might attempt it and *You Won't Let Me Know* delivered with a Ray Bryant-like nonchalance. The excellent *Back Country Suite* is appropriately bucolic, offering orthodox bop on *Scamper* and *Highway 49* but elsewhere showing how best to broach the subject of musical description. *New Ground* is a rolling blues, *Train* avoids the simulated locomotive clichés but still makes the journey, while *January* has an almost contrived sense of apathy. The Baptist church creeps into *The Promised Land,* while *Spring Song* shows that even the Back Country has cocktail lounges. Allison's laconic post-Hoagy Carmichael drawl mixes no-hope pessimism with hip self-realisation on *One-Room Country Shack*, but for more obvious vocal mayhem there is the brother CD, **Local Colour** (Prestige OJCCD 457-2). **BMcR**

Karrin Allyson 1962

Azure-Te **Allyson** (v, p); **Kim Park** (as, ts); **Paul Smith**, **Laura Caviani** (p); **Danny Embrey**, **Rod Fleeman** (g); **Bob Bowman**, **Gerald Spaits** (b); **Todd Strait** (d); guests on selected tracks: **Claude 'Fiddler' Williams** (v); **Stan Kessler** (t); **Mike Metheny** (flh); **Randy Weinstein** (h); **Bryan Hicks** (v). Concord Ⓕ CCD-4641 (61 minutes). Recorded 1993.

⑧ ❽

In her third release for Concord, jazz diva Karrin Allyson and her fellow KC mates effectively prove that "everything's up to date in Kansas City". A gifted young singer who is a bona fide musician (she is an excellent pianist), Allyson, like the young Ella Fitzgerald, conjoins evocative sophistication with girlish delight in a beguiling style that sizzles with sensual as well as musical allure. When she sings *Blame It on my Youth* and *Good Morning, Heartache* you believe her. And, happily, as she moves mountains, dramatic and musical, she does so without resorting to histrionic plays to the balcony.

Allyson's cast of Kansas Citians is excellent. On the pleading *Gee Baby (Ain't I Good to You)*, the filigrees of the legendary Claude 'Fiddler' Williams taunt and tease. For *Bernie's Tune*, gritty horn lines launch Stan Kessler's soaring trumpet and the tandem vocal acrobatics of Allyson and Bryan Hicks. Adding bright moments to the home-town affair are pianist Paul Smith and the exceptional saxophonist Kim Parks. The coup-de-grace is Allyson's tribute to KC's rich jazz legacy via a blithe bop-inflected romp through Charlie Parker's *Ornithology* and its pop palimpsest, *How High the Moon*. In today's vocal pantheon, Allyson's is a unique presence. **CB**

Franco Ambrosetti

1941

Gin and Pentatonic **Ambrosetti** (t, flh); **Lew Soloff, Michael Mossman** (t); **Alex Brophy, John Clark** (frh); **Steve Coleman** (as); **Michael Brecker** (ts); **Howard Johnson** (bs, tba); **Kenny Kirkland, Tommy Flanagan** (p); **Buster Williams, Dave Holland** (b); **Daniel Humair** (d). Enja Ⓕ ENJ-4096 2 (68 minutes). Recorded 1983/1985.

⑧ ❽

Compiled from his much-acclaimed 1983 sextet recording **Wings** and the later **Tentets**, **Gin and Pentatonic** provides an excellent introduction to the work of jazz-playing business executive Franco Ambrosetti. Although his neo-bop style has been compared with that of Freddie Hubbard, Ambrosetti's purity of tone (particularly on flügelhorn) his flawless balance and control at high tempos, (enabling him to rip through a tune's changes without apparent effort) also bring Kenny Wheeler to mind. Ambrosetti's compositions are, however, utterly individual, and provide the meat of this compilation, being excellent platforms not only for Ambrosetti himself, but for his all-star **Wings** band. Michael Brecker, always burly and sinewy, sounding more engaged in an unalloyed jazz setting than he frequently does in more fusion-based fare, is a perfect front-line foil, John Clark's french horn provides valuable extra tone and texture, Kenny Kirkland is exhilarating throughout and Buster Williams's sonorous, full-bodied bass drone is an excellent anchor. Long-time associate Daniel Humair is the powerhouse behind each band and is particularly effective on the George Gruntz material - unsurprisingly, given the three Europeans' long association in Gruntz's concert band. The tentet recordings conjure up less immediate excitement than the sextet material, but are nevertheless faultlessly - if unspectacularly - arranged, and are particularly notable for providing an intriguing glimpse of altoist Steve Coleman in his pre-M-Base, Mel Lewis/Thad Jones band period. Overall, a highly enjoyable, exuberant but tasteful collection from a European master. **CP**

AMM

The Nameless Uncarved Block **Lou Gare** (ts, vn); **Keith Rowe** (g, electronics); **John Tilbury** (p); **Eddie Prévost** (d). Matchless Ⓕ MR 20 (74 minutes). Recorded 1990.

⑧ ❽

AMM will soon be celebrating three decades together, although the personnel has altered somewhat over the years, as has the direction and possibly the intent of their music. Even though totally improvised, it is somewhat distinct from free jazz, although that is the way they started out in the sixties when Prévost, Gare and Rowe began exploring instinctual methods of structuring sound. After years of experimentation they are now able to create not just a language (as do most new musics) but an environment; a way of defining space and filling it with meaningful sounds. The *idea* of jazz may create a subtle tension in the listener's mind; the saxophone and piano produce tones which we may identify with jazz (although Tilbury, particularly, is trained and experienced in 'classical' New Music), but the context is unfamiliar. In fact, they desire to create new contexts, intentionally confusing their own contributions and our responses: each instrument might be used percussively *or* melodically, or in a way to make it unrecognizable, as individual details mesh into a complex fabric free of conventional form (which is why they work in such large time-frames: the three pieces here clock in at 29, 37, and seven minutes). The album's title is apt; the gradually exposed sounds are frequently layered like the grain in rock. Sometimes the musicians seem to be excavating unformed sounds from a bottomless quarry, other times they are sculpting them into abstract shapes. This is music not of virtuosity, but concentration and risk, and AMM has reached a point of success where, regardless of its newness, the sounds have a feeling of inevitability - not of compositional precision, but of Nature. **AL**

Albert Ammons

1907-1949

The First Day **Ammons, Meade Lux Lewis** (p). Blue Note Ⓜ CDP7 984502 (74 minutes). Recorded 1939.

⑧ ❼

Ammons shares this record with his boogie-woogie contemporary Meade Lux Lewis, and the difference in their approaches is at once obvious: whereas Lewis's slow blues appear to be largely improvised, Ammons's creations seem to have been thought through, planned in detail—and there is a great deal of detail in pieces like *Boogie Woogie Stomp* or the superb *Bass Goin' Crazy*, where the left hand launches a series of bold invasions into the right hand's home ground. The contrast of steady pulse and flamboyant adventure, so characteristic of the idiom, is for Ammons a particularly rich source of ideas. Some of them are almost visual in their effect; without too much effort the listener can see a stocky, good-humoured man strolling amiably but purposefully along, say, Lenox Avenue, joyfully rattling the money in his pockets.

Ammons also evinces an interest in reshaping traditional themes and earlier compositions, such as *Easy Rider Blues*, *Backwater Blues* and *Suitcase Blues*, and in later years he had some success with boogie-woogie translations of more outré material, as in *Swanee River Boogie*. Although more conventional in design, Ammons's 1941 duets with Pete Johnson are classics of their kind; they can be found on **Barrelhouse Boogie** (RCA Bluebird ND88334), together with recordings by Lewis and Jimmy Yancey. **TR**

Gene Ammons
1925-1974

Young Jug **Ammons** (ts); **Billy Massey** (t); **Matthew Gee, J.J. Johnson** (tb); **Sonny Stitt** (bs); prob. **Willie Jones, Christine Chatman, Junior Mance, John Houston** (p); **Leo Blevins** (g); **Leroy Jackson, Lowell Pointer, Gene Wright, Ernie Shepherd** (b); **Wesley Landers, Ike Day, Teddy Stewart, Rob Wilson** (d) **Tom Archaia** (ts). Chess Ⓜ GRP 18012 (60 minutes). Recorded 1948-52.

⑧ ❻

Ammons, son of pianist Albert, is sometimes dismissed as a forerunner of populist players such as Lou Donaldson and Grover Washington, but for the black audience who appreciated his soulful tenor he personified the boundary of jazz and r&b. As a teenage star of the Billy Eckstine big band, he partnered Dexter Gordon (later, like Dexter, spending nearly a decade out of circulation) and for some years toured with Sonny Stitt. The equal of Gordon in combining Parker's influence with a strong allegience to Lester Young, he was famous for ballads in a simplified version of the style established by Hawkins and Chu Berry.

This material, some of the first under Ammons's own name (though he also recorded prolifically for Mercury and Prestige during the same period), shows his great qualities applied to a number of current ballads (*My Foolish Heart*, *Somewhere Along the Way*) as well as standards already long in the tooth. But these were almost all issued on 78rpm singles with a more up-tempo B-side such as *Jug Head Ramble* (a title incorporating Ammons's nickname) or *More Moon* (remaking a hit from his brief stay with Woody Herman).

Inferior production mars the first four tracks, including the witty *Swingin' for Xmas*, but these can be programmed out or could, indeed, have been put at the end of the programme by the producer. **BP**

Franck Amsallem
1972

Out A Day **Amsallem** (p); **Gary Peacock** (b); **Bill Stewart** (d). OMD Ⓕ CD1532 (65 minutes). Recorded 1990.

⑥ ❽

Ignoring the obvious presence of two Americans for the moment, this album is typical of what the French jazz scene has been churning out for some years now: highly competent, stylistically contemporary and almost wholly derivative piano trio music (in Amsallem's case, the originals include Bill Evans, Chick Corea and Herbie Hancock). There is absolutely nothing wrong with this record (Amsallem, by the way, wrote seven of the nine songs on the album), but it hardly takes us anywhere new. Gary Peacock plays beautifully—his solo work is for me the highlight of the album—and Stewart is the perfect drummer, discreetly feeding the other two but never allowing things to drift. In a club, this would be a pleasant and diverting set. Under the harsher spotlight of a CD, it stands up as a good set of performances, but nothing to get too excited about. **KS**

Cat Anderson
1916-1981

Cat Anderson Plays W.C. Handy **Anderson** (t, v); **Booty Wood** (tb); **Norris Turney** (as); **Harold Ashby, Gerald Badini** (ts); **André Persiany, Raymond Fol, Philippe Baudoin** (p); **Aaron Bell, Michel Gaudry** (b); **Sam Woodyard** (d). Black & Blue Ⓕ 59.163-2 (55 minutes). Recorded 1978-79.

⑧ ❽

The razor blade-like notes of Cat Anderson were part of Duke Ellington's imprimatur for the best part of three decades. Usually Ellingtonians did not sound as good away from the Ellington band as they did within it; Anderson was an exception, and this wonderfully flourishing album makes one wonder what might have been. The excellent material—Handy collected the best tunes—lets Cat and his associates play comfortably within their limits, the outbursts of stratospheric notes husbanded in a miserly fashion. Much use is made of mutes and Anderson reveals himself to be both dextrous and tasteful.

He is generously supported by his sidemen—Booty Wood's muted solos on *Careless Love* and *Beale Street Blues* are masterful. Ashby preaches on *St Louis Blues* and sings on his horn in *Hesitating Blues*, no doubt inspired by the spanking but rather repetitive drumming of Sam Woodyard. Persiany's piano is also most effective. But Anderson predictably towers over the proceedings with a dazzling display of trumpet expertise and good taste. The influence he took from Armstrong is much in evidence and this sterling album is indeed a worthy match for Armstrong's similar essay on Handy's tunes. **SV**

Ernestine Anderson 1928

Hello Like Before **Anderson** (v); **Hank Jones** (p); **Ray Brown** (b); **Jimmie Smith** (d). Concord Ⓕ CCD 4031 (38 minutes). Recorded 1976.

⑦ ❽

Anderson has been a professional singer now for 50 years, having started in the early forties with Russell Jacquet and gone on to sing with Lionel Hampton and Johnny Otis, among others. By the mid-fifties she had developed away from her r&b roots, spending time in Europe and evolving a modern approach to standard repertoire which jazz-based audiences found pleasing. This new career withered with the onset of the sixties, and she spent more than a decade in England before landing in Los Angeles. After a few gigs around and about, she was invited to appear at the 1975 Concord Jazz Festival. Her set there effectively re-launched her Stateside career and led directly to *Hello Like Before*, her first album for Concord and still arguably her best, though there have been many since.

A large part of the reason for this success is the superbly sympathetic and imaginative support she receives from Hank Jones, one of the greatest jazz accompanists of any era. There is not a moment on this disc when Jones is not supplying delightful instrumental commentary and subtle shadings of his own to Anderson's supple and winning ways with a lyric or a melody. The singer herself avoids bombast or interpretative clichés, chooses her standards with care (even *'Tain't Nobody's Business* sounds fresh here), and manages to sustain that magical intimacy between singer and audience which is the essence of good vocalizing. **KS**

Fred Anderson 1929

Destiny **Fred Anderson** (ts); **Marilyn Crispell** (p); **Hamid Drake** (perc). Okkadisc Ⓕ OD12003 (67 minutes). Recorded 1994.

Now an elder statesman of the Chicago scene, Fred Anderson was among the AACM's prime movers in the mid-sixties. His later groups, often co-led with trumpeter Billy Brimfield, provided a valuable testing-ground for a rising generation of players: notable alumni have included reedsmen Douglas Ewart and Chico Freeman and trombonist George Lewis. Anderson's fluent, big-toned sound seems to encompass the tenor tradition, although he has named Gene Ammons, Chu Berry, Don Byas and Lester Young as particular favourites and reported too that he sharpened his technique by constantly practising Charlie Parker tunes. Those influences were woven into a distinctive, personal style that one writer has suggested is the 'missing link' between late fifties Ornette Coleman and early AACM saxophonists such as Roscoe Mitchell and Joseph Jarman (on whose 1967 **Song For** Anderson guested).

Unfortunately, discs by Anderson himself have been extremely rare: even this CD, his first new recording in nearly 15 years, comes from a concert that was nominally under Crispell's leadership. Yet Anderson's is often the dominant voice, simply through the magnificent authority of his playing. The disc's six improvisations run the gamut from vigorous excitement to reflective calm, with Anderson's sudden foray into Trane-like balladry on *Destiny 5* leading to the most inspired sequence of this absorbing trio encounter. **GL**

Ivie Anderson 1905-1949

With Duke Ellington and his Famous Orchestra **Anderson** (v) with personnels including **Ellington** (p); **Arthur Whetsol**, **Cootie Williams** (t); **Rex Stewart** (c); **Lawrence Brown**, **Tricky Sam Nanton**, **Juan Tizol** (tb); **Johnny Hodges**, **Otto Hardwicke** (as); **Barney Bigard** (cl, ts); **Ben Webster** (ts); **Harry Carney** (bs); **Wellman Braud**, **Billy Taylor**, **Jimmy Blanton** (b); **Sonny Greer** (d). Jazz Archives Ⓑ 157352 (65 minutes). Recorded 1932-40.

⑧ ❻

Ivie Anderson was the best singer that Duke Ellington ever had. It is curious that Ellington, whose flair for choosing players is legendary, saddled himself for the most part with a series of dire vocalists. But in Ivie he found a true Ellingtonian voice. It is a strange, matter-of-fact kind of voice, not at all conventionally beautiful but fragile and oddly touching. Her very first record (and the first number on this CD) was the famous *It Don't Mean A Thing If It Ain't Got That Swing*, a piece whose cheery message is surrounded by a weird, faintly menacing orchestral aura, in the midst of which Ivie pops up like a not entirely well-intentioned elf.

There is a coolness about Ivie's voice that gives an ironic edge to her love-songs and a watchful reserve to the good-time numbers. She was unique and inimitable and might have become a jazz diva, had her life not been blighted by asthma. This collection of 22 songs represents her reasonably well, although I cannot understand why it leaves out *I Got It Bad*, one of her best performances. But it does have *All God's Chillun, I'm Checkin' Out - Go'om Bye* and *Truckin'*. **DG**

Ray Anderson

1952

Every One Of Us **Anderson** (tb, v); **Simon Nabatov** (p); **Charlie Haden** (b); **Ed Blackwell** (d). Gramavision ℗ R2 29471 (46 minutes). Recorded 1992.

⑥ ❻

Every time a new trombonist expands the possibilities of the instrument, one thinks it cannot go any further. People once thought that Jack Teagarden had done all there was to be done. Then Tommy Dorsey arrives. Then J.J. Johnson. Jimmy Cleveland turned out to be faster than J.J. Johnson, but he was so fast he couldn't do much else, and after that it seemed that nobody could face the challenge of going further technically, until Ray Anderson came along and produced a technique that went higher, lower, faster than seemed previously possible. A lot of people think he is too tricky to be good—a gimmick man. A lot of other people think he is just wonderful. I think he is probably a wonderful musician with elements of the poseur in him, and with a technique like his, which seems capable of doing things you had not thought worth trying, you would be justified in sounding like a poseur occasionally. Anyway, one thing is certain. It cannot go any further than this. Or can it ...? **MK**

Azurety **Anderson** (tb, tba); **Christy Doran** (g); **Han Bennink** (d). hatART ℗ CD 6155 (56 minutes). Recorded 1994.

⑧ ❽

Like his fellow-trombonist Roswell Rudd, Anderson is able to work convincingly in an impressive number of musical situations. This dynamic trio is just one of them, but it allows Anderson tremendous scope for his ideas. This is not to downplay the contributions of either Bennink or Doran, who emerge as equal partners here. It is just that Anderson's voice on his instrument is so developed and clear that his eloquence is often mesmerizing. The ease with which he and Bennink deliver an easy-swinging statement of the theme to Ellington's *Just Squeeze Me*, Anderson by the means of passing tones suggesting by sure touches what the rest of the band would be doing if they were there, is breathtaking. He is equally persuasive on the tuba, as his introduction to *The Waters/Dixon Line* demonstrates, and although he is not the type of player to ignore the comic possibilities in the lower-pitched instrument, he brings it a plasticity and expressiveness only perhaps Howard Johnson could approach.

Doran seems to be having a lot of fun on *Waters/Dixon* as well, apeing Hendrix, Buddy Guy and others, but his adaptability is also on display across this disc, from absolutely free to the most subtle chording. Bennink, as ever, does not disappoint. A trio which fits happily together and a programme which entertains. **KS**

Krister Andersson

About Time **Andersson** (ts, cl); **Ion Baciu** (p); **Torbjorn Hultcrantz**, **Markus Wikstrom** (b); **Leif Wennerstrom**, **Jan Robertson** (d); **Malando Gassama** (perc). Flash Music ℗ FLCD1 (50 minutes). Recorded 1993.

⑧ ❽

Although small in terms of overall population, the Scandinavian countries continue to produce a wealth of high quality jazz players and Krister Andersson is one of the most accomplished soloists to emerge from the Swedish jazz scene. He plays tenor throughout the six tracks on this CD, adding an extra clarinet line to strengthen the theme statements on *About Time*. His powerful, expressive sound is reminiscent of both Lucky Thompson and Sonny Rollins; like them he has enormous stamina. On *How High The Moon* he opens with an astonishing seven minutes of sustained invention which has all the confidence and imagination of a true jazz master. *Markus' Blues* (by Wikstrom) shows that the 12-bar format can still provide jazz soloists with a stimulating basis for improvisation. The programme closes with an arresting tenor and drums duet, *All Of A Sudden*, the kind of thing which takes great nerve and confidence, but Anderssen and Leif Wennerstrom are equal to the task. **AM**

Ernie Andrews 1927

No Regrets **Andrews** (v), **Houston Person** (ts), **Junior Mance** (p), **Jimmy Ponder** (g), **Ray Drummond** (b), **Michael Carvin** (d). Muse Ⓕ MCD 5484 (51 minutes). Recorded 1992.

⑥ ❼

This album, produced by Houston Person, brings back Ernie Andrews after a long time away from the recording studio and settles him in the musical milieu for which his voice was created: a small-group mainstream jazz setting redolent in blues feeling. In that sense, his most obvious antecedent might well be Jimmy Witherspoon, except that he has been around almost as long as Spoon and has always been closer to the jazz tradition than the latter, having started his career at Birdland and recorded with, among others, Harry James, Cannonball Adderley and Benny Carter.

The music here is made up of standards (*Sweet Lorraine*, *Until The Real Thing Comes Along*), with a couple of less obvious choices (a Lucky Millinder ditty, *Sweet Slumber*, for example) thrown in to keep it interesting, and Andrews works closely with his backing group to make sure that it is not merely a singer-plus-band date but a properly collaborative effort. The sidemen respond with spirited work, and both Mance and Person excel in a way which does not detract from the confident but curiously vulnerable light baritone which Andrews possesses. **KS**

Julian Argüelles 1966

Phaedrus **Argüelles** (ss, ts); **John Taylor** (p); **Mick Hutton** (b); **Martin France** (d). AhUm Ⓕ 010 (63 minutes). Recorded 1990.

⑧ ❽

Like fellow ex-Loose Tubes saxophonists Iain Ballamy and Tim Whitehead, Julian Argüelles has firmly established himself since the big band's demise in the front rank of the UK's younger jazz players. Late-eighties work with units led by Mike Gibbs and Kenny Wheeler revealed him as an adaptable, lively but dependable sideman, and his début recording as a leader is considerably enlivened by the presence of a third representative of Gibbs's and Wheeler's generation, pianist John Taylor. The sympathetic interplay between saxophone and piano, particularly on the impressionistic, discursive Argüelles originals which constitute the bulk of the album, is uniformly impressive, Taylor's luminous delicacy the perfect foil for Argüelles's earnest, intimately conversational tenor style. The session ballads, whether Arguelles's own or (a standout track) Chris McGregor's *Maxine*, work better than either the brisk stop-start title-track or the Rollins-influenced bustler *Red Rag*; Martin France is a touch over-reliant on skittering embellishment at the expense of strict timekeeping. Overall Phaedrus is an impressive début, a demonstration of the efficacy of the Loose Tubes experience as a foundation for a career in jazz composition and improvisation **CP**

Steve Argüelles 1963

Steve Argüelles **Argüelles** (d); **Julian Argüelles** (as, ts); **Stuart Hall** (g, vn); **Kim Burton** (acc); **Mick Hutton** (b). AhUm Ⓕ 007 (52 minutes). Recorded 1990.

⑥ ❽

Drummer Steve Argüelles came to prominence as part of the 21-piece big band Loose Tubes, and that aggregation's openness to all manner of musical influences, particularly from South Africa, South America and the Caribbean, has clearly left its mark on him. Like the music of another Loose Tubes spin-off group Human Chain, the originals on this, the elder Argüelles brother's début album as leader, are eclectic, jaunty and light-hearted. Sly quotations from, and humorous references to everything from calypso through fairground music to Country - even the echoey sound of the Shadows - litter the album. The result is a disquieting heterogeneousness which is easier to experience as superficial pastiche rather than as the meaningful assimilation of a variety of interesting sounds into a coherent musical statement. The album too frequently degenerates into a mere rag-bag of apparently unrelated sounds—an occupational hazard for musicians attempting to occupy the ill-defined territory between so-called 'world' music and jazz—for its very real strengths to be consistently appreciated. **CP**

Louis Armstrong 1901-1971

Portrait of the Artist as a Young Man, 1923-1934 **Armstrong** (c, t, v); with a collective personnel featuring: **Joe Oliver, Elmer Chambers, Howard Scott, Elmer Chambers, Joe Smith, James Tate, Bill Wilson, Homer Hobson, Henry 'Red' Allen, Otis Johnson, Leon Elkins, George Orendorff, Harold Scott, Zilner Randolph, Ellis Whitlock, Jack Hamilton, Leslie Thompson** (c, t); **Honore Dutrey, Charlie Irvis, Aaron Thompson, Charlie Green, Edward 'Kid' Ory, Eddie Atkins, Roy Palmer, Johnny Thomas, Fred Robinson, Jack Teagarden, J. C. Higginbotham, Tommy Dorsey, Lawrence Brown, Luther Graven, Preston Jackson, Keg Johnson, Lionel Guimaraes** (tb); **Johnny Dodds, Jimmy Dorsey, Albert Nicholas, Jimmy Noone, Buster Bailey** (cl); **Sidney Bechet,**

Don Redman, Angelo Fernandez, Stump Evans, Boyd Atkins, Joe Walker, Jimmy Strong, Charlie Holmes, Bert Curry, Crawford Wethington, Leon Herriford, Willie Stark, Les Hite, Marvin Johnson, Lester Boone, George James, Scoville Brown, George Oldham, Pete DuConge, Henry Tyree (cl, as, ss, bs); **Coleman Hawkins, Norvai Morton, Albert Washington, Happy Caldwell, Teddy Hill, William Franz, Charlie Jones, Albert 'Budd' Johnson, Alfred Pratt** (ts, cl, C-ms, bss); **Lil Armstrong, Clarence Williams, Fletcher Henderson, Fred Longshaw, Richard M. Jones, Hersal Thomas, Teddy Weatherford, Earl Hines, Joe Sullivan, Luis Russell, Justin Ring, Gene Anderson, Buck Washington, L.Z. Cooper, Harvey Brooks, Henry Prince, Charlie Alexander, Teddy Wilson, Herman Chittison** (p); **Bill Johnson, Bud Scott, Johnny St. Cyr, Buddy Christian, Charlie Dixon, Frank Etheridge, Mike McKendrick** (bj); **Rip Basset, Lonnie Johnson, Mancy Carr, Dave Wilborn, Eddie Lang, Lonnie Johnson, Will Johnson, Jimmie Rodgers, Ceele Burke, Bill Perkins, Maceo Jefferson** (g); **John Hare, Pops Foster, Joe Bailey, John Lindsay, John Oldham, German Arago** (b); **Charlie Jackson, Ralph Excudero, Pete Briggs, Reggie Jones** (tba); **Baby Dodds, Kaiser Marshall, Jimmy Bertrand, Tubby Hall, Zutty Singleton, Paul Barbarin, Stan King, Lionel Hampton, Yank Porter, Oliver Tines** (d); **Harry Hoffman, Carroll Dickerson** (vn); **Eva Taylor, Margaret Johnson, Maggie Jones, Bessie Smith, Bertha 'Chippie' Hill, Hociel Thomas, Mau Alix, Clarence Babcock, Lillie Delk Christian, Seger Ellis, Jimmie Rodgers** (v). Columbia/Legacy Ⓜ 57176 (four discs: 248 minutes). Recorded 1923-1934.

✓ ⑩ ❽

This extraordinary four-disc boxed set reveals a ripe but still maturing Louis Armstrong during a singularly significant phase when he consolidated and coined jazzdom's basic grammar and syntax virtually single-handedly. It duplicates a good deal of the repertoire to be found on some of the other sets below, but it is an extremely handy way to obtain a quick overview of this crucial period in Armstrong's career. It is an 11-year odyssey during which we glimpse such Armstrong ports-of-call as King Oliver and Fletcher Henderson, and collaborations with such fellow legends as Bessie Smith, Maggie Jones, Clarence Williams, Sidney Bechet, Johnny Dodds, Lonnie Johnson, Earl 'Fatha' Hines and Lionel Hampton. The discographic survey commences in 1923 with King Oliver's Creole Jazz Band and *Chimes Blues*, the first Armstrong solo committed to wax, wrapping up in 1934 with *Song of the Vipers*, recorded in Paris with a European cast.

Along the way, Armstrong's seemingly innate capacity to swing, his penchant for dividing quarter-notes into eights, and his inimitable 'vocalized' instrumental style and 'instrumentalized' vocals are all present and accounted for. So, too, is the trumpeter's contagious *joie de vivre*. For Louis, as well as his cohorts and audiences, music was a means of joyful transcendence. Trips to the summit abound—there's the zesty *Struttin' with Some Barbecue* (1927) with his Hot Five in Chicago; the hand-in-glove Armstrong-Hines duet on *Weather Bird* (1928); the landmark *Ain't Misbehavin'* (1929) from **Hot Chocolates**, the Andy Razaf/Fats Waller revue whose broad appeal helped make Armstrong a pop as well as jazz star; the deeply felt *Knockin' a Jug* (1929), the first important inter-racial jazz date featuring Jack Teagarden, Eddie Lang and Kaiser Marshall; a rollicking *I'm a Ding Dong Daddy* with Lionel Hampton's exuberant drumming; and an upbeat *I've Got the World on a String* (1933) where Teddy Wilson's sprightly break sets up the maestro's warm gravelly vocal and stentorian trumpeting. In all, it is a priceless time capsule of one of the era's great personalities and jazz's most seminal stylist. Sound quality, which beats any previous Columbia issues of Armstrong's material, ranges from good to excellent. **CB**

The Complete Recordings of Louis Armstrong and The Blues Singers **Armstrong** (c, t, v); **Charlie Green** (tb); **Buster Bailey** (cl, ss); **Charles Irvis** (tb); **Sidney Bechet** (cl, ss); **Aaron Thompson** (tb); **Lil Armstrong** (p); **Fred Longshaw** (harm, p); **Don Redman** (cl, as) **Coleman Hawkins** (ts); **James P. Johnson** (p); **Hersal Thomas** (p); **Richard M. Jones** (p); **Artie Starks** (cl); **Jimmy Noone** (cl); **Earl Hines** (p); **Tommy Dorsey** (tb); **Jimmy Dorsey** (cl); **Fred Robinson** (tb); **Jimmy Strong** (cl); **Joe Venuti** (vn); **Arthur Schutt** (p); **Eddie Lang** (g); **Clarence Williams Blue Five**; **Red Onion Jazz Babies**; **Bill Jones' Southern Serenaders**; **Fletcher Henderson Orchestra**; **Perry Bradford's Jazz Phools**; **Armstrong's Hot 5**. Affinity Ⓜ CD AFS1018-6 (six discs: 366 minutes). Recorded 1924-30.

✓ ⑩ ❹

By the time Armstrong joined Fletcher Henderson in 1924 he was jazz music's most avant-garde figure. He had also undertaken what were meant to be backroom duties as an accompanist to singers, but as this boxed set of six CDs shows he almost always stole the show. The Clarence Williams Blue Five and its related Red Onion Jazz Babies were fertile ground for him. Behind or around the likes of the jaunty Eva Taylor or the more bluesy Alberta Hunter he waged a running musical battle with Sidney Bechet or Buster Bailey and, on titles such as *Mandy Make Up Your Mind* and *Cake Walkin' Babies*, gave masterful trumpet recitals that pre-date the Hot Five records by almost a year. He also enhanced the work of impressive blues artists such as Sippie Wallace and Victoria Spivey as well as lending stature to lesser talents such as Maggie Jones, Trixie Smith, Hociel Thomas and Margaret Johnson. With poorer singers like Nolan Welsh, he produced solos that turned routine performances into essential listening. He deflected attention from the poor intonation of Virginia Liston, the eccentric timing of Blanche Calloway and even the 'little girl lost' bathos of Lillie Delk Christian.

Where his true majesty is most evident, however, is with artists of equal stature. His preaching cornet behind Ma Rainey on *Countin' the Blues*, his dramatic response to the superbly strident Chippie Hill on *Low Land Blues* or *Pleadin' For The Blues*, or his sensitivity in matching the inherent sadness of Clara Smith on *Shipwrecked Blues* all bear the mark of genius. These are masterpieces of blues collaboration, but there are nine titles with Bessie Smith that represent the pinnacle of art. There is the definitive *St Louis Blues*, the impossibly moving *Reckless Blues* and even the bravura rivalry of *Cold In Hand Blues*. All save *Second Fiddle* are incomparable.

Colour is added with novelties from Grant and Wilson, a badly recorded Perry Bradford, a Hot Five-inspired Butterbeans and Susie, and the incongruous Jimmy Rodgers. In spite of major contributions from Armstrong, the Billy Jones, Baby Mack and Seger Ellis items are of rarity value only and it must be pointed out that, had the transfer/recording assessment been based on the Columbia or Okeh items only, the sound quality rating would have been upped to seven. **BMcR**

Highlights From His American Decca Years **Armstrong** (c, t); **Howard Scott, Elmer Chambers, Leonard Davis, Gus Aiken, Louis Bacon, George Thow, Toots Camarata, Shelton Hemphill, Red Allen, Otis Johnson, Bernard Flood, Frank Galbraith, Gene Prince, Billy Butterfield, Bernie Privin, Aaron Izenhall, Carl Poole, Yank Lawson, Melvin Solomon, Paul Webster, Andy Ferretti** (t); **Roy Palmer, Kid Ory, Charlie Green, Harry White, Jimmy Archey, Bobby Byrne, Joe Yukl, Don Mattison, George Matthews, George Washington, J.C. Higginbotham, Wilbur De Paris, Claude Jones, Norman Green, Henderson Chambers, James Whitney, Jack Teagarden, Will Bradley, Morton Bullman, Lou McGarity, Cutty Cutshall, Phil Giardiana, Jack Satterfield, Trummy Young** (tb); **Ralph Escudero** (tba); **Johnny Dodds, Buster Bailey, Hank D'Amico, Edmond Hall** (cl); **Barney Bigard, Bingie Madison, Jimmy Dorsey, Albert Nicholas, George Koenig, Jack Greenberg, Art Drellinger, Milton Chatz** (cl, ts); **Sidney Bechet** (ss); **Don Redman, Charlie Holmes, Henry Jones, Jack Stacey, Pete Clark, Rupert Cole, Sid Stoneburn, Jules Rubin, Sid Cooper, Johnny Mince, Milt Yaner, Hymie Schertzer, George Dorsey, Hilton Jefferson** (as); **Coleman Hawkins, Greely Walton, Fud Livingston, Skeets Herfurt, Joe Garland, Carl Frye, Prince Robinson, Bill Stegmeyer, Art Rollini, Josh Jackson, Bill Holcombe, Al Klink, Lucky Thompson** (ts); **Paul Ricci, Dave McRae** (bs); **Earl Hines, Lil Armstrong, Fletcher Henderson, Luis Russell, Bobby Van Eps, Dick Cary, Dave Bowman, Joe Bushkin, Billy Kyle, Bill Doggett, Bernie Leighton** (p); **Bud Scott, Johnny St Cyr, Charlie Dixon, Lee Blair** (bj), **Roscoe Hillman, Bernard Addison, Lawrence Lucie, Carl Kress, Norman Brown, Danny Perri, Everett Barksdale, Carmen Mastren, George Barnes** (g); **Pops Foster, Jim Taft, Wellman Braud, Hayes Alvis, John Simmons, Bob Haggart, Arvell Shaw, Trigger Alpert, Joe Benjamin, Bob Bushnell, Jack Lesberg, George Duvivier, Sandy Clock, Squire Gersh** (b); **Baby Dodds, Kaiser Marshall, Paul Barbarin, Ray McKinley, Sidney Catlett, Zutty Singleton, Johnny Blowers, Cozy Cole, Jimmy Crawford, Joe Morris, Ed Grady, Barrett Deems** (d); **The Mills Brothers, Ella Fitzgerald, Billie Holiday, Louis Jordan, Bing Crosby, Velma Middleton** (v); **Sy Oliver Choir, Gordon Jenkins Choir**. GRP Ⓜ 26382 (two discs: 124 minutes). Recorded 1924-57.

⑧ ❽

Spanning the whole of Armstrong's career from the Fletcher Henderson big band in 1924 to his **Musical Autobiography** in the late fifties, this is an essential selection of his best work. The anthology is produced by Orrin Keepnews, whose knowledge of his subject, sure hand in juxtaposing the material, and access to first-rate source material make this one of the essential jazz collections. The Hot Five and Seven are best represented elsewhere (see below), and sensibly this release does not seek to duplicate other groupings of Armstrong's earliest work. The core of the collection, and the major section of Armstrong's life represented on these two CDs, is the big band he led (in effect Luis Russell's band fronted by Armstrong) from the early thirties until the mid-forties. The majority of the first disc is highlights of their most memorable sessions, from the trumpet fireworks of *Struttin' With Some Barbecue* to examples of their successful formula for Louis's vocals (band intro, trumpet statement, vocal and soaring trumpet out-chorus) like *I'm Confessin'* and *I'm In The Mood For Love*. Disc Two combines Armstrong's move back to small group jazz and the birth of the All Stars with many of his collaborations with other singers and entertainers. Few Dixieland revivalists could compete with the heat and energy of *Muskrat Ramble* from Boston Symphony Hall, and the only dubious selection is the final hokum of *King Of The Zulus*, which might better have been replaced by one of the more musical highlights of the **Autobiography**. **AS**

Hot Fives And Sevens, Volumes 1-4 **Armstrong** (c, t, v); with a collective personnel including: **Bill Wilson** (c); **Homer Hobson, Henry 'Red' Allen** (t); **Kid Ory, Hy Clark, Honore Dutrey, Jack Teagarden, J.C. Higginbotham, Fred Robinson** (tb); **Johnny Dodds, Don Redman, Albert Nicholas, Charlie Holmes** (cl, as); **Boyd Atkins** (cl, ss, as); **Joe Walker** (as, bs); **Albert Washington, Happy Cauldwell, Bert Curry, Teddy Hill** (ts); **Jimmy Strong** (cl, ts); **Lil Armstrong** (p, v); **Earl Hines, Joe Sullivan, Luis Russell, Gene Anderson** (p); **Johnny St. Cyr, Rip Bassett, Mancy Cara, Eddie Condon** (bj, g); **Lonnie Johnson, Eddie Lang** (g); **Peter Briggs** (tba); **Pops Foster** (b); **Baby Dodds, Tubby Hall, Zutty Singleton, Kaiser Marshall** (d); **Paul Barbarin** (d, vb); **Hoagy Carmichael, Joe Edwards, Susie Edwards, May Alix** (v), **Carroll Dickerson** (vn, dir). JSP Ⓕ CD312/3/4/5 (four discs, oas: 72, 67, 70, 68 minutes). Recorded 1925-31.

✓ ⑩ ❽

These four CDs contain what is undoubtedly one of the most important bodies of recorded work in the entire history of jazz. The first three volumes cover the two-and-a-half years during which all the

Hot Fives and Sevens titles were recorded in Chicago, the city to which Armstrong returned after his year with Fletcher Henderson (see below). There are priceless masterpieces to be heard here: the perfect *West End Blues* of course, but also gems such as *Potato Head Blues, Fireworks, Wild Man Blues* and the slightly later Armstrong-Hines duet *Weather Bird*. The Hot Five was essentially a recording band (it only appeared in public twice) but it represented the important period when Louis stepped outside the traditional New Orleans ensemble, focusing attention on the soloist. Strictly speaking, and despite the album titles, half of Volume Three and the whole of Volume Four are not by the Hot Five and Seven but by later bands put together by Carroll Dickerson, Luis Russell and others to back Armstrong. But no matter; the chronology and the continuing magic is complete. Volume Three ends with the splendid *Knockin' A Jug* by a racially mixed group (and marks the first time Louis and Jack Teagarden recorded together) while Volume Four has two very rare takes of *Rockin' Chair* and *I Can't Give You Anything But Love* in addition to the originals. The remastering throughout has been done by John R.T. Davies and must be rated as a high point even by his own superior standards in the field of record restoration. There is no doubt that these issues (and two further JSP CDs by Armstrong which continue the chronology) are the best available collections of these important recordings. **AM**

Louis Armstrong 1928-1931 **Armstrong** (t, v); with various groups including: **Henry Allen**, **Ed Anderson**, **Zilner Randolph** (t); **Fred Robinson**, **J.C. Higginbottom**, **Lawrence Brown**, **Preston Jackson** (tb); **Jimmy Strong**, **Don Redman**, **Albert Nicholas**, **Charlie Holmes**, **Teddy Hill**, **Les Hite** (reeds); **Earl Hines**, **Luis Russell**, **Buck Washington**, (p); **Mancy Cara**, **Eddie Condon** (bj); **Lonnie Johnson**, **Bernard Addison** (g); **Pops Foster**, **John Lindsay** (b); **Pete Briggs** (tba); **Zutty SIngleton**, **Paul Barbarin**, **Lionel Hampton**, **Tubby Hall** (d). Hermes Ⓜ HRM 6002 (63 minutes). Recorded 1928-31.

⑧ ❽

A chronological selection of 19 numbers recorded over the years in question, the period from the last Hot Five to the first of the big bands. This is not a disc for Armstrong specialists, but it would form a useful part of a general jazz collection, containing as it does such timeless works as *West End Blues*, *Black and Blue*, *I'm Confessin'*, the first *Mahogany Hall Stomp* and *Rockin' Chair* (with vocal by Hoagy Carmichael).

It need hardly be said that Armstrong's trumpet playing regularly touched sublime heights at this period, before the show-band routines had had a chance to become ingrained. And to anyone who associates Louis with gravel-voiced singing, his high, husky crooning of the late twenties will come as a delightful surprise. The music was digitally remastered not from old 78 copies but from clean acetate test pressings, and the result sounds remarkably fresh and unprocessed. **DG**

Satchmo: A Musical Autobiography **Armstrong** (t, v); **Edmond Hall**, **Barney Bigard** (cl); **Jack Teagarden**, **Trummy Young** (tb); **Bud Freeman** (ts); **Billy Kyle** (p); **Arvell Shaw**, **Squire Gersh** (b); **Sid Catlett**, **Barrett Deems** (d); **Velma Middleton** (v); **Sy Oliver** (arr, cond) and others. Jazz Unlimited Ⓕ JUCD 2003-05. (three discs: 209 minutes). Recorded 1947-57.

✔ ⑧ ❻

The idea of re-creating a large number of Armstrong's earlier hits came to fruition in 1956, and it paid off, because, unexpectedly, Armstrong plays even better on numbers like *Cornet Chop Suey* than he did on the original versions. The mass of this music gives a better idea of his imagination, humour and majesty than any other collection of CDs which come to mind. Along with the W.C. Handy and Waller sets on CBS, this music makes up the very finest collection of latter-day Armstrong. The best tracks are the ones by a version of his All Stars (Hall, Young and Kyle) augmented by a saxophone section. These recreate such hits of the thirties as *Lazy River*, *That's My Home* and *Sunny Side Of The Street*. The Hot Fives and Sevens of the twenties are well reinterpreted (not copied) with Edmund Hall on particularly fine form. Velma Middleton does a fair job of recalling some of the classic blues singers who Louis accompanied, although her work is best regarded as a foil for Armstrong's obbligati rather than for its own merit. Most of these tracks were studio recorded in 1956-57 and it is only a handful (the ones featuring Teagarden and Bigard) which come from the earlier period. The earlier tracks were often truncated by Decca, who made the original issues, but here they are restored to their full lengths. *Froggie Moore* was not in the original set and has been taken from the only copies located, both of which suffered from added reverberation. This is the only track which defied the rejuvenating recording techniques of sound engineer Dave Bennett, who has otherwise been able to do an excellent job. **SV**

The California Concerts **Armstrong** (t, v) with, in 1951: **Jack Teagarden** (tb, v); **Barney Bigard** (cl); **Earl Hines** (p); **Arvell Shaw** (b); **Cozy Cole** (d); **Velma Middleton** (v); in 1955: **Trummy Young** (tb, v); **Barney Bigard** (cl, v); **Billy Kyle** (p); **Arvell Shaw** (b); **Barrett Deems** (d); **Velma Middleton** (v). MCA/GRP Ⓜ 46132 (four discs: 184 minutes). Recorded 1951/55.

✔ ⑨ ❻

The fifties are generally regarded as a time of revived fortunes for Armstrong and these remarkable live recordings do nothing at all to gainsay such received opinions. Both sets of performances were famous in their own right as single LP releases, but this newly-remastered four-CD collection gives us the full story of the 1951 L.A. Civic Auditorium concert as part of a Gene Norman *Just Jazz* package, and also fills out the picture on a remarkable night's music at the Crescendo Club in early 1955.

The Civic concert features the original All-Stars line-up and shows the full extent of its fire and panache prior to the disaffection and subsequent departure of Hines and Teagarden. While Louis is clearly the leader, there is a sense of the co-operative give-and-take about this ensemble's performances which had been replaced by a carefully-guided spotlight on Armstrong by the time of the 1955 performances. Hines is a busy pianist, whether comping or soloing, and pushes the trumpeter all the way. Teagarden does such glorious things to the trombone that he's worth the price of the set by himself and at no stage does he sound like Armstrong's sideman. This is not to denigrate the 1955 sets at the Crescendo, because they have different plus points. But the people playing with Louis there—and I would include Bigard, who is present on both dates—know that they are his sidemen, and adapt their roles accordingly.

There is a wonderful sense of spontaneity (even though all the routines were well-grooved, and solos rehearsed) which the presence of an audience always evoked in Armstrong. His great fifties studio sessions may be more momentous events (and amongst those I would include the long-unavailable **Satchmo Plays King Oliver** on Audio Fidelity), but these concerts, familiar repertoire and all, tell us the real story. **KS**

Satch Plays Fats **Armstrong** (t, v); **Trummy Young** (tb); **Barney Bigard** (cl); **Billy Kyle** (p); **Arvell Shaw** (b); **Barrett Deems** (d); **Velma Middleton** (v). Columbia Ⓜ 450980-2 (38 minutes). Recorded 1955.

⑥ ❽

This version of the All Stars, in which Trummy Young's broad and sometimes vulgar gestures acted as both counterweight and goad to the maestro, was actually a much more balanced band than its predecessor with Jack Teagarden (it is a pity that there is no satisfactory album available from the period when clarinettist Edmund Hall had replaced Bigard). Many of these Fats Waller standards had been featured by Armstrong in years gone by, but few were in his active repertoire at the time of this recording. There are, of course, vocals on every track (Middleton appears on three, and has *Squeeze Me* to herself) and Louis's are better than average for this period, but it is the distilled majesty of the trumpet that compels attention. These latter-day versions of *Ain't Misbehavin'* and *Black and Blue* compare with his 1929 originals as the wisdom of middle age to the impetuosity of youth.

Humphrey Lyttelton's accompanying notes—clearly *not* "taken from the original analogue release"—detail exactly how that release differed from the present version, which omits Armstrong's overdubbed trumpet behind his voice, and replaces several previously edited takes. Despite this and the short playing time, the representation of Louis at a late peak is unbeatable. **BP**

Art Ensemble Of Chicago

The Art Ensemble 1967-68 **Lester Bowie** (t, perc); **Roscoe Mitchell**, **Joseph Jarman** (reeds, perc); **Malachi Favors Maghostut** (b, perc); **Philip Wilson**, **Thurman Barker**, **Robert Crowder** (d); **Charles Clark** (b). Nessa NCD-2500A-E. (five discs: 304 minutes). Recorded 1967-68.

✔ ⑧ ❽

Throughout the seventies and eighties, the Art Ensemble of Chicago was one of jazz's (or as they prefer, Great Black Music's) most innovative and exhilarating ensembles; their importance in the evolution of the music certainly ranks them with such groups as Jelly Roll Morton's Red Hot Peppers, Louis Armstrong's Hot Fives and Sevens, the classic quartets of John Coltrane and Ornette Coleman, and Miles Davis's quintets of the fifties and sixties. Their first works were in many ways their most iconoclastic, and much of the shocking experimentalism that subsequently influenced so many musicians came from the original concepts of Roscoe Mitchell. Until recently we have only had sketchy documentation of the group's crucial formative period, but thanks to the efforts of Chuck Nessa, a longtime supporter of the Art Ensemble, we now have a more complete picture of their amazing discoveries. Some of the previously unreleased material from this five-CD collection comes from rehearsal tapes (the sound quality is remarkably fine considering the source) where the original quartet—Mitchell, Lester Bowie, Malachi Favors and Philip Wilson, Joseph Jarman not yet having joined—are in the very process of creating a truly new music from Mitchell's ideas. In questioning every conceivable musical parameter, they are forming a new language with its own inherent drama, humour and form. The quartet's colours and dynamics are stunning, the ensemble relationship always coherent regardless of the broad range of individual emotions and unconventional instrumental voices. Listening to the newly released versions of *Number 1* and *Number 2* alongside those issued on LP, it is obvious that the four achieved an amazing unity of purpose. Multi-sectional, intricate and still flowing in design, the group improvisations cohere around quickness and appropriateness of response, as incongruous sounds and extremes of timbres blend subtly or clash vehemently, suggesting layers of irony and dramatic immediacy. By the last recordings here, issued on LP as **Congliptious**, the Art Ensemble (plus Jarman) was intact, sure in their methods and message, and ready to conquer Europe. This music remains as shocking and satisfying today as when it was initially created, and these recordings are essential to anyone wishing to understand one of the great post-bebop revolutions in jazz. **AL**

Full Force **Lester Bowie** (t); **Joseph Jarman** (af, f, cl, bcl, snino s, ss, as, ts, bs, bss, pic, bn, whistle, conch shell, cel, vb, gongs, cgas); **Roscoe Mitchell** (f,cl, ss, as, ts, bs, bss, pic, glockenspiel, gongs, cga); **Malachi Favors Maghostus** (melodica, b, perc, v); **Famoudou Don Moye** (whistles, conch shells, bikehorns, d, perc, bells, gongs, etc.). ECM Ⓔ1167 (829 197-2) (43 minutes). Recorded 1980.

⑧ ❿

After a spell of prolific music-making in France (many of which sessions are currently out of catalogue), the Art Ensemble returned to the US in 1972. Recording opportunities at home remained sporadic, but finally an agreement with the Munich-based ECM label brought a series of new releases that appeared between 1979 and 1985. **Nice Guys**, **Full Force**, the live **Urban Bushmen** and **The Third Decade** were typically erratic works, with passages of brilliant ensemble interplay (*Dreaming of the Master*) interspersed with longeurs and occasional ill-judged stabs at populism (*JA, Funky AECO*). **Full Force**, free of these latter traits, is the most consistent of the ECM albums and makes an attractive introduction to the group's versatile polystylism.

Full Force itself is a collective improvisation, all fast colours and humorous asides, while *Magg Zelma* is a more structured excursion into similar territory, its gentle array of "little instruments" the prelude to a series of stately, then agitated, horn passages. Other tracks hew closer to conventional form: *Charlie M*, Lester Bowie's Mingus tribute, is a smouldering ensemble prowl; Joseph Jarman's cheery *Old Time Southside Street Dance* is lit by volatile saxophones. Despite the later increase in their output, **Full Force** remains one of the Art Ensemble's more engaging sets. **GL**

Thelonious Sphere Monk: Dreaming of the Masters Volume 2—featuring Cecil Taylor **Lester Bowie** (t, flh, perc); **Joseph Jarman** (ss, as, ts, bs, fl, syn, perc); **Roscoe Mitchell** (as, ts, bss, f, pic, perc); **Malachi Favors Maghostut** (b, perc, belaf); **Famoudou Don Moye** (d, perc, ch, various percussion, bells etc.); **Cecil Taylor** (p). DIW Ⓔ 846E (62 minutes). Recorded 1990.

⑦ ❿

After their early masterpieces, the AEC went on to refine and sharpen their procedures, but there is little evidence for a broadening of scope or any significant change in direction. Thus many of their albums from the seventies and eighties are excellently executed, mostly superbly engineered, and quite often lacking focus and urgency. It becomes increasingly rare to find anyone within the band with a burning musical issue to get across to the listener, and the musical parodies and reconstructions become increasingly central to the group's raison d'être. The significant work achieved by all three of the horn players—Bowie, Jarman and Mitchell—is mostly to be found in their own projects, away from the AEC.

This album, dating from a flurry of activity for the DIW label as the eighties sputtered to an end and the nineties staggered in behind them, finds them with a broader canvas than usual and a number of intriguing solutions to some of the constraints and problems posed by their collective make-up. The question of form is both directly addressed here (especially in two of the pieces involving Taylor, *Excerpt from Fifteen* and *Caseworks*) or flagrantly ignored (the third piece with Taylor, *Intro to Fifteen*, is a clear example), with provocative results. Taylor here sounds unusually 'connected' to a group which is not his own, and much excellent music is made along the way. The Monk compositions, *'Round Midnight* and *Nutty*, add little to anyone's view of Monk, but are fun nonetheless and illustrate the measures each AEC member has individually had to take to renew the band's music: Bowie leads the line, but no-one 'solos' anymore. This avoids falling into solo conventions that even their late seventies albums suffer from and allows the form to be more truly plastic.

An absorbing listen, then, although *Intro to Fifteen* is certainly neither Taylor's or the AEC's finest moment on records, and at 18 minutes in length, is perilously close to self-indulgence. **KS**

Georges Arvanitas

1931

Arvanitas Trio with Francis Darizcuren **Arvanitas** (p); **Francis Darizcuren** (vn); **Jacky Samson** (b); **Charles Saudrais** (d). EPM Ⓔ 982252 (60 minutes). Recorded 1992.

⑥ ❽

Marseilles-born Arvanitas is one of the many fine post-war French pianists. He has worked with a variety of Americans, from Albert Nicholas to David Murray, by way of Chet Baker and Ben Webster. A valuable accompanist, his trio has worked together since the late sixties and here they provide Basque violinist Darizcuren with exemplary support, sensing with accuracy the need to increase or decrease the tension. The violinist is an excellent technician (not always the case with all jazz violinists) who can double-stop with accuracy, notably in the theme statement of the 12-bar *Ça Alors*. He receives a written accolade from Stephane Grappelli in the accompanying booklet and there is a careful version of Reinhardt's *Nuages* in the 15-tune programme. *Digital Dream* is an unaccompanied violin solo making use of electronic delay devices and, although credited to Darizcuren, the entire theme of Bud Powell's *Parisian Thoroughfare* crops up in the middle. In fact something seems to have gone slightly awry with the composer listing in places; *Cute, You're So Cute* is actually Neal Hefti's tune *Cute* and not a Darizcuren original while *To Big Mike* turns out to be a medley of known songs. Arvanitas briefly switches to electric piano but he comes into his own on *Claude et Catherine*, a fine piano solo full of the post-Bud Powell and Hank Jones feeling that we associate with this excellent pianist. **AM**

Harold Ashby

1925

The Viking Ashby (ts); **Norman Simmons** (p); **Paul West** (b); **Gerryck King** (d). Gemini Ⓕ GMCD 60 (49 minutes). Recorded 1988.

⑧ ❽

Ashby deputised for various members of the Duke Ellington sax section over a period of years before he gained a permanent place, taking over from the departed Jimmy Hamilton at the 1968 Newport Jazz Festival. He makes no secret of his admiration for the late Ben Webster; the two recorded together and, for a time, shared an apartment. Inevitably Ashby sounds like Ben at times, especially when producing his ravishing version of *I Got It Bad* (included here amongst the eight tracks, four of them being Ashby originals). The music is uncomplicated, enjoyable at various levels and is, in many ways, the epitome of contemporary mainstream jazz. Ashby was attending the Oslo Jazz Festival when this recording was made and he is supported by a fine rhythm team, then working as accompanists to singer Joe Williams. The session took place in Oslo's Rainbow Studio, a location which has been the venue for many other well recorded jazz albums put out by Gemini. The power of Harold's playing has been expertly captured, together with that breathy approach to ballads which is an ever-present legacy of his continuing admiration for Webster. **AM**

Arne Astrup

Seven Brothers Astrup (ts); **Paul Hindberg** (cl); **Louis Hjulmand** (vb); **Mogens Petersen** (p); **Frits von Bulow** (g); **Jorgen Johnbeck** (b); **Hans Sorensen** (d). Olufsen Ⓕ DOCD 5126 (61 minutes). Recorded 1989-90.

⑥ ❻

Tenor player Astrup is best-known internationally for his exemplary discographical work on such major figures as Gerry Mulligan and Stan Getz. As is often the case, however, his own abilities on the saxophone have gone largely unrecognized outside his native Denmark. This is a shame, because not only does his career span close on 50 years of playing, but he is a well-schooled and warm player in the progressive tradition of the post-war years. This album features his Septet and at times it sounds more like the late-forties Goodman small-groups than a post-bop band. Still, this fact should hinder no-one's enjoyment of a smoothly-swinging and urbane collection of arrangements. The great majority of pieces here are originals, though Parker's *Scrapple From The Apple* gets a re-appraisal, courtesy of Paul Hindberg's arrangement. Hindberg's own playing is very much in the shadow of Goodman, while Astrup's has a friendly personality of its own. **KS**

Eden Atwood

1969

There Again Atwood (v); **Dave Berkman** (p); **Michael Moore** (b); **Ron Vincent** (d); with **Marian McPartland** (p) on two tracks; **Chris Potter** (ts) on four tracks. Concord Ⓕ CCD 4645 (56 minutes). Recorded 1994/95.

⑥ ❿

This is Atwood's third album for Concord in quick succession, and signifies a step towards musical maturity. Her first two showed her to have a clean, acceptably versatile, technically competent voice which shone most brightly on medium tempo swingers. She showed no particular aptitude for the slower ballads also attempted on those discs. On **There Again** she still sounds most comfortable on these swingers, with *You're My Thrill* having a nicely balanced combination of flirtatiousness and sheer enjoyment of the situation, and *In Love In Vain* showing her ability to inject irony into a situation.

But progress has been made with the ballads: *The Nearness of You* succeeds quite acceptably, as does *Music That Makes Me Dance*. *It Never Entered My Mind*, quite frankly, still has a "danger—deep water" sign in front of it for her, although she makes an honest attempt at rendering it. She just does not yet have the inner intensity to make songs such as this burn. Yet there is much to enjoy in her singing, and the more straightforward songs of love, lust and life are delivered with nothing less than panache. Atwood has come a long way, has a long way still to go, and it will be interesting for we listeners to trace her journey on the albums undoubtedly still to come. **KS**

Lovie Austin

1887–1972

1924–1926 **Austin** (p); **Tommy Ladnier, Natty Dominique** (c); **Kid Ory** (tb); **Johnny Dodds, Jimmy O'Bryant** (cl); **Eustern Woodfork** (bj); **W.E. Burton** (d, perc); **Edmonia Henderson, Ford & Ford, Priscilla Stewart, Viola Bartlette, Henry Williams** (v). Classics Ⓜ 756 (73 minutes). Recorded 1924-26.

⑧ ❷

Although active on the vaudeville circuit, Austin and her fine groups were frequent visitors to the Paramount recording studios. She made outstanding sides with the major blues singers, but the two years covered by this CD present her at her finest, in the company of her Blues Serenaders and playing many of her own compositions. Austin was that rarity among piano leaders in that she took no solos. She was a cajoler rather than a challenger and she was happiest in her ensemble role, calibrating each selection and guaranteeing that neither tuba nor string bass were missed. Her arrangements were rudimentary but effective and the likes of *Steppin' On The Blues* and *Mojo Blues* were models of concision. Sound balances varied even on the original recordings and, if she is too dominant on *Too Sweet*, the contrast occurs when Woodfork's banjo backs her on the final session. When the piano is favoured, as behind Dodds and Ory on *Jackass Blues*, she is more able to present her 'solo' piano voice.

Later in her life she became a musical director in Chicago theatres, worked as accompanist in a dancing school and, in 1961, actually recorded again (Prestige/Bluesville Original Blues Classics OBCCD 510). Nevertheless, it was the Serenaders's titles, in the company of masters like Ladnier, Dodds and Ory, for which she will be remembered. **BMcR**

Teodross Avery

1973

In Other Words **Avery** (ss, ts); **Roy Hargrove** (t, flh); **Charles Craig** (p); **Reuben Rogers** (b); **Mark Simmons** (d). GRP Ⓕ GRP 97982 (72 minutes). Recorded 1994

⑧ ❽

Every so often a young player emerges on whom high expectations are placed at every stage of his or her career. Avery's career is still in its infancy, but this first album suggests why so much is expected of him. Not yet 21 at the time of this recording, Avery's reputation as a remarkable young talent is the Bay Area tradition of Benny Green and Joshua Redman had preceded him eastwards to Berklee College of Music in Boston, where he formed the nucleus of the group that appears here. There are two striking things about the album. One is the melodic quality of Avery's playing - notable in the themes of his own writing, like *Our True Friends*, one of nine of his own compositions on the disc, and in his individual and similarly melodic interpretation of those themes. The language is, like that of so many saxophonists of his generation, Coltrane-inspired. The dialiect is his own. The second striking thing is Avery's rapport with pianist Craig, whose clean touch displays similar clarity of thought and melodic invention. The presence of Hargrove on three tracks is a bonus, especially his less-familiar flugelhorn playing, which is the focus of *Positive Role Models*, a title which (perhaps too) neatly sums up the artistic thrust of the album. The UK release has a bonus track, for anyone who wants this much of a new thing. **AS**

Albert Ayler

1936-1970

Spiritual Unity **Ayler** (ts); **Gary Peacock** (b); **Sunny Murray** (d). ESP Ⓜ1002-2 (30 minutes). Recorded 1964.

✔ ⑩ ❻

Ayler had experience with the r&b field before spending almost three years with military bands in Europe. On release, he decided not to return to America and for some time worked in Sweden, where he made his first somewhat inchoate recordings, wrestling unsuccessfully with bebop. A period with Cecil Taylor and a return to the US helped to clear his mind and to formulate a style that was to make him one of jazz's outstanding innovators on the tenor saxophone. *Spiritual Unity* was Ayler's **Saxophone Colossus** and **Giant Steps** and it provides an ideal example of his style. It uses very basic, almost folk-like tunes and shows how each slender thematic starting point projects his solos on their path. There are inevitable variations and, whereas *The Wizard's* development circles back to a simple paraphrase of the original, the *Spirits* solo is departmentalized into thematic sub-areas, each using the same harmonic base, yet all exploring at different levels of melodic density and emotional power. *Ghosts II* is the better of the two takes that offer further examples of Ayler's improvisational method, although it is *Ghosts I* that perhaps emphasizes the aptness of his primitive sound and unique phrase shapes. On all he is superbly complemented by Peacock, who shoulders most of the responsibility for rhythmic and harmonic movement, and Murray, who provides the textural stratum while swinging in a detached, almost subliminal manner. The three men make this a very important jazz CD. **BMcR**

Spirits Rejoice **Ayler** (ts); **Donald Ayler** (t); **Charles Tyler** (as); **Henry Grimes, Gary Peacock** (b); **Sunny Murray** (d); **Call Cobbs** (h). ESP-Disk Ⓜ ESP 1020-2 (33 minutes). Recorded 1965.

⑩ ❹

As was true during his brief career, critical discourse on Ayler still tends to emphasize the intensity and dark spirituality of his music, with little attention paid to the the humour of which he was capable when playing with other horns (though it must be acknowledged that listening to Ayler has always been a guessing game, inasmuch as no one can be certain of what was intended as irony and what was evidence of madness). Along with *Bells* from the same year, *Spirits Rejoice* is where Ayler's humour first came to the fore, showing up not only in the allusions to *Le Marseillaise* on the title-track and the echoes of Salvation Army bands throughout, but also in the way that Ayler's solos vacillate between ecstasy and what could be interpreted as self-mockery. Then still in Ayler's thrall, Tyler is often virtually indistinguishable from him, a similarity compounded by the poor recording quality (the sound here is better than on the original LP, however) and the tendency of both saxophonists to pitch their solos in the altissimo register. The bassists are practically inaudible except during their solos, but Murray's drum interjections are strongly felt, as are Donald Ayler's fractured trumpet solos, which have a hint of Booker Little to them, although delivered at twice the speed. Cobbs's silent-film harpsichord is present only on *Angels*, a rubato ballad on which Ayler—exiled from the jazz canon by those who prefer to pretend that the sixties never happened—recalls no one so much as Sidney Bechet, with his oversized vibrato and the operatic scale of his emotion. You cannot get more 'in the tradition' than that. **FD**

In Greenwich Village **Ayler** (ts, as); **Donald Ayler** (t); **Michel Sampson** (vn); **Joel Freedman** (vc); **Bill Folwell, Henry Grimes, Alan Silva** (b); **Beaver Harris** (d). Impulse! Ⓜ MCAD-39123 (37 minutes). Recorded 1966-67.

✔ ⑩ ❽

In the spring of 1966 the Albert Ayler quartet was joined by violinist Michel Sampson and in November this new five-piece toured Europe. Several concerts from this tour have appeared on record, although in many cases the sound quality is poor. Fortunately, Ayler's new label Impulse! recorded the group live shortly after their return to New York; on December 18 (with the addition of second bassist Henry Grimes) and again on February 25, with Alan Silva replacing Grimes and cellist Joel Freedman added. Widely regarded as his definitive album, **In Greenwich Village** certainly marks a watershed in Ayler's evolution. It is tempting to hear the November *Truth Is Marching In* as the majestic climax to that brief period, from 1964-67, when Ayler produced nearly all of his greatest music. Here are the marching tunes, the fanfares, the abrupt group free-for-alls, the squealing overblowing and ripe, vibrato all gathered together with thundering drums and frantic, swirling violin for a last procession of raggedy grandeur.

The disc's other great track is *For John Coltrane*, from the February concert. Accompanied only by the basses and Freedman's intense cello, Ayler turns to alto saxophone, his lines soaring with fluent, melodic grace. The ethereality of the piece seemed to bespeak a transformation of Ayler's visceral energies into a feeling for space and light. But although changes were imminent in his music, in the event they were to take a very different turn. **GL**

Love Cry **Ayler** (as, ts); **Don Ayler** (t); **Call Cobbs** (h); **Alan Silva** (b); **Milford Graves** (d). Impulse! GRP Ⓜ 11082 (54 minutes). Recorded 1967-68.

⑧ ❿

This is the last good album Ayler made before his precipitous decline. In an odd sense, it is a little like a 'greatest hits' package, with six of the eight tunes being straightforward unison statements of the main theme, plus a little sprinkling of trumpet obbligato thrown in for good luck. On the original LP issue of **Love Cry** this impression was all the more intense, because that album carried only *Universal Indians* as a track containing any significant degree of improvisation by Ayler or his brother. The rest of it we could all presumably sing along with. And good clean fun it all was, too.

This CD reissue redresses this balance by including another edit of *Universal Indians* (same take, just more of it), plus a previously unissued track, *Love Cry 11* (not to be confused with *Love Cry*, to which it bears no resemblance). Both get quite wild enough, thereby demonstrating what a superbly apposite drummer for the Aylers Graves really was. This new material puts the bite back into the overall message and puts this album in a position much more central to the Ayler tradition. A fitting valé to a major artist, even if he did not see it that way himself at the time.

Compared to the dire low-fi to be found on earlier, non-Impulse! Aylers, this one sounds like it was recorded in Paradise. **KS**

Azimuth

Azimuth '85 **John Taylor** (p, org); **Kenny Wheeler** (t, flh); **Norma Winstone** (v). ECM Ⓕ 1298 (827 520-2) (44 minutes). Recorded 1985.

⑥ ❿

Azimuth is one of those groups which so closely defines the ECM ethos. Just like Eberhard Weber's early efforts, or Terje Rypdal's continuing odyssey of sound, they create both the intellectual and sonic environment for that Cathedral-like ECM resonance to emerge in all its glory. The space the music naturally has enhances this quality to the point that every note in each chord, every melodic filament of the greater whole, is etched unerringly across your mental palette.

It is possible that all this was once challenging to the listener; now it seems comforting, or comfortable, like a well-worn jacket which fits perfectly. A quality product which serves you well. No mood or emotion becomes overpowering; nothing seems ill thought-out, or the subject of an irresistable impulse. If you like musical understatement, wistfulness and elliptical melodic shapes conveying faintly other-wordly notions and sentiments, then this album will strongly appeal. It is not New Age music, because it has bucketloads more musical ideas in one minute than a whole New Age album uses up in 60, and it has three superbly talented improvising musicians involved. However, if one was not careful, the end result could superficially be confused with New Age, Wheeler's eloquence notwithstanding.

KS

Alice Babs

1924

Far Away Star **Babs** (v); **Duke Ellington Orchestra**; **Nils Lindberg Orchestra**. Bluebell Ⓕ ABCD005 (36 minutes). Recorded 1973/1976.

④ ❽

No-one has ever accounted for Ellington's Achilles' heel—the ability to select what appeared to be totally unsuitable singers for his orchestra. Babs was the shining example of the exception to the rule. Her extraordinary voice enables her to be equally at home with pop music, Mozart or Ellington, and she has a feeling for jazz which never lets her down. Even when she has scat exchanges with the trumpets in the band on *Spacemen* her jazz sense never falters, and she has all the abilities of the more established Ellingtonian soloists.

Babs's voice is truly unique and in the four numbers with the 1973 Ellington band her voice highlights the fabric of the orchestral ensembles behind her. This effect is particularly evident on the beautiful *Far Away Star* and on *Jeep's Blues* she is as lyrical as the normal incumbent of that work, Johnny Hodges, used to be.

The tracks with Lindberg use mostly Ellington material and include his best ballad, *Warm Valley* and a second version (the first is with Ellington) of the beautiful *Serenade To Sweden*, a fortuitous tribute to Miss Babs's native land.

SV

Benny Bailey

1925

For Heaven's Sake **Bailey** (t); **Tony Coe** (ts, ss, cl); **Horace Parlan** (p); **Jimmy Woode** (b); **Idris Mohammad** (d). Hot House Ⓕ HHCD1006 (53 minutes). Recorded 1988.

⑧ ❽

Born in Cleveland, Ohio, Benny Bailey worked with Jay McShann, Dizzy Gillespie and Lionel Hampton before settling in Europe in 1953 to become one of the most sought-after session trumpet players on the entire continent. He is a faultless section leader and a hugely inventive soloist. Curiously, the reputation of being a successful man at the top of his profession has caused him to become invisible to jazz commentators; if he had been in and out of jail for a series of lurid offences the press would have beaten a path to his door.

Although he has spent his life in recording studios, this album is one of the few to be issued under his own name. For an example of Benny Bailey's exceptional jazz talent you need only to hear the first number, Roy Eldridge's *Little Jazz*; swinging, resourceful, witty, without a trace of vulgarity or empty show. Everyone on the date plays superbly and there is a great feeling of relaxed enjoyment about the proceedings. If this had been recorded in New York and issued on Blue Note it would have had five-star reviews everywhere. Since it was made in London and issued by a small British company it was largely overlooked. Fortunately for us it is still available.

DG

Derek Bailey

1931

Figuring **Bailey** (g); **Barre Phillips** (b). Incus Ⓕ CD05 (58 minutes). Recorded 1987-88.

⑩ ❽

Bailey is one of the very few British-born jazz musicians who has been an influence on his peers worldwide. His career began in the most commercial circles, and he even played in the pit at the London Palladium. Having decided that he wanted to take a more creative path, he became involved with the Spontaneous Music Ensemble and other members of the London's free improvisation movement. This CD, a culture shock for newcomers, takes the listener to the heart of his style. There is no episodic continuity but his essentially chromatic music is played with scrupulous accuracy. Ideas are thrown up, flourish briefly and then end abruptly as these musicians move to the next exposition. As a duo, Bailey and Phillips play together superbly: they listen to each other yet never completely tailor their lines to those of their team-mate. Bailey's work has been described as "avant-garde bottleneck" and, following his convoluted, slurring path through a solo, it is not difficult to see why this should be so. An essential avant-garde purchase. **BMcR**

Judy Bailey 1935

Sundial Bailey (p, arr); **James Morrison** (tb); **Graeme Lyall** (as); **Sandy Evans**, **Paul Williams** (ts); **Craig Scott** (b); **Simon Barker** (d); **Erana Clark** (v). ABC Jazz Ⓔ 514 978-2 (75 minutes). Recorded 1993.

⑤ ❽

Judy Bailey first made an impact in Australian jazz circles in the early sixties, when her distinctive piano came to be heard amongst the progressive players coalescing around the El Rocco in Sydney's King's Cross. She and Bryce Rhode both brought a fresh and exciting openness to their playing which announced the casting aside of the hopeless pursuit of Powell-like brilliance and intensity and the turning to a new balance between composition and improvisation.

This latest album from Bailey shows her concerns to have developed but not radically altered since then. She still has a consuming passion for sound, especially the sound of the piano, and her harmonic choices, even on a relatively routine excursion through Ellington's *Do Nothing 'Til You Hear From Me*, constantly bring a smile to the lips. Which is just as well, as Duke's soulful ballad is singularly ill-served by Erana Clark's overly-mannered, showbizzy vocals. Other lapses of taste on the album include a spirited but ultimately pointless trio reinvention of *Waltzing Matilda* and a truly Amateur-Night level vocal from Clark on *Smoke Gets In Your Eyes*. In between all this, however, there is a great deal of excellent and oft-inspired music-making, with the most scintillating playing generally coming on the Bailey originals, of which there are nine here. A flawed and uneven disc, but one with enough good things to be going on with. **KS**

Mildred Bailey 1907-1951

The Rockin' Chair Lady Bailey (v) with: **The Casa Loma Orchestra**; **Her Alley Cats** (Bunny Berigan [t]; Johnny Hodges [as]; Teddy Wilson [p]; Grachan Moncur [b]); **The Delta Rhythm Boys**; small group with **Herman Chittison** (p); **Dave Barbour** (g); **Frenchy Covetti** (b); **Jimmy Hoskins** (d); **Harry Sosnick & His Orchestra** (Billy Butterfield [t]; Jack Jenney [tb]; Jimmy Lytell [cl]; Sal Franzella [bcl]; Billy Kyle [p]; Carmen Mastren [g]; Charlie Barbour [b]; O'Neil Spencer [d]); **Vic Schoen & His Orchestra** (John Best [t]; Murray McEachern, Ed Kusby, Hoyt Bohannon, Sy Zenter [tb]; Wilbur Schwartz, Ted Nash [as]; Johnny Rotella [ts]; Rudy Herman [bs]; Willy Usher [p]; Al Hendrickson [g]; Joe Mondragon, Irv Cottler [d]). MCA Ⓜ GRP 16442 (63 minutes). Recorded 1931-50.

✔ ⑩ ❽

If it had not been for Billie Holiday, there is little doubt that Mildred Bailey would now be regarded as *the* jazz voice of the thirties, the young Ella notwithstanding. Her voice was light and sensual, her sense of rhythm remarkably supple, her diction clear. This collection not only bears out the opening sentiment, but also produces a handy snaphot guide to the majority of her entire recording career. She first made a name as featured vocalist with The Paul Whiteman Orchestra (she was with him from 1929-34); the earliest recording in this set, from 1931 and using the Casa Loma Orchestra as backing, is cast in the Whiteman style of the day and shows Bailey's singing to be deeply rooted in the declamatory, emotive style then in vogue on Broadway. By 1935 her jazz phrasing is fully evolved, her use of blues-inflected swoops and glides is idiomatic: the only left-over from Broadway is an occasional broad vibrato or shake at the finish of a note (she was certainly not alone in using this technique). By 1941, such decoration has been judged superfluous and discarded, and the sessions from that year reveal an artistry which is perfect and an interpretive depth which is completely fulfilling. Indeed, the versions of *Rockin' Chair* (her one big hit, back in 1930) and *Georgia On My Mind* have rarely been bettered, such is their sense of ease and their remarkable quiet eloquence. In all there are nine tracks from 1941 on this collection, and every one deserves the status of a classic.

Finally, a note of commendation to transfer engineers Steven Lasker and Erick Labson at MCA Studios, who have done an exceptional job in giving us such a clear, full sound. **KS**

Chet Baker 1929-1988

The Pacific Jazz Years Baker (t, v); with various personnels including: **Don Fagerquist** (t); **Frank Rosolino** (tb); **Bob Brookmeyer** (vtb); **Art Pepper**, **Bud Shank**, **Herb Geller** (as); **Stan Getz**,

Phil Urso, Herb Geller, Jack Montrose, Bill Holman, Bill Perkins (ts); **Gerry Mulligan** (bs); **Russ Freeman, Pete Jolly, Bobby Timmons** (p); **Carson Smith, Red Mitchell, Leroy Vinnegar, Monty Budwig** (b); **Chico Hamilton, Larry Bunker, Bob Neel, Shelly Manne, Mel Lewis** (d); **Jack Montrose, Bill Holman, Bob Zieff** (arr); **Annie Ross** (v). Pacific Jazz Ⓜ CDP7 89292-2 (four discs: 226 minutes). Recorded 1952-57.

⑧ ❼

Baker hit musical highs all through his career, but there is little doubt that they arrived most consistently during the fifties. The trumpeter made his deepest impact during his initial stay in the Gerry Mulligan Quartet, and that group's initial recordings propelled Baker into the international spotlight. The famous *My Funny Valentine* (made for Fantasy at the instigation of Dave Brubeck) is not included here, although you get an excellent live version, almost twice as long as the studio one, which is every bit as intense. Much of the material in this compilation has been available on CD in various forms in the past few years, but this is a very handy way to gather together a representative sampling of the trumpeter at his best or near-best, amongst musicians sympathetic to his art and stimulating to his soul.

Baker's association with Mulligan lasted less than 12 months; his more long-term partnership with Russ Freeman gets a healthy representation here, as well as the dates with Stan Getz, Art Pepper, Phil Urso and Herb Geller. The larger ensembles, used mostly as a foil for Baker's melodicism, function cleanly and with appropriate spirit, while the much-lauded 1957 reunion with Mulligan is given three tracks (for a review of the complete session, see below). Baker had a unique gift and many of the recordings sampled here finds that gift displayed to its fullest advantage. That, plus the useful booklet and sturdy packaging of the four discs, suffering less than usual from the EMI art department's idea of meaningful design, makes this a convenient summary of Baker's art. **KS**

Chet Baker & Crew **Baker** (t, v); **Phil Urso** (ts); **Bobby Timmons** (p); **Jimmy Bond** (b); **Peter Littman** (d); **Bill Loughbrough** (perc). Pacific Jazz Ⓜ CDP7 81205 2 (64 minutes). Recorded 1956.

⑧ ❽

In the fifties Baker became an international jazz star largely on the strength of a still fresh-sounding series of recordings made under the auspices of Pacific Jazz producer Richard Bock. Here we catch one of his best groups from the period, a unit that had toured Europe and the US prior to this recording. It's no surprise then that it exhibits a high degree of cohesion and empathy. Ex-Herman-ite Urso also adds an edge, while Bobby Timmons adds a significant presence. The disc contains hauntingly cool West Coast-style tracks like Urso's *Halema*, a wistful melody with Baker's gorgeous balladry in full flight. But in lines like the quintet's steely take on Gerry Mulligan's *Revelation*, there is a heels-dug-in quality where Urso's urgent tenor and Baker's Miles-ish trumpet crackle together. For *To Mickey's Memory* (based on *I'll Remember April*) the quintet is augmented by the chromatic tympani of Bill Loughbrough; it's also a take that bears comparison to Blakey's and Silver's mid-fifties *Jazz Messengers*. Among the bonus tracks on this CD reissue is a buoyant limning of Mulligan's *Line For Lyons*, with a perfectly beautiful Baker vocal. **CB**

The Italian Sessions **Baker** (t); **Bobby Jaspar** (ts, f); **Amadeo Tommasi** (p); **René Thomas** (g); **Benoit Querson** (b); **Daniel Humair** (d). RCA Bluebird Ⓜ 2001-2 (55 minutes). Recorded 1962.

⑧ ❹

By 1962, Baker was living in Italy, where he was reunited with two players from his 1955 Paris dates in an international sextet boasting a great Belgian guitarist, Swiss drummer and Belgian tenor saxophonist. Baker is in exceptionally good lip; the heavy Miles Davis influence often imputed to him is virtually nowhere in evidence. Instead, he sounds indebted (like Miles) to Dizzy Gillespie, judging by his crackling uptempo work on Monk's *Well, You Needn't*, his aggressive attack and singing vibrato on Tommasi's *Ballata in forma di blues*, his fat brass timbre on Pettiford's uptempo *Blues in the Closet*. Even on the slow ballads *These Foolish Things* and *Over the Rainbow*, Baker's introspective playing has substantial body.

Fellow soloists Jaspar, Thomas and Tommasi set the hard-bop tone, different from the laid-back groupings Baker habitually appeared in. Bird's calypso *Barbados* even has a shout chorus at the end. Many jazz fans, Americans especially, think fluent European jazz musicians are a recent phenomenon, but this crew speaks the language with no awkward accent. They challenge Baker, who rises to the task. About the only thing wrong with this session is the tinny, echo-ridden recorded sound. Chet doesn't even get to sing ... **KW**

& Paul Desmond Together: The Complete Studio Recordings **Baker** (t, v); **Paul Desmond** (as); **Jim Hall** (g); **Bob James, Kenny Barron, Roland Hanna** (p); **Ron Carter** (b); **Steve Gadd, Tony Williams** (d). Epic Ⓜ 472984-2 (56 minutes). Recorded 1974-77.

⑥ ❽

Baker and Desmond did not record much together, and were not the most obvious of partners, being too much like each other for comfort, so one imagines that the reason for this CD—a compilation from three other Epic records—is mostly nostalgic. Baker and Desmond are both comparatively recently dead, so there is a kind of wispy logic in teaming them retrospectively. Baker was always seen as a tough survivor who played fragile, dreamy trumpet, while Paul Desmond had more the corporate image—Mr Nice Guy in the Brubeck set-up—but against expectations it is Baker who comes across as the stronger soloist here, more forceful and more memorable. Nearly 20 minutes of the 60 is devoted to one piece, Rodrigo's *Concierto de Aranjuez*—strange, the appeal this piece has had for jazz musicians. **MK**

The Touch Of Your Lips **Baker** (t, v); **Doug Raney** (g); **Niels-Henning Ørsted Pederson** (b). SteepleChase Ⓕ SCCD 31122 (43 minutes). Recorded 1979.

⑧ ❻

Baker's restless life-style was clearly an expensive road to ultimate self-destruction, causing him to be ever-ready to make records, especially during his years in Europe. For that reason one has to be circumspect in one's choice from the dozens of albums which continue to appear under his name, but this one may be purchased with safety. Recorded in Copenhagen, it is one of the warmest and most intimate examples of Baker's craft on one of his very good days. Doug Raney (son of Jimmy) is ideal in this context, with a warm sound and expert knowledge of chords, while NHØP is a tower of strength and dependability. When one considers that there is no fixed-pitch instrument in this trio, there are no intonation problems, nor do Raney and NHØP experience any harmonic clashes. Chet's trumpet sound is fragile on the ballads, and one immediately warms to his work; even the very occasional cracked note evokes a feeling of sympathy in the listener, for this is great trumpet playing in the tradition of Bix, Bobby Hackett and Miles Davis. Baker sings on the title track and on *But Not For Me*, indulging in a chorus of scat on the latter. The vocals neither add to nor diminish the value of a recommended CD on which the clarity of the recording adds to the intimacy of the music. **AM**

Ginger Baker 1937

Going Back Home **Baker** (d); **Bill Frisell** (g); **Charlie Haden** (b). Atlantic Ⓕ 782652-2 (45 minutes). Recorded 1994.

⑧ ❾

What's going on? Is this really the man who played in Cream all those years ago? Yes, it is. Baker was a jazzer long before he stumbled into r&b and, later, rock. His personal odyssey has since seen him deeply involved in many musical styles, including the African beat a good 15 years before it was hip. Here he closes the circle and plays rinky-tink variations like someone who never went away. This is another power trio, but of a very different ilk to the Baker-Bruce-Clapton one who would deliver high-volume jams on *Spoonful* for 15 minutes. Here the irresistible momentum of Baker's stroll is matched by the deep hue of Haden's beautiful tone and powerful rhythm. Frisell, meanwhile, remains a light and agile performer, content to react to the directions fed him by the other two members of the trio. This relationship works admirably because all three players have the imagination and empathy to investigate unusual angles in mutually enhancing ways, especially when it comes to such latter-day jazz standards as *Straight, No Chaser* and *Ramblin'*. An impressive showing for all three musicians. **KS**

Kenny Baker 1921

The Boss Is Home **Baker, Derek Healey, Bruce Adams, Simon Gardner** (t); **Don Lusher, Bill Geldard, Richard Edwards** (tb); **Roy Willox, Alan Barnes, Vic Ash, Dave Willis, Eddie Mordue** (reeds); **Brian Dee** (p); **Dave Green** (b); **Ralph Salmins** (d). Big Bear Ⓕ ESSCD 224 (70 minutes). Recorded 1993.

⑧ ❻

The weekly broadcasts by Kenny Baker's Dozen during the fifties brought succour to beleaguered European jazz fans who were, by union restrictions, denied live American jazz. This recreation of the days of the Dozen, recorded live at Ronnie Scott's in Birmingham, builds nicely on the original and manages to be contemporary while holding on to the nostalgic spirit.

These spirited performances blow away the usual 'show band' ennui of what have become known as graveyard groups. Baker always chose his material well and here it varies from *Street Of Dreams*, *Stumbling* (with its startling explosion of trumpet from Bruce Adams) and *When Sunny Gets Blue* to an unhackneyed clutch of Ellingtonia which includes the little-heard *Golden Cress,* arranged by Baker for the trombone of Don Lusher, to the shouting *In A Jam*, which includes one of several solos on the album by Richard Edwards, an emergent trombone great.

Baker is liberal with solo space and his team of soloists, youngsters and veterans alike, respond magnificently to produce a triumph of melodic, swinging mainstream jazz. **SV**

Kenny Ball 1930

Strictly Jazz **Ball** (t); **John Bennett** (tb); **Dave Jones** (cl); **Colin Bates, Ron Weatherburn** (p); **Diz Disley, Tony Pitt, Paddy Lightfoot** (bj); **Vic Pit** (b); **Ron Bowden** (d). Kaz Ⓜ CD19 (75 minutes). Recorded 1960-62.

⑤ ❻

Some listeners might quibble with the title, but Ball is synonymous with the Dixieland end of the 'Trad' phenomenon in sixties Britain, and this album collates much of his best work from the dawn of that period. The liner insert contains no personnel or recording details, but most of this material dates from Ball's recordings for Pye or Enja, including one 'live' concert from Liverpool's Empire Theatre.

The banjo is relentless and dominant, but Jones plays a full and accomplished clarinet, while Ball and Bennett supply energetic and full-ranged brass work, consistent with Ball's background in larger bands with great demands on iron-lipped trumpeters. Weatherburn is the star pianist, and Bowden relaxes from the straightjacket of the fifties Chris Barber band which he had joined at its inception. Missing are Ball's great hits, *Samantha* and *Midnight in Moscow*, but the album has a full sweep of the early Dixieland repertoire from *Ole Miss* to *Ostrich Walk*. *High Society* has Ball's party piece of shadowing the classic clarinet choruses on trumpet. **AS**

Iain Ballamy
1964

All Men Amen **Ballamy** (ss, as); **Django Bates** (p, kbds, frh); **Steve Watts** (b); **Martin France** (d, perc). B&W Music Ⓕ BW065 (45 minutes). Recorded 1994.

⑧ ❽

Although somewhat under-recorded as a leader (his previous album, **Balloon Man**, featuring the same personnel as above, was released in 1989), Iain Ballamy has established himself as a highly individual voice since the demise of Loose Tubes. His is a light-toned, breathily intimate saxophone sound more overtly beholden to, say, Warne Marsh or even Paul Desmond than to the more usual model for eighties UK players, John Coltrane; his romantic, deeply contemplative style often brings Charles Lloyd to mind. His playing on this album, however, like that on the US-made **Meeting In Brooklyn** featuring pianist John Donaldson as leader of a stellar rhythm section, is immediately recognizable as quintessential Ballamy, whether he is contributing keening soprano over Django Bates's luminous, rippling piano, or warbling alto, delicately propelled by Martin France's skittering drums and Steve Watt's rock-solid bass. Although Ballamy is a fine interpreter of standards— particularly ballads—all the material here is original, and there are signs on pieces such as *Meadow* (given great textural depth by the use of Bates's horn and embellished with hunting noises for atmosphere) that he is developing into a considerable composer, especially adept at writing tender, at times wistfully plaintive, vehicles for his alternatively rhapsodic and meditative saxophones. **CP**

Gabe Baltazar
1929

Back In Action **Baltazar** (as); **Tom Ranier** (p); **Richard Simon** (b); **Steve Houghton** (d). VSOP Ⓕ #85 CD (MODE 201). (64 minutes). Recorded 1992.

⑥ ❽

A Hawaiian native, Baltazar had early experience with Howard Rumsey. He was Stan Kenton's lead alto for five years from 1960, and in the sixties worked with Terry Gibbs, Gil Fuller and Oliver Nelson. A return to Hawaii took him out of the recording limelight but this CD marks a reasonably auspicious return from the wilderness. The programme, with three of his pleasingly melodic originals, is imaginative and Baltazar shoulders most of the solo responsibility. Time has lent a greater opulence to his tone but his improvisations remain as logical and melodically sensitive as ever. There is evidence of the occasional faulty note production but he never seems to lose his direction. His most challenging work is on *Ruby, My Dear*, where his unpredictable line and adroit tempo changes add genuine colour, or on *Dream Dancing*, where an inventive outing also emphasises the warmth and relaxation of his style. The three little-known men who comprise the rhythm section do a good job and seem to have the needs of the alto saxophonist uppermost in their minds. Baltazar could be said to be back. **BMcR**

Billy Bang
1947

Live at Carlos 1 **Bang** (vn, clave); **Roy Campbell** (t); **Thurman Barker** (mba, perc); **Oscar Sanders** (g); **William Parker** (b); **Zen Matsuura** (d); **Eddie Conde** (cgas). Soul Note Ⓕ 21136-2 (47 minutes). Recorded 1986.

⑧ ❼

Billy Bang's gutsy violin playing combines the hard-bowing drive of Stuff Smith with the new sound worlds opened up by Ornette Coleman and AACM innovator Leroy Jenkins. Outcome: a potent blend of swing, blues and freewheeling abstraction. Bang has been leading groups since the early seventies, his versatility evident in left-field projects such as the solo **Distinction Without a Difference** (not yet on CD) and **Outline No 12**, which features his writing for a large string ensemble. His small-group recordings have also foraged across a range of styles, their eclecticism held together by Bang's zippy rhythmic bounce.

Live at Carlos 1 extends this diversity, from the stinging jazz swing of *Thank You, M'am* through African, Latin and Middle Eastern influences, even dropping into a credible reggae groove on

Sinawe Mandelas. The attractive violin/trumpet/marimba line-up, inspired in part by Eric Dolphy's **Out To Lunch** (reviewed below) was first tried by Bang on his 1984 LP, **The Fire From Within**. Although the trumpet is not well-recorded, the colours glow more vividly on **Carlos 1** and there is more spice in the rhythm. Bang himself is in inspired form; his bravura playing galvanizes the mellow *Abuella*, then blossoms into rhapsody for *Rainbow Gladiator*. Jazz populism with flair and a sensuous kick. **GL**

Paul Barbarin 1899-1969

Paul Barbarin and His New Orleans Jazz **Barbarin** (d); **John Brunious** (t); **Bob Thomas** (tb); **Willie Humphrey** (cl); **Lester Santiago** (p); **Danny Barker** (bj); **Milt Hinton** (b). Atlantic Ⓜ 790977-2 (48 minutes). Recorded 1955.

⑦ ❻

Already a professional by 1915, Barbarin arrived in Chicago in 1917. He worked with King Oliver and Jimmie Noone and earned a considerable reputation for his uncomplicated but propulsive drum style. In 1928 he joined Luis Russell and became part of one of the most dynamic rhythm sections of its day. The band was ultimately taken over by Louis Armstrong, but Barbarin remained very much its heartbeat. In the late forties he returned to New Orleans to lead his own bands and this CD presents a typically professional 1955 edition. Swing era inflections are discernible in Brunious's accomplished style, but he is a highly effective ensemble leader. Thomas's forthright trombone adds the tailgate muscle and Humphrey's flowing solos and coherent contrapuntal skills complete a fine front line. Despite being a drummer's band, the four-man rhythm section is strategically understated. Barker and Hinton apply a light touch, but it is the leader's jaunty two-beat drum style at its core that most imparts the feeling of good-humoured buoyancy. The list of drummers influenced by Barbarin would be short, but as groups grew in size in the twenties, he played an important part in providing a workable vernacular for the new jazz language. **BMcR**

Chris Barber 1930

In Concert (Volumes 1 and 2) **Barber** (tb, v); **Pat Halcox** (t); **Monty Sunshine** (cl); **Johnny Duncan** (g); **Eddie Smith** (bj); **Dick Smith** (b); **Ron Bowden, Graham Burbridge** (d); **Ottilie Patterson** (v, p). Dormouse Ⓕ DM23CD (two discs, oas: 63 and 71 minutes). Recorded 1956/58.

⑧ ❽

Although he gained great popularity from the British 'Trad' boom of the fifties and sixties, Barber has always shown that his musical interests lay far beyond the endless permutations of *The Saints* and the wearing of funny hats. He has led a band for more than 40 years and has been instrumental in enticing American guests as diverse as Louis Jordan, John Lewis, Trummy Young, Alex Bradford, Dr John and Wild Bill Davis to perform with his band. These two CDs are inextricably linked (although available separately) if only because the 1958 concert at Birmingham Town Hall is spread across both. All of the material comes from 'live' performances and retains the freshness of this popular line-up, prior to the departure of Monty Sunshine. In fact Sunshine's sub-tone clarinet is a strong feature of the music, adding warmth to *Mood Indigo* on Volume One (Barber's various bands have always had a particular empathy for Duke Ellington's earlier works; Volume Two, for instance, contains *Rockin' In Rhythm*). Pat Halcox sounds like a mainstream soloist on *You Took Advantage of Me* (Volume Two) and both discs feature the singing of Ottilie Patterson. The band's repertoire is drawn from a wide variety of sources, plus a most attractive Barber original in *New Blues* (Volume One). Transfers from the original three LPs to the two CDs have been well handled by Mike Brown. **AM**

Concert For The BBC **Barber** (tb, v); **Pat Halcox** (t), **Ian Wheeler** (cl, as); **John Crocker** (cl, as, ts); **Roger Hill** (g); **Johnny McCallum** (bj, g); **Vic Pitt** (b), **Norman Emberson** (d). Timeless Ⓕ CDTTD509/10 (62 minutes). Recorded 1982.

⑥ ❻

The piano-less banjo-propelled rhythm section of the Barber band has become more sophisticated over the years, but it is in the front line that fundamental change has taken place. *Perdido Street Blues* is an interesting case of metamorphosis because it retains the clarion clarinet solo from the Johnny Dodds original while adding a booting contemporary tenor solo from John Crocker.

The two reed players Crocker and Ian Wheeler are versatile in their various roles, and the employment of a guitar soloist (Roger Hill) adds yet another colour to the solo strength. Barber

himself seems to sing more than play on this occasion, but when he does sing the obbligato playing of Pat Halcox is sensitive and creative.

This is the Barber band caught at its very best. It represents what is probably the most potent and imaginative latter-day use of a traditional jazz line-up. **SV**

Gato Barbieri

1934

In Search Of The Mystery **Barbieri** (ts); **Carlo Scott** (vc); **Sirone (Norris Jones)** (b); **Bobby Kapp** (d). ESP-Disk Ⓜ 1049-2 (40 minutes). Recorded 1967.

⑦ ❽

Barbieri's increasing determination to use his Argentinian musical heritage has led to a progressive dilution of jazz content as his career progressed. With Don Cherry in Europe and on records in the Sixties he had given notice of becoming a major talent. This 1967 album, while still not the finished article, shows him as an exciting saxophonist with a brilliant grasp of multiphonics and with the technique to project them. Initially a John Coltrane devotee, Barbieri had already charted his own course and titles like *In Search Of The Mystery* and *Obsession No. 2*, while not always exploiting the rhythmic freedom made available, demonstrate an array of tonal colours as he takes his tenor into ranges normally associated with high-note trumpet men. The motif-based brick-building tradition of the free formers may not be greatly developed here, but Barbieri tends to evoke the feeling of solo evolution by repeating phrases in which either minute timbral adjustments or more violent changes of pitch occur. Rather than being the album that might have opened the door for a musical giant, it now appears as something of a pinnacle from which a very good player retreated. **BMcR**

Guy Barker

1957

Isn't It? **Barker** (t, flh); with collective personnel of: **Jamie Talbot** (ss); **Peter King** (as); **Nigel Hitchcock** (as, ts); **Julian Joseph**, **Stan Tracey** (p); **Jim Mullen** (g); **Alec Dankworth** (b), **Clark Tracey** (d). Spotlite Ⓕ SPJ-CD 545 (68 minutes). Recorded 1991.

⑧ ❽

In the light of his considerable expertise as a trumpet player and his obvious accomplishments as a jazz soloist it is surprising that until this year (1995) it was left to the independent labels (Spotlite and Miles Music) to record Barker as a group leader. A great deal of care went into the production of this album and Spotlite's Tony Williams was clearly anxious to give Barker the settings and the musical colleagues to bring out the best in this world-class player. Almost every track sees a change in instrumentation; *Goodspeed*, for example, puts Barker with Peter King and Nigel Hitchcock (both playing altos) while Hoagy Carmichael's lovely *I Get Along Without You Very Well*, like *Amandanita*, is just trumpet and rhythm section. Two of the most startling performances are duets. The breadth of Barker's knowledge of jazz tradition comes to the fore on *In A Mist*, a transcription of a Bix Beiderbecke piano piece for just trumpet and bass. Guy's accuracy in pitching here is complete while the burnished tone, one of his strongest features, is well in evidence. *Lament For The Black Tower* is the second duet, this time Barker with Stan Tracey, who composed the tune (this is Tracey's only appearance on the CD). *Black Tower* is music-making of the highest quality, but the entire album is a credit to all concerned, musicians and producer. Barker's move to a major company notwithstanding, this remains his best effort to date. **AM**

Dale Barlow

Wizards of Oz **Barlow** (ts); **Paul Grabowsky** (p); **Lloyd Swanton** (b); **Tony Buck** (d). EmArcy Ⓜ 834 531-2 (44 minutes). Recorded 1988.

⑥ ❻

Wizards of Oz no longer exist as a working band and this album is now over six years old, but its reissue on EmArcy is justified by the high level of artistry attained by these young Australians. Barlow is the player with an international platform, following his outings with Blakey, but Grabowsky is equally impressive. The style of this quartet is pleasingly different from most of the po-faced neo-bop orthodoxy coming out of many of the young US players.

Both Barlow and Grabowsky demonstrate a close affinity to various editions of Keith Jarrett's quartets, yet their music is at the same time both more relaxed and more adventurous than Jarrett's has in time become. Which is only natural—these are still young men, and Jarrett's wild days are long behind him. Buck and Swanton respond enthusiastically to the proddings of the two main soloists (who, between them, also composed all the songs on the date), but Buck's at times frenetic drumming is not well served by a recording mix which seems reluctant to place him on such occasions at the forefront of the music. Still, this is a solid and entertaining post-bop workout. **KS**

Bob Barnard 1933

At The Winery **Barnard** (t); **Paul Williams** (cl, ts); **Chris Taperell** (p); **Wally Wickham** (b); **John Morrison** (d). ABC Jazz Ⓜ 836 195-2 (47 minutes). Recorded 1985.

⑤ ❺

Early experience in Melbourne brass bands was put to good use when Barnard became a leading figure in Australia's traditionalist revival during the fifties and sixties. He formed his own band in 1974 and toured America as a solo artist in 1985; throughout the eighties he was first-call trumpet by all like-minded American tourists in the antipodean continent. The session heard on this CD could have taken place at any time in the last 40 years. Barnard is a good trumpeter with a fierce attack, originally inhabiting stylistic territory somewhere between Bobby Hackett and Freddy Randall but later a stylist in his own right. His stance is mainstream in the narrow sense and here he is well supported by Williams's all-purpose tenor and, more specifically, Dixieland-slanted clarinet. Pianist Taperell does well on a poor instrument and the rhythm duo function well throughout. Barnard's singing is devoid of any genuine jazz feeling, but this is a representative example of the open-minded attitude that Australians have always had to pre-bop jazz, since the days when Graham Bell and Ade Monsbourgh gave the British scene a shot in the arm in the late forties and early fifties. **BMcR**

Alan Barnes 1959

Thirsty Work **Barnes** (as, bs); **Martin Shaw** (t); **Iain Dixon** (ts); **Andy Panayi** (ts, bs, f); **David Newton** (p); **Paul Morgan** (b); **Mark Taylor** (d). Fret Ⓕ FJCD106 (63 minutes). Recorded 1993.

⑧ ❻

Barnes is one of those happy musicians who can apparently play in any style. His collaborations with guitarist Gary Potter in their Django Reinhardt-styled group and with trumpeter Bruce Adams in an abrasive bebop quintet are only two manifestations of his extraordinary talents. Here he is in an ideal setting with hand-picked musicians, the most notable of whom is Barnes's alter-ego, pianist David Newton.

Barnes wrote or had a hand in all the arrangements and chose his material from a wide range which includes blues, sambas and ballads. He acknowledges the influence of people like Monk and Mingus, but really these are just starting points for his great imagination and inventive skills. The 11-minute title-track does, however, pick up that great juggernaut Mingus sound, aided by a sinister bottom register tenor and baritone theme. Full of clever touches as well as driving solos, it is not a moment too long and has a wistful and sparsely accompanied trumpet solo from Shaw. Newton is a master accompanist and soloist and his work with Morgan obviously inspires the other soloists. Barnes, revealed here on disc with his baritone for the first time, shows a remarkable agility on the lower-pitched horn.

Barnes has already made many good albums, but this is his best yet. It marks another confident step in the career of a man who is already a world-class jazz musician. **SV**

George Barnes 1921-1977

Carl Kress and George Barnes—Two Guitars **Carl Kress, George Barnes** (g); **Bud Freeman** (ts). Ⓕ Jass J-CD-636 (71 minutes). Recorded 1962/1963.

⑥ ❻

When it came to guitarists, Kress and Barnes believed there was safety in numbers. Both recorded with other guitarists in tandem (Barnes with Earl Backus, Kress with Tony Mottola) and George actually made an LP for Mercury on which he was joined by no less than ten other guitarists. Most of the tracks here were recorded at a New York club called Chuck's Composite and were closely miked to catch every nuance, including the squeaking of a stool! There is never any doubt about the identities of the guitarists, for it is Barnes who plays the single-note lines and Kress who keeps the rhythm going, often sounding like a bass. The notes refer to the parallel with the Eddie Lang/Lonnie Johnson duets (Kress also made some duet recordings with Lang), but there is a slickness here which, after a time, leads to a certain sameness of approach. There is not a note out of place, and the way the two work together on a harmonically complex song such as *Gone With The Wind* is perfection itself, but in the final analysis this is music for guitarists. Even the addition of Bud Freeman's tenor on five titles does little to change the overall sound or concept. (The Freeman titles may well be from Bud's own United Artists studio album with Kress and Barnes.) **AM**

Charlie Barnet 1913-1991

Cherokee **Barnet** (ts, as, ss); with a collective personnel including: **Bob Burnet, Billy May** (t); **Bill Miller, Nat Jaffe** (p); **Phil Stephens** (b); **Cliff Leeman** (d) RCA Bluebird Ⓑ ND 90632 (33 minutes). Recorded 1939/1940.

Barnet always led a hard-swinging band which, by virtue of the fact that it copied other people's music, remained in the second rank. Given that the first rank in this case was Ellington and Basie, Barnet's was still a prodigious musical force. Because his arrangers were so well chosen and the music then so well played, many of Barnet's tracks retain a notable freshness and, for example, the version of *Flying Home* included here has much more cohesion and clarity than the contemporary ones by the tune's composer Lionel Hampton. The spirit of the band was instilled by the leader, and long-term support was provided by the outstanding trumpeter Bob Burnet, pianist Bill Miller and arranger Billy May. Barnet's own saxophone playing was distinctive and forceful and originals by him like *The Count's Idea*, *Leapin' At The Lincoln* and *Afternoon Of A Moax* (included here) show a lively and inventive mind at work. Barnet was a distinguished band leader who, because he was of independent means, was able to do a lot for jazz in the big band field during his life. A good sample of his distinctive output is included here, but it is to be regretted that better and more generous CDs of his music have been deleted. **SV**

Drop Me Off in Harlem **Barnet** (ss, as, ts, ldr); with a collective personnel of: **Peanuts Holland**, **Irving Berger**, **Joe Ferrante**, **Chuck Zimmerman**, **Al Killian**, **Jimmy Pupa**, **Lyman Vunk**, **Art House**, **Roy Eldridge**, **Johnny Martel**, **Jack Mootz**, **Holland Killian**, **Everett McDonald**, **George Seaberg**, **Ed Stress**, **Paul Webster**, **Art Robey**, **Dennis Sandole** (t); **Russ Brown**, **Kahn Keene**, **Wally Baron**, **Bill Robertson**, **Eddie Bert**, **Ed Fromm**, **Spud Murphy**, **Bob Swift**, **Porky Cohen**, **Tommy Pederson**, **Ben Pickering**, **Charles Coolidge**, **Gerald Foster**, **Dave Hallett**, **Burt Johnson**, **Bill Haller**, **Frank Bradley**, **Lawrence Brown** (tb); **George Bone**, **Conn Humphries**, **Murray Williams**, **Buddy DeFranco**, **Ray De Geer**, **Harold Herzon**, **Joe Meisner**, **Les Robinson** (as); **Kurt Bloom**, **James Lamare**, **Mike Goldberg**, **Andy Pinot**, **Ed Pripps**, **Denny Dehlin**, **Dave Mathews** (ts); **Danny Bank**, **Bob Polland**, **Bob Dawes** (bs); **Bill Miller**, **Dodo Marmarosa**, **Al Haig**, **Sheldon Smith** (p); **Tommy Moore**, **Turk Van Lake**, **Barney Kessel** (g); **Jack Jarvis**, **Bob Elden**, **Russ Wagner**, **Andy Riccardi**, **Howard Rumsey**, **Morris Rayman**, **Irv Lang** (b); **Cliff Leeman**, **Harold Hahn**, **Mickey Scrima** (d); **Frances Wayne**, **Peanuts Holland**, **Art Robey**, **Kay Starr** (v). MCA/Decca Ⓜ GRD-612 (57 minutes). Recorded 1942-46.

⑧ ❽

Saxophonist and big band leader Charlie Barnet catapulted to the front ranks of the swing era with hits such as *Cherokee* (1939) and *Old Black Magic* (1942), the latter heard here with Frances Wayne's soulful vocal, and the still sleek *Skyliner* (1944). Barnet, like Benny Goodman, also deserves credit for featuring black jazz stars as early as 1937 when trumpeter Frankie Newton joined the band. On this disc we hear such prominent Afro-American jazz players as trumpeters Roy Eldridge, Al Killian and trombonist Lawrence Brown.

In 1942 Barnet, who had just finished a successful tenure with Bluebird, signed with American Decca for a productive stint that was to see some of the band's best work. A generous leader who allowed his men plenty of elbow-room to strut their stuff, Barnet was also a first-rate soloist whose robust tenor, Hodges-inflected alto and pioneering work on soprano still impress. Indeed, the Decca sessions reveal an inspired, no-nonsense band which had discipline and élan a-plenty.

The title track, Ellington's *Drop Me Off in Harlem*, propelled by pianist Dodo Marmarosa, guitarist Barney Kessel and drummer Harold Hahn plus Eldridge's wailing trumpet, is a gem, as is the exotic Ralph Flanagan arrangement of the insinuating Gulf Coast Blues. In all, a poignant reminder of one of the great jazz swing bands. **CB**

Joey Baron

Raised Pleasure Point **Baron** (d); **Steve Swell** (tb); **Ellery Eskelin** (ts). New World Ⓕ 80449-2 (77 minutes). Recorded 1993.

⑥ ❽

Joey Baron is best known for his work with John Zorn's various projects, but he occasionally strikes out on his own as a leader. This is one such recent excursion. Some of Zorn's own obsessions flow over into this record, especially the one of two melody instruments interchanging snippets of a theme while playing at around 1,000 mph. This makes for some good clean fun and keeps everyone on their toes, musicians and listeners alike. It also points perhaps to the ultimate source of much of this music—Ornette Coleman. So this is from the tradition, then, whatever Baron does with the beat.

It is impossible to approach this music on a level playing field without a sense of humour, so do not play **Raised Pleasure Point** if you're in a bad mood: it will only make you feel worse. However, if you have more than an hour to spare to listen to three guys having a whale (and wail) of a time going from what sound like carefully-prepared pieces to clearly unpremeditated rants, then this is for you. It is not the most essential of releases for modern music followers, but it is more than mildly diverting, if only for its humour, which on occasion rises to Zappa-esque heights. **KS**

Bill Barron

1927-1989

The Next Plateau **Barron** (ts, ss); **Kenny Barron** (p); **Ray Drummond** (b); **Ben Riley** (d). Muse Ⓕ 5368 (43 minutes). Recorded 1987.

⑧ ❽

Kenny Barron's older brother was always an underrated player, perhaps to some degree because he never fell under Coltrane's critically accepted sway. He first received some recognition in the late fifties with stylistically opposed leaders Philly Joe Jones and Cecil Taylor and within a few years was co-leading an exciting band with trumpeter Ted Curson, proving his linear approach (similar to that of, say, Joe Henderson, a decade younger) was adaptable inside and outside chord changes. By the time of this, his final album, his tone had deepened, reaffirming his roots in Coleman Hawkins's muscularity, and his linearity was modified to emphasize intervals rather than chords, the results approaching the feel of early Ornette. But this date is solidly in the mainstream, aided by a sturdy rhythm section. Barron had long been a writer of interesting tunes; here, *This One's For Monk* acknowledges one of his compositional influences, alluding to several Monk themes including *Misterioso* and *We See* (a.k.a. *Manganese*). In fact, Barron's writing and playing are so rich in allusions (a tad of Rouse here, a dash of Dexter there) as to reinforce the breadth of his conception. A remarkably consistent player of invention and integrity, Barron fortunately left behind a few—too few—recordings like this one to treasure. **AL**

Kenny Barron 1943

The Only One **Barron** (p); **Ray Drummond** (b); **Ben Riley** (d). Reservoir Ⓕ 115 (66 minutes). Recorded 1990.

⑧ ❹

Barron is one of those jazz pianists who is too good for their own good: too tasteful, too devoted to the needs of the leaders he has worked for to call attention to himself. Those employers have included Bill Barron, Dizzy Gillespie, Yusef Lateef, Ron Carter, Freddie Hubbard and Stan Getz. His style is distinguished less by flash than by exquisite touch, absence of wasted motion, authentic lyricism and a strong feel for the blues with little recourse to hard-bop funk licks (which he does in fact trot out for the Latinized head of *Love for Sale*). The title track is an affectionate counterfeit of a romping Monk tune.

Taste is the hallmark of Riley's drumming too, and his animated and animating touch with wire brushes is quietly displayed. Riley is so discreet on *Sunny Side of the Street* that he is more felt than heard. Drummond is one of the most reliable, supportive and swinging bassists around, a huge man who handles the bull fiddle as effortlessly as a ukulele. Alas, as with most modern sessions done at Rudy van Gelder's legendary New Jersey studio, the bass was recorded using a pickup instead of a microphone, and has an ugly, unnatural sound. **KW**

Gary Bartz 1940

Shadows **Bartz** (ss, as); **Willie Williams** (ts); **Benny Green** (p); **Christian McBride** (b); **Victor Lewis** (d). Timeless Ⓕ SJP 379 (69 minutes). Recorded 1991.

⑥ ❻

Like Marlon Brando's character in **On the Waterfront**, Bartz could have been a contender. He was one of the most promising saxophonists to emerge in the sixties, displaying both roots and a maverick streak in his work with Roach, Blakey and Tyner and on his own now-deleted Milestone albums; but he fused out after a stay with Miles Davis and was a virtually forgotten man for much of the seventies and eighties. More recently Bartz has mounted a mild comeback, with each succeeding release on SteepleChase, Candid and Timeless finding him in stronger voice. **Shadows**, one of the most recent, is the best, although still short of the young Bartz's blowtorch intensity (hear his *Vision* solo on McCoy Tyner's **Expansion**, Blue Note B21Y-84338, for what might have been). The old hortatory streak emerges here on Coltrane's *Song of the Underground Railroad*, Tyner's *Peresina* and Wayne Shorter's *Children of the Night*, not to mention the loopy humour of choosing *Holiday for Strings* as a closer. Willie Williams, who has gained notice as part of Art Taylor's Wailers, is a fine front-line partner, and the rhythm section is as reliable as expected. **BB**

Paul Bascomb 1910-1986

Bad Bascomb **Bascomb** (ts); **Eddie Lewis** (t); **Frank Porter**, **Tommy Waters** (as); **Harold Wallace** (bs); **Duke Jordan** (p); **James McCrary** (b); **George DeHart** (d) **Bascomb, Porter** (v). Delmark Ⓕ DD-431 (49 minutes). Recorded 1952.

⑦ ❼

Paul, tenor-playing brother of trumpeter Dud Bascomb, shared sideman duties with him in the Erskine Hawkins band when it was at its zenith in the early forties, and successfully ran his own small groups for the next 30 years, mostly in and around Chicago and Detroit. Bascomb recorded intermittently for the United label, both as a leader and as a sideman, and it is a measure of his musicianship and dedication that he sticks to his stylistic guns all through these sides. His roots are in the swing era, just as Louis Jordan's were, and so the occasional jump-style touch is no mere lip-service to the then-burgeoning r&b scene, but more a harking back to Jordan's own golden era. All the playing is polished and well-rehearsed, and there is no hint of bad taste: indeed, as a self-confessed Coleman Hawkins fan, Bascomb on *Body and Soul* tries an interesting re-working of the Hawk's classic by going medium-tempo, dispensing with the melody and jamming on the chords. Oddly enough, in the process he sounds like Jack McVea on the 1944 JATP sides.

Of course this type of playing was dreadfully recherché by 1952, as even greats like Webster and Hawkins themselves discovered, so Bascomb's name has not endured as it might have. These sides demonstrate the unfairness of this neglect, no more so than on tracks like *More Blues-More Beat*, where Ellington's *Jam With Sam* receives a jump-style re-write. For the quite astonishing fluency of his improvising ideas, try his solo on the previously-unissued *Nona*: this is the equal of what Jacquet was doing for Norman Granz at this time. Bascomb is well worth hunting down in your specialist shop. **KS**

Count Basie

1904-1984

Count Basie: The Original American Decca Recordings **Basie** (p); **Buck Clayton**, **Carl Smith**, **Harry 'Sweets' Edison**, **Ed Lewis**, **Bobby Moore**, **Shad Collins** (t); **George Hunt**, **Dan Minor**, **Benny Morton**, **Dicky Wells** (tb); **Eddie Durham**, (tb, g); **Lester Young**, **Herschel Evans** (cl, ts); **Chu Berry** (ts); **Caughey Roberts**, **Earl Warren** (as); **Jack Washington** (as, bs); **Freddie Green** (g); **Walter Page** (d); **Jo Jones** (d); **Jimmy Rushing**, **Helen Humes** (v). MCA/Decca Ⓜ GRD-3-6112 (three discs: 186 minutes). Recorded 1937-39.

✓ ⑨ ❾

This superbly remastered collection of classics from the first editions of the legendary Basie Band, recorded during its 1937-39 Decca contract, provides a dynamic snapshot of the rumbunctious juggernaut that in terms of its insinuating rhythms and bluesy, riff-based arrangements captured the essence of big band swing more persuasively than the plusher, more polished dynamics of either Ellington or Lunceford.

In the course of the three discs (one each for 1937, 1938 and 1939), we witness the band's growing maturity, the addition of key personnel like guitarist Freddie Green, and the rounding of its initial rough edges; by 1939, ensembles had clicked and everyone played consistently in tune. Throughout, the band kept swinging and having fun. Indeed, a sense of *joie de vivre* is everywhere evident, a tribute to Basie's loose, relaxed leadership. We also hear such stalwarts of the blues-inflected Kansas City style as singers Jimmy Rushing and Helen Humes, saxmen Lester Young, Herschel Evans, Earl Warren and Chu Berry, and trumpeters Buck Clayton and Harry 'Sweets' Edison. That group of soloists is still close to unrivalled in big band history. In pianist Basie, guitarist Green, bassist Walter Page and drummer Jo Jones, we also savour one of the great rhythm sections of jazz. Additionally, we get to hear such staples of the big band tradition as *One O'Clock Jump* and *Jumpin' at the Woodside*.

The package is accompanied by Steven Lasker's expert liner notes, a generous sampling of photos, and comprehensive discographic information. **CB**

The Essential Count Basie, Volume 1 **Basie** (p, ldr) with: **Carl Smith**, **Buck Clayton**, **Shad Collins**, **Ed Lewis**, **Harry Edison** (t); **Dan Minor**, **Dickie Wells**, **Benny Morton** (tb); **Earl Warren** (as); **Jack Washington** (as, bs); **Lester Young**, **Buddy Tate** (ts, cl); **Freddie Green** (b); **Walter Page** (b); **Jo Jones** (d); **Jimmy Rushing**, **Helen Humes** (v). Columbia Ⓜ 460061-2 (47 minutes). Recorded 1936/1939.

✓ ⑩ ❼

Apart from the very first, all 16 tracks here date from 1939, one of the peak years for the first Basie band. With the world's finest rhythm section and an unrivalled cast of soloists this was the band which defined the meaning of 'swing'. There are several famous classics here, including the Lester Young feature *Taxi War Dance*, the double-length *Miss Thing* and the archetypal Jimmy Rushing up-tempo blues, *Baby Don't Tell On Me*. The first track is the even more famous (and classic) *Lady Be Good* from the 1936 Jones-Smith Inc. quintet date, Lester Young's first recording session and one of the finest things he ever did.

With music of this unquestioned stature the important point is the quality of the edition. This one seems to have been compiled on the basis of taking something from every Basie session recorded by Columbia in 1939 (between 1936 and 1939 Basie was contracted to Decca), and the job is well done. Nothing vital is missing, except perhaps for *Shoe Shine Boy* from 1936. Moreover, the transfers are good and the notes comprehensive. Of course this only represents a tiny part of Basie's 60-year recording career. **DG**

Verve Jazz Masters 2 **Basie** (p, org); **Paul Campbell**, **Wendell Culley**, **Joe Newman**, **Charlie Shavers**, **Reunald Jones**, **Thad Jones**, **Snooky Young**, **Fip Ricard**, **Al Aarons**, **Sonny Cohn**, **Don Rader** (t); **Henry Coker**, **Benny Powell**, **Jimmy Wilkins**, **Bill Hughes**, **Grover Mitchell**, **Urbie Green** (tb); **Marshall Royal** (as, cl); **Bill Graham** (as); **Ernie Wilkins**, **Eric Dixon** (as, ts); **Frank Wess** (as, ts, f); **Paul Quinichette**, **Floyd Johnson**, **'Lockjaw' Davis**, **Frank Foster** (ts); **Charlie Fowlkes** (bs); **Freddie Green** (g); **Jimmy Lewis**, **Gene Ramey**, **Eddie Jones**, **Buddy Catlett** (b); **Gus Johnson**, **Sonny Payne** (d); **Eddie Durham**, **Buster Harding**, **Neal Hefti**, **Wilkins**, **Foster**, **Quincy Jones** (arr); featured guests: **Roy Eldridge** (t); **Lester Young**, **Illinois Jacquet** (ts); **Jo Jones** (d); **Jimmy Rushing**, **Joe Williams** (v). Verve Ⓜ 519 819-2 (66 minutes). Recorded 1952-63.

⑧ ❽

One could argue that most of Basie's worthwhile achievements reflect the profound influence of the blues. The excellent **Plays The Blues** (Verve 513 630-2) compilation only overlaps the present selection by three titles (and only one in the same version), but nine of these 16 items adhere to the 12-bar format. With only one sixties track, the whole album dates from the period when the blues expression was still central to the band's output. This was the band which Basie formed in 1952 after a couple of years working with a small group, and its personnel rapidly developed into a superbly cohesive unit, less loose that the thirties band but more punchy. The four sextet tracks here are drawn from the big-band, including three rare items with Basie on organ and tenorman Quinichette, who is heard in remakes of *Every Tub* and *Blue And Sentimental*; the other 1952 tenor, Lockjaw Davis, is also backed by organ on *Paradise Squat* (a remake of *Mr Roberts' Roost* from the forties).

Later arrivals Foster and Wess join trumpeter Newman as most prolific soloists, and the band proves its continuity with the thirties by its spontaneous head arrangements on the closing Newport Jazz Festival tracks from 1957 with Jones and Young. **BP**

At Newport **Basie** (p, ldr); **Wendell Culley**, **Joe Newman**, **Reunald Jones**, **Thad Jones** (t); **Henry Coker**, **Benny Powell**, **Bill Hughes** (tb); **Marshall Royal**, **Bill Graham**, **Frank Foster**, **Frank Wess**, **Charlie Fowlkes** (s); **Freddie Green** (g); **Ed Jones** (b); **Sonny Greer** (d); with featured guests: **Roy Eldridge** (t); **Lester Young**, **Illinois Jacquet** (ts); **Jo Jones** (d); **Jimmy Rushing**, **Joe Williams** (v). Verve Ⓜ 833 776-2 (57 minutes). Recorded 1957.

⑨ ❼

Norman Granz, the founder and original owner of Verve, recorded close to the entire 1957 Newport Jazz Festival, and a goodly amount of it was eventually released on Verve, including such oddities as an LP with the young Cecil Taylor's Quartet on one side and the Gigi Gryce/Donald Byrd Jazz Lab on the other.

This Basie CD has been a long time in the making, but is worth the wait, because it finally reunites nearly all the material played by the Basie band in their set at the festival (there is still a fugitive track, featuring Joe Williams joined by Sarah Vaughan, which has never been issued) originally released over one-and-a-half vinyl albums. Thus we have as an added delight the songs crooned by Joe Williams with the band, as well as a rip-roaring Basie outfit charging through *Blee Blop Blues* like an express train.

But the real treasures are the guest stars, with Lester Young making a rare return to form very late in his creative life on three tracks, Roy Eldridge shining on his features, and Illinois Jacquet bringing it all back home on a stirring *One O'Clock Jump*. Jimmy Rushing and Jo Jones also make worthy contributions and the atmosphere throughout is electric. This is a band which really revelled in playing, and it is also fascinating to hear such a well-drilled group playing tight arrangements but also making room for such stellar solo talent. The sound is adequate: everyone is audible, in roughly the right amounts. **KS**

The Complete Atomic Mr Basie **Basie** (p); **Joe Newman**, **Thad Jones**, **Wendell Culley**, **Snooky Young** (t); **Benny Powell**, **Henry Coker**, **Al Grey** (tb); **Marshall Royal** (cl, as); **Frank Wess** (as, ts); **Frank Foster**, **Eddie 'Lockjaw' Davis** (ts); **Charlie Fowlkes** (bs); **Freddie Green** (g); **Eddie Jones** (b); **Sonny Payne** (d); **Neal Hefti** (arr); **Joe Williams** (v on one track). Roulette Ⓜ 8 28635 2 (57 minutes). Recorded 1957.

✔ ⑩ ❽

A change of record company often signals an alteration in style, policy and recorded sound. Such was the case when Basie left Norman Granz's label and signed with the new Roulette concern. This remains a most important album, the first for Roulette and also the first time an entire Basie record had been devoted to the compositions and arrangements of one man. The very album title became an identifying term for a vital period of Count's post-war musical history. Packed with soloists (but with the greatest of them seated at the piano) this was one of the finest swing bands the world has ever known. Neal Hefti's writing captures all the special nuances for which this Basie orchestra was famous; the unparalleled ability to swing, irrespective of tempo, the splendid internal balance and a nonpareil reed section under the leadership of Royal. *Li'l Darlin'* remains an object lesson in dynamics and on how to swing at just 18 bars to the minute. This is the edition to collect, for it contains five additional tracks to the original LP (although it must be said that the original 11 titles are still the most impressive) and, more importantly, has been remixed back to the original gorgeous mono, restoring the opening bars of *Kid From Red Bank*, invariably missing from the unsatisfactory stereo tapes. **AM**

Django Bates 1960

Summer Fruits (and unrest) **Bates** (p, kbds, peck-horn, g, v, arr); **Sid Gauld**, **Chris Batchelor** (t); **Dave Laurence** (frh); **Roland Bates** (tb); **Richard Hemy** (btb); **Sarah Waterhouse** (tba); **Eddie Parker** (f); **Sarah Homer** (cl, bcl); **Iain Ballamy**, **Steve Buckley**, **Mark Lockheart**, **Barak Schmoo**, **Julian Arguelles** (reeds); **Stuart Hall** (g, bj); **Steve Watts** (b); **Mike Mondesir** (elb); **Martin France** (d, perc); **Thebe Lipere** (perc). JMT Ⓕ 514 00X-2 (57 minutes). Recorded 1993.

⑧ ❽

Surprisingly, this is described as the keyboardist/composer's first album under his own name, although he previously recorded with his so-called "Powder Room Collapse Orchestra". In addition he was already well-known, of course, as a driving force behind both Loose Tubes and Human Chain. The latest edition of the latter group, with saxist Ballamy and now Mike Mondesir on bass, is responsible for four of the 11 tracks here, including my current favourite (*Hyphen-*) and my favourite title (*Food For Plankton (in detail)*). The remainder are by a 19-piece band of relatively standard instrumentation which inevitably recalls the best of Loose Tubes, down to including a faster version of their *Sad Afrika*. Bates's often diatonic writing is attractively melodic but investigates hidden byways (the *Armchair March* theme reappears during the closing *March Hare Dance*). Even a couple of 'circus'-type pieces, initially resembling other writers' parodies of the genre end up being charmingly challenging. The author's cryptic annotations of these items include one just characterized as "Sickly sweet (but irresistible)", and one or two other touches might merit the verdict "Corny humour (but funny)" because they are so well carried off. This music is alive with so many possibilities that it demands attention. **BP**

Alvin Batiste 1937

Bayou Magic **Batiste** (cl); **Emile Vinette, Maynard Batiste** (p); **Chris Severn** (b); **Herman Jackson** (d); **Edith Batiste** (v). India Navigation Ⓕ IN1069CD (60 minutes). Recorded 1988.

⑨ ❾

Though a virtuoso clarinettist, Alvin Batiste has rarely recorded and is little-known to the wider jazz public. In the fifties he played with Ed Blackwell, Ray Charles, Ornette Coleman and Ellis Marsalis, but has spent most of the last 30 years teaching in the Baton Rouge area. Not until the eighties did he begin to record regularly, playing with both Clarinet Summit and the American Jazz Quintet and releasing his début as a leader, **Musique d'Afrique Nouvelle Orleans,** in 1984.

Bayou Magic, its successor, is a peerless display of jazz clarinet played with breathtaking facility. Unlike **Musique d'Afrique**, which draws both on Batiste's involvement with classical music and his deep interest in mysticism, **Bayou Magic** is more a conventional jazz set. His clarinet seems essentially bop-oriented but he has evolved a highly personal eclecticism that incorporates influences from funk (*Bayou Magic*) to freeform (*Aerophonics*) and is superbly at ease on Maynard Batiste's gorgeous ballad, *Son Song*.

Batiste favours the higher registers but his tonal control covers the instrument's range, whether negotiating supple timbral inflections or abrupt intervallic leaps. He is a fine composer too, the askew sprightliness of *Picou* and *Venus Flow* brought out by the excellent rhythm section. The CD's only drawback is the lack of documentation—no recording date, no insert-notes, no mention of the synthesizer (or electric clarinet) that is heard on two tracks. **GL**

Mario Bauzá 1911-1993

944 Columbus **Bauzá** (ldr); **Victor Páz, Michael Mossman, Daniel Colette** (t); **Manny Durán** (t, flh); **Gerry Chamberlain, Bruce Eidem, Don Hayward** (tb); **Rolando Briceno** (as, ss); **Pete Yellin** (as, cl); **Enrique Fernadez** (ts, f); **Dioris Rivera** (ts, f); **Pablo Calogero** (bs, bcl); **Marcus Persiani** (p); **Joe Santiago** (b); **Bobby Sanabria** (d); **José Mangual Jr., Carlos 'Patato' Valdes, Joe Gonzales, José Alexis Diaz** (perc); **Graciela, Rudy Calzado** (v). Messidor Ⓕ15828-2 (48 minutes). Recorded 1993.

⑦ ❽

Bauzá assumed an important role in the most successful of all jazz fusions. He played for and led Afro-Cuban jazz bands, using the best elements of each idiom and detracting from none. He initially studied clarinet in Havana and recorded in New York with Antonio Maria Romeu in 1926. He moved to America in 1930, switched to trumpet and worked with, amongst others, Chick Webb, Fletcher Henderson and Cab Calloway. In 1941 he joined Machito as lead trumpet, became musical director and ushered the band along the Afro-Cuban jazz trial.

Cubop is what is heard on **944 Columbus**. The powerful trumpet of the ageing leader is absent but the celebration of his music permeates every title. Mossman is the pick of the arrangers; the driving mambo of *Cubauzá* contrasting with the almost Ellingtonian bolero of *Lourdes Lullaby*. Irving Berlin's *Heatwave* assumes a Latin cloak and Chico O'Farrill's excellent reed writing elevates *Congratulations To Someone* to the seriously good category. Bauzá left Machito in 1976, led his own band through the eighties and was not averse to adding salsa to his musical menu. The solos on **944 Columbus** are not spectacular but the band epitomizes the still thriving spirit of the Afro-Cuban movement. **BMcR**

Jim Beard

Lost At The Carnival **Beard** (p, syn, perc); **Jon Herington** (elg, hca, perc); **Bill Evans** (ts, ss); **Stan Harrison** (cl, bcl, f, af); **Ron Jenkins** (elb); **Steve Rodby** (b); **Scooter Warner, Mike Mecham, Billy Ward** (d). Lipstick Ⓕ LIP 89027-2 (55 minutes). Recorded 1994.

⑥ ❽

Jim Beard is best known for his straight-ahead funk and fusion work with John McLaughlin, John Scofield, Bob Berg, The Brecker Brothers, Pat Metheny and others. Here, while he retains the funky agenda, he adopts something of a concept album approach, using the textures, moods and styles of the carnival both to flavour and unify his programme. To this end, several tracks are prefaced or closed with fairground organ, *Chunks And Chairknobs* being a whimsical march-like piece dominated by woodwinds, while *Holiday* is reminiscent of a fifties palais band.

If this seems a recipe for banality, the discordant aural assault of the carnival actually gives Beard a licence to create all manner of harmonic and stylistic colourations, much as Charles Ives used the collision of contrasting ensembles to create polytonal effects. For example, although *Poke* is in essence a four-chord Latin vamp, the insertion of flattened thirds and fifths quickly undermines its superficial innocuity. The set is dotted with jazz solos from Beard's piano and Evans's saxes, but the main attraction for jazz listeners is likely to be in the subversive totality of Beard's concept. **MG**

Sidney Bechet

1897-1959

The Legendary Sidney Bechet Bechet (ss, cl); with a collective personnel of: **Tommy Ladnier, Sidney de Paris, Red Allen, Charlie Shavers** (t); **Rex Stewart** (c); **Mezz Mezzrow, Albert Nicholas** (cl); **Happy Cauldwell, Lem Johnson** (ts); **Teddy Nixon, Sandy Williams, J.C. Higginbottom, Claude Jones** (tb); **Hank Duncan, Cliff Jackson, Jelly Roll Morton, Sonny White, Earl Hines, James Tolliver, Willie 'The Lion' Smith** (p); **Teddy Bunn, Lawrence Lucie, Charlie Howard, Bernard Addison, Everett Barksdale** (g); **Wilson Myers, Elmer James, Wellman Braud, John Lindsay** (b); **Morris Morland, Manzie Johnson, Zutty Singleton, Kenny Clarke, Sid Catlett, Baby Dodds, J.C. Heard, Arthur Herbert** (d). RCA Bluebird Ⓜ ND86590 (86 minutes). Recorded 1932-41.

✔ ⑧ ❽

On the first number in this collection, *Maple Leaf Rag*, Sidney Bechet never once stops playing. This is a fair indication of his personality, both musical and personal. A forceful and truculent individual, Bechet never willingly shared the limelight, even with Louis Armstrong, and this trait of character is reflected in the unstoppable flow of his playing. It probably explains, too, why he took up the soprano saxophone quite early in his career, relegating the clarinet to second place; the soprano is louder.

In the period covered by these 22 tracks Bechet's playing was at its best—bravura, florid, headlong and unfailingly inventive. The solo breaks in the aforementioned *Maple Leaf* would defeat most players today, even after much practice—but Bechet made them up on the spur of the moment. *High Society*, from Jelly Roll Morton's 1939 Victor session, is a famous performance in which the traditional clarinet solo is taken first by Bechet (on soprano) and then by Albert Nicholas (on clarinet)—a contest which ends in a dead heat. Equally praised as a classic of the genre is the recording session which featured Earl Hines, Baby Dodds and Rex Stewart and produced *Blues In Thirds, Ain't Misbehavin'* and two versions of *Blue For You, Johnny*.

The band billed as 'Sidney Bechet and his New Orleans Feetwarmers' had a somewhat transient personnel but produced many authentic jazz classics, including *Shake It and Break It*, *Wild Man Blues* and *Stompy Jones*, all included in this anthology.

The CD transfers are in mono and perfectly satisfactory, bearing in mind the variable quality of the originals. **DG**

Sidney Bechet In New York 1937-40 Bechet (cl, ss); **Louis Armstrong** (t, v); **Charlie Shavers** (t); **Claude Jones** (tb); **Sammy Price, Luis Russell** (p); **Teddy Bunn, Bernard Addison** (g); **Richard Fulbright, Wellman Braud** (b); **Zutty Singleton** (d); **O'Neil Spencer** (d, v); **Trixie Smith, Coot Grant, Kid Wesley Wilson** (v). JSP Ⓔ CD 338 (69 minutes). Recorded 1937-40.

⑧ ❽

Bechet bought his first straight soprano saxophone in London in 1919 during his first visit to Europe. Almost single-handedly he put the instrument on the jazz map, frequently using it on record with various Clarence Williams recording units. He worked with Noble Sissle's band for a number of years and the opening tracks here come from his closing period with the band. In fact there is probably more of Bechet's clarinet to be heard here than soprano; on both instruments he manifested a biting, attacking tone and had a tendency to dominate other front-line players, even trumpeters. Here he has to allow Shavers and Armstrong pride of place in the ensembles, although it must be said that all the musicians play with considerable sensitivity on the date with Trixie Smith and the other singers. The 1940 date with Louis Armstrong achieves classic status, even though Bechet said later that he was disappointed with the date because Louis ignored the previously agreed arrangements. **Perdido Street Blues** has superb work from Sidney and Louis, but the whole session is a memorable achievement. The CD has been lovingly remastered by John R. T. Davies who has achieved the best possible sound. In addition, the disc includes both original and alternative takes of Sissle's *Characteristic Blues* and Armstrong's *Down In Honky Tonk Town*. **AM**

Jazz Classics, Volumes 1 and 2 Bechet (cl, ss); with various groups comprised of: **Sidney De Paris, Max Kaminsky, Bunk Johnson, Frankie Newton** (t); **Vic Dickenson, George Lugg, Sandy Williams, J.C. Higginbotham, Jimmy Archey** (tb); **Albert Nicholas** (cl) **Art Hodes, Meade Lux Lewis, Cliff Jackson, Don Kirkpatrick** (p); **Teddy Bunn** (g); **Pops Foster, John Williams** (b); **Manzie Johnson, Big Sid Catlett, Danny Alvin** (d); **Fred Moore** (d, v). Blue Note Ⓜ 789384/85 2 (two discs, oas: 39 and 43 minutes). Recorded 1939-51.

✔ ⑩ ❽

It is a shame that the running time here is a couple of minutes more than a single CD can cope with, because combining these famous two separate volumes onto one disc would have made a great deal of sense. As it is, the old LP order (disorder?) has been preserved across the two discs, so the listener hops from date to date and constantly refers to the reproduced LP sleeve notes to find out what is going on. Not that this should detract one jot from the enjoyment of some of the most exhilarating jazz ever committed to wax (these all date from the pre-tape era). Bechet was rarely below peak form anyway, but the combination of above-average recorded sound and considerably above-average fellow musicians makes the magic come tumbling out on virtually every track. Just to look at the track listing on Volume One is enough to gladden the heart—an imperiously swinging *Muskrat Ramble* featuring De Paris, Dickenson and Art Hodes, followed by the deep blues cry of *Blue Horizon* with the same band, then *Weary Blues* with Max Kaminsky followed by the immortal 1939 recording of *Summertime* with Teddy Bunn, Meade Lux Lewis and Big Sid. This really is one version of musical paradise.

One of the most striking musical factors consistently on display here is just how disciplined and swinging Bechet's rhythm sections were. Even when Bunk Johnson is fluffing notes on the lead line in 1945, Cliff Jackson, Pops Foster and Manzie Johnson are registering levels of rockin' rhythm which border on the ecstatic. This is simply not typical for New Orleans bands, but is rarely absent from a Bechet session anywhere in his career. One can only conclude that it is his own vitality which translates itself to his sidemen when they are of the calibre mentioned above. But above all it is the ever-persuasive voices of Bechet's soprano and clarinet which dominate, and rightly too. A personality so strong as to be overwhelming, he was often at his best with musicians not quite his equal (only a handful could get close anyway) but strong enough to stick to what they do best and not get in his way, and this is what the majority of tracks here contain. Bechet is an inspired and bewitching presence throughout these two records, and they should be a part of every jazz collection. **KS**

The King Jazz Story, Volume 1 **Bechet** (ss, cl); **Mezz Mezzrow** (cl); **Hot Lips Page** (t, v); **Sammy Price, Fitz Weston** (p); **Pops Foster, Wellman Braud** (b); **Sid Catlett, Baby Dodds, Kaiser Marshall** (d); **Pleasant Joe, Coot Grant, Douglas Daniels** (v). Storyville Ⓜ STCD 8212 (77 minutes). Recorded 1945-1947.

⑧ ❽

Some of Bechet's most majestic playing was recorded for Mezzrow's King Jazz label. His most notable compositions here are *Delta Mood*, a heart-breaking and lyrical slow blues, and *Where Am I?*, a similarly melancholy and delicate theme. Bechet soars above the simple ensembles with an authority reminiscent of some of Armstrong's finest blues performances of the late Twenties.

"I'm a genius," Mezzrow claimed at one point in his comments on these sessions, "and Sidney Bechet helps me prove it." The reverse is palpably the case and Bechet takes full advantage of one of the most bountiful recording opportunities of his career. It is hard to over-estimate the importance of these tracks (the ones on the four companion volumes, STCD 8213, 8214, 8215 and 4104 are just as good) in the traditional mainstream field. **SV**

Jazz At Storyville **Bechet** (ss); **Vic Dickenson** (tb); **George Wein** (p); **Jimmy Woode** (b); **Buzzy Drootin** (d). Black Lion Ⓜ BLCD 760902 (57 minutes). Recorded 1953.

⑧ ❻

By this period of his career, Bechet had finally achieved the kind of lasting fame that Armstrong was enjoying, though not in Bechet's case while remaining based in the US. For the last decade of his life he was based in France, where he was viewed as a sort of musical Merlin and where his well-meaning backing bands were several stages less competent than the worst of Armstrong's big-bands.

Back home his reputation was seriously diminished, like that of most of the classic and mainstream players at the time, and Bechet's last US visit is documented here through the then Boston-based promoter George Wein's invitation to appear at his club and on his Storyville record label. Contrary to current discographies, the CD combines all of the two ten-inch LPs, with *Ole Miss* occupying the second half of *Bugle Blues*.

The local rhythm section is competent but rather ill-served by the recording, whereas the still imperious Bechet—although probably sharing a single microphone with Dickenson—is better registered than on many of the French albums. There is scarcely any division between Bechet's ensemble leads and his solos, but the stimulating inclusion of Dickenson provides a challenge and a counterweight to the saxophonist's sweeping style. **BP**

Gordon Beck

1938

For Evans' Sake **Beck** (p); **Jack DeJohnette** (d); **Dave Holland** (b); **Didier Lockwood** (vn). JMS Ⓕ 059-2 (59 minutes). Recorded 1991.

⑥ ❽

Gordon Beck was a familiar figure on the modern British scene in the sixties, playing with Tubby Hayes and for a time leading the house trio at Ronnie Scott's. However, work with Phil Woods's European Rhythm Machine brought him valuable European exposure, and since the late seventies he has forged many continental connections. It is from such an association—with French record producer Jean-Marie Salhani—that this recording emanates. The title is every bit as revealing of the contents as it might seem. Beck's informative inlay note makes no secret of its author's admiration for Bill Evans and neither does the music, most of it composed by Beck. However, although Evans might be a cornerstone of Beck's style, other pianists who absorbed Evans have had an effect on his playing.

Thus the album's two most dramatic tracks—the splintered, occasionally Monkish *Try This* and the taut, virtuosic *Trio Type Tune Two*—carry strong echoes of Chick Corea's trio work from the sixties and eighties. Another vigorous outing, *Not The Last Waltz*, honours McCoy Tyner, an influence from the other end of the modern piano spectrum. The set has its routine moments, but Beck's most spirited performances speak eloquently of his often under-valued talent. DeJohnette and Holland are muscular and flawless, and Didier Lockwood adds rococo flourish to a reworked *All The Things You Are*. **MG**

Harry Beckett

1935

All Four One **Beckett**, **Chris Batchelor**, **Jon Corbett**, **Claude Deppa** (flh); **Alastair Gavin** (p); **Fred T Baker** (b); **Tony Marsh** (d); **Jan Ponsford** (v). Spotlite Jazz Ⓕ SPJ-CD 547 (53 minutes). Recorded 1991.

⑧ ❼

An early fan of Miles and Dizzy, Harry Beckett came to London from his native Barbados in 1954, first making his mark working with Charles Mingus on the 1961 film *All Night Long*. In the subsequent three decades he has played with many of the UK's leading ensembles, including small groups led by Graham Collier and Stan Tracey, plus big bands such as the Brotherhood of Breath, the London Jazz Composers Orchestra and the Jazz Warriors. He has also led several groups of his own, notably Joy Unlimited, and currently co-leads the Anglo-Italian Quartet, but little of his best work is available on CD.

All Four One features a recent Beckett project, the Flügelhorn 4+3. Although a versatile player, adept at free jazz, bebop, even West African Highlife, Beckett's own music has a graceful romanticism at its core which is well-suited to the soft tones of the flügelhorn. His playing typically mixes this with darting excursions into a more abstract language of gruff expostulation and avuncular chuckles. He is also known as a composer of attractive tunes, and *All Four One* underlines the point, with the bright *Time of Day* and a musing *The Shadowy Light* being outstanding. Singer Jan Ponsford adds a powerful vocal to the ballad *Enchanted* and Beckett closes an amiable set with a rousing flourish on Mingus's *Better Get it in Your Soul*. **GL**

Bix Beiderbecke

1903-1931

Bix Beiderbecke and the Chicago Cornets **Beiderbecke** (c) with a collective personnel of: **Jimmy McPartland**, **Muggsy Spanier** (c); **Al Gande**, **George Brunies**, **Miff Mole**, **Tommy Dorsey**, **Guy Carey** (tb); **Don Murray**, **Volly DeFaut** (cl); **Jimmy Hartwell** (cl, as); **Frank Trumbauer** (c-ms); **George Johnson** (ts); **Rube Bloom**, **Paul Mertz**, **Mel Stitzel**, **Dick Voynow** (p); **Bob Gillette** (bj); **Marvin Saxbe** (bj, g, cymbal); **Min Leibrooke** (tba); **Vic Moore**, **Vic Berton**, **Tommy Gargano** (d). Milestone Ⓜ MCD-47019-2 (76 minutes). Recorded 1924.

⑧ ❹

Nineteen of these 28 tracks are the first recordings Bix made, 15 of them by the Wolverines, the dedicated band of young white musicians who had been captivated by the work of the Original Dixieland Jazz Band. All the titles were made for the Gennett company under fairly primitive recording conditions in the 'pre-electric' days, so we miss the magic, shimmering Beiderbecke cornet sound of the later Okeh discs. Nevertheless, it is apparent that Bix stands head and shoulders, musically speaking, above his colleagues, always ready with an apt turn of phrase and playing with an assurance which belies his age. By the end of 1924 he had left the Wolverines. This CD includes two titles featuring his replacement Jimmy McPartland, who has clearly learned Bix's solos but who at the time lacked the singular qualities which highlighted Beiderbecke's work. The disc also contains seven titles by the Bucktown Five, a lusty little band fronted by the then 17-year-old Muggsy Spanier. The CD is virtually the equivalent of a two-LP set Milestone issued in 1974 (the Bucktown Five's *Someday Sweetheart* replaces an alternative take of *Buddy's Habits*). The sound seems to have been improved, although some of the titles have a built-in swish from the 78s used for dubbing. **AM**

Volume 1: Singin' The Blues **Beiderbecke** (c, p) with **Frank Trumbauer and his Orchestra**: **Sylvester Ahola** (t); **Miff Mole**, **Bill Rank** (tb); **Jimmy Dorsey** (cl); **Don Murray** (cl, ts, bs); **Frank Trumbauer** (c-ms); **Adrian Rollini** (bs); **Paul Metz**, **Frank Signorelli** (p); **Eddie Lang** (g); **Joe Venuti** (vn); **Howdy Quicksell** (bj); **Chauncey Moorhouse**, **Vic Burton** (d); Columbia Ⓜ 466309-2 (61 minutes). Recorded 1927.

✔ ⑩ ❽

Of all the current Beiderbecke reissues this is undoubtedly the best collection on a single CD. At the age of 24 Bix was at the height of his powers and on these sessions he was working with some of his finest contemporaries. Unimpeded by ornate arrangements or fumbling sidemen, he was able to relax into that bright, clipped eloquence which has been captivating listeners ever since.

Bix Beiderbecke's cornet is one of the authentic voices of jazz. It has become a cliché to describe his tone and articulation as 'bell-like', but in this case the cliché is exact. His improvised line has the same kind of brisk confidence as that of the young Armstrong (his near-contemporary) and listening to it brings the same feeling of satisfaction, of following an unerring and elegant mind. There are many classics among these 20 pieces, including *Singin' The Blues*, *I'm Coming Virginia*, *Riverboat Shuffle*, and *Way Down Yonder in New Orleans*. The high point is always the cornet solo, but another unique voice can also be heard—the floating C-melody saxophone of Frank Trumbauer, Lester Young's first idol. The disc also contains a few examples of Bix's piano playing, including his best-known keyboard piece, *In A Mist*. **DG**

Volume 2: At The Jazz Band Ball **Beiderbecke** (c); with: **Chicago Loopers, Willard Robison and his Orchestra; His Gang; New Orleans Lucky Seven; Frank Trumbauer and his Orchestra; Russell Gray; Lou Raderman**. Columbia Ⓜ 466967-2 (70 minutes). Recorded 1927-28.

④ ❻

There are two kinds of Bix Beiderbecke compilations. One kind tries to trawl the best stuff from all over, no matter how often it has reappeared, while the other tries to be all-inclusive and give the collector every whiff of Bix it can, no matter how dreadful the records are in other respects, or how little a whiff of Bix is actually provided. This record is the second kind. It throws in everything he recorded or may have recorded between October 1927 and April 1928, two takes in some cases, and only a few of these are really good, familiar ones, like *Sorry* and *Since My Best Gal Turned Me Down*. Without Bix, most of them would just be dated dance music. In fact, most of them are dated dance music *with* Bix. *Oh Gee! Oh Joy!* with Lou Raderman's band is claimed to be a hitherto unknown Bix performance, as are *Why Do I Love You?* and *Ol' Man River*, but for all Bix does on them, it doesn't really matter. Annotator Michael Brooks goes into realms of detail about authenticity, and into contortions of embarrassment about the racist lyrics of *Mississippi Mud*. The fact is that Bix didn't make many good records, and rather a lot of poor ones, many of which are on this CD. If anyone cared to take Columbia to court for including this set under their Jazz Masterpieces label, it would be an interesting case. **MK**

Richie Beirach

1947

Self Portraits **Beirach** (p, prepared p). CMP Ⓕ CD 51 (48 minutes). Recorded 1990.

⑥ ❽

Since coming to prominence in the irreproachably authentic jazz setting of the Stan Getz Quartet in 1972, Beirach has proved an ingenious and idiosyncratic post-bop improviser. His debt to the modern jazz piano masters is clear, but he is also fascinated by the harmonies and textures of Webern, Debussy, Bartók and others, as was apparent in his 1992 set of rather cute re-harmonizations of jazz standards in Concord's Maybeck Hall series. Though leavened by the occasional jazz figure, the classical influences are to the fore in this bracing collection of eight autobiographical improvisations.

Perhaps the fullest picture of Beirach's range of expression emerges in *Darkness Into Air*, which merges creeping, spectral whole-tone figures with more animated passages, where the stillness is ruptured by strafing upper-register glissandi. *A Quiet Normal Life*, which overdubs relatively dynamic standard piano to lively prepared piano, is also a strenuous exception in a set which generally unfolds gradually, humming with glowering, supenseful dissonance. This music evokes a chastened, interior world, attractively distant from the rather cosy, gallery-pleasing epigrams of the Maybeck recital. **MG**

Bob Belden

1956

The Music of Sting—Straight To My Heart **Belden, Tony Kadlek, Jim Powell, Tim Hagans** (t, flh); **Peter Reit, John Fedchock, George Moran, Bob Stewart, Marcus Rojas** (frh, tb, tba); **Chuck Wilson, Mike Migliore, Tim Ries, Rick Margitza, Ron Kozak, Glenn Wilson, Bobby Watson, Kirk Whalum** (f, reeds, ww); **Joey Calderazzo, Marc Copland, Benny Green, Kevin Hays** (p); **Doug Hall, Adam Holzman** (syn); **Pat Rebillot** (org); **John Hart, John Scofield, Fareed Haque, Jimi Tunnell** (g); **Darryl Jones, Jay Anderson** (b); **Dennis Chambers, Jeff Hirshfield** (d); **Jerry Gonzales, Abraham Adzeneya, Ladji Camara, Jerry Gonzales, David Earle Johnson** (perc); **Dianne Reeves, Phil Perry, Mark Ledford, Jimi Tunnell** (v). Blue Note Ⓕ CDP7 95137-2 (61 minutes). Recorded 1991.

⑥ ❽

Belden, a graduate of North Texas State University and the Woody Herman band, has made his name with a trio of jazz covers of celebrity pops and classics. Latterly he has done Prince and jazzed-up *Turandot*, but his first major project dealt with Sting, appropriately enough a writer noted for his use of jazzy chords and dynamics.

Ironically, given Belden's self-proclaimed iconoclasm, he actually produces little we have not heard before. The spirit of Gil Evans and Miles Davis is evident in various places, but most extensively in *Roxanne*, which opens like *Gone, Gone, Gone* from **Porgy and Bess** before picking up a rock beat and sounding like mid-seventies Gil; similarly, *Shadows In The Rain* is a blend of spacious Bitches Brew-type textures and Evans-like horn writing. Elsewhere, perhaps with the exception of Jimi Tunnell's powerful reading of *I Burn For You*, various vocalists show that Sting had the best idea of how his songs should sound. And there is Belden's problem: the straight renditions fail to improve on the

originals, the more oblique covers might as well be other tunes. He does, however, provide work for good jazz soloists, and it is probably significant that transmuting *Dream Of The Blue Turtles* into *Impressions*, and letting Calderazzo and the Pat Martino-esque Hart have their head, was one of the best ideas he had.
MG

Louie Bellson
1924

Hot **Bellson** (d); **Robert Millikan, Brian O'Flaherty, Larry Lunetta, Danny Cahn, Glenn Drewes** (t); **Clark Terry** (flh); **Don Mikkelson, Hale Rood, Clinton Sharman, Keith O'Quinn** (tb); **Joe Roccisano, Don Menza, Jack Stuckey, George Opalisky, Kenny Hitchcock** (reeds); **John Bunch** (p); **Jay Leonhart** (b). MusicMasters Ⓔ 5008-2-C (50 minutes). Recorded 1987.

⑥ ❽

Bellson is a moveable feast, forming a big band wherever he hangs his hat. Here it was in New York and, apart from veterans like Roccisano and Menza (who probably came with Bellson from Los Angeles for the visit), Clark Terry and John Bunch, he has an exuberant crew of younger musicians. Bassist Jay Leonhart makes a perfect partner for the leader's modest but incisive drumming.

Four of Bellson's not inconsiderable compositions are included, including *The Peaceful Poet*, a showcase for Menza and *Walkin' With Buddy*, dedicated to Rich and featuring Clark Terry. Like *Caravan*, which also features both Terry and Menza, the track runs for almost eight minutes. Roccisano wrote *Hookin' It*, a wailing feature for himself, and the title-track is borrowed from Bob Florence. It is impressive to find that Bellson can stick his library under his arm, fly to New York and conjure from the Big Apple a big band as good as this, which sounds so polished and convincing that it might have been together for years.
SV

Tex Beneke
1914

Jukebox Saturday Night: The 1946 Glenn Miller Orchestra Live at the Hollywood Palladium **Beneke** (ts, ldr); **Bobby Nichols, Graham Young, Steve Steck, Whitey Thomas** (t); **Jimmy Priddy, Paul Tanner, John Halliburton, Bobby Pring** (tb); **John Graas** (frh); **Sol Livero, Freddy Guera** (cl, as); **Manny Thaler** (as, bss); **Stanley Aaronson, Vince Carbonne** (ts); **Gene Bergen, Gene Shepherd, Phil Cogliano, Earl Cornwall, Stan Harris, Jasper Hornyak, Joseph Kowalewski, Stan Kraft, Richard Motylinski, Norman Forrest, Michael Violooky, Carl Ottobrino** (vn); **Henry Mancini** (p, arr); **Bobby Joe Gibbons** (g); **Rollie Bundock** (b); **Jack Sperling** (d); **Artie Malvin, Lillian Lane, Murray Kane, Gene Steck, Steve Steck, 'The Crew Chiefs'** (v); **Bill Finegan, Jerry Gray, Norman Leyden** (arr). Vintage Jazz Classics Ⓔ.VJC 1039 (73 minutes). Recorded 1946.

⑤ ❹

'Ghost' bands are a major area of controversy among jazz lovers. How could anyone fill the shoes of the great leaders of the past, like Ellington or Basie? And how does the attempt to keep a living commercially-based band on the road square with the jazz repertory movement that tries faithfully to recreate the classic performances of the long-gone? At least Tex Beneke's leadership of Miller's band had some advantages. It was set up immediately after the war by the Miller estate and re-employed many of Miller's sidemen as they re-entered civvy street from the Army/Air Force Band.

Composer/arranger Henry Mancini added new charts based on popular songs to the book, but Beneke was employed by Helen Miller to play the old arrangements from both the pre-war band and the AAF group. The results are unspectacular but swinging, with the amiable Beneke hooting through tenor solos that sound jazzy in this rather puddingy context, but which are strangely isolated from, say, the contemporaneous JATP concerts. Apparently Beneke was keen to invoke some bop charts, but there's little sign of this as the band swan through Miller favourites like *Moonlight Serenade* and *Sun Valley Jump*.
AS

Tony Bennett
1926

The Tony Bennett–Bill Evans Album **Bennett** (v); **Bill Evans** (p). Fantasy Ⓜ OJCCD 439-2 (35 minutes). Recorded 1975.

⑥ ❽

This must have been a challenging album to make, and it says a lot for both Tony Bennett and Bill Evans that it came off as well as it did. With no rhythm section to lean on, the singer relies entirely on the pianist for rhythmic and harmonic support. Yet Bill Evans's style was one which took a great many of the basic ingredients for granted. He did not play time with the left hand and his chords were full of ambiguity, suspensions and inversions. In the event, a form of compromise seems to have been reached, in which he plays a simplified accompaniment to the vocal and opens out for solo passages.

As you might expect from these two, the material is chosen with exquisite taste—*My Foolish Heart, When In Rome*, *Waltz For Debby* (with lyric by Gene Lees), and so on. Yet for all the intelligence and discernment that obviously went into the project, the final result is not as satisfying as one might expect. I think the problem lies with Tony Bennett's voice, which is too 'public' for such a small-scale undertaking. He is always at his best when singing quite forcefully, but when he puts on the pressure he sounds too big for the context. **DG**

Han Bennink 1942

Clusone 3 **Bennink** (d); **Michael Moore** (as, cl); **Ernst Reijseger** (vc). Ramboy Ⓕ 01 (66 minutes). Recorded 1990-91.

⑧ ❹

Dutch jazz is notorious for its irreverent humour, and no Dutch improviser is nuttier than Bennink, who may hurl his cymbals like frisbees or build a small fire inside his hi-hat. But Bennink—who has recorded with Eric Dolphy, Major Holley, Peter Brotzmann and (often) with alter ego Misha Mengelberg—doesn't let his antics disrupt the music's flow. He is one of the most powerfully swinging jazz drummers, even (or especially) using wire brushes, as on Herbie Nichols's tunes *117th St* and *Sunday Stroll* here. A musician of uncommon presence, Bennink evokes big-beat masters like Sid Catlett and gets a beautiful, tough sound from his drum kit.

The Clusone trio is his handpicked band. Moore, an American living in Amsterdam, has a clean, sleek clarinet sound, feisty alto sax style and a passion for fetching tunes, like Neal Hefti's lovely *Girl Talk* or his own plaintive *Debbie Warden*. Reijseger, perhaps the most technically adept jazz cellist, can sound like a drunken blues guitarist or a jazz bassist on amphetamines. Sometimes this CD sounds like a tenor/bass/drums LP on 45rpm. The music ranges from the lyrical to the bopping to the outward-bound; virtually all of it swings like crazy. **KW**

George Benson 1943

Compact Jazz **Benson** (elg, v); **Clark Terry**, **Ernie Royal**, **Snooky Young** (t); **Jimmy Owens** (t, flh); **Garnett Brown** (tb); **Alan Raph** (btb); **Arthur Clarke**, **George Marge** (ts); **Pepper Adams** (bs); **Eric Gale** (elg); **Herbie Hancock**, **Paul Griffin** (p); **Jimmy Smith** (org); **Buddy Lucas** (hca); **Ron Carter**, **Bob Cranshaw** (b); **Chuck Rainey** (elb); **Billy Cobham**, **Jimmy Johnson Jr**, **Leo Morris**, **Donald Bailey** (d); **Jack Jennings** (cga, vb); **Johnny Pacheco** (cga). Verve Ⓜ 833 929-2 (55 minutes). Recorded 1967-69.

⑥ ❻

The opening *Billie's Bounce*, by a quintet featuring Ron Carter and Herbie Hancock, is a model example of Benson's straight-ahead jazz playing, and sufficient inducement alone to buy this CD. The ensemble is supple and responsive, Benson has a vigorous and strongly focused solo, and Hancock catches the fire, his excursion forming the perfect complement to Benson's. Things deteriorate later, but not before another three tracks by the same group from the 1967 **Giblet Gravy** album have passed. None of these cook with the bristling invention of the opener, but none suffer from the incipient mass-market strategies of *That Lucky Old Sun*, the first of four tracks from the 1968 **Goodies** album. There, in contrast to the democratic setting of the small group, Benson's guitar and vocals are rigidly framed by shrill big-band rhythm and blues textures. The small-group *Doobie Doobie Blues* and a wild card, *Tuxedo Junction* with Jimmy Smith, are mild exceptions, but the string-shrouded *I Remember Wes* leaves no doubt about the way things were going. Within a year, Benson had been adopted by Creed Taylor to fill the shoes of his inspiration Wes Montgomery; soul-jazz celebrity was just around the corner. **MG**

Breezin' **Benson** (g, v); **Phil Upchurch** (g); **Ronnie Foster** (elp, moog); **Jorge Dalto** (p, clav); **Stanley Banks** (b); **Harvey Mason** (d); **Ralph MacDonald** (perc); **orchestra**. Warner Bros Ⓜ 27334-2 (39 minutes). Recorded 1976.

⑥ ❻

This is often claimed to be the biggest-selling jazz album of all time. It may well be, but a more accurate description would perhaps be the biggest-selling jazz-inflected album. There is no way of doubting Benson's jazz pedigree (he even appeared as a sideman on a Benny Goodman small group date), and he still contributes some very tasty solos (*Six to Four* is especially effective) to this record, but there is also no doubting the fact that Benson took what Wes Montgomery was doing a few steps further. He plays largely within the contemporary popular styles, stating the melodies in a quite unadorned way, then moves on to some easeful improvisation, letting the rhythm section do most of the cooking. In doing so, he set the pattern for thousands of imitators in the years to come, and a close listen to the original here (for this is the original, significantly different from what Montgomery did before) reveals a good deal more toughness and bite in Benson's guitar work than what could be found in that of his followers. In that sense at least, Benson has often been given short shrift for what he did on this album. But then the material weighs against him here, being largely lightweight and arranged to stay that way, whatever interest he can generate after the themes are dispensed with. **KS**

Ed Bentley

Bolla **Bentley** (org), **Dave Lewis** (ts), **Jim Mullen** (g), **John Piper** (d), **Francis Piper** (perc), **Louise Markham** (v). Prestige Ⓕ CDSGP 003 (59 minutes). Recorded 1990.

⑤ ❽

Bentley, an organist born in Ghana and settled in London, has made a record of two parts: the first part, tracks one to seven, is a swinging date in the tradition of Jimmy Smith, Jack McDuff and the rest, with fine tenor playing from Dave Lewis and some outstanding blues-based guitar from Jim Mullen. There is little need to doubt the reason for Bentley's band being called the Blue Note Quartet; if this had been released on Blue Note in 1965 it would have passed muster. The New York label, Muse, are still releasing records just like this.

The other part (tracks eight to twelve) of the date is not something you'd find on a mid-sixties Blue Note album. It features vocalist Louise Markham, who has a good voice and clear diction, but no special message to deliver. When the material she sings includes things like *Black Coffee*, *'Round Midnight* and *The Man I Love*, all sung definitively by many others, I find it hard to justify its inclusion in what is already a full programme of music. **KS**

Cheryl Bentyne

Something Cool **Bentyne** (v); with various groups including: **Mark Isham** (t, elec perc); **Bob Militella** (ts); **David Goldblatt**, **Corey Allen** (p); **Larry Bunker** (vb); **David Torn** (g); **John Patitucci**, **Chuck Domanico**, **Doug Lunn** (b); **Kurt Wortman** (d); **Lisa Johnson**, **Steve Scharf**, **Ray Tischer**, **Mathew Cooker** (strings). Columbia Ⓕ CK 48506 (45 minutes). Recorded 1992.

⑥ ❽

This album, dedicated to the memory of June Christy, in all truth hovers near the borders of jazz, but it has more jazz elements than those of any other musical style, easy listening included. Bentyne, a recent member of The Manhattan Transfer, has a moderate range and a pleasantly impure timbre, wedded to a secure technique. She has the ability to make a melodic line glide rather than stagger along, and the arrangements, suitably atmospheric (ballads like *Moonray* are particularly evocative), esoteric and almost new-age-ish at times, suit her approach very nicely.

Backing musicians do not get a lot to do here, with Mark Isham landing the biggest supporting role, his trumpet adding a useful obbligato from time to time. In the fifties, an album like this would have been proudly labelled 'mood music' by its record company, and a legion of listeners would have known what to expect. These days, such a label tends to denigrate, but I mean no such disrespect if I describe it so. This is a well-crafted and enjoyable album of nineties mood music, made by talented professionals. **KS**

Bob Berg

1951

Riddles **Berg** (ts, ss, rec); **Gil Goldstein** (acc); **Jim Beard** (kbds, org, p, elp); **Jon Herington** (g, elg, mand); **Victor Bailey**, **John Patitucci** (elb); **Steve Gadd** (d); **Arto Tuncboyaciyan** (v, perc). Stretch Ⓕ GRS 00112 (50 minutes). Recorded 1994.

⑧ ❽

At a time when his peers were almost universally embracing fusion, Berg's unfailingly melodic soloing on Sam Jones's 1978 **Visitation** was one of the delights of seventies hard bop. In due course he turned to fusion, first with Miles Davis and then in several albums with the Denon label. The first of these, **Short Stories**, spawned a minor fusion classic in *Friday Night At The Cadillac Club*, but sadly this early promise was not fulfilled on later Denon issues.

However, signing with Stretch has marked an artistic renaissance for Berg, and although his first Stretch album, in which he revisited hard bop, didn't match his seventies work, **Riddles**, his second, is his most satisfying since **Short Stories**. In an appealingly varied programme which offers an impressively integrated fusion of folk, funk, world music and jazz, Berg's sound and melodic creativity seem fully restored, the new settings providing the ideal foil for his bristling, raw-toned inventions. A good deal of thanks for the success of the date are due to the compositions and arrangements (notably by Berg, Chick Corea and Jim Beard) from which Berg's solos emerge as perfectly placed organic elements. **MG**

Karl Berger

1935

Conversations **Berger** (p, vb); **Ray Anderson** (tb); **Carlos Ward** (as, f); **Mark Feldman** (vn); **James 'Blood' Ulmer** (g); **Dave Holland** (b); **Ingrid Sertso** (v). In & Out Ⓕ IOR 77027-2 (72 minutes). Recorded 1994.

⑥ ❽

Initially a bop pianist in home town Heidelberg, Berger adopted the vibraphone and followed free pioneers Ornette Coleman and Don Cherry to Paris. His next stop was America and he worked briefly with both of these luminaries. He became involved in education and is currently in a major musical post in Frankfurt.

As this CD demonstrates, he is still very much a practising musican and composer, with the piano rejoining the vibes in his performance equation. This excellent series of duo *Conversations* show that he uses whatever best suits the job. Both piano and vibes are effective in the gentle dialogues he has with Ward but crisp vibraphone lines seem more appropriate to the tête-à-tête that unites him with Sertso's voice on *Why Is It*. His piano on *Bemsha Swing* is a model of good design and execution while the musical badinage he has with Anderson proclaims that unforced humour favours neither instrument. *North* takes calm piano into polemic territory with Ulmer's quarrelsome guitar, while Berger's reflective piano on *Lover Man* shows his genuine sympathy for Feldman's romantic violin recitation and for Ramirez's original theme. Long gone are the free-form aspirations but, in their place, there is a maturity and depth that transcends the choice of instrument. **BMcR**

Jerry Bergonzi

1947

Vertical Reality **Bergonzi** (ts); **Andy LaVerne** (four tracks) (p); **Mike Stern** (five tracks) (g); **George Mraz** (b); **Billy Hart** (d). Musidisc Ⓕ 500642 (55 minutes). Recorded 1994.

⑥ ❾

This may be Bergonzi's album, but for five of the eight tracks Mike Stern steals it away from him. Why? Because Bergonzi is a supremely competent saxophonist who can play up a storm but who possesses few distinguishing traits. He has a muscular post-Coltrane tone, a style which is Coltrane and Brecker entwined (with perhaps some Joe Henderson thrown in for ballast), and a relentless swing. He is one of those players for whom the word 'brisk'—or perhaps even brusque—could have been coined. So he does not invite the listener's affection; rather, his respect. Stern is more ready to insinuate himself into your consciousness, more able to pause in a solo and take off in a different direction, or on a different phrase. His touch is commendably varied, so he is capable of rhythmic emphases which escape Bergonzi in their subtlety.

The tracks with LaVerne are more conventional in execution, but hardly lessen the problem. LaVerne is the more interesting soloist, especially on *Lover Man* where Bergonzi abandons all attempts to retain some form of continuity with the theme's message and opts for a punchy workout on familiar ideas. A less than scintillating album, then. **KS**

Bunny Berigan

1908–1942

Portrait of Bunny Berigan **Berigan** (t) with: **Eddie Miller**, **Bud Freeman**, **Forrest Crawford** (ts); **Claude Thornhill**, **Cliff Jackson Joe Bushkin** (p); **Grachan Moncur**, **Mort Stulmaker** (b); **Edgar Sampson** (cl, as), **Dave Barbour**, **Eddie Condon** (g); **Dave Tough**, **Cozy Cole**, **Ray Bauduc** (d); **Connee Boswell** with **The Dorsey Brothers Orchestra**; **Paul Hamilton and his Orchestra**; **Frankie Trumbauer and his Orchestra**; **Glenn Miller and his Orchestra**; **Gene Gifford and his Orchestra**; **Benny Goodman and his Orchestra**; **Bud Freeman and his Windy City Five**; **Tommy Dorsey and his Orchestra**; **Bunny Berigan and his Blues Boys**; **Bunny Berigan and his Boys**; **Bunny Berigan and his Orchestra**. ASV Living Era Ⓜ AJACD5060 (69 minutes). Recorded 1932-37.

⑧ ❻

Throughout his short life Berigan was inspired by the trumpet playing of Louis Armstrong; he added a special kind of poetry of his own and the result was a style which fitted bands large and small. His unbreakable attachment to alcohol was ultimately his downfall and this excellent and representative selection from his extensive discography gives a good idea of what jazz lost when he was cut down at the age of only 36. With either muted or open trumpet, he could enhance the work of vocalists, but a fine example of his power and bottled-up excitement with a big band is included here in the shape of Benny Goodman's classic *King Porter Stomp*. His own small recording units produced little masterpieces; the four titles with his Blue Boys in 1935 have marvellous solos by pianist Cliff Jackson and tenor saxist Eddie Miller as well as Bunny himself. His service with Tommy Dorsey the masterly *Marie* included here, but for many it was his own version of *I Can't Get Started* which epitomized his best work, as a trumpeter and a vocalist. Fittingly, it is the closing track on a collection in which the transfers are good, although some surface noise remains from the original 78rpm sources. **AM**

Tim Berne

1954

Fractured Fairy Tales **Berne** (as, v); **Herb Robertson** (t, c); **Mark Feldman** (vn, bar vn); Hank Roberts (vc, v, electronics); **Mark Dresser** (b); **Joey Baron** (d, electronics). JMT 834 431-2 (55 minutes). Recorded 1989.

⑦ ❼

Starting in 1979 from a loosely adapted Braxton/Hemphill/John Carter base, Berne's recordings have grown more unpredictable all along. With several of his crucial early albums unavailable on CD, attention falls on this promising band. Unlike many ad-hoc aggregations, this one has the advantage of familiarity; it is an enhancement of the trio Miniature (Berne, Roberts, Baron) and the same personnel that made Berne's second CBS disc, **Sanctified Dreams**, with the addition of the galvanic violinist Feldman (Feldman, Roberts, and Dresser, by the way, have their own string trio, Arcado). Such common experience allows for the concise, intuitive group activity of *Now Then*, stretching a freebop line into new parameters without breaking the thread. Nothing stays the same for too long here, the arrangements are constantly broken apart for various instrumental re-groupings. Thus *Hong Kong Sad Song/More Coffee* begins with three separate layers of activity—wah-wah brass, col legno percussion, and a mournful Ornette-ish theme—before expanding into a taut Berne solo, a staggered string trio, and so on. *SEP* is a smoky blues with unusual twists and a duo between stinging Feldman and sputtering Robertson. Not all this imaginative; a couple of the tunes meander a bit. But this is a band with bite, still under development. **AL**

Bill Berry 1930

Bill Berry's L.A. Big Band **Berry** (c); **Cat Anderson, Gene Goe, Blue Mitchell** (t); **Jack Sheldon** (t, v); **Britt Woodman, Jimmy Cleveland, Benny Powell, Tricky Lofton** (tb); **Marshall Royal, Lanny Morgan** (as); **Richie Kamuca, Don Menza** (ts); **Jack Nimitz** (bs); **Dave Frishberg** (p); **Monty Budwig** (b); **Frank Capp** (d). Concord Ⓕ CCD-4027 (49 minutes). Recorded 1976.

⑧ ❽

Berry is a bop cornettist who first formed a rehearsal band in New York in the fifties. Like many musicians in that pre-synthesizer era he migrated to California because that was where studio work then abounded. He reformed his band there and drew into it a glittering assembly of jazz stars. The musicians played, as Jack Sheldon said "for fun and 30 bucks". Berry's talents as an arranger and a leader enabled him to shape the band into one of the best in the country. His experience in Duke Ellington's trumpet section and the presence of other ex-Ellington men in his band (Anderson and Woodman) enabled him to re-create Ellington's music more convincingly than any other band (better even than the Ellington ghost band led by Duke's son Mercer). Like Juggernaut, a similar L.A. band led by Frankie Capp and Nat Pierce, he had the benefit of the playing of Marshall Royal, one of the finest lead alto players in the business. Berry knows that the way to keep musicians happy is to give them plenty of solos, and there are rewarding features here for Anderson (*Boy Meets Horn*) and Sheldon (*Tulip Or Turnip*) as well as a plethora of good solos all round on the rest of the tracks. **SV**

Chu Berry 1910-1941

Berry Story **Berry** (ts); **Roy Eldridge, Irving Randolph** (t); **Hot Lips Page, Wingy Manone** (t, v); **George Matthews, Keg Johnson** (tb); **Benny Goodman, Buster Bailey** (cl); **Joe Marsala** (cl, as); **Doc Rando** (as); **Lionel Hampton** (vb, p, v); **Jess Stacy, Horace Henderson, Benny Payne, Conrad Lanoue, Clyde Hart** (p); **Allen Reuss, Lawrence Lucie, Dave Barbour, Jack Lemaire, Danny Barker, Zeb Julian** (g); **Israel Crosby, Milt Hinton, Artie Shapiro, Jules Cassard** (b); **Gene Krupa, Cozy Cole, Leroy Maxey, Danny Alvin, Sid Catlett** (d). EPM/Jazz Archives Ⓑ ZET 738 (68 minutes). Recorded 1936-39.

⑧ ❽

During the 1930s absence of Coleman Hawkins in Europe, musicians who had worked with both the great man and Berry hailed the latter as the reigning champion of the Hawkins school of tenor. Like most of his contemporaries, he ignored the challenge of Lester Young and instead mastered Hawkins's fluency and power, falling short only occasionally in terms of imagination.

The selection covers many of his small-group recordings while a sideman with Fletcher Henderson and Cab Calloway (he was still with Calloway at the time of a fatal road accident). It omits alternate takes and the 1941 Commodore session (currently only in a Mosaic box) and includes such cherished favourites as Wingy Manone's *Jumpy Nerves* and the Lionel Hampton date that produced *Sweethearts On Parade* and *Shufflin' At The Hollywood*. His partnership with Eldridge, fellow Henderson and Calloway sideman, was continued in much after-hours jamming, which is celebrated in *Sittin In'* (a *Tiger Rag* variant) and a two-tempo version of *Body And Soul*, whose success provoked Hawkins' subsequent masterpiece. A highly rhythmic player (and author of the popular *Christopher Columbus* riff), Berry's originals here include *Maelstrom*, which was later vocalized by Calloway as *Jive*. A reminder that Berry's neglect is unjust, this album deserves a follow-up volume. **BP**

Eddie Bert 1922

Encore **Bert** (tb) with a collective personnel of: **J.R. Monterose** (ts); **Joe Puma** (g); **Hank Jones** (p); **Clyde Lombardi** (b); **Kenny Clarke** (d) Denon/Savoy Ⓜ SV-0229 (35 minutes). Recorded 1955.

⑩ ❾

J.J. Johnson's speed on the trombone eventually led him to compromise the tone of the instrument, and the 'pea-shooter' sound persevered for some years. Eddie Bert, already a veteran, was the first to combine the new style with the proper tonal values of the horn. No doubt his studies with Benny Morton and Trummy Young helped him in this. He is the ultimate veteran, having been a stalwart section man and soloist in the big bands of Norvo, Barnet, Herman, Goodman, Monk, Hampton,

Elliott Lawrence, Thad Jones-Mel Lewis and just about everyone but Duke Ellington. At the time of the current CD he was effective in the Mingus quintet, and working with such tasteful musicians as Puma and Jones was obviously a great delight to him. He is an eloquent player who today still (though now in his seventies) plays with great power and imagination. Everybody knows his name, but not enough people make a fuss about him. This is as good a collection of trombone solos as you will find anywhere with Bert showing himself to be very much a match for his pals Jay and Kai (see below). He is credited on the liner as composer of *Conversation* (a track with a boisterous Rollins-like solo from Monterose). When Pete Rugolo recorded the tune with Shorty Rogers and Milt Bernhart he took composer credit. Bert has a lovely open tone and is also an excellent player with the mutes. Don't worry about the playing time; feel the quality of the material. **SV**

Ed Bickert 1932

Third Floor Richard **Bickert** (g); **Neil Swainson** (b); **Terry Clarke** (d); **Dave McKenna** (p). Concord Ⓕ CCD 4380 (53 minutes). Recorded 1989.

⑧ ❽

Bickert's apparent preference for spending most of his time in his native Canada probably accounts for his modest international reputation. He made important contributions to some fine Paul Desmond albums, but **Third Floor Richard** is a wide-ranging, comprehensive picture of his talents. On the basis of a few tracks, one might be excused for thinking he was a somewhat introvert soloist with a penchant for dreamy, wistful ballads. That is only part of the story. When the tempo is up and with guest Dave McKenna laying down a percussive keyboard backing, Bickert turns into a hard-driving soloist capable of producing long and interesting lines with no loose musical ends. The 11 tracks contain some beautiful and unhackneyed material including a tune which even its composer, Duke Ellington, seems to have forgotten, for he seldom recorded it: *Tonight I Shall Sleep (With A Smile On My Face)*. Harry Warren's *I Know Why (And So Do You)* is a duet by McKenna and Bickert; on all the other tracks Swainson and Clarke provide ideal support. Concord may have many guitarists in their catalogue but none better than Ed Bickert. **AM**

Acker Bilk 1929

Acker and Humph **Humphrey Lyttelton** (t, cl); **Acker Bilk** (cl, v); **Dave Cliff** (g); **Dave Green** (b); **Bobby Worth** (d). Calligraph Ⓕ CLGCD 027 (68 minutes). Recorded 1992.

⑧ ❽

Outgrowing the hype and publicity which pushed him to fame in the fifties and sixties, Bilk has surreptitiously metamorphosed from being an icon of the Trad boom into a hard swinging mainstream clarinettist and jazz vocalist. Traces of his early influence from George Lewis remain, and his vocals are Armstrong-inspired, but he yet contrives to have his own sound, as did that other British original Sandy Brown.

Bilk has made several good albums with musicians ranging from Al Fairweather and Bruce Turner to Stan Tracey, but this one with Lyttelton stands out amongst them. Lyttelton has always had an affinity for clarinet and alto saxophone players and the ensembles he creates with Bilk call to mind the best of the 'jump' sessions of the thirties.

The sometimes delicate moods created, as on *When You And I Were Young, Maggie,* are much aided by the replacement of a piano by guitarist Cliff, most sophisticated in both solo and accompaniment. Green leads as a bass player should and provides a resounding mattress for the two horns to bounce their ideas on. Amongst the fresh and appropriate material chosen, Bilk fashions a delicate version of Bechet's poignant *Southern Sunset*, a tune unknown to him until Lyttelton played him the original record shortly before the session. **SV**

Walter Bishop Jr 1927

What's New **Bishop** (p); **Peter Washington** (b); **Kenny Washington** (d). DIW Ⓕ 605 (46 minutes). Recorded 1990.

⑥ ❽

Bishop is of the same generation as Bud Powell and Al Haig, being just three years younger than both men, and a stylist with his roots deep in bop. He was Charlie Parker's preferred pianist for much of the last five years of the saxophonist's life. His own solo career, however, has never been high-profile, and he has usually appeared in other people's bands.

This lively trio album, made in New York five years ago, will help redress the balance a little. Although the *un poco loco* tempo of the opening *I'll Remember April*, an obvious Powell tribute, is a little beyond Bishop in terms of finding him creating new ideas and patterns at that sort of pace, the rest of this pleasingly varied programme enchants and impresses. Certainly, the treatment of

Wayne Shorter's *Speak No Evil* is enterprising, with all three musicians swinging in unison and finding a light-as-air feel to glide on. That and Kenny Dorham's *Una Mas* are perhaps the standouts. *Crazy She Calls Me*, a solo feature, finds Bishop in Tatum territory and coping quite well, but the world was not waiting for another flat and uninspired version of the old Ellington warhorse, *Things Ain't What They Used To Be*. **KS**

Cindy Blackman 1959

Telepathy Blackman (d); **Antoine Roney** (ss, ts); **Jacky Terrasson** (p); **Clarence Seay** (b). Muse Ⓕ MCD 5437 (51 minutes). Recorded 1992.

⑧ ❽

A busy, bustling drummer in the Tony Williams mode, Cindy Blackman proved on the stellar hard-bop session **Code Red** that she was not only a tastefully rumbustious musician but also a fine composer. On this later session, featuring a working band rather than an ad hoc studio grouping, she again demonstrates both skills in abundance, but there is a maturity about her work present only sporadically in previous recordings, Where **Code Red** was something of an assault on the ears—albeit a surprisingly subtle one at times—**Telepathy** bears all the hallmarks of a more considered piece of work. The drum performance still bristles with press rolls, sudden felicitous side drum interventions and delicate cymbal work, but there are signs that, instead of favouring the headlong charge, Blackman has now recognized the virtues of a carefully planned campaign. Thus up-tempo material driven by tumbling drums and fleshed out by Antoine Roney's grainy, long-spun lines and Jacky Terrasson's spiky, delightfully unpredictable playing is tellingly juxtaposed with whisper-soft material; percussive originals with an intelligent version of Monk's *Well, You Needn't* and a wonderfully hectic romp through Miles Davis's *Tune Up*. Where previous albums have tended to be enjoyable showcases for individual virtuosity, **Telepathy**, as its name suggests, is all about communication within the quartet, and although not as immediately accessible as some of Blackman's earlier work, richly rewards repeated listenings. **CP**

Ed Blackwell 1929-1992

What It Is? Blackwell (d); **Graham Haynes** (c), **Carlos Ward** (f, as), **Mark Helias** (b). Enja Ⓕ ENJ 7089 2 (63 minutes). Recorded 1992.

⑨ ❾

Ed Blackwell was an exceptionally versatile, melodic drummer who graced every record he played on. Though best known for his early sixties recordings with Ornette Coleman, he stayed close to the music's cutting edge, his discography in the seventies and eighties including dates with players such as Anthony Braxton, Joe Lovano, David Murray and the Coleman alumni group, Old and New Dreams. What It Is?, taped live in California just two months before his death from kidney failure, is a rare excursion as leader for Blackwell and features his Ed Blackwell Project. The date brings the best from the players; bassist Mark Helias is rock-steady and also takes several bravura solos, as does the impressive Haynes on cornet, notably on Pettiford Bridge. Carlos Ward plays eloquently and contributes four of the disc's six compositions. Blackwell shines on The Mallet Song, a ceremonial exchange of drum solos and brief ensemble unisons. His drumming throughout is wonderfully alert and buoyant, a dancing pulse that he threads through the music with a master's deftness of touch. **GL**

Eubie Blake 1883-1983

Memories of You Blake (piano rolls); **Gertrude Baum**; **Steve Williams** (one piano roll each). Biograph Ⓕ BCD 112 (50 minutes). Recorded 1915-73.

A professional ragtime pianist at 15, Blake first recorded in 1917. He had a long association with singer Noble Sissle and together they took the first Negro musical to Broadway in 1921. Most of their recordings in the twenties concentrated on the cabaret side of their music, but after a lengthy period of retirement from public playing Blake emerged to launch a second recording career. Naturally the latter-day records were the real thing, but Blake was now 86 and time had taken its toll. Most of the rolls on this CD present Blake from the 1917 to 1921 period and make a fine job of documenting the more youthful end of his musical life. As with many ragtime rolls, the timing is somewhat regimented and as (*Dangerous Blues* demonstrates) the odd difficult phrase is negotiated rather stiffly. Blake was an accomplished player however, and a more legato feeling is engendered on *Memphis Blues* and *Good Fellow Blues*. This stride element in his style was to become more significant as his career progressed and is more evident on the final two tracks that took him back to a roll-recording piano for the first time in 52 years. They show that this great musical figure still knew how to present *Wild About Harry* and *Memories of You*, his two great compositional hits, to maximum advantage. **BMcR**

Ran Blake

1935

The Short Life Of Barbara Monk **Blake** (p); **Ricky Ford** (ts); **Ed Felson** (b); **Jon Hazilla** (d). Soul Note Ⓕ 1127 (42 minutes). Recorded 1986.

⑧ ❽

Blake's music, usually so intricate, individual and insular, is allowed to interact with a sensitive rhythm section and a forthright tenor saxophonist. The result is, quite naturally, unlike his highly charged solo discs, but still evocative and satisfying. A harmonically and structurally original artist, he sacrifices a measure of freedom to blend with the others but maintains the unorthodox voicings that prove him a movement of one, and his oblique solos are balanced by Ford's more direct statements. The programme reflects the leader's Third Stream idealism and eclecticism, with two versions of a brief Sephardic melody, a mournful Greek folk song by Mikis Theodorakis, a lightly Latin swinger (where his Monkish interjections come to the fore) and Stan Kenton's theme song. But there is a consistent emotional undercurrent too, a leitmotif of death, specifically in the tender waltz dedicated to Thelonious's daughter, a quizzical meditation on a friend's suicide (*Pourquoi, Laurent?*), and the brooding *Impresario Of Death*. Still, the mood is never bleak optimism being registered in the lush Strayhornesque ballad *In Between* and a clash of keys on *I've Got You Under My Skin*. As always, Blake's music is both subtle and richly rewarding. **AL**

Art Blakey

1919-1990

The History of Art Blakey and the Jazz Messengers **Blakey** (d); **Kenny Dorham**, **Clifford Brown**, **Bill Hardman**, **Lee Morgan**, **Freddie Hubbard**, **Woody Shaw**, **Valery Ponomarev**, **Wynton Marsalis** (t); **Howard Bowe**, **Curtis Fuller**, **Robin Eubanks** (tb); **Sahib Shihab**, **Lou Donaldson**, **Jackie McLean**, **Bobby Watson** (as); **Musa Kaleem**, **Hank Mobley**, **Benny Golson**, **Wayne Shorter**, **Carter Jefferson**, **Dave Schnitter**, **Bill Pierce** (ts); **Ernie Thompson**, **Branford Marsalis** (bs); **Walter Bishop**, **Horace Silver**, **Sam Dockery**, **Bobby Timmons**, **Cedar Walton**, **Walter Davis**, **James Williams** (p); **Laverne Barker**, **Curley Russell**, **Doug Watkins**, **Spanky DeBrest**, **Jymie Merritt**, **Reggie Workman**, **Mickey Bass**, **Dennis Irwin**, **Charles Fambrough** (b); **Kevin Eubanks** (g); **John Ramsey** (d); **Tony Waters** (cga). Blue Note Ⓜ CDP7 97190-2 (three discs: 202 minutes). Recorded 1947-81.

✔ ⑧ ❽

This is the best survey of Blakey's Messengers, spread over 34 years and taken principally from his Blue Note albums (some of the later tracks have been leased from Prestige, Timeless and Roulette). A glance at the collective personnel listed above gives a good idea of the important young musicians who benefited from their experience with the Messengers. Two of the earliest tracks in this chronological survey were taped one night at Birdland in New York by an ephemeral quintet containing both Clifford Brown and Horace Silver. The next tracks are by one of the first and best-known Blakey units, a co-operative quintet containing Kenny Dorham and Hank Mobley. This is classic hard-bop, with great interaction between Art and the front line men. Inevitably over the years there were changes, and the arrival of Lee Morgan and Benny Golson gave the band a new character with tunes such as *Blues March* and *Moanin'* (both included here), but it was the sixties units with the three-piece front line and Wayne Shorter contributing eminently suitable arrangements which shifted Art's group onto a new plane of excellence. The third disc introduces Bobby Watson and Wynton Marsalis, but it also reminds us of the fine band with trumpeter Ponomarev and tenor saxist David Schnitter. Throughout this well-compiled set Blakey steers his various bands like a true leader and the bright sound and good transfers help to give the music maximum presence. **AM**

Art Blakey's Jazz Messengers With Thelonious Monk **Blakey** (d); **Monk** (p); **Bill Hardman** (t); **Johnny Griffin** (ts); **Spanky DeBrest** (b). Atlantic Ⓜ 781332-2 (44 minutes). Recorded 1957.

⑧ ❻

Few drummers could relax when they played with Monk. Blakey could and the bond between him and the pianist meant, in the early days at least, that when Monk really hit his stride, Blakey was on drums. Griffin also had more than a grasp of the music and the coming together of the three men on this date meant that it was set fair to succeed. It did beyond expectation, and it would be hard to find a better monument to both Monk and to the hard bop era. Monk's tunes are built like Rome, and he and Blakey set up a continual onslaught of inspired creation. Griffin's solos have a life of their own and it is only the young trumpeter to whom Blakey feels the need to give the occasional supercharging from the drums.

Many of the groups in which Monk played were flawed for various reasons—ften because the musicians were intimidated by the music. This one is as nearly without flaw as makes no matter. It also confirms that the sparse and concise early versions of the Messengers were far better than the sprawling later bands. Unfortunately the recording quality is not as good as the music. **SV**

Paris 1958 **Blakey** (d); **Lee Morgan** (t); **Benny Golson** (ts); **Bobby Timmons** (p); **Jymie Merritt** (d). RCA Bluebird Ⓜ 61097-2 (65 minutes). Recorded 1958.

⑧ ❻

The coming of age of the 'new' Jazz Messengers is documented by this remarkable evening at the Club St. Germain, which originally filled three LPs (leaving as much material again yet to be reissued on CD). The valuable anecdotal notes recount that the recording was 'disguised' as a live broadcast—indeed, the opening track was first issued as *Blues March For Europe No. 1*. Presumably the Parisian radio station was as baffled by the dedication as Blakey's American record company of the time.

Interestingly, the band's success with this tune and *Moanin'* on their first trip to Europe preceded the issue of the studio versions, which were done less than eight weeks earlier. These versions are longer and more unbuttoned, with Blakey doing his well-known trick of pushing his soloists to their apparent limits and then some, the catchy material being ultimately subservient to the drummer's interplay with Golson and the 20-year-old Morgan Timmons sounds more dated, but Art is also heard taking fours on *Now's The Time* and he solos on Monk's *Evidence*.

Less well-known than his various Birdland albums, this set is one of the best from the remarkably consistent Blakey. The awkward edits before the closing themes of *Now's The Time* and *Whisper Not* are retained from previous issues, but are about the only blemishes on a splendid set. **BP**

Free For All **Blakey** (d); **Freddie Hubbard** (t); **Wayne Shorter** (ts); **Curtis Fuller** (tb); **Cedar Walton** (p); **Reggie Workman** (b). Blue Note Ⓜ CDP7 84170-2 (37 minutes). Recorded 1964.

✔ ⑩ ❿

I do not know what was bugging Blakey the day this album was made, but boy does he beat the stuffing out of both his drum kit and the band on the title track! Things get to such a pitch of passion that Shorter, the first soloist, sounds like he is about to drown during the last verse of his solo, and hands over to Curtis Fuller in the manner of a man who has just gone the distance with the then-Cassius Clay. Fuller simply cannot cope with the barrage, and while Hubbard skips joyfully over the worst that Blakey can do to him (including a 6/8 snare roll that lasts for five bars and blots everyone else out), the only possible way out of all this is a drum solo. And when it comes, it has the manic exultation of a man just escaped from prison. Or hell.

The rest of the date, the Latin-based *Pensativa* aside, lowers the emotional temperature only by degrees, so that *Hammer Head*, a Shorter line cast in the mould of so many Messengers two-beat anthems, sounds distinctly threatening, and *Hubbard's Core*, a fast-ish, scalar composition, comes across as a speedboat in choppy seas as Blakey thrashes away underneath the soloists, creating a tricky polyrhythmic base for them to slither on.

This may not be a typical Messengers date, but it's one of the great Blakey albums, with only Riverside's *Caravan* able to get anywhere near it for emotional intensity. **KS**

Album of the Year **Blakey** (d); **Wynton Marsalis** (t); **Bobby Watson** (as); **Billy Pierce** (ts); **James Williams** (p); **Charles Fambrough** (b). Timeless Ⓕ SJP 155 (43 minutes). Recorded 1981.

✔ ⑧ ❻

Yes, the title is presumptious, but the Jazz Messengers did produce an excellent set when they cut this date in a Paris studio shortly before a wholesale turnover in personnel. The balance toward new material (originals by Watson and his wife, Williams and Fambrough) plus the inclusion of jazz classics (by Parker and Shorter) not previously identified with Blakey, underscore this edition of the Messengers' distance from a fixation in the past. Marsalis is vivid and technically impeccable, but only one of a group of strong soloists, and the charged contribution of the others drives home the point that they (especially Watson and Williams) were the real architects of Blakey's resurgence in the last decade of his life. For the leader's part, the expected energy is present, plus substantially more shading than he could manage as his hearing loss progressed. Fambrough's big-enough bass is too far forward in the mix, which is not the comment one generally makes about Blakey albums and a tribute of sorts to Fambrough's muscular attack. That caveat aside, it is hard to fault this definitive snapshot of why the Jazz Messengers remained important well into their fourth decade. **BB**

Pierre Blanchard

1956

Music for String Quartet, Jazz Trio, Violin and Lee Konitz **Blanchard** (vn); **Lee Konitz** (ss, as); **Herve Cavelier**, **Vincent Pagliarin** (vn); **Michael Michelakakas** (va); **Herve Derrien** (vc); **Alain Jean-Marie** (p); **Cesarius Alvim** (b); **André Ceccarelli** (d). Sunnyside Ⓕ SSC 1023D (43 minutes). Recorded 1986.

⑥ ❽

Unlike the majority of jazz-string collaborations, where the latter are used merely to provide a lush backdrop for a soloist (occasionally successfully, as with Art Pepper's *Winter Moon*), Pierre Blanchard's project does demand a fair degree of musical interaction and mutual commitment. This can work, as Stan Getz and Eddie Sauter's **Focus** amply demonstrates, but here, despite the best efforts of violinist/composer Blanchard himself and his guest soloist Lee Konitz, the participants never quite gel. The most successful pieces are the least jazz-based, the ones for which the strings set the agenda, the jazz players apparently finding it easier to accommodate themselves to the strings than vice versa. Thus two extended, more classically-oriented pieces, *Mani-pulsations*, and *XVIII Brumaire*, with their tricky tempo-changes and more complex rhythms, are intriguing failures; the jazz pieces, particularly John Coltrane's *Moment's Notice*, render the strings almost embarrassingly redundant at worst and over-polite at best. There are some rewarding moments in the session—one which Konitz apparently requested, having always wanted to record with strings—but these come chiefly in passages mainly featuring either strings or jazz instruments; their combination merely accentuates the strings' rigidity on the one hand and Konitz's occasionally startlingly astringent tone on the other. **CP**

Terence Blanchard 1962

The Billie Holiday Songbook **Blanchard** (t); **Bruce Barth** (p); **Chris Thomas** (b); **Troy Davis** (d); **Jeannie Bryson** (v). Columbia Ⓕ 475926-2 (57 minutes). Recorded 1993.

⑥ ❽

This project is neither an attempt at recreation nor, fortunately, an exercise in deconstruction. Blanchard takes a dozen songs associated with Billie Holiday and plays them in his own style with his own rhythm section, backed by an orchestra of strings, woodwind and French horns. Five pieces also feature the vocalist Jeannie Bryson, who delivers good, plain readings. All the songs are, of course, reharmonized according to contemporary practice, which bleaches out the pristine simplicity of strong, lively tunes like *Nice Work If You Can Get It*, but adds new colour to the more dirge-like ones, such as *Good Morning Heartache*. The inevitable *Strange Fruit* receives an interesting and effective treatment, with Bryson speaking the words while Blanchard simultaneously plays the melody, such as it is. The orchestral arrangements by Miles Goodman are subtle, sophisticated and infinitely better than anything Billie Holiday herself ever received in this line. An interesting and enjoyable set. **DG**

Carla Bley 1938

Escalator over the Hill **Bley** (p, org, cel, ch, v); **Enrico Rava**, **Michael Snow** (t); **Don Cherry** (t, v); **Michael Mantler** (t, vtb, kbds, perc); **Sam Burtis**, **Jimmy Knepper**, **Roswell Rudd** (tb); **Jack Jeffers** (b-tb); **Bob Carlisle**, **Sharon Freeman** (frh); **Jack Buckingham**, **Howard Johnson** (tba); **Souren Baronian**, **Peggy Imig**, **Perry Robinson** (cl); **Jimmy Lyons** (as); **Gato Barbieri** (ts); **Chris Woods** (bs); **Don Preston** (syn, v); **Karl Berger** (vb); **Sam Brown**, **John McLaughlin** (g); **Leroy Jenkins** (vn); **Nancy Newton** (va); **Calo Scott** (vc, v); **Charlie Haden**, **Ron McClure**, **Richard Youngstein** (b); **Jack Bruce** (elb, v); **Paul Motian** (d, perc); **Roger Dawson** (cgas); **Bill Morimando** (orch bells, celeste); **Paul Jones**, **Sheila Jordan**, **Jeanne Lee**, **Linda Ronstadt**, **Viva** (v). JCOA Ⓜ 839-310-2 (two discs: 121 minutes). Recorded 1968-71.

✔ ⑩ ❽

Given Bley's description of her *Genuine Tong Funeral* (recorded by an augmented Gary Burton band in 1968) as a "dark opera without words", *Escalator over the Hill* qualifies as her dark opera with words—libretto courtesy of Paul Haines, whose poetry frequently suggests Paul Bowles overtaken by whimsy. 'Opera' literally means story, but the story told by Haines amounts to little more than existential posturing. Even so, the principal singers—Jack Bruce, the unlikely Paul Jones, late of the Manfred Mann Band, and the perhaps even less likely Ronstadt—make surprising sense of it all, though the real story is Bley's flair in casting according to type a variety of emotive improvisers, including the garrulous Rudd, the solemn Haden and the fire-breathing Barbieri. Until this and *Funeral*, Bley was prized as a gifted miniaturist, having made her mark with compositions for her ex-husband Paul's piano trio. *Escalator* suggested the full size of Bley's talents as a composer and orchestrator. Some of the most beguiling moments are provided by a 'Desert Band' featuring Cherry and Lee; these can be listened to as a preview of Cherry's adventures in World Music. One complaint: shrunk to fit a jewel box, the facsimile of the original LP booklet reduces the libretto to a squint and the lavish session photography to a series of meaningless blurs. **FD**

Carla Bley Live **Bley** (p, org, glspl); **Michael Mantler** (t); **Steve Slagle** (ss, as, f); **Tony Dagradi** (ts); **Gary Valente** (tb); **Vincent Chancey** (frh); **Earl McIntyre** (tba, btb); **Arturo O-Farrill** (p, org); **Steve Swallow** (b); **D. Sharpe** (d). Watt Ⓕ 12 (815 730-2) (41 minutes). Recorded 1981.

⑧ ❻

As it gradually becomes apparent that Carla Bley's band may be the best sounding band lead by any pianist-composer since Duke Ellington died, it makes more sense to search out records like this. More than a dozen years old now, but sounding as fresh as a shower of rain, and with all the characteristics you come to expect from Carla Bley – great slabs of sound, sudden blasts of exotic air, odd interludes on organ, bits that sound like circus music, bits of gospel, bits of Gary Valente's force-10 trombone (always sounding a bit similar, but nobody cared that Tricky Sam Nanton always played more or less the same solo for Duke), bits of parody, jokes ... but all joined together by something more basic than logic. And only ten people producing such a grand sound! **MK**

Fleur Carnivore **Bley** (p); **Lew Soloff, Jens Winther** (t); **Frank Lacy** (frh, flh); **Gary Valente** (tb); **Bob Steward** (bb); **Daniel Beaussier** (ob, f); **Wolfgang Puschnig** (as, f); **Andy Sheppard** (cl, ts); **Chistof Lauer** (ss, ts); **Roberto Ottini** (ss, bs); **Karen Mantler** (h, org, vb, ch); **Steve Swallow** (b); **Buddy Williams** (d); **Don Alias** (perc). Watt Ⓔ 21 (839 662-2) (56 minutes). Recorded 1988.

⑧ ❽

One came to expect Carla Bley to be touring and recording with small to medium-sized groups during the eighties. This CD, recorded live at the Montmartre in Copenhagen, returned her to the fruitful area of the bigger band. This 15 piece, equipped with excellent original Bley material, takes her back into pure jazz territory. Her arrangements are imaginative, with the four-man rhythm section sounding much larger and with Valente's trombone voice smearing across the lower reaches of the ensemble almost as a trade mark. The trumpet/horn section also achieves a remarkable depth, matching the reeds with its dancing lilt. *Fleur Carnivore* was written to commemorate the tenth anniversary of Duke Ellington's death and something of the great man's approach to leading permeates the whole session. Each soloist is accommodated in a way that suits him. Puschnig chooses the title track to show his ease with an attractive tune, and even becomes Hodges-like in his theme statement in the third movement of *The Girl Who Cried Champagne*. Valente shines in the same piece, and also in *Song Of The Eternal Waiting Of Canute*, where the horns pace his throaty utterings. Soloff is his usually confident solo self and Lauer deals several heavy tenor hands in a score that demands such treatment. Although too little is heard of Bley's quirky piano, her talent as composer, arranger and leader has rarely been so effectively displayed. **BMcR**

Paul Bley

1932

With Gary Peacock **Bley** (p); **Gary Peacock** (b); **Paul Motion, Billy Elgart** (d). ECM Ⓔ 1003 (843 162-2) (34 minutes). Recorded 1968.

⑧ ❻

Canadian-born Bley has had a long and occasionally influential career. He has been in the habit of being around when important things were happening—making an album for Mingus's Debut label when in his early 20s; forming a band for a club date in late-fifties L.A. which turned out to be the entire Ornette Coleman Quartet plus himself on piano; being one of the formative members of the Jazz Composers' Guild in mid-sixties New York; making a crazy album for avant-garde label ESP (titled **Barrage**) which nonetheless was one of the first New Wave records, and holds up quite well today; marrying such talents as Carla Bley and Annette Peacock, and premièring their early work on his records; and getting involved in the electronic rush of the early seventies before, like Keith Jarrett, beating a hasty retreat to his former acoustic style.

This album is quintessential mid-period Bley; all the major stylistic traits are in place, including a tendency to lose his accompanists at ultra-slow tempos. Although it does not have the emotional depth of the currently unavailable **Ramblin'** (Charly/Affinity), it shows his versatility (the repertoire here ranges from Jerome Kern to Ornette) and has two excellent versions of two classic Annette Peacock pieces, *Gary* and *Albert's Love Theme*. Gary Peacock's presence is also a considerable asset.

The is clearly out of tune and the recording somewhat shallow, but the listener's enjoyment should not be affected too much by this. Pretty lousy playing time though, especially when there is other material available, from the contemporaneous **Ballads** album, to beef it up with. **KS**

Open, To Love **Bley** (p). ECM Ⓔ 1023 (827 751-2) (43 minutes). Recorded 1972.

✔ ⑨ ❾

Paul Bley has the rare distinction of being one of jazz's most recorded and, at the same time, most underrated pianists. Crucially influential but seldom credited as such, his music over the past four decades has addressed and altered our perception of rhythm and harmony. This solo disc, which is really an extension of many of the concepts he explored in sixties trios, frees him from jazz conventions of form and phrasing to expand possibilities of expression. It also marked his rediscovery of the acoustic piano after a long period of working with electronics. Thus his tone and subtle pedal effects are lovely (and captured marvelously by the excellent engineering). The thematically unified programme, consisting of moody, atmospheric pieces by Bley and two former wives, Carla Bley and Annette Peacock, is a mirror of Bley's introspective nature and commitment to absolute spontaneity. The sparse textures throughout are a reflection of the material (whether the poignancy of Carla's *Closer*, the fragility and exposed vulnerability of Annette's *Open, To Love*, or his own abstracted view of *I Can't Get Started*) and an indirect homage to the laconism of Monk and Count Basie in an entirely different context. Bley's remarkable lyricism, chromaticism, modulations, and rubato combine in a moving, unique voice. **AL**

Solo Piano **Bley** (p). SteepleChase Ⓔ SCCD 31236 (68 minutes). Recorded 1988.

⑩ ❾

From the tumble of notes that opens *If I Loved You*, it is clear that this is top-form Bley; a sure touch and a precision of thought that has become ever-sharper over the years. Every note is 'just so'. **Tears**, a 1983 solo album for the French label Owl, was similarly exact, but implacable in mood, fraught with desolation. There is a hint of that here in a mournful *Tin Tin Deo*, but overall **Solo Piano** is a far friendlier record, its abstractions spiced with blues, romance and a touch of dry wit.

One of Bley's great talents is succinctness. His improvisation is so well-focused that each track becomes a reverie almost from the first note. Moods and styles flit through his playing in playful profusion: *Gladys* is rolling boogie; *If I Should Lose You*, subtle rumination; *Slipping*, abstract fun. He alters *You Go To My Head* beyond recognition, yet his own *Mariona* turns out to be *Fools Rush In*. There are one or two excursions inside the piano, notably the collage of twangs that leads into *And Now The Queen*. Mostly, though, his radicalism is diffident; a slight shift of tempo, a new harmonic twist—but all shaped with the loving care that comes from 40 years' experience. **GL**

Jane Ira Bloom

1953

Art & Aviation **Bloom** (ss); **Kenny Wheeler**, **Ron Horton** (flh, t); **Kenny Werner** (p); **Rufus Reid**, **Michael Formanek** (b); **Jerry Granelli** (d). Arabesque Ⓕ AJ 107 (58 minutes). Recorded 1992.

⑨ ❾

Like Steve Lacy, Jane Ira Bloom has forged an estimable career by focusing her considerable talents on the soprano saxophone. It is a decision that has paid handsome dividends. So, too, has her decision to concentrate on a repertory centred on her own work. Indeed, the Yale composition graduate has written for the Pilobolus Dance Theater, New York's Improvisational Dance Ensemble and, as heard here in *Most Distant Galaxy*, the National Aeronautics and Space Administration.

Bloom is genuinely a contemporary composer-performer as much influenced by Charles Ives as Charles Mingus or Ornette Coleman. She's one of a very few saxophonists to have successfully incorporated live electronics as an artistic rather than commercial adjunct, a facility aptly demonstrated in the cosmic-foray lighting up *Gateway to Progress*. In a Bloom performance, composition and improvisation seem as one. Bloom's inspired vision elicits the best from her co-voyagers. In the galvanizing title track, Bloom, Wheeler, Formanek and Granelli chart the heavens with audacity and awe. Equally impressive is the cleverly titled *Hawkins' Parallel Universe*, Bloom's plastique re-limning of *Body and Soul*. **CB**

Hamiet Bluiett

1940

Nali Kola **Bluiett** (bs, f); **Hugh Masekela** (t, flh); **James 'Plunky' Branch** (ss); **Donald Smith** (p); **Billy 'Spaceman' Patterson** (g); **Okeryema Asante** (d); **Chief Bey** (d); **Tito Sompa** (d); **Seku Tonge** (d); **Quincy Troupe** (author and poet). Soul Note Ⓕ 121 188-2 (48 minutes). Recorded 1987.

⑦ ❽

Bluiett had experience with St Louis's Black Artists Group before moving to New York in 1969. There he played a prominent part in the eighties 'loft movement'. He established himself as the marauding samurai of his instrument, vocalizing his passion on the baritone sax, dredging honks from his very soul and using overtones with superb control. The eighties found him to be a cornerstone of the World Saxophone Quartet and leader of the Telepathic Arkestra, Rainshout and the Clarinet Family. His open mind made him amenable to most musical situations and this CD is a typical challenge. The absence of a bass player ensures a free harmonic plain over which he can roam and the driving drum barrage becomes a buoyancy factor. This is never more evident than on *Enum*, a piece with changing time signatures and with Bluiett ranging freely across them. His switch to flute on *Ganza* offers a different response to the same situation as he wheezes an extremely creative path over the hot coals of the drum bed. The presence of three horns does change the emphasis on *Nali Kola*, perhaps bringing the music back from the pan-tonal sound canvas so adeptly provided by the drummers. The master drummers do set the tone of the whole session, however, and in so doing, they help Bluiett to show yet another facet of his multi-talented approach to jazz. **BMcR**

Arthur Blythe

1940

Retroflection **Blythe** (as); **John Hicks** (p); **Cecil McBee** (b); **Bobby Battle** (d). Enja Ⓕ 8046 2 (69 minutes). Recorded 1993.

⑥ ❽

Blythe emerged in New York's seventies loft movement a prodigy of 34 and an erstwhile member of California's freer music scene. His earliest records announced an original talent with a style that tempered chromatic irreverance with flowing rubato and, in the eighties, he led a superb combo with cellist Abdul Wadud and tuba player Bob Stewart as well as working effectively with Gil Evans. Unfortunately, the conservatives saw his expansive style as their link with the loft extremists and, after joining Columbia, he was saddled with some projects that compromised his talent. Although a recipient of electronic enhancements, Blythe continued to work in straight-ahead jazz situations and, in the nineties, showed more desire to do so.

This CD presents a typical working date, live at the Village Vanguard and with Blythe comfortably set in a musical debating club where everyone has a say. His compositions are well in evidence; *Peacemaker* and *Faceless Woman* show how his writing relates to the structural consistency of his solos. His ferocious blues playing on *JB's Blues* displays his more atavistic side and the **Retroflection** session appropriately embraces the more basic elements of his musical past. Blythe's playing in 1993 is harnessed to tunes but it has an inner freedom that makes it timeless. **BMcR**

Jimmy Blythe

1901-1931

Johnny Dodds & Jimmy Blythe 1926–1928 **Blythe** (p); prob. **Freddie Keppard**, **Punch Miller**, **Louis Armstrong**, **Natty Dominique** (c); **Roy Palmer** (tb); **Junie Cobb** (cl); **Johnny Dodds** (cl, as); **Bud Scott** (bj); **Jimmy Bertrand**, **Baby Dodds**, **Buddy Burton** (wbd); **Jasper Taylor** (d, wbd). Timeless Ⓜ CBC 1-015 (66 minutes). Recorded 1926-28.

⑧ ❽

Kentucky-born Blythe moved to Chicago in his teens, studied with Clarence Jones and became one of the most ubiquitous figures on the South Side scene. Early solo recordings suggest the proxy influence of the Harlem stride piano school, but at heart he was very much a blues player. His technique was adequate for the tasks he set himself and his sense of timing was suited to the rolling gait proposed by his style. Arhythmic passages confirmed his confidence and his two-handed method ideally accommodated his unpretentious creative process.

This CD sets his barrelhouse piano in various combo situations and lusty solos on *Poutin' Paper* and *Idle Hour Special* can be seen as vital parts of the ensemble fabric. Their natural momentum is in itself a stimulant but the way in which he drives the entire ensemble on *Adam's Apple* gives a clearer indication of his inspirational skills. His sympathy for vocalists is found on *Messin' Around*, but it is his relaxed interaction with Dodds on *Buddy Burton's Jazz* that draws attention to his more subtle contrapuntal talents. He was dead at 30 but the rhythmic basis of his style seems to have lived on, firstly through Chicago's hard boppers and then beyond. **BMcR**

Sharkey Bonano

1904-1972

Sharkey Bonano **Bonano** (c, t, v); **Julian Lane**, **Santo Pecora**, **Moe Zudecoff**, **George Brunies** (tb); **Meyer Weinberg** (cl, as); **Irving Fazola**, **Joe Marsala** (cl); **Dave Winstein** (ts), **Armand Hug**, **Clyde Hart**, **Joe Bushkin** (p), **Bill Bourjois** (bj, g), **Frank Frederico**, **Eddie Condon** (g), **Ray Bonitas**, **Thurman Teague**, **Artie Shapiro**, **Hank Wayland** (b), **Augie Schellange**, **Ben Pollack**, **George Wettling**, **Al Sidell** (d); **Johnnie Miller's New Orleans Frolickers; Monk Hazel and His Bienville Roof Orchestra; Santo Pecora And His Back Room Boys.** Timeless Jazz Ⓜ CBC1-001 (70 minutes). Recorded 1928-37.

⑥ ❻

Although Bonano's musical career centred on his home town New Orleans, he was one of jazz's nomads. This CD documents his career in the twenties and thirties, a time when he also worked with Jean Goldkette, Larry Shields and Ben Pollack. He was a lyrical trumpeter; he had an ample, warm tone, a discreet vibrato and he built his solos with taste and logic. Suspect intonation did not help his singing, but his colourful way with a vocal did add spice to many of his performances. He was happiest in a Dixieland set-up and it is significant that this issue has him working with tailgate specialists Pecora and Brunies and with clarinettists Sidney Arodin, Fazola and Marsala, who knew their way around a New Orleans ensemble. His way of combating the arrival of the swing era was to pretend it was not happening. His fine solo on the 1928 *High Society* could be transplanted into the 1936 version without trouble and, with Fazola and Marsala reneging and his rhythm team accepting the new stylistic rules, he was forced to make some concessions on the Sharks of Rhythm titles in the thirties. After World War II the revivalist movement allowed him to return to his first love, and his last musical days were spent entertaining tourists in the Crescent City. **BMcR**

Joe Bonner

1948

Suite for Chocolate **Bonner** (p); **Khan Jamal** (vb); **Jesper Lundgaard** (b); **Leroy Lowe** (d). SteepleChase Ⓕ SCCD 31215 (57 minutes). Recorded 1985.

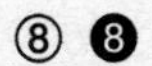

Taking a light, spacious airiness somewhat reminiscent of Ahmad Jamal's fifties work and imbuing it with enough bluesy funkiness to prevent it from too firmly occupying the middle of the road, **Suite for Chocolate** is a highly accessible and consistently pleasing session. Particularly effective is the combination of the two front-line instruments, lending an attractive chiming quality to the group's overall sound. Both Joe Bonner and Khan Jamal are highly accomplished, versatile musicians, the former as at home playing free jazz with Richard Davis as he was contributing rippling piano to Pharoah Sanders's unique sound; the latter commuting between Sunny Murray's free jazz, Ronald Shannon Jackson's jazz-rock in the Decoding Society and Billy Bang's complex and highly arranged units. This wealth of experience, brought to bear on a selection of Bonner originals notable for their clean melodic lines and unpretentious directness, lifts the session above the undemanding and excessively easy-going set it appears to be on first acquaintance. Bonner in particular, his style a compelling and unusual mixture of almost lushly romantic mellifluousness and biting percussive effects, is especially effective at injecting tension into superficially unremarkable tunes by occasionally teasingly slipping into double-time, and overall **Suite for Chocolate** showcases a considerable improvisational talent which deserves wider exposure. **CP**

Earl Bostic

1913-1965

Blows A Fuse **Bostic** (as) with various groups including: **Blue Mitchell** (t); **John Hardee**, **John Coltrane**, **Stanley Turrentine**, **Benny Golson** (ts); **Jaki Byard** (p); **Al Casey**, **Mickey Baker** (g); **Jimmy Cobb** (d). Charly Ⓜ CDCHARLY 241 (58 minutes). Recorded 1946-58.

⑧ ❻

Some may still view Bostic's fifties best-sellers as undemanding forerunners of Kenny G, but in terms of style if not sales, Maceo Parker would be a better comparison (coincidentally, James Brown originally worked for the same label as Bostic, and borrowed his arrangement of *Night Train*, heard here.) The altoist was into his 30s, with much playing and arranging experience behind him, before recording under his own name. As heard in five early tracks recorded for Sam Goody, he is fluent all over the instrument but with a musical policy close to Louis Jordan's (check the novelty vocal *Cuttin' Out*). His jazz ambitions surface on the better recorded 1949-50 material, the title-track being based directly on *Stompin' At The Savoy*, while *Disc Jockey Nightmare* is the dazzling *Man I Love* showpiece he used as a Lionel Hampton sideman.

His 1951 version of *Flamingo*, with its growly alto throughout and its groovy off-beat (from Jimmy Cobb!) was a hit, so none of the later sidemen get a look in solowise. It requires some insight to realize that this is the saxophonist admired by Coltrane and others for his technical mastery, but his imagination was also superior to that of most rhythm-and-blues players. **BP**

Boswell Sisters

It's the Girls **Connee and Helvetia Boswell** (v); **Martha Boswell** (v, p) with various accompaniment, including: **Manny Klein** (t); **Tommy Dorsey** (tb); **Jimmy Dorsey** (cl, as); **Arthur Schutt**, **Martha Boswell** (p); **Eddie Lang** (g); **Joe Venuti** (vn); **Joe Tarto** (b); **Stan King** (d). ASV Living Era Ⓜ CDAJA 5014 (62 minutes). Recorded 1925-31.

⑥ ❺

The American popular music factory of the twenties and early thirties, while offering only a back-door entrée to Bessie Smith and her black sisters, boasted a flourishing department of white women whom it would describe as blues singers—apparently meaning that they lent their material, whether formally blues or not, a blue tone and often a Southern accent. The best of this group were the New Orleans-born Boswell Sisters.

Connee shared with Bing Crosby (whom she would occasionally partner on record) a deep warm voice, a way with languorous sliding notes and great rhythmic assurance. She recorded a number of solos, some included here, such as *Time On My Hands* with the Victor Young Orchestra. But the Boswells's métier was their vivacious and elaborate harmonizing, often deployed through several changes of tempo, as on *Heebie Jeebies*, *Shout, Sister, Shout!* and the bravura *Roll On, Mississippi, Roll On*. Such numbers, which make up about a third of this collection, were accompanied with matching verve by a contingent from the Dorsey Brothers Orchestra, and ever since they were first issued these performances have been admired for the pointed contributions of Klein, Jimmy Dorsey, Venuti and Lang. Others have more staid orchestral settings, or employ Martha's piano, as on their 1925 début *I'm Gonna Cry* (*Cryin' Blues*). This quaint performance, with its mock-instrument effects in the manner of the Mills Brothers, has a funny-hat air that gives no hint of the thoroughly modern millinery they would strut in just five years later. **TR**

Jean-Paul Bourelly

Tribute To Jimi **Bourelly** (g, v); **T. M. Stevens** (b); **Alfredo Alias** (d); **Kevin Johnson**, **Irene Datcher** (v). DIW Ⓕ DIW-893 (73 minutes). Recorded 1994.

⑧ ❿

This album is decidedly not for jazz purists. On it, Jean-Paul Bourelly comes closer to recreating the sound and passion of Jimi Hendrix's music than anyone else since the master died in 1970. It is uncanny: Bourelly is not only able to reconstruct Hendrix's sound, he can also get frighteningly close approximations of his phrasing, precise rhythms, his little hesitancies, his searing intensity, his audaciousness. What has all this got to do with jazz? Well, Hendrix was one of the supreme improvisers of his generation, his music was thoroughly based in the blues and his music profoundly influenced subsequent jazz musicians as much as rock, funk or fusion. Bourelly, a guitarist with impeccable jazz credentials and a string of associations with top-flight jazz musicians, brings his wide knowledge and abilities to this project and breathes new life into an important musical legacy. His version of Hendrix's *Machine Gun* here is spine-tingling, almost savage, and it takes on a doppelgänger relationship to the famous 'live' Hendrix original at Fillmore East.

This is certainly one way to reinvigorate the jazz tradition, and if you want to see how inventive it can get without resorting to rap and sampling, try Bourelly's version of *Power of Soul*, where he uses just fragments of Hendrix's original composition to create a mesmerizing and wildly catchy, utterly new piece of music. This is a CD to revive your faith in both the past and the future. **KS**

Lester Bowie 1941

The Great Pretender **Bowie** (t); **Donald Smith** (p, org); **Fred Williams** (b); **Phillip Wilson** (d); **Hamiet Bluiett** (bs); **Fontella Bass**; **David Peaston** (v). ECM Ⓕ 1209 (829 369-2) (43 minutes). Recorded 1981.

⑧ ❾

The Great Pretender is the record with which Lester Bowie first caught the ear of the pop audience. This was due chiefly to the title-track, an epic, passionate and often hilarious account of The Platters' old r&b hit. Earlier Bowie albums had delved into various African-American music traditions with versions of *Hello Dolly*, *St Louis Blues (Chicago Style)* and the gospel tune *God Has Smiled On Me*. Drawing here on his own soul roots, Bowie fashions a lavish arrangement, complete with falsetto ooh-oohs plus hiccoughing baritone saxophone, and runs through a spectaular arsenal of trumpet effects–smears, stabs, gurgles, chortles and a gamut of vocalising techniques–all spiced with his typically puckish humour.

Inevitably the rest of the album is a little anticlimactic, although *Rios Negroes'* sensuous lyricism and the cool sound-painting of *Rose Drop* impress. Bowie's flamboyant personality tends to dominate proceedings; the trumpet playing, for which he draws on the complete span of black music history, is often brilliant, but the frequent recourse to humour can wear thin. **GL**

Lester Bowie's Brass Fantasy: The Fire This Time **Bowie**, **E.J. Allen**, **Gerald Brazel**, **Tony Barrero** (t); **Vincent Chancey** (frh); **Frank Lacy**, **Louis Bonilla** (tb); **Bob Stewart** (tba); **Vinnie Johnson** (d); **Famoudou Don Moye** (perc). In & Out Ⓕ IOR 7019-2 (75 minutes). Recorded 1992.

⑧ ❽

Lester Bowie has been the one member of the Art Ensemble of Chicago to create a public persona large (and popular) enough away from the group to be perceived as Lester Bowie, trumpeter and showman, rather than "that guy from the Art Ensemble". The records and concerts given under his name, or that of his Brass Fantasy, have a distinct personality, and freely indulge his rollicking sense of fun and irony. The Brass Fantasy has, of course, got more than half-a-decade's experience behind it now, and inevitably the personnel has experienced change. From the evidence of this, its latest record, made live in concert in Switzerland, the band's enthusiasm and verve continues to grow apace rather than diminish.

Bowie is still very much the focal point and the band's repertoire remains as eclectic as ever (Michael Jackson and Jimmie Lunceford rub shoulders on this disc), but there is no dissipation of spirit and no fossilising of the structures through which the wholly brass-bound music is created. This means that the arrangements (from a multitude of pens) really work and continue to challenge the players in useful ways. E.J. Allen's ten-minute piece *Journey Towards Freedom* may well be the standout composition and performance here, but there is plenty more to enjoy. The sound, especially for a live recording, is vivid and full. **KS**

Ronnie Boykins 1935-1980

Ronnie Boykins **Boykins** (b, bb); **Joe Ferguson** (ss, ts, f); **Monty Waters** (as, ss); **James Vass** (as, ss, f); **Daoud Haroom** (tb); **Art Lewis**, **George Avaloz** (perc). ESP-Disk Ⓜ 3026-2 (44 minutes). Recorded 1975.

⑥ ❹

Associated for many years with Sun Ra, Boykins latterly worked with Roland Kirk, Sarah Vaughan and Steve Lacy. He was a very effective servant for the Arkestra and his superbly rounded tone, accurate pitching and seemingly effortless pizzicato mobility stamped him as one of jazz's most outstanding bassists. His arco tone was pleasingly clean and, as *The Will Come, Is Now* and *Starlight At The Wonder Inn* on this CD show, he builds solos that have the legato feeling of a saxophone line. This release also provides the opportunity to judge him as a composer and demonstrates that he works in a style that would not immediately suggest a bass player. His arrangements are functional rather than detailed, but he knows how to turn unison saxophone and solo bass into balanced counterpoint. The solo strength at his disposal is something of a limiting factor and, not surprisingly, the emphasis is centred on the leader's bass. His sousaphone is heard on *The Third*, but it is rather pedestrian and poorly recorded. Fortunately there is enough here to confirm Boykins as a brilliant bassist, as well as a man who makes the most of the troops at his disposal. **BMcR**

Charles Brackeen
1940

Worshippers Come Nigh **Brackeen** (ts); **Olu Dara** (c); **Fred Hopkins** (b); **Andrew Cyrille** (d, perc); **Dennis Gonzalez** (perc). Silkheart Ⓔ SHCD 111 (56 minutes). Recorded 1987.

⑧ ❽

Initially a pianist and violinist, Brackeen moved to California in 1956 and worked as a tenor saxophonist with Dave Pike and Joe Gordon. He moved to New York in 1966, married pianist JoAnne Grogan and worked alongside Don Cherry and Ed Blackwell before becoming involved with the loft movement and the likes of Dara, Frank Lowe and with his own Melodic Art-tet. This CD, with a title from the Attainment session added to the original LP, is an excellent introduction to Brackeen's comprehensive, musical talents. He wrote all of these consistently strong themes, as well as fashioning arrangements to give the impression of a larger unit. The size illusion is further fuelled by the fullness of Hopkins's generously-toned bass lines and Cyrille's kicking, group-conscious drumming. Both play for the soloists and the horn men respond well. Brackeen is a successful escapee from the mighty influence of John Coltrane, his dry-toned and economical approach especially evident on *Bannar* and *Cing Kong*. Dara is a talent that blossomed in the eighties and his fiery horn really ignites *News Stand* and the title-track. Fine solos apart, the distinct, organizational guide lines of the arrangements offer a performance to make one of the freer jazz forms accessible to the sceptics. **BMcR**

Joanne Brackeen
1938

Take A Chance **Brackeen** (p); **Eddie Gomez** (b); **Duduka Da Fonseca** (d); **Waltinho Anastacio** (perc, v). Concord CCD Ⓔ 4602 (64 minutes). Recorded 1993.

⑥ ❽

A product of the West Coast's largely unsung late-fifties scene, Brackeen moved to New York and worked with the Messengers, Joe Henderson and Stan Getz and as well as a string of small groups showcasing her mature piano style. This CD, her second dedicated to the music of Brazil, owes its existence to her tours of the country with Getz. It shows that her technical assurance is a major advantage and, rather than be restricted by the choice of material, she draws strength from the alternatives it offers.

The be-bop basis of her style is evident as she marauds through *Frevo*; her lithe lines are conducive to a perfect bossa nova reading of *Recado Bossa Nova* while her reflective improvisation on *Estaté* largely ignores the Brazilian connection. Her waltz-time duet *On The Island* recalls the Bill Evans Gomez duets and shows that the spirit of Brazil can thrive without Latin percussion, while *Mountain Flight* has her playing with an airy buoyancy that could ride comfortably with any rhythmic foundation. There are three Brackeen originals and all are extensions of her creative soloing process. Their choice of harmonies suit the Brazilian muse and all three exhibit a latent power that suggests the very talented Brackeen could break out at will. **BMcR**

Don Braden
1964

After Dark **Braden** (f, ts); **Scott Wendholt** (t, flh); **Noah Bless** (tb); **Steve Wilson** (as); **Darrell Grant** (p); **Christian McBride** (b); **Carl Allen** (d). Criss Cross Ⓔ 1081 CD (65 minutes). Recorded 1993.

⑦ ❽

This is not Braden's latest album (he has a 1994 quartet date on Landmark) but it is still his best, most varied and resourceful effort. Part of the reason for this is that the expanded front line gives him so many more options, and on the five originals he takes appropriate advantage. Braden, a graduate of the Betty Carter, Wynton Marsalis and Tony Williams groups, is a skilled soloist, but more importantly to his long-term career he writes tunes with a clear personality and his arrangements nicely illuminate the interesting corners of each song's harmonic structure. Which puts me in mind just a little of Wayne Shorter, and although there is a deal of difference between the two saxophonists, stylistically and otherwise, the implication is clear for his future development.

Meanwhile, there is this album, and there is little here to fault. Everything is tastefully and intelligently done, and Braden is skilfully supported by Wendholt, Bless and Wilson, while the rhythm section has such a nice groove to it (McBride, a particular delight, is very sweetly recorded) that it is possible to listen through each track taking them in alone and not get bored. If you're concerned over the viability of the young jazz mainstream, try this for size. **KS**

Bobby Bradford
1934

Comin' On **Bradford** (c); **John Carter** (cl); **Don Preston** (p, syn); **Richard Davis** (b); **Andrew Cyrille** (d). hatART CD6016 Ⓔ (75 minutes). Recorded 1988.

In the mid-sixties cornettist/trumpeter Bobby Bradford joined forces with reedsman John Carter to co-lead the New Art Ensemble, a West Coast-based quartet that further explored the free jazz territory first opened up by their mutual acquaintance Ornette Coleman. That group broke up in 1974 but Bradford and Carter continued to work together, often playing support on each other's projects. **Comin' On** captures one of their final collaborations before Carter's death in 1991; a Hollywood club performance on which they front a rhythm section well-versed in the more lyrical areas of free jazz.

Compared to the New Art Ensemble, this music has more colours, more textures (thanks in part to Preston's dashing swathes of synthesizer), while the two leaders are now so attuned that their every exchange is a mercurial delight. Carter, who by this time was playing clarinet exclusively, is arguably the more adventurous of the pair, but Bradford is the more graceful player, his lines spun with a melodic logic and rythmic flexibility that hint at his bop roots. His poise on the title track, the elegance he brings to *Ode to the Flower Maiden*, the fire and urgency he displays throughout, together with his distinctive, blues-inflected tone, all reaffirm his status as a master stylist of contemporary jazz. **GL**

Ruby Braff

1927

Hi-Fi Salute To Bunny **Braff** (c); **Benny Morton** (tb); **Pee Wee Russell** (cl); **Dick Hafer** (ts); **Nat Pierce** (p); **Steve Jordan** (g); **Walter Page** (b); **Buzzy Drootin** (d). RCA Victor Ⓜ 118520 2 (53 minutes). Recorded 1957.

⑧ ❼

This record, an early attempt at a 'concept' album, quite neatly sums up the hybrid nature of Braff's talent and appeal. He has an instrumental style which forges together elements of Armstrong, Beiderbecke and others, but his phrasing fits very comfortably over the free-flowing common time which is at the root of swing, plus he has a sufficiently sophisticated technique and harmonic imagination to incorporate elements of later jazz styles with which to add colour and drama to his playing. In making this album a tribute to a technically and lyrically gifted trumpeter from an earlier age, Braff has given himself the room to roam freely through repertoires and styles as it suits him. This is very much to the music's advantage, giving it a Basie-ish rhythmic drive, a modified Dixieland-cum-mainstream ensemble, and (for the most part) swing-style solos. If nothing else, this means that men as disparate as Hafer and Russell sound equally at home, and each element gels convincingly. Russell is particularly persuasive at slower tempos (his spot on *I Can't Get Started* being a highlight), but Braff excels at all tempos and plays with great conversational poise, as well as an attractively burnished brass tone. That he is also a fine ensemble lead is amply demonstrated.

The only drawback discernible on this album is the decision by RCA Victor's producer on the session to bathe Braff in excessive reverb, spoiling the otherwise commendably clean, sharp and balanced recording quality. If that can be ignored, then some fine music making will come your way. The CD reissue has an extra track from the session, *Did I Remember*, originally released on LPM 1644 due to lack of space on the original LP. **KS**

Bravura Eloquence **Braff** (c), **Howard Alden** (g), **Jack Lesberg** (b). Concord Ⓕ CCD-4423 (59 minutes). Recorded 1988.

⑦ ❽

All of Braff's albums for Concord reach a high standard, and the one under consideration is singled out purely because Braff, Alden and Lesberg are as near to being without flaw as it is safe for improvising jazz musicians to be. Braff's forte is melodic improvisation, and ideas tumble from him as though he were a singing waterfall. He has a piquant dash of be-bop in his work which places him rather ahead of more conventional trumpet players. Like most musicians of small physical stature - Hackett, Berry and so on - Braff plays the trumpet-cornet, which is more of a cornet than a trumpet. It could be argued that he has lost some of the element of surprise which spiced his style in the fifties and sixties, but in middle-age he remains an eloquent and refreshingly creative improviser.

Howard Alden is a young guitarist who is something of a throwback, basing his virtuoso playing firmly in the music of three or four decades ago. He was the perfect partner for Braff and it is to be regretted that, due to Braff's restless personality, the two men no longer work as a team. **SV**

Leandro Braga

E Por Que Nao? (And Why Not?) **Braga** (p); **Bob Mintzer** (f, ts); **Steve Nelson** (vb); **Romero Lubambo** (g); **David Finck**, **Jose Pienasola** (b); **Ignacio Berroa** (d); **Giovanni Hidalgo** (perc). Arabesque Jazz Ⓕ AJ104 (47 minutes). Recorded 1991.

⑥ ❽

Braga is one of the newer generation of musicians who are equally at home in Latin and jazz-based music, rhythms and forms. The resultant mix is potent and bodes well for the future. He is an assured technician and has clearly picked his cohorts carefully. Mintzer and Nelson, of course, have jazz credentials from any number of sources, and David Finck shows himself to be a thoroughly modern bass player in both technique and in thought. A ballad like *My Little One* displays Braga's touch and poise and gives a clear pointer towards Bill Evans as one of his sources of inspiration, while both the title tune and *Not A Chance* are exciting because the mix of jazz and Latin is so adept and fluid that it is not a case of them co-existing but melding into a new musical language. Which is just possibly a new phase for the broad church of jazz, some 50 years after Dizzy's first recorded efforts to explore the dialogue between the two musics. Braga has some way to go to find the perfect balance, but he and his musicians here exude an easy familiarity with the two cultures which is the perfect building block for the future. **KS**

George Braith

1939

Double Your Pleasure **Braith** (braith-horn, ts); **Ronnie Mathews** (p); **Tarik Shah** (b); **Mark Johnson** (d); **Jimmy Lovelace** (d). King Ⓔ KI-CJ 114 (66 minutes). Recorded 1992.

⑥ ❽

Circus tricksters simultaneously playing three trumpets have never much impressed the jazz world, but the impact of Roland Kirk and his one-man saxophone section was widely felt. Players on both sides of the Atlantic began concomitantly playing different saxophones simultaneously. One such player was Braith, who also played the stritch, Kirk's alto variant, as well as the ancient c-melody sax. During the sixties he was featured on several Blue Note and Prestige sessions, mainly in the company of organists such as Billy Gardner and John Patton. Little has been heard of him on record since that time, but this CD has him in good company and showing undiminished enthusiasm. His self-designed Braith-horn has two bodies but only one bell, and the effect is similar to Kirk's two-horn excursions. Moreover, Braith is a practised jazzman; he knows how to swing and he builds uncomplicated solos that accept the limitations of the instrument while showing genuine inventive flair. His approach to the tenor confirms that he is in no need of gimmicks to get his message across, but delivery of that message is made easier by the sparkling Mathews piano and by the support of Shah and Johnson. **BMcR**

Anthony Braxton

1945

Live **Braxton** (ss, as, cbs, f, cl, cbcl); **Kenny Wheeler** (t); **George Lewis** (tb); **Dave Holland** (b); **Barry Altschul** (d). RCA Bluebird (US) Ⓜ 6626-2 (63 minutes). Recorded 1975-76.

⑧ ❼

Braxton's first great quartet, with Wheeler, Holland and Altschul, worked together for nearly five years, and their level of commitment and communication was crucial, no doubt inspiring Braxton to expand the conceptual range of his composing for small group. This disc is doubly valuable in that the three performances from the 1975 Montreux Festival are not only spellbinding examples of the unit's tenacity, concentration and invention, but are in fact the only ones currently available on CD. Wheeler's lyricism balanced Braxton's raging quixotism beautifully, while Holland was telepathic and inhumanly capable of handling the music's complexities. Altschul, a vastly underrated percussionist, set the standard for the subtle colours and lucid propulsion necessary to buoy Braxton's structures. The group remained together only an additional six months after Lewis replaced Wheeler, but (as the three performances from Berlin, 1976, show) the level of virtuosity soared. Both versions had wit and energy in abundance, whether the music essayed a drone environment allowing pointillistic interplay, a quicksilver neo-bop line (that swings like crazy) or a circus march including a frantic Charleston episode. It should be mentioned that there is a better, more fully documented concert recording of the second quartet (Dortmund 1976, on hatART) available, but until the excellent Arista and Moers recordings of the first quartet are reissued, this is all there is. Note too, that this disc would have received higher marks but for the sloppy production. There are some harsh edits audible and the track indexing is not only inconvenient but misnumbered. There is also an incorrect statement unedited from the original liner notes, mentioning the composition for chamber ensemble and two soloists (Braxton and Lewis) which was part of the double LP set but is not included here, now apparently lost in limbo forever. There are spectacular recordings of later Braxton music in all its variegated forms, but for the important early quartets this is the best we have for now. **AL**

Eight (+3) Tristano Compositions 1989—For Warne Marsh **Braxton** (as, sps, f); **John Raskin** (bs); **Dred Scott** (p); **Cecil McBee** (b); **Andrew Cyrille** (d). hatART Ⓔ CD 6052 (75 minutes). Recorded 1989.

⑧ ❾

Throughout the eighties Braxton concentrated mainly on his own compositions with their attendant pulse tracks; his excursions into jazz standards had been rewarding but rare. This CD represents his first investigation into the music of Lennie Tristano. Being essentially a free player, his solos produced on his own material tended to be organic parts of the whole work. Here he is a far more orthodox improviser. There are starting points and climaxes, his solos have balance and a consistent inner logic and his improvisations take place not because he is obliged to, but because the tune offers options that he is prepared to pursue. There are some very testing tempos here and where it would be easier to parade favourite phrases as you coast through changes, Braxton thinks at speed on *Two Not One*, *Lennie's Pennies* and *Victory Ball*, building well-articulated solos, free from clichés and invested with a rich strain of musical ideas. His readings of *How Deep Is The Ocean* and *Time On My Hands* are fine examples of cogent development and they project an emotional involvement not always transmittable on flute. Raskin is solid in support, Scott makes an impressive recording début and McBee and Cyrille play as well as their reputations suggest they should. **BMcR**

Willisau (Quartet) 1991 **Braxton** (f, cl, cbcl, ss, as); **Marilyn Crispell** (p), **Mark Dresser** (b), **Gerry Hemingway** (d, mba). hatART Ⓕ 4 61001/04 (four discs: 259 minutes). Recorded 1991.

✔ ⑩ ❿

The last few years have brought a rich harvest of Braxton's music on record. As well as the Tristano tribute (see above), outstanding discs have included a trio date with Tony Oxley and Adelhard Roidinger, three quartet concerts from his 1985 UK tour and an excellent big-band CD, **Eugene** (1989). The jewel in the crown is this four-CD set from his current quartet, which was released by Hat Hut Records to celebrate his first 25 years in creative music.

The two studio CDs offer a broad spectrum of Braxton's quartet writing. They include four new pieces plus several examples from the earlier *23* and *40* series of quartet compositions. *40M* and *40B* (the latter graced here with an alto solo that rides on a slipstream of happiness) both show Braxton's love for twisting, speedy bebop-derived lines, while the feinting *23M* recalls the unpredictable phrasing of Warne Marsh, one of his several saxophone heroes. Of the new pieces, *161* stands out as a lovely example of ensemble lyricism, here gathered around the creaking sonorities of a contrabass clarinet.

The use of 'pulse tracks' and 'collage forms' has been a major factor in Braxton's music since the early eighties. The two live CDs show just how much these structural innovations have changed the shape of his quartet concerts, where the main compositions are now played at the same time as various kinds of improvisation and/or extracts from other Braxton works, which the members of the quartet are free to quote from almost at will. The result is a brilliant flow of colours, dramas and flashing interplay; loving tangles that alternate with outbursts of fiery intensity or dreamy solos or droll exchanges. However complex the ground-plan, the quartet are so well-attuned to it and to each other that the music remains gloriously alive as it dances through its maze of choices. **Willisau (Quartet) 1991** places the Braxton quartet in a small-group lineage which includes the Armstrong Hot Fives and The Ornette Coleman Quartet and in which jazz is recast anew and the tradition carried forward. **GL**

The Brecker Brothers

Collection, Volumes 1 and 2. **Randy Brecker** (t, flh); **Michael Brecker** (ts); **David Sanborn** (as); **Don Grolnick**, **Doug Riley**, **Mark Gray**, **Paul Schaeffer** (kbds); **Steve Khan**, **Hiram Bullock**, **Barry Finnerty**, **Bob Mann**, **Jeff Mironov**, **David Spinozza** (elg); **Will Lee**, **Neil Jason**, **Marcus Miller** (elb); **Harvey Mason**, **Steve Gadd**, **Chris Parker**, **Terry Bozzio**, **Richie Morales**, **Alan Schwartzberg**, **Steve Jordan** (d); **Ralph McDonald**, **Sammy Figueroa**, **Rafael Cruz**, **Manolo Badrena**, **Airto** (perc); **George Duke** (syn); **Victoria** (tamb); **Kash Monet** (perc, v); **Jeff Schoen**, **Roy Herring** (v); **Bob Clearmountain** (handclaps). RCA Novus Ⓜ ND 90442/ 83076 (two discs, oas: 71 and 69 minutes). Recorded 1975-81.

✔ ⑧ ❽

There are surely few listeners who can recall such Brecker Brothers abominations as *Finger Lickin' Good* and *Lovely Lady* without head-shaking disbelief, but it seems that once some critics got hold of a good angle they refused to let go. As a result, the brothers' pioneering and intelligent jazz-rock has often been thrown out with the bathwater. Luckily, populist concessions are absent from this valuable retrospective on the first edition of the siblings' band, 1975-81.

Although one could argue with the amount of space given to the rather pallid George Duke-produced items from the early eighties, the 22 selections in these two volumes offer a good representation of the group's strikingly individual and influential fusion of the rhythm and soul of Sly Stone, Stevie Wonder, Cream, Hendrix and others with the harmonic and improvisatory richness of post-bop jazz. Perhaps the set's strongest suit is the inclusion of the whole of the legendary 1978 album **Heavy Metal Bebop**, with its rough but detailed live renditions of such classics as *Some Skunk Funk* and *Squids*. The studio originals are here too, for comparison, and so is the splenetic *Rocks*, with some tough jockeying between Michael Brecker and David Sanborn. Digitally remastered and offered at mid-price, these discs of long-unavailable material offer a long overdue opportunity for critical revision. **MG**

Willem Breuker

1944

De Onderste Steen **Breuker** (cl, bcl, ss, as, ts, rec, v); **Andy Altenfelder**, **Kees Klaver**, **Boy Raaymakers**, **Gerard V.D. Vlist** (t); **Gregg Moore** (tb); **Bernard Hunnekink** (tb, tba); **Willem de Manen** (tb, v); **Iman Soeteman**, **Jan Wolff** (frh); **Dil Engelhardt**, **Lien de Wit** (f); **Andre Goudbeek**, **Bob Driessen** (as); **Maarten van Norden** (ts); **Peter Barkeman** (ts, bs); **Hank de Wit** (bsn); **Bert van Dijk**, **Emil Keijzer**, **Reinbert de Leeuw** (p); **Leo Cuypers** (p, melodica); **Henk de Jonge** (p, acc, syn); **Louis Andriessen** (p, org, h); **Michel Waisvisz** (hca, syn); **Johnny Meyer** (acc); **Sytze Smit** (vn); **Maarten van Regteren Altena**, **Arjen Gorter** (b); **Han Bennink**, **Martin van Duynhoven**, **Rod**

Verdurmen (perc); **Frits Lambrechts**, **Olga Zuiderhoek** (gamelan); **Mondrian Strings**; **Ernö Ola String Quartet**; **Daniël Otten String Group**; **Amsterdam Philharmonic Orchestra / Anton Kersjes**. Entr'acte Ⓕ CD2 (69 minutes). Recorded 1972-91.

⑨ ❽

Dutchman Willem Breuker's early influences were Arnold Schoenberg, marching bands and free jazz. In 1967 he co-founded Holland's ICP (Instant Composers' Pool) with Han Bennink and Misha Mengelberg, but later found its bias towards free improvisation too restricting. In 1974 he set up his own label, BVHaast, and formed his long-standing big band, the Kollektief, whose repertoire takes in the history of jazz, plus waltzes, marches, film scores, theatre music, folk tunes, pop hits and occasional forays into the classical canon—all of which the band may play straight or tongue-in-cheek or ruthlessly satirize, their madcap air balanced by precisely drilled ensembles.

De Onderste Steen, a collection of mostly unreleased material from the last 20 years, makes a marvellous entrée to Breuker's eclectic creativity. It may not all be jazz—few of his records are—but two of the best tracks fit the description. *Besame*, a Breuker clarinet solo, is an hilarious fantasia that mixes free jazz squalls and duck quacks with abrupt snatches of popular classics; *Duke Edward Misère*, a sombre threnody for Ellington with growling solo trumpet, demonstrates (as does *Hawa-Hawa*) Breuker's gift for successfully integrating large string ensembles into big band jazz. Other tracks feature tangos, TV themes, gamelan, accordion, comic rhythm and blues and, in most instances, Breuker thumbing his nose at bourgeois notions of culture. **GL**

Dee Dee Bridgewater 1950

Keeping Tradition **Bridgewater** (v); **Thierry Eliez** (p); **Hein Van De Geyn** (b); **André Ceccarelli** (d). Verve Ⓕ 519 607-2 (57 minutes). Recorded 1992.

⑧ ❽

Dee Dee Bridgewater is almost unique among 'jazzy' modern jazz singers in that she treats songs as songs and not as raw material. Even when she departs quite radically from the original melody the departure remains in the spirit of the piece—so *Fascinatin' Rhythm* for instance has a scat chorus full of rhythmic tricks. Furthermore, she has the knack of swinging simply, bouncing the melody line off the rhythm section without tearing it to bits. Would-be jazz singers should listen to the way she lays out the tune of *Lullaby of Birdland*, as a demonstration of how to do it. Ms Bridgewater now lives in France and the splendid trio on this disc is her regular band there. Together they have made a superb vocal album. **DG**

Ronnell Bright 1930

Bright's Spot **Bright** (p); **Leonard Gaskin** (b); **Kenny Burrell** (g). Denon/Savoy Ⓜ SV-0220 (31 minutes). Recorded 1956.

⑧ ❽

Bright worked as Sarah Vaughan's accompanist for a time during the fifties and made a handful of albums under his own name. He later played piano with the California-based Supersax unit (a group dedicated to playing transcriptions of Charlie Parker's recorded solos) and more recently has turned to acting. The stage's gain has been jazz's loss, for although not an innovator he was nevertheless a very fine pianist in the long tradition of 'utility' players, from Teddy Wilson to Hank Jones. He has a light, graceful touch and the ability to make the notes stand out with clarity. Although this was not a regular working trio the three men function so well together that the unit is as compact as almost any of the better-known established piano-guitar-bass triumvirates (the Clarence Profit Trio of the early forties comes to mind). Three of the eight tunes are originals, the other five good-quality standards including a sensitive reading of *If I'm Lucky.* Kenny Burrell fits into the group sound very well and takes some melodic solos. The playing time is ludicrously short (this is a straightforward transfer of an LP to the CD format) and can only be marginally justified by the price bracket. **AM**

Nick Brignola 1936

It's Time **Brignola** (ss, as, ts, bs, cl, acl, bcl, f, pic); **Kenny Barron** (p); **Dave Holland** (b). Reservoir RSR Ⓕ CD 123 (64 minutes). Recorded 1991.

⑥ ❽

Since leaving Berklee College of Music, Brignola has been something of a stylistic nomad. He has worked with Herb Pomeroy and Woody Herman's Big Band as well as with Latinesque Cal Tjader and Sal Salvador. He also took up the more modern challenge of Ted Curson and for some time led his own rock/jazz fusion band. He has been back in the bop world for some time now and this CD is typical of his current work. It does, however, have an important extra dimension. With overdubbing, Brignola plays all the horn parts in a one-man reed section that has tonal depth, is clearly articulated and is imbued with a naturally buoyant swing. To omit a drummer was a conscious decision by the leader, but it was a strategic omission. Barron and Holland are a powerhouse team and some of the horn parts come over as if deliberately designed to sound like a snare fill or a ride cymbal substitute. Brignola also displays his solo versatility with excellent soprano on *Walkabout*, graceful clarinet on *I Thought About You* and boppish alto on *How Tasteful of You*. It is not surprising that it is on his first-choice baritone that he is most prominent; his gruff but faintly edgy sound lending a certain urgency to all he plays and, in particular, dominating *'Round Midnight* in a one-man, five-horn contrapuntal tone poem. **BMcR**

Alan Broadbent 1947

Live At Maybeck Hall **Broadbent** (p). Concord Ⓕ CCD 4488 (57 minutes). Recorded 1991.

⑨ ❾

New Zealand-born Alan Broadbent is a consummate jazz pianist whose immense talent can perhaps be seen as a logical extension of a line tracing Art Tatum, Bud Powell, Lennie Tristano and Bill Evans. Although classically trained, Broadbent came under the sway of Bill Evans and sojourned in the US, studying at Berklee School of Music. Coming to prominence as Woody Herman's pianist/arranger in the late sixties, Broadbent settled in Los Angeles to become a top jazz studio player/writer whose continuing associations include Charlie Haden's Quartet West and singer Natalie Cole.

As a leader, Broadbent's trio sessions with bassist Buster Smith and drummer Frank Gibson Jr for example **Another Time** (Trend), or **Everything I Love** (Discovery) are passionate, thoughtful and exquisitely wrought. But this intimate solo set recorded live in the cosy Maybeck Recital Hall in Berkeley, California, Broadbent makes his piano a veritable orchestra without sacrificing either rhythmic momentum or shifting textural densities. While the set incorporates his virtuoso technique and sophisticated architectonics, it is Broadbent's sinewy lyricism that emerges as the ultimate authorial seal. Superb playing and sound! **CB**

Bob Brookmeyer 1929

Back Again **Brookmeyer** (vtb); **Thad Jones** (flh); **Jimmy Rowles** (p); **George Mraz** (b); **Mel Lewis** (d). Sonet Ⓕ SNTCD-778 (43 minutes). Recorded 1978.

⑧ ❻

Brookmeyer's accomplishment within jazz is of considerable magnitude and the variety of his talents is so great that he is in danger of being undervalued for each of them. He is the man who has made most expressive use of that brass step-child, the valve trombone. He wears it like a comfortable pair of carpet slippers and exploits all its quirks with skill and passion. His Kansas City roots ensure that he swings hard and unpretentiously and he is one of the best trombone soloists playing today. He is also a pianist and composer of considerable substance.

The title refers to Brookmeyer's return from a long period of what is euphemistically referred to as ill health. His playing has metamorphosed from the muscular and heated improvisations of the sixties into a more subtle and laid-back approach. One misses the sudden violent eruptions into blues phrases of earlier years. Nonetheless we find him here in good form, with a group of long-time associates from the very top echelons. His writing for the date is most imaginative and there is a fetching version of *Willow Weep For Me*, where Brookmeyer's arrangement manages to create new melodies while never actually stating the original one. **SV**

Cecil Brooks III 1961

Hangin' With Smooth **Brooks** (d); **Phillip Harper** (t); **Justin Robinson** (as); **Craig Handy** (ts); **Benny Green** (p); **Peter Washington** (b); **Kenneth Davis** (elb). Muse Ⓕ MCD 5428 (54 minutes). Recorded 1990.

⑦ ❼

The musicians of the neo-classical jazz movement have taken the hard-bop pioneers of the fifties as role models. Their instrumental schooling ensures accurate intonation and clean-lined improvisational methods. They have studied on-stage communication, audience awareness and are well dressed by any standards. To some, the pure perfectionism of such an outlook sounds like a formula for the vapidly unexciting and it takes CDs such as this to re-establish the more appealing virtues of animation, spontaniety and the leader's own special 'swing with simplicity'. Brooks's aggressive drumming at the heart of his well-integrated rhythm section certainly guarantees the right foundation for such a stance and he gets the full backing of his young band. Both saxophonists preach their personal religions most effectively on the *Work Song*-style *Swamp Thang*, Harper makes best use of the intriguing changes on *Accustomed To Her Face*, while Green's Silver-ish piano really rocks on *Don't Forget The Forgotten*. The negative contention that such musicians are not extending jazz boundaries is true but this is mainstream jazz played with flair and imagination by young aspirers. Their Berlin Wall may yet fall; after all, Brooks is also associated with the M-Base collective. **BMcR**

Tina Brooks

1932-1974

True Blue **Brooks** (ts); **Freddie Hubbard** (t); **Duke Jordan** (p); **Sam Jones** (b); **Art Taylor** (d). Blue Note Ⓜ CDP8 28975-2 (50 minutes). Recorded 1960.

⑦ ❽

Brooks (his nickname 'Tina' being a corruption of the childhood soubriquet 'Tiny', and thus pronounced in the manner of McCoy Tyner's surname) had a brief recording career in the early sixties, with just one album, this one, being released during his lifetime (all of his sessions as a leader for Blue Note are now available in a Mosaic boxed set). His style is not dissimilar to Hank Mobley's, with a pleasing combination of what was then called 'soul' in jazz circles and a hard bop harmonic tilt, but his lines are more convoluted, more wide-ranging than Mobley's. Brooks can easily deceive you into thinking not much is going on (most of the songs here are relatively pedestrian reworkings of standard changes), but if a decent degree of concentration is levelled at it, this music is rewarding for head, heart and feet. Of the others around for this session, Hubbard plays cleanly and with taste, his attractive tone and good intonation a constant pleasure, and while Jordan keeps to a supportive role, that big, woody tone and driving rhythm of Sam Jones's bass cannot be suppressed.

Music like this got rapidly lost in the quick-fire evolution of jazz at the beginning of the sixties. While not being earth-shattering, it is worth rediscovering. The CD has alternative takes of two tracks to take the playing-time up to an acceptable level. **KS**

Peter Brötzmann

1941

Machine Gun **Brötzmann** (ts, bs); **Willem Breuker** (ts, bcl); **Evan Parker** (ts); **Fred Van Hove** (p); **Peter Kowald** (b); **Buschi Niebergall** (b); **Han Bennick** (d); **Sven-Ake Johansson** (d). FMP Ⓕ CD 24 (62 minutes). Recorded 1968.

✔

⑧ ❹

This CD was a musical landmark. It followed John Coltrane's **Ascension**, Ornette Coleman's **Free Jazz** and Albert Ayler's **New York Eye And Ear Control** but was unlike any of them. Brötzmann, a former Dixielander, was making a statement for European Free Music that was utterly dramatic, faintly unsure of its direction and ear-shatteringly loud. Brötzmann, Parker, Van Hove, Kowald and Bennink have all played better elsewhere but the real impact here is by the entire ensemble, clamouring their collective anti- establishment discord. There are solos from a young Parker at his most discursive, Van Hove in combat with the rhythm team and Breüker using raw emotion as his calling card. It is Brötzmann, however, who has the most to say; his typical solos on both takes of *Machine Gun* are frenetic to the brink of hysteria, inchoate to order, and are delivered with a power and a bombast that suggests the demented rather than the abandoned. His seventies trio with bassist Harry Miller and drummer Louis Moholo may well have contained work by a more creative saxophonist, but Brötzmann was a harbinger of musical anger, confrontation and the consciously ugly long before the world had heard of punk. In the process, **Machine Gun** provided ground rules for much of the wildest of the music to follow. **BMcR**

Clifford Brown

1930-1956

Memorial Album **Brown** (t); **Lou Donaldson** (as); **Gigi Gryce** (as, f); **Charlie Rouse** (ts); **Elmo Hope**, **John Lewis** (p); **Percy Heath** (b); **Philly Joe Jones**, **Art Blakey** (d). Blue Note Ⓜ CDP7 85126-2 (40 minutes). Recorded 1953.

⑧ ❽

Brown was the musical successor to Fats Navarro and, although not featured on records until the first of these sessions, was sufficiently precocious to have been encouraged by Navarro, who died in 1950. He was also praised by both Gillespie and Parker while barely out of his teens and, though dedicated to a decidedly healthier lifestyle than Navarro, he died even younger. His inspiration, though, was crucial to the early work of Lee Morgan (whom he, in turn, encouraged directly) and Freddie Hubbard.

These sessions, done while he was stepping into Navarro's shoes with the Tadd Dameron band, show what all the enthusiasm was about. Most immediately revealing are the up-tempo tracks *Cherokee* (which became sufficiently associated with him to be re-recorded by the quintet he co-led with Max Roach) and *Brownie Speaks*; the latter's alternate chords make it quite an obstacle course, but Clifford seems to have ample time to construct a rounded statement. His work at slower speeds shows even more clearly his great melodic imagination and the way his almost too-bright tone is modified by brilliantly varied articulation. Not only more prolific on record than Navarro, he promised to be even more creative. **BP**

The Complete Paris Sessions, Volumes 1-3 **Brown** (t) with the following collective personnel: **Art Farmer**, **Quincy Jones**, **Walter Williams**, **Fernard Verstraete**, **Fred Gerard** (t); **Al Hayes**, **Jimmy Cleveland**, **Bill Tamper**, **Benny Vasseur** (tb); **Gigi Gryce**, **Anthony Ortega**, **Clifford Solomon**, **Henry Bernard**, **Henry Jouot**, **Andre Dabonneville**, **William Boucaya** (reeds):

Henri Renaud (p); **Jimmy Gourley** (g); **Pierre Michelot** (b); **Alan Dawson, Jean-Louis Viale, Benny Bennett** (d). Vogue Ⓜ 15461/63-2 (three discs, oas: 65, 68 and 59 minutes). Recorded 1953

✔ ⑧ ❽

The band Lionel Hampton brought to Europe in the autumn of 1953 had a very high proportion of young, comparatively unknown musicians, men such as Quincy Jones, Art Farmer, Alan Dawson, Gigi Gryce and, of course, Clifford Brown. Thanks to the perspicacity of French pianist Henri Renaud, then acting as a consultant to the Vogue label, arrangements were hastily made to record this burgeoning talent in all manner of sessions, from large Franco-American big bands to quartets. These three CDs (available separately) comprise all the titles from the period on which Brown solos, a remarkable body of work completed in just over two weeks, all of it carried out without Hampton's knowledge or permission. A lot of the writing is by Gryce, a composer and arranger of considerable skill and originality as well as being a very capable alto soloist. But it is Brown whose rich, warm-toned trumpet attracts the ear, from the two takes of the opening big band *Brown Skins* (a two-tempoed excursion over the *Cherokee* chords) on Volume One to the 13 titles by a quartet on Volume Three. There are fine sextet and octet pieces too, with Renaud playing his distinctive understated piano on nearly every performance on the three CDs. On the second volume you can hear Brownie actually learning a tune (*Venez Donc Chez Moi*) which appears in completed form on Volume Three. These are essential records, especially for those who recognize Brown as one of the greatest of all jazz trumpeters. **AM**

Jazz Immortal **Brown** (t); **Stu Williamson** (vtb); **Zoot Sims** (ts); **Bob Gordon** (bs); **Russ Freeman** (p); **Joe Mondragon, Carson Smith** (b); **Shelly Manne** (d); **Jack Montrose** (arr). Pacific Jazz Ⓜ CDP7 46850-2 (30 minutes). Recorded 1954.

⑧ ❼

Jazz Immortal finds Clifford Brown in a more relaxed setting than he had previously been accustomed to. Recorded for the Pacific Jazz label while he was working in Los Angeles with Max Roach, the album hews closer to a typically laid-back West Coast ambience than to the more intense bop Brown was playing with the drummer. The resulting music has an easy going charm and, while not among his more brilliant achievements, is still very enjoyable.

Four Brown tunes are included. *Daahoud* and *Joy Spring*, recorded just a few weeks before the definitive versions with Roach, retain a distinctive, balmy appeal. *Tiny Capers* and *Bones For Jones* are less well-known, the latter a rarity that Brown recorded only this once. The arrangements are by tenorman Jack Montrose, who also contributes the attractive *Finders Keepers*. His charts, although not demanding, work well and make good use of ensemble textures. Manne lays down a gentle swing and Sims glides through the date with effortless propriety. The highlight, not surprisingly, is Brown's trumpet playing, which is unstintingly vivacious and melodic—a joy spring, indeed.

The CD adds an alternate take of *Tiny Capers* in place of the track *Bones For Zoot*, which appeared on previous LP issues but does not include Brown. **GL**

The Complete EmArcy Recordings **Brown** (t) with a collective personnel including: **Maynard Ferguson** (t); **Joe Maini, Herb Geller** (as); **Sonny Rollins, Walter Benton, Harold Land, Paul Quinichette** (ts); **Herbie Mann** (f); **Richie Powell, Kenny Drew, Jimmy Jones, Junior Mance** (p); **Keter Betts, George Morrow, Joe Benjamin, Curtis Counce** (b); **Max Roach, Roy Haynes** (d); **Dinah Washington, Sarah Vaughan** (v); **Quincy Jones** (arr, cond). Featured albums: **Clifford Brown/Max Roach Quintet with Harold Land; Helen Merrill with Strings; Clifford Brown All-Stars / Herb Geller; All-Star Live Jam Session / Clark Terry; Clifford Brown with Strings**. EmArcy Ⓜ 838 306-2 (ten discs: 604 minutes) . Recorded 1954-56.

⑩ ❼

This set is not the perfect introduction to Clifford Brown—for that you would be better advised to turn to the slim-line two-CD set of Brown with Max Roach on the Mercury label (526 373-2). Yet this is every bit as important a body of music as the Verve Billie Holiday collection, the RCA Jelly Roll Morton set, or the Verve Charlie Parker box. The reason is simple: Brown carved a new and brilliant trumpet style out of the old bones of bebop, created a challenging body of work in just four years of recording, and substantially influenced every jazz trumpet player to come after him. Without him, people as significant in the music as Lee Morgan, Booker Little, Freddie Hubbard, Blue Mitchell, Woody Shaw and Wynton Marsalis would never have got past first base, for it was his fallen mantle they, in turn, picked up.

The sessions so lovingly and thoughtfully packaged here span just 19 months, and come at the end of his playing life (he died in a car crash in June 1956, four months after the last session here). Undoubtedly the perfect vehicle for his artistry was the quintet he co-led with Roach, regardless of whether Land or Rollins was the tenor player. In Max Roach he had a drummer-partner with the musical intelligence to develop each rhythmic area, punctuate each newly-minted phrase, and generally shape the music with an eye to its overall form. Richie Powell (Bud's younger brother) was a prodigiously talented pianist with a real gift for accompaniment and an arranger's ear. These players, with Brown's rich, optimistic sound and fresh melodies, made a unique combination which has not suffered through endless imitation. The group in many ways was the soul of mid-fifties modern jazz.

The other sessions included here range from great fun (the two discs with Dinah Washington) to intriguing cocktails (Clifford as featured soloist with Sarah Vaughan and Helen Merrill) to timeless interpretive beauty (Clifford with strings). All of this material (sans alternative takes) has been available on single CDs as originally issued on vinyl, and the Vaughan and Washington dates have recently been reissued, but the **With Strings** album and all the original LP compilations of the Brown-Roach are not currently available separately on CD. This boxed set is itself a limited edition, so if you are a Clifford Brown fan, get it while it lasts. Annotation and transfer standards are exemplary. **KS**

The Beginning And The End **Brown** (t) with, on two tracks (1952): **Chris Powell** (v, perc); **Vance Wilson** (as, ts); **Duke Wells** (p); **Eddie Lambert** (g); **James Johnson** (b); **Osie Johnson** (d). On remaining tracks (1956): **Ziggy Vines**, **Billy Root** (ts); **Sam Dockery** (p); **Ace Tisone** (b); **Ellis Tollin** (d). Columbia Ⓜ 477737 2 (35 minutes). Recorded 1952/56.

⑧ ❻

Brown's career on record lasted for four years and three months. Fortunately for us his unique talents were always recognized and he packed an abnormal amount of recordings into that period. His death at the age of 26 was a hammer blow to jazz. Perhaps unusually for such a virtuoso he was a simple, outgoing man, very modest and liked by all who came into contact with him. He was, after Gillespie, one of the most influential modern trumpet players and, had he not died, his life could very well have assumed Armstrong proportions. The fact that his wellspring was in the playing of Fats Navarro and Gillespie is almost irrelevant, for he moved so far away from those two.

The first pair of tracks here, done in Chicago with Chris Powell's Blue Flames (Powell was a Jamaican singer at the bottom of the Cab Calloway league) are of little musical interest, being two sides of a calypso-styled 45rpm single with less than a minute of Brown's solo work between them. However, the substance of the album is in *Walkin'*, *Night In Tunisia* and *Donna Lee*. These come from a jam session at a musical instrument shop in Philadelphia called Music City on June 25, 1956. Brown plays luminous trumpet solos with the local musicians. Nobody approaches his aura but the two tenor players, Billy Root and the legendary Ziggy Vines, are of interest.

Brown left the club at the end of the session to go back out on the road. A couple of hours later he and fellow-travellers pianist Richie Powell and Powell's wife Nancy were killed when their car skidded off the Pennsylvania Turnpike. **SV**

Donald Brown

1954

The Sweetest Sounds **Brown** (p); **Steve Nelson** (vb); **Charnett Moffett** (b); **Alan Dawson** (d). Jazz City Ⓕ 660 53 008 (65 minutes). Recorded 1988.

⑥ ❽

Ex-Messenger Brown has appeared in a number of settings as a leader, but never seems quite to have settled in his own groove as a stylist. On this album he self-avowedly sets out to pay respects to some of the pianists he has admired, such as Ahmad Jamal, Gene Harris and Ramsey Lewis, and this he does nicely, but his own personality, though conducive to the production of a relaxed, swinging record, hardly stamps itself upon the listener's memory. This said, there is a great deal of pleasure to be derived from listening closely to what Moffett and Dawson are doing, for they create a wonderful rhythmic matrix; clean, light and sweetly powerful, so buoyant as to seemingly float at times. Vibist Nelson also contributes some spirited playing on the tracks where he appears, adding usefully to the colour and character of the music. Brown himself comes across rather diffidently here, but as a player capable of much more when he wants to stretch out. **KS**

Jeri Brown

1954

A Timeless Place **Brown** (v); **Jimmy Rowles** (p, v); **Eric Von Essen** (b). Justin Time Ⓕ (56 minutes). Recorded 1994.

⑦ ❽

Brown's début disc, **Mirage**, had its moments and showed considerable courage in the way the vocalist was prepared to embark on long improvisatory excursions more often associated with saxophones or guitars. Here she has moved to different territory, although it is scarcely less unusual. The whole album is given over to her interpretations of the songs of Jimmy Rowles. The composer is also the pianist (as he is on Norma Winstone's latest album, **Well Kept Secret** (Hot House), which duplicates some of this repertoire to very interesting effect, especially as Winstone is the lyricist for the title track here), and he plays superlatively. Brown has an exceptionally large range, a full voice with a burnished sound to it, and a happy, involved manner to her singing. She occasionally lapses into arch or over-stylized phrasing or articulation, but for the most part her vocals communicate sincerely and without flash. She is a good scat singer, yet keeps this aspect of her work under control. On one track, *Baby Don't Quit Now*, she duets with Rowles, whose non-voice blends satisfyingly with Brown's polished approach. Brown's voice is very closely miked, and some extra-musical sounds (tongue, lips and breathing; some pages being turned) are the result, but these are not unduly irksome. Recorded sound is otherwise fine. **KS**

Lawrence Brown 1907-1988

Everybody Knows Johnny Hodges/Inspired Abandon **Brown** (tb); **Hodges** (as); **Ray Nance**, **Cat Anderson**, **Rolf Ericson**, **Herbie Jones** (t); **Buster Cooper**, **Britt Woodman** (tb); **Russell Procope** (as, cl); **Paul Gonsalves**, **Jimmy Hamilton**, **Harold Ashby** (ts); **Harry Carney** (bs); **Jimmy Jones** (p); **Ernie Shepard**, **Richard Davis** (b); **Grady Tate**, **Gus Johnson**, **Johnny Hodges Jr** (d). Impulse! Ⓜ GRP 1162 (69 minutes). Recorded 1964-65.

⑥ ❽

Brown was one of the most distinctive trombone stylists ever, and his total of nearly 30 years in the Ellington band capitalized on both his swing phrasing and his sensuous, cello-like ballad work. By the time of the above recordings he had also shouldered the role of plunger-mute specialist created by Joe Nanton.

The above issue combines two mid-sixties LPs, the second of which, **Inspired Abandon**, was issued under Brown's name; the key organisational figures, though, are Hodges with his original material and the absent Duke, whose tunes are re-created on both albums. Only four tracks employ a 15-piece band, the rest being by either a scarcely less full 12-piece or an octet which recalls Hodges's earlier small-group recordings (Brown was never accorded this treatment, and only ever made one other album in his own right). The trombonist is well featured on both albums, while also heard on four tracks (including *Main Stem*, not indicated in the otherwise comprehensive notes) is his egregious section-mate Buster Cooper, who points up the uniqueness of Brown. Replacements in the rhythm-section give it a rather insensitive feel, while Richard Davis's bass on the second album is mixed so forward that the graphic equaliser is essential to enjoyment. **BP**

Marion Brown 1935

Why Not? **Brown** (as); **Stanley Cowell** (p); **'Sirone' (Norris Jones)** (b); **Rashied Ali** (d). ESP-Disk Ⓜ ESP 1040-2 (37 minutes). Recorded 1966.

⑦ ❼

Though he has made some fine music over the years, Marion Brown's best work is not yet on CD. It is particularly regrettable that neither his ECM and Impulse! albums nor the 1985 set **Recollections** are currently available. In comparison, **Why Not?**, which was only Brown's third album as a leader, has a rather tentative feel, though there is still much here to enjoy.

A 'New Thing' advocate, Brown worked in the mid-sixties with Archie Shepp, Sun Ra and John Coltrane (he was on **Ascension**). The latter was a major influence, as is clear from *La Sorella*, where Brown's phrases are suspended Trane-like over Stanley Cowell's scampering piano (Cowell's fine solo spot on this track is nothing like McCoy Tyner). There are traces too of Albert Ayler on *Homecoming*, where military themes are interspersed with snatches of free jazz.

What differentiates Brown from his contemporaries is that he mostly eschews extremes of register and tonal distortions, playing with a light-toned fluency that points back to Johnny Hodges (with whom he played in the late fifties). This melodic grace became more pronounced on later records, but is already evident in both *La Sorella*'s airy flow and the heartfelt balladry of *Fortunato*. Rashied Ali provides strong support but the lacklustre recording quality makes the bass sound somewhat indistinct. **GL**

Ray Brown 1926

Bass Face **Brown** (b); **Benny Green** (p); **Jeff Hamilton** (d). Telarc Jazz Ⓕ Cd-83340 (68 minutes). Recorded1993.

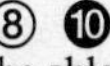

Brown has been at the top of the jazz bass-playing tree for more than 45 years. It is pleasing to be able to report that this fact has not meant a latter-day resting on his many laurels. This disc, recorded 'live' at Kuumba Jazz Center in California, kicks off with a version of *Milestones* which is set at an absolutely ferocious pace. Needless to say, Brown not only makes the tempo with ease, he becomes the very heart of the rhythmic thrust.

In his years with talents such as Oscar Peterson and Milt Jackson, Brown showed himself to be the master of every musical situation he found himself in, from sensitive accompaniment on ballads to thrusting blues walking on the funky stuff. Here, with the astonishingly gifted and perfectly simpatico pianist Benny Green (already a leader on a number of fiery sessions for Blue Note), Brown investigates an unusually wide range of moods and feels. The title track is straight out of the slinky-slow mode trademarked years ago by Peterson and Basie, while *In The Wee Small Hours of The Morning* finds Brown swapping between bow and fingers with effortless dexterity.

It's a relief to report that Telarc have caught that gorgeous bass tone exactly, and that the audience is well-behaved. You may be listening to what amounts to a recreation of the Peterson-Brown-Thigpen band, but that is not important. It's a great trio. It's a great trio record. For which Brown, as boss and elder statesman, must take all due credit. **KS**

Rob Brown

1962

Youniverse **Brown** (as); **Joe Morris** (g); **Whit Dickey** (d). Riti Ⓕ CD 3 (65 minutes). Recorded 1992.

⑧ ❽

As an alto saxophonist coming of age in the eighties, Brown was drawn to the music of Ornette Coleman, Eric Dolphy and Roscoe Mitchell, and is now using their innovations to develop his own voice. Thinking intervallically rather than harmonically, he has the ability to sustain phrases along unusual melodic contours, and the equally unorthodox guitarist Morris is a good match, providing ambiguous chordal clusters and complementary lines that tangle with Brown's in attractively complex ways. The lack of a bass or piano opens the trio textures considerably and they reply with pungent implied harmonies and loose polyrhythms. The music flirts with freedom but maintains a firm grasp on ensemble principles, and they are not afraid of varied dynamics or delicacy (thanks largely to Whit Dickey's perceptive drumming); sheer energy seldom threatens to get the best of them. Brown supplies the finely etched tunes, although the improvisations are liable to wander far afield. Some pieces use this to their advantage: *Sonic Film*, for example, teeters on the fulcrum balancing melody and indistinct pitch, ending only after the brief, tender theme finally arrives; *Svengali* toys with a hypnotic four-note motif. Others, like the title-song, reflect a more direct Ornette flavour. Either way, **Youniverse** offers an auspicious beginning for these talented, thoughtful players. **AL**

Ted Brown

1927

Free Wheeling **Brown** (ts); **Art Pepper** (as); **Warne Marsh** (ts); **Ronnie Ball** (p); **Ben Tucker** (b); **Jeff Morton** (d). Vanguard Ⓜ 662089 (41 minutes). Recorded 1956.

⑧ ❽

Playing in Warne Marsh's shadow must have been a difficult experience for Ted Brown; after their short-lived two-tenor quintet broke up 1957 he moved to New York, took a day job, and all but retired from the music scene. He recorded only once in the seventies (an excellent date with Lee Konitz, **Figure and Spirit**, on Progressive) and twice in the eighties (under his own name for the Dutch label Criss Cross). Interestingly, his playing has always been of high quality, with a similar taste for long bar-stretching lines and circuitous imagery but lacking Marsh's capricious melodic and rhythmic genius, as if never willing to take that dangerous next step. This was Brown's first session as a leader, and what distinguishes it is the company he keeps. The rhythm section, adhering closely to Tristano's principles, is a rather stodgy affair, but the horns are exhilarating. Recorded less than a month after Pepper and Marsh's underrated contemporary date, the addition of Pepper to Brown and Marsh's working band is a welcomed spice. Three of the tunes (two of Ball's and Marsh's *Long Gone*) reflect Tristano's stamp of intricacy, the others are from Tin Pan Alley. The horns' unison chorus on *Broadway* is an act of homage to Lester Young. The fact that Brown can hold his own with two of the best, most individualistic post-war saxophonists is a recommendation in itself. **AL**

Tom Browne

1955

Browne Sugar **Browne** (t); **Michael Brecker** (ts); **Dave Grusin**, **Robert Mounsey**, **Bernard Wright** (kbds); **Ronald Miller** (g); **Marcus Miller**, **Francisco Centeno** (b); **Buddy Williams** (d); **Sue Evans**, **Erroll Bennett** (perc). GRP Ⓜ D 9517 (37 minutes). Recorded 1978.

⑤ ❻

Browne is a fine trumpeter with a clear lineage in his playing back to Freddie Hubbard, Lee Morgan and, ultimately, Clifford Brown. He has a beautiful open tone and a gift for stating even the simplest melody with grace and feeling. This was his first album, and it was made before he hit it big internationally with the funk piece *Funkin' For Jamaica* which made him a hot chart property for a few years. The musical settings are very much par-for-the-course fusion, but Browne always displays his jazz feel whenever he plays. On a track like *Herbal Scent*, an attractive piece written by Marcus Miller, Browne sings the melody on his horn in exactly the way Clifford Brown did on his **With Strings** album. It is the same process, only the settings have been updated. Browne always attempted to get some jazz onto his albums: his 1981 album **Yours Truly** (not currently on CD) included excellent quintet versions of *Lazy Bird* and *Naima*, for example. This one contains more than enough jazz feel to justify its inclusion here, the ubiquitous GRP arrangements notwithstanding. **KS**

Dave Brubeck

1920

Octet **Brubeck** (p); **Dick Collins** (t); **Bill Smith** (cl); **Paul Desmond** (as); **David van Kriedt** (ts); **Bob Collins** (bs); **Jack Weeks** (b); **Cal Tjader** (d); **Jimmy Lyons** (narr). Fantasy Ⓜ OJCCD O101-2 (48 minutes). Recorded c.1946-50.

⑧ ❻

The cool jazz that swept California in the fifties is traditionally heard as stemming from Miles Davis's **Birth of the Cool** sessions. The Brubeck octet apparently anticipated cool as well—apparently, as the dates of their recordings are uncertain. But at least some charts date from 1946. Most octet members, Brubeck included, were composer Darius Milhaud's students at Mills College near San Francisco in the mid-forties. Brubeck's arrangement of *The Way You Look Tonight* employs counterpoint and the pastel harmonies West Coast cool would soon adopt; Smith's *Ipca* could easily fit into the Miles nonet's repertoire. Some of the music is more self-consciously arty. *How High the Moon*, performed in various jazz styles, and fatuously narrated, comes off sophomoric. But on Smith's *Schizophrenic Scherzo*, no matter how formal the voice leading or forward-looking the frequent textural shifts, the phrasing swings. Even van Kriedt's *Fugue on Bop Themes*, which is not very boppish, floats on cool's light, driving pulse. Brubeck's own playing is less heavy than it became later, though hints of his mature style are evident.

Prescient though this music was, cool musicians rarely cite them as an inspiration. Nevertheless, these sides give evidence that in jazz—as in other fields of research—good ideas often arise simultaneously from different quarters. **KW**

Jazz At Oberlin **Brubeck** (p); **Paul Desmond** (as); **Ron Crotty** (b); **Lloyd Davis** (d). Fantasy Ⓜ CDR1VM 007 (38 minutes). Recorded 1953.

⑦ ❻

This live recording was made early in the quartet's life and legend has it that it was a troubled session; Brubeck and Desmond are alleged to have quarrelled, Crotty was working out his notice and Davis had a fever. Ironically the outcome was better than might have been expected. The tightly-knit formula was breached possibly because of this atmosphere, and there is little doubt that it was the element of internal warfare that gingered up all four players. The gifted Desmond was particularly inspired and his light-toned and lilting improvisations on *These Foolish Things* and *The Way You Look Tonight* are as inventive as anything he ever did. On the latter title there are even examples of ill-formed, thin notes as excitement seems to take over. Brubeck is his normal self; controlled and exploratory at first but too often allowing his solos to run into a cliché-laden barrage with little trace of swing. Davis's brushes do their best to give shape to these tirades but, with Crotty content to stick to the script rather than direct from the back, it is difficult to avoid the odd static moment.

The days of Joe Benjamin, Eugene Wright and Joe Morello were still some time off, but this CD documents the music of the quartet of the period and must always be rated amongst as its very best. **BMcR**

Dave Digs Disney **Brubeck** (p); **Paul Desmond** (as); **Norman Bates** (b); **Joe Morello** (d). Columbia Ⓜ 471250 2 (51 minutes). Recorded 1957.

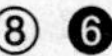

It seems likely that Brubeck's best recordings all featured Desmond and Morello. When this album was recorded his quartet was just reaching its ultimate maturity. It is often considered that it finally did this when bassist Eugene Wright joined, but this is to undervalue Bates, who made up what he lacked in Wright's technical abilities with good jazz sense and feeling. Brubeck depended mightily on Desmond's unflagging improvisations and beautiful tone. If ever there was authority without the big fist, then it was in the alto player's deceptively limpid-sounding solos. Here they are almost without flaw. The Disney songs (made up from *Give A Little Whistle*, *Some Day My Prince Will Come* and others of the genre) work surprisingly well and Brubeck adapts them skilfully to his rhythmic methods. Perhaps, appropriately to Disney, there is just that little touch too much polish. Brubeck's earlier **Jazz Goes To College** for the same label had, along with a couple of other concert recordings, offered more warts but also more challenge to the four players, a challenge rumbustiously taken up. For those who prefer their Brubeck compiled, the luxury version (with the music, from the Fantasy, Columbia and Brubeck archives, chosen by Brubeck himself) is available on the four-CD set **Time Signatures** (Columbia 472776-2), while the economy route is available for the price of the two-CD set, **Jazz Collection** (Columbia 480463-2). **SV**

Jazz Impressions of Eurasia **Brubeck** (p), **Paul Desmond** (as), **Gene Wright** (b), **Joe Morello** (d). Columbia Ⓜ 47129-2 (40 minutes). Recorded 1958.

This album was recorded and released just prior to the explosion of popularity Brubeck enjoyed through the unprecedented success of **Time Out**. It was chosen to accompany **Time Out** (reviewed below) because it was one of Brubeck's first themed albums. The concept was still quite fresh and the group's response to the ideas mapped out by Brubeck is relaxed, sensitive and imaginative. The pianist's own playing has his by-now familiar vices and felicities on unembarrassed display and there seems to be a greater intensity of vision and unity of purpose to many of his solos. An often busy player (although he always accompanied Desmond with wonderful empathy), he uses space and sustained tones to great dramatic effect, especially in *The Golden Horn* and *Calcutta Blues* (which anticipates Keith Jarrett's explorations of Near Eastern scales by a good 15 years). Many people would find his obsessive reiterating of a rhythmic and harmonic motif for an entire chorus in *The Golden Horn* simply too much, but it is an exciting idea, and if it had been an early Cecil Taylor solo, everyone would still be cheering. Poor old Dave just isn't hip, so he gets the sackcloth and ashes.

There are many good things to be heard here, not least the compositions themselves (Brubeck didn't only write *The Duke* and *In Your Own Sweet Way*), and for once nobody could accuse Desmond of carrying the date. **Eurasia** is a quiet triumph for Brubeck. **KS**

Time Out **Brubeck** (p); **Paul Desmond** (as); **Gene Wright** (b); **Joe Morello** (d). Columbia Ⓜ 460611-2 (39 minutes). Recorded 1959.

⑧ ❼

It was Stan Kenton who opened up the colleges and high schools as places receptive to jazz, and by the fifties Dave Brubeck was spear-heading the follow-up wave. His working quartet with the late Paul Desmond became immensely popular as a result (and, such is the perverse way of the world, largely unpopular with 'true' jazz enthusiasts). **Time Out** was an honest attempt to explore time signatures other than 4/4 for use in jazz extemporization and, thanks to the inclusion of Desmond's tune *Take Five*, the original LP issue became one of Brubeck's biggest and most durable sellers. Musically it remains of interest, and not just for curiosity value. Signatures such as 9/8 (for *Blue Rondo à la Turk*) and 6/4 (for *Pick Up Sticks*) are still unusual in jazz, but it must be pointed out that Brubeck cheated slightly; although theme statements observe the unexpected meters, the quartet often reverts to common time for the solo choruses. Nevertheless, **Time Out** is a praiseworthy attempt to push the boundaries of jazz outwards, and in the charming *Strange Meadow Lark* we have a most attractive Brubeck composition (to which words were subsequently added by Brubeck and Carmen McRae for the **Tonight Only!** album). **AM**

Bill Bruford

1948

Feels Good To Me **Bruford** (d, perc, tuned perc); **Dave Stewart** (kbds, syn, p); **Allan Holdsworth**, **John Goodsall** (elg); **Annette Peacock** (v); **Jeff Berlin** (elb); **Kenny Wheeler** (flh). Editions EG/Virgin Japan Ⓜ VJD-28051 (48 minutes). Recorded 1977.

✓ ⑧ ❽

Given the predominant rhythmic tilt and the background of the players, it is tempting to file this session under art-rock. By 1977 Bill Bruford had made a splash as a member of Yes and King Crimson, and he protests that he approached this as a rock session. Yet the evidence of the record suggests that that description needs qualifying. For one thing, **Feels Good To Me** is replete with improvisations as satisfying as any in post-bop jazz. Allan Holdsworth, one of the most original but under-valued guitarists of his generation, has an extraordinary impact on several tracks, playing densely chromatic lines with an inspiration and creativity he has rarely bettered. Kenny Wheeler also has a number of lyrical solos.

The record's not inconsiderable appeal to jazz lovers might end there, but it has other strengths. In such suite-like forms as *Adios A La Pasada* there is a level of textural, metric and dynamic contrast often absent from jazz, and themes like *Beelzebub* and *If You Can't Stand The Heat* ... have all the harmonic and rhythmic sophistication and velocity of bebop without the idiomatic clichés. The whispered passion and coiled menace of Annette Peacock's vocals and the thoroughly musical bass-playing of Jeff Berlin are no less attractive parts of the package. The analogue recording sounds as well in digital as the music does in the nineties. **MG**

Rainer Brüninghaus

1949

Continuum **Brüninghaus** (p, syn); **Markus Stockhausen** (t, picc t, flh); **Fredy Studer** (d). ECM Ⓕ 1266 (815 679-2) (45 minutes). Recorded 1983.

⑦ ❿

Brüninghaus first came to international attention on Eberhard Weber's epochal **Colours of Chloë**, and played with the bassist on and off for most of the seventies. **Continuum** remains his best and most cohesive effort to date as a leader and is a remarkable document, in its own unassuming way. The rather eccentric instrumentation has its own logic, and one is not aware, while listening, of the lack of any one sound or texture. This is largely due to Brüninghaus's rhythmic and colouristic dexterity on his various keyboards, plus his meticulous organization of both the music and the musicians within it. On *Strahlenspur*, for example, the keyboards, piccolo trumpet and drums all occupy separate registers as well as having their own clear sonic and timbral differences. This would all be to no avail if the music itself was vacuous, but this is thankfully not the case. Brüninghaus's melodies are catchy and hummable, his keyboard work wide-ranging and always exquisitely tasteful, while Stockhausen (Karlheinz's son) has both technique to burn and a wonderful combination of rhythmic freedom and melodic expressivity, in the same way that Booker Little did in a different musical context. Some of the tracks are a little long. The recording quality is stunning. **KS**

Ray Bryant

1931

Through The Years, Volumes 1 and 2 **Bryant** (p); **Rufus Reid** (b); **Grady Tate** (d). EmArcy Ⓕ 512 764/ 933-2 (two discs, oas: 62 and 61 minutes). Recorded 1992.

⑧ ❽

No pianist has a wider-ranging knowledge of the jazz and blues tradition than Bryant, a fact which caused him to be called for many recording sessions backing artists as diverse as Miles Davis,

Coleman Hawkins, Elmer Snowdon, Sonny Rollins and Buck Clayton. His trio worked with Carmen McRae in the late fifties (a sure sign of his knowledge of tunes) and he had a hit record with his composition *Little Susie*. These two CDs were made to mark his 60th birthday, each comprising ten splendidly melodic tunes which get sensitive and apt treatments. Volume One includes his own *Cubano Chant* and certainly the best version of his *Blues Changes*, the attractive tune which gave an identity to the altered blues chords in bars one to four of the chorus. Volume Two contains his own bounding *Cold Turkey* and a beautifully controlled *Li'l Darlin'*, played just a shade faster than Basie's version and with Wendell Culley's original trumpet solo woven into the fabric of the song. With numbers such as *Django, Blue Bossa, Moanin', Misty, 'Round Midnight* and *Whisper Not* distributed over the two CDs, one realises that Bryant has lived through one of the finest eras of jazz composition. The work of Reid and Tate is exemplary and both discs are unreservedly recommended. **AM**

Willie Bryant 1908–1964

Willie Bryant & His Orchestra **Bryant** (ldr, v); **Edgar Battle** (t, vtb); **Benny Carter, Otis Johnson, Taft Jordan, Jack Butler** (t); **George Matthews, Eddie Durham** (tb); **Glyn Paque** (cl, as); **Johnny Russell, Ben Webster** (ts); **Charles Frazier** (ts, f); **Teddy Wilson, Roger 'Ram' Ramirez** (p); **Arnold Adams** (g); **Ernest 'Bass' Hill** (b); **Cozy Cole** (d). Jazz Archives Ⓑ 157682 (68 minutes). Recorded 1935-36.

⑤ ❼

As a musician Bryant was a useful song and dance man. A failed trumpeter, his musical input into his own band was negligible and his sentimental speaking and vocal style had little to do with jazz. Fortunately for music, he did need to keep faith with audiences at Negro dance halls like the Apollo. As a result, he employed a string of outstanding soloists and used skilled arrangers such as Benny Carter, Edgar Battle and Teddy Wilson to give style and credibility to his bands. These he led from 1934 to 1938 and from 1945 to 1948; the first was the better and all of the titles here are from that period. The CD offers love songs and comedy numbers as well as straight instrumentals, but more significantly it allows a good look at most of the soloists. Wilson's sparkling piano, Webster's fast maturing tenor and Paque's clarinet and alto all impress. Matthews's trombone is authoritative rather than inspired but Jordan's trumpet and Louis Armstrong-ish vocal style are well captured on *All My Life*. When Bryant quit the band-leading business he worked as a disc jockey and actor and actually served as master of ceremonies at the Apollo. It was for his first band, however, that he is best remembered. **BMcR**

Jeanie Bryson

Tonight I Need You So **Bryson** (v); **Claudio Roditi** (t); **Jay Ashby** (tb); **Paquito D'Rivera** (as); **Don Braden** (ts); **Steve Nelson** (vb); **Vic Juris** (g); **Ted Brancato**, **Danilo Perez** (p); **Christian McBride** (b); **Ignacio Berroa**, **Ron Davis** (d); **Rudy Bird** (perc). Telarc Jazz Ⓔ CD 83348 (63 minutes). Recorded 1994.

⑥ ❽

Bryson's 1993 début album for the same label, **I Love Being Here With You**, was reviewed more in terms of who she is, rather than what she is. It appeared soon after the death of Dizzy Gillespie and the publicity focused on Bryson's announcement that she was his child. Critics therefore generally overlooked the arrival of a remarkable vocal talent, and a first-rate album, enriched by Kenny Barron and Ray Drummond. This is even more accomplished, and airs some of the best lyrics and compositions by the singer's mother, Connie Bryson. Bryson's voice has a delicate warmth that invests all her lyrics with a strong sense of personal involvement. Even standards like *Willow Weep For Me* and *Honeysuckle Rose* benefit, but when she turns her attention to material as varied as *What Can a Miracle Do?* (a Luther Vandross piece made famous by Dionne Warwick) or Stevie Wonder's *Too Shy To Say*, she produces something exceptional. The latter track is almost chamber jazz, with just Brancato's piano and McBride's arco bass. McBride is the lynch-pin of the album, his seldom-heard electric bass underpinning the fusion rhythms with the same precision his conventional bass brings to the rest. The album ends on a magnificent reading of Freddie Hubbard's *Skydive*, with new Connie Bryson lyrics and outings for D'Rivera, Roditi and Ashby that show the vocalist holding her own with some powerhouse soloists. **AS**

Milt Buckner 1915 – 1977

Green Onions **Buckner** (org, p, vb, v); **André Persiany** (p); **Roy Gaines** (g); **Roland Lobligeois** (b); **Panama Francis** (d); **Sam Woodyard** (d). Black & Blue Ⓕ 59 087 2 (55 minutes). Recorded 1975-76.

⑤ ❼

A multi-instrumentalist, Buckner began his professional career in 1932 with the Don Cox band. He had several spells with Lionel Hampton but from the middle fifties worked mainly as leader of his own small groups. His main claim to fame was his "block-chord" or "locked-hands" piano method; the playing of patterned, parallel chords in a way that gave his style tremendous power and colour. Thanks to the recording studio, this CD (featuring his best-known disciple, Persiany). has plenty of atmosphere. Nothing of any great musical note occurs; the leader's organ continually sets up rocking moods, Gaines teases with his blues-based guitar, Persiany plays solos on *Green Onions*, *Sleep* and *Pour Toutes Mes Soeurs* that could be mistaken for the leader's but it is really the late-night blues club ambience that makes this session attractive. In later years Buckner tended to concentrate on his organ playing, and that is the case here. He swings prodigiously on all three instruments but does not really have much to say. **BMcR**

Miroslav Bukovsky

Wanderlust **Bukovsky** (t); **James Greening** (tb); **Tony Gorman** (cl, ts); **Carl Orr** (g); **Alister Spence** (p, kbds); **Adam Armstrong** (b, elb); **Fabian Helva** (d); **Greg Sheehan** (v, perc); **Alan Dargin** (didgeridu). ABC Jazz Ⓔ 518 650-2 (76 minutes). Recorded 1993.

⑥ ❽

Bukovsky is a young veteran of the Australian jazz scene and this new album is a measure of the maturity he has discovered as well as a measure of the strength in depth of contemporary jazz in Australia. These guys (the band is in fact called Wanderlust) do not really have to give anything to their Stateside or European counterparts in terms of musicianship or inspiration. While there seems a natural avoidance of extremes in this and other Australian jazz, there is enough going on in the middle ground to make each record an absorbing listening experience. These players have a natural combination of exuberance and ease which is as natural an expression of the Australian psyche as Paul Hogan's smile.

Bukovsky has a pleasingly pure trumpet sound and an excitingly eclectic ear which introduces not only Alan Dargin's virtuoso didgeridu variations during *Only Connect* but a whole range of local and international colours between *Bronte Café*, *Dakar* and *Game of Gulf*. *Ornettelogic* shows signs of pastiche rather than inspiration but, that apart, the music is theirs all the way through. Bukovsky has gone to great lengths to make this a group record, and there are accordingly plenty of solos and collective contributions from all concerned. *MDD*, a 'love song to Miles', according to Bukovsky, is taut and full of the keening melancholy for which that icon was famed. **KS**

Chas Burchell

1925-1986

Unsung Hero **Burchell** (ts); **Clark Terry** (t, flh, v); **Brian Wood** (t); **Bob Hirschman** (tb); **Ronnie Scott**, **Geoff Carter** (ts); **Mike Hennessey**, **Matt Ross**, **Bernard Eppy** (p); **Alan Simmons** (b); **Al Merritt**, **Mike Scott**, **Alec Adams** (d). In & Out Ⓔ IOR 7026-2 (70 minutes). Recorded 1962-93

⑥ ❺

Chas Burchell was a well-kept secret on the British jazz scene. A few collectors knew of his debut album from the 1969 Richmond Festival, or his handful of other discs, and could attest to the agile quality of his Warne Marsh-inspired playing. His death in 1986 went all but unnoticed (the 1993 track here is a tribute by his former band) so this retrospective album is a long-overdue tribute, compiled by Burchell's long-term colleague and pianist, journalist and write Mike Hennessey. Chas was undaunted by a splendid (if rather poorly recorded) partnership with Clark Terry, who appears on a couple of tracks, and overall he dominates the proceedings with the fluency of his thought and execution. This is an excellent document of an obscure player who deserved to be better-known during his lifetime. **AS**

Dave Burrell

1940

Plays Ellington and Monk **Burrell** (p); **Takashi Mizihashi** (b). Denon Ⓔ DC-8550 (47 minutes). Recorded 1978.

⑧ ❽

Although an adept player of freer jazz (his past credits include stints with Archie Shepp, Pharoah Sanders, Beaver Harris and Sunny Murray) Dave Burrell here concentrates (like latter-day Shepp) on reinterpretations of the work of two masters, Duke Ellington and Thelonious Monk. "Ellington" actually refers to material played, not necessarily composed, by the great band leader, since Burrell's set not only includes Billy Strayhorn's *Lush Life* but also his tender Johnny Hodges feature *A Flower is a Lovesome Thing*. There are stately, near-reverential treatments of *In A Sentimental Mood* and *'Round Midnight* and an occasionally over-dramatic bass feature on *Come Sunday*, where Burrell restricts himself to an accompanying role, but it is on the Monk staples *Straight, No Chaser* and *Blue Monk* that the pianist's virtuosity is truly allowed free rein. On the majority of the other tracks, which rarely stray far from the melody, the listener's chief pleasure derives from discovering just how much individual idiosyncrasy Burrell can display within the tight limits he has set for himself; in the aforementioned Monk standards, operating with fewer restrictions, he employs splashes of dissonance, hypnotic repetition, sly allusions and all-round Monkish quirkiness to superb effect, bringing great harmonic and dynamic variety to a highly accomplished session. **CP**

Kenny Burrell

1931

Guitar Forms **Burrell** (g, elg); **Gil Evans** (arr, cond); **Roger Kellaway** (p); **Ron Carter**, **Joe Benjamin** (b); **Grady Tate**, **Elvin Jones**, **Charlie Persip** (d); **Willie Rodriguez** (cga); **Johnny Coles**, **Louis Mucci** (t); **Jimmy Cleveland**, **Jimmy Knepper** (tb); **Andy Fitzgerald** (f, engh); **Ray Beckenstein** (af, f, bcl); **George Marge** (engh, f); **Richie Kamuca** (ts, ob); **Lee Konitz** (as); **Steve Lacy** (ss); **Bob Tricarico** (ts, bsn, f); **Ray Alonge**, **Julius Watkins** (frh); **John 'Bill' Barber** (tba). Verve Ⓜ 825 576-2 (39 minutes). Recorded 1964-65.

⑥ ❽

As its title suggests, **Guitar Forms** sets out to explore the stylistic scope of the guitar. Its range of idiom actually tends to be rather selective—there is no representation for atonality or the new guitar sonorities rock had introduced by the mid-sixties—and its moods tend to blandness, but within its limitations the programme is attractively varied. The brevity of many of the nine tracks—most last three or four minutes—enhances the sense of contrast between the pieces. The music falls into two broad categories, reflecting the dualism of Burrell's guitar style: on the one hand lie his small group jazz talents, showcased by the country blues of *Downstairs*, the urban blues of *Terrace Theme* and the brisk swing of *Breadwinner*, and on the other lie his classical finger-style skills, displayed in a transcription for solo guitar of part of Gershwin's Prelude No. 2 and in five concerto-like settings by Gil Evans. Evans cannot resist the temptation to recall **Sketches of Spain**, and *Lotus Land* shimmers in an Iberian heat haze, but he also fleshes out a bossa nova (*Moon And Sand*), a couple of ballads that show Burrell's pretty lyricism, and a jaunty reading of *Greensleeves*. At times the latter has the lubricity of shopping mall music, but like many other items here it also features some excellent jazz. **MG**

Don Burrows

The First Fifty Years **Burrows** (f, alto f, cl, ss, as, bs, ldr); various groups, collective personnel including: **Wally Norman**, **Ken Brentnall**, **James Morrison**, **Bob Barnard** (t); **John Bamford** (tb, vb); **Bob McIvor** (tb); **Rolf Pommer**, **Frank Smith**, **Charlie Munro**, **Bernie McGann** (as); **Errol Buddle** (f, cl, ts, ob, bn); **Graeme Lyall**, **Bob Bertles**, **Lee Hutchings**, **Dale Barlow** (ts); **John Sangster** (vb, d); **Tony Ansell** (kbds); **Jack Allan**, **Billy Walker**, **Terry Wilkinson**, **Judy Bailey**, **Roger Frampton**, **Julian Lee**, **Paul Grabowski**, **Kenny Powell** (p); **George Golla** (g); **Ron Hogan**, **Ed Gaston**, **Jack Thorncroft**, **Craig Scott**, **Doug De Vries** (b); **Paul Baker** (elb); **Joe Singer**, **Jack Dougan**, **Alan Turnbull**, **Laurie Thompson**, **David Jones** (d); **Norman Erskine** (v); on two tracks **Luiz Bonfa** (g); on one track each **Stephane Grappelli** (vn); **Chris Hinze** (af). ABC Jazz Ⓜ 514 295-2 (five discs: 371 minutes). Recorded 1944-92.

⑥ ❽

Burrows is to Australian jazz what Sidney Nolan was to Australian fine art: he is the one everyone overseas has heard of. As such, he has been a worthy ambassador, for he has always combined high levels of professionalism and technical competence with unfailing good taste. With the clarinet as his first instrument his own stylistic predilections have never wandered very far away from updated variations on the West Coast music of the fifties, although his first models were clarinet-wielding big band leaders such as Goodman and Herman.

Probably due to the lack of recording opportunities, the first 20 years of Burrows's career is served by disc number one, while the following 28 are spread across discs two to five. His achievements are many and varied, and he has dabbled in a range of ventures which have brought different cultural colours to the basic jazz vein of his output (hence the appearance of Luiz Bonfa): he has even moved successfully into the deploying of electronics in his music. But the byword with Burrows is 'taste', and this is exemplified by his use, for over 30 years, of the guitarist George Golla, a massively skilful musician whose playing makes Jim Hall's sound impassioned. Burrows's own emotional temperature, by the evidence of this set, comes across as 'moderate', and this approach is emphasized in his work after the mid-sixties by his increasing preference for the flute. There is fire to be found in this collection, but it usually emanates from one of the sidemen, such as James Morrison on *The Flintstones Theme*. Which leads me to wonder rather uncharitably whether the set as a whole might have made more of an impact if there had been less music in it, making the focus tighter. Burrows is rarely at his best in a jam session, and some of those could have been dropped without loss.

Incidentally, the work of the mercurial John Sangster is scattered liberally through this set. Presently not represented as a leader on CD, he is one of the most venturesome and original of all Australian musicians of any generation, often utilizing an extensive range of ethnic musics in any given project, and his work in the Burrows groups of the sixties is worth seeking out. **KS**

Abraham Burton

1972

Closest To The Sun **Burton** (as); **Marc Cary** (p); **Billy Johnson** (b); **Eric McPherson** (d). Enja Ⓕ ENJ-8047 2 (65 minutes) Recorded 1994.

⑦ ❽

Burton came the public's attention while a member of Art Taylor's Wailers, and just a handful of gigs with his own band convinced Enja artist and talent scout Gust William Tilis that this was a young altoist who had to be recorded immediately. The first track, a speedy workout on Jackie McLean's *Minor March*, will amply demonstrate the soundness of Tilis's instincts. Burton is part of the neo-classicist wave, but inhabits a more radical section of it than many. His style seems to have coalesced around a period of sixties progressive American jazz, with Coltrane's influence clearly discernible. His playing the alto helps distance him from that overwhelming stylistic mantle and allows aspects of Dolphy and McLean to beneficially inflect the whole.

Burton plays with tremendous passion and complete commitment. His pianoless trio version of *Laura* exhibits his way with the phrasing of a melody. Burton has mastered the art of underplaying: he doesn't crowd the listener with unneccessary ornament. What you hear is what should be there, dictated by the song's architecture and meaning. What you also hear is deep feeling. In communicating this he is greatly helped by Cary and the rest of the rhythm section. His own compositions are not so distiinguished, but—what the heck; he's young. Lots of time yet. There's plenty about his music to enjoy in the meantime. **KS**

Gary Burton

1943

Hello Hotel **Burton** (vb, mba, org); **Steve Swallow** (b, p). ECM Ⓕ1055 (835 586-2) (36 minutes). Recorded 1974.

⑧ ❾

Vibraphonist Gary Burton was a teenage prodigy who made his first recordings with country guitarist Hank Garland. After studies at the Berklee School of Music he toured with George Shearing and recorded under his own name for RCA. A two-year tenure with Stan Getz expanded his reputation, thus making it possible to organise the notable 1967 quartet with Larry Coryell, Steve Swallow and Bob Moses. Other Burton albums include Pat Metheny, John Scofield and Makoto Ozone. The intimate small-group settings have allowed Burton to establish a distinctively open-ended style that contrasts with the more percussive mallet pioneers Lionel Hampton and Milt Jackson; Burton has also succeeded in incorporating the seemingly contradictory influences of European classical and American country and folk music.

Here, in a cosy and consistently satisfying date from 1974 released under the co-leadership of Burton and bassist Steve Swallow, we find Burton the inspired conversationalist. We also hear Burton on organ and marimba and Swallow on piano, in rare but happily felicitous departures from their usual roles. Throughout, moods and textures shift with kaleidoscopic abandon. There are ethereal moments as in the poignant *Chelsea Bells* (*For Hern*) and *Impromptu*. But there are tracks like *Hello Hotel* and *Sweet Henry* where the effectively overdubbed mixes dance with dashes of rock and country. Pity about the playing time, however. **CB**

Matchbook **Burton** (vb); **Ralph Towner** (g). ECM Ⓕ 1056 (835 014-2) (39 minutes). Recorded 1974.

⑥ ❽

For Burton, even more than for his peers, being a Flower Power role model was a hard act to follow. His 1967 quartet with Larry Coryell had set a performance pattern and for some time he used similar groups with guitarists such as Mick Goodrick, John Scofield and Pat Metheny in the guitar chair. Later the gifted Burton toured in duo with Chick Corea, Steve Swallow and Towner. This CD comes from that era and promises more than it actually delivers. Both men are masters of their own genre and they come together quite effectively. Regrettably, this is one of those inoffensive items; meanderingly unpremeditated, it replaces the themes not with cogent alternatives but with pretty variations. The interaction of vibraphone and guitar works better than had the piano/vibes combination, but neither player throws down the gauntlet. There is an element of duelling implicit in the more challenging *Icarus* and *Matchbook* to suggest what might have been achieved, but even the outstanding *Goodbye Pork-Pie Hat* comes over as if it might have been a blueprint for a larger personnel or a more detailed examination. Sadly, one can almost imagine the looks of delight around the Studio Bauer as these gentle improvisational traceries were woven. **BMcR**

Joe Bushkin

1916

The Road To Oslo and Play It Again, Joe **Bushkin** (p,v, flh); on 11 tracks: **Johnny Smith** (g); **Milt Hinton** (b); **Jake Hanna** (d); **Jack Parnell Orchestra; Bing Crosby** (v on two tracks); on nine tracks: **Warren Vache** (t); **Al Grey, Dan Barrett** (tb); **Phil Bodner** (cl); **Howard Alden** (g); **Major**

Holley (b); **Butch Miles** (d); string section arranged by **Glenn Osser**. DRG Ⓕ 8490 (69 minutes). Recorded 1977/86.

⑤ ❻

The CD title uses the names of the two original LPs, one on United Artists and one on RCA Victor, which have been combined for this reissue. Bushkin's jazz credentials are impeccable; he worked with the bands of Bunny Berigan, Joe Marsala, Muggsy Spanier, Tommy Dorsey and Benny Goodman as well as leading his own trio and writing some successful songs. In 1977 he was Bing Crosby's musical director on a tour which took in Norway and Britain (and culminated in Crosby's death on a Madrid golf course); the first 11 tracks were made during the tour, topped and tailed by short appearances by Bing. Bushkin talks engagingly and plays a lot of attractive piano, albeit aiming his work more at the showbiz element rather than the outright jazz audience. Johnny Smith is featured on a so-called Norwegian song titled *Sunday Of The Shepherdess* which turns out to be the same tune as *Ack Varmeland Du Skona*, or *Dear Old Stockholm*. The remaining tracks were made in a studio nine years later and repeat four of the songs including, inevitably, *Oh Look At Me Now*, Bushkin's perennial hit. Occasionally the brilliant keyboard work which marked his work with Berigan and Marsala (and his own Commodore sessions) bursts through and even less occasionally the small band is featured (Vaché on *What's New?,* Bodner on *It Had To Be You*, etc.) but much of the music is pleasant rather than profound. **AM**

Jaki Byard

1922

Phantasies II **Byard** (p, ldr); **Roger Parrett**, **Graham Haynes**, **Jim White** (t); **Carl Rienlieb**, **Steve Swell**, **Rick Davies**, **Steve Calial** (tb); **Bob Torrence**, **Susan Terry** (as); **Jed Levy**, **Bruce Revels** (ts); **Don Slatoff** (bs); **Peter Leitch** (g); **Ralph Hamperian** (b); **Richard Allen** (d); **Vincent Lewis**, **Diane Byard** (v). Soul Note Ⓕ 121175-2 (42 minutes). Recorded 1988.

⑥ ❻

Byard has been a respected figure in the music since at least the early fifties, when he was a Boston legend and, due at least in part to his reluctance to hit the road, something of a well-kept Boston secret as far as the wider jazz public went. His move to New York and subsequent appearance on a string of albums on the Prestige label at the opening of the sixties established an international profile which his role as a sideman with Charles Mingus during the early part of that decade rapidly developed. His own albums were somewhat hit-and-miss affairs, although none is without interest or musical ambitions, and some—notably the 1968 **Jaki Byard Experience** with Roland Kirk (Prestige LP, nla)—are close to being classics. Yet his best playing was invariably found on other people's albums, and for a long time he failed to record under his own name. Soul Note have made strenuous efforts to put that right over the past decade, and this quite typical Byard album reveals the breadth of his ambitions and the problems inherent in realizing them.

One of his most basic quandaries is that he is both one of the world's great eclectics and a musician of genuine originality. Hence, many of his compositions flick from a pastiche of an earlier style to a profound reflection from deep within his soul. On this album his arrangements of other people's works (as well as his approach to his own) show a driving need to switch from style to style, often more than once within the same piece. His band respond admirably to his direction, and much passionate music-making is the result. Countless references to previous jazz landmarks are also there to be uncovered by the diligent, although at times one longs for an undiluted shot of pure Byard. But then perhaps eclecticism is the core of his achievement, making the tribute to B.B. King, electric guitar blues and all, as much pure Byard as is his own *Concerto Grosso* or the decidedly off-centre version of Sondheim's *Send in the Clowns*, with off-pitch vocals to boot. **KS**

Don Byas

1910-1972

Walkin' **Byas** (ts); **Bent Axen** (p); **Niels-Henning Ørsted Pedersen** (b); **William Schiopffe** (d). Black Lion Ⓜ BLCD 760167 (53 minutes). Recorded 1963.

Under-recognized today, Byas was by the mid-forties one of the four leading tenor players, along with Hawkins, Young and Ben Webster, and for a brief moment the most popular of the four. He sacrificed his status and popularity by joining the first US jazz group after World War II to tour Europe and then remaining there. His achievement was to extend the harmonic explorations of Coleman Hawkins and, improbably enough, to do so with a chunky Chu Berry-like tone which ought to have been less mobile than Hawkins. The impact of his early records after leaving Count Basie in 1943 (he had replaced Lester Young) was as dramatic as those of Parker, whom he had probably influenced as he certainly did Coltrane. Since dates done then for Savoy are unavailable at this writing, it is instructive to turn to this later session from Copenhagen's Montmartre Club.

The recording balance is better than on the companion volume **A Night In Tunisia**, while the version here of that tune (the only one tackled on both sets) is superior. Byas's own playing shows his extraordinary fluency (e.g. the ending of *Don't Blame Me*), while his inventive powers are even further out than 20 years earlier. **BP**

Charlie Byrd

1925

Moments Like This **Byrd** (g); **Ken Peplowski** (cl); **Bill Douglass** (b); **Chuck Redd** (d, vb). Concord Jazz Ⓕ CCD-4627 (61 minutes). Recorded 1994.

⑧ ❽

Byrd has never been rated in most critical circles as a profound jazzman, but his finger-style work has appealed to many. He shot to international fame with the first of Stan Getz's bossa nova albums but later LPs in the genre showed that his playing lacked the easy fluidity of the true Brazilian guitarists. Nevertheless his semi-jazz approach is a valid part of our music and this entirely pleasant album has many virtues, commencing with a good choice of material which takes in *Wang Wang Blues, Rose Of The Rio Grande* and numbers by Ellington and Bechet. A considerable asset is the fine, warm-toned clarinet-playing of Peplowski, who goes from strength to strength in all manner of contexts; he is certainly a more individual soloist on clarinet than on tenor. Chuck Redd makes his recording début as a vibraphonist on six tracks and there is an air of quiet professionalism about the whole CD. Byrd, it would seem, is at his most impressive when the jazz is not too demanding. **AM**

Donald Byrd

1932

At The Half Note Cafe **Byrd** (t); **Pepper Adams** (bs); **Duke Pearson** (p); **Laymon Jackson** (b); **Lex Humphreys** (d). Blue Note Ⓜ CDP7 46539-2 (64 minutes). Recorded 1960.

⑧ ❽

While obtaining his MA at the Manhattan School of Music in the fifties, Byrd became a ubiquitous figure on the Prestige, Blue Note and Riverside labels. In fact, an over-saturation of Byrd, whether as leader or sideman, became a problem. The critical reaction was to take him for granted, but the scribes were not without grounds. Endless recording opportunities did sometimes expose a paucity of new ideas as an over-exposed trumpeter resorted to favourite phrases rather than reach for the structural re-evaluation that more preparation would have made possible. By 1960, this situation had changed somewhat. Byrd was recording less and, as this CD suggests, had more time for the necessary groundwork. The arrangements he uses are little more than standard hard-bop frames, but Pearson and the two horns organize their solos well. Byrd's contribution to *My Girl Shirl* is an especially incisive piece of improvising and his *Portrait Of Jennie* outing is delivered with a grace often missing in his earlier work. Both of Byrd's excellent compositions, *Soulful Kiddy* and *Cecille,* are fundamentally blues. They round out a live performance that speaks volumes for the trumpeter's self awareness. It was as if he had realized that he should no longer allow the prolix habits of before to dominate. **BMcR**

Free Form **Byrd** (t); **Wayne Shorter** (ts); **Herbie Hancock** (p); **Butch Warren** (b); **Billy Higgins** (d). Blue Note Ⓜ CDP7 84118-2 (38 minutes). Recorded 1961.

⑧ ❼

Byrd's career has been long and varied, and a goodly proportion of its latter-day output falls outside the scope of this guide, being buried deep in the musical vocabulary of seventies funk and soul.

No such demarcation disputes here: this is classic Blue Note jazz of the period and an unusually thoughtful album at that. Byrd, one of the most well-rounded players on the New York scene at the time (he later gained a doctorate of music and ran his own music courses), demonstrates a keen interest in a variety of musical styles and disciplines here. He ranges from the baptist beat of the opener, *Pentacostal Feelin',* to the delicacy of pianist Hancock's ballad *Night Flower* and the disciplined, stimulating experimentation of the title track, where the basic framework for the eleven-minute piece is a tone-row which can be—and is—interpreted in any number of ways. Shorter and Hancock, impressive elsewhere on the date, excel in such an environment and contribute some of their strongest playing. Byrd shows himself willing to take chances, bending notes and accelerating in and out of rhythm at will, although his musical language remains firmly based in Clifford Brown. A stimulating and intelligently-prepared album, with good sound for the period. **KS**

Don Byron

Tuskegee Experiments **Byron** (cl, bcl); **Edsel Gomez**, **Joe Berkovitz** (p); **Richie Schwanz** (m); **Greta Buck** (vn); **Bill Frizell** (g); **Lonnie Plaxico**, **Reggie Workman** (b); **Kenny Davis** (elb); **Ralph Peterson Jr**, **Phereoan akLaff** (d); **Sadiq** (poet). Elektra Nonesuch Ⓕ 979280-2 (62 minutes). Recorded 1990-91.

✔ ⑧ ❽

Initially marked out for his classical background, Byron paints on a very broad canvas. His New York upbringing avails him many choices and tapping into the town's Klezmer tradition was only one. On this CD, that aspect is clearly evident and the way that it interacts with Frisell's raw freedoms and with inescapable jazz undertones completes the package. Jewish romanticism is most evident when percussionists are not involved, but when Peterson and akLaff appear to discourage flowing rhetoric, Byron responds to their goading by applying his own rules. He challenges each tune on his own terms, uses slurs and note distortions and juggles the points of emphasis. The spirit of the material affects him in different ways; his irreverent treatment of *Main Stem* cuts a jagged swathe across Ellington's flowing jam session sward while his dedication to Diego Rivera suggests an affinity with the artist's powerful style. Fortunately, Byron seems as much at home with the pathos of Buck's violin as he is with Frisell's carousing guitar and subsequent albums such as **Music For Six Musicians** (Nonesuch 59354-2) point to **Tuskegee** as providing a working pattern for development. If in the process jazz becomes a more potent factor, this musical maverick seems less than prepared to discount the kosher element entirely. **BMcR**

George Cables 1944

Night And Day **Cables** (p); **Cecil McBee** (b); **Billy Hart** (d). DIW Ⓕ 606 (49 minutes). Recorded 1991.

⑧ ❽

A bandsman with, amongst others, Art Blakey, Sonny Rollins, Cannonball Adderley, Joe Henderson and Dexter Gordon, Cables has tended to be categorized as a sideman rather than a leader. His solo work has always been individualistic, but forever tailored to the needs of the leader for whom he is working. With this CD we hear Cables in charge of his own musical destiny, able to choose an imaginative programme and to arrange each tune as seems appropriate. McBee and Hart are themselves assertive players, but the internal balance of the trio is built around the highly accomplished playing of its leader.

Initially influenced by Thelonious Monk and Herbie Hancock, it is the latter's flowing treble improvisations that are most suggested by Cables's style, although Monk-ish interjections on titles such as *I Thought About You* and *Doxy* show how he views certain harmonic structures. When soloing, his storytelling right hand is never a separate entity; it darts above and between each imaginatively built new framework, while on pieces like *Very Early* it matches the signposting duties of the left hand and of McBee's bass. The Cables of 1991 has genuine creative flair, a secure technique and appears to be blossoming into a leader in his own right. **BMcR**

Uri Caine

Sphere Music **Caine** (p); **Graham Haynes** (t); **Don Byron** (cl); **Gary Thomas** (ts); **Kenny Davis**, **Anthony Cox** (b); **Ralph Peterson** (d). JMT Ⓕ 514 007-2 (66 minutes). Recorded 1992.

⑧ ❽

The pointillistic clarinet and piano reading of *'Round Midnight* might be more obviously avant-garde, but the most genuinely novel element in this fine set of high-intensity modern jazz is the juxtaposition of the liquid tones of Don Byron's virtuoso clarinet with the burning sixties-style hard bop of *Mr B.C.* Elsewhere the clarinet seems perfectly suited to convey the rollicking, whimsical humour of *Jelly*. However, although Byron may be the most noticeable player, the musicianship, craftsmanship and interplay of the band as a whole is no less worthy of remark. The leader, a New Yorker making his mark on the scene, plies a familiar but nonetheless creative and exciting line in McCoy Tyner-style piano to especially good effect on the opening two tracks, abetted with masterly flair by Ralph Peterson, who has obviously learnt well from Tony Williams how to add stop-go drama to the flow of such music. Gary Thomas's tenor, heard on three tracks, might be a more conventional timbre but there is nothing hackneyed about the tart harmonic syntax he has developed. Fittingly for a début, this album is full of vigour, but there is no question of the maturity of the players. **MG**

Joey Calderazzo 1965

To Know One **Calderazzo** (p); **Branford Marsalis** (ss, ts); **Jerry Bergonzi** (ts); **Dave Holland** (b); **Jack DeJohnette** (d). Blue Note Ⓕ CDP7 98165-2 (67 minutes). Recorded 1991.

⑦ ❽

Calderazzo is young enough to look upon McCoy Tyner and Herbie Hancock as old masters, and it is the music of these two giants which remains the pervading influence on his own style. He has chosen musicians who know and understand that legacy (Holland and DeJohnette, of course, are of a similar generation as the older men, and share the Miles Davis experience with Hancock) and Bergonzi does his utmost to raise the ghost of Coltrane. The album's more interesting and original moments come when Marsalis, whether on soprano or on tenor, is playing with Calderazzo: their imaginations seem more at odds and therefore able to stimulate each other to better and more resourceful playing. Having DeJohnette and Holland around is also a major asset.

Calderazzo is still assembling a complete musical identity, but he has bags of ability, a very good ear for what others are doing, and an individual touch on the instrument. Definitely one to watch. **KS**

Cab Calloway

1907-1994

Cruisin' With Cab Calloway (v); with the following collective personnel; **R.Q. Dickerson, Lamar Wright, Reuben Reeves, Doc Cheatham, Ed Swayzee, Mario Bauza, Irving Randolph, Dizzy Gillespie, Jonah Jones, Russell Smith, Shad Collins, Paul Webster** (g); **DePriest Wheeler, Harry White, Claude Jones, Keg Johnson, Tyree Glenn, Quentin Jackson, Fred Robinson** (tb); **Thornton Blue, Andrew Brown, Walter Thomas, Arville Harris, Chauncey Haughton, Chu Berry, Jerry Blake, Hilton Jefferson, Ted McRae, Irving Brown, Al Gibson, Rudy Powell, Ike Quebec, Bob Dorsey** (reeds); **Earres Prince, Bennie Payne, Dave Rivera** (p); **Morris White, Danny Barker** (bj, g); **Tyree Glenn** (vb); **Jimmy Smith, Al Morgan, Milt Hinton** (b); **Leroy Mazey, Cozy Cole** (d). Topaz Ⓜ TPZ 1010 (65 minutes). Recorded 1930-43.

⑧ ❻

Although Cab Calloway was first and foremost an entertainer, his bands contained some of the best musicians of the day. Some of them resented the antics of the leader and the requirement to play nonsense songs such as *Minnie The Moocher* and *Kicking The Gong Around* every night, but many of them stayed with Cab for years. This 20-track compilation gives an accurate picture of the band and the inclusion of three instrumental broadcast items bring out the surging power of the ensemble. On *Cupid's Nightmare* (which lasts for nearly six minutes) there is an easily recognizable solo from Dizzy Gillespie; the following tenor passage by Chu Berry has what sounds like a groove-skip from, presumably, the original acetate. Berry, in fact, is featured at length on the studio-recorded *Ghost Of A Chance*, included here, a highlight of the tenorist's career on record. Many musicians of the period spoke well of the Calloway band and it must have rated highly, for Cab took over at the Cotton Club in 1931 when Duke Ellington left. The transfers from source material have been well carried out by compilers Tony Watts and Colin Brown. **AM**

Best Of The Big Bands Calloway (v); **Lammar Wright, Doc Cheatham, Shad Collins, Mario Bauza, Dizzy Gillespie** (t); **De Priest Wheeler** (tb); **Eddie Barefield, Arville Harris, Garvin Bushell, Andrew Brown, Chauncey Haughton** (cl, as); **Walter Thomas** (cl, ts); **Chu Berry** (ts); **Bennie Payne** (p); **Morris White** (g, bj); **Danny Barker** (g); **Al Morgan, Milt Hinton** (b); **Leroy Maxey, Cozy Cole** (d). Columbia Ⓜ 466618-2 (47 minutes). Recorded 1932-42.

⑥ ❼

Cab Calloway's exuberant celebrations of Harlem low life in the thirties have had a mixed jazz press. Sterner commentators regard the vocal arabesques of *Reefer Man* or the evergreen *Minnie The Moocher* as vulgar vaudeville routines obscuring the vigorous, nervy playing of the orchestras he led; others argue that he amusingly and stylishly embodies the vital connection between jazz and the linguistic extravagance of black street culture and thus stands early in the line that leads to Slim Gaillard, beat poetry and rap.

This collection draws on a decade of Calloway's work (although this is not apparent from the notes, which provide no recording data) and shows his band developing from the studied exoticism of an Ellington Cotton Club orchestra, as in the 1932 sides like *Beale Street Mama*, to the more conventional but by no means subdued swing ensemble heard in *Take The "A" Train* or *Minnie The Moocher* (not the original 1931 recording, but one from 1942).

Though numerous first-rate musicians served under Calloway (the 1939-40 line-up heard in *Bye Bye Blues* and *Pickin' The Cabbage* has the momentous trumpet section of Dizzy Gillespie and Mario Bauza, soon afterwards to be the architects of the Afro-Cuban movement), they were rarely given much solo space; the spotlight was fixed upon the leader, chanting and ululating with an almost cantorial virtuosity that few listeners (those stern parties aside) will fail to find exhilarating. **TR**

Roy Campbell

1952

New Kingdom Campbell (t); **Ricardo Strobert** (as, f); **Zane Massey** (ts); **Bryan Carrott** (vb); **William Parker** (b); **Zen Matsuura** (d). Delmark Ⓕ DE 456 (65 minutes). Recorded 1991.

⑤ ❻

Campbell was taught by Lee Morgan and shows many elements of Morgan's exciting yet audience-oriented style. The timbre of this group is unusual, with vibes taking the conventional piano or guitar role of supplying chords, and, through Carrott's comping on tracks like *Thanks To The Creator,* bringing a light airy quality to the sound. Where Campbell plays open horn, he has a full tone and a strong personal presence. On three tracks he works with just bass and drums, his delicate muted playing on bassist Parker's composition *Angel* showing an introspective side to his character, nodding in the direction of Miles Davis, but clearly showing Campbell's originality. Strobert, who plays impassioned alto, particularly on *Thanks To The Creator*, is a schoolteacher. His playing is more alert and arresting than Massey's, although Massey contributes a solo feature, *Peace,* with just Parker and Matsuura's feathery brushwork that almost steals the album. **AS**

Conte Candoli

1927

Lighthouse All-Stars: Jazz Invention **Candoli** (t); **Bob Enevoldsen** (tb); **Bob Cooper** (ts); **Bud Shank** (as); **Claude Williamson** (p); **Monty Budwig** (b); **John Guerin** (d). Contemporary Ⓜ CCD 14051-2 (53 minutes). Recorded 1989.

⑦ ❽

Candoli's credentials go back through the big bands of Woody Herman, Stan Kenton, Terry Gibbs and Charlie Barnet. He was in Doc Severinsen's 'Tonight Show' band and has worked continually in film and television studios. As such a record suggests, he is an extremely versatile trumpeter and this CD places him amongst his West Coast peers. Musical director Cooper provides loose arrangements that allow players to relax into their solos rather than compete with each other and, although the concept of 'cool' oversees this live concert, there is an element of latent passion lurking beneath the surface. The record is published under the collective title of The Lighthouse All-Stars, but Candoli in particular is the man to add the cutting edge, which he does most effectively through his adroitly re-worked *Topsy* solo. This, therefore, is an appropriate disc to select as a showcase for his talents. *Woody'n You* is very much his tribute to his mentor Dizzy Gillespie and he ensures that there is no showboating. He does take *Broadway* somewhat by storm but he employs his own special brand of good judgement to make the hackneyed *Bernie's Tune* a model of creative discretion. 'Good taste' when applied to Candoli's trumpet is never a euphemism for mediocrity. **BMcR**

Frankie Capp

1931

Juggernaut **Capp** (d, ldr); **Bill Berry**, **Gary Grant**, **Blue Mitchell**, **Bobby Shew** (t); **Buster Cooper**, **Alan Caplan**, **Britt Woodman** (tb); **Marshall Royal**, **Bill Green** (as); **Richie Kamuca**, **Plas Johnson** (ts); **Quinn Davis** (bs); **Nat Pierce** (p); **Chuck Berghofer** (b); **Al Hendrickson** (g). Concord Ⓕ CCD-4040 (50 minutes). Recorded 1977.

⑧ ❽

Motivated by the example of the Ellington-inspired Bill Berry's L.A. Big Band (see above), Pierce and Capp drew on the same pool of Hollywood studio musicians to create a band which was designed to follow the Basie philosophy. Juggernaut immediately became better than the contemporary Basie band and, despite the fact that it was not recorded as often as it should have been, it put considerable heart into the West Coast jazz scene.

Most of the library was chosen and arranged by pianist Nat Pierce, a man who literally lived for jazz. Enlivened even more by the skilful drumming of Capp and by a team of soloists who, apart from being as strong as any which could have been put together anywhere, simply wanted to play jazz, it is not surprising that Juggernaut became one of the most consistently invigorating big bands of the seventies and eighties. The album bubbles over with exuberant solos from Buster Cooper, Blue Mitchell and, notably on Pierce's arrangement of *Dickie's Dream* where they follow each other one by one, soloists from all the sections. Pierce's brilliant ability to mirror the heart and soul of any other pianist—in this case Basie—is the catalyst to a 'live' album which captures the concert presence to perfection. **SV**

Una Mae Carlisle

1915-1956

1944 **Carlisle** (p, v); with a collective personnel including: **Ray Nance** (t); **Budd Johnson** (ts); **Snags Allen** (g); **Basie Robinson** (b) **Shadow Wilson** (d) (on eight tracks); **Billy Butterfield** (t); **Vernon Brown** (tb); **Bill Stegmeyer** (cl); **Bob Haggart** (b); **George Wettling** (d) (on four tracks); **Doc Cheatham** (t); **Trummy Young** (tb); **Walter Thomas** (ts); **Cedric Hardwick** (b); **Wallace Bishop** (d) (on three tracks). Two tracks have **Maxine Sullivan** (v) with three violinists; **Ken Billings** (p); **Everett Barksdale** (g); **Cedric Wallace** (b). Last four tracks are **Savannah Churchill** (v); **Russ Case** (t); **Will Bradley** (tb); **Jimmy Lytell** (cl); **Frank Signorelli** (p); **Carmen Mastren** (g); **Haig Stevens** (b); **Chauncey Morehouse** (d). Harlequin Ⓕ HQ CD 19 (61 minutes). Recorded 1942-44.

⑦ ❼

Carlisle's early career thrived under the auspices of Fats Waller, and it was Waller who, when she returned from an ill-fated stay in Europe, re-launched her Stateside career by duetting with her on his hit *I Can't Give You Anything But Love*. After that, she was ready to go out as a solo act again, and the forties saw a string of respectable hits on the Beacon label, allied with her own shows on radio and TV, and regular appearances in films. By the mid-fifties persistent ill-health led to retirement, and soon after came her premature death.

Carlisle's vocal style owes less to Billie Holiday than often thought; her delivery is measured, her voice lighter in timbre, while her characteristic sound is one with a smile on its face. Today her most famous session is one from 1941 with Lester Young guesting, but the standard of material on that date is very poor indeed, and the songs chosen for her work with Beacon in 1944 give her infinitely more opportunities to shine. Naturally, a more balanced picture of her talent emerges, especially her ability to give apt delivery to any half-decent set of lyrics.

The two Sullivan tracks would be unbearable were it not for the singer's sweet voice. The songs are as bad as the string arrangements. Savannah Churchill is a different matter. Her Dixieland backing is appropriate to her half-jazz, half-showbiz delivery. Her discs were big sellers in their day, with the mildly risqué *Fat Meat* (the last track here) selling over 200,000, and while the material sometimes borders on corn, the band swings well enough, in its own clumsy sort of way. **KS**

Larry Carlton

1948

On Solid Ground **Carlton** (elg, elb, kbds); **Dean Parks** (elg); **Terry Trotter, Alan Pasqua, Rhett Lawrence, David Foster, Brian Mann** (kbds); **John Robinson, Rick Marotta** (d); **Abraham Laboriel, Nathan East, John Pena** (elb); **Kirk Whalum** (ts); **Paulinho Da Costa, Michael Fisher** (perc). MCA Records Ⓕ MCAD-6237 (55 minutes). Recorded 1988.

④ ❽

Many listeners will have been introduced to Larry Carlton's distinctive fusion of the blues style of B.B. King with the harmonic sophistication of Joe Pass and Wes Montgomery through his hot, stylish contributions to albums by The Crusaders (see below) and Steely Dan in the seventies. In such contexts, often as a cameo soloist in others' arrangements, his solos shone like gems, but given limitless space to flex his chops as in this set, Carlton finds it harder to sustain the tension. All the trademarks are here: the singing bluesy bends, the trilling arpeggios, the funky riffing, the jazzy chromaticism; but the taut, incisive quality of his best work as a sideman is missing. The inclusion of two old standards—Eric Clapton's *Layla* and Steely Dan's *Josie*—and an overdose of mawkish rock ballads reminiscent of Hank Marvin do nothing to help his case. The guitar playing is representative enough, but it seems that by the late eighties Carlton was locked into an endless rehearsal of his best licks. **MG**

Janusz Carmello

1994

Portrait **Carmello** (pkt t); **Keith Hutton** (tb); **Jimmy Woods** (as); **Phil Bancroft** (ts); **Gordon Cruickshank** (bs); **Brian Kellock** (p); **John Hartley** (b); **Tony McLennan** (d); **Jimmy Deuchar** (arr). Hep Ⓕ CD 2044 (54 minutes). Recorded 1989.

⑥ ❻

The full personnel only appears on one track, Jimmy Deuchar's version of the Ellington/Strayhorn *Daydream*. For the rest of the album, Carmello displays his very considerable talent as a pocket trumpet soloist, either with rhythm or just with Brian Kellock's eloquent piano.

When Carmello first arrived in Britain in 1973, with a reputation acquired in his native Poland and previous port-of-call Italy, he struggled hard for every gig he could find, playing in pick-up bands in pubs one minute and opening supermarkets with New Orleans marching bands the next. As he garnered experience (and friends) everywhere he went, he grew in stature as a musician. This is a joyous showcase for his mature style. His affinity for (and technical mastery of) Clifford Brown's style shines through on *Tiny Capers* and *Joy Spring*. He includes two of his own compositions but is at his most original when deconstructing standards from the inside. No-one could find a hint of a tired trad warhorse in his *Saints* and his delicate exploration of Neal Hefti's *Lil' Darlin'* evokes the ghost of Basie's whole band in its carefully-chosen open spaces. **AS**

Hoagy Carmichael

1899-1981

Stardust & Much More **Carmichael** (v, p) **Bix Beiderbecke, Bubber Miley** (c); **Manny Klein, Ray Lodwig** (t); **Benny Goodman** (cl); **Jimmy Dorsey, Sidney Arodin, Arnold Brilhart** (as, cl); **Bud Freeman** (ts); **Min Leibrook** (bs); **Joe Venuti** (v); **Red Norvo** (xyl); **Eddie Lang** (g); **Harry Goodman** (tba); **Artie Bernstein** (b); **Gene Krupa** (d). RCA Bluebird Ⓜ ND 88333 (67 minutes). Recorded 1927-60.

⑥ ❽

There is very little Hoagy Carmichael material available on CD at the time of writing. Notably absent are the archetypally quirkish and laid-back forties and fifties recordings. This collection consists mainly of early pieces in which the young Hoagy sings a chorus in the middle of a lively twenties band number. Indeed, the main interest of much of the disc lies in the work of the players detailed above. Nevertheless it is fascinating to hear the characteristic Carmichael back-porch style evolving, from the puppyish *Washboard Blues* of 1927 to the relaxed ease of *Moon Country* in 1934. The 1960 items consist of a couple of versions of *Stardust*—piano, vocal and speech—which open and close the programme. The recordings have been very well transferred from the 78 original, using the NoNoise process. **DG**

Mike Carr

1937

Good Times and The Blues **Carr** (org); **Dick Morrissey** (ts); **Jim Mullen** (g); **Mark Taylor** (d). Cargogold Ⓕ CGCH191 (54 minutes). Recorded 1993.

Carr also plays piano and vibraphone, but it is as an organist that he has made the greatest impact on the British jazz scene. He has worked with a number of powerful American soloists such as Coleman

Hawkins, Johnny Griffin, Don Byas, Buddy Tate, Illinois Jacquet and Eddie Davis, but he has always had a natural affinity for the playing of Dick Morrissey and guitarist Jim Mullen. This is the best example on record of the threesome, plus the alert, energetic but tasteful drumming of Mark Taylor. Carr lays down a constantly swinging, propulsive background for the soloists, using the organ pedals to produce a moving bass line. Morrissey has always possessed the ability to create solos which communicate with even non-specialist audiences and some of his most impressive playing in a pure jazz context will be found here. Mullen is a very creative player who traces out fast-moving single note lines like a second horn. Carr wrote all ten tunes here, which includes his boppish tribute to the late Vic Feldman, *Viva Victor*, and a very attractive ballad, *Freedom Song*. Good, unselfconscious modern-mainstream jazz. **AM**

Barbara Carroll 1925

This Heart Of Mine **Carroll** (p, v); **Art Farmer** (t); **Jerome Richardson** (ts, as); **Jay Leonhart**, **Frank Tate** (b); **Joe Cocuzzo** (d). DRG Ⓕ 91416 (67 minutes). Recorded 1993.

⑥ ❻

Carroll's career goes back to the forties when she led a bop trio in New York and invited the likes of Charlie Parker and Stan Getz to share her stage. A family-raising sabbatical interrupted her musical activities but her career resumed in the mid-seventies at no apparent artistic cost. As this CD demonstrates, she is very much at home with horn players and she exploits the difference between Farmer and Richardson very effectively. As a soloist herself she shows similar adaptability, with titles like *The Way You Look Tonight* and *Sweet Lilacs* explaining why she was known as "the first girl to play bebop". In contrast, she nurtures themes such as *Some Other Time* and *Never Let Me Go* to proffer the romantic's concern for a well-turned phrase and to endorse her awareness of the composer's intention. Her supper-club sing/speak vocals on *I Wanna Be Yours* and *Rain Sometimes* show how she guards her shallow range and suspect intonation but both confirm her oblique sense of timing and the way in which she deliberately torments an overly sentimental lyric. Like the Carroll of her 1949 record début, however, this talented lady is first and foremost a jazz pianist and she does her best work at the keyboard. **BMcR**

Benny Carter 1907

Complete Recordings 1930-40, Volume 1 **Benny Carter** (as, ts, cl, t, p, v, arr); playing with and leading various groups, including **The Chocolate Dandies**; **McKinney's Cotton Pickers**; **The Ramblers**. Charly CD AFS Ⓜ 1022-3 (three discs: 213 minutes). Recorded 1930-37.

⑧ ❻

The very first number gives a good indication of what is to come: Carter composed the tune, wrote the arrangement, sings the vocal and plays the alto solo. On the ensuing 69 tracks he also plays trumpet, tenor, clarinet and piano—sometimes several in the course of one three-minute piece. For sheer all-round brilliance nobody in jazz has ever been able to top Benny Carter.

The groups to be heard on this hugely entertaining collection vary from full-blown big bands to quartets, almost always with Carter as leader, arranger and principal soloist. The word to describe his whole manner is 'debonair'—stylish, charming, self-assured and never a bore. His alto playing grows more delectable with the passing years, so that you begin to get irritated with his constant and determined displays of versatility, astounding although they are. This is particularly true of the big-band numbers recorded during his period in London during 1936-37, where he plays three instruments per tune as a matter of routine. On the other hand, there is a little throw-away performance of *When Lights Are Low* (composer Benny Carter) (with an enchanting vocal chorus by Elisabeth Welch) in which Benny Carter the alto saxophonist delivers a stunning demonstration in the art of playing a straight melody and making it swing. At moments like this you hear him speaking in his own voice, forgetting the virtuosity for the moment, and it is irresistible.

In later years he wisely concentrated his playing on the alto and came to be regarded as one of the great alto triumvirate—Hodges, Carter, Parker—an eminence he would never have achieved if he had continued to present himself as the man who could do everything. That is why I cannot rate this set as part of an essential jazz collection, although it is so enjoyable that it is worth having in any case. **DG**

Cosmopolite **Carter** (as); **Bill Harris** (tb); **Oscar Peterson** (p); **Herb Ellis**, **Barney Kessel** (g); **Ray Brown** (b); **J.C. Heard**, **Buddy Rich**, **Bobby White** (d). Verve Ⓜ 521 673-2 (78 minutes). Recorded 1952/54.

⑩ ❻

This album comprises all the Verve Carter material which features Oscar Peterson in a supporting role. On four 1954 tracks Bill Harris is added to the basic quartet format. It complements—and supplements—the previous Norgran/Clef/Verve compilation, **3, 4, 5—The Small Group Sessions**, which found Carter in superb form and accompanied by, among others, Teddy Wilson, Jo Jones and Louie Bellson. The Peterson trio were Carter's accompanists on the last three tracks of that collation, and this CD picks up where that finished.

That there is empathy here is hardly to be doubted. On ballads, Peterson's group act as the softest and plushest of musical suspensions for Carter's rich tone and elegant phrasing to glide upon, while medium and faster tempos find Carter being driven harder than usual. Happily, he responds with alacrity, showing that he could swing as hard as Hodges when he needed to. His powers of paraphrase are as sharp as ever here, and his ability to deliver miraculously balanced phrases over the course of an entire solo is fully exploited. This may not be spectacular jazz, but if you are looking for that, then Carter is the wrong place to start anyway. What you get here is beautifully crafted, sophisticated music played with complete commitment by a born communicator. What you get here is sheer pleasure. **KS**

Jazz Giant **Carter** (as, t); **Frank Rosolino** (tb); **Ben Webster** (ts); **André Previn**, **Jimmy Rowles** (p); **Barney Kessel** (g); **Leroy Vinnegar** (b); **Shelly Manne** (d). Contemporary Ⓜ OJCCD 167-2 (39 minutes). Recorded 1957.

⑧ ❽

From the forties Carter established himself as the first important black composer of Hollywood background music, initially (for 20 years, that is) 'ghosting' for white writers but paving the way for such as Quincy Jones, Oliver Nelson and J.J. Johnson. In the meantime jazz saxophone became largely a sideline for him, although you would scarcely know it from his recordings of the fifties onwards.

His mellifluous alto is surprisingly urgent when pushed by Manne's trio and Kessel's rhythm-guitar, while his trumpet on two tracks exhibits a similar broad tone reminiscent of Charlie Shavers but with more direct phrasing. The repertoire consists of well-worn tunes from the twenties, with the exception of Edgar Sampson's *Blue Lou* and two delightfully simple Carter originals which bridge the gap between the genuine old material and the then current backward-looking Horace Silver approach.

The additional horns on most tracks add a suitably timeless feel and, although there is a difference of dialect between Webster and the punchy, mobile Rosolino, you are unaware of the actual generation gap. Fellow film composer Previn (relieved on two numbers by the understated Rowles) contents himself with Petersonisms, but hardly distracts from this beautifully relaxed date. **BP**

Further Definitions **Carter**, **Phil Woods** (as); **Coleman Hawkins**, **Charlie Rouse** (ts); **Dick Katz** (p); **John Collins** (g); **Jimmy Garrison** (b); **Jo Jones** (d). Impulse! MCAD 5651-2 (34 minutes). Recorded 1961.

⑧ ❽

The original idea for this session was to re-interpret some of the music which Carter and Hawkins had recorded in Paris with Django Reinhardt before the war. Because of Carter's outstanding arrangements the group had moved beyond that concept before a note had been blown. In the event only lip-service was paid to the earlier occasion and the new originals which Carter had written for the date stand out as some of the best mainstream of the period. Carter's ballad *Blue Star* is a beautiful example of his writing with the four saxes knitting into a most impressive section—perhaps one would not have expected such individuals to be able to suborn themselves so well to a common cause. The rhythm section is ideal, and Katz shows himself to be a versatile accompanist and soloist. The match between scoring of the highest quality and similarly first division sax solos is quite outstanding, with the unlikely matching of Hawkins and Woods seeming to inspire both players. It is interesting to hear *The Midnight Sun Will Never Set*, normally a feature for Woods with the Quincy Jones band, scored by Carter to feature himself and Hawkins. The music is near-perfect. It is a pity that the meagre playing time could not have been augmented by adding the subsequent volume to this disc. **SV**

Central City Sketches **Carter** (as, t, arr); with **American Jazz Orchestra**; **John Eckert**, **Virgil Jones**, **Bob Milikan**, **Marvin Stamm** (t); **Eddie Bert**, **Jack Jeffers**, **Jimmy Knepper**, **Britt Woodman** (tb); **Bill Easley**, **John Purcell** (as, f); **Loren Schoenberg** (ts); **Lew Tabackin** (ts, f); **Danny Bank** (bs, b cl); **Dick Katz** (p); **Remo Palmieri** (g); **Ron Carter** (b); **Mel Lewis** (d); **John Lewis** (p). MusicMasters Ⓕ CIJD60126X (72 minutes). Recorded 1987.

✔ ⑩ ❿

Recorded a few months before his 80th birthday, this was Carter's first big band album in two decades and the first in at least that long to show him off to full advantage as both a soloist and composer. His blues choruses on *Easy Money*, to cite one example among many, show that Carter remains one of jazz's most dazzling improvisers—still in full possession of the roseate, almost Marcel Mule-like tone that has been his signature for over half a century, but surprisingly modern in his harmonic values and rhythmic placements. The programme offers a Carter retrospective, with material ranging from *Lonesome Nights*, *When Lights Are Low*, *Symphony in Riffs* and *Blues in My Heart* (unaccountably burdened with a doubled-up and dated-sounded 'contemporary' beat—Carter's only injudicious revision) from the thirties, to the varied six-piece title suite finished just in time for the recording session (the melodic accelerations of the section subtitled *Promenade* are especially winning). The set is also a reminder of the key role played by the now-defunct AJO in the jazz repertory movement of the eighties, with music director Lewis spelling Katz on four numbers, including Carter's no-doze arrangement of the Fred Waring warhorse, *Sleep*. **FD**

Betty Carter 1930

'Round Midnight **Carter** (v); **Norman Simmons** (p); **Lisle Atkinson** (b); **Al Harewood** (d). Roulette Ⓜ CDP7 95999-2 (42 minutes). Recorded 1969.

⑦ ❻

Betty Carter sang with Charlie Parker as a teenager, was dubbed Betty Bebop by Lionel Hampton and toured with Ray Charles during the sixties. She began leading her own trio in 1969 and today (1995) still works in that manner. The trio heard on this CD was her first group, and this recording, live from Judson Hall in New York, is typical of her work at the time. She successfully breathes bebop into everything she sings, an easy task with the likes of *'Round Midnight* and a good scat vehicle like *Surrey With A Fringe On Top*, but not quite so simple with *Ev'ry Time We Say Goodbye* or *My Shining Hour*.

A considerable amount of preparation goes into her arrangements, she makes no concessions to popularity and, when she succeeds, she produces brilliant pieces of bop improvisation. Little attempt is made to dignify the lyrics; if Carter needs to override them for creative purposes, she literally ignores their meaning—in Carter we have a jazz musician first and a singer second. She has chosen her rhythm section with skill; Simmons was previously with Carmen McRae for nine years and he is an accompanist par excellence. **BMcR**

The Audience With Betty Carter **Carter** (v); **John Hicks** (p); **Curtis Lundy** (b); **Kenneth Washington** (d). Verve Ⓕ 835684-2 (two discs: 93 minutes). Recorded 1979.

⑨ ❾

Ten years to the night after the Judson Hall concert that produced the **'Round Midnight** and **Finally** CDs, Betty Carter recorded a second live date for what many people now regard as her masterpiece. **Audience** is certainly one of the finest live jazz vocal performances on disc and confirms her feeling that "an audience makes me think, makes me reach for things I'd never even try for in a studio".

She is backed, as before, by a trio of super-alert young talents; but, ten years the wiser, her singing now has an extra degree of sophistication and daring. The extremes of tempo she likes have become almost surreal—she tears up a manic *My Favorite Things*, yet sinks beautifully into a lugubrious *Everything I Have Is Yours*. Her intervallic swoops are so dramatic, so startling, those low, gruff notes dragged across the syllables are like an erotic caress. She can also inhabit a song as never before, time virtually suspended as she delves into *Spring Can Really Hang You Up The Most*.

Her scatting runs like a grain through the music, from rapid fire delivery to lullaby coo. The totally improvised *Sounds (Moving On)* is a tour-de-force, perhaps the most brilliant scat on record, although its 25-minute length could be considered indulgent. **GL**

James Carter 1969

Jurassic Classics **Carter** (ss, as, ts); **Craig Taborn** (p); **Jaribu Shahid** (b); **Tani Tabbal** (d). DIW/Columbia Ⓕ 478612-2 (57 minutes). Recorded 1994.

⑦ ❿

Carter is a phenomenal sax player, fully capable of going within the space of a few bars from the most outrageous smears of expressionistic rant to almost tender, rhapsodic melodicism. He is a 'full-on' player in much the same manner as Rahsaan Roland Kirk, Sonny Rollins, George Adams and David Murray are: when it starts to tumble out there is simply no stopping it, and a ceaseless torrent of ideas comes rushing at the listener while the rhythm section be-bops along. This is the second album for DIW made with this line-up, and to be honest there is not much to choose between the two. Carter, a veteran of Lester Bowie's and Julius Hemphill's groups, is such an in-your-face player that it would be idle to expect a complete re-think in the 12 months between recording sessions. The other players do what is required: they give Carter good, responsive support, keep out of his way and keep the rhythm moving along. Taborn solos from time to time, but has not acquired the sort of distinctive voice possessed in abundance by Carter. So if you are going to buy this, it will be for one reason only: you think you will enjoy hearing a modern-day saxophone colossus shredding a few jazz standards (by Monk, Ellington, Coltrane, Rollins) in the name of good clean fun. **KS**

John Carter 1929-1991

Castles of Ghana **Carter** (cl, v); **Bobby Bradford** (c); **Baikida Carroll** (t,v); **Benny Powell** (tb); **Marty Ehrlich** (bcl, perc); **Terry Jenoure** (vn, v); **Richard Davis** (b); **Andrew Cyrille** (d, perc). Gramavision Ⓕ R2 79423 (49 minutes). Recorded 1985.

⑨ ❾

John Carter's five-suite magnum opus *Roots and Folklore: Episodes in the Development of American Folk Music* displays a breadth of vision rare in modern jazz. Over the course of five CDs, Carter and his octet trace the evolution of African-American music from its origins in the ancient kingdoms of West Africa (**Dauwhe**), along the bloody passage of the transatlantic slave roots (**Castles of Ghana**, **Dance of the Love Ghosts**), to the rural communities of the American South (**Fields**) and the later black migrations to the cities of the North (**Shadows on a Wall**). Elements of country blues, rhythm & blues, gospel and other 'roots' musics are woven into this narrative, but Carter does not attempt to recreate these styles. Rather he uses the manifold possibilities of freedom-based music (inspired by his old associate Ornette Coleman) to evoke a series of moods, scenes and incidents that tell the story of his people's travails.

Castles of Ghana—the reference is to the fortified trading posts that were used as "holding stations for captives awaiting shipment"—is a particularly moving work that conjures up crepuscular feelings of pensiveness and desolation. The ensemble playing is superb—disconsolate reeds, growling brass, a throb of African percussion—whilst Carter's clarinet is masterful (he gave up his other reeds in the early seventies to concentrate on the clarinet and became its leading modern jazz virtuoso). His exquisite work on this album embraces the floating lines of *Evening Prayer*, the restless flutters of *Conversations* and, on *Capture*, an a cappella solo of truly breathtaking facility. **GL**

Ron Carter

1937

Telephone **Carter** (b); **Jim Hall** (g). Concord Ⓕ CCD 4270 (46 minutes). Recorded 1984.

⑦ ❽

Carter's curriculum vitae would fill this entry without reference to the details of the music. Stalwart of more than a thousand albums in various fields of music, he remains one of jazz's finest string bassists. Work with Chico Hamilton, Thelonious Monk, Miles Davis, The New York Jazz Quartet and V.S.O.P. barely scratches the surface, but his duo recordings with Jim Hall and Cedar Walton give perhaps the most positive exposure to his personal style. This CD with Hall affords him room to breathe while at the same time testing his concomitant skills. It is one of his most successful duos because his brilliant ability as an accompanist does not overshadow his solo exploits and his desire to stretch out is suitably accommodated. The ductile *Indian Summer* is an ideal vehicle for him: it shows how cunning re-routing can take a pretty tune into fertile new territory while retaining the spirit of the original. His aptitude for contrapuntal playing is emphasized on *Alone Together* and *Choral And Dance*, non-gladiatorial confrontations which reflect well on both men, while *Telephone* gives evidence of Carter's facility in unison passages. The richness of his full tone is never better demonstrated than on his journey through the range on *Stardust*. He remains the complete jazz bassist. **BMcR**

Al Casey

1915

Buck Jumpin' **Casey** (g); **Rudy Powell** (cl, as); **Herman Foster** (p); **Jimmy Lewis** (b); **Belton Evans** (d). Swingville Ⓜ OJCCD-675-2 (48 minutes). Recorded 1960.

⑥ ❻

Casey was still attending high school when he started working with Fats Waller in 1934, but his allegiance to Waller's music remains strong. This is a reissue of an LP made at a time when Casey and the rhythm section were all working with tenor saxophonist King Curtis's band, a unit in which Al was called upon to play electric guitar. For this Prestige-Swingville date he went back to unamplified guitar and it is a pleasure to hear the instrument throughout all nine tracks. The opening *Buck Jumpin'* revives memories of Waller (this was one of Casey's features with Fats) and the presence of another ex-Wallerite, Rudy Powell, helps to give the music period charm. On *Casey's Blues* Powell comes on like a reedy Pete Brown, but elsewhere his tone is sweeter and on *Ain't Misbehavin'* his clarinet sound is mellow. Casey relishes the up-tempos and the ballads (*Body and Soul* is a gem) so while the music may not be too significant, it happily conjures up a past era. The CD has two previously unissued titles: *Gut Soul* is a blues which may have been previously rejected due to some unsteady tempos and a chopped-off ending. **AM**

Philip Catherine

1942

Moods Volumes 1 and 2 **Catherine** (g); **Tom Harrell** (t, flh); **Michel Herr** (kbds); **Hein Van De Geyn** (b). Criss Cross Ⓕ 1061/62 (two discs, oas: 60 and 62 minutes). Recorded 1992.

⑧ ❽

These two volumes are separate CDs, but they stem from the same date and are clearly meant to be heard in tandem: indeed, anyone who enjoys one album will certainly enjoy the other. Catherine's career has seen him gradually move away from a wild and woolly musical youth at the opening of the seventies with such people as Jean-Luc Ponty and Charlie Mariano, and into the arms of musical conservatism. Yet this is not necessarily a process we need mourn, because his playing is as expressive and rewarding today as it ever was. He is just a lot more subtle in the way he goes about it. The absence of a drummer on this date should be a giveaway, and may even put some people off without so much as a cursory listen, but the fascinating dialogue between Harrell and Catherine should by itself be enough to satisfy anyone, let alone the lyrical beauty which both men continually exhibit on both volumes. Van De Geyn's bass offers exemplary support, which is as it should be, given the extra weight his role assumes in the absence of a drummer, while Herr, who appears on five tracks in all, fulfils his discreetly colouristic function sensitively. Harrell's idea organization in his solos is a thing to treasure all of itself, while Catherine manages to wring so many contrasting moods and nuances from the simplest melodic line or the most casual harmonic substitution that these discs will continue to give satisfaction for years to come. Both Harrell and Catherine, by the way, contribute a number of highly evocative original themes. **KS**

Oscar 'Papa' Celestin

1884 – 1954

New Orleans Classics **Celestin, 'Kid Shots' Madison, Guy Kelly, Ricard Alexis** (c); **William Ridgley, August Rousseau, Ernest Kelly** (tb); **Willard Thoumy** (cl, as, ts); **Manual Manetta, Jeanette Salvant** (p); **John Marrera** (bj); **Simon Marrera** (b); **Abby Foster** (d, w); **Paul Barnes** (cl, as); **Earl Pierson** (ts); **Charles Gills, Ferdinand Joseph** (v); **Sid Carriere** (ss, ts); **William Matthews** (tb); **Clarence Hall** (cl, ss, as); **Oliver Alcorn** (cl, ts); **Josiah Frazier** (d); **Narvin Kimball** (bj); **Sam Morgan's Jazz Band**. Azure Ⓕ AZ-CD-12 (73 minutes). Recorded 1925-28.

✔ ⑦ ❽

Celestin founded the Original Tuxedo Orchestra in 1910 and worked in and around New Orleans for more than 20 years. He excelled as a leader, although as a soloist he was something of an artisan. His plunger solo on the 1926 *My Josephine* is perhaps most typical, showing him as a good but comparatively straight player, a tweaker of melodies rather than an improviser. Since most of the records made when he returned to jazz in 1946 are feeble revivalist fare, this CD offers his very best work. The personality of the excellent 1925 band is obvious, but it was certainly influenced by King Oliver, using Oliver-style two-cornet breaks on *Original Tuxedo Rag* as well as *Mable's Dream*-style trumpet conversations and a swannee-whistle obbligato on *Careless Love*. The introduction of brass bass and a larger personnel took the 1927 band further along the Oliver path, this time capturing much of the Savannah Syncopators' gambolling mobility. The solo work by Alexis, Celestin and Hall make *It's Jam Up* one of the best titles, but a further lightening of the band's rhythmic approach in the 1928 session took the Tuxedos to greater sophistication. Sadly, no further records were seen for 19 years. **BMcR**

Joe Chambers

1942

Phantom Of The City **Chambers** (d); **Philip Harper** (t); **Bob Berg** (ts); **George Cables** (p); **Santi DeBriano** (b). Candid Ⓕ 79517 (59 minutes). Recorded 1991.

⑦ ❽

Despite being one of the most active and impressive drummers of the sixties, Chambers's visibility has dropped considerably over the past decades. Except for his role in Max Roach's Mboom, he has been something of a phantom; this is in fact his first recording as a leader in the US since the seventies. Given the challenging musical environment he inhabited earlier in his career, the mainstream nature of this return is a disappointment. For one thing, his work as a composer is slighted. He contributed a number of evocative, engagingly constructed compositions to albums by Bobby Hutcherson, for example, and on his own dates took advantage of a wider timbral palette, including piano/organ duets and pieces for multiple percussion. In his two tunes here, a tender ballad (*For Miles*) and the genial *Nuevo Mundo*, there is none of the 'free counterpoint' or expansive harmonic profile of his best work. Berg, the featured soloist, is solid in the mid-period Coltrane mode and sets off sparks on Joe Henderson's *In And Out*. Philip Harper, although of a younger generation, has most of the proper moves down. Cables, with whom Chambers recorded as far back as 1971 for Muse, is fluid throughout. But even though this is a pleasant, occasionally potent date, it does not reflect the breadth of Chambers's experiences or the depth of his talents. **AL**

Paul Chambers

1935-1969

Just Friends **Chambers** (b); **Freddie Hubbard** (t); **Cannonball Adderley** (as); **Wynton Kelly** (p); **Jimmy Cobb, Philly Joe Jones** (d) Charly LeJazz Ⓑ CD24 (40 minutes). Recorded 1959.

⑥ ❻

Chambers had a prolific career on record, thanks to the 12-inch LP boom of the mid-fifties onwards. Only 23 years old at the time of this session, he already had several previous albums issued under his name (further material from the period has appeared since), and had done dozens of sessions for other artists. Unfortunately, neither of his two outstanding Blue Note albums is currently available on CD.

If Jimmy Blanton made the pizzicato bass a melodic instrument emerging from the rhythm section, Chambers specialized in emulating the solo style of bop and post-bop horn players, while his functional rhythm playing was superbly driving and inventive without drawing attention to itself. Both facets are displayed in this album, and featuring the bass on every track seems, for once, justified by the results.

Done in Chicago at the same time as Adderley's quintet album featuring Coltrane in place of the callow Hubbard, this is a simplified version of Miles's late-fifties approach to blues and standards. His new rhythm section with Cobb is one of the chief delights (Jones replaces Cobb on three tracks out of six), but the solo work of Chambers and Adderley on every track and Kelly on *Just Friends* is what is most memorable. **BP**

Thomas Chapin

Safari Notebook **Chapin** (f, ss, as); **Tom Harrell** (t, flh); **Peter Madsen** (p); **Kiyoto Fujiwara** (b); **Reggie Nicholson** (d). Arabesque Ⓕ AJ 0115 (63 minutes). Recorded 1994.

⑥ ❽

This is Chapin's second album as a leader for Arabesque, although he has appeared on numerous albums in a sideman role. A veteran of many nights at the Knitting Factory, but just as comfortable stretching the sonic boom at CBGB's, Chapin held down a job with the Lionel Hampton band for six years before moving on to an equally rewarding sojourn with Chico Hamilton. From that list it is clear he is nothing if not versatile, and although both this and the previous Arabesque album tend to suggest his natural niche is at the more exotic end of modern mainstream, this is not meant to portray him as a player without vision or imagination. **Safari Notebook** is a loosely-connected series of tunes which give little pictures of places in Africa. As such it is not a borrowing of native music but more a musician's impressions of the people, the landscapes and the cityscapes he was moving through.

As with many albums being made by players who have arrived on the scene in the past decade, this is one which could conceivably have been made any time in the past 20 years, although the giveaway on its contemporaneity is the control and crafting which is evident is everyone's playing. Chapin solos with plenty of fire, but avoids long, self-indulgent solos and formless raves: each piece has a pleasant sense of forward motion. Harrell plays with engagement, while pianist Madsen also impresses with his measured support. A good, thoughtful and at times exciting album. By the way, this, to my ears, sounds like it is mastered in mono, not stereo. Strange ... **KS**

Ray Charles

1930

Soul Brothers/Soul Meeting **Charles** (p, as); **Billy Mitchell** (ts); **Milt Jackson** (p, vb, g); **Skeeter Best** (g); **Oscar Pettiford** (b); **Connie Kay** (d): on five tracks **Charles** (p, as); **Jackson** (p, vb); **Kenny Burrell** (g); **Percy Heath** (b); **Art Taylor** (d) Atlantic Jazz Ⓜ 781951-2 (two discs: 94 minutes) Recorded 1957/58.

⑧ ❻

A famous pairing (and originally one which had Jackson's name first) and two justly prized albums from it, recorded almost exactly a year apart. The first session is steeped in the blues from beginning to end, but the ghosts of Charlie Parker and Kansas City also hover, each performance sharing that familiar loping beat and the phraseology of bop which was Parker's most immediate musical legacy. Jackson is of course a peerless blues improviser on the vibes, but also exhibits considerable dexterity as a pianist, while Charles gets some uniquely persuasive solos out of his alto in a style somewhere between Parker and Pete Brown. Billy Mitchell, then known for his work with Dizzy's big band, is meaty and alert in his solos. What is most memorable about the first date in particular, however, is the atmosphere of relaxed co-operation. This really does sound like an after-hours session where everything is mellow, everyone inspired. Even Jackson's guitar playing (on *Bags' Guitar Blues*) has an earthy conviction about it.

The second session is a little smoother, partly because Kenny Burrell is a smooth guitarist and takes some of the themes with Jackson and Charles, but mostly because Mitchell is absent and Charles only gets his alto out of the case on one track (on *X-Ray Blues*). Still, there is much to admire, not least Jackson and his unstinting inventiveness across a blues sequence.

This is probably Charles's best jazz work. However, if you want to combine the two sides of his genius in one set, Rhino/Atlantic have a superb two-CD compilation, **Blues+Jazz**, currently available. It has two tracks from the sessions reviewed here. By the way: the CD booklet with my copy of **Soul Brothers/Soul Meeting** has the two sets of liner notes mixed up because the page sequence has been muddled. Read with care! **KS**

Teddy Charles

1928

The Teddy Charles Tentet **Charles** (vb); **Art Farmer** (t); **Eddie Bert** (tb); **Jim Buffington** (frh); **Don Butterfield** (tba); **Gigi Gryce, Hal Stein** (as); **Robert Newman, J.R. Monterose** (ts); **George Barrow, Sol Schlinger** (bs); **Hall Overton, Mal Waldron** (p); **Jimmy Raney** (g); **Addison Farmer, Teddy Kotick, Charles Mingus** (b); **Joe Harris, Ed Shaughnessy** (d). Atlantic Ⓜ 790983-2 (68 minutes). Recorded 1956-59.

⑧ ❽

A reasonably fluent, although not innovative vibist, Charles was nevertheless an important instigator and focal point for the fifties modernist movement, straddling the West Coast (Shorty Rogers, Jimmy

Giuffre, Charles Mingus) and East Coast (Teo Macero, George Russell, Charles Mingus) scenes. This tentet (different recording sessions account for the collective personnel above) was an outgrowth not only of the famous Miles Davis nonet, but also lesser-known groups like Mingus's Composers Workshop and Charles's own New Directions quartet. It was a vehicle for some of the period's most progressive composer/arrangers, attempting to integrate improvisation with classically-influenced writing and greater juxtaposition of material and mood. The most inventive and convincing charts are George Russell's brisk and exciting *Lydian M-l* (an early exercise in his new harmonic concept) and Mal Waldron's confrontational *Vibrations*. Gil Evans, Jimmy Giuffre, and Bob Brookmeyer each contribute a chart exploring harmonic movement or formal reorganization in a jazz setting. Charles's own *Word From Bird* is rather ponderous; his *The Emperor* at least offers altered chords from *Sweet Georgia Brown* for the soloists' familiarity. Much of this music remains fresh and feisty today; and all of it is of historical interest.
AL

Doc Cheatham
1905

At The Bern Jazz Festival **Cheatham** (t); **Roy Williams** (tb); **Jim Galloway** (ss); **Ian Bargh** (p); **Neil Swainson** (b); **Terry Clarke** (d). Sackville Ⓕ CD2-3045 (58 minutes). Recorded 1983-85.
⑧ ❽

Doc Cheatham is one of the most experienced jazz musicians still playing. He has worked with innumerable bands, including six years with Cab Calloway during the thirties. An immensely popular figure internationally, he appeared at the Bern Festival in Switzerland with a Scot, a Canadian rhythm section and England's fine trombonist Roy Williams. The six titles from that concert are supreme examples of mainstream jazz with everyone not only on top form but determined to work as a group. Doc inevitably takes on the role of leader when it is called for, but this is very much a combined effort. Galloway's piping soprano weaves through the ensembles, never once sounding like a Bechet clone, and the 'unknown' Ian Bargh (unknown, that is, to non-Canadian jazz lovers) is a two-handed revelation. Roy Williams demonstrates his class and the two choruses he plays on *Polka Dots and Moonbeams* are perfect in conception and execution, while he displays an apt turn of phrase and Ellingtonian effects on *Creole Love Call*. But it is Doc who, at the age of 78, is the star, a position reinforced on the final three tracks recorded in Toronto some time later. *My Buddy*, from the Toronto dates, is an immensely satisfying performance. The Bern concert was digitally recorded, the Toronto dates analogue; in all cases the sound is excellent.
AM

Don Cherry
1936

The Avant-Garde **Cherry** (t); **John Coltrane** (ts, ss); **Charlie Haden, Percy Heath** (b); **Edward Blackwell** (d). Rhino/Atlantic Ⓜ 790041-2 (36 minutes). Recorded 1960.
⑩ ❽

In 1967, when this session was first released, its title was even less accurate than when it was recorded. By 1960, Cherry was thoroughly conversant with the freebop method of his usual partner Ornette Coleman, whose influence here is paramount—he wrote three of the five tunes—so the music sounds comfortably lyrical, not radical. Despite the co-billing, this was obviously Cherry's date. All of the players save Coltrane had recorded with Don under Coleman's leadership, Cherry wrote one tune (Coltrane none), and usually solos first. The trumpeter's lines loosely imply chord changes, but never as systematically as harmony-obsessive Coltrane's do. The rhythm section, with either bassist, has a light, springy feel.

The Avant-Garde was the first album recorded (but not first released) on which Coltrane plays soprano—not that you would know it, his sinewy playing is so assured. The album also contains some uncommonly splendid Cherry. He has always been more intuitive than chops-oriented, with a raw, raspy, airy brass sound, but his harmon-muted improvisation on *The Blessing* is one of his loveliest, most limber and inspired on record. Cherry obviously had fond memories of the date; he revived its *The Blessing* and *Bemsha Swing* (by Thelonious Monk) and much of its feel for 1989's **Art Deco** (see below). A shame two alternative live takes were not included, especially when the playing-time is taken into account.
KW

Symphony For Improvisers **Cherry** (c); **Gato Barbieri** (ts); **Pharoah Sanders** (ts, pic); **Karl Berger** (vb, p); **Henry Grimes**, **J.F. Jenny-Clark** (b); **Ed Blackwell** (d). Blue Note Ⓜ CDP8 28976-2 (39 minutes) Recorded 1966.
⑦ ❽

Cherry made three of his best and most consistent records for Blue Note in the mid-sixties; this is the only one of them currently on CD. Remarkably similar personnel share them. As is the way of the world, the first (**Complete Communion**) was probably the best, the second (this one) almost as good, the third (**Where Is Brooklyn?**) somewhat lagging behind, the format by then getting a little frayed at the edges. Cherry is often best when having a strong central personality to bounce delightedly off, and here that role is played (in more than one sense) by Barbieri, who is still revelling in what was an early creative peaking of his powers. In this he is duplicating the role he inhabited on **Complete Communion**, but the space is shared with Sanders (although on side one Pharoah sticks to piccolo, thus clearing the centre ground a little, while on side two Barbieri plays on the first two tunes, Sanders on the latter two). The music is in the form of two suites (suiting the two sides of the old LP format), the themes only very loosely associated, the cues mostly quite blatantly signalled by Berger or Cherry himself blurting out a snippet of the next piece as a rallying cry. In a typically thoughtful piece of programming, Blue Note have given us just two index points to the whole CD.

Still, the music is there for all to hear, and on *Manhattan Cry*, the piece which starts side two (or Movement Two, according to the CD running order), Cherry makes one of his most convincing and technically secure ballad statements, with not a saxophone or piccolo within earshot. Barbieri also solos strongly. The concluding two pieces with Pharoah on board find the band sounding a deal more hesitant, with the tenor player unable or unwilling to shift his ground to accommodate Cherry's concepts.

KS

Art Deco **Cherry** (t); **James Clay** (ts); **Charlie Haden** (b); **Billy Higgins** (d). A&M Ⓕ CD 5258 (56 minutes). Recorded 1988.

✔

⑧ ❾

Cherry's involvement with projects that are consistently beneath him has led to much justifiable concern for his musical future. World music has never fitted the extrovert free-form pioneer to any real degree of comfort; indifferent concert, club and record performances had in the eighties become frequent occurrences and this 1989 release, with its return to previous musical territory, came as a breath of fresh air. It breaks no new ground; there are three Ornette Coleman tunes, one by Thelonious Monk and several standards. He has chosen a tried and trusted rhythm duo and teamed himself with a no-nonsense Texas tenor man. Perhaps the most important thing is that Cherry sounds enthusiastic, more technically secure than he has for some time and seemingly happy to revert to his old Atlantic style, or at least a reasonable facsimile of it. In the process, he presents jazz that falls somewhere between Old and New Dreams and the original Coleman Quartet. Credit is due to Haden and Higgins but also Clay, who makes no attempt to go into unsuitable territory but provides a bluesy realism, in particular to *When Will The Blues Leave?*, *Bemsha Swing* and *I've Grown Accustomed To Her Face*. On this album it seemed Cherry had finally come in from the cold, although subsequent concerts have once again raised old doubts.

BMcR

Ed Cherry

1954

First Take **Cherry, Jon Faddis** (t); **Paquito D'Rivera** (cl); **David Jensen** (ts); **Kenny Barron** (p); **Peter Washington** (b); **Marvin 'Smitty' Smith** (d). Groovin' High Ⓕ 519 942-2 (67 minutes). Recorded 1993.

⑦ ❾

Cherry played guitar in Dizzy Gillespie's touring band for what seemed like decades, although in fact it was a mere 14 years. For this, his first album as leader, he chose Peter Washington and Marvin 'Smitty' Smith as the rhythm section and a cast of four guests: Kenny Barron, Paquito D'Rivera, Jon Faddis and David Jensen. Together they make an enjoyable and varied programme, with D'Rivera's clarinet solo on his own composition *Lorenzo's Wings* the outstanding item, closely followed by Ed's own interpretation of Duke Ellington's *In A Sentimental Mood.* Altogether an excellent début, well worth hearing. I urge you to read Cherry's little reminiscence of Gillespie in the booklet. The man is a natural born writer.

DG

Cyrus Chestnut

1962

Another Direction **Chestnut** (p); **Christian McBride** (b); **Carl Allen** (d). Alfa Jazz Ⓕ ALCR-317 (48 minutes) Recorded 1993.

⑦ ❽

Chestnut has in recent years become one of that select group of pianists who are first-choice for virtually anybody's recording session. Like Kenny Barron, Hank Jones and Tommy Flanagan, Chestnut has spent time giving miraculous support to some of the best singers in jazz (in Chestnut's case, the most regular employer has been Betty Carter) while at the same time being ubiquitous in the recording studios. Also like them, he is the younger generation's answer to that well-known producer's problem: how do we make this new horn player sound even better? Hire Cyrus. On the other hand, the CD market is not exactly overflowing with releases headlined by him, this being his first and recorded in spring 1993 for the Japanese company, Alfa Jazz (although there has since been another for Atlantic), a label with reasonable overseas distribution.

When it comes to his own session, Chestnut has opted for the best in terms of fellow-players, with McBride in particular making his own imperious mark on the music. The programme is heavily loaded in favour of standards—some of them dating back to the twenties. Chestnut impresses in the way Peterson in his prime did—he just has so much time to do what he does, whatever the tempo. Nothing is forced; it is beautifully placed and impeccably played. The other bonus is that he doesn't overplay and distort a song's proportions. All of which makes this an impressive and very pleasant outing in the post-war modern-mainstream tradition.

KS

Herman Chittison

1909-1967

Herman Chittison 1933-41 **Chittison** (p, v); **Ikey Robinson** (g, v); **Arita Day** (v). Classics Ⓜ 690 (63 minutes). Recorded 1933-41.

⑤ ❻

Chittison was of the generation which grew up in the shadow of the great stride pianists and came to honour Art Tatum. He had a wide and varied experience, working with comedian Stepin' Fetchit, accompanying Louis Armstrong and making some fine sides with Willie Lewis's orchestra. He spent the years 1934-40 in Europe, and the majority of this 'classics' volume was recorded in Paris. The first two tracks here, where a rather distant-sounding Chittison accompanies the dully derivative vocalising of Ikey Robinson and his equally uninspiring guitar, can safely be given a miss, but the real thing can be found in a sprightly solo workout on Waller's *Honeysuckle Rose*. While Chittison here is by no means as technically secure as Tatum or even Waller himself, he is a superior craftsman with more than a hint of Jelly Roll in his left hand, which is rhythmically closer to ragtime in its emphasis and weightings than Waller and his ilk were by the early thirties. Some of these tracks are taken at ill-advised tempos, and Chittison is a lot more impressive when he slows down and allows himself a little more time to direct his fingers rather than let them fall into pre-conceived patterns. An example of this is *You'll Be My Lover*, where the tempo is hardly slow (it bounces along nicely at the sort of speed Teddy Wilson was most comfortable at: 'sprightly' is the best way to put it), but Chittison can for once think more subtly than usual.

The two tracks where he accompanies Arita Day find him virtually overwhelming a small-voiced and none-too-confident chanteuse: the lure of Tatumesque arabesques are, for Chittison, irresistible. Things improve by the 1938 solo sessions, where a fully mature and more finely-balanced Chittison style has emerged, and although it may owe too much to Tatum to be of more than historical interest, it is mighty prettily executed, for all that. **KS**

Charlie Christian

1916-1942

The Genius of the Electric Guitar **Christian** (g); with a collective personnel of **Benny Goodman** (cl, ldr); **Alec Fila**, **Irving Goodman**, **Jimmy Maxwell**, **Cootie Williams** (t); **Cutty Cutshall**, **Lou McGarity** (tb); **Gus Bivona**, **Skippy Martin** (as); **Georgie Auld**, **Pete Mandello** (ts); **Bob Snyder** (bs); **Lionel Hampton** (vb); **Fletcher Henderson**, **Count Basie**, **Johnny Guarnieri**, **Dudley Brooks** (p); **Artie Bernstein** (b); **Nick Fatool**, **Harry Jaeger**, **Jo Jones**, **Dave Tough** (d). Columbia Ⓜ CK 40846 (49 minutes). Recorded 1939-1941.

⑨ ❼

Initially recorded and released under Benny Goodman's name, these classic sessions now stand at the center of the abbreviated but prophetic canon of jazz guitar pioneer Charlie Christian. Born in Dallas but raised in Oklahoma City, Christian got his professional start with Alphonso Trent's sextet. On a tip from Mary Lou Williams, entrepreneur John Hammond 'auditioned' the youngster, lining him up for the Goodman juggernaut on the spot. The simpatico with Goodman was immediate and profound. Indeed, on each of these BG tracks the clarinettist made sure that his new 'discovery' had ample room to stretch out.

Christian was the right guitarist at the right time to take advantage of the possibilities of the technologically evolving electric guitar. Thanks to amplification, Christian could be heard above the band. Technology, though, was only part of the story. Influenced by the flowing lyricism of Lester Young and the riff-style blues of the American Southwest, Christian gave the guitar a jazz persona. On *Rose Room*, his insinuating single-note lines swing with bluesy looseness and disciplined panache. The more brightly paced *Seven Come Eleven* shows off Christian's swinging virtuosity, and like the 1941 take on *Air Mail Special*, antecedents of boppish things-to-come. The guitarist brought a new edge to Goodman's already stellar small group forays, inspiring Goodman anew: on all these selections the clarinettist sounds terrific. The one big-band track, *Solo Flight*, is an ebullient feature for Christian. Thanks to well-executed digital remastering, sound quality is excellent. **CB**

Solo Flight **Christian** (g); **Buck Clayton**, **Cootie Williams** (t); **Benny Goodman** (cl); **Lester Young**, **Georgie Auld** (ts); **Lionel Hampton** (vb); **Fletcher Henderson**, **Johnny Guarnieri**, **Count Basie** (p); **Freddie Green** (g); **Artie Bernstein**, **Walter Page**, **Walter Iooss** (b); **Nick Fatool**, **Jo Jones**, **Harry Jaeger**, **Gene Krupa**, **Dave Tough** (d); **Benny Goodman Orchestra**. Vintage Jazz Classics Ⓜ VJC-1021-2 (76 minutes). Recorded 1939-41.

✔ ⑧ ❻

The influence of Christian on jazz and way beyond is quite incalculable and it was affected by a career of less than two years in the national spotlight before he was hospitalized with terminal tuberculosis. His CV is almost identical to that of bassist Jimmy Blanton, who likewise catapulted his instrument into the second half of the century before dying in 1942.

Two months before Blanton hooked up with Ellington, Christian joined Benny Goodman, with whom all his formal appearances and recordings were made. While sporadic jazz use had been made of the amplified guitar in the preceding few years, it was Charlie who saw that it could be a major voice rivalling the saxophone and, while having little in common stylistically with Lester Young, his 'new sound' was at the time as revolutionary as Young's. Christian's slender output has been reissued in a more cavalier fashion than that of almost any other major figure. So it is a pleasure to turn to these broadcast versions of the studio material recorded with Goodman, plus one originally unreleased Goodman studio rehearsal set (with the added bonus of glorious playing from Young, Clayton and the Basie rhythm-section) which first appeared on Jazz Archives JA6 and JA42. **BP**

Live Sessions At Minton's Playhouse **Christian** (g); with, on four tracks: **Joe Guy** (t); **Thelonious Monk** (p); **Nick Fenton** (b); **Kenny Clarke** (d); on one track: unknown (t); **Don Byas** (ts); **Monk** (p); **Fenton** (b); **Clarke** (d); on three tracks: **Dizzy Gillespie** (t); **Don Dyas** (ts); **Kenny Kersey** (p); **Fenton** (b); **Clarke** (d). Jazz Anthology Ⓑ 550012 (38 minutes). Recorded 1941.

⑧ ❻

Charlie Christian was the man who invented modern jazz guitar and whose work with the Benny Goodman Sextet was a revelation to musicians and jazz lovers. He was a frequent habitué of the New York 'after hours' clubs with the young Turks of the day and we are fortunate that a college student, Jerry Newman, took his primitive disc recorder along to locations such as Clark Monroe's Uptown House and Minton's Playhouse to record the events. The tracks here enable us to hear Christian's improvisations at considerably greater length than he was allowed on the Goodman records, and *Swing To Bop* (based on *Topsy*) opens this fine collection with a superb guitar solo. The personnel listed above, taken from the insert card, is somewhat tentative; for example, there are a number of other horns to be heard playing the final notes behind Don Byas's rich-toned *Stardust*. But the sound generally is clear and jazz owes Newman a lot for his work in documenting events (other items from his archives featuring Art Tatum, Billie Holiday, Lips Page and many others have been released on Xanadu and Onyx but are not currently available on CD). This release also enables us to study the work of the Minton's 'house' band containing Thelonious Monk and Kenny Clarke plus a notable guest, Dizzy Gillespie, who plays well on two versions of *Stardust*, open on the first, muted on the second, and a thinly disguised *Take The 'A' Train,* re-labelled *Kerouac.* **AM**

Jodie Christian

1932

Experience **Christian** (p); **Larry Gray** (b); **Vincent Davis** (d). Delmark Ⓕ DD 454 (59 minutes). Recorded 1991-92.

⑧ ❽

This album is a delight. Christian has been a musician to reckon with since the fifties and has had an international reputation since the early sixties, but this record is, quite incredibly, his first as a leader. Equally comfortable with the likes of Coleman Hawkins, Eddie Harris, Roscoe Mitchell, Dizzy Gillespie and Stan Getz, his sheer adaptability, plus a desire to stay put in Chicago rather than spend his life touring, has kept him from a more high-profile career. If nothing else, **Experience** should win him some of the attention he has deserved and not received for far too long.

Six of the ten tracks are solo piano performances, and the pianist who springs to mind—not because of any stylistic overlap, but rather because of a similarly robust touch and imaginative harmonic approach—is Jaki Byard. Christian is much less intent on covering the entire history of the music on one album, but his playing reveals an equal knowledge of the history of each selection, be it a standard (*They Can't Take That Away From Me*), a Goodman signature tune (*Goodbye*) or a bop anthem (*All The Things You Are*). An accomplished and invigorating record. Four of the compositions are Christian originals, with the sensuous ballad *Reminiscing* probably the pick of them. **KS**

Christie Brothers Stompers

Collective personnel: **Ken Colyer** (c); **Dickie Hawdon** (t); **Keith Christie** (tb); **Ian Christie** (cl); **Pat Hawes**, **Charlie Smith** (p); **Ben Marshall** (bj); **Nevil Skrimshire** (g); **Micky Ashman**, **Denny Coffee** (b); **George Hopkinson**, **Bernard Saward**, **Pete Appleby** (d); **Bill Colyer** (wshbd); **Neva Raphaello** (v). Cadillac Ⓕ SGC/MEL CD 20/1 (68 minutes). Recorded 1951-53.

⑧ ❻

The Christie Brothers—Keith (1931-1980) and Ian (born 1927)—formed their band in the early part of 1951 to make records for the Esquire label using men from the Humphrey Lyttelton and Crane River groups. The records were successful and the Christie Brothers Stompers became a regular unit. All their subsequent recordings were for the now-defunct Melodisc label and this 23-track CD comprises all the Melodisc sides, including two that were withdrawn quickly (for technical reasons) and *Old Grey Bonnet*, originally rejected. In addition there are four privately-recorded titles, one with Neva Raphaello singing the vocal. Ken Colyer played cornet with the Christies until he left on his much-publicized trip to New Orleans. Colyer is present here on nine of the tracks, his place taken on the others by Dickie Hawdon. The years have dealt kindly with the music of the Stompers simply because it was created by dedicated young men who also believed that jazz was something to be enjoyed. Kid Ory was perhaps the band's principal hero (and Keith Christie plays some of his best solos on record here; his subsequent move into the 'modern' field with John Dankworth and Ted Heath tended to diminish his importance as a soloist) but there is a high degree of originality within the general constraints of the New Orleans format. Pat Hawes, who plays piano on all but four of the tracks, has written the most informative notes, Charlie

Crump has remastered the original Melodisc 78s and the attractive gate-fold packaging contains facsimiles of historic posters and photographs. Recommended. **AM**

June Christy

1925-1990

Something Cool **Christy** (v); **Orchestras / Pete Rugolo** (arr). Capitol Ⓜ CDP7 96329-2 (69 minutes). Recorded 1953-58.

⑧ ❽

June Christy's voice, bright and clear but with a slight haze at the edges, could have been made for her time. It fits the American fifties to perfection: outwardly happy and contented but clouded with a vague sense of unease. She began her career as a vocalist with Stan Kenton's Orchestra in the late forties and, although she gave it up as a permanent job in 1948, most of her best subsequent work was done with ex-Kenton players and arrangers, such as Pete Rugolo and Bill Holman.

This background determined the general tone of her work, which brings to the classic American song a certain detachment and deliberation. The accompaniments on this and other recordings tend to be far more dissonant than was usual at the period, and sometimes her interpretations seem on the verge of turning popular song into a species of art song. A case in point here is the title piece of this CD, a touching dramatic monologue with overtones of Tennessee Williams. These 24 tracks include the whole original **Something Cool** album, about half of **This is June Christy** and numerous previously unreleased singles. The sound is excellent. **DG**

Clarinet Summit

In Concert At The Public Theatre **Alvin Batiste, John Carter, Jimmy Hamilton** (cl); **David Murray** (bcl). India Navigation Ⓕ IN 1062 CD (74 minutes). Recorded 1983.

⑧ ❽

There is some doubt regarding the date of this recording. The notes imply the end of 1981 or 1982 but Bruyninckx suggests 1983. What is certain is that Clarinet Summit did not become a committed group until 1984 and that the concert from which this recording came acted as an inspiration for its formation. It features three B-flat clarinets and one bass clarinet and embraces three generations of jazz evolution. Hamilton is from the latter stages of the swing era, Batiste and Carter from the free-form revolution and Murray a young post-Aylerian from the loft movement. Above all, it is a coalition of equal skills; the players are dealt a programme of challenging arrangements and 'heads' alike and show themselves to be in the mood for creativity. A *Whispering* quote colours *Groovin' High*, the *Snag It* riff intrudes into *Jeep's Blues* as styles are effortlessly amalgamated. There is a beautiful harmony of spirit on *Mood Indigo* and Murray parades his false upper register mastery on *Sweet Lovely*. Everyone has his solo as well as a contrapuntal say in a masterful concert; Carter is clean-lined and stately, Batiste warmer-edged, Hamilton impishly flowing and Murray gruff-voiced at the quartet's heart. It says much for this outstanding unit that identification is sometimes a problem. **BMcR**

John Clark

1944

Il Suono **Clark** (frh); **Lew Soloff** (t); **Dave Taylor** (btb); **Alex Foster** (ts); **Jerome Harris** (g); **Anthony Jackson** (contrabass g); **Kenwood Dennis** (d). CMP Ⓕ CD 59 (53 minutes). Recorded 1992.

⑤ ❽

Clark has been around a fair time, first coming to my attention, at least, on Gil Evans's early-seventies albums (one of the tracks, *Buster's Move*, is dedicated to Evans). His methods here are not so far removed from those of latter-day Evans; taking material from other sources (here we have an extended workout on the old sixties hit, *Mustang Sally*) and investing them with a completely new life and identity through a few deft arranging strokes and a lot of committed playing from the troupe.

If there is a fault with this disc, it is the unvarying sound of Clark's lead. The burnished timbre of the French horn and the sheer amount of time Clark spends in front of the microphone tends to dissipate the music's impact, especially when the second most frequent soloist, guitarist Jerome Harris, is not exactly Mr Exciting. Considering he had the presence of Foster and Soloff (Foster solos to effect on *Groove from the Louvre*), things could have been more variegated throughout more of the programme. Still, the drumming of Dinnard is a pleasure, even when there is nothing much else going on. **KS**

Sonny Clark

1931-1963

Sonny Clark Trio **Clark** (p); **Paul Chambers** (b); **Philly Joe Jones** (d). Blue Note Ⓜ B21Y 46547 (49 minutes). Recorded 1957.

In his relatively brief recording career from February 1953 (with Teddy Charles) to October 1962, Clark established himself as probably the most fluent of the post-Bud Powell pianists: this CD is the best example of his work in trio context. He is in fast company here, with Jones keeping up the pressure especially on the faster-paced numbers such as *Bebop*, but Clark is the master of the situation. He had a brittle sense of touch and a way of slithering from one phrase into the next with the easy facility of a saxophonist. He was the progenitor of a keyboard style in which the left hand made the most telling stabs at the relevant chords while allowing the right to trace out long, serpentine lines. The original LP has been fleshed out with extra takes of *I Didn't Know What Time It Was*, *Two Bass Hit* and the attractive Tadd Dameron tune, *Tadd's Delight*. Clark recorded with all of the great drummers of the fifties, Art Blakey, Max Roach, Louis Hayes, Dannie Richmond, Art Taylor and Elvin Jones amongst them, but in the final analysis the interplay between Sonny and Philly Joe Jones on sessions such as this achieved a close and very special cohesion. **AM**

Kenny Clarke

1914-1985

Bohemia After Dark **Clarke** (d); **Donald Byrd** (t); **Nat Adderley** (c); **Cannonball Adderley** (as); **Jerome Richardson** (ts, f) **Horace Silver**, **Hank Jones** (p); **Paul Chambers** (b). Denon/Savoy Ⓜ SV-0107 (42 minutes). Recorded 1955.

⑥ ❽

Clarke is the frequently-undersung drummer who developed the style of Jo Jones in ways crucial to the evolution of bebop; he was the original percussionist in both the Gillespie band and the Modern Jazz Quartet. From 1956 he was based in Europe, where he later fronted his own big band, but in the 18 months or so after leaving the MJQ and before leaving New York he appeared on around 100 jazz albums. Often, as here, he concentrated on accompaniment almost to the exclusion of solo work.

This early example of the studio 'blowing session' finds Clarke the nominal leader of front-line players recently arrived in New York (in Cannonball's case, only a matter of days before). Among the simple but catchy material, the most memorable tune is Oscar Pettiford's title-track. Each of the Adderleys has a brief ballad feature (Nat's actually done a couple of weeks later) and, while they and Byrd show obvious promise and poise, they were soon to become much more rounded players.

Denon's remastering has drawn attention to some distortion on *Hear Me Talkin' To Ya* (not the Johnny Dodds tune), but otherwise the sound is good for the period. **BP**

Clarke-Boland Big Band en concert avec Europe 1 **Clarke** (d); **Francy Boland** (p); **Benny Bailey**; **Art Farmer**, **Derek Watkins**, **Idrees Sulieman** (t); **Aake Persson**, **Nat Peck**, **Erik Van Lier** (tb); **Derek Humble**, **Johnny Griffin**, **Sahib Shihab**, **Tony Coe, Kenny Clarke** (saxes); **Jimmy Woode** (b); **Kenny Clare** (d). Trema Ⓕ 710413/14 (two discs: 101 minutes). Recorded 1969.

⑧ ❽

The brainchild of jazz promoter Gigi Campi, who decided in 1960 to programme a big band for mardi gras in Germany as an antidote to "traditional junk carnival music", the Clarke-Boland big band is notable chiefly for the ease with which the US and European musicians gel within it. Their début recording, indeed, was entitled **Jazz is Universal**, but this live recording documents their sound almost a decade later, in concert in Paris, the band comprising eight Americans, five British players, a Swede, a Dutchman and a Belgian, Francy Boland himself. Their overall sound and approach are celebratory rather than innovative, their material chiefly straightforward platforms for the roaring bustle and thunderous attack in which the band specialised, but it is the quality of the soloists which grabs and holds the attention. Benny Bailey and Art Farmer, and—more eccentrically—Tony Coe, who provides a startlingly original interpretation of *Gloria*, are all outstanding, as are Johnny Griffin and the self-effacing co-leader himself, Francy Boland. No new ground is broken on either disc of this high-energy set, but most of the old ground is covered with some panache, and the masterful way Kenny Clarke—always a genius at discreetly fitting into any group context—adapts his drumming to a big-band context is worth the price of admission alone. **CP**

Stanley Clarke

1951

Journey to Love **Clarke** (elb, perc); **Chick Corea** (p); **George Duke** (kbds); **David Sancious**, **Jeff Beck**, **John McLaughlin** (g); **Lenny White**, **Steve Gadd** (d); **Jon Faddis**, **Lew Soloff**, **David Taylor**, **Peter Gordon**, **Allen Rubin**, **Thomas Malone**, **John Clark**, **Earl Chapin**, **Wilmer Wise** (brass). Epic Ⓜ 468221-2 (39 minutes). Recorded 1975.

⑧ ❽

Being, along with Miles Davis and Sly Stone, one of the seminal jazz-rock figures of the seventies, Stanley Clarke consolidated an already precociously substantial reputation made with Chick Corea's Return to Forever with a series of commercially successful fusion albums throughout that decade. **Journey to Love** in many ways encapsulates both the strengths and weaknesses of the jazz-rock form in particular and the decade's music in general. So-called progressive rock at the time was somewhat burdened by an over-concentration on the spuriously 'cosmic', both in theme and electronic effects; jazz was prone to tender the commercial strengths of rock—its immediacy and punch, its accessible, unsophisticated approach to harmony—an exaggerated respect. Thus

Clarke's considerable strengths such as his virtuosic pioneering of the 'hammered' electric bass, producing a strangulated, percussive sound that would reverberate throughout the eighties; his ability to lay down a fearsomely taut rhythm for the brass to punctuate and wailing guitars to soar over, are too frequently diluted by dreamy vocals (another seventies affliction) and an over-reliance on rock's unsubtle, inflexible beat. The bass guitar playing of Clarke himself and the lead guitar playing of his featured soloists Jeff Beck and John McLaughlin is always vital and exciting, and Chick Corea's acoustic piano brings a touch of class to a two-part John Coltrane tribute, but overall **Journey to Love** is perhaps better viewed as a wildly above-average rock album rather than a jazz recording.
CP

James Clay
1935

A Double Dose Of Soul **Clay** (f, ts); **Nat Adderley** (c); **Vic Feldman** (vb); **Gene Harris** (p); **Sam Jones** (b); **Louis Hayes** (d). Riverside Ⓜ OJCCD-1790-2 (53 minutes). Recorded 1960.

⑥ ❻

Clay is from Texas and has the big tenor sound associated with others from that state, men such as Buddy Tate, Herschel Evans, Arnett Cobb and Budd Johnson. He created enough of an impact on his first visit to Los Angeles in 1956 to get Miles Davis interested in employing him (for non-musical reasons the job never materialized). It is his tenor sound which is immediately impressive, big and soulful as it is, but his improvisations do not always live up to that initial imprint as he allows time to pass while he assembles his ideas. The occasional reed squeaks are also disturbing. On flute he is much more assured, creating long, flowing lines with ease and a fine delivery. Nat Adderley plays cornet on the tenor tracks and produces two splendid choruses in the middle of his solo on the blues *Pockets*; tightly muted, he is supported by just Sam Jones's purposeful bass line. The rhythm section is an inspiration with fine Gene Harris piano. Vic Feldman plays vibes on the flute tracks, two of the tunes being his compositions.
AM

Buck Clayton
1911–1991

Jam Sessions From The Vaults **Clayton, Billy Butterfield, Ruby Braff, Joe Newman** (t); **J.C. Higginbotham, Urbie Green, Henderson Chambers, Bennie Green, Dicky Harris** (tb); **Tyree Glenn** (tb, vb); **Lem Davis** (as); **Coleman Hawkins, Buddy Tate, Julian Dash** (ts); **Charlie Fowlkes** (bs); **Kenny Kersey, Sir Charles Thompson, Al Waslohn** (p); **Steve Jordan, Freddie Green** (g); **Walter Page, Milt Hinton** (b); **Bobby Donaldson, Jo Jones** (d); **Jimmy Rushing** (v). Columbia Ⓜ 463336 2 (52 minutes). Recorded 1953-56.

⑥ ❻

Clayton was one of the most individual and important trumpeters from the swing era, and his solos and arrangements greatly enhanced the reputation of the Count Basie Band. A key figure in the establishment of mainstream jazz as an identifiable sub-category, he was the titular head of many star-studded studio jam session groups, of which those for Columbia, produced by George Avakian and John Hammond, are the most important. This release is a reissue of an LP called **All The Cats Join In**, with the important difference that all five titles are alternative takes to those used previously and the playing time is boosted by *After Hours*, which Columbia had not previously put out. Clayton plays a vital part in organizing the music, devising background riffs for soloists, setting the most suitable tempos but never hogging the solo microphone. The level of solos is sometimes uneven and there are examples of uncertainties which would have been duly edited out of these takes, had they been issued previously, but all that is of minor importance to the overall enjoyment and impact of the music. Coleman Hawkins, Ruby Braff and Urbie Green in particular are in fine form and it is to be regretted that, at the time of writing, Sony/Columbia have yet to transfer to the compact disc format any of the other five **Buck Clayton Jam Session** originally issued on LP. That, it seems, has been left to Mosaic.
AM

Ben And Buck **Clayton** (t); **Ben Webster** (ts); **Henri Chaix** (p); **Alain Du Bois** (g); **Isla Eckinger** (b); **Romano Cavicchiolo** (d). Sackville Ⓕ SKCD2-2037 (65 minutes). Recorded 1967.

⑧ ❻

This was virtually the last occasion on which Clayton played at the height of his powers. Immediately after this concert he suffered a medical collapse with the result that he never played effectively again. He and Webster play so well here that it is to be regretted that more privately-recorded concert performances like this have not surfaced on CD. Delicate and incisive are words which it is hard not to use when writing about Clayton and he was the leading mainstream trumpeter of the two decades before this Baden concert. He plays beautifully throughout and, as always, manages to make *I Want A Little Girl* sound as though he was playing it for the first time. Webster is similarly on good form, bustling through *In A Mellotone* and playing exquisitely on *My Romance*.

Henri Chaix's group is world-class and the pianist probably deserves inclusion in this guide with his trio. But there is enough of him here, sandwiched between the masters, for the listener to assess his proficiency.
SV

Jay Clayton

1941

Live At Jazz Alley **Clayton** (v); **Julian Priester** (tb); **Stanley Cowell** (p); **Gary Peacock** (b); **Jerry Granelli** (d). ITM Pacific Ⓔ ITMP 970065 (61 minutes). Recorded 1987.

⑥ ❽

Jay Clayton is best known as an abstract and experimental vocalist, but this set, recorded live at a Seattle club, finds her singing mainly standard material. In scat numbers, such as Gillespie's *Birks' Works*, her phrasing and almost vibrato-less voice are often reminiscent of Miles Davis in his **Kind Of Blue** period, and free from the self-conscious hipness that overtakes most jazz vocalists in these circumstances. But the best things here are the ballads, especially *My Foolish Heart*, in which she sings the melody with great restraint, alongside a wonderfully sensitive obbligato by Priester, and *But Beautiful*, with lovely piano from Cowell. The recording is particularly good, discreetly capturing the live atmosphere and maintaining perfect balance throughout. **DG**

Clementine

Mes nuits, mes jours **Clementine** (v); **André Villeger** (ss, ts); **Kenny Drew** (p); **Niels-Henning Ørsted Pedersen** (b); **Alex Riel** (d). Orange Blue Ⓔ OB 007 (54 minutes). Recorded 1990.

⑥ ❽

Clementine is a young Parisienne singing in the tradition of intimate, small-voiced French singers of the fifties and sixties. She chooses her material with care, not pushing her voice too hard and using its natural charm to beguile the listener into the moods she is projecting. She also has excellent taste in her choice of accompanists (previous albums have found her in the company of Ben Sidran and Johnny Griffin), and all four players here provide sympathetic and insightful support. The repertoire is a combination of old standards like *Everything Happens to Me, Makin' Whoopee* and *When Sunny Gets Blue* and more obviously jazz-derived pieces such as Coltrane's *Naima* with lyrics by Mimi Perrin, or Ben Sidran's *It Didn't All Come True.* It is fascinating to listen to records like this because there is simply no tradition for this type of singing in Britain, and a patchy one at best in America. The majority of the record is sung in English, and there is no doubt that it is a jazz date. It has a unique charm and should be sampled at least once by those with an ear for the unusual. **KS**

Rosemary Clooney

1928

Blue Rose **Clooney** (v); **The Duke Ellington Orchestra** (Clark Terry, Willie Cook, Cat Anderson [t]; Ray Nance [t, vn]; Quentin Jackson, Britt Woodman, John Sanders [tb]; Jimmy Hamilton [cl, ts]; Russell Procope [as, cl]; Johnny Hodges [as]; Paul Gonsalves [ts]; Harry Carney [bs, cl, bcl]; Ellington [p, ldr]; Jimmy Woode [b]; Sam Woodyard [d]). CBS Ⓜ 466444 (39 minutes). Recorded 1956.

⑧ ❽

Although not a jazz singer *per se,* Rosemary Clooney not only knows what jazz is about but has made some very successful latter-day albums with the Concord stable (Scott Hamilton, Warren Vaché, Dave McKenna et al - see below) and the full Woody Herman band. But **Blue Rose** occupies a special place in her discography and the sympathy she shows for the music and the magnificent Ellington orchestra is manifest. A lot of play was made at the time of the initial issue over the fact that the band recorded its parts in Chicago, leaving Rosie to dub in her vocals a few weeks later in New York. In fact this has nothing to do with the success of the album (particularly in the light of the tape surgery which today is standard practice in every studio). Miss Clooney's voice has a warmth which is immediately appealing, while her pitching and diction are exemplary. Her version of *Sophisticated Lady* here must rank as one of the finest interpretations of this ballad. But the programme does not depend only on the expected Ducal war-horses; there are excellent readings of fairly obscure songs such as *I'm Checkin' Out -Goom Bye, Hey Baby* and *Me And You.* Duke wrote a song especially for the occasion, which gives the album its title: it provides a wordless vehicle for the singer. Rosemary is absent from one title, a magnificent reading of Billy Strayhorn's *Passion Flower* by Johnny Hodges, surely one of his most intense and involving showcases on record. Recommended. **AM**

Tribute To Billie Holiday **Clooney** (v); **Warren Vaché** (c); **Scott Hamilton** (ts); **Cal Collins** (g); **Nat Pierce** (p); **Monty Budwig** (b); **Jake Hanna** (d). Concord Jazz Ⓔ CCD 4081 (42 minutes). Recorded 1978.

⑧ ❽

Rosemary Clooney is one of the great generation of American singers which served its apprenticeship with bands during the swing era, and she always showed great affinity with the jazz side of classic American song. Had she been contracted in the fifties to a label such as Capitol we might now have a string of superb albums from her, made when her voice was in its prime. Unfortunately, her label was Columbia, where she suffered under the regime of trivia-king Mitch Miller. It was not until her late middle age that Miss Clooney was able to begin recording consistently good material in the congenial surroundings of the Concord repertory company—Scott Hamilton, Warren Vaché and pals.

This disc is one of the best of many, a sparkling set of ten numbers associated with Billie Holiday, but with no hint of pastiche. In particular, she sings *Ev'rything Happens To Me* with wonderful simplicity and control of ironic tone. The playing is excellent throughout, especially from Nat Pierce, whose piano introductions alone could be used as object lessons in how to be an accompanist. **DG**

Arnett Cobb

1918-1989

Blow Arnett, Blow **Cobb**, **Eddie 'Lockjaw' Davis** (ts); **Strethen Davis** (org); **George Duvivier** (b); **Arthur Edgehill** (d). Prestige Ⓜ OJC 794-2 (37 minutes). Recorded 1959.

⑩ ❻

It has been a long wait, but at last some of the best Arnett Cobb has crept onto CD. Cobb was maligned in the same way that Illinois Jacquet still is, and for much the same reasons. A Texas tenor (from Houston), he was Jacquet's replacement in Lionel Hampton's roaring big-band after the two of them had previously been section mates in the Milton Larkins band. While with Hampton Cobb had a hit with *Flying Home No. 2* (Jacquet, of course, had recorded *No. 1* with Hamp) and by the late forties he was leading his own rip-snorting small group. Between them, he and Jacquet had launched the honking tenors school, garnering the critical damnation that went along with it.

But Cobb was not a johnny-one-honk. He had a massive, caressing tone on ballads, a fierce attack on swingers, and endless inventiveness (of the pre-bop variety) when it came to constructing an orderly and melodically interesting solo. Yet his calling card remained his unique ability to send shivers down the listener's spine when he opened a solo with a searing tenor moan, signalling his readiness for some heavyweight action. On this album, the first long-playing disc he made (a bad car accident had put him out of action for part of the fifties), the action comes thick and fast: in fact, on both *Go Power* and *Go Red, Go*, things get so heated that both tenor men start excitedly yelling to each other during their respective solos. In a no-holds-barred session, Lockjaw Davis keeps pace with the older man on the screamers, while both saxophonists play with big-toned sensitivity on their ballad features. The backing group is adequate for the job and the recording quality perfectly acceptable. If you are a fan of the tenor sax, then this is definitely one to treasure. **KS**

Junie Cobb

1896-c.1970

The Junie Cobb Collection 1926–1929 **Cobb** (cl, ts, ss, vn, v); **Jimmy Cobb** (c, t); **Johnny Dodds**, **Angelo Fernandez** (cl); **George James** (as, bar); **Tiny Parham**, **Jimmy Blythe**, **Alex Hill**, **Earl Frazier** (p); **Bill Johnson** (b); **Walter Wright** (bb); **Eustern Woodfork** (bj); **Clifford Jones** (d, k); **Jimmy Bertrand** (d, x, w); **Harry Dial** (d); **W.E. Burton**, **Thomas A. Dorsey** (v). Plus four titles by **Kansas City Stompers** (without Cobb). Collectors Classics Ⓜ COCD 14 (74 minutes). Recorded 1926–29.

⑥ ❹

Arkansas-born multi-instrumentalist Junius C. Cobb had his musical awakenings in New Orleans. His next move took him to Chicago where he became a central figure on the South Side and in the free-wheeling jazz scene that blossomed there in the late twenties. He enjoyed prestigious stints with King Oliver and Jimmie Noone, but in the main it was his casual, on-the-spot recordings that earned him his quiet corner in jazz history.

His best instrument was clarinet; on this CD, he is heard playing excellent straight man to the creatively devious Johnny Dodds on *Chicago Buzz*, crafting more shapely solos on *Barrell House Stomp* (sic) and *Shake That Jelly Roll* and wringing true blues feeling from *South African Blues*. His spikey soprano seeps into *Panama Blues*, his good-time violin scrapes to good effect on *Shake That Jelly Roll* and his bar-room vocals fit the mood ideally. His slap-tongue effects on tenor are mercifully brief but the simple lyricism of his style made him an ideal blues player on the horn. With trumpet-playing brother Jimmy he was among the rough diamonds of the twenties recording scene. Their mutually homespun music was without artifice but it had an ingenuous quality that was instantly appealing to the audiences that filled Chicago's dance clubs and speakeasys. **BMcR**

Billy Cobham

1944

The Best of Billy Cobham **Cobham** (d); **Randy Brecker** (t); **Garnett Brown**, **Glenn Ferris** (tb); **Michael Brecker** (ts); **Tommy Bolin**, **John Abercrombie**, **John Scofield**, **Cornell Dupree** (g); **Jan Hammer**, **George Duke**, **Milcho Leviev** (kbds); **John Williams**, **Lee Sklar**, **Alex Blake** (b). Atlantic Ⓜ 781558-2 (45 minutes). Recorded 1973-76.

⑥ ❽

Although Billy Cobham's seventies brand of bustling fusion was extraordinarily important, particularly for drummers, for whom he became (and remains) a super-hero, from a nineties perspective it is not immediately apparent what all the fuss was about. The up-tempo material showcases Cobham's unique technique and sheer physical stamina, but is less interesting either for its melodic content or for the quality of the soloing it inspires. The medium-tempo numbers settle quickly into solid, attractive grooves, but lack direction and punch, despite the usually inspirational presence of players such as George Duke, the Brecker brothers and John Abercrombie. It would be tempting to dismiss Cobham's output as unremarkable music played remarkably fast, or in impressively tricky time-signatures, were it not for its undeniable visceral impact when experienced live. Perhaps more importantly, the all-pervasive nature of its influence in the eighties, accustoming the ear to virtuoso fusion music of its type, has retrospectively (and unfairly) lessened its impact. Certainly Billy Cobham is one of contemporary jazz-fusion's great drummers, but perhaps his most sympathetic recording environment remains the Mahavishnu Orchestra. **CP**

Tony Coe

1934

Nutty **Coe** (cl, ss, ts); **Chris Laurence** (b); **Tony Oxley** (d). Hat Hut Records Ⓕ hatART CD 6046 (73 minutes). Recorded 1983.

⑧ ❽

A virtuoso player on several reeds, Tony Coe's remarkably catholic range of activities has included working with Humphrey Lyttelton, Count Basie, Derek Bailey and Franz Koglmann; recording film scores with Henry Mancini; and a little crooning with the Melody Four; a madcap trio he runs with Lol Coxhill and Steve Beresford. No one disc can be described as representative of such a versatile talent, but **Nutty**, recorded live at the Willisau Jazz Festival (and officially credited to Coe, Oxley and Co.), offers a wonderful display of instrumental bravura in the challenging context of extended improvisation.

Coe transforms *Body and Soul* into a tide of barbed tenor fragments, makes a witty extract of Monk's *Nutty* and winds a skein of supple clarinet lines through Bill Evans's *Re: Person I Knew*. Laurence engages the leader in some daunting exchanges and takes a couple of characterful solos; Oxley's subtle, pitter-patter scurries of percussion dart intrepidly to the thick of the action. **Nutty** shows three players using freedom and invention to re-fire the tradition with a new sense of adventure. Hat Hut have generously squeezed the original double album onto a single CD, though at the cost of losing one track (*Gabriellissima*). **GL**

Al Cohn

1925-1988

Nonpareil **Cohn** (ts); **Lou Levy** (p); **Monty Budwig** (b); **Jake Hanna** (d).Concord Ⓕ CCD-4155 (43 minutes). Recorded 1981.

⑧ ❽

Had he not given up so much of his time to writing, Cohn could have become the most powerful of the group of saxophonists to which he belonged. Indeed, the leaders of that group, Zoot Sims and Stan Getz, each insisted that Cohn was their favourite tenor soloist.

Cohn's wide-ranging blues-based style is shown at its best here with a truly *simpatico* West Coast rhythm section that could not have been bettered. He swings, grunts and roars through a well-chosen repertoire which includes two of his own numbers, two by Johnny Mandel and one each by Billy Strayhorn and Gary McFarland. Cohn's firm treatment of Mandel's beautiful *Unless It's You* also inspires a fine solo from Lou Levy, and Al's unusual treatment of Weill's *This Is New* must have been the inspiration for the version which Getz added to his repertoire a few months later.

There was never anything flashy in Cohn's playing and his are invariably trenchant improvisations which, when called for, swing with great fire. His ballad performances have the same qualities and are totally devoid of superfluous embellishment or sentiment. **SV**

Vinnie Colaiuta

1953

Vinnie Colaiuta **Colaiuta** (d, kbds, b, syn, loops, perc); **Jeff Beal** (t, flh); **Steve Tavaglione** (ts); **Ron Moss** (tb); **Michael Landau, Dominic Miller, Mike Miller** (g); **David Sancious, David Goldblatt, Chick Corea, Herbie Hancock** (kbds, syn); **Neil Stubenhaus, Pino Palladino, Sting, John Patitucci, Tim Landers, Sal Monilla** (b); **Bert Karl** (perc). Stretch Ⓕ GRS 00132 (58 minutes). Recorded 1994.

⑧ ❽

Although Colaiuta's Berklee training and stints with such exacting writers as Frank Zappa, Allan Holdsworth and Chick Corea ought to leave no doubt of his rhythmic competence, this début issue does leave the impression that he feels he has something to prove. The studied polymetric effects of the opening track, for example, seem to be designed as much to impress as entertain. More generally, Colaiuta seems to be striving rather too hard to be clever, contemporary and creative, employing such a wide variety of fashionably outré devices, including samples, world music and techno-industrial noise, that he becomes a musical chameleon, a jack-of-all-trades which, as a session drummer, he has no doubt had to be).

However, despite the absence of a unifying stylistic personality, the record does offer several good isolated moments, among them Steve Tavaglione's sinewy Breckerosity on *Private Earthquake* and the

Nefertiti-like *Slink*, plus the dense, accomplished jazz-rock ensembles of *Bruce Lee*. Nevertheless, to discover the full range of expression available to the contemporary drummer, Colaiuta might investigate Leon Parker's captivating **Above & Below** (Epicure), discussed elsewhere in this volume. **MG**

Cozy Cole

1906-1981

1944 Cole (d); with a collective personnel of: **Joe Thomas**, **Lamar Wright**, **Emmett Berry**, **Frankie Newton**, **Shad Collins** (t); **Trummy Young**, **Ray Conniff**, **Tyree Glenn** (tb); **Eddie Barefield**, **Earl Bostic** (as); **Coleman Hawkins**, **Ben Webster**, **Walter 'Foots' Thomas**, **Budd Johnson**, **Don Byas** (ts); **Earl Hines**, **Johnny Guarneri**, **Teddy Wilson** (p); **Teddy Walters**, **Remo Palmieri** (g); **Billy Taylor**, **Slam Stewart** (b). Classics Ⓜ 819 (69 minutes) Recorded 1944.

✔ ⑩ ❻

The list above looks like a roll-call of swing small-group greats, and it is a tribute to Cole's talents as a drummer and organizer of men that he could get them all into a studio and get them to play so well. Cole made his name in the late twenties in New York and recorded with Jelly Roll Morton before playing in Blanche Calloway's band. After success in other groups, he returned in 1938 to the Calloway aggregation, now very famous and run by Blanche's brother, Cab. He stayed there until war broke out, and after a later spell with Louis Armstrong's All-Stars he freelanced as a leader, working in film studios as well as straight jazz situations.

Cole was ever the immaculate swing-style drummer who could hold down a swinging beat and drive on the most leaden-footed soloist. In the company he keeps here, there is no need for that, and all is sweetness and light. These sessions, all in the year before bop started to get widely recorded, is almost a swan-song from the Indian summer of small-group swing. That does not make these tired performances, or in any way corny. But there is an added touch of poignancy that all this perfection would soon be swept away in the post-war flood. **KS**

Holly Cole

Blame It On My Youth Cole (v); **Aaron Davis** (p); **David Piltch** (b) with, on two tracks, **Johnny Figo** (vn); **Robert Stevenson** (bcl). EMI Manhattan Ⓕ B21Z 97349 2 (39 minutes). Recorded 1991.

⑥ ❽

The young Canadian singer Holly Cole has in her short career constantly crossed between different styles of music. Consequently, although she's made five records as a leader, much of her output (including her latest album **Temptation** where she gives her own interpretations to seventeen Tom Waits songs), falls outside the scope of this book. **Blame It On My Youth** may not be her latest, but it has a high quotient of jazz (as opposed to jazz-inflected) performances, and although she can't do much with Chaplin's *Smile* (few can), she weaves a magical spell on the Disney-derived *Trust In Me*, and her early take on Waits's *Purple Avenue* stays in a jazz ballad tradition more than her later effort does.

The piano-bass support is exactly syncronised with her lazy phrasing and exact articulation; both instruments tend to stay in the middle and lower registers, which suit her rather breathy voice. An imaginative effort; it remains to be seen whether she will build a career in its image, or move on to other pastures. **KS**

Nat King Cole

1917-1965

Hit That Jive Jack: The Earliest Recordings Cole (p, v), **Oscar Moore** (g, v), **Wesley Prince** (b, v). MCA/Decca Ⓜ MCAD-42350 (46 minutes). Recorded 1940-41.

⑧ ❽

These 16 sides from Nat Cole's brief tenure with American Decca (before he signed with Capitol in 1943) reveal his inimitable vocal style as well as his lithe and influential approach to jazz piano. As a vocalist, there is an indelible 1940 version of *Sweet Lorraine* showing off Cole's caressing intimacy, immaculate diction and razor-sharp intonation; ironically, an almost note-for-note replication of the Cliff Burwell-Mitchell Parrish standard would become Cole's first big hit for Capitol. There are also catchy novelty tunes like *Hit That Jive, Jack*, the template for such subsequent Cole hits as *Straighten Up and Fly Right*. There are also bluesy jive numbers like *Scotchin' With the Soda* where Cole, Moore and Prince sing in unison.

We also catch a glimpse of Cole the trend-setting pianist who evolved a soloistic style based on fluid right-hand runs set against spartan left-hand chordal tracings. In effect, Cole was one of the vital links connecting such important thirties pianists as Earl Hines to the bebop revolutionaries of the forties like Bud Powell. Also significant was Cole's format of piano-guitar-bass, a setting emulated by Oscar Peterson, Ahmad Jamal and even Art Tatum. In the often-overlooked guitarist Oscar Moore, one hears the Charlie Christian-inflected antecedents of bebop guitar, whose melody-and-chord style also anticipates players like Johnny Smith and Les Paul. **CB**

Jazz Encounters Cole (p, v); **Dizzy Gillespie**, **Bill Coleman**, **Ernie Royal** (t); **Bill Harris** (tb); **Buddy DeFranco**, **Benny Bailey** (cl); **Benny Carter** (as, arr); **Flip Phillips**, **Coleman Hawkins**, **Charlie Barnet** (ts); **Billy Bauer**, **Oscar Moore**, **Irving Ashby**, **Johnny Moore** (g); **Eddie Safranski**, **John Kirby**, **Art Shapiro**, **Joe Comfort** (b); **Buddy Rich**, **Shelly Manne**, **Max Roach**, **Nick Fatool** (d); **Pete Rugolo**, **Paul Weston** (arr); **Kay Starr**, **Jo Stafford**, **Nellie Lutcher**, **Woody Herman**, **Johnny Mercer** (v). Capitol Ⓜ 96693-2 (61 minutes). Recorded 1945-50.

⑥ ❻

Cole is heard here in varied jazz and pop settings. He plays on all 21 tracks; his trio with bass and guitar is the core band on most of them. It is a grab-bag, but suggests Cole's range as pianist, crooner and comic. As accompanist, he feeds the Metronome All-Stars soloists' bop chords in taut rhythm, and lays down frilly arpeggios for pop singer Jo Stafford on *I'll Be with You in Apple Blossom Time*. The influence of Earl Hines's creative irrationality is evident in Nat's solo on the Metronomes' *Leap Here* (alternate take) and in the left-hand runs that conclude his spot on the Capitol International Jazzmen's *Riffamarole* (alternate).

A third of the cuts feature Cole's singing (maybe bantering is a better word) with guests including singer Nellie Lutcher. His sense of humour was as light as his voice, and devoid of eye-rolling degradation, no matter how vaudevillian the material. There is a bizarre, hipster's *Mule Train* sung with Woody Herman, where the special-effects mule sounds like a robot dog barking in a sewer pipe. With ever-jocular Johnny Mercer he travesties Burke and van Heusen's *Harmony*, hammering out clinkers on a tack-piano. Not a great record, but an entertaining one. **KW**

Big Band Cole Cole (v); **John Anderson**, **Joe Newman**, **Wendell Culley**, **Thad Jones**, **Snooky Young**, **Henry Coker**, **Al Grey**, **Benny Powell** (t); **Marshall Royal**, **Frank Wess** (as); **Frank Foster**, **Billy Mitchell** (ts); **Charlie Fowlkes** (b); **Gerald Wiggins** (p); **Freddie Green** (g); **Eddie Jones** (b); **Sonny Payne**(d); **Dave Cavanagh** (arr, cond); **King Cole Trio** (Cole, Irving Ashby [g], Joe Comfort [b]); **Stan Kenton Orchestra**; **Pete Rugolo, Shorty Rogers** (arr). Capitol Ⓜ CDP7 96259-2 (45 minutes). Recorded 1950/1958.

✔ ⑧ ❽

It has often been suggested that Nat King Cole turned into an entirely different person when he stopped playing piano and became a stand-up ballad singer, but this is absurd. All the musicality that went into making him the finest jazz pianist of his generation was still there, and can be heard in every vocal performance he ever recorded. For jazz lovers, this is the one to get. Originally issued under the title **Welcome to the Club**, it features Nat with the Count Basie Orchestra (minus Basie himself, for contractual reasons).

There is always drama inherent in the combination of solo voice and orchestra, and the contrast between Nat's warm, unhurried tones and the purring ferocity of the great swing machine brings it out magnificently. **DG**

Richie Cole

1948

Side By Side Cole (as, v); **Phil Woods** (as); **Eddie 'Lockjaw' Davis** (ts); **John Hicks** (p); **Walter Booker** (b); **Jimmy Cobb** (d). Muse Ⓕ MCD 6016 (52 minutes). Recorded 1980.

⑥ ❽

This is an ideal CD through which to discover Cole because, while still at school, the young saxophonist studied with his partner here, Woods. After Berklee, he worked with Buddy Rich and Lionel Hampton and since the mid-seventies has led combos of his own. As a player he has always come over better on live dates. His Woods-like style has its wayward as well as its humorous moments; his search for the correct improvisational route sometimes takes him into musical forests from which he is pressed to extricate himself. He could have sounded a trifle lightweight alongside Woods (and the heavyweight Davis, who appears on just one track), but their presence does mean that he can neither coast or showboat. His tough, swaggering tone is distinctive and, if Woods sounds cleaner, more controlled and more obviously creative, it is not the one-sided contest it might have been. Cole is certainly not overawed; *Naugahyde Reality* is his brief free jazz send-up, while it is his alto that winds up the tension on *Scrapple From The Apple*, produces the tastefully concise reading of *Polka Dots and Moonbeams* and in the juxtaposed *Eddie's Mood* and *Side By Side* proves that, when the chops are up, he can match even the likes of Woods. **BMcR**

Bill Coleman

1904-1981

Bill Coleman 1929-1940 Coleman (t); with various personnel including: **Frankie Newton** (t); **Dicky Wells** (tb); **Joe Hayman**, **Willie Lewis** (cl); **Cecil Scott** (cl, ts, bs, bss); **John Williams**, **Harold McFerran**, **George Johnson** (as); **Christian Wagner** (cl, as); **Gene Sedric** (cl, as, ts); **Edgar Courance**, **'Big Boy' Goudie** (cl, ts); **Don Frye**, **Herman Chittison**, **Garnet Clark**, **Emil Stern**, **Jean Ferrier** (p); **Fats Waller** (p, cel, v); **Al Casey**, **Django Reinhardt**, **Joseph Reinhardt**, **Oscar Aleman**, **John Mitchell** (g); **Stephane Grappelli** (vn, p); **Billy Taylor**, **Charlie Turner**, **Eugene d'Hellemmes**,

June Cole, Wilson Myers, Lucien Simoens (b); **Rudolph Williams** (bj, g); **Mack Walker** (tba); **Lloyd Scott, Harry Dial, William Diener, Jerry Mengo, Ted Fields, Tommy Benford** (d); **Greta Keller** (v); **Luis Russell and His Orchestra; Cecil Scott and His Bright Boys; Fats Waller and His Rhythm; Willie Lewis and His Entertainers/Orchestra; Benny Carter and His Orchestra**. Jazz Archives Ⓑ 157 822 (72 minutes). Recorded 1929-40.

⑧ ❻

Coleman paid his first visit to Paris in 1933 and, although he travelled far and worked in a number of countries, he always returned to France, living there for the last 33 years of his life. This is an excellent summary of his pre-war activities in the US and Europe, his clean, clear-toned trumpet being heard with the big bands of Luis Russell and Benny Carter as well as Fats Waller And His Rhythm. But it was in Paris that he made his first records as leader, fronting splendid little bands containing other expatriate Americans such as Herman Chittison, drummer Tommy Benford and the intriguing piano of Garnet Clark. With the latter he is heard on a delicious version of *Stardust*, followed on the CD by an equally felicitous *I'm In The Mood For Love* played as a duet with Chittison. But there were Europeans who could hold their own with Bill, notably Grappelli and Reinhardt. Also present on a couple of tracks is the Argentinian guitarist Oscar Aleman, a man whose solos are highly original. This album also contains the rare tracks with the Austrian singer Greta Keller; the transfers to CD have been well done. However, the *Sweet Sue* listed as being with the Willie Lewis orchestra turns out to be the Coleman/Dicky Wells version from July 1937. **AM**

George Coleman

1935

My Horns of Plenty **Coleman** (ss, as, ts); **Harold Mabern** (p); **Ray Drummond** (b); **Billy Higgins** (d). Birdology Ⓕ 511 922-2 (63 minutes). Recorded 1991.

⑥ ❽

Coleman is indissolubly linked with two great mid-sixties recordings, Herbie Hancock's **Maiden Voyage** and Miles Davis's **My Funny Valentine**. Yet it is odd that this fine player is rarely given his fair share of the credit for the success of those ventures. Coleman, born in Memphis, is of the same generation as Booker Little and Frank Strozier, and in the late fifties played with Little in the Max Roach Quintet. By the time he graduated to the Miles Davis Quintet, replacing Hank Mobley, his was a highly personal style combining elements of Coltrane, Getz, Young and perhaps Jacquet, using a sophisticated harmonic and rhythmic palette to create a great deal of understated lyrical beauty. From that point on he played mostly with leaders like Elvin Jones or with his own groups, and has carved a solid if unspectacular career.

This present set is good but not at the same level as his work on the above-mentioned albums, where his impassioned lyricism is at times transcendent. The shadow of Coltrane hovers a little closer than in the past, not helped by a decidedly toppy recorded sound which imparts less than the usual warmth to his tenor tone (he plays tenor on the majority of tracks here). Mabern is very busy throughout, and is perhaps not the ideal partner. However, a Coleman disc is always full of thoughtful, uncompromising improvisation with little reliance on cliché, so those who like their sax to be modern mainstream with a touch of flair will be satisfied by this one. **KS**

Ornette Coleman

1930

Beauty Is A Rare Thing **Coleman** (as, ts); **Eric Dolphy** (as, f, bcl); **Don Cherry** (c, pocket t); **Freddie Hubbard** (t); **Charlie Haden, Scott LaFaro, Jimmy Garrison** (b); **Billy Higgins, Ed Blackwell** (d); **Bill Evans** (p); **Contemporary String Quartet**. Rhino/Atlantic Jazz Ⓜ R2-71410 (six discs: 427 minutes). Recorded 1959-61.

⑩ ❽

Listening to this music today, it is hard to hear it as revolutionary, not because its value or profundity has lessened (it hasn't), but because what was shocking once is now so familiar, what was called by some 'anti-jazz' has become a pervasive influence on so much contemporary music. In retrospect it is easier to hear how with such simple means Ornette extended the hyper-reality of Charlie Parker into a new formal consideration, redesigning, as one album cover aptly put it, the *shape* of the music to come by erasing barlines, loosening rhythms and reducing harmony to an incidental by-product of the creation of pure melody. And as a melodist, Coleman is a master storyteller—à la Lester Young. Each of the individual Atlantic LPs may be available singly, but among the advantages of this collection (other than the six previously unreleased numbers, the Japanese-only **To Whom Who Keeps A Record**, and the so far unreissued Gunther Schuller-composed pieces from **Jazz Abstraction**, all included here) is the opportunity to experience classic performances in a fresh, revealing context. One point that jumps out is that, for all of the freedom Ornette's procedures supposedly granted each player, this is an amazingly interdependent *ensemble*. In the liner notes Don Cherry reminds us of how thoroughly prepared the musicians were in order to deal with this freedom, and how organized the music was, although the details and—the truly revolutionary aspect—the form was spontaneously improvised. Yet another is the brilliant and absolutely crucial contribution of Charlie Haden, who was literally inventing the role of 'free' bassist on the spur of the moment. But it is Ornette's vision and courage which comes through the strongest. That it ultimately and forever changed how and what we hear as jazz is secondary; separately or together, it is the music for its own sake—imaginative, joyful, bluesy, funny, ecstatic and essential—that must be heard. **AL**

The Shape of Jazz to Come **Coleman** (as); **Don Cherry** (c); **Charlie Haden** (b); **Billy Higgins** (d). Atlantic Ⓜ 781317-2 (38 minutes). Recorded 1959.

✔ ⑩ ❽

Today this music sounds so clear and flowing it is hard to believe people at the time thought it cacophonous. They did so because Ornette Coleman's new conception of jazz simply bypassed bebop's predetermined patterns of chord changes and bar lengths and left each player (in Coleman's words) "free to contribute what he feels in the music at any given moment". The result was not the anarchy that some feared but, on Coleman's classic Atlantic recordings, a new kind of spontaneous group rapport plus improvisation that, based on melody, roamed freely.

The Shape of Jazz to Come was Coleman's début recording for Atlantic and the first to feature his regular quartet (for various reasons, they had not all played on his two previous albums for Contemporary). This was a vital plus. Coleman and Cherry's then near-telepathic understanding is complemented here by the group's ability to hang together even when horns, bass and drums are playing independent lines. A striking example is *Lonely Woman*, one of Coleman's best-known compositions, where the horns announce the dirge-like theme over racing drums and a separate accented bass line. Coleman's brief solo here, with its vocalized cry and asymmetrical phrases, typifies his breakdown of conventional form to give voice more directly to feeling. The ultimate introduction to Ornette from this period is the boxed set **Beauty Is A Rare Thing** (reviewed above), but if that is too daunting, then this is a perfect beginning. **GL**

Free Jazz **Coleman** (as); **Eric Dolphy** (bcl); **Don Cherry** (pocket t); **Freddie Hubbard** (t); **Charlie Haden, Scott LaFaro** (b); **Ed Blackwell, Billy Higgins** (d). Atlantic Ⓜ 781364-2 (54 minutes). Recorded 1960.

✔ ⑩ ❽

Alto saxophonist Ornette Coleman's double-quartet one of the most important jazz albums of the post-war period. Its significance lies in the crystallization of Coleman's truly revolutionary improvisational approach that, to paraphrase Coleman, picks up where Charlier Parker stopped. By marginalizing the customary chord-changes undergirding bop, as well as swing and Dixieland and the contemporary mainstream, Coleman advanced a 'free jazz' approach that privileged melody, its pitches and intervals, as the improvisor's basic materials. In 1960, Coleman's *outré* free-form abstractions, with their bluesy wails and microtonal deviations from the tempered scale, created a *cause célèbre*. Today, while still bristling with the raw energy of Coleman's then-radical dialogues, **Free Jazz** is much more comprehensible, more clearly a part of the tumultuous sixties zeitgeist which saw cinema, art and rock as well as jazz transformed from the inside out.

By doubling his quartet (with Don Cherry's puckish pocket trumpet, Charlie Haden's plummy bass and Billy Higgins's tap-dancing drums), Coleman set up dialectic force-fields based in part on the players contrasting styles. With only a few brief pre-written themes, the thirty-seven minute collective improvisation unfolds with alternating ensemble and solo segments where melodic and rhythmic motifs bounce like billiard balls. Interestingly, the overall impression is now one of amiable exploration. And for those who think of free jazz as nothing but inchoate shrieks and howls, it's a happy reminder of how lyrical and bluesy Coleman's music could be. This CD reissue includes the seventeen-minute first take of Free Jazz, appropriately titled *First Take*, which makes for fascinating comparisons. Of course all this material is in the boxed set reviewed above, but for those listeners on a more restricted budget, the single CD version is an essential purchase. **CB**

At The Golden Circle, Volumes 1 and 2 **Coleman** (as, t, vn); **David Izenzon** (b); **Charles Moffett** (d). Blue Note Ⓜ CDP7 84224/25-2 (two discs, oas: 39 and 44 minutes). Recorded 1965.

⑨ ❻

Sometimes jazz history and some people's perception of it is affected by the sequence in which recordings are issued. Coleman's Town Hall concert had given the jazz world a brief glimpse of his trumpet and violin work. For those who did not hear him on his European tour, the **Golden Circle** issue was their first exposure to these new elements. Coleman had re-assembled his pre-sabbatical trio for the tour and united the classically devoted Izenzon and the propulsive Moffett into an ideal team. His own alto skills remain undiminished. He makes *The Riddle* a melodic 'free fall', he builds *Faces And Places* from scantily related melodic statements, while on *Antiques* he shows how he moves away from his strong parent themes, elaborating on each idea before moving to the next. On *Dawn* we are treated to another superb Coleman dirge, full of bluesy implications and Texas rhythm & blues know-how. Both violin and trumpet appear on *Snowflakes And Sunshine* and confirm that they are 'like his alto' in a way that his formal (non jazz) compositions are not. The violin hints at a more radical departure in style and shows that a theme taken on the instrument is not so much rebuilt as given a new state. The trumpet parts are rhythmically more similar to the alto; they adopt the same chromatic stance but do not aspire to the same controlled methods of execution. Both are important espects of Coleman's art and these two CDs occupy a significant place in his portfolio. **BMcR**

In All Languages **Coleman** (as, ts, t); **Don Cherry** (t); **Charlie Haden** (b); **Billy Higgins** (d); also with **Primetime** (Charlie Ellerbe, Bern Nix [g]; Jamaaladeen Tacuma [b]; Denardo Coleman, Calvin Weston [d]). Caravan of Dreams Ⓕ 008 (72 minutes). Recorded 1987.

⑦ ❽

1987, the year this album was recorded, saw the 30th anniversary of Ornette's original L.A. quartet. This celebratory album is Ornette's marking of the career calender. On it, he re-convenes the quartet for what, on the initial vinyl-only release, was disc one, and proceeds to a set on (vinyl only) disc two with his current (1987) band, Prime Time. For CD purposes, there is just one disc, containing both bands, and the quartet comes first on it.

In a situation not that dissimilar to Miles Davis's, Ornette tends to play the same style of solo no matter what is going on behind and around him. This can be viewed as a good or bad thing, depending on your point of approach to the music, but there can be no doubt that both bands are equally attuned to what their leader is doing. The extreme brevity of the pieces (most clock in at between two and three minutes, with the longest being just four-and-a-half minutes in duration) means very little waste, and few bouts of over-enthusiasm from the sidemen. So the focus is squarely on the leader, who responds with spirited playing. The textures of Prime Time are predictably denser, there being two electric guitarists and two drummers to complicate matters, but the music still coheres nicely. For long-term Coleman devotees, there is nothing new here, but for those who tune in to harmolodics only once a decade, this will be a pleasant surprise. **KS**

Virgin Beauty **Coleman** (as, vn, t); **Charles Ellerbe**, **Bern Nix**, **Jerry Garcia** (g) **Al MacDowell**, **Chris Walker** (elb); **Calvin Weston** (d); **Denardo Coleman** (d, kbds, perc). Columbia Portrait Ⓕ RK 44301 (45 minutes). Recorded 1987-88.

✔ ⑧ ❽

Perhaps Coleman's most accessible recording, although oddly one of his most overlooked. If the synthesis of funk and free jazz that he achieved in the name of harmolodics on 1975's **Dancing in Your Head** was the freshest thing some of us had ever heard, this item from 12 years later sounded to many like the freshest thing they had ever heard before. A closer listen to **Virgin Beauty** reveals delightful new wrinkles. The synthesized, playfully static backdrop to Coleman's rolling alto on *Healing the Feeling* is an example of his son Denardo's increased production savvy, as is the double-tracking that allows Ornette to play trumpet and alto duets with himsèlf here and there. Spread over the stingy length of this disc are tempos and rhythms new to jazz, or at least uncommon to it: the camel lope on *Three Wishes*, the hoedown feeling on the irresistible *Happy Hour* and the lick borrowed from Wilson Pickett on *Bourgeois Boogie*. Coleman's shapely, unaccompanied introduction to *Unknown Artist* ranks as one of his most lyrical solos on record. The Grateful Dead's Jerry Garcia guest stars on three tracks and blends in so nicely with Prime Time regulars Ellerbee and Nix that you do not even notice him. **FD**

Steve Coleman 1956

The Tao Of Mad Phat **Coleman** (as, p); **Andy Milne** (p, kbds); **David Gilmore** (g, g syn); **Reggie Washington** (elb); **Oliver Gene Lake Jr** (d, perc); **Roy Hargrove** (t); **Josh Roseman** (tb); **Kenny Davis** (b); **Matthew Garrison** (elb); **Junior 'Gabu' Wederburn** (perc). RCA Novus Ⓕ 63160 2 (76 minutes). Recorded 1993.

✔ ⑧ ❽

The principles that fuel the M-Base ethic are more consistent with the inspirational sources that motivated Jelly Roll Morton, Louis Armstrong and Charlie Parker than are the academic ground rules nurturing the neo-classical boppers or any other revivalist movement. The Five Elements heard here are part of Brooklyn's M-Base world and they take as their starting point the rhythms of their own black youth. By their very circumstances, this means the pulsating and often unsubtle heartbeat of soul and funk as much as it does the jazz tradition of Ornette Coleman and John Coltrane. The outcome can be heard clearly on this CD as Coleman's men, recorded live before a studio audience, show how they have synthesized both extremes to produce a 1993 music that is their own. The acoustic *Incantation* presents their jazz basics, but it is items such as *Laid Back Schematics* and the title-track that best demonstrate Coleman's outstanding improvisational skills in a style born of namesake Ornette's free jazz, but painted on a soulful canvas. Steve Coleman's moments of greatest inspiration may be found in the non-electronic fabric of Dave Holland's small groups (see below), but the altoist is very much at home in the different rhythmic environment on offer here. **BMcR**

Def Trance Beat (Modalities of Rhythm) **Coleman** (as); **The Five Elements** (Andy Milne [p, kbds]; Reggie Washington [b]; Gene Lake [d, perc]); on three tracks, add **Ravi Coltrane** (ts). RCA Novus Ⓕ 63181 2 (69 minutes). Recorded 1994.

⑨ ❿

Coleman has always been a rigorous theorist, unafraid to investigate the musical application of his ideas. This has led him into some notable cul-de-sacs, some of which have been sheer hard work for the listener with no concomitant pay-off of pleasure. This album is different: his ideas spontaneously combust into a compelling tapestry of technique, passion and plain old excitement. The title is an apt one, for the whole basis of the music is profoundly rooted in the swirling matrix of rhythm created by the intricately plotted intersections of drum, piano, bass and saxophone. This is not, as has been suffered in the past, some warmed-over cod-funk workout; this is genuinely challenging music, with a wild excitement about the resultant melding together of timbre, tone and punctuation. When tenor player Ravi Coltrane is added to the chemistry, the effect can be close to overwhelming, the richness of the scoring and the solos like a Fauvist painting.

This challenging album is an important step forward for Coleman, and is a fascinating synthesis of many contemporary musical developments. Essential contemporary listening. **KS**

Johnny Coles 1926

New Morning **Coles** (flh); **Horace Parlan** (p); **Reggie Johnson** (b); **Billy Hart** (d). Criss Cross Ⓕ 1005 CD (42 minutes). Recorded 1982.

⑦ ❽

This, amazingly enough, is the only CD ever released under Coles's leadership, and only the fourth recording session under his name. Not a very impressive strike-rate in a career dating back to the fifties, but then it is not the flügelhornist's fault that he plays beautiful but unfashionable modern jazz, and has too often been dismissed as yet another Miles Davis disciple. This was not helped by his prominent role on the Gil Evans albums of the fifties and sixties which did not have Miles on them.

But this is to overlook Coles's considerable talents, his clear inheritance from Clifford Brown, and his successful establishment of a distinct musical voice by the early sixties. On this quartet date he plays with unquenched conviction, is consistently inventive in his choice of melodic paths through the chords of the pieces played, and still possesses a tone combining a lovely warmth with a bell-like clarity not usually associated with the flügelhorn, which can often sound more than a little sleepy. While Coles is outstandingly inventive on his erstwhile employer Charles Mingus's ballad *Sound of Love*, he also has the drive to make an uptempo swinger like his own *Mister B* an exciting event. The rhythm team gives excellent support. **KS**

Buddy Collette 1921

Jazz Loves Paris **Collette** (fl, cl, as, ts); **Frank Rosolino** (tb); **Red Callender** (tba); **Howard Roberts** (g); **Red Mitchell** (b); **Bill Richmond, Bill Douglass** (d). Speciality Ⓜ OJCCD 1764-2 (42 minutes). Recorded 1958.

⑤ ❼

Collette was one of Charles Mingus's earliest colleagues and partners, but Mingus himself opined that Collette, a man of great and diverse abilities, had played in the studios too long and lost his way in the music. Certainly this album, made not so long after Collette had left the very popular Chico Hamilton group (he was replaced by Eric Dolphy), suffers from an extremely low emotional temperature. It is immaculately turned out, but the only players with a spark in their work are Rosolino and Roberts. One would be inclined to point to the repertoire as being the main culprit, but although it is a rather weak concept to jazz-up songs about Paris, the actual song choice is not at all bad. Yet the arrangements are so polite as to be offensive, and although the ensemble work is as immaculate as Bel Ami's coiffure, it has all the punch of a Jean Sablon vocal. Rosolino is a trombonist who is impossible to pin down for a whole session, and earns a few cheers, as does a recalcitrant Roberts in his solo spots, but as for the rest, I shall stick with *La Bohème*. **KS**

Alice Coltrane 1937

Journey in Satchidananda **Coltrane** (p, h); **Pharoah Sanders** (ss); **Tulsi** (tamboura), **Cecil McBee**, **Charlie Haden** (b); **Rashied Ali** (d); **Majid Shabazz** (perc); **Vishnu Wood** (oud). Impulse! Ⓜ MCAD 33119 (37 minutes). Recorded 1970.

⑥ ❽

After John Coltrane's death in 1967, the Impulse! label embarked on a number of recordings with his wife, Alice, who had been the pianist in his last working group. The music on her records bears little relation to that of her husband but, taken on its own terms, offers considerable pleasures. Alice often binds her compositions together with a nicely bluesy ostinato from the double bass (with much of her work performed over drones, this is a logical way of propelling an otherwise static music forwards), and there are plenty of cheery lines here from the virtuoso McBee. Another near-constant factor on her albums, at least up until around 1972, was Pharoah Sanders. On this record he sticks exclusively to soprano sax, keeps his improvising highly disciplined, and provides a much-needed focal point to the washes of sound the leader conjures. Probably Coltrane's greatest weakness here is her own rather unmemorable soloing (which is odd, because prior to meeting her husband she soloed tidily with Terry Gibbs, among others). This record is at its least-inspired on *Something About John Coltrane* , which is as vague as its title and seems interminable. *Isis and Osiris*, however, where her harp directs from the background, is a treasure. The playing time is ridiculous. **KS**

John Coltrane

1926-1967

Blue Train **Coltrane** (ts); **Lee Morgan** (t); **Curtis Fuller** (tb); **Kenny Drew** (p); **Paul Chambers** (b); **'Philly' Joe Jones** (d). Blue Note Ⓜ CDP7 46095-2 (43 minutes). Recorded 1957.

✓ ⑧ ❽

Coltrane made his professional début at 19 and spent much of his early career in the rhythm & blues bands of Cleanhead Vinson and Earl Bostic. Spells with Dizzy Gillespie and Johnny Hodges honed his big-band disciplines until, in 1955, he joined Miles Davis. The implications of that partnership are well documented in this CD, made while he was briefly with Thelonious Monk. The triumphs of **Giant Steps** are nearly two years ahead, but this is one of the first sessions to hint at the awesome authority that would attend his later work. Playing with Monk placed moderately strict harmonic restrictions on him and it is as if, on this album in particular, he sees leadership of his own session as a licence to extend the melodic aspect of his style. His detailed horizontal progress can still sound like three men playing in a telephone booth but there is an excitement and power in the music that transcends all other issues. His improvisations have already broken free of standard structures, but fortunately Miles Davis's colleagues, Chambers and Jones, know what is expected of them. The presence of the outstanding Morgan and journeyman Fuller is of little significance on a session that is increasingly being acknowledged as the first landmark in Coltrane's group-leading exploits. **BMcR**

Soultrane **Coltrane** (ts); **Red Garland** (p); **Paul Chambers** (b); **Arthur Taylor** (d). Prestige Ⓜ OJCCD021 (40 minutes). Recorded 1958.

⑧ ❽

The conservative listener is more likely to find pre-1961 Coltrane preferable to the later work where his tendency to prolixity was so often given its head. The intense and precise nature of his inventions on albums such as this one and on the contemporary ones he made with Miles Davis (see below) brought a succinct and powerful new manner of improvising into jazz. Most of Coltrane's important innovations had become apparent by the time of this session, made with two thirds of the Davis rhythm section (for some reason Taylor replaced Philly Joe Jones).

The intensity of Coltrane's feeling is offset by the elegant piano playing of Red Garland, sounding much more relaxed playing for Coltrane than he did for Davis, who was apt to be more proscriptive about how his pianists played.

Having said that Coltrane is succinct, so he is, but some of the tracks are quite long, with *Good Bait* running for 12 minutes. *I Want To Talk About You* lasts for 11 minutes and is the earliest recording of a tune that Coltrane was later to play almost nightly. It is a beautiful blues ballad composed by Billy Eckstine and is particularly suitable for the keening melodicism with which the tenorist imbues it. This is arguably Coltrane's best work before the **Giant Steps** album which opened another phase of his career a year or so later. **SV**

Giant Steps **Coltrane** (ts); **Cedar Walton, Tommy Flanagan, Wynton Kelly** (p); **Paul Chambers** (b); **Lex Humphries, Art Taylor, Jimmy Cobb** (d). Atlantic Jazz Ⓜ 781 337-2 (63 minutes). Recorded 1959.

✓ ⑩ ❽

When Coltrane's contract with Prestige expired at the end of 1958 he moved to Atlantic, an organization which had resources to allow him to spend more time on the production of albums. **Giant Steps** is arguably one of the three most important LPs Coltrane ever made. All seven tunes were not only written by Coltrane but all were highly original and each has become part of the larger jazz repertoire. Here at last he was able to present his music in a considered and comprehensive manner. He was ridding himself of the overpowering obligation of a repeated chord progression; instead the music uses scales, allowing the soloist more options, more possibilities to branch out into a fresh direction. Throughout **Giant Steps** his enormous instrumental technique (he could cruise comfortably through more than three octaves on a tenor) is allied to a most fertile imagination to produce music of supreme quality. Not only are there headlong assaults at fast tempo (*Giant Steps* itself is a perfect example) but there is the tender, moving ballad approach of *Naima*. The LP has been lovingly transferred to CD and adds alternative versions of five of the tunes, three of them actually recorded at an earlier session with a different rhythm section, all of which makes for fascinating listening. **AM**

My Favorite Things **Coltrane** (ss, ts); **McCoy Tyner** (p); **Steve Davis** (b); **Elvin Jones** (d). Atlantic Jazz Ⓜ 782346-2 (41 minutes). Recorded 1960.

✓ ⑧ ❼

Coltrane's first issued workout on soprano sax (**The Avant-Garde** with Don Cherry was recorded earlier, released later), *My Favorite Things* remained a staple of Coltrane's live performances thereafter. As a popular song with graceful modal chord changes and an insinuating, incantatory melody, it was perfect for his gifts, although one should note that the 14-minute version here is less expansive than renditions he would play on the bandstand in future years. The influence of nasal-sounding Asian and Mid-Eastern reed instruments on Coltrane's soprano is often noted, but the similarities in tone and range between soprano and trumpet suggest the valve instrument's influence also; indeed, the soprano ballad feature *Ev'ry Time We Say Goodbye* betrays Miles Davis's stamp (later it was to become associated with Chet Baker).

An uptempo swing through Gershwin's *Summertime*, with Trane on tenor, is in the splashy style of his emerging classic quartet, which at this point lacked only bassist Jimmy Garrison. Jones's polyrhythmia and Tyner's billowing extended chords, both designed to restrict a soloist as little as possible, were already developing. Coltrane's art was often about process; **My Favorite Things** finds him poised at the beginning of a key phase of his development. **KW**

Coltrane's Sound **Coltrane** (ss, ts); **McCoy Tyner** (p); **Steve Davis** (b); **Elvin Jones** (d). Atlantic Jazz Ⓜ 781419-2 (50 minutes). Recorded 1960.

✔

⑧ ❻

There is a lot of exceptional Coltrane in the mass of pre-Impulse! material, including **Traneing In**, **Settin' the Pace**, **Coltrane Jazz** and especially the present set. This album is hardly unknown, containing as it does the ballad **Central Park West**, the mysterious blues **Equinox** and Coltrane's afro-vamp arrangement of **Body and Soul** which manages the impossible task of moving this classic out from under the looming shadow of Coleman Hawkins's version. While the above compositions/ arrangements have entered the realm of jazz standards, the tracks that give us Coltrane's take on bebop are equally valuable. *Liberia* is his reworking of *Night in Tunisia*, *Satellite* his *How High the Moon*, and bonus-track *26-2* his theme on the chords of *Confirmation*. There is also a blistering *The Night Has a Thousand Eyes* with an exultant Elvin Jones, plus an alternative take of *Body and Soul*. McCoy Tyner was still developing, and could have used a better studio piano, but it is otherwise hard to fault this view of Coltrane from the sessions that also produced **My Favourite Things** and **Coltrane Plays the Blues**. At the time of going to press, Rhino/Atlantic are readying for release a deluxe seven-CD boxed set of the complete Coltrane Atlantic recordings, including previously unheard rehearsals and studio chat. **BB**

Africa/Brass, Volumes 1 & 2 **Coltrane** (ts, ss); **Booker Little**, **Freddie Hubbard** (t); **Britt Woodman** (tb); **Carl Bowman**, **Charles Greenlee**, **Julian Priester** (euph); **Jimmy Buffington**, **Julius Watkins**, **Donald Corrado**, **Bob Northern**, **Robert Swisshelm** (frh); **Bill Barber** (tba); **Eric Dolphy**, **Pat Patrick**, **Garvin Bushell** (reeds); **McCoy Tyner** (p); **Reggie Workman**, **Art Davis** (b); **Elvin Jones** (d). Impulse! Ⓜ MCAD 42001 (68 minutes). Recorded 1961.

⑧ ❼

John Coltrane's first sessions for his new label saw his quartet (with Workman on bass) augmented by a large ensemble of mostly brass pieces. The original **Africa/Brass** LP comprised three tracks (*Africa, Greensleeves, Blues Minor*). In the mid-seventies three more tracks (*Song Of The Underground Railroad* and alternate takes of *Africa* and *Greensleeves*) were released on **The Africa/Brass Sessions Volume Two**, then another two (*The Damned Don't Cry* and a second alternate take of *Africa*) appeared on the double-LP compilation **Trane's Modes**. This CD comprises the six tracks from the two **Africa/Brass** LPs but does not include the two from **Trane's Modes**. The documentation is a disgrace, with innumerable errors in the personnel listing. Now that MCA has re-launched the Impulse! catalogue, the news is that this session is earmarked for a properly comprehensive reissue, possibly on two CDs. Until then this will have to suffice.

The music itself is fascinating and boasts what was at the time some of Coltrane's strongest tenor playing. The large ensemble is used sparingly and the arrangements (by Coltrane, Tyner and Dolphy) are minimal—for long stretches the quartet plays unaccompanied—although there are moments of tremendous excitement as Coltrane's tenor soars and screams above the stabbing brass lines. *Africa* is the most adventurous track, its implied rhythms based on a two-note bass figure and its semi-improvised ensemble making it, as Brian Priestley has noted, "far more expressionist and collectivist" than nearly all previous jazz. *Greensleeves* , a modal setting in 6/8, is the first of several unlikely tunes to follow *My Favourite Things* as a feature for Coltrane's bewitching soprano. *Blues Minor* is a bright swinging piece with exultant tenor. *Song Of The Underground Railroad* , with its sax-and-drums axis, anticipates the frenetic *Chasin' The Trane* of six months later. **GL**

Impressions **Coltrane** (ss, ts); **Eric Dolphy** (bcl); **McCoy Tyner** (p); **Reggie Workman**, **Jimmy Garrison**, (b); **Elvin Jones**, **Roy Haynes** (d). Impulse! Ⓜ MCAD 5887 (35 minutes). Recorded 1961-63.

⑨ ❼

The two most important tracks, *India* and *Impressions*, were recorded during Coltrane's Village Vanguard stint of November 1961. It was a watershed period when the saxophonist was expanding his modal explorations in terms of group size and duration of solos, and was an approach marked by freer yet disciplined cascades of carefully constructed motive blocks connected by dazzling streaks of scalar lightning.

For the exotic *India*, Coltrane's classic quartet with Tyner, Garrison and Jones was augmented by bass clarinettist Dolphy and bassist Workman. By placing his soprano over the drone-like gestures of the two basses, Coltrane intensified the modal as well as Eastern resonances. However, it was Dolphy's uninhibited improvisational flights that eventually exerted an ever-increasing influence on Coltrane.

Still, the most significant track was the quartet version of *Impressions* in which Coltrane's tenor burns non-stop for over 14 minutes in one of jazzdom's most keenly examined and imitated solos. Indeed, along with his forays on Miles Davis's **Kind of Blue** album, Coltrane's sequence of utterly stunning variations on *Impressions* constitute a summing-up of the possibilities of modality as dense and comprehensive as what Bach did for classical harmony in the *Goldberg Variations*. Two short studio tracks from 1963, *Up Against The Wall* and *After The Rain*, complete the album. **CB**

Coltrane Live at Birdland **Coltrane** (ss, ts); **McCoy Tyner** (p); **Jimmy Garrison** (b); **Elvin Jones** (d). Impulse! Ⓜ MCAD-33109 (39 minutes). Recorded 1963.

✔ ⑩ ❻

Coltrane Live at Birdland is one of the few jazz records to capture faithfully the unique blend of universal love laced with righteous anger which characterised sixties black consciousness. Recorded in late 1963, a year after **Ballads** and a year before **A Love Supreme**, the album, despite its title, contains only three live tracks; the now-classic *Afro Blue* which in Leroi Jones/Amiri Baraka's words renders "an almost unintelligible lyricism suddenly marvellously intelligible"; *I Want To Talk About You*, an impassioned but subtle extemporization featuring a lengthy unaccompanied tenor coda; and *The Promise*, another soprano excursion reaching heights of fervent intensity practically unparalleled outside of Sufi devotional music. Recorded six weeks later, the two studio tracks, *Alabama*, a tremendously moving lament for the schoolchildren killed by the bombing of a church in Birmingham, Alabama, and *Your Lady*, a plagently lyrical song referring to Alice McLeod (later to be Alice Coltrane), are less overtly passionate than the live tracks. Nevertheless, in their tightly controlled power, they demonstrate as well as any other of this quartet's recordings just why many regard the band as the finest in jazz history. For sheer dynamism, energy and commitment, they are unmatched, their four-way musical empathy is little short of miraculous, and Coltrane himself, ceaselessly pushing at the boundaries of the possible, imbues every note with an extraordinary amalgam of passion and spirituality; **Live at Birdland** captures a unique band at the height of its considerable powers. **CP**

A Love Supreme **Coltrane** (ts); **McCoy Tyner** (p); **Jimmy Garrison** (b); **Elvin Jones** (d). Impulse! Ⓜ GRD 155 (33 minutes). Recorded 1964.

✔ ⑩ ❽

With **Giant Steps** in 1959 and *Chasin' the Trane* two years later, Coltrane redefined the standards by which a musician would be judged a master on his horn. But with *A Love Supreme*—a turbulently lovely four-part work ending with what Coltrane explicitly intended to be heard as a prayer—he altered public perception of the jazz musician from hipster's hipster to seeker of higher truths. In a paradox central to Coltrane's mystique, this was both his most intensely personal album and the one which most struck a chord with audiences. With the possible exception of **Kind of Blue** (to which Coltrane was, of course, a significant contributor), **A Love Supreme** is the one jazz album most likely to be found in the collections of people only casually interested in jazz. As an indication of **A Love Supreme**'s musical staying power, it continues to yield new insights after hundreds or even thousands of hearings. Has anyone ever pointed out, for example, that the eight-bar theme subtitled *Pursuance*, the springboard for one of Coltrane's most vocalized and furious solos, borrows its intervals from Miles Davis's *Nardis*, much as *Impressions* borrowed from Davis's *So What*?

Insofar as the religious reawakening that Coltrane describes in his sleeve-note can be likened to that of an evangelical Christian, **A Love Supreme** can be taken to be his public testimony. Usually hailed as a culmination of sorts (it does represent an apex for this quartet, although Tyner's piano was becoming increasingly superfluous), the album might also be regarded as the beginning of a new chapter, its truncated and/or elementary songforms suggesting Coltrane was attempting to simplify his approach even as his solos took on greater complexity. Perceived this way—as a masterpiece disassembled into a work-in-progress—**A Love Supreme** renders inevitable everything that followed in the not-quite-three years that Coltrane had to live.

This latest reissue, the first along with **Ballads** (GRD 156) and **And Johnny Hartman** (GRD 157) from the revitalized Impulse! label, comes with appropriately lavish packaging, plus a 20-bit remastering process direct from the two-track master which finally makes a decent stab at aural exactitude after many half-hearted attempts on previous MCA reissues. **FD**

The Major Works of John Coltrane **Coltrane** (ts); **Freddie Hubbard**, **Dewey Johnson** (t); **John Tchicai**, **Marion Brown** (as); **Archie Shepp**, **Pharoah Sanders** (ts); **Donald Garrett** (bcl, b, perc); **McCoy Tyner** (p); **Jimmy Garrison**, **Art Davis** (b); **Elvin Jones**, **Frank Butler** (d, perc); **Juno Lewis** (perc, v); **Joe Brazil** (f). Impulse! Ⓜ GRP 21132 (two discs: 142 minutes). Recorded 1965.

⑧ ❻

The 11-piece group on *Ascension* remains a unique entry in Coltrane's discography, and an achievement that in the succeeding years inspired much emulation but considerably less success. Unlike his 1961 **Africa/Brass** sessions (reviewed above) which were akin to conventional soloist-with-big-band albums, Trane here developed the approach of Coleman's **Free Jazz** but, where the latter's horn ensembles were head-arranged in "harmolodic unison", *Ascension*'s soloists are separated by ferocious passages of collective improvisation from seven horns. These include both Shepp, then at his most far-reaching, and Coltrane's partner in live appearances from this date onwards, Pharoah Sanders.

Two versions of *Ascension* were issued, the first being withdrawn and replaced at Trane's request by *"Edition II"*—and Marion Brown has confirmed that this better-focused recording was the second performance, contrary to speculation. Both are included, occupying somewhat more than half the playing-time, which is completed by three sextet and octet pieces originally issued as album title-tracks: *Om, Kulu Sé Mama* and *Selflessness*. These are anti-climactic, compared to the intense yet channelled energy of *Ascension*, but historically they are significant for introducing African percussion into a free-jazz context. Tyner, who left Coltrane two months later, has a fine swan-song on *Kulu*. **BP**

Meditations **Coltrane** (ts, bcl); **Pharoah Sanders** (ts); **McCoy Tyner** (p); **Jimmy Garrison** (b); **Elvin Jones, Rashied Ali** (d). Impulse! Ⓜ MCAD 39139 (37 minutes). Recorded 1965.

✔ ⑩ ❽

1965 was, for Coltrane, a year of turbulent change which ended in the dissolution of the classic early-sixties quartet. It was also a year of a few triumphs and a number of near-misses. This album is definitely one of the triumphs. It remains the only instance of Jones and Ali recording together, and the resultant rhythmic maelstrom on *The Father and the Son and the Holy Ghost* makes for some of the most intoxicating listening in the history of recorded jazz. Add to this Coltrane in the frame of mind to contribute some of his most highly-disciplined playing to what is a concept album which takes **A Love Supreme** another step further, plus Pharoah Sanders in two solos of mind-bending ferocity, and you have a highly coherent and overwhelmingly powerful record.

As with **A Love Supreme**, the music is organized as a suite of contrasting parts (this one has five movements) which leads from the turbulence and chaos of *The Father* to the hard-won musical and emotional resolutions to be found in the last piece, *Serenity*. In between, all manner of things are displayed, including one of the most gorgeously sensual ballad readings of Coltrane's career on *Love*, a volcanic Tyner solo on *Compassion*, and a wistful, disturbing five-minute reading of the final theme by Coltrane which suggests not so much serenity as an unconfined yearning. This is Coltrane's most carefully-prepared and completely satisfying latter-day recorded statement. **KS**

Expression **Coltrane** (ts, f); **Pharoah Sanders** (picc, f, tamb); **Alice Coltrane** (p); **Jimmy Garrison** (b); **Rashied Ali** (d). Impulse! Ⓜ Ⓡ Ⓟ 11312 (51 minutes). Recorded 1967.

⑧ ❽

By 1967 the devotional preoccupations which Coltrane had announced in such early sixties pieces as **Spiritual** and 1964's **A Love Supreme** (see above) had become all-consuming. It might have seemed that the unbridled energy of the 1965 **Ascension** was a final cathartic exorcism of his search for higher things, but the pursuit continued into his final months and, in **Expression**, was often surprisingly sanguine.

Although on a rhythmic level the music is uniformly rubato and harmonically often threatens to break free of its loose modal basis, there are moments of relative serenity, such as on the short, elegaic *Ogunde*, or in the opening minutes before Coltrane builds up a fervent heard of steam, and also throughout *To Be*, where his use of flute dictates a lower volume and more lyrical aesthetic. But even when the pressure builds the music is rarely entirely free, acquiring form through variations of tone and texture and, when Coltrane's tenor is dominant, always shaped by his virtuosic command of phrasing and dynamics. The rewards of this music may not be immediately apparent, but as the final chapter in one of the most ceaselessly progressive careers in modern jazz it will be of interest to all who have relished Coltrane's earlier, more readily accessible work. **MG**

Ravi Coltrane

1965

Grand Central: Tenor Titans **Coltrane** (ss, ts); **Antoine Roney** (ts); **Jacky Terrasson** (p); **Jeff Chambers** (b); **Ralph Penland**. Alfa Jazz Ⓔ ALCD-313 (59 minutes). Recorded 1993.

⑦ ❿

This is fun. Ravi, son of John and Alice, co-leads this studio group with Antoine Roney, brother of Wallace, and as his name comes first on both albums the band has made, the album is entered under him in this book. Roney has already débuted under his own name (see below), but Ravi Coltrane is still biding his time, despite extensive appearances on others' records. There is little doubt that this and its 1992 predecessor, **Sax Storm** (also on Alfa), give us his best recorded playing to date, and the presence of both Roney and a fiercely swinging rhythm section led from the front by piano *enfant terrible* Jacky Terrasson helps enormously. So: does he sound like the famous one? Yes and no. He has the slightly vulnerable tone of the mid-fifties Trane, but his phrasing is closer to the Joshua Redman version of Rollins. He has a firm grasp of harmony, pushing through the changes and substitutions at a terrific rate even on a harmonically simple piece such as Victor Feldman's *Joshua*. Roney shows himself to be no slouch either, bringing a slightly more bustling, harder-edged personality to the music, creating a finely-balanced foil for the other horn man.

Both of them acquit themselves well at slow tempos, with Larry Clinton's *My Reverie* and Victor Young's *Stella By Starlight* coming in for some sumptuously rapturous playing, with both Roney and Coltrane avoiding the temptation to double-time and destroy the moods created. The album closes with a re-creation of *The Chase*, the old Dexter Gordon-Wardell Gray warhorse, and as noted at the beginning, much fun is had. This is good modern mainstream music with no strings attached. **KS**

Ken Colyer

1928-1988

Marching Back To New Orleans: The Decca Years, Volume 7 Colyer (t, v); **Bob Wallis**, **Sonny Morris** (t); **Mac Duncan**, **Mick Clift** (tb); **Ian Wheeler** (cl); **Dave Keir** (as); **Derek Eastern** (ts); **Johnny Bastable** (bj); **Dick Smith** (b); **Mo Benn** (tba); **Stan Greig**, **Colin Bowden**, **Neil Millet** (d). Lake Ⓕ LACD21 (59 minutes). Recorded 1955/1957

⑥ ❹

Sincerity was the watchword for 'The Guvnor', as Colyer was known to fans of the British New Orleans revival. He found it in the music of Mutt Carey and George Lewis, and jumped ship in New Orleans in 1952 to meet and play with some of the surviving pioneers of their style of jazz. This album catches Ken in his heyday, during the mid-fifties. Seven tracks are by his influential small band with Duncan and Wheeler, oozing sincerity and displaying a cross-section of his repertoire from *Hiawatha Rag* to a storming *Red Wing*. Remastered from none-too-hi-fi Decca originals by Paul Adams, the set is dominated by a stately *Dallas Blues* that goes a long way to prove that Great Yarmouth could produce a heartfelt blues style.

The balance of the disc is by Ken's Omega Brass Band, the first European attempt to recreate the marching bands of New Orleans. It comes close in its ragged excitement to the spirit of the original, although modelled on Bunk Johnson's somewhat old and staid approach rather than the looser Eureka or Young Tuxedo bands. The album is a good introduction to Colyer, avoiding both the clinical precision of his first band with Chris Barber and the stodgy decline of his later years. **AS**

Eddie Condon

1905-1973

The Original Decca Recordings Condon (g); **Max Kaminsky**, **Billy Butterfield**, **Yank Lawson** (t); **Bobby Hackett**, **Wild Bill Davison** (c); **Jack Teagarden** (tb, v); **Lou McGarity** (tb); **Brad Gowans** (vtb); **Pee Wee Russell**, **Edmond Hall**, **Tony Parenti** (cl); **Bud Freeman** (ts); **Ernie Caceres** (bs); **Joe Dixon** (cl, bs); **Joe Sullivan**, **Gene Schroeder**, **Joe Bushkin** (p); **Clyde Newcombe**, **Bob Haggart**, **Sid Weiss**, **Jack Lesberg** (b); **George Wettling**, **Dave Tough**, **Johnny Blowers** (d); **Lee Wiley** (v). MCA/Decca Ⓜ GRD-637 (61 minutes). Recorded 1939-46.

⑧ ❻

This album includes the four tracks originally recorded in 1939 as an album called **Chicago Jazz**, plus a further 16 titles done between 1944 and 1946. Unfortunately the set is not as complete as the album implies. One classic, *Aunt Hagar's Blues*, is omitted without reason, and some lesser titles which featured James P. Johnson and Ralph Sutton are also overlooked.

The earlier quartet have spiky solos from Russell and powerfully-fisted piano from Joe Sullivan, but it is the later tracks which really displayed that Condon's music was not by any means all hell-raising. The ballads here are without exception quite outstanding in the jazz of the forties. They include Wiley's beautiful version of *Someone To Watch Over Me* and Condon's unlikely composition *Wherever There's Love* with its fine Teagarden solo. Teagarden, Hackett and Butterfield share the superlative instrumental *When Your Lover Has Gone*, Hackett has *My One And Only,* Bushkin, at his most delicate, takes the first half of *The Man I Love* whilst Butterfield glories in the rest.

There are plenty of very hot numbers, notably the pair with Wild Bill Davison and the previously unissued take of *I'll Build A Stairway To Paradise* which features Hall and Lawson. Thanks to the good quality of the clean-up job, Condon's rhythm guitar can actually be heard (most often it could not). He had a faultless feel for time, which no doubt was a major factor in the success of many of his recordings. **SV**

Harry Connick Jr

1968

When Harry Met Sally... Connick (v, p); **Benjamin Jonah Wolfe** (b); **Jeff 'Tain' Watts** (d); **Frank Wess** (ts); **Jay Berliner** (g), **Marc Shaiman** (arr, p). Columbia Ⓕ CK 45319 (38 minutes). Recorded 1989.

⑥ ❽

The Harry Connick Jr phenomenon raises a number of thorny issues. Is he really a jazz singer? Is he really a jazz pianist? And since so many jazz commentators have answered such queries with a resounding "no", just where should the blue-eyed Crescent City crooner be classified?

The Sinatra comparison is an obvious starting point. Indeed, in his singing and playing, Connick has affected Sinatra's nonchalant cool and blasé world-weariness with obvious success, at least for the general public. He has also surrounded himself with jazz players and big band charts cut from the same cloth as the post-war hits of the Basie Band. Not insignificantly, Connick has helped re-popularize a batch of venerable tunes from the catalogue of the classical American song. Indeed, his soundtrack album for *When Harry Met Sally*, the romantic comedy starring Billy Crystal and Meg Ryan, includes *It Had To Be You, Our Love Is Here To Stay, But Not For Me, Stompin' at the Savoy, Autumn In New York, Don't Get Around Much Anymore, I Could Write A Book, Let's Call The Whole Thing Off* and *Where or When*. It is not surprising then that many musicians feel grateful to Connick for having once more made the world safe for standards, at least some of the time.

The album, while launching Connick's star, reveals an attractive if somewhat cloying voice. Settings range from solo piano and trio to big band. Finally, whatever his shortcomings, it is useful to keep in mind that Connick is still a very young man.The question is whether a matinée idol can also become a bona fide artist. We shall see. **CB**

Chris Connor

1927

As Time Goes By **Chris Connor** (v); **Hank Jones** (p); **George Mraz** (b); **Keith Copeland** (d). Enja Ⓕ ENJ 7061-2 (69 minutes). Recorded 1991.

⑧ ❽

Although she was 62 when she recorded it, this is one of Chris Connor's finest performances and almost certainly the best currently available. The pitch of her voice has dropped quite markedly since her sixties heyday, but the attractively hazy quality remains. She sings far more simply than before, which is actually an improvement, because she swings more.

Like June Christy, with whom she is often compared, Chris Connor takes an undemonstrative, almost detached line with her lyrics and this has the paradoxical effect of bringing them to the fore. Even *As Time Goes By* sounds fresh when she sings it, and it would be difficult to find a better version of Rodgers and Hart's pugnacious *Everything I've Got*. Much of the credit for this set must go to Hank Jones. All aspiring jazz pianists should be required to spend a stipulated number of hours listening to him carefully; this would ensure that they at least know what good accompaniment sounds like. **DG**

Bill Connors

1949

Of Mist and Melting **Connors** (g); **Jan Garbarek** (ss, ts); **Gary Peacock** (b); **Jack DeJohnette** (d). ECM Ⓕ 1120 (847 324-2) (48 minutes). Recorded 1977.

⑦ ❽

Connors first came to international notice in Return to Forever, and spent most of the seventies swapping between acoustic and electric guitars. On this album he favoured the former, and this helps distance him from any pervasive Forever influence; not that such a thing could be expected with Peacock and DeJohnette down in the boiler room.

The guitarist is hardly a soloist of the first order; although a superb technician, able to bring a wide degree of nuance from his instrument, he does not have the presence or ideas of a McLaughlin or Abercrombie. Perhaps that is what Garbarek was there for; if that is the case, then he does what is asked of him, and keeps the dialogue with a decidedly hot rhythm section bubbling away. Connors seems happiest when supplying textures for Garbarek to solo across, or for him to declaim Connors's melodies. Whatever, there is plenty of room for DeJohnette to get his rocks off, and on the opening track, *Melting*, he does in thrilling style.

Not essential listening—all the sidemen have reached greater heights elsewhere—but a pleasant and absorbing collection, and very much of a piece with ECM's then-philosophy of atmospherics and muscle seamlessly combined. That still doesn't explain, though, why we have to pay full price for the CD reissue of a 19-year-old album. **KS**

Junior Cook

1934-1992

On A Misty Night **Cook** (ts); **Mickey Tucker** (p); **Walter Boker** (b); **Leroy Williams** (d). SteepleChase Ⓕ SCCD31266 (65 minutes). Recorded 1989.

⑧ ❽

Florida-born Cook spent several years in the Horace Silver Quintet, where he was always in danger of being overlooked due to the strong solo work of the leader and trumpeter Blue Mitchell. But Junior was always a highly skilled player and a soloist whose lines had great continuity. These aspects are highlighted here on what is certainly his best album under his own name. Cook responds well to strong thematic material and makes telling use of the Tadd Dameron title tune which, although strongly associated with John Coltrane through the **Mating Call** album on Prestige, soon becomes Cook's own property. He also resurrects a forgotten but very attractive Cannonball Adderley tune, *Wabash* (from the **Cannonball In Chicago** Mercury release), and turns it into one of the strongest performances on the CD. But the programme is full of delights, especially for those of us who cherish unhackneyed show tunes; Cook plays two superb Arthur Schwartz songs here, *By Myself* and *Make The Girl Love Me*, the latter from **A Tree Grows in Brooklyn** (a fact not mentioned anywhere on the package, which contains no programme notes whatsoever). An excellent rhythm section (Tucker is a most helpful accompanist) and splendid engineering by Jim Anderson make this a truly memorable release. **AM**

Al Cooper

1911-1981

Al Cooper and The Savoy Sultans 1938-41 **Cooper** (cl, as, bs); **Pat Jenkins** (t); **Sam Massenberg** (t); **Rudy Williams** (as); **Ed McNeil**, **Sam Simmons**, **Irving 'Skinny' Brown** (ts); **George Kelly** (ts, v); **Paul Chapman** (g, v); **Oliver Richardson**, **Cyril Haynes** (p); **Grachan Moncur** (b); **Alex 'Razz' Mitchell** (d); **Helen Proctor**, **Evelyn White** (v). Classics Ⓜ 728 (72 minutes). Recorded 1938-41.

⑧ ❻

Talent-spotted by John Hammond when leading a band in upstate New York, Al Cooper auditioned for the Savoy Ballroom and made an immediate impression. The name Savoy Sultans was adopted and a residency was begun in 1937; there were few changes in personnel and the band stayed at 'The Track' for many years. This CD nicely represents their most productive period and presents them as the ideal dance band for the Harlem crowd. They were, however, very much more than that. The rhythm section (with Cooper's half-brother Moncur on bass) was outstanding, leading the whole band to swing incessantly. The simple arrangements were ideal for the band and Dizzy Gillespie, who occasionally guested, once described them as the "most exciting band ever". Williams was the outstanding soloist, happy with the Johnny Hodges testimony on *Jeep's Blues* but singularly driving on *Jumpin' The Blues* and *Stitches*. The band, which finally broke up in 1946, will be remembered as a great dance band that also played for listeners and it is no coincidence that six titles on this issue include the word 'jump'. **BMcR**

Bob Cooper

1925-1993

Tenor Sax Jazz Impressions **Cooper** (ts); **Michael Fahn** (vtb); **Ross Tompkins**, **Carl Schroeder** (p); **Chuck Berghofer**, **Bob Magnusson** (b); **John Guerin**, **Jimmie Smith** (d). Trend Ⓕ TRCD-543 (55 minutes). Recorded 1979/86.

⑧ ❽

The fact that it took seven years to accumulate enough tracks under his own name to compile a Bob Cooper CD is a reflection on one of jazz's more serious oversights. Because Cooper persistently graced the bands of other leaders (Shorty Rogers, Capp-Pierce Juggernaut and others) he was not accorded his correct ranking in the tenor hierarchy. He comes somewhere between Zoot Sims, Stan Getz and Al Cohn. His playing is characterized by technical fluency, a Sims-like swing and a penchant for blues phrases which all four men share.

Cooper was one of those consistent players who never recorded a bad solo, and this was his best album since his 1954 **Kenton Presents** session for Capitol (not yet issued on CD). Strayhorn's *Kissing Bug* draws out his best blues playing and gives Michael Fahn a chance to shine and make one wonder if he is to be the next Brookmeyer—he is that good. **SV**

Jim Cooper

1949

Nutville **Cooper** (vb, belaphon); **Ira Sullivan** (t, ts, ss); **Bob Dogan** (p); **Dan DeLorenzo** (b); **Charlie Braugham** (d); **Alejo Poveda** (perc). Delmark Ⓕ DD 457 (63 minutes). Recorded 1991.

⑦ ❼

Chicago has always had its own strangely personal jazz scene. This CD presents the virtually unknown Cooper with the superb multi-instrumentalist Sullivan and even has Paul Serrano, one of the city's unsung trumpet heroes, as its engineer. Cooper is from the Gary Burton generation but with his own way of approaching the improvising process. He responds in a way that is appropriate to the material; taking the gentle Latin route on *Cantor Da Noite*, a strong attack to *Bemsha Swing* and on *Nutville* giving his fine solo a distinctive edge by the use of the belaphon, an African xylophone. Pianist Dogan solos well and leads a useful rhythm section but it is Sullivan that makes the biggest impression. As always, he switches horns throughout a session with no detrimental effect to his playing of them. The difference between his approach to his two saxophones on *Autumn Nocturne* is typical, with his soprano soulfully reverential and his tenor assertively matter-of-fact. In contrast, the breathy tonal quality of his tenor is emphasized on *Mallethead*, while he selects the oddly changing time signatures of *Sui Fumi* to provide the stimulant for a really authoritative soprano outing. His stylish trumpet playing is captured on *Tanga* and on the title track, displaying a mode of improvising some distance from his saxophone work. The session belongs to the admirable Cooper but Sullivan does tend to steal his thunder. **BMcR**

Marc Copland

Ilg/Copland/Hirschfield: What's Goin' On **Dieter Ilg** (b); **Copland** (p); **Jeff Hirschfield** (d). Jazzline Ⓕ JL 11138-2 (63 minutes). Recorded 1993.

⑧ ❽

The most striking aspect of this excellent trio's work—the installation of rock beats underneath a jazzy harmonic conception—is, of course, not essentially new, but by retaining acoustic instruments, especially acoustic bass, they have developed an attractively fresh perspective on piano jazz. In its original form the Marvin Gaye title-track was hardly a model of harmonic sophistication, but before the first minute of the trio's version is out, Copland's cheeky sideslips and polytonalisms prick up the ears of the jazz-minded and scupper any possibility of the track leaping into the Soul 100. *Scrapple From The Apple* suffers similarly glorious indignities at the hands of an ostinato vamp, a tart reharmonization and piano figures which suggest Richie Beirach, and two originals in a similar vein, *Bigfoot* and *Take It To The Bridge*, are further examples of the delights awaiting the jazz piano trio which escapes the tyranny of the Broadway song form and triplet bass lines.

However, it is not all pranks and japes. Pleasure is balanced by the pain of limpid, Jarrett-esque readings of *Young And Foolish*, *In The Wee Small Hours Of The Morning* and Dori Caymmi's poignant *Photograph*. **MG**

Chick Corea

1941

Now He Sings, Now He Sobs **Corea** (p); **Miroslav Vitous** (b); **Roy Haynes** (d). Blue Note Ⓜ CDP7 90055-2 (70 minutes). Recorded 1968.

✔ ⑩ ❻

This was one of the most welcome reissues of the late eighties. It presents Corea at the height of his powers and, thanks to the diligent Michael Cuscuna, brings together his trio's entire March 1968 session in one digitally remastered package. Previously it was available only as two LP issues divided by a decade.

The impeccable production and presentation is the perfect complement to the music: if Corea has fallen into mannerism in recent years, he is captured here in his first prime, and the results are unselfconscious, impassioned and devoid of contrivance. His influences are clearly apparent, but so is his incipient individualism. Thus *My One And Only Love*, *Windows* and *Pannonica* are infused with the poetry of Bill Evans, *Matrix* and the first section of *Steps—What Was* are exhilarating rollercoasters in the manner of McCoy Tyner, *Steps*' second section illustrates Corea's proto-Hispanicism and suggests a sketch for the later standard *Spain*, and the abstractions of *Fragments* and *Gemini* prefigure his work in the seventies improvising group Circle (see below).

The musicianship is first class throughout, Vitous and Haynes enjoying an uncommon empathy with Corea and shadowing his lithe, agile lines with wit and vigour. Their pushing and pulling of the time on the title-track is just one in a seemingly endless variety of excitements. **MG**

Early Circle **Corea** (p, cel, perc); **Anthony Braxton** (ss, as, f, cl, cbcl); **Dave Holland** (b, co, g); **Barry Altschul** (d, perc). Blue Note Ⓜ 7 84465 2 (55 minutes). Recorded 1970.

⑦ ❻

Over the course of a 30-year career Corea has proven to be a chameleon, changing colours and stylistic approaches to blend into vastly different surroundings. His brief but incisive period with the co-operative Circle, separating episodes with the eclectic Miles Davis and his own electric Return To Forever, was undoubtedly the most experimental. Corea's considerable talents—including curiosity tempered with taste, and ever-present lyricism even in abstract climes—served him well in this context. There is a surefootedness about his playing, a crispness to his phrasing, an overall sense of design, a poise that belies the unstructured environment. A free-floating *Ballad* brings out his Impressionist harmonies (which do not translate well, unfortunately, to the celeste on the two *Chimes*), and he is able to soften the sharp edges of Holland's boppish *Starp* and Braxton's intricate *73°–A Kelvin* without blunting the aggressive attack. You can hear the musicians searching for common ground, feeling their way cautiously towards formal consensus, in the short duets and the extended, spontaneous *Chimes*; four months later their familiarity would crystallize in the **Paris Concert** (ECM 1018/19). Ultimately, Braxton's spirit of adventure proved incompatible with Corea's populist leanings, and led to the break-up of the group. **AL**

Piano Improvisations, Volumes 1 and 2 **Corea** (p). ECM Ⓕ 1014, 1120 (811 979-2, 829 190-2) (42 and 40 minutes, oas). Recorded 1971.

⑧ ❿

There is a feeling of joy running through much of the music on these two CDs, products of the same recording session in April 1971. Whatever Corea's personal circumstances at the time, there is no doubt that these albums represented something akin to a liberation. To understand why, it may be worth recalling that in 1971 solo piano recitals were a rarity, rather than the norm. Corea, being one of the few modern pianists of the time fully equipped to take full advantage of being solo (Jarrett had just done the same thing for ECM, and Paul Bley did so shortly after), plays through a programme of his own music (plus one Monk piece, *Trinkle Tinkle*, on Volume Two) and simply revels in the interpretative freedom he finds for himself.

It is salutary to compare his solo piano version of *Sometime Ago*, a composition also covered on the group album **Return to Forever** shortly after. With the latter, the piece is rushed, as if the group cannot wait to get to the major-key groove of the main theme, which Flora Purim delivers with panache. Here, Corea paces the work beautifully, and returns repeatedly to the central section of the piece, the minor, Spanish-feel refrain. The major chorus is used only as relief. It is eight minutes of real magic, with no punches pulled.

Both discs contain plenty of uncompromising, gritty playing across a large range of subjects and styles, with the focus held sharp throughout. **KS**

Chick Corea Akoustic Band **Corea** (p); **John Patitucci** (b); **Dave Weckle** (d). GRP Ⓕ GRD-9582 (60 minutes). Recorded 1989.

⑧ ❽

Chick Corea—despite having earned praise for his early seventies adventures with Dave Holland, Barry Altschul and Anthony Braxton—fell from favour among jazz purists for his crossover endeavours with the seventies Return To Forever and the mid-eighties Chick Corea Elektric Band. In 1989, however, the pianist's Akoustic reconfiguration of his bebop roots amazed even those who had perhaps written Corea off as another casualty to the fiscal lures of fusion. Released on the crossover-minded GRP label for whom Corea had organised his successful Eleckric Band, the newly forged Akoustic Band features bassist John Patitucci and drummer Dave Weckle, prime movers in Corea's plugged-in unit. And although Corea is the fulcrum around whom the music turns, the pianist's younger colleagues establish themselves as figures to reckon with, especially Patitucci whose agile technique and resonant sound evoke the legacy of the young Scott La Faro with Bill Evans.

Corea is simply dazzling. From the Monkish twists of *Bessie's Blues* and boppish drive of *Autumn Leaves* to the languor of *Sophisticated Lady* and rakish lilt of *Someday My Prince Will Come*, the pianist's capacity for genuine invention and surprise startle at each turn. There are also crisp readings of Corea's own standards *Spain, Circles and Morning Sprite*, as well as his provocatively free *T.B.C.* (*Terminal Baggage Claim*), which reconnects the pianist to his sonic voyages with the aforementioned Holland, Altschul and Braxton. **CB**

Larry Coryell

1943

Shining Hour **Coryell** (g); **Kenny Barron** (p); **Buster Williams** (b); **Marvin 'Smitty' Smith** (d). Muse Ⓕ MCD 5360 (50 minutes). Recorded 1989.

⑥ ❽

Coryell achieved notoriety in the vanguard of fusion in the late sixties, but since the early eighties he has been working his way back to the modern mainstream. Several straight-ahead dates for Muse have resulted, and this one has him yoked to a top-drawer rhythm section. Coryell seizes the opportunity forcefully, perhaps sometimes too forcefully. *Apathy Rains*, rendered thoughtfully on acoustic guitar and piano, is elegant enough, but at faster tempos the combination of a brittle tone, an over-enthusiastic attack, a sometimes uncertain rhythmic sense and vague formal design tends to produce inconclusive, only partially satisfying solos. There is no doubting the intensity of such spirited assaults as that on *Floyd Gets A Gig*, but sometimes Coryell seems to mistake speed for musicality, and ends up sounding frantic rather than vigorous. This is ironic when Miles seems one of the session's chief inspirations. Indeed, renditions of such unusual guitar fare as *Nefertiti* and *The Duke* help to distinguish a session which otherwise offers little out of the ordinary. Perhaps because of its loose, modal flavour, Herbie Hancock's *The Sorcerer* is one of the most successful tracks here, providing a sympathetic environment for Coryell's McLaughlin-like ideas. **MG**

Eddie Costa

1930-1962

Eddie Costa Quintet **Costa** (p, vb); **Art Farmer** (t); **Phil Woods** (as, p); **Teddy Kotick** (b); **Paul Motian** (d). VSOP Ⓕ #7CD (31 minutes). Recorded 1957.

⑧ ❻

At the time of his death in a tragic road accident, Costa was recognized as one of the most individual keyboard players of his day. He favoured a hard, driving two-handed style, making full use of the lower half of the piano as much as the top half, unlike a number of his contemporaries who relied on bass players to fill out the roots of the chords. Of the comparatively few records under his own name his Jubilee trio set (with Vinnie Burke and Nick Stabulas) is overdue for translation to CD, but this album, recorded for the Mode label originally, is welcome. It features Costa leading an efficient, well-rehearsed quintet with some searing alto solos from Phil Woods and carefully considered statements from Art Farmer. Costa lays down a propulsive backing on piano which would stir the most recalcitrant of soloists into action. Like Horace Silver and Dave McKenna he seemed capable of playing the complete rhythm section's part on the piano keyboard. He plays vibes on two tracks, a finely-etched version of Brubeck's *In Your Own Sweet Way* and a delicately sketched out *I Didn't Know What Time It Was*. On both titles Phil Woods plays very capable piano support. Motian is recorded a little too prominently in places but generally the balance and the transfers are acceptable. The playing time of the original LP (and this CD) is so meagre that the Top Rank label once issued it in the UK as a ten-inch album without any loss of tracks. **AM**

Curtis Counce

1926-1963

You Get More Bounce with Curtis Counce! **Counce** (b); **Jack Sheldon** (t); **Harold Land** (ts); **Carl Perkins** (p); **Frank Butler** (d). Contemporary Ⓜ OJCCD 159-2 (51 minutes). Recorded 1956-57.

⑧ ❽

To refute the notion that all fifties California jazz was cool and creamy, critics cite Counce's hard-bop quintet, which swung aggressively à la New York's Art Blakey and Horace Silver. The Clifford Brown/Max Roach quintet is even more of a role model (as a fast, mildly intricate *Mean to Me* and the underrated Butler's attentive drumming make clear), although that East Coast band was founded in California. But it's important not to oversimplify; *Complete*'s jaunty walking and open latticework arrangement suggest quintessential West Coaster Shorty Rogers's *Martian* pieces more than Blakey's Messengers.

Born in Kansas City, Counce retained that city's taste for relaxed, unfettered swing. A key player on the L.A. scene in the fifties (he died prematurely of a heart attack), Counce epitomizes the decade's exemplary pre-amplification bass stylings, when players were expected to have a plump, robust tone and propulsive approach. Brown/Roach veteran Land, who had a long, productive subsequent career, and Perkins, who had a tragically short one (dying at 29, in 1958), lack nothing in blues authority or soul. Trumpeter Sheldon brings a warm, full tone to ballads (like *Stranger in Paradise*), but crackles hot as well. This facsimile edition's tacky cheesecake cover is a period classic. **KW**

Stanley Cowell

1941

We Three **Cowell** (p); **Busfer Williams** (b); **Freddie Waits** (d). DIW Ⓕ 807 (66 minutes). Recorded 1987.

⑧ · ❽

Cowell has been deeply involved with projects such as Music Inc., the seven-piece Piano Choir and the CBA Ensemble. A University of Michigan graduate, he has worked with Marion Brown, Max Roach and the Heath Brothers and is currently himself a teacher. He is a fine composer and arranger and both of these talents are evident on this trio session. It is as a pianist in the intimacy of this group, however, that he makes his mark and, in choosing Williams and Waits, he has given himself the best possible opportunity. All of the tunes were written by members of the trio and they maintain a high standard. This trio really succeeds because all three men are virtuosi. Williams swings as do few bassists, his solos have shape and purpose and in the ensemble he never hesitates to re-direct. Waits is one of that rare breed of drummers, a percussionist that can play not only the tune but also his own version of it. In spite of this, Cowell remains the star in this stellar company. He plays sparklingly daring runs yet still manages to remain relaxed, even at the most daunting up-tempos. In addition he still manages to rock gently with the medium tempo *Sienna* and to play with genuine sensitivity in his two fine readings of his own *Winter Reflections*. **BMcR**

Ida Cox

1889-1967

I Can't Quit My Man **Cox** (v); **Hot Lips Page**, **Henry 'Red' Allen** (t); **J.C. Higginbotham** (tb); **Edmond Hall** (cl); **James P. Johnson**, **Fletcher Henderson**, **Cliff Jackson** (p); **Charlie Christian** (g); **Artie Bernstein**, **Billy Taylor** (b); **Lionel Hampton**, **Jimmy Hoskins** (d). Affinity Ⓜ CD AFS1015 (55 minutes). Recorded 1939-40.

⑥ ❻

This album offers a rare chance to hear a leading blues singer of the twenties who retained her abilities long enough to give an accurate account of her style in relatively good recording conditions. On the 1939 sessions Cox's deliberate, unornamented delivery is faithful to her past and her accompanists play with the accents of the day, yet there is nothing uncomfortable about the collaboration; indeed, *Death Letter Blues* matches anything in Cox's discography. There was little of nostalgia in these sessions: *Pink Slip Blues* and *Hard Time Blues* allude to contemporary events, while in the sprightly *One Hour Mama* the singer forsakes the measured pace typical of the songs of her heyday. The 1940 session, which has 'Red' Allen rather than Page, and a different rhythm section, has a decidely modern flavour, especially in *You Got To Swing and Sway*, which has attractive solos by all the front line.

The 11 tracks produced at these three dates are supplemented by rejected takes (eight in all) of six of them, different only in detail. These may be valuable only to specialists, but the core material is music of ready appeal and enduring value. **TR**

Lol Coxhill

1932

The Dunois Solos **Coxhill** (ss). Nato Ⓕ 95 (42 minutes). Recorded 1981.

⑧ ❽

Over the years the idiosyncratic Coxhill has recorded with birds, bagpipes, a loose floorboard, punk rockers and a curious nostalgic trio called The Melody Four. Obviously, there is more than a trace of Dada in his blood, but as a serious improviser he has developed a personal vocabulary quite unbeholden to Steve Lacy, Wayne Shorter, Evan Parker or any other soprano saxist you care to name. For pure, undiluted Coxhill, this solo album is hard to beat, consisting of two low-key, sustained improvisations, aptly titled *Distorted Reminiscences* and *Further Developments*. Like a hazy memory, this music has no prearranged beginning or ending; Lol's elusive logic allows free association, a wide range of references, connections and diversions. It is fascinating to stroll with him along these winding melodic paths, which twist and climb or dip at unexpected intervals, widen or narrow as notes pinch or broaden with vibrato. He gets a lovely, singing quality from the horn as, despite the occasional pitch bending and smear, he is a lyrical improviser above all, often with a touch of the pastoral or melancholy. Given his comedic talents, he is not always taken seriously, and so in mixed groups somewhat resembles Pee Wee Russell among the Condon gang. In fact he admits an affinity to Pee Wee, crediting the quixotic clarinettist with his awareness of the "spaces between the notes." And like Russell, he is a vastly underrated nonconformist of marvellous artistry. **AL**

Hank Crawford 1934

Midnight Ramble **Crawford** (as, ep); **Charlie Miller**, **Waymon Reed** (t); **Dick Griffin** (tb); **David 'Fathead' Newman** (ts); **Howard Johnson** (bs); **Dr. John** (p, org); **Calvin Newborn** (g); **Charles 'Flip' Green** (b); **Bernard Purdie** (d). Milestone Ⓜ MCD-9112-2 (39 minutes). Recorded 1982.

⑧ ❽

The former music director of Ray Charles's big band, Crawford is among the most consistent of performers. Any of the half-dozen or so similar albums he has made for Milestone in the last ten years would do just as nicely as this one, which is the choice here mainly because it was the prototype. Even then, it follows the pattern set on the r&b-influenced albums that Crawford made for Atlantic in the sixties, when he was still with Charles. Nothing wrong with that. If not exactly essential jazz library items, those albums were classics of their unpretentious genre. So is **Midnight Ramble**, if only for testifying to Crawford's knack for making four or five horns roar like a dozen—a trick arrangers used to learn on the road with jump bands forced by circumstances to play the same venues as the big swing bands. This album and those which have followed also show off Crawford's singing tone and straightforward but lusty approach to improvisation. He is an especially winning ballad player, as demonstrated here by *Street of Dreams* and Gamble and Huff's pretty *Forever Mine*. Crawford is a soul man from the old school: like Charles himself, he knows that the way to make it *really* funky is to make it *s-l-o-w*. **FD**

Ray Crawford 1924

Smooth Groove **Crawford** (g); **Johnny Coles** (t); **Cecil Payne** (bs); **Junior Mance** (p); **Ben Tucker** (b); **Frankie Dunlop** (d). Candid Ⓜ 79028 (43 minutes). Recorded 1961.

⑦ ❻

Crawford, a consistently interesting and intelligent guitarist, has never really had the chance to establish himself in the limelight. Originally trained as a saxophonist, he played back in the early forties with Fletcher Henderson, but ended up in hospital with tuberculosis and after his recovery switched to the guitar. As the fifties began he joined Ahmad Jamal, playing with him for six years, only to leave the trio not long before Jamal's big break with his Pershing Lounge album. After that, Crawford moved on to New York and gravitated towards the Gil Evans circle, playing on and off for him for a number of years. It was his outstanding work on Evans's **Out Of The Cool** (see below) which led Candid proprietor Nat Hentoff to invite him to record this album. Like Cal Massey and others, Crawford was to see the original Candid label go broke before his album was released. This, then, is its first issue.

The music is tightly organized, each player contributing a clearly-defined personality to a role created for them by Crawford. This is no mere blowing session. Crawford himself has a pleasing edge to his sound, and a willingness to dig in and groove which justifies the album's title. Coles, another under-recorded alumnus of the Evans band, plays exquisitely throughout, while Payne alternates winningly between warmth and bustle. Dunlop is outstanding in the rhythm section. All five tunes are Crawford originals, and all are carefully crafted pieces. This is a very worthy effort which certainly did not deserve to dwell in darkness for nearly 30 years. **KS**

Marilyn Crispell 1947

Marilyn Crispell/Anthony Braxton - Duets, Vancouver 1989 **Crispell** (p); **Braxton** (reeds). Music and Arts Ⓕ CD 611 (46 minutes). Recorded 1989.

⑧ ❽

The idea that academic musical studies and jazz do not mix is refuted in the work of Marilyn Crispell. A graduate of the New England Conservatory, she studied classical piano but was won over to jazz by listening to John Coltrane and Cecil Taylor. Since the conversion, she has developed into one of the most outstanding of all free jazz pianists, and one whose idea of improvisation is realized in her own mind as instant composition.

This CD shows a special side to her often ferocious playing. Working with Anthony Braxton (whom she first met in 1979) moderates her overtly passionate approach and demands that she conciously organizes her solo utterances, even if not diluting them in terms of creative potency. The music here is presented as a continuous performance, comprising four primary structures with pulse tracks added. For both performers, the line between the formal and the spontaneous is hard to draw, although it is Crispell's line that most communicates as being free from pre-conceived ideas. She solos throughout with true invention and, together with the gifted saxophonist, carries her improvisational elements into superbly balanced counterpoint. Her most typical work is found on *No. 36* but it pays her the greatest compliment to say that it is as a pair that these musicians excel. She has successfully recorded solo albums, but in this situation she demonstrates her ability to listen to a colleague and to show how to best use the dynamic contrasts between horn and keyboard.

BMcR

Sonny Criss

1927-1977

Portrait of Sonny Criss **Criss** (as); **Walter Davis** (p); **Paul Chambers** (b); **Alan Dawson** (d). Prestige Ⓜ OJCCD-655-2 (32 minutes). Recorded 1967.

⑧ ❻

As a teenager Criss grew up in Los Angeles, playing with bands led by men such as Howard McGhee and Billy Eckstine. The visit of Charlie Parker to the city at the end of 1945 gave Criss a new hero to worship and his earliest recordings have the strained, urgent sound of Parker before his nervous breakdown. After a period of residency in Europe in the early sixties, Criss returned to the US where Prestige's Don Schlitten set up a number of recording sessions; this New York date is certainly one of the best, despite the miserly playing time. Criss's tone is big and expressive, especially so on ballads where an admiration for Benny Carter seems to have overtaken the Parker mantle. There is a memorable reading of *God Bless The Child* and a suitably wistful air on pianist Walter Davis's tune *A Million More Times*. But the spirit of Parker still looms large on the up-tempo numbers, especially the hectic *Wee* (or *Allen's Alley*) where the occasional slight reed-squeak adds to the "you are there" sense of excitement. Walter Davis is a most helpful pianist and Alan Dawson's drumming simply cannot be faulted. Strongly recommended.

AM

Bing Crosby

1904–1977

Bing Crosby And Some Jazz Friends **Crosby** (v); featured with: **Louis Jordan and His Tympany Five**; **Connee Boswell**; **Bob Crosby's Bob Cats**; **Georgie Stoll Orchestra**; **Joe Sullivan**; **Louis Armstrong**; **Tommy Dorsey Orchestra**; **Jack Teagarden Orchestra**; **Eddie Condon Orchestra**; **Lionel Hampton Orchestra**; **Lee Wiley**; **Victor Young Orchestra**; **Woody Herman's Woodchoppers**; **John Scott Trotter Orchestra**. MCA/Decca Ⓜ GRP 6032 (60 minutes). Recorded 1934-51

⑦ ❽

A giant of popular music, Crosby was also a good-natured comedian and an extremely successful film actor. His involvement in jazz began when he was a member of the Rhythm Boys with Paul Whiteman in the twenties and his association with players such as Bix Beiderbecke, Frankie Trumbauer and Eddie Lang began then, resulting in his lifelong enthusiasm for the music. He was not a jazz singer in the true sense, but when in the right company and with the right material he fitted well into the jazz milieu. The more maudlin aspects of his style are exposed here on 'square' performances such as *Someday Sweetheart* and *Pennies From Heaven* but on *Yes, Indeed!* and *When my Dreamboat Comes Home*, with brother Bob's Bob Cats, or *After You've Gone*, with the Condon mob, he demonstrates plenty of jazz virtues in a rollicking Dixieland atmosphere. His timing could never be said to give his music the cutting edge of true jazz singing, but his relaxed, richly legato style had a rhythmic strength of its own. If nothing else, *The Waiter And The Porter And The Upstairs Maid, I Ain't Got Nobody* and *Gone Fishing* are classics from the jazz fringe and they stamp him as probably the most jazz-inspired one-handicap golfer.

BMcR

Bob Crosby

1913-1993

South Rampart Street Parade **Crosby** (ldr); with a collective personnel of: **Yank Lawson**, **Shorty Sherock**, **Phil Hart**, **Max Herman**, **Zeke Zarchy**, **Lyman Vunk**, **Andy Feretti**, **Billy Butterfield**, **Charlie Spivak**, **Sterling Bose** (t); **Ward Silloway**, **Buddy Morrow**, **Artie Foster**, **Warren Smith**, **Elmer Smithers**, **Mark Bennett**, **Jim Emert**, **Ray Conniff**, **Floyd O'Brien** (tb); **Gil Rodin** (cl, as, ts); **Matty Matlock** (cl, as); **Irving Fazola** (cl); **Noni Bernardi**, **Bill Stegmeyer**, **Joe Kearns**, **George Koenig**, **Art Mendelsohn**, **Art Rando** (as); **Eddie Miller** (ts, cl); **Dean Kincaide** (ts); **Gil**

Bowers, **Bob Zurke**, **Joe Sullivan**, **Jess Stacy** (p); **Nappy Lamare** (g, v); **Bob Haggart** (b, arr); **Ray Bauduc** (d). MCA/Decca Ⓜ GRP 16152 (62 minutes). Recorded 1936-42

⑧ ❻

Bing's younger brother Bob was invited to front a band formed of musicians who had all left the Ben Pollack orchestra. His pleasant although innocuous singing is not heard here, but he was nevertheless an important figure in the undoubted success of this unique band, unique because it played an orchestral form of Dixieland at a time when nearly every other big band was producing swing music. All but one of the 20 tracks here are by the Crosby Orchestra as opposed to the Bob Cats small group (the only non-orchestral track is the Haggart-Bauduc duet *Big Noise From Winnetka*). Seldom has a band produced such zestful music, bouncing along on the steady beat laid down by Bauduc's fine drumming. A lot of the success is due to the consistently excellent arangements of Haggart and the outstanding solos from Eddie Miller, Irving Fazola and a wealth of memorable trumpeters. The underrated Sterling Bose, plunger-muted, is superb on *I'm Prayin' Humble*, for example. Pianists Bob Zurke and Jess Stacy are strongly featured on *Little Rock Getaway* and *Complainin'* respectively. The transfers are generally good, although they are evidently taken from a variety of sources. **AM**

Pat Crumly

1942

Flamingo **Crumly** (ss, as, ts, f); **Guy Barker** (t); **Richard Edwards** (tb); **John Pearce** (p); **Alec Dankworth**, **Simon Woolf** (b); **Simon Morton** (d); **Bosco DeOliveira** (perc). Spotlight Ⓕ SPJ-CD 550 (74 minutes). Recorded 1993.

⑧ ❽

Like his earlier Spotlite album **Behind the Mask**, **Flamingo** is a showcase for a somewhat neglected talent. Pat Crumly is equally at home in rock, r&b and jazz, having decorated the albums of Eric Burden, Alan Price and Jimmy Witherspoon while developing a jazz sound rooted in bop and the blues. He is inspired by, but by no means slavishly imitative of, Cannonball Adderley and Phil Woods. Like the latter, on his favoured horn—alto—Crumly produces freewheeling, uninhibited solos laced with tart astringency, but he also plays driving if slightly querulous tenor, agile soprano and (on one track, *It Might as Well be Spring*) pure-toned, sure-footed flute. The material on this, as on **Behind the Mask**, consists of carefully selected standards from the likes of Rodgers and Hart (*Bewitched*), Kern and Fields (a storming version of *The Way You Look Tonight*) and Henry Mancini (a lithe alto treatment of *The Days of Wine and Roses,* packed with felicitous touches), interspersed with attractive Crumly originals. The album's centrepiece is its title-track, in Crumly's words "a pleasing update of the Mingus chart" first heard on the bassist's 1957 album **Tijuana Moods**. His core quartet is augmented on this, his own bustling *Eucalypso* and the sinewy opener for tenor, *Nightwalk*, by the classy, bright sophistication of Guy Barker and the warm but gutsy trombone of Richard Edwards. Crumly demonstrates on this album just how strong the current UK jazz scene is. **CP**

The Crusaders

1970-1990

Chain Reaction/Those Southern Knights **Wilton Felder** (s, elb); **Nesbert 'Stix' Hooper** (d); **Joe Sample** (p, kbds); **Wayne Henderson** (tb); **Larry Carlton**, **Arthur Adams** (elg); **Robert 'Pops' Popwell** (elb); **The Crusaders** (v). MCA Ⓜ MCAD 5841 (69 minutes). Recorded c. 1975-76.

⑥ ❻

The Crusaders have often been used to warn of the evils attending the fall of jazz into dance-floor temptation, and certainly their guileless two and four-bar funky riffs were a long way from the Messengers-style hard bop they had studied as The Jazz Crusaders through the sixties. But they had their moments, and this generously-timed double-decker illustrates both the best and worst aspects of their work.

Pleading shortage of space, the package omits two tracks from **Chain Reaction** and one from **Those Southern Knights**. In the case of **Chain Reaction**, it could have omitted more without significant loss, since much of the set sounds like a series of entrées to not very appetizing main courses. Over half the tracks run for three-and-a-half minutes or less, and most consist of underdeveloped, prematurely faded riffing. By contrast, **Those Southern Knights** is refreshingly confident and expansive. Impelled by the new, hard-grooving bassist Robert Popwell, it features well-rounded compositions and strong solos from Sample, Henderson and Carlton. Purists might have thought the music diluted enough by this stage, but there was worse to come: a few moments spent with the top ten soul-pop of *Street Life* (1979) puts **Southern Knights** into perspective as one of the best examples of the post-Jazz—but still jazzing—Crusaders. **MG**

Ronnie Cuber

1941

Cubism **Cuber** (bs, ts); **Joe Locke** (vb); **Michael Formanek** (b); **Bobby Broom** (g); **Ben Perowsky** (d); **Potato Valdez** (cga). Fresh Sounds Ⓕ FSR-CD188 (49 minutes). Recorded 1991.

Was a man ever blessed with a more appropriate surname? Cuber is perhaps best-known as a funk and pop session player, but his masterly treatments of the Latin style comfortably earn him the right to exploit the punning Caribbean potential of his name. His versatility should not be a surprise, since eclecticism has long been his stock-in-trade: before tackling the bespoke demands of the New York studios in the seventies, he played in big bands with Maynard Ferguson and others, and in organ combos with George Benson.

Cuber's Blue-Note-inspired Latin, bop and rhythm & blues tunes make no major stylistic departures, but it is hard to imagine such familiar idioms being delivered with more spirit, authenticity and polish. The period material and robust delivery combine to create the atmosphere of a sixties club somewhere on the wrong side of the tracks, the scene set perfectly by the sophisticated yet unpretentious opener, *Arroz Con Pollo*. The use of vibes and guitar in place of piano adds exotic tonal colour, and there are fine solos all round—from Cuber's chesty Coltrane-through-Pepper Adams bari, Joe Locke's urbane but earthy vibes and the perpetually inspired Bobby Broom, still improving on the style George Benson abandoned in the late sixties. **MG**

Bill Cunliffe

A Rare Connection **Cunliffe** (p) with the following collective personnel; **Clay Jenkins** (t, flh); **Bruce Paulson** (tb); **Bob Sheppard** (ts, bcl); **Dave Carpenter** (b); **Peter Erskine** (d); **Kurt Rasmussen** (perc). Discovery Ⓕ 77007 (55 minutes). Recorded 1993.

⑧ ❽

Cunliffe won the 1989 Thelonious Monk Jazz Piano Award around the time he was working with the Clayton-Hamilton Jazz Orchestra (which also included trumpeter Clay Jenkins). In the notes to this CD he is reported as saying "my intention was to take the language of traditional bebop jazz and bring it into the nineties." He has a delicate, expressive touch and a post-Bill Evans approach. Despite some Coltrane-inspired tenor from Sheppard this is not hard bop music; in fact, it sounds like a logical extension of the jazz associated with the West Coast movement of the fifties. A considerable asset is the presence of Peter Erskine, one of the most tasteful, intelligent and musical drummers since the late Shelly Manne. The music flows evenly with no awkward breaks in the mood. Cunliffe wrote seven of the tunes but his approach to the standards *Stella By Starlight* and the latterday Jerome Kern song *Nobody Else But Me* is very personal. *A Rare Connection* is a piano trio number of great charm (aided by some subdued synthesizer) and is a clear indication of Cunliffe's considerable keyboard control. **AM**

Ted Curson 1935

Plenty of Horn **Curson** (t); **Bill Barron** (ts); **Kenny Drew** (p); **Jimmy Garrison** (b); **Roy Haynes**, **Danny Richmond**, **Pete LaRoca** (d). On two tracks **Eric Dolphy** (f) replaces Barron. Old Town/Boplicity Ⓜ CDBOP 018 (40 minutes). Recorded 1961.

⑦ ❼

Curson first gained attention in 1960 as a member of Charles Mingus's Jazz Workshop at New York's Showplace. He, along with Eric Dolphy and Booker Ervin, was to become a permanent part of Mingus's front line for close on a year. Since then he has led his own bands and over the years has enjoyed a close working relationship with tenorist Bill Barron, brother of pianist Kenny. Curson made a number of albums in the sixties, and their value ranges from excellent to more-or-less interesting. The present album was his leadership début, and is certainly his freshest, brightest recording of the sixties. There is surprisingly little evidence here of his stay with Mingus (although drummer Richmond and Dolphy, present on two and three tracks respectively, are physical traces of the link), and Curson sticks for the most part to a style not that far removed from early Lee Morgan, although his brighter tone occasionally hints at Don Cherry.

Bill Barron, here like Dolphy to provide support rather than compete for time at the mike, contributes effectively to the more harmonically adventurous themes, but tends to drift through the blues-based numbers. Curson's *Ahma (See Ya)* has an opening arpeggio uncannily combines elements of John Coltrane's 1959 *Giant Steps* and Wayne Shorter's *E.S.P.* of six years later, and Barron's solo on this track could even be Shorter himself. The album does not have the emotional depth of Curson's 1964 **Tears For Dolphy**, but does have a clear identity, a firm creative focus, and plenty to interest the curious. **KS**

King Curtis 1934-1971

Soul Battle **Curtis**, **Oliver Nelson**, **Jimmy Forrest** (ts); **Gene Casey** (p); **George Duvivier** (b); **Roy Haynes** (d). Prestige Ⓜ OJCCD 325-2 (47 minutes). Recorded 1960.

⑥ ❽

It is King Curtis who plays the brief but fiery tenor saxophone solos on pop classics such as *Yakety Yak* by the Coasters, Little Eva's *Locomotion* and Chubby Checker's *Let's Twist Again*. Most records under his own name are also in the r&b/soul mould, and this is the only traceable CD example of his jazz playing available at press date. It reveals him to be a player typical of his origins and background;

he was born in Fort Worth, Texas, where he began his career in small clubs and dance halls. Like all Texas tenor players, he had a broad, juicy tone and strong leanings towards the blues. He sounds entirely at home in the company of two acknowledged jazz soloists, which only goes to show how unstable such categories can be.

The whole CD is highly enjoyable in a relaxed, rambling kind of way. Jimmy Forrest, in particular, was a superb blues player and is heard in top form here. The rhythm section is exceptionally good. **DG**

Andrew Cyrille

1939

My Friend Louis **Cyrille** (d); **Hannibal** (t); **Oliver Lake** (ss, as); **Adegoke Steve Colson** (p); **Reginald Workman** (b). DIW Ⓕ DIW-858 (63 minutes). Recorded 1991.

⑧ ❽

Master percussionist Andrew Cyrille is best known for his 11-year (1965-75) stint with Cecil Taylor, a role that established him as a pioneering influence on free jazz drumming. In recent years he has played across the spectrum of modern jazz, an in-demand figure who has graced records by (for instance) Muhal Richard Abrams, Anthony Braxton, John Carter and David Murray. He has also worked as a solo percussionist, in duos with improvisers such as Jimmy Lyons and Vladimir Tarasov, and has led his own group Maono (a Swahili word for 'feelings'), whose late-seventies-early-eighties albums for Soul Note (notably the fine **The Navigator**) deserve a CD issue.

The album's dedicatee is South African drummer Louis Moholo. Its music is relatively 'inside' with a loose, friendly quintet ease in the repertoire, although the quintet are razor-sharp when they need to be, as on Cyrille's convoluted *Shell*. Hannibal's trumpet, all fire and quicksilver, is a good foil for Lake's acerbic reeds, and Colson's gentle pianism complements Workman's firm melodic pulse. Cyrille himself brings a stream of felicitous touches, fierce and playful by turn, fringed with a stinging patter of cymbal cross-rhythms. Whether he is brushing ballads with a delicate lustre or rapping out the township bop of *My Friend Louis*, he has the gift to make his drum kit sing and dance. **GL**

Meredith D'Ambrosio

1941

South to a Warmer Place **d'Ambrosio** (v); **Eddie Higgins** (p); **Don Coffman** (b); **Danny Burger** (d); **Lou Colombo** (t). Sunnyside Ⓕ SSC 1039 D (65 minutes). Recorded 1989.

⑦ ❼

John Coltrane so liked d'Ambrosio's voice that in 1963 he invited her to tour with his quartet. She declined the offer so we can only speculate as to how her intimate singing style would have fitted with the saxophonist's pyrotechnics. It was more than 20 years later (motherhood intervened) before d'Ambrosio finally made her mark in the jazz world with a series of intriguing, erratic records for the Sunnyside Label. **South to a Warmer Place** is the best of these.

Her love of wincingly cute lyrics is held in check on a set that comprises mostly high-class romantic standards such as *The Touch of Your Lips, Dream Dancing* and *More Than You Know*. After trying several instrumental settings on previous albums with varying degrees of success, d'Ambrosio sounds completely at home with this lightly-swinging trio. Coffman and Burger (plus Colombo, who guests on four of the 17 tracks) offer discreet support, while husband Higgins threads bright piano lines through the songs, his slashes of colour a perfect foil for her low voice and quietly compelling style. **GL**

Tadd Dameron

1917-1965

Fontainebleau **Dameron** (p, comp); **Kenny Dorham** (t); **Henry Coker** (tb); **Sahib Shihab** (as); **Joe Alexander** (ts); **Cecil Payne** (bs); **John Simmons** (b); **Shadow Wilson** (d). Prestige Ⓜ OJCCD 055-2 (31 minutes). Recorded 1956.

✓ ⑧ ❻

Tadd Dameron is the least well known of the great jazz composers. Many of his themes became jazz standards during the bebop era (*Ladybird*, *Our Delight*, etc.) and his small-group recordings with bands including Fats Navarro, Wardell Gray and Alan Eager are among the finest of their period. He also provided some superb arrangements for the young Sarah Vaughan. But Dameron found few opportunities to develop his talent for composition, in particular for orchestration.

The title piece of this disc is the most substantial work he succeeded in completing. Typically, it is scored for the smallest possible line-up and the shortage of rehearsal time is sometimes painfully obvious, but a distinct atmosphere comes through nonetheless. The effect is not unlike that of Monk's early Blue Note sessions, produced under similar circumstances, although the melodies and harmonic structures are unmistakably Dameronian. *Fontainebleau* is that rare thing, a completely through-written jazz composition (like Ellington's *Harlem*). It is in three linked sections—*Le Foret*, *Les Cygnes*, *L'Adieu*—and Dameron was inspired to write it after visiting Fontainebleau while he was in Paris for the 1949 jazz festival. Although there are no improvised solos, it could only ever be performed by jazz musicians. Interestingly, Dameron recorded *Fontainebleau* again in 1962, with a full band and proper rehearsal, but the result has nothing like the personality and depth of the 1956 original. The remaining five tracks are rather sketchy performances, presumably because time was running out, but the title piece is a classic.

The original recording quality was far from brilliant, but the CD transfer has improved matters somewhat. **DG**

Dameronia

Live At The Theatre Boulogne—Billancourt, Paris **Don Sickler** (t, cond); **Virgil Jones** (t); **Benny Powell** (tb); **Clifford Jordan** (ts); **Cecil Payne** (bs); **Walter Davis Jr** (p); **Larry Ridley** (b); **Kenny Washington** (d). Soul Note Ⓕ 121202-2 (67 minutes). Recorded 1989.

⑥ ❽

Drummer Philly Joe Jones struck on the idea of having a band dedicated to the music of the late Tadd Dameron, a pianist and composer whose multi-dimensional music had fitted most circumstances and had served the bebop pioneers ideally. The problem was that most of the scores had been lost and it was not until 1982 that Jones, together with transcribers Don Sickler and John Oddo, set about producing a 'book'. The result was Dameronia, an excellent band and a triumphant celebration of Dameron's music.

Sadly, Jones died in 1985, but this new manifestation of the band came about in 1989, using seven players involved in the early eighties. This CD pays tribute to Dameron's memory and, at the same time, produces music of immediate appeal. The choices of tempo are sympathetic, the themes get a chance to breathe and the mood of the composer is never shattered. The reeds as a team are especially effective but solo interludes, provided by Jordan's tenor on *Philly J.J.*, Wess's almost Hodges-like alto on *Soultrane* and Powell's shapely trombone on *Gnid* and *Good Bait*, lend further substance to music that makes it difficult to believe that Dameron has been gone for 30 years. **BMcR**

Eddie Daniels

1941

To Bird With Love **Daniels** (cl); **Fred Hersch** (p, elp); **Roger Kellaway** (p); **John Patitucci** (b); **Al Foster** (d); **Steve Thornton** (perc). GRP Ⓕ 95442 (53 minutes). Recorded 1987.

⑥ ❾

Initially a saxophonist, Daniels was six years with the Thad Jones-Mel Lewis Orchestra. In more recent times, he has concentrated on clarinet and has been featured in the Benny Rides Again group with Gary Burton. This CD takes him on an entirely different route. He plays tunes associated with Charlie Parker and does so with consummate artistry. He has a superb technique, a pure tone and he swings effortlessly. He is creative at all tempos but does move into double time when not always appropriate and his tempo choices for *East Of The Sun* and *Just Friends* are suspect. More significantly, his style is not entirely suitable for Parker's music. His phrase shapes do not sit naturally wlth bebop and, not surprisingly, it is his respectful *Old Folks* reading and the loping perambulations of *Repetition* that show him at his best. In a duet with Kellaway, he takes *Why Do I Love You?* to the brink of contemporary chamber music. Daniels remains a gifted player whose technical accomplishments sometimes cloud his creative vision. **BMcR**

Lars Danielsson

...Continuation **Danielsson** (b); **John Abercrombie** (g); **Adam Nussbaum** (d) L+R Records Ⓕ CDLR 45085 (58 minutes) Recorded 1993.

⑦ ❽

Continuation is both the name of this début album from the young Swedish bass player and also the name of the trio which plays on it. Danielsson has an exceptionally wide list of career credits, having played with Herbie Hancock, John Scofield, Michael Brecker, Mike Stern, Bob Berg, Bill Evans, Muhal Richard Abrams, Flora Purim and Victor Lewis, among others. His technique is in the tradition of Scott LaFaro, his sense of time a cross between the late bassist and Dave Holland, while his sound is clear and resonant.

Abercrombie enjoys the space this set-up allows him, producing solos and interplay which come across as utterly involved. His overall contribution shows him to be listening closely to what is going on around him, and he gets plenty of bite into his tone and execution. Nussbaum is his usual sensitive and immaculate self. If you intend purchasing this, then be warned that you will have to be someone who enjoys bass solos. Although Danielsson doesn't take many, there is the occasional one. All such things are made up for by the wonderful way he can walk that bass; just try the middle section of *Flykt* for a demonstration of this fine, fine art. **KS**

Palle Danielsson 1946

Contra Post **Danielsson** (b); **Joakim Milder** (ss, ts); **Rita Marcotulli** (p); **Goran Klinghagen** (g); **Anders Kjellberg** (d). Caprice Ⓕ Cap 21440 (58 minutes). Recorded 1994.

⑥ ❽

Although he has recorded with many different leaders, this is Danielsson's first album under his own name; it features the quartet he has led on a number of tours. Rita Marcotulli is Italian, the other musicians are Swedish and most of the tracks were recorded at Norway's outstanding Rainbow Studios in Oslo. At times the music takes on the precious feeling of an ECM session (and the clarity of Jan Erik Kongshaug's recording certainly places it in the ECM class as far as technical reproduction is concerned). One is tempted to say that self-indulgence takes over on some of the pieces, which tend to sprawl as if waiting for the hint of a climax, but it must also be said that others build well (although *Not Yet* cuts off in mid-flight) and Marcotulli's *7 Notes, 7 Days, 7 Planets,* based on a repeated, hypnotic seven-note phrase is pleasingly orthodox in construction. The opening track (a fine unaccompanied bass solo) and the guitar-bass duets were taped at Danielsson's own residence, south of Stockholm, and have a warmth and intimacy of their own: the duet version of *Monk's Mood* is a highlight. Danielsson has worked and recorded with men such as Zoot Sims, Al Cohn, Peter Erskine, Jan Garbarek, Keith Jarrett, Bill Evans, Charles Lloyd, Barney Wilen and the outstanding Knut Riisnaes but one must assume that this CD represents his own preferred musical environment. **AM**

Harold Danko 1947

Alone But Not Forgotten **Danko** (p), **Marc Johnson, Michael Moore** (b); **Joe LaBarbera** (d), **Bob Dorough** (v); **John LaBarbera** (arr). Sunnyside Ⓕ SSC 1033D (46 minutes). Recorded 1985-86.

⑦ ❽

Harold Danko came up through the ranks of the latter-day Woody Herman Herds, as did the three other instrumentalists present here. This album, however, betrays little of that legacy, as it was made with the firm idea of being a romantic record. Hence the lack of rip-roaring up-tempo numbers (something Danko is pretty good at) and the prevalence of undulating melody lines, rich harmonic shifts and exotic rhythms. Most of the pieces are Danko's own, but he makes some excellent choices from others' pens, including Cal Tjader's charming waltz, *Liz Ann*, and Bill Evans's *Laurie*, although the latter is graced with a typical Bob Dorough vocal.

Danko's thorough grounding in harmony makes this an ever-interesting experience, as he finds endlessly apposite vertical substitutions and fresh melodic ways through sets of chords, making this an album of inner voices in more than one way. The rhythm team move as one with him and nothing happens here which does not evidence a high quality of input from all concerned. **KS**

John Dankworth 1927

The Roulette Years **Dankworth** (as, ldr); **Ron Simmons, Leon Calvert, Kenny Wheeler, Gus Galbraith, Dickie Hawdon, Derrick Abbott, Stan Palmer, Colin Wright, Bob Carson** (t); **Tony Russell, Eddie Harvey, Ray Premru, Laurie Monk, Danny Ellwood, Garry Brown** (tb); **Ron Snyder** (tba); **Roy East, Peter King** (as); **Danny Moss, Art Ellefson** (ts); **Vic Ash** (ts, cl); **Bob Efford** (bcl); **Frank Reidy** (bcl, as); **Ronnie Ross, Alex Leslie** (bs); **Alan Branscombe, Dave Lee** (p); **Spike Heatley, Kenny Napper, Eric Dawson, Ronnie Stephenson, Kenny Clare** (d). Roulette Ⓜ CDP7 96566 2 (75 minutes). Recorded 1959/61.

⑥ ❽

After the dissolution of the Seven, Dankworth formed a big band which became the first British orchestra of its type to get a recording contract with an American label. The 18 titles here are representative of the often Basie-inspired writing by Dankworth and his arranger Dave Lindup, but there are also some excellent scores by Dickie Hawdon and Tony Russell. The opening *Curtain Up* starts innocuously but builds steadily to an exciting climax and is a heartening introduction. Hawdon's crackling Clifford Brown-inspired trumpet is perhaps the band's strongest solo voice and his feature, *Tribute To Chauncey*, stands comparison with any comparable band of the time. Some of the leader's writing is deceptively lightweight, almost as if it had been conceived as film music, but invariably the solos and the might of the ensemble add strength. Just occasionally one is conscious of the lack of inspiration from the rhythm section, but this was a very good band and the solos by Hawdon and Danny Moss in particular have not dated. The CD contains two previously unissued tracks in Dave Lee's feature *Blue Furs* and Dave Lindup's *Caribé*. The remastering is excellent. **AM**

James Dapogny

1940

Original Jelly Roll Blues **Dapogny** (p); **Jon-Erik Kellso, Paul Klinger** (c); **Bob Smith** (tb); **Mike Walbridge** (tba); **Kim Cusack** (cl, as); **Peter Ferran** (cl, ss, as); **Russ Whitman** (cl, ts); **Rod McDonald** (bj, g); **Wayne Jones** (d). Discovery Ⓕ 74008 (61 minutes). Recorded 1993.

⑥ ❻

Dapogny's Chicago Jazz Band is one of the leading traditional bands in the US, with a long history and recordings for Jazzology dating from the early eighties. It is also, most importantly, a repertory band, and its unique strengths stem from the personal and scholarly interests of its leader. Jim Dapogny, as well as having edited the monumental Smithsonian edition of Jelly Roll Morton's piano music, is a fervent advocate of the live performance of Morton's oeuvre, bringing his considerable keyboard, arranging and bandleading skills to bear in playing this music sympathetically and well. Here his band is a model of revivalism, with none of the stilted rhythm often found in this type of group. The beat is laid back and relaxed, not least due to Dapogny's own keyboard work. He is a far more subtle and expert player of Morton's piano style than virtually anyone else playing today, with the possible exception of Butch Thompson. But his real achievement was to apply his musicological skills to create new arrangements in the style of various sizes of Morton bands for pieces that only survive in piano versions, like *Seattle Hunch* and *Chicago Breakdown*. **AS**

Carlo Actis Dato

Ankara Twist **Actis Dato** (ts, bs, bcl); **Piero Ponzo** (as, bs, bcl, f); **Enrico Fazio** (b); **Fiorenzo Sordini** (d, perc). Splasc(h) Ⓕ 302-2 (72 minutes). Recorded 1989.

⑧ ❽

Tarantellas, saltarellos and istampitas may mean nothing to most jazz listeners, but they're the life blood of Carlo Actis Dato. One of a generation or more of Italian (that includes Sicilian and Sardinian) musicians who look to their roots music for inspiration, Actis Dato has arranged original material based on various dance forms—some dating back to medieval times—using ostinatos, repetition and cyclical themes. The rhythms are infectiously buoyant and reflect the intermingling of different cultures in historical Italy, with Greek and Balkan influences as well as an audible Moorish presence. In a vivid sense, Actis Dato and cohorts draw on folk traditions rather than those of jazz (that is, in their fluent improvising the details are less important than heightening the moment, extending the spirit of the tune. Invention takes a back-seat to intensity) and Actis Dato is an intense soloist, especially on baritone saxophone, where he is liable to erupt à la Mount Vesuvius. Fellow reedman Ponzo is an apt, engaging foil, and together the saxes twist lines around the bass and drums with an almost satiric abandon. There is nothing in this music that you could call profound, but taken in small doses, it is intoxicating. **AL**

Kenny Davern

1935

Dick Wellstood and His All-Star Orchestra Featuring Kenny Davern **Davern** (ss, cl); **Dick Wellstood** (p); **Bobby Rosengarden** (d). Chiaroscuro Ⓕ 129 (78 minutes). Recorded 1973/81.

⑧ ❼

Do not be confused by the billing. The 'orchestra' consists solely of Wellstood's 88s, and he and Davern are equal partners. Half the disc is a reissue of a Chiaroscuro LP of the same name, Wellstood duetting with Davern's soprano sax; the other half is a Chaz Jazz LP by the Blue Three, with Davern on clarinet and adding Rosengarden's drum patter. The repertoire is a heavy on Jelly Roll, as might be expected, with singular excursions into the ODJB, Tin Pan Alley, and even Monk. The latter's *Blue Monk* is one of two informal homages to Pee Wee Russell (Russell having performed this with Monk at Newport), with Davern's clarinet essaying Pee Wee-like pitch bending, unpredictable swoops and groans. On the second, *Oh Peter* from the 1933 Rhythmakers date, Davern growls à la Pee Wee while Wellstood evokes Joe Sullivan's flash. Together with Rosengarden, the three stalk each other like bloodhounds. Other trio highlights include a leisurely stroll through *Indiana*; a *Tiger Rag* that begins as a rag and ends as a stop, without the cornball dixie-isms; and *Please Don't Talk About Me*... with a passage so evanescent the tune nearly evaporates. Without the drummer, the duo is more intimate, despite the brassier tone of the soprano and Wellstood's rolling orchestral chords. Davern does a terrific job approximating Armstrong's power on *Wild Man Blues*, elsewhere offering fluid commentaries without overt Bechet-isms, with Wellstood *Wallering* in and out of stride. Of course, Davern's playing in Soprano Summit was marvellous, but this disc is special too. **AL**

Lowell Davidson

1941-1990

Lowell Davidson Trio **Davidson** (p); **Gary Peacock** (b); **Milford Graves** (d). ESP-Disk Ⓜ ESP 1012-2 (45 minutes). Recorded 1965.

⑥ ❺

This is Davidson's only record as a leader, and although it was announced as part of the initial ESP programme back in the mid-sixties, it was in fact never released. So 1993 marked its first appearance, three years after the pianist's death. It certainly did not deserve so harsh a fate, being absorbing music balanced stylistically around halfway between Paul Bley and Cecil Taylor. Davidson quite clearly had considerable technical facility, a formed compositional sense, and an awful lot of bad luck.

His partners on this disc, both considerably more celebrated than him and both still successfully pursuing their careers, give Davidson strong support. Peacock plays in the manner still associated with him today, although he is understandably a little more free with his phrasing here than with Jarrett and Co. Graves, ubiquitous on early ESP-Disk albums and a fine free drummer, makes a lively and not altogether inappropriate contribution, although I feel that a player such as Barry Altschul or Tony Williams would have helped Davidson a little more. **KS**

Anthony Davis 1951

Hemispheres **Davis** (p); **Leo Smith** (t, perc); **George Lewis** (tb); **Dwight Andrews** (f, picc, cl, ss, cond); **J.D. Parran** (cl, cbcl); **Shem Guibbory** (vn); **Eugene Friesen** (vc); **Rick Rozie** (cb); **David Samuels** (vb, mba); **Pheeroan akLaff** (d, perc). Gramavision Ⓕ R2 79428 (39 minutes). Recorded 1983.

⑨ ❽

The remarkable breadth of Anthony Davis's music is rare for one ostensibly identified as a jazz artist, which shows how confining such labels can be. From the critical and public success of his opera, *X*, to chamber trio improvisations, a violin concerto, programmatic tone poems for mixed ensembles, impressionistic solo piano recitals, and appearances as sideman on jazz dates, it is apparent Davis draws on multiple sources for inspiration. On the surface, **Hemispheres** would seem to have little connection to jazz. Composed to a commission from the modern choreographer Molissa Fenley, the suite's five movements speak with a harmonic language more familiar to classical than jazz listeners, and the intricate rhythmic emphasis (structured around contrasting complex metres and layers of heavily accented rhythms) reflect Davis's interest in Stravinsky as well as music from Africa, Bali and Java. But there are precedents in the music of Mingus and Ellington—in fact, one can hear the fourth movement as an extended Ducal meditation on an exotic theme, with intimations of Ray Nance's violin, Lawrence Brown's trombone, and Duke's piano; or Leo Smith's solo entrance in the second movement atop a suggestion of big band riffing, echoes of New Orleans polyphony resonating within the classical counterpoint. The fluidity of Davis's scoring is masterful, the music accomplished and highly evocative, regardless of how you categorize it. **AL**

Charles Davis 1933

Reflections **Davis** (ts); **Barry Harris** (p); **Peter Washington** (d). Red Ⓕ RR 123247 (48 minutes). Recorded 1990.

⑥ ❽

Despite his lack of prominence Charles Davis is a veteran and gifted baritone saxophonist who has spent most of his career as a key sideman with people as diverse and Billie Holiday, Dinah Washington, Kenny Dorham, Sun Ra, Steve Lacy and the Thad Jones-Mel Lewis Jazz Orchestra. He is also a distinctive exponent of the soprano, but here restricts himself to tenor. His association with Barry Harris has persisted for some years and the latter's ascendancy in interpreting the music of Thelonious Monk is reflected in Davis's composition, *Monking*. There seems to be as much of Monk and Bud Powell about Harris's playing of his own composition *To Duke With Love* as there is Ellington. The rest of the pieces, all substantial, are composed by Davis. *Miriam's Delight* evokes Monk even more strongly since there is much of Monk's tenor player Charlie Rouse in Davis's own work here. The influence of Coltrane (with whom Davis once worked) is minimal, and indeed Davis's softer tone is more out of Hawkins via Hank Mobley.

Barry Harris's piano playing is something to savour on every track; he must surely be one of the most gifted of the bop pianists. Like those of Davis, his solos are both strongly constructed and unfailingly imaginative. **SV**

Eddie 'Lockjaw' Davis 1921-1986

The Eddie 'Lockjaw' Davis Cookbook Volume 1 **Davis** (ts); **Jerome Richardson** (f, ts); **Shirley Scott** (org); **George Duvivier** (b); **Arthur Edgehill** (d). Prestige Ⓜ OJCCD-652-2 (41 minutes). Recorded 1958.

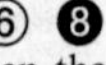

Lockjaw was, like several of his contemporaries such as Gene Ammons, a living bridge between the tenor tradition of the thirties and the post-rhythm & blues of the fifties. Temperamentally, rhythmically and sometimes tonally close to Illinois Jacquet, Davis seemed more complex; yet, despite his stylistic link with the tortuous phrasing of Paul Gonsalves, his choppy terseness gave him a direct line to the populace. Appropriately, he was the virtual founder of the tenor-and-organ trio, using players such as Bill Doggett on record as early as 1949 and fronting a regular trio from 1954 onwards. The five years in which the keyboardist was Shirley Scott represented Lockjaw's popular peak, and her relatively subdued approach and awareness of dynamics providing a suitable contrast to his brusque attack. Although his up-tempo playing is most immediately compelling, the heart of his work is the ballads (here *But Beautiful*) and slow blues (*In The Kitchen*, themeless but mistakenly credited to Johnny Hodges).

On most tracks guest Richardson is restricted to flute, played as it was before Lateef and Kirk showed everyone how. Davis's preceding album, where the guests were Count Basie and Joe Newman, might be more desirable if transferred to CD, but meanwhile this will do nicely. **BP**

Miles Davis

1926-1991

Birth Of The Cool **Davis** (t); **Kai Winding, J.J. Johnson** (tb); **Junior Collins, Sandy Siegelstein, Gunther Schuller** (frh); **John Barber** (tba); **Lee Konitz** (as); **Gerry Mulligan** (bs); **Al Haig, John Lewis** (p); **Joe Shulman, Nelson Boyd, Al McKibbon** (b); **Max Roach, Kenny Clarke** (d); **Kenny Hagood** (v). Capitol Ⓜ CDP7 92862-2 (36 minutes). Recorded 1949/50.

✔ ⑩ ❼

This is the nine-piece band which lasted two weeks in public, made a total of a dozen 78 rpm sides and has had an influence on jazz lasting more than four decades. So much has been written about the music and the circumstances which brought this particular grouping of musicians and arrangers together that further comment now is largely superfluous. This CD brings together all 12 titles (inexplicably not in chronological order of sessions, let alone individual titles) and, while the transfers have not magically added anything that was not on the Dutch Capitol LP—the best previous manifestation of the music—then it has not taken anything away either. There is still so much to study, understand and enjoy here that, like the best in any art form, it has proved to be timeless. Johnny Carisi's handling of the traditional blues form in *Israel* is an object lesson in ingenuity; Davis's *Boplicity* (a collaboration with Gil Evans) is musical poetry while Mulligan's handling of *Darn That Dream* makes Kenny Hagood's accurate singing all the more remarkable. No self-respecting jazz collection can claim to be complete without this important music and, despite the meagre playing time, the CD is strongly recommended. **AM**

Chronicle **Davis** (t); with a collective personnel of **J.J. Johnson, Benny Green** (tb); **Lee Konitz, Jackie McLean, Dave Schildkraut** (as); **John Coltrane, Sonny Rollins, Lucky Thompson, Charlie Parker, Zoot Sims, Al Cohn** (ts); **Milt Jackson** (vb); **Thelonious Monk, Red Garland, Horace Silver, John Lewis, Walter Bishop Jr, Tommy Flanagan, Ray Bryant, Sal Mosca** (p); **Billy Bauer** (g); **Percy Heath, Paul Chambers, Charles Mingus, Oscar Pettiford** (b); **Kenny Clarke, Philly Joe Jones, Art Taylor, Art Blakey, Max Roach, Roy Haynes** (d). Prestige Ⓕ 8PCD 012-2 (eight discs: 522 minutes). Recorded 1951-56.

✔ ⑧ ❻

This set contains the complete recordings in 17 sessions which Davis made for Prestige. It also chronicles the first major movement in jazz after the bebop and cool periods. When the first recordings were made Davis had suffered a setback in his playing, brought on by the euphemistic "personal problems". The opening session, with Sonny Rollins on tenor and John Lewis on piano, has one flawed masterpiece in *Blue Room*. An early session under Lee Konitz's name had cool music more typical of the altoist, and was followed by more sessions with Sonny Rollins. On the second of these Charlie Parker also played tenor, and although Bird was not on his normal inspired form, these tracks are not nearly as bad as has sometimes been suggested. A session with Cohn and Sims was more interesting for Cohn's compositions and arrangements than for the solos, and it was not until the subsequent sessions that Davis is heard playing with the command and confidence which were to be with him for the rest of his career. There are some stark but appealing quartet blues in the early sessions, and indeed blues pieces abound until the emergence of the classic quartet with Coltrane.

The recordings with Milt Jackson and Monk are amongst the best examples of a post-swing jam session and the inclusion of long alternate takes of *The Man I Love* and *Bags' Groove* is totally justified by the excellence of the music. The final three discs are given over to the quintet with Coltrane and Red Garland—a virtual jazz crucible and one of the most influential small groups since Louis Armstrong's Hot Five. The intensity of invention produced in the reworking of such a host of good and unhackneyed standards is breath-taking and the high standards rarely falter. While appreciating the quintet as a unit, the piano playing of Red Garland should be especially noted as some of the best in a career which often took him away from the limelight.

And the fuse was by this time well alight on the bomb that John Coltrane was carrying. **SV**

'Round About Midnight **Davis** (t); **John Coltrane** (ts); **Red Garland** (p); **Paul Chambers** (b); **Philly Joe Jones** (d). Columbia Ⓜ 460605-2 (39 minutes). Recorded 1955-56.

✔ ⑩ ❽

For anyone seeking a single representative album of the classic Miles Davis Quintet of the mid-fifties, this is it. All the individual strengths and stylistic innovations which made this one of the most influential bands in jazz history are summed up in these six numbers.

The poignant, lost quality of Miles's trumpet sound, indispensable background music to fashionable life in the late fifties, commands the attention, even when surrounded by such strong musical personalities as Coltrane and Philly Joe. This effect is particularly striking when he plays through a harmon mute directly into the microphone, as he does here in *'Round Midnight, All of You* and *Bye Bye Blackbird*. His phrases are simple in outline but generate an extraordinary feeling of tension because of the way he poises them over the light, springy beat. This in itself was a complete departure from the clenched, nervous rhythms of bebop. Everything about this record sounds as fresh today as when it first appeared, even though endless imitation has reduced some of its most original strokes to clichés.

This is the original Columbia mono LP transferred to CD and the playing time is short, although there are several more pieces from the same sessions which might also have been included. The digital transfers are very effective. **DG**

Miles Ahead **Davis** (f); **Gil Evans** (arr); **Bernie Glow**, **Ernie Royal**, **Taft Jordan**, **Louis Mucci**, **John Carisi** (t); **Willie Ruff**, **Tony Miranda**, **Jimmy Buffington** (frh); **Frank Rehak**, **Jimmy Cleveland**, **Joe Bennett** (tb); **Tom Mitchell** (btb); **Bill Barber** (tba); **Lee Konitz** (as); **Danny Bank** (bcl); **Romeo Penque**, **Sid Cooper**, **Eddie Caine** (fl, cl); **Wynton Kelly** (p); **Paul Chambers** (b); **Art Taylor** (d). Columbia Ⓜ CK 53225 (37 minutes). Recorded 1957.

✔ ⑩ ❽

According to George Avakian's notes this was recorded on a two-track machine which Columbia had acquired just days before the 1957 recording date, thus capturing binaurally something which couldn't come out in stereo then. Not until now, in fact, and this CD confirms what you always knew—that if it is not the finest jazz big band record ever made, then nobody ever made a better. Three odd things emerge. One is that there were no saxophones among the 19, except for Lee Konitz. Another is that, at less than 40 minutes, it was pretty short even for an LP. The third is that the star of the record is not Miles Davis, but Gil Evans, whose writing is the wonderful river that carries Davis's frail boat towards the sea. Davis's fragile, poignant sound is really just a foil for the ever-changing colour of the Evans sound, which moves faster and more flexibly than Miles ever does. This is the **Birth of the Cool** in its maturity. One other odd thing: even on his greatest record, jazz composer Gil Evans wrote none of the tunes. **MK**

Porgy And Bess **Davis** (t, flh); **Ernie Royal**, **Bernie Glow**, **Johnny Coles**, **Louis Mucci** (t); **Dick Hixon**, **Frank Rehak**, **Jimmy Cleveland**, **Joe Bennett** (tb); **Willie Ruff**, **Julius Watkins**, **Gunther Schuller** (frh); **John 'Bill' Barber** (tba); **Phil Bodner**, **Romeo Penque**, **Jerome Richardson** (f); **Julian 'Cannonball' Adderley** (as); **Danny Bank** (bs, bcl); **Paul Chambers** (b); **Philly Joe Jones**, **Jimmy Cobb** (d). Columbia Ⓜ 450985 2 (51 minutes). Recorded 1958.

✔ ⑧ ❽

This, the second orchestral collaboration between Miles Davis and Gil Evans on Columbia, re-emerged as a digitally remastered CD in 1991, and the new incarnation offers a significant improvement in clarity over the analogue issue. Mercifully, it also escapes the idle meddling accorded the original digital reissue of **Miles Ahead**, where several of the originally-issued takes were supplanted by alternatives. This **Porgy** is not without its problems however, and although they are small, they exemplify Columbia's casual neglect of the masterpieces in its charge. By now, surely, the blurb could note that Daniel Banks plays bass clarinet as well as baritone, and offer some account of the vagaries of the mixing on *Here Comes De Honey Man*, where at 21 seconds the right channel volume suddenly leaps up. Charles Smith's original note does, however, illuminate the chief business of the record, namely the singularity and sensitivity of Evans's orchestral conceptions, and the aptness of his adaptations of themes from Gershwin's folk-opera for Miles Davis's style. By this time Miles had devised an unassailable rationale for his circumscribed technique and cool aesthetic, and the settings here suit it well. He is able to exercise his lyric intensity on such as *Prayer*, or swing lightly at a sympathetic medium tempo over simple, sometimes modal harmonies of the sort heard on *It Ain't Necessarily So* without fear of meeting a *Donna Lee* or an *Ornithology*. **MG**

Kind of Blue **Davis** (t); **Julian 'Cannonball' Adderley** (as); **John Coltrane** (ts); **Bill Evans**, **Wynton Kelly** (p); **Paul Chambers** (b); **Jimmy Cobb** (d). Columbia Ⓜ 460603-2 (45 minutes). Recorded 1959.

✔ ⑩ ❽

Few albums have been granted the destiny this one received. Recorded when each of its participants was at a personal peak of one kind or another, it is both a celebration of what has gone before in their careers and a door opening on the next ten years of small-group modern jazz.

Davis, with the help of pianist Evans (and the input of arranger Gil Evans), prepared a set of charts for the recording sessions which, for the most part, abandoned the conventional song structures and bop changes, substituting instead a series of interrelated scales, or modes. This allowed the soloist the freedom to develop any improvisational angle he chose, and it is fascinating to hear the quite different approaches taken by the four main soloists to music they had not had a chance to get accustomed to before the sessions. Miles revels in the new space he finds for himself, becoming even more rhythmically daring than before, using pauses and sudden ringing notes to great effect. Adderley is stimulated to some remarkably fresh invention. His usual busy style is modified somewhat and his choice of notes more judicious than before. Coltrane, especially on the medium-tempo *So What* and

Freddie Freeloader, invents complications for himself, but also relies heavily on thematic improvisation—a comparative rarity in his work.

Bill Evans sounds like a man reborn, and gives a perfect performance, whether as accompanist or as soloist. His playing, more than any others', dictates the extraordinary mood of the album (Wynton Kelly is present on *Freddie Freeloader* and generally sticks to the Evans approach, albeit with a touch more funk), and it is no accident that Miles chose him as collaborator.

There is little need to enumerate the many felicities of this unique record, although I would mention one personal favourite—Coltrane's heartstopping entrance to, and exquisite lyricism during, his *Flamenco Sketches* solo.

KS

The Complete Concert: 1964 **Davis** (t); **George Coleman** (ts); **Herbie Hancock** (p); **Ron Carter** (b); **Tony Williams** (d). Columbia Ⓜ 471246-2 (two discs: 120 minutes). Recorded 1964.

⑨ ❽

Originally marketed as two separate releases, the landmark **My Funny Valentine** and **Four and More**, this new compilation of the entire 1964 Carnegie Hall concert is almost pure pleasure. The one caveat is Columbia's decision not to re-sequence the tracks in accordance with their placement in the original programme; as a result, the second disc (the original **Four**) is one up-tempo tune after another. Even more spurious is the repetition of Mort Fega's 're-introduction' of the group in the middle of each disc, a deceptive dodge suggesting that the original concert consisted of four parts!

Otherwise, this is one of Davis's great straight-ahead acoustic bands at the apex of its powers. There is the justly celebrated rhythm section of Hancock, Carter and Williams. Equally significant is the incandescent and yet lyrical tenor saxophone of George Coleman, inexplicably one of the least appreciated of prominent ex-Davis sidemen. Indeed, there is an argument to be made that it is Coleman that gives this particular Davis group its transcendent and distinctive sound. The repertory of timeless standards, in spite of the sequencing, includes *All of You*, *Stella by Starlight*, *All Blues*, *Walkin'* and *So What*. There is also a brilliant extended exploration of the poignant *My Funny Valenine,* with Coleman's nonpareil solo, and the dashing *Four*.

CB

The Complete Live At The Plugged Nickel, 1965 **Davis** (t); **Wayne Shorter** (ts); **Herbie Hancock** (p); **Ron Carter** (b); **Tony Williams** (d). Columbia Ⓜ CXK 66955 (seven discs: 454 minutes). Recorded 1965.

⑧ ❻

Over two nights at Chicago's Plugged Nickel Club, just before Christmas in 1965, Columbia's microphones picked up every nuance and every shade of every set by one of the best Miles Davis quintets, hovering on the cusp between hard-swinging conventional jazz, the opening up of time and form that constituted Miles's flirtation with freer music, plus some presaging of jazz rock. Not issued at the time, highlights were released in the form of two LPs nigh on two decades later. Now, as we become eager to understand more about Miles, how he worked, what he did and his role in the development of the music, it is fitting to follow on the 1992 release of the bulk of this material on Japanese Columbia with a US issue of every remaining scrap. As a document, this is as comprehensive and useful as the GRP release of Louis Armstrong's **California Concerts**, an equally warts-and-all presentation of a master at work.

Musically, despite the formulaic repetition of the set-list from one house to the next, the variety and invention of the quintet makes listening through the several hours of material a valuable exercise. There is a trap in the study of recorded jazz that makes one view a particular performance as definitive. This album debunks that view, with radically different readings of standards like *My Funny Valentine*, neither of them conforming to the studio or earlier live versions, but both showing an inventive and ever-changing approach. Here, as on *Stella By Starlight*, the melody itself often counts for little, Davis and Shorter's own melodic gifts substituting paraphrase and fragmentation for the coherence of the original. Carter's bass proves to be the lynch-pin of the band, anchoring harmony and time with understated confidence. Williams adds flamboyant and complex textures on drums, particularly apparent in the two takes of *Agitation*, the first marked by Miles's rapid-fire phrases running all over the horn in parallel with the shifting drum rhythms. Hancock frequently lays out, leaving just bass and drums to carry the soloist. His own solos are understated, too, if masterly, and he adds just the right level of support for Miles in transition and Shorter on the verge of becoming a major soloist.

AS

Miles Smiles **Davis** (t); **Wayne Shorter** (ts); **Herbie Hancock** (p); **Ron Carter** (b); **Tony Williams** (d). Columbia Ⓜ 471004 2 (42 minutes). Recorded 1966.

✔

⑩ ❿

Hancock and Williams came into the band in 1963 and Shorter joined in 1964. These changes presaged a considerable shift in the way that Davis approached his music. He seemed willing for the dynamic Williams to assume the emotional reins and for Shorter and Hancock to have a greater say in the choice of material and in writing duties. Commencing with **E.S.P.** (Columbia 467899-2), his recording sessions concentrated on a new book and a new freedom. Davis, hospitalized during the period, had been able to re-assemble his group without loss when he returned to the scene and this CD endorses the kind of unity that the new line-up had established. The programme includes three originals by Shorter and one by Davis, and finds both horn players reacting in their own way to the rhythmic challenges thrown down by Williams. Eddie Harris's *Freedom Jazz Dance* is typical, with Davis taking an economical, open solo, using space as a vital element and allowing Williams front line status in a virtual trumpet/drum duo. Shorter makes a similar impact, both as a player and composer, and *Footprints*, with its adroit use of a five-note vamp in the *So What* manner, was perhaps his most memorable contribution. The same title also elicited from Davis a timeless performance, confirming that the trumpeter had again moved on as a creative force. **BMcR**

A Tribute to Jack Johnson **Davis** (t); **Steve Grossman** (ss); **Herbie Hancock** (kbds); **John McLaughlin** (g); **Michael Henderson** (elb); **Billy Cobham** (d). Columbia Ⓜ CK 47036 (53 minutes). Recorded 1970.

✓ ⑧ ❻

The personnel given above is that listed on some pressings of the original LP and on the CD reissue. Yet Sonny Sharrock has confirmed that the echoplex guitar solo toward the end of *Yesternow* is indeed his, and several other musicians are suspected to have participated in the recording sessions. Exact personnel is just one of the mysteries surrounding this television film documentary tribute to a boxer who dabbled in music by a trumpeter who dabbled in the ring. *Right Off*, the first of the two lengthy performances here, has the crunch of a studio jam, yet producer Teo Macero, probably pieced it together from several different sessions, just as he did the spacy *Yesternow*, which more obviously betrays signs of such after-the-fact editing.

Jack Johnson avoids the bombast of **Bitches Brew** and **Live Evil**, the empty noodling of **On the Corner** and (save for parts of *Yesternow*) the pleasant tinkering of **In a Silent Way**. Yet it is not completely satisfying as jazz *or* rock; if you wanted to explain to someone why fusion is not rock & roll, all you would need to do is play this and tell him to concentrate on Billy Cobham's tight drumming. For all of that, the album has its electrifying moments, most of them coming either from the superb McLaughlin or when Davis aims for his upper register on *Right Off*. **FD**

On the Corner **Davis** (t, org?); **Dave Liebman**, **Carlos Garnett** (ss, ts); **Teo Macero?** (sax); **Bennie Maupin** (bcl); **Chick Corea** (elp); **Herbie Hancock**, **Harold I. Williams** (elp, syn); **David Creamer**, **John McLaughlin** (g); **Colin Walcott** (sitar); **Michael Henderson** (b); **Jack DeJohnette**, **Billy Hart** (d); **Badal Roy**, **Don Alias**, **James Mtume Foreman** (perc). Columbia Ⓜ CK 53579 (55 minutes). Recorded 1972.

⑥ ❻

On first release, **On the Corner** was greeted with open hostility by critics and musicians, and indifference on the part of record buyers. In retrospect, it is apparent they were all listening for things that were not there: harmonic motion, prominent trumpet, clear demarcation between soloist and rhythm section. Miles said in his autobiography that in the seventies he wanted his music to be more African, less European. This loud electric band—strings, keyboards, percussion and trumpet played (like the guitars) through a wah-wah pedal—functions more like an African drum choir than a jazz group, with each player adding another layer to the polyrhythmic weave. With vamps that go on forever, these pieces appear to be about stasis rather than progress, but that is an illusion; it is just that the rate of change tends to be slow. Soloists bubble up to and then slip back under the fluid surface.

If that description suggests an unlikely kinship between this street funk and the emerging minimalism of such composers as Steve Reich, who are also indebted to African percussion ensembles, give Miles the last word (from the Autobiography), "I got further and further into the idea of performance as process ... I never end songs, they just keep going on." (The question-marks over some of the personnel and instrumentation are a result of them never being adequately identified, either by Miles or the record company.) **KW**

Decoy **Davis** (t, syn); **Branford Marsalis**, **Bill Evans** (ss); **John Scofield** (g); **Robert Irving III** (syn, prog); **Darryl Jones** (b); **Al Foster** (d); **Mino Cinelu** (perc). Columbia Ⓜ 468702 2 (40 minutes). Recorded 1984.

⑧ ❻

The penultimate Columbia Miles Davis album, featuring two tracks recorded live in Montreal with one of his strongest electric bands, **Decoy** is one of the trumpeter's most straightforwardly accessible recordings. Although his relaunched career really took off with the (arguably inferior but more wine-bar-friendly) **You're Under Arrest** album of the following year, **Decoy** firmly established Davis as the most widely influential jazz figure of the eighties. Many have argued that his whole-hearted embracing of popular music's synthesized sound, hammered bass and unsubtle beats had stifled his creativity, but **Decoy** provides one of the best counter-arguments to this viewpoint. As in another underrated Davis album, **Agharta**, the leader's genius is manifest in subtle dynamic and textural shifts rather than, as previously, in flaring improvisational brilliance or an affecting poignancy of tone. In John Scofield he has his most sympathetic guitar foil since John McLaughlin, both Bill

Evans and Branford Marsalis are supremely competent without being remarkable, and Robert Irving's synthesizer and programming work sets off the front line to perfection. The rhythm section is taut and dependable without ever lapsing into the robotic monotony frequently characterizing music of this sort. **Decoy** is a late peak in a protean career which is perhaps only paralleled in jazz by that of Ellington's.
CP

Amandla **Davis** (t); **Kenny Garrett** (as, ss); **Rick Margitza** (ts); **Joe Sample** (p); **George Duke** (kbds, arr); **Joey DeFrancesco** (kbds); **John Bigham** (kbds, g, prog arr); **Michael Landau, Foley McCreary, Jean-Paul Bourelly, Steve Khan, Billy Patterson** (g); **Marcus Miller** (b, kbds, g, ss, bcl, d, arr); **Ricky Wellman, Omar Hakim, Al Foster** (d); **Don Alias, Mino Cinelu, Paulinho Da Costa, Bashiri Johnson** (perc); **Jason Miles** (prog). Warner Bros Ⓕ 925 873-2 (43 minutes: DDD). Recorded 1989.

⑧ ❿

Becoming bored with Miles's latest usually meant one was bored with life, or that one was merely nostalgic for his earlier work. Different listeners had different sticking-points, but even some who had gone along with him right up to the mid-eighties jumped off when he began adopting pre-recorded backgrounds. Despite their occasional use in **Jack Johnson** and **Get Up With It**, Miles almost invariably worked with a live band in the studio, even when less creative and less forward-looking souls had all but abandoned the interactive approach.

All the backings on **Amandla**, with the exception of the bass and drums of the Gil Evans-like *Mr Pastorius*, were prepared in advance and masterminded (apart from two tracks) by the ubiquitous Marcus Miller. His melodic hooks are often simplistic but, as in *Jo-Jo* (very reminiscent of the slightly earlier **Tutu** album), his textures are less blatant than Miles's later touring bands, and the drums are often played with brushes. Many of the other musicians listed play on only one or two items—fortunately, in the case of the bland Joe Sample—but Kenny Garrett distinguishes himself throughout and Davis, taking it easy and mostly muted, still creates the old magic.
BP

Richard Davis

1930

One For Frederick **Davis** (b); **Cecil Bridgewater** (t); **Ricky Ford** (ts); **Roland Hanna** (p); **Frederick Waits** (d). Hep Ⓕ CD 2047 (74 minutes). Recorded 1989.

⑧ ❽

In the front rank of jazz bass players since the late fifties and equally at home in classical and rock settings (his contribution to Van Morrison's **Astral Weeks**, in particular, is a stunning piece of virtuosity), Richard Davis assembled this group of like-minded individuals for a tour of Japan in 1989. It brings its considerable collective musical experience—Waits's previous collaborations range from stints with Johnny Hodges to Cecil Taylor; Hanna's from Benny Goodman to James Newton—to bear on a repertoire broadly representative of small-group jazz from the sixties to the present. The quintet thus moves from Benny Golson, Horace Silver and Kenny Dorham tunes to Monkish Davis originals and a relaxed Bridgewater vehicle with all the ease and confidence born of technical mastery and familiarity with the material. Hanna is sly and delightfully eccentric without ever sliding into gratuitous idiosyncracy; the front line performs with controlled gusto and acerbic bite; Davis—as ever—is lithe, supple and simply one of the great bass soloists in the music (although a slow, bowed *Ev'ry Time We Say Goodbye* reveals occasional pitch problems). The album's dedicatee, Freddie Waits, who died shortly before its release, is faultless; sensitive to naunce but always propulsive. Recorded at New York's Sweet Basil the album showcases a great band swinging and relaxed in a congenial setting.
CP

Sammy Davis Jr

1925-1990

The Wham of Sam **Davis Jr** (v) with **The Marty Paich Dek-tette**: **Jack Sheldon, Al Porcino** or **John Audino** (t); **Stu Williamson** (tb); **Vince DeRosa** (frh); **William Hood, Bud Shank, Bill Perkins** (reeds); **Red Callender** (tba); **Joe Mondragon** (b); **Mel Lewis** (d); **Marty Paich** (arr, cond). Warner Bros Ⓜ 245637-2 (37 minutes). Recorded 1963.

⑥ ❽

Sammy Davis Jr as a jazz singer? For the vast majority of his career, frankly, no. But the jazz basis of his style would surface from time to time, no doubt guided by Sinatra's lead, and on this, his first session for Reprise after terminating his American Decca contract, he opted for arrangements and accompaniment from Paich and his unit which are not just jazz-drenched, they are jazz from go to whoa. With such tight, sophisticated and insightful arrangements of standards like *My Romance*, *Thou Swell*, *Can't We Be Friends?* and *Blame It On My Youth*, Davis Jr has firmly embraced the sort of territory often explored by Mel Tormé, and carries the whole thing off with no little panache. His way with lyrics remains essentially superficial, preferring mostly to skate elegantly across the rhythm patterns they present to him, but his phrasing and his habit of paraphrase owes everything to jazz stalwarts such as Armstrong, Lester Young, Billie and Ella.

Obviously scared to death about their new star's intentions, Reprise never issued these tracks as a single LP, but scattered them through Davis Jr's first batch of albums for them, leavening them with his more usual fare. This, then, is the first release of the Dek-Tette material as originally intended. **KS**

Walter Davis Jr 1932-1990

Illumination **Davis** (p); **Charles Sullivan** (t); **Carter Jefferson** (ts); **Jeremy Steig** (f); **Milton Frustino** (g); **Buster Williams** (b); **Bruno Carr**, **Art Blakey**, **Tony Williams** (d); **Nana** (perc). Denon Ⓕ DC-8553 (71 minutes). Recorded 1977.

⑥ ❻

As might be expected from a pianist whose career took off while he was playing with Charlie Parker and subsequently included stints with Dizzy Gillespie, Max Roach and the Jazz Messengers, the late Walter Davis Jr was as at home playing bop and hard bop as with Latin and other 'world' rhythms. Unfortunately, as a leader his undoubted virtuosity fatally lacks the restraint and discipline imposed by the demands of fitting into someone else's design, and **Illumination** is therefore a somewhat sprawling, over-frenetic affair, lacking in both variety and balance. Tempos, typically, are too rushed for musical clarity, and on the first session (the CD combines two 1977 dates) a distinctly substandard, tinny piano does not help matters, rendering Davis's upper-register work almost painful to the ear. Moreover, the recording's problems are compounded by Davis's apparent inability to keep quiet while he is playing, resulting in many tracks being disfigured by an irritatingly tuneless background humming. The second session features three solo piano pieces, an overblown, faintly ridiculous and utterly misguided attempt at *Abide with Me*, an over-embellished sub-Tatumesque *Just One of Those Things* and a rather gloomy version of Bud Powell's *I'll Keep Loving You*. His collaborators on the group tracks, despite their stellar status, are hampered by both the headlong rush of the tempos and by the cluttered natures of the arrangements, although Buster Williams's fat, almost furry bass sound is a joy throughout and Charles Sullivan's pure-toned trumpet, despite its use on a sickly rendition of Nino Rota's *Theme from La Strada*, is also noteworthy. Overall, however, these are two fatally flawed, if commendably energetic, sessions. **CP**

Wild Bill Davis 1918

At Birdland **Davis** (org); **Floyd Smith** (g); **Chris Columbus** (d). Columbia Ⓜ 471427-2 (49 minutes). Recorded 1955.

Although Wild Bill Davis was not the first jazz musician to turn to the Hammond organ, he was certainly the principal figure on the instrument in the late forties and early fifties. His trio dealt in excitement and was at its best when appearing in front of an enthusiastic audience. This CD was recorded during Davis's lengthy series of engagements at New York's 'Birdland' club, where he was a most popular figure. Issued originally as an Epic LP, the CD format retains the 'end-of-set' routine so the theme song *Linger Awhile* occurs in the middle and at the end. It was Wild Bill who wrote the "one more time" arrangement of *April In Paris* for Count Basie and the trio's version is included here, along with such foot-tapping favourites as *Lullaby of Birdland*, *Night Train* and *Jumpin' At The Woodside*. The music is seldom profound, but was hardly meant to be. The slightly claustrophobic atmosphere of the club might account for the closed-in relationship of the three instruments in the recording. **AM**

Wild Bill Davison 1906-1989

Stars Of Jazz Volume 1 **Wild Bill Davison** (c); **Jim Beebe** (tb); **Barney Bigard** (cl); **Art Hodes** (p); **Eddie Condon** (g); **Rail Wilson** (b); **Hillard Brown** (d). Jazzology Ⓕ JCD-62 (56 minutes). Recorded 1972.

⑥ ❻

By the time of this recording Davison, Bigard and Hodes had reached old age. Davison's style had matured and solidified, Bigard had never regained the bloom of his youthful playing and Hodes was the only one of the three who remained truly creative. The fiery attack and power which had gained Davison his nickname made him an exciting lead player, and earlier battles fought alongside Sidney Bechet and Edmond Hall showed him at his best in this role. But he also had the lyricism of an Irish tenor, his ballad playing moving but never cloying. His opening statement on *Just A Closer Walk With Thee* shows him at his expressive best, and his lead in the brief ensemble which follows it has a Bixian sense of form. His subsequent solo when the tempo doubles is genuinely hot and nicely underpinned by Condon. On such occasions one does not notice the limitations of Wild Bill's technique, but they matter little because he made so much of his limited palette. Jim Beebe is a good journeyman trombonist out of Jack Teagarden and Floyd O'Brien, while Hodes's piano playing at this concert was outstanding. Apart from *Grandpa's Spells*, which is a piano feature, the rest of the numbers are the usual Dixieland warhorses. **SV**

Doris Day

1922

Doris Day With Les Brown **Day** (v); **Les Brown Orchestra.** CBS Ⓜ 466958 (52 minutes). Recorded 1945-46.

⑥ ❻

The Les Brown band was always immaculate and tasteful with a good helping of jazz feeling. While it may seem unlikely on the strength of some rather cloying film roles ("I knew her before she was a virgin," said Oscar Levant), the same description applies to Miss Day.

Day is typical of the superb talents who were the big-band girl vocalists of the forties (Jo Stafford, Frances Wayne and June Christie were others). This well-chosen collection omits her biggest hit with Brown, *Sentimental Journey*, but splendid collaborations with the band like *Aren't You Glad You're You?* and *Come To Baby Do* show Day's impressive musicality and sense of time in combination with powerful work from the band, spiced with good instrumental solos. None of the soloists is identified, but the expressive tenor on a typically fine ballad like *We'll Be Together Again* is probably Ted Nash.

Apart from making the case for Day to be treated seriously as an excellent singer, the album is a fine showcase for one of the most immaculate and impressive of the big bands. Because of the skills involved all round, the music has hardly dated. **SV**

Blossom Dearie

1926

Once Upon a Summertime **Dearie** (v, p); **Mundell Lowe** (g); **Ray Brown** (b); **Ed Thigpen** (d). Verve Ⓜ 517 223-2 (36 minutes). Recorded 1958.

⑧ ❽

It is hard to be anything but subjective when it comes to Blossom Dearie. One either likes what she does or hates it.Whatever your stance, this reissue is the best possible case for the defence, because it is probably her best album and is certainly from her best period, the late fifties.

Her voice is small, and she makes little attempt to sing out with it, choosing instead to go for a special intimacy with the listener. At times this can result in performances which can sound a little too cutesy (*Doop-Doo-De-Doop (a Doodlin' Song)* definitely fits into this category). But then again, that intimacy makes her renditions of *Tea for Two* and *It Amazes Me* extraordinary in the way she persuades the listener that she is engaged in a one-to-one monologue with no-one else in the world but them. These are genuinely moving performances.

Her backing musicians are models of discretion and support, the recording balance and ambience is perfect for her, and one couldn't wish for a better representation of her art. **KS**

Santi Debriano

Obeah **Debriano** (b); **Jerry Gonzalez** (t); **Sonny Fortune** (f, as); **Kenny Barron** (p); **Paul Meyers** (g); **Billy Hart** (d). Freelance Ⓕ CD 008 (53 minutes). Recorded 1987.

⑥ ❼

Panamanian Debriano has been successful as a sideman with a string of modern jazz big names for many years now, so it is no surprise that someone felt it was time he had his own record out. It is a worthy offering, cast in the mould of the things McCoy Tyner was doing for most of the seventies—intense, uncompromising modern jazz with fierce polyrhythms and themes stripped for improvising action. Fortune is in good form throughout the date and the music picks up every time he enters. Debriano has a fine tone, a decided melodic bent, and excellent time. He and Hart make a combustive team which Barron rides in his usual imperturbable manner. Gonzalez plays cleanly and well, but at the time of this date had not emerged as an especially original trumpeter.

The programme is quite well paced, with Debriano keeping to the rhythm section most of the time: *Anima* and *Evolution* are virtually all bass. A nice album. **KS**

Dedication Orchestra

Spirits Rejoice **Guy Barker**, **Harry Beckett**, **Claude Deppa**, **Jim Dvorak**, **Kenny Wheeler** (t); **Dave Amis**, **Malcolm Griffiths**, **Radu Malfatti**, **Paul Rutherford** (tb); **Django Bates** (peckhorn); **Dave Powell** (tba); **Neil Metcalfe** (f); **Lol Coxhill** (ss, ts); **Ray Warleigh** (as, f); **Elton Dean** (as); **Evan Parker**, **Alan Skidmore** (ts); **Chris Biscoe** (bs); **Keith Tippett** (p); **Paul Rogers** (b); **Louis Moholo** (d, v); **Phil Minton**, **Maggie Nicols**, **Julie Tippetts** (v). Ogun Ⓕ OGCD 101 (75 minutes). Recorded 1992.

⑧ ❽

In the early sixties London became home-base for a number of South African musicians fleeing apartheid. Prominent among these exiles were bassist Harry Miller and the group the Blue Notes, which included Johnny Dyani, Mongezi Feza, Chris McGregor, Louis Moholo and Dudu Pukwana. Their infectious township swing and explosive free-form galvanized London's modern jazz scene and, in 1970, they also provided the core of McGregor's Brotherhood of Breath, one of the first and finest of the free jazz big bands.

Spirits Rejoice was co-organized by Moholo, now the Blue Notes' sole survivor, as a tribute to his colleagues and features a selection of their tunes performed by a 24-piece orchestra of leading UK improvisers. The music, fiercely celebratory, moves with exceptional power and grace, the large personnel adding lustre to the textures and an extra kick to the rhythms. The range of moods takes in Pukwana's ballads *B My Dear* and *Hug Pine*, Miller's lively *Dancing Demon*, Feza's joyful *Sonia* and the noble kwela lilt of his *You Ain't Gonna Know Me 'Cause You Think You Know Me*. Moholo's *Woza*, the album's climax, flies with a passion that is intensely moving. The Brotherhood and the Blue Notes have a fine memorial in **Spirits Rejoice**. **GL**

Joey DeFrancesco 1971

Live At The 5 Spot **DeFrancesco** (org, t); **Jim Henry** (t, flh); **Robert Landham** (as); **Illinois Jacquet**, **Houston Person**, **Grover Washington Jr**, **Kirk Whalum** (ts); **Jack McDuff** (org); **Paul Bollenback** (g); **Byron Landham** (d). Columbia Ⓕ 474045 2 (75 minutes). Recorded 1992.

⑥ ❿

DeFrancesco is no longer with Columbia, but his last album for the label is still pretty much his most engaging and representative. It has the advantage of capturing the young man live in front of an appreciative crowd and in the company of some heavyweight mainstream artists. DeFrancesco himself is a player with a very strong beat, good ears and the rare ability to play with real sensitivity for those around him. His backing of Jacquet on the latter's ballad feature, *Embraceable You*, has a wonderful balance between discreet support and gentle prodding. The instrument does not blare or flare. In his own solo, he humanizes it with expert control of vibrato, tone and colour, making it unusually communicative. Generally speaking, he is not especially original in his improvisations, but he is immensely accomplished and clearly enjoys getting a whole band to turn up the heat in unison. This has come in handy on his recent records with John McLaughlin's Free Spirits.

Four tenors on *every* track would be a mite overwhelming, but fear not: there is never more than one saxophonist per track, so the variety is pleasingly consecutive. Washington takes a nicely funky solo on *Work Song*, while Houston Person gently asserts his balladry credentials on *Moonlight In Vermont*. DeFrancesco's unusually wide range for a Hammond man is indicated by the inclusion of Kirk Whalum's workout on Coltrane's *Impressions*, but the set—and the album—ends up back home in a sprightly blues duet with Jack McDuff. You would have to be a dedicated Hammond hater not to enjoy what is on offer here. **KS**

Buddy Defranco 1923

Chip Off The Old Bop **Buddy DeFranco** (cl); **Larry Novak** (p, syn); **Joe Cohn** (g); **Keter Betts** (b); **Jimmy Cobb** (d). Concord Jazz Ⓕ CCD 4527 (58 minutes). Recorded 1992.

⑧ ❿

From being an icon of the swing era, the clarinet has declined almost to the status of an oddity in contemporary jazz. And yet the leading players form a wonderfully varied and individual bunch, from the darkly lyrical Kenny Davern to the mercurial Eddie Daniels. But of all the jazz clarinettists living none is more brilliant than Buddy DeFranco. This is the latest in a long line of recordings stretching back to the late forties, and it is as good as any of them.

With his tone of polished glass and his impeccable technique, DeFranco makes every solo an object of wonder and fascination for the listener and of despair for aspiring clarinet players. It used to be said that his playing was 'cold', which was never true, although there is a kind of icy deliberation in the way he constructs his phrases. But listen to these versions of the ballads *If You Could See Me Now* and *You're Blasé* and hear how warm his tone can be. DeFranco is joined on this disc by the guitarist Joe Cohn, a partnership which shows great promise for the future. **DG**

Jack DeJohnette 1942

Album Album **DeJohnette** (d, p, kbds); **John Purcell** (ss, as); **David Murray** (ts); **Howard Johnson** (tba, bs); **Rufus Reid** (b). ECM Ⓕ 1280 (823 467-2) (43 minutes). Recorded 1984.

⑧ ❿

By 1984 drummer-keyboardist Jack DeJohnette, an important member of the jazz-rock and fusion revolution due to his tenures with Charles Lloyd and the electrified Miles Davis, had expanded his acoustic horizons through vital collaborations with Keith Jarrett, John Abercrombie and Stan Getz. In the mid-seventies, DeJohnette originated his band Special Edition to explore the implications of his varied musical associations in a context where the leader's compositional designs often played as important a part in the music's substance as improvisation.

In this evocative date dedicated to his mother (who had just passed away), DeJohnette creates dazzling spells. On *New Orleans Strut*, for example, there's a rolling Cajun-influenced beat backdropped with the leader's concertina-like atmospherics and simmering drums. The Crescent City mood also extends to *Festival*, where tumultuous group fireworks evoke traditional New Orleans music's collective approach to improvisation. Here, in contrast to later configurations of Special Edition, DeJohnette is among players who are his musical equals. Bassist Reid is the veritable anchor mooring DeJohnette's overdubbed drum and keyboard tracks. The vibrant horn section of Purcell, Murray and Johnson is simply magnificent. DeJohnette's meticulously-crafted compositions are full of fascinating detail (which the group articulates brilliantly), yet they are also expansive and exuberant in outlook. Instead of referring back to Miles, DeJohnette's rich ensemble sonorities and bracing harmonies use Ellington and Mingus as their touchstones. In all, a highly satisfying session. **CB**

Peter Delano

1976

Bite Of The Apple **Delano** (p) with the following collective personnel; **Tim Hagans** (t); **Dick Oatts**, **Chuck Wilson** (f); **Gary Bartz** (as); **Chris Potter**, **Craig Handy** (ts); **Richard Locker**, **Tomas Ulrich** (vc); **Joe Locke** (vb); **Eddie Gomez**, **Marc Johnson**, **Gary Peacock**, **Peter Washington** (b); **Joe Chambers**, **Jeff Hirshfield**, **Victor Lewis**, **Adam Nussbaum**, **Bill Stewart** (d); **Ray Mantilla** (conga). Verve 521 869-2 (72 minutes). Recorded 1994.

⑥ ❽

This is pianist Delano's second CD for the Verve label, featuring various groupings of instrumentalists including several well-known younger players from the New York recording scene. The music is very efficiently played but the listener's enthusiasm may be tempered by those occasions when pure technique takes over and the music takes on a relentlessness which sometimes sounds superficial. The most impressive titles are the ones taken at slower pace or with more intimate instrumentation. *Heartfelt* has the pleasing sound of two cellos behind Chuck Wilson (playing alto and flute) while *Sunrise Remembered* is a beauty, played by just Delano and Joe Locke on vibes. **AM**

Barbara Dennerlein

1961

That's Me **Dennerlein** (org, syn); **Ray Anderson** (tb); **Bob Berg** (ts); **Mitch Watkins** (g); **Dennis Chambers** (d). Enja Ⓕ ENJ 7043-2 (64 minutes). Recorded 1992.

⑧ ❿

This really is an organ record for people who hate Hammond B3 organs. It demonstrates quite convincingly that organs can be fun, and that they do not all have to sound like Jimmy Smith the morning after. Dennerlein has a number of things going for her, prime among them real taste in the choice of sidemen on her records: this is by no means the first time either Ray Anderson or Mitch Watkins, both very superior musicians, have recorded with her, and the results have never been less than stimulating.

She also composes most of her own material, and is sufficiently adept at it to bring an unusual breadth of outlook to her repertoire. She plays with enormous drive and enthusiam: all her albums have that energy and it emanates from her outward to the other musicians, rather than the other way around. Her bass lines, all created on the pedals, invariably swing like crazy. On this, her last album for Enja, Dennerlein's normal group is joined by saxophonist Berg, and he does not waste time getting acquainted. His solos bristle with ideas and his section playing helps keep the whole thing moving along at a bright clip. Although she has moved to Verve and has released her début album, **Take Off!** there, this remains her best record to date. Recording quality is first-rate. **KS**

Karl Denson

Herbal Turkey Breast **Denson** (ss, as, ts); **Ron Stout** (t); **Deron Johnson** (p); **Nedra Wheeler** (b); **Tom White** or **Bruce Cox** (d); **Milton Commeaux** (perc). Minor Music Ⓕ MM 801032 (52 minutes). Recorded 1993.

⑦ ❽

With a first album called **Blackened Red Snapper** and a second celebrating the delights of turkeys, Denson obviously enjoys his grub. Luckily for us, the inspiration he derives from food communicates itself liberally in his music.

This second album for Minor Music sports a similar band to the first, and if there may not be a great deal to choose between the two sessions, this latter one is perhaps more assured, more relaxed. Denson is settling into the role of session leader and his own playing is less that of a person attempting to lead from the front. The style of the music is by and large neo-bop, embracing as it does most of the innovations of the modern jazz mainstream up to the point of Miles's late-sixties desertion of acoustic jazz for the greener pastures of jazz-rock and fusion. Denson himself has a persuasive tone and attack on all three of the saxophones he uses, although it is perhaps on alto that he is at his most natural. His phrasing is fresh, his ideas clear and well-executed: his band is sufficiently experienced with his music to respond deftly and imaginatively to the character of each piece. Denson's other major soloist, trumpeter Stout, has the full and lively tone and range of a Hubbard or Morgan, but has fashioned his own personality on the instrument, while pianist Johnson is alive to every angle the front men may want to explore. The least impressive music here probably occurs on the *Crown Jewels Suite*, which perhaps needs a larger musical unit to further flesh out the ideas, but no matter; this is a satisfying and stimulating album from a resourceful and well-matched outfit. **KS**

Philippe Deschepper 1949

Sad Novi Sad **Deschepper** (g); **Steve Swallow** (elb), **Jacques Mahieux** (d); **Martin Fredebeul** (ss); **Michel Godard** (tba); **Gerard Marais** (g); **Jean-Luc Ponthieux, Henri Texier** (b). Ida Ⓕ 008 CD (45 minutes). Recorded 1986.

⑥ ❽

French guitarist Deschepper came to modern jazz quite late, having originally been content to play banjo in trad bands. He is of a generation which has grown up under the influence of people like John Scofield, John Abercrombie and Bill Frisell, and certainly these players are almost tangible presences on this disc. It does not stop the album from being highly enjoyable in its own very laid-back way. The pacing is excellent, with different guests giving different slants on the music on each track. Swallow brings his usual combination of lyricism and drive to the band, and although much is made of atmospherics by Deschepper, the occasional solo catches fire. Pleasant, a little dreamy, and immaculately turned out. **KS**

Paul Desmond 1924-1977

East Of The Sun **Paul Desmond** (as); **Jim Hall** (g); **Percy Heath** (b); **Connie Kay** (d). Discovery Ⓜ DSCD 840 (43 minutes). Recorded 1959.

✔ ⑧ ❽

The fact that Desmond spent most of his career trapped within the Dave Brubeck Quartet has tended to obscure his proper eminence in jazz. He should be ranked with Stan Getz, Lee Konitz, Al Cohn and Phil Woods. His cool veneer diverted attention from the passion and exhilaration of his best work. This quartet was in fact a late development from the by-then defunct cool school, and its music was played with a light touch and delicacy which easily upstaged the contemporary music of Brubeck's group. Desmond and Hall rarely played better than in their five recording sessions together and this, the first of them, was the best. The exquisite *For All We Know* is flanked by a pastoral *Greensleeves*, an eloquent reading of John Lewis's fine blues *Two Degrees East, Three Degrees West*, and a bouncing *I Get A Kick Out Of You* which is as near to muscle as this team gets. Percy Heath and Connie Kay from the Modern Jazz Quartet, well versed in such intimate surroundings, make a perfect rhythm team. **SV**

Two of a Mind **Desmond** (as); **Gerry Mulligan** (bs); **John Beal, Wendell Marshall, Joe Benjamin** (b), **Connie Kay, Mel Lewis** (d). RCA Bluebird Ⓜ ND 90364-2 (41 minutes). Recorded 1962.

✔ ⑩ ❼

I originally intended giving this a slightly less than perfect rating, as my memory of it was that it had some outstanding tracks, but somehow didn't quite sustain itself to the end. I was wrong. On re-hearing it, I am happy to declare it perfect. By that, I don't mean that every note is perfectly articulated and each phrase is the best possible phrase in its context; I just mean that there is a perfect fusion of intentions and the realization of them. Desmond and Mulligan make a beautiful ensemble sound together and find exciting and different routes to that sound in each selection. They both also play inventively and resourcefully, clearly inspiring each other to reach for more in each solo. Their interplay is uncanny, and the contrast between their instrumental approaches keeps the record continually on the boil.

Why does this album work better than Desmond's other RCA dates of the same period? And why is it also better than the Verve album these two made together in 1957? Firstly, this date has neither piano nor guitar, and the resulting clarity of texture leaves the listener with ample room to follow the two lead men in every detail. It also brings an intimacy to their efforts which would have been hard to sustain with a harmony instrument added. As for the second question, it may be that both players are better at creating something new out of a group of old standards than they are at playing the blues, and the first album had its fair share of blues-based numbers. It also wasn't very well recorded.

Summation: this is a classic, and bears not just repeated listening, but years of familiarity. The tender, rapt eight-minute version of *Stardust* included here is as good a thing as either player has ever done, separately or together. **KS**

Easy Living **Desmond** (as); **Jim Hall** (g); **Eugene Wright, Gene Cherico, Percy Heath** (b); **Connie Kay** (d). Bluebird Ⓜ ND82306 (60 minutes). Recorded 1964.

⑥ ❽

The sound of Paul Desmond is the sound of the alto saxophone playing the melody on *Take Five* by the Dave Brubeck Quartet, and therefore one of the best-known jazz sounds in the world. Desmond recorded so much with Brubeck, and so little elsewhere, that the two are indivisible in the public mind. This is one of the limited number of albums under his own name.

Paul Desmond was one of the very few alto saxophone players of his generation not to succumb to the overwhelming power of Charlie Parker; indeed everything about his playing is the exact opposite of Parker—the one livid, impulsive and gritty, the other pale, considered and possessed of an unearthy purity of tone. Desmond's tone on this CD is of such an airy consistency that it could almost be mistaken for times for a flute. But it has to be said that there is nothing wrong in being unorthodox, and Desmond's sound is all of a piece with his elegant and witty phrasing.

It may be significant that, released from Brubeck's dogged piano, he chose for his accompanist that most delicate and mercurial of guitarists Jim Hall. Together they create variations on good standard tunes (such as *Bewitched* and *That Old Feeling*) for which the word 'charming' might have been coined.
DG

Laurent DeWilde

Off The Boat **DeWilde** (p), **Eddie Henderson** (t), **Ralph Moore** (ss, ts), **Ira Coleman** (b), **Billy Hart** (d). Ida Ⓕ 015 CD (38 minutes). Recorded 1987.

⑥ ❽

This is an inconsistent album, but when it sparks there are some unified and fully realized tracks with the power to move the listener. The opening track, *Assaulted Peanuts*, finds Henderson lacking and DeWilde doing nothing startling, but the touching ballad *Odd and Blue* has a lot more to offer, with the pianist finding meaningful points to make and Moore, on soprano, really singing his lines. Moore is in good shape on every track, regardless of which instrument he is has chosen, and is one of the album's main selling-points. Henderson shows he is still a formidable player, his solo on the extra-speedy Ignatz's Brick demonstrating the talent of seeming to have loads of time at high speed to execute his ideas. But he seems only partially engaged on some tracks, occasionally content with borrowed ideas when he should be pushing ahead with his own. A good album, then, with its fair share of pluses, but with a couple of minuses to look out for, including a rather feeble playing time for a full price album.
KS

Vic Dickenson

1906-1984

Gentleman of the Trombone **Dickenson** (tb, v); **Johnny Guarneri** (p); **Bill Pemberton** (b); **Oliver Jackson** (d). Storyville Ⓕ STCD 5008 (58 minutes). Recorded 1975.

⑧ ❽

The trombone seems to be one of those instruments in jazz which attract individualists. Dickenson can certainly be numbered in those ranks. He made a late start to soloing after spending most of the thirties in big band trombone sections, but his work with Lester Young for Commodore and Aladdin, amongst other dates, certainly launched his highly vocalized and good-humoured style. He has been leading his own small groups since the late forties and this group is typical of his favoured environment. Guarneri is a pianist capable of emulating any pre-bop style you care to name, always soloing with wit and drive, while the bass and drums have been around plenty of top-grade swing outfits.

Dickenson is in typically relaxed form here, using his mutes to snake and angle his line through the chord changes with the maximum of sly ease. His swing, like Teagarden's, is seemingly lazy but highly infectious. He sings on a couple of tracks, which I guess is extra value for money, but his trombone playing, with its charming twists and exhortations, is the main event for every pair of ears here. The CD reissue, by the way, has three extra tracks not released on the original vinyl version.
KS

Walt Dickerson

1931

Divine Gemini **Dickerson** (vb); **Richard Davis** (b). Steeplechase Ⓕ SCCD 31089 (34 minutes). Recorded 1977.

⑥ ❽

Even after all these years, there is really only one choice for the best Walt Dickerson album, and this is not it. However, while the owners of the Prestige masters continue to overlook the CD début of his 1962 masterpiece, **To My Queen**, this fine album will do nicely. The dialogue between these two highly creative and resourceful players is utterly involved, and if you have the powers of concentration to stick with two such un-percussive instruments for the duration, then what they create together is utterly involving, too.

Dickerson has a special gift of touch on his instrument, coaxing a variety of sound and personalized statement from it which even so attuned a technician as Gary Burton cannot match. Davis is simply one of the most gifted players of his generation, regardless of instrument. Together they perceive and highlight angles of each other's music, across two rather long tracks and two quite short ones, which banish larger questions of form and dynamics. The sound is very good, but full price seems a lot to ask for this, still just sneaking over 30 minutes of music 18 years after initial release.
KS

Al DiMeola

1954

Electric Rendezvous **Al DiMeola** (g); **Jan Hammer** (syn); **Anthony Jackson** (b); **Steve Gadd** (d); **Mingo Lewis** (perc); plus, on one track: **Phillipe Saisse** (syn); **Paco De Lucia** (g). Columbia Ⓜ 668216-2 (35 minutes). Recorded 1982.

⑥ ❽

Launched into the limelight as the replacement for Bill Connors in Chick Corea's Return to Forever (and that at the tender age of 19), electric guitar prodigy DiMeola for many years exemplified the development of jazz-rock after its initial cloudburst. For the music's detractors, his staggering ability —a combination of rapid-fire staccato single note runs and finger-breakingly pianistic chord voicing—was all the music had to say for itself, while for fusion's fiercest supporters his chops-heavy playing and composition represented the perfect blend of rock intensity and jazz exploration (and, indeed, its inclusiveness—DiMeola's music easily accommodates Flamenco melodies and Brazilian rhythms without so much as a mention of the dreaded "world music").

Released in 1982, and hence pitched halfway between his arguably over-referential early albums (with McLaughlin and Coryell writ large all over the young guitarist's playing) and the primarily acoustic, quasi-New Age recent albums, **Electric Rendezvous** represents Di Meola's oeuvre perfectly. Latin ballads, rock shuffles, a fiery duet with Flamenco superstar De Lucia and progressive rock-like, tempo-changing mini-epics, all with portentous titles like *God Bird Change* and *Jewel Inside a Dream*, define Di Meola perfectly. At its heart, and as much an influence on today's young Heavy Metal guitar hot shots as their jazz counterparts, is Di Meola's trademark Les Paul and Marshall sound; not jazz's critically best-received, but certainly one of its most popular. **SH**

Gene DiNovi

1928

Renaissance of a Jazz Master **DiNovi** (p); **Dave Young** (b); **Terry Clarke** (d). Candid Ⓕ CCD 79708 (62 minutes). Recorded 1993.

⑥ ❽

DiNovi was born in Brooklyn and is of the generation which came to maturity with the heady sounds of be-bop swirling in their heads. His self-professed early influences include George Wallington, Dodo Marmarosa, Ellington and Basie at the piano, with Charlie Parker exerting a large overall grip on his musical thinking, but later he came to appreciate Nat Cole, Teddy Wilson and Art Tatum. This stood him in good stead at the time, for he was able to record with both Benny Goodman and Fats Navarro, and it certainly gave him the resources to become long-term accompanist to a number of outstanding singers, including Tony Bennett, Peggy Lee, Lena Horne and Anita O'Day. A move to Toronto in the seventies after a number of years in the California studios took him out of the mainstream but ironically gave him the opportunity to record under his own name for the first time.

Candid came on to the scene after DiNovi had put out two good piano records, and this is his first release with a wide distribution. He now plays in a style most closely related to that of George Shearing. His rhythm is firmly rooted in the symmetry of phrasing to be heard in Teddy Wilson and Nat Cole, while his harmonic thinking reflects his early love of bop. Nothing startling happens on this record, but there is no dull or unimaginative playing either. A typical track is *It Never Entered My Mind*, where DiNovi is able to communicate honestly without unnecessary artifice or elaboration. This is a quietly impressive trio outing by a man whose pianisms deserve respect. **KS**

Joe Diorio

1936

Rare Birds **Diorio**, **Mick Goodrick** (g). Ram Records Ⓕ RMCD 4505 (75 minutes). Recorded 1993.

⑧ ❽

Recordings from Joe Diorio seem to come along like buses—none for a decade then three in a row. **Rare Birds** is one of three recordings Diorio made during visits to Italy in 1992 and 1993, but where the other two—one solo, one with bass—are rather subdued, this one, in duo with a like-minded fellow guitarist, is a hot one. Although he played in earlier years with Getz, Freddie Hubbard, Eddie Harris and others, Diorio is perhaps best known to guitarists around the world for his *Intervallic Designs* guitar manual, and those whose interest was aroused by that volume now have a fresh opportunity to hear the theory in practice. Indeed, the duo's treatments of such standards as *Green Dolphin Street*, *Out Of Nowhere*, *Well, You Needn't* and *Blue In Green* are rich in quartal harmony and abstruse chord substitution, and this is one element which helps distinguish this date from so many routine jazz guitar duets. But the session also thrives on imaginative use of texture and arrangement, exploiting the contrasts between block chords and walking bass, between chord and solo and two-voice counterpoint, between functional harmony and pointillistic free improvisation; and by doing it all in an adversarial but co-operative spirit, the duo are able to sustain interest in a format that otherwise often induces polite boredom in its audiences. **MG**

Dirty Dozen Brass Band

Live: Mardi Gras At Montreux **Gregory Davis** (t); **Efrem Towns** (tb); **Kevin Harris** (ts); **Roger Lewis** (bs, ss); **Kirk Joseph** (bb); **Jenell Marshall** (snare, v); **Lionel Batiste** (bd). Rounder Ⓕ CD2052 (47 minutes). Recorded 1985.

⑥ ❻

Initially little more than a skiffle group, the Dirty Dozen arrived at their present size and shape in 1975. Their New Orleans origins are obvious in every note they play and they are as ideally suited to march amongst their concert audiences as they once did around the streets of the Crescent City. As this CD shows, their music is a wonderfully homogenized mixture of traditional, New Orleans jazz, r&b, hard bop and swing era riffs. Their ineluctable bounce is superbly captured on Mardi Gras in New Orleans, *It Ain't What You Think* and *Lickity Split*, but it is the way they boogie through *Night Train* or take a quasi-serious look at a tune like *Blue Monk* that draws attention to a wider stylistic range than is at first apparent. Little profundity is intended or achieved from the band's soloists but, like Marshall's occasional vocal, they are often used as a means to stir the audience. In addition a liberal seasoning of humour adds to their vivacity and the response from the audience at this 1985 Montreux Festival is typical. Whether the Dozen should be considered a jazz band is immaterial. They are a permanent fixture on the jazz tour and a large number of serious jazz musicians stand at the side of the stage to listen and stomp. **BMcR**

Bill Dixon

1925

Son Of Sisyphus **Dixon** (t, p); **John Buckingham** (tba); **Mario Pavane** (b); **Laurence Cook** (d). Soul Note Ⓕ 121138-2 (39 minutes). Recorded 1988.

⑩ ❽

Trumpeter, composer, educator and a painter of international repute, Bill Dixon's tiny discography is a poor indication of his talent. A major figure in the sixties avant-garde, he worked with Cecil Taylor and Archie Shepp, co-founded the New York Contemporary Five and recorded in **Intents and Purposes**, one of the decade's most original and beautiful albums. Neither that LP nor his two fine seventies records for the Italian Fore label are currently available, but thanks to a later association with Soul Note at least two Dixon masterworks are now on CD; the live **November 1981** and his latest set **Son Of Sisyphus**.

Dixon's music has been described as painterly, although its attention to the details of form, line, texture and colour are as much the mark of a composer (and testament to a rigorous instrumental technique). Like his paintings, his music is abstract; titles such as *Thoughts* and *Considerations* indicate its reflective quality, an impression reinforced by his liking for darker sonorities (tuba and bass here). Much of **Son Of Sisyphus** sounds deep in thought, notably tracks such as *Fusama Codex*, *Mandala per Mandala* and *Negoro Codex*, where his elegaic trumpet wanders through shadowy thickets of low-register support. In contrast, *Vecctor* is skittering group empathy; *Schema VI-88* a delve into brass timbres, all gargles and leonine growls. Dixon also plays telling piano on two brief duos with bass, *Sumi-E* and the valedictory *Silences For Jack Moore*, its grief imbued with the dignity of the blues. **BMcR**

Johnny Dodds

1882-1940

Johnny Dodds 1926-40, Volume 1 **Johnny Dodds** (cl); **Louis Armstrong**, **George Mitchell**, **Natty Dominique** (c); **Kid Ory**, **Roy Palmer** (tb); **Jelly Roll Morton**, **Earl Hines**, **Jimmy Blythe**, **Lil Armstrong** (p); **Johnny St Cyr**, **Bud Scott** (bj); **Baby Dodds**. **Jimmy Bertrand** (d, wbd). Affinity Ⓜ CD AFS 1023-3 (three discs: 193 minutes). Recorded 1926/27.

⑧ ❻

There were better technicians and more sophisticated exponents of the clarinet, but Dodds was the best all-rounder and set much of the method of ensemble playing for the instrument. His abilities within a group are best displayed on four tracks by Jimmy Bertrand's Washboard Wizards where he and Armstrong form the front line. It is interesting to hear Armstrong trying to change his style on six tracks by Dodds's Black Bottom Stompers because he was under contract to another record company and was trying to avoid being recognized—as a consequence his playing is inhibited on these tracks when compared to his magnificent work on *I'm Going Hunting* with Blythe. Dodds flowers with chalumeau performances of great beauty on *Wild Man Blues* and *Melancholy*.

Eight tracks by the New Orleans Wanderers/Bootblacks feature the estimable George Mitchell, while Dodds's performance on *Perdido Street Blues* is one of the finest of his career. Coming from obscure sources, some of this material has had to be taken from worn recordings, but where the source is good the transfers are excellent. **SV**

Bill Doggett

1916

Dame Dreaming **Doggett** (org); **Clifford Scott** (as, ts); **Billy Butler** (g); **Edwyn Conley** (b); **Shep Shepherd** (d). King Ⓑ KCD 532 (32 minutes). Recorded 1956.

Charly Records put out a very good compilation of Doggett King Records material, but that is now deleted and we are left with the rather appalling situation as represented by the current holders of the King CD chalice. At least this was originally released as an LP, rather than being a compilation CD, but that hardly excuses the playing-time (even at budget price) or the appalling lack of information on the sleeve (although the personnel information is buried in the unreadably reproduced original sleeve notes, reduced from LP size to CD with no adjustment for the decrease in size—a step up from the earlier King CDs, which had no sleeve notes at all).

The 'theme' behind this album is typical mid-fifties tastelessness: a concept album of interpretations of songs with women's names. The treatment given them is typical tenor-and-organ, and if the theme (and the tacky cover) is ignored, then it is really quite pleasant. Doggett ventures no further than Wild Bill Davis had already gone by 1956, and most of the tracks don't break the three minute barrier, but in its own utterly unambitious way this is pleasant music, and the warm tenor playing of Shep Shepherd is not without its felicities. **KS**

Niels Lan Doky

1963

Misty Dawn **Doky** (p); **Niels-Henning Ørsted Pedersen** (b); **Alex Riel** (d). Columbia Ⓕ 477460-2 (54 minutes). Recorded 1993-94.

⑦ ❽

Doky, a native of Denmark, spent most of the eighties in New York, where he got to play with a wide selection of the music's front-runners, including John Scofield, Joe Henderson, Woody Shaw, Charlie Haden and Ray Brown. He now spends his professional career swapping between the two sides of the Atlantic, and has to his credit over 14 albums under his own name. This is the latest, and is typical. Although these three have not made a trio album before, they are old colleagues, and their playing sits together seamlessly. NHØP hardly needs any introduction, although it is worth remembering that he was playing in a trio with Bud Powell when he was just 16, while Alex Riel is probably best known internationally for being the drummer on Eric Dolphy's **Last Date**.

The music here is very much in the tradition of modern piano trios such as Bill Evans, Chick Corea and Herbie Hancock, although a partiality to quasi-classical music effects in his own compositions suggests the more pronounced duality of his musical experience and origins. NHØP plays beautifully throughout, eschewing the impulse to overplay and fill in too many gaps, while Riel is the soul of sensitive drive. Hardly music to change the world, but no less enjoyable for that. **KS**

Eric Dolphy

1928-1964

Far Cry **Dolphy** (fl, as, bcl); **Booker Little** (t); **Jaki Byard** (p); **Ron Carter** (b); **Roy Haynes** (d). Prestige New Jazz Ⓜ OJCCD 400-2 (48 minutes). Recorded 1960.

⑨ ❼

This was not Dolphy's first album as a leader, but it is the best studio album he made for Prestige. Part of the reason for this lies in the unusual unity of conception generated over the first four pieces, and part of it lies also in the increased level of daring in his own playing (this is understandable, as Dolphy had earlier that same day participated in the recording of Ornette Coleman's **Free Jazz** album (see above). Yet, in the final analysis, it is the overall contributions of Dolphy's colleagues Booker Little and Jaki Byard which give **Far Cry** its added dimensions. Little and Dolphy were a perfect musical blend, with each man giving to the music something the other lacked, and it is no accident that they went on to form a co-led band before Little's untimely death from leukaemia late in the following year.

Byard is another case altogether. His is also a perfect musical fit here, but he is generally happy to accompany and support. However—and this is crucial—he contributes two memorable compositions (both expressing a nostalgia for Charlie Parker) which, combined with Dolphy's own *Far Cry*, form a kind of suite of meditations on the deceased altoist. On all three, Little and Dolphy discover a near-telepathic blend which is both moving and unique while continually hinting at sounds beyond the scope of the conventions they are playing within here (cf. the final tones of *Far Cry* itself). Their interplay on *Ode to Charlie Parker* is extraordinary.

If the rest of the album cannot quite match these exceptional standards, there is still much to enjoy, although the unaccompanied alto solo, *Tenderly*, has little of the tautness and urgency to be found in other unaccompanied Dolphy solos, and *It's Magic*, an intentionally humorous bass clarinet showcase, unintentionally dissipates the mood the album had achieved elsewhere. The CD version has an extra track, *Serene*, not on the original LP release. **KS**

Memorial Album **Dolphy** (b, cl, as); **Booker Little** (t); **Mal Waldron** (p); **Richard Davis** (b); **Ed Blackwell** (d). Prestige Ⓜ OJCCD-353-2 (31 minutes). Recorded 1961.

✔ ⑧ ❽

Eric Dolphy is one of the towering figures of the early sixties avant-garde. Influenced by a deeply-felt appreciation of African and Indian music as well as contemporary 'classical' music, Dolphy evolved a fluid improvisational approach which oscillated between these two poles and bebop. Dolphy also benefited from working with Chico Hamilton, Charles Mingus and John Coltrane, leaders whose experimental temperaments allowed him to range far and wide. As an important member of John Lewis's Orchestra U.S.A., Dolphy also had direct exposure to the third-stream concepts of Gunther Schuller and the more dissonant tonalities of such 'conservatory' avant-garde composers as Edgard Varèse.

Here, in the last of an original three-album release recorded in July 1961 at the Five Spot in New York City, we catch Dolphy in a probing, neo-boppish date with co-leader Booker Little, the protean bebop trumpeter who died shortly after the session at the age of 23; thus the **Memorial** title. Throughout, one senses Dolphy straining against and yet revelling in each tune's bebop parameters. In Dolphy's gritty *Number Eight*, the composer projects his alto through the defined stylistics of Charlie Parker into the limitless horizons first glimpsed by Ornette Coleman. For Little's ebullient *Booker's Waltz*, Dolphy flails against the in-the-pocket rhythm section on bass clarinet, an instrument he proved to be a viable jazz voice. In the process, we witness the fragmentation of bop into what would be variously called "free jazz" and " the new thing." The sole caveat is that, some 30 years after the music was played and ten years after the advent of CD, OJC are still giving us a disc with playing time which was only average even in the days of vinyl. Why hasn't the whole of the Five Spot material (including the bits on **Here And There**) been re-programmed onto three—or even two—well-filled CDs? **CB**

Conversations **Dolphy** (as, bcl, f); **Woody Shaw** (t); **Clifford Jordan** (ss); **Sonny Simmons** (as); **Prince Lasha** (f); Bo**bby Hutcherson** (vb); **Richard Davis**, **Eddie Kahn** (b); **Charles Moffett**, **J.C. Moses** (d). Celluloid Ⓜ CELD-5014 (34 minutes). Recorded 1963.

⑩ ❷

Along with its companion volume from the same sessions, **Iron Man**, **Conversations** is rivalled only by **Out To Lunch** as Dolphy's most mature statement as a leader. It's also the most varied: each of four selections features different line-ups.

Conversations includes a couple of his most charming performances; the merry mariachi-cum-calypso *Music Matador* by Lasha (later Lawsha), for three reeds, flute, bass and drums, and a lilting, definitive take on Fats Waller's *Jitterbug Waltz*, for quintet. Featuring Dolphy on flute, it showcases Hutcherson, who has never sounded better than with Dolphy, while *Music Matador* affords an excellent example of Eric's goose-cry bass clarinet and his knack for making spectacular dramatic/comic entrances. On an intense and slowly unfolding *Alone Together*, for bass clarinet and doublebass, Dolphy's and Davis's joint attention to silence and open space comments on the title. The leaping staccato intro and outro to a solo alto version of the standard *Love Me* look ahead to Anthony Braxton's and Roscoe Mitchell's angular styles, and to the late-sixties Chicago vanguard's penchant for solo-horn recitals in general.

There are severe problems with this reissue: the remastered sound is tinny and distant; **Iron Man** would easily have fitted onto the same CD, where it belongs. The disc seems to be withdrawn in the US but available in Europe, where part of these sessions, at least, is also available on the budget Charly Le Jazz label (CD14) (with even worse sound reproduction)! Even so, this is essential music. **KW**

Out to Lunch **Dolphy** (f, bcl, as), **Freddie Hubbard** (t), **Bobby Hutcherson** (vb), **Richard Davis** (b), **Tony Williams** (d). Blue Note Ⓜ CDP7 46524-2 (43 minutes). Recorded 1964.

✔ ⑩ ❽

Dolphy's last studio recording as leader is now widely regarded as his masterpiece. **Out to Lunch** has taken its place alongside titles such as **Free Jazz** and **Unit Structures** as a landmark of early modern jazz. It is Dolphy's most advanced set, notable particularly for its radical experiments with rhythm. The catalyst here was the young Tony Williams, then marking out a path between the polyrhythmic complexities of Elvin Jones and Sunny Murray's total freedom. What little regular pulse there is on **Out to Lunch** tends to be carried by Richard Davis's roaming bass, while Williams disrupts and dislocates the beat with counter-rhythms, abetted by sudden percussive flurries from Hutcherson's vibes.

Dolphy and Hubbard both negotiate this tricky new terrain surefootedly, although it is the leader who more often grabs the attention; the quizzical bass clarinet expostulations on *Hat and Beard*; the rapid, feisty flute on *Gazzelloni*; the alto's collage of fragmentary phrases on the title-track, or its wildly humorous slurs on *Straight Up And Down*. Solos, though, are all succinct, facets here of a brilliantly integrated group music. Dolphy's growing sophistication as a composer (most evident on the lovely *Something Sweet, Something Tender*) plays its part, but it is the group interaction—the way they hold the music together even as they take it apart—that makes **Out to Lunch** so contemporary and so compelling. **GL**

Last Date **Dolphy** (f, bcl, as); **Misja Mengelberg** (p); **Jacques Schols** (b); **Han Bennink** (d). EmArcy/Limelight Ⓜ 510 124-2 (46 minutes). Recorded 1964.

✔ ⑧ ❻

Eric Dolphy is generally agreed to have been one of the major talents in modern jazz, yet somehow he is not much talked about these days, perhaps because he was overshadowed by his contemporary John Coltrane. Perhaps, too, Coltrane was the sort of talent that could influence people, whereas Dolphy's style did not incite imitation (certainly, it is hard to think of anyone who could be said to be a Dolphy stylist). His passionate improvising on all three of his main instruments, harmonically shrewd and rhythmically daring though it was, also tended to have a slightly gurgling quality which was not immediately beautiful. The best track on this album (not his last date, incidentally, but a transcription from a Dutch television programme), recorded with a Dutch rhythm section, is his long flute feature *You Don't Know What Love Is*, which is still quite striking; it is hard to gurgle on a flute and he does not. But the music as a whole is quite spacious and thoughtful and if you had to have a record called **Last Date** (he died only a month later), then this isn't a bad way to be remembered. You can hear Dolphy's voice at the end, extracted from from an interview in the programme, saying: "When you hear music, after it's over, it's gone in the air. You can never capture it again." An odd inclusion, perhaps, when you can hear records like this again and again, but then only a jazz musician is aware of quite how much stuff does go into the walls of jazz clubs and never re-emerges. **MK**

Arne Domnerus

1924

Dompan at the Savoy **Domnerus** (as, cl); **Ulf Johansson** (p); **Sture Åkerberg** (b); **Aage Tanggaard** (d). Phontastic Ⓟ PHONT NCD 8806 (60 minutes). Recorded 1990.

④ ❻

A pleasant enough session which takes Domnerus away from his long-time partner Bengt Hallberg and teams him with young pianist Ulf Johansson, ambling through 12 standards by Duke, Hines, Waller, etc. The Swedes can do this sort of thing standing on their heads, and there are no real surprises except for the occasional tasty trombone solo by Ulf Johansson and a vocal on *Exactly Like You* from the same man which comes as a shock if you are not expecting it. He also does a chorus of scatting, and if you have never heard a Swedish pianist scatting, this is your big chance. **MK**

Lou Donaldson

1926

Sentimental Journey **Donaldson** (as); **Dr Lonnie Smith** (org); **Peter Bernstein** (g); **Fukushi Tainaka** (d); **Ray Mantilla** (perc). Columbia Ⓟ 478177 2 (55 minutes). Recorded 1994.

⑧ ❽

When Donaldson erupted onto the New York scene, hailed inevitably as the 'new' Charlie Parker (with the 'old' one still playing ...) he appeared on Blue Note sessions in the heavyweight company of men such as Horace Silver, Thelonious Monk, Milt Jackson and Clifford Brown. Although he clearly acknowledged the blanket influence of Bird, his tone was fuller with a tinge of sweetness in place of the sour sound produced by some other Parker devotees. Over the years he has worked consistently, although his many records on Blue Note, Argo/Cadet, Timeless and Milestone have varied from uncompromising jazz to funk by way of the blues. This is his first album for a major label and Columbia must be given credit for allowing Lou to come up with an uncompromising set using his regular group and orthodox material. On the title track (the old Les Brown signature tune) he has a very attractive broad sound, while on *Messin' Around With C.P.* he takes off like a bebop rocket (the C.P. of the title is Charlie Parker). *Midnight Creeper* uses an attractive broken rhythm similar to that of Lee Morgan's *Sidewinder* and Bird's *My Little Suede Shoes* showcases his fine guitarist Peter Bernstein. Lonnie Smith (not to be confused with keyboard player Lonnie Liston Smith) has been with Donaldson for years and his Hammond work is exactly in context. An additional star for musical quality may be added by those with fond memories of albums featuring sax and B3. **AM**

Dorothy Donegan

1924

Live At The 1991 Floating Jazz Festival **Donegan** (v); **Dizzy Gillespie** (t); **Jon Burr** (b); **Ray Mosca** (d). Chiaroscuro Ⓟ CRD 318 (73 minutes). Recorded 1991.

⑥ ❻

Initially a church organist, Donegan graduated to the night club circuit. She appeared in the *Sensations of 1945* film and worked in Broadway plays. She was an attraction at the Embers in the forties as her syle developed from its early boogie influences, felt the impact of bebop and embraced the Art Tatum message. Summarily dismissed by the Jepsen discography as a fringe player, she has consistently made her presence felt in the jazz world. It is true that some of her appeal is based on her extravagant actions on stage but her antics can not conceal her musical talent. This CD offers the full range of her style, with her singing mercifully restricted to one title. Her classical aspirations are humorously paraded in a *Warsaw Concerto* that leads her into *Secret Love*, *Just In Love* and finally *Lover*. Her ability as an orthodox stride pianist is captured on *Things Ain't What They Used To Be* and the presence of Tatum is felt throughout, most especially on *Tea For Two* and *Lover*, where her clean articulation and strong left hand give her access to the master's powerful swing. Gillespie guests on *Sweet Lorraine*, and a reminder of her roots is provided by *Bumble Bee Boogie*. She is not a jazz major but she has created her own specialist niche in the jazz world. **BMcR**

Pierre Dørge

1946

Even The Moon Is Dancing **Dørge** (g, balafon, v); **Harry Beckett** (t, flh); **Kenneth Agerholm**, **Niels Neergaard** (tb, african hn); **Soren Eriksen**, **Doudou Gouirand** (ss, as); **Jesper Zeuthen** (as); **John Tchicai** (ts, v); **Morten Carlsen** (ts, ney, taragot, bs, cl, zurna); **Irene Becker** (p, syn); **Bent**

Clausen (vb, perc); **Hugo Rasmussen** (b); **Johnny Dyani** (b, p, v); **Marilyn Mazur** (d, perc, kalimba); **Ahmadu Jarr** (f, perc). SteepleChase Ⓕ 31208 (69 minutes). Recorded 1985.

⑨ ❽

The eighties were an explosive period for mid-sized ensembles led by composers rethinking the jazz tradition. Many of the most adventurous outfits sprang up in Europe, and the New Jungle Orchestra from Denmark created their own niche by highlighting relevant aspects of world music. Leader Pierre Dørge had studied African and Asian musics first-hand in Gambia and Nepal; his guitar serves a similar role to that in Nigerian juju music, as commentator and, often, as conductor. The New Jungle Orchestra's unique sound is partially due to its instrumentation (which includes African horns, balafon (a wooden/gourd xylophone), and thumb piano; Turkish oboe and flute; the Hungarian clarinet-like taragato), and to key musicians such as 'talking bassist' Johnny Dyani, tenor saxist John Tchicai and trumpeter Harry Beckett, all of whom are fluent in a variety of folk styles. But primarily the NJO is a groove band; Dørge's arrangements feature loose textures, vibrant solos over pervasive percussive vamps, and infectious, buoyant rhythms—such as the 14-beat melody on *Mirjam's Dadadance* or the intertwining African and Caribbean motifs on *Even the Moon is Dancing*. The choice of *The Mooche* as the opening track on this, their debut album, was a symbolic one, not only paying homage to Dørge's predecessor in exotica, Duke Ellington, but reminding us of jazz's roots in the extended instrumental timbres and ensemble polyphony of non-American, non-European musics. **AL**

Kenny Dorham

1924-1972

Matador/Inta Somethin' **Dorham** (t); **Jackie McLean** (as); **Bobby Timmons, Walter Bishop** (p); **Teddy Smith, Leroy Vinnegar** (b); **J.C. Moses, Art Taylor** (d). Blue Note Ⓜ CDP7 84460-2 (77 minutes). Recorded 1961/62.

⑥ ❻

Although McKinley Dorham had all the right credentials (regular trumpeter in the Charlie Parker Quintet in the forties, replacement for Clifford Brown in the Max Roach group and a string of memorable appearances on record with men such as Sonny Rollins, Hank Mobley, Thelonious Monk and Andrew Hill as well as being an original Jazz Messenger) he failed to achieve the universal recognition that he deserved. Many of his own bands were musicianly but ephemeral, and this CD catches the quintet he fronted with Jackie McLean in the early sixties, both in the studio (the six titles with Timmons) and playing 'live' at the Jazz Workshop in San Francisco (six titles with Walter Bishop). It must be said at once that the 'live' tracks are better if only because Bishop is a more helpful and sympathetic group pianist. But all of the music is laced with the spirit of bebop, an area of jazz in which Dorham was an experienced and expert performer. Kenny was an original composer and *Una Mas* from the San Francisco session predates his Blue Note studio version. McLean produces solos of great intensity with the spirit of Charlie Parker not too far away. On the 'live' date fate was smiling on Dorham, who succeeds in playing his solos with virtually none of the instrumental fluffs which sometimes marred his work. Add an extra star for the 'live' titles which were issued first as a Pacific Jazz LP (the **Matador** studio material was first issued on United Artists). **AM**

Jimmy Dorsey

1904-1957

Contrasts **Dorsey** (cl, as); with the following collective personnel; **George Thow, Toots Camarata, Joe Meyer, Shorty Sherock, W.C. Clark, Ralph Munzillo, Nate Kazebier, Johnny Napton, Shorty Solomson, Jimmy Campbell, Paul McCoy, Bill Oblak, Ray Linn, Bob Alexy, Phil Napoleon, Marky Markowitz** (t); **Bobby Byrne, Don Mattinson, Joe Yukle, Bruce Squires, Sonny Lee, Jerry Rosa, Nat Lobovsky, Al Jordan, Phil Washburn, Andy Russo, Billy Pritchard, Nick DiMaio** (tb); **Dave Matthews, Rud Livingstone, Skeets Herfurt, Jack Stacy, Leonard Whitney, Charlie Frazier, Non Bernardi, Milt Yaner, Herbie Haymer, Sam Rubinwich, Frank Langone, Don Hammond, Babe Russin, Chuck Gentry, Bill Covey, Bob Lawson** (reeds); **Bobby Van Eps, Freddy Slack, Joe Lippman, Johnny Guarnieri, Dave Mann** (p); **Roc Hillman, Guy Smith, Allen Reuss, Tommy Kay** (g); **Slim Taft, Jack Ryan, Bill Miller** (b); **Ray McKinley, Buddy Schutz** (d); **June Richmond, Helen O'Connell, Bob Eberly** (v). MCA/Decca Ⓜ GRP 16262 (63 minutes). Recorded 1936-43.

⑧ ❽

Jimmy was the less rumbustious of the battling Dorseys and the bands he led never seemed to attract the same attention as Tommy's. But in many ways his bands were more adventurous; he commissioned arrangements from Dizzy Gillespie and in the forties had jazzmen such as Serge Chaloff, Stan Getz, Al Haig, Johnny Mandel and Herb Ellis on the payroll. This CD dates from a slightly earlier period and while the music is clearly intended for the dancing public there is much to recommend. Jimmy broke new ground by bringing in a coloured singer (June Richmond, prior to her term of service with Andy Kirk's band), heard here on a couple of tracks, including her success, *Darktown Strutters' Ball*. But Dorsey suffered from his record company's desire to produce cover versions of Benny Goodman hits during the late thirties. The policy seems to have changed at the end of 1940 and this issue makes it clear that from the recording of *Dolomite* onwards, Jimmy seemed determined to go his own way. The brass hits hard and with fine soloists such as tenor saxist Herbie Haymer and trumpeter Nate

Kazebier Dorsey's output improves. In fact the closing *King Porter Stomp,* with its flaring trumpet solo from Ray Linn and big-toned tenor from Babe Russin, would do credit to any swing band of the period. **AM**

Tommy Dorsey 1905-1956

And His Clambake Seven: The Music Goes Round & Round **Dorsey** (tb); with a collective personnel of: **Sterling Bose, Max Kaminsky, Pee Wee Irwin, Yank Lawson, Jimmy Blake, Charlie Shavers, Ziggy Elman** (t) **Joe Dixon, Johnny Mince, Buddy DeFranco** (cl); **Sid Block, Bud Freeman, Skeets Hurfurt, Babe Russin, Boomie Richman** (ts); **Dick Jones, Howard Smith, John Potoker, Teddy Wilson** (p); **Bill Schaeffer, Carmen Mastren, Sam Herman** (g); **Gene Traxler, Sid Block, Billy Bauer** (b); **Dave Tough, Maurice Purtill, Graham Stevenson, Cliff Leeman, Alvin Stoller** (d); **Edythe Wright, Hughie Prince, Hanna Williams** (v). RCA Bluebird Ⓜ ND 83140 (64 minutes). Recorded 1935-47.

⑦ ❻

One thing Dorsey's bands always had was an identity, and this is as true of his small groups as of the big bands. The Clambake Seven was formed in 1935 to allow Dorsey an outlet for his high spirits, and it would be a very basic mistake indeed to assume that in forming this band Dorsey was attempting the same sort of innovation and serious music-making Goodman managed with his trios and quartets of the same period. This band was a good-time outfit full of excellent jazz musicians playing in a Dixie style which was already slightly behind the times, but not that far to be perceived as a bad joke. It was a good joke in which both the band and the listener can join. The Clambake Seven was strong on vocals and on clearly-stated melodies where the trombone combined fruitily with the trumpet and tenor, and the clarinet wove driving, rhythmic embellishments. Dorsey may have had a retro approach to making music and little inclination to take his own improvisation too seriously, but his ability to carry a melody rivalled Teagarden's and Armstrong's, and his fabled discipline made for superbly tailored band performances.

The vocalist on most of these tracks, Edythe White, was not the most technically assured of the period, but her full voice has its own charm, and she at least manages to phrase in line with the rest of the band. She left Dorsey in late 1939. Hanna Willams, present on the last two tracks from 1947, is a thorough professional and sings deliciously on *But I Do Mind If Ya Don't*, which also has a tasty eight bars from Wilson. The four late-forties tracks chosen here show a different style of small-group music, quite similar to that being played at the time by Lips Page, Jonah Jones and their ilk, but it is the earlier material which most will regard as typical. **KS**

The All-Time Hit Parade Rehearsals **Dorsey, Walter Benson, Nelson Riddle, Tex Satterwhite** (tb); **Sal La Perche, Mickey Mangano, Dale Pearce, George Seaburg** (t); **Buddy De Franco** (cl, as); **Gail Curtis, Mickey Sabol** (ts); **Bruce Branson** (bs); **Dodo Marmarosa** (p); **Bob Bain** (g); **Sid Block** (b); **Joe Park** (tba); **Buddy Rich** (d); **Bobby Allen, Bonny Lou Williams, The Sentimentalists, Judy Garland, Frank Sinatra** (v). Hep Ⓜ HEPCD39 (68 minutes). Recorded 1944.

⑧ ❽

During World War II Tommy Dorsey led one of the most successful (and expensive) dance orchestras. In the summer of 1944 he was in Los Angeles for a series of engagements including the weekly NBC radio show "The Lucky Strike All-Time Hit Parade". This CD comprises 24 titles taken from previously unavailable dress rehearsals for eight of the shows, well recorded and remastered and featuring guest singers Judy Garland (on *I May Be Wrong*) and Frank Sinatra (on *I'll Walk Alone* and *If You Are But A Dream*) as well as Dorsey's regular vocalists. The CD is particularly valuable for it comes from a period when a recording ban was in force in the US; here are the earliest recordings by the band with Buddy Rich back on drums, after his discharge from the Marines. Heard on a number of tracks is the brilliant clarinet of Buddy De Franco, and Dorsey features his unique ballad trombone style on songs such as *Dancing In The Dark* and *Embraceable You*. There are some fine arrangements by Sy Oliver, Bill Finegan and Axel Stordahl and Bonny Lou Williams sings the seldom-heard verse to *I Can't Give You Anything But Love*. Dodo Marmarosa is heard on Dean Kincaide's arrangement of *Boogie Woogie*, introduced by Jose Iturbi. With the Bluebird Dorsey Archive currently in confusion on disc, this is a good summary of his band's strengths. **AM**

Double Six Of Paris

Les Double Six **Mimi Perrin** (v); on all tracks, with collective personnel of: **Monique Guerin, Louis Adelbert, Jean-Claude Briodin, Claude Germain, Eddy Louiss, Ward Swingle, Jean-Louis Conrozier, Roger Guerin, Christiane Legrand, Jacques Denjean** (v); various piano trio accompaniments, featuring: **Rene Urtreger, Georges Arvanitas** (p); **Art Simmons, Pierre Michelot** (b); **Daniel Humair** (d). Open/OMD Ⓕ CD 1518 (68 minutes). Recorded 1959-1962.

⑦ ❼

The Double Six was the brainchild of Mimi Perrin, an effervescent musical personality with great stage presence but, more crucially for the CD listener, a highly sophisticated arranger's ear. The group was formed in 1959 and first recorded that same year. The fruits of those sessions, and the follow-up disc featuring Quincy Jones compositions, are all contained on this generous CD reissue, overseen by Mimi Perrin herself.

The group, which was never more than six in number, used to double-up in the studio via double-tracking, thus allowing extremely rich voice arrangements: their style may have grown out of the King Pleasure/Eddie Jefferson/Lambert-Hendrick-Ross tradition of vocalizing previously intrumental jazz performances, but their music reached a degree of formal sophistication much in advance of any of their models. In a genre which was mostly given over to happy-go-lucky, fun-time entertainments, the diversity of moods, the ambition of the project and the sheer charm of the vocal blend were elements which remained virtually unique to this group. On this disc, a listen to *Naima* (ironically, a solo Perrin vocal) will illustrate the unusual emotional range of the group, while *Scrapple From The Apple* shows not only their extraordinary versatility and scrupulous accuracy, but also their ability to capture the real flavour of the original. Ok—it's all in French, but non-French speakers can still enjoy the glories of the vocals, unaffected by literal meaning. **KS**

Boots Douglas
1908

Boots & His Buddies, 1935–37 **Douglas** (d, ldr); **Theodore Gilders**, **Percy Bush**, **Douglas Byers**, **Charles Anderson** (t); **Johnny Shields** (tb); **Alva Brooks**, **Wee Demry** (as); **Baker Millian**, **David Ellis** (ts); **A.J. Johnson** (p); **Jeff Vant** (g); **Walter McHenry** (b); **Celeste Allen**, **Israel Wicks**, anon. vocal trio (v). JSP Ⓕ CD 327 (70 minutes). Recorded 1935-37.

④ ❻

The world of the territory bands during the twenties and thirties is shadowy. Many bands, like 'T' Holder's, did not record, and others are only spottily represented on record and in oral histories. There were two great bands from San Antonio, Texas. One was led by Don Albert from New Orleans, an urbane trumpeter who imported talent from his home town, cut some good discs, and survived as a working musician into the international festivals of the seventies. The other was led by Boots Douglas, and is more obscure. Apart from its regular recordings in the mid-thirties, little else survives, none of its star players having gone on to fame elsewhere. The performances are propulsively driven by the leader's straight-ahead drumming, giving a sense of the sound of a working band. Some arrangements are stocks (thinly disguised with new names, like *San Antonio Tamales* for *Angry*) and some section playing, such as on *Jealous*, is ragged. Singer Celeste Allen (a man) lacks Jimmy Rushing's strength, but there is an earthy, honest quality about the band that makes it compulsive listening. As you hear the musicians shouting encouragement to trumpeter Charles Anderson, or as they storm through *Riffs* or *The Vamp*, your mind's eye conjures up the long-dead dancers and a little light is shed on a dark corner of jazz history. **AS**

Kenny Drew
1928-1993

This Is New **Drew** (p); **Donald Byrd** (t); **Hank Mobley** (ts); **Wilbur Ware** (b); **G.T. Hogan** (d). Riverside Ⓜ OJCCD 483-2 (43 minutes). Recorded 1957.

⑥ ❻

Kenny Drew's classical training was apparent in his very obvious understanding of the keyboard and his careful approach to slow tunes. He worked with several important leaders, including Lester Young, Charlie Parker, Coleman Hawkins and Buddy De Franco. He was with Art Blakey when this session took place and it may have been Riverside's idea to create in the studio a Jazz Messengers-type of group. The music is well played but lacks the explosive excitement which a few of Blakey's gigantic press-rolls behind the soloists might have created. Drew himself is very much in control of the keyboard, even at the fastest of tempos; his playing has an easy fluidity and continuity not always found in the playing of bebop pianists. Byrd has several praiseworthy solos and the music actually sounds better now than it did to me when it was first released; at that time it was judged against a monthly barrage of new hard bop issues. **AM**

Kenny Drew Jr
1958

Portraits of Charles Mingus & Thelonious Monk **Drew** (p); **Lynn Seaton** (b); **Marvin 'Smitty' Smith** (d). Claves Jazz Ⓕ 50-1194 (61 minutes). Recorded 1994.

⑧ ❽

Drew is the son of the late Kenny Drew (see above), an excellent and wholly reliable pianist who worked with men such as Lester Young and Buddy De Franco. Drew Jr is classically trained and came to jazz via rhythm and blues, pop music and his father's records. Actually he does not sound like Kenny Sr and is, in some ways, a more impressive player. This is certainly his best album, beautifully recorded with two excellent rhythm men in support on eight of the ten tunes, five each by Monk and Mingus. *Light Blue* and *Weird Nightmare* are unaccompanied solos; the notes incorrectly state that *Trinkle Tinkle* is also a solo. The formal training comes out in Kenny's superb digital control and acute gradation of touch. Yet he also appreciates the humour which lurks just beneath the surface of Monk and Mingus's work and is not above bringing in a bit of two-handed stride-style playing. But it is the care which has gone into both the selection and the interpretation of the music which is impressive. Not many would tackle Monk's *Skippy* or dig out comparative Mingus rarities such as *Eclipse*, *Farewell*, *Farewell* or *Weird Nightmare*, the latter played as a thoughtful ballad. Drew has also worked with the exciting Mingus Big Band on and off record which helps to add authenticity to his interpretations of Charles's music. Recommended to all interested in contemporary jazz piano. **AM**

Paquito D'Rivera 1948

Havana Café **D'Rivera**, (cl, as, ss); **Fareed Haque**, **Ed Cherry** (g); **Danilo Perez** (p); **David Finck** (b); **Jorge Rossy** (d); **Sammy Figueroa** (p). Chesky Ⓕ JD60 (58 minutes). Recorded 1991.

⑧ ❽

Paquito D'Rivera is a fiery saxophonist-clarinettist whose uniquely exciting style reflects the combined influences of bebop, the music of Latin and South America, and the brio of his hometown of Havana.

The precocious son of one of Cuba's finest reed players, the conservatory-trained D'Rivera, while working in theatre and radio orchestras as a teenager, 'studied' jazz by listening to Willis Conover's "Jazz Hour" on Voice of America. He also played in Orquesta Cubana de Musica Moderna out of which Irakere, Cuba's foremost modern jazz band, was formed. In 1980 D'Rivera defected to the US to pursue his muse free from Castro's constraints.

On this consistently satisfying 1991 date Rivera is surrounded by some of New York's best young Latin players, and in the tradition of Art Blakey and his often youthful Jazz Messengers, the open exchange of ideas between two generations of inspired players works wonders.

Guitarist Fareed Haque's *The Return*, a gear-shifting power glide for Paquito's soaring soprano, and pianist Danilo Perez's percolating *Havana Café*, a showcase for the leader's caffeinated alto, are among several provocative charts contributed by D'Rivera's young colleagues. Also striking are the intimate clarinet features, Claudio Roditi's charming *Bossa do Brooklyn*, and Paquito's own solo piece, *Contradanza*. **CB**

Billy Drummond

Native Colours **Drummond** (d); **Steve Wilson** (ss, as); **Steve Nelson** (vb); **Renee Rosnes** (p); **Ray Drummond** (b). Criss Cross Ⓕ 1057 (63 minutes). Recorded 1991.

⑥ ❽

Drummond is a youngish drummer from an area of Virginia that has nurtured several recent arrivals on the jazz scene, including James Genus, Sam Newsome and Steve Wilson. The band Out of the Blue gave Drummond and his soon-to-be-wife Renee Rosnes important early exposure, and the pair (plus altoist Wilson) went on to work in Buster Williams's quintet. This familiarity comes through clearly on Drummond's début as a leader, which is a fine forum for his spirit, taste and flexibility. Substantial thought apparently went into the date, to judge from the nice balance of three Rosnes originals plus titles by Bobby Hutcherson, Walter Bishop and Ornette Coleman as well as the now-obligatory Monks and the hip standard *Yesterday's Gardenias*. Bassist Ray Drummond (no relation) fits in well with the spousal rhythm section, Wilson has a full sound and avoids cliché, and the often too-ruminative Nelson is in an assertive mood. The contribution of Rosnes, as player and writer, plus the good programming choices, brings the date a notch above the current neoclassical norm. **BB**

Ray Drummond

Continuum **Drummond** (b); with **Randy Brecker** (t); **Kenny Barron** (p); **John Scofield** (g); **Steve Nelson** (vb); **Marvin 'Smitty' Smith** (d); **Mor Thiam** (perc). Arabesque Jazz Ⓕ AJ0111 (68 minutes). Recorded 1994.

⑧ ❽

This is Drummond's second album for the Arabesque label and is his best so far as leader. He has played on very many albums under the direction of others but for this CD he has chosen tunes by the late Scott LaFaro, Oscar Pettiford, Stanley Cowell and Billy Strayhorn, from which it will be seen that this is by no means another of those self-indulgent collections of ephemera. Scofield (ex-Miles Davis) plays extremely well in this context; in fact this is some of his most impressive work, heavily blues-inflected and working well as a member of the group. One of the most memorable pieces here is Pettiford's *Blues In The Closet*, played as a guitar and bass duet (with Smith discreetly marking the passage of time) closely followed by a fine version of *Sophisticated Lady* played by just Drummond and vibraphonist Nelson. Ray Drummond is one of the younger generation of bass players who believes in continuing the great tradition of the instrument. Not for him the freak notes (played the wrong side of the bridge) or over-amplifications. In all a very enjoyable CD of sensible contemporary jazz. **AM**

George Duke 1946

Brazilian Love Affair **Duke** (kbds, syn, v); **Byron Miller**, **Jamil Joanes** (elb); **Ricky Lawson** (d); **Roberto Silva** (d, perc); **Airto**, **Chico Batera**, **Sheila Escovedo** (perc); **Roland Bautista** (elg); **Toninho Horta** (g, elg); **Milton Nascimento** (g, v); **Jerry Hey** (t, flh); **William Reichenbach**, **Raul De Souza** (tb); **Larry Williams** (ts, as, f); **Flora Purim**, **Josie James**, **Lynn Davis**, **Zéluiz**, **Flavio Faria**, **Lucia Turnbull**, **Lucinha Lins**, **Simone** (v). Columbia Legacy Ⓜ EPC 471283 2 (49 minutes). Recorded 1979/80.

⑧ ❽

George Duke had an early and close involvement with jazz, playing in the late sixties and early seventies with Don Ellis, Jean-Luc Ponty, Frank Zappa and Cannonball Adderley, but he fell sharply from grace in the eyes of critics, if not the general public, when he joined the disco gravy train in the mid-seventies. Thus this frequently creative session came as a surprise and went a good way to restoring his stock with the jazz crowd.

For one thing it features a generous allowance of Duke's well-structured, highly musical solo work on Fender Rhodes (especially effective on *Sugar Loaf Mountain*) and Moog synth, and some resonant, melodic trombone from Raul De Souza. In addition, with the exception of a couple of dirges by Milton Nascimento, the arrangements are crisp, intelligent and colourful, and generally infused with the rhythmic verve associated with Brazilian music. Furthermore, although Brazil provided the stimulus for the record, this is no mere exercise in cultural colonialism: perhaps as a result of his disco experience, Duke was able to conceive a spirited and individual fusion of funk and Brazilian impulses. The result is hardly profound, but it can be very exciting. The set appears in digitally remastered form as part of Columbia's Contemporary Masters series. **MG**

Dutch Swing College Band

Digital Dixie **Rod Mason** (t, bb); **Dick Kaart** (tb); **Bob Kaper** (cl, as); **Peter Schilperoort** (cl, ss, bs); **Fred Murray** (p); **Henk Bosch Van Drakesteyn** (b); **Huub Janssen** (d, wbd). Philips Ⓜ 800 065-2 (52 minutes). Recorded 1981.

⑤ ❽

Formed in 1945 by Schilperoort and pianist Fred Vink, the DSCB were born in the Dutch Swing College, a school that had been founded the previous year. The music they played has always been open-minded Dixieland with mainstream affiliations. They have recorded with Sidney Bechet and Joe Venuti and toured with the likes of Jimmy Witherspoon, Billy Butterfield, Hot Lips Page and Albert Nicholas. This CD, recorded at the North Sea Jazz Festival, was the first made after the arrival of British trumpeter Mason and is typical DSCB fare. Schilperoort on clarinet and soprano is the strongest soloist but Mason, with the outstanding Louis Armstrong cadenza on *West End Blues* and driving solo work elsewhere, runs him close. Murray sounds more at home in the boppish climate of *Green Dolphin Street* than with the Dixieland, Kaper's thin-toned clarinet noodles gently but Kaart's trombone is somewhat pedestrian. The whole is better than the parts, however, and the rhythm section do a proficient job. Mason's horn and Schilperoort's reeds earn the extra half star. **BMcR**

John Eardley 1928-1991

From Hollywood to New York **Eardley** (t); **J.R. Monterose** (ts); **Pete Jolly**, **George Syran** (p); **Red Mitchell**, **Teddy Kotick** (b); **Larry Bunker**, **Nick Stabulas** (d). NewJazz/Prestige Ⓜ OJCCD 1746-2 (41 minutes). Recorded 1954/55.

⑧ ❽

Having joined Gerry Mulligan's quartet in 1954, Eardley is often compared with his predecessor Chet Baker, but Eardley had his own distinctive crackling attack and fatter, sassier tone, and he wasn't nearly so enamoured of slow ballads. He's closer to Clifford Brown than to the other C.B. Despite the presence of Mulligan stalwarts Mitchell and Bunker on the 1954 Hollywood session, the music throughout is closer to emerging East Coast hard bop than West Coast cool.

Most of the tunes from these two sessions move at medium-to-fast tempos—an exception being Tadd Dameron's lovely *If You Could See Me Now*. *Demanton* is Eardley's romp on *Sweet Georgia Brown*'s chords; on *Hey There*, he carefully balances rests and jaunty lines, deftly structuring his solo without aiming toward an explosive climax. Like the rest of the New York session, the tune features the little-recorded, throaty tenorist J.R. Monterose, whose presence is a plus.

In recent years Eardley has lived in Germany and Belgium, and been associated with the WDR Big Band in Cologne. Of late he has testified to the subtle influence on his playing of Bix Beiderbecke (who sat beside Jon's father in Paul Whiteman's trumpet section), but that influence is undetectable here. **KW**

Charles Earland

1941

Unforgettable **Earland** (org); **Kenny Rampton** (t); **Clifford Adams** (tb); **Eric Anderson** (ss, ts); **Houston Person** (ts); **Oliver Nevels** (g); **Gregory Williams, Buddy Williams** (d); **Laurence Killian** (perc). Muse Ⓕ MCD 5455 (46 minutes). Recorded 1991.

✔ ⑦ ❽

Earland has been working the same musical area for most of his career, hitting the chitlin circuit in the sixties and having commercial success at the end of that decade. This latest offering from him does not break with tradition, sticking with loping, easy feels and blues-drenched phrases. Producer Houston Person appears on tenor on three numbers; otherwise, the excellent saxophonist with Earland's working band, Eric Alexander, dominates solo space along with the organist.

This album is a cut above the average, if only for the reason that it was recorded a couple of months after Earland had suffered a near-fatal heart attack and been nursed back to health by his wife, Sheila, the album's dedicatee. The music is lovingly coaxed along by the organist throughout; there is also a happy absence of crass, fabricated climaxes as well as long, aimless jams where everyone gets a solo because there is no other way to fill the album up. There is one 12-minute piece, Carlos Santana's *Europa*, but this is at a bright, happy tempo and none of the solos sound too long. A fine, tasteful organ-and-sax disc, not generous on playing time, but it's all meat and no potatoes. **KS**

Earthbound

Unity **Alexandros** (p); **Alex Foster** (ss); **Andy McKee** (b); **Victor Jones** (d); **Steve Thornton, Cosa Ross** (perc). Leo Ⓕ CD LR 189 (62 minutes). Recorded 1992.

⑥ ❻

Alexandros has his own small New York recording studio and his powerful, free piano is at the heart of Earthbound. He is a personal friend of Cecil Taylor and the group takes its inspiration from the Taylor small group. Fortunately the leader's Greek background and his enthusiasm for bravura free piano are factors that coalesce more naturally than might seem likely. His flowingly propulsive clusters are supported by left-hand chordal patterns that make for their own brand of organization. This carries over into the ensemble and provides a modus operandum for the group. Foster has a Jimmy Lyons-like feeling for space and, although some distance from the former Taylor alumnus in terms of style, he produces carousing melodic outbursts that display similar dramatic intent. Despite the formal programme, there is no thematic continuity in his solos; prime motifs are allowed to develop until, almost arbitrarily, time is right for further musical mutation. Jones, McKee and Thornton make for an arhythmic support team and, even when Ross makes the unit a sextet, there is no congestion. The permanency of such a group must be in some doubt but this CD has the excitement and quality to foster hope that they will survive. **BMcR**

Billy Eckstine

1914-1993

Imagination **Eckstine** (v); with a big band including: **Pete Candoli, Don Fagerquist** (t); **Bud Shank** (f, as); **Gerry Wiggins** (p); **Red Callender** (b); **Larry Bunker** (d); **Pete Rugolo** (ldr, arr); remainder unidentified. EmArcy Ⓜ 848 162-2 (40 minutes). Recorded 1958.

⑦ ❽

Back in the mid-forties, Eckstine led the first big bebop band, employing such Young Turks as Charlie Parker, Fats Navarro, Dexter Gordon and Art Blakey. Although he joined the 'establishment' later to become one of the most popular (and most imitated) baritones of his day, he never lost touch with his jazz background. While this album consists of a dozen good standards, his approach is clearly that of a man who knows how to phrase correctly and, moreover, how to keep that powerful vibrato under control. Occasionally arranger Rugolo allows Billy to take off with just a small group behind him, as on *What A Little Moonlight Can Do* for example, but much of the time it is Eckstine pitching his wares at the wider audience. *Gigi*, from a different session, has been added to the ll tracks which comprised the original LP, but EmArcy have failed to discover any more personnel details. There is a good trombonist to be heard and a guitarist who might well be the late Howard Roberts. Kiyoshi Tokiwa has remastered the original tapes with skill. **AM**

No Cover, No Minimum **Eckstine** (v, t); with big band including: **Charlie Walp** (t); **Bucky Manieri** (tb); **Charlie McLean, Buddy Balboa** (saxes); **Buddy Grievey** (d); **Bobby Tucker** (p, arr). Roulette Ⓜ CDP7 98583-2 (65 minutes). Recorded 1960.

✔ ⑩ ❽

This was Eckstine's first and best live album, and arguably his greatest album ever. He is forever associated with the revolutionary big band he put together in the mid-forties after leaving Earl Hines, but in fact the support he gets here is much more sympathetic and far less distracting. Here, we have Eckstine in prime voice in front of a (thankfully inaudible) Las Vegas audience, cossetted in perfect little-big-band arrangements penned by long-term associate Bobby Tucker. His repertoire is a judicious mix of pieces long identified with him and newly-covered songs, some of them at that stage still fresh from Broadway (*I've Grown Accustomed to Her Face*, for instance). All through, that oft-imitated and never-matched voice, deep and sensual in a way Nat King Cole never attempted to be, handles every challenge effortlessly. This is a stunning display of sustained vocalizing, the intimacy of the Tucker arrangements only throwing it into further relief. Eckstine is often omitted when it comes to lists of Great Jazz Singers. He should not be, and this album is living proof of it.

The entirely remixed CD reissue is an enormous improvement over the old vinyl set, both in terms of recording balance and sound improvement and in terms of playing time. We have no less than 13 extra tracks here. Now that is value for money. **KS**

Harry Edison

1915

Jawbreakers **Edison** (t); **Eddie 'Lockjaw' Davis** (ts); **Hugh Lawson** (p); **Ike Isaac** (b); **Clarence Johnston** (d). Riverside Ⓜ OJCCD-487-2 (42 minutes). Recorded 1962.

Over the years the music created by these two ex-Basie stars tended to be predictable but nevertheless enjoyable. This is a well-transferred reissue of their first album together, and it retains the freshness of that early meeting. This was Edison's regular quintet, with Davis taking tenor saxist Jimmy Forrest's place for the day; the rhythm section performs with the assurance of a regular trio. There can have been few major jazz soloists with more immediately recognizable sounds than Edison and Davis, each in his own way making telling use of a fairly limited vocabulary. Harry's tightly-muted opening statement on his blues *Moolah* is a case in point, for this is in effect a compendium of his favourite phrases, yet he creates a sense of tension which is riveting for the listener. The eight tunes hold a few surprises, such as the way the two produce the theme statement on Miles Davis's tune *Four*. All in all, a fine example of mainstream jazz played by experts of the genre. **AM**

Teddy Edwards

1924

Together Again! **Edwards** (ts); **Howard McGhee** (t); **Phineas Newborn Jr** (p); **Ray Brown** (b); **Ed Thigpen** (d). Contemporary Ⓜ OJCCD-424-2 (40 minutes). Recorded 1961.

⑦ ❽

An extremely well-equipped player, Edwards had to wait unfairly long to be recognised. He figured in the West Coast bebop scene of the mid to late forties, which is when he first worked with McGhee. The trumpeter went on to sudden fame, prestigious bookings and a long spell out of action through drug addiction; Edwards stayed in California, healthy and obscure. But by 1961 he was building a name, and when McGhee dropped into Los Angeles for an engagement, their reunion was unquestionably a meeting of equals. It proved a wonderfully relaxed affair, although something more than the amiable blow through well-worn standards that such meetings often turn into. Edwards is an excellent blues player, but he had already demonstrated that on **Teddy's Ready** (currently unavailable on CD). Here, apart from Charlie Parker's *Perhaps*, he chooses other structures, bustling through the boppish changes of *Up There* and bringing a dry, unsentimental sensitivity to *Misty*. McGhee plays dextrously throughout, usually muted, developing the ballad *You Stepped Out of a Dream* and his own *Sandy* with taste and imagination, qualities shared by the rhythm section. The album's undimmed vitality stems less from the players' individual achievements than from its air of fellowship and mutual appreciation. **TR**

Mark Egan

1951

Beyond Words **Egan** (b); **Toninho Horta**, **Steve Khan** (g); **Bill Evans** (ss); **Clifford Carter** (syn); **Danny Gottlieb** (d); **Don Alias**, **Manolo Badrena**, **Gordon Gottlieb** (perc). Blue Moon Ⓕ R279171 (50 minutes). Recorded 1991.

Bassist Mark Egan is an important member of the first generation of jazz-oriented musicians who have devoted the majority of their efforts to the so-called fusion school. Indeed, Egan has been a central part of groups led by such popular and varied performers as guitarist Pat Metheny, saxophonist David Sanborn, and the Brazilians Airto Moreira and Flora Purim.

Here, as in the work of his previous units South Dade and Elements, Egan has evolved an attractive electronic palette through the use of such custom-instruments as the Pedulla double-neck 4 and 8 string bass guitar. Like Metheny, he is a lyrical player whose pieces unfold with kaleidoscopic swirls of genuine improvisation, gentle but no less dynamic Latin-rock rhythms, plus an often poignant ethnic music ambience that have made his efforts popular with world music and New Age as well as jazz audiences.

As suggested by the tune titles such as *Campfire Stories*, *Swept Away* and *The Bamboo Forest*, there is a strongly picaresque dimension to Egan's broadly-stroked sketches. His soundscapes are largely confined to a narrow range of postcard-pretty pastels; still, there is a palpable element of sincerity—Egan's music is heartfelt. So, although deviating from the usual criteria associated with jazz, Egan (as well as Metheny, et al) is again raising the question, "what is jazz?" **CB**

Marty Ehrlich

1955

The Traveller's Tale **Ehrlich** (ss, as, cl, bcl); **Stan Strickland** (ss, ts, v); **Linsday Horner** (b); **Bobby Previte** (d). Enja Ⓕ 6024-20 (54 minutes). Recorded 1989.

⑧ ❽

A graduate of the New England Conservatory Of Music, Ehrlich has worked in the testing musical workshops of George Russell, Gunther Schuller and Ran Blake. He is a young veteran of nearly 50 recording dates and his name has not altogether inappropriately been linked with the Knitting Factory, New York's own cosmopolitan music academy. Five of the eight compositions and all of the functional arrangements here are by Ehrlich and they serve the quartet well. *Alice's Wonderland* is especially imaginative and yet, like the remainder, it never obstructs the individual contributions. For their part, the rhythm duo are consciously obtrusive. Both behind the written unisons and the most detailed solos their fractured progress provides the kind of accent displacement to stimulate the horns. Ehrlich and Strickland respond well. Ehrlich's solos are imaginatively varied; they do not take a wildly convoluted route but, like the plaintive alto on the title track, use the freer harmonies of the avant-garde in a way that colours and enhances them. No attempt is made to shock and there are sequences where simplicity becomes its own virtue. Behind Strickland's idiosyncratic vocal on *The Reconsidered Blues*, Ehrlich's clarinet pulls on its Pee Wee-ish cloak to warm the agonizingly vunerable voice. It is typical of the way in which Ehrlich chooses whatever approach or whatever of his many horns suits the situation. **BMcR**

8 Bold Souls

Sideshow **Robert Griffin** (t, flh); **Isaiah Jackson** (tb); **Aaron Dodd** (tba); **Mwata Bowden** (cl, bs); **Edward Wilkerson Jr** (ts, arr); **Naomi Millender** (vc); **Harrison Bankhead** (b); **Dushun Mosley** (d). Arabesque Jazz Ⓕ AJO 103 (66 minutes). Recorded 1991.

⑧ ❽

A third generation AACM member, Edward Wilkerson Jr may be best known for his involvement in the three-piece Ethnic Heritage Ensemble, but his gargantuan orchestra Shadow Vignettes and this flexible octet are the primary outlets for his distinctive compositions. In terms of length and compositional breadth, his pieces could be considered tone poems; they frequently evolve through contrasting episodes and integrate solos within the dramatic atmospheres Wilkerson strives to create. *Black Herman* is a case in point, with a calm, dark, moving dirge framing a surprisingly upbeat boppish line that houses his tenor solo. The arrangement of Ornette Coleman's *Lonely Woman* creates its own ebb and flow, growing out of a striking cello and bass introduction. *Glass Breakers* reveals the main source of his inspiration—the trombone theme and assisting horn harmonies, especially the trumpet and clarinet voicings, are lessons learned from Ellington. A tenor saxist of brawn and swagger, Wilkerson is out of the Hawkins/Webster/Shepp lineage, and each of the other Bold Souls have their own noteworthy talents. In writing for the ensemble he favours deep, rich velvet sonorities; as the arrangements drift from scene to scene, textures, the timbres, and colours are sure to shift as well. These pieces seldom shout, but you may find yourself seduced by their unexpected curves and noir-ish moods. **AL**

Roy Eldridge

1911-1989

Heckler's Hop **Eldridge** (t, v); with a collective personnel including **Robert Williams**, **Eli Robinson** (tb); **Benny Goodman** (cl); **Scoops Carey** (as); **Joe Eldridge** (as, arr); **Chu Berry**, **Dave Young**, **Prince Robinson**, **Franz Jackson** (ts); **Jess Stacy**, **Teddy Cole**, **Clyde Hart**, **Kenny Kersey** (p); **John Collins**, **Danny Barker** (g); **Israel Crosby**, **Truck Parham**, **Artie Shapiro**, **Ted Sturgis** (b); **Gene Krupa**, **Zutty Singleton**, **Sid Catlett**, **Panama Francis** (d); **Helen Ward**, **Gladys Palmer**, **Laurel Watson** (v). Hep Ⓜ HEPCD1030 (66 minutes). Recorded 1936-39.

⑧ ❻

Eldridge was not alone in providing hints of the bebop to come, for the same might be said of Red Allen, the undervalued (especially on CD) Charlie Shavers, and even Ellington's Rex Stewart. But Roy was the idol of young Dizzy Gillespie who, during the period of the above recordings, was busy succeeding to what had been Eldridge's chair in the Teddy Hill band.

While not the most complete trumpeter of the thirties, he was certainly the most fiery and, by this time, the most aware of his debt and implicit challenge to Louis Armstrong. Much of his phraseology was Armstrong played faster, while the coda of his famous *After You've Gone* (later re-made with Gene Krupa's band) refers explicitly to the Armstrong/Hines *Weather Bird* duo.

This collection usefully collects his early small-group work, if his Chicago-based eight-to-ten-piece band may be described this way. Some dubious vocals (easily overshadowed by Roy's own on *You're A Lucky Guy*) are intermingled with impressive trumpet features. The standouts are eight tracks with Chu Berry, the first four under Krupa's leadership; the five duplicated on Berry's own album have less surface noise there, but the instrumental sound is more faithful here. **BP**

After You've Gone **Eldridge** (t, v); with a collective personnel including **Sidney De Paris**, **Yank Lawson**, **Elmon Wright** (t); **Ted Kelly**, **Sandy Williams**, **Gerald Wilson**, **Vic Dickenson**, **Wilber De Paris** (tb); **Buster Bailey** (cl), **Joe Eldridge**, **Andrew Gardner**, **Porter Kilbert**, **Sahib Shihab** (as); **Chu Berry**, **Hal Singer**, **Franz Jackson**, **Tom Archia**, **Ike Quebec**, (ts); **Cecil Payne**, **Ernie Caceres** (bs); **Teddy Cole**, **Ted Brannon**, **Dave Bowman**, **Buster Harding**, **Duke Jordan**, **Rozelle Gayle** (p); **John Collins** (g), **John Kirby**, **Ted Sturgis**, **Billy Taylor**, **Rodney Richardson** (b); **Harold West**, **Cozy Cole**, **Lee Abrams**, **Sid Catlett** (d). MCA/Decca Ⓜ GRP 16052 (64 minutes). Recorded 1936-46.

✓ ⑩ ❻

After Gene Krupa broke up his band in the spring of 1943, Roy Eldridge fronted various small groups, then joined Artie Shaw. After leaving Shaw he formed his own big band which failed, not for musical reasons but simply because the climate was not right for a new big band. This recommended CD covers that period, opening with seven titles from a November 1943 Chicago date (three of the tracks are previously unissued) which contain some of Roy's most exciting solos, including the exceptional *The Gasser* which builds and builds. Ike Quebec is on tenor, making his record début on this session. The big band titles are designed principally as showcases for Eldridge, who rises to the occasion, as always. The Armstrong influence is strong at times but the heated tone is uniquely Eldridge, especially on numbers such as *St Louis Blues* and *After You've Gone*. *Embraceable You* is by Roy and a big-but-efficient studio band. The final track is a version of *Christopher Columbus*, the only number to appear from Roy's first date as leader (in 1936) by what is, in fact, a small group taken from the Fletcher Henderson band. The transfers to CD are good, with the instrumentalists clearly defined. Strongly recommended. **AM**

Uptown: Roy Eldridge With The Gene Krupa Orchestra **Eldridge** (t, v); **Krupa** (d, ldr); with musicians including: **Anita O'Day** (v); **Sam Musiker** (cl, as, ts); **Frank Rosolino**, **Tommy Pederson** (tb); **Ralph Blaze** (g); **Ray Biondi** (g); **Ed Mihelich** (b) and others. CBS Ⓜ 4663102 (73 minutes). Recorded 1941-49.

⑥ ❻

Although workmanlike, Gene Krupa's band remained outside the group of top swing bands. Krupa's library was often unimaginative and avowedly commercial, and it was mainly the solo work of Eldridge and Anita O'Day (referred to in Downbeat as "Krupa's fem chirper") which gained the band a place in history. Eldridge was a notably volatile performer throughout his career and was often filled with remorse after some of his more explosive excesses. There were remarkably few of these during his time with Krupa and some of his solos here were quite masterful. The reworking of his feature from the thirties, *After You've Gone*, though flashy, is a trumpet tour-de-force which contained, for 1941, a virtuoso exploration of the instrument's upper reaches. *Rockin' Chair* (a hit at the time) and *Skylark* similarly deserve their places in posterity. O'Day and Eldridge did not get along, but they worked well together. The singer was still evolving her style during her stay with Krupa, but impresses wherever she appears. The famous *Let Me Off Uptown* has a fiery Eldridge solo, but some of the more obscure titles like *Kick It* are even more effective, and also employ the contrast between O'Day's fey voice and Eldridge's pithy trumpet. Some of the arrangements are good, notably the surreal *The Walls Keep Talkin'* which again has fetching O'Day and serrated Eldridge trumpet. **SV**

Roy and Diz **Eldridge**, **Dizzy Gillespie** (t); **Oscar Peterson** (p); **Herb Ellis** (g); **Ray Brown** (b); **Louis Bellson** (d).Verve Ⓜ 521 647-2 (76 minutes). Recorded 1954.

⑩ ❻

The two LPs which made up the original release of this material back in the fifties have been subject to many fluctuations of critical standing: presently, this late-autumn 1954 L.A. session is generally seen as an OK date where neither trumpeter really takes off and delivers a sermon from the Olympus of trumpet playing. But perhaps that view is too coloured by the idea of challenge, of contest and of the need to have an ultimate victor. For all Eldridge's fabled competitiveness, and Gillespie's ability to cut other trumpeters, there is a great deal of playing here distinguished by a clear desire to create a performance which is more coherent than mere endless choruses trying to top the other guy. A track like *Trumpet Blues*, basically an idea rather than a tune (the idea is to give the two horns a chance to trade choruses and bounce off each other's lines), shows both men slowly warming to the task, creating balanced statements, mindful of light and shade, and also creating background riffs from time to time.

Similarly, the *Ballad Medley* features some truly outstanding and sensitive interpretations of quality material. Eldridge's naked emotionalism brings out the most sincere side of Gillespie's balladry and curbs his tendency to mug, while Gillespie's wonderful technical control pushes Eldridge to form his notes and phrases with especial care. This is not to say that both players have too much respect for each other not to ruffle a few feathers, but no-one is out for blood, even on a warhorse such as *I've Found a New Baby*, and the listener benefits from the friendly rivalry and exploration of each trumpeter's limits. It is a co-operative, and one by which the listener benefits dramatically. Don't be put off by those who always know better: this is the real thing, down to the last note. **KS**

Little Jazz: The Best of the Verve Years **Eldridge** (t, flh, v); **Joe Ferrante**, **Bernie Glow**, **Ernie Royal**, **Nick Travis** (t); **Jimmy Cleveland**, **J.J. Johnson**, **Fred Ohms**, **Kai Winding**, **Benny Morton**, **Vic Dickinson** (tb); **Eddie Barefield** (cl); **Sam Marowitz**, **Hal McKusick**, **Benny Carter**, **Johnny Hodges**, **Sonny Stitt** (as); **Aaron Sachs**, **Eddie Shu**, **Coleman Hawkins**, **Ben Webster** (ts); **Danny**

Bank (bs); **Oscar Peterson, Dave McKenna, Dick Wellstood, Billy Strayhorn, Bruce Macdonald, Hank Jones, Ronnie Ball** (p); **Oscar Peterson** (org); **Barney Kessel, Barry Galbraith, Herb Ellis** (g); **Ray Brown, John Drew, Walter Page, John Simmons, Jimmy Woode, Benny Moten, George Duvivier** (b); **Jo Jones, J.C. Heard, Gene Krupa, Alvin Stoller, Buddy Rich, Sam Woodyard, Eddie Locke, Mickey Sheen** (d); **Anita O'Day** (v); **The Orchestras of Gene Krupa, George Williams, Russell Garcia and Johnny Hodges**. Verve Ⓜ 523 338-2 (77 minutes). Recorded 1952-60.

⑨ ❽

If anyone deserved the nickname 'Little Jazz', it was trumpeter extraordinaire Roy Eldridge. Although often pegged as the link between Louis Armstrong and Dizzy Gillespie, Eldridge should be recognized as their co-equal, the prime innovator of the swing trumpet tradition and an indefatigable spirit whose rhythmic finesse, melodic inventiveness and *joie de vivre* always lifted the bandstand. In this splendid collection culled from his varied projects for Norman Granz's Verve label between 1952 and 1960, we catch 'Little Jazz' in an array of settings. There is a 1956 reprise of Eldridge's first big hit as a member of the 1941 Gene Krupa Band, *Let Me Off Uptown*, featuring Roy's snappy vocal exchange with a sassy Anita O'Day and a cooking Krupa-led studio band. There are tips-of-the-hat to the Armstrong tradition where Roy and his Central Plaza Dixielanders elevate *Bugle Call Rag* and *Ja-Da*. Although string dates are not everyone's cup of tea, Roy's heart-on-sleeve limning of *How Long Has This Been Going On?* is a show-stopper embellished by Russ Garcia's Orchestra. The quintet date with Eldridge confrere Coleman Hawkins is another grabber. For barn-burners, the romp through *Allen's Alley* with Sonny Stitt, Oscar Peterson's trio and Jo Jones shows that Roy could bop with the best. With 19 great tracks, many with star colleagues from Granz's Jazz at the Philharmonic, Eldridge jumps with poignant joy whatever the tempo or format. **CB**

Eliane Elias

1960

Cross Currents Elias (p); **Barry Finnery** (g); **Eddie Gomez** (b); **Jack DeJohnette, Peter Erskine** (d); **Café** (perc). Denon Ⓕ CY 2180 (62 minutes: DDD). Recorded 1987.

⑧ ❽

Elias has no fewer than six albums on the market at present, with the later ones on Blue Note and Manhattan for the most part emphasizing her Brazilian heritage rather than her strong jazz credentials. This earlier Denon date, her second for the label, shows why we should be excited about her talent and rather concerned that, for the time being, she has put the jazz side of her playing more or less under wraps. To open with a flawless rendition of Bud Powell's *Hallucinations* at the sort of tempo Bud himself would use to scare other pianists off with is pretty impressive. To follow it up with an attractively funky riff-based title song with plenty of meaty improvisation to boot means that this album is not about potential, but about already-realized talent. Elias has the ability to send her improvised lines in any direction at any moment, has a highly-developed dynamic sense so that any phrase she plays carries many meanings, and has a tidy elegance which may be a leftover of the inevitable Bill Evans influence, but more truly indicates the high quality of her musical thought. To enjoy the sheer confidence of her playing, go no further than her version of Mingus's *Peggy's Blue Skylight*. Let's hope she comes back onto this course on future albums. **KS**

Kurt Elling

1967

Close Your Eyes Elling (v); **Edward Peterson, Von Freeman** (ts); **Laurence Hobgood** (p, syn); **Dave Onderonk** (g); **Eric Hochberg, Rob Amster** (b); **Paul Wertico** (d). Blue Note Ⓕ CDP 830645 2 (64 minutes) Recorded 1994.

⑥ ❾

Young Chicagoan Elling takes the opportunity, during his list of dedicatees, to mention Eddie Jefferson, Jon Hendricks and Mark Murphy "who taught me how to sing Jazz", and indeed it is difficult to envisage this album existing without the prior example laid out by that triumvirate, although the ghost of Sinatra also hovers. Elling has a voice with plenty of texture, and he uses its limitations to his own advantage, pushing it, bending it, growling with it, straining it, using an expressive falsetto, so you get a clear impression that he has done a lot of homework to get this far. He has taken a leaf out of Hendricks's book by adding lyrics to previously instrumental works (Wayne Shorter's *Dolores* becomes *Dolores' Dream*, a delirious and funny recounting of a romantic interlude) as well as singing pieces with lyrics already intact (the title song, *Wait 'Til You See Her* and *Ballad of the Sad Young Men*). He can scat and slur with the best of them but his diction is mostly excellent.

The supporting players stick very much to the background, with the tenors appearing on just three tracks between them. It is not too important, because there is plenty going on out front. **KS**

Duke Ellington

1899-1974

Early Ellington: The Complete Brunswick and Vocalion Recordings of Duke Ellington 1926-1931 Ellington (p); **Bubber Miley, Louis Metcalf, June Clark, Arthur Whetsol, Freddie Jenkins, Cootie Williams** (t); **Joe Nanton** (tb); **Juan Tizol** (vtb); **Prince Robinson, Otto Hardwick,**

Rudy Jackson, **Harry Carney**, **Barney Bigard**, **Johnny Hodges** (cl, ss, as, ts, bs); **Fred Guy** (bj); **Teddy Bunn** (g, bj); **Bennie Payne** (p, v); **Mack Shaw** (tba); **Wellman Braud** (b); **Sonny Greer** (d, v); **Bruce Johnson** (wbd); **Harold Randolph** (kz); **Joe Cornell** (acc); **Bill Robinson** (v, spch, tap); **Dick Robertson** (v). MCA Ⓜ GRP 36402 (three discs: 204 minutes). Recorded 1926-31.

⑧ ❻

This issue demonstrates simultaneously the strengths and weaknesses of a single label reissue policy for as prolific a recording artist as Ellington. Only passing references in Stephen Lasker's admirably detailed notes make clear that during the same period Ellington recorded for Okeh, Victor, Columbia and a handful of lesser labels. For this reason, despite the formidable span of material included here, and the opportunity to hear the orchestra coalesce from near chaos to slick professionalism, great chunks of the story are missing, and Jabbo Smith's alternative vision of *Black and Tan Fantasy* (for example) or Adelaide Hall's glowing, wordless *Creole Love Call* need to be sought elsewhere.

If incompleteness is a weakness in the set, the benefits (as compared to the comprehensive but technically flawed reissues on Classics 39, 542, 550, 559, 569, 577 and 586) are the uniformly high quality of the originals (many from Jerry Valburn's unique collection, or from original metal masters) and excellent (if slightly 'toppy') re-mastering. Lasker's painstaking and occasionally over-pedantic research, adhering to the spelling "Whetsel", for instance, makes the whole document remarkably illuminating. During the course of the five years spanned by this set, Braud and Greer redefined the rhythm section to something akin to Luis Russell's New Orleans beat, and Bigard and Miley recorded much of their finest work. The high points are too many to list, but this set is indispensable as the best-produced cross section of Ellington's work as his genius emerged. **AS**

Early Ellington (1927-1934) **Ellington** (p, ldr); with a collective personnel of: **Bubber Miley**, **Louis Metcalf**, **Arthur Whetsol**, **Freddy Jenkins**, **Cootie Williams**, **Louis Bacon** (t) **Joe Nanton**, **Lawrence Brown** (tb), **Juan Tizol** (vtb), **Johnny Hodges** (cl, ss, as), **Otto Hardwick** (cl, ss, as, bss), **Barney Bigard**, **Rudy Jackson** (cl, ts), **Harry Carney** (cl, as, bs), **Fred Guy** (bj, g), **Wellman Braud** (b), **Sonny Greer** (d), **Adelaide Hall**, **Cootie Williams** (v). RCA Bluebird Ⓜ ND 86852 (72 minutes). Recorded 1927-1934.

✔ ⑩ ❽

When I went to lectures on mediaeval French in my three years at university, the lecturer stood up on the first day and said: "I know why you're all here. You're here out of duty. You think mediaeval French is a sort of old-fashioned and primitive stage on the way to modern French. This is emphatically not so. It's a living language in its own right, and in some ways vastly superior to modern French..."

Dan Morgenstern has the same message about Duke in his notes for this CD. "Our common perspective on jazz, which adversely affects our openness to the music's rich heritage, is so reflexively historical that we hear the past not for its own sake, but merely as an overture to the present. But had Ellington through some misfortune ceased to record in 1934 he would nonetheless be a figure to reckon with in the annals of jazz. This music needs no historical footnoteing to be appreciated ..."

He is absolutely right. More than half these 22 numbers are little classics. From *Washington Wobble* to *Old Man Blues*, from *Creole Love Call* to *Mood Indigo*, they are all worth burning on the memory. As Morgenstern says again, after a Fletcher Henderson record you wish the soloists could have gone on a lot longer; with these Duke sides you know he has got it just right. The odd thing is that Duke himself did want to change things, over and over again. The *East St Louis Toodle-Oo* on this CD was recorded in 1927 and was already his fourth crack at it. *Rockin' In Rhythm* is on here from a 1931 version; he was rejigging that tune 40 years later ...

Yes, it does sound dated. That clanking banjo ... those piping clarinets ... that busy-bee double bass ... but through it all comes the sound of a genius taking his first steps, mixing his first colours, stretching his first muscles, and you fall under the spell all over again. **MK**

Reminiscing in Tempo **Ellington** (p); **Arthur Whetsol**, **Bubber Miley**, **Freddie Jenkins**, **Cootie Williams**, **Wallace Jones**, **Harold 'Shorty' Baker**, **Francis Williams**, **Al Killian**, **Shelton Hemphill**, **John Cook**, **Clark Terry**, **William 'Cat' Anderson** (t); **Rex Stewart** (c); **Ray Nance** (t, c, vn); **Joe 'Tricky Sam' Nanton**, **Lawrence Brown**, **Claude Jones**, **Tyree Glenn**, **John Sanders**, **Britt Woodman**, **Quentin Jackson** (tb); **Juan Tizol** (vtb); **Johnny Hodges**, **Barney Bigard**, **Otto Hardwick**, **Ben Webster**, **Jimmy Hamilton**, **Russell Procope**, **Al Sears**, **Paul Gonsalves**, **Bill Graham**, **Harry Carney** (reeds); **Fred Guy** (g, bj); **Lonnie Johnson** (g); **Wellman Braud**, **Hayes Alvis**, **Billy Taylor**, **Jimmy Blanton**, **Oscar Pettiford**, **Junior Raglin**, **Jimmy Woode** (b); **Sonny Greer**, **Fred Avendorf**, **Sam Woodyard** (d); **Baby Cox**, **Ivie Anderson**, **Kay Davis**, **Mahalia Jackson** (v). Columbia/Legacy Ⓜ CK 48654 (77 minutes). Recorded 1928-60.

✔ ⑩ ❽

Hard to believe, but with all of the Ellington that has found its way onto CD, there is no single collection that has a broad focus on the orchestra's work in the thirties. While CBS/Sony, which owns most of Ellington's output from the period, has done well by small-group Ellingtonia, its only survey of the full band with a thirties focus is this anthology, produced in conjunction with a 1991 public television special. The other company covering the Ellington band in this period, Classics, has stuck to its year-by-year chronicling, thereby keeping each individual CD's focus quite narrow. Fifteen of the 20 tracks on this current title date from 1930-41 and such essential items as the complete *Reminiscing in Tempo*, the new conceptions of *East St Louis Toodle-Oo* and *Black and Tan Fantasy*,

Merry-Go-Round, It Don't Mean a Thing and *Sophisticated Lady* are included, plus soundtrack versions of *The Labourers, Cotton Tail* and *Don't Get Around Much Anymore,* plus an unissued take of *Grievin'*. *The Mooche* on the front end of the anthology, plus four later titles (including *On a Turquoise Cloud* with Kay Davis and *Come Sunday* with Mahalia Jackson) make for something of a lopsided survey; but until Columbia sorts itself out, this collection becomes essential by default. Sound is greatly improved from early CBS reissues. **BB**

The Duke's Men—Small Groups Volumes 1 & 2 Selected collective personnel under leaderships: **Rex Stewart, Ellington, Johnny Hodges, Barney Bigard, Cootie Williams, The Gotham Stompers**; including: **Rex Stewart** (c); **Cootie Williams, Freddie Jenkins** (t); **Lawrence Brown, Joe 'Tricky Sam' Nanton** (tb); **Juan Tizol** (vtb); **Barney Bigard** (cl); **Johnny Hodges** (ss, as); **Otto Hardwick** (as, bss); **Harry Carney** (bs); **Duke Ellington, Tommy Fulford** (p); **Bernard Addison, Fred Guy, Brick Fleagle** (g); **Wellman Braud, Billy Taylor, Hayes Alvis** (b); **Sonny Greer** (d); **Mary McHugh, Jean Eldridge** (v). Columbia Ⓜ CK 46995/48835 (two two-disc sets, oas: 128 and 119 minutes, oas). Recorded 1934-39.

✔ ⑩ ❻

While all the major developments and monumental achievements in Duke Ellington's career were reached through the vehicle of his Orchestra, some of the most sublimely happy episodes took place within his various small group aggregations. These recording groups took on different names during the thirties and forties, but all operated under the Duke's aegis and relied on him to give the numbers their distinctive aura. Although not always based on blues changes, most of the numbers had blues phrasings grafted onto them by the soloists, and the minor voicings gave Ellington a chance to display his endless variety. The smaller numbers of musicians present also meant that the limited recording facilities could do the rhythm sections more justice, and the added drive evident here is welcome.

Many of these tracks are classics of long standing (Volume Two favours Hodges, while the earlier title shows off the trumpeters more), but there are felicities in most performances, and we are given delicious draughts of Hodges soprano on the early sides in particular. Cootie Williams growling his way through Juan Tizol's *Caravan*, Rex Stewart returning the compliment on *The Back Room Romp* plus Hodges making joyful noises on *Tea and Trumpets* and soulful sounds on *Jeep's Blues* and the famous *Wanderlust* are joys not be missed, but then these sides are one of the great miniature collections in jazz. Sony/Columbia US, often rightly criticized for their slap-dash approach to their jazz reissue programme, got it right here, from the improved sound through to the good playing times and the excellent notes by Helen Oakley Dance, who presided over many of these sessions. **KS**

Fargo, North Dakota November 7, 1940 **Ellington** (p, arr); **Rex Stewart** (c); **Wallace Jones** (t); **Ray Nance** (t,v); **Joe 'Tricky Sam' Nanton, Juan Tizol, Lawrence Brown** (tb); **Johnny Hodges** (as); **Otto Hardwick** (cl, as); **Ben Webster** (ts); **Harry Carney** (bs); **Freddie Guy** (g); **Jimmy Blanton** (b); **Sonny Greer** (d); **Billy Strayhorn** (arr); **Ivie Anderson, Herb Jeffries** (v). Vintage Jazz Classics Ⓜ 1019/20-2 (two discs: 155 minutes). Recorded 1940.

✔ ⑩ ❽

Ellington was on the road as usual—Winnipeg the night before, Duluth the night after—when the band stopped in Fargo for a typical evening playing five sets for dancing. Typical except that two fans brought a borrowed disc-cutter, and with Duke's permission recorded as much of the show as possible, breaking away only to change discs. The Fargo recordings are justly prized for vividly documenting a good night by a great band—by common consent Duke's best—in which bassist Blanton and tenorist Webster temporarily took their places among the orchestra's longtime stars (as detailed in Andrew Homzy's excellent notes, Fargo appears to have been Nance's Ellington début).

Some players listened to playbacks on their breaks, and were delighted by the good sound the amateur engineers got, off-microphone vocals aside. The hectic ambience of a night at a local ballroom comes across, replete with great solos, missed cues, a local radio announcer talking in the background during one set, and Duke's everyday but astoundingly rich mix of pop tunes, ballads, concertos and flagwavers, all featuring breathtaking reed and brass voicings. Incidentally, one of the recordists was Jack Towers, who later went on to become an expert at cleaning up valuable but noisy old recordings like this. **KW**

The Blanton-Webster Band **Ellington** (p, cond); **Wallace Jones, Cootie Williams** (t); **Ray Nance** (t, v); **Rex Stewart** (c); **Tricky Sam Nanton, Lawrence Brown** (tb); **Juan Tizol** (vtb); **Johnny Hodges** (as, ss, cl); **Otto Hardwick** (as, bs); **Barney Bigard, Chauncey Haughton** (cl, ts); **Ben Webster** (ts); **Harry Carney** (bs, as, cl); **Billy Strayhorn** (p); **Fred Guy** (g); **Jimmy Blanton, Junior Raglan** (b); **Sonny Greer** (d); **Ivie Anderson** (v). RCA Bluebird Ⓜ ND 85659 (three discs: 209 minutes). Recorded 1940-42.

✔ ⑩ ❻

Towards the end of 1939 the 21-year old bass virtuoso Jimmy Blanton joined Duke Ellington and his Famous Orchestra; in January 1940 Ellington added a fifth saxophone to the band in the substantial form of Ben Webster. Thus was completed the band which, over the following two years, produced some of the finest work Ellington ever recorded and thus, by definition, some of the greatest masterpieces in the history not only of orchestral jazz but of twentieth-century music.

This set contains 66 numbers from those years, including all the great works such as *Ko-Ko, Bojangles, Harlem Airshaft, Concerto For Cootie, Cottontail*, etc. It is astonishing to recall that these hugely sophisticated pieces were written, rehearsed and recorded in the midst of a full schedule, during which Ellington and the band worked long hours every night in ballrooms, hotels and amusement parks, often travelling hundreds of miles between engagements.

Whole books of scholarly exegesis have been written around Ellington the composer, his musicians and his manner of working, and there is no room here to begin a summary. The one quality which emerges from all his work, and especially from these pieces, is a kind of breathing humanity. The sound of the Ellington orchestra is the sound of a huge, many-tongued human voice. It is not a thing of pinpoint accuracy or snappy effects, but of depth and warmth and endless invention. The music merits a large and comprehensive CD package such as this, but if you are looking for a reasonable one-volume anthology you will find it in **Duke Ellington: The Essential Recordings** (Charly/Le Jazz CD2). **DG**

Black, Brown & Beige **Ellington** (p); **Cat Anderson**, **Harold 'Shorty' Baker**, **Shelton Hemphill**, **Taft Jordan**, **Rex Stewart**, **Francis Williams** (t); **Ray Nance** (c, vn, v); **Lawrence Brown**, **Wilbur DeParis**, **Tommy Dorsey**, **Claude Jones**, **Joseph 'Tricky Sam' Nanton** (tb); **Jimmy Hamilton** (cl, ts); **Johnny Hodges**, **Russell Procope** (as); **Al Sears** (ts); **Harry Carney** (bs, bcl); **Billy Strayhorn** (p, arr); **Freddie Guy** (g); **Bob Haggart**, **Al Lucas**, **Oscar Pettiford**, **Alvin 'Junior' Raglin**, **Sid Weiss** (b); **Sid Catlett**, **Sonny Greer** (d); **Marian Cox**, **Kay Davis**, **Marie Ellington**, **Al Hibbler**, **Joya Sherrill** (v). RCA Bluebird Ⓜ 6641-2-RB (three discs: 181minutes). Recorded 1944-46.

✔ ⑩ ❼

Picking up where **The Blanton-Webster Band** left off, this surveys the orchestra's output through 1946, beginning with studio recordings of portions of *BB&B*, "the tone parallel to the American Negro" debuted at Ellington's first Carnegie Hall concert, in 1943. (The entire concert is available on Prestige PCD-34004-2 and there is an almost-complete studio version of *BB&B* from the mid-sixties on Volume Ten of The Private Concerts, Saja 91234-2.) *BB&B* was initially greeted less than enthusiastically, the problem being (as Ellington himself might have put it) that it was neither tulip nor turnip—neither a fullblown, organic symphonic work nor conventional jazz, even by Ellington's standards. Yet *BB&B* fully deserves the reputation it has subsequently acquired as not merely the most ambitious of Ellington's extended works, but perhaps the most majestic. It hardly suffers from the trimmings it receives here. The fanfare that announces the section called *Work Song* is one of the most stirring passages in modern music, and there are few passages even in the rest of Ellington's work as haunting or as finely measured as the guitar-and-bass tremolos behind Hodges on *Come Sunday*. This set also presents the complete *The Perfume Suite*, as much Billy Strayhorn's work as Ellington's and one of several numbers here illustrating the influence Strayhorn was beginning to exert on his mentor, especially in terms of the melodic use of dissonance. The three-minute masterpieces include *Blue Cellophane* and *Transblucency*, the latter spawned from Ellington's earlier *Blue Light* and featuring Hamilton and Kay Davis in an incredible duet between clarinet and coloratura. What else? Generous samples of irresistible jive such as *(Otto, Make That) Riff Staccato*, the maestro's own updatings of ten of his classic pieces from the thirties, a handsome showcase for fellow bandleader Dorsey on *Tonight I Shall Sleep* and inimitable solos by Hodges, Nanton, Carney, Stewart, Brown and the rest—ample evidence of Ellington's ability to weather wartime shortages, union recording bans and the deaths or defections of several key sidemen. The digital remastering is a little boxy, although better than on **The Blanton-Webster Band**. **FD**

The Great Ellington Units **Ellington** (p, ldr); with collective personnel including: **Rex Stewart** (c); **Cootie Williams**, **Ray Nance** (t); **Lawrence Brown** (tb); **Juan Tizol** (vtb); **Barney Bigard** (cl); **Johnny Hodges** (ss, as); **Ben Webster** (ts); **Harry Carney** (bs); **Jimmy Blanton** (b); **Sonny Greer** (d). RCA Bluebird Ⓜ ND 86751 (69 minutes). Recorded 1940-41.

✔ ⑩ ❻

The short duration of the 78 rpm record left Ellington no alternative but to become the master of the three-minute form. It is arguable that his subsequent lengthier works never matched his superbly concentrated reordings of 1940, but it is indisputable that his genius spilled from the big band recordings to those of the small groups of that outstanding period. Earlier Ellington small groups had passion, fire and joie de vivre, but the 1940 ones achieved those qualities and added a greater degree of subtlety and sophistication.

The casual perfection of Johnny Hodges's alto playing on *Good Queen Bess* and *Squaty Roo* is the epitome of swing or 'jump' music, while the lush exotica of *Day Dream* offers an early example of the potent new element brought to Ellingtonia by composer Billy Strayhorn. Barney Bigard's ripe clarinet is at its best on six tracks under his name, and the eccentric cornettist Rex Stewart, already undervalued as a horn player, reveals himself as an original and memorable jazz composer with his *Menelik (The Lion Of Judah)*, which includes a turbulent display of his freak abilities on cornet, and *Poor Bubber*, the wistfully melancholic tribute to his forebear in the Ellington band, Bubber Miley.

It is difficult to find a weak point amongst the 22 tracks on offer here, although it is a point of some irritation that two of the eight Barney Bigard tracks recorded for RCA at this time were omitted from this disc, although CD technology would certainly have allowed a further six minutes' worth of music. **SV**

Ellington At Newport **Ellington** (p); **Willie Cook**, **Clark Terry**, **Cat Anderson** (t); **Ray Nance** (c); **Britt Woodman**, **Quentin Jackson**, **John Sanders** (tb); **Russell Procope** (as, cl); **Johnny Hodges** (as);

Paul Gonsalves (ts); **Jimmy Hamilton** (ts, cl); **Harry Carney** (bs); **Jimmy Woode** (b); **Sam Woodyard** (d). Columbia Ⓜ 472385 2 (44 minutes). Recorded 1956.

✓ ⑧ ❼

Things looked somewhat bleak for big bands in the early fifties, but in 1953 Woody Herman assembled the Third Herd, by 1955 the 'Atomic' Basie band line-up was in place and in 1956 Johnny Hodges returned to Ellington to begin a period of personnel stability for the Duke. On this CD, Hodges gives a superb reading of his beloved *Jeep's Blues* but it was Gonsalves whose one single performance really changed the band's fortunes. His 27 electrifying choruses on *Diminuendo And Crescendo In Blue* sent the 1956 Newport Jazz Festival audience into a state of near delirium and re-established the Ellington Orchestra in the eyes and ears of the world. The incredible atmosphere is genuinely captured on this CD, as some 7000 fans stood on their seats, cheered and whistled and seemed almost mesmerized as Anderson added his killer touch at the end of the performance. Ellington's *Newport Jazz Festival Suite* had earlier warmed up the audience with characteristic contributions from the likes of Hamilton, Nance, Procope, Terry and the band's masterful pianist. It had all been a normally immaculate Ducal presentation until that fateful moment when, at around midnight on July 7th 1956, Gonsalves stood up to solo. An act that somehow re-directed the band, it also sparked Ellington's compositional enthusiasm and led the band into a new and highly successful phase.

BMcR

Such Sweet Thunder **Ellington** (p, ldr); **Cat Anderson, Clark Terry, Willie Cook** (t); **Ray Nance** (c, vn); **John Sanders, Britt Woodman, Quentin Jackson** (tb); **Johnny Hodges, Russell Procope, Paul Gonsalves, Jimmy Hamilton, Harry Carney** (reeds); **Jimmy Woode** (b); **Sam Woodyard** (d); **Billy Strayhorn** (arr). Columbia Ⓜ 469140-2 (36 minutes). Recorded 1956-57.

⑧ ❼

Ellington consolidated his orchestra's return to favour at the 1956 Newport Festival with two new suites: *A Drum is a Woman*, his bizarre re-telling of jazz history, and the Shakespeare-inspired *Such Sweet Thunder*, which has the more attractive music. Some critics have complained that the suite's links with Shakespeare are pretty tenuous. More to the point is Ralph Gleason's comment that "*Such Sweet Thunder* runs the Ellington gamut ... Every single moment of it is well done."

One novel outcome of the Duke's encounter with the Bard was a new 14-line musical form written in imitation of the sonnet. The four examples on *Such Sweet Thunder* work well, with *Sonnet for Caesar*, which features beautiful, rapt clarinet from Jimmy Hamilton, among the disc's highlights. The remaining music, although more conventional in form, shows plenty of felicitous Ducal touches (check the horns' funky prowl on the title-track), while nearly every piece has a showcase solo from a leading player. Johnny Hodges's languorous alto has made *The Star-Crossed Lovers* (a Billy Strayhorn tune) the suite's best-known track, but Harry Carney's baritone stroll through *The Telecasters* is hardly less sensual.

Such Sweet Thunder does not strike me as an Ellington masterpiece. However, it is well-crafted, consistently charming and lifted at times by real inspiration. A "concord of sweet sounds" for all but the most strategem-minded.

GL

Money Jungle **Ellington** (p); **Charles Mingus** (b); **Max Roach** (d). Blue Note Ⓜ CDP 7 46398 2 (57 minutes). Recorded 1962.

⑧ ❻

Money Jungle is a Summit Meeting which almost foundered. Mingus walked out of the session, refusing to play with "that drummer" (Roach, in fact, was an old comrade and friend) and it was Ellington who cajoled him into returning to the studio. Almost any recording session with Mingus had its moments of tension and this on-edge feeling is present here. This time it actually works to the advantage of the resultant music.

The CD version contains the complete programme of music (13 tracks) and plays for more than twice the duration of the original United Artists LP. There are three established Ellington works (*Caravan*, *Solitude* [two takes] and *Warm Valley*) which are, by comparison with the rest of the material, 'safe'. It is on numbers such as the explosive title-track (where Mingus, attacking his instrument with something close to violence, goads Ellington into some unusually fiery and searching playing) the blues *Switch Blade* (which fades out at the end of the fourth bar of a chorus) and the beautiful *Fleurette Africaine* that the interaction between these three instrumental masters is heard at its best and most dynamic. Roach senses the shape and direction of Duke's music to perfection (the two had recorded once before, in 1950) while Mingus's playing, despite some coloratura passages, is magnificent. *REM Blues* turns out to be a familiar riff, sometimes known as *Blues For Blanton*. The remix engineer has improved the sound from the original muddy LP production. The only drawback is that the original (and very successful) LP track sequence has been abandoned on the CD reissue. Those readers who have kept their turntables in good condition may prefer to hunt down a copy of the now-deleted contemporaneous vinyl reissue, which has most of the added music and a closer approximation of the original track order.

AM

The Far East Suite—Special Mix **Ellington** (p, arr, ldr); **Cat Anderson, Herbie Jones, Mercer Ellington, Cootie Williams** (t); **Lawrence Brown, Chuck Connors, Buster Cooper** (tb); **Johnny Hodges** (as); **Russell Procope** (cl, as); **Jimmy Hamilton** (cl, ts); **Paul Gonsalves** (ts); **Harry Carney**

(bs, bcl); **John Lamb** (b); **Rufus Jones** (d); **Billy Strayhorn** (arr). RCA Bluebird Ⓜ 366551 2 (61 minutes). Recorded 1966.

✓ ⑩ ❽

One of the last great Ellington albums, and the last to be issued before the final great edition of his band began to disperse. However, drummer Sam Woodyard (who played on earlier, then-unissued recordings of parts of the suite) was unavailable and it was left to Rufus Jones, a newcomer to Duke, to add his personal touch to this 'exotic' repertoire.

Titled after Ellington's first Middle East and Japanese tours, material was written during a two-year period, and equates the inspiration of foreign climes with sixties modal jazz (which could be described as descending from *Caravan*, written in 1936!). As always, Duke and co-writer Billy Strayhorn managed to absorb outside influences in a way that spiced up the Ellington sounds yet remained faithful to its own traditions. And, as usual, it is the relative freedom afforded to the players that both complicates and facilitates the balancing act. Gonsalves's features on *Tourist Point of View* and *Mount Harissa* could be pronounced typical, while *Blue Pepper* and *Isfahan* have typical Hodges solos (despite the thematic link between *Isfahan* and *Harissa*). But they are also highly individualized, as are Duke's piano contributions to *Harissa*, *Depk*, *Amad* and *Ad-Lib On Nippon*.

The reason for the so-called "special mix" is explained in the sleeve-notes by reissue producer Orrin Keepnews: the two-track tape machine used to create a stereo master from the four-track session tapes had not been aligned properly, creating a slight but noticeable tonal distortion. Keepnews located the original session tapes, thankfully clear of all distortion, and remixed from them. During this process he discovered the four alternative takes included here, which are a considerable bonus. The remix has also subtly but markedly improved what was always a rather brittle sound on previous LPs and CD reissues, thus helping the various elements in the Ellington tonal palette to blend more sweetly. A masterpiece for the twenty-first century. **BP**

New Orleans Suite **Ellington** (p); **Cootie Williams**, **Money Johnson**, **Cat Anderson**, **Mercer Ellington**, **Al Rubin**, **Fred Stone** (t, flh); **Booty Wood**, **Julian Priester** (tb); **Dave Taylor**, **Chuck Connors** (btb); **Russell Procope** (cl, as); **Johnny Hodges** (as); **Norris Turney** (cl, as, f); **Harold Ashby** (cl, ts); **Paul Gonsalves** (ts); **Harry Carney** (cl, bcl, bs); **Wild Bill Davis** (org); **Joe Benjamin** (b); **Rufus Jones** (d). Atlantic Jazz Ⓜ 781376-2 (43 minutes). Recorded 1970.

⑧ ❽

The five-part *New Orleans Suite* was commissioned by George Wein for performance at the 1970 New Orleans Jazz Festival. At first glance, Wein's choice of the Washington D.C. born/New York-honed Ellington may seem odd. However, as Stanley Dance notes in the informative liners, Ellington had been entranced and subsequently open to and influenced by Crescent City players since first hearing Sidney Bechet in 1921 declaim *I'm Coming, Virginia*. When Ellington's Washingtonians moved to New York, the gutsy swingingness of Louis Armstrong made its impact. So, too, did the hiring of clarinetist Barney Bigard and bassist Wellman Braud in late 1927, two New Orleans masters with credentials including Armstrong, King Oliver and Jelly Roll Morton.

For this wonderful 1970 studio recording made just after the *Suite*'s successful première in New Orleans, Ellington interspersed four additional but related *Portrait* segments saluting Louis Armstong, Mahalia Jackson, Sidney Bechet and ex-Ellingtonian Wellman Braud. Among the Suite's gems are the rollicking *Second Line* and the frothy *Aristrocracy à la Jean LaFitte*, where Harry Carney's dainty baritone saxophone (yes, dainty!) waltzes gracefully with Fred Stone's lithe flügelhorn. The opening *Blues for New Orleans* showcases Wild Bill Davis's wailing Hammond B-3 organ and the bluesy alto saxophone of Johnny Hodges, who died on May 11, 1970, and to whom the album is dedicated. **CB**

Don Ellis

1934-1979

Autumn **Ellis** (t, ldr); **Glenn Stuart**, **Stu Blumberg**, **John Rosenberg**, **Bob Harmon** (t); **Ernie Carlson**, **Glenn Ferris**, **Don Switzer** (tb); **Ira Schulman**, **Frank Strozier** (as); **Sam Falzone**, **John Klemmer** (ts); **John Magruder** (bs); **Pete Robinson** (kbds); **Ray Neapolitan**, **Dave Parlato** (b); **Ralph Humphrey** (d); **Gene Strimling**, **Lee Pastora** (perc). On three tracks add **Ron Starr** (as, f); **Terry Woodson** (tb); **Doug Bixby** (tba); On two tracks add **Mike Lang** (kbds), **Roger Bobo** (tba) Columbia Ⓜ 472622-2 (58 minutes). Recorded 1968.

⑦ ❻

From the mid-sixties to the early seventies, Don Ellis's big bands combined post-Kenton extended charts and experimental forms with complex rhythms, rock energy, electricity, high-voltage soloists and, toward the end, a string section, achieving a fair amount of popularity in so doing. **Autumn** is the only one of the representative albums from that period available on CD, and gives a good idea of what all the shouting, pro and con, was about. Ellis loved bombastic arrangements and some of the effects and affectations (especially his electronically-modified trumpet) do not wear well today, but his ambition and talent was such that a banal passage was likely to be followed by something quite remarkable. An extreme example is the six-part *Variations For Trumpet*, which includes plush themes far beyond anything Claude Thornhill might have envisioned, as well as a swinging 7/4 Latin section with four polyrhythmic percussionists. Most impressive here are *K.C. Blues*, a straight-ahead bash with an excellent Frank Strozier introduction and a transcribed Charlie Parker episode that anticipates Supersax, and *Indian Lady*, which whips up a firestorm of excitement. As their titles indicate, *Scratt And Fluggs* and *Pussy Willow Stomp* are intended as comic relief, and *Child Of Ecstasy* is a brief, atmospheric showpiece with a 12-tone row or two hidden in the arrangement and enough trumpet pyrotechnics by Glenn Stuart to chill the blood of even Maynard Ferguson. Other outstanding soloists in the band at this time were altoist Strozier, tenorman John Klemmer (fresh from his days in Chicago, when he was breathing fire and not the thinner New Age air), trombonist Glenn Ferris, adventurous keyboardist Pete Robinson and tuba virtuoso Roger Bobo. History should not forget that Ellis himself was a trumpeter of enormous facility, if extremely uneven taste, best when he could scatter bright, penetrating variations of swing phrasing upon the band's contrapuntal sections. At those moments, the Don Ellis Orchestra was truly exciting. **AL**

Herb Ellis

1921

Nothin' But The Blues **Ellis** (g); **Roy Eldridge**, **Dizzy Gillespie** (t); **Stan Getz**, **Coleman Hawkins** (ts); **Oscar Peterson** (p); **Ray Brown** (b); **Stan Levey**, **Gus Johnson** (d). Verve Ⓜ 521 674-2 (58 minutes). Recorded 1957/1958.

⑧ ❽

The first eight tracks of the album are by a piano-less quintet made up from Ellis, Eldridge, Getz, Brown and Levey. Years after the session the musicians involved talked about it with pleasure, and it remains one of Ellis's favourites of his own recordings. So it should. This is an unpretentious collection of swinging mainstream, powered by the leader's abiding love of the blues. Everyone lets his hair down and the music flows and flows. Solos from Getz and Eldridge, moving into the centre for the occasion, are invariably inspired, but not as much as Ellis, a modest man who for once lets his aura pervade the whole session. There is much harking back to the classic Goodman sextet, with *Big Red's Boogie Woogie* notable both for a good drenching of Charlie Christian and for the punching Goodman-like riffs. Brown, a great stalwart on the session, opens *Tin Roof Blues* with an almost inaudible bass intro and later in the piece Stan Getz, who often made a virtue from blowing blues into a ballad, turns *Tin Roof* itself into a ballad for his solo.

Four interesting fragments have been added to make up the weight of the CD. These were recorded for the French film *Les Tricheurs* and feature individual performances from Eldridge and Getz (again), Gillespie and Hawkins. **SV**

Pee Wee Ellis

Twelve And More Blues **Ellis** (ts, bs); **Dwayne Dolphin** (b); **Bruce Cox** (d). Minor Music Ⓕ MM 801034 (72 minutes). Recorded 1993.

⑦ ❽

Ellis is one more of the excellent hornmen to have emerged from the James Brown band over recent years to begin carving a career under his own banner, and while Maceo Parker may have made the greater public impact, this album demonstrates a deeper grounding in the bop tradition than anything Parker may have come up with to date.

For a start, the album, recorded live in Cologne last year, features the same trio line-up favoured by Sonny Rollins on his epochal **Live at the Village Vanguard** (see below), and the first two tracks (*There Is No Greater Love* and *Doxy*) are actually taken from the Rollins performing book. Ellis's tenor sound is a likeable amalgam of Rollins and early Archie Shepp, while his phrasing has the rhythmic regularity of Lockjaw Davis plus a number of enjoyable twists from more contemporary concepts. *Doxy* may be a pedestrian effort compared with the manic genius of Rollins's classic 1961 live version with Don Cherry, but the pedestrian strolls with admirable humour and takes the listener with him every step of the way. No little part of the reason for this stems from the supple rhythms and emphases of the bass-drums team of Dolphin and Cox, who are commendably supportive of Ellis throughout. The sax player, by the way, sticks mostly to tenor on this album, essaying on the larger horn just once, on the walking blues *In The Middle*, where he offers a sensible sonic variation in quite a long programme. This is a good-humoured and engaging album with little of the humdrum about it and plenty of well-directed improvisational energy, and as such it deserves your attention. **KS**

Sidsel Endresen

Exile **Endresen** (v); **Hans Petter Molvaer** (t); **Django Bates** (p); **Jens Bugge Wesseltoft** (kbds); **David Darling** (vc); **Jon Christensen** (d). ECM Ⓕ 1524 (521 721-2)(56 minutes). Recorded 1993.

⑦ ❿

Endresen is like fifties Helen Merrill translated into the bleak and harsh realities of the fin-de-siècle nineties, except that she also touches on borderline figures of folk and pop like Mary Travers, Nico and Buffy Sainte-Marie. The compositions here are mostly shared between herself and Jon Eberson, with Django Bates contributing the music to one of the most complex and fully-fleshed piece, *Stages I, II, III*. The music is spare, with long stretches of pianissimo, and Jon Christensen has certainly been much busier on other days in the studio. This is a borderline entry for this guide, but then often it is the music on the edge of a style which has the widest resonance, because it constantly hints at other dimensions. By this I am not endorsing 'crossover' but suggesting that strong talents with a clear idea of what they are at can sail close to the wind in any form. Whichever way she is coming from, Endresen can sail closer than most. Her key talent is the quiet distillation of experience as if it was already past experience when in fact it is still happening. That is a special talent, a special intensity and an acquired taste. It will be worth your while to acquire the taste for this record. **KS**

Lena Ericsson

Doodlin' **Ericsson** (v); **Arne Domnerus** (as, cl); **Ulf Johansson** (p); **Rune Gustafsson** (g); **Bo Stief** (b); **Aage Tanggaard** (d). Phontastic Ⓕ NCD 8808 (63 minutes). Recorded 1990.

⑧ ❽

From the opening notes of the first track *Days of Wine And Roses*, which she sings gently over Gustafsson's guitar, it is obvious that Miss Ericsson is going to cause a lot of re-thinking of the vocal stakes. She takes her place as a worthy companion to Domnerus and the other Swedes, indisputably at the head of European jazz musicians and, in Miss Ericsson's case, able to see off many of the Americans.

Her voice is full and her confident control of it remarkable. She has a good range and an imposing skill with dynamics. She can hit hard on the blues and fine-tune nuances in her ballads with the skill of a Vaughan or a Fitzgerald, and yet she is very much an original. She seems little troubled by the difficulties Scandinavians often have with lyrics in English and her histrionics on *Doodlin'* are not as intrusive as they are in others' versions. The flying version of *Love For Sale* with only drum accompaniment is more spectacular than moving, and one has to go to the next track, the Laine-Dankworth *It's Not Easy*, for one of her superb ballad performances.

She would be good even without the fine accompanists, but it should be noted that Domnerus, Gustafsson and Johansson take powerful and potent solos throughout. **SV**

Peter Erskine

1954

Sweet Soul **Erskine** (d); **Randy Brecker** (t); **Joe Lovano** (ts, ss); **Bob Mintzer** (ts); **Kenny Werner** (p, org, syn); **John Scofield** (elg); **Marc Johnson** (b). BMG Novus Ⓕ PD 90616 (75 minutes). Recorded 1991.

⑧ ❽

Erskine's work with Weather Report and Steps Ahead in the late seventies and early eighties could hardly have prepared his listeners for the directions he has taken in recent years. For one thing he has returned to the swinging, often standard material of his apprenticeship; but he has also ventured into experimental areas that were circumscribed by the Weather Report he served, including an involvement with theatre music.

This richly varied session touches all his favourite musical bases without overbalancing, as some of his earlier efforts did, in favour of composition. The programming covers a wide and satisfying emotional range, from the poignant, tiptoeing balladry of William Walton's *Touch Her Soft Lips and Part* through the tart abstractions of three Vince Mendoza pieces to the slow-burning gospel funk of the title track and the surprisingly authentic-sounding Shorterisms of *To Be Or Not To Be*. Erskine's talents as a percussionist have long been evident, but *Sweet Soul* proves him a composer of exceptional ability. Kenny Werner stands out from a group of top-drawer soloists for his treatments, thrilling and witty respectively, of his own *Press Enter* and Brubeck's *In Your Own Sweet Way*. The direct to two-track digital sound is irreproachable. **MG**

Booker Ervin

1930-1970

The Song Book **Ervin** (ts); **Tommy Flanagan** (p); **Richard Davis** (b); **Alan Dawson** (d). Prestige Ⓜ OJCCD 779 (38 minutes). Recorded 1964.

⑧ ❽

Astonishingly, none of the masterpieces made by Ervin around this time featuring a quartet made up by the above bassist and drummer but with Jaki Byard on piano is currently on CD (buy, beg or borrow **The Freedom Book** or **The Space Book**, for starters, should you ever spot them). In the meantime, this fine session will do nicely. Flanagan is hardly a drag—he comps sensitively, solos fleetly, and generally helps direct affairs—but he does not have the off-the-wall imagination which is Byard's in abundance and which was the catalyst which made this particular group explode with creative vitality.

A Texas tenor, Ervin made his first impact in New York with the Charles Mingus band which included John Handy, and was a charter member of the later Mingus group with Dolphy and Ted

Curson. His style was sufficiently original and individual, his stance sufficiently uncompromising, for him to have a difficult time trying to sustain a career as leader of his own groups, and even the quartet lauded above was never more than a studio band. **The Song Book** was recorded in February 1964, just two months after **The Freedom Book**, and Ervin's playing burns with the same intensity and unfussed directness. The programme is all standards—a distinct change from most of his sessions, which concentrated on his own material. His version of Ellington's *Come Sunday* is stripped of any grandiloquence, and communicates straight to the heart; a most moving personal statement on a much-abused melody. *All The Things You Are*, *Our Love Is Here To Stay* and *Just Friends* get chirpy treatments at medium tempo, while *Yesterdays* is a real lament, as the lyrics imply. Ervin sounds perfectly comfortable with the music and the company he is keeping here, and with no other horn to distract us, we can hone in on his remarkable tenor voice. **KS**

Setting The Pace **Ervin** (ts); **Dexter Gordon** (ts); **Jaki Byard** (p); **Reggie Workman** (b); **Alan Dawson** (d). Prestige Ⓜ OJC 24123-2 (77 minutes). Recorded 1965.

⑨ ❽

Ervin's early death quieted a horn of great authority and power. A celebrated stint with Mingus and a cache of excellent albums on his own, most assisted by the impeccably creative rhythm team of Byard, Richard Davis and Dawson, had preceded this remarkable evening's (actually early morning's) work, as chronicled by David Himmelstein's surrealistic liner notes and initially released on two LPs (intact here bar one track), **Setting The Pace** and **The Trance**. Suffice to say, extreme conditions and near-exhaustion sometimes lead to exceptional results, as they do here. On a pair of marathon excursions, Ervin locks horns with Gordon, the tenor duellist par excellence, and both are inspired to breathtaking heights. On *Setting The Pace* Booker's harsh cry swells to a wail at climatic points, or he envelops chords with sheets-of-sound after Dexter elaborates on his original 1947 solo; Booker is impressive on *Dexter's Deck* but Gordon owns the tune, taking a full nine minutes to weave a patchwork quilt of quotes and oblique ideas. On *The Trance* and *Speak Low* Ervin seems relieved that Dexter's not around, and the latter receives a fascinatingly uncharacteristic reading, in two tempos simultaneously with the rhythm pulled like taffy. Workman and Dawson do yeoman's service and Byard is a hero; his solos are full of unexpected delights and it is nearly as rewarding to follow his comping (echoes of Ellington and Monk), with splashed chords, punched notes, huge rolling tremolos, broken and rebuilt rhythm schemes. Two LPs of awesome performances on a single CD make for rare value. **AL**

Ellery Eskelin 1959

Forms **Eskelin** (ts); **Drew Gress** (b); **Phil Haynes** (d). Open Minds Ⓕ 2403 (62 minutes). Recorded 1990.

⑧ ❽

Eskelin's adventurous outlook separates him from the great majority of saxists of his generation. Unwilling to recycle the encyclopedia of post-bop licks, he is working hard on an individual voice, exploring extreme chromaticism and unruly rhythmic accents within a still recognizable song form. It is an approach reminiscent of Sonny Rollins in his most open period. Although a gutsy, unfettered album of solo sax gave his sense of fantasy free rein, he works best with the support of longtime collaborators Gress and Haynes (together with trumpeter Paul Smoker, they have recorded as a co-operative band named Joint Venture). The bassist and drummer are remarkably attuned to the music's flow no matter where it goes, and are equally adept at subtle pressure to redirect the action. There is plenty of irony in this programme; the titles (*Blues*, *In Three*, *Ballad*, *Latin*) may be generic but the forms are deceptively re-cast and the playing has real personality. *Blues* shows off Eskelin's alternately melismatic and fragmented phrasing and a fountain of ideas, one after the next; Dizzy's *Bebop* features un-boppish phrasing and a free middle, while Ellington's *African Flower* receives a lean, fragrant reading (especially Haynes's hypnotic drumming). A good introduction to musicians worth watching in the future. **AL**

Ethnic Heritage Ensemble

Ancestral Song **Kahil El'Zabar** (sansa, d, perc, v); **Joseph Bowie** (tb, mba, perc); **Edward Wilkerson** (cl, ts, perc). Silkheart Ⓕ 108 (63 minutes). Recorded 1987.

⑧ ❽

A second-wave AACM group, the Ethnic Heritage Ensemble has since the mid-seventies reflected the purer strains of African influence on jazz. Led from its inception by the talented multi-percussionist Kahil El'Zabar, the trio's evocative instrumentation and open, flowing compositions allow them to explore the relationship between the folk sources of African music and those of American urban experience. A good example of this is *Loose Pocket*, which begins with Wilkerson's bluesy tenor inflections and an El'Zabar vocal; when the percussionist shifts to the drum set the laidback theme becomes a hard bop riff and Bowie's trombone rips off a hot solo. El'Zabar is an excellent conga player as well as trap drummer, but the focus here is the sansa (or mbira, an African thumb piano). Its buzzing, bell-like sonorities introduce and unify the various phrases which serve as loose thematic structures. Bowie, who is also leader of the avant-funk dance band Defunkt, has been a member since 1986; he adds percussion, including a moving marimba part to *Papa's Bounce*, to his trombone contributions. Reedman Wilkerson supplies most of the fireworks. A formidable tenor saxist with a narrative style, his playing throughout is notable for its slippery tonal maneuvres and melodic ingenuity. Wilkerson's own groups, 8 Bold Souls and Shadow Vignettes, are also highly recommended. **AL**

Kevin Eubanks

1957

Spirit Talk **Eubanks** (g, elg); **Robin Eubanks** (tb); **Kent Jordan** (f); **Dave Holland** (b); **Marvin 'Smitty' Smith** (d, perc, v); **Mark Mondesir** (d). Blue Note Ⓕ CDP7 89286 2 (53 minutes). Recorded 1993.

⑦ ❽

Eubanks's musical career began with rock; he recorded in Europe with Chris Hinze but in the early eighties found himself comfortable in the jazz company of men such as Ronnie Matthews, Sam Rivers, Chico Freeman and Wynton Marsalis. More recently he has been involved in several M-Base sessions, although he is guarded about any permanent commitment to them. His 1991 **Turning Point** (Blue Note CDP7 98170 2) marked his début as a leader of a pure jazz date and seemed to shut the door on the fuzak gloss of his distant past. This fine CD enlarges on that project and uses the accomplished trombone of brother Robin on five titles. Despite the use made of the horns, it is Kevin Eubanks who dominates. His ease of execution, his relaxed rhythmic application and his ability to construct coherent solos is demonstrated throughout. On the acoustic instrument he allows himself a degree of romanticism, but if his electric guitar is marginally more dramatic, there is no real diversity of style. Sparing use is made of multi-tracking but most of the best musical conversations that take place are between guitar and trombone on *Union* or guitar and flute on *Going Outside*. If anything, Kevin Eubanks sounds more comfortable in a pure jazz setting and in the company of long-term working colleague Holland. **BMcR**

Robin Eubanks

1959

Karma **Eubanks** (tb, etb, rap.v); **Earl Gardner** (t); **Greg Osby** (as); **Kevln Eubanks** (elg); **Renée Rosnes**, **Kenny Werner** (kbds); **Lonnie Plaxico** (elb); **Marvin 'Smitty' Smith** (d); **Kimson Albert** (rap.v); **Mino Cinelu** (perc); **Dave Holland** (b); **Branford Marsalis** (ts); **Cassandra Wilson** (v). JMT Ⓕ 834 446-2 (63 minutes). Recorded 1990.

✔

⑦ ❽

An important aspect of the M-Base ethic of the eighties was its promotion of rap. Eubanks, a man of instrumental experience with Sun Ra, McCoy Tyner's Big Band, Abdullah Ibrahim and Geri Allen as well as Patti LaBelle and Talking Heads, was one of the best M-Base rappers. As this CD shows, his rap oratory swings, but also reminds the listener that while bad rap is self-indulgent space-filling, a piece such as *Karma* is poetic and meaningful. Eubanks is also an outstanding trombone player who has moved some distance from the clean-lined articulation of the bop masters. His vocalized tone has a throat-clearing quality that adds depth to his playing and his solos move from the rich legato ease of *Maybe Next Time* to the busy declamatory rebuilding of Monk's *Evidence* or his own *Pentacourse*. His natural flair for shapely improvisation is matched by his good taste as a composer and he is a frequent guest on the recording dates of his M-Base colleagues. **BMcR**

Bill Evans

1929-1980

At The Village Vanguard **Evans** (p), **Scott LaFaro** (b), **Paul Motian** (d). Riverside Ⓜ FCD-60-017 (65 minutes). Recorded 1961.

✔

⑩ ❿

This CD contains nearly all the material originally released on two separate LPs, **Sunday at the Village Vanguard** and **Waltz For Debby**. In addition to this, alternative takes of the same songs have been released on later compilations. To my ears, this composite CD is still better value for money than buying the CD equivalents (also currently available, with alternative takes added) of those two original releases.

For many people, the Evans trio with LaFaro and Motian reached a peak which the pianist never scaled again. The reason why this may be the case is a simple one: this trio has all the freshness and intensity of youth—there is a palpable delight in discovery going on all the time here, shared between the three players. Whatever the later Evans oufits had, that freshness had gone. Perhaps it went with the death of LaFaro. Perhaps something else happened. Luckily for us, these recordings catch the trio at their best. The dialogue between the three players is extraordinary, the depth of interpretation always surprising, no matter how many times you play these selections. Evans is famed for his harmonic sophistication and LaFaro for his virtuosity, but what impresses most from all three men here is their ability to make their instruments truly *sing*. Any track will show this, but *All of You* perhaps best of all. **KS**

Undercurrent **Evans** (p); **Jim Hall** (g). Blue Note Ⓜ CDP7 90583-2 (53 minutes). Recorded 1962.

⑧ ❻

The 1962 pairing of two of improvised music's transcendent lyricists remains one of the great exemplars of jazz as the art of intimate conversation. Indeed, the hand-in-glove interactions lacing up such standards as *Stairway to the Stars* and *Darn That Dream* are classic examples of focused spontaneity. There are, of course, absolutely haunting balladic dialogues such as the ethereal *I Hear a Rhapsody* and Hall's smouldering *Romain*. An element of reflective plaintiveness is also central to the atmospherics of the enchanting waltz called *Dream Gypsy*. The big surprise, given Evans's deserved reputation as a contemplative melodist, is his and Hall's unabashed displays of swinging abandon in robustly up-tempo versions of *I'm Getting Sentimental Over You* and, amazingly, *My Funny Valentine*, in 1962 almost always treated as one of the jazz world's foremost balladic gauntlets for slow-motion rhapsodizing.

The disc also includes stellar alternative takes of *My Funny Valentine* and *Romain*, plus a whimsical twirl through John Lewis's lovely three-quarter-time *Skating in Central Park*, in which Evans and Hall exhibit their poignant skills as introspective yet romantic minimalists. The sound, never that good to start with, is less murky than on previous issues. **CB**

Conversations With Myself **Evans** (multi-tracked p). Verve Ⓜ 821 984-2 (44 minutes: AAD). Recorded 1963.

⑧ ❻

Strange that the two most convincing early examples of overdubbing in jazz should have been started in the same month. Unlike its serendipitous use in Mingus's **Black Saint And The Sinner Lady**, it was clearly integral to the conception of this Evans album produced by Creed Taylor. Two tracks tucked away at the end of the original album seem to represent an early phase of the project, before the problem of getting the parallel piano tracks absolutely in tune was solved, but they include the desolate modal improvisation *N.Y.C.'s No Lark* (dedicated to the late Sonny Clark, of whose name the title is an anagram) and are now followed by two bonus items.

Both pianist and producer worked hard to achieve an orchestral texture in which the 'lead' piano sounds are mixed upfront while the more accompanimental parts are suitably backgrounded. Some of the tinkly bits seem in retrospect to be errors of judgement but, rather than being oppressive, on the whole the combination of up to three keyboard tracks enhances both the material and what Evans does with it. This is certainly superior to his later overdubbed albums and, although ultimately less typical than his trio or even solo work, **Conversations** is essential Evans. **BP**

Empathy/A Simple Matter Of Conviction **Evans** (p); **Monty Budwig, Eddie Gomez** (b); **Shelly Manne** (d). Verve Ⓜ 837 757-2 (73 minutes). Recorded 1962/66.

✔ ⑧ ❽

Manne built his early reputation as a powerful big band drummer (Kenton, Herman, Shorty Rogers) but after taking up residence in California his true value as an imaginative, sensitive painter of rhythmic sounds in small groups emerged. He was particularly adept at working with pianists (notably Russ Freeman and André Previn), and the two LPs he did with Bill Evans can only make the listener wish they had made more records together. Both LPs are combined here, a feast of sensitive playing by two masters of their instruments. The first date produced half a dozen standards (although one would be hard-pressed to find any other version of Berlin's *The Washington Twist* or *Let's Go Back To The Waltz)* and **Empathy** is certainly a most apt title. The way Manne and Evans interlock on *With A Song In My Heart* is nothing short of brilliant (coincidentally Manne made a fine duet version of this same tune with Russ Freeman) but the clever "stop-start" approach to Frank Loesser's *I Believe In You* is the highlight in a consistently fine programme. The second session was actually the first time Evans and Gomez had recorded together, but the magic is repeated. No other drummer Evans recorded with had such an acute appreciation of the variety of sounds capable of being produced from his kit, and this obviously inspired the pianist. The clear recording balance allows us to hear all the subtle nuances of the music-making. **AM**

Bill Evans At Town Hall, Volume 1 **Evans** (p); **Chuck Israels** (b); **Arnold Wise** (d). Verve Ⓜ 831 271-2 (53 minutes). Recorded 1966.

⑧ ❽

At the centre of this absorbing concert is the unaccompanied 13-minute tribute Evans dedicated to the memory of his father who had died two weeks before the date of the concert. In keeping with the cerebral nature of much of Evans's playing, this is not overtly emotional, but its compositional depth repays repeated listening. The central section of the piece is built around two song themes, but they are almost irrelevant in the tissue of finely crafted lines that Evans runs together into his solo. In the piece, the boundaries between improvisation and composition become blurred, and the listener is caught up in Evans's ever-deeper dissection of his ideas. In sharp contrast, the rest of the concert is stimulating ensemble playing, containing some of Chuck Israel's best work, less brittle than La Faro, who had preceded him, and less technically perfect than Gomez, who was to follow. The trio romps through a mixture of Broadway show tunes and standards, the CD carrying three tracks in addition to the original LP release, one of which is the previously unreleased tribute to his manager Helen Keane, Evans's own *For Helen*. In an original note to part of this session, Leonard Feather wrote of Evans's "almost mystical ability for drawing even more out of a song than the composer put into it." This album is the perfect exemplar of that observation. A point of clarification: Volume Two (presumably meant to be the Evans Trio with Orchestra which made up the other half of the concert) has never been issued. **AS**

Bill Evans

1958

Push Evans (ss, as, ts, kbds); **Keith O'Quinn, Conrad Herwig, Gary Smulyan, Barry Bryson, Dave Stahl, Michael Davis, Chris Botti** (brass); **Chuck Loeb, Jeff Golub, Nick Moroch, Max Risenhoover** (g); **Clifford Carter, Bruce Hornsby, Philippe Saisse, Bob James** (kbds); **Chris Ming Doky, Victor Bailey, Marcus Miller, Mark Egan** (b); **Billy Ward** (d); **Evans, Clifford Carter, Max Risenhoover, K.C. Flight, Jimmy Bralower, Michael Colina** (programming). Lipstick Ⓕ LIP 89022-2 (61 minutes). Recorded 1993.

⑥ ❽

While never quite matching the expressive range and harmonic sophistication of such other post-1980 Miles Davis reedmen as Bob Berg, Gary Thomas and Kenny Garrett, Bill Evans did make a number of striking contributions to Miles's late bands, among them several memorably fine solos on **We Want Miles.** There followed a couple of patchily successful fusion dates recorded live in Japan, but it was not until 1993, and **Push**, that his early promise was realized.

In the fashion of the day, **Push** has Evans teamed up with an assortment of acid jazz, rap, hip-hop and techno specialists. The album was studio-produced, which allowed for close attention to detailed arrangement, and it is in large part this aspect which occasions the record's success. The clarity of the sound and the imaginative and precise interplay between synths, variously-toned electric guitars and horns on the Sanborn-ish *Road To Ruin*, for example, is more significant than the melodic or harmonic content of the tune. Having said that, the more focused setting does draw out the best of Bill Evans, as his feverish soprano on *London House* illustrates. **MG**

Gil Evans

1912-1988

Gil Evans & Ten Evans (p, arr); **Louis Mucci, Jake Koven, John Carisi** (t); **Jimmy Cleveland** (tb); **Willie Ruff** (frh); **Bart Varsalona** (btb); **Steve Lacy** (ss); **Lee Konitz** (as); **Dave Kurtzer** (bs); **Paul Chambers** (b); **Nick Stabulas, Jo Jones** (d). Prestige Ⓜ OJC CD 346-2 (33 minutes). Recorded 1957.

⑩ ❽

Evans already had close on two decades in the music business under his belt when he came to make this, his first album as a leader, just four months after completing the sessions on his first album in collaboration with Miles Davis, **Miles Ahead** (the **Birth of the Cool** sessions were never conceived as an album, and Evans, while still the guiding spirit, was only one of a number of arrangers there).

This record has its own character, quite distinct from **Miles Ahead**, and Evans makes judicious use of a number of soloists, himself included, with Steve Lacy and Jimmy Cleveland being the most persuasive in that role. The man Gerry Mulligan termed Svengali chose here a diverse set of tunes and gave them all the gift of his unique soundscapes. With Evans, at least in this phase of his career, it is always the choice of instruments balanced off against each other, and the inner voicings of the harmonic paths they follow, which gives the music its often startling identity. His added ability to home in on the part of a tune which will give the most dramatic re-working of its essence is starkly etched on *Just One of Those Things*, taken at a moderately brisk tempo, where the melody is virtually ignored throughout. It is the descending chords behind the theme which attract Evans, and he brings them to the fore. In jazz, only Ellington had a comparable orchestral imagination and love of subtle sonorities. **KS**

Out Of The Cool Evans (p, arr, cond), **Johnny Coles, Phil Sunkel** (t); **Jimmy Knepper, Keg Johnson, Tony Studd** (tb); **Bill Barber** (tba); **Ray Beckenstein, Eddie Caine, Budd Johnson, Bob Tricarico** (reeds); **Ray Crawford** (g); **Ron Carter** (b); **Charlie Persip, Elvin Jones** (d, perc). Impulse! Ⓜ MCAD-5653 (38 minutes). Recorded 1960.

✔ ⑩ ❽

Evans believed in giving as much creative freedom as was practical to his musicians, and as a consequence the quality of his work depended to some extent on the quality of his soloists. Recorded at a time when he was working for another company with Miles Davis, he was well served by the men on this session.

Like Ellington, Evans often reworked chunks of previous composition. *La Nevada*, which runs for 15 minutes, is a simple four-bar theme which Evans had used before. Its use for the development of a string of solos makes it a text book for arrangers as Evans places the soloists under pressure at certain points and raises and then relaxes tension. Some of the filigree figures scored (for example for bassoon) behind the soloists are supreme examples of the orchestrator's art. At the time Evans used Coles as a Davis clone with enormous success. Bewildered at first when Evans gave him no direction as to how to play his feature role on *Sunken Treasure,* Coles nevertheless produced a classic improvisation—one could not sense that he was at the outer limits of his perception of Evans's music and was shortly to give it up. In Knepper Evans had the services of the most creative trombonist of the time; his poised and eloquent variations on *Where Flamingos Fly* make this one of the most outstanding statements on the instrument.

The miniaturization of the sleeve notes from the original LP is disastrous, making notes and personnel indecipherable. In another seeming oversight, MCA/Impulse! have also not bothered to include the extra track from this session, Horace Silver's composition *Sister Sadie,* which first saw the light of day on a mid-seventies vinyl reissue of this music. **SV**

The Individualism Of Gil Evans **Gil Evans** (p, arr, cond); **Johnny Coles, Thad Jones** (t); **Jimmy Cleveland** (tb); **Al Block** (f); **Phil Woods** (as); **Wayne Shorter** (ts); **Kenny Burrell** (g); **Paul Chambers, Richard Davis, Milt Hinton** (b); **Elvin Jones, Osie Johnson** (d). Verve Ⓜ 833 804-2 (68 minutes). Recorded 1964.

✔ ⑩ ❽

Nowhere else, not even in the music he wrote and conducted for Miles Davis, does the genius of Gil Evans come over more strongly than it does on this disc. Like Duke Ellington, he created a unique and instantly recognizable sound from an orchestra and could write parts for soloists with such understanding of their style that it is often impossible to tell where the written part ends and the improvisation begins.

That is the case here with his reworking of Kurt Weill's *Barbara Song*, in which Wayne Shorter's tenor saxophone gradually emerges from a kind of orchestral mist, delivers a meditative solo and sinks back again. Throughout the piece the instrumental textures change like cloud formations, slowly altering their patterns of light and shade. His mastery of orchestration was astounding: like Debussy, he could voice a phrase for piccolo and tuba in such a way that you are convinced you can hear the ghostly harmonies between. At the same time his music is full of rhythmic energy. Harmonically, *Las Vegas Tango* shimmers like a desert mirage but it is lifted and kept airborne by the drumming of Elvin Jones, doing exactly what he always did for John Coltrane.

This CD release is virtually twice as long as the original vinyl issue, with five previously unissued pieces included, some of them in newly-restored mixes and removing previous edits, all of which work was done under the supervision of Evans himself. **DG**

Svengali **Evans** (p, elp, arr); **Tex Allan, Marvin Peterson, Richard Williams** (t); **Sharon Freeman, Peter Levin** (frh); **Joseph Daley** (tb, tba); **Howard Johnson** (tba, flh, bs); **Dave Sanborn** (as); **Billy Harper** (ts, f); **Trevor Koehler** (ss, bs, f); **David Horowitz** (syn); **Ted Dunbar** (g); **Herb Bushler** (elb); **Bruce Ditmas** (d); **Susan Evans** (perc). ACT Ⓜ 9207-2 (41 minutes). Recorded 1973.

⑧ ❽

When Evans began leading a live band, which he had seldom done before the seventies, the distillation of textures and careful plotting of structure was substantially loosened. Fortunately, he used creative players who, rather than splitting the seams of his scores, on the whole enhanced his original conception. The above album, recorded live at two concerts but with little audience noise, shows the process at work. For instance *Zee Zee*, perhaps the simplest composition of the lot, becomes a soaring improvisation by Peterson, but probably neither would stand up without the other. The same applies to *Cry of Hunger*, written by and featuring Harper, which is not only arranged by Evans but reorganized by him at the editing stage, as the new liner note by Howard Johnson points out.

The other four pieces are remakes in one way or another. Both Gershwin's *Summertime* and Evans's *Eleven* (a.k.a. *Petits Machins*) distantly resemble the versions arranged by Gil for Miles Davis, but turning them over to Dunbar and Williams respectively makes them very different, and the backgrounds are changed accordingly. Harper's *Thoroughbred* and George Russell's *Blues In Orbit* are closer to the Evans recordings of a couple of years earlier (reissued on Enja 3069-2), but these versions have a sharper edge. **BP**

Jon Faddis

1953

Legacy **Faddis** (t); **Harold Land** (ts); **Kenny Barron** (p); **Ray Brown** (b); **Mel Lewis** (d). Concord CCD-4291-2 (42 minutes). Recorded 1985.

⑧ ❽

Trumpeter Jon Faddis was a precocious 18-year-old 'young lion' when he moved to New York from his hometown of Oakland, California, to join Lionel Hampton's band in New York City in 1971. Once in the Big Apple, his powerful high-register, keen reading skills and Gillespie-derived solo style led to important tenures with the Thad Jones-Mel Lewis Orchestra, Gil Evans and Charles Mingus. Faddis's most significant association, though, was with Gillespie himself. Indeed, Gillespie included his virtuosic protégé in any number of concert, club and recording engagements.

On this sterling 1985 date, Faddis deploys his clarion sound, stratospheric probes and fleet technique in heartfelt salutes to some of the greats of jazz's trumpet 'legacy'. On *West End Blues* we sense the presence of Louis Armstrong, whereas on *Little Jazz* it is Roy Eldridge who 'appears'. With *A Child Is Born*, Faddis pays poignant tribute to former colleague Thad Jones. For *Night in Tunisia* and *Things to Come*, Faddis honours mentor Dizzy Gillespie with dazzlingly boppish flights.

Throughout, Faddis is ably supported by the superb rhythmic team of Kenny Barron, Ray Brown and Mel Lewis, while Harold Land's smouldering tenor provides an apt front-line foil on lines such as *Li'l Darlin'* and *Whisper Not*. In the liner notes, Dizzy Gillespie writes that "this new album of Jon's is terrifying!" Amen! **CB**

Don Fagerquist

1927-1974

Eight By Eight **Fagerquist, Ed Leddy** (t); **Bob Enevoldsen** (vtb); **Vince DeRosa** (frh); **Herb Geller** (as); **Ronnie Lang** (bs); **Marty Paich** (p); **Buddy Clark** (b); **Mel Lewis** (d). VSOP Ⓔ #4CD (34 minutes). Recorded 1957.

⑧ ❽

This is an example of West Coast jazz at its best. All its finest qualities—technical skill, lyricism and passionate improvising—are here in abundance. Fagerquist's playing, although here in a small 34 minute bottle, is amongst the finest of jazz wines, and this collection of ballads and standards is the noblest part of his legacy, for although he was much in demand as a sideman, notably with Les Brown, he recorded shamefully little in relation to the size of his talent. His work is essentially mellow, reminding one very much of Clifford Brown without the fireworks. The eminent West Coast personality Marty Paich was responsible for all the arrangements; consequently they are stamped with his seal of excellence. His piano soloing and accompanying is both fiery and immaculate.

Herb Geller, here not far behind Art Pepper, is a potent alto soloist who works predictably well as a foil to the trumpet, whilst Enevoldsen is a consistently inspired and original voice on valve trombone. An elementary finger calculation reveals that the album should be titled **Eight By Nine**. **SV**

Georgie Fame

1943

Three Line Whip **Fame** (org, v); **Guy Barker** (t); **Peter King** (as); **Alan Skidmore** (ts); **Steve Gregory** (ts, f); **Anthony Kerr** (vb); **Tristan Powell** (g); **Steve Gray** (kbds); **Brian Odgers** (b); **James Powell** (d); **Kaz** (v). Three Line Whip Ⓔ TLW 001 (50 minutes). Recorded 1993.

⑧ ❽

As a sample of Georgie Fame's mature work, this self-published CD would be hard to beat. From the very beginning he staked out his territory—an area embracing, among others, Mose Allison, Count Basie, Jon Hendricks and the Hammond organ groovers—and has been exploring it with taste and intelligence for the past 30 years. His colleagues here are all members of the informal repertory company which he regularly calls upon for his various projects. They represent two generations of British jazz at its most distinguished, with King, Barker and Kerr especially prominent. The Powell brothers, drummer and guitarist, are Fame's own talented sons. The programme consists mainly of Fame originals, sung in his distinctive husky, vibratoless voice and underpinned by his discreetly throbbing Hammond. The solos are excellent, without exception, and fit perfectly into the atmosphere of hip relaxation which Fame seems able to create at will. **DG**

Tal Farlow

1921

A Sign of the Times **Farlow** (g); **Hank Jones** (p); **Ray Brown** (b). Concord Ⓔ CCD-4026 (40 minutes). Recorded 1977.

⑥ ❽

Tal Farlow emerged in the late forties to deify guitar technique, bebop and otherwise, and his digital dexterity earned him the nickname 'The Octopus'. In the late-fifties, after a few busy years, he withdrew from full-time performance and worked as a signwriter, but he returned in the mid-seventies, and this recording was evidence of that renascence. By then, the years had perhaps taken their toll on the celebrated technique, since his timing is often wayward, his articulation imprecise. However, the guitaristic tricks remain intact. Most of these are commonplace now, and outnumbered by the catalogue of electric guitar techniques that grew from rock, but his production of a bongo drum effect on the damped strings of the guitar—heard here on *Stompin' At The Savoy*—is still intriguing. More routine is his skilful use of harmonics on *You Don't Know What Love Is* and often stuttering bebop fluency. The programme is mostly standards, but several are imaginatively arranged: *You Don't Know What Love Is* is the most striking, opening with a lugubrious two-bar ostinato divided into alternating bars of 5/8 and 3/8. It is completely out of character with the rest of the tune, which swings in a conventional way, but it adds welcome drama to an otherwise rather bland set. The modest playing time reflects the recording's analogue origins. **MG**

Art Farmer

1928

Portrait Of Art Farmer **Farmer** (t); **Hank Jones** (p); **Addison Farmer** (b); **Roy Haynes** (d). Contemporary Ⓜ OJCCD 166-2 (42 minutes). Recorded 1958.

✓ ⑩ ❽

Despite a commendably consistent and high-level career (or perhaps because of it), Farmer has always been underrated. By the time of this album he had worked for Lionel Hampton and Horace Silver and was currently with Gerry Mulligan, as seen in *Jazz On A Summer's Day*. Possessing an individual tone and a manner often compared to early Miles, his choice of notes was markedly different even by the time of his first major recordings with Wardell Gray.

This is one of the great quartet albums irrespective of artist and, like Farmer's later **Sing Me Softly Of The Blues** (which has sadly yet to be reissued on CD), it is highly representative of the trumpeter's work during the period in question. Everyone plays at the top of their game, with a puckish but sensitive Jones contrasting pleasantly with the ebullient Haynes, who was on the point of joining Thelonious Monk. The session includes a couple of ballads that are gentler than Miles's (and more interesting than anything by Chet Baker), alongside more challenging material by George Russell and Benny Golson. Blues and rhythm changes are attacked without pre-set themes and, from the opening a cappella Farmer solo, here is an album to treasure. **BP**

Live at the Half Note **Farmer** (flh); **Jim Hall** (g); **Steve Swallow** (b); **Walter Perkins** (d). Atlantic Jazz Ⓜ 790666-2 (38 minutes). Recorded 1963.

⑧ ❼

Farmer is one of those players beloved of other musicians and of critics for his impeccable musicianship, taste and invention, but never fully appreciated by the wider world because his music is unspectacular, almost diffident, to the casual listener. First heard from in the late forties, by the time of this recording Farmer had fully mastered every aspect of his art. The Jazztet, an excellent group he co-led with Benny Golson, was in the recent past, and his band with Jim Hall was currently one of the most intriguing in modern jazz. The 'live' context here allows all four musicians to stretch out, and they respond enthusiastically. Hall, sometimes a rather remote player, sounds fully engaged with the rest of the group and comes up with some stupendous ideas, both while soloing and while backing Farmer. The flügelhornist delivers well-constructed solos, playing with great warmth and enthusiasm (his solo on the up-tempo *Swing Sping* must be one of his most spirited), and in this he also receives superb backing from Swallow and Perkins. A memorable engagement at the Half Note then, with only one sour note to strike: considering the rather embarrassing playing-time and the policy on other Atlantic CD jazz reissues (Coleman, Coltrane) of including extra material it seems miserly in the extreme to give not a single extra second of music on this reissue. **KS**

Soul Eyes **Farmer** (flumpet); **Geoff Keezer** (p); **Kenny Davis** (b); **Lewis Nash** (d). Enja Ⓕ ENJ 7047-2 (66 minutes). Recorded 1991.

⑧ ❽

Since his emergence as a soloist in the early fifties Farmer has been the epitome of the sure-footed, tasteful jazz trumpeter. Whether he plays trumpet, flügelhorn or the clumsily named flumpet—a combination of the two—is of no consequence. His solos always merit 'impeccable' and the other adjectives so tirelessly retreaded in praising his direct forebear, Buck Clayton. But, unlike Clayton, Farmer rarely stretches himself to any outer limits, and there is never any chance that he will fall off his well-considered perch. He has graced many big bands, notably that of Quincy Jones (see below), but in the small group used here he has full control over his material and ranges freely over the changes of a varied set of jazz compositions from Strayhorn, Monk, Golson, Joe Henderson and Mal Waldron.

Geoff Keezer, a man to watch, plays the type of sizzling and aggressive piano which is more likely to produce blood on the floor than are the leader's poised and tidy variations. Keezer shows his power in a solo on Henderson's *Recorda Me* which sounds robust enough to have frightened Farmer from the stage. **SV**

Joe Farrell

1937-1986

Vim 'n' Vigour **Farrell** (ts, ss, f); **Rob Van Den Broeck** (p); **Harry Emmery** (b); **Louis Hayes** (d). Timeless Ⓕ CDSJP-197 (45 minutes). Recorded 1983.

⑧ ❽

Saxophonist/flautist Joe Farrell was one of the most accomplished and versatile players of the seventies and eighties. Although he had absorbed the basics of bebop, his fascination with the more melodic side of the modal approach of Miles Davis and John Coltrane led him to a distinctly lyrical yet steely style. Farrell also possessed a remarkable versatility that allowed him to productively mesh in settings as varied as the big bands of Maynard Ferguson and Thad Jones-Mel Lewis, the fusion of Chick Corea's original Return to Forever and the dynamic small group of drummer Elvin Jones. Farrell also achieved a degree of commercial success with a series of albums in the early seventies for CTI including **Outback** and **Moon Germs**.

Here, in a highly satisfying straight-ahead date recorded in Holland in 1983, Farrell's swinging modal approach soars. There is a throbbing tip-of-the-hat to Sonny Rollins, *Three Little Words*, in which Farrell's tenor skips in tandem with co-leader Louis Hayes's 'dialoguing' drums. There are impressive soprano forays, Farrell's serpentine *Arab Arab* and Coltrane's aptly tagged *Miles' Mode*. Farrell's fleet flute work is spotlighted on the Latin-inflected *Besame Mucho*. On the exuberant title-track, his smoking tenor stamps out a dazzling set of modern blues choruses that jump with stylish modern jazz élan. **CB**

Pierre Favre

1937

Singing Drums **Pierre Favre, Paul Motian, Fredy Studer** (d, perc); **Nana Vasconcelos** (perc, v). ECM Ⓕ 1274 (823 639-2) (42 mins). Recorded 1984.

⑧ ❽

Wholly self-taught, Swiss drummer and percussionist Favre has drawn together each of his successive influences into a non-idiomatic, almost contemporary classical style which is entirely his own. Initially going down the mainstream path alongside the likes of Philly Joe Jones and Bud Powell, in the mid-sixties Favre went on to join all the European noisemakers busy offering their own version of urban America's New Thing: Evan Parker, Peter Brötzmann, Irene Schweizer and Manfred Schoof and so on (especially of note: Favre's contribution to the latter's seminal, blistering **European Echoes**). But where other European free jazz drummers, most remarkably Han Bennink, have continued to explore the endless possibilities offered by (and the endless problems encountered in) spontaneous music-making, Favre has instead looked to non-Western cultures for inspiration. Mastering a myriad of esoteric instruments, he allows tuned gongs, bowed cymbals and crotales to get a look in on *Singing Drums*, his 1984 paean to the joys of banging things to make music. He is joined on seven of his own compositions by three other master drummers: the American Paul Motian, ex-Bill Evans sideman and one of the finest drummer-composer bandleaders in jazz history, the underrated Fredy Studer, one-time sideman of Stockhausen's trumpeter son Markus, and the Brazilian Nana Vasconcelos, whose berimbau soloing in particular is known to jazz audiences worldwide for its contribution to the music of Pat Metheny, Jan Garbarek and Andy Sheppard. The music they make together ranges from tone poem to pan-global swing; its diversity and beauty will shock anyone who has ever groaned at the words 'drum solo'. **SH**

Victor Feldman

1934-1987

The Artful Dodger **Feldman** (p); **Chuck Domanico, Monty Budwig** (b); **Colin Bailey** (d); **Jack Sheldon** (t, v). Concord Ⓕ CCD-4038 (40 minutes). Recorded 1977.

⑧ ❻

Britain lost one of its most talented jazz musicians when Feldman decided to work in the US in 1955. His achievements there were numerous in both the popular music and jazz fields: he played piano with the Cannonball Adderley Quintet, worked as an accompanist to Peggy Lee, wrote and played for Miles Davis, to name a few. Although he confines himself to the keyboard on this CD, the extent of his musicianship is overwhelming. He wrote four of the tunes and leads a most exciting trio which contains another British-born immigrant in Colin Bailey whose fast hands and feet contribute so much to the drive and accuracy of the music. *A Walk On The Heath* is a beautiful Feldman waltz and the treatment of Stevie Wonder's *Isn't She Lovely?* is jazz from start to finish. On two tracks Feldman switches to Fender Rhodes piano, one being the closing version of his *Haunted Ballroom*, which ends eerily with the sound of a ten-year-old Feldman taking a drum solo with the Glenn Miller Band in October 1944 at a London concert. This CD is a well-transferred copy of what was a splendid LP. **AM**

Eric Felten

T-Bop **Felten, Jimmy Knepper** (tb); **Joshua Redman** (ts); **Jonny King** (p); **Paul LaDuca** (b); **Jorge Rossy** (d). **Tom Everett, Evan Dobbins** (tb); **Paul Henry** (b). Soul Note Ⓕ 121196-2 (75 minutes). Recorded 1992.

⑦ ❽

Eric Felten is young, but he was brought up steeped in the jazz tradition, having a grandfather who played with the territory bands in the twenties and an aunt who graced Ina Ray Hutton's outfit, while his father is still a music teacher. All of which gave him the great commonsense to contact Jimmy Knepper when he had this album to make. Knepper, one of the instrument's great individuals and most neglected voices, adds his inimitable magic to the whole date, although he only solos on five of the ten cuts. His velvety tone and oddly-phrased, bleary arpeggiated style comes across like an old friend in unfamiliar company here, although Felten himself has a very cleanly-phrased and visceral style, showing not only the technical assurance of a J.J. Johnson fan but the love of a big open brass tone which doubtless comes from an appreciation of the opposite tradition, that of Bill Harris and Roswell Rudd.

Redman makes a worthy contribution, as does the admirable rhythm section, but the spotlight rightly falls on the two slide trombonists. Felten takes two duets with bass only, in which he demonstrates admirable maturity, but one of the most beautiful moments on the disc occurs when Knepper's singing tone comes floating out of the simple two-part harmony ensemble vamp of *Hold Back the Dawn*. Knepper's highly vocalized approach is one which he has held intact for over 30 years, and although this album is not his show, he steals it more than once. It is a tribute to the younger player's generosity of spirit that he is prepared to let the old stager be there to do it in the first place. **KS**

Maynard Ferguson

1928

A Message From Newport **Ferguson** (t, vtb); **Joe Slaney Jr, Clyde Reasinger, Bill Chase** (t); **Slide Hampton, Don Sebesky** (tb); **Jimmie Ford** (as); **Willie Maiden, Carmen Leggio** (ts); **Jay Cameron** (bs); **John Bunch** (p); **Jimmy Rowser** (b); **Jake Hanna** (d). Roulette Ⓜ CDP7 93272-2 (44 minutes). Recorded 1958.

⑧ ❻

Ferguson's iron lips and phenomenal range on the trumpet helped give the 1950-53 Stan Kenton band its 'wall-of-sound' reputation. After a stint with the Paramount film company's studio band, he formed his own orchestra, essentially a young outfit with plenty of talent in the writing and playing departments. Men such as Jaki Byard, Don Ellis and Wayne Shorter all worked with Ferguson, and this CD is perhaps the best representative example of what was, in effect, a 'small' big band. Despite what the title suggests, these nine tracks were recorded in a studio and not at the Newport Jazz Festival. Trombonist Slide Hampton wrote five of the originals, the best of which is the masterly *Frame For The Blues*. Two more are from Don Sebesky, with one apiece by Willie Maiden and Bob Freedman; all were designed for this brassy, exciting, enthusiastic band. With men such as Bill Chase and Jake Hanna on lead trumpet and drums respectively the power and accuracy of the ensemble is never in doubt. There are several good soloists to be heard, but just occasionally (as on *The Fugue*) Jimmie Ford almost gets submerged by the band, possibly due to incorrect microphone placing. **AM**

Si! Si!—MF **Ferguson, Don Rader, Gene Goe, Nat Pavone** (t); **John Gale, Kenny Rupp** (tb); **Lanny Morgan** (as), **Willie Maiden, Don Menza** (ts, ss, f, cl); **Mike Abene** (p); **Link Milliman** (b); **Rufus Jones** (d). Roulette Ⓜ CDP7 95334-2 (61 minutes). Recorded 1962.

This combination of most of two earlier albums gives a wider cross-section of Ferguson's material than any other. These tracks show off a good big band playing a most original library, and it is doubtful if his band was ever so consistently good again. This is not to dispute that his 'Big Bop Nouveau' is one of the most exciting playing today. The library was contributed by writers like Ernie Wilkins, Marty Paich and Ferguson sidemen Don Sebesky, Willie Maiden and Mike Abene. The band was full of talent. A lot of the coruscating sounds which dogged some of his later albums are absent, and as a result the high quality of some of his soloists is allowed to break through. Ferguson is a unique phenomenon on his instrument, and his high note work has sometimes been allowed to obscure the fact that he is able to swing a band more than any other leader. Apart from the leader, the most notable soloist is Lanny Morgan, who plays well throughout but is outstanding on the fresh-sounding Ernie Wilkins chart *Morganpoint*. Don Rader's title-track pits Rader and Ferguson in an expressive trumpet conversation and features typically powerhouse section work. After Morgan, Don Menza is the most effective of the reeds, and Frank Hittner impresses with his baritone on *Great Guns*. **SV**

Rachelle Ferrell

First Instrument **Ferrell** (v)with: on six tracks **Eddie Green** (p); **Tyrone Brown** (b); **Doug Nally** (d); on one track add **Alex Foster** (ss); one track **Terence Blanchard** (t); **Gil Goldstein** (p); **Kenny Davis** (b); **Lenny White** (d); one track **Wayne Shorter** (ts); **Michel Petrucciani** (p); **Stanley Clarke** (b); **Lenny White** (d); **Pete Levin, Gil Goldstein** (syn). Blue Note Ⓕ CDP8 27820 2 5 (57 minutes). Recorded 1989/90.

⑥ ❽

As a great deal of jazz makes use of the popular song as its basis for improvisation, singers often find themselves restricted by the original lyrics in their attempts to find the freedom enjoyed by instrumentalists. I would not say that Rachelle Ferrell has completely solved the problem but she comes much closer to a satisfactory resolution than most. Of course she could have based her entire programme on originals, but instead of that she shows what can be achieved by using the words and music of writers such as Cole Porter, Frank Loesser, Richard Rodgers, Gene DePaul, etc., as well as two pieces of her own. The results are sometimes startling for she has the vocal equipment to soar up through the octaves with great accuracy. On *What Is This Thing Called Love?* she cuts down the supporting group to just Doug Nally's drums, stays in tune, skates around the melody with ease and even manages to insert a quotation from *Hot House*. At rest, so to speak, she reveals the warm, sensuous voice and extracts great feeling from ballads such as *My Funny Valentine* and Cy Coleman's *With Every Breath I Take*. She is at her most self-indulgent, and least successful, on the live performance of *Autumn Leaves* where her shrieks and yodels delight the groundlings just as Flip Phillips and Illinois Jacquet did with JATP. **KS**

Bobby Few

1935

Mysteries **Few** (p, v). Miss You Ⓕ 12 2122 (71 minutes). Recorded 1992.

⑤ ❽

A Brook Benton accompanist and Albert Ayler sideman, Few is a man of many parts. He came to Europe in 1969 and Paris has remained his home base for 26 years. While there, he has recorded with the likes of Archie Shepp, Frank Wright, Sunny Murray and Noah Howard, and the eighties found him a member of Steve Lacy's impressive sextet. This CD presents a rare solo performance, with *The Umbrella Man* the only title not written by him. It shows him to be a talented composer and puts the emphasis on the lyrical side of his personality. The romantic *Like A Waterfall* is the only descriptive piece and there are none of the wild chromatic outbursts heard on his freer mid-seventies work or, more recently, that with Lacy. Low spots are his vocals on the Mose Allison-type *Mysteries* and the Tom Lehrerish nonsense of *Let's Play Dice*, but his piano truly captures the genuine Baptist rock of *Church People*, while *Die With Love* is a beautiful and plaintive tribute to Frank Wright. To hear him deliver orthodox chordal patterns with the authority associated with Abdullah Ibrahim is a surprise but Few has always been a positive player and the absence of a rhythm section ensures that he tells his own story in his own manner. **BMcR**

Barry Finnerty

Straight Ahead **Finnerty** (g); **David Kikoski** (p); **Mike Richmond** (b); **Victor Lewis** (d); **Chuggy Carter** (perc). Arabesque Ⓕ AJ0116 (62 minutes). Recorded 1994.

⑦ ❿

Finnerty is no spring chicken, and his début comes after 20 years of professional music-making, but that does not mean that this album should be ignored. Suffering the fate of many jobbing guitarists, he has made money playing music away from jazz and been discounted when he has come to companies with jazz ideas for albums or songs. His style of playing is not that far removed from Emily Remler, and he swings every bit as fluently as the late and gifted mainstream player. His range is quite broad within the ambit mentioned above, and he is not afraid of beefing up, cranking up and going for broke on, say, *Carnaval*, or Joe Henderson's old stormer, *Inner Urge*. He also improvises fluently on *Count Up*, his own version of Coltrane's ferocious set of changes, *Countdown*.

The supporting musicians do well, although poor David Kikoski has to labour with a piano that has an octave of its range in a distinctly *desafinado* shape. Victor Lewis is, as usual, immaculate but busy enough for you to know he is there. **KS**

Ella Fitzgerald

1918

The Original American Decca Recordings **Fitzgerald** (v) with her **Savoy Eight**, her **Famous Orchestra**, **Louis Armstrong**, **Louis Jordan**, **The Chick Webb Orchestra**, **The Sy Oliver Orchestra**, **The Bob Haggart Orchestra**, **The Ink Spots**, **The Delta Rhythm Boys**; **Billy Kyle**, **Ellis Larkins**, **Hank Jones** (p); **Ray Brown** (b). MCA/Decca Ⓜ GRP26192 (two discs: 119 minutes). Recorded 1938-55.

✔

⑧ ❽

This is a sensible overview of Ella's recordings during the years indicated above. The Decca sessions were much hotter than her later famous sessions for Verve and some of the contrived alliances, notably with Armstrong and her boy-friend Louis Jordan, worked very well. The many tasteful ballads, a rare form during the 1940s, are sung with great brio and Ella's scat workouts, including *Flying Home*, *Lady Be Good* and others included here, are the original benchmarks for the style. Although a good number of the songs, from *A Tisket, A Tasket* (1938) to *Hard Hearted Hannah* (1955) were popular hits, all the 39 tracks are high in jazz interest and consistency. "Man, woman and child," said Bing Crosby, "Ella's the greatest." On this showing that is a reasonable motion for debate. The tracks included from the fifties demonstrate Fitzgerald's ability to overcome any musical obstacle or constriction imposed upon her by an increasingly distant record company management. She imparts something special to every performance.

Erudite essays by Dan Morganstern and a comprehensive discography grace the lavish but rather clumsy book which contains the discs. The fact that the two discs are packaged together vertically makes the set impossible to file with other discs on conventional shelves. A recent Brubeck issue on Columbia was in a similar format: manufacturers should resist this trend. **SV**

Ella and Louis **Fitzgerald** (v); **Louis Armstrong** (t, v); **Oscar Peterson** (p); **Herb Ellis** (g); **Ray Brown** (b); **Buddy Rich** (d). Verve Ⓜ 825 373-2 (54 minutes). Recorded 1956.

⑦ ❽

While it would be impossible to deny the professionalism and sheer class of these performances, it must be said that the setting and the material favours Ella rather than Louis. Of the 11 songs making up this first Verve collaboration, Armstrong had never previously recorded nine of them and (perhaps significantly) was never to record them again. Louis, like Billie Holiday, actually seemed to thrive on the trite and the banal; the sophisticated melodies and lyrics of Berlin, the Gershwins, etc., seem to defeat him at times, and *Tenderly* is pitched in a key which may have suited Miss Fitzgerald but is frankly beyond Louis's comfortable range. Having said all that, the music is ideal for those mellow moments when the listener wants to hear some of the greatest jazz personalities at their most relaxed. Louis's occasional trumpet solos and obbligatos are never less than apt while the conjunction of the Oscar Peterson Trio and Buddy Rich makes for the most flawless platform. Ella, of course, is superb (was she ever otherwise at this time?) and makes a passable imitation of Louis himself at the end of *Tenderly*. Just less than a year later Norman Granz assembled virtually the same group (with the substitution of Louie Bellson for Rich) in the same studio with equally memorable results. **AM**

The Best Of the Song Books **Fitzgerald** (v) with orchestras of **Nelson Riddle**, **Billy May**, **Duke Ellington**, **Buddy Bregman**, **Paul Weston** and various small groups including **Ben Webster** (ts); **Stuff Smith** (vn); **Paul Smith** (p); **Barney Kesel** (g); **Joe Mondragon** (b); **Alvin Stoller** (d). Verve Ⓜ 519 804-2 (63 minutes). Recorded 1956-64.

✔ ⑩ ❽

No two people will ever agree on which 16 numbers constitute the 'best' of a gigantic undertaking like Ella Fitzgerald's **Song Book** albums, but this is as good and varied a selection as any so far attempted. Included are the obligatory *Ev'ry Time We Say Goodbye* and *Our Love Is Here To Stay*, two songs which now exist for most people solely in Ella's versions, and the complete *Bewitched, Bothered And Bewildered*, restoring some of Lorenz Hart's mildly risqué sallies ("Horizontally speaking, he's at his very best ...") and running to just over seven minutes. Over the years the songbooks have acquired the reputation of presenting 'definitive' versions of songs by the great American songwriters, but if 'definitive' means a straight and undeviating reliance on the songsheet this is not the case. Ella brings to the songs the elasticity of time and melody that only a superb jazz singer can manage. For a prime example, hear *Between The Devil And The Deep Blue Sea*, in a setting by Billy May, or *Hooray For Love*—or, indeed, any of the pieces included here. **DG**

The Complete Song Books **Fitzgerald** (v); accompanied by **Duke Ellington and his Orchestra**, **The Nelson Riddle Orchestra**, **The Billy May Orchestra**, **The Buddy Bregman Orchestra**, **The Paul Weston Orchestra**; plus the following small-group musicians: **Ben Webster** (ts); **Stuff Smith** (vn); **Paul Smith**, **Oscar Peterson** (p); **Barney Kessel**, **Herb Ellis** (g); **Joe Mondragon**, **Ray Brown** (b); **Alvin Stoller** (d) Verve Ⓕ 519 832-2 (16 discs: 932 minutes) Recorded 1956-64.

⑩ ❽

First things first: it is certain that Norman Granz had clear ideas on how Ella Fitzgerald's recording career should develop when he wrested her from Decca and started this series with the **Cole Porter** project in 1956, but it is doubtful that even he realized what the eventual size of one of popular music's most comprehensive and enduring achievements would be. It boggles the mind even today, and the most remarkable aspect of the whole thing is its consistency. There is simply nothing here which is not top-quality or, as Ellington noted, "beyond category". The arrangers, the musicians, the conductors; all involved gave of their best and exerted restraint, flair and good taste at every turn. But not even the best-intentioned project can succeed without a central object worthy of the care and attention. In Ella, Granz had an artist who simply never let him down, and who responded creatively to every situation he constructed for her. Considering the track record of many other popular and jazz singers when it came to consistently giving of their best in the studio, this alone is a remarkable feat.

Of course a lot of the arrangements are couched in the commercial pop rather than jazz idiom, with string sections and Latin percussionists, so it is at least arguable that many of the **Song Book**'s sides fall outside the scope of this Guide. That is to reckon without Ella, for everything she does as a singer— her phrasing, her attack, her expression, her moulding of notes, her humour—is thoroughly imbued with jazz feeling. She is taking these songs and giving them a definitve intepretation, rather than using them as a vehicle for self-promotion.

All the Songbooks have their own highlights and utilize great musicians (Benny Carter is featured, for example, during the **Harold Arlen Song Book**), but one is slightly different from the rest. The **Duke Ellington** project had Duke and his orchestra on hand, plus extra sessions with a small-group which remain some of the brightest treasures in Ella's recording career. Feelings remain mixed about the sides with Duke's orchestra, but too much has been made of the suggestion that Duke and Strayhorn didn't make new arrangements of the songs chosen. A close listen suggests this to be not entirely true, and anyway, the old ones sound beautiful behind her and the band plays with great spirit.

It is worth noting that, for those prospective purchasers who are understandably nervous about investing a substantial amount of money in such a large set as this, most of the **Song Books** remain available as separate entities, although they do not come with the dazzling packing and information granted the boxed set. **KS**

At the Opera House **Fitzgerald** (v); **Oscar Peterson** (p); **Herb Ellis** (g); **Ray Brown** (b); **Jo Jones** (d); plus in three tracks; **Roy Eldridge** (t); **J.J. Johnson** (tb); **Sonny Stitt** (as); **Stan Getz, Coleman Hawkins, Illinois Jacquet, Flip Phillips, Lester Young** (ts); **Connie Kay** (d). Verve Ⓜ 831 269-2 (59 minutes). Recorded 1957.

✔ ⑩ ❽

Ella Fitzgerald's long association with promoter, producer and manager Norman Granz resulted in a string of classic recordings for Verve, plus frequent Jazz at the Philharmonic tours. The short sets she sang on Granz's star-crammed road-shows allowed her to pull out all the stops on stage; she and Peterson's quartet attack *Goody Goody*, Benny Goodman's 1936 novelty hit (which she had recorded in 1952), with some of the raw exuberance of Elvis Presley's 1954 Sun Sessions (the comparison may strike some as odd, but Fitzgerald's jazz roots were in the raucous dance-hall variety, not supper-club fare).

This CD documents two concerts, recorded a week apart (one in stereo, one mono), on which she performed almost identical programmes. It is an ideal situation for observing the creative leeway she took within relatively fixed arrangements. Selections include rhythm tunes where she scats magnificently (an *Oh, Lady Be Good!* with riffing guest horns), relaxed uptempo romps (*It's All Right with Me*) and classic ballads (*Moonlight in Vermont*, Arlen's *Ill Wind*). Too much of Fitzgerald's pre- or non-songbook work is dismissed as frivolous, but only by those who underestimate the ecstatic mode in jazz. On these concerts, she is in gorgeous voice and high spirits. **KW**

Mack The Knife—The Complete Ella in Berlin **Fitzgerald** (v); **Paul Smith** (p); **Jim Hall, Barney Kessel** (g); **Wilfred Middlebrooks, Joe Mondragon** (b); **Gus Johnson, Alvin Stoller** (d). Verve Ⓜ 519 564-2 (50 minutes). Recorded 1960.

⑧ ❼

The **Song Books** were vital to her career portfolio but Fitzgerald was very much a working singer. She was on the Norman Granz circuit and live performances provided an alternative example of her artistry. **Ella In Berlin (Mack The Knife)**, performed in the Deutschlandhalle in front of 12,000 people, is a perfect example. The basics do not change; her faultless intonation is a source of constant wonder, her control of vibrato is exemplary and her ability to swing is never in doubt. The challenge of a live date gives her a keening edge, however, and on this CD she really entertains.

She does a Sinatra-style massacre of *Lady Is A Tramp*, she mugs through the forgotten lyrics of *Mack The Knife* and her supremely confident readings of *Misty* and *The Man I Love* show how effortlessly she stamps her own personality on other people's material. Her subtle Jimmy Rushing-type reconstruction of *Just One Of Those Things* improves on the original, while her unforced humour throughout provides alternatives, not desecrations. Her scat singing has always been a tad perfunctory but the ease with which she discriminates between the bop lines of Charlie Parker and Dizzy Gillespie on *How High The Moon* is masterful. In 1960, Fitzgerald was up and singing. More was to come. **BMcR**

Tommy Flanagan

1930

Lady Be Good...For Ella **Flanagan** (p); **Peter Washington** (b); **Lewis Nash** (d).Groovin' High Ⓕ 521 617-2 (61 minutes). Recorded 1993.

⑦ ❾

These songs, all drawn from the repertoire of Ella Fitzgerald, were recorded as a tribute shortly before she underwent such traumatic surgery last autumn. Flanagan was the most notable of the excellent pianists who worked as her accompanist and musical director; his tenure with the singer was for most of the two decades until 1978. Flanagan's style grew out of be-bop and could be described as being near to Hank Jones at one end and Erroll Garner at the other. He is a subtle player who also likes to attack, and his love of open melody makes his work very pleasing and accessible. He is also capable of generating a swing which is fluid and not bound by muscle, so that the dynamic range of his albums tends to be very great. Today he must be regarded as a mainstream player and all these tunes, some of them long regarded as hackneyed elsewhere, are treated with a freshness which makes them attractive all over again. Fitzgerald's famous improvisation on *Lady Be Good* is rehearsed in a second version of the tune, and Flanagan pulls it on like a comfy slipper. On the other hand, Gershwin's *Isn't It A Pity?* isn't so well known, and this ballad performance is one of the many high points of this delightful set. Bassist Peter Washington and drummer Lewis Nash are similarly subtle players; like Flanagan himself, they benefit from the excellent recording. **SV**

Bob Florence

1932

The Limited Edition—State Of The Art **Florence** (ldr, kbds, arr); **George Graham, Charley Davis, Warren Luening, Steve Huffsteter, Larry Ford** (t, flh); **Chauncey Welsch, Rick Culver, Charlie Loper, Herbie Harper** (tb); **Don Waldrop** (btb): **Lanny Morgan, Kim Richmond** (ss, as, f, cl); **Dick Mitchell, Bob Cooper** (ts, f, cl); **Bob Efford**; (f, bcl); **John Lowe** (bs, cl); **Tom Warrington** (b); **Peter Donald** (d); **Alex Acuna** (perc). BBC/Prestige Ⓜ CDPC797 (56 minutes). Recorded 1989.

⑥ ❽

Although Florence is one of the hardest working arrangers active in the Los Angeles area, his name is seldom found in jazz reference books. Yet his big studio bands invariably play exciting music, featuring solos by men such as Pete Christlieb, Nick Ceroli, Bill Perkins, Bob Cooper, etc. He also earned himself a Grammy nomination in 1982 for his album **Westlake**. This CD is a typically efficient Florence release, this time making use of five standards as well as four original compositions. *Moonlight Serenade* is turned into a samba, while *Stella By Starlight* is a swirling showcase for the altos of Morgan and Richmond. Steve Huffsteter is featured playing flügelhorn throughout *Silky* and

Bob Efford's baritone adds dignity to *Auld Lang Syne*, which also benefits from a most sympathetic Florence arrangement. The band may lack an instantly recognizable style, but it packs an impressive punch, well captured in the recording; Nimbus are credited with the mastering. **AM**

Marty Fogel

Many Bobbing Heads, At Last **Fogel** (cl, ss, ts); **David Torn** (g); **Dean Johnson** (b); **Michael Shrieve** (d, perc). CMP Ⓕ CD 37 (47 minutes). Recorded 1989.

⑥ ❽

Fogel and guitarist David Torn had been playing together for nearly 20 years, primarily in the Upstate New York Everyman Band, at the time of this recording, which is the kind of avant/world/fusion one might expect from players who count Lou Reed and Don Cherry among their past associates. Most tracks are either by the saxophonist (heard mostly on tenor) or are collective creations by the band, and are frequently enhanced by the studio soundplay of engineer/co-producer Walter Quintus, who provides the typically excellent and appropriately overheated CMP sound to this high-energy date. While one might wish for a bit less eclecticism at times, Fogel and Torn are always pushing, never simply lolling in the exotic moods; and the one cover, *Cherry's Guinea*, is a bashing beauty. Michael Shrieve, best known for his work with Santana, also gives a good accounting of his more creative impulses. The electric trappings of this music should not scare away acoustic music fans, particularly those who lean toward the more exploratory end of the jazz spectrum. **BB**

Ricky Ford

1954

Ebony Rhapsody **Ford** (ts); **Jaki Byard** (p); **Milt Hinton** (b); **Ben Riley** (d). Candid Ⓕ CCD 79053 (56 minutes). Recorded 1990.

⑦ ❽

Ricky Ford is a 40-something tenor saxophonist whose diverse credits include traditionalists Lionel Hampton and Duke Ellington as well as modernists Charles Mingus, Danny Richmond and Abdullah Ibrahim. Therefore it is not surprising that his style is an amalgam of the old and new, as well as something blue. One hears in Ford's extended solo intro to *Mon Amour* the motivic probing and at times the intense vibrato of Sonny Rollins. The Rollins signature is invoked further when the rhythm section enters and Ford's tenor at first pushes ahead and then pulls back from the centre of the pulse. Also, there are echoes of Coleman Hawkins's brusque assertiveness in Ford's rough-and-tumble *Independence Blues* and *Ebony Rhapsody*.

On Ford's haunting limning of the Ellington classic *In A Sentimental Mood* there are refractions of the lush balladry of Ben Webster, as well as the more astringent Rollins, especially on the tune's bridge. Cast as a duo with Milt Hinton, *Mood* is also a vibrant example of the bassist's ever-buoyant comping and solo work **CB**

Mitchel Forman

Now And Then **Forman** (p); **Eddie Gomez** (b); **Jack DeJohnette** (d). BMG Novus Ⓕ 163165-2 (48 minutes). Recorded 1992.

⑥ ❿

This album is subtitled "a tribute to Bill Evans", and a glance at the personnel and song titles will confirm this. A cursory listen to the opening *Waltz For Debby* will indicate that the tribute is heartfelt and is also painstaking in its efforts to create the rarified atmospheres of the best Bill Evans trios. Forman is a gifted player with a beautiful touch and extended harmonic knowledge to call upon. That he subsumes it to pay tribute to an obvious influence is perhaps ultimately more frustrating than anything else, because one gets constant hints throughout this programme that other musical thoughts are waiting to be pursued to their own logical ends, and the ghost of Evans maybe does not need such determined summoning.

This is not to say that the album is hard to enjoy. It is beautifully crafted, expertly played, and the interaction between the trio members is exemplary. Much music is being played. But perhaps Forman should have waited until a later point in his recording career to launch such a retrospective as this. He may just have come up with a fresher angle. As it is, the most consistent response a listener is likely to get from track after track here is an unwelcome comparison with the Evans original. There is only one winner when you play that game. **KS**

Michael Formanek

1958

Low Profile **Formanek** (b); **Dave Douglas** (t); **Ku-Umba Frank Lacy** (tb); **Marty Ehrlich** (cl, bcl, as, ss); **Tim Berne** (as); **Salvatore Bonafede** (p); **Marvin 'Smitty' Smith** (d). Enja Ⓕ ENJ 8050 2 (77 minutes). Recorded 1993.

⑦ ❽

Californian bassist Formanek paid his dues in the seventies with Joe Henderson, Dave Liebman and Herbie Mann. He worked in Europe during the eighties and has since established himself as a first call player in New York. The bonus is that the nineties have seen him emerge as a successful leader in his own right. His arrangements show an awareness of his soloist's requirements and their presentation needs.

This CD is a perfect example. He has a stylistically varied team and he showcases them with genuine style. He wrote and arranged every title and the way in which he encourages the flow of Ehrlich's bass clarinet on *Rivers* is in total contrast to the jocular mood of the Lacy-driven *Groogly* or to the subtle stimulation he provides for Berne's alto on *Great Plains*. The trumpet and trombone team bask in the latitude available on *Paradise Revisited* and the manner in which the horns alternate the lead in the all-ins on *Shuddawuddacudda* shows that the implications of John Coltrane's **Ascension** and Ornette Coleman's **Free Jazz** have been fully grasped. He has a superb pizzicato solo on *Great Plains* but it is the adroit way in which his varied charts unite the band that establishes his real status. **BMcR**

Jimmy Forrest

1920-1980

Most Much! **Forrest** (ts); **Hugh Lawson** (p); **Tommy Potter** (b); **Clarendon Johnson** (d); **Ray Barretto** (cga). Prestige Ⓜ OJCCD-350-2 (50 minutes). Recorded 1961.

⑥ ❻

Born in St Louis, Missouri and apprenticed in bands such as those of Andy Kirk and Jay McShann, it was inevitable that Forrest would emerge as one of those powerful, big-toned tenors. He worked in the Duke Ellington orchestra for seven months (1949-50) and succeeded in turning parts of a couple of Ducal tunes (*Happy-Go-Lucky-Local* and *That's The Blues, Old Man*) into a best-selling 'original' which he called *Night Train*. **Most Much!** is certainly the best album he did for Prestige, and the CD version adds two tracks to the original LP programme which were previously only issued on a separate album. Forrest, like Charlie Parker, had a way of infusing every tune he played with deep blues inflections. The opening *Matilda* is a somewhat repetitious calypso, but the rest of the nine-tune programme is nicely varied. The title tune is a powerful blues by Forrest in which time passes all too quickly; even the potentially lachrymose *I Love You* emerges as a fine jazz performance after the theme has been disposed of. A special mention must be made of the helpful, tasteful conga drumming of Barretto throughout the session. **AM**

Sonny Fortune

1939

Monk's Mood **Fortune** (as); **Kirk Lightsey** (p); **David Williams** (b); **Joe Chambers** (d). Konnex Ⓕ KCD 5048 (58 minutes). Recorded 1993.

⑩ ❿

In the past I have often found Fortune a hard player to warm to, his brilliant tone and fleet technique somehow by-passing my emotions. This date, however, is something special. Maybe it was the repertoire, or the personnel, or good planning, or just plain luck. Whatever it was, this has such a positive focus and is so full of humour, commitment and inspired twists that it makes you hear Monk's songs as if they were new once again. Not that Fortune and Co. wilfully pull them about and generally shred their original forms; that they most decidedly do not do. But they sound utterly at home with not only the changes and the rhythms, but the also attitude—what Bill Evans once described as Monk's "angle"—which is essential in keeping to the spirit of the work. Too many Monk covers obey the letter and lose the spirit. This one gets it just right, and the interplay between Fortune and Lightsey is worthy of Monk and his most distinguished horn men.

Fortune has gone on to make a further Monk album, **Four In One**, for Blue Note, again in tandem with the admirable Lightsey. Make no mistake: this Konnex date is the one to get. It has the extra-special glow. **KS**

Frank Foster

1928

No 'Count **Foster** (ts); **Frank Wess** (ts, f); **Benny Powell, Henry Coker** (tb); **Kenny Burrell** (g); **Eddie Jones** (b); **Kenny Clarke** (d). Denon/Savoy Ⓜ SV-0114 (36 minutes). Recorded 1956.

⑥ ❽

Foster had a cutting edge to his sound which later became fashionable with the hard bop saxophone players. This distinguishes him from the equally inventive Wess, who has a slightly softer, more mainstream attack. Foster must be regarded as a product of the Dexter Gordon school of thought, whilst Wess came from Hawkins and Byas.

Foster is an inventive musician who has also distinguished himself as an arranger. All the horns in the front line were part of the fine Count Basie band of the time, and it was their contemporary thinking (and in Foster's and Wess's case, writing) which, grafted on to the Basie rhythm style, gave that band its powerful character.

But Foster and his band were of the second bebop generation and although there is a leavening here of Basie type blues, the more stimulating numbers are Foster's originals. These are good themes beautifully voiced and, thanks to the quality of Rudy Van Gelder's recording, Foster's playing crackles with a fire not normally captured on his early Basie records.

The trombones, released from Basie's section, show how well they could solo. Kenny Burrell was an ideal guitar choice, for he is a player possessed of natural jazz feeling, and his presence in the rhythm section in lieu of a pianist adds freshness to the band's sound. **SV**

Pete Fountain 1930

Swingin' Blues **Fountain** (cl); **Bill Bachman** (t); **Jimmy Weber** (t); **Mike Genevay** (tb); **Tom Gekler** (tb); **Earl Vuiovich, Bob Molinelli** (p); **Johnny Gimbel** (vn); **Les Muscott** (bj, g); **Ed Firth** (bb); **Olivery Felix** (b); **Charlie Lodice** (d). Ranwood Ⓕ RDS 1002 (67 minutes). Recorded 1990.

④ ❻

One of the original members of the Basin Street Six, Fountain has long been a mainstay of tourist Dixieland in New Orleans. A club owner, he has worked copiously with Tony Almerico and Al Hirt and gained nationwide popularity on the Lawrence Welk Show. Fountain has a good tone in all registers, and is a natural swinger in a style that falls between Benny Goodman and Irving Fazola. As this CD shows, his rhythm sections often chug along in a polite but somewhat leaden manner, but in the process they draw attention to Fountain's own fluency and easy way with a tune. There is certainly little solo challenge from his sidemen here. Bachman plays a tidy lead and puts together neat solos, Gimbel carves out some quaint jazz fiddle, while Genevay stays close to the safety of the theme in most of his rather clumsy solos. The real point is the exposure of Fountain, as a practised ensemble player or as a warm sounding and fluent soloist, bouncing through the medium tempo of *Deep Purple* or bubbling with enthusiasm on *Alice Blue Gown* and *Running Wild.* It is 'good time' jazz with little content and even less emotional involvement, but it is all very well done. **BMcR**

Roger Frampton

Pure Piano **Frampton** (p). Tall Poppies Ⓕ TP 019 (60 minutes). Recorded 1989-90.

⑥ ❼

Frampton has for over two decades been a leading light in the Australian music scene, moving freely between jazz, classical music and avant-garde. Born in England, he went to Australia in 1966 and has rarely been out of the local limelight since. His singular approach to music has tended to keep him from achieving the consistent exposure his talent deserves and which seemed would come his way while he was a member of the Jazz Co-Op in the early seventies.

This present album, the third solo recital on Tall Poppies but the first with any appreciable connection to jazz (the other two were extended investigations of quartertone music), certainly demonstrates both the vast imagination he possesses and the effortless technique at his disposal. If it has a reference point in past jazz history, the two 1971 solo albums by Chick Corea on ECM are perhaps the closest in approach. Frampton calls his work on this album "real-time composition", which he defines as "free improvisations which are intended for repeated listening." While some of the work here recalls the free-ranging idea-association one finds in, say, Copland's *Piano Fantasy*, and other pieces the gradual disintegration of a motivic idea in the manner of Cecil Taylor, there is an ascetic sensibility often present with Frampton which is rare in the work of the other two men. The music here rewards close listening. **KS**

Panama Francis 1918

Gettin' In The Groove **Francis** (d); **Francis Williams, Irvin Stokes** (t); **Norris Turney** (as, cl); **Howard Johnson** (as); **George Kelly** (ts, arr); **Red Richards** (p); **John Smith** (g); **Bill Pemberton** (b). Black & Blue Ⓕ 233320 (66 minutes). Recorded 1979.

⑥ ❻

Francis worked with the Lucky Millinder band in the early forties, spending plenty of time at the Savoy in Harlem. This medium-sized band sets out to create the kind of music that Millinder, Al Cooper's Savoy Sultans, Erskine Hawkins and dozens of other bands provided for dancers during that period. Under Francis's careful hands (and feet) the band bounces along and produces an infectious beat suitable for dancing, but also potent as a tapestry against which soloists can perform. Nearly everyone solos here (it is unfortunate that we do not hear a solo from John Smith, the guitarist who

replaced Al Casey with Fats Waller years ago); Norris Turney turns in a fine tribute to Johnny Hodges on his own *Checkered Hat* and Francis Williams takes the trumpet role once played by Taft Jordan on the exciting *Harlem Conga*, a tune associated with Chick Webb. Panama calls the band his Savoy Sultans and pays tribute to the original Sultans by including such Al Cooper tunes as *Stitches*, *Rhythm Doctor Man*, *Frenzy* and *Second Balcony Jump*. The music may be eclectic but it is all played with verve.
AM

Aretha Franklin

1942

Aretha's Jazz **Franklin** (v, p); 1968 tracks with orchestras arranged and conducted by **Quincy Jones**: **Ernie Royal, Snooky Young, Bernie Glow, Richard Williams, Joe Newman** (t); **Jimmy Cleveland, Benny Powell, Urbie Green, Thomas Mitchell** (tb); **George Dorsey, Frank Wess** (as); **Seldon Powell, King Curtis** (ts); **David 'Fathead' Newman** (f, ts); **Pepper Adams** (bs); **Spooner Oldham** (org); **Junior Mance** (p); **Joe Zawinul** (elp, org); **Kenny Burrell, Jimmy Johnson** (g); **Ron Carter** (b); **Tommy Coghill, Jerry Jemmott** (elb); **Bruno Carr, Roger Hawkins** (d); 1972 tracks with unidentified ensembles, soloists including **Phil Woods** (as); **Billy Preston** (p). Atlantic Jazz Ⓜ 781230-2 (35 minutes). Recorded 1968/72.

⑥ ❼

Franklin, from Memphis, Tennessee, had a Baptist church background and as a teenager featured in her father's gospel troupe. In something of a career turnaround, she signed for Columbia records in 1960 and made a string of jazz-based albums with remarkably inappropriate arrangements and song selections. It took a move to Atlantic and an astute return to her natural musical habitat for her to register her first popular success. Since then her career has rarely faltered, though in recent years she has veered in style more towards the popular mainstream.

This disc takes selections first released on two different albums, **Aretha Franklin: Soul '69** and **Hey Now Hey (The Other Side of The Sky)**. The former record features thoroughly Basie-inspired charts from Quincy Jones and concentrates squarely on the blues. Franklin, utterly at home with the idiom, responds with some blues shouting the like of which had not been heard in a jazz context since the death five years previously of Dinah Washington. It may not be supper jazz, but Jimmy Rushing would recognise a kindred spirit. Of the three 1972 tracks, *Somewhere* veers more towards the type of pop arrangement singers from Andy Williams to Diana Ross were then experimenting with, probably with the success of Roberta Flack in mind. However all is retrieved in a swinging double-tracked vocal workout with a jazz big-band on *Moody's Mood* before the date is wrapped up with a long, slow blues, *Just Right Tonight*, on which Billy Preston excels with a long, mood-setting opening solo.
KS

Rebecca Coupe Franks

1963

Suit of Armour **Franks** (t, flh); **Joe Henderson** (ts); **Kenny Barron** (p); **Buster Williams** (b); **Leni Stern** (g); **Ben Riley** (d); **Carolyn Brady** (perc). Justice Ⓕ JR 0901-2 (62 minutes). Recorded 1991.

⑤ ❽

Coming from a family of trumpeters, Franks's interest in jazz was stimulated by hearing Miles Davis, Clifford Brown and Blue Mitchell. This 1991 CD was her first for Justice and 1992 saw her beginning to make her mark as a featured soloist on the festival circuit. The CD features seven of her imaginative compositions and teams her with one of the tenor majors and a very fine rhythm section. She is certainly not over-awed, but the real Franks has still to surface; the influence of her hard bop heroes at present is all pervading: her Miles-ish use of mutes on *Afternoon In Paris* and the title-track seems designed to keep it so. Open, her tone is a trifle light but she has good ideas and puts together shapely solos on *Beginning To See The Light* and *Elephant Dreams*. Apart from her own efforts, the best solos come from Williams and Barron, with Henderson sounding less than fully interested and on *U-Bitch*, in particular, seeming almost to coast. The serious collector will be aware that the Davis, Brown and Mitchell originals are available but Franks is a trumpeter of promise.
BMcR

Bud Freeman

1906-1991

Great Original Performances 1927-40 **Bud Freeman** (ts, cl); **Jimmy McPartland, Bobby Hackett** (c); **Max Kaminsky, Bunny Berigan** (t); **Floyd O'Brien, Jack Teagarden, Tommy Dorsey** (tb); **Brad Gowans** (vtb); **Joe Venuti** (vn); **Pee Wee Russell, Benny Goodman; Frank Teschemacher** (cl); **Dave Matthews** (as); **Adrian Rollini** (bs, s); **Dave Bowman, Joe Sullivan, Jess Stacy, Claude Thornhill** (p); **Eddie Condon, Dick McDonough** (g, bj); **Jim Lannigan, Artie Bernstein, Artie Shapiro** (b); **Gene Krupa, Cozy Cole, Sid Catlett, Dave Tough** (d). Jazz Classics In Digital Stereo Ⓕ RPCD 604 (63 minutes). Recorded 1927-40.

⑧ ❻

Robert Parker's techniques for turning old 78s into stereo have produced some turkeys, but this is not one of them. His successful rejuvenation of these tracks is fortuitous, for he has made a remarkably good choice from Freeman's best work. Freeman was the next major tenor sax innovator after Coleman Hawkins. His playing was lighter than Hawk's and probably had a considerable sway on the development of Lester Young's 'cool' style (Freeman plays 'cool' here on Ray Noble's 1935 *Dinah*, which has weathered the years surprisingly well). The McKenzie-Condon Chicagoans of 1927 are represented by *China Boy*, there is some nice Freeman clarinet in his quintet with Bunny Berigan, polished big band things with Noble and Dorsey, a couple of tracks by Bud's Summa Cum Laude Orchestra, and all eight classics from the 1940 Famous Chicagoans' session which included both Jack Teagarden and Pee Wee Russell, as well as some of the finest collective ensemble playing on record. Also included is the 1933 version of *The Eel*, a performance which confirmed that Freeman was an important and progressive soloist in the thirties. Some people have unkindly suggested that Freeman spent the rest of his life re-working *The Eel*; be that as it may, Freeman made a substantial contribution to jazz, and it is well illustrated here. **SV**

Chicago/Austin High School Jazz In Hi-Fi **Freeman** (ts) with, on four tracks: **Jimmy McPartland** (t); **Pee Wee Russell** (cl); **Dick Cary** (p); **Al Casamenti** (g); **Milt Hinton** (b); **George Wettling** (d); on two further tracks sub **Billy Butterfield** for **McPartland** (t); add **Tyree Glenn** (tb); on five tracks: **Billy Butterfield** (t); **Jack Teagarden** (tb, v); **Peanuts Hucko** (cl); **Gene Schroeder** (p); **Leonard Gaskin** (b); **George Wettling** (d). RCA Victor Ⓜ 113031 2 (44 minutes). Recorded 1957.

⑥ ❽

Another worthy release in the fine RCA Germany reissue programme of fifties LPs which rarely these days get the chance to reappear as originally conceived. This stereo workout, from three different 1957 sessions, uses Freeman's soubriquet Summa Cum Laude Orchestra to cover the disparate personnel, but really just a re-convening of jam sessions from the past with old mates. Everybody knows what their role is and goes on to fulfil it, with the two trumpeters sounding particularly at ease. Freeman is content to add the second or third line to the ensemble passages, but usually takes the first solo on a piece, and his full, instantly recognizable tone is captured superbly. Even Russell's acrid sound, often punished harshly by unsympathetic engineers, has a properly balanced body behind the edge it undoubtedly possesses.

The lessening of energy which comes with middle-age is quite noticeable here, but that is largely compensated for by unselfish ensemble joys and a general glow of warm happiness from every player. McPartland in particular keeps his tone ringing and bright, his rhythm sharp as a tack. On the five tracks featuring Teagarden, the crisp ensemble work is supplemented by the trombonist's wonderfully graceful solo work, while on Freeman's anthem, *Prince of Wails*, Butterfield gets in a spirited chorus. And if Schroeder does not have Cary's sensitivity as an accompanist, then two Teagarden vocals make up any deficiency. **KS**

Chico Freeman

1949

Spirit Sensitive **Freeman** (ss, ts); **Jay Hoggard** (vb). **John Hicks** (p); **Cecil McBee** (b); **Billy Hart, Don Moye** (d); **Jay Hoggard** (vb). India Navigation Ⓕ IN 1045CD (64 minutes). Recorded 1979.

⑧ ❽

Son of Chicago tenorman Von Freeman and a seventies member of the AACM, Chico Freeman's career has been rather erratic, the promise of his brighter moments never quite flowering into sustained achievement. A relatively conservative player, he is a good stylist, happy in most areas of the tradition, yet seemingly disinclined to forge a strong music of his own. He does excel at playing ballads, however, as the ten that comprise **Spirit Sensitive** make clear.

Freeman plays with great restraint and tenderness, his phrasing eloquent, his tone incorporating the barest hint of breathy vibrato. He gets sensitive support too, especially from the responsive McBee. Their duo track, a haunting *Autumn In New York*, is among the disc's high spots, as are the gentle reveries *A Child is Born* and *Carnival* (the latter featuring vibes and wistful soprano).

This CD has four more tracks than the original LP, including *Lonnie's Lament* and *Wise One*, where the Coltrane influence in Freeman's playing is to the fore. Regrettably, this generosity does not extend to the documentation, which omits recording details and composer credits. **GL**

Luminous—Chico Freeman and Arthur Blythe at Ronnie Scott's Club **Freeman** (ss, ts); **Blythe** (as); **John Hicks** (p, kbds); **Donald Pate** (b); **Victor Jones** (d); **Norman Hedman** (perc). Jazz House Ⓕ JHCD 010 (62 minutes). Recorded 1989.

⑦ ❽

Freeman has made many records where he has shared the heading with other luminaries (including his dad), and this live pairing with altoist Arthur Blythe is a good example of the results. Freeman's debt to Coltrane is more evident in his soprano playing than with the lower pitched horn, but his cooler approach to the instrument allows a distinctive voice to emerge. On *Footprints*, he manages to sound unlike both Coltrane and the piece's composer, Wayne Shorter. Blythe is a freer spirit, and his readiness to pile on the heat is evident from bar one of his first solo. Although, as is usual with a club recording, things tend to go on a little, the moments (or minutes, depending on your cravings for variety) when you are wishing for the next tune to start, or at least someone else to step up for the next solo, are relatively few, which means that the leaders here are playing consistently well. Freeman's long-term pianist John Hicks enjoys the spotlight in a number of excellent solos alongside those of the two horns.

As is often the case at Ronnie's, the audience is rather talkative at times **KS**

Von Freeman 1922

Walkin' Tuff **Freeman** (ts); **Jon Logan, Kenny Prince** (p); **Carroll Crouch, Dennis Carroll** (b); **Wilbur Campbell, Mike Raynor** (d). Southport ℗ 0010 (69 minutes). Recorded 1989.

⑧ ❼

Von Freeman is a great saxophonist and a Chicago legend; that his reputation has seldom escaped the Windy City's borders is due to sheer neglect on the part of the recording industry. A contemporary and peer of Illinois Jacquet, Dexter Gordon and Gene Ammons, he was not recorded as a leader until he was 50, and there have been precious few discs since then. This is a casual date, split between two competent rhythm sections (energized only by the presence of Campbell, another of the unsung legends of Chicago's post-bop community), that captures Freeman's unpredictability and peculiarities in a congenial setting. His tone is full of vigour and vinegar, in fact his playful idiosyncracies of pitch are part of his charm and individuality, and he is unafraid to honk, squawk, or squeal expressively. *Bruz, George And Chico* (dedicated to his musician brothers and son) displays the convoluted logic of his lines, and the extreme chromaticism and jittery multi-noted phrases of *Blues For Sunnyland* lead to Dolphy. But *Every Tub* reveals his true roots in Herschel Evans and Lester Young, while the unaccompanied *How Deep Is The Ocean* rivals Rollins for melodic intimations and ingenuity. The interest level drops dramatically when Von stops playing—the pianists are self-effacing and the bass solos tedious—but fortunately he is well featured, and should be heard. **AL**

Don Friedman 1935

At Maybeck **Friedman** (p). Concord Jazz ℗ CCD-4608 (63 minutes). Recorded 1993.

Friedman has worked, and sometimes recorded, with a number of important leaders including Dexter Gordon, Jimmy Giuffre, Shorty Rogers, Booker Little and Joe Henderson but his most fully realized work has always been as the leader of his own trio or, as here, as a true soloist. He has always worked closely to the manner of expression exemplified by Bill Evans (his earliest trio recordings for the Riverside label were remarkably similar in concept to Evans's albums which were appearing on the same label at the same time). This is probably his best solo album to date and he seems to have been inspired by the Maybeck piano (a Yamaha S-400B) and the attentive, appreciative audience. Unlike some of his other solo albums, there is a very positive approach here and a lack of self-indulgence. From the opening notes of *In Your Own Sweet Way* the listener knows he is in for a memorable musical experience. Friedman's careful gradation of touch and accurate digital work makes it easy to understand why he has worked for some time as a teacher. At the same time his classical training manifests itself too, notably on his thoughtful original *Memory For Scotty*. But it is the manner in which he works out his musical ideas, developing them into a logical whole, which makes this such an important album of contemporary keyboard jazz. **AM**

David Friesen 1942

Remembering The Moment **Friesen** (b); **Julian Priester** (tb); **Jim Pepper** (ts); **Mal Waldron** (p); **Eddie Moore** (d). Soul Note ℗ 121278-2 (68 minutes). Recorded 1987.

⑦ ❼

This CD is that unlikely animal, a progress report from Portland, Oregon. Pepper and the leader were natives of that city and The Hobbit was, for some years, the hub of its jazz activities. Recorded at the club, this innocuous-sounding quintet, faced with a somewhat hackneyed programme, completes a gentle metamorphic exercise by turning base musical metal into unexpected gold. Fortunately the rhythm section knew each other well and had more than five years of touring as a trio behind them. They draw full benefit from such familiarity and are able to provide the horns with a more than adequate rhythmic brace. Stylistically, all men occupy the modern mainstream area and, with a live date's usual solo licence, they have room to explore. Friesen's creative flair is well in evidence on *Night In Tunisia* and *All Blues*, Moore parades the tunefulness of his drumming on *Autumn Leaves* and Pepper, Priester and Waldron have cogent comments to make on all of the album's three titles. The listener can easily imagine being in the Hobbit on a hot June night as five genuine professionals go about their business. On the surface it could look predictable but this is the nuts and bolts of the jazz life. **BMcR**

The Fringe

It's Time For The Fringe **George Garzone** (ts, ss); **John Lockwood** (b); **Bob Gullotti** (d). Soul Note Ⓕ 121205-2 (66 minutes). Recorded 1992.

⑦ ❽

Formed in Boston in the early seventies, this group has enjoyed an underground following for more than twenty years. This, their sixth album, explains why. The trio's musical outlook is free and all of the pieces at this concert were conceived on the spot. Appropriately all composer credits are given as by The Fringe, and in the main they are simple melodic hooks on which the players hang their personal statements. Garzone is both an inventive and lyrical player, able to put the right tonal flavour into his tenor and soprano work; his tenor on *Peace For L.A.* shows him also capable of subtlety, strength and an in-built sense of time. Circular breathing and the other contemporary saxophone tools are in his performance kitbag but there is no gratuitous showboating. Lockwood has a singing tone and a fine melodic flair, while the busy Gullotti gets his ride cymbal ringing with Billy Higgins-like intensity. He is a drummer who thinks ahead, both for himself and his colleagues, and his deliberately out-of-tempo passages greatly add to the rhythmic intensity. There is a strong feeling of relaxation, even in the more passionate moments, and this, allied to the freely melodic aspect of Fringe jazz, could make it more accessible to those suspicious of the more incontinent free players. **BMcR**

Bill Frisell

1951

Lookout For Hope **Frisell** (g, elg, bj); **Hank Roberts** (vc, v); **Kermit Driscoll** (b); **Joey Baron** (d). ECM Ⓕ 1350 (833 495-2) (45 minutes). Recorded 1987.

⑦ ❿

Frisell was always destined to be an unconventional player. His early interests were varied and he tapped into Jimi Hendrix and the creative side of pop. He studied under Mike Gibbs at Berklee College and came to Europe with the trombonist's big band. There he met Eberhard Weber and in the late seventies and early eighties became something of a house guitarist at ECM. As this CD shows, he has managed to produce a personal synthesis of influences, never forgetting Wes Montgomery, but using the implied power of rock, as well as the texture-conscious sound production of the ECM ethic. In fact the title-track demonstrates Frisell nursing rich tonal fluctuations with considerable artistry and showing how he is prepared to get his results by any means available. Performances like *Little Brother Bobby* and *Lonesome* have charm rather than depth and in his more clinical moments there is a certain New Age preciousness about his work. He is at his best, as on Remedio's *The Beauty* or *Hackensack*, when he rakes the thematic entrails and reminds the listener of the music's dirt road origins. The most important aspect of his playing is that he is now an original; he has made available new techniques and provided ground-rules to promote another generation of guitarists. **BMcR**

Have a Little Faith **Frisell** (g); **Don Byron** (cl, bcl); **Guy Klucevsek** (acc); **Kermit Driscoll** (b); **Joey Baron** (d). Elektra Nonesuch Ⓕ 79301-2 (61 minutes). Recorded 1993.

④ ❿

Frisell's eclecticism continues to become more all-embracing as his career broadens. Here we have some rather dicey re-arrangements of Aaron Copland's suite from his ballet, *Billy The Kid*, a crazy-mixed-up elaboration of Charles Ives's 'Col. Shaw' from his *Three Places in New England*, plus retreads of songs by Bob Dylan, Madonna, Sonny Rollins, Stephen Foster and Muddy Waters.

Eclecticism is fine, just as long as it contributes something fresh to the original subject—even if that is merely a good-humoured send-up. To these ears, the Copland and Ives adaptations add little if anything to the original works (just as piano transductions of symphonies often have you longing for the full colour of the real thing), and it is only among the popular song rewrites, inconsistent as they are, that things get going. *Just Like a Woman* is not strong enough to stand on its own two musical feet, judging by this instrumental version, badly missing the emotion of Dylan's words, but Muddy's *I Can't be Satisfied* receives a wonderful arrangement here, utterly different in instrumentation, but similar in intent to Muddy's own. Madonna escapes censure, while Rollins inspires a similarly quirky sense of humour to his own.

A long programme, and one to dip into, rather than digest at one sitting. **KS**

Dave Frishberg

1933

Can't Take You Nowhere **Frishberg** (p, v). Fantasy Ⓕ 9651-2 (54 minutes). Recorded 1986.

⑧ ❽

Frishberg is the most talented of the several jazz singer/songwriter/instrumentalists currently active. An accomplished pianist, (early in his career he had accompanied Carmen McRae and recorded with Bud Freeman and Jimmy Rushing, among others) Frishberg sometimes bases his songs on tunes by other musicians (the barrelhouse title-track's melody comes from two blues by Tiny Kahn and Al

Cohn). On this concert recording from San Francisco, he does a medley of songs by his hero Frank Loesser, plays compositions by Ellington, Berlin and Porter sans vocals, and showcases some of his own best melodies and lyrics, including *My Attorney Bernie* and a touching evocation of homesickness, *Sweet Kentucky Ham*, which demonstrate his verbal facility, wit, and eye (or ear) for telling detail (he studied journalism in college).

As a singer, Frishberg is an acquired taste, with a narrow range, adenoidal timbre, and a conversational delivery indebted to his early champion Blossom Dearie (she had a minor hit with his *I'm Hip*, co-written with Bob Dorough, which Frishberg hams up here). But his confidential delivery enhances the quiet humour of his lyrics—which is why he interprets his songs better than technically superior singers such as Rosemary Clooney or Susannah McCorkle. **KW**

Fred Frith

1949

Step Across the Border **Frith** (g, b, vn, d, perc, v, keys, homemade instr); **Tim Hodgkinson** (bcl); **Jean Derome, John Zorn** (as); **Haco** (p, v); **Bob Ostertag** (syn, sampler, tapes); **Lasse Hollmer** (kbds); **Zeena Parkins** (kbds, v, d); **Eino Haapala** (g); **Pavel Fajt** (g, v, perc); **Iva Bittova** (vn, v); **Tom Cora** (cel, d, v); **Tina Curran, Bill Laswell, Rene Lussier** (b); **Hans Bruniusson, Eitetsu Hayashi, Fred Maher, Kevin Norton** (d). East Side Digital Ⓔ 80462/RecRec 30 (74 minutes:). Recorded 1979-89.

⑧ ❻

Frith works mostly in the fields of art rock and non-idiomatic (i.e. non-jazz) improvisation, but there are good reasons to consider him a fellow-traveller with jazz. He has helped shape modern electric guitar concepts, notably by attaching alligator clips to the strings directly over the pickups—"preparing" the guitar to get ringing doubled overtones and to warp the distance between intervals, creating artificial scales. He has also been allied with key figures on the New York and Amsterdam jazz scenes, such as John Zorn (as bassist in Zorn's loud thrash band, Naked City) and Han Bennink, with whom he plays duo.

A true internationalist, Frith, born and raised in England, has lived in New York and Munich, and his bands often reflect a conscientious ethnic/gender mix. This soundtrack from a documentary portrait finds him in more than a dozen settings: solo, duos with Zorn, Cora, Hodgkinson and others; with Skeleton Crews (Frith, Cora, Parkins); playing a few rock songs, improvising with collaborators from England, the US, Quebec, Sweden, Japan and the Czech Republic, occasionally using homemade mutant guitars. Always a resourceful, sound-conscious guitarist, Frith has a flair for appealing but not too simple melodies, some relying on East European scales, and is an original, tuneful electric bassist and good fiddler. **KW**

Curtis Fuller

1934

Blues-ette **Fuller** (tb); **Benny Golson** (ts); **Tommy Flanagan** (p); **Jimmy Garrison** (b); **Al Harewood** (d). Denon/Savoy Ⓜ SV-0127 (37 minutes). Recorded 1959.

⑥ ❽

Fuller is to the post-bop era what J.J. Johnson was to early bop; in other words, he ignored the fact that the trombone should have appeared clumsy and inappropriate, and made it work alongside the fleet and flowing trumpeters and saxophonists who defined these styles. Naturally, Fuller was as influenced by Johnson as almost every other player of his generation, but he also aimed for the simplicity and obliquity of Miles Davis—perhaps more successfully in his early work than later. Displaying a most attractive tone, often aided by a felt mute, he aims straight for the melodic core while the rhythm-section opens each piece by loping along in the two-to-the-bar style which Miles had recently reintroduced. Meanwhile Golson, lately graduated from the Jazz Messengers, offers the piquant contrast of a multi-noted style influenced equally by Don Byas/Lucky Thompson and his teenage colleague, John Coltrane. The material has a suitable modern-mainstream feel for the period, with the début recording of Golson's B-minor blues *Five Spot After Dark* (a.k.a. *Nightlife*) being followed by Charlie Shavers's *Undecided*. It is, of course, reprehensible that Denon have failed to include on a single CD another of Fuller's equally short-running LPs for the same label, although, as part of their new recordings programme, they recently issued a CD called **Bluesette Part 2**. **BP**

Slim Gaillard

1916-91

Laughing In Rhythm: The Best of the Verve Years **Gaillard** (v, g, p); with a collective personnel of **Taft Jordan** (t); **Bennie Green** (tb); **Buddy Tate, Ben Webster** (ts); **Dodo Marmarosa, Dick Hyman, Maceo Williams, Cyril Haynes** (p); **Pepe Benque** (bj); **Bam Brown, Ernie Sheppard, Clyde Lombardi, Ray Brown** (b); **Herbie Lovelle, Charlie Smith, Milt Jackson** (d); **Jim Hawthorne** (barks). Verve Ⓜ 521 651-2 (65 minutes). Recorded 1946-53.

As half of the twosome Slim & Slam (with Slam Stewart), Gaillard had a major hit in the late thirties with *Flat Foot Floogie*. Such giddy commercial heights were never reached again, but he did enjoy some ten years of wide popularity, and the period covered by this disc seems to represent something of a peak in terms of his overall musical activities. Certainly the live 'suite' later titled *Opera In Vout*, which comes from a spring 1946 JATP concert, shows both Gaillard and his partner Bam Brown working at comic white heat in 12 minutes of inspired mayhem, much of which revolves around either verbal gymnastics or sly take-offs of then-popular jazz musicians and singers. It also confirms his largely neglected talents as a guitar improvisor (also to be found at length on the out-of-print **Slim Gaillard at Birdland** (Hep), taken from radio airshots in the early fifties). Studio-bound moments of comic anarchy on this disc include the almost Dada-istic *Chicken Rhythm* and *Serenade To A Poodle*, with their animal imitations and deliberately idiotic lyrics. At moments like these, Gaillard was jazz's equivalent of The Goons. Other performances find the formulas wearing a trifle thin, but Gaillard's good humour usually wins through on even the most mundane material. Two tracks here, by the way, see their long-delayed début: *Genius* and *Federation Blues*. The latter is a heartfelt moan directed at the Musician's Union as controlled at that time by James C. Petrillo (a good enough reason for its quick suppression), while *Genius*, an altogether more remarkable piece featuring Gaillard multiple-tracked on all instruments (including tap-dancing), was damned by association, being another number from the same withdrawn EP. Hopefully that will have piqued your interest enough to take the time to explore this fascinating period-piece. **KS**

Galapagos Duck

The Voyage of The Beagle **Tom Hare** (t, flh, f, ss, as); **Greg Foster** (tb, hca, didgeridu); **Bob Egger** (kbds); **Mick Jackman** (kbds, vb, mba); **John Conley** (elb, g, didgeridu); **Mal Morgan** (d, perc). ABC Jazz Ⓜ 512 380-2 (52 minutes). Recorded 1983.

⑤ ❻

Formed in the early seventies, Australia's Galapagos Duck were an incongruous mixture of that country's Dixieland tradition, the occasional almost mainstream solo, and an awareness of post-**Silent Way** electronics. They enjoyed considerable local success and made their first recording, **Ebony Quill**, in 1973. By the time this session took place in 1983, only Hare of the original line-up remained but he had added alto, soprano and flute to his instrumental arsenal. The programme here is made up of the band's look at various countries in the world. *Tattooed Warriors* and *The Emu Dance* in particular capture their subjects rather well. There are good solos from Hare's flügelhorn on *St. Elmo's Fire*, his useful Sanborn-ish alto on *The Voyage Begins* and his soprano on *Latin Doll*. Foster's forthright trombone shines on strongest on *The Voyage Ends*. The Duck, whose name has a Spike Milligan rather than a historical origin, have avoided commercializing their act outrageously but they are not unaware of what the general public enjoy. Certainly titles such as *In A Brazilian Forest* would not cause too much excitement in a local supermarket. **BMcR**

Jim Galloway

1936

Jim Galloway and Art Hodes: Recorded Live at Cafe des Copains **Galloway** (saxes); **Art Hodes** (p), Music & Arts Ⓕ CD-610 (69 minutes). Recorded 1988.

⑧ ❽

This is a little gem of a record. By emigrating from Scotland to Canada, Jim Galloway has ensured this his soprano playing has never been in the centre of things, but he has recorded over the years with some mighty fine pianists such as Dick Wellstood, Jay McShann and Ralph Sutton, and it is reasonable to assume that such men would not have entered the cruel spotlight of a duo relationship if they were not sure of their partner. With this partnership, you could assume that the nerves were on Galloway's side. Not only was Hodes a living legend, but his technique is not exactly flamboyant; when all you have as a safety net is Hodes's rather sparse keyboard playing, you have to fly right. Galloway does fly right; his soloing throughout is fluent and ear-catching, while Hodes's backing is immensely satisfying—like all pianists who do not have technique to fall back on (Stan Tracey is another example), he has to think more than most, and a lot of the textures and patterns he supplies are not ones that would occur to more facile pianists. They enjoyed playing this date; the audience enjoyed it, and the players respond to the audience. The tunes are mostly standards (*I Would Do Most Anything*, *Some of These Days*, etc.) although Hodes's two solos are both more modern (*The Preacher*) and more ancient (*Tomorrow's Blues*). **MK**

Hal Galper

1938

Dreamsville **Galper** (p); **Steve Gilmore** (b); **Bill Goodwin** (d). Enja Ⓔ ENJ-5029 2 (38 minutes). Recorded 1986.

⑧ ❽

This trio constituted one of the most consistently entertaining rhythm sections of the eighties, delighting audiences worldwide with their performances behind Phil Woods and Tom Harrell in the former's superb quintet, and on this recording they show off all the musical empathy they acquired in that process. In a well-paced programme (albeit not of CD length), Galper provides alternately chunkily percussive and glowingly burnished piano as appropriate on such rousing familiar fare as Richard Rodgers's *Surrey with a Fringe on Top* and less frequently performed material like J.J. Johnson's wistful *Lament*. Although much of the album—particularly the barnstormers *Once I Loved* and the closing *Sweet Pumpkin*, along with Jimmy McHugh's stalwart *Don't Blame Me*—appears to prioritize straightforward stretching out by all three men, the Henry Mancini title-track hints at the considerable resources of subtlety upon which the trio can draw when necessary, its lush romanticism shaded with darker moments, its tempo shifting, its texture rich and varied. Overall, this is a feisty, tight trio performance packed with spontaneous musical felicities; Gilmore is vigorous but thick-toned, Goodwin smart as a whip and the leader is, as always, unfussily virtuosic, his improvisations assertive without being bombastic. **CP**

Ganelin Trio

Poco-A-Poco **Vyacheslav Ganelin** (p, basset); **Vladimir Chekasin** (reeds); **Vladimir Tarasov** (d). Leo Ⓔ CD LR 101 (61 minutes). Recorded 1978.

✔ ⑦ ❼

The Ganelin Trio was formed in Russia in 1971, a mixture of American avant-garde, Willem Breuker laugh-in and European free improvisation. To this potent brew they added their own Russophian folk extras and an indomitable spirit as they faced sceptics, both home and abroad. This CD is from a session that took place before any other Ganelin issues appeared in the West. The music is equally dramatic, however, with Chekasin at his most potent, demonstrating throughout his impressive range, control of the false upper register and ability to build detailed solos from the most meagre of thematic germs. Tarasov is a comparable powerhouse, a muscular drummer who reads his colleagues well while balancing his work from whisper to shout with both taste and rhythmic subtlety. Ganelin himself is a comparative conservative, seemingly happier when harmonically positive themes are on the table. The trio is best judged as a whole, however, and it is then that the contrast between the group's surface fury and its more formal approach to structure becomes apparent. The projection of individual passion is undeniable but it cannot disguise the fact that the Ganelin's music is well prepared, even if only in outline form, and that the jazz world suffered a considerable loss when Ganelin emigrated to Israel and the group folded in 1987. **BMcR**

Jan Garbarek

1947

Afric Pepperbird **Garbarek** (ts, bss, cl, f, perc); **Terje Rypdal** (g, bugle); **Arild Andersen** (b, thp); **Jon Christensen** (perc). ECM 1007 (843 475-2) (41 minutes). Recorded 1970.

⑦ ❾

Born in Norway and influenced by John Coltrane at an early age, Garbarek was discovered by and later worked with George Russell. This CD offers the result of his first session for a major label and, as with Archie Shepp (another of his influences), it starts a recording career at a 'way out' point from which he later retreated. It shows an eclectic interest in the American scene of the time and takes him from the Chicagoan 'little instruments' soundscape of *Skarabee* to the headlong, freely improvised tirades of *Beast of Kommodo*, *Blow Away Zone* and the title-track. He interacts consistently with his powerful group and, although inevitably the focal point, does not insist on total domination. On *Skarabee* he meets the need to be controlled in the false upper register superbly, on *Afric Pepperbird* he uses the bass saxophone like a subtle bludgeon, while on *Kommodo* his tenor strokes his personal conflagration from spark to free-ranging blaze, with an abrasive Shepp-like tone sounding the fire warning. Creativity was already a high priority and, although at this stage he was a player looking for a personal direction, he was already a very impressive jazz musician. **BMcR**

Paths, Prints **Garbarek** (ss, ts, wood f, perc); **Bill Frisell** (g); **Eberhard Weber** (b); **Jon Christensen** (d, perc). ECM Ⓔ 1223 (829 377-2) (51 minutes). Recorded 1981.

⑧ ❿

Path, Prints is one of Jan Garbarek's most meditative and discreetly eloquent recordings. " More abstract than much of his later, deeply folk-rooted anthemic work, its considerable power derives more from the variety of textures and moods created by the free interplay of the four musicians involved than from melody or rhythm. As the titles suggest—*Kite Dance*, *Considering the Snail*, *Still*, etc.—**Paths, Prints** is largely impressionistic, evoking subtle effects through nuance, quiet shifts of mood and hypnotically insistent repetition, rather than through unambiguous melodic statement. Garbarek mostly plays soprano saxophone—although he does contribute an affecting introduction to *Footprints* on wooden flute and a deceptively simple four-note tenor figure to *Ar*—and the combination of this pure-toned, plangent instrument with Bill Frisell's absorbed, deeply ruminative electric guitar sound is one of the album's chief attractions. Eberhard Weber is a superb anchor, his singing bass often carrying the pieces' closest approximation to the melodic line, allowing Garbarek, Frisell and the uniformly excellent Jon Christensen a freedom to embellish of which they take full and telling advantage. Not Garbarek's best work but very close to it, and an album of some importance in defining the ECM sound. **CP**

Twelve Moons **Garbarek** (saxes); **Rainer Bruninghaus** (kbds); **Eberhard Weber** (b); **Manu Katche** (d); **Marilyn Mazur** (perc); **Agnes Buen Garnas, Mari Boine** (v). ECM Ⓔ 1500 (519 500-2) (76 minutes). Recorded 1992.

⑤ ❿

Garbarek has come a long way from the high-energy approach he adopted at the beginning of his solo career, over 25 years ago. In between, he has skirted the bottomless pit of twee-ness associated with ECM's more atmospherics-oriented musicians, but has never really fallen. Part of the reason for this is his continuing interest in folk music, both from his own and from other lands. **Twelve Moons**' title-track is derived quite considerably from this interest; the knotty rhythms derived from these sources, plus the unpredictable melodic leaps, allows the musical associations to resonate rather than implode into fey pastiche.

Elsewhere, though, this album is much softer than its predecessor, **I Took Up The Runes**, and I am not sure that is a good thing. Garbarek can be an incendiary soloist when the mood takes him, and the mood took him sufficiently to light up most of **Runes**. Here his concerns seem to lie with the overall sound and shape of his compositions and the way the group conjures this. When the drums are absent, things congeal rather quickly for lack of forward propulsion. They are what make *Twelve Moons* and the other long track, *Gautes-Margjit* , such enjoyable listening, giving a decided splash of sensuality to Garbarek's often severely ascetic vision, and spurring him to his most distinguished playing of the date. **KS**

Red Garland

1923-1984

A Garland of Red **Garland** (p); **Paul Chambers** (b); **Art Taylor** (d). Prestige Ⓜ OJCCD-126-2 (42 minutes). Recorded 1956.

⑧ ❽

Texas-born Red Garland received his first musical training on clarinet and alto saxophone. Though he studied alto with Prof. Buster Smith, Charlie Parker's early mentor, a three-year boxing career provided a sabbatical that eventually led to piano. In the decade following the Second World War Garland worked with a host of stylistically varied players, including Billy Eckstine, Charlie Parker, Fats Navarro, Coleman Hawkins, Flip Phillips and Miles Davis. When he joined the latter's quintet in 1955, he soon won international recognition for his spare yet harmonically and rhythmically supple playing.

While influenced by fellow pianists Count Basie, Nat King Cole, Art Tatum, Erroll Garner, Ahmad Jamal and Bud Powell, Garland synthesized these and other contrasting sources into a uniquely individual style which was lean without being austere, sprightly (especially at medium tempos) and always swinging. A player of impeccable taste, Garland is an exemplar of Buckminster Fuller's "dymaxium principle" of doing more with less. Here, with poignant and self-effacing support from bassist Paul Chambers and drummer Art Taylor, Garland fashions exquisite medium-up interpretations of standards such as *A Foggy Day* and *September in the Rain*. There is a flag-waver, Parker's *Constellation*, where the boppish influence of Powell is evident, and there are thoughtful ballads like *Little Girl Blue* where the effect is like that of a subdued and meditative Garner. In all, a superb demonstration of the timeless talents of one of the jazz piano giants. **CB**

Erroll Garner

1921-1977

Body and Soul **Garner** (p); **John Simmons** (b); **Shadow Wilson** (d). Columbia Ⓜ 467916-2 (60 minutes). Recorded 1951-52.

⑥ ❻

It is hard to think of pianists who have always insisted on appearing solo or just with rhythm section—even Bill Evans had a stint with Miles Davis—but to find Garner playing with horns you probably have to go back to the forties. It was not that he disliked other soloists; just that he did not need them. He played the piano but he thought like a big band—as you listen to these trio sides from the early fifties, you can hear him mentally orchestrating the tunes as he goes through his three minutes on each: single note middle eight here, sax section eight bars here, brass effects here …

Garner always stood aside from the jazz mainstream because of this, and because he gained wide popularity, and because critics had trouble placing him, but he always had the most important jazz

virtues such as wit, invention, swing and surprise, and you get a goodly rationing of all those on this sampler of his early, pre-fame stuff. The rhythm section is unobtrusive. All his rhythm sections were unobtrusive. They had no choice.
MK

Concert By The Sea **Garner** (p); **Eddie Calhoun** (b); **Denzil Best** (d). Columbia Ⓜ 451042-2 (44 minutes). Recorded 1955.

✔ ⑧ ❻

This is one of the very few jazz albums to get into the 'Billboard' pop charts (no. 12 in 1958) and is a strong candidate for the best-selling jazz piano record ever. It sold in its millions and could be found, along with Brubeck and Sinatra, on the shelves of people who would never have called themselves jazz fans.

All this is very easy to understand. Garner's style is tuneful, dramatic, by turns witty and swooningly romantic, full of virtuosity smilingly presented. It is also unique; even the most unpractised ear can recognize Erroll Garner after a few bars. All his trade-marks are on display in this live recording; the chugging left hand (like rhythm guitar), the bouncing right-hand fingers, the filigree treble. There are also several examples of his speciality, the "keep-'em-guessing introduction". These can go on for several minutes, with great, portentous chords, meaningful pauses and misleading hints until, at the least expected moment, the tune comes blithely tripping out. It never failed to raise a storm of applause, as it duly does here.

It is almost impossible to deliver a judgement on Erroll Garner's music because there is nothing else remotely like it. Even his technique was so unorthodox that classically trained pianists declare it to be impossible. Along with all his other gifts he was completely ambidextrous; this plus his intuitive grasp of the most complex harmonies made it impossible for him to be precisely duplicated.
DG

Solitaire **Garner** (p). Mercury Ⓜ 518 279-2 (72 minutes) Recorded 1955.

✔ ⑩ ❼

This and its companion piece **Afternoon of an Elf**, which has been and gone on CD already, are the product of one spring day's work in the studio when Garner was not only nursing an injury to one hand (he had a finger in a splint), but was also uncommonly inspired. And for once, the sound quality is pretty good, too. It has often been said that Garner hardly needed a rhythm section because his left hand was one in itself. Here there is no rhythm section, and although **Solitaire** concentrates for the most part on the reflective side of his playing (**Elf** highlighted the more dynamic aspects), not once do you wonder where the bass and drums got to.

As usual, Garner re-casts his choice of standards to the point where he virtually reinvents them, and with *Over The Rainbow* he launches into over ten minutes of incredibly rich pianistic embroidery and fantasy. Garner may have been a player who by and large stuck to a particular form in his performances—intro, theme, extemporization, theme and cadenza—but then most jazzmen do not even think as far about form as Garner did, and although his model in this may have been Tatum, he was a great deal more imaginative in the way he applied this form to his own performances. His imagination is at its peak when he plays solo, and this collection is Garner on top form, playing solo. His *A Cottage For Sale* is a good illustration of this, where the stages of his treatment of the song flow seamlessly into each other, sounding for all the world like an intimate conversation between the pianist and his listener. An apt way to describe the song's lyrics.

There are four extra tracks here, originally released on the LP **Erroll!** (the **Afternoon of an Elf** CD has the rest of the **Erroll!** solo pieces on it). None of the performances is below a formidably high standard.
KS

Kenny Garrett

Black Hope **Garrett** (as, ss); **Joe Henderson** (ts); **Kenny Kirkland** (p, syn); **Donald Brown** (syn); **Charnett Moffet** (b); **Brian Blade** (d); **Don Alias** (perc). Warner Bros. Ⓕ 945017-2 (66 minutes). Recorded 1992.

✔ ⑦ ❽

Another messenger from the Art Blakey finishing school, Garrett was the saxophonist in Miles Davis's last group and, with the trumpet giant's health failing, was the group's most creative spokesman. His duties with Davis put some emphasis on the blues but Garrett's own recording dates have presented a more cosmopolitan face, using material from various jazz strains with the emphasis on the bop vernacular rather than the rareified Davis dialect. This CD is typically non-specific and shows that he fits easily into most of his contemporary stances. *Jackie And The Bean Stalk* and *Books And Toys* have him driving an orthodox hard bop quartet; on *Tacit Dance Computer G* and the gladiatorial *Bye Bye Blackbird* he jousts with the eloquent Henderson, while on three titles he enjoys the comfort of a percussion-assisted Latinesque ride. The recently-left Davis world is conjured up on *Two Step* and *Bone Bop*, in particular, and he closes the album with a brief but heartfelt alto solo. The various line-ups used throughout make a nonsense of stylistic wars, and if you were to leave a CD in a time capsule to be opened in the year 2300, this would be as honest an example of jazz from 1992 as you could find.
BMcR

Michael Garrick

1933

A Lady In Waiting **Garrick** (p); **Dave Green** (b); **Alan Jackson** (d). Jazz Academy Ⓕ JAZA 1 (76 minutes). Recorded 1993.

⑧ ❽

Garrick's talents are so diverse that there is a tendency to forget that he is a fine pianist in his own right. His work as composer, group leader (he once had both Shake Keane and the late Joe Harriott in his sextet), jazz educator and poet are well known and this is a timely reminder of his expertise at the keyboard and also his maturity as a soloist. There is a grace to his playing but just beneath the surface is the strength necessary to drive home tunes such as *Oleo* and *Tea For Two*. There are salutes to the three pianists with John Lewis's blues *Two Degrees East, Three Degrees West*, Herbie Hancock's lovely *Dolphin Dance* and Monk's *'Round Midnight,* but there are also six movements from Garrick's own *The Royal Box,* a suite which Michael has also arranged for a big band. In the accompanying notes Humphrey Lyttelton makes the point that this is a trio in the truest sense of the term with all three men making important contributions to the whole. Garrick, Green and Jackson have worked together frequently over a long period of time and this close empathy is manifest in the music. Recommended. **AM**

Giorgio Gaslini

1929

Multipli **Gaslini** (p); **Roberto Ottaviano** (ss, as, bcl); **Claudio Fasoli** (ss, ts); **Bruno Tommaso** (b); **Giampiero Prina** (d). Soul Note Ⓕ 121220-2 (45 minutes). Recorded 1987).

⑧ ❽

Gaslini is more than just the best-known, most accomplished jazzman in Italy; he is a world-class artist who has toured extensively and recorded over 50 albums with his own groups and musicians like Anthony Braxton, Roswell Rudd, Jean-Luc Ponty and Steve Lacy. A thoughtful, fluent pianist, his individual approach is that of a conceptualist, as his challenging programmes of music by Monk, Robert Schumann and Albert Ayler prove. On the aptly titled **Multipli** he explores the variety of voicings, textures and moods available to the quintet à la Andrew Hill or Stan Tracey. His airy arrangements make excellent use of Ottaviano and Fasoli, a matched pair of blithe spirits. The title tune offers them space and open harmonies, and they use the freedom with great restraint. Gaslini's classical touch and quizzical demeanour is evident on *Interni*, and there is an echo of *Harlem Nocturne* in Fasoli's tenor, although the contrast of moods never jolts. It is likely Jelly Roll Morton would not recognize his *Chicago Breakdown*, as the horns reconstruct the theme from fragments while Tommaso layers in tactile arco effects. *Piano Sequenza* juxtaposes an Ayleresque dirge with march-like material, and *Ornette Or Not* captures the inherent optimism of its namesake. In sum, a stylish and fresh perspective from an underrated musician. **AL**

Charles Gayle

1939

Consecration **Gayle** (ts, bcl); **William Parker** (vc, vn); **Vattel Cherry** (b); **Michael Wimberley** (d). Black Saint Ⓕ 120138-2 (68 minutes). Recorded 1993.

⑧ ❽

In a jazz world cosily reassured by the neo-classicist movement, Gayle is one of the ultimate 'outcats'. Born in Buffalo, NY, he had early piano lessons but is self-taught on saxophone. He jammed with the likes of Archie Shepp and Pharoah Sanders in the sixties but then, as now, was basically a loner. He moved to New York City in the seventies and has played on streets and in subways ever since. His more recent association with the Knitting Factory has brought him to more serious notice and he now has the beginning of a recording portfolio.

This CD does not feature his idiosyncratic piano but it suggests that, whether he used tenor, bass clarinet or blow torch, his music would have the same incendiary qualities. His style does owe something to Albert Ayler's world of the sixties but he sets his own guidelines and is indisputably virtuosic. Thoughts of the field holler are evoked on *O Father*; *Rise Up* is an unashamed *cri de coeur*, while *Justified* has an ineluctable rhythmic thrust that is almost frightening. His bass clarinet on *Thy Peace* navigates more gentle waters but it is his wild freedoms, intimidating power and melody demolitions that have made him one of jazz's most potent non-conformists. **BMcR**

Gianni Gebbia

Outland **Gebbia,** (ss, as, prepared sax); **Lelio Giannetto** (b); **Vittorio Villa** (d); **Massimo Simonini** (turntables, kbds, objects, v). Splasc(h) Ⓕ 315-2 (55 minutes). Recorded 1990.

⑦ ❽

Gebbia is one of a new generation of unheralded, adventurous Italian (in his case Sicilian) jazz musicians influenced by the flood of various post-war styles. One common decision has been to blend folk musics and local colour into their improvising, and Gebbia is comfortable in such modal surroundings, often at rhapsodic tempos. He can also spray notes at will and is unafraid of noise for its own sake. His primary sax is the soprano, and there is little doubt that the music of Steve Lacy, Anthony Braxton and Wayne Shorter helped point him in that direction. But his search for additional colours has led him on previous recordings to include didjeridu (an Australian aboriginal wind instrument) and Sicilian voices, as well as electronics of his own devising. Here, Simonini is the wild card, manipulating turntables and found-sound samples to play havoc with the trio. His electronics seldom mirror the acoustic instruments; he is most effective and most shocking injecting a sampled melismatic vocal on the North African-tinged *Shamal*, sound splurges in *Zero In Geometry*, or cartoonish hi-jinks in *Outland*. The sometimes over-extended performances may evoke atmosphere in lieu of invention, but Gebbia's music should be of interest to those looking for an alternative to conventional (i.e. American) jazz. **AL**

Herb Geller

1928

That Geller Feller **Geller** (as); **Kenny Dorham** (t); **Harold Land** (ts); **Lou Levy** (p); **Ray Brown** (b); **Lawrence Marable** (d). Ⓕ FSR CD 91 (35 minutes). Recorded 1957.

⑥ ❺

There is very little Geller around on CD, so this album (not especially well transferred to the small disc from the larger format, and ageing just a little) is probably worth hunting down. Recorded in 1957 for the tiny Californian Bel Canto label, when his American career was peaking (he later moved to Europe), this shows a tidy arranger's mind and an ebullient Parker-influenced soloist. Geller in fact is head and shoulders above his fellow horns on this disc, who both sound as if it is the morning after the night before (I have rarely heard Land sound so uninspired), but perhaps fewer tracks and more room for stretching out would have lit the fire more consistently. When there are three front men and a pianist all capable of and looking for the solo spotlight, it makes for considerable congestion and some rather brief and inconsequential flurries.

The selections show imagination, with Geller's originals holding up well while a very rare outing for an attractive Bud Powell composition, *The Fruit*, makes one of the more forceful marks on the listener's memory, with Dorham rising to his best playing of the date. All in all, a superior West Coast session which does not quite make classic status. **KS**

Stan Getz

1927-1991

Stan Getz At The Shrine **Getz** (ts); **Bob Brookmeyer** (vtb); **John Williams** (p); **Bill Anthony** (b); **Art Mardigan**, **Frank Isola** (d). Verve Ⓜ 513 753-2 (70 minutes). Recorded 1954.

⑧ ❻

This Los Angeles concert was recorded when the group had matured into a singularly fine improvising band. Getz paid the lowest wages he could get away with and was lucky to enrol such giants of the time as Brookmeyer and Williams. Having taken Bob Brookmeyer into his band Getz let the valve trombonist hold sway with a powerful influence over both the band's repertoire and over Getz's own playing. The spirit of Kansas City jazz reigned within a neo-bop group. There was always more to Getz's talents as a leader than has been acknowledged and the sensitive selection of material reaches its acme in Al Cohn's *Tasty Pudding*, a mournful theme which should have become a jazz standard. Brookmeyer the composer is represented by *Open Country*; Johnny Mandel, briefly in the quintet on trombone before Brookmeyer, by the stomping *Pernod*. The concert was recorded during a tour which included the Gerry Mulligan Quartet, wherein Brookmeyer, Anthony and Isola had all done time. In fact Isola was still a member of Mulligan's group, and there was some friction between leaders over the drummer's appearance on the two studio recorded tracks here, a fetching version of the superior ballad *We'll Be Together Again* and a romping version of Basie's *Feather Merchant*. Getz emerged butterfly-like from his 'cool' period at this time, and this is a fine example of his Brookmeyer-inspired commitment to mainstream jazz. Finally, CDs displaying the original piano style of John Williams are to be winkled out like truffles. The opportunity to pick this one up from above ground should not be missed. **SV**

Stan Getz & J.J. Johnson at the Opera House **Johnson** (tb); **Getz** (ts); **Oscar Peterson** (p); **Herb Ellis** (g); **Ray Brown** (b); **Connie Kay** (d). Verve Ⓜ 831 272-2 (73 minutes). Recorded 1957.

✔

⑩ ❻

None other than Johnson himself has recently alluded to the "circus atmosphere" that surrounded many Jazz at the Philharmonic performances. In this case, the excitement was fully earned, the natural product of imaginatively matching some extrovert and more restrained players. The blends of Getz and Johnson as featured voices, the Peterson trio and Kay in support, and this front line with this rhythm section inspires each member of the sextet to memorable contributions. Great ballad features balance more hard-driving jams in an environment in which *My Funny Valentine* inspires burning creativity. They sounded so nice, Norman Granz recorded them twice—in stereo at Chicago's Opera House, then eight days later in mono at the Los Angeles Shrine Auditorium—and released both versions in similar packaging without indicating the difference. The CD has the entire superior Chicago set, plus four of the L.A. tracks. **BB**

Focus **Stan Getz** (ts); **John Neves** (b); **Roy Haynes** (d); **The Beaux-Arts Quartet** and other unidentified strings; **Hershey Kay** (dir). Verve Ⓜ 821 982-2 (38 minutes). Recorded 1961.

✔ ⑩ ❽

Focus is unlike any other saxophone-and-strings record ever made. Getz and the composer Eddie Sauter devised an entirely new musical form for this one record, and it was never subsequently taken up by anyone, not even Getz himself. Sauter wrote what amounted to a complete composition for small string orchestra, plus bass and drums, with a lot of space in it, and left Getz to complete the picture. The result is a glowing work of remarkable cohesion and depth, yet one which can be enjoyed by absolutely anyone.

The time-honoured way of writing for saxophone and strings is to treat the saxophone like a ballad singer, packed around with strings in the form of a soft cocoon or pillow. There is absolutely nothing wrong with this method, as Ben Webster, Zoot Sims and many others have proved over the years, but **Focus** showed that it was not the only way. Whereas most string arrangers drew their inspiration from the nineteenth-century Romantics, Sauter seems to have drawn his mainly from Bartók. The result is a spiky, energetic work, relieved by moments of deep, contemplative calm. One of the seven movements (*I'm Late, I'm Late*) is cast in the form of a mini-double concerto for Getz and his favourite drummer, Roy Haynes. Another (*I Remember When*) is a kind of pastoral idyll. It is almost impossible to believe that music of such clarity, emotional breadth and formal elegance can have been created by a method so untried and risky.

For Getz himself **Focus** represented a crucial moment, the moment when everything about his playing began to grow and deepen. It spread like some vast, luxuriant plant until, by the end of his life, it had outgrown the confines of jazz itself. **DG**

The Girl From Ipanema—The Bossa Nova Years Getz (ts); with the following collective personnel: **Doc Severinsen, Bernie Glow, Joe Ferrante, Clark Terry, Nick Travis** (t); **Ray Alonge** (frh); **Tony Studd, Bob Brookmeyer, Willie Dennis** (tb); **Gerald Sanfino, Ray Beckenstein, Eddie Caine, Babe Clark, Walt Levinsky, Romeo Penque** (f, cl, bcl); **Hank Jones, Steve Kuhn** (p); **Jim Hall, Tommy Williams, Keter Betts, George Duvivier, Don Payne, Gene Cherico** (b); **Johnny Rae** (d); **Jose Paula** (tamb); **Carmen Costa** (cabassa); **Charlie Byrd, Luiz Bonfa, Kenny Burrell, Laurindo Almeida, Joao Gilberto** (g); **Gene Byrd** (g, b); **Antonio Carlos Jobim** (g, p); **Gary Burton** (vb); **Luiz Parga, Jose Paulo, Buddy Deppenschmidt, Bill Reichenbach, Paulo Ferreira, Jose Carlos, Dave Bailey, Milton Banana, Joe Hunt, Helcio Milito, Edison Machado, Jose Soorez** (d, perc); **Maria Toledo, Astrud Gilberto, João Gilberto** (v). Verve Ⓜ 823 611-2 (four discs: 221 minutes). Recorded 1962-64.

⑩ ❻

Getz was not the first jazz musician to involve himself in Brazilian music but he probably did more to popularize it internationally than any other. Although his first LP in the Brazilian idiom did not actually carry the words 'bossa nova' anywhere on its sleeve, it nevertheless sparked off interest in this blending of the music of North and South America. This four-CD set (complete with booklet) brings together all of the bossa nova music which Getz recorded for the Verve label and is virtually the equivalent of five LPs (**Jazz Samba**, **Big Band Bossa Nova**, **Jazz Samba Encore**, **Getz/Gilberto** and **Getz/Almeida**) plus various other tracks including five previously unissued performances. The best tracks are in the majority, that is the small band titles where Stan blends so beautifully with the guitar work of João Gilberto, Charlie Byrd and Laurindo Almeida as well as providing ideal support to the voices of João and Astrud Gilberto and the fine singing of Maria Toledo. At a time when jazz seemed in danger of turning in on itself, Getz came up with albums of pure melody, allied to the intriguing, shifting rhythms of Brazil. This is the definitive collection of bossa nova material by the master, including the original versions of songs such as *Desafinado* and *The Girl From Ipanema*. Much of this music was recorded on 30 ips tape initially and the discovery of the original master tapes in most instances means that the intimate group sounds have been retained in pristine condition. A classic collection. **AM**

Sweet Rain Getz (ts); **Chick Corea** (p); **Ron Carter** (b); **Grady Tate** (d). Verve Ⓜ 815 054-2 (37 minutes). Recorded 1967.

✔ ⑩ ❾

Sweet Rain was a revelation on its first issue, some 27 years ago; it showed an abrupt change for Getz, away from any involvement in the by then evaporated bossa-nova craze, away from the sometimes lightweight elegance of the quartet with Burton, towards a new interest in more flamboyant expressivism. On Corea's piece *Litha*, for example, he continually distorts his tone, creating boiling, bubbling rages of notes as the composition alternates between its two halves, one at medium, one at fast tempo. That this piece is modal in the manner of Miles and Coltrane, and that the rhythm section here has the elasticity of both men's groups, cannot also have been coincidental. Getz was reacting, in his own way, to the prevailing spirit of the times.

The rhythm section is exemplary in its support, with Grady Tate producing drumming which is both memorable and enjoyable in its own right while not being distracting. Corea paces Getz with amazing exactitude, feeding him ideas, moods, alternatives, while also being prepared to react to his every nuance. Carter is impeccable. With *O Grande Amor* and *Con Alma*, Getz is re-interpreting old territory, but he seems intent on doing so from a radically different vantage point. The title-track, a Mike Gibbs composition, brings forth a performance of unearthly beauty. **KS**

The Dolphin **Stan Getz** (ts); **Lou Levy** (p); **Monty Budwig, Victor Lewis** (d). Concord Ⓕ CCD-4158 (46 minutes). Recorded 1981.

⑨ ❽

Recorded live at San Francisco's Keystone Korner in May 1981 as Getz was in the process of setting up residence in the Bay area, this remains one of the tenor saxophonist's most evocative testaments to the capacity of jazz as a medium of transcendent melodic expression.

The repertoire, with its lyric lines and provocative harmonic grids, is perfection; so too is Getz's rhythm section. Indeed, if jazz is music's quintessential form for intimate and yet dynamically interactive conversation, discussants Getz, Levy, Budwig and Lewis provide a textbook example of mainstream interlocution elevated to the level of art. Two of the loveliest examples of Getz's melodic invention are his exquisite readings of Johnny Mandel's haunting ballads, *A Time For Love*, and *Close Enough For Love*. Clifford Brown's bebop anthem *Joy Spring* unfolds with similar mellifluence, albeit at a loping medium gait. Throughout the rhythm tandem of Levy, Budwig and Lewis whispers powerfully. Levy also deserves credit for his exuberant yet disciplined solo work which provides an effective foil for Getz's inspired limning. Also of note are Getz's poignant rhapsodizing on *My Old Flame* and his lithe Latinizations of Luiz Eca's sleek title-track and *The Night Has a Thousand Eyes*. Regardless of tempo or rhythmic pattern, Getz again proves himself a sublime yet always swinging classicist. **CB**

Anniversary **Getz** (ts); **Kenny Barron** (p); **Rufus Reid** (b); **Victor Lewis** (d). EmArcy Ⓕ 838 769-2 (70 minutes). Recorded 1987.

✔ ⑧ ❽

This Copenhagen concert exemplifies what Stanley Dance dubbed "mainstream" jazz—standards and blues played in a style which naturally and seamlessly combines the values of swing (the genre) and hard bop. Barron and Lewis are among the most creatively sympathetic accompanists in modern jazz, always suggesting new ideas to the soloist. Like Reid they frame everything in terms of emphatic but relaxed swing. The burping, amplified bass sound is about the only real problem, endemic to period concert recordings.

By 1987, Getz's gorgeous tone had deepened slightly—as with many tenor players, his sound became more lustrous as he approached 60—and he sounds as elegant as ever, with delicacy and manly grace at odds with the popular image of Getz the prickly, difficult leader. *Stella by Starlight* is buoyant, a warhorse played without the cynicism repetition can breed. Billy Strayhorn's meditation on his own mortality, *Blood Count*, gets an especially plaintive reading, yet the pathos Getz mines is more ennobling than self-pitying. Some jazz musicians sound like they love their instruments, some like they love themselves. Whatever his failings, Getz played like he loved music, loved art. There is a good sequel from the same concert, *Serenity*, but *Anniversary* is the cream. **KW**

Mike Gibbs

1937

The Only Chrome Waterfall Orchestra **Gibbs** (kbds); **Derek Watkins, Ian Hamer, Kenny Wheeler, Henry Lowther** (t, flh); **Chris Pyne** (tb); **Ray Warleigh, Charlie Mariano, Stan Sulzman** (as); **Tony Coe** (ts. bcl); **Alan Skidmore** (ts); **Philip Catherine** (g); **Steve Swallow** (b); **Bob Moses** (d). AhUm Ⓕ 009 (39 minutes). Recorded 1975.

⑩ ❽

Gibbs is the most important and original British-based composer and his work can only be compared to that of Gil Evans. Like Evans he has mastered the ability to draw the best from his soloists. His complex writing here is typical of his output. At the time he was much involved with John McLaughlin's Mahavishnu Orchestra and his writing reflects the period, making much use of ostinato figures and multi-tempos. The strength and character of Gibbs's compositions are his most notable qualities, and his themes are both unique and memorable. Included here are Gibbs classics like *To Lady Mac In Retrospect*, *Tunnel Of Love* and *Unfinished Sympathy*, all of which Gibbs continues to rework with great success.

The voicing of the orchestra is another primary strength and his use of exotic elements like Mariano's nadhaswaram is always done with purpose and not simply for effect.

Everybody seems to want to work for Gibbs, and he has difficulty accommodating all of his pre-eminent soloists. Tony Coe's tenor is set against a beautifully constructed orchestral choir for his feature on *Antique*. Of the ones who are granted solo space he, Catherine and Mariano are the most potent. This CD, not his latest but still his most impressive, cannot be recommended too highly. **SV**

Terry Gibbs

1924

Dream Band **Gibbs** (vb); **Al Porcino, Ray Triscari, Conte Candoli, Stu Williamson** (t); **Bob Enevoldsen, Vern Friley, Joe Cadena** (tb); **Joe Maini, Charlie Kennedy** (as); **Bill Holman, Med Flory** (ts); **Jack Schwartz** (bs); **Pete Jolly** (p); **Max Bennett** (b); **Mel Lewis** (d). Contemporary Ⓜ CCD-7647-2 (53 minutes). Recorded 1959.

⑥ ❹

Terry Gibbs's natural effervescence was one of the vital elements of the late-forties Woody Herman Herd, and whenever he has had the opportunity he has put together a big band for a record or club date. Most of the tracks here come from once-a-week engagements at the Seville Club in Hollywood where the owner could only afford a quartet. The fact that all the high-powered players were prepared to play at the club for minimum payment is an indication of the collective enthusiasm of the men involved. This is a very exciting band playing very exciting music; the only drawback being that much of the programme is cast in the same mould as regards tempo and general atmosphere. There is a relentlessness to the music (spread across no less than five albums now, for those who are interested in the complete output), which is a little wearying in bulk. The best way to approach such discs is to pick out three or four titles at one sitting rather than sit through close to an hour of sustained excitement. Gibbs solos on nearly every track but there are plenty of others voices to be heard (*Avalon* sports both Richie Kamuca and Bill Perkins on tenor). Spread over the five albums (of which this is the first) are arrangements by Bill Holman, Med Flory and Bob Brookmeyer, plus others by Marty Paich, Manny Albam and Al Cohn. Wally Heider's engineering has caught the in-person spirit to perfection.
AM

Harry 'The Hipster' Gibson

Boogie Woogie In Blue **Gibson** (p, v); **Slim Gaillard** (g); **John Simmons**, **Tiny Brown** (b); **Sidney Catlett**, **Zutty Singleton** (d). Musicraft Ⓜ MVSCD 63 (36 minutes). Recorded 1944-46.
③ ❻

Gibson was a local sensation in the jazz world in the early forties when his frenetic boogie-based piano playing, married to his rather self-consciously hip vocals, gave him a string of recording successes and residencies in jazz clubs across America. Like his contemporary Slim Gaillard (heard on four tracks here) he fell out of favour at the end of the decade when his patented brew of pepped-up humour was overtaken by the more earthy attractions of the burgeoning r&b scene. Unlike Gaillard, he did not enjoy an Indian summer later in life, so he remains locked in a strange sort of time warp, like clothes fashions, where style is everything and, just as quickly, merely a diverting anachronism. There is little in the word-play which rises above a sort of schoolboy delight in dealing with mildly risqué, naughty-boy subjects (*Who Put The Benzedrine In Mrs Murphy's Ovaltine?* may have looked good on paper, but wears the joke thin well before its three minutes of fame is up), and the musical content on the vocal numbers is not too distant from nursery rhymes. You need a genius of Fats Waller's dimensions to get away with such musical gruel, and unfortunately for Gibson, he was only mildly talented. For train-spotters and nostalgia freaks only.
KS

Astrud Gilberto
1940

Look To The Rainbow **Gilberto** (v); with orchestras arranged and conducted by **Gil Evans, Al Cohn**; **The Walter Wanderley Trio**. Verve Ⓜ 821 556-2 (45 minutes). Recorded 1966.
⑧ ❽

Astrud Gilberto is one of the few popular singers of modern times to use absolutely no vibrato whatsoever. It was this which created that first impression of pubescent artlessness, an effect confusingly and delightfully at odds with the sophistication of the songs she sang. She chose the right moment to appear. In 1963, the year of her hit recording of *The Girl From Ipanema*, bookstalls happened to be doing a brisk trade in paperback copies of *Lolita*.

This CD consists largely of her third and best solo album, with arrangements by Gil Evans. As one might expect, the settings are bold and original: one piece features that strange and plangent Brazilian folk instrument, the berimbau, or musical bow, while another reproduces the sound of a carnival band which moves across the stereo picture from right to left (it was a year before the same effect appeared on the Beatles's **Sergeant Pepper**, to be hailed as a unique stroke of genius). The early to mid-sixties was Evans's great period, when his instinct for instrumental timbre and texture was drawing unimagined riches from studio orchestras judiciously laced with jazz soloists. One of these was Johnny Coles, who plays a delectable trumpet solo, in the Michel Legrand song *I Will Wait For You*. Evans was an agonizingly slow writer, which explains why two of the numbers are arranged in his style by Al Cohn, with a flair that goes beyond pastiche. The six tracks added for this CD edition come from Astrud Gilberto's fourth album **A Certain Smile, A Certain Sadness**, accompanied by Brazilian organist Walter Wanderley.
DG

João Gilberto

1931

The Legendary João Gilberto **Gilberto** (v, g); with orchestras arranged and conducted by **Antonio Carlos Jobim, Walter Wanderley**. World Pacific Ⓜ CDP7 93891-2 (76 minutes). Recorded 1958-61.

⑧ ❻

On this compilation you will find the original versions of the songs later recorded by Stan Getz with Gilberto and others, and it soon becomes clear that the Getz/Gilberto classics were expansions of these already-established arrangements.

The beauty of Jobim's melodies, the gently insinuating voice of Gilberto and the subdued but springy bossa nova rhythm make these performances irresistible, and it is easy to understand the attraction such music must have held for jazz musicians in the early sixties. In particular, the harmonies of songs like *Chega De Saudade* and *O Pato* are far more tempting than those of most jazz originals being turned out at the time. **DG**

Dizzy Gillespie

1917-1993

The Complete RCA Victor Recordings **Gillespie** (t, v); with a collective personnel of **Dave Burns, Elmon Wright, Lammar Wright, Benny Bailey, Matthew McKay, Ray Orff, Willie Cook, Benny Harris** (t); **Taswell Baird, William Shepherd, Ted Kelly, Andy Duryea, Sam Hurt, Jesse Tarrant, J.J. Johnson, Charles Greenlea** (tb); **John Brown, Howard Johnson, Ernie Henry** (as); **James Moody, Joe Gayles, Don Byas, Big Nick Nicholas, Budd Johnson, Yusef Lateef** (ts); **Cecil Payne, Al Gibson** (bs); **Milt Jackson** (vb); **John Lewis, Al Haig** (p); **John Collins, Bill DeArango** (g); **Ray Brown, Al McKibbon** (b); **Joe Harris, J.C. Heard, Kenny Clarke** (d); **Chano Pozo** (cga, perc, v); **Sabu Martinez** (perc); **Kenny Hagood, Johnny Hartman, Joe Carroll** (v); **The Teddy Hill Orchstra; The Lionel Hampton Orchestra; The Metronome All-Stars**. RCA Bluebird Ⓜ 66528 2 (two discs: 129 minutes). Recorded 1937-49.

✔ ⑧ ❽

There are three 1937 tracks by the Teddy Hill band featuring Gillespie, and one from Hampton's studio aggregation where Gillespie is prominent. There are also two takes each of two numbers from the Metronome All-Stars of 1949. The rest of the collection comes from the big bands and small groups led by Gillespie which recorded for Victor between February 1946 and July 1949. The recordings reflect typical major-label reactions to a recently underground phenomenon, combining the ground-breaking pieces such as *Night In Tunisia*, *Manteca* and *Good Bait* with the more lightweight (and hopefully more commercially successful) clowning in which Gillespie loved to indulge. That said, the bulk of the music is quintessential early bop, with Gillespie's post-California septet replacing the L.A.-mired Parker with Don Byas, who is impressive on both takes of Monk's *52nd Street Theme*, while the innovative charts of the big band also feature key tracks with congas by Chano Pozo.

Gillespie's Victor sides as a leader are pre-dated by his small-group Musicraft recordings of 1945 (see below), but it is on Victor that the big band first appeared and continued to flourish. Many of the charts from this collection have become hallmarks of the bop style and deserve their classic status. This is an important reissue, charting The Way Ahead for all those who cared to listen at the time. Sound quality, never that good on the originals, is enhanced by some deft transfer techniques. **BP**

Shaw 'Nuff **Gillespie** (t, v, ldr) with personnel including: **Dave Burns, Kenny Dorham** (t); **Charles Greenlea** (tb); **Charlie Parker, Sonny Stitt, Howard Johnson, Scoops Carey** (as); **Dexter Gordon** (ts); **Leo Parker, Pee Wee Moore** (bs); **Milt Jackson** (vb); **Clyde Hart, Al Haig, John Lewis** (p); **Remo Palmieri** (g); **Curly Russell, Slam Stewart, Ray Brown** (b); **Sid Catlett, Cozy Cole, Kenny Clarke, Joe Harris** (d); **Gil Fuller** (v). Musicraft Ⓜ MVSCD-53 (58 minutes). Recorded 1945/46

✔ ⑧ ❻

After leaving the Billy Eckstine Orchestra in 1944, Gillespie settled into playing in the clubs along New York's 52nd Street. It was the street that hosted jazz of every persuasion, but more significantly allowed old to either blend or contrast with new. It was left to the recording studios to document the proposed merger and this CD provides an insight into the way in which the emerging boppers tended to distance themselves from most of the swing era giants. Outstanding swing players like Slam Stewart suddenly sounded very pedestrian; of the outsiders, only the likes of Catlett and Hart seemed to fully grasp the new requirements. For his part, Gillespie was playing magnificently; he has stunning solos on *Blue 'N' Boogie*, *Hot House* and *Oop Bop Sh'Bam*. Parker's contributions to *Dizzy Atmosphere* and *Groovin' High* are no less impressive as both men advance jazz into a new era of complex harmonic investigations and more oblique rhythmic patterns. These developments notwithstanding, Gillespie's recent experience with Eckstine had fired his interest in presenting bop on a wider canvas. On five titles he insinuates his bop lines into an existing tradition with only the minimum of adjustment to the big band frameworks required to accommodate him. Some of the music on this disc is duplicated on the Savoy label Gillespie reissue, **Groovin' High**. The sound quality is better here, and you also get an extra 20 minutes of music. **BMcR**

Dizzy Songs **Gillespie** (t); **Don Byas** (ts); **Hubert Fol** (as); **Bill Tamper**, **Nat Peck** (tb); **Arnold Ross**, **Raymond Fol**, **Wade Legge** (p); **Joe Benjamin**, **Pierre Michelot**, **Lou Hackney** (b); **Bill Clark**, **Pierre Lemarchand**, **Al Jones** (d); **Joe Carroll** (v). Vogue Ⓜ 115464 2 (74 minutes). Recorded 1952/53.

⑩ ❽

These 24 delightful tracks (four of them alternative takes) date from Dizzy's visits to Paris in 1952 and 1953. Coming as they did hard on the heels of his combative and radical big-band bebop of the late forties, they revealed for the first time his flair for melody and relaxed swing. The heart of the collection is a series of improvisations on standard tunes, such as *Somebody Loves Me* and *Sweet Lorraine*, in which Dizzy is virtually the only soloist. The tone is broad and juicy and the melodic line remarkably un-boppish, apart from a sparing use of double-tempo phrases and the odd flattened fifth or augmented ninth. From the moment of its foundation in 1948, Vogue records and their jazz director Charles Delaunay made a point of recording visiting American musicians in informal settings and with the minimum of 'production'. The results added up to a valuable and distinctive body of work, of which these sessions are among the very best. **DG**

Diz and Getz **Gillespie** (t) **Stan Getz**, **Hank Mobley** (ts); **Oscar Peterson**, **Wade Legge** (p); **Herb Ellis** (g); **Ray Brown**, **Lou Hackney** (b); **Max Roach**, **Charlie Persip** (d). Verve Ⓜ 835 559-2 (48 minutes). Recorded 1953/54.

⑧ ❻

Eight of these tracks were made in Los Angeles while Getz and Gillespie were on tour with a Stan Kenton package show and Max Roach was working at the Lighthouse with Howard Rumsey's All Stars. With the efficient and reliable Peterson Trio providing a foundation it was easier to find common ground with songs such as *Exactly Like You* rather than try to produce new, original material, and the two best tracks are the opening ones, both of which are Ellington compositions. On *It Don't Mean A Thing* the ultra-fast tempo puts the soloists on their mettle and it is surprising to find how well Getz (at his coolest is the early-fifties) rises to the challenge. Gillespie was apparently never off form in or out of a recording studio, and his solo work throughout is noteworthy, especially his control with a mute. He plays conga drum on part of *Siboney* and does not sing (despite the notes). *One Alone* was recorded in New York the following year by Dizzy's regular band, a fairly lightweight number with a short solo from the tenor player listed as "Earl Mabley"! A useful example of how Gillespie invariably succeeded in pulling together seemingly disparate elements on recording sessions, this compact disc is typical of the 'all star' dates organized by Norman Granz. **AM**

Dizzy Gillespie At Newport **Dizzy Gillespie** (t, v); **Lee Morgan**, **Ermit Perry**, **Carl Warwick**, **Talib Daawud** (t); **Melba Liston**, **Al Grey**, **Chuck Connors** (tb); **Ernie Henry**, **Jimmy Powell** (as); **Billy Mitchell**, **Benny Golson** (ts); **Pee Wee Moore** (bs); **Wynton Kelly**, **Mary Lou Williams** (p); **Paul West** (b); **Charlie Persip** (d). Verve Ⓜ 513 754-2 (73 minutes). Recorded 1957.

⑧ ❽

Although Gillespie has been the subject of many CD collections it is unlikely that there has been a more lively and humour-filled one than this. He leads a spirited, loose big band and his own playing is at its most mature and uncompromising. It was soon after this period that he understandably drew in his horns as far as trumpet playing was concerned, so that we are privileged to enjoy one of his last flat-out performances. The atmosphere of the open air concert adds to the excitement of this most vivid of concerts. This group, about to be disbanded, was the remains of the one Gillespie put together for State Department tours and had lost only one major soloist—altoist Phil Woods. The solos of Al Grey and Billy Mitchell were driven by the supercharged drumming of Persip. Confirmation that Wynton Kelly was a good big band pianist as well as a soloist comes in his playing behind Gillespie on the magnificent interpretation of *I Remember Clifford*. Mary Lou Williams replaces Kelly to play three extracts from her *Zodiac Suite*. Both her writing and playing are fresh and contemporary, and the band roars back in response to her piano solos. The ten-minute re-creation of *Cool Breeze*, more like a hot tornado, roars along at a tremendous tempo, with Al Grey indulging in the double-tempo soloing which he uses to try to convince his audiences that he is playing bebop rather than straight mainstream. There is no such doubt about the flaring Gillespie solo which follows and builds ecstatically as the band (and Kelly) build the tension behind him. Gillespie drops out to let the newly-emergent Lee Morgan solo with considerable fire on *Night In Tunisia*. **SV**

Duets with Sonny Rollins and Sonny Stitt **Gillespie** (t); **Sonny Rollins** (ts); **Sonny Stitt** (as, ts); **Ray Bryant** (p); **Tommy Bryant** (b); **Charlie Persip** (d). Verve Ⓜ 835 253-2 (60 minutes). Recorded 1957.

⑧ ❼

Gillespie's career has so far been inadequately covered by CD issues and reissues. Whole sections of his best period lie undisturbed in various record companies' vaults while inferior performances have been repeatedly reissued. In the absence of vast swathes of masterpieces recorded for Verve, Philips

and Solid State (who between them own such gems as **An Electrifying Evening**, **Perceptions**, **The New Continent** and **At the Village Vanguard**, to name a mere handful), we can buy this as a good representation of Gillespie, relaxed and jamming with friends.

This is a better buy than its companion-piece, **Sonny Side Up**, recorded a week later with the same personnel, if only because extra material on the CD adds no less than 20 extra minutes to the original LP, while **Sonny Side** is still only a mediocre 38 minutes in duration (**Sonny Side**, however, does have the famous and heartstopping unaccompanied Rollins solo on *The Eternal Triangle*.) The music itself is fine: Diz is full of good notions and his execution is magnificent. In a period when he could often be ruminative during solos, he lights up here. Stitt is a more comfortable partner than Rollins, in the sense that he better fits in with Gillespie's conception of the overall performance, but Rollins is in the typically aggressive, searching form of this period. The rhythm section is exemplary, with Bryant additionally contributing some neat solos. Recording sound is much improved. **KS**

Dizzy Gillespie's Big 4 **Gillespie** (t); **Joe Pass** (g); **Ray Brown** (b); **Mickey Roker** (d). Pablo Ⓜ OJC 443-2 (44 minutes). Recorded 1974.

✔ ⑩ ❻

Gillespie's personality cost him the respect of many critics and listeners, who considered him not serious enough once jazz grew more introverted and abstract. Yet Gillespie was as intellectual an improviser as any of his successors, and he remained a deeply moving ballad player. The present set, one of producer Norman Granz's most inspired showcases for Gillespie in the trumpeter's Pablo period, gets an after-hours feeling by using Pass's guitar rather than piano. Even a flagwaver like *Russian Lullaby* sounds intimate, though it and the rest of the date are hardly lacking in energy. The rhythm section (Granz's usual suspects) play as well here as they did anywhere, and the trumpeter unleashes cliché-free improvisations that were as fresh and challenging as any trumpeter's of the period. There is a brief and lovely *September Song*, a delicate *Jitterbug Waltz*, and a *Hurry Home* that was one of the first things to hit my sound system when I learned of Gillespie's passing. **Big 4**, which tended to go unnoticed like much of Gillespie's later playing, argues that his later years were also filled with music of great beauty. **BB**

Max + Diz: Paris 1989 **Gillespie** (t); **Max Roach** (d). A&M Ⓕ CD 6404 (two discs: 126 minutes). Disc Two includes a 33 minute interview. Recorded 1989.

⑨ ❽

This heartfelt reunion of two of the legendary pioneers of bebop, and therefore of modern jazz, is a wondrous affair. Recorded before an appreciative audience on March 23, 1989 at the Maison de la Culture de la Seine Saint-Denis, Bobigny in Paris, we hear two masters 'conversing' in their native tongue of bebop. While there are palpable recollections of past glories, it is far from being an 'oldies but goldies' trek down memory lane. Indeed, one is struck time and again by the freshness of conception, the risk-taking, the timeless universality of drummer Max Roach and trumpeter Dizzy Gillespie. There are highly personalized renditions of standards like Monk's *'Round Midnight* and Denzil Best's *Allen's Alley*, and we catch one of the finest scat singers in jazz history, Mr Gillespie, vocalizing in tandem with Mr. Roach's 'talking drums' on Dizzy's *Oo Pa Pa Da*. The bulk of the concert is devoted to what one can assume, given the determinedly impromptu nature of the event, are spontaneous dialogues such as *The Arrival, Versailles* and *Place de la Concorde*.

There is also a wonderfully warm and revealing interview with Dizzy and Max; one of its highlights is the playback of the infamous early-fifties TV performance of Diz and Charlie Parker being introduced by an uncomprehending host, Earl Wilson, and then playing *Hot House*. Here we catch Dizzy and Max commenting on Wilson's inept and implicitly racist intro, but also fondly recalling their association with Parker. **CB**

John Gilmore

1931

Blowing In From Chicago **Gilmore**, **Clifford Jordan** (ts); **Horace Silver** (p); **Curly Russell** (b); **Art Blakey** (d). Blue Note Ⓜ 8 28977 2 9 (47 minutes). Recorded 1957.

⑧ ❽

Although he actually co-leads this session with Clifford Jordan, it is listed here under John Gilmore's name as one of those rare occasions where he is out from under the shadow of Sun Ra. This was in fact the recording début of both saxophonists, fresh out of the Windy City; Jordan was born there, Gilmore brought there as an infant, and they were classmates under the legendary music instructor Captain Walter Dyett at DuSable High School. Chicago has a rich tradition of muscular, extroverted tenor saxists, including Gene Ammons, Johnny Griffin, Eddie Harris and Von Freeman (all of whom studied under Dyett), and Gilmore and Jordan fill the bill at this stage of their careers. With the dead-on New York rhythm section of Silver, Russell and Blakey, this is a prototypical hard-bop date, capturing a level of excitement you seldom hear today (due at least in part to engineer Rudy Van Gelder's classic Blue Note sound). Both saxists are well-versed in bebop lore, as the quotes and licks sprinkled throughout *Billie's Bounce* show, yet the variety of tunes authored by Gigi Gryce, Jordan and Silver prevent them from playing by rote. Jordan's tone is a touch grainier than it would later become, and his lines tend to tumble forward from exuberance; Gilmore's sinewy phrasing barely anticipates his subsequent freer approach. The only complaint I can muster is against the constant, annoying sizzle of Blakey's ride cymbal; otherwise, this is a classic fifties blowing date well worth hearing. **AL**

Egberto Gismonti 1947

Danca Das Cabecas **Gismonti** (g, p, wood f, v); **Nana Vasconcelos** (perc, berimbau, corpo, v). ECM Ⓕ 1089 (827 750-2) (50 minutes). Recorded 1976.

✔ ⑧ ❽

Gismonti was on the leading edge of world-music synthesis that has recently opened jazz to diverse ethnic influences. A trained pianist and self-taught guitarist who studied with Nadia Boulanger and played pop music in his native Brazil, he was drawing on diverse compositional and improvisational resources long before such eclecticism became fashionable. While he has made several later recordings for ECM in solo, duo and quartet formats, as well as with the trio Magico, his first album for the label remains his most intense and expressive. In ten keenly-shaped yet spontaneous-sounding pieces, played primarily on eight-string guitar, Gismonti moves in focused bursts of melody, sometimes ruminative, sometimes explosive, with Vasconcelos's percussion slipping in and out for just the right emphasis. While the atmospherics associated with such music are present, there is also more impulse and grit than usual, making **Danca Das Cabecas** more appealing to jazz fans, and a definitive example of how the jazz spirit can inform the creative music of other cultures. **BB**

Jimmy Giuffre 1921

The Jimmy Giuffre 3 **Giuffre** (cl, ts, bs); **Jim Hall** (g); **Ralph Peña, Jimmy Atlas** (b). Atlantic Ⓜ 790981-2 (47 minutes). Recorded 1956-57.

⑧ ❻

Giuffre, the contributor of the famous *Four Brothers* to Woody Herman's Second Herd, a composition which defined a whole period of that band's history, has led a varied career. After a stint with Herman he settled on the West Coast and became a Lighthouse All-Stars regular, also moonlighting as a honkin' rhythm & blues tenor player in Shorty Rogers's apocalyptic (and unattributed) studio band, Boots Brown and His Blockbusters. By 1956, when this album was made, Giuffre had carved out a fascinating contemporary niche for himself, operating at low voltage—and low volume—in this drummerless, pianoless trio. The achieved intimacy had a great deal to do with the quick public acceptance of his work, and with the initial release of this LP he had a minor hit on his hands. The song *The Train and the River*, here given its first recording, became a talking-point of both the 1957 CBS TV special, *The Sound of Jazz*, and Chuck Wein's film of the 1958 Newport Jazz Festival, *Jazz on a Summer's Day*.

This CD reissue has greatly improved the recording sound, and in the process has helped delineate the interplay and natural balance between the three equal participants in this music. Giuffre's breathy, low-register clarinet playing, although derided at the time, has a wonderful, casual warmth, Hall wraps Giuffre's lines in a continual thread of golden chords, and Peña perfectly anticipates every shift of musical direction. In retrospect, the only change between this group and the radical trio of 1961 is in the style, not the process.

The CD contains two tracks from a previously unissued session, recorded a year after the initial LP. Now that Neshui Ertegun, the CD's producer, is gone, one wonders whether the whole session, or any other Giuffre Atlantic, will ever see the light of day. **KS**

1961 **Giuffre** (cl); **Paul Bley** (p); **Steve Swallow** (b). ECM Ⓕ 1438/39 (849 644-2) (two discs: 92 minutes). Recorded 1961.

⑩ ❽

This set is a reissue of the Verve albums **Fusion** and **Thesis**, recorded in March and August of 1961 by the Jimmy Giuffre Three. Giuffre had already led a drummerless trio with Jim Hall and Ralph Pena some five years earlier, but the three studio albums he made with Bley and Swallow (the Columbia album **Free Fall** followed in 1962) represented a more radical break with jazz tradition. Free, abstract, with no regular tempo, these records went farther out than anyone (except perhaps Cecil Taylor) had then ventured. And whereas other free players of the period tended towards the fiercely declamatory, The Giuffre Trio created quiet, alert, sensitive music that set out the blueprint for a freeform chamber jazz.

Although **Free Fall** (not currently available on any format) was the record on which, to quote Giuffre "I let everything go", the impulse towards abstraction is already well advanced on the two 1961 records. Even so, the mostly improvised music here always starts from a head and often explores a specific mood or idea. The trio's interplay shows unusual empathy and their attention to textural detail, together with the spacious feel of their music, anticipates the early experiments of the AACM. A further bonus is the presence of four Carla Bley tunes, notably the bright, Monkish *Ictus* and a dreamy *Jesus Maria*.

ECM have done a splendid job of enhancing the sound quality and have also added three previously unreleased tracks. However, *Used To Be*, a track from the **Fusion** LP, has mysteriously vanished and the original version of *Trudgin'* (also from **Fusion**) has been replaced by an alternative take, again without explanation. These anomalies aside, **1961** makes newly available two LPs which were among the first masterpieces of a truly post-bebop jazz. **GL**

Globe Unity Orchestra

Rumbling **Kenny Wheeler** (t); **Albert Mangelsdorff** (tb); **Paul Rutherford** (tb); **Steve Lacy** (ss); **Evan Parker** (ss, ts, saw); **Gerd Dudek** (ts); **Alexander Von Schlippenbach** (p); **Peter Kowald** (b, bb); **Paul Lovens** (d, pc, saw). FMP Ⓕ CD 40 (69 minutes). Recorded 1975.

✔ ⑧ ❻

In 1966, Von Schlippenbach composed *Globe Unity* to fulfil a commission from RIAS Berlin, and in doing so provided the performing orchestra with a name. Since that date, the GUO have been a rarely heard and sparsely recorded band, full of brilliant soloists and performing a highly appropriate 'book'. Despite the inevitably inconsistent personnel they have proved to be one of the world's more successful aggregations, undertaking the difficult task of reconciling free jazz with the tradition of a large orchestra. This CD presents a slightly pared-down edition of the band but one that parades all the trademarks of the full unit. They make full use of ferocious collective 'all-ins', but these are balanced by moves to the *sotto voce* area, and room is even found for silence. All of the impressive solo roster gets to have a say and some of the background parts are as freely improvised as the solos they support. The music is at times arhythmic, in the theme statement of *Alexander Marschbefehl* consciously vertical, and occasionally even deliberately static. On Monk's *Evidence*, at Lacy's instigation they actually produce a swing-era momentum; in all cases they seem to adopt the stance that seems appropriate to the matter in hand. Be it shrill counterpoint by reeds in the false register, guttural conversations by trombones or strident solo trumpet, nothing which occurs here seems out of place from a band that displays subtlety and bravado in about equal parts. **BMcR**

Vinny Golia

Commemoration **Golia** (pic, f, cl, ss, bs, bss); **Mark Underwood**, **John Fumo**, **Marissa Benidict**, **Rob Blakeslee** (t, flh); **Mike Vlatkovich**, **Bruce Fowler**, **George McMullen**, **Phil Teele** (tb); **William Roper** (tba); **Emily Hey** (pic, f); **Kim Richmond**, **Steve Fowler**, **Bill Plake**, **David Ocker** (reeds); **Wayne Peet** (p, syn, cond); **Harry Scorzo**, **Jef Gauthier** (vn); **Greg Adamson**, **Matt Cooker**, **Jonathan Golove**, **Dion Sorrell** (vc); **Ken Filiano**, **Joel Hamilton** (b); **Alex Cline** (d, perc); **David Johnson**, **Brad Dutz** (vb, mar, perc); **Stephanie Henry** (cond). 9 Winds Ⓕ NWCD 0150/60 (two discs: 120 minutes). Recorded 1991/92.

⑧ ❼

One of the best-kept secrets in jazz, California visual artist, composer and multi-instrumentalist Vinny Golia's Large Ensemble has been active since 1982, having recorded two multi-LP sets and three CD releases, to little or no acclaim. One of the problems may be that Golia's provocative writing owes little to the prevailing canons of big band orthodoxy; the addition of strings, mallet instruments and unusual wind and brass combinations (*Mahlow*, for example, features tuba, bass trombone and bass saxophone) makes the Large Ensemble more of a chamber music group than a swinging big band, although they can swing when called upon to do so. Most of the 11 compositions on this two-disc set take their time to brew, which allows Golia gradually to integrate soloists into the music rather than have them interrupt its progress. Golia's sombre moods and sharply etched up-tempo lines inhabit a territory somewhere between the orchestral conceptions of Charles Mingus and Anthony Braxton, but the way he orchestrates for alternately subtle and dramatic colour and texture is entirely his own. A case in point is *Tumulus Or Griffin*, which begins as if an illustration of Gothic architecture and builds to a fantastic multi-layered climax. As a painter, Golia has a trained eye for line, contrast and chiaroscuro; his ear is no less acute. **AL**

Benny Golson

1929

This is for You, John **Golson** (ts); **Pharoah Sanders** (ts); **Cedar Walton** (p); **Ron Carter** (b); **Jack DeJohnette** (d). Timeless Ⓕ CDSPJ 235 (43 minutes). Recorded 1983.

⑦ ❼

Benny Golson's playing career falls into two distinct phases, themselves separated by a dozen or so years in which he virtually gave up performing to work as a composer and arranger. The best of his earlier recordings, often made in the company of Art Farmer, have yet to reappear on CD. **This is for You, John** is a particularly enjoyable album from his later period, which commenced in the late seventies. It is also among the more personal of the many recorded tributes to John Coltrane, for Golson had been Coltrane's regular jamming partner when the pair were growing up in forties Philadelphia. Most of the tracks touch on the tenorists' friendship in some guise, from *Page 12*'s recreation of the complex bebop lines they played together as young men to *Times Past*'s evocation of the lilting, surging tunes on which Coltrane liked to fashion his more rhapsodic solos. The Trane link is underlined by the presence of Pharoah Sanders, whose abrasive tone is an excellent foil for the leader's more liquid sound.

Golson's ballad feature, *A Change of Heart*, reveals his talents as both player and composer. A floating dream of a tune, so subtly shaped it sounds almost abstract, he performs it with such deftness—of phrasing, timing—that it recalls of one of his chief tenor influences, the great Lucky Thompson. Lehar's *Vilia*, also recorded by Coltrane, makes an unlikely but charming finale. **GL**

Eddie Gomez

1944

Gomez **Gomez** (b); **Yasuaki Shimsu** (ts); **Chick Corea** (kbds); **Katumi Watanabe** (g); **Steve Gadd** (d). Denon Ⓕ DC 8562 (46 minutes). Recorded 1984.

⑥ ❽

Because of the difficulties of smooth articulation on the instrument, the bass remained the least viable of the solo jazz instruments until the arrival of Jimmy Blanton in 1940. From then on virtuosi like Ray Brown, Charles Mingus and Red Mitchell gradually expanded the instrument's voice to a point where the grand masters of today, Gomez very much amongst them, have an almost saxophone-like fluidity in their lines. However, the bass does not have the emotional palette of the saxophone, and showcase albums like this one are to be taken as rare wine.

Gomez has an equal eloquence throughout the full range of his instrument and demonstrates that it is not just possible, but desirable to use amplified acoustic bass in preference to the purpose-built electric bass. Like his successor and peer Marc Johnson, Gomez developed as an individual voice in the Bill Evans trio. Evans had already matured the ill-fated Scott La Faro there, and there is no doubt that his closely-knit trios, developed over the years rather than months, had a profound effect on the bassists. Gomez's tone is plump and full and his arco work on the out-of-tempo *Zimmerman* is a dark contrast to the powerfully plucked basses on the multi-dubbed *Mez-Ga*, a duet with Gadd.

Corea plays delicate acoustic piano solos on a couple of the tracks and it is only on his own *Ginkakuji* that he employs his multitude of electronics. **SV**

Nat Gonella

1908

Nat Gonella and His Georgians **Gonella** (t, v); **Bruts Gonella**, **Johnny Morrison** (t); **Albert Torrance**, **Ernest Ritte** (cl, as); **Pat Smuts**, **Don Barrigo** (ts); **Harold Hood**, **Monia Liter** (p); **Jimmy Mesene** (g); **Charlie Winter**, **Tiny Winters** (b); **Bob Dryden** (d). Flapper Ⓜ PAST CD9750 (66 minutes). Recorded 1935-40.

⑥ ❺

After some years in the trumpet section of British dance-bands led by Billy Cotton, Roy Fox and Lew Stone, Gonella formed his own slightly smaller ensemble, the Georgians. Their repertoire suggests a showband like Cab Calloway's, mixing standards like *Nagasaki* and *On the Sunny Side of the Street* with novelty hot numbers such as *Someone Stole Gabriel's Horn* or the hillbilly song *The Man Who Comes Around*. Torrance, Smuts and Hood contribute sprightly swing solos a little in the manner of sidemen in Fats Waller's or Skeets Tolbert's groups, but the dominant character of the music lies in Gonella's trumpet playing, deeply influenced by Louis Armstrong's, and his unobtrusive London-accented singing. Occasionally, as in *Tiger Rag*, he matches the excitable audacity of the young Armstrong, but more often he and his companions show the decent restraint that has thwarted so much promising English jazz.

This is not an outstanding selection of Gonella's work, and the remastering is muddy, but it gives an adequate picture of his band's repertoire and style. Three 1940 tracks are by the New Georgians, with similar instrumentation but an entire change of personnel. **TR**

Paul Gonsalves

1920-1974

Gettin' Together **Gonsalves** (ts); **Nat Adderley** (c); **Wynton Kelly** (p); **Sam Jones** (b); **Jimmy Cobb** (d). Jazzland Ⓜ OJCCD 203-2 (40 minutes). Recorded 1960.

⑧ ❽

It is hard to think of a jazz musician who was as generally underestimated as Gonsalves was. He emerged from the saxophone section of the Duke Ellington Orchestra to become famous for one of his least trenchant solos, the 27 choruses which he blew on Duke's *Diminuendo and Crescendo in Blue* at the 1956 Newport Jazz Festival, and was forever more linked to up-tempo tenor marathons. In truth Gonsalves was one of the more creative musicians within the Ellington ranks and although he was firmly rooted in the Ben Webster tradition, he brought consistently fresh thought to Ellington's works.

He made half a dozen outstanding albums away from the Ellington influence, and this one is probably his best. His supporting musicians came from the Miles Davis (Kelly and Cobb) and Cannonball Adderley (Jones and Nat Adderley) quintets, and Kelly in particular is responsible for the virtuous tenor playing which results. There are exquisite tenor ballad performances of *I Surrender, Dear* and *I Cover The Waterfront*, and a most refreshing treatment of *Yesterdays*. That the other musicians also enjoyed the invigorating surroundings is evinced by the way they and Gonsalves pile into the up-tempo pieces here. Perhaps this was Gonsalves's true masterpiece. **SV**

Jerry Gonzalez

1949

Rumba Para Monk **Gonzalez** (t, flh, perc); **Carter Jefferson** (ts); **Larry Willis** (p); **Andy Gonzalez** (b); **Steve Berrios** (d, perc). Sunnyside Ⓕ SSC 1036D (72 minutes). Recorded 1988.

⑧ ❽

A conscious attempt to demonstrate Thelonious Monk's often neglected indebtedness to Cuban rhythms, **Rumba Para Monk**, courtesy of its uncontrived arrangements and the enthusiastic commitment of all its participants, triumphantly vindicates the truth of the late composer/pianist's assertion that "Jazz is New York man. It's in the air." A passionate and eloquent champion of all Latin Musics, Jerry Gonzalez, a New York-based Puerto Rican, has managed a rare feat; he has produced a tribute album which genuinely grants the listener a new perspective on the work of its dedicatee. A representative example of Monk's compositions—*Monk's Mood*, *Nutty*, *Ugly Beauty* among them—are filtered through Latin arrangements and instrumentation, and the result is a joyous celebration not only of the durability and versatility of the tunes themselves, but also of the subtle power and infectious exuberance of Latin rhythms, ranging from (as the album's excellent liner notes point out) the mozambique employed on *Bye-Ya* to the guiro on *Little Rootie Tootie*. This last is a particular delight, featuring Gonzalez's muted trumpet over percussive train effects and Larry Willis's pianistic 'bell', but throughout Gonzalez's respect for and sensitivity to the nuances of Monk's tunes are demonstrated in a series of startlingly idiosyncratic but entirely appropriate arrangements. The quality of the soloing occasionally does not quite fulfil the promise inherent in the arrangements, but this is a minor quibble, given the originality and sheer panache of the project as a whole. **CP**

Brad Goode

1964

Shock Of The New Goode (t); **Lin Halliday, Ed Petersen** (ts); **Jodie Christian** (p); **Fareed Haque** (g); **Dennis Carroll, Angus Thomas, Rob Amster** (b); **Jeff Stitely, Paul Wertico, Bob Rummage** (d). Delmark Ⓕ DD 440 (44 minutes). Recorded 1988.

⑥ ❼

A first-call trumpeter for session work and club dates around Chicago, Goode has made a reputation for himself at a young age because of his crisp technique, versatility and ability to keep up with fast company. He acknowledges Clifford Brown as a major influence and constructs clean, curving lines often reminiscent of Red Rodney. His début album, however, like many début albums, is a mixed bag. In an effort to display his various interests, Goode has included a fusion novelty number and a pair of trumpet-plus-strings tunes that border on muzak. The straight-ahead blowing tunes reveal Goode's real potential. *The New Blues*, for example, allows him to flaunt his bright, brash tone and fluent chops. There is a version of *Old Folks* that erases any lingering sentiment, with Goode biting and smearing notes in his solo. A reliable Chicago piano veteran, Jodie Christian, gets little space to showcase his sophisticated wares, but of most interest may be Lin Halliday. One of those locals who fell between the cracks, he is an attractively insular player with a dry, whispery tone and a habit of phrasing like a man looking over his shoulder. Halliday's playing may entice fans of obscure bop tenors like J.R. Monterose and Allen Eager to listen up here. **AL**

Benny Goodman

1909-1986

The Birth Of Swing **Benny Goodman** (cl); **Bunny Berigan, Pee Wee Irwin, Mannie Klein, Sterling Bose** (t); **Red Ballard, Jack Lacey, Murray McEachern** (tb); **Toots Mondello, Hymie Schertzer** (as); **Art Rollini, Vido Musso** (ts); **Frank Foeba, Jess Stacey** (p); **George Van Eps, Allan Reuss** (g); **Harry Goodman** (b); **Gene Krupa** (d). RCA Bluebird Ⓜ ND 90601/3 (three discs: 205 minutes). Recorded 1935/36.

✔ ⑧ ❽

There is a case for claiming that swing, as a musical and social phenomenon, was born on July 1, 1935. On that day Benny Goodman's new and still struggling band recorded Fletcher Henderson's arrangement of Jelly Roll Morton's *King Porter Stomp*. By any standards this three-minute work is a little masterpiece, from Bunny Berigan's opening trumpet solo, through constant changes of texture and dynamics, to the exultant riff ending. When success broke over Goodman and the band later that year it was numbers like this that the crowds wanted, and which set the pattern for the following decade.

These three discs contain the band's entire output in its first two years of existence and there is a freshness about the best pieces that was rarely recaptured later. The combination of Henderson's elegant imagination and Goodman's fanatical attention to detail produced a stream of wonderfully sharp-edged and uplifting performances: *Down South Camp Meeting*, *When Buddha Smiles*, *Somebody Loves Me*, etc. The other main arranger was Jimmy Mundy, whose *Swingtime In The Rockies* could stand as the archetype of riff-based dance numbers. Notable soloists during this period, apart from Berigan and Goodman himself, include Jess Stacey, Jack Teagarden and the heavyweight Vido Musso. The vocalists here were both teenagers at the time: Helen Ward was the band's regular singer and Ella Fitzgerald guested on the last session of 1936.

Admittedly this is a hefty package, representing only a brief period in Goodman's career, and it just misses a number of important events, such as the arrival of Harry James and the arranger Eddie Sauter. What we need is a really good one-volume anthology for the general listener which covers the entire Victor years, but there is not one (the two single-volume Harry James sets which cover subsequent Goodman events miss the best of this one); so this remains an essential item. **DG**

The Small Bands, Volumes 1 and 2. **Goodman** (cl); **Teddy Wilson** (p); **Lionel Hampton** (vb, d, v); **Gene Krupa**, **Buddy Schutz** (d); **John Kirby** (b); **Helen Ward** (v). RCA Bluebird Ⓜ ND 85631/82273 (two discs, oas: 69 and 69 minutes). Recorded 1935-39.

⑩ ❻

Although these two CDs cover a number of years, they are so much of a piece that they are best reviewed together. A great deal has been claimed for the Goodman small groups over the years, but now that half a century has passed since their creation and circumstances have altered entirely, it is perhaps easier to get a wider perspective on them. Certainly, they are not as revolutionary as they once seemed (and were not even the first racially mixed band, just the first famous one); even the 'chamber music' tag that their music was landed with seems as much the result of media hype as anything the musicians themselves thought about creating.

With that out of the way, though, it is possible to delve into what to this day remains an aural treat. The precision of these bands, the perfect balance between their constituent parts either as a trio or as a quartet, remains astonishing. Listening to Krupa on these sides, it is difficult to understand why he is so often dismissed as a cloth-eared show-off. At all times he plays *for* the group, not over it, and with the same ebullience as that from which Hampton creates his driving, exiciting contributions. Goodman, of course, combines an immaculate technique with a real zest for playing, while with Wilson around, nobody misses the absence of a bass player on all but just four cuts. The repertoire choice shows infallible good taste, as do the arrangements, where Goodman invariably chooses not to be the 'star', and allows a real interplay between all participants.

But I have a complaint: why was the decision taken to leave out the two tracks with vocals by Martha Tilton, *Silhouetted in the Moonlight* and *Bei mir bist du Schön*, which would have made this collection complete, at least as far as master takes go? Helen Ward's vocal numbers were included in Volume One, after all, and there is enough CD space left. It makes this collection as frustratingly short of perfection as the Jelly Roll Morton Bluebird box was. We will just have to wait for both RCA Jazz Tribune Volumes (which contain all the alternative takes as well) to be transferred to CD. So far only Volume One has made the transition **KS**

Live At Carnegie Hall **Goodman** (cl); **Harry James**, **Ziggy Elman**, **Bobby Hackett**, **Gordon 'Chris' Griffin**, **Cootie Williams**, **Buck Clayton** (t); **Red Ballard**, **Vernon Brown** (tb); **Johnny Hodges** (ss, as); **Hymie Schertzer**, **George Koenig** (as); **Babe Russin**, **Arthur Rollini**, **Lester Young** (ts); **Harry Carney** (bs); **Lionel Hampton** (vb); **Jess Stacy**, **Teddy Wilson**, **Count Basie** (p); **Allan Reuss**, **Freddie Green** (g); **Harry Goodman**, **Walter Page** (b); **Gene Krupa** (d); **Martha Tilton** (v). Columbia Ⓜ 450983 2 (two discs: 103 minutes). Recorded 1938.

⑨ ❹

Goodman's commercial success in the late thirties aroused the latent snob that lurks in the bosom of so many jazz musicians. As well as being an outstanding jazz clarinettist, Goodman was also an accomplished classical performer and, perhaps because of this, felt the need to legitimize the jazz side of his music by fronting a jazz concert in Carnegie Hall. This CD provides authentic documentation of 'The Night of January 6, 1938', a vital date in American musical history. Goodman was himself inspired, fully involved in *One O'Clock Jump*, in spikey reverence to Larry Shields on *Sensation Rag*, in parody of Ted Lewis on *When My Baby Smiles at Me* and totally at ease with Count Basie and Duke Ellington's men on the jammed *Honeysuckle Rose*.

His elegant trio and quartet performances with Hampton, Wilson and Krupa make a major contribution and his big band takes care of all the heavy duty parts. Hackett pays homage to Bix Beiderbecke on *I'm Coming Virginia*, James tips his hat to Louis Armstrong on *Shine* while Krupa tears into the amazing *Sing Sing Sing*. The Ellington message is delivered by the Duke's men on *Blue Reverie*, there are excellent solo interludes by Young, Basie, Hodges and Brown, showboating efforts from Elman and Griffin and pleasant vocal interludes by Tilton. Despite the daunting prospects that

the concert must have presented, the outcome was tremendously successful. Carnegie is now a regular venue for such concerts, but this ground-breaking effort should be in every collection, despite the low-fi sound. **BMcR**

Benny Goodman Sextet Featuring Charlie Christian (1939-41) **Goodman** (cl); **Christian** (g); **Cootie Williams** (t); **Georgie Auld** (ts); **Lionel Hampton** (vb); **Fletcher Henderson**, **Johnny Guarnieri**, **Dudley Brooks**, **Kenny Kersey**, **Count Basie** (p); **Artie Bernstein** (b); **Nick Fatool**, **Harry Jaeger**, **Jo Jones**, **Dave Tough** (d). Columbia Ⓜ CK 45144 (55 minutes). Recorded 1939-41.

⑧ ❽

Oklahoman Charlie Christian was among the first guitarists to effectively employ amplification as a means of equalizing volume levels with horn players, pianists and drummers. With the decibel playing-field thus levelled, Christian, who like all swing era guitarists had been limited to four-to-the-bar comping, suddenly had the technical means for viable soloing. That Christian should have become the leader of this loud mini-revolution is a consequence of the entrepreneurial acumen of John Hammond who in 1939 brought Christian to Goodman's attention. And while Christian had the right musical stuff, it took the national platform provided by Goodman's band to make the transition possible.

These landmark tracks also figured significantly for Benny Goodman, who expanded on the success of his mid-thirties trio and quartet recordings with the sextet and septet sides of 1939-41 with Christian. What may surprise some first-time listeners is Christian's rather limited role, but considering that the enlarged Goodman small groups featured not only the leader, but also Lionel Hampton, Count Basie and Cootie Williams, what becomes clear is Goodman's generosity in sharing the spotlight on tracks whose average length is only three minutes. Yet even in the half-chorus breaks of *Poor Butterfly* we hear "the father of modern jazz guitar" clearly anticipating things to come. We also hear a supple accompanist whose relaxed rhythmic pulse bears comparison to Freddie Green, for 50 years the heartbeat of the Basie Band. **CB**

B.G. In Hi-Fi **Goodman** (cl); with **Chris Griffin**, **Ruby Braff**, **Bernie Privin**, **Carl Poole**, **Charlie Shavers**, **Bobby Donaldson** (t); **Will Bradley**, **Cutty Cutshall**, **Vernon Brown** (tb); **Hymie Schertzer**, **Paul Ricci** (as); **Boomie Richman**, **Al Klink** (ts); **Sol Schlinger** (bs); **Mel Powell** (p); **Steve Jordan** (g) **George Duvivier** (b); **Jo Jones, Bobby Donaldson** (d). Capitol Ⓜ CDP7 92864-2 (64 minutes). Recorded 1954.

⑧ ❽

At the time of these November 1954 sessions Goodman was leading a small group containing Shavers and Powell, so the big band was just a studio-assembled unit. Many of the dozen arrangements were taken from the old book and had been scored originally by Fletcher Henderson, but this excellent band of professionals attacks them with enthusiasm, so what might well have been a tired re-creation emerges as a thrillingly fresh experience. Braff was added as a soloist only, the remaining solos being taken by Brown on trombone, Richman (fine, rich-toned tenor), Powell and Goodman himself. Benny clearly felt happy with the band, for his solos are scintillating, sailing high over the ensemble and contributing to the building excitement on tunes such as *Jumpin' At The Woodside*. The eight small groups titles are gems, with marvellous piano from Powell and Braff in great form on *Rock Rimmon. Rose Room* and *What Can I Say After I Say I'm Sorry* are minor classics; here the instrumentation is reduced to clarinet, piano and drums only. The CD contains four previously unissued tracks (including a superb quintet version of *Slipped Disc*), and the music is programmed in chronological order of recording. Capitol's high standard of recording and CD transfer makes this a most attractive issue. **AM**

Mick Goodrick

1945

Biorhythms **Goodrick** (elg); **Harvie Swartz** (b, elb); **Gary Chaffee** (d). CMP Ⓕ CD 46 (54 minutes). Recorded 1990.

⑥ ❽

Mick Goodrick is hardly a jazz household name, having been anchored in Boston by a teaching gig for some two decades, but any of the post-1970 crop of guitar heroes associated with Berklee School—Abercrombie, Scofield, Frisell, Stern, Metheny and the like—will vouch for his skill and influence. Goodrick's music straddles several worlds, from the monochrome asceticism heard on **In Pas(s)ing** (a recently reissued 1978 set for ECM) to the more visceral, funkier style heard in his later recordings with Jack DeJohnette's Special Edition and Gary Thomas's Seventh Quadrant.

All shades of his wide-ranging style are represented here, from the chorale-like chord solo which opens the set through the sometimes awkward funk of *Thramps* (Swartz does not sound too happy with the electric bass) to the nineties bop of *H.D.&L.* and the atonal, pointillist textures of the aptly titled *Something Like That Kind Of Thing.* Occasionally Goodrick's guitar sounds shrill, his phrasing a mite effortful, but the set's rough edges lend it a certain charm and it remains the most comprehensive statement yet from a father figure of what may be recognized as the seventies school of Boston guitar players. **MG**

The Goofus Five

1926-1927 **Chelsea Quealey** (t); **Abe Lincoln, Al Philburn** (tb); **Bobby Davis** (cl, ss, as); **Sam Ruby** (ts); **Adrian Rollini** (bsx, gfs); **Irving Brodsky, Jack Russin** (p); **Tommy Feline** (bj); **Herb Weil** (d); **Ernest Hare, Les Reis, Ted Wallace, Beth Challis** (v). Timeless Historical Ⓜ CBC 1-017 (73 minutes). Recorded 1926/7.

⑥ ❼

Needless to say, The Goofus Five rarely played as a quintet, and invariably recorded with between seven and eight pieces. As a small group within the larger dance-band, the California Ramblers, they were a disciplined, driving good-time unit with an unusually propulsive rhythm section given a good deal of its life by the extraordinary Adrian Rollini, who was soon to carve an indelible niche on a series of classic recordings with Bix Beiderbecke. Rollini aside, the jazz content is relatively light. In Quealey the group had a good trumpet lead with a full tone and the ability -probably learned from Beiderbecke- to carry a melody gracefully. That said, his improvisation is pretty basic, although it is still a few steps ahead of either Lincoln or Davis, who sound hesitant every time they move away from the simplest paraphrase of the melody.

The Goofus Five, for all their limitations, are a very enjoyable unit, and while all the vocalists without exception have little to offer the listener, the instrumental side of things will bring a smile to your face and get you tapping your foot. **KS**

Dexter Gordon

1923-1990

On Dial: The Complete Sessions **Gordon, Wardell Gray, Teddy Edwards** (ts); with a collective personnel of: **Melba Liston** (tb, arr); **Charlie Fox, Jimmy Bunn, Jimmy Rowles** (p); **Red Callender** (b); **Chuck Thompson, Roy Porter** (d). Spotlite Ⓜ SPJCD 130 (63 minutes). Recorded 1947.

⑧ ❻

When these titles were recorded Gordon was *the* tenorman-in-residence at Los Angeles's Central Avenue jazz establishments. He was already dubbed 'Vice-Pres' and was having a considerable influence on all local saxists, including the young Art Pepper. Producer Ross Russell placed on record the two-tenor 'battle' *The Chase* which was a nightly show-stopper at the Bird-In-The-Basket restaurant when Gordon and the brilliant Wardell Gray locked horns. A week prior to the *Chase* record date Russell formed a quintet around Dexter using a trombonist from Gerald Wilson's big band in the dual role of arranger and soloist; even at this early stage in her career Melba Liston gives a very clear indication of her talent. Later quartet sessions for Dial produced some gorgeous ballads, including a fine *Talk Of The Town*. On the last Gordon date before the recording ban came into force at the end of December 1947, Ross Russell tried to recreate the initial excitement of *The Chase* but this time with Dexter and Teddy Edwards but some of the magic had evaporated and *The Duel* lacks the impact of the earlier battle; the session comes to a close with *Blues In Teddy's Flat* played by just Edwards and the rhythm section. Gordon was hardly an under-recorded soloist but these Dial tracks have a special place in his discography, freezing in time a most important and exciting period of post-war jazz development. This CD contains all surviving alternative takes and benefits from excellent programme notes contained in a separate booklet. **AM**

Dexter Blows Hot and Cool **Gordon** (ts); **Jimmy Robinson** (t); **Carl Perkins** (p); **Leroy Vinnegar** (b); **Chuck Thompson** (d). Boplicity Ⓜ CDBOP 006 (39 minutes). Recorded 1955.

⑥ ❻

Californian Gordon made his first mark on the music in the mid-forties, being one of the first second-wave boppers to create a distinct personality on the tenor (as opposed to the alto) saxophone. His big tone and fluent rhythm marked him out from the freneticism of much of the playing going on around him, and his slow-burning style would have been a natural for the 'cool' jazz movement of the fifties. By then, however, he had hit big personal setbacks, many of them associated with drugs, and much of the fifties were wasted. This date, for the tiny Dootone label, was an island in a sea of problems, and is also notable for featuring the much-revered and little-recorded Carl Perkins on piano.

Listening to this music today, the similarity to Lester Young in terms of note choice, ballad interpretation and rhythmic placement is more noticeable than it perhaps was at the time. Both *Cry Me A River* and *Don't Worry About Me* are cast in a completely Lesterian mould. Elsewhere, at brighter tempos, Dexter's style becomes more composite, his individuality more secure. Perkins contributes some bright solos and some very heavy comping. **KS**

Go! **Dexter Gordon** (ts); **Sonny Clark** (p); **Butch Warren** (b); **Billy Higgins** (d). Blue Note Ⓜ CDP7 46094-2 (38 minutes). Recorded 1962.

⑧ ❽

Dexter Gordon sounds exactly like what he was; a big, confident, forceful man. There was little subtlety in his playing, but prodigious swing, ingenuity, joie de vivre and an engagingly obvious sense of humour. This is one of the glories of jazz, the fact that it is a medium which so directly expresses the personality. In Dexter's case this took the form of a curiously deliberate articulation, each phrase delivered with a delighted thump, only just in time. The humour found expression in a succession of unlikely quotations, fitted with devilish cunning into whatever tune happened to be receiving attention at the moment. In this set, for instance, you will find bursts of *Mona Lisa*, *My Heart Stood Still*, *The Mexican Hat Dance*, *Five O'Clock Whistle* and *Three Blind Mice*.

Go! comes from Dexter's very best period, the early sixties. It is entirely typical and a delight from beginning to end. The rhythm section is particularly good, Sonny Clark being one of the sharpest-eared pianists in the business. On more than one occasion he picks up the melodic thread at the end of Dexter's solo and keeps it spinning intact—a rare feat. The sound is exceptionally good, as is usual with Blue Note at this time. **DG**

Billie's Bounce **Gordon** (ts); **Tete Montoliu** (p); **Niels-Henning Ørsted Pedersen** (b). SteepleChase Ⓕ SCCD 36028 (51 minutes). Recorded 1964.

⑧ ❼

A visit to Europe in 1962 was so successful that Gordon decided to stay. He remained for 15 years and the Jazzhus Montmartre in Copenhagen became something of a home to him. A series of live recordings with his European rhythm section were made by SteepleChase and they prove that the pioneer of bop tenor was still playing very well. As this CD shows, his big tone complements his unforced lyricism and his swaggering, confident delivery takes control of up-tempo items like *Billie's Bounce*. His approach to ballads varies. Titles such as *Satin Doll* are met head-on, their natural cadence largely ignored and Gordon's aggression giving them Bird-like stridency. The gentle balladeer appears more rarely but, even when he does, there is no suggestion of sentimentality. Either way, all are decked out with his famous and ubiquitous quotes, propelled with the ease of an orator so that only rarely do they become an irritant. This release, with Montoliu at the heart of a good support team, is one of the best in a good series. Perhaps inevitably the full set duplicates some titles, although Gordon manages to have something different to say in each version. His occasional returns to 'home' in the sixties were hailed as mini-triumphs, but here Gordon plays unselfconsciously to a live audience in his then home town. **BMcR**

Honi Gordon

1936

Honi Gordon Sings **Gordon** (v); **Ken McIntyre** (f, as); **Jaki Byard** (p); **Wally Richardson** (g); **George Duvivier** (b); **Ed Shaughnessy** (d). Prestige Ⓜ OJCCD 1783-2 (34 minutes). Recorded 1962.

⑤ ❺

Honi Gordon's recording career has not been extensive. She recorded with the family vocal group (the Gordons) for Mingus's Debut label in 1953 and continued to record from time to time for Mingus over the next decade and a half. Her father George Gordon directed his family singers and was a poet of sorts. His aim was to merge poetry and melodic line into compositions that stimulated spontaneous improvisation. His most convoluted piece on this album is *My Kokomo*; a relative of the poetry-meets-jazz vocalese of Lambert, Hendricks and Ross.

The nine tracks on offer here are Honi's only album under her own name, but it is a tribute to her vocal skills that she has a stellar backing group, with Byard and Richardson outstanding. Her voice is accurate but veers towards blandness, not helped by a narrow, lowish range. Even so, in a low-key way she navigates the twists and turns of her father's tortuous compositions, and her singing lingers in the mind like melancholy mist. At this distance in time she sounds most accomplished on the standards *Ill Wind* and *Why Try To Change Me Now?* (the latter with brilliant Byard moments). George Gordon's work sounds too contrived for comfort. **AS**

Joe Gordon

1928–1963

West Coast Days **Gordon** (t); **Richie Kamuca** (ts); **Russ Freeman** (p); **Monty Budwig** (b); **Shelly Manne** (d). Fresh Sounds Ⓕ FSCD 1030 (57 minutes). Recorded 1960.

⑥ ❹

Gordon was a player who made a nonsense of the East and West divide in American jazz by being prominent in both arenas. He worked in his native city of Boston with Sabby Lewis and Georgie Auld and gigged alongside visitors such as Charlie Parker, Lionel Hampton, Art Blakey and Don Redman. He was in Dizzy Gillespie's big band for the 1956 tour of the Middle East and in 1958 he moved to California. There he teamed up with Harold Land, Dexter Gordon and Barney Kessel before becoming a permanent member of Shelly Manne's quintet. This CD suggests that his tidy articulation and lightly ringing tone was better suited to the reserved temper of the West Coast's brand of hard bop. His approach to *Summertime* is typical, with an improvisation that keeps well in the centre of the thematic safety net. An essential lyricism ensures his almost saxophone-like fluency and one senses that he is guarded against the dramatically angular phrase. The undulating contours of the *Poinciana* line surprisingly inspire a greater show of motive power but the Gordon on this live Lighthouse Club date is trading mainly in understatement. He certainly made better recordings but these are, as yet, unavailable on CD. The bonus here is two 1960 titles by a Richie Kamuca Quartet with Scott LaFaro. **BMcR**

Dusko Goykovich

1931

Soul Connection **Goykovich** (t, flh); **Jimmy Heath** (ts); **Tommy Flanagan** (p); **Eddie Gomez** (b); **Mickey Roker** (d). Enja Ⓕ ENJ-80442 (71 minutes). Recorded 1993.

⑧ ❽

Goykovich was born in what was then Yugoslavia and found his way across the Atlantic with Marshall Brown's International Youth Band after working for some years in Germany. He studied at Berklee College and subsequently worked with the orchestras of Maynard Ferguson, Woody Herman and Kenny Clarke-Francy Boland. He is, with Rolf Erison and the late Jimmy Deuchar, one of the three leading post-war European jazz trumpet soloists, and **Soul Connection** is certainly his best small group recording. Made in New York, it has a virtually unbeatable rhythm section and, on five of the nine tracks, a very on-form Jimmy Heath. Dusko received help and encouragement as a young player from Miles Davis and this album is dedicated to "Miles and his spirit". It is the spirit, rather than the letter, of Davis's teachings which is manifest here. All but *I'll Close My Eyes* are Goykovich originals and his *Ballad For Miles* is one of the most sensitive and moving of all the tributes to the trumpeter. The originals have a haunting Balkan feeling, beautifully interpreted by the full group. This is an excellent example of post-hard bop jazz by five quite outstanding musicians. The recording quality captures the music with clarity and sympathy, making this a highly recommended release.

AM

Teddy Grace

1905-1993

Teddy Grace Grace (v); **Bobby Hackett**, **Charlie Shavers**, **Max Kaminsky** (t); **Jack Teagarden**, **Sonny Lee**, **Brad Gowans** (tb); **Buster Bailey**, **Pee Wee Russell** (cl); **John Sandola**, **Bud Freeman** (ts); **Dave Barbour**, **Eddie Condon** (g); **Frankie Froeba**, **Billy Kyle**, **Dave Bowman** (p); **Haig Stephens**, **Delmar Kaplan**, **Pete Peterson** (b); **Al Sidell**, **O'Neil Spencer**, **Morey Feld** (d). Timeless Ⓜ CBC1-016 (62 minutes). Recorded 1937-40.

⑧ ❻

Teddy Grace was a well-connected Southern belle who, for a dare, stood up to sing with the band at a country club dance. Within a year she was a professional vocalist and a few years later made her recording début. That was 1937. For three years she recorded with the best (see above) and then stopped. The rest of her extraordinary story is told in the notes to this CD, so fascinating that they are one of the reasons for buying it. She had a sweet voice and an inborn sense of swing almost at the Peggy Lee level. But her real talent was for the blues. I can think of no white woman who sings the blues as easily or as authentically as Teddy Grace; in this regard she is the female equivalent to Jack Teagarden. They were both Southerners, and this leads to the reflection that geography, rather than race, could be the determining factor. Whatever the case, this collection rehabilitates an important lost voice.

DG

Robert Graettinger

1923-1957

City Of Glass **The Ebony Band / Gunther Schuller**. Channel Crossings Ⓕ CCS 6394 (64 minutes). Recorded 1993.

⑧ ❻

One of the phantoms of modern jazz, Bob Graettinger's brief career consisted of the dozen or so compositions and arrangements he scored for Stan Kenton's Progressive Jazz and Innovations In Modern Music orchestras. Few people—from the musicians themselves to most of the critics and certainly the majority of listeners—would admit to understanding or enjoying Graettinger's idiosyncratic music, full of sharp dissonance and abrupt, colliding rhythms. Kenton himself was a staunch supporter of Graettinger, however, and today, more than 40 years and several musical revolutions later, his vision now seems to be one of the most imaginative and prophetic of his time. *City Of Glass* was Graettinger's masterpiece, and Gunther Schuller offers us both the original composed in 1948 and the second expanded version, adding strings, from 1951. Influenced by Stravinsky, Bartók, Schoenberg and especially Varèse's blocks of sound and clashing textures, *City Of Glass* reflects Graettinger's view of an architecture of the future, seen from a cubist's multiple perspectives and through various stages of illumination—as well as the psychological problems man may have in existing there. The music is alien territory to most jazz fans, but *City Of Glass*, as well as Pete Rugolo's *Mirage* and *Conflict* and Franklyn Marks's *Trajectories* (also written for Kenton and performed here) are really examples of a new kind of chamber music in which classical ambitions and jazz devices coexist. Equally shocking are Graettinger's arrangements of *April In Paris*, devoid of sentimentality, and an enigmatic *Portrait of Laura*. The excitement in his *Incident In Jazz* and *Thermopylae* arises from the tension between episodes of swing and non-swing, bracing polyphony, unusual melodic contours and the almost antagonistic rhythms and harmonies. Although it may have seemed puzzling or chaotic at the time, this music now sounds distinctive and dramatic; Bob Graettinger and the others who shared his vision deserve to be re-examined in a new, more favourable light.

AL

Bob Graf

1927-1981

Bob Graf At Westminster **Bob Graf** (ts); **Ron Ruff** (ts, fl); **Jimmy Williams** (p); **Bob Maisel** (b); **Al St James** (d). Delmark Ⓕ DD 401 (41 minutes). Recorded 1958.

⑥ ❹

Bob Graf was an authentic Brother; that is to say he was a member of Woody Herman's Second Herd saxophone section in 1950-51. Before that he had preceded Wardell Gray in Count Basie's small band, although he did not record with it. His best-known solo with Herman is probably on Al Cohn's *Music To Dance To*, recorded in June 1950. He had a warm, round tone, similar to those of Allen Eager and Brew Moore, and ultimately derived, like the whole Brothers sound, from early Lester Young.

The reason for Graf's obscurity probably lies in his dislike of the road. After spending some time on the West Coast he returned to his home town of St Louis and remained there until his death. This live session was recorded with a local band at the city's Westminster College. The other front-line player, Ron Ruff, is a Brothers-inspired tenor who presents a somewhat paler version of the style. The real interest lies in Graf's solos, particularly his solo feature, *Street Of Dreams*, which displays his elegant turn of phrase to great effect. Both tenors are slightly off-mike, which does not help in conveying the mixture of smoothness and energy in Graf's tone and articulation, but otherwise the technical quality is satisfactory. **DG**

Jerry Granelli

1940

Another Place **Granelli** (d); **Julian Priester** (tb); **Jane Ira Bloom** (ss); **David Friedman** (vb, mba); **Anthony Cox** (b). VeraBra vBr Ⓕ 2130 2 (51 minutes). Recorded 1992.

⑧ ❽

San Franciscan drummer Granelli has been making fine music with others—including Vince Guaraldi, Ralph Towner and John Handy—for over 30 years. As it is, this is by no means Granelli's first album—there are two worthy attempts on the ITM label—and it demonstrates most forcefully that Granelli is of the Paul Motian school to the extent that he is offering much more than sheer physical and percussive presence to the music. Here, he supplies the concept and shapes this unusually resourceful band in a manner which continually offsets the soloists in the most provocative light. This enables each composition to be fully fleshed out and paced so that each performance is properly formed and balanced.

Additionally, it is a treat to have Julian Priester back on record. This man has been in the shadows for far too long, and here he is given a setting which perfectly suits his velvet tone and angular melodic conception. Both Bloom and Friedman also solo imaginatively, with Friedman adding a distinctive colour through his extensive use of the marimba. This is first-rate modern music, played with immense style and no little commitment, with improvisatory egos nicely in check. **KS**

Stephane Grappelli

1908

Grappelli Story **Grappelli** (vn, p); with the following collective personnel: **Bill Shakespeare**, **Stan Andrews** (t); **Dennis Moonan**, **Frank Weir** (reeds); **Charlie Pude**, **Frank Baron**, **George Shearing**, **York de Sousa**, **Maurice Vandair**, **Raymond Fol**, **Marc Hemmeler**, **Michel Legrand** (p); **Django Reinhardt**, **Roger Chaput**, **Eugene Vees**, **Jack Llewellyn**, **Chappie D'Amato**, **Syd Jacobson**, **Joe Deniz**, **Dave Wilkins**, **Alan Hodgkins**, **Rene Duchaussoir**, **Pierre Cavalli**, **Leo Petit**, **Diz Disley**, **Ike Isaacs**, **Philip Catherine**, **Larry Coryell** (g); **Harry Chapman** (h); **Arthur Young** (novachord); **Reg Conroy**, **Roy Marsh**, **Michel Hauser** (vb); **Louis Vola**, **George Senior**, **Hank Hobson**, **George Gibbs**, **Joe Nussbaum**, **Coleridge Goode**, **Benoit Quersin**, **Pierre Michelot**, **Guy Pedersen**, **Lennie Bush**, **Eberhard Weber**, **Lisla Eckinger**, **Andrew Simpkins**, **Nils-Henning Ørsted Pedersen** (b); **Eugene Pini**, **Stanley Andres** (vn); **Tony Spurgin**, **Al Philcock**, **Jock Jacobson**, **Dave Fullerton**, **Jean-Louis Viale**, **Jean-Baptiste 'Mac Kac' Reilles**, **Alan Levitt**, **Daniel Humair**, **John Spooner**, **Kenny Clare**, **Rusty Jones** (d); **Beryl Davis** (v). Verve Ⓜ 515 807 2 (two discs: 174 minutes). Recorded 1938-92.

⑧ ❻

A comprehensive survey of Grappelli's work, culled from sources available to PolyGram and commencing with some Quintet Of The Hot Club sides made for Decca during a visit to London in 1938. The conjunction of Grappelli and Reinhardt was unique; it is brought into sharp focus with two duets, *It Had To Be You* (on which Stephane doubles on piano and violin) and the intimate *Nocturne*. Guitars have always figured prominently on Grappelli's recording dates, but subsequent to the break between the two principals, the chugging sound of the string-laden QHCF has usually been replaced by the lighter effect of a more orthodox rhythm section. A brief revival of the Grappelli-Reinhardt partnership in 1946 (again in London for Decca) produced the lovely *Nuages*, but Stephane was already looking for new inspiration. His strong sense of melody and a hard, aggressive approach on the faster tempos is well demonstrated here. An indication of the violinist's awareness of jazz in the wider sense is evident in his choice of material which takes in Sonny Rollins's *Pent Up House* and John Lewis's *Django* from a fine 1962 session represented here. *Darling je vous aime beaucoup* is quite hilarious and has a deliberately funny vocal by Grappelli. In the seventies Steph did an LP with George Shearing (the two worked together frequently in the early forties), the source of two tracks

immediately preceding the 1979 *Sweet Chorus*, which sets the violinist in between youngsters Philip Catherine and Larry Coryell. Overall Grappelli's work is in a class of its own, albeit a little florid at times, but few other musicians have enjoyed such a long and distinguished career in jazz. A recommended issue with generous playing time.
AM

Milford Graves
1941

Percussion Ensemble **Graves** (d, perc); **Sunny Morgan** (d, perc). ESP-Disk Ⓜ 1015-2 (35 minutes). Recorded 1965.

⑧ ❼

An important second-generation free drummer, Graves worked with the New York Art Quartet, Albert Ayler, Don Pullen and the Jazz Composer's Orchestra in the sixties. More recently he has been involved in teaching, but this CD reissue shows him in the naked spotlight of the percussion duo. Fortunately, the sound separation is good and Graves comes at the listener from the right speaker. All of his trade-marks are here; his mobility around his entire kit and his expert use of the auxiliary percussion paraphernalia to flesh out the textures. There is obviously no orthodox thematic continuity, a fact emphasized by the absence of tune titles (well, they are all called *Nothing*), but both men pursue a policy of storytelling on the drums. Neither uses points of strict punctuation and it is instructive to hear how both create the feeling of abstract calibration that was to offer a state of free flow to horn players soloing above it. Although a lesser-known figure, the late Sunny Morgan comes over as a player of near-equal stature.
BMcR

Georg Gräwe
1956

Chamber Works 1990-92 **Gräwe** (p); **Horst Grabosch** (t); **Melvyn Poore** (tba); **Michael Moore** (cl, bcl); **Phil Wachsmann** (vn); **Ernst Reijseger** (vc); **Anne Le Baron** (harp); **Hans Schneider** (b); **Gerry Hemingway** (d); **Phil Minton** (v). Random Acoustics Ⓕ 003 (50 minutes). Recorded 1991/1992.

⑧ ❽

Georg Gräwe's music is difficult to categorize; in fact, the name of his self-produced record company, Random Acoustics, might be the best clue to how he views the problem himself. One of a younger generation of Europeans who are equally adept at improvisation and composition, Gräwe is working in an area where those two disciplines overlap, or blur. As an improvising pianist, he can be best heard in the Gräwe/Reijseger/Hemingway trio (they have recorded for hat Art, Music & Arts and other labels). But as a composer, he has written memorable pieces for the ten-piece GrubenKlangOrchestra, and contingents of smaller groups, as on **Chamber Works 1990-92**. Although many of Gräwe's compositional techniques are based in contemporary classical procedures, by using musicians well versed in free improvisation he obtains striking results from small details and intimate gestures. Both *15 Duets* and *Flavours A* here are good examples. On the former, the six musicians improvise in the various possible duo combinations, but their statements are kept so brief as to create a music of constantly changing colour, character and perspective. Likewise, *Flavours A* consists of violin, tuba and piano whispering aphorisms and minuscule variations of pitch and timbre. *Variations Q* is a reworking of a piece for the larger ensemble, performed by a livelier, more interactive quartet. Gräwe acknowledges the musicians's contributions of what he calls "extended interpretation" in bringing his music to life.
AL

Wardell Gray
1921-1955

Memorial Volumes 1 and 2 **Gray** (ts); **Clark Terry**, **Art Farmer** (t); **Sonny Criss**, **Frank Morgan** (as); **Dexter Gordon** (ts); **Teddy Charles** (vb); **Al Haig**, **Phil Hill**, **Jimmy Bunn**, **Hampton Hawes**, **Sonny Clark** (p); **Tommy Potter**, **John Richardson**, **Billy Hadnott**, **Harper Crosby**, **Dick Nivison** (b); **Roy Haynes**, **Art Mardigan**, **Chuck Thompson**, **Larry Marable** (d); **Robert Collier** (cga). Prestige Ⓜ OJCCD-050/51-2 (two discs, oas: 59 and 64 minutes). Recorded 1949-53.

⑧ ❻

In 1949 Gray recorded his most popular track (the blues *Twisted* which was later lyricized by Annie Ross) and must have seemed well on the way to becoming the most successful bop-tinged tenorman of the next decade. By comparison with Gene Ammons and Dexter Gordon, who had reinforced a basic Lester Young approach with the harder sound of Charlie Parker, Gray (like Sonny Stitt) softened the Parker style with reminiscences of Young. Sadly, Gray followed Stitt along the drug trail and spent the first half of the fifties under-employed on the West Coast until his untimely death.

For the CD edition, each volume (available separately) includes several additional takes originally available only on unofficial issues, the inferior sound being carried over where presumably the masters have been lost. But this is by far the best representation of Gray's slender discography. Vying with the *Twisted* session, a 1952 date with the young Art Farmer and Hampton Hawes has everyone on form, while a 19-minute jam with fellow Basie sideman Terry and friendly rival Dexter is energizing. The Milt Jackson-influenced Charles's sextet date has the first jazz recordings of latterly rehabilitated Frank Morgan, then just 19, but the best news throughout is Gray. **BP**

Bennie Green
1923-1977

Blows His Horn **Green** (tb); **Charlie Rouse** (ts); **Cliffe Smalls** (p); **Paul Chambers** (b); **Osie Johnson** (d); **Candido** (cga). Prestige Ⓜ OJCCD-1728-2 (40 minutes). Recorded 1955.

④ ❻

The advent of the LP may have given musicians a chance to stretch out, but it also led to a lot of not bad not good two-frontline-plus-rhythm blowing sessions. Fashionably there was also a conga player, who came in for the faster numbers and laid out on the ballads, unless they doubled the tempo on the ballad whereupon he would stub out his cigarette and leap into action. The advent of J.J. Johnson is also supposed to have liberated the trombone, but in hindsight Johnson's dry, gentlemanly tone led to a lot of slightly desiccated stylists like Bennie Green, and the trombonists who now shine out of the fifties are those who like Jimmy Knepper went their own way, not J.J.'s. This record never really gets anywhere, nor really tries; it is a museum piece, to be placed in a glass case marked "Mid-fifties modern jazz sophisticated horns 'n' rhythm session" and got out and dusted occasionally, so that we can marvel at what people found exciting in those days. **MK**

Benny Green
1963

That's Right **Green** (p); **Christian McBride** (b); **Carl Allen** (d). Blue Note Ⓕ CDP7 84467-2 (53 minutes). Recorded 1992.

⑧ ❽

Blue Note shepherded a line of good pianists which included Bud Powell, Thelonious Monk, Horace Silver and, on occasion, Bobby Timmons. There is no one in the younger generation who deserves to continue that line better than Green, despite the fact that there appear to be more good young pianists about than players of the other instruments. Perhaps it is because Green refers back more firmly to earlier days. It is no criticism to note that his work often reflects elements from Powell, Timmons, Gerald Wiggins and Erroll Garner. The trio, beautifully recorded in this studio session, is a mighty one indeed, with the formidable McBride capable of completely suborning himself to the needs of the piano. When he shares the limelight one is forcefully reminded of some of the duets between Duke Ellington and Jimmy Blanton, and this is appropriate for McBride is obviously one of the major bassists of to-day and of a similar stature to Blanton. *That's Right,* with its muscular single-note lines and explosive chords, harks back to Timmons with Blakey and both this and McBride's rugged blues in 3/4, *Hoagie Meat,* have prodigious bass solos to complement the stalwart piano. This is not Green's latest album, but it remains equal to anything released under his name. **SV**

Bunky Green

Healing The Pain **Green** (ss, as); **Billy Childs** (p); **Art Davis** (b); **Ralph Penland** (d). Delos Ⓕ DE 4020 (66 minutes). Recorded 1989.

⑧ ❽

Delos is an American company more usually asociated with classical music recordings than jazz, but we can all be grateful that they crossed the great divide and made this one. Green is not exactly a household name, although he has been making records since the sixties at least, most notably for the old Chess/Argo/Cadet group based in Chicago. He went through a stage of playing quite funky music which won him few friends among jazz pundits, but he has always been an intelligent and articulate man who could express with absolute clarity exactly what he was trying to achieve on any given piece of music. This album carries a dedication to his parents, both of whom died shortly before the sessions for it were held, and the choice of tracks is certainly dominated by that dedication, whether it is *The Thrill is Gone*, *I Concentrate on You* or *Goodbye*. Tempos are for the most part slow, and a mood of longing and despairing love hangs over Green's playing. The album is very moving, and Green plays with terrific intensity of a type more normally associated with latter-day Art Pepper. Although he plays both soprano and alto, he favours the latter. He long ago carved a highly individual style on both instruments, and is capable of both the simplest and most complex of improvisational approaches. A fine album. **KS**

Grant Green
1931-1979

Idle Moments **Green** (g); **Joe Henderson** (ts); **Bobby Hutcherson** (vb); **Duke Pearson** (p); **Bob Cranshaw** (b); **Al Harewood** (d). Blue Note Ⓜ CDP7 84154-2 (64 minutes). Recorded 1963.

Grant Green made many fine albums for Blue Note (many of which are currently on CD), but this is the best. It has a certain indefinable, but quite tangible, atmosphere to it, something which existed just for the hours these musicians assembled for this project. The title-track, which opens the album, properly sets the mood: it is a very slow blues-based line written by pianist Duke Pearson, and one with intriguingly altered changes which suggest other things to the soloist and, ultimately, the listener. If anyone wanted to define music for the small hours, then this is it. Each soloist plays in the most relaxed, soulful manner, completely free from artifice or grandstanding, each digging a little further into the mood. It is 15 minutes long, but not for a second does it drag, so perfectly is it judged.

The rest of the date keeps up the standard, with an energetic, forward-reaching feel to *Jean de Fleur*, an enigmatic and tautly elegiac atmosphere to one of the most successful readings of John Lewis's *Django* outside the original, and a distinctly hard-boppish edge to the medium-tempo *Nomad*. In all, a remarkably unified session, with fresh, unhackneyed improvising and a special group 'feel' to the whole proceedings. There really must have been something in the air that night. The record has been marked a half-star short due to the inclusion of 20 minutes' worth of alternative takes which disrupt the flow of the original album, and really should have been added at the end of the CD programme.

KS

Sonny Greenwich

1936

Live at Sweet Basil **Greenwich** (g); **Fred Henke** (p); **Ron Seguin** (b); **Andre White** (d). Justin Time Ⓕ JUST 26-2 (60 minutes). Recorded 1987.

⑧ ❽

Jazz guitarists are a dime a dozen these days, and Coltrane-influenced saxophonists come even cheaper. But Greenwich, a reclusive Canadian who performed briefly with John Handy and Wayne Shorter in the sixties, and who seems to pop up every ten years or so, just when you have abandoned hope of ever hearing him again, is worth his weight in gold as a Coltrane-influenced guitarist. He is also one of very few jazz musicians to have realized the harmonic potential of Stephen Sondheim's music—witness his spiralling interpretat rane-like you can imagine the rise and fall of his breath. *You Go To My Head*, this live set's ballad, is not nearly as mesmerizing, but the faster numbers are satisfying emotional workouts, and you would be able to tell that *Libra Ascending*—perhaps the most effervescent of them—was dedicated to Coltrane even without reading Greenwich's brief sleeve note. Occuping a niche just to the left of Grant Green and just to the right of Sonny Sharrock, Greenwich is an elusive figure who always leaves you wanting to hear more.

FD

Al Grey

1923

Al Meets Bjarne **Grey** (tb); **Bjarne Nerem** (ts); **Norman Simmons** (p); **Paul West** (b); **Gerryck King** (d). Gemini Ⓕ GMCD 62 (60 minutes). Recorded 1988.

⑧ ❽

Grey's considerable playing experience takes in employment with the big bands of Lucky Millinder, Benny Carter, Lionel Hampton, Dizzy Gillespie and Count Basie as well as numerous tours with JATP. As a group leader he favours the trombone-tenor front-line and has worked with partners such as Jimmy Forrest and Buddy Tate, but few have bettered this one-off session with Norway's outstanding mainstreamer, the late Bjarne Nerem. Backed by the rhythm section then working with singer Joe Williams (which also supported Harold Ashby on his Gemini date—see above) the two men create fine music in a variety of moods and tempos. Nerem gets close to the spirit of Lester Young in places and produces a superlative version of *Blue and Sentimental*. Grey makes adroit use of mutes, especially the rubber plunger, but his brazen open sound gets close to the tone we associate with Bill Harris. The title tune is a beautifully relaxed blues and the sound of the quintet has been well captured in this session held in Oslo's Rainbow studio.

AM

Carola Grey

1969

The Age of Illusions **Grey** (d); **Ralph Alessi** (t, f); **Peter Epstein**, **Ravi Coltrane** (ss, ts); **Mike Stern** (g); **Carlton Holmes** (p, kbds); **Cliff Corman**, **Dario Eskenazi** (p); **Ed Schuller**, **Calvin Jones**, **Gene Perez** (b); **Jeff Andrews**, **Gregg Jones** (b); **Café**, **Bobby Sanabria** (perc). Jazzline Ⓕ JL 11139-2 (47 minutes). Recorded 1994.

⑧ ❽

Carola Grey, a 25-year-old German now resident in New York, is an exemplar for her sex. It is an admirable and remarkable achievement for a woman to master and rise to prominence in such a traditionally male environment, and as her stylish and authoritative drumming shows, she has done it on the strength of sheer talent and drive.

Although the music makes no great stylistic departures, there is never a routine or automatic moment in an attractively varied programme which ranges from furious hard bop to jazz ballads to jazz-rock. This freshness derives in large part from the superb soloists with which Grey has surrounded herself, outstanding among them Epstein (especially in casually brilliant Coltrane mode on the opening blues tribute to Philly Joe Jones) and Alessi, who also wrote the storming *All The Things* paraphrase *Aldo Thin Suar*. Coltrane Jr proves a match for the latter and is poignant on the ballad *Colour*. Grey, needless to say, matches her band move for move and more. **MG**

Della Griffin

Travellin' Light **Griffin** (v); **Houston Person** (ts); **Randy Johnson** (g); **Stan Hope** (p); **Cameron Brown** (b); **Michael Carvin** (d). Muse Ⓕ MCD 5496 (49 minutes). Recorded 1992.

⑥ ❻

For many years Della Griffin played drums and sang in her own band at various Harlem clubs, keeping a career going during the twilight years for jazz in the seventies and eighties. She was something of a local legend but not known beyond her home patch. A traffic accident ended her percussion playing and she relaunched her career as a singer, aiming at a wider audience than her quarter of Manhattan. Her début album is produced, with great taste, by Person, whose 20 years with Etta Jones have taught him how to back a singer, and it is his contributions in particular that make this more than an ordinary album. He builds up a rapport with Griffin that is a model of how to accompany a singer without stealing the limelight, yet to play so ravishingly in what Buck Clayton called the 'windows' as to command attention. Griffin's voice has echoes of Billie Holiday's style and phrasing, although it is fanciful to suggest she sounds as Billie might have, had she lived another few decades, despite a 'lived-in' tone, and the sense of worldly experience with which she delivers her lyrics. Hope is outstanding in a strong rhythm section, and this is a commendable first album. **AS**

Dick Griffin

A Dream For Rahsaan & More **Griffin** (tb) with **Gary Bartz** (as); **Stanley Cowell** (p); **Cecil McBee** (b); **Idris Muhammed**, **Billy Hart** (d); **Don Smith** (f, p); **Clifford Jordan**, **Bill Saxton** (ts); **Hubert Eves** (p); **Calvin Hill** (b); **Freddie Waits** (d); **Lawrence Killian** (perc). Konnex Ⓕ KCD 5062 (65 minutes). Recorded 1979/1985.

⑤ ❺

Griffin has primarily been associated with Rahsaan Roland Kirk, having been one of the longest-serving members of his band. Hence the dedication, and although the energy level here is not in the same power station, the approach and style is roughly equivalent, with simple, singable melodies given a rough and ready treatment and used as vamps for improvisation. The only problem is, multiphonics notwithstanding, Griffin is not a particularly gripping improviser, and his solos seldom have much sense of form or forward momentum. Bartz sticks pretty much to a supporting role, and the most impressive soloist is, predictably, Cowell, even though his piano is recorded so harshly as to be offputting.

The second set, although recorded six years previously, has a marginally better sound, and Griffin's writing is better showcased with the larger ensemble. The piano on this one is out of tune, which is a shame, as the pianist is interesting. The writing is rather dull, often sounding like a backdrop for an absent lead line or soloist. Pharoah Sanders would have known what to do with it. Or Rahsaan. **KS**

Johnny Griffin

1928

The Congregation **Griffin** (ts); **Sonny Clark** (p); **Paul Chambers** (b); **Kenny Dennis** (d). Blue Note Ⓜ CDP7 89383-2 (37 minutes). Recorded 1957.

⑧ ❼

Griffin is still active, both 'live' and in the recording studio, and continues to produce good and varied albums, but the ones which made his reputation are those he recorded as a sideman with both the Blakey and Monk groups and a string of burning dates for Blue Note in the late fifties, the most famous of which, **A Blowing Session** (featuring both Coltrane and Mobley), is currently unavailable on CD. So **The Congregation**, from the same year as the triple-tenor album, will have to serve as substitute. And no mean substitute it is, with Sonny Clark (at that time more or less permanently nailed to Van Gelder's piano stool when it came to Blue Note sessions) at the keyboard and Paul Chambers providing pulsation. Griffin, one of the great speed merchants (he and Lockjaw Davis ran a terrifying twin-tenors band for a few years), surprisingly opts for medium swingers on five of the six tunes here, but his busy, bustling style and unburnished tone retains sufficient bite and content to keep the listener happy and involved. Besides, the medium tempos give Griffin the perfect excuse to double-up at will.

To say this is typical late fifties Blue Note fare is not to denigrate it, but give it a proper perspective. If you like hard bop, then this is a safe bet. This CD reissue is the album's first appearance in true stereo, and there is a seven-minute bonus track, *I Remember You*. Which makes the original LP playing-time desperate. **KS**

Henry Grimes

1935

The Call **Grimes** (b); **Perry Robinson** (cl); **Tom Price** (d). ESP-Disk 1026-2 (34 minutes). Recorded 1965.

✓ ⑧ ❼

A Juilliard student, Grimes's early musical grounding was in r&b bands. He later worked with Anita O'Day, Gerry Mulligan and Sonny Rollins before getting involved with sixties avant-garde. This CD comes from that period and portrays Grimes as an outstanding talent. *For Django* is evidence of his writing talent but, whether racing out behind the clarinet line or soloing with strength and genuine harmonic originality, it is his highly original bass playing that stands out. Both arco and pizzicato work excel and in the former role he deploys notes, bent in the manner of a horn, avoiding the string player's normal slurs and achieving the changing density associated with the saxophone. Robinson is at times rhythmically predictable but he was an important figure in changing the vernacular of his instrument, producing a new sound in the process. On *For Django* and *The Call*, in particular, he shows his talent for taking fragments of the theme and working them in theoretical circles, from germ ideas and free development, back to the original. While he is doing this, Grimes and Robinson provide a rhythmic contradiction, yet they do achieve a form of integration in the process. Grimes was amongst the first of the free bassists to demand this front line status. **BMcR**

Tiny Grimes

1916-1989

Tiny In Swingville **Grimes** (g); **Jerome Richardson** (f, ts, bs); **Ray Bryant** (p); **Wendell Marshall** (b); **Arthur Taylor** (d). Prestige Swingville Ⓜ OJCCD 1796-2 (40 minutes). Recorded 1959.

⑦ ❽

A one-time drummer, pianist and dancer, Grimes became one of the pioneers of the amplified guitar. He adopted the instrument in the late thirties and by 1943 had reached a level of technical proficiency sufficient to persuade Art Tatum to include him in the pianist's first trio. He recorded *Tiny's Tempo* with Charlie Parker in 1944 and graced the rock & roll world with his Rockin' Highlanders in the early fifties. His métier, however, was small, blues-based bands with their roots in the swing era. This CD, from the period of the mainstream revival, documents this fact and finds him with similarly inclined musicians. No attempt is made to emulate the facility demonstrated with Tatum or Parker; this is the blues. There is the turbulent, down home tradition on *Homesick* and *Down With It*, while everybody's really jumpin' on *Durn Tootin'*. Grimes solos well in either guise, building his lines with a care born of past experience and communicating a real blues feeling at all tempos. Richardson's bluesy flute, booting tenor and authoritative baritone are added value, but it is the superb rolling piano from Bryant and the excellent rhythm section that give most inspiration. The superficial listener could find this 'ordinary' but the jazz heard here is by five men doing what they know best and doing it extremely well. **BMcR**

Don Grolnick

Nighttown **Don Grolnick** (p); **Randy Brecker** (t); **Joe Lovano** (ts); **Marty Ehrlich** (bcl); **Steve Turré** (tb); **Dave Holland** (b); **Bill Stewart** (d). Blue Note Ⓕ CDP7 98689-2 (57 minutes). Recorded 1991.

⑧ ❽

Pianist-composer Don Grolnick, though perhaps best known for his provocative fusionistic writing and playing with the Brecker Brothers Band of the mid-seventies, is also a no-nonsense modernist whose acoustic piano attack borrows from the spartan solo style of Bill Evans as well as the thumping chordal accompaniments of McCoy Tyner. Here, in an astringent post-bop date, Grolnick has penned a gallery of compelling soundscapes. There is *Heart of Darkness*, where Lovano's steely tenor walks the pianist's mean streets with a noirish swagger worthy of the hard-boiled Humphrey Bogart, and *Genie*, a magic carpet ride through swirling, mysterious atmospheres 'shot' in the aural equivalent of stutter-frame, cyber-space, quasi-slow-motion.

There is also a standard, Cole Porter's *What Is This Thing Called Love?*, a dynamic dream-trek veering between a Latinized matinée stroll across Roseland's dance floor and a desperate marathon chase down Broadway in the wee small hours of the morning.

Throughout, there are powerful ensemble and solo contributions by Randy Brecker's smouldering trumpet, Steve Turré's blaring trombone, as well as Lovano's haunting tenor. Grolnick's decision to add the reedy raspiness of Marty Ehrlich's bass clarinet is another master-stroke. Cementing it all are the supple and ESP-like rhythmatics of bassist Dave Holland, drummer Bill Stewart and Grolnick—superb! **CB**

Steve Grossman

1951

Standards **Grossman** (ts); **Fred Hanks** (p); **Walter Booker** (b); **Masahiro Yoshido** (d). DIW Ⓕ DIW-908 (57 minutes). Recorded 1985.

⑦ ❽

Grossman's period in the Miles Davis's band in 1970 is his most-quoted biographical fact. He also worked with Lonnie Liston Smith and Elvin Jones, but was certainly one of the first formerly orthodox saxophonists to be classified as a jazz/rock fusionist. The eighties saw him record many scratch sessions, with him playing powerfully but with too little preparation before reaching the studio. The fault applies rather less with **Standards** and little is also heard here of Grossman the fusionist. This is the Rollins-inspired hard bop tenor saxophonist, demonstrating a considerable mastery of his horn and a sense of timing that pays scant attention to normal bar division. He does however show several faces. *When I Fall In Love* has him luxuriating back to the Ben Websterish world of the sixties; the theme is reshaped, paraphrased and adjusted rather than developed. *Autumn Leaves* and *Mr Sandman*, in contrast, are explored in an oblique manner with Grossman building away from the theme and using each motif as a stepping-stone to the next, rather than as an immediate route back to the harmonic base. The rhythm section is faithfully guided by Booker's bass and the light-fingered logic of Henke, but as a team it is functional rather than inspired, and seems to ignore Grossman's more extravagent excursions in the rhythmic void. **BMcR**

George Gruntz

1932

Blues 'n' Dues Et Cetera: The New York Sessions **George Gruntz** (p, ldr); **Marvin Stamm, Bob Millikan, Randy Brecker, Michael Mossman, Jon Faddis, John D'earth, Wallace Roney, Ray Anderson, Art Baron, Dave Taylor, Dave Bargeron** (t); **John Clark, Jerry Peel** (flh); **Dave Bargeron, Jim Pugh** (euph); **Howard Johnson** (tba); **Chris Hunter, Bob Mintzer, Bob Malach, Jerry Bergonzi, David Mann, Alex Foster, Roger Rosenberg** (reeds); **John Scofield** (g); **Mike Richmond** (b); **Adam Nussbaum** (d). Enja Ⓕ 6072-2 (67 minutes). Recorded 1991.

⑧ ❿

Formed in 1972 with Gruntz as music director and chief writer/arranger, the George Gruntz Concert Jazz Band is an exuberant players' ensemble in which an annually shifting international cast of handpicked improvisers are given plenty of elbow-room for gritty, no-nonsense treks on the wild side. It is also a highly disciplined unit combining the best attributes of both Basie and Ellington along with the modernistic palette of Gil Evans. Indeed, Gruntz's ability to incorporate even 'rap'—as he does in *Rap for Nap* with trombonist/ jazz-rapper Ray Anderson—is reminiscent of Evans's capacity to creatively amalgamate the big band heritage and the latest of pop music trends with equal amounts of irony and appreciation.

Like Evans, Gruntz uses post-bop electric guitar to advantage on tracks like the mysterioso *Forest Cathedral*, featuring the wailing John Scofield. Gruntz's organization is also open to newcomers like trumpeter Wallace Roney, who is given prime time on *Datune*.

Throughout, the GGCB's experimentalism is balanced with its appreciation of tradition and its sense of joie de vivre. Indeed, the GGCB's capacity to surprise and tickle as well as to swing like mad is frequently astonishing. **CB**

Dave Grusin

1934

The Gershwin Connection **Dave Grusin** (kbds, ldr); **Sal Marquez** (t); **Eddie Daniels** (cl); **Eric Marienthal** (as); **Gary Burton** (vb); **George Gershwin, Chick Corea, Don Grusin** (kbds); **Lee Ritenour** (g); **John Patitucci** (b); **Dave Weckl, Sonny Emory** (d); **David Nadien** (concertmaster) **Ettore Strata** (cond). GRP Ⓕ GRD-2005 (60 minutes). Recorded 1991.

⑦ ❽

Pianist/composer Grusin is one of the key figures of the eighties West Coast fusion movement. He is a top TV and film composer with an Academy Award for Robert Redford's *The Milagro Beanfield War* (1988). He is also a successful producer whose GRP label, co-founded with partner Larry Rosen, was one of the recording industry's great eighties success stories although both men have subsequently departed the label.

Here, Grusin's affection for what Alec Wilder calls "The American Popular Song" is refracted through often poignant settings for Gershwin classics like *'S Wonderful* and *Our Love Is Here To Stay*. The stylistic range runs from a hauntingly modal *My Man's Gone Now*, with a quintet featuring Grusin's Tyneresque flurries, Marquez's crackling trumpet and Marienthal's plaintive alto, to a more fusionistic launch for *There's a Boat Dat's Leavin' Soon for New York*. Also appealing are buoyant readings of *Soon* with Daniels's eloquent clarinet, and *Fascinating Rhythm* with Burton's quicksilver vibes.

The tracks, like the bulk of GRP's commercially successful studio-massaged jazz, are highly choreographed. Yet Grusin's arrangements are attractive, and there is much spontaneity. For contrast, there are two solo piano tracks, one by Gershwin, a poignantly articulated *That Certain*

Feeling via piano roll; and, *Nice Work If You Can Get It* in which Grusin's acoustic ruminations bespeak a man who like Gershwin has had the good fortune to achieve his own fair piece of 'nice work'. **CB**

Gigi Gryce

1927-1983

Nica's Tempo Gryce (as); **Art Farmer** (t); **Jimmy Cleveland, Eddie Bert** (tb); **Gunther Schuller, Julius Watkins** (frh); **Bill Barber** (tba); **Danny Bank, Cecil Payne** (bs); **Horace Silver, Thelonious Monk** (p); **Oscar Pettiford, Percy Heath** (b); **Kenny Clarke, Art Blakey** (d); **Ernestine Anderson** (v). Denon/Savoy Ⓜ SV-0126 (43 minutes). Recorded 1955.

⑧ ❻

Gryce was one of the brightest and most original writers to emerge in the fifties, but he was also an extremely competent and original alto soloist, combining the language of Charlie Parker with a warmth of tone which was distinctive. This is a reissue of an LP made originally for the small Signal label before its purchase by Savoy. On six titles Gryce uses a nine-piece band which uses the precise instrumentation of the epoch-making Miles Davis **Birth of the Cool** band and even employs three of the men who appeared on the Davis dates, viz. Bill Barber, Gunther Schuller and Kenny Clarke. The richly satisfying sound of the ensemble (capable of spanning three-and-a-half octaves) is compelling, particularly on Gryce's tunes *Speculation* and *Smoke Signal*. There are interesting lines written for all the players, including the tuba. Ernestine Anderson sings capably on two tracks, but her presence adds little to the overall value simply because Gryce has such a fine band of soloists and so many interesting ideas of his own. The final four tracks are by a Gryce-led quartet which includes Monk on piano, a unit which plays three lesser-known Monk tunes, *Shuffle Boil*, *Brake's Sake* and *Gallop's Gallop* as well as Gryce's own *Nica's Tempo*. It is unusual to hear Thelonious playing a tune by another jazz musician, and this intriguing session is often overlooked in assessments of the pianist's work. **AM**

Vince Guaraldi

1928-1976

Jazz Impressions of Black Orpheus Guaraldi (p); **Monty Budwig** (b); **Colin Bailey** (d) Fantasy Ⓜ OJC CD 437-2 (39 minutes). Recorded 1961.

Guaraldi was never really given an even break by the critics of the time. While he himself would never have claimed to be a moving spirit of the music, or someone with a truly original, creative voice, he brought great taste and discernment to whatever he did, and the arrangements on this album of the music from the 1959 film, *Black Orpheus*, combine the lithe elegance of Brazilian music with the drive and dynamism of piano trio jazz. His style was rooted deep in the West Coast of the fifties (he didn't spend three years with Cal Tjader for nothing), but his instinct for melody set him apart and eventually led to him having a major hit single, which is included on this album. An example of his genuine empathy with Brazilian music, and his equally real sensitivity as a pianist, is his reading here of Jobim and Bonfa's beautiful *Manha de Carnaval*, recorded before the deluge of cover versions let loose by the Getz/Byrd labum of the following year. The second side of the original LP (the last four tracks here), by the way, has nothing to do with the film or Brazil. **KS**

Lars Gullin

1928-1976

Volume 1: With Chet Baker Gullin (bs); **Baker** (t); **Arne Domnerus** (as, cl); **Rolf Billberg, Bjarne Nerem** (ts); **Dick Twardzik, Gunnar Svensson, Rune Ofverman** (p); **George Reidel, Jimmy Bond** (b); **Egil Johansen, Peter Littman, Nils-Bertil Dahlander** (d); **Caterina Valente** (v) and others. Dragon Ⓕ DRCD 224 (74 minutes). Recorded 1955-56.

⑧ ❽

One of the most original of the European giants, Gullin was one of the most eloquent of all the baritone players. Unusually his playing was not obviously influenced by Harry Carney or Gerry Mulligan, and unlike them he didn't emphasize the barrel-chested quality of the instrument, preferring to play it with smooth flexibility as though it was a tenor. All of his work was of a high standard which has not dated and his playing seemed unimpaired by the narcotics which bedevilled so much of the rest of his life. This album serves as a fine collection of his inventive sounds, both as soloist and composer, and is also to be relished for the way in which it illustrates him at home in his natural habitat, playing with other world-class Swedes like Rolf Billberg and Arne Domnerus. Chet Baker and Dick Twardzik, on the European visit which was to take Tzwardik's life six days after his work here, slipped easily into Gullin's company, and both are at their most confidently creative on the under-rated Bob Zieffs *Brash*. They shine again on *I'll Remember April*, which contains the only flaw in the album, a listless scat vocal by the usually excellent Caterina Valente The reviewer has for some years pursued every available recording of Gullin's and has yet to be disappointed. Dragon are providing a welcome service in keeping so much of his work in their catalogue. **SV**

Trilok Gurtu
1951

Living Magic **Gurtu** (d, perc, v); **Jan Garbarek** (ss, ts); **Daniel Goyone** (kbds); **Nicolas Fiszman** (b, g); **Tunda Jegede** (kora, v); **Shanthi Rao** (veena); **Nana Vasconcelos** (perc). CMP Ⓕ CD 50 (43 minutes). Recorded 1990-91.

⑧ ❿

Gurtu came to prominence in the late seventies and early eighties in a succession of striking partnerships with jazz musicians, including Charlie Mariano, Barre Phillips, Nana Vasconcelos and Jan Garbarek. The latter two appear to good effect on this record.

Gurtu, born in Bombay and with a formidable course of instruction in classical Indian music behind him, has come to jazz through hearing records, and his own albums tend to veer one way or the other, with a solidly jazz-based content or music predominantly displaying Indian music characteristics. This is an album closer to jazz than to eastern music, and a heady mix it turns out to be. Gurtu's complete mastery of even the most remote time signature gives this music considerable rhythmic depth and complexity, suggests a logical musical role or area for each instrument to play within, and gives the soloist a remarkably rich tapestry of sound to glide over or dig into, as the whim (or the arrangement) takes them. Of the improvisors, only Garbarek need detain us for long, but when he takes centre stage, the album locks into top gear and really earns its grading.

KS

Bobby Hackett
1915-1976

Coast Concert/Jazz Ultimate **Bobby Hackett** (c); **Jack Teagarden**, **Abe Lincoln** (tb); **Matty Matlock** (cl); **Peanuts Hucko** (cl, ts); **Ernie Caceres** (cl, bs), **Dick Owens**, **Gene Schroeder** (p); **Billy Bauer** (g); **Jack Lesberg** (b); **Phil Stephens** (b, tba); **Nick Fatool**, **Buzzy Drootin** (d). Dormouse Ⓕ DMI CDX02 (67 minutes). Recorded 1955-57.

⑧ ❽

This coupling together by the late Brian Hainsworth of these two matchless albums celebrates the pairing of Hackett and Teagarden; surely (Armstrong-Teagarden excluded) the epitome of Dixieland jazz. Teagarden and Hackett were possessed of the finest brass tones in their fields, their jazz being characterized by its easy relaxation. The tumbling lyricism of Hackett graces every one of these tracks, and he finds himself in ideal company. In his later years Teagarden (who had strong feelings about melodic improvisation) fell back more and more on cliché but, apart from a standardized version of *Basin Street Blues*, here he was happily free of it. The two sessions overflow with good things, but it is the ballad features for the two leaders which stand out. These include *I Guess I'll Have To Change My Plans*, *New Orleans* and *It's Wonderful* (the latter not to be confused with Gershwin's *'S Wonderful*, also played here). On *I've Found A New Baby* Teagarden repeats his party trick of playing the slide of the trombone only, holding a glass over the hole where the bell should be. There is also accomplished baritone playing from Ernie Caceres, his warm clarinet elsewhere confirming that he was one of the best reed players. Other bit-players who impress are Hucko, Matlock and Lincoln, whilst the rhythm section of Schroeder, Bauer, Lesberg and Drootin is exemplary.

SV

Charlie Haden
1937

"Closeness" Duets Haden (b): **Ornette Coleman** (as); **Keith Jarrett** (p); **Alice Coltrane** (hp); Paul Motian (d). A&M Ⓜ CDA 0808 (39 minutes). Recorded 1976.

⑧ ❼

With the current absence of the first Liberation Music Orchestra from the CD format, this is the earliest example of Haden's work as a leader which is readily available to the public. As such it is both absorbing and instructive, because it becomes in one sense a guided musical tour of Haden's past, and in another sense a virtuosic display of the type Haden has no desire to include in one of his large-group recordings, where other concerns are paramount.

Thus you get a lot more of Haden the instinctual player here, trading felicities with his four partners, conjuring extraordinarily full musical landscapes behind their statements of his themes (this is especially true of the duet with Alice Coltrane, *For Turiya*), and indulging in energetic dialogue within the improvised sections. The most immediate quality to be appreciated on a Haden album is the depth and beauty of his rich, dark tone. It is instantly identifiable and inimitable. The second unique quality he possesses is an enormous authority in his playing. He rarely opts for complicated, helter-skelter lines in his own work, preferring the simplicity of the perfect choice of note. His authority resides in the fact that invariably he does make the perfect choice.

Each duet is utterly different in tone and content, and this is what Haden wished: each reflects the past work carried out with these artists, and in the case of the duet with Ornette, Haden's theme consciously imitates those wild, exciting Coleman tunes of the L.A. years. A disc for those with wonder in their souls.

KS

The Ballad of the Fallen **Haden** (b, ldr); **Don Cherry** (pt t); **Michael Mantler** (t); **Gary Valente** (tb); **Sharon Freeman** (frh); **Jack Jeffers** (tba); **Steve Slagle** (f, cl, ss, as); **Jim Pepper** (f, ss, ts); **Dewey Redman** (ts); **Carla Bley** (p, glockenspiel, arr); **Mick Goodrick** (g); **Paul Motian** (d, perc). ECM Ⓕ 1248 (811 546-2) (52 minutes). Recorded 1982.

⑧ ❾

If Spanish Civil War songs inspired Charlie Haden to record his first Liberation Music Orchestra album, it was the more immediate fact of US involvement in El Salvador that spurred him to re-form the orchestra a dozen years later and make a second album. **The Ballad of the Fallen** takes its title from a poem found on the body of a Salvadorean student murdered by the US-backed National Guard. When set to music it became a popular folk song; it is played here as an instrumental. The disc also includes resistance songs from Chile and Portugal, several more Spanish Republican tunes and three new pieces—Haden's *Silence* and *La Pasionaria* and Carla Bley's ominously-titled *Too Late*.

Bley plays as central a role here as she did on the first album. Her arrangements fashion a cohesive style for music that ranges from the desolation of *Too Late* (her duet with Haden) to the brass-led defiance of *The People United Will Never be Defeated*. It is a better-recorded set than Liberation Music Orchestra; the arrangements are smoother, the solos more focused. But its moods are sombre, lacking the raucous sixties optimism that gave the first album its extraordinary lift. Haden's bass remains a small flame of hope—tender, reflective, always melodic. **GL**

Bob Haggart

1914

Lawson/Haggart Jazz Band-Singin' the Blues **Haggart** (b); **Yank Lawson** (t); **George Masso** (tb); **Joe Muranyi** (cl, ss); **John Bunch** (p); **Bucky Puzzarelli** (g); **Jake Hanna** (d). Jazzology Ⓕ JCD 193 (69 minutes). Recorded 1990.

⑥ ❽

Bass player, composer, arranger and frequent poll winner, Haggart was a Bob Crosby Band original before moving to the world of radio and television. In 1968 he was, with Lawson, instrumental in the formation of the World's Greatest Jazz Band; a unit devoted to keeping the Crosby spirit alive. Despite the unfortunate name foisted upon it, the WGJB employed the likes of Billy Butterfield, Vic Dickenson, Bud Freeman, Bob Wilber and Ralph Sutton during its 13-year life. The band on this CD is its logical successor and features several musicians with WGJB experience. The choice of material does appear a trifle hackneyed but, with Lawson adroitly ignoring the Bix Beiderbecke connection on the title track, all the soloists de-Wallering *Blue Turning Grey* and the smooth trombone of Masso irradicating the earthy Kid Ory memory on *Muskrat Ramble* the Lawson/Haggarts put their own brand on everything. Haggart, with his full tone and supple rhythmic instructions, is at the heart of an ideal rhythm section and they are two guest appearances from the pleasing Barbara Lea. The 'Legendary Lawson/Haggart Jazz Band' is certainly a better and more descriptive label than the World's Greatest Jazz Band. **BMcR**

Jerry Hahn

1940

Time Changes **Hahn** (g); **David Liebman** (ss); **Phil Markowitz**, **Art Lande** (p); **Steve LaSpina** (b); **Jeff Hirschfield** (d). Enja Ⓕ ENJ-9007-2 (51 minutes) Recorded 1993.

⑥ ❽

Hahn made a terrific impact in the mid-sixties as a member of the John Handy group with Michael White on violin which became one of the decade's major jazz successes. He continued into the seventies with the Jerry Hahn Brotherhood but by mid-decade was back in his hometown of Wichita, Kansas, teaching at the University and writing about music. This is his first headlining album in over 20 years, and it finds his sound and conception largely intact, the continuity with his youth still discernible. He describes himself as "a jazz player who loves the blues", and a direct affinity with latter-day John Scofield is immediately apparent here, even though they may have arrived at similar conclusions from vastly different starting-points. There is plenty of space to compare, with the two pianists between them managing just five appearances over ten tracks (saxophonist Liebman is on just two). Frankly, Hahn is at his best just accompanied by bass and drums, where he has the most flexibility of support and can go whichever way he wants. His serpentine improvising lines and his elusive sound do not always sit with the immediate sonics and harmonic patterns of the piano, and on the bright-tempo *The Method*, pianist Markowitz quite simply cannot make the tempo. That problem aside, this is a useful return to the studio by Hahn, with the ballads perhaps impressing most. **KS**

Al Haig

1924-1982

Ornithology **Haig** (p): **Jamil Nasser** (b); **Frank Gant** (d). Progressive Ⓕ PCD 7024 (42 minutes). Recorded 1977.

Haig was one of the first (and best) of the young pianists who took to bebop in the mid-forties. He worked and recorded with, among others, Charlie Parker, Stan Getz and Wardell Gray, turning in beautifully crafted solos in which compression was the name of the game. After a period of time away from the limelight he came back in the seventies as a fully mature concert performer, and it is a source of regret that many of his finest albums for the Interplay and Spotlite labels have either not been transferred to the CD format or, in the case of the Interplays, are available only in Japan. This is a CD version of an LP titled **Reminiscing**, boosted by the addition of *Body And Soul* which is actually a feature for Nasser. Despite this, there is enough of Haig's wonderfully apt interpretations of classic bebop tunes such as *Shaw 'Nuff*, *Marmaduke* and *Blue Bird* to make this a memorable album. The delicacy of his work on Ellington's *Daydream* reminds us of another dimension and the only question mark hangs over the prominence given to Nasser in the instrumental balance. Haig came up with bass players such as Tommy Potter and Curley Russell, whose throbbing lines kept a respectful distance from the piano in terms of audio perspective. Nasser is a fine technician (Haig rated him very highly), but on a programme made up principally of bebop tunes the strong bass presence is sometimes anachronistic.

AM

Pat Halcox

1930

There's Yes! Yes! Yes! In Your Eyes Halcox (t); **Bruce Turner** (cl); **John Beacham** (tb); **Ray Smith** (p); **Jim Douglas** (g); **Vic Pitt** (b); **Geoff Downes** (d). Jazzology Ⓕ JCD-186 (42 minutes). Recorded 1989.

⑥ ❹

After 40 years with the Chris Barber band it is not surprising that Halcox is rarely considered as an individual soloist out of Barber's métier. Freed from the tyranny of a banjo-dominated rhythm section he shows himself to be a free-thinker with a melodic priority much like Buck Clayton's—this feeling is particularly evoked on *All By Myself* and *She's Funny That Way*.

The inclusion of Bruce Turner is a most welcome one, for both Halcox and Turner are long overdue for an album like this. Turner confines himself to clarinet capturing Barney Bigard's sound and values with inspired grace on his feature, *Black And Blue*. The acoustic guitar solos from Jim Douglas are trenchant and skilled. The material for this session at the Bull's Head in Barnes has been well chosen and ensures that the music throughout is always refreshing.

SV

Adelaide Hall

1904-1993

Hall of Memories: Recordings 1927-39 Hall (v); with a collective personnel of: **Bubber Miley**, **Louis Metcalf**, **Jabbo Smith**, **Pike Davis**, **Demas Dean**, **Charlie Teagarden**, **Manny Klein**, **Wardell Jones**, **Shelton Hemphill**, **Ed Anderson**, **Bill Coleman**, **Bobby Martin** (t); **Joe Nanton**, **Herb Flemming**, **George Washington**, **Henry Hicks**, **Billy Burns** (tb); **Henry Edwards** (tba); **Jimmy Dorsey** (cl); **Carmello Jejo**, **Albert Socarras**, **Gene Mikell** (cl, as); **Harry Carney** (cl, as, bs); **Rudy Jackson**, **Frank 'Big Boy' Goudie** (cl, ts); **Joe Garland** (cl, ts, bs); **Otto Hardwicke** (ss, as, bs); **Willie Lewis**, **George Johnson** (as); **Joe Hayman** (as, ts, bs); **Crawford Wethington** (as, bs); **Raymond Usera** (ts, vn); **Duke Ellington**, **George Rickson**, **Joe Turner**, **Francis Carter**, **Art Tatum**, **Edgar Hayes**, **Herman Chittison** (p); **Fats Waller**, **Fela Sowande** (org); **Larry Gomar** (vb); **Fred Guy**, **Benny James** (bj); **Dick McDonough**, **John Mitchell** (g); **Wellman Braud**, **Hayes Alvis**, **Louis Vola** (b); **Sonny Greer**, **Jesse Baltimore**, **O'Neill Spencer**, **Ted Fields** (d). Conifer Ⓜ CDHD 169 (54 minutes). Recorded 1927-39.

⑥ ❹

Adelaide Hall's career is a paradox. Many jazz musicians, singers and entertainers lost ground by coming to Europe in the twenties and thirties, whereas Adelaide (in common with very few others, Josephine Baker being one) used her European move to prolong and sustain a career that had already teamed her with some of the world's finest jazz musicians before she left the US. This disc is an excellent cross-section of her pre-war work, from her wordless vocals with Ellington's orchestra to her duos with Fats Waller at HMV's mighty Compton organ. Her delivery lacks the edge of Alberta Hunter, but she had the same vaudevillean ability to interpret a song. Her best work here is with the piano duet backing of Francis Carter and either Joe Turner or Art Tatum, where the uncluttered setting allows her lyrics to shine, but gives plenty of space for some first-rate piano stride. The transfers (by John R.T. Davies) make the most of the source material available, but not all the selection was as well recorded in the first place as the Victors of Ellington or Millinder, so the overall quality is a little uneven.

AS

Bob Hall

1942

Alone With The Blues Hall (p, v); **Tom McGuinness** (g, b); **Rob Townsend** (d); **Hilary Blythe**, **Linda Adams** (v). Lake Ⓕ CD44 (54 minutes). Recorded 1995.

⑥ ❽

Hall has established himself as one of Britain's leading boogie woogie pianists, and his encyclopaedic knowledge of the genre, coupled with his technical facility, means that he combines authentic performances of less well known works by the likes of Montana Taylor, Peter Johnson and Cripple Clarence Lofton with original compositions of his own. The core of this album is a set of unaccompanied piano solos, with Johnson's *Blues on the Downbeat* and Lofton's *Sixes and Sevens* standing out. Hall's blues singing is a shade lightweight, though pleasant enough, and the tracks of his own vocals and those with backing singers are peripheral to the main strengths of this disc. Solo, or backed up by McGuinness (whose steel guitar playing has a suitably plaintive ring) and Townsend, Hall has the right timing and feel in his playing to keep the spirit of boogie alive. His original compositions explore all the ingredients that make boogie a varied rather than a narrowly similar genre, from single-note bass patterns to walking basses and train-like chords, and suggest that Hall is a worthy companion to the boogie composers of yore whose works he brings back to life so vividly. **AS**

Jim Hall

1930

All Across the City **Hall** (g); **Gil Goldstein** (p, syn); **Steve La Spina** (b); **Terry Clarke** (d). Concord Ⓟ CCD-4384-2 (57 minutes). Recorded 1989.

⑧ ❾

Jim Hall is among the gurus of modern jazz guitar. Just ask John Abercrombie, John Scofield or Pat Metheny, and "Jim Hall" is always mentioned in the first-rank of crucial influences. A veteran whose collaborations with giants like tenor saxophonist Sonny Rollins and pianist Bill Evans are among the classics of recorded jazz, Hall possesses a warm, intimate sound, a uniquely sophisticated yet understated harmonic palette, and a rare gift for flowing lyric invention. He's also one of jazzdom's most effective accompanists.

In this 1989 outing, Hall evokes the boppish side of his melodism in a striking take on Monk's *Bemsha Swing*. But, significantly, there are new twists that indicate that Hall has been listening to his younger colleauges on the tumultuous New York scene. Gil Golstein's stop-start *R.E.M. State*, a dashingly novel composition in the mode of the late Gil Evans, balances through-composed and free episodes. Hall's own piece, the urban soundscape *All Across the City*, is an aural analogue to Seurat's masterful painting, *Sunday Afternoon On The Island of Grande Jatte*, while the guitarist's puckish *Drop Shot* bubbles with good cheer.

Hall's inclusion of Goldstein's adroitly deployed electronic (and acoustic) keyboards marks a turning point for the guitarist, although you can rest assured that there is nothing even remotely close to 'fusion' involved here. Also impressive are bassist La Spina and drummer Clarke, two *simpatico* and long-standing Hall colleagues. **CB**

Bengt Hallberg

1932

Yellow Blues **Hallberg** (p). Phontastic Ⓟ PHON-CD 7583 (60 minutes). Recorded 1987.

⑧ ❽

Sweden's Bengt Hallberg is one of the most gifted, technically accomplished and least prejudiced pianists jazz has produced. From his early recordings with American visitors such as Clifford Brown and Stan Getz, his work with fellow Swedes Lars Gullin and Arne Domnerus and his own solo and trio albums he has established a reputation as a musician of world class. **Yellow Blues** was recorded at the Royal Academy of Music in Stockholm (Hallberg is a member of the Academy) and 17 of the 18 tracks are adaptations of the music of the Värmeland province of Sweden (the other track is the title blues, written by Bengt). Varmeland is obviously rich in composers and native folk music; Hallberg's treatments of the pieces are so ingenious, so inventive and so beautifully played that this is a CD which deserves the largest of audiences. Bengt's use of accelerando and rallentando, his most expressive sense of touch and continuity of ideas sets him apart from many jazz pianists. He includes a version of *Ack Värmeland Du Skona* (better known in jazz circles as *Dear Old Stockholm*, the song he recorded with Stan Getz in 1951). Gert Palmcrantz's engineering has perfectly captured the full range of the piano. **AM**

Rich Halley

Umatilla Variations **Halley** (ts, guiro, bell); **Rob Blakeslee** (t); **Vinny Golia** (cl, bcl); **Troy Grugett** (b, perc); **Phil Sparks** (b); **William Thomas** (d, perc). 9 Winds Ⓟ NWCD 0163 (74 minutes). Recorded 1993.

⑤ ❽

Unlike the fifties American West Coast Scene, its nineties equivalent stretches from Seattle to Los Angeles and beyond. It also differs in style concentration; no longer centred on one set of ideals, it is now flourishing by virtue of its flexibility. 9 Winds is one of the main independent record companies to document contemporary happenings in Oregon and California and musicians such as Halley,

Golia and Blakeslee are prominently featured. All three are members of Lizard Brothers, featured on this CD under the nominal leadership of Halley.

With a day job, Halley is technically an amateur but the professionalism of his playing and the quality of his writing suggest something entirely different. Imaginative arrangements on the likes of *Rattlesnake And Spider* mark his comfort with orthodox voicings, while an item like *Inequilaterality* makes use of the fierce collective. His own solos are not afraid to visit both ends of his range and he builds them with discernment. A solo like *Rattlesnake* shows his unpredictability, on *Stubble* he is reflective, while *Inequilaterality* portrays his irascible self. The fifties devotion to quality musicianship has survived but the Lizards confirm that the interim 40 years have taught today's West Coasters to use the less conservative aspects of jazz. **BMcR**

Lin Halliday

1939

East of The Sun **Halliday** (ts); **Ira Sullivan** (t, flh, ts, f); **Jodie Christian** (p); **Dennis Carroll** (b); **George Fludas** (d). Delmark Ⓕ DE 45864 (64 minutes). Recorded 1992.

⑤ ❼

Halliday, originally from Arkansas, has been playing professionally for more than three decades, and his career has seen him settled in places as far apart in America as Hollywood, Wisconsin, Nashville and New York (where in the early sixties he was a member of the Maynard Ferguson band). His style relies heavily on Rollins and Mobley for the way in which he approaches thematic development or negotiates chord changes, his sound also nestling closely between these two players. So much so that, for all Halliday's skill and commitment, the flood of echoes from other people's solos gets in the way of a proper perception of his talents. Nevertheless, he is a fluent and knowledgeable saxophonist who is expertly supported by a rhythm section in which pianist Jodie Christian is a standout. Multi-instrumentalist Ira Sullivan spreads himself rather thinly on this date, and has been heard to better advantage elsewhere. **KS**

Chico Hamilton

1921

Gongs East! **Hamilton** (d); **Eric Dolphy** (as, f, cl, bcl); **Dennis Budimir** (g); **Nathan Gershman** (vc); **Wyatt Ruther** (b). Discovery Ⓜ DSCD 831 (38 minutes). Recorded 1958.

⑧ ❽

The Chico Hamilton Quintet was one of the most popular modern jazz units of the fifties; in addition to appearing in the noted jazz documentary *Jazz on a Summer's Day* (1958), it was also featured, dramatically as well as musically, in Alexander Mackendrick's stunning film noir study of Big Apple corruption, *The Sweet Smell of Success* (1957). Hamilton, reflecting experiences with such lyrical artists as Lester Young, Lena Horne and Gerry Mulligan, built his highly appealing fifties quintets around a chamber-music-like approach, with its inclusion of such then-unusual instruments as cello, flute and bass clarinet. Hamilton also introduced such emerging talents as Paul Horn, Eric Dolphy, Ron Carter and, at a later stage, Charles Lloyd, Gabor Szabo and Larry Coryell.

Here, in an ebullient yet carefully modulated session from 1958, Hamilton's group weaves its way through highly choreographed charts that include plenty of elbow-room for Dolphy, the date's principal soloist. Although Dolphy was soon to become an important figures of the nascent avant- garde, here we meet a disciplined player who, while taking chances, meshes perfectly with the Third Stream tendencies of compositions such as Nat Pierce's *Far East* in which Dolphy's flute melds with Nathan Gershman's cello before romping over the changes. Fred Katz's *Nature By Emerson* is a reflective ballad in which Dolphy's surprisingly glossy alto evokes the legacy of Johnny Hodges. Hamilton, while finessing the subtle rhythmic textures, adds nuance and colour through his expert brush and stick work. **CB**

Man From Two Worlds **Hamilton** (d); **Charles Lloyd** (f, ts); **George Bohanon** (tb, four tracks); **Gabor Szabo** (g); **Albert Stinson** (b). Impulse! Ⓜ GRP 11272 (68 minutes). Recorded 1962/63.

⑥ ❼

There lurk behind this title not one but two separate albums, recorded more than a year apart. The earlier (and better) disc was called **Passin' Thru**, and represented one of Lloyd's earliest exposures on record. Since being part of the original Gerry Mulligan Quartet, Hamilton had specialized in bringing to the fore a formidable number of gifted young players—Buddy Collette, Paul Horn, Eric Dolphy, Ron Carter, Charles Lloyd and Gabor Szabo up to this point, with Larry Coryell to follow in short order. In that sense, Lloyd in this band was part of an ongoing process. As the group's musical director, he had a great opportunity to formulate his ideas, and this on-the-job experience was soon to pay enormous dividends when he formed his own quartet featuring young Keith Jarrett and Jack DeJohnette. *Forest Flower*, the composition which did it for Lloyd at Monterey in 1965 (see below), is here in a stiff and rather unconvincing version, hampered by the inflexible sonics of Szabo's wooden-sounding guitar. In fact Szabo, soon to go on to considerable commercial success, is the weak link in general on the 1963 cuts, his intonation often suspect and his role ill-defined.

The earlier **Passin' Thru** avoids these problems through Hamilton's more assertive playing and the presence of trombonist George Bohanon, who can carry the ensemble lines with Lloyd and give Szabo a more chordal and rhythmic role. Szabo also solos more conventionally, avoiding the self-conscious gipsy imitations which were soon to overcome him. Lloyd plays with terrific drive, his every solo full of earthiness and the excitement of discovery. This is Hamilton's chamber jazz concept working at its best, and it is still worth hearing today. **KS**

The Dealer **Hamilton** (d); **Arnie Lawrence** (as); **Larry Coryell** (g); **Ernie Hayes** (org); **Richard Davis** (b); on one track, add **Archie Shepp** (p). Impulse! Ⓜ MCAD-39137 (42 minutes). Recorded 1966.

⑧ ❽

This album is so much of its time (mid-sixties) and its place (West Coast) that you can almost smell the joss-sticks. Unlike a lot of his output, which leans towards discreet chamber jazz, this Chico Hamilton-led session is informal, humorous and almost excessively relaxed—a Happening, in short. Shepp contributes light-hearted (if not light-fingered) barrel-house piano to his own tongue-in-cheek *For Mods Only*, with Davis and Hamilton impeccable both here and throughout the session, while the date's other participants, Larry Coryell (on his first jazz-based recording, one of many young players Hamilton encouraged over the years), Arnie Lawrence and Ernie Hayes are enthusiastic and somewhat wayward, as befits their youth and relative inexperience. The material ranges from a multi-textured rousing opener *The Dealer*, through an unusual-sounding *The Trip* (the former probably not about cards, the latter equally unlikely to refer to a holiday excursion) to Coryell's moody, shuffling *Larry of Arabia* and the extraordinary *Thoughts*, where a murmured chant gives way to a strident alto feature of considerable power. Although Impulse! probably did not overwhelm producer Bob Thiele with gratitude for this session at the time, as a period-piece it has undeniable charm and considerable novelty-value. **CP**

Scott Hamilton

1954

Race Point **Hamilton** (ts); **Gerry Wiggins** (p); **Andy Simpkins** (b); **Howard Alden** (g); **Jeff Hamilton** (d). Jazz Concord Ⓕ CCD 4492 (58 minutes). Recorded 1992.

⑧ ❽

Scott Hamilton is a swing tenor player who happens to have been born long after the swing era was officially declared dead and buried. His very existence challenges all kinds of hallowed assumptions about jazz and progress. His steady growth as an artist refutes charges of pastiche, and his evident success and popularity act as a constant irritant to advanced opinion. In the course of 15 years he has recorded 26 albums under his own name, not to mention many with other artists, such as Rosemary Clooney and Ruby Braff.

I have chosen **Race Point** because it is one of the more recent and because it features him in two contexts—with a full rhythm section and in duet with guitarist Howard Alden. I could equally well have nominated a dozen others. To paraphrase Philip Larkin, you do not have to attend a course of lectures to appreciate Scott Hamilton. The virtues in his playing are joyously evident: fluency, warmth, drive, wit and a feeling of immense well-being. **DG**

Gunter Hampel

1937

The 8th of July 1969 **Hampel** (p, vb, bcl); **Anthony Braxton** (as, cbcl, snino s); **Willem Breuker** (as, ts, bcl, ss); **Arjen Gorter** (b); **Steve McCall** (d); **Jeanne Lee** (v). Birth Ⓕ 001 (68 minutes). Recorded 1969.

⑧ ❽

American and European free jazz scenes have gone separate ways in recent decades (although one should not oversimplify; cross-pollination quietly continues), but there was a short period, beginning in 1969 with a wave of Chicago avant-gardists taking up residence on the continent, when the intermingling of style and players was common. This historic meeting of Chicagoans Braxton and McCall, New Yorker Lee, Holland's Breuker and Gorter (still working together in Breuker's Kollektief) and German multi-instrumentalist Hampel, shows how total that blending could be.

Some of this music is rumbunctious and dissonant in the prevailing free-jazz manner, but not all of it. Atmospheric improvising was already common among the Chicagoans, who often set the tone. But it is Lee's cool, almost uninflected singing, with or without words, which really gives this date its distinctive flavour. The free scene produced few singers and fewer good ones; Lee is the best of the lot. There were not many free vibraphonists either—the instrument is not particularly assertive—but Hampel was always one of the best and most outgoing (his dippy, syncopated piano figure underpinning on *We Move* is less satisfying). This CD reissue adds alternative takes to four out of five tunes. **KW**

Lionel Hampton

1909

1937-38, 1938-39, 1939-40 **Hampton** (vb, p, d, v); **Ziggy Elman**, **Cootie Williams**, **Jonah Jones**, **Harry James**, **Walter Fuller**, **Irving Randolf**, **Dizzy Gillespie**, **Henry 'Red' Allen** (t); **Benny Carter** (t, as, cl); **Rex Stewart** (c) **Lawrence Brown**, **J.C. Higginbotham** (tb); **Mezz Mezzrow**, **Eddie**

Barefield, **Edmon Hall** (cl); **Omer Simeon** (cl, as); **Johnny Hodges**, **Russell Procope**, **Earl Bostic**, **Toots Mondello** (as); **Vido Musso**, **Herschel Evans**, **Budd Johnsonn**, **Chu Berry**, **Coleman Hawkins**, **Ben Webster** (ts); **Edgar Sampson**, **Harry Carney** (bs); **Jess Stacy**, **Clyde Hart**, **Billy Kyle**, **Spencer Odum**, **Joe Sullivan** (p); **Allan Reuss**, **Danny Barker**, **Charlie Christian**, **Wesley Prince**, **Al Casey**, **Freddie Green**, **Oscar Moore** (g); **Harry Goodman**, **John Kirby**, **Billy Taylor**, **Milt Hinton**, **Artie Bernstein** (b); **Gene Krupa**, **Cozy Cole**, **Sonny Greer**, **Jo Jones**, **Alvin Burroughs**, **Sidney Catlett**, **Zutty Singleton**, **Nick Fatool** (d). Classics Ⓜ 524, 534, 562 (three discs, oas: 72, 70 and 70 minutes). Recorded 1937-40.

✔ ⑩ ❼

What makes the Hampton Victors such a special studio series is the large number of musicians involved. It anticipates the Jazz At The Philharmonic mix-and-match policy while showcasing one of the most remarkable of all jazz musicians. Hampton is heard on these three CDs as the master vibraphone player, superbly relaxed on *Singin' The Blues,* fiercely attacking on *Hot Mallets*, lyrically poetic on *I Surrender Dear* and endlessly inventive in almost every solo he takes. His honestly forthright drumming is heard to good advantage on *Drum Stomp* and *Big Wig In The Wigwam*, while his excellent but underrated singing is never better displayed than on *Object Of My Affections* and *After You've Gone*. His somewhat boring piano playing blights *Rock Hill Special* and *Central Avenue Breakdown*, but compensation for these is found in his special contrapuntal moments. His vibes work with Berry on *Sweethearts On Parade*, his response to Catlett's rhythmic thrust on *Haven't Named It Yet* or his rhythmic freedom over the Carter-arranged reeds on *I'm In The Mood For Swing* speak for themselves. In addition, the trumpets boast the sometimes brash Elman, the powerful Jones, the smouldering Williams, the bubbling Gillespie and the irascible Stewart. Carter stars on trumpet, clarinet and alto and there are also outstanding reed contributions from Hodges, Berry, Hawkins, Bailey and the unsung Mondello. **BMcR**

Flying Home **Hampton** (vb, p, v); **Ernie Royal**, **Karl George**, **Joe Newman**, **Cat Anderson**, **Roy McCoy**, **Joe Morris**, **Lamar Wright Jr**, **Snooky Young**, **Wendell Culley**, **Dave Page**, **Al Killian**, **Jimmy Nottingham** (t); **Fred Beckett**, **Sonny Craven**, **Harry Sloan**, **Al Hayes**, **Booty Wood**, **Vernon Porter**, **Andrew Penn**, **Allen Durham**, **Abdul Hamid**, **John Morris**, **Jimmy Wormick** (tb); **Marshall Royal** (cl, as); **Ray Perry** (as, vn); **Earl Bostic**, **Gus Evans**, **George Dorsey**, **Herbie Fields**, **Bobby Plater**, **Ben Kynard** (as); **Illinois Jacquet**, **Dexter Gordon**, **Al Sears**, **Arnett Cobb**, **Fred Simon**, **Jay Peters**, **Johnny Griffin** (ts); **Jack McVea**, **Charlie Fowlkes** (bs); **Milt Buckner**, **John Mehegan**, **Dardanelle Breckenridge** (p); **Irving Ashby**, **Eric Miller**, **Billy Mackel** (g); **Vernon Alley**, **Vernon King**, **Charles Harris**, **Ted Sinclair** (b); **George Jenkins**, **Fred Radcliffe**, **George Jones** (d); **Dinah Washington** (v). MCA/Decca Jazz Ⓜ MCAD-42349 (50 minutes). Recorded 1942-45.

✔ ⑧ ❽

Hampton left Benny Goodman to form his own band in 1940, but remained under contract to RCA through the following year. This anthology captures the beginning of his successful period with Decca, and producer Orrin Keepnews does an admirable job of salvaging Hampton's more substantial performances from the period without totally neglecting the boisterous side of his music that made him such a commercial success (and such an important figure in the jazz-to-r&b transition of black popular music). A glance at the personnel reveals that the Hampton band was a breeding ground for both young modernists and the mainstream yeomen who would keep bands like Ellington's and Basie's going for the next several decades. Among the essential titles included here are *Flying Home* with the classic Illinois Jacquet solo and *Flying Home No. 2* with Arnett Cobb, flagwavers Hamp's *Boogie Woogie* (featuring the leader's two-finger piano) and *Hey! Ba Ba Re Bop*, plus Dinah Washington's salty *Blow Top Blues* with a septet taken from the band. Pianist Milt Buckner, who contributed several arrangements, is the unsung hero of this affirmative and very swinging collection. **BB**

The Paris Session 1953 **Hampton** (vb); **Walter Williams** (t); **Al Hayse**, **Jimmy Cleveland** (tb); **Mezz Mezzrow** (cl); **Clifford Scott**, **Alix Combelle** (ts); **Claude Bolling** (p); **Billy Mackell** (g); **William Montgomery** (b); **Curley Hamner** (d). Vogue Ⓜ VG 655609 (55 minutes). Recorded 1953.

⑧ ❻

The band that Hampton brought to Europe in 1953 was full of young men who were destined for greatness; players such as Clifford Brown, Art Farmer, Quincy Jones, Gigi Gryce and Alan Dawson. Hampton decreed that there should be no unathorized recording dates during the tour; fortunately this stipulation was ignored and even while this "authorized" jam session was taking place in one Paris studio, a big band using much of the rest of the Hampton orchestra was at work in another. But this was no mere jam session, it was a high-powered social occasion and, surprisingly, the music matched the event. Hampton was given complete freedom in terms of material and lengths of tunes (*Free Press Oui* which uses the chords of *I Found A New Baby*, runs for nearly 13 minutes). He also insisted on bringing in Mezzrow while the two French musicians, Combelle and Bolling, emerged as stars in their own right. The five full-group performances have solos of a generally acceptable standard from everyone, even if things get a little out of hand at times. But the three tracks by just Hampton, Billy Mackell and William Montgomery achieve classic status. **AM**

Reunion at Newport, 1967 **Hampton** (vb, p, d, v); with a collective personnel of **Snooky Young, Jimmy Nottingham, Joe Newman, Wallace Davenport** (t); **Al Grey, Garnett Brown, Britt Woodman, Dave Gonzalez, Walter Morris** (tb); **Benny Powell** (btb); **Ed Pazant, George Dorsey, Frank Foster, Dave Young, Jerome Richardson** (saxes); **John Spruill, Tete Montoliu, Oscar Dennard, Milt Buckner** (p); **Billy Mackel** (g); **George Duvivier, Peter Badie** (b); **Steve Little** (d); **Eddie Chamblee** (d); **Illinois Jacquet, Eddie Chamblee** (ts); **Eddie Chamblee** (d); **Scoville Brown** (cl); **Bobby Plater** (as); **Curtis Lowe** (bs); **Maria Angelica** (castanets). RCA Bluebird Ⓜ 66157-2 (71 minutes). Recorded 1956/1967.

⑥ ❹

The Newport set was originally released under the title **Newport Uproar!**, which still seems entirely appropriate when re-appraising this CD. For 50 years Hampton has been leading a take-no-prisoners big band with feet firmly in both the chutzpah and jazz camps. Some bands have been better than others, depending mostly on who the soloists and section leaders were at any given time. This band was a special one, pulled together as a one-off for the Newport Festival and containing many old Hampton hands. The excitement is palpable and the recording balance certainly lets you know there was an excited crowd present. The set is nicely varied, with *Thai Silk* being a romantic setting for Hampton and *Meet Benny Bailey* bringing out the best in Joe Newman. By the time the inevitable *Flying Home* is reached, everybody is suitably tired and emotional, and Illinois Jacquet boots them all home in vintage style. The encore, a reprise of *Greasy Greens*, adds little to the first version. The sound, always poor on vinyl, is still very thin.

The last five tracks bring onto CD a most peculiar disc, probably the weirdest thing Hamp has ever made. The album was cut in Madrid while the band was on the Spanish leg of a seven-month tour of Europe and the Near East (they had played to 19,000 in a Barcelonan bull ring the week before). Hamp had spent a reputed 48 hours in a Flamenco nightspot and had come across Maria Angelica there. As Hamp said, "I dug her the most. I said to myself, 'Man, you got to get this together with the band.' So we did." Well, not quite: the recording quality is primitive in the extreme, Maria's castanets dominate the whole date, and Flamenco Swing was still a fledgling art when this date happened. The presence of Tete Montoliu on two tracks aids things considerably, but, as David Drew Zingg wrote in the original liner notes, "This is a crazy, mixed-up album." Amen. Hamp must have *really* dug that castanet player.

KS

You Better Know It!!! **Hampton** (vb, v); **Clark Terry** (t); **Ben Webster** (ts); **Hank Jones** (p); **Milt Hinton** (b); **Osie Johnson** (d). Impulse! Ⓜ GRP 11402 (40 minutes). Recorded 1964.

⑥ ❽

The most profound jazz events of the late 1930s were probably the prolific small band recording sessions led by Lionel Hampton and Teddy Wilson. The fastidious Wilson wisely let his lie. The more ebullient Hampton had a shot at recreating some of his on these tracks. As re-lived history they are a failure. The tight meniscus of the earlier performance is lost and even Ben Webster can only make a hollow fist at Chu Berry's original exultant *Sweethearts On Parade*. *Ring Dem Bells* has replaced the original springy rhythmic mattress with a good time shuffle. Hampton sings on these two, phrasing his voice like a trumpet player would. Terry plays a notably poised and dexterous trumpet solo on *Bells*, miles from the controlled ferocity of Cootie Williams on the original version. However, taken as contemporary mid-sixties mainstream, the two sessions here produce relaxed, loping jazz with Webster and Terry near to their best - how could they not be with Mad Lionel ever-ready to propel them over such a flawless rhythm team?

Five of the ten tracks are contemporary themes. They include two Manny Albam originals, Neil Hefti's *Cute* and Bobby Scott's *A Taste Of Honey*, the last of which which draws shimmering ballad performances from Hampton and Webster.

SV

Slide Hampton

1932

Dedicated to Diz **Hampton** (tb, ldr, arr); **Jon Faddis, Roy Hargrove** (t, flh); **Steve Turré** (tb); **Douglas Purviance** (btb, tba); **Antonio Hart** (ss, as); **David Sanchez** (ss, ts, f); **Jimmy Heath** (ts); **Danilo Perez** (p); **George Mraz** (b); **Lewis Nash** (d). Telarc Jazz Ⓕ CD 83323 (72 minutes). Recorded 1993.

⑦ ❻

Slide Hampton and the Jazz Masters, to give this group its full title, was born in early 1993 of an idea shared by Slide Hampton and Dizzy Gillespie's manager Charles Fishman. It was conceived as a small big band (12 pieces) which could perform the compositions associated with the masters such as Gillespie, Parker, Ellington and Monk, all in imaginative new arrangements specially tailored for the band by Slide Hampton. It was a great idea on paper, and the resulting CD (recorded live at the Village Vanguard) shows that Hampton has created an unusually persuasive book.

This should hardly surprise the long-term follower of Hampton's career. A good if unspectacular soloist, Hampton's forte has always been creating charts honed to perfection for forces such as the one assembled on this date. He first came to prominence with Lionel Hampton, Lloyd Price and Maynard Ferguson, and in 1959 he formed his Octet, a group which brought him considerable attention and which crystallized his clean, powerful approach to arranging, one which, like Gerry Mulligan, left considerable room for good soloists to stretch out. His later group, World of Trombones, understandably had less room for solos (there were nine trombonists to cater for), but in recent years he has been performing mostly with quintets. Thus it is good to welcome him back to his natural milieu on this date. The recording quality may not be wonderful (it is about par for the Vanguard), and the band may be a little rough in places, but it is all there, and the soloists—all of whom can claim a meaningful association with Gillespie—create a worthwhile tribute to a great man and his music. **KS**

Herbie Hancock

1940

Maiden Voyage **Hancock** (p); **Freddie Hubbard** (t); **George Coleman** (ts); **Ron Carter** (b); **Tony Williams** (d). Blue Note Ⓜ CDPB21Y 46339-2 (42 minutes). Recorded 1964.

✔ ⑩ ❽

Hancock made many fine albums in the sixties, and this one is so often paraded in front of the public as a genuine jazz classic (and just as regularly debunked by those anxious to appear better informed) that one could be forgiven for wondering why it would need yet another recommendation. The answer to that runs along the lines of the type of music played by the band on **Maiden Voyage**. It is generally quiet, relaxed, contemporary mid-sixties jazz, aware of the turmoil of change around it but happy to stay within clear parameters. Of course four-fifths of the line-up were in the Miles Davis quintet at the time, but this is the least Milesean album of all the ones this rhythm section made with this trumpeter. The members of the group are clearly comfortable with each other, and there are no unseemly dramas: mutual support is the rule. Hancock's compositional and arranging skills see to that.

George Coleman in particular solos strongly, his warm, clear tone and truly original melodic sense combining to create a series of timeless improvisations. Being relatively unadventurous musically, Coleman in general is underrated, and his period with Miles (he was the one between Mobley and Shorter), which saw him at his peak, won him few friends. This is a shame: he was capable, on occasion, of playing to Getzian standards. This is one of the occasions. No-one else falls below such relative values on their own instruments. Need I reiterate it? I will, anyway: a classic. **KS**

Mwandishi: The Complete Warner Bros. Recordings **Hancock** (p); **Johnny Coles**, **Joe Newman**, **Ernie Royal**, **Eddie Henderson** (t); **Garnett Brown**, **Benny Powell**, **Julian Priester** (tb); **Ray Alonge** (frh); **Joe Henderson**, **Joe Farrell** (ts, f); **Benny Maupin** (ss, bcl, af); **Arthur 'Babe' Clarke** (bs); **Eric Gale**, **Billy Butler**, **Ron Montrose** (g); **Patrick Gleason** (syn); **Buster Williams**, **Jerry Jermott** (b); **Albert 'Tootie' Heath**, **Bernard Purdie**, **Billy Hart** (d); **George Devens**, **Leon Chancler**, **Jose 'Capito' Ares**, **Victor Pontoja** (perc); **Candy Love**, **Sandra Stevens**, **Della Horne**, **Victoria Domagalski**, **Scott Beach** (v). Warner Archives Ⓜ 9 45732-2 (two discs: 124 minutes). Recorded 1969-72.

⑧ ❽

This splendid collection of Hancock's three LPs for Warner's highlights a significant moment in the vaunted pianist-composer's career. Coming off a six-year stint with Miles Davis when the trumpeter made the transition from acoustic to electric, Hancock put together galvanizing sextets that probed various strategies for incorporating everything from funk to free jazz. The first Warner date from 1969, **Fat Albert Rotunda**, is built from themes Hancock penned for Bill Cosby's highly successful 'Fat Albert' TV cartoon series. Here, as in most of the tracks of the three dates, Hancock successfully exploits the electric Fender-Rhodes piano. Also of note are the leader's witty three-horn charts, the insouciant rhythms and the charged soloing of Joe Henderson, on alto flute as well as tenor, and trumpeter Johnny Coles. From the 'ah-ha' funk of *Wiggle-Waggle* to the lyric balladry of *Tell Me a Bedtime Story*, Hancock's gritty sextet remains persuasive and just plain fun.

On his second Warner's date, **Mwandishi** (1970), a revamped Hancock sextet with Benny Maupin's bass clarinet and Eddie Henderson's plaintive trumpet embarked on a far more spiritual quest. As indicated by titles such as *You'll Know When You Get There*, the music was an open-ended affair that drew on the zeitgeist of the period's avant-garde. The music's kaleidoscopic colours and insinuating rhythms also took inspiration from Africa (significantly, each member of the group adopted a Swahili name). African rhythms also inform **Crossings** (1972), Hancock's final Warner's date. In the five-part *Sleeping Giant*, Hancock returns to some of the funkier aspects of *Fat Albert*. while with Benny Maupin's *Water Torture* an eerie and highly dramatic piece unfolds in sparkling detail. The addition of Patrick Gleason's sweeping Moog synthesizer is another defining element. Throughout, Hancock impresses his signature by dint of his sharing leadership as well as compositional and pianistic élan. **CB**

Headhunters **Hancock** (elp, clav, syn, pipes); **Bennie Maupin** (ss, ts, saxello, bcl, af); **Paul Jackson** (elb, marimbula); **Harvey Mason** (d); **Bill Summers** (perc). Columbia Legacy Ⓜ 471239 2 (42 minutes). Recorded 1973.

✔ ⑧ ❽

When he left Miles Davis, Herbie Hancock (driven perhaps by pressure of reputation) felt he ought to produce a jazz masterpiece. The esoteric, critically well-received 'space music' of his early seventies sextet resulted, but when these records reduced parties to silence, Hancock chose a more populist path and, ironically, turned out a seminal recording. In essence, **Headhunters** was an attempt to produce an instrumental paraphrase of the music of Sly Stone, James Brown and other soul artists, and Hancock's grasp of the infectious polyrhythmic counterpoint typical of that style is confirmed by the funk staple *Chameleon*. Soul has its dull moments too, and they are here in the corny update of *Watermelon Man* and the drowsy tone poem *Vein Melter*. However, although the aim had been to produce dance music, jazz kept surfacing, and *Sly*, the best track here, provides a fresh and invigorating modal setting for Hancock's polytonal jazz style. Jackson's motoring dotted crotchet bass lines and Mason's restless bass drums and urgent 16th-note hi-hat and cymbal figures are a wonder in themselves, but Hancock ices the cake with improvisation as volatile as any he produced in a straight-ahead context. In the midst of this careering, hothouse jazz, the insistent funky clavinet becomes an irritating superfluity. **MG**

A Jazz Collection **Hancock** (p); **Wynton Marsalis**, **Freddie Hubbard** (t); **Wayne Shorter** (ss, ts); **Chick Corea** (p); **Ron Carter** (b); **Tony Williams** (d). Columbia Ⓜ 467901-2 (76 minutes). Recorded 1977-82.

⑧ ❽

This album covers a cross-section of Hancock's jazz activities between his hit singles *Chameleon* (1973) and *Rockit* (1983). Three groups are represented, most notably VSOP, Hubbard and Shorter being teamed with the ex-Miles rhythm section of Hancock, Carter and Williams in a powerful *Nefertiti*. The same rhythm section backs Wynton Marsalis in an early eighties touring band (caught here in Japan) while the disc is rounded out with some sublime piano duos between Hancock and Corea.

Some critics felt Hancock lost touch with jazz when he struck commercial success in disco and funk, but on this showing he is as assured and original as in his dominant performance in Tavernier's film *'Round Midnight*. The tune of that name is the most impressive of the Marsalis quartets, with some deft manipulation of the tempo resulting in a power surge of acceleration out of Monk's ballad. Wynton over-uses one device of punching out a series of descending high notes, but his playing on this and Monk's *Well, You Needn't* is otherwise impressive. For sheer uninhibited joy, musicality and quick-fire exchange of ideas, nothing compares with the Corea/Hancock duet on *Liza*, where the two pianists seem to operate as one, recreating the magic of their concert appearances. **AS**

Mr Hands **Hancock** (p, kbds, syns, d); **Bennie Maupin** (ts); **Wah Wah Watson** (g); **Paul Jackson**, **Byron Miller**, **Jaco Pastorius**, **Ron Carter**, **Freddie Washington** (b); **Harvey Mason**, **Leon 'Ndugu' Chancler**, **Alphonse Mouzon** (d); **Bill Summers**, **Sheila Escovedo** (perc). Columbia Ⓜ 471240-2 (41 minutes). Recorded 1982.

⑥ ❽

By the early eighties, Hancock's funk flirtation had been fully exploited. After the popular success initiated by the hit album **Headhunters** and solidified by a string of chart-topping albums and singles, he accepted that his jazz roots had spread into areas that embraced the VSOP message, the acoustic duets with Corea and even a solo acoustic piano recording for Sony Japan, as well as the overriding fusion ethic of the early seventies. On this album all of the tunes are by Hancock, and this gives him a firm controlling hand in a very varied programme. The emphasis remains on dance qualities inspired by Sly Stone, but titles like *Calypso* are pure jazz aimed at the heads of the jazz cognescenti rather than at the dancing feet of club dwellers. Certainly *Just Around The Corner* and *Shiftless Shuffle* present a synthesis of both elements, with creative solos over a strong rhythmic base: clearly, Hancock was not trading in comfort music. He relished the challenge the electronic world offered, but he was a jazzman of such stature that it became a foregone conclusion that he would successfully surmount any difficulties of integration between the two musical streams. Meanwhile, anyone who can sit through this album oblivious of the music's dance potential would have to be in need of orthopaedic assistance. **BMcR**

Craig Handy

1962

Introducing Three for All + One **Handy** (ts, ss); **David Kikoski** (p); **Charles Farnbrough** (b); **Ralph Peterson** (d). Arabesque Ⓕ AJ 0109 (53 minutes). Recorded 1993.

⑧ ❽

Tenor saxophonist Craig Handy is a rollicking modernist, a big-toned player whose arabesques reflect the melodic wit and rhythmic panache of Sonny Rollins as well as the loping neo-bop swingingness of Dexter Gordon. Like Rollins, Handy has a zesty imagination capable of reconfiguring pop standards such as *Spinning Wheel*, Blood, Sweat & Tears' mega-hit, rendered here as a harmonically spartan Rollins-esque trio track for tenor, bass and drums. It is pithy and perky, and bubbling with Handy's distinctive barrel-chested brio.

The University of North Texas alumnus uses Gordon-like broad-strokes in the balladic stroll through Gordon Jenkins's *P.S. I Love You*. For Marvin Hamlisch's *One!*, his tenor slashes with sheets-of-sound abandon while the lean Jarrett-like jabs of pianist Kikoski keep things bright and swinging. His foray on Farnbrough's lithe *Amy's Waltz* spotlights this Coltrane-inflected soprano. Also impressive are the trio version of Joe Henderson's harmonically challenging *Isotope* and the quartet take on Kikoski's haunting lamentation, *Chant*. Handy, as evidenced in the roller-coaster ride called *To Woo It May Concern* and in the solo flight, *West Bank: Beyond the Berlin Wall*, is a composer to reckon with as well. **CB**

John Handy III

1933

Centrepiece **Handy** (as, cl, v); **Julie Carter** (vn, v); **Tarika Lewis** (vn, v); **Sandi Poindexter** (elvn, v); **Flip Nunez, Bill Bell** (p); **Herbie Lewis, Arlington Houston** (b); **Eddie Marshall, Dexter Story** (d); **John 'Buddy' Conner** (v). Milestone Ⓕ MCD 9173-2 (45 minutes). Recorded 1989.

② ❽

After making blues records in his youth, Handy moved to New York in 1958. Two spells with Charles Mingus preceded the forming of his own unique quintet with violinist Mike White and guitarist Jerry Hahn in 1965. This was the group that had great success at the Monterey Jazz Festival of that year but began his gradual move firstly toward Indian musical outlooks and then on to jazz/rock. Like other recent CDs, this issue does not enhance his jazz reputation. Handy plays uncomplicated, commercial saxophone with scant attention paid to good taste and with little improvisational commitment. The arrangements are all by Handy but they do nothing to elevate the music to a more serious plane. There is a hint of substance in *Jeep's Blues* and *Centrepiece* has some neat vocalese, but the likes of *Summertime* and *My Funny Valentine* are cute vocal bores. Even *Mood Indigo* is trivialized, despite Handy's understated clarinet solo, and the whole thing implies a feeling of 'good time' which it never quite delivers. Sadly, this is Handy's sole current CD. Those interested in a more involved Handy will have to turn to Mingus or the 'Monterey' quintet LPs. **BMcR**

Roland Hanna

1932

Impressions **Hanna** (p); **Major Holley** (b); **Alan Dawson** (d). Black & Blue Ⓕ 59 753-2 (54 minutes). Recorded 1979.

⑥ ❻

'Sir' Roland Hanna is another of the gifted products of America's Rust Belt, being born and raised in Detroit. Initially self-taught, he progressed eventually to Juilliard, from whence he graduated to professional life. His most famous stint as a sideman is the early sixties one with Charles Mingus, but for years now he has divided his time between work as a leader and sessions with the New York Jazz Quartet.

This trio date is of the typical Black & Blue tradition, recorded in their "open air studio" in Nice. All three musicians stretch out and play what they please, and with such a disciplined team as this, the results are just fine. Hanna's style, whether solo (as on *Body and Soul* here) or in a trio, remains essentially a 'modern conservative' one, with roots as much in Milt Buckner and Art Tatum as in Powell or Monk. This makes his foray into Coltrane's *Impressions* that much more interesting; the return to the piano from the saxophone of this sliver from Debussy's *L'Isle Joyeuse* has a peculiarly apposite excitement, set to a sprightly jazz rhythm by the superb Alan Dawson. **KS**

Bill Hardman

1933-1990

What's Up **Hardman** (t); **Junior Cook** (ts); **Robin Eubanks** (tb); **Mickey Tucker** (p); **Paul Brown** (b); **Leroy Williams** (d). SteepleChase Ⓕ SCCD 31254 (68 minutes). Recorded 1989.

✔ ⑦ ❾

Converted from swing-era influences by hearing Charlie Parker as a teenager, Hardman became a 'first call' trumpeter who graced the bands of Jackie McLean, Art Blakey, Charles Mingus and Horace Silver throughout the fifties and sixties. In the next decade he led Brass Company and began a fruitful musical association with Junior Cook. In his earlier days his bubbling lines made him sound like a bop version of Freddie Jenkins, but as he matured, more of the hard bop lean burn became apparent. This CD is by his working band, augmented by Eubanks, and it documents the music of Hardman's last few years with some accuracy. The programme, with only one Hardman original, is well chosen, and the trumpeter continually demonstrates his adaptability. His easy lyricism is heard on *I Should Care*, his puckish humour on *Whisper Not* and his-well chosen aggression on *Yo What's Up*. His five blues choruses on *Room's Blues* are well engineered and full of genuine feeling: as all of this session develops, it becomes obvious that this is a commodity always available in Hardman's musical storehouse. It all makes for a performance that gives no hint of the trumpeter's imminent and untimely demise. **BMcR**

Roy Hargrove

1970

With The Tenors Of Our Time **Hargrove** (t, flh); **Ron Blake** (ts. ss), **Cyrus Chestnut** (p); **Rodney Whitaker** (b); **Gregory Hutchinson** (d); with guests **Johnny Griffin**, **Joe Henderson**, **Branford Marsalis**, **Joshua Redman**, **Stanley Turrentine** (ts). Verve Ⓕ 523 019-2 (74 minutes). Recorded 1994.

⑧ ❽

Hargrove, one of the outstanding neo-classicists, spent much of the late eighties as a teenage background figure, sitting in at jam sessions around the New York scene. He was a prominent member of Generations in 1989 and distinguished himself with the first and best edition of Jazz Futures in 1991. Now the leader of his own groups, he has developed considerably since that time. His confident trumpet may reveal a trace of Lee Morgan's bristling libido but it is tempered with a relaxed lyricism and a style that is very much his own.

On this CD he is matched by a team of the most daunting tenor saxophonists possible. Not once is he fazed, and on several occasions there is a drop in creative tension when his solo ends. He is entirely graceful as he presents his thoughts on *Once Forgotten*, he tells his story on *Never Let Me Go* with some stealth, he bustles through *Shades Of Jade*, while on *Valse Hot* he projects his solo as if oblivious of bar divisions. His superb tone on both trumpet and flügelhorn complements the ideas he relentlessly delivers and supports the theory that Hargrove is the best of the young trumpet tigers in the post-Marsalis era. **BMcR**

Billy Harper

1943

Black Saint **Harper** (ts); **Virgil Jones** (t); **Joe Bonner** (p); **David Friesen** (b); **Malcolm Pinson** (d). Black Saint Ⓕ 0001 (41 minutes). Recorded 1975.

⑧ ❽

I first encountered Billy Harper's playing on a Lee Morgan LP released in 1972; his tenor solos were thoughtful, articulate, unusually contoured and immediately impressive. They include one solo teeter-tottering on a repeated honk that brought to mind Arnett Cobb and their shared 'Texas tenor' roots. It was only later that I noticed the album's two most attractive compositions were from Harper's pen. One of them, *Croquet Ballet*, a waltz with challenging melodic twists and turns, appears on this disc. But this has proven indicative of Harper's career since then. Although this and a pair of Japanese LPs from the late seventies enhanced his reputation, he remains better known as a valuable sideman in groups led by Max Roach, Art Blakey, Thad Jones/Mel Lewis, Gil Evans and Randy Weston than as a leader himself. One wonders why. This is enormously exciting music. Extending the concept of Coltrane's arpeggiated 'sheets of sound', Harper flexes his muscles on the opening *Dance, Eternal Spirit, Dance!* Here, and on the anthemic *Call Of The Wild And Peaceful Heart* (where the unusual 9/8 meter creates a surging momentum) it is trumpeter Jones's task to relieve the tension Harper's chromatic exuberance builds, with pianist Bonner a romantic foil, comping in the rich, ringing style McCoy Tyner popularized during this period. Worthy of rediscovery. **AL**

Herbie Harper

1920

Two Brothers **Herbie Harper** (tb); **Bill Perkins** (ts, bs, f); **Larry Koonse** (g); **John Leitham** (b); **Laurance Marable** (d). VSOP Ⓕ #80 CD (51 minutes). Recorded 1989.

⑧ ❽

The combination of saxophone and trombone as a front line is a mightily rewarding one, and the expected clash between the similar ranges of trombone and tenor seldom happens. Brookmeyer and Getz made the most memorable pairing, but the leaders of the Harper-Perkins Quintet are joyously compatible. This group has a completely fresh sound, spiced by the use of a guitar instead of a piano.

The album is also important because it gives Harper, trombonists' trombonist par excellence, a rare chance to be heard at length. His beautiful tone, developed from long years in big bands and the studios, is better than ever, and his smooth legato work is set off by Perkins's astringent tenor (Perkins, who had previously followed his Rollins muse, was at this time re-orienting because he had discovered that his fans wanted his older Lester Young-based style). Unique treatments of Russ Freeman's *The Wind*, Brookmeyer's *Dirty Man* and Hefti's *Fred* are only the beginning, while *The Touch Of Your Lips* in a most imaginative treatment is just one of a selection of unhackneyed standards.

The rhythm section is ideal and a just celebration of this quintet demands more space than is available, so this pressing recommendation will suffice. **SV**

Tom Harrell

1946

Moon Alley **Harrell** (t, flh); **Kenny Garrett** (as, f); **Kenny Barron** (p); **Ray Drummond** (b); **Ralph Peterson** (d). Criss Cross Ⓕ 1018 CD (52 minutes). Recorded 1985.

⑦ ❿

Due to the non-appearance of a record from a 1982 session, this CD was Tom Harrell's second as a leader. Few players come to their début album, as he did in 1984, with such a good track record. He had toured as a member of the Stan Kenton and Woody Herman trumpet sections, he had worked with Horace Silver and with Lee Konitz and had just begun what proved to be a long stint with saxophonist Phil Woods. Here the appropriately-named *Change of Pace* shows Harrell can be effortlessly lyrical when playing slowly but he is never better than as the thrusting duellist at medium tempo. He is not deliberately gladiatorial, but he conducts his own cut and thrust with fellow hornman Garrett and, perhaps even more specifically, with his backroom men. This particular trio of supporters form an outstanding rhythm section; they keep a tight rein on the collective timing but throughout are a listening and caring team. This is hard bop with an acceptable softening at the corners. Harrell is seemingly incapable of playing an angular or ugly phrase, his solos are designed to accommodate this fact, and he remains a player who never coasts. **BMcR**

Barry Harris

1929

Live At Maybeck Recital Hall **Harris** (p). Concord Ⓕ CCD-4476 (53 minutes). Recorded 1990.

⑧ ❽

Although solidly grounded in bebop, Harris has always shown that he does not suffer from tunnel vision as far as music is concerned. This fine album from Concord's 'Maybeck Hall' series of unaccompanied pianists at work and in front of a small audience is strongly recommended. Solo piano is challenging for the pianist (richly satisfying for the listener), but Harris is obviously at home in this setting. One of his early LPs for Riverside was a solo album, with one title, an original named *Mutattra*, giving a clue to Barry's idol if you reverse the spelling. There are graceful ruminative readings of songs such as *It Could Happen To You* and *Gone Again*, a tribute to Monk in the opening chorus of *All God's Children* (before the tempo shifts up to about 80 bars a minute) and a moving version of the Bud Powell Ballad *I'll Keep Loving You*. Just as dramatic is Harris's total recall of *Parker's Mood*. A short ballad medley opens with a splendid version of Richard Rodger's *It Never Entered My Mind* which slides surprisingly but logically into the *Flintstones* theme! The closing track is a tune Art Tatum liked to play, *Would You Like To Take a Walk?*, a fitting end to a fascinating solo recital. **AM**

Beaver Harris

1936

Beautiful Africa **Harris** (d); **Grachan Moncur III** (tb); **Ken McIntyre** (as, bn, f); **Rahn Burton** (p); **Cameron Brown** (b). Soul Note Ⓕ 121002-2 (40 minutes). Recorded 1979.

⑥ ❽

After moving to New York from Pittsburgh in 1962, Beaver Harris played for a remarkable number of leaders, including Sonny Rollins, Albert Ayler, Roswell Rudd and Thelonious Monk. His spell as the driving force behind Archie Shepp's explosive quintet was the most noteworthy, but Harris was always an extremely adaptable drummer. In 1968 he formed the 360° Music Experience with Moncur and pianist Dave Burrell, and this highly musical CD gives a fine example of Harris's own propulsive style as well as the group's well-balanced musical stance. All of the players here were at one time associated with the free-form leaders of the sixties, but all play better in this more orthodox musical environment. The tunes were written by group members and, apart from the odd pan-tonal flourish from McIntyre and Burton, the treatment they receive is straight-ahead jazz. Burton shows the odd flash of Horace Silver on *African Drums* and *Love And Hate*. Moncur is selectively laconic on *Love And Hate* and at his loose-limbed best on *Baby Suite*, while McIntyre's flute lights up *Aladdin's Carpet*. Brown makes good solo statements on *Love And Hate* and *Baby Suite* and Harris is relaxed and swinging throughout. *Drums For Milan* is just what it claims to be, but there is no percussion overkill. **BMcR**

Bill Harris

1916-1973

Woody Herman Live 1957 Featuring Bill Harris, Volume 1 **Herman** (cl, as, v); **Bill Berry**, **John Coppola**, **Bill Castagnino**, **Andy Peele**, **Danny Styles** (t); **Harris**, **Bobby Lamb**, **Willie Dennis** (tb); **Jay Migliori**, **Jimmy Cook**, **Bob Newman** (ts); **Roger Pemberton** (bs); **John Bunch** (p); **Jimmy Gannon** (b); **Don Michaels** (d). Status Ⓕ STCD107 (56 minutes). Recorded 1957.

✔

⑧ ❻

Two of the trombonists who held sway in the thirties, J.C. Higginbotham and Dickie Wells, were responsible for the schools of the following decade, variously led by Bill Harris and J.J. Johnson.

Harris eschewed Johnson's machine gun-like precision for an emotional shaggy-dog style of trombone playing which, at its best, was one of the most exciting sounds in jazz. Harris was a man full of contradictions. On the one hand he was shy and retiring, while on the other he was an incurable practical joker and a blustering giant of a trombone soloist who could transform a performance with a few violent smears on his horn. He was also a formidable section leader. His introspective ballad performances, represented here by *Let's Talk*, managed to be exquisite as well as powerful.

The CD under review is particularly apposite since it provides an opportunity to hear Harris playing lead in the section as well as soloing. Take into account that Bobby Lamb and Willie Dennis were uncommonly devoted disciples and that the Herman band, little known in this version, was on particularly good form, then this Status volume, one of two, becomes essential listening. The recording quality is good for a live session and it is further remarkable in that it was recorded on a single mike suspended over the band. **SV**

Bill Harris

1925-1988

The Fabulous Bill Harris **Harris** (g, v, recitation); with, on one track **Howard University Ensemble**. VSOP Ⓕ 66CD (62 minutes). Recorded 1957-86.

⑧ ❽

Not to be confused with the trombonist of the same name, Bill Harris made a considerable impression on many listeners with his solo acoustic guitar albums for the EmArcy label in the late fifties. This CD has nothing to do with any earlier releases and comes from a variety of dates and locations including the Kennedy Centre, New York's Village Gate and San Francisco's Blues Alley. The choice of material is wide-ranging, taking in Django Reinhardt (an impressive *Nuages* running for nearly 11 minutes), Bach (Segovia's arrangement of the Prelude in D Minor), John Coltrane (*Syeeda's Song Flute*) and Big Bill Broonzy (*Key To The Highway*). A couple of (fortunately) short tracks which should have been left on the editing room floor are devoted to Harris's recitations on the subject of Ma Rainey and jazz bands. Harris also has some difficulties with playing the complex line of *Syeeda's Song Flute*, but overall there is enough good, orthodox acoustic guitar playing here to justify the rating. **AM**

Craig Harris

1953

Shelter **Harris** (tb, didjeridu); **Edward E.J. Allen** (t); **Don Byron** (cl, bcl); **Anthony Cox** (b); **Pheeroan AkLaff** (d); **Rod Williams** (p); **Tunde Samuel** (v). JMT Ⓕ 870008-2 (43 minutes). Recorded 1986.

⑦ ❽

"Why weren't there any trombonists on Coltrane's Ascension?" Craig Harris once asked, and in so doing identified himself with those trombonists like Roswell Rudd and Grachan Moncur III who redefined the horn in the light of its earliest jazz progenitors. Harris himself blows burry, hot trombone, nurtured in dynamic bands led by Abdullah Ibrahim, Sun Ra and David Murray. But these experiences also taught him the value of arranging and scene setting, and at times the music on Shelter is reminiscent of the modernist side of the Blue Note catalogue circa 1964-65. That is, the piquant voicings and slippery, shifting metres of tunes like *Cootie* and *Sound Sketches* are impressive, although they seem to keep the band from erupting into a Mingus-like frenzy. Harris is partial to programmatic themes for his albums, here connecting the plight of underdeveloped Third World countries with that of the American homeless. Tunde Samuel's vocals on *Africans Unite* and *Shelter* may remind you of Leon Thomas, as the band finds an infectious groove and builds a rewarding head of steam. Harris makes good (if slightly restrained) use of his quality personnel; Byron's background in klezmer bands lets him slide through and around the modalities effortlessly and Allen's best workout is in a late-Miles mode on *Sound Sketches*. Attractive music just short of outstanding. **AL**

Eddie Harris

1936

Artist's Choice: The Eddie Harris Anthology **Harris** (ts, ets, p, reed t, v); with a collective personnel including: **Benny Bailey**, **Joe Newman**, **Snooky Young**, **Ray Codrington**, **Don Ellis** (t); **Bennie Powell** (btb); **King Curtis**, **Fathead Newman** (ts); **Haywood Henry** (bs); **Jodie Christian**, **Cedar Walton**, **Milcho Leviev** (p); **Richard Abrams** (elp); **Joe Diorio** (g); **Melvin Jackson**, **Leroy Vinnegar**, **Ron Carter**, **Rufus Reid** (b); **Richard Smith**, **Billy Higgins**, **Billy Hart**, **Grady Tate**, **Paul Humphrey** (d); **Ray Barretto** (perc). Rhino/Atlantic Ⓜ 271514-2 (two discs: 150 minutes). Recorded 1961-77.

⑥ ❼

Chicagoan Harris started on piano and clarinet but soon shifted to saxophone. Stationed in Germany during his stint in the army he came into contact with Don Ellis, Leo Wright, Quincy Jones, Cedar Walton and Don Menza, among others, and this helped set him on the road to the type of music he would become famous for. His first hit, the *Theme From 'Exodus'*, was recorded for Vee Jay records; this propelled him into a Contract with Columbia which failed to work for either party. By 1965 he was with Atlantic, which was to be his company for the next decade or more. There he recorded *Freedom Jazz Dance* (a complex line over a simple vamp, and a title which Miles Davis also recorded) and *Listen Here*, the latter being another substantial hit. He was to have another million-seller in tandem with Les McCann with *Compared To What*? (not in this selection), pulled from the **Live at Montreux** album (see below) and released as a single. After that, business stayed much the same.

Harris has a light, alto-like tone and a phenomenally complete technique. He has a thorough grasp of modern jazz history and is able to play in virtually any style he likes, but he tends to stick for the most part to mixing jazz-funk rhythm and phraseology together with the occasional harmonic sequence or line which would not have been out of place in early-sixties progressive jazz. As such he is something of an enigma, as is this collection, which mixes the hits (including the original Vee-Jay recording of the *Exodus* theme) with his rigorous workouts on Coltrane's *Giant Steps* and *Steps Up*, which Harris describes as "another intervallic tune" and features Don Ellis on his last recording session. Whichever your preference (and you may just like the lot), there is never

the chance of mistaking Harris for anyone else; nor is there the chance of finding him playing music he has no interest in or commitment to. Both qualities are rare and should be accorded due respect. It is only to be expected that the sound quality is variable over such a long stretch of recording time, especially when it comes to the horrible bass sounds that studios insisted on producing in the late seventies.
KS

There Was a Time (Echo of Harlem) **Harris** (ts); **Kenny Barron** (p); **Cecil McBee** (b); **Ben Riley** (d). Enja Ⓕ 6068-2 (59 minutes). Recorded 1990.

⑨ ❽

"Under-achiever" is a dubious term which has entered the language via the social sciences; applied to oneself, it amounts to self-flattery masquerading as self-flagellation. But there is no other word for Harris, a tenor saxophonist with a paradoxical combination of gifts: a tone as airy as Paul Desmond's, an attack as bruising as Gene Ammons's and an understanding of harmonic relationships almost as keen as Sonny Rollins's. Since scoring a hit single with a jazz version of the theme from the movie *Exodus* in 1961, Harris has mostly given his audience the sort of tepid funk he presumes them to want. Over the decades, he has indulged in electronics, stand-up comedy, scat and mouthpiece gimmickry of a sort that enabled him to do an eerie Billie Holiday impersonation on one of his live albums. Every once in a while, however, he refrains from this, and when he does, there are few improvisers whose work is as viscerally or intellectually satisfying. Most of his better recordings are out-of-print on vinyl and have never been available on CD. The CD listed here might be the best Harris album of all, if only for the push he receives from a superb rhythm section and the gem of a solo he turns in on Victor Young's *Love Letters*—a solo which creates the illusion of being delivered in a rush, though Harris is phrasing well behind the beat.
FD

Gene Harris

1933

Black And Blue **Harris** (p); **Ron Eschete** (g); **Luther Hughes** (b); **Harold Jones** (d). Concord Ⓕ CCD-4482 (63 minutes). Recorded 1991.

⑥ ❽

Gene Harris began as a blues and boogie pianist in the Albert Ammons and Pete Johnson mould, and his playing is still dominated by the rollicking blues licks on which his fifties successes with The Three Sounds rested. He also developed a tendency to extravagant pianistic gestures, and that, together with the piano-guitar-bass-drums line-up heard here, probably owes much to his admiration for Oscar Peterson. This programme mixes unreconstructed blues and gospel-inflected items like *C.C. Rider* and *Nobody Knows You When You're Down And Out* with the sorts of show tunes that Harris began to introduce into his repertoire in the late fifties. However, true to form, Harris turns any tune he touches into a honorary blues. Even *Blue Bossa*, one of the most successful tracks here, bends to the Harris treatment, which involves a subtle hi-hat backbeat, firm four-beat bass, and florid, bluesy tremolos from the piano. For all the clichés, the result is vibrant, infectiously joyous night-club jazz, bereft of pretension.
MG

Donald Harrison

1960

Full Circle **Harrison** (as, v); **Cyrus Chestnut** (p); **Mark Whitfield** (g); **Dwayne Burno** (b); **Carl Allen** (d). Bellaphon/Sweet Basil Ⓕ 660 55 003 (53 minutes). Recorded 1990.

⑦ ❽

Born in New Orleans, Donald 'Duck' Harrison studied at Southern University and the Berklee College of Music. More significantly, he joined the Art Blakey Academy when he became a Jazz Messenger in 1982. His current work suggests that it is his place of birth and his sojourn with the drummer that most make him the player heard on this CD. His melodic delivery on *Bye Bye Blackbird* displays a character that is uniquely of the Crescent City. The related jump blues style of *Hold It Right There* has the same roots, and contrasts to his ease with *Let's Go Off*, an orthodox hard bop 12-bar that could have come from the Blakey repertoire.

Harrison is already a versatile player, his intonation is accurate, he plays with relaxation and has an unforced improvisational manner. He is at home with the Latin elements here and on *Nature Boy* he shows that he is as aware of a tune's structure as he is of its changes. The balladeer is heard on *Good Morning Heartache* and on his own *Infinite Heart*. On both he moves well away from the parent theme

and demonstrates how to produce a replacement as pleasing as the original. Chestnut and Allen are at the heart of a highly sympathetic support team for one of the truly original young saxophone voices. **BMcR**

Nancy Harrow

Lost Lady **Harrow, Vernel Bagneris** (v); **Phil Woods** (cl, as); **Dick Katz** (p); **Ray Drummond** (b); **Ben Riley** (d). Soul Note Ⓕ 121263-2 (48 minutes). Recorded 1993.

⑥ ❼

Harrow has made a number of albums over the years, starting with her Candid and Atlantic efforts at the dawn of the sixties, and continuing with albums such as this and its immediate predecessor, **Secrets** (Soul Note). Yet she has been passed over without comment in the major jazz encyclopaedias and dictionaries. Which is doubly odd in that her latter-day career has seen her blossom into a songwriting talent to be reckoned with. There is nothing original in the style of the pieces she has created here—they are in the broad tradition of Porter, Gershwin, Rodgers and Hart and their ilk—but the unusual element is that this album was conceived as a whole, in order to tell the story to be found in a Willa Cather novella, *A Lost Lady*. To do this she has created two narrating voices and used Vernel Bagneris to take the male narrating role.

Harrow has a small voice and a relatively rudimentary technique, although her ear is good and she sings in tune. Bagneris, a good live performer, seems less at ease in front of a studio mike and rather too aware of the words he has to deliver, but his good feeling communicates itself. The supporting musicians play with taste and sensitivity. A good record, interesting from its own point of view, but not one which will change your life. **KS**

Antonio Hart

1969

It's All Good **Hart** (ss, as, ts, syn); **Darren Barrett** (t, syn); **Carlos McKinney** (p); **Tassili Bond** (b); **Nasheet Waits** (d); with guests **Robin Eubanks** (tb); **Gary Thomas** (ts); **Steve Nelson** (vb); **Collin Barrett** (b); **Kahli Kwami Bell, Andrew Davies** (perc) and **Akua Dixon-Turre, Gayle Dixon, Regina Carter, Ron Lawrence, Judith Issell, Clarisa Howell** (strings). RCA Novus Ⓕ 163183-2 (64 minutes). Recorded 1994.

⑦ ❽

This, Hart's third album for Novus, is comfortably his best. A fine, passionate player who previously showed his indebtedness to Cannonball Adderley perhaps a little too readily has now matured into a musician on the cusp of a fully-formed voice of his own. Of course those with the disposition to carp could accuse Hart of being entirely retro in his vision, and there would be difficulty in denying this but, equally, when the music reaches this type of quality, then such a comment becomes irrelevant, for the music becomes enjoyable wholly for the qualities it possesses, rather than the musical culture it reflects. Hart has developed particularly in the area of dynamics, both in stating a theme and in soloing. He no longer needs to career along in top gear quite so much, and can find multiple ways to get drama from sudden understatement, just as Lester Young and many others have done before him. His ability suddenly to thicken or purify his tone also helps in this respect. Hart has developed the inner stillness which all great melodists possess, from Webster to Getz to Hodges, and although the occasional piece here still has the rather undigested sense of pastiche (*Puerto Rico* suffers heavily in this respect), much of the album needs no such special pleading for its existence.

The other musicians all perform adequately, but the spotlight is firmly on Hart. The strings, by the way, only accompany (discreetly, too) on two tracks, and the synthesizers on one (*Missin' Miles*, which has a sampled soul beat and a Milesian muted trumpet for good measure). A note to the Novus cover art people: this is not your first foray into tiny coloured lettering out of black backgrounds (one particularly horrific Fats Waller reissue comes to mind as well). In the interests of disseminating information to the public, please make it your last! **KS**

Billy Hart

Amethyst **Hart** (d); **John Stubblefield** (ss, ts); **David Kikoski** (p); **Marc Copland** (kbds); **Mark Feldman** (vn); **David Fiuszynski** (g); **Santi Debriano** (b). Arabesque Ⓕ Jazz AJ01505 (67 minutes). Recorded 1993.

⑤ ❼

Hart made a considerable impact as the drummer in Mwandishi Herbie Hancock's pre-**Headhunters** sextet, along with Bennie Maupin and Eddie Henderson. He already has a couple of albums as leader to his credit, but this latest one is the only date to be current on CD. It is a good record, played by expert musicians, but there is little on it which cuts through in a way that makes you glad you bought it. For the most part, there are themes played across a variety of vamps or suspended tempos, then everybody lines up for their solos, then the theme is re-stated, then the track stops. Only Debriano's *El Junque* and Feldman's *Asylum* have what could be termed a definable atmosphere which calls to be

explored by the players, but then little is done to develop that atmosphere while everyone tries to keep out of each soloist's way. The shortest of the seven tracks on the album is just a handful of seconds less than seven minutes, while four of them are comfortably over ten. With that sort of length, more thought needed to be put into the overall shape of the music if the album was not to pall long before it finished.
KS

Johnny Hartman

1923-1983

I Just Dropped By To Say Hello **Hartman** (v); **Illinois Jacquet** (ts); **Hank Jones** (p); **Kenny Burrell**, **Jim Hall** (g); **Milt Hinton** (b); **Elvin Jones** (d). Impulse! Ⓜ MCAD-39105 (33 minutes). Recorded 1965.

⑧ ❽

Hartman made less than half a dozen albums, and must have counted himself lucky to survive the outrageous liner note to this one, flatulently written by some long-forgotten disc jockey ("I cannot say that I have liked and played every recording that Johnny Hartman has made ..."). Judged by this album and the relaxed and lyrical one he recorded with John Coltrane (recently reissued in a cleaned-up and lavishly-packaged version), he was a good jazz singer whose warm bass-baritone showed the influence of Billy Eckstine and Joe Williams in its pitch, also spreading out to include Sinatra's phrasing. The songs are well-chosen and most of them rarely sung—*Stairway To The Stars*, *If I'm Lucky* and *A Sleepin' Bee* are well delivered and Hartman even manages to create an original version of *In The Wee Small Hours Of The Morning*. The voice is richly melodic and the timing that of a jazz musician born and bred. The accompaniment is spiced by the two guitarists. Jones solos with his usual light touch on the title track, and Jacquet is suitably voluptuous whenever he enters.
SV

Michael Hashim

The Billy Strayhorn Project: Lotus Blossom **Hashim** (ss, as); **Michael Le Donne** (p); **Dennis Irwin** (b); **Kenny Washington** (d). Stash Ⓕ ST-CD-533 (65 minutes). Recorded 1990.

⑧ ❿

As might be expected from a quartet containing three members (Michael Hashim, Michael Le Donne and Kenny Washington) of the Widespread Depression Orchestra, which exists to bring the music of Depression Era America to nineties audiences, this album of Billy Strayhorn originals is sensitive yet exuberant, channelling the great composer/arranger's music through modern sensibilities without compromising its integrity one whit. Hashim's quartet commendably avoids the more familiar Strayhorn fare (*Lush Life*, *Take the 'A' Train* and *Blood Count* are all absent), restricts themselves to concentrated quartet readings of a sample representative enough to include early (1938 and 1939) pieces (*Something to Live For*, *I'm Checkin' Out*, *Goom'bye*, and *Grievin'*), Hodges-type ballad features (*After All*, *Lotus Blossom*, *Charlotte Russe*, *My Little Brown Book*) and a sprinkling of more straightforward mid and up-tempo swingers (*Smada* and *The Intimacy of the Blues*). On both alto and soprano Hashim has a beautifully pure, smooth sound reminiscent of, yet not over-indebted to Johnny Hodges, but he is capable also of the booting, gutsy improvisational flights which constitute much of his later organ-trio work with Le Donne and Washington. His rhythm section is quite superb, Le Donne luminous in the ballads, percussively quirky elsewhere; Toshiko Akiyoshi and Mel Lewis sideman Dennis Irwin is supple and dependable, while Washington is never anything but a thinking drummer, constantly alive to the smallest nuance. An excellent album, and especially fascinating when compared and contrasted with Joe Henderson's award-winning Strayhorn tribute, **Lush Life**.
CP

Stan Hasselgard

1922-1948

The Permanent Hasselgard **Hasselgard**, **Benny Goodman** (cl); **Rolf Ericson** (t); **Tyree Glenn** (tb); **Wardell Gray** (ts); **Red Norvo** (vb); **Arnold Ross**, **Teddy Wilson**, **Barbara Carroll**, **Kjeld Bonfils** (p); **Barney Kessel**, **Billy Bauer**, **Chuck Wayne**, **Al Hendrickson** (g) and others. Phontastic Ⓕ PHONT NCD 8802 (70 minutes). Recorded 1945-48.

⑧ ❻

Although it includes less of Hasselgard's recordings with Benny Goodman than other albums, the Phontastic gives a comprehensive portrait of the clarinettist's short career since the first dozen tracks were done in Sweden before he left for the U.S.A. These show him to be an accomplished Goodman disciple as yet untouched by bebop, and they also display the very high jazz standards which Hasselgard and the other Swedish musicians had achieved.

It was in 1947 that Hasselgard emigrated to the U. S. and eventually, in a most extraordinary move by Goodman, became co-opted into the Benny Goodman Septet as second clarinet. By then he had become a confident bop player, more comfortable in this role than many other exponents who tried so hard to popularise the clarinet as a bop instrument (Goodman made a half-hearted attempt. It is interesting to compare Hasselgard and Goodman on the second version of *All The Things You Are* where they each solo and then duet. It seems likely that Goodman hired the young man so that he could study Hasselgard's bebop playing at close hand). The last track, *Cottontop*, introduced by Hasselgard himself, was recorded less than a week before his death and shows him completely fluent in the bop idiom. **SV**

Hampton Hawes

1928-1977

This is Hampton Hawes, Volume:1 The Trio **Hawes** (p); **Red Mitchell** (b); **Chuck Thompson** (d). Contemporary Ⓜ OJCCD 316-2 (42 minutes). Recorded 1955.

⑧ ❻

Hampton Hawes's reputation is based mainly on his palmy days in the fifties when he emerged as one of the brightest, sparkiest and most sought-after pianists on the West Coast, where his percussive, bluesy modern style was in complete contrast to what we are told is typically West Coast—cool, unemotional and cerebral. He was treated by the record company as an exciting discovery in the mid-fifties, and some of that excitement still comes through. But he has an even greater stake to fame than that; the book he left behind him, *Raise Up Off of Me*, which is the most harrowing yet truthful and humorous account of the jazz life as lived by a black man in white America. This session dates from the happy days when he was on the up and up and not yet dogged by drugs and prison, and is a pleasant enough set, although looking back at a collection issued on LP at the time called **West Coast Piano** it's easy to see that he was but one of a bunch of talented men—Pete Jolly, Russ Freeman, Dick Twardzik and so on. Still, Hawes, on this first date for Contemporary, reveals a winning swagger in his playing. History it may be, but enjoyable history nonetheless. **MK**

As Long As There's Music **Hawes** (p); **Charlie Haden** (b). Verve Ⓕ 513 534-2 (70 minutes). Recorded 1976.

⑧ ❻

This album grew out of the series of duets Charlie Haden recorded for release on the two albums, **"Closeness" Duets** (A&M, see above) and **The Golden Number** (Artists' House). When Hawes died in May 1977 of a cerebral haemorrhage, Haden went back to the session tapes and found sufficient material to release this critically-acclaimed album. This is its first appearance on CD. It comes with three extra tracks, all alternative readings of songs present on the LP version. Haden and Verve have commendably added the extra tracks to the end of the CD, thereby not interrupting the playing order of the original album.

The extra intimacy of the duet format allows an especially direct link between the two musicians, and both are sufficiently inventive and sensitive to thrive from such a link. Haden's clear thematic logic impresses in each of his solos here, while the insouciance of Hawes's lines keep his clear, vibrant musical personality in perfect focus throughout. Their easy gambol through Ornette's *Turnaround* is a particular joy, but the two Hawes originals, the ballad *Irene* and the latin-tinged *Rain Forest*, both have a disarming simplicity emanating from their subtle sophistication. **KS**

Coleman Hawkins

1904-1969

The Complete Recordings, 1929-41 **Hawkins** (ts); accompanied by: **his Orchestra**, **All Star Jam Band, Trio and the Chocolate Dandies**; **Mound City Blue Blowers**; **Henry 'Red' Allen**; **Horace Henderson**; **Benny Goodman**; **The Ramblers**; **Michel Warlop**; **The Berries**; **Benny Carter**; **Jack Hylton**; **Metronome All Star Band** and **Count Basie**. Affinity Ⓜ CD AFS1026-6 (six discs: 430 minutes). Recorded 1929-41.

⑧ ❻

The comprehensive treatment accorded here to Hawkins's early work is amply justified, for the tenor giant was as fundamental to jazz saxophone as Armstrong to jazz trumpet. The title of this otherwise exemplary boxed set is slightly misleading, since recordings by the Fletcher Henderson band, with Hawk still a member until 1934, are excluded. What is here is everything else, including that band's six tracks led by Horace Henderson and small groups from the band (led by Hawkins himself and Red Allen).

Already by 1933 Hawk had perfected a couple of personal styles, the rhythmic but flowing 'hot' approach that others had merely attempted on saxophone, and the luxuriant balladry, for example on *I've Got To Sing A Torch Song* (disc two), which—with only Armstrong as inspiration—he created from the ground up. After Hawkins's five-year stay in Europe, the ballad style flowered with the artistic and sales success of *Body and Soul* (disc five) This was greeted as a triumph within the enclosed jazz world, but was largely ignored by record producers and, without the fascinating multiple takes of the 1940 Commodore session, the last period covered would be thin indeed.

Three CDs' worth, forming the core of the set, document the European sojourn. Because he was justly treated as a star in Europe, he was recorded more often and frequently accorded more space on individual tracks, seeming to expend more energy to make up for sometimes inadequate accompaniments. Although a natural outgrowth of his commanding musical personality, this bore fruit triumphantly in the sessions with fellow-expatriate pianist Freddie Johnson and in examples of

Hawkins's little-known composing ability, such as *A Strange Fact* and *Netcha's Dream* (both with The Ramblers). Even the several recordings with Benny Carter, also in Europe for two years, find Hawk carrying all before him, for instance on the famous *Crazy Rhythm*.

Hawkins's historical position as the fount of all worthwhile saxophone playing is underlined by the contrast of the opening track, *Hello Lola* (which clearly influenced Bud Freeman, the earliest convincing 'non-Hawkins' stylist) with *One O'Clock Jump* and *Feedin' The Bean* from the closing sessions. These latter make a convincing case for Hawk's parentage of the Southwestern blues/riff style which begat Lester Young, prior to founding that player's influential 'anti-Hawkins' school. But it is unnecessary to listen for such academic reasons—each of the 142 tracks has something worth hearing, mostly from Hawk himself. **BP**

Hollywood Stampede **Hawkins** (ts); with a collective personnel: **Howard McGhee, Miles Davis** (t); **Vic Dickenson, Kai Winding** (tb); **Sir Charles Thompson, Hank Jones** (p); **Allan Reuss** (g); **Oscar Pettiford, John Simmons, Curley Russell** (b); **Denzil Best, Max Roach** (d). Capitol Ⓜ CDP7 92596-2 (49 minutes). Recorded 1945/47.

✓ ⑩ ❽

The dozen titles which Coleman Hawkins recorded for Capitol in Hollywood at the beginning of 1945 are amongst the very finest he made throughout his long and fruitful career. He had recently been working in New York with Thelonious Monk and was clearly very interested in the new ideas of the incipient boppers, Howard McGhee amongst them. McGhee, Thompson, Best and Pettiford comprised Hawk's regular band at the time and the library contained a number of pieces which, in retrospect, effectively bridged the gap between swing and bebop. Tunes such as *Rifftide and Stuffy* became closely identified with Hawkins but the programme also contained sumptuous ballad readings such as the superlative *What Is There To Say?*, a close contender for second place after *Body and Soul* as one of Hawk's most impressive performances. These 12 tracks demonstrate again what a high standard Capitol had achieved in recording terms by 1945. The clarity and immediacy of this music, although in mono, is actually superior to a lot of later stereo recordings. The CD is fleshed out with four tracks done two years later for Aladdin Records by an ephemeral band that Hawkins took on a number of bookings. Musically these are good, although the recording quality is a little lower. Miles Davis solos on *Bean-A-Rebop*, but the most memorable moments are when the leader solos. **AM**

Encounters Ben Webster **Hawkins, Ben Webster** (ts); **Oscar Peterson** (p); **Herb Ellis** (g); **Ray Brown** (b); **Alvin Stoller** (d). Verve Ⓜ 823 120-2 (36 minutes). Recorded 1957.

⑩ ❽

This album, a classic latter-day Hawkins set, comes from a mammoth recording session in October 1957 which also produced the album **The Genius of Coleman Hawkins** (Verve 825 673-2). The difference between the two is that Webster is absent from **The Genius**. On the set under consideration Hawkins and Webster manage to keep competitiveness to a minimum, and the resultant music has a relaxed, quiet warmth which is wholly beneficial. The opening track, *Blues for Yolanda*, contains a blistering Hawkins solo which reaches a climax wherein the tenorist is literally shrieking high-note phrases on his horn. Webster, unperturbed, follows with a disarmingly relaxed, beautifully poised effort which nevertheless keeps the listener spellbound. For the rest of the record, both saxophonists produce gloriously sensuous ballad readings (Hawkins, aware of Ben's mastery in this area, is much less dismissive of melodic expression than he usually was by this stage of his career) and lightly swinging medium-tempo interpretations of standards such as *You'd Be So Nice To Come Home To* and *Shine on Harvest Moon*. The rhythm section extends a level of support all the more extraordinary for its discretion and complete absence of showiness.

The only carp I have here is that, with a playing-time which hardly begins to stretch CD capacity, and with a late-seventies vinyl reissue of this material setting a laudable precedent of including all the material from this pairing, there are two tracks left off here, one of them being the bewitchingly pretty Hawkins original, *Maria*. Both tracks were originally assigned back in the fifties to **Coleman Hawkins and his Confrères**, but surely they could have been added to this set? They were the only tracks on that album with Webster present. **KS**

With Roy Eldridge At The Opera House **Hawkins** (ts); **Eldridge** (t); **John Lewis** (p); **Percy Heath** (b); **Connie Kay** (d). Verve Ⓜ 521 641-2 (74 minutes). Recorded 1957.

⑧ ❽

For many years these recordings posed a great puzzle. They were on two LPs, with some numbers in mono and others in stereo, and several were identical on both discs. In fact, two concerts were recorded, one in Los Angeles and one in Chicago, and they are both on this CD. Hawkins plays superbly, using that rather irrascible mode of address that he adopted in the 1950s. His long, heavily accented lines pursue the harmonies relentlessly through every conceivable permutation, and it is quite impossible to resist the power of his biting tone and unremitting swing. Eldridge, too, seems in a somewhat peppery mood. He resorts even more than usual to sudden stratospheric shrieks, the kind that had had such an effect on his young acolyte, Dizzy Gillespie, and hurls himself into solos with a recklessness which would bring instant disaster to a lesser artist. The blistering effect of these two is heightened by the suave self-possession of the rhythm section, which is actually three-quarters of the Modern Jazz Quartet. And that is where the great attraction lies; jazz played by artists of this age and calibre is a drama of character and personality as much as anything else. They reveal themselves through the music. A long additional track features others on the same concert bill - JJ Johnson, Stan Getz, Lester Young, Oscar Peterson - but it is the interplay between Hawkins and Eldridge that really matters. **DG**

Hawk Eyes **Hawkins** (ts); **Charlie Shavers** (t); **Ray Bryant** (p); **Tiny Grimes** (g); **George Duvivier** (b); **Osie Johnson** (d). Prestige Ⓜ OJCD 294-2 (46 minutes). Recorded 1959.

⑧ ❻

As Hawkins entered his last decade his tenor sound was angry, harsh and stripped of adornment. This coincidentally allowed him, in sound at least, to keep up with the contemporary hard-boppers. The exception here is in a softly wistful statement of *La Rosita*. However, the 14-minute blues *C'mon In* is a towering and menacing example of his craft at its best. Opening with teak-like tenor over double bass, the piece builds gradually until Shavers enters with a blood vessel bursting solo which, for him, is pretty well stripped down to essentials. His second solo on the piece is an unexpectedly delicate and tasteful essay. Bryant was a couple of generations younger than Hawkins, but he was already a veteran of Jo Jones's trios; here he shows complete maturity in everything he does. *I Never Knew* is a previously unissued track which must have been excluded from the original for space reasons and not for any dip in quality, for it has a marvellously buoyant and driving solo from Hawk, plus robust but tasteful piano, while Shavers wrestles himself to the floor with a brazen solo which has a fleeting but effective touch of half-valving at its conclusion. You could never fall asleep to this album, but if somehow you managed such a feat, the remarkable honk with which Hawk starts his second tirade on *I Never Knew* would abruptly awaken you and your neighbours. **SV**

Wrapped Tight **Hawkins** (ts); **Bill Berry**, **Snooky Young** (t); **Urbie Green** (tb); **Barry Harris** (p); **Buddy Catlett** (b); **Eddie Locke** (d). Impulse! Ⓜ GRD-109 (44 minutes). Recorded 1965.

⑧ ❽

The two crucial adjectives in biographer John Chilton's description of this Coleman Hawkins session are "lethargic" and "desultory", and even producer Bob Thiele noted in an interview the following year that the great tenorman's breath control was not what it once had been, leading to his substituting rapid flurries for his trademark sweeping phrases. While these comments are undoubtedly true, perceptive and fair, **Wrapped Tight**, despite rather wasting a stellar brass section on routine background work and never remotely stretching anyone involved, remains, like a lot of later Hawkins, a strangely compelling album. Its attraction is in part attributable to the sheer emotional charge carried by the great instrumentalist; even at his most relaxed and informal, his often bleary but frequently still rhapsodic sound inexplicably moving in its world-weary querulousness. The material is pretty unremarkable, contain the usual Hawkins mix of tender ballads (*Beautiful Girl*), standard fare (*Red Roses for a Blue Lady*) and blues (*Wrapped Tight*), and of the band, only Barry Harris gets to solo in a discreet Teddy Wilson-ish rippling style, but overall, despite its faults, this is an enjoyable example of sixties Hawkins. **CP**

Supreme **Hawkins** (ts); **Barry Harris** (p); **Gene Taylor** (b); **Roy Brooks** (d). Enja Ⓕ ENJ-9009-2 (65 minutes). Recorded 1966.

⑧ ❽

Recorded live in Baltimore in 1966, at a time when his playing was reported to be erratic at best, **Supreme** catches Coleman Hawkins on a night that gloriously reaffirms his greatness. It's true that the gruffly muscular tone has taken on a querulous edge, that the bustling rhythmic assurance has been infiltrated by a degree of hesitancy, but in their place has come an economy of means that bespeaks a man still at the peak of creativity. Every pared-down, beautifully-weighted phrase has the rightness of a Zen painter's brush-stroke, the wisdom of 45 years' playing distilled into the *essence* of tenor mastery. What's more Hawkins sounds like he's enjoying himself, his grizzled lyricism imparted with the playfulness of an old dog who knows there are no more tricks to learn. The set comprises mostly standards – *Lover Come Back to Me*, Monk's *In Walked Bud* – plus a lovely reading of Quincy Jones's ballad *Quintessence*; the pick-up rhythm trio, with Gene Taylor, Roy Brooks and Hawkins's then-regular pianist Barry Harris, provide sensitive support. Inevitably, there's a version of *Body and Soul*, through which Hawk ambles with a gruff inventiveness, the site of the warrior's most historic victory transformed by this new cause for celebration. **Supreme** is an apposite title. **GL**

Erskine Hawkins

1914-1993

and His Orchestra 1936-38 **Hawkins**, **Wilbur 'Dud' Bascomb**, **Marcellus Green**, **Sammy Lowe** (t); **Edward Sims**, **Robert Range** (tb); **William Johnson** (as); **Jimmy Mitchelle** (as, v); **Paul Bascomb**, **Julian Dash** (ts); **Haywood Henry** (cl, bs); **Avery Parrish** (p); **William McLemore** (g); **Leemie Stanfield** (b); **James Morrison** (d); **Billy Daniels**, **Merle Turner** (v). Classics Ⓜ 653 (67 minutes). Recorded 1936-38.

⑥ ❼

At the age of 20, Hawkins went with the Alabama State College band to New York. Two years later he assumed the band's leadership and began recording almost immediately. He continued to lead a big band until the early fifties and, significantly, his last orchestra contained several of the sidemen who had started with the 'Bama State Collegians and who are featured extensively on this CD. As a band, it was not significant: Lowe was a useful arranger in the Sy Oliver manner and most of the remaining charts were by Parrish. They enjoyed considerable popularity with black audiences, but items such as *I'll Get Along Somehow* are almost mawkishly sentimental. The band were at their most comfortable with medium tempo items like *Uproar Shout* or *Big John Special*. The outstanding soloists were the forthright Dud Bascomb, the fleet Dash and the gifted Parrish but, not surprisingly, most of the solo space fell to the leader. In his more restrained moments Hawkins played powerful, Louis Armstrong-inspired trumpet, but there were times, as on *Dear Old Southland*, where he became incontinently exhibitionistic. The final four titles, with a fuller ensemble, are the strongest and arguably represent the Hawkins orchestra at its peak. **BMcR**

Louis Hayes

1937

Light And Lively **Louis Hayes** (d); **Charles Tolliver** (t); **Bobby Watson** (as); **Kenny Barron** (p); **Clint Houston** (b). SteepleChase Ⓕ SCCD 31245 (66 minutes). Recorded 1989.

⑧ ❽

One of the finest small-band drummers in jazz, Louis Hayes provided the drive behind two leading hard-bop groups of the early sixties—the Horace Silver and Cannonball Adderley Quintets—and later played with the bands of Oscar Peterson and McCoy Tyner, as well as co-leading a group with Freddie Hubbard and Joe Henderson. Such a curriculum vitae speaks for itself.

No-one can get quite so many gradations of tone out of a top cymbal as Louis Hayes, nor generate more propulsion by simply playing four even beats to a bar. Although he is by no means self-effacing, Hayes never dominates the proceedings, even when he is the leader, and plays with as much finesse on slow ballads as on his speciality, a walking mid-tempo. The entire rhythm section on this session is a thing of beauty, like a well-made watch. It could serve as an excellent study-model for young players. **DG**

Tubby Hayes

1935-1973

For Members Only **Tubby Hayes** (ts, fl); **Mick Pyne** (p); **Ron Matthewson** (b); **Tony Levin** (d). Master Mix Ⓕ CDCHE 110 (71 minutes). Recorded 1967.

✔ ⑧ ❽

Tubby Hayes possessed an awesome talent. The combination of a remarkably fast brain and a flawless technique manifested itself in a garrulous, pugnacious, completely unstoppable flow. These 12 numbers by his last quartet all come from BBC Radio Two live sessions and benefit from the presence of enthusiastic studio audiences. There is an added sparkle to everyone's playing, Tubby's in particular.

Of all the posthumous Tubby Hayes releases, this is probably the best. It reveals what a complete artist he was, both as a composer and a player. The slow ballad *Dedicated To Joy* is especially good, as is the characteristically bravura *Off The Wall*. This was the time when new and looser forms were being explored by jazz musicians, and towards the end of his life Tubby Hayes was cautiously expanding his horizons in this direction. Probably his most complete achievement in this area was the extended composition *Mexican Green*, which he recorded with Fontana. The version here is every bit as good as the one released on LP, if not better. **DG**

Graham Haynes

1960

The Griots' Footsteps **Haynes** (c, kbds); **Steve Williamson** (ts, ss); **Cheick Tidiane-Seck**, **Don-Dieu Divin**, **Luis Manresa** (kbds); **Laroussi-Ali Djamel** (g); **Brigitte Menon** (sitar); **Lyra Menon** (tbra); **Vincent Othieno**, **Noel Ekwabi** (b); **Brice Wassy** (d,v); **Jorge Amorim**, **Daniel Moreno**, **Chief Udoh Essiet** (perc). Verve Ⓕ 523 262-2 (60 minutes). Recorded 1994.

⑥ ❻

Haynes is one of the more conceptually savvy jazz funksters, with an ear for fluid forms and plausible syntheses of different traditions. On this session, recorded in Paris with an aggressively international cast, his limber cornet soars over a near-cinematic montage of string-synth washes, de-natured blues, organ riffs, South Indian string drones, talking drum and ethnofunk beats. The players develop their complex rhythmic interaction by ear, which is why Haynes's music breathes more freely than the electric jazz of contemporaries like his one-time associate Steve Coleman. But Haynes is also a sound democrat: some background textures are thick and juicy, some banal synth clichés. It is a little closer to Jon Hassell than seventies Miles.

Graham's fan Don Cherry pioneered this jazz-meets-the-Third-World stance, and Haynes echoes Cherry's declarative pentatonics and vulnerable, human tone. He also has a younger man's chops. This disc is far from perfect: it is way too long, and dead patches abound. That said, the cornettist crafts shapely phrases even when harmonic motion is nil—sometimes following the arabesques of sung Islamic prayers—and executes complex bent-note figures without self-congratulation. He is worth hearing even in an uneven setting. **KW**

Roy Haynes
1926

Te Vous! Haynes (d); **Donald Harrison** (as); **Pat Metheny** (g); **David Kikoski** (p); **Christian McBride** (b). Dreyfus Ⓕ FDM 36569-2 (53 minutes). Recorded 1994.

⑥ ❽

Haynes is very much a drummer for any occasion. He is hardly a leader of note but his well publicised spells with Lester Young, Miles Davis, Thelonious Monk and Sarah Vaughan make him a much sought after sideman. In more recent times work with Stan Getz, Ted Curson and Chick Corea have underlined his versatility and he has been a familiar face on the world tour.

This CD puts him in fast company and gives a clear indication of his present stance. He is an elegant drummer, a player of tunes who occupies sound space with care. The recording balance does him full justice and he conducts his own volume controls, throttling right back behind Metheny on *John McKee*, *If I Could* and *Blues M45*, easing the way for Kikoski on *Like This* and *Trinkle, Tinkle* and setting the cruise control further up behind Harrison's swinging lines on *James*, *Trigonometry* and *Good For The Soul* in particular. His solos on *John McKee* and *Trigonometry* take the form of persuasive soliloquies rather than bombastic tirades, but it is his ensemble self, floating comfortably across bar divisions, jousting with bassist McBride while still providing exemplary group punctuation, that makes him the master of such combo situations. **BMcR**

Jimmy Heath
1926

Nice People Heath (ts, arr); with a collective personnel including: **Clark Terry, Freddie Hubbard, Donald Byrd** (t); **Nat Adderley** (c); **Curtis Fuller** (tb); **Dick Berg, Julius Watkins, Jim Buffington** (frh); **Don Butterfleld** (tba); **Cannonball Adderley** (as); **Tom MacKintosh** (ts); **Pat Patrick** (bs); **Wynton Kelly, Cedar Walton, Herbie Hancock, Harold Mabern** (p); **Kenny Burrell** (g); **Paul Chambers, Percy Heath** (b); **Al Heath, Connie Kay** (d). Riverside Ⓜ OJCCD-6006-2 (53 minutes). Recorded 1959-64.

⑥ ❻

All three Heath brothers Jimmy, Percy and Al, play on some of these sessions; the ten titles are drawn from the six LP's which Jimmy made for Riverside and six of the numbers were written by him. Heath is a fine tenor soloist with a rich, warm tone who was once known as Little Bird, when he played alto but on tenor he is more of an individual. His writing has always been functional and with the workman-like approach of a man who knows what it is like to play his part in a group. There is a healthy regard for the brass instruments here, with careful use of french-horns and tuba on some tracks. A couple are uncomplicated excuses for extended solo playing such as *Nice People* (based on the chord sequence of *Indiana*) and *All The Things You Are* which benefits from the presence of guitarist Kenny Burrell. The most interesting piece is *The Picture of Heath*, expertly played by a ten-piece band and featuring a short chase passage by Nat Adderley and Clark Terry. This is, unfortunately, the sole track taken from Jimmy's fine **Really Big** LP, certainly the best of all his Riverside albums. The sound is generally very good although the early stereo, with the band parted neatly down the middle, sounds quaint by today's standards. **AM**

Ted Heath
1900-1969

Headin' North Collective personnel includes **Bobby Pratt, Bert Courtley, Duncan Campbell, Eddie Blair** (t); **Don Lusher, Johnny Keating, Keith Christie** (tb); **Les Gilbert, Roy Willox, Ronnie Chamberlain** (as); **Henry McKenzie** (cl, ts); **Danny Moss, Don Rendell, Bob Efford** (ts); **Ralph Dollimore, Frank Horrox, Stan Tracey** (p); **Johnny Hawksworth** (b); **Ronnie Verrell** (d); **Johnny Keating, Kenny Graham, Reg Owen, Ken Moule, Ralph Dollimore, Ronnie Roullier** (arr). Memoir Ⓕ CDMOIR 505 (62 minutes). Recorded 1952-63.

⑥ ❽

Ted Heath created the finest and most impressive dance band in Britain. The fact that his recordings sold well enough in the US to warrant several tours of that country is an indication of the band's popularity there too. A hard task-master, Heath always produced perfectly played music by a band which looked as good as it sounded, for it flourished in the days when the public still wanted to dance to 'live' music. Although Ted gave employment to many jazz writers and soloists (vide the listed partial personnel above) he was enough of a businessman to know that the majority of his record buyers and paying customers at

dance halls and concerts were not committed jazz fans. This CD is made up of 'singles', records made for juke boxes and radio play. Only one of the 24 tracks lasts for more than three minutes and, within those constraints, a great deal of good music is to be heard. But it was only very rarely that Heath gave the band its head (**Our Kind Of Jazz** and **Spotlight On The Sidemen** are two Decca LPs in the genre which would benefit from conversion to CD) and it is only occasionally on **Headin' North** that the true jazz potential of this fine orchestra is realized. **AM**

Mark Helias

1950

Desert Blue Helias (b); **Herb Robertson** (t); **Ray Anderson** (tb); **Marty Ehrlich** (as, ts, clt, bcl); **Jerome Harris** (g); **Anthony Davis** (p, syn); **Pheeroan AkLaff** (d). Enja Ⓕ CD 6016-2 (51 minutes). Recorded 1989.

⑧ ❽

As might be expected from a musician whose career includes stints with the Yale Philharmonic Orchestra, Anthony Braxton, Nu and Slickaphonics, Mark Helias is as at home with the hammered electric bass associated with funk as with the more complex acoustic bass figures favoured by the avant-garde, and **Desert Blue** effectively showcases the whole spectrum of his instrumental and compositional talent. The material ranges from slinky blues numbers through rumbustious funk to semi-abstract pieces (an arco bass and bass clarinet duo is particularly memorable); moreover, Helias's virtuosic adaptability is emulated by that of his sidemen. Anthony Davis is a delight throughout, constantly eccentric and unpredictable even in the tightest of formats; Marty Ehrlich has a passionate, plangent sound on saxophones and is also an exceptional clarinet and bass clarinet player; Hank Robertson, despite lapses into misguided musical humour, demonstrates great versatility on both trumpet and cornet; Pheeroan akLaff more than justifies his ranking in the top flight of contemporary drummers, whether he is providing a driving funk beat or subtly embellishing a free-jazz meditation. Poll-winning trombonist Ray Anderson and guitarist Jerome Harris—often seen with Sonny Rollins bands in recent years—adorn the unusually tasteful funk-based tracks, but it is, unsurprisingy, the overall musical vision of Helias himself, impressive both for its range and for the performances it elicits with almost Mingus-like sureness from the sidemen, which makes **Desert Blue** such a rich and rewarding album. **CP**

Julius Hemphill

1940-1995

Big Band **Hemphill** (ss, as); **David Hines**, **Rasul Saddik** (t); **Frank Lacy**, **David Taylor** (tb); **Vincent Chancey**, **John Clark** (frh); **Marty Ehrlich** (ss, as, f); **John Purcell**, **John Stubblefield** (ss, ts, f); **J.D. Parran** (bs, f); **Jack Wilkins**, **Bill Frisell** (g); **Jerome Harris** (elb); **Ronnie Burrage** (d); **Gordon Gottlieb** (perc); **K. Curtis Lyle** (narr). Elektra/Musician 960831-2 (61 minutes). Recorded 1988.

⑧ ❻

Through much of the early part of his recording career, Julius Hemphill favoured lean, uncluttered settings for his eloquent alto—frequently duos with like-minded cohorts such as Oliver Lake or Abdul Wadud, or piano-less trios or quartets with cello replacing bass. His moody, lavish compositions for the World Saxophone Quartet were an outgrowth of his early overdubbed solo works, programmatic 'audiodramas' like *Blue Boye* and *Roi Boye and the Gotham Minstrels*. Such extravagant gestures are carried over into his writing for big band, with unusual instrumentation put to unconventional use. Most accessible are the ballads; *For Billie* finds his piquant lead alto awash in muted brass and five flutes, while the winding melody of *Leora* must conjure with a minimal, static background reminiscent of Steve Reich. Cagey freebop lines contrast with noirish episodes in *At Harmony* and *C/Saw*—the latter indebted in some structural way to Coltrane's *Bessie's Blues* (is there a hidden clue in the title?). But on the debit side are *Bordertown*, a visit to Hemphill's Texas roots via a strained soprano line, refracted harmonies, and a backbeat that threatens to go on forever, and *Drunk On God*, a lengthy pastiche of styles meant to illuminate a shamanistic poem. Altogether, an ambitious but flawed programme. **AL**

Eddie Henderson

1940

Flight of Mind Henderson (t); **Larry Willis** (p); **Ed Howard** (b); **Victor Lewis** (d). SteepleChase Ⓕ SCCD 31284. (61 minutes). Recorded 1991.

⑤ ❻

The influence of Miles Davis, which marked Henderson's work so strongly during his years with Herbie Hancock's Mwandishi sextet, is still obvious when the trumpeter employs Harmon mute, as he does on *L+M* (based on *Love for Sale*) and a tender *Goodbye* (dedicated to his recently-deceased son), or when the mood turns Moorish, as it does on *Torre-Adore*. Elsewhere, tonal and melodic notions recall Freddie Hubbard, without the excessive high-register reaching, while there are more personal touches like the muttered coda on the title-track and the rubato theme statement of Puccini's "Un Bel di Vedremo". A surfeit of slow tempos drags down the overall impact of this session, which provides too little opportunity for the fine rhythm section to stretch. The after-hours mood is effective, however, and such uncommon tunes choices as Hubbard's *Lament for Booker* and the Puccini add a few nice wrinkles. Henderson is a practising psychiatrist who continues to play well for a part-timer without moving into the realm of the exceptional. **BB**

Fletcher Henderson

1897-1952

A Study In Frustration Selective personnel: **Fletcher Henderson**, **Horace Henderson** or **Fats Waller** (p); **Louis Armstrong**, **Rex Stewart**, **Red Allen**, **Roy Eldridge** (t); **Charlie Green**, **J.C. Higginbotham**, **Jimmy Harrison**, **Benny Morton** (tb); **Buster Bailey** (cl); **Don Redman**, **Benny Carter**, **Russell Procope**, **Hilton Jefferson** (as); **Coleman Hawkins**, **Ben Webster**, **Chu Berry** (ts); **John Kirby**, **Israel Crosby** (b); **Walter Johnson**, **Sid Catlett** (d). Columbia Ⓜ 57596 (three discs: 194 minutes). Recorded 1923-38.

⑧ ❻

Henderson was an unlikely man to be the one who evolved and formalized the conventional line-up of the big band in jazz—trumpets, trombones, reeds and rhythm section. In his personal life and as a band leader Henderson was largely ineffectual, his brother was a much better pianist, and colleagues like Don Redman and Benny Carter were much better band leaders. In another place it could be argued that most of the credit which accrued to Henderson should have gone to Don Redman, who wrote magnificent arrangements for the band and undoubtedly provoked Henderson's compositional innovations.

Never mind that; it was all done under Henderson's name, and it was he who gave house room to Louis Armstrong, Coleman Hawkins, Roy Eldridge and Chu Berry at the burgeoning point of their careers. Henderson chose musicians well and wrote good arrangements for them to play. Even the earliest of these 64 tracks, done before there were any major soloists, holds much of interest. Armstrong electrified the band when he joined in 1924 and on the nine tracks on which he is featured shows by his tone, ideas and abilities to swing that he was light years ahead of the rest of the band, which sounds leaden by contrast. Later Coleman Hawkins matured within the band and created the first chapter in the history of the tenor saxophone. His 1933 *Queer Notions*, featuring himself and trumpeter Red Allen, (the only two musicians in the band who could really understand the composition) was a decade ahead of its time and the first example of avant-garde jazz. In the later bands the emergent Roy Eldridge and Chu Berry treat the music like a great playground for their solos. It is amazing to find such a body of well-written music with such a consistently high level of soloists.

Henderson eventually abandoned his own orchestra and took his arrangements to Benny Goodman, who added another dimension to them and made all the money. **SV**

Louis With Fletcher Henderson **Henderson** (p); **Elmer Chambers**, **Howard Scott**, **Louis Armstrong** (t); **Charlie Green** (tb); **Don Redman** (cl, as, ts); **Cecil Scott** (cl, as); **Buster Bailey** (cl, bcl, sop, as); **Coleman Hawkins** (cl, ts, c-mel, bss); **Charlie Dixon** (bj); **Ralph Escudero** (tba); **Kaiser Marshall** (d). Forte Records Productions Ⓜ F-38001/03 (three discs: 201 minutes). Recorded 1924-25.

✔ ⑩ ❻

Louis Armstrong spent a year with Fletcher Henderson's orchestra, and this three-CD set, of Canadian origin, contains all known 65 tracks of Louis with Henderson, including rare alternative takes from collectors labels such as Puritan, Domino and Paramount. Henderson wanted a 'hot' soloist in his band to replace trumpeter Joe Smith; Louis was riding the crest of a popularity wave in Chicago through his work with King Oliver. It was an incredible experience for Louis to be subjected to the discipline of a big dance band made up principally of schooled musicians but it was a two-way exchange, for Henderson's arranger Don Redman had to devise ways of making the stilted ensemble loosen up and swing. To play through the three discs is to hear not only the emergence of Armstrong as a big band soloist but also the growth of a big band jazz style. Louis takes plenty of solos but all (with one exception), are muted, as if Fletcher was not prepared to alter the overall tone colour of his band too drastically. From the first tracks (*Manda* and *Go 'Long Mule*), where Armstrong's solos are tentative in approach, to the closing *TNT* and *Carolina Stomp*, the band gets better and more prominence is given to other soloists such as Bailey, Hawkins and Green. A great deal of care has gone into the preparation of this most important package with John R.T. Davies involved in the transfers. We are not likely to hear better sound reproduction of these historic sides. **AM**

Tidal Wave **Henderson**, **Horace Henderson** (p, arr); **Russell Smith**, **Bobby Stark**, **Rex Stewart**, **Irving Randolph**, **Henry 'Red' Allen** (t); **Claude Jones**, **Benny Morton**, **Keg Johnson** (tb); **Buster Bailey** (cl); **Russell Procope**, **Harvey Boone**, **Edgar Sampson**, **Hilton Jefferson**, **Benny Carter** (cl, as); **Coleman Hawkins**, **Ben Webster** (cl, ts); **Clarence Holiday**, **Lawrence Lucie** (g); **John Kirby**, **Elmer James** (b, tba); **Walter Johnson** (d). MCA/Decca Ⓜ GRD-643 (61 minutes). Recorded 1931-34.

⑧ ❽

With a decent press agent, Fletcher Henderson might have been annointed 'King of Swing'. Indeed, by the mid-1920s, Henderson was leading the archetype for all swing groups at New York's fabled Roseland

Ballroom. Though starting out and functioning primarily as a dance band, Henderson's ensemble got an important jazz boost with the addition of Louis Armstrong in 1924-25. Also pivotal was arranger Don Redman, whose charts bubbled with riffs and call-and-response exchanges that would become hallmarks of the 1930s big band sound. When Redman left in 1927, Henderson took over the principal arranging chores, developing a lean yet supple approach that swung with power and panache.

In this sparkling compilation of 21 tracks from the band's 1931-34 tenure with Decca, we catch a well-drilled ensemble, a stable of outstanding soloists and a batch of Henderson charts like *Sugar Foot Stomp* that still make your feet want to dance. Among the soloists, Coleman Hawkins, then establishing the tenor sax as a front-line solo 'voice', was central to the band's success. Trumpeters Red Allen and Rex Stewart and a young Benny Carter on alto sax also shine. Ironically, the title track was written and arranged by Russ Morgan. Though a clever novelty number demonstrating the reeds' digital dexterity, it throws into relief (as do the charts of brother Horace and Carter) Henderson's sleek, power-packed take on tunes such as *Wrapping' It Up* and *Shanghai Shuffle*. Indeed, Henderson classics like *Down South Camp Meetin'* (heard here in its original 1934 incarnation) would soon help make swing Amercia's popular music and Benny Goodman its 'King'. **CB**

Horace Henderson

1904

Horace Henderson and His Orchestra 1940 **Henderson** (p); **Emmett Berry, Harry 'Pee Wee' Jackson, Gail Brockman, Nat Bates** (t); **Harold Johnson** (t, v); **Ray Nance** (t, vn); **Edward Fant, Nat Atkins, Joe McLewis, Leo Williams, Archie Brown** (tb); **Dalbert Bright** (as, cl); **Willie Randall, Howard Johnson, C.Q. Price** (as); **Elmer Williams** (ts); **Dave Young** (ts); **Mosey Gant** (ts); **Bob Dorsey, Lee Pope** (ts); **Leonard Talley** (bs); **Hurley Ramey, Leroy Harris** (g); **Jessie Simpkins, Israel Crosby** (b); **Oliver Coleman, Debo Mills** (d); **Viola Jefferson** (v). Classics Ⓜ 648 (69 minutes). Recorded 1940/1941.

⑥ ❻

Horace Henderson, brother of Fletcher, led big bands for more than 40 years. He was a useful pianist, an accomplished arranger and over the years he provided charts for Benny Goodman, Don Redman, The Casa Loma Orchestra, Rommy Forsey and Earl Hines as well as for his better-known brother. This CD offers the only sides made by Horace Henderson's working band, a band that he had recently 'inherited' from Nat Towles. His arrangements were in some ways more subtle than Fletcher's; *Do-Re-Mi* and *I Still Have My Dreams* give an idea of the contrasts in his style; the former a texturally aware fun number and the latter a reserved version of the inter-section call and response system. His soloists were impressive, with Nance's violin particularly strong on *Kitty On Toast*, Young's tenor flying the Coleman Hawkins colours on *Shufflin' Joe* and Berry conspicuous throughout, especially on the declamatory *Turkey Special*. Henderson's own piano also displays understated finesse, perhaps rather obviously striding on *Flying A Whing-Ding* but elsewhere taking the more judicious Teddy Wilson route. Crosby's Blantonian bass and some of the trombone parts remind one of the great forties Ellington Band; for a short time this Henderson Orchestra, with its close attention to collective dynamics, could be discussed in the same breath. Four Fletcher Henderson titles from 1941 complete the programme. **BMcR**

Joe Henderson

1937

The Blue Note Years with a collective personnel of: **Henderson** (ts); **Hubert Laws** (f); **Leo Wright, Eric Dolphy, James Spaulding, Jerry Dodgion, Jerome Richardson, Steve Wilson** (as); **Jerome Richardson, Eddie Daniels** (ts); **Pepper Adams** (bs); **Kenny Dorham, Blue Mitchell, Lee Morgan, Carmell Jones, Donald Byrd, Freddie Hubbard, Woody Shaw, Snooky Young, Al Porcino, Denny Moore, Marvin Stamm** (t); **Johnny Coles** (flh); **Curtis Fuller, Garnett Brown, Tony Studd, Benny Powell, Jimmy Knepper, Bob Burgess, Julian Priester** (tb); **Grant Green, Eddie Wright** (g); **Bobby Hutcherson** (vb); **Herbie Hancock, McCoy Tyner, Andrew Hill, Duke Pearson, Barry Harris, Tommy Flanagan, Horace Silver, Steve Kuhn, Cedar Walton, Roland Hanna, Renée Rosnes** (p); **Freddie Roach, Larry Young** (org); **Butch Warren, Gene Taylor, Eddie Khan, Bob Cranshaw, Richard Davis, Teddy Smith, Steve Swallow, Ron Carter, Herbie Lewis, Buster Williams, Ira Coleman** (b); **Tony Williams, Pete LaRoca, Roy Brooks, Al Harewood, Roy Haynes, Billy Higgins, Clarence Johnston, Albert 'Tootie' Heath, Elvin Jones, Roger Humphries, Mickey Roker, Joe Chambers, Mel Lewis, Al Foster, Billy Drummond** (d). Ⓜ CDP7 89287-2 (four discs: 278 minutes). Recorded 1963-90.

⑨ ❽

Since hitting the scene in 1962 with Brother Jack McDuff, Henderson has built a body of work placing him at the post-war tenor sax summit with such titans as Sonny Rollins, John Coltrane and Stan Getz. Henderson's singular style, while drawing on Rollins's rhythmic serendipity, Coltrane's sheets-of-sound and Getz's ethereal lyricism, also calls on rhythm 'n' soul and the "harmolodic" free-falls of Ornette Coleman. However, it's the saxophonist's pliant sound—at once bluesy and hip, as well as lush and cool—that makes Henderson immediately identifiable. In this four-hour, four-disc boxed anthology culled from Henderson's initial dates for Blue Note in 1963 to a 1990 session with pianist Renée Rosnes, Henderson emerges as a consistently engaged and innovative player able to respond with apt élan whatever the setting or style.

Henderson's Blue Note oeuvre encompasses seven albums as a leader and 30 albums as a sideman. Here, 26 of the 36 tracks consist of dates led by Kenny Dorham, Blue Mitchell, Grant Green, Andrew Hill, Lee Morgan, Freddie Roach, Horace Silver, Duke Pearson, Pete LaRoca, Larry Young, Bobby Hutcherson, McCoy Tyner, Herbie Hancock and the Thad Jones-Mel Lewis Orchestra, all from the sixties. The package is thus as much a retrospective of Blue Note's glory years as of Henderson. Among the gems are Henderson-penned standards *Blue Bossa* and *Recorda Me* from **Page One** (1963), the saxophonist's Blue Note début as a leader, and a rousing *Isotope* from **The State of the Tenor, Volume 1** (1985). Definitive. **CB**

The Milestone Years **Henderson** (ts); with various groups comprising: **Mike Lawrence**, **Woody Shaw**, **Oscar Brashear** (t); **Nat Adderley** (c); **Grachan Moncur lll**, **Julian Priester**, **Curtis Fuller** (tb); **Jeremy Steig**, **Ernie Watts** (f); **Hadley Caliman** (f, ts); **Lee Konitz** (as); **Kenny Barron**, **Don Friedman**, **Joe Zawinul**, **Mark Levine**, **Joachim Kühn** (p); **Herbie Hancock**, **George Cables**, **Hideo Ichikawa**, **George Duke** (p, elp); **Alice Coltrane** (p, hp); **Patrick Gleeson** (syn); **Michael White** (vn); **George Wadenius**, **James Blood Ulmer**, **Lee Ritenour** (g); **Ron Carter**, **Victor Gaskin**, **Stanley Clarke**, **Kunimitsu Inaba**, **Dave Holland**, **Charlie Haden**, **J.F. Jenny-Clark**, **David Friesen** (b); **Ron Carter**, **Alfonso Johnson** (elb); **Louis Hayes**, **Jack DeJohnette**, **Roy McCurdy**, **Lenny White**, **Motohiko Hino**, **Leon Chancler**, **Daniel Humair**, **Harvey Mason** (d); **Airto Moreira**, **Carmelo Garcia**,. **Bill Summers** (perc); **Flora Purim** (v). Milestone Ⓕ 8MCD-4413-2 (eight CDs: 587 minutes). Recorded 1967-76.

⑦ ❽

Henderson's improvisatory style has changed little since his introduction to the recording studio by Kenny Dorham in 1963 (see above). On this collection, made for the Milestone label over the best part of a decade, he reveals a wide interest in a multiplicity of settings for his music and his playing, but his identity remains static. This in part explains why his years at Milestone were for the most part financially unrewarding—popular music, with jazz following in its wake, went through cataclysmic changes, and many musicians changed with it to stay afloat—and why, ultimately, his stylistic intransigence has lately paid off in a big way. By then, he had certainly paid his dues, as the simple fact of him being a sideman for most of the years contained within this box points out.

Henderson excels in both the hard-bop milieu he responded so positively to while in the Horace Silver band, and in the relative freedom which modality can bring to a player. His playing on compositions recorded previously for both Blue Note and Silver, such as *Mamacita*, *The Kicker* and *Mo' Joe*, has a warmth and relaxation which can sometimes on more straightforward sessions be replaced by diffidence and a reliance on personal cadences. This is most clearly evident in his work on the Lighthouse Cafe gig with his working band from 1970, where the general fire and excitement to be found around him does not seem to translate to the leader; perhaps leadership and solo duties did not sit easily with him. Either way, his next live date for the label, with a pick-up rhythm section in Japan in the summer of 1971, produced arguably his best playing for Milestone, and his best since the remarkable **Inner Urge** on Blue Note from 1964.

Later Milestone studio efforts switch sometimes uneasily between electric and acoustic stools, seemingly attempting to follow the paths opened up by Miles Davis, Herbie Hancock and Tony Williams. Henderson plays with undiminished vigour, and his choice of musicians is ever perspicacious, but it is at times hard to escape a period-piece feeling to the musical forms and patterns being investigated. The ballad *Black is the Colour* elicits warm, tender sax playing from Henderson, but the arrangement sounds second-hand, all swirls and sound-cushions à la Miles, 1969-1970. The October 1973 effort, **Canyon Lady**, finds a variation to this sequence, placing as it does Henderson in front of a set of fine Latin-based big and mid-sized band arrangements, and the saxophonist responds with great sensitivity. A similarly oblique departure took place in the same month, when Henderson joined up with Alice Coltrane and Michael White for **The Elements**, a record anticipating world music by more than a decade. Another live date—recorded in Paris and released as one side of **Black Narcissus**, with weird electronic additions by Patrick Gleeson—and a studio session marrying fusion beats with acoustic band arrangements completes Henderson's Milestone years, and the sense of momentum which began the package has largely evaporated. This fascinating collection gives a general clue to what happened to the majority of jazz musicians between 1967 and 1976, especially when you consider the anodyne version of *My Cherie Amour* to be found on **Black Miracle**, the tenorist's last album for the label. Henderson always plays well, always stays true to his own music, but the latter half of his career here is the musical equivalent of trying on endless new suits in an attempt to get an image the wearer is happy with. Perhaps the first one was the best after all. **KS**

The State of the Tenor: Live at the Village Vanguard **Henderson** (ts); **Ron Carter** (d); **Al Foster** (d). Blue Note Ⓜ CDS 828 879 2 (two discs: 108 minutes). Recorded 1985.

⑥ ❽

Recorded live at New York's Village Vanguard in the tenor-bass-drums format pioneered by Rollins in **Way Out West** and **At the Village Vanguard** (both 1957), Henderson turns in a crowning performance where genuine risk-taking is filtered through the tenorist's encyclopaedic knowledge of his instrument's heritage and his virtuosic technique. It is a journey whose varied points of departure include Monk's *Boo Boo's Birthday*, Parker's *Cheryl*, Silver's *Soulville* and Henderson originals like *The Bead Game* and *Isotope*. There are also hauntingly rendered standards like *Stella by Starlight* and *All the Things You Are*.

Just as remarkable as Henderon's individual accomplishment is the hand-in-glove interplay between the tenorman and bassist Ron Carter and drummer Al Foster. Indeed, the trio's boldness of conception and execution is gracefully sustained for the duration of the two discs. A stellar achievement, and now available as a mid-price slimline two-CD pack. **SV**

So Near, So Far (Musings For Miles) **Henderson** (ts); **John Scofield** (g); **Dave Holland** (b); **Al Foster** (d). Verve Ⓕ 571 674-2 (73 minutes). Recorded 1992.

⑥ ❽

In this Miles tribute, Henderson and his producers have concentrated on less well-worn if not completely overlooked Miles tunes. Thus, in place of *So What*, *All Blues*, *Blue And Green*, *Nardis* and the like, such infrequent visitors to the repertoire as *Miles Ahead, Flamenco Sketches, Teo, Side Car, Circle* and *So Near, So Far* get rare and (given the pre-funk Milesian inspiration) generally rarified inspections. In an album which seems mellow even at quick tempos, the treatment of the orchestral piece *Miles Ahead* is intriguing, the suave sonorities of the big group transferring quite convincingly to the smaller ensemble. As far as performance is concerned, Scofield is consistent if routine, and Holland is a particularly melodic and appealing soloist. Henderson, a widely influential and recently much-fêted stylistic cousin to Coltrane, is at his best on the outstanding *Swing Spring*, still plying the signature licks that he perfected on Blue Note in the sixties, although playing perhaps with less timbral variety and bite than in those days. This album garnered generally ecstatic reviews on release, but despite the unusual material, the dust is likely to settle on a thoroughgoing if unexceptional sixties-style session. **MG**

Scott Henderson

Spears **Henderson** (g); **Pat Coil** (kbds); **Brad Dutz** (mallets, perc); **Gary Willis** (elb); **Steve Houghton** (d). Relativity Ⓕ 88561-1030-2 (44 minutes). Recorded 1988.

⑥ ❽

Led Zeppelin was one of Scott Henderson's earliest and strongest musical influences, and the rock-blues sonorities of that group have informed both his playing and writing, especially on Tribal Tech's last three albums, **Nomad**, **Tribal Tech** and **Illicit**. This record comes from an earlier period, when Henderson's jazz influences were more prominent. Although Henderson relishes the power and immediacy of rock, it is clear from his playing in this group, or with Chick Corea's Elektric Band or The Zawinul Syndicate, that he has a firm grasp of bebop and the Coltrane idiom. Thanks—or no thanks—to record company advice, his music acquired a dense, homogenous texture on the later albums. **Spears**, by contrast, is lightly woven and varied. It has arrangements with plenty of dynamic shading, a broad instrumental palette, detailed but airy compositions and sharply focused solos. Weather Report, Jaco Pastorius's Word Of Mouth band and Chick Corea's jazz-rock are discernible in the writing, and Gary Willis has almost certainly studied Pastorius's bass guitar style. However, Henderson's tone and melodic concept often suggest a loose, bluesy, reading of Allan Holdsworth. The opening track, *Caribbean*, is a particularly effective example of both his writing and soloing. **MG**

Jon Hendricks

1921

Freddie Freeloader **Hendricks, Judith Hendricks, Aria Hendricks, Kevin Fitzgerald Burke, Al Jarreau, George Benson, Bobby McFerrin, The Manhattan Transfer** (v); **Randy Sandke, Wynton Marsalis, Lew Soloff** (t); **Britt Woodman, Al Grey** (tb); **Jerome Richardson** (as); **Frank Foster, Stanley Turrentine** (ts); **Joe Temperley** (as, ts, bs); **Andy Stein, Al Rogers** (vn); **Barry Finclair** (va); **Larry Goldings, Tommy Flanagan** (p); **Romero Lumbambo** (g); **Andy McCloud, George Mraz, Tyler Mitchell, Rufus Reid** (b); **Clifford Barbaro, Jimmy Cobb, Duffy Jackson** (d); **Ron McBee** (perc); **Margaret Ross** (hp); **Count Basie Orchestra**. Denon Ⓕ 81757 6302-2 (59 minutes). Recorded 1989-90.

⑧ ❽

Too many of Hendricks's projects, with and without Lambert and Ross, have been undermined by questionable intonation and the sameness of albums dominated by vocalese. This project had the budget to bring in talented guest singers and strong instrumental soloists, ensuring stronger vocals and welcome variety from track to track. Hendricks also chose his material well—*Jumpin' at the Woodside* and two originals with the Basie band; the title-track with McFerrin, Jarreau and a very agile Benson taking one solo apiece; Stanley Turrentine's *Sugar* with the composer and Wynton Marsalis blowing; a pair of Monk tunes with support from Tommy Flanagan's trio; and a pair of Armstrong classics for his own family-based vocal group. Everyone had a lot of fun, as well as the necessary studio time to keep vocal clams to a minimum. Brian Lee, who did much of the original engineering, also did an unobtrusive job of mixing the various parts, which were often recorded separately. Hendricks still has the knack for setting lyrics to instrumental solos; additionally in this case, one can listen without wincing through stretches of faulty execution. **BB**

Michele Hendricks

Me And My Shadow **Hendricks** (v); **James Williams, David Leonhardt** (p); **Ray Drummond** (b); **Marvin 'Smitty' Smith** (d). Muse Ⓕ MCD 5404 (59 minutes). Recorded 1990.

④ ❽

Hendricks's third album, like its predecessors, finds her contrasting scat singing with ballads. She has inherited her father's (Jon Hendricks) agility and accuracy of voice and this enables her to use scat without the embarrassment which often accompanies the forays into the genre by so many others (perhaps Armstrong was the only one secure in the style). Ballads are Miss Hendricks's forte. *But Beautiful*, treated conventionally, is a beautiful reading and *Misty*, treated at twice its normal tempo, comes off with great success. The rolling ostinato with which James Williams opens *Summertime* confirms that this is to be a collection of most individual interpretations. The singer is fortunate in having the backing of such a skilled regular group and she can relax into it as a member of it, rather than as a cabaret singer with accompaniment. **SV**

Ernie Henry

1926-1957

Seven Standards and a Blues **Henry** (as); **Wynton Kelly** (p); **Wilbur Ware** (b); **Philly Joe Jones** (d). Riverside Ⓜ OJC 1722-2 (40 minutes). Recorded 1957.

⑦ ❽

Ernie Henry is a footnote in the jazz history books. From 1947 to the mid-fifties he was a sideman with the likes of Tadd Dameron, Max Roach, Illinois Jacquet and Dizzy Gillespie, until his career peaked with his recorded solos on Monk's *Ba-Lue Bolivar Ba-lues-are* and *Brilliant Corners*. A year (and less than a handful of recordings) later, he was dead at 31. As he was still developing as a musician, we can only speculate on what would have been his mature voice, but what can be heard, if only momentarily, on recordings like this is inviting. Like John Jenkins and Jackie McLean, Henry was discovering personal alternatives of tone and phrasing to the overwhelming influence of Bird. He flashes the requisite bop chops on *I Get A Kick Out Of You* and *Lover Man* (the occasional intonation problems add charm), but seems more comfortable with the sentiments of *Soon* and *Like Someone in Love*, staying close to the melody and singing through his horn. The respectful way he plays *Sweet Lorraine* without trying to modernize his phrasing is reminiscent of Benny Carter, and his most winsome passages occur as he stretches out on the blues *Specific Gravity*. The reliable rhythm section keeps everything on an even keel and, thanks to the succinctness of Henry's solos, there are plenty of opportunities to enjoy Ware's warm and pithy playing. **AL**

Woody Herman

1913-1987

Blues On Parade **Herman** (cl, as, v); with the following collective personnel: **Clarence Willard, Kermit Simmons, Steady Nelson, Mac MacQuordale, Bob Price, Cappy Lewis, John Owens, Ray Linn, George Seaburg, Billie Rogers, Charlie Peterson** (t); **Joe Bishop** (flh); **Neal Reid, Toby Tyler, Bud Smith, Vic Hamman, Jerry Rosa, Tommy Farr, Walter Nimms** (tb); **Murray Williams, Don Watt, Joe Estrin, Ray Hopfner, Joe Denton, Herb Tompkins, Eddie Scalzi, Jimmy Horvath, Sam Rubinowich** (as); **Saxie Mansfield, Bruce Wilkins, Pete Johns, Ronnie Perry, Nick Caiazza, Sammy Armato, Mickey Folus, Herbie Haymer, Pete Mondello** (ts); **Skippy De Sair** (bs); **Nick Hupfer** (vn); **Horace Diaz, Tommy Linehan** (p); **Chick Reeves, Hy White** (g); **Walter Yoder** (b); **Frank Carlson** (d). MCA/Decca Ⓜ GRD-606 (60 minutes). Recorded 1937-42.

⑧ ❻

Herman's first band was a co-operative unit formed out of the Isham Jones orchestra. This 20-track CD documents the growth of 'The Band That Plays The Blues in near-chronology and contains two previously unissued tracks (although some doubt exists over whether or not this particular take of *Farewell Blues* was included on an old Coral LP). From those earlier beginnings, when Woody was playing (and sometimes singing) such pieces as Morton's *Doctor Jazz*, to the final track, a 1942 Dizzy Gillespie composition and arrangement titled *Down Under*, is a fascinating evolutionary study. The band got stronger and more exciting (try *Woodsheddin' With Woody*, for example) and much of the library came from within the Herman ranks, particularly from the busy pen of flügelhorn player Joe Bishop. The CD contains a number of Woody's winners, commencing with the original 1939 version of *Woodchoppers' Ball* and, of course, the famous *Blue Flame*. There are two titles by the Woodchoppers (including *River Bed Blues*) and two more by the Four Chips which allow us to hear the leader's attractive, Jimmy Noone-like clarinet to advantage. A number of CDs exist comprising Herman selections from the American Decca archive, but this one is probably the best and certainly the most comprehensive. **AM**

Best of the Big Bands **Woody Herman** (cl, as, v); with **The First Herd** (Sonny Berman, Chuck Frankhauser, Ray Wetzel, Pete Candoli, Conte Candoli, Shorty Rogers, Carl Warwick, Conrad Gozzo [t]; Bill Harris, Ralph Pfeffner, Ed Kiefer [tb]; Sam Marowitz, John LaPorta [cl, as]; Pete Mondello, Flip Phillips [ts]; Skippy DeSair [bs]; Ralph Burns [p, arr]; Jimmy Rowles [p]; Marjorie Hyams [vb]; Billy Bauer [g]; Chubby Jackson [b]; Dave Tough, Don Lamond [d]); **The Second Herd** (Shorty Rogers, Ernie Royal, Bernie Glow, Stan Fishelson, Marky Markowitz [t]; Earl Swope, Ollie Wilson, Bob Swift [tb]; Sam Marowitz [as]; Herbie Steward [as, ts]; Stan Getz, Zoot Sims [ts]; Serge Chaloff [bs]; Fred Otis [p]; Gene Sargent [g]; Walter Yoder [b]; Don Lamond [d]; Ralph Burns [arr]). Columbia Ⓜ 466 621-2 (52 minutes). Recorded 1944-47.

⑤ ❻

Of all the great big-band recordings, Woody Herman's First and Second Herd classics for Columbia have consistently been some of the most ill-treated and sloppily presented on CD. This disc is the only current release covering the crucial mid-to-late forties period of studio recordings (a better one, though still far from perfect, has recently been deleted by the British Charly label), and although the playing time is acceptable, the choice of material is scandalously idiosyncratic. A simple illustration will suffice: on this disc we are presented with a jokey re-arrangement of Khachaturian's *Sabre Dance* from his "Gayaneh" Ballet. It's close to embarrassing. This is chosen (along with other oddities) in preference to *The Good Earth*, *Bijou*, *Your Father's Moustache*, *Wild Root*, *Steps*, *Igor*, *Fan It*, *Sidewalks of Cuba*, *Lady McGowan's Dream* (either part), *Panacea*, *Woodchopper's Ball*, *Back Talk*, *Four Brothers* or any section of *Summer Sequence*. None of the above sides are currently on CD.

What *is* here includes *Apple Honey*, *Caldonia*, *Blowin' Up A Storm*, *Goosey Gander*, *Happiness Is A Thing Called Joe*, *Everywhere* and *Northwest Passage*. Considering the unusually good sound on the original 78rpm recordings, the remastering is, at best, adequte, while the complete lack of recording dates or personnel is shoddy in the extreme. Until the excellent old vinyl boxed set, **The Thundering Herds** (or a decent approximation of such) makes its debut on CD, this miserable ekeing-out of some of big-band jazz's most prized treasures will have to suffice. **KS**

Keeper Of The Flame **Herman** (cl, as, v); **Ernie Royal**, **Bernie Glow**, **Stan Fishelson**, **Red Rodney**, **Shorty Rogers** (t); **Earl Swope**, **Bill Harris**, **Ollie Wilson**, **Bob Swift** (tb); **Sam Marowitz** (as); **Al Cohn**, **Zoot Sims**, **Stan Getz**, **Gene Ammons**, **Buddy Savitt**, **Jimmy Giuffre** (ts); **Serge Chaloff** (bs); **Terry Gibbs** (vb); **Lou Levy** (p); **Chubby Jackson**, **Oscar Pettiford**, **Joe Mondragon** (b); **Don Lamond**, **Shelley Manne** (d); **Mary Ann McCall** (v). Capitol Ⓜ CDP7 98453-2 (58 minutes). Recorded 1948-49.

✔ ⑩ ❽

Woody Herman formed his Second Herd, featuring the celebrated three-tenors saxophone section, in 1947. It recorded its first sides for Columbia in great haste in December of that year, in order to beat a recording strike due to begin on January 1, 1948. The strike dragged on for most of the year, and it was not until December 1948 that the band could record again, this time for Capitol. This disc contains its complete Capitol recordings.

So much for history. The one undeniable classic here is *Early Autumn*, composed by Ralph Burns as a kind of afterthought to his suite *Summer Sequence* and featuring the tenor saxophone of the 21-year-old Stan Getz. The effect of this one piece is difficult to overestimate, not only on Getz, or even on the tenor saxophone style, but on the direction taken by modern jazz during the fifties. Together with the Miles Davis band of the same period (also recorded by Capitol), it defined the ideals of restraint and purity of tone which were summed up in the term 'cool'. Alongside this, and complementary to it, was the influence of bebop. There was a brief popular craze for bebop at the time, which found its expression mainly through the medium of fashion accessories like berets and dark glasses and a few musical trade-marks, such as Gillespie-type scat vocals. Probably the best of all these pop-bop records was Herman's recording of George Wallington's *Lemon Drop*, an exhilarating, headlong affair featuring brief but crackling solos by Chaloff, Swope, Rodney, Gibbs and Herman.

This disc is important both for its musical excellence and its historical significance. **DG**

Woody's Winners **Woody Herman** (cl, as); **Gerald Lamy**, **Dusko Goykovich**, **Bobby Shew**, **Don Rader**, **Bill Chase** (t); **Henry Southall**, **Frank Tesinsky**, **Donald Doane** (tb); **Gary Klein, Sal Nistico, Andy McGhee** (ts); **Tom Anastas** (bs); **Nat Pierce** (p); **Anthony Leonardi** (b); **Ronnie Zito** (d). Columbia Ⓜ 468454 2 (44 minutes). Recorded 1965.

⑧ ❽

Each edition of the Herman Herd usually managed to produce a blockbuster and **Woody's Winners** is certainly that. The infectious elation captured here is all the more imposing when one remembers that the Herman Herd delivered this kind of punch to its live audiences every night.

Nat Pierce was the spark plug, both in rehearsing and arranging for the band, and his rolling piano, mixing elements of stride, Basie and Ellington styles, is better displayed on this album than on any other. Herman's facetious identification of Pierce as Mary Lou Williams has caused reviewers and listeners difficulties ever since. The ten-minute *Opus De Funk*, Pierce's arrangement of Horace Silver's tune, swings as fiercely as any big band performance one can recall, and apart from good solos by

Pierce, Klein and Duskovich, it contains a powerful one from Henry Southall which has gone unacknowledged (and remains so on this CD reissue) since the album was first released on LP. The trio of ballads is quite overwhelmed by the quintet of flag-wavers. **SV**

The 40th Anniversary Carnegie Hall Concert **Herman** (c, as, v); **Pete Candoli, Conte Candoli, Alan Vizutti, Nelson Hatt, John Hoffman, Dennis Dotson, Bill Byrne, Danny Styles** (t); **Phil Wilson, Jim Pugh, Dale Kirkland, Jim Daniels** (tb); **Stan Getz, Flip Phillips, Al Cohn, Zoot Sims, Jimmy Giuffre, Sam Marowitz, Frank Tiberi, Gary Anderson, Joe Lovano, John Oslawski** (reeds); **Jimmy Rowles, Nat Pierce, Ralph Burns, Pat Coil** (p); **Billy Bauer** (g); **Chubby Jackson, Rusty Holloway** (b); **Don Lamond, Jake Hanna, Dan D'Imperio** (d); **Mary Ann McCall** (v). RCA Bluebird Ⓜ 86878-2 (90 minutes). Recorded 1976.

⑧ ❽

Woody Herman's 40th Anniversary fête at Carnegie Hall on November 20, 1976, was a bash that anyone present will never forget. Combining Woody's youthful New Thundering Herd and an all-star line-up of Herman alumni, it was an apt retrospective and a consequently poignant reminder of the literally hundreds of ex-Herman sidemen who had gone on to distinguished and highly productive individual careers.

The recording perfectly captures the evening's electricity. It also captures Woody's heartfelt reminiscences, including a tribute to the then recently deceased Bill Harris, a mainstay of Herman's trombone section and the composer of the haunting *Everywhere*, magnificantly rendered by Jim Pugh. Also stirring is the eponymously tagged *Four Brothers* with Stan Getz, Zoot Sims, composer Jimmy Guiffre and Al Cohn, the latter two taking the parts of the departed Herbie Steward and Serge Chaloff. Getz's shimmering reprise of *Early Autumn* with composer Ralph Burns at the piano is another gem, as is Alan Broadbent's kaleidoscopic arrangement of *Blues in the Night* with Woody's poignant vocal and Joe Lovano's smoking tenor. In the latter part of his career Woody added soprano saxophone to his battery; here, it is heard to advantage in Gary Anderson's Latinized re-framing of Aaron Copland's *Fanfare for the Common Man*.

In all, it is a celebration that, while appropriately nostalgic, is nonetheless a musically valid representation of the variegated and ever-fascinating persona of the singular Woodrow Charles Herman. **CB**

Vincent Herring

1966

Don't Let It Go **Herring** (ss, as); **Scott Wendholt** (t); **Cyrus Chestnut** (p); **Jesse Yusef Murphy** (b); **Carl Allen** (d). MusicMasters Jazz Ⓕ 65121-2 (54 minutes) Recorded 1994.

⑧ ❿

Herring is a young musician who is maturing at a frightening rate. Lucky enough to be discovered while still a teenager and installed in Nat Adderley's band for close to five years, his natural affinity with brother Cannonball's sound and style was perhaps heightened more than would otherwise have been the case. Nevertheless, he was leading his own dates at the dawning of the 1990s and a steady progression of albums (and record labels) now reach the point where clear signs of maturity are evident on every level. Interestingly, Herring does it here with musicians who have often cropped up on his records before, including the fine pianist Chestnut and the accomplished drummer and leader Carl Allen.

What has happened to Herring now that he has reached this stage is, as Benny Golson points out in his long and detailed liner notes, he has developed his own sound and his own personal mix of the past. He has also been writing some uncommonly good songs for his band to play. Often in the minor key, they stay within a relatively restricted harmonic ambit, but are beautifully arranged between the members of the group, and the melodies are fresh. Herring no longer goes hell-for-leather from the first note of a solo, and his pacing of all aspects of the music on this disc is exemplary. The album hangs together as a single identity very well indeed. Of his band, pianist Chestnut perhaps stands out due to his unerring choice of chord voicings and his wonderfuly weighted hands, but no-one is below par, and the group works beautifully as a complete unit. An understated yet rewarding record, and an important step forward for Herring. **KS**

Fred Hersch

Sarabande **Hersch** (p); **Charlie Haden** (b); **Joey Baron** (d). Sunnyside Ⓕ SCC 1024-D (51 minutes). Recorded 1986.

⑥ ❻

Hersch has been making a reputation for himself around New York for a number of years now, and has recorded two or three albums as a leader, as well as having some of his non-jazz material recorded for RCA. The measure of his reputation comes with the company he keeps here: Haden is in a class of his own as a creative bassist, and Joey Baron has a formidable reputation. The programme, as the name suggests, concentrates on the feelings evoked by the sarabande dance, "a slow, stately dance", Hersch writes on the sleeve, "in 3/4 time". Hence we have dreamy and touching performances of

Jimmy Rowles's *The Peacocks*, Bill Evans's *Blue in Green* and Hersch's own title song. The 3/4 time signature is by no means ubiquitous, and some of the tracks find Hersch to be a very busy pianist indeed, but by and large the title is not inappropriate. This is a superior piano trio record, with some touching moments, but it rarely *sings* its song.
KS

Conrad Herwig
1959

New York Hardball **Herwig** (tb); **Richie Beirach** (p); **Ron McClure** (b); **Adam Nussbaum** (d). Ken Music/Bellaphon Ⓕ 660 56 002 (43 minutes). Recorded 1989.

✔ ⑧ ❽

American college bands have been attacked with boring regularity for producing technically accomplished but characterless musicians; Conrad Herwig, who studied at North Texas State, is one player who proves conclusively the foolishness of that position. Clark Terry warned us, when Herwig was in his big band, to "be on the lookout for a new giant" and now, thanks to Ken Music, which has recorded three dates led by Herwig, the work of one of the most individual and gifted of contemporary musicians is being more widely heard. Like Woody Shaw on the trumpet, he has transferred Coltrane's technically demanding polytonal vocabulary to the trombone with impressive rigour; in addition he has absorbed some of the language of Bartók, Berg and others. Allied to that is an extraordinary control and facility, a range of timbral resources as expressive as that of the human voice and a thematic sense so powerful that it enables him to render chromatic material as musically as if it were a mere pentatonic. This recording is also marked by unusually cohesive ensembles, and fine playing by Herwig's mentor, the vastly underrated Richie Beirach. There is barely a dull moment here, but the throwaway brilliance of Herwig's arrangement of *I'm Getting Sentimental Over You* is a particularly good place to start.
MG

John Hicks
1941

Naima's Love Song **Hicks** (p); **Bobby Watson** (as); **Curtis Lundy** (b); **Victor Lewis** (b). DIW Ⓕ DIW 823 (47 minutes). Recorded 1988.

⑦ ❽

Hicks became part of the New York scene in 1963 and quickly progressed his career. Being comfortable with singer Betty Carter, in the all-action Jazz Messengers or as part of a Woody Herman Herd, he has long been part of the jazz scenery. In the eighties he was often found in the freer atmosphere of groups led by Arthur Blythe, David Murray and Hamiet Bluiett. This CD has him firmly back 'inside' in the company of the highly accomplished Lundy and Lewis and playing host to the redoubtable Watson. With this line-up, it is a session that could almost be pre-reviewed and it does nothing to betray such confidence. Hicks's own versatility has added to his stature and he is now a readily identifiable pianist whatever the material in hand. *Someday Soon* sustains his creative flow impressively, *On The One* highlights the chordal strength that underpins his whole style, while *Soul Eyes* shows how much emotion he can push through cold ivory. Tracing his lineage would take you from Teddy Wilson through Bud Powell to Tommy Flanagan, although to make such a superficial comparison is merely a critical tool. He has his own box of tricks and each musical component produced bears the Hicks trademark.
BMcR

Eddie Higgins

Those Quiet Days **Higgins** (p); **Kevin Eubanks** (g); **Rufus Reid** (b). Sunnyside Ⓕ SSC 1052D (57 minutes). Recorded 1990.

⑦ ❺

Higgins is a pianist whose touch and conception immediately communicates itself as someone who came up in the fifties, rather than a later era. His models are not Hancock, Tyner, Evans and Corea; from him you hear the tidiness of structure, the articulation of Tatum, Powell, Shearing and Garner. This is not his first album: that was made in 1957. But it is the first in some time. On it, he breaks with the convention (or tyranny) of the piano-bass-drums format and opts for a guitar and bass instead. This was an inspired idea, for it opens up the music to more unusual influences on its direction in each piece, and it also makes the musicians work together in freshly-minted ways, rather than rely on pavlovian sequences and reactions.

All three musicians thrive in this situation, with Eubanks in particular sounding free and swinging, his lines seeking out unusual harmonic nuances in a similar way to Jim Hall's methodology. Higgins himself plays through this set of originals and old favourites with enormous confidence.

For Bill Evans fans looking for a change of scenery.
KS

Andrew Hill

1937

Judgment! **Hill** (p); **Bobby Hutcherson** (vb); **Richard Davis** (b); **Elvin Jones** (d). Blue Note Ⓜ CDP8 28981 2 (48 minutes). Recorded 1964.

⑩ ❽

Of all the great artists to have had significant parts of their careers documented by Blue Note recordings, Andrew Hill has been by far the worst served in the reissue stakes. Even his two fine albums made at the dawn of this present decade for the reborn label have been deleted, while not only the entire extent of his unissued material lies inactive and unheard in the Blue Note vaults, but the vast bulk of his brilliant series of sixties releases are either deleted or await their 15 CD minutes in the sun. Thankfully, **Point of Departure** (see above) remains available (probably due to the presence of one Eric Dolphy and one Joe Henderson), but of the rest, just this one remains. Grab it while you can, because the music is little less than sensational. And if you need any convincing, play either the opener, *Siete Ocho* (logically, a piece in 7/8), which goes directly from a theme-over-ostinato bass and Hutcherson solo to a boiling explosion of drums from Elvin Jones. If you still feel obstinate about it, try the ballad *Alfred*, dedicated to Blue Note's founder, Alfred Lion. It is one of the most beautiful tunes to have come out of jazz in the past 50 years, is an ingenious construction worthy of Monk, and must melt even the most obdurate potential buyer's heart.

After those two, anything else would necessarily have a sense of anti-climax, but each extra piece has reasons for further fascination, if you give it a chance. The title track, for example, has a wonderfully sinuous and insinuating melody. Hill has a unique pianistic voice, has an identifiable compositional style, and is worth the effort of discovering. As we go to press, news has arrived from EMI announcing the reissue of Hill's **Smokestack** album. Now, if only Blue Note could get around to **Compulsion!** **KS**

Point Of Departure **Hill** (p); **Kenny Dorham** (t); **Eric Dolphy** (f, as, bcl); **Joe Henderson** (f, ts); **Richard Davis** (b); **Tony Williams** (d). Blue Note Ⓜ CDP 84167-2 (51 minutes). Recorded 1964.

✔ ⑩ ❽

Andrew Hill's still underrated yet superb body of work for Blue Note from 1963-70 epitomized the movement which sought to combine elements of freedom (primarily an evasion of the tyranny of bar lines and rhythmic regularity) with an expansive concept of composition (including unusual, often juxtaposed metres, modal areas rather than strict chord changes, and less rigid rhythmic relationships). An excellent pianist with an individual, mosaic-like manner, he nevertheless recorded with eight different instrumental combinations during this period, expanding and diversifying his expressive ambitions. **Point Of Departure** is especially noteworthy for the quality of the compositions and the contributions of the ensemble. Dolphy, in his characteristic way, extends Hill's often ambiguous harmonic framework even further; Henderson's probing, focused style is more attuned to the music's intricacies—a dramatic contrast to Dolphy's jolting expressionism. Dorham responds to the freedom offered with a moving introspection; Davis and Williams are responsible for the relaxed feel and flow. But Hill's organization of voicings, colours, and polyrhythms (more an extension of Herbie Nichols than Monk in this regard) is masterful—this music is not just written, it is scored for sextet; a music of nuance, complexity and consequence. **AL**

Shades **Hill** (p); **Clifford Jordan** (ts); **Rufus Reid** (b); **Ben Riley** (d). Soul Note Ⓕ SN 1113 CD (44 minutes). Recorded 1986.

⑩ ❾

After leaving Blue Note in 1970, Andrew Hill continued to record for a number of labels, but it was not until 1986's **Shades** for Soul Note that he made an album to stand alongside the best of his sixties work.

Hill has cited Tatum, Powell and Monk as primary influences. Memories of Monk are certainly to the fore on **Shades**, both in the tribute *Monk's Glimpse*, its dancing lines punctuated by percussive stabs, and in the skipping phrases of *Chilly Mac*. Yet Hill remains very much his own man, his shifting tempos and fragmented lines the surface-play of a deeply thoughtful music that can be lit by flashes of lyricism or darkened by turbulent anxiety. On **Shades** the moods are mostly happy, thanks in part to Clifford Jordan's warm-toned tenor, which sails through the music with a beautiful delicacy. Reid and Riley are also superb, the latter's cymbals consistently whisking up the beat. They are heard to best advantage on the two trio tracks, *Tripping* and *Ball Square*, where Hill is at his most probingly idiosyncratic. The real gem, though, is *La Verne*, a dedication to his wife that Hill has recorded several times. Here Jordan's deft, swinging phrases coax a new tenderness from the tune, casting a spell of rhapsodic magic that envelops even Hill's more private solo. **GL**

Buck Hill

1928

I'm Beginning to See the Light **Hill** (ts); **Jon Ozment** (p); **Carroll Dashiell** (b); **Warren Shadd** (d). Muse Ⓕ MCD 5449 (52 minutes). Recorded 1991.

⑦ ❽

Born and bred in Washington D.C., Hill was playing professionally at the age of 15. He worked at several clubs in his home town during the fifties and recorded with Charlie Byrd in 1959. He played sporadically during the sixties but emerged in the next decade to establish himself as a leading saxophone light in Washington. There is little doubt that, by shunning the limelight of New York, he has retarded a promising career but, as this CD shows, he is a talented player. His solo on *Lullaby Of Loosdrecht* gives notice of his structural awareness, *Warm Valley* is a model of tonal consistency while the urgent *Mitzi* shows that he knows how to bear down on the beat. The title-track is taken with good-humoured swing and, like most of his playing, exhibits an inner strength. He can be a busy player but there are few superfluous arpeggios and he is concerned mainly with providing the bare bones of each musical story. To add interest, he uses the odd very personal phrase shape and ensures that his stories take some unpredictable turns. Despite his absence from the main arena, he does have albums such as this to campaign for him. **BMcR**

Teddy Hill

1909-1978

Uptown Rhapsody **Hill** (ts, ldr, v); **Bill Dillard, Bill Coleman, Roy Eldridge, Frankie Newton, Shad Collins, Dizzy Gillespie** (t); **Dicky Wells** (tb); **Russell Procope** (cl, as); **Howard Johnson** (as); **Chu Berry, Robert Carroll** (ts); **Cecil Scott** (ts, bs); **Sam Allen** (p); **John Smith** (g); **Richard Fulbright** (b); **Bill Beason** (d); **Beatrice Douglas, Bill Dillard** (v). Hep Ⓜ HEPCD 1033 (72 minutes). Recorded 1936-37.

⑧ ❻

Roy Eldridge and Dizzy Gillespie played their first solos on record with Teddy Hill (and in Dizzy's case, these were his first-ever recordings); it was also Hill who, in 1940, became manager of Minton's club in Harlem where the young beboppers tried out their first musical experiments. This CD comprises all 26 issued sides by the Hill band, splendidly remastered by John R.T. Davies and programmed in chronological order. It helps to place the band in perspective, for although it may not have possessed the 'name' value of other Harlem bands of the period, it had more than its fair share of soloists, particularly in the brass department. Eldridge rips off a fine solo on the opening *Lookie, Lookie, Lookie Here Comes Cookie* and Gillespie's exciting chorus on *King Porter Stomp* just over a year later shows where his allegiance lay at the time. The final six tracks are by the band which Hill brought to Europe, with Dillard, Collins and Wells joining in on the classic Paris sessions with Django Reinhardt. But the work of pianist Sam Allen should not be overlooked, nor the fine solos from Chu Berry on the first session. **AM**

Earl Hines

1903-1983

The Chronological Earl Hines and his Orchestra 1928-32 **Hines** (p, v); **Shirley Clay, George Mitchell, Charlie Allen, George Dixon, Walter Fuller** (t); **William Franklin** (tb, v); **Louis Taylor** (tb); **Lester Boone, Toby Turner, Cecil Irwin, Darnell Howard, Omer Simeon** (reeds); **Claude Roberts** (bj, g); **Lawrence Dixon** (g); **Hayes Alvis** (bb, v); **Quinn Wilson** (b); **Benny Washington, Wallace Bishop** (d); **Alex Hill, Irwin, Alvis, Reginald Foresythe** (arr). Classics Ⓜ 545 (71 minutes). Recorded 1928-32.

⑥ ❻

Hines was the first pianist to deliver his instrument from the inheritance of ragtime. For all their captivating right-hand melodies, James P. Johnson and Hines's contemporary Fats Waller were bound by the regular beat of their left-hand rhythm section. But the influence of Armstrong's trumpet lines on Hines's right (he claimed his distinctive style was formed before working with Louis, but he can hardly have been unaware of his records) also liberated his left, forcing it to become less regular and to dialogue with the right hand.

In 1928 he was not quite as adventurous as subsequently (*A Monday Date*, especially in the QRS version, recalls Waller), but this playing was absolutely revolutionary in the context of the times. What distinguishes this reissue is the gathering together—seemingly for the first time ever—of the eight QRS sides and the four Okehs, all performed unaccompanied and all within a couple of weeks of his 25th birthday. His early big-band tracks which follow are crude indeed by comparison, and not a patch on later editions. But, even despite the surface noise of the opening tracks and the frequent distortion of the piano sounds, their historical importance is matched by their joyous dynamism. **BP**

Earl Hines and His Orchestra 1932-34 and 1937 **Hines** (p); with the following collective personnel: **Charlie Allen, George Dixon, Walter Fuller, Milton Fletcher** (t); **Louis Taylor, William Franklin, Trummy Young, Kenneth Stuart** (tb); **Darnell Howard, Omer Simeon** (cl, as); **Cecil Irwin, Jimmy Mundy, Budd Johnson** (ts); **Lawrence Dixon** (g); **Quinn Wilson** (b); **Wallace Bishop** (d); **Walter Fuller, Herb Jeffries, Valaida Snow, Madeline Green** (v). Archives Of Jazz Ⓑ 3801022 (44 minutes). Recorded 1932-37.

⑥ ❻

These 16 titles were recorded when Hines and his orchestra were the star attractions at Chicago's Grand Terrace. Some of the earlier material is trite (*Why Must We Part?* is a lachrymose ballad which was presumably on the then-current 'plug' list), but invariably Hines's own piano interludes lift the entire level of the performances.

This was a good band with a fine trumpet soloist in Walter Fuller (he also sings effectively) and a pleasing tenor soloist, Cecil Irwin. On *Cavernism*, Jimmy Mundy's first arrangement for Hines, there is a splendid violin chorus from Darnell Howard, and on one of the 1934 sessions there are a couple of vocals by Herb Jeffries. But it is Hines himself who invariably catches the ear with his immensely assured solo work. Perhaps the best tracks of all are *Love Me Tonight* and *Down Among The Sheltering Palms*: these are piano solos of great value. The whole CD interlocks well with the Hines chronology on the Classics label, for these are alternative takes, some of them very rare, thereby avoiding duplications. Inevitably there are a few clicks and pops on the tracks dubbed from test pressings, but the overall sound is good. **AM**

Grand Reunion **Hines** (p); **Roy Eldridge** (t); **Coleman Hawkins** (ts); **George Tucker** (b); **Oliver Jackson** (d). Verve/Limelight Ⓜ 528 137-2 (two discs: 91 minutes). Recorded 1965.

✔ ⑨ ❽

Hines's valuable and influential career is very strangely represented on CD at present. His earliest recordings as a leader (see above) are quite freely available, but much from the decade which saw him at his popular peak, starting with his long residency at Chicago's Grand Terrace (which began in 1935) and continuing until the demise of the big band which had people like Billy Eckstine, Art Blakey and Charlie Parker (among many others) pass through its ranks, is poorly documented. Only the French label, Classics, has taken on the task of a complete chronological reissue, and their sound quality leaves something to be desired. RCA has deleted the invaluable Bluebird CDs. Moving on from there, the Vogue material from 1949 is on CD, but the sound quality is dim indeed.

Conversely, the decade of recording following his 1964 rediscovery is very well covered, although most of the releases find him alone at the piano. Which is just one more reason to welcome the reissue of this superb set of Village Vanguard performances by a truly all-star small band. Hines allows himself to function as a trio leader, an accompanist and a soloist in a fiery quintet (Eldridge and Hawkins take it in turns to sit in with the group on ballads, and combine fruitfully on the jam numbers like *Sweet Georgia Brown* and *C-Jam Blues*). Hines is at once very modern and archly antique in his playing on these sides: his solos abound with strange twists, unevenly-paced and formed phrases, plus whole clusters and flurries of notes, while his very full accompaniment is either undiluted four-to-the-bar swing (often with a walking left hand) or heavyweight versions of Basie-like jabs. No matter - he digs away at the horns to provoke some heated and exciting work from both men, though Hawkins, then in his last handful of years, has lost some of his fire.

The session is well recorded and the booklet carries an excellent set of liner notes (newly written) by Chris Albertson, in addition to the clearly reproduced original notes to both LP volumes by Dan Morgenstern and Ira Gitler respectively. **KS**

Plays Duke Ellington **Hines** (p). New World Ⓕ 361/62-2 (two discs: 121 minutes). Recorded 1971-75.

✔ ⑩ ❽

Hines's last great phase began in 1964, when critic Stanley Dance persuaded him to begin performing solo; the unaccompanied recordings he made in this period are the distillation of everything he had ever learned and played: masterworks. Hines had always been a radical. More than any other pianist he liberated the left hand from stride and ragtime's march-rooted oompah patterns—a bass-register revolution more profound than his oft-cited, 'trumpet-style' right hand. On *Squeeze Me*, Earl's antic left alternately clonks asymmetrical runs like Bud Powell and bounces classic stride patterns; Hines compresses decades of jazz history into one cut, one style. His independence of hands, most striking on *Caravan*, harks back to early days when he patterned each hand's moves after a different Pittsburgh piano hero.

This is not typical late Hines in that he was unfamiliar with many of the 20 Ellington tunes he essayed, some of them rather obscure (you can hear him turning a page of music early on in *Take Love Easy*). But he stretches out enough to get comfortable—a couple of tracks run ten minutes—and his excursions highlight the similarities between his stride-rooted, bass-jabbing style and Duke's. It is a painless history lesson, and a thoughtful appreciation of a composer and pianist Hines greatly admired. **KW**

Terumasa Hino

1942

Triple Helix **Hino** (t); **Masabumi Kikuchi** (p); **James Genus** (b); **Masahiko Togashi** (perc). Enja Ⓕ ENJ-8056 2 (58 minutes). Recorded 1993.

⑦ ❽

This inspired meeting of old friends from the Tokyo scene of the 1960s was recorded before a rapt audience at the Second Yamaha Jazz Festival in Hamamatsu, Japan. It was, however, the first time that trumpeter Terumasa Hino, pianist Masabumi Kikuchi and percussionist Masahiko Togashi had actually played together. It was a moment worth waiting for. Along with the young American bassist James Genus, the quartet crackles with an energy reminiscent of the acoustic mid-sixties Miles Davis. Although Hino, Kikuchi and Togashi are listed as co-leaders, Hino is the informing presence. A Davis devotee who edited a set of transcriptions of Davis solos, Hino has adapted such Davis trademarks as the skittering high register flurries, the mid-range half-valve smears and low regiter growls. But with his big, brassy signature sound and the experience picked up through associations with such stalwarts as Jackie McLean, Gil Evans, Dave Liebman and Elvin Jones, Hino has emerged as one of the most original of the post-Miles trumpeters.

Hino, although a virtuoso with an impressive high range, is an economical player who deploys space as a means of punctuation and dramatic emphasis. His darting lines and aerial stunts on *Blue Monk* and his own tempestuous *Trial* are that much more effective because they so often seem to pop in from out of nowhere. As he demonstrates with his laser sharp *Sapphire Way*, Hino is also an impressive ballad player. Throughout, Hino's heroic horn is given effectively lean yet strong support by the admirable Kikushi, Togashi and Genus. **CB**

Milt Hinton

1910

Laughing At Life **Hinton** (b, v) with the following collective personnel; **Jon Faddis** (t, flh); **Harold Ashby** (ts); **Richard Wyands, Derek Smith** (p); **Lynn Seaton, Brian Torff, Santi Debriano, Rufus Reid** (b); **Alan Dawson, Dave Ratajczak, Terry Clarke** (d). Columbia Ⓔ 478178 2 (54 minutes). Recorded 1995.

⑥ ❽

Hinton made his first records in 1933 and is arguably the most recorded bass player in the history of jazz. That in itself is remarkable but even more noteworthy is the fact that, at the age of 84, he has such a 'modern' sound and forward-looking approach. There are, for example, four trio tracks here (two with Smith and Dawson, two with Wyands and Ratajczak) which are propelled along with enormous power by Milt who obviously enjoys playing in this context. He takes three pleasant, if lightweight, vocals and on the closing *The Judge And The Jury* leads a four-man bass 'choir' of musicians, all considerably younger than himself. Yet he remains one of the most respected of all New York-based musicians, for he has been a part of so many developments in jazz. The men chosen for this CD are people he admires greatly and the opening *Child Is Born* featuring Milt and Jon Fadds is beautiful. Harold Ashby plays his part on four tracks, including a gorgeous *Prelude To A Kiss*; in the absence of Ben Webster one gets the impression that Ashby was Milt's second choice. Good, varied mainstream music; add another star if you are not averse to the occasional bass solo. **AM**

Les Hite

1903 -1962

Louis Armstrong and his Orchestra 1930-31 **Armstrong** (t, v); **Hite** (as, bs); **Leon Elkins, George Orendorff, Harold Scott, McClure 'Red Mac' Morris** (t); **Lawrence Brown, Luther Graven** (tb); **Leon Herriford, Willie Start, Marvin Johnson** (as); **William Franz** (ts); **Charlie Jones** (cl, ts); **L.Z. Cooper, Harvey Brooks, Henry Prince** (p); **Ceele Burke, Bill Perkins** (bj, g); **Reggie Jones** (bb); **Joe Bailey** (b); **Lionel Hampton** (d, vb). Classics Ⓜ 547 (40 minutes). Recorded 1930/31.

④ ❼

During his career, only 14 titles were actually issued under Hite's name. Those, with the likes of T-Bone Walker and Dizzy Gillespie in the line-up, were in the forties. Hite retired from music to launch his own business in 1945, but before that had been a musician for well over 20 years. The most significant part of this time was during the thirties, when he led the band at Frank Sebastian's New Cotton Club, backing players such as Louis Armstrong and Fats Waller as well as playing on soundtracks and making personal appearances in Hollywood film studios. This CD contains 12 sides featuring the Hite band backing Armstrong; the period covered is barely eight months but the band, with Lawrence Brown on trombone and Lionel Hampton on drums and vibraphone, was not always make-weight. Armstrong's genius is detailed elsewhere but Hite's band did complement the master and make a few points of its own. The saxophones were fashionably pedestrian and at their most dreary on *In The Market For You*. An Hawaiian guitar destroys the mood of *I'm Confessin'* but Brown enriches the four titles on which he appears. Throughout the remainder, the band matches Armstrong's steely trumpet rubato with a cushion that highlights his majestic delivery. It seems somewhat dated in comparison, but does an effective and highly professional job. The star rating is based purely on the backing band's contribution. **BMcR**

André Hodeir

1921

Solal et son orchestre jouent Hodeir **Solal** (p); **Tony Russo, Bernard Marchais, Eric LeLann, Roger Guerin** (t); **Jacques Bolognesi, Christian Guizien** (tb); **François Jeanneau, Jean-Pierre Debarbat, Jean-Louis Chautemps, Pierre Gossez, Jacques DiDonato** (cl, bcl, saxes); **Cesarius Alvim** (b); **André Ceccarelli** (d). Carlyne Ⓔ 008 (40 minutes). Recorded 1984.

⑧ ❽

A brilliant commentator on jazz as well as a skilled musician, Hodeir has acknowledged that the primary influences on his composing and arranging have been Ellington, the writing for the Miles Davis Nonet and Monk. It is somewhat easier to follow the structuralist methods through his rearrangements of jazz standards (on Savoy and Epic discs from the fifties, not yet on CD). His original material, of the kind heard here, is often adroit if not particularly lyrical, notable for a sophisticated harmonic language and striking architectural design. He has been fortunate to have capable musicians as advocates, as Solal, who contributes sparkling solos to two tunes, proves. But Hodeir's touch emerges in the writing: the contrast between Jeanneau's tenor and the exclamations from other instruments (ending with a bass solo!) in *Catalyse*, the section of soprano saxes in *Transplantation I*, the variety of settings for DiDonato's Jimmy Hamilton-styled clarinet in *Arte Della Commedia Dell'*, the baroque counterpoint and sprightly variations of *D Or No*. Two arrangements of Monk tunes are really unintentional acts of homage to Hall Overton. True to the original, *Crepuscule With Nellie* contains no solos; points are made with the wit of Hodeir's scoring and detailed inner voicings. *Coming On The Hudson* presents a counter-theme even before Monk's melody is introduced. Interesting music that tries hard to combine the cerebral and the swinging. **AL**

Art Hodes

1904-1993

Pagin' Mr Jelly **Hodes** (p). Candid Ⓕ 79037-2 (58 minutes). Recorded 1988.

⑧ ❼

How ironic that a white, Russian-born, Chicago-bred pianist in his 80s became one of the last masters of a disappearing style of blues playing. Always a competent, devoted disciple of South Side pianists ranging from the sophisticated, especially Earl Hines, to the earthy, in this case the equally incomparable Jimmy Yancey, Hodes's art grew more personal, more pleasingly idiosyncratic with age. This intimate programme, dedicated to another of Hodes's idols Jelly Roll Morton, finds him approaching the ragtime-influenced pieces like *Grandpa's Spells* with a calm, crisp articulation and only a touch of whimsy, although still likely to highlight an unusual progression in the bass line or add his own tag. He takes a few more liberties with the non-Morton material, joking with quotes in *Ballin' The Jack* and coaxing bluesy passages out of the march-step *High Society*. He really shines on the blues, however, whether his own tribute *Gone Jelly Blues* or *Mamie's Blues* (here mistakenly credited to Morton; he attributed it to Mamie Desdume)—both gorgeously slow, sparse and saturated with atmosphere. Like Yancey, he is unafraid to take his time, alter the dynamics of his phrases, or find a particularly tart harmony and let it ring, much as Monk would do. Hodes never dazzled with his technique, but his vast experience allowed him to interpret this material with a wealth of associations, allusions, and simple eloquence. It may not be trendy, but it is timeless, and as Art used to say, "The records got released, and no-one got hurt." **AL**

Johnny Hodges

1907-1970

Used to be Duke **Hodges** (as); **Harold 'Shorty' Baker** (t); **Lawrence Brown** (tb); **Jimmy Hamilton** (cl, ts); **John Coltrane** (ts); **Harry Carney** (bs); **Call Cobbs**, **Richie Powell** (p); **John Williams** (b); **Louis Bellson** (d). Verve 849 394-2 (48 minutes). Recorded 1954.

⑧ ❼

Johnny Hodges's 42-year stint with the Ellington orchestra was interrupted just once: from 1951 to 1955 he led his own small ensembles, recording several fine albums for the Norgran label. These LPs were reissued by Verve, then in 1989 resurfaced, still on vinyl, as a Mosaic box-set. Presumably Verve will eventually release all of this material on CD, but to date **Used to be Duke** is the only disc to have appeared.

A strong Ducal influence pervaded Hodges's Norgran dates. **Used to be Duke** is atypical in having only one Ellington tune (*Warm Valley*), but a line-up that includes four of Hodges's ex-orchestra colleagues (Baker, Brown, Carney, Hamilton) is par for the course. The blues exerts a strong influence. The masterly *Sweet as Bear Meat* is taken at what Stanley Dance has called "a relaxed, sauntering tempo" of a kind almost peculiar to Hodges; the punchier riffing of *Burgundy Walk* and the title-track reflects the fifties taste for r&b. Hodges brings an urbane elegance to the blues, while *Warm Valley* is all melting balladry, and the zestful *Sunny Side of the Street* finds him slipping in and out of double-time with consummate ease. There is nothing superfluous in his playing, just a stream of supple phrases, beautifully poised and unfailingly melodic. **GL**

Back to Back/Side by Side **Hodges** (as); **Harry Edison**, **Roy Eldridge** (t); **Lawrence Brown** (tb); **Ben Webster** (ts); **Duke Ellington**, **Billy Strayhorn** (p); **Les Spann** (g, f); **Sam Jones**, **Al Hall**, **Wendell Marshall** (b); **Jo Jones** (d) Verve Ⓜ 823 637-2/821 578-2 (two discs, oas: 46 and 52 minutes). Recorded 1958/59.

⑩ ❽

One of the most significant late-period small-groups, **Back to Back** and 16 minutes of **Side by Side** came from the same sessions, with Duke on the piano and billed accurately as co-leader. Until such time as they are combined on a single CD, both original albums need to be recommended.

All seven tracks on the first and one item on the second (Waller's *Just Squeeze Me*) are old warhorses, composed by neither Hodges nor Ellington but freshened remarkably by the combination of the altoist with ex-Basie-ite Edison (and indeed Duke with Jo Jones). Hodges knew how to play simple with supreme effectiveness, and the skeletal arrangements on such as *Wabash Blues* or *Loveless Love* take much of their flavour from Ellington's piano. Of the two Ducal themes on **Side by Side**, he lifts the entire performance of *Stompy Jones* by his dialogue with Jones, while the other, *Goin' Up*, is a 1943 Ellington item never previously recorded in the studio and marking Duke's first use of the flute.

Six septet items on **Side by Side** recall the group Hodges led during the first half of the fifties, but the addition of Verve contract artists Eldridge and Webster is an undoubted plus. Two laid-back standards (*Let's Fall In Love* and the unusually structured *Just a Memory*) are a diversion from the main course of four blues at different tempos. A reminder that Hodges virtually founded instrumental rhythm & blues in the late thirties is Strayhorn's repetition of a single figure throughout the joyous *You Need To Rock*. **BP**

And Wild Bill Davis **Hodges** (as); with, on disc one: **Wild Bill Davis** (org); **Dickie Thompson**, **Mundell Lowe** (g); **Milt Hinton**, **George Duvivier** (b); **Osie Johnson** (d); on disc two: **Lawrence Brown** (tb); **Bob Brown** (ts, f); **Wild Bill Davis** (org); **Dickie Thompson** (g); **Bobby Durham** (d). RCA Jazz Tribune Ⓜ ND 89765 (two discs: 79 minutes) Recorded 1965/1966.

⑧ ❼

Hodges made a large number of albums with Wild Bill during the sixties, spreading them between two companies—RCA and Verve. Few of them are available in any form at the present time, so we must welcome such reissues. The first CD is a 1965 studio session and finds Hodges at his most relaxed and sumptuous, his tone beautifully captured by the RCA technicians and faithfully balanced against the might of Davis's instrument. Wild Bill occasionally threatens to overwhelm anyone within earshot, and once or twice is a little too adept at imitating Fats Waller's organ timbres, but apart from that he is enthusiastic and supportive, often showing surprisingly attentive and discreet backing to Hodges. The lack of a second horn is in fact a bonus, allowing Hodges all the room he needs.

The second CD stems from an engagement at Grace's Little Belmont, Atlantic City, where Davis had a residency and from whence came a contemporaneous live album featuring the organist's trio with tenorist Bob Brown on a couple of tracks. Until recently this was available on American Bluebird as a single CD, which had a previously unissued version of *Just Squeeze Me* to bolster a not overwhelming amount of playing time. The music here is not so finely balanced, or finely recorded (too much stereo separation, a fair amount of bottom-end distortion and far too much audience chatter) as the 1965 session, but it has its moments, especially a sprightly *Good Queen Bess*. But why have BMG France put this out with the extra track missing, especially when, as the playing time now stands, this entire package could have been fitted onto one CD? **KS**

Jay Hoggard

1954

In The Spirit **Hoggard** (vb), **James Newton** (f), **Dwight Andrews** (bcl), **Mark Helias** (b), **Ed Blackwell** (d). Muse Ⓕ MCD 5476 (56 minutes). Recorded 1992.

⑧ ❽

Hoggard is an accomplished vibraphonist who has been recording under his own name since his early twenties without ever making a very consistent impression. On this occasion, however, he has found a viable concept and assembled a group worthy of it. 1994 saw the 30th anniversary of the death of Eric Dolphy, and of his last great album **Out To Lunch**. Hoggard's new set is a tribute to Dolphy, with an original number in his honour, an Oliver Nelson blues associated with him (*Stolen Moments*) and the Dolphy piece from **Out To Lunch** called *Gazzelloni*, inspired by the Italian flute virtuoso.

The instrumentation throughout recalls Dolphy's own version of the latter, with the use instead of a trumpet of both flute and bass clarinet, and marks Hoggard's return to the influence of Bobby Hutcherson rather than the more faceless playing heard from him lately. With robust contributions from Helias and Ed Blackwell on one of his last sessions, this is a varied and stimulating album. Other material includes Thelonious Monk's *Bye-Ya* and Anthony Davis's *Andrew*, which—although we're not told—I imagine is dedicated to Andrew Hill, with whom Dolphy also recorded in his final year. **BP**

Allan Holdsworth

1946

Metal Fatigue **Holdsworth** (g); **Jimmy Johnson**, **Gary Willis** (elb); **Chad Wackerman**, **Gary Husband**, **Mac Hine** (d); **Alan Pasqua** (kbds); **Paul Williams**, **Paul Korda** (v). Cream Ⓕ CR 270-2. (38 minutes). Recorded 1985.

⑥ ❽

Allan Holdsworth's music has been notoriously variable in quality. Although his improvisations have rarely been less than acceptable, and often quite brilliant, his compositions have usually been a disappointment. This inconsistency plagues all his recordings, so that some of his best work has been as a sideman, with Soft Machine and Bruford (see above). This recording is no exception, and four-fifths of it can safely be disregarded. However, moments on a couple of tracks render it essential to all Holdsworth followers. Most of the compositions are hampered by vaguely organized material and several feature shapeless vocals, but within the generality are several magic moments that show why Holdsworth is one of the handful of original British jazz guitarists. The outstanding points here are his chord work and fills around the vocals on the title-track, and his beautifully developed solo on *Devil Take The Hindmost*. More than anything since his work with Bruford, the latter encapsulates the main elements of his style—a Coltrane-inspired polytonal vocabulary, an acutely lyrical sensibility, exquisitely expressive use of the tremolo arm, and a fast and fluent legato style made possible by the use of overdrive and extra light strings. **MG**

Billie Holiday

1915-1959

The Voice Of Jazz **Billie Holiday** (v); **Roy Eldridge**, **Buck Clayton**, **Bunny Berigan**, **Jonah Jones**, **Frankie Newton** (t); **Bobby Hackett** (c); **Benny Morton**, **Dickie Wells**, **Jack Teagarden**, **Trummy Young** (tb); **Benny Goodman**, **Cecil Scott**, **Irving Fazola**, **Artie Shaw**, **Edmund Hall**, **Buster Bailey** (cl); **Hilton Jefferson**, **Johnny Hodges**, **Tab Smith**, **Benny Carter** (as); **Lester Young**, **Ben Webster**, **Joe Thomas**, **Babe Russin** (ts); **Teddy Wilson**, **Joe Bushkin**, **Sonny White** (p); **Lawrence Lucie**, **Dave Barbour**, **Al Casey**, **Freddie Green**, **John Collins**, **Allan Reuss**, **Bernard Addison** (g); **John Kirby**, **Milt Hinton**, **Artie Bernstein**, **Walter Page** (b); **Cozy Cole**, **Jo Jones**, **Gene Krupa**, **J.C. Heard**, **Yank Porter** (d). Affinity Ⓜ CD AFS BOX 1019-8 (eight discs: 559 minutes). Recorded 1933-40.

✔ ⑩ ❽

Billie Holiday's achievement was to take popular songs, purge them of sentimentality and raise them to expressive heights unimagined by their composers. She had the techniques and instincts of a jazz musician, and is both the greatest jazz singer and the greatest interpreter of American song.

This boxed set contains Billie's earliest and best records, most of them made in an informal, small-band setting, surrounded by the best jazz musicians of her generation. The finest pearls in the collection are those pieces where Lester Young plays as Billie sings. Their lines are so close together you expect them to trip each other up, but they never do; they simply move as one, gracefully and in perfect accord. Apart from Armstrong in his prime, there is no more optimistic, spirit-lifting sound in jazz.

These discs follow Billie's career into its second stage, when she was being taken up by the intelligentsia and characterized as a tragic figure, a wronged woman and a kind of universal human doormat. Her repertoire changes suddenly and quite markedly to slow, doom-laden ballads, torch songs of the most despairing kind, and of course, the famous *Strange Fruit*, a poem set to music on the subject of lynching in the Deep South.

In all, there are 189 tracks here; some are alternate takes, but not many. Because there are so many great classics here, it really is worth getting the full set rather than seeking a one-volume anthology, none of which are particularly good. The remastering and presentation here is also greatly in advance of the single-CD series issued by the owners of the masters, Columbia, so it is a worthwhile investment from every point of view. **DG**

The Quintessential Billie Holiday, Volume 9. **Holiday** (v); **Bill Coleman**, **Shad Collins**, **Roy Eldridge**, **Emmett Berry** (t); **Benny Morton** (tb); **Jimmy Hamilton** (cl); **Leslie Johnakins**, **Eddie Barefield**, **Ernie Powell**, **Lester Boone**, **Jimmy Powell**, **Hymie Schertzer** (as); **Benny Carter** (as, cl); **Georgie Auld**, **Lester Young**, **Babe Russin** (ts); **Sonny White**, **Eddie Heywood**, **Teddy Wilson** (p); **Ulysses Livingston**, **John Collins**, **Paul Chapman**, **Al Casey**, **Gene Fields** (g); **Wilson Myers**, **Ted Sturgis**, **Grachan Moncur**, **John Williams** (b); **Yank Porter**, **Kenny Clarke**, **Herbert Cowans**, **J.C. Heard** (d). Columbia Ⓜ CK 47031 (55 minutes). Recorded 1940-42.

✔ ⑩ ❻

For those torn between the early, smooth-voiced Holiday or the later, tortured one, on this last volume from her first Columbia period she is poised between the two. The music can be decidedly melancholic: *Solitude* and *Am I Blue?* are effectively slightly too slow, and the suicide-themed *Gloomy Sunday* is ages away from the blithe young Billie of a few years earlier. She was now 26.

Still, the swinging small groups follow her established model. Eight of 18 tracks are with Teddy Wilson, including a fine *I Cover the Waterfront* where the introductory verse swings as hard as the rest. There are classics here: the original *God Bless the Child*, Holiday's own fine lyric; a buoyant *It's a Sin to Tell a Lie*; the fussing-over-baby charmer *Mandy Is Two*, words by Johnny Mercer, no piece for a juvenile; one of Lady's rare blues, albeit a fancy one—W.C. Handy's *St. Louis Blues*. Her melismatic phrasing is so personal, it's odd to hear her bend conventional blue notes there.

Critics may complain about Holiday's lacklustre material, but this fairly representative slice is clinker-free (not even *Jim* sounds corny). We sometimes talk of early and late Holiday as different people; this Billie is both, and integrated: the soaring voice of youth seasoned with a deeper personal understanding. **KW**

The Complete Original American Decca Recordings **Holiday** (v); with a collective personnel of: **Joe Guy**, **Rostelle Reese** (t); **Lem Davis** (as); **Bob Dorsey** (ts); **Joe Springer**, **Billy Kyle**, **Bobby Tucker** (p); **Tiny Grimes**, **Jimmy Shirley**, **Mundell Lowe** (g); **Thomas Barney**, **Billy Taylor**, **John Levy**, **John Simmons** (b); **Kelly Martin**, **Kenny Clarke**, **Denzil Best** (d); **Louis Armstrong** (v). MCA/Decca Ⓜ GRP 26012 (two discs:151 minutes). Recorded 1944-50.

✔ ⑩ ❽

For once an album title is correct; these are the complete recordings Billie made for Decca, including nine previously unissued tracks and others which only saw the light of day briefly on Japanese or

German LP compilations. All of the music has been lovingly restored to near-perfect conditions (allowing, in some instances, for worn source material) and the 80-page booklet which is part of the package is packed with relevant information on personnels, actual times of the sessions, background stories by supervisor/producer Milt Gabler and many rare photographs. Billie's Decca recordings have often received short shrift from critics but this set of 50 tracks, made over a five-and-a-half year period, makes it clear that Miss Holiday was singing as well as she ever did during her career, often better in fact, and the strings and studio bands were not Decca's idea but Billie's. She saw herself as a star and demanded star treatment, and was no longer content with a casual gig with a handful of jazzmen grouped around Teddy Wilson's piano. There are gems to be found here, apart from the expected *Lover Man* and *Porgy* (plus a previously unissued take of *My Man*); the 1947 version of *Easy Living*, for example, is the equal of the 'classic' 1937 record of the song even though there are no instrumental solos. And the two tracks on which Billie duets with Louis Armstrong are beyond category. This set renders all other compilations from the Decca period obselete and is essential in the overall assessment of Billie's unique artistry. **AM**

The Complete Billie Holiday on Verve **Holiday** (v); with a selected collective personnel of **Howard McGhee, Buck Clayton, Joe Guy, Charlie Shavers, Joe Newman, Harry 'Sweets' Edison, Roy Eldridge, Joe Wilder** (t); **Trummy Young, Jimmy Cleveland** (tb); **Buddy DeFranco** (cl); **Tony Scott** (cl, p); **Willie Smith, Benny Carter** (as); **Illinois Jacquet, Wardell Gray, Charlie Ventura, Coleman Hawkins, Lester Young, George Auld, Flip Phillips, Paul Quinichette, Budd Johnson, Ben Webster, Al Cohn** (ts); **Danny Bank** (bs); **Red Norvo** (xyl); **Milt Raskin, Ken Kersey, Bobby Tucker, Oscar Peterson, Carl Drinkard, Beryl Booker, Sonny Clark, Billy Taylor, Jimmy Rowles, Wynton Kelly, Mal Waldron, Hank Jones** (p); **Dave Barbour, Tiny Grimes, Barney Kessel, Freddie Green, Jimmy Raney, Billy Bauer, Kenny Burrell, Barry Galbraith, Billy Byers** (g); **Charles Mingus, Curly Russell, Al McKibbon, Ray Brown, Red Mitchell, Leonard Gaskin, Artie Shapiro, John Simmons, Aaron Bell, Joe Mondragon, Joe Benjamin, Milt Hinton** (b); **Davie Coleman, J.C. Heard, Jackie Mills, Alvin Stoller, Elaine Leighton, Cozy Cole, Chico Hamilton, Larry Bunker, Jo Jones, Don Lamond, Osie Johnson** (d); **Ray Ellis and his Orchestra**. Verve Ⓜ 517 658-2 (ten discs: 722 minutes). Recorded 1945-59.

⑧ ❼

Critics have had a field day with the post-war career of Billie Holiday. There are two basic positions adopted: the first is that her career was spoiled by the overly commercial backdrops given her by American Decca in the forties, and by the time she got back to small-group jazz recordings with Norman Granz, her voice was shot to pieces. The second position is that her later recordings are a triumph of spirit and artistry over acute physical and personal handicaps, and in fact offer deeper insights into the human condition than any of her earlier recordings. Both positions reveal more about the critics who form these opinions than about the artistry of Holiday. For she, along with just a handful of jazz singers, deserves to have her entire recorded output accorded the same degree of study and hard-won insight usually reserved for the very greatest figures in their respective fields, be that Mozart, Picasso or Rilke, Armstrong, Parker or Ellington.

This collection covers a greater time-span than any other single-label set can (the Columbia is from 1933 to 1942; the Decca from 1944 to 1950, while the Commodore sides cover just a handful of years), and therefore shows a more complete picture of the aritst and than any other. The earliest concert sides on disc one (all taken from Jazz At The Philharmonic appearances from the forties) find her in perfect voice and in mostly outgoing and ebullient mood, whatever the character of the songs perfomed. Her various accompaniment is also variously successful, although Charles Mingus is conspicuous on bass on the very first track, *Body and Soul*, from 1945. Verve's attempt to be exhaustive in its coverage of Holiday's Verve years has led to the inclusion of an entire disc (disc 4) and all but three tracks from disc 6 which for the first time bring home-made Holiday rehearsal tapes before the public. The sound quality is not very good, although the insights are facintating for the dedicated Holiday fan. It is definitely not for casual listening, however.

Also available here is the 1956 Carnegie Hall concert, which generally finds her in good voice and well focused on her material, and the 1957 Newport Jazz Festival set where her voice is scratchy and her delivery uncertain. The set ends with the sessions she made with a Ray Ellis orchestra which contains both sympathetic obbligato jazz soloists and a string section, thereby combining, to her way of thinking at this stage of her career, the best of both worlds.

As a document of jazz history, this is a vital set to acquire. As a ten-disc set of entertainment for those more inclined to a casual approach to music, it is something to avoid. The standard of presentation, packaging and documentation (there is a 220-page booklet included in the set) is exemplary, and an object lesson to all those who would care to embark on similar enterprises. **KS**

The Billie Holiday Songbook **Holiday** (v); with a collective personnel of: **Buck Clayton, Harry 'Sweets' Edison, Roy Eldridge, Joe Newman, Charlie Shavers** (t); **Tony Scott** (cl); **Willie Smith** (as); **Al Cohn, Coleman Hawkins, Paul Quinichette** (ts); **Carl Drinkard, Wynton Kelly, Oscar Peterson, Bobby Tucker, Mal Waldron** (p); **Kenny Burrell, Herb Ellis, Freddie Green, Barney Kessel** (g);

Aaron Bell, Ray Brown, Red Callender, Milt Hinton, Carson Smith (b); **Chico Hamilton, Gus Johnson, Don Lamond, Lenny McBrowne, Ed Shaughnessy** (d). Verve Ⓜ 823 246-2 (46 minutes). Recorded 1952-58.

⑥ ❻

This CD collects together many of Billie Holiday's best-known songs, including *God Bless the Child, Don't Explain, Strange Fruit, Billie's Blues* and *Fine and Mellow*. These are not the original versions, however, but later re-recordings that Holiday made for Verve in the fifties, and the convenience of having so much familiar material on a single CD must be balanced against the fact that, in nearly every case, the earlier versions are artistically stronger, and are certainly less problematic for the listener, since Holiday's voice was still in full bloom and her intonation had not started to break down into the croaks that became common by the mid-fifties.

Most of the tracks on **Songbook** come from 1956. There are impressive versions of *Don't Explain* and *God Bless the Child*, and her late hit *Lady Sings the Blues*, written for Holiday by pianist Herbie Nichols, makes a welcome appearance. Overall, though, this is a disquietening collection, given both the state of Holiday's voice and the preponderance of her more lugubrious tunes about unrequited or abused love, those "embarrassing anything-for-a-man songs" (to quote Alice Walker) that teeter along a thin line between artistry and pathos. Holiday's Commodore sessions, although currently out of catalogue, or one of the above Columbia series would make a more readily enjoyable, and certainly less emotionally fraught, introduction to her music. **GL**

Dave Holland

1946

Extensions **Holland** (b); **Steve Coleman** (as); **Kevin Eubanks** (g); **Marvin 'Smitty' Smith** (d). ECM Ⓕ 1410 (841 778-2) (59 minutes). Recorded 1989.

⑧ ❾

Holland was born in Wolverhampton but left the UK for America in 1968 at the behest of Miles Davis. He swiftly established himself as a leading talent on bass and cello and hit an early peak with his 1972 LP **Conference of the Birds**, made with Anthony Braxton and Sam Rivers. In the eighties Holland led his own group (originally a quintet that featured Kenny Wheeler and Julian Priester) and recorded a series of well-received albums for ECM. Recent releases such as **Triplicate** and **Extensions** show him moving away from the previous, Mingus-inspired ensembles towards a more fluid, expansive form of music.

Holland has cited Ornette Coleman's strong melodic lines as a major influence on his composing and it is not difficult to hear the Coleman Quartet's Atlantic LPs as a model for **Extensions**. Eubanks adds watercolour daubs of chords at times, but often saxophone, bass and guitar simply play lines, lending the music an attractive sense of space and flow as snippets of melody float and circle over a skittering pulse. Steve Coleman's alto has never sounded more eloquent and his funk-driven *Black Hole* jumps and jolts with elastic charm. But it is Holland who lays the foundation of the record's success. His bass, and his compositions (notably the lovely *Procession*), sparkle with grace and intelligence in ECM's pellucid acoustic. **GL**

Red Holloway

1927

Locksmith Blues **Holloway** (as, ts); **Clark Terry** (t, flh); **Gerald Wiggins** (p); **Phil Upchurch** (g); **Richard Reid** (b, elb); **Paul Humphrey** (d). Concord Ⓕ CCD 4390 (51 minutes). Recorded 1989.

⑦ ❽

Red Holloway came to jazz almost as a second choice. A Chicago native, his natural home was in the r&b field and he presented this persona on the majority of his early records. He was very much at home backing blues singers or in the organ/tenor groups of the sixties, although he moved increasingly towards jazz. The most concerted move came about in his five-year collaboration with Sonny Stitt, but there have been other sessions with equally uncompromising jazz musicians. The productive two saxophone partnership was ended by Stitt's death, but this CD is typical of the latter type of pairing, teaming Holloway with trumpet giant Clark Terry.

The session draws concessions from both sides. It pits Terry's sauve balladeering and puckish tune rebuilding against Holloway's more considered and slightly pedestrian style. *Happiness Is A Thing Called Joe* features Holloway's lone horn and it shows him well able to modify, paraphrase and generally re-model a standard. At times the luxurious tone on tenor takes him to the brink of bathos

but he somehow manages to avoid the plunge and, if his improvisations are overtly romantic, they are never without charm. In contrast, his approach to the blues is altogether more earthy, whether up-tempo and driving or surgingly low-down. Perhaps playing the blues in this self-made world between r&b and jazz is Holloway's successful secret. There are certainly few contenders for a crown he wears with ease. **BMcR**

Christopher Hollyday

1970

Christopher Hollyday **Hollyday** (as); **Wallace Roney** (t); **Cedar Walton** (p); **David Williams** (b); **Billy Higgins** (d). Novus Ⓕ PD 83055 (62 minutes). Recorded 1989.

⑦ ❽

Memorizing Charlie Parker solos at 14, Hollyday joined America's growing school of neo-classicists without being a member of the Jazz Futures academy. Boston born and still only 19 when this record was made, he represents the school of players devoted to the perpetuation of the bop and hard bop messages. Whether a more personal route to self expression is more desirable is immaterial, because this CD, his fourth issued session, shows him capable of meeting the required standards of execution. He is very much at home with the outstanding rhythm section here and is also equal to the challenge of a soloist of Roney's quality. For his part, Hollyday is not an empty copyist and his solos, while using the grammar of men like Jackie McLean, project his own brand of personal expression. Moreover, they are not delivered in a polite, glib manner; the faintly acerbic tone and a degree of edge-roughening lends depth to what he has to say. At the time of writing, it could be said that his subsequent releases have not yet been up to the standard of this fine effort. **BMcR**

Bill Holman

1927

Bill Holman Band **Holman** (ts, arr); **Carl Sanders**, **Frank Szabo**, **Don Rader**, **Bob Summers** (t, flh); **Jack Redmond**, **Bob Enevoldsen**, **Rick Culver**, **Pete Beltran** (tb); **Lanny Morgan**, **Bob Militello** (ss, as, f); **Bob Cooper**, **Dick Mitchell** (ss, ts, f); **Bob Efford** (bs, bcl); **Rich Eames** (p); **Barry Zweig** (g); **Bruce Lett** (b); **Jeff Hamilton** (d). JVC Ⓕ 3308-2 (59 minutes). Recorded 1987.

⑦ ❽

One of the best-respected and in-demand big band arrangers of the last 40 years, Holman has written for, among others, Maynard Ferguson, Buddy Rich, Woody Herman, Sarah Vaughan, films and television, although the bulk of his best and most adventurous work was done in the fifties for Stan Kenton (which can be heard on the highly recommended Mosaic multi-disc set **Stan Kenton—The Complete Capitol Recordings of the Holman and Russo Charts**). Due to the unavailability on CD of **The Fabulous Bill Holman** (originally on Coral), this JVC session offers the best example of latter-day Holman. He was accused of swinging too hard for Kenton's taste, and he maintains that standard here in the punchy style of postwar mainstream arranging he helped develop. Characterized by ingenious sectional scoring, his charts balance brilliance with tact, agility with craft. Although a fine composer on his own, as shown on the flagwaving *Front Runner* and the quirky *The Real You*, he likes to take a familiar piece of material and open its seams, inserting counter-themes and bravura episodes. This works well with *St Thomas*, highlighting Holman's gift for thematic variation, and *I Mean You*, with its piquant three-soprano front line. The approach is less successful on a pop song like *Isn't She Lovely?* and the intimate elegy *Goodbye Pork Pie Hat*. The orchestra plays the charts with crisp precision; the soloists may not exhibit the personality of his collaborators of the Kenton days, but they remain faithful to the character of the music. **AL**

Richard 'Groove' Holmes

1931-1991

Blues All Day Long **Holmes** (org); **Cecil Bridgewater** (t); **Houston Person** (ts); **Jimmy Ponder** (g); **Cecil Brooks III** (d); **Ralph Dorsey** (perc). Muse Ⓕ MCD 5358 (40 minutes). Recorded 1988.

⑦ ❽

In the absence of the certified classic **Groove**, recorded in 1961 for Richard Bock's Pacific Jazz and featuring Ben Webster on sax, which has been both released and deleted on CD, this is as good a taste of the B3 solid sender as you are likely to hear. It finds him in utterly tyical musical territory, mixing smoothly-rolling blues numbers with tasteful performances of old standards. It also finds him with a distinctly superior bunch of supporting stars, with saxophonist Person also doubling as producer. The treatment of *These Foolish Things* shows a deal of forethought and draws a sustained and touching ballad display from Person, with his caressing of the melody being particularly affecting.

Holmes always saw himself as a distinct cut above the average Hammond groove merchant, and his skilful deployment of a large sonic range on his instrument shows that he worked hard for that distinction. Even the boogaloo-type treatment of *Killer Joe* finds him experimenting with sound in a refreshing rather than a clichéd way, driving along the beat with deft touches and slick footwork. Bridgewater responds by playing a deeply bop-rooted solo in the manner of his better work with Max Roach. By and large, this is typical of the overall approach taken by Holmes and his sidemen, and it makes for an intelligent and above-average organ-plus-horns workout. Holmes made albums after this, but it remains a high point in his output. **KS**

Bertha Hope

Elmo's Fire **Hope** (p); **Eddie Henderson** (t); **Junior Cook, Dave Riekenberg** (ts); **Walter Brooker** (b); **Leroy Williams** (d). SteepleChase Ⓕ SCCD 31289 (56 minutes). Recorded 1991.

⑧ ❽

In many respects a re-creation of the small-group session of an earlier era—quirky boppish themes delivered in a slightly sour ensemble sound followed by a brisk round of solos before a theme restatement—**Elmo's Fire** nevertheless has three great strengths. The first is the playing of Bertha Hope herself; a considered, unspectacular but intriguing soloist, she proceeds through her subtle extemporizations with almost cat-like care and delicacy. This approach works extremely well on her own compositions, an extended blues and a relaxed bossa nova, and brings new life to her late husband's faintly Monkish minor classics *Bellarosa* and *Elmo's Fire*. The second is the presence of tenor saxophonist Junior Cook, one of the finest and most neglected of the bop-influenced mainstream players. His most obvious influence is Dexter Gordon, whom he closely resembles not only in tone and overall approach, but also in his predilection for unexpected but felicitous musical quotations. On **Elmo's Fire**, he demonstrates his grandiloquent, foggy sound to perfection. The third is the inclusion in the quintet's repertoire of Elmo Hope's tricky, idiosyncratic compositions, like those of Herbie Nichols never quite accorded the acclaim they deserved during his life, but nevertheless sounding fresh as ever over a quarter-century after his premature death. Eddie Henderson has an unusual, smeary trumpet sound, but it is appropriate in this context, and all those present contribute to a quietly competent but surprisingly subtle album. **CP**

Elmo Hope

1923-1967

Elmo Hope Trio **Hope** (p); **Jimmy Bond** (b); **Frank Butler** (d). Contemporary Ⓜ OJCCD0477-2 (44 minutes). Recorded 1959.

⑧ ❼

"Elmo truly had a touch of genius. I was in awe of him." If Harold Land's tribute to the still little-known Hope sounds a shade extravagant, listen to the pianist's trenchant contributions (as player and composer) to Land's classic album **The Fox** and to his own records, such as the two-volume **Last Sessions** or this trio set, made during a four-year stay in Los Angeles at the close of the fifties.

Hope's major influences were Bud Powell (a childhood friend) and Thelonious Monk, although as with those men (and the similarly neglected Herbie Nichols) his style was a distinctly personal distillation of bebop. His abrupt right-hand runs, in which strings of notes seem almost to jostle against each other, give a bright rhythmic bounce, heard to good advantage on **Trio** on the blues-based *B's A-Plenty* and the Latin-ish *Something For Kenny*, which also boasts a striking hands-on-kit solo by the redoubtable Frank Butler. The album's highlight is a reading of the Van Heusen-Burke standard *Like Someone in Love*, its dreamy tread cueing a series of skittish feints at the melody line by Hope. He is not a spectacular player, but the cumulative effect is richly inventive. **GL**

Claude Hopkins

1903-1984

Monkey Business **Hopkins** (p, ldr); with a collective personnel of: **Albert Snaer, Sylvester Lewis, Shirley Clay, Jabbo Smith, Lincoln Mills** (t); **Ovie Alston** (t, v); **Fernando Arbello, Fred Norman, Floyd Brady, Vic Dickenson** (tb); **Edmond Hall** (cl, as, bs); **Gene Johnson, Chauncey Haughton, Ben Smith** (as); **Bobby Sands** (ts); **Walter Jones** (g); **Henry Turner, Abe Bolar** (b); **Pete Jacobs, George Foster** (d); **Orlando Roberson, Baby White** (v). Hep Ⓜ HEPCD 1031 (64 minutes). Recorded 1934.

⑥ ❻

Hopkins had an eventful and interesting early life which included a tour of Europe with Sidney Bechet and Josephine Baker in 1925. During the thirties he led one of Harlem's most popular dance bands, with long residencies at the Cotton Club and Roseland Ballroom. The 23 titles comprising this reissue date from this period, and while Hopkins himself was very modest about the band's solo strength in later years (he singled out Edmond Hall as the only outstanding soloist) it was, from these recordings, a very efficient unit with a light ensemble sound and a crisp attack, particularly in the popular 'call and response' ensemble passages. Ovie Alston was a good Armstrong-inspired trumpeter and singer, while Hall performed well on both clarinet and baritone. But Hopkins's own piano playing (well featured here on *Three Little Words*, for example) was everything that a band leader's keyboard work should be. In Bobby Sands he had a most impressive Hawkins-like tenor saxophonist, and the 1937 titles benefit from the solo playing of Shirley Clay, especially on the fine *Church Street Sobbin' Blues*. Inevitably there are several vocal tracks (Orlando Roberson's falsetto singing will appeal immediately to connoisseurs of the unusual) but the fine remastering has enabled us to get a truly representative taste of pre-war Harlem. **AM**

Glenn Horiuchi

1955

Oxnard Beet **Horiuchi** (p); **Francis Wong** (f, ts); **Taiji Miyagawa** (b); **Leon Alexander** (d, vb). Soul Note Ⓕ 121228-2 (49 minutes). Recorded 1989.

⑥ ❻

Horiuchi is part of a movement, based primarily in California and also including saxophonist Fred Ho and pianist Jon Jang, that uses jazz to make a statement about Asian-American culture. As with the others, Horiuchi makes pointed references in his composition titles, but the music is fairly straightforward, applying scales from Japanese music together with Latin and more straight-up jazz rhythms. Otherwise, the most overt Asian touch is Francis Wong's deep-toned flute; his tenor, similarly round, comes across as a more familiar bellicose voice. Horiuchi the pianist generally avoids flash, preferring a heavy touch that reinforces the assertive drum patterns of Alexander. The music has weight without totally sacrificing buoyancy, relying a bit too much on repeated vamp patterns while staying just this side of monotony. With less methodical solos from Wong and the leader, the music might soar a bit more, though it still has admirable personality and reveals an area of cross-fertilization that remains largely unexplored in jazz. **BB**

Shirley Horn

1934

You Won't Forget Me **Shirley Horn** (v, p); **Charles Ables**, **Buster Williams** (b); **Steve Williams**, **Billy Hart** (d); on one track each: **Miles Davis**, **Wynton Marsalis**, (t); **Buck Hill**, **Branford Marsalis** (ts); **Toots Thielemans** (hca, g). Verve Ⓕ 847 482-2 (71 minutes). Recorded 1990.

⑧ ❽

Thanks to several recent and stunning sessions for Verve, veteran singer-pianist Shirley Horn has ascended to the top echelons of the contemporary jazz world. Significantly, she has done it with an essentially traditional mainstream style and repertory. Though her success has had an 'overnight' aspect for the general public, the fact is that Horn has refined her style and built her library through a long and distinguished career that began in earnest during her student days at Howard University.

For this 1990 date, Horn teams with various 'stars', a format generally more noted for its commercial rather than musical payoffs. Here, however, Horn transcends the business-as-usual expectations of the genre for a set of absolutely striking collaborations. With Wynton Marsalis, she waxes with bluesy yet refined whimsy on *Don't Let the Sun Catch You Cryin'*; with Toots Thielemans, she wistfully recalls a *Beautiful Love*; with Branford Marsalis, she poignantly confesses *It Had to Be You*; while with Miles Davis she sizzles on the plaintive *You Won't Forget Me*. One of the most fascinating dimensions of Horn's vocal style is that she never shouts, or emotes for the fans in the last row of the balcony. As her incisive and spare piano style reveals, Horn is a musician. When she sings, it is with the instincts of an instrumentalist who also happens to be a keen observer of the human situation. **CB**

Lena Horne

1917

Stormy Weather **Lena Horne** (v); with **Charlie Barnet and his Orchestra; Artie Shaw and his Orchestra**; plus studio groups arranged and conducted by: **Lou Brigg**, **Horace Henderson**, **Phil Moore**, **Lennie Hayton**. RCA Bluebird Ⓜ ND90441 (66 minutes). Recorded 1941-58.

⑥ ❽

Although of the same generation as Billie and Ella, and with a similar early musical background, Lena Horne has never been fully accepted in jazz circles. This is partly because, being a celebrated beauty, she acquired film star status early in life and rarely performed in a pure jazz context. Nevertheless, her whole style has that loose, lightly swinging approach that characterizes the kind of singer jazz musicians love listening to.

This selection, drawn from the earlier part of Lena's career, begins at the time when she was Charlie Barnet's resident singer, continues through her period in cabaret (notably at the politically conscious Café Society) and end at the height of her career as a best-selling album artist. The bulk of the performances date from the mid-forties, musically her best decade. She seems to have had a special affinity at the time with the work of Harold Arlen and there are some splendid versions of his songs here, in particular a beautiful, swinging *As Long As I Live*. **DG**

Wayne Horvitz

Miracle Mile **Horvitz** (kbds, p); with **The President**: **J.A. Deane** (tb); **Doug Weiselman** (cl, ts); **Denny Goodhew** (saxes); **Stew Cutler**, **Bill Frisell**, **Elliot Sharp** (g); **Ben Steele** (g, sampler); **Kermit Driscoll** (elb); **Bobby Previte** (d). Elektra Nonesuch Ⓕ 79278-2 (48 minutes). Recorded 1991.

✔

⑩ ❽

Wayne Horvitz is one of the talents to have emerged unscathed from the Knitting Factory in New York, moving on now from small local labels to a deal with a major like Elektra. Where this has no doubt helped most is in the recording budget, for this ambitious album is very fully realized indeed. Each of the eight tracks here is an individual entity, with no great continuity between them past the musical forces employed. Horvitz often uses riffs, ostinato lines and repetitious slivers to keep the music moving on (in fact, *Variations on a Theme by W.C. Handy*, the theme being *St Louis Blues*, is entirely taken up by progressive modifications of riffs and lines which run the length of the piece). *Yuba City*, in contrast, uses repetition merely as a backcloth to hang the often fierce improvising and sound-painting he elicits from his group. *An Open Letter to George Bush* sounds more like a lament for a vanished America, à la Charlie Haden's Liberation Music Orchestra recordings, reiterating simple but moving harmonies, while the title track has an enigmatic progression on keyboards, a fifth interval in the treble clef having its harmonic base constantly modified by where the pedal points land. A sax takes an impassioned solo in the B section of the song.

This is jazz from a very different angle, but it is essential listening for those interested in what those who today are stretching the form are actually achieving. **KS**

Steve Houben

1950

City of Glass Houben (fl, ss, ts); **Diederick Wissels** (p); **Jan De Haas** (d). Miss You Ⓕ 12 2010 (71 minutes). Recorded 1989.

⑥ ❽

There are plenty of excellent modern musicians in France, Belgium and the like, playing very palatable and occasionally inspiring music, just waiting to be discovered by a wider international audience. Steve Houben is one. Although a frequent visitor to the US and someone who has played in groups with people like Bill Frisell and Chet Baker, this still-young Belgian is not known widely outside his own country. It is everyone else's loss, because he is a tidy composer, capable of a tasty range of moods, a highly accomplished saxophonist with good tone and excellent intonation, and a disciplined group leader. This trio is highly rehearsed, and not just in terms of playing the right notes: all the dynamics and pulses in the music are beautifully controlled. The music is eclectic, and occasionally borders on the Weather Report end of fusion, but has its own quite self-contained character. The album's title has nothing to do with Stan Kenton.

If this was on ECM, it would command attention. Buy without fear. **KS**

Kid Howard

1908-1966

George Lewis Ragtime Band of New Orleans Howard (t); **Jim Robinson** (tb); **George Lewis** (cl); **Alton Purnell** (p, v); **Lawrence Marrero** (bj); **Alcide Pavageau** (b); **Joe Watkins** (d, v). American Music Ⓕ AMCD 24 (52 minutes). Recorded 1953.

⑥ ❻

Initially a drummer, Howard played in the twenties with Chris Kelly and Isaiah Morgan. The former gave him cornet lessons, and by the end of the decade he was leading his own band on the instrument. In the thirties he worked with Jim Robinson and Capt John Handy. When the New Orleans revival began, Howard joined George Lewis on his first recording session with a full band in 1943. This CD was made at a time when he was working only intermittently and was no longer the powerful Armstrong-inspired player he had been in the thirties. He was now a more diffident performer, with a querulous vibrato and a lacklustre delivery. Fortunately the Lewis band at the time would not have welcomed a powerhouse player, and for all his technical frailty, Howard integrated perfectly. His uncomplicated lead was rhythmically assured and the somewhat thin tonal quality of his trumpet suited this particular front line well. He is exposed on slower items like *Tin Roof Blues* and *Just A Closer Walk*, but when the tempo moves up on the likes of *Sensation Rag* and *Precious Lord*, he contributes considerably to the overall balance of the ensemble. Ironically, following a serious illness in 1960, he landed a Preservation Hall spot and, up to the time of his death, played as well as at any time in the previous 20 years. **BMcR**

Noah Howard

1943

At Judson Hall Howard (as, bells); **Ric Colbeck** (t); **Dave Burrell** (p); **'Sirone' (Norris Jones)** (b); **Catherine Norris** (vc); **Robert Kapp** (d). ESP-Disk Ⓜ 1064-2 (38 minutes). Recorded 1966.

⑧ ❻

Born in New Orleans, Howard's early influences were Johnny Hodges and Charlie Parker. After hearing Ornette Coleman, he moved to California and teamed up with other second-generation free form players such as Byron Allen and Sonny Simmons. This CD was made after his move to New York in 1965 and rates with any recording he ever made. His enthusiasm for free playing was on the up and his early eclecticism had provided him with a very personal style. His playing displays a sense of the dramatic and, in both *This Place Called Earth* and *Homage to Coltrane*, passages of motif declension building are juxtaposed with fiery and longer-lined forays. The *Homage* owns little to Coltrane but it does have the same spiritual intensity, and in this he is particularly helped by Kapp's

Graves-like drum torrent. There is a real input from Colbeck, a highly talented young British trumpeter who later committed suicide, as well as from Burrell, whose modification of the Cecil Taylor message is of intrinsic value to the group. Not surprisingly Howard dominates and, although his later work with Archie Shepp, Sun Ra, Sonny Sharrock and Frank Wright has distinct merit, October 1966 in Judson Hall was a very special occasion. **BMcR**

Freddie Hubbard 1938

The Artistry of Freddie Hubbard **Hubbard** (t); **Curtis Fuller** (tb); **John Gilmore** (ts); **Tommy Flanagan** (p); **Art Davis** (b); **Louis Hayes** (d). Impulse! Ⓜ MCAD-33111 (43 minutes). Recorded 1962.

⑧ ❿

"If someone were to ask how rising young jazzmen in New York were playing on a good get-together in 1962, this album would provide a succinct answer," is Dan Morgenstern's assessment of **The Artistry of Freddie Hubbard**, and 30 years on it is possible to add that the music has also triumphantly stood the test of time. A front line consisting of two Jazz Messengers, Hubbard and Curtis Fuller, augmented by John Gilmore, long-time Sun Ra associate, backed by a first-class rhythm section and engineered by Rudy Van Gelder, promises a great deal and delivers in spadesful. Three Hubbard originals—*Bob's Place*, a quintessential hard-bop vehicle; *Happy Times*, a bubbling, joyous theme; and *The Seventh Day*, a more complex affair incorporating punning references to sevenths and rests—are complemented by two classics, *Caravan* and *Summertime*, and provide excellent springboards for exuberant, youthfully ebullient improvisation from all participants. Hubbard, equally assured at either extreme of the trumpet's range, and possessed of an exhilarating, crackling, fiery tone, demonstrates just why so many tipped him at the time as the new trumpet prospect; Fuller is slyer in approach, but just as virtuosic and exciting; Gilmore shows why he is frequently seen as Coltrane's major influence, exhibiting an obsessive fascination with small cycles of notes and playing with passionate intensity throughout. Overall, this is a definitive early-sixties East Coast jazz session, faultlessly recorded. **CP**

Breaking Point **Hubbard** (t); **James Spaulding** (fl, as); **Ronnie Mathews** (p); **Eddie Khan** (b); **Joe Chambers** (d). Blue Note Ⓜ CDP7 84172 2 (47 minutes). Recorded 1964.

⑧ ❽

Hubbard has always been a formidable player, right from his arrival in New York in 1958, but during 1964 and 1965 he seems to have hit some sort of personal peak, because his playing on a range of albums, both as sideman (Dolphy, Andrew Hill, etc.) and as leader, is outstandingly resourceful. **Breaking Point** is an entirely apt summation of that resourcefulness and reflects the level of inspiration Hubbard was consistently finding. The inspiration on this album is spread equally between the compositions (all bar one by Hubbard—the other is by drummer Chambers) and the choice of personnel (his newly-established working band of the time). The compositions are by no means the usual humdrum head lines, designed to be over with as soon as possible: they are often made up of two or more sections (the title-track), or the predominant mood is continually altered as new elements are introduced during the length of the piece (*Far Away*). Hubbard himself is in burning, declamatory form, chock-full of ideas and with some heavy emotional loads to deliver. His beautiful tone and incredible control allows a very wide range of emotions to be communicated, often through bent notes and growls. Although pianist Mathews also impresses, the other key player here is Chambers, a drummer with amazing musical intelligence and the technique to follow his imagination. **KS**

Born To Be Blue **Hubbard** (t); **Harold Land** (ts); **Billy Childs** (kbds); **Larry Klein** (b); **Steve Houghton** (d); **Buck Clark** (perc). Pablo Ⓜ CD 2312134-2(41 minutes). Recorded 1981.

⑤ ❽

With the CTI label a thing of the past and Creed Taylor's A&R requirements behind him, the Hubbard of the eighties declined to make further disco-oriented, choir-or-violin-enhanced records. Initially, his return to the hard bop field had its problems; this CD, made some five years after the launch of VSOP, shows that he had still to stamp his authority on such projects. Some of the empty trills remained to remind the listener of the fusion years but there is enough of the vintage Hubbard to be heard on titles such as *True Colours* and *Joy Spring*. Unfortunately, the surprisingly diffident support afforded by Land and Childs does not challenge the trumpeter. He certainly would have relished greater musical stimulation, but there is still the bristling attack, the fund of impudent ideas transcending the concept of bar divisions and, above all, the distinctively rounded brassy tone. The session as a whole presents one of the truly outstanding jazz trumpeters playing without the conviction found in his finest work. Better was to come. **BMcR**

Topsy **Hubbard** (t); **Kenny Garrett** (as); **Benny Green** (p); **Rufus Reid** (b); **Carl Allen** (d). Enja Ⓕ 7025 2 (63 minutes). Recorded 1989.

This is the most successful Hubbard session for quite some time, and at least part of the reason lies in the repertoire. Since the late sixties, such pop songs as were included on his albums (and those of many other artists) had been recent 'chart' material, which has seldom proved either suitable or stimulating—an honourable semi-exception in this respect being the Sting song *Fragile* on **Times Are Changing** (Blue Note). Here the first four tunes are from the thirties (including the Basie-popularized title-track and *As Time Goes By*) while the most recent are fifties items, such as *All Of You* and J.J. Johnson's *Lament*.

Hubbard adopts a relaxed approach, whatever the tempo, and the rhythm section combines youth and experience to inspiring effect; as a result, the trumpeter is not overly flamboyant but warms to his task most satisfyingly. It may well not have been his own choice but the marketing considerations of the Japanese producer that dictated the Miles Davis-associated harmon-mute on every track; nevertheless the emotional spectrum is quite wide. Add the excellent work of guest altoist Garrett on his three numbers, and what seems at first glance an unambitious assignment is carried out with all Hubbard's considerable authority. **BP**

Spike Hughes

1908-1987

High Yellow **Hughes** (b); with the following collective personnel: **Norman Payne**, **Chick Smith**, **Jimmy Macaffer**, **Bruts Gonella**, **Billy Higgs**, **Billy Smith**, **Red Allen**, **Shad Collins**, **Leonard Davis**, **Bill Dillard**, **Howard Scott**, **Leslie Thompson** (t); **Leslie Thompson**, **Lew Davis**, **Bill Mulraney**, **Dickie Wells**, **Wilbur De Paris**, **George Washington** (tb); **Harry Hines**, **Billy Amstell**, **Dave Shand**, **Philip Buchel**, **Harry Hayes**, **Buddy Featherstonehaugh**, **Benny Carter**, **Howard Johnson**, **Wayman Carver**, **Coleman Hawkins**, **Chu Berry** (reeds); **Billy Mason**, **Billy Munn**, **Eddie Carroll**, **Luis Russell**, **Red Rodriguez** (p); **Alan Ferguson**, **Lawrence Lucie** (g); **Ernest Hill** (b); **Ronnie Gubertini**, **Bill Harty**, **Sid Catlett**, **Kaiser Marshall** (d); **Claude Ivy** (chimes). Largo Ⓕ 5129. (60 minutes). Recorded 1930-33.

⑧ ❻

It simply was not possible to confine Spike Hughes's talents and enquiring mind to just one musical form and his three-year involvement with jazz at the commencement of the thirties probably gave him all he wanted, although he continued to write provocative and valuable criticism for years after laying down his bass. By the closing months of 1930 his jazz interests had moved away from the 'white' small groups of Red Nichols and Venuti-Lang; he had become enamoured of the orchestral works of Duke Ellington. Hughes was able to deploy his arranging talents to greater effect and his best-selling record of the day was the two-part *Harlem Symphony* included here, a release devoted to Spike's own compositions and including nine of the 14 tracks he recorded in New York in May 1933 with what was, in fact, Benny Carter's orchestra. This had a stellar personnel which included Coleman Hawkins, Chu Berry, Red Allen, Dickie Wells and Sid Catlett. Largo have grouped together the seven pieces (including *Harlem Symphony, Six Bells Stampede* and *Elegy*) used in the ballet *High Yellow*, first staged in June 1932. This was certainly the very first conjunction of ballet and jazz but the titles made in New York are likely to have the strongest appeal, especially tracks such as *Donegal Cradle Song* and *Arabesque,* with their magnificent contributions from Hawkins. All tracks have been carefully remastered and restored by John R.T. Davies. **AM**

Daniel Humair

1938

Edges **Humair** (d); **Jerry Bergonzi** (ss, ts); **Aydin Esen** (p); **Miroslav Vitous** (b). Label Bleu Ⓕ LBLC 6545 (50 minutes). Recorded 1991.

⑧ ❽

Geneva native Humair, one of the great jazz drummers on any continent, usually displays his skills as an accompanist, or in such collective groups as the Kuhn/Jenny-Clark/Humair trio or Quatre. This disc gives him a rare opportunity to function as a leader; rather than monopolizing the situation, he has done an inspired job of blending performers and material. The talented international quartet plays music from a variety of jazz composers (including Joachim Kühn, Franco d'Andrea, Michel Portal and George Gruntz) and interprets each piece, rather than merely using them as excuses for casual blowing. What results is an uncommonly balanced programme where we appreciate Humair's empathy for each soloist. The empathy is real: he and Bergonzi have grown to know each other, and pianist Esen is also moved to more interesting playing than on his own Columbia album. Vitous, who works with Humair in Quatre, lets his bold ideas pivot through the structures naturally over the drummer's flowing time. Humair, one of the most beautiful drummers to watch when he plays, conveys the dance-like grace of his conception, even in the heat of a performance like *Monitor*. **BB**

Helen Humes

1913-1981

Songs I Like To Sing! **Humes** (v); **Al Porcino**, **Ray Triscari**, **Stu Williamson**, **Jack Sheldon** (t); **Harry Betts**, **Bob Fitzpatrick** (tb); **Art Pepper** (cl, as); **Ben Webster**, **Teddy Edwards** (ts); **Bill Hood** (bs); **André Previn** (p); **Barney Kessel** (g); **Leroy Vinnegar** (b); **Shelly Manne** (d). Contemporary Ⓜ OJCCD-171-2 (42 minutes). Recorded 1960.

⑦ 

Humes emerged from near-retirement in 1959 to make appearances and recordings that were greeted with fervent enthusiasm even by sober critics. The sweetness, accuracy and musicality of her voice had not declined since her time with Count Basie's orchestra in the thirties, nor been coarsened by the raucous blues that maintained her career after World War II—a period excellently documented on **Be-Baba-Leba** (Whiskey, Women and... RBD 701).

For this album, arranger Marty Paich booked a 14-piece band of leading West Coast players; Sheldon, Pepper and Webster take most of the solos. Humes dresses a classy selection of standards, such as *Don't Worry 'Bout Me*, *You're Driving Me Crazy* and *Love Me or Leave Me*, without fuss or frippery, allowing the lyrics to tell their tales and adding a judicious minimum of decoration. *My Old Flame* and three others are arranged for jazz quintet (with Webster as tenor soloist) and string quartet. Humes's first recordings were racy blues, and her best-known number *Million Dollar Secret* (reprised here) another, yet she resisted being typecast in that idiom, maintaining that her favourite songs were ballads. She promoted that side of her repertoire on several subsequent recordings, all of them good, but none as spontaneously happy as **Songs I Like To Sing!**

TR

Alberta Hunter

1895-1984

Young Alberta Hunter: The 1920s and 1930s **Alberta Hunter** (v); **Charlie Shavers** (t); **Louis Armstrong**, **Elmer Chambers** (c); **George Brashear** (tb); **Buster Bailey**, **Don Redman**, **Ernest Elliott** (cl); **Sidney Bechet** (cl, ss); **Lil Armstrong**, **Fletcher Henderson**, **Eddie Heywood**, **Eubie Blake** (p); **Fats Waller** (org); **Buddy Christian**, **Charlie Dixon**, **Wellman Braud** (b). Jass Ⓕ J-CD 6 (67 minutes). Recorded 1921-40.

⑥ ❹

Clarity of diction, forceful delivery, a voice that is sweet and hard by turns, and the ability to bring a narrative song to life made Alberta Hunter one of the very best of the classic blues singers. She wrote *Downhearted Blues*, which she performs here, though less forcefully than most of the other pieces on the disc. Alberta was in Europe for the late twenties and early thirties, and this collection draws together the best of her American work from either side of that visit. The later sides, from 1939 and 1940, are a pointer to her mature style. Chief among them are four solos with pianist Eddie.Heywood, which range from the mournful *The Love I Have for You* to the gutsy *My Castle's Rockin'*. At her best, she acts out a vocal character, and her reading of *Fine and Mellow* is the opposite to Billie Holiday's tragic lament,yet avoids sacrificing the song's intensity. Only the transfers let this collection down, as they are muddier than the few of these tracks that have surfaced in other anthologies.

AS

Charlie Hunter

Bing, Bing, Bing! **Hunter** (8-string g); **Dave Ellis** (ts); **Jay Lane** (d); with guests **Jeff Cressman** (tb); **Ben Goldberg** (cl); **David Phillips** (pedal steel g); **Scott Roberts** (perc). Blue Note Ⓕ CDP 8 31809 2 (56 minutes). Recorded 1995.

⑤ ❽

Guitarist Hunter came to jazz through rock, rap and funk, discovering it on his own through the records of Charlie Christian and Charlie Parker. His own career path took him into the industrial rap band the Beatnigs and then on to the Disposable Heroes of Hiphoprisy, who reached a zenith by supporting U2 on tour. A move into jazz gave him more musical rewards, and the Charlie Hunter Trio is now his main pursuit.

The album betrays the eclecticism which is at the root of Hunter's approach to music, and much of it has exact parallels in the music of a parade of musicians such as Eddie Harris, John Scofield, Ry Cooder, John Coltrane, Jimi Hendrix and George Benson, just to touch on a few. The trio play together as a fully integrated team, the music is clear and precise, and drummer Jay Lane is particularly impressive. Hunter certainly offers us one solution to the problem of where to take contemporary jazz next, but he's not the first person to have thought of it.

KS

Bobby Hutcherson

1941

Components **Hutcherson** (vb); **Freddie Hubbard** (t); **James Spaulding** (as, f); **Herbie Hancock** (p); **Ron Carter** (b); **Joe Chambers** (d). Blue Note Ⓜ CDP8 29027-2 (41 minutes). Recorded 1965.

⑧ ❽

Vibraphonist Bobby Hutcherson is a player deserving far greater recognition. Originally inspired by Milt Jackson, Hutcherson, while borrowing from Jackson's inmitable blues-cum-bop bag, has developed a remarkably broad and pliant style. The Los Angeles native received his initial baptisms with Curtis Amy, Charles Lloyd, Al Grey and Billy Mitchell. It was his 1961 move to New York and a batch of outstanding Blue Note dates with protean players such as Jackie McLean, Grachan Moncur III, Grant Green, Andrew Hill and Eric Dolphy that put him on the map. Here, in his second date for Blue Note as a leader, Hutcherson's compelling breadth is revealed in tandem with some of Blue Note's then youngest and hottest new stars.

The first four tracks, Hutcherson originals, speak with an edgy, no-nonsense neo-bop voice reminiscent of Blakey's Jazz Messengers. On the title tune, ensembles snap like a whip, unleashing inspired solo flights. A contrast is *Tranquillity*, a shimmering soundscape whose introduction features a surprisingly ethereal Hutcherson. *Little B's Poem* is a charmingly lithe waltz with Spaulding's breezy fluting, while *West 22nd Street Theme* is a slow stroll featuring Hutcherson's and Hubbard's bluesy bopisms. Most surprising are the remaining four tunes by Joe Chambers, galvanizing amalgams of bop and free jazz that alternately groove, float, flutter and fly to the heavens. In all, it is a diverse and alluring set spotlighting the multi-dimensional Hutcherson and a group of peers whose alert simpatico and derring-do still raise goose bumps. **CB**

Solo/Quartet **Hutcherson** (vb, mbas); **McCoy Tyner** (p); **Herbie Lewis** (b); **Billy Higgins** (d). Contemporary Ⓜ OJCCD 425-2 (45 minutes). Recorded 1981-82.

⑧ ❽

Hutcherson made his reputation with a long sequence of brilliant albums for the Blue Note label, starting in the early sixties and coming to an end with the demise of the original Blue Note jazz programme in the mid-seventies. Of those 15 or so vinyl releases, just two—**Components** and **San Francisco**—are currently available (the other Blue Note now available is **Oblique**, a mid-sixties session which went unissued at the time, and is certainly not essential Hutcherson). The L.A.-based vibes player has since continued his recording career with Contemporary, Landmark and Timeless.

This early-eighties session contains most of the best things about Hutcherson's playing. On what was originally the first side of an LP, but now is just the first three tracks of a CD, Hutcherson plays solo, with a deal of double-tracking utilized as well. His musical thinking has always been much broader than that of someone who just waits for his turn to solo, and he uses this natural arranger's sensibility to brilliant effect on the pieces where the vibes, glockenspiels and marimbas are built up track by track into cohesive and swinging wholes. The remarkable thing about these tracks is that they remain utterly transparent in texture and completely devoid of clutter. The quartet sides are more conventional in concept, and Hutcherson's roots in the Milt Jackson vocabulary more clearly evident, but his originality of approach is just as certain, as is the intensity of vision he brings to everything he does. Hutcherson's is a major voice in the music and this album is a significant achievement in his career. **KS**

Cruisin' The Bird **Bobby Hutcherson** (vb); **Ralph Moore** (ts, ss); **Buddy Montgomery** (p); **Rufus Reid** (b); **Victor Lewis** (d). Landmark Ⓕ LCD 1517-2 (53 minutes). Recorded 1988.

✔ ⑧ ❽

This is just the record to play to anyone who is fond of announcing the imminent death of jazz. Everything about it is distinguished; the bass and the drums function together with the ease and familiarity of a long-standing relationship, the piano lays down clear but unobvious harmonies, and both front-line soloists play with relaxed brilliance. You might expect a band of veterans like Hutcherson to perform at this level, in this timeless style which is beyond fashion, but Ralph Moore was born in 1956, the year Rollins made **Saxophone Colossus**. Hence the reason to be cheerful about the future.

In form, this is a simple quintet blowing session, recorded over two days, made up of originals and standards and very lightly arranged. The result is sparkling music. Hutcherson's whole career is dotted with such works and they have rarely received the praise they deserve. **Cruisin' The Bird** is one of the great jazz records of the eighties **DG**

Dick Hyman

1927

Music From My Fair Lady **Hyman** (p); **Ruby Braff** (c). Concord Jazz Ⓕ CCD 4393 (53 minutes). Recorded 1989.

✔ 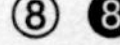

Hyman is a repository of early jazz and jazz-related piano styles, which made him the perfect composer to work on Woody Allen's period comedy *The Purple Rose of Cairo*, one of several films he has scored. Stylistic diversity is Hyman's strength; in the fifties he worked with swing veteran Red Norvo, modernist Tony Scott, and Dixieland revivalists. In the sixties, he was one of the first to record on synthesizer.

His partnership with cornettist Braff, dating from 1974, brings out Hyman's best. In person, he is quiet and composed, Braff an outspoken cut up. Before the microphones, they switch personalities: Braff plays with warm elegance (a weakness for witty quotes notwithstanding); Hyman prods him using any workable strategy.

This is the most satisfying of their duo albums, not least because Lerner and Loewe's 1956 show may have been the last Broadway musical with more than two songs worth whistling. Hyman can break into Waller-style stride (a fast *With a Little Bit of Luck*), careen like Earl Hines (*I'm an Ordinary Man*), walk 4/4 bass lines (*Wouldn't It Be Loverly*), or echo Darius Milhaud's chromatic Brazilian pieces of the twenties (*Rain in Spain*). But there is nothing musty about their playing fifties music, twenties style, in the eighties: it breathes fresh air. **KW**

Abdullah Ibrahim

1934

Echoes From Africa **Ibrahim** (p, v); **Johnny Dyani** (b, v). Enja Ⓔ 3047 2 (32 minutes). Recorded 1979.

⑧ ❽

Although best known as a solo pianist and group leader, Ibrahim also has a number of duo albums to his credit. These include sets with Gato Barbieri, Johnny Dyani, Max Roach, Archie Shepp and Carlos Ward. **Echoes From Africa** is the second of his two records with Dyani, a fellow South African totally conversant with Ibrahim's musical roots and whose bass has an elemental power to match the leader's driving piano.

Namhanje, a traditional folk song, shows how well they work together, the piano's rich rolling drama underpinned by a strong bass pulse as their voices sing out in exhortation. *Lakutshonilanga*, by Mackay Davashe, shares the plaintive beauty of Ibrahim tunes such as *The Wedding*, although here the pianist embroiders the melody line with tiny percussive dissonances that point to his love for Thelonious Monk's music. Ibrahim's own *Zikr* is devotional music, a genre he has been exploring since his conversion to Islam in 1968: over growling arco bass, the men's hushed voices rise up in undulating lines of prayer.

The CD's drawback is a playing time of only 32 minutes. Enja should consider coupling **Echoes Of Africa** with Ibrahim's and Dyani's 1973 **Good News From Africa**, as both LPs could be accommodated on a single disc.

GL

Ekaya **Ibrahim** (p, ldr); **Dick Griffin** (tb); **Carlos Ward** (f, as); **Ricky Ford** (ts); **Charles Davis** (bs); **Cecil McBee** (b); **Ben Riley** (d). Blackhawk Ⓔ BKH 50205 CD (38 minutes). Recorded 1983.

⑧ ❼

Capetown-born Adolph Johannes Brand converted to Islam in 1968 and became Abdullah Ibrahim, but by that time he had already become known internationally as Dollar Brand. No matter, it is the music which is important and this CD, released originally on the Ekapa label, features the group which calls itself Ekaya which means "home" in several South African languages. There is a very strong thread of African music in the six titles and the work of the American jazzmen is exactly in context. In fact Carlos Ward sounds for all the world like a native-born South African (he was, in fact, born in the Panama Canal Zone); it is Ward who is one of the strongest featured voices here, playing with the verve and dancing quality found in the work of the late Kippie Moeketsi, a remarkable South African alto saxist. Ibrahim has surrounded himself with men who are very sympathetic to his work (five of the six tunes and all of the arrangements are by the pianist); and the rhythm work of Ben Riley is so imaginative that one realises he was never given sufficient scope when working with groups such as the Thelonious Monk Quartet or the Lockjaw Davis-Johnny Griffin band. Inevitably Ibrahim is not featured at length with the group, but his personality manifests itself throughout this fascinating programme of genuine Afro-American music.

AM

African River **Ibrahim** (p); **Robin Eubanks** (tb); **John Stubblefield** (f, ts); **Horace Alexander Young** (ss, as, picc); **Howard Johnson** (bb, tba, bs); **Buster Williams** (b); **Brian Adams** (d). Enja Ⓔ CD 6018 2 (46 minutes). Recorded 1989.

⑧ ❽

In retrospect, Ibrahim's somewhat prodigious output must be rated as inconsistent; outstanding solo albums such as **African Piano** (Japo CD 600002) and **Ode To Ellington** (West Wind 2020 CD) must be weighed against poor items where the pianist's insistent chordal emphasis has led him into somewhat static areas. His work with the American free-players in the late sixties occasionally lacked direction and his more recent partnership with Carlos Ward often foundered through no fault of his own. Fortunately, more is now being heard of his arranging skill in medium-sized groups and this CD is a superb example. Despite the American emphasis in the personnel, the arrangements consistently capture the South African 'high life' spirit. The piano plays a prominent part and there is a textural depth that speaks of the leader's wide musical experience, as well as his awareness of the need to surprise in jazz writing. There is something of the Ellington tone poem about *Joan—Capetown Flower* and evidence of Ducal voicings on other titles. Ibrahim's own hypnotic fervour remains an important ingredient in titles such as *Toi-Toi* and *Chisa* but, with quality solos in particular from Williams on *African River*, Eubanks on *Joan* and *Duke 88*, Young on *Duke 88* and Stubblefield and Johnson literally throughout, this is a perfectly balanced mixture of the prepared and the extemporized.

BMcR

No Fear, No Die (s'en fout la mort) **Ibrahim** (p); **Frank Lacy** (tb); **Horace Alexander Young III** (f, ss, as); **Ricky Ford** (ts); **Jimmy Cozier** (bs, cl); **Buster Williams** (b); **Ben Riley** (d). Enja/Tip Toe Ⓔ 88815-2 (45 minutes) Recorded 1990.

⑧ ❿

On this, the soundtrack album to Claire Denis's eponymous film, Ibrahim combines his twin fascinations for Ellington and African music into a compelling, lazy, sensuous tapestry of sound. The opening track, *Calypso Minor*, sets a brooding, spare mood similar to that often caught in later years by Ellington when he was casting a spell of mystery and vauge unease. Ford does a manful impersonation of Gonsalves, Lacy of Britt Woodman. This theme, with its dominant ostinato bass pattern, gets a reprise at the end, this time in brighter colours and re-titled *Calypso Major*. The music is pellucid, every note has its proper place, and Ibrahim gives us the core of its meaning.

The Ellington connection gets even stronger on the second track, *Angelica*, one of Duke's tunes which first saw the light of day on his 1963 small-group date with Coltrane. This is a jolly treatment of a colourful theme, and it stresses the Latin and West Indean rhythmic angle inherent in the melody.

On this disc Ibrahim manages to convey the best of both his dominant musical worlds, avoiding the siren calls of both - imitation of a master or the repetition of static patterns past the point of interest and into tedium. His writing for his group is consistently resourceful, bringing especially bright colours to the unison themes, while his own piano playing is concise, taut and heavy with meaning. The horns all deliver their section work convincingly. Of the soloists, only Ford really pulls his weight, but this is a small drawwback to a generally very positive and enjoyable programme of music. **KS**

ICP Orchestra

Performs Nichols And Monk **Misha Mengelberg** (p, arr); **Ab Baars** (ss, as); **Michael Moore** (as, cl); **Wolter Wierbos** (tb); **Maurice Horsthuis** (va); **Ernst Reijseger** (vc); **Han Bennink** (d); **George Lewis** (tb) on Monk programme only; **Toon de Gouw** (t); **Garrett List** (tb); **Larry Fishkind** (tba); **Sean Bergin** (as); **Paul Thermos** (as); **Steve Lacy** (ss) on Nichols programme only. ICP Ⓕ 026 (72 minutes). Recorded 1984/86.

⑩ ❽

The ICP Orchestra was originally formed in the seventies as a Dutch version of Globe Unity, although under the guidance of the remarkable Misha Mengelberg it grew into a more versatile and still volatile ensemble. These two stimulating sessions expand upon the small group arrangements of tunes by Thelonious Monk and Herbie Nichols recorded under Roswell Rudd's leadership in 1982. As a pianist Mengelberg is fully capable of mirroring Monk's inimitable timing and acidic harmonies, but as an arranger his own brilliant vision intrudes—or example, in the unrelated atonal episode which interrupts the swinging performance of *Four In One* or the non-tempered, atmospheric introduction to *Misterioso*—preventing these versions from remaining merely rote recreations. Mengelberg himself perfectly characterizes the musicians' contributions as "uninhibited," and their tart, often thematically tangential solos slip in and out of context in these always unpredictable arrangements. Mengelberg may extend vamps, eliminate chord changes, adopt even more outrageous harmonies than in the original, and add extreme splashes of colour by use of instruments like cello, tuba and soprano sax, but he is ever-faithful to the *spirit* of Monk's unique style and wit. His radical redesign of Nichols's pieces do no harm to their inherent lyricism, and the presence of Steve Lacy acts as an additional grounding force. But there is nevertheless a constant tension, a pulling apart and reformation, that energizes the arrangements and identifies Mengelberg's brilliance and individuality. Like John Zorn at his best, Mengelberg is able to recontextualize the originality of the music in a time when our ears have grown accustomed to dissonance and rhythmic quirks—an essential antidote to musty neo-conservative revivalist attitudes. **AL**

Irakere

Live At Ronnie Scott's **Jesus 'Chuchu' Valdes** (p, ldr); **Juan Monguia**, **Adalberto Moreno** (t); **Orlando Valle**, **Caesar Lopez**, **Carlos Averhoff** (reeds); **Carlos E. Morales** (g); **Carlos del Puerto** (b); **Oscar Valdes** (v, perc); **Enrique Pla, Miguel 'Anga' Diaz** (perc). World Pacific Ⓕ CDP7 80598-2 (61 minutes). Recorded 1991.

⑦ ❼

Here, the exuberant 11-strong Irakere is caught live in a tumultuous 1991 date recorded at Ronnie Scott's Club, London's fabled jazz mecca. Led by Jesus 'Chuchu' Valdes, the juggernaut's peppery pianist and chief composer, Irakere is an open-ended yet disciplined ensemble with lots of wide open spaces for soloists to range and roam freely.

Since its establishment in Havana in 1973, Irakere has been an incubator for fine soloists such as Paquito D'Rivera and trumpeter Arturo Sandoval, who both defected in the early eighties for solo careers in the US. That tradition continues, especially in the inspired work of saxophonists Carlos

Averhoff and Caesar Lopez, and flautist Orlando Valle. In a programme of Valdes originals, the band smokes with Caribbean fire. Even on the ballad *When My Heart Sings* there is a larger-than-life, heart-on-sleeve lyricism that sets everything in motion. On *Looking Up*, the band struts with an infectious street-wise swagger keyed to Lopez's surging alto à la Gil Evans-vintage David Sanborn.

Valdes, who attacks the keyboard with a brio similar to that of Monty Alexander and Michel Camillio, is a constant source of soloistic heat, especially in the tempestuous *Neurosis* in which he includes a number of Maynard-isms in an oblique but no less sincere tip-of-the-hat to fellow bandleader Maynard Ferguson. **CB**

Mark Isaacs

For Sure **Isaacs** (p); **Adam Armstrong** (b); **Andrew Gander** (d). ABC Jazz Ⓕ 518 397-2 (47 minutes). Recorded 1993.

⑦ ❽

Isaacs, an Australian pianist who has travelled extensively and sufficiently impressed his peers to have fronted a previous trio album in New York with Dave Holland and Roy Haynes, here puts together a disc which is simultaneously very gentle on the ear yet curiously disturbing. The reasons for this are not hard to locate: his chord voicings, for example, on the title-track, are unusually open, his improvisation deliberately lazy, rendering a dreamlike quality to a track which in fact has a surging latin rhythm. His touch, as revealed on Pat Metheny's song *Never Too Far Away*, owes something to Bill Evans, but his note placement—slightly after the beat, and sometimes even dragged very slowly across the beat—is his own. Certainly Evans rarely deviated from a relatively staid rhythmic conception.

The trio here is admirably meshed, with Armstrong's well-recorded bass having a resonance and appositeness usually reserved for only the very best bassists. Gander does nothing wrong and adds much fire to the trio on the right occasions. Isaacs's technical limitations are plain to hear on his version of Coltrane's *Giant Steps*, where his fingers simply cannot keep pace with the scorching tempo set by Gander, but he more than makes up for that by producing a haunting eight-minute-long piano trio version of Gil Evans's *Las Vegas Tango* (strange that no-one else thought of doing it).

This man has a quietly original piano voice, and that puts him ahead of 90 per cent of current jazz pianists. Give him a listen if only for that reason. **KS**

Itchy Fingers

Full English Breakfast **Matt Wates** (as); **Pete Long** (as, cl); **Andy Panayi** (ss, as, ts); **Dave O'Higgins** (ts); **Mike Mower** (ts, bs, cl, f). Enja Ⓕ ENJ-7085 2 (51 minutes). Recorded 1992.

⑧ ❽

In contrast to their previous (third) album, **Live in Europe**, **Full English Breakfast** presents the UK's leading saxophone quartet with the opportunity to exploit a range of studio techniques, most importantly overdubbing, to produce their most intricate and polished work to date. Time signatures can be anything from 7/8 through 15/16 to 4/4 (and that is just one piece, *The Dome*), and the intricacy of leader/composer Mike Mower's arrangements occasionally militates against his band achieving the exuberant informality characterizing the work of say, Bobby Watson's 29th Street Saxophone Quartet, but this album generally hits a workable balance between composition and improvisation. Thus, alongside the elaborate formality of *Svea Rike*, a Mower composition commissioned by a Swedish classical saxophone quartet and containing a bare minimum of improvisation, Itchy Fingers are versatile enough to present *This Time's Hard*, a 5/8 piece held together by a drum machine and climaxing in an absorbing tenor duel between Andy Panayi and the uniformly excellent Dave O'Higgins. They then follow that with *The Crillon Controller*, featuring a bluesy, airy alto solo from Matt Wates. Overall, the album is at its most enjoyable on tracks like these last two—and, in particular, a highly intelligent version of *Night In Tunisia*, when the band lets its hair down a bit; the prevalence of tricksy arrangements elsewhere tends to over-egg the pudding somewhat, but then full English breakfasts are traditionally hard to digest, if ultimately extremely nourishing. **CP**

Cliff Jackson

1902–1970

Carolina Shout **Jackson** (p). Black Lion Ⓜ BLCD 760194 (49 minutes). Recorded 1961-62.

⑥ ❼

Although born in Culpeper, Virginia, pianist Cliff Jackson's life was always inextricably bound up with New York City. In the twenties and thirties he was involved with the Apollo Theatre and the Lenox Club, while after the Second World War he was house pianist at Nick's, Ryan's and the RX Room. These locations were wholly appropriate because Jackson was one of the genuine members of the New York 'walking' left hand or 'stride' piano school.

As this CD shows, the needs of the Apollo 'pit' and accompaniment of club conversation did mean that the pure style was occasionally modified. The creative intrigue of James P. Johnson and the rhythmic subtleties of Fats Waller are side-stepped and the flagrantly propulsive energy of the swing era creeps in. A suitable mixture of the reverential and the mischievous attends the mentor's material in *Carolina Shout* and *Honeysuckle Rose*. Stride vibes are secreted into the soft underbelly of *I'm Coming, Virginia* and *Someday Sweetheart* and the swing era is avenged as *Who's Sorry Now* and *You Took Advantage Of Me* assume stride proportions. Jackson was never as technically secure as his mentors Johnson and Waller or, indeed, Ralph Sutton, Dick Wellstood or Butch Thompson. He was an honest artisan and the only possible gait open to him was 'striding'. **BMcR**

D.D. Jackson

1967

Peace-Song **Jackson** (p); **David Murray** (ts); **John Geggie** (b); **Jean Martin** (d). Justin Time Ⓕ JUST 72-2 (66 minutes) Recorded 1994.

⑦ ❽

Canadian pianist Jackson has come to attention through his work with bands such as Billy Bang's and Kip Hanrahan's, has worked with Jane Bunnett and Dewey Redman, and has put in time around the New York scene, including the Knitting Factory. He has also been a stable part of David Murray's quartet and octet, so it is logical that the tenorist should be present for Jackson's first record as a leader. With a player of such commanding power, Jackson has to work hard to impose his own concepts, but he is a musician with sufficient energy and robustness of purpose that Murray is channelled in the direction the leader wants. That direction makes use of a stylistic foundation which touches base with Monk, Jarrett, Byard and especially Don Pullen, who incidentally had been one of his tutors. No wonder the group swings.

The music on this record could be described as straight-ahead, high-spirited modern jazz which is not obsessively looking over its shoulder in search of tradition and pedigree. It is just happy to be here. I am happy it is here, too. **KS**

Ed Jackson

1959

Wake Up Call **Jackson** (as, arr); **James Zoller** (t, f); **Tom Varner** (frh); **Clark Gayton** (tb); **Rich Rothenberg** (ts); **John Stetch** (p); **Dave Jackson** (b); **Steve Johns** (d); **Jamie Baum** (f). New World CounterCurrents Ⓕ 80451-2 (70 minutes). Recorded 1994.

✔ ⑧ ❽

New York saxophonist/composer Jackson has been making appearances on recordings since the beginning of the eighties, enjoying stints with Jaki Byard's Apollo Street Stompers and Roy Haynes's quintet before making international waves with the 29th Street Saxophone Quartet. This is his début as a leader, and it has a great deal more going for it than the vast majority of débuts. His musical language is fully formed as both a composer and an improviser. He understands the sonorities of the instruments he combines here in superb arrangements, mostly with his own originals but also, with notable imagination, to Monk's *Played Twice* (John Stetch contributes the arrangement for the Richard Rodgers standard, *Have You Met Miss Jones?*).

In some respects Jackson conjures memories of Charles Mingus's Jazz Workshop alchemy in the way he combines his own material with re-thought standards he has particular affection for. He is interested in extended form as well as an individual balance between scored and improvised sections. There is also a healthy amount of interchange and dialogue between all the musicians involved: this is not an exercise in the horns queueing up for their solo spots either side of a theme statement. Much more happens than that, and the unwinding of each tale told is a consistent stimulation to the listener. This is not 'difficult' music at all, but it rewards close attention and repeated hearings. **KS**

Javon Jackson

For One Who Knows **Jackson** (ts); **Jacky Terrasson** (p); **Fareed Haque** (g); **Peter Washington** (b); **Billy Drummond** (d); **Cyro Baptiste** (perc). Blue Note Ⓕ CDP 8 30244 2 (50 minutes). Recorded 1995.

⑧ ❿

Jackson is a young tenor player who has made a quick but deep impression: his work with Elvin Jones in particular had marked him out as one to watch. This leadership debut is imbued with tremendous authority and confidence. The combination of Jackson's direct, no-nonsense tone and aggressive rhythmic phrasing with Terrasson's explosion of pianistic ideas, both as accompanist and soloist, is electrifying, and the opening track, *For One Who Knows (For Freddie Hubbard)*, rudely pushes the listener into the type of forward-looking, exciting modern music Blue Note used to expect in the mid-sixties from such artists as Wayne Shorter, Andrew Hill and Hubbard himself.

Jackson has picked a finely-integrated band which can empathise with every mood he dips into. His version of *Etcetera* has that indefinable sense of ease that Joe Henderson can bring to latin-tinged mid-tempo ballads, and this ambience is only possible with a band which works closely in support of its leader. Jackson has sufficient confidence in its abilities to just state the melody and then let bass player Washington take a leisurely but concise solo. Jackson's own jauntiness often touches on the type of spirit also found in mid-fifties Rollins, making it entirely apt that he attempts a cover version of an overlooked Rollins piece from his classic **Worktime** album, *Paradox*. This he does with just bass and drums (Drummond sounding particularly Elvin Jones-ish), thereby extending the parallel deep into **Village Vanguard** territory.

This debut is not just impressive. Jackson is already a long way past the issue of technique and deep into the important one: meaning. **KS**

Milt Jackson

1923

Plenty, Plenty Soul **Jackson** (vb); **Joe Newman** (t); **Jimmy Cleveland** (tb); **Cannonball Adderley** (as); **Frank Foster**, **Lucky Thompson** (ts); **Sahib Shihab** (bs); **Horace Silver** (p); **Percy Heath**, **Oscar Pettiford** (b); **Art Blakey**, **Connie Kay** (d); **Quincy Jones** (arr). Atlantic Jazz Ⓜ 781269-2 (42 minutes). Recorded 1957.

⑧ ❽

The star of the Modern Jazz Quartet, and before that a sideman with Dizzy Gillespie and Woody Herman, Jackson is still the vibraphonist most able to sound like a wind instrument, rather than a novelty effect whose main appeal is visual. The two sessions here feature all-star sextet and nonet line-ups within which Jackson's status as a 'horn-player' is triumphantly confirmed, especially in the larger group where Blakey's 'big band' drumming is a challenge and a complement to all concerned. The brief but pithy comments of Adderley and Basie sidemen Newman and Foster are excellent. In particular, Thompson's solos on the sextet sides exemplify his peak period, which includes other sessions with Jackson for Atlantic and Savoy.

Jones's arrangements are crucial to the mellow sound of both sets, including the only up-tempo number *Boogity Boogity*, which has the same melody as his more famous ballad *The Midnight Sun Never Sets*. Nat Hentoff's updated notes are definitive, on both Jackson and the then-new term 'soul', though the booklet fails to include Silver in the sextet line-up. Happily, the overdubbing which enables Milt to duet with himself briefly on *Blues At Twilight*, lost in at least one earlier reissue, is duly restored. **BP**

Bags & Trane **Milt Jackson** (vb); **John Coltrane** (ts); **Hank Jones** (p); **Paul Chambers** (b); **Connie Kay** (d). Atlantic Jazz Ⓜ 781368-2 (57 minutes). Recorded 1959.

⑧ ❽

The vibraphone does not need a better interpreter than Milt Jackson. His robust and direct manner with the instrument is much more astute than the fey approach evinced by Gary Burton and more incisive than that of the voluble Lionel Hampton. Atlantic provided a myriad of settings for Jackson when he was under contract to them at the beginning of the sixties—this one in late 1959 came a couple of months after a similar pairing of Jackson with Coleman Hawkins. The resultant music is often stark and economical, more like hessian than silk. On the other hand benign warmth flows through the jumping *Three Little Words* and Coltrane is at his softest on *The Night We Called It A Day*. He moves happily in Jackson's blues-drenched homeground and plays more open and less self-conscious tenor than was often the case, producing a virtuous set of mainstream tear-ups which is probably the nearest Coltrane ever came to a frolic. It would have been difficult to improve on the rhythm trio. Three tracks, Jackson's *Blues Legacy*, the standard *Stairway to the Stars* and a stalwart version of Harry Edison's *Centrepiece*, which previously appeared elsewhere on vinyl, have been added to the original album. **SV**

The Prophet Speaks **Jackson** (vb); **Joshua Redman** (ts); **Cedar Walton** (p); **John Clayton** (b); **Billy Higgins** (d). On three tracks **Joe Williams** (v). QWest/Reprise Ⓕ 245591-2 (74 minutes). Recorded 1994.

⑧ ❿

Jackson is now comfortably into his seventies, but there is no lessening of his creative fire: the flow of improvisatory ideas is as strong as ever. This may not be the greatest record he has been involved in, but it is a very good one and equal to any he has made under his own name for many years. This is in part due to the superb empathy to be found within the rhythm section, Walton and Higgins moving as one with Jackson at every turn in the music. As for the vibist himself, he always plays to his strengths, with the blues and balladry being two which get ample coverage here. Jackson has an uncanny ability to make his instrument sing a melody, his gradations of touch and his minute rhythmic shifts giving great expressivity to the simplest line. Examples of such moments abound throughout the programme.

Jackson often has guest saxophonists on his dates, and this time it is Joshua Redman, who makes his presence felt in an entirely appropriate way on six of the 12 tracks, two of which also have the veteran singer Joe Williams vocalizing with unusual restraint and directness. Redman makes full use of his versatility, concentrating on the blues-based part of his style and using a full, sensuous tone to good expressive effect. In this he fulfils the function once taken up by, say, Jimmy Heath on some of Jackson's sixties albums (one of which has been included as a filler on last year's Impulse! reissue, **Statements**). Its also nice to see Jackson continuing his long-standing affair with Monk's music, both *Off-Minor* and *Blue Monk* getting the treatment here. **KS**

Oliver Jackson

1933-1994

Billie's Bounce **Jackson** (d); **Irvin Stokes** (t); **Norris Turney** (as); **Claude Blake** (p); **Ali Jackson** (b). Black & Blue Ⓕ 59 183 2 (70 minutes). Recorded 1984.

⑤ ❽

A stalwart of the Detroit modern scene of the forties, Jackson formed a duo with Eddie Locke in 1948 and for five years worked as a variety act called Bop and Locke. He moved to New York in 1956 and, after playing at the Metropole for a time, found himself being called repeatedly for mainstream gigs. He played with leaders such as Buck Clayton, Benny Goodman and Earl Hines, and in 1969 formed the JPJ Quartet. In more recent years he had been a member of George Wein's Festival All Stars.

This CD gives a good impression of his driving and always swinging style. There remains an edge to his playing that reminds the listener of his bop beginnings, but he is an ideal partner for the uncomplicated trumpet of Stokes and the gently flowing alto of Turney. Appropriately, the odd drum bombs are dropped on *Billie's Bounce* and *Yardbird Suite*, while the softly contoured aspects of *I Don't Know About You* are exploited in a more relaxed manner. Jackson's timing is very good, his ride cymbal always suitably pushy. This musicianly, if unspectacular, session shows him to have been an all-round professional. **BMcR**

Willis Jackson

1928-1987

Bar Wars **Jackson** (ts); **Charles Earland** (org); **Pat Martino** (g); **Idris Muhammad** (d); **Buddy Caldwell** (perc). Muse Ⓕ MCD 6011 (46 minutes). Recorded 1977.

✔ ⑩ ❿

Willis 'Gator' Jackson (he got his nickname from a hit 45 he had with the Cootie Williams band in 1948, *Gator Tail*) started his career as an out-and-out bar-walking honker. His early sides certainly lack nothing in excitement, but are rather short on invention (a goodly sample of his work at this time is available on **Call of the Gators**, Delmark CD DD460). Possibly realizing that this approach would limit his long-term career, he developed his playing much in the same way as did the daddy of all honkers, Illinois Jacquet. By the time this 1977 Muse album, Jackson had long achieved mastery of the idiom he worked in; the tenor-and-organ combo.

Bar Wars gets top rating simply because tenor-and-organ records do not come better than this. Jackson's full, warm tone is ideally captured by—who else?—Rudy van Gelder, he plays the ballads in way which suggests direct descent from the Herschel Evans-Gene Ammons school of sax playing (there is a beautiful version of *Blue and Sentimental* here), and on the medium-tempo swingers he is exciting without being repetitious and boorish. In all this he is superbly backed by Earland, who shadows his every phrase, and Pat Martino, who contributes some very tasty solos indeed. It was also an inspired day for Idris Muhammad at the drum kit. The CD contains two extra tracks, both alternative takes of numbers on the original vinyl release. **KS**

Illinois Jacquet

1922

Flying Home **Jacquet** (ts); **Russell Jacquet, Joe Newman** (t); **J.J. Johnson, Henry Coker** (tb); **Ray Perry** (as); **Leo Parker, Maurice Simon** (bs); **Sir Charles Thompson, John Lewis, Cedric Heywood** (p); **John Collins** (g); **Al Lucas** (b); **Shadow Wilson, Jo Jones** (d); **Lionel Hampton Orchestra**. RCA Bluebird Ⓑ ND90638 (36 minutes). Recorded 1947-67.

⑧ ❽

Like his contemporary 'Lockjaw' Davis, Jacquet was prominent on the juke-boxes of black bars in the forties. He was 19 when he made his famous solo contribution to Hampton's *Flying Home* in 1942, and he started leading his own bands a couple of years later. Further hits created by his solos with Basie and Jazz At The Philharmonic led to his signing by one of the few major labels, RCA Victor, when he was still only 25.

Ten singles by his eight-piece group from this period form the backbone of this budget-price reissue. Jacquet himself is featured almost to the exclusion of his colleagues, but his taut tone and sensuous swing travel well across the almost 50-year gap. Arrangements by Jimmy Mundy and J.J. Johnson for the five-man horn section—trombonist Henry Coker is missing from the sleeve details—make valiant attempts at rabble-rousing, and often succeed in sounding like a much larger group. But they are firmly put in their place by the inclusion of the closing track, the saxophonist's 1967 guest spot with Hampton's 18-piece band on an extended re-run of the title-number: this Newport Festival performance has the kind of organized delirium that made the reputation of both men in the first place. **BP**

Flying Home—Best Of The Verve Years **Illinois Jacquet** (ts); with the following collective personnel: **Russell Jacquet, Joe Newman, Elmon Wright, Lammar Wright, Harry Edison, Roy Eldridge** (t); **Henry Coker, Matthew Gee** (tb); **Ernie Henry, Earle Warren, Count Hastings, Cecil Payne, Ben Webster** (reeds); **Carl Perkins, Hank Jones, Johnny Acea, Sir Charles Thompson, Jimmy Jones** (p); **Count Basie, Hank Jones, Gerry Wiggins, Wild Bill Davis** (org); **Freddie Green, Oscar Moore, John Collins, Joe Sinacore, Irving Ashby, Herb Ellis, Kenny Burrell** (g); **Blakey,**

Shadow Wilson, Jimmy Crawford, Osie Johnson, Al Bartee, Jo Jones, Johnny Williams (d); **Chano Pozo** (perc). Verve Ⓜ 521 644-2 (80 minutes). Recorded 1951-58.

⑧ ❻

On the basis of some deliberately orchestrated crowd-rousing solos, principally with early editions of Norman Granz's JATP units, Jacquet has been unjustly dismissed in some critical circles as a musician of little consequence. In fact his playing contains all the elements of a significant soloist in the great tenor tradition, taking in the strength of Hawkins, the breathiness of Webster on ballads and the inventive melodic continuity of Lester Young. This excellent compilation from his Verve years, put together by Brian Priestley, plays for just a few seconds under one hour and 20 minutes and contains some of his best titles, including two by a studio-assembled big band (*Boot 'Em Up* and *Bluesitis*) and the lengthy *Kid And The Brute,* where he shares the tenor spotlight with Ben Webster. It also contains *Lean Baby* and *Port Of Rico*, made in 1952 with Count Basie (as a sideman) playing organ. These titles triggered off a host of sessions featuring tenor and organ. Three tracks come from a neglected album (never issued in Britain) pairing Jacquet with Roy Eldridge and the quality of the supporting musicians throughout is exemplary. A fine issue. **AM**

The Blues: That's Me! **Jacquet** (ts, bn); **Wynton Kelly** (p); **Tiny Grimes** (g); **Buster Williams** (b); **Oliver Jackson** (d). Prestige Ⓜ OJCCD 614-2 (41 minutes). Recorded 1969.

⑦ ❼

Jacquet, the inventor of tenor saxophone hysteria back in the early forties and a big star by the end of that decade, had become a reformed character by the time of his long series of records for Norman Granz in the fifties. On those, his Texas tenor tone and swagger was placed in the context of other jazz legacies, in particular those of his predecessors in the Basie band, Lester Young and Hershel Evans. Unfortunately, little of his vast Verve fifties output is on CD (see above).

This date is not entirely typical: his preferred company for much of the sixties and seventies was organist Milt Buckner, and he rarely uses musicians born of the sixties, but here we find ex-Miles pianist Kelly and young tyro Williams on bass. Yet it all gels the way it should, bound together by the common language of the blues. Kelly has the disadvantage of playing a poorly-tuned instrument, but still solos spiritedly: Jacquet seems impervious to any form of setback and plays with great conviction, both at the ultra-slow tempo of the long title-track and the racy clip of *Still King*. His bassoon playing on *'Round Midnight* is tuneful, dignified and astonishingly natural. Tiny Grimes lays out on this track, but pulls his weight elsewhere. **KS**

Jean-Marc Jafet

Agora **Jafet** (b); **Stephane Belmondo** (t); **Denis Leloup** (tb); **Eric Seva** (ss); **Jean-Yves Candela** (p, syn); **Marc Bethoumieux** (acc, syn); **Thierry Eliez** (syn); **Sylvain Luc** (g); **André Ceccarelli, Thierry Arpino, Francois Laizeau** (d); **François Constantin** (perc). JMS Ⓕ 18639-2 (57 minutes) Recorded 1993.

⑥ ❻

Jafet has been a presence on the French jazz and studio scene for many years. This album stands out partly for its melding of fusion and jazz techniques, partly for the fact that Jafet has composed all 12 pieces, with each title carrying a separate dedication. So, in a way, this is a form of testimony to his life, past and present. Although the above list gives the impression that there is a large cast, each track has different instrumental permutations, with some players only appearing once or twice on the whole album (Seva, Eliez and Arpino all manage one visit each).

The synthesizers are used discreetly to colour the music rather than dominate it, and in the main, acoustic instruments are left to do the soloing and theme statements, Luc's electric guitar being the sole exception. Jafet is consistent in keeping to the background, supplying flawless and lyrical bass lines to each composition. Of the soloists, Luc is perhaps the most fluent, his lines often soaring over rich polyrhythms. Excellent and sophisticated music drawing on many contemporary strands of music-making, but with a jazz heart. **KS**

Ahmad Jamal

1930

At The Pershing **Jamal** (p); **Israel Crosby** (b); **Vernell Fournier** (d). Chess Ⓜ MCAD 9108 (58 minutes). Recorded 1958.

⑦ ❼

A number of pianists, prominent among them Erroll Garner and Oscar Peterson, came to fame without any CV of years spent toiling behind famous hornmen before striking out on their own. Like them, Jamal soon received endorsement from hornmen—in his case, from Miles Davis, no less—and went on to become extremely influential, possibly more than even Garner or Peterson. This was because of his updating of Garner's block-chords to make them compatible with post-bop of all kinds, his dramatic use of space and his ability to ride on top of the rhythm section instead of driving it like his more swing-derived forebears.

That he appeared to be "taking it easy" (an accusation also sometimes levelled at Miles) is easily understood when listening to his classic trio with fellow Chicagoan Crosby, who débuted with

Fletcher Henderson in 1936. The simplified Latin rhythm of *Poinciana*, a revision of Jamal's 1955 version with guitarist Ray Crawford, is so hypnotic that the pianist's imaginative ideas can be displayed rather than developed. On some tracks the same approach combines with upper-register tinkling and over-obvious changes of dynamics to be positively annoying, but elsewhere the subtle chord voicings sustain interest, and they quite clearly interested a new generation of pianists sufficiently for them to adopt a similar approach. **BP**

The Awakening **Jamal** (p); **Jamil Nasser** (b); **Frank Gant** (d). Impulse! Ⓜ MCAD 5644 (41 minutes). Recorded 1970.

⑧ ❼

Jamal's most famous album is his live date at The Pershing, **But Not For Me** (see above), and that record certainly caught him at his first peak. There is plenty of recorded evidence to suggest that the pianist reached a second peak at the close of the sixties, when his style was freer and more adventurous, but his framework was basically unaltered. Virtually all of this work is not currently on CD (**Extensions**, on Argo/Chess, and **At The Top**, on Impulse! are two cases in point), but **The Awakening** fits comfortably into this grouping.

Jamal, a superb technician, is also master of the vamp (a single figure which is sustained or repeated for large sections of a piece), and uses many vamp variants to pace and organise familiar material in new and imaginative ways. On this disc Jamal uses vamps, pedal tones and pianistic pauses in his inimitable fashion, but he also plays a great deal more piano than in the past. A vehicle such as *I Love Music* is almost entirely a piano solo, couched in Tatum-like swirls of notes: just the middle section picks up the trio at a sedate tempo, which Jamal pulls about almost to breaking. Herbie Hancock's *Dolphin Dance* is made to sound as if it were written for Jamal, so natural is its treatment, while Oliver Nelson's *Stolen Moments* is given great respect and played with power and dignity. **KS**

Chicago Revisited—Live at Joe Segal's Jazz Showcase **Jamal** (p); **John Heard** (b); **Yoron Israel** (d). Telarc Jazz Ⓕ CD 83327 (60 minutes). Recorded 1992.

⑧ ❽

Thirty-four years after the residency at Chicago's Pershing lounge where Jamal's best-selling album, including a seven-minute *Ponciana*, was recorded, this is an attempt to re-create the chemistry by eavesdropping on another live Chicago session by Jamal's trio. In the intervening years, Jamal produced a steady stream of recordings, most of them above average, despite some less artistically successful forays into fusion. This album restates his importance as a jazz pianist of distinction. Jamal acknowledges Erroll Garner as an early influence, and refines Garner's sense of drama into a unique blend of pianistic flair and minimalism. On a straight-ahead bop track like Clifford Brown's *Daahoud*, Jamal invests his relentlessly swinging performance with continual dramatic touches, but underlying them is a sense of dynamics that builds on a potent use of quiet. When bass and drums still almost to silence, Jamal wills his listeners to concentrate, and he produces constantly inventive motifs to decorate the clear development of his dramatic ideas. His improvisation is not a headlong rush, but the imposition of such compositional devices as form, dynamics and thorough melodic restatement on an apparently spontaneous process. Eavesdropping, we hear his ideas develop, how he throws them to Heard and Israel to work on further, and how he pulls the whole thing together with the light touch of the experienced dramatist. Not so much Chicago revisited, but a statement of the far-from-wasted years of experience since the Pershing in 1958. **AS**

Bob James

1939

Explosions **James** (p, tapes, samples); **Barre Phillips** (b); **Robert Pozar** (d, perc). ESP-Disk Ⓜ 1009 (35 minutes). Recorded 1965.

⑩ ❼

Unless you knew otherwise, there is no way you would connect the man who made this album with the one who has in the past two decades added a new dimension to the concept of wallpaper music in jazz. James came to jazz in the early sixties as a thoroughly schooled musician, and his first album (**Bold Conceptions**, Mercury 1962) demonstrated the sort of imaginative re-thinking of bop formulas which a number of pianists (Jaki Byard, Roger Kellaway) were playing around with at that time. This, his next effort, is about as far removed from that as the Globe Unity Orchestra is from Fletcher Henderson. For four out of the five tracks there is not a single metric jazz beat kept by the trio (the one exception has the trio playing cocktail jazz as an ironic comment on the taped radio commercials being used at the same time). All but one track uses taped electronic effects and what was then called 'musique concrète', but is now probably best known as 'found art' or 'samples'—that is, sounds and noises taken from the natural world. If this all sounds very esoteric, it is; but James and his trio keep such an iron grip on the form and drama of each piece that the album is completely gripping from beginning to end.

A point of clarification: the CD release perpetuates a titling confusion from the original vinyl issue. Track one, *Explosions*, is mis-titled *Peasant Boy*; track three, *An On* (the only completely acoustic performance, and mis-spelt here as *And On*), is mis-titled *Explosions*; track four, *Peasant Boy*, is mis-titled *An On*. The other two tracks are actually what they say they are. **KS**

Jon Jang

Self Defense! **Jang** (p); **John Worley Jr** (t, flh, perc); **Jeff Cressman** (tb, perc); **Melecio Magdaluyo** (as, ss, f, perc); **Francis Wong** (ts, f, dizi); **Jim Norton** (bcl, ss, f, dizi); **Mark Izu** (b, sheng); **Anthony Brown** (d, perc); **Susan Hayase** (taiko). **James 'Frank' Holder** (perc). Soul Note Ⓕ 121 203-2 (75 minutes). Recorded 1991.

⑧ ❽

Along with saxophonist Fred Houn and pianist Glenn Horiuchi, pianist/composer Jang is at the forefront of the flourishing Asian-American jazz movement. Each writes extended works which express their community's dissatisfaction with the subtle and not-so-subtle forms of racism that have pervaded post-Second World War US society. Here, titles like *Never Give Up!* (dedicated to Jesse Jackson and the Rainbow Coalition), *Redress* and *Reparations Now!* from his 30-minute *Concerto for Jazz Ensemble and Taiko*, relate Jang's socio-political agenda. But the music itself warrants attention as an original blend of multicultural elements. Jang's orchestrations include Asian instruments like the sheng (a Chinese bamboo mouth organ), dizi (flute), and taiko (Japanese drum) to fascinating effect. His multiple flute and piano voicings in *Never Give Up!* may be reminiscent of Toshiko Akiyoshi, but the rhythmic impetus is via Mingus, and on Dizzy's *A Night In Tunisia* Japanese drum riffs join with the Latin percussion. The Asian influence is heard even more directly through the pentatonic scales of Jang's *Concerto* and the traditional Chinese and Japanese tunes *Butterfly Lover's Song* and *Ichikotsu-cho*, respectively. Such ambitious arranging—along with strong soloists like Wong, Magdaluyo, Brown and Jang himself—should help bring the music's message to a larger audience. **AL**

Denise Jannah

A Heart Full Of Music **Jannah** (v); **Rick Margitza** (ts); **Cyrus Chestnut** (p); **George Mraz** (b); **Billy Hart** (d); **Martin Verdonk**, **Lucas Van Merwijk** (perc). Timeless Ⓕ CDSPJ 414 (57 minutes). Recorded 1993.

⑤ ❽

Jannah, from Surinam, is a good young singer who has passed through formal training in Hilversum University and has now embarked on a career as a jazz performer. This is not her first album, and he experience of recording shows through in the confidence she gives to her delivery. She has little interpretive depth at this stage of her life and on ballads her technique can be questioned, with her habit of continually attacking a note from underneath becoming a little worrying. Is she doing it deliberately or is she plain out of tune? Anyway, her personality is very pleasant, as is the voice itself, and she is given good if unremarkable backing by stellar talents which include an attentive Cyrus Chestnut and a superbly assured George Mraz. Jannah clearly means business, and this disc would indicate the possibility that she will yet achieve memorable results. **KS**

Guus Janssen

Dancing Series **Janssen** (p); **Herb Robertson** (t); **Wolter Wierbos** (tb); **Vincent Chancey** (frh); **Ab Baars** (ss, ts, cl); **Paul Termos** (as); **Jacques Palinckx** (g); **Maurice Horsthuis** (va); **Ernst Reyseger** (vc); **Raoul van der Weide** (b); **Wim Janssen** (perc). Geestgronden Ⓕ 1 (64 minutes). Recorded 1988.

⑧ ❽

As a composer, Holland's Guus Janssen does not have the reputation of fellow countrymen Maarten Altena, Willem Breuker or Misha Mengelberg, but he certainly shares their predilection for provocation and humour. His ensemble includes a couple of American ringers in Robertson and Chancey, but the rest are among Holland's best—and they have to be to negotiate the high-wire balancing and razor-sharp axe-juggling of Janssen's deliciously unpredictable scores. The tongue-in-cheek titles survey dance forms from the seventeenth-century French passepied to street beat Hip Hop, but audience participation may not be advisable. Moods, colours, tempos and rhythms all change at the drop of a beat, with quick cutting à la cinematic montage; incongruous episodes are bashed together or flow in bizarre compromise, repetitious riffs collide with hasty polyphony or sizzling solo outbursts. Highlights are a noirish ballad (*Slow Fox*), a phantasmagorical *Mambo* and a satirical *Jojo Jive*, heavy on the growl and wah-wah brass and slappy doo-wah rhythms. On the debit side are an inchoate *Incourante* and an over-parodied pair of *Pogo*s which succumb to mumbling, terrorist landmines and cavalry fanfares. Still, highly recommended to those listeners unafraid of the whimsical deconstruction and reconstruction of conventional jazz. **AL**

Joseph Jarman

1937

Song For **Jarman** (as, recitation); **Bill Brimfield** (t); **Fred Anderson** (ts); **Christopher Gaddy** (p, mba); **Charles Clark** (b); **Thurman Barker**, **Steve McCall** (d). Delmark Ⓕ DD 410 (51 minutes). Recorded 1966.

⑧ ❼

This, Jarman's recording début as a leader, predates the formation of the Art Ensemble of Chicago by nearly two years. The disc's personnel, while never a working band as such, reflects the period's emphasis on experimenting with varying instrumental combinations. Anderson and Brimfield are longtime partners; adding them to Jarman's active quartet completely changed its emotional balance. Jarman has always been partial to theatrical presentations, and even on disc the drama of this music is palpable. The opening version of Anderson's *Little Fox Run* is forceful and determined, with the two drummers providing a rhythmic torrent and the cumulative power of the horns a squalling force of nature. Limited to the quartet, *Non-Cognitive Aspects Of The City* integrates Jarman's existential poetry with a sensitive, highly-organized and changing environment of related activity—Gaddy's florid piano gestures, Clark's power and arco prowess, Jarman's wailing post-Dolphy alto eventually soothing harsh nerves. On both *Adam's Rib* and *Song For* the tension is thick, with emotions barely held in check despite the growing flux of details. The return of *Little Fox Run*, as encore, now sounds like a shout of affirmation and exuberance. The tragically early deaths of Gaddy and Clark would destroy this group and send Jarman to Europe with the Art Ensemble. In subsequent albums under his own name Jarman's vision would expand and blossom; still, this vibrant music documents a portion of the vital musical experimentation within the early days of Chicago's AACM. **AL**

Al Jarreau

1940

Al Jarreau: 1965 **Jarreau** (v); **Cal Bezemer** (p); **Gary Allen** (b); **Joe Abodeely** (d). Bainbridge Ⓜ BCD2037 (43 minutes). Recorded 1965.

⑦ ❼

This engagingly rough recording catches Al Jarreau when he was still a graduate student in psychology at the University of Iowa and moonlighting as a jazz singer at the Tender Trap in nearby Cedar Rapids. It also places Jarreau with the Tender Trap's house rhythm section, with whom he worked regularly. It is not surprising, then, that there is a gritty yet relaxed kind of serious fun at work.

Jarreau's wonderfully supple voice shines throughout, and what a pleasure it is to hear a jazz vocalist who sings in tune and who really swings. Jarreau, at age 25, had also developed into an effective story-teller whose renderings of tunes like *This Masquerade Is Over* and *Come Rain or Come Shine* connect with a dramatic impact that is neither over-the-top nor too close-to-the-vest. And in a genre in which scatting is assumed to be the essential criterion necessary to be called a jazz singer, it is refreshing to hear Jarreau take flight, as with *Stockholm Sweetnin'*, in a musically convincing manner derived from the bop-crobatics of Jon Hendericks and Dave Lambert. Although Jarreau went on to develop an intriguing repertory of mouth and body sounds, here the focus is straight-ahead. Pianist Bezemer, bassist Allen and drummer Abodeely also deserve credit for their restrained and sensitive support. **CB**

Keith Jarrett

1945

Fort Yawuh **Jarrett** (p); **Dewey Redman** (ts, musette); **Charlie Haden** (b); **Paul Motian** (d, perc); **Danny Johnson** (perc). Impulse! Ⓜ MCAD 33122 (42 minutes). Recorded 1973.

⑧ ❻

When Jarrett was younger, before his varied interests and lofty pronouncements obscured matters, his inspirations were easy to hear: the Ornette Coleman quartet's harmonic rambling, and pianist Paul Bley's adaptation of it; Coltrane's and Bill Evans's free-tempo ballads; gospel piano and the rolling-chord grooves of Ramsey Lewis and Vince Guaraldi.

On this live Village Vanguard set, different tracks highlight different sources: *De Drums* is the pop-piano finger-snapper, where Motian's defiantly loose pulse forestalls monotony. (*If the*) *Misfits* (*Wear It's*) theme is explicitly Ornette-ish, no surprise as Redman and Haden are longtime Coleman sidemen. Redman is well displayed with an impassioned multiphonic played/sung tenor on *Misfits*, and a short, deft solo on his usually intractable double-reed musette, on *Fort Yawuh*.

The music is eclectic, but because each member of the quartet has a strong personality, they sound like a band (Johnson was not a regular, and plays an ancillary role). The pianist's trademark rubato phrasing is everywhere evident, but his ruminations are less ponderous and prone to self-parody than elsewhere. The stylistic gulf between Jarrett's 'American' and 'European' seventies quartets is not as great as commonly assumed. But on a good night like this, the Yanks had more juice. **KW**

Belonging **Jarrett** (p); **Jan Garbarek** (ss, ts); **Palle Danielsson** (b); **Jon Christensen** (d). ECM Ⓕ 1050 (829 115-2) (47 minutes). Recorded 1974.

✔ 

Keith Jarrett's biographer Ian Carr refers to **Belonging** as "one of the greatest quartet recordings in jazz because everything about it is superlative: the compositions, the free-flowing interplay, the level of inspiration and the brilliantly focused improvising of all four musicians." This is a verdict with which contemporary jazz aficionados wholeheartedly agreed, **Belonging** and Jarrett immediately garnering a clutch of awards across Europe, Japan and the US. Recorded in two days after minimal rehearsal, all the tracks—first takes—are perfect vehicles for demonstrating both the soloists' strengths (Garbarek's sonorous, anthemic keening, Jarrett's intense lyricism) and the truly astonishing empathy characterizing the Scandinavian rhythm section. Jarrett's slower compositions, *Blossom* and the beautiful two-minute title-track, verge on sound-poetry; his up-tempo pieces are jaunty and often irresistibly joyous. The album as a whole is a faultless vindication of Jarrett's reputation for producing complex and subtle but wholly accessible music, delightful to jazz specialists and casual listeners alike. The quintessential European-quartet Jarrett recording, it not only gave its name to this particular band but set new standards for quartet jazz. Simply indispensable. **CP**

The Köln Concert **Jarrett** (p). ECM Ⓕ 1064/65 (810 067-2) (66 minutes). Recorded 1975.

✔ ⑧ ❻

Well, this is it. This is the live solo recording by Keith which showed that one man could sustain a whole record, that one man improvising without a touch of electronics could capture a generation, that one man dancing between the borders of jazz and classical music could make friends with both sides, but above all it is the record which sold millions for ECM and thus funded the rise of one label and the style of music which became associated with it. When you think of the players before Jarrett who had shown allegiance to both jazz and classical music, and how they have been forgotten or abandoned (Jacques Loussier, Gunther Schuller, Phil Sunkel, etc.), you get a measure of just how resourceful Keith Jarrett was. This is still hypnotic, shifting, beautiful music. Will it ever sound dated? I suspect not. **MK**

At The Deer Head Inn **Jarrett** (p); **Gary Peacock** (b); **Paul Motian** (d). ECM Ⓕ 1531 (66 minutes). Recorded 1992.

⑧ ❾

The nineties have seen Jarrett take a new angle on himself. By that I do not mean he has de-constructed his music or re-invented himself or anything quite so drastic. But it would seem that he has done a lot of thinking about his own output, because it tends to be more clearly delineated into 'types' or 'streams' than previously. Hence we get a Jarrett album of old masters classical music interpretations, or a Jarrett album of standards interpretations, or we get a Jarrett solo recital. Less often, we may get an album of his compositions, most of which fall loosely into an 'art music' approach. Clearly the man's pursuits are as varied as ever, but what seems less in evidence is a working unit playing his own tunes (like the old quartets did) or just setting to and seeing what happens (like on the classic **Changes** album from 1983).

There is nothing wrong with any of this: it is merely an observation on where Jarrett may be heading as a musician. Certainly at the present time his albums of standards interpretations outweigh the rest, and this one is the current pick of the bunch. Which is just slightly odd, because it is not the usual Standards trio with DeJohnette, but a throwback to the seventies band which featured Paul Motian so consistently. This does the music no harm at all, Motian's rhythmic colour and propulsion unerringly centring the musical spotlight on the soloist. There is a great sense of peace and well-being in this 'live' set, recorded at one of Jarrett's teenage haunts: no-one forces the pace or distorts the contours of the music. Everything breathes naturally, so to speak. Examples abound, but *You Don't Know What Love Is* is spellbinding. So—grunts and squeaks aside, this is exemplary music-making. **KS**

Bobby Jaspar

1926-1963

Memory of Dick **Jaspar** (ts, f); **Sacha Distel** (g); **Rene Urtreger** (p); **Benoit Quersin** (b); **Jean-Louis Viale** (d). EmArcy Ⓜ 837 208-2 (41 minutes). Recorded 1955.

⑥ ❻

Jaspar certainly counts as one of Belgium's most impressive jazzmen; at one point in the late fifties he made a successful career move to New York and played with a string of top-line leaders, including Miles Davis and Donald Byrd. This early session finds him in excellent form, accompanied by guitarist Distel, who was later to have quite a career in another musical style.

The predominant mood here is cool, with Jaspar displaying a notable penchant for Getzian phrasing and sound, while often also betraying an interest in harmonic structures more closely associated with the Byas/Hawkins saxophone lineage. His solos are seamlessly unfolded, his ideas strong and his poise unblemished. His flute outings are pretty but less musically substantial, and it is with the tenor that he delivers his most cogent and inspired lines. The backing group, at the time of this recording functioning around Paris as the Bobby Jaspar Quintet, is solid but unexceptional, with Distel being the only other point of interest away from the leader; which in itself is disappointing, considering the substantial talents Urtreger manages to hide here in the interests of group solidarity. Playing time is not brilliant, but then Jaspar CDs are something of a rare breed, so get what you can while you can. The Dick of the title song, by the way, was pianist Dick Twardzik, who had died in Paris shortly before these sessions. **KS**

André Jaume 1940

Musique Pour Huit: L'oc **Jaume** (as, ts, f); **Jean-François Canape** (t, flh); **Yves Robert** (tb); **Jacques Veille** (btb); **Michael Overhage**, **Heiner Thym** (vc); **François Mechali** (b); **Gerard Siracusa** (d). hatART Ⓕ 6058 (55 minutes). Recorded 1981.

⑧ ❽

This French multi-reed player has shown his prowess on a wealth of discs from his own CELP label, where he favours duos (partners have included Jimmy Giuffre, Charlie Mariano, Daniel Humair and Raymond Boni) and trios (notably one with Joe McPhee and another, exploring Ornette material, with Charlie Haden) that inspire his increasingly intimate style. But this earlier date gives a broader, more imaginative view of his original music. The striking compositions present a tug-of-war between arranged and freely improvised elements, performed by musicians sensitive to the spontaneity of the moment but who may miss that last measure of urgency. The strings bring a post-Bartók chamber music feel to pieces like the slightly melancholy *Blue Note* and *L'oc*, a tone poem of stark themes and shifting textures. Jaume's playing at this stage is reminiscent of Archie Shepp's reconsideration of the tradition, with split notes and stretched tones striking sparks. Most impressive, however, is the music's concentration on ensemble interplay and uncommon ideas, as the unusual instrumentation offers fresh colours. It is a pure, European concept, the kind of sound and perception that probably would not occur to an American jazzman. **AL**

Jazz at the Philharmonic

Jazz at the Philharmonic: The First Concert (1944) Collective personnel: **Shorty Sherock** (t); **J.J. Johnson** (tb); **Illinois Jacquet**, **Jack McVea** (ts); **Nat King Cole** (p); **Les Paul** (g); **Red Callender**, **Johnny Miller** (b); **Lee Young** (d). Verve Ⓜ 521 646-2 (63 minutes). Recorded 1944.

⑨ ❻

This, the inaugural JATP concert (and one which set in train a highly successful series of Granz promotions which would continue for over 25 years), happened to inspire some of the most typical jam session playing of any JATP set. The line-up may not be the most spectacular of impresario Norman Granz's career (his 1946 concert series, currently reissued under Charlie Parker's name, had Coleman Hawkins and Lester Young on the same bill, plus Parker and Willie Smith, with Buck Clayton, Al Kilian and Dizzy Gillespie variously keeping trumpet fans happy), but the music is absolutely irresistible. The rhythm generated by Nat Cole and Les Paul in tandem with Red Callender on bass and Lester's brother Lee Young on drums is impossible not to tap your feet to. Cole and Paul, by the way, indulge in a continuing series of one-upmanship games from track to track which have both men laughing out loud at various points, and it is arguable that in their own solos not only do they occasionally outshine the two tenors and J.J., but they play some of the best jazz of their lives.

But of course it is Illinois Jacquet who became a tenor-sax hero (or zero, depending on your point of view) by his high-note screeches and frenziedly expressionistic solos here. What he was doing was nothing new for him - after all, his *Flying Home* with Hamp was already two years in the past - but the sheer intensity and ebullience he brings to his work here is breathtaking. He also invents some pretty meaty normal-register work and his solos are consistently well-formed. The other tenor, Jack McVea, is a fine Lester Young-style swing player who refuses to be intimidated by Jacquet and who on *Tea For Two* takes a driving and eloquent solo. Johnson, overtaken by all the excitement, plays with little of his later poise but is enjoyable nonetheless. Shorty Sherock appears on a couple of tracks and does nothing to lower the temperature. For anyone interested in locating the soul of jazz circa 1944, then this is no bad place to start. In fact, I'd even go so far to say it is required listening. **KS**

J.A.T.P. In Tokyo Collective Personnel - i) **JATP All-Stars**: **Roy Eldridge**, **Charlie Shavers** (t), **Bill Harris** (tb), **Willie Smith**, **Benny Carter** (as), **Ben Webster**, **Flip Phillips** (ts), **Oscar Peterson** (p), **Herb Ellis** (g), **Ray Brown** (b), **J.C. Heard** (d); ii) **Oscar Peterson Trio**: **Peterson** (p), **Ellis** (g), **Brown** (b) iii) **Gene Krupa Trio**: **Benny Carter** (as), **Oscar Peterson** (p), **Gene Krupa** (d); iv) **Ella Fitzgerald** with **Raymond Tunia** (p), **Ellis** (g), **Brown** (b), **Heard** (d) and **The JATP All-Stars**. Pablo Live Ⓜ 2620-104-2 (2 discs, 144 minutes). Recorded 1953.

⑧ ❻

JATP was a jazz institution all over the world for close on twenty years (they even made it to Australia in 1960). Norman Granz, a bright and resourceful man with the drive and taste to want only the best and want them onstage all at the same time found a formula which the world's audiences responded to enthusiastically until the whole idea of the jam session withered and died in the white heat of sixties change. Granz recorded JATP extensively and released many hours' worth of concerts on his Norgran, Clef and Verve labels, much of which has never been transferred to CD (although at the present time, Verve are rumoured to be preparing a deluxe boxed set of the entire forties JATP tapes in their possession). Granz, however, kept much of the material back, and when he started his Pablo label in the seventies, he began issuing selected concerts. This was one of them, and possibly the best of the Pablo bunch. It follows time-honoured JATP procedure, starting with a jam session, moving on to a ballad medley, then giving over to small group sessions (here it's the Peterson and Krupa groups). After the interval Ella would come on for a set, to be joined at the end by the jam session all-stars for a last-number rave-up. A simple formula, but one which worked for years and gave us all many memorable moments. Hearing people such as Willie Smith and Benny Carter, at length, on the same stage together, or Roy Eldridge and Charlie Shavers doing battle, is something to treasure. No-one does such unselfconscious things today, and jazz is the poorer for it. **SV**

The Jazz Crusaders

Freedom Sound **Wayne Henderson** (tb); **Wilton Felder** (ts); **Roy Gaines** (g); **Joe Sample** (p); **Jimmy Bond** (b); **Stix Hooper** (d). Pacific Jazz Ⓜ CDP7 96864-2 (47 minutes). Recorded 1961.

⑧ ❽

The irony of a band with the name Jazz Crusaders being in the vanguard of those deserting jazz for commercial funk in the seventies is given a further twist by the content of this, their début album, for it concentrates on the sort of jazz—gospel-tinged hard bop with an emphatic backbeat—which became relatively commercial in the eighties, filling dance floors and sparking something of a jazz revival among the young. **Freedom Sound** was recorded by this group of mainly Houston-born musicians on their arrival on the West Coast, and it combines an infectious freshness and enthusiasm with the relaxed, comfortable groove that results from long association. It is full of ringing, declamatory themes impeccably played, including the anthemic title tracks and the rousing opener *The Geek*—even the theme from the film *Exodus*—but the chief attraction is the group's overall sound, which is clean and neat with tasteful, tuneful soloing and well-judged, imaginative arrangements set against the crispest rhythm section imaginable. In that sense, little changed in these men's careers, because those elements were at the heart of their later successes. The CD contains two bonus tracks, extended alternative takes of *MJS Funk*—a reference to the band's previous name, the Modern Jazz Sextet—and *Coon*. **CP**

The Jazztet

Blues On Down **Art Farmer** (t); **Tom McIntosh** (tb); **Benny Golson** (ts); **Cedar Walton** (p); **Tommy Williams** (b); **Albert Heath** (d). Chess Ⓜ GRP 18022 (67 minutes). Recorded 1960/61.

⑦ ❽

The Jazztet was a band which should have made it big. Its leaders Art Farmer and Benny Golson had been sidemen in all the right bands, including Gerry Mulligan for Farmer and Art Blakey for Golson, both men were first-rate soloists, and Golson was a seriously gifted composer. The band inhabited a stylistic area defined by Blakey, the Adderleys and the type of well-drilled group J.J. Johnson was running, and all those groups were conspicuously successful. So what happened? It seems to have been a case of the times moving on just when these guys caught up. With the advent of Ornette, with Coltrane's emergence as a leader, with Sonny Rollins's reinvention and Miles's blossoming under modality, what Golson and Farmer had to offer - beautifully-crafted small-group arrangements of quality material, and a mainstream approach to improvisation which was conspicuous in its lack of flash and shallowness - was not what was in demand. So the band broke up after a few years and a number of fine albums, some for Chess/Argo and the remaining ones for Mercury.

Does the reissued music live up to the memories, then? By and large, yes. These men are playing uncompromising jazz, they express themselves with conspicuous taste and an admirable clarity, and the rhythm section settle to a groove at every tempo. What's more, the front line are invariably in tune. This is warm, sophisticated music with much to offer the careful listener, and it wears its age very well. Any track will demonstrate this, but Golson's *Five Spot After Dark* is an especially good place to start. **KS**

Eddie Jefferson

1918-1979

Letter From Home **Jefferson** (v); **Clark Terry**, **Ernie Royal**, **Joe Newman** (t); **Jimmy Cleveland** (tb); **James Moody** (f, as); **Johnny Griffin** (ts); **Arthur Clark** (bs); **Barry Galbraith** (g); **Joe Zawinul**, **Wynton Kelly**, **Junior Mance** (p); **Sam Jones** (b); **Osie Johnson**, **Louis Hayes** (d). Riverside Ⓜ OJCCD 307-2 (38 minutes). Recorded 1962.

⑥ ❻

There have been a number of claimants for the position of 'first' in the field of what became known as 'vocalese'; that is, the adding of words to a recorded jazz solo, but it seems likely that Jefferson was the originator. King Pleasure (born Clarence Beeks) seems to have beaten Eddie to the punch only in terms of getting on record first.

Cannonball Adderley, who often worked in an informal A&R capacity for the old Riverside label, was behind the making of this album, which includes Adderley's *Ja-Da*-like tune *Things Are Getting Better*, and while there are some of Jefferson's 'vocalese' excursions, there are also a number of straightforward examples of Eddie's attractive and musicianly singing. He was associated with James Moody for some time (he was Moody's vocalist and road manager in the late fifties) and *Back In Town* (based on *I Cover The Waterfront*) and *I Feel So Good* (or *Body And Soul*) use Moody's recorded solos as the basis for Jefferson's singing. One of the best vocalese tracks here is *Bless My Soul*, a very accurate transcription of Charlie Parker's stunning solo on his Savoy recording of *Parker's Mood*. Ernie Wilkins wrote all of the arrangements and most of the instrumental solos are by Johnny Griffin, although Jimmy Cleveland gets a chorus to himself on the title-track. Incidentally, Manhattan Transfer included their version of Jefferson's *Body And Soul* on a latter-day tribute (see below). **AM**

Billy Jenkins

1954

Scratches of Spain **Jenkins** (g, vn); **Chris Batchelor**, **John Eacoti**, **Skid Solo** (t); **Iain Ballamy**, **Steve Buckley**, **Dai Pritchard** (saxes); **Dave Jago** (tb); **Ashley Slater** (v, btb, tba); **Dave Cooke** (elg); **Django Bates** (kbds); **Jimmy Haycraft** (vb); **Jo Westcott** (vc); **Tim Matthewman** (elb); **Simon Edwards** (b); **Dawson**, **Steve Argüelles**, **Roy Dodds** (perc). Babel Ⓕ BDV 9404 (39 minutes). Recorded 1986.

⑤ ❼

Jenkins has been a part of the London jazz scene for a good fifteen years, having previously graduated from the 'art-rock' scene of the late seventies and early eighties. This part of his career is perhaps best summed up by the albums he made with the band Burlesque. Most of his jazz and improvisational work has been performed, issued or published under the auspices of his own Voice of God Collective; much of it carries a double edge where the listener is not quite sure whether the joke is on the musicians or the audience.

The Babel label itself is jokey in the same way as *The Beano*. Jenkins's album plagiarises the distinctive Gil Evans/Miles Davis **Sketches of Spain** cover and the insert-note has schoolboy jokes like "bigtime saxophones" and "juvenile trombone". It may well once have amused Molesworth, but few others nowadays will have a great deal of patience with it. The mostly joyful music is much better than one might have expected: Jenkins plays wailing guitar and clapped-out violin, the latter some way advanced from the Stuff Smith demolition school of virtuoso playing. The personnel reads like a spin-off of Loose Tubes and includes Django Bates on keyboards. The arrangements are mannered but lifted by some robust solo contributions. Ashley Slater's trombone enlivens *Benidorm Motorway Services* and there are powerful saxophone solos on *Bilbao*. Dai Pritchard contributes three minutes of beautifully played clarinet to *Barcelona* which is indistinguishable from the work of the late Jimmy Hamilton. After that the track, pinned by a martial drum rhythm, quickly becomes tiresome. The best track is *Cooking Oil*, a moving piece dominated by arco cello from Jo Westcott. **SV**

Leroy Jenkins

1932

The Legend of A.I. Glatson **Jenkins** (vn); **Anthony Davis** (p); **Andrew Cyrille** (perc). Black Saint Ⓕ 120022-2 (37 minutes). Recorded 1978.

⑧ ❼

A pioneering figure in contemporary violin music, Leroy Jenkins found his musical direction when he joined Chicago's AACM in 1965. There he gained the confidence to go beyond his classical training and devise new personal languages for improvisation. In the late sixties he played with Anthony Braxton and Leo Smith, then in 1971 co-founded the Revolutionary Ensemble with Sirone and Jerome Cooper. That group broke up in 1977, but Jenkins has since been active on many fronts; he has played solo concerts, composed for the JCOA, toured with Cecil Taylor, experimented with electronics and led several of his own ensembles.

The Legend of A.I. Glatson is the only one of his four early Black Saint releases currently on CD. While the 1983 chamber-jazz **Mixed Quintet** is perhaps his most accessible music, **A.I. Glatson** is a thrilling record. The title-track is densely textured, through-composed; in contrast *Tuesday's Child* is typical AACM pointillism, tiny squeaks and sighs in a hushed sound space. The grave lament *Albert Ayler* catches the violinist at his most rapturous, while his punning *Brax Stone* tribute features a charming duet of pizzicato violin and dancing percussion. Jenkins's keening tone, steeped in the blues, has an astringency that some may find initially daunting, but there is always a broad spectrum of creativity to enjoy in his music. **GL**

J.F. Jenny-Clark

1944

Unison **Jenny-Clark** (b); **Christof Lauer** (s); **Joachim Kühn** (p); **Walter Quintus** (elecs). CMP Ⓕ CD 32 (46 minutes). Recorded 1987.

⑤ ❽

Jenny-Clark has had a long and successful career playing with musicians loosely associated with the avant-garde of both Europe and America. He has a complete technique, a big, dark and woody tone, and a slippery imagination. This record starts with overdubbed solo basses on a track called *Scott*, and the playing style points to it being a tribute to the late Scott LaFaro, a clear model (along with Gary Peacock) for at least a portion of Jenny-Clark's technique. The music does not stay there, however: it mixes and matches the bass player with a varied selection of instruments and environments, including some which give an unusual range of alternatives to the idea of overdubbed basses. Both Kühn and Quintus show themselves to be remarkable partners for Jenny-Clark, interpreting his musical needs and providing apt foils in every situation. This may ultimately be a record for specialists, or those with an already-acquired taste for the double-bass, but once that step is taken, there is much here to admire. **KS**

Ingrid Jensen

1967

Vernal Fields **Jensen** (t); **Steve Wilson** (ss, as); **George Garzone** (ts); **Bruce Barth** (p); **Larry Grenadier** (b); **Lenny White** (d). Enja Ⓕ ENJ-9013 2 (65 minutes). Recorded 1994.

⑥ ❽

Jensen is a young trumpeter with a full brass tone and a fiery attack. She has picked a very talented team to back her on her début album, with Steve Wilson already forging a successful solo career and Lenny White being a well-established master of the drums. Jensen's version of *Ev'ry Time We Say Goodbye* shows what she has learned from Art Farmer (someone she has seen play many times in Vienna) about how to caress a ballad. She is equally adept at taking a standard and giving it a fresh face, as she does with *I Love You*, where a vamp over a suspended chord gives it the type of suspense so beautifully exploited by Miles on mid-tempo ballads in the early sixties.

Jensen operates in a modern mainstream style, not moving very far from the type of music being created by Davis, Hubbard, Morgan, Farmer and their ilk in the sixties. She does it well, has a impressive maturity of thought and execution, and we will undoubtedly hear more from her. **KS**

Antonio Carlos Jobim

1927

Antonio Carlos Jobim **Jobim** (g, p, v, arr, comp); with various groups comprising: **João Gilberto** (g, v); **Luiz Bonfa**, **Oscar Castro Neves**, **Helio Demiro** (g); **Stan Getz** (ts); **Stu Williamson** (t); **Jimmy Cleveland**, **Milt Bernradt** (tb); **Bud Shank**, **Leo Wright** (as, fl); **João Donato**, **CC Mariano** (p); **Tommy Williams**, **Luiz Maia**, **George Duvivier**, **Joe Mondragon** (b); **Milton Banana**, **Paulo Ferreira**, **Jose Carlos**, **Paulo Braga** (d); **Astrud Gilberto**, **Maria Toledo**, **Elis Regina** (v); **Claus Ogerman**, **Marty Paich** (arr). Verve Compact Jazz Ⓜ 843 273-2 (54 minutes). Recorded 1963-87.

⑧ ❻

Of all the marriages between jazz and Latin American music, that with bossa nova was by far the most successful. There are two main reasons for this: bossa nova is built on virtually the same harmonic-melodic basis as the standard American song, and the beat is smooth and supple enough to allow jazz soloists to swing. Bossa nova was never a primitive folk form, except insofar as it derives distantly from the samba. It was the work of a sophisticated group of musicians and poets, led by Jobim and Vinicius de Moraes.

The bossa nova craze of 1962-64 owed much to Jobim's lilting, seductive melodies, and also to the fact that Brazilian Portuguese is the most sensuous sounding language on earth. Both these qualities are well conveyed by this compilation. The four tracks featuring Stan Getz inevitably stand out, in particular the gorgeous first version of *O Grande Amor*, a song which was to remain in his repertoire for many years. Jobim's own piano versions of his tunes tend to blandness but they come alive when sung, especially in the sibilant, lubricious whisper of João Gilberto. **DG**

Jan Johansson

1931-1968

Longing Collective personnel: **Lennart Aberg** (ldr, cond); **Lars Lindgren**, **Bertil Lovgren**, **Bosse Broberg**, **Jan Allan** (t); **Sven Larsson**, **Runo Ericksson** (btb); **Lennart Aberg**, **Joakim Milder**, **David Wilczewski**, **Erik Nilsson**, **Rune Falk**, **Arne Domnerus**, **Claes Rosendahl**, **Jan Kling** (reeds, f); **Bobo Stenson** (p); **Rune Gustafsson** (g); **Dan Berglund**, **George Riedel** (b); **Egil Johansen** (d). Phono Suecia Ⓕ PSCD 74 (62 minutes). Recorded 1966/93.

⑧ ❽

The 13 tracks comprising this CD are actually played by the Swedish Radio Jazz group but, fittingly, it is Jan Johansson's name which is displayed most prominently. Swedish pianist-composer Johansson was killed in a road accident in 1968 at the age of just 37. He played both on and off record with Stan Getz and Oscar Pettiford but it was as a writer that the Jazz Group remembered him. This outstanding band interprets Jan's music with expertise and care well above the line of duty, achieving a unique ensemble blend to produce some of the freshest and most intriguing voicings. Johansson had a love and understanding of Scandanavian folk music and this element of his work is present here. There are no spurious attempts to manufacture a North American dialect, for this is original music written and played by men with an all-round knowledge of jazz. The tone colours are gorgeous, the solo playing of men such as Aberg, trumpeters Jan Allan and Bosse Broberg and the piano work of Bobo Stenson are all exactly in context. Scandinavia continues to produce quality jazz of such originality that only those with tunnel vision fail to recognize the fact. The final track, *Langtan* (Longing), dates from 1966 and was written for the Mai Zetterling film **Night Games**. It makes a fitting postscript to an important release. **AM**

Bunk Johnson

1889—1949

1944 **Johnson** (t); **Jim Robinson** (tb); **George Lewis** (cl); **Lawrence Marrero** (bj); **Alcide 'Slow Drag' Pavageau** (b); **Sidney Brown** (bb); **Baby Dodds** (d); **Myrtle Jones** (v). American Music Ⓕ AMDC 3 (61 minutes). Recorded 1944.

✓ ⑦ ❹

Jonnson's penchant for embellishing the truth led to misconceptions regarding his music. It is most unlikely that he played with Buddy Bolden. He was, however, a prominent figure in the jazz of New Orleans. He left that city in 1915, toured with minstrel shows, circus and theatre bands before dental problems forced him to retire in the mid-thirties. His discovery, rehabilitation and revived recording career was an important landmark in jazz history. This CD helps explain why Johnson was never entirely happy with the circumstances in which he found himself. He was a professional musician who resented being seen as a folk figure and he preferred to play pop tunes of the day such as *You Wore A Tulip* and *There's Yes! Yes! In Your Eyes* rather than *Tiger Rag*, *The Saints* or other items from the traditional repertoire. He was further disenchanted by the choice of musicians in the band and he certainly considered himself superior to his front line partners. The amazing thing is that the outcome of the American Music sessions is basically good. The ensemble integration on *Darktown Strutter's Ball* and *Panama* is beautifully balanced and Johnson's simplistic but heartfelt solos on *Careless Love* and *Alabama Bound* are the work of an emotionally fired and skilful musician. What he sounded like in valve trombonist Frank Duson's Band in 1910, we will never know. **BMcR**

Charlie Johnson

1891-1959

The Complete Charlie Johnson Sessions **Johnson** (p, arr); **Gus Aiken**, **Leroy Rutledge**, **Jabbo Smith**, **Thomas Morris**, **Sidney De Paris**, **Leonard Davis** (t); **Regis Hartman**, **Charlie Irvis**, **Jimmy Harrison**, **George Stevenson** (tb); **Ben Whittet** (cl, as); **Edgar Sampson** (as, cl, vn, arr); **Alec Alexander** (ts, cl); **Benny Waters** (as, ts, arr); **Benny Carter** (cl, as, arr); **Bobby Johnson** (bj); **Cyrus St Clair, Billy Taylor** (bb); **George Stafford** (d); **Monette Moore** (v). Hot 'N' Sweet Ⓜ FDC 5110 (78 minutes). Recorded 1925-29.

⑦ ❻

His first band having been formed in 1918, Johnson was already established when he took a band into the newly opened Small's Paradise Club in New York City in 1925. This CD covers Johnson's entire recorded output, although his tenure at the club was very much longer. The 1925 band was somewhat primitive, with Hartman a rustic but well featured soloist and Sampson's reed scoring predictable and clumsy. Matters had improved greatly by 1927, however, with Waters bringing greater co-ordination to the arrangements and the considerable talents of Smith breathing fire into titles like *Charleston Is The Best Dance Of All* and *Birmingham Black Bottom*. The organizational skills of Carter were employed in 1928, but later that year those duties had returned to Waters and to a now more accomplished Sampson in what was the best Johnson band to record. De Paris excelled whether open or tightly·muted and he is outstanding on *The Boy In The Boat* and *Hot Bones And Rice*, where he preaches through a plunger with a passion perhaps rivalled only by King Oliver or Bubber Miley. Despite this, he is matched here blow-for-blow by Harrison. The trombonist's innovatory importance has been cursorily dealt with in most jazz histories but, although it must be weighed against that of George Brunies, Miff Mole, Charlie Green and Jack Teagarden, the 1928 Harrison had progressed jazz playing on his instrument beyond the stage achieved by his rivals. This CD highlights his declamatory style, his naturally coherent sense of solo construction and his effortless swing. More importantly, it demonstrates the immediacy of his playing and the way in which his improvisations evolved on each recording date. Sadly, with Harrison replaced by Washington, Johnson's last recording was in 1929. He remained at Small's until 1938 but, disillusioned with music, retired in 1940. **BMcR**

Howard Johnson

1941

Howard Johnson's Nubia: Arrival **Johnson** (cl, bcl, bs, v); **Sarah Seidel** (f, v); **Johannes Georg Bahlmann** (p); **Sabine Worthmann** (b, v); **Wolff Reichert** (d, chimes); **Dumisani Mabaso, Kojo Samuels** (perc). Verve Ⓕ 523 985-2 (63 minutes). Recorded 1994.

⑥ ❽

Having waited 30 years to make an album under his own name, baritonist and tuba player extraordinaire Howard Johnson has taken the somewhat unpredictable decision to make his début record a tribute to the much-recorded Pharoah Sanders. Thus all but four of the nine songs are Sanders originals, while Johnson's own efforts are so steeped in the Sanders mould as to make little difference. Despite Johnson's own liner notes professing his sincere enthusiasm for the Little Rock tenor man, one wonders still why this is so. It certainly makes it nigh impossible to identify telling individual characteristics which Johnson brings to the job of being a leader for a change.

Be that as it may, his band, Nubia, is a competent and well-integrated unit made up of young players from Europe and Africa, and they respond spiritedly to the modal challenges of Pharoah's music.

Johnson himself plays with fire and imagination, and the whole disc makes one wonder what would have happened if these people had made music cut to their own cloth. Certainly, Sabine Worthmann's *Gasheia* suggests there is a worthwhile album in there waiting to come out. **KS**

James P. Johnson

1894-1955

Carolina Shout **Johnson** (p); **Don Wilke** (player p) Biograph Ⓕ BCD 105 (46 minutes). Recorded 1988 from piano rolls cut 1917-25.

④ ❽

Most of the great pianists of the twenties, including Duke Ellington and Fats Waller, enhanced their craft by analyzing the piano rolls cut by James P. Johnson. By stopping the mechanism of a player piano, it was possible to figure out the fingering and chord structures used by "the Father of Stride Piano" in his own set-pieces like *Steeplechase Rag*, *Twilight Rag* and *Harlem Strut*. The title-track was Johnson's most celebrated contribution to the Harlem rent party circuit, a fiendishly difficult multi-thematic composition, played here at a far more modest tempo than the headlong dash of Johnson's own disc, cut in 1921, or the 1941 version by his star pupil Waller. The slower tempo is advantageous in understanding the structure of the piece and hearing Johnson's dramatic right hand voicing against the mobile tenths of his left.

Few piano roll recordings escape a slightly mechanical, stilted feel. This disc is better than most at infusing life into the performances, and the first-rate sound quality illuminates many of the subtleties in Johnson's playing not immediately obvious from the discs he cut in this pre-electric recording era. His *Eccentricity* is a charming piece in 3/4 time, while the closing track reminds us that Johnson was the man who composed the original *Charleston*. **AS**

Snowy Morning Blues **Johnson** (p); **Eddie Dougherty** (d). MCA/Decca Ⓜ GRP1 6042 (58 minutes). Recorded 1930-44.

⑧ ❽

Although a decade younger than the long-lived Eubie Blake, Johnson is acknowledged as the great master of the 'Harlem stride' piano style. Like Blake, he composed several of the early standard songs to come from the jazz milieu (such as *Old-Fashioned Love* and *If I Could Be With You*) and solo piano showstoppers. Among the latter, the classic *Carolina Shout* inspired not only Ellington and Basie in their formative years as pianists, but also his student Fats Waller, who did the most to popularize his style and material.

The set begins with four 1930 solo tracks, including a subtle transformation of the then-new *What Is This Thing Called Love?* while the remaining duo sessions from 1944 consist of tunes by Johnson himself and Waller (the first jazz figure to be celebrated on record immediately after his premature death). While the Wallers are slightly less imaginative than the versions Johnson made without the doughty Dougherty, they underline the imagination both pianists brought to bear on their own and others' material. Rhythmic and textural nuances may go unnoticed behind the melodic variation and surging swing, but they do much to illustrate the difference between the more stilted ragtime and this early jazz style. **BP**

J.J. Johnson

1924

The Eminent Jay Jay Johnson, Volumes 1 and 2 **Johnson** (tb); **Clifford Brown** (t); **Hank Mobley** (ts); **Jimmy Heath** (ts, bs); **John Lewis, Wynton Kelly, Horace Silver** (p); **Charles Mingus, Paul Chambers, Percy Heath** (b); **Kenny Clarke** (d); **Sabu** (perc). Blue Note Ⓜ CDP7 81505/06-2 (two discs, oas: 38 and 61 minutes). Recorded 1953-55.

✔ ⑨ ❺

If Johnson's output in the late forties had been about convincing fellow musicians and critics that bebop was feasible on the slide trombone, his work in the early fifties did very much more than prove it. Volume One here is a truly full marks performance, although both CDs can be rated as good as anything he has ever done. Traditional trombone techniques have long since been abandoned and there are even moments when Johnson embraces an almost saxophone-like cadence. On Volume One his fluency and trumpet-like articulation light up *Turnpike* and *Get Happy*, *Loverman* confirms his infallibly accurate intonation while *It Could Happen To You* could be taken as a model for a concert feature number. The presence of the young and confident Brown is an added bonus. Volume Two embraces two sessions. The first, with Johnson the only horn, provides *Time After Time* and *Too Marvellous For Words* as evidence of his harmonic insight and both justify the description of instant composition. The strong hands of Silver are introduced to good effect on the second recording date but Johnson's *Pennies From Heaven* (originally issued version) and the superbly restrained *You're Mine You* solos are standouts and are as fine an example of trombone improvisation as one could find. At this juncture the Johnson career looked to be set fair. **BMcR**

The Great Kai and J.J. **Johnson**, **Kai Winding** (tb); **Bill Evans** (p); **Paul Chambers, Tommy Williams** (b); **Roy Haynes**, **Art Taylor** (d). Impulse! Ⓜ MCAD-42012 (42 minutes). Recorded 1960.

⑧ ❽

Although the partnership started almost accidentally (Bennie Green was the original choice to duet with Johnson on the first LP—on Savoy—by the trombonists) J. J. and Kai got a lot of mileage out of the group. They had gone their separate ways when Impulse! reassembled the duo at the end of 1960 for this album, but to hear them sliding smoothly into the routines makes it sound as if the group was still gigging. The vibratos are beautifully matched, the dynamics are superbly rehearsed and executed and the choice of material ideal for the instrumentation. Winding is on the right channel throughout with J.J on the left, a fact which has to be remembered occasionally when the two start carving the solos up into four bar lengths. *I Concentrate On You* is a masterpiece of mute swapping and there is humour too in *Going, Going Gong!*, an upated sequel to the previous *Gong Rock* from the duo's Bethlehem LP. The rhythm sections are perfect in this context and the solos by Bill Evans, although fairly brief, are gems of lucidity and compression. This was a little band which succeeded in combining marvellous musicianship with good humour and a lot of jazz playing. Impulse! have thoughtlessly reproduced the original LP sleeve note a quarter of its size, but it is worth getting out a magnifying glass to read it, for it is both literate and informative. It was written by pianist Dick Katz, who once worked with Jay and Kai. **AM**

Proof Positive **Johnson** (tb); **Harold Mabern**, **McCoy Tyner** (p); **Toots Thielemans** (g); **Arthur Harper**, **Richard Davis** (b); **Frank Gant**, **Elvin Jones** (d). Impulse! Ⓜ GRP 11452 (41 minutes). Recorded 1964.

⑦ ❼

Johnson is the author of several major big-band jazz scores: Miles Davis and Gil Evans recorded *Lament*, while Dizzy Gillespie commissioned and recorded an entire album of his music, **Perceptions**. Until recently, this side of his art was represented on CD by the excellent **Say When** album of mid-sixties recordings for RCA, but this is now deleted. **Proof Positive** is from a similar period, but finds Johnson stretching out unexpectedly in the opposite direction. Here he is prepared to take long solos and push himself to the limit in improvising. Being the only horn, he has deliberately put himself under scrutiny, and in general he comes out ahead. The long opening track, Davis's *Neo* (aka *Teo*), finds Johnson soloing all the way, and while the group which plays on all but one track here—Mabern, Harper and Gant—are somewhat conservative and possibly ill at ease, Johnson is quite happy to dominate proceedings. Which is all to the good, because he is remarkably versatile and consistent, moving from ballads (*Gloria*, *My Funny Valentine*) to funky jazz waltzes (*Blues Waltz*) to medium tempo swingers (*Stella By Starlight*, *Lullaby of Birdland*) without once stepping out of character or showing signs of strain or distortion of his basic musical personality. He also proves to be a lot more dynamic than the common perception: it was the imitators who lacked his range, his fire and precision, and got the J.J. Johnson school of trombone playing a bad name. The originator was always something else: the proof positive is here. **KS**

Vivian **Johnson** (tb); **Rob Schneiderman** (p); **Ted Dunbar** (g); **Rufus Reid** (b); **Alira Tana** (d). Concord Ⓕ CCD 4523 (56 minutes). Recorded 1992.

⑧ ❽

One of Johnson's latest recordings, this is a set of ten ballads dedicated to the memory of his late wife, Vivian Johnson. Perhaps inevitably, it is a somewhat subdued affair in which there is little call for his renowned ability to nip around on the instrument as though it had valves attached. On the other hand, it is extraordinary how little his tone and ballad style have changed over the years. There is no essential difference between these performances and the two ballads on his 1953 Blue Note date with Clifford Brown—smooth, expressive and subtly shaded.

The immaculatedly polished rhythm section deserves mention for its ability to maintain variety, flow and interest at these leisurely tempos. **DG**

Pete Johnson

1904-67

Pete's Blues **Johnson** (p); **Hot Lips Page** (t); **J.C. Higginbotham**, **Clyde Bernhardt** (tb); **Albert Nicholas** (cl); **Don Stovall** (as); **Ben Webster**, **Budd Johnson** (ts); **Jimmy Shirley** (g); **Al Hall**, **Abe Bolar** (b); **J.C. Heard**, **Jack Parker** (d); **Etta Jones** (v). Denon/Savoy Ⓜ SV-0196-2 (38 minutes). Recorded 1946.

⑥ ❼

For 1946 this was rather an ingenious concept record. Johnson opens the session with a piano solo and is joined by musician after musician, track by track, until an octet has been assembled. The order of the day is blues, and all the participants contribute characteristic solos. The last five tracks feature a mostly different and more Basie-like eight-piece band, but the emphasis on blues and boogie material never weakens.

This is a pleasant record that gives a fair impression of Johnson in one of his common contexts, but the listener concerned to hear him in the round will need to look further. The authoritative boogie-woogie duets with Albert Ammons are on **Barrelhouse Boogie** (RCA Bluebird ND88334), but Johnson's most influential pieces, the ones that boogie-woogie practitioners still test themselves by, are the early forties solos and trios like *Dive Bomber*, *Death Ray Boogie* and *Kaycee Feeling*, which combine thematic invention and rhythmic intensity. These are presently most easily found on **Genius of Boogie Woogie** (Giants of Jazz CD53053), an inexpensive compilation which also has work by Albert Ammons, Meade Lux Lewis, Jimmy Yancey and others. **TR**

Pete Jolly

1932

Pete Jolly Trio And Friends **Jolly** (p); **Chuck Berghofer** (b); **Larry Bunker** (d); add **Howard Roberts** (g) on four tracks; substitute **Nick Martinis** for Bunker (d); **Orchestra**. VSOP Ⓕ #78CD (59 minutes). Recorded 1962-64.

⑧ ❽

Jolly has been a jazz mainstay on the West Coast for more than four decades, working with Shorty Rogers's Giants, his own trio, innumerable recording units and all manner of studio and film line-ups. His crisp note production is a model of technically correct piano playing, but he is also a fine jazz soloist with a driving, percussive syle at fast tempos and an appealingly melodic approach to ballads. This CD contains items from all three LPs he made for the Ava/Choreo label in the early sixties, opening with his own *Little Bird* which he co-wrote with arranger Dick Grove and Ava chief Tommy Woolf. The best titles are certainly the trio ones, which include an extended *Alone Together* and interpretations of Ellington's *I'm Beginning To See The Light* and Rollins's *Oleo*. He is the only soloist on the big band tracks where a concerto grosso effect is achieved with the trio in front of the brass, reeds and strings. Jolly's style has changed remarkably little over the years and while he is not a style-setter, he is nevertheless one of the most consistent and swinging pianists of the post-war years. **AM**

Elvin Jones

1927

Heavy Sounds **Jones** (d, g); **Richard Davis** (b); **Frank Foster** (ts); **Billy Green** (p). Impulse! Ⓜ MCAD 33114 (42 minutes). Recorded 1968.

⑥ ❽

After Jones left the John Coltrane Quartet at the close of 1965, he ran a number of small group line-ups, but most of them featured tenor player Frank Foster, who contributes tasty solos here. Jones had made an album as sole leader for Impulse!, **Dear John C**, plus a dual-leaders album with bassist Jimmy Garrison (neither yet on CD) while still with Coltrane, but this present set was a good deal looser and more relaxed, with the spotlight more firmly on the drummer and bassist (pianist Green, for example, is absent entirely from a very loose and spacious *Shiny Stockings*). The old standby *Summertime*, a vehicle for a Davis-Jones duet, is a little too long in the sun at 11 minutes, and Jones is not altogether comfortable with Davis's more outré gambollings; but at least we get a good solo out of the drummer (though not as breathtaking as *The Drum Thing* on Coltrane's **Crescent**). The unaccompanied guitar intro from Jones on *Elvin's Guitar Blues* sounds like it is from another record, so inappropriate is its conception and execution, but the rest of the track is a deliciously relaxed, concise blues, with Foster soloing beautifully. The album ends with a perfectly judged reading of *Here's That Rainy Day*, with Foster and Green both making spare, telling contributions. Finally, it is worth listening out for Jones's delightful brushwork on many of the above tracks. **KS**

It Don't Mean A Thing **Jones** (d); **Nicholas Payton** (t); **Delfeayo Marsalis** (tb); **Sonny Fortune** (ts, f); **Willie Pickens** (p); **Cecil McBee** (b); **Kevin Mahogany** (v). Enja Ⓕ ENJ 8066 2 (59 minutes). Recorded 1993.

⑦ ❽

Jones came to prominence on the Detroit scene with brothers Hank and Thad. His style, a composite of Max Roach's bebop tradition, Art Blakey's aggression and his own massive inspiration, recommended him to John Coltrane. From 1960, he was the ideal drummer for the tenor giant, delivering the cross rhythms and irregular accents that released him from the role of 'pulse provider' and put him in competition with his leader. After leaving Coltrane in 1965 he began leading his own groups, the name Jazz Machine was adopted and this CD, not so named, offers an example of the musical style he fostered.

Each of the players responds to Jones's special brand of turmoil in his own way. The mixture of off-centre rhythmical shifts and oblique snare accentations adds drama to Fortune's plaintive flute on *Zenzo's Spirit*. It also adds body to McBee's inventive bass on *It Don't Mean A Thing*, leaving no doubt that neither would have sounded as substantial with a routine percussionist. Never routine, Jones is a master of propulsive playing. This pushes Payton to his best work on *Fatima's Waltz* and, although Marsalis responds rather less positively, one cannot discount the inhibition factor. Jones is one of the great drum innovators, a jazz icon who must seem daunting to a young musician. **BMcR**

Etta Jones

1928

Reverse The Charges Jones (v), **Philip Harper** (t); **Houston Person** (ts); **Benny Green** (p); **Christian McBride** (b); **Winard Harper** (d); **Sammy Figueroa** (perc). Muse Ⓕ MCD 5474 (41 minutes). Recorded 1991-92.

⑥ ❻

The collaboration between Jones and Person has been long-lasting and fruitful, and just a few bars of their exchanges here on *Undecided* show an intuitive musical understanding. Etta's voice has thickened as she enters the nineties but she has an individual delivery, marked by a characteristic way of ending phrases that sounds like a trill on up-tempos and a sob on heart-rending ballads. Influenced early in her career by Billie Holiday, she can take a song like *P.S. I Love You* and make it her own. The phrasing owes something to late period Billie, but the tone and emotional projection are all Jones.

What really marks this album out as exceptional is the backing band. It contains one genuine star in pianist Benny Green and his masterful choruses on *Undecided* and Petersonesque flurries elsewhere mean that no track is without a constant tissue of interest from the keyboard. Winard and Philip Harper both bring a lot to the album, and Philip's muted trumpet work is a particular strength. I have never understood the appeal of *Ma, He's Making Eyes At Me*, but at least this album contains a reading of it that suggests why it holds such fascination for some singers and saxophonists. **AS**

Hank Jones

1918

Quartet-Quintet Jones (p); **Donald Byrd, Matty Dice** (t); **Eddie Jones** (b); **Kenny Clarke** (d). Denon/Savoy Ⓜ SV-0147 (41 minutes). Recorded 1955.

⑧ ❽

No other jazz pianist has been more consistent on record than Hank Jones. From his early brushes with the boppers he has emerged as one of the finest accompanists and soloists of the last four decades. However, for the full flavour of Jones's work it is best to turn to a small-group recording, and this CD comes from the heyday of the Savoy Records period under the managerial control of Ozzie Cadena. Jones and Kenny Clarke, with Wendell Marshall or Eddie Jones on bass, played on most of the sessions as a 'house' rhythm section. There were occasions when the rhythm section was more rewarding to hear than the featured leader but here the honours are even. Byrd, then aged 22, was making a name for himself on record and the ease and fluency of his work here (especially on *Don't Blame Me*) makes it understandable why he was a popular choice with A&R men. Jones's backings are always perfectly in context but the most out-going work by all concerned will be found on the long blues *An Evening At Papa Joe's*. Matty Dice, who appears on *Joe's* and *And Then Some*, has a rougher-edged tone than Byrd, but does not deserve the obscurity that was his fate; these are amongst his very, very few appearances on record. Good remastering retains that exclusive 'Savoy' sound. **AM**

Jo Jones

1911-1985

Jo Jones Special Jones (d); **Emmett Berry** (t); **Benny Green, Lawrence Brown** (tb); **Lucky Thompson** (ts); **Rudy Powell** (as, cl); **Nat Pierce, Count Basie, Pete Johnson** (p); **Freddie Greene** (g); **Walter Page** (b). Vanguard Ⓕ 662 132 (42 minutes). Recorded 1955.

✔ ⑧ ❽

Given instruction by Fess Whatley drummer Wilson Driver, Jones worked with Walter Page's Blue Devils in Oklahoma city and with Jeter-Pillar's Orchestra in St. Louis. He was in the film *Jammin' The Blues* in 1944, made many tours with Jazz At The Philharmonic and, in later years, was in constant demand when swing-based rhythm sections were assembled for club, concert or record dates. His status as one of jazz music's greatest drummers, however, stems from the pre-eminent part he played in the 'All-American Rhythm Section' of the Count Basie Orchestra. This CD features that rhythm quartet as well as players steeped in that tradition. It shows how Jones discounted the bass drum as a pulse provider and used his gapped hi-hat to produce a lighter, more flexible rhythmic impetus. It features his superb work with brushes, his dragged rim-shot timing and his bass drum endorsements as well as other devices that inspired the bebop drummers. Basie (or Pierce), Green, Page and Jones almost breathed as one man in the Count Basie Orchestra and they slot into that groove on this session. Recorded at the time when the forgotten men of the 'mainstream' were being given an opportunity to record, this session has outstanding solo work by Thompson, Green and Berry. **BMcR**

Jonah Jones

1909

At The Embers Jones (t); **George Rhodes** (p); **John Browne** (b); **Harold Austin** (d). RCA Victor Ⓜ 18523-2 (46 minutes). Recorded 1956.

⑥ ❽

Looking back, it seems almost outlandish that a good mainstream trumpeter, playing straightforward, swinging versions of the best tunes, should have been not only vastly popular but a fashionable figure of New York nightlife—yet that was Jonah Jones in the later fifties. His quartet was virtually a fixture at the Embers Club, and his albums sold literally in millions. This one epitomizes his approach—terse, muted theme statement, slightly florid piano solo, possibly a half-chorus of drums, trumpet solo and the theme again to round it off. Rarely does any number exceed four minutes. Jones was born in 1909 and inevitably, given his age, an Armstrong adherent. He is particularly fond of the long, Louis-style glissando, which he uses rather liberally, and he has acquired some of the Master's clipped authority. This is music designed to be played in a social context, not listened to in hushed reverence, but this does not make it an inferior product. The relevant distinction is that between decorative art and fine art. This is good decorative art. **DG**

Leroy Jones

1958

Mo' Cream From The Crop **Jones** (t, flh, v); **Lucien Barbarin** (tb); **Ed Frank** (p); **Bill Huntington**, **Walton Payton** (b); **Shannon Powell** (d); **Matt Perkins** (perc). Columbia Ⓕ 477751 2 (62 minutes). Recorded 1994.

⑧ ❿

Leroy Jones is one of the younger generation of New Orleans musicians, along with Kermit Ruffins and the Dirty Dozen Brass Band, who play traditional New Orleans music in a style clearly influenced by modern jazz. He worked almost exclusively around the city, mainly in the music bars along Bourbon Street, until 1990, when he joined the touring band of Harry Connick Jr. He was eventually given the opening spot in Connick's show, leading his own band, of which this is the début album. They play a mixture of standards and Jones originals, together with the obligatory New Orleans anthem *Bourbon Street Parade*, in a brisk and genial style that fluctuates between Louis Armstrong and Clifford Brown. It sounds like an incongruous mixture, but it works very well. This CD is notable for a splendid, high-spirited version of the old Armstrong-Fletcher Henderson number *How Come You Do Me Like You Do?* **DG**

Oliver Jones

1934

A Class Act **Jones** (p); **Steve Wallace** (b); **Ed Thigpen** (d). Justin Time Ⓕ Just 41-2 (50 minutes). Recorded 1991.

⑤ ❽

For many years involved as an accompanist to pop singer Ken Hamilton, Jones did not return to full-time jazz involvement until 1980. Since then he has made a considerable name for himself on the festival circuit. This CD is typical of his output and shows him to be a player with a dazzling technique. His solos are well-designed and when the mood takes him he can swing remorselessly. He is most at home, however, with the less tempting challenge of very positive themes like *Everybody's Song But My Own* or *Very Early*. In the former he relaxes to let the melody breathe through his improvisation, while in the latter he rocks gently in waltz time. He is never totally convincing with the Baptist rock of *Tippin' Home From Sunday School* or *Hymn to Freedom* and he is just a shade heavy handed with *Stan Pat Calypso*. Where he is least impressive is in his showboating approach to titles like *Mark My Time* or *Scrambled*, where his style recalls Oscar Peterson and the lack of content found in that giant's early work is replicated. He is well supported by Wallace and Thigpen, a logical choice in the circumstances, and together they have produced a proficient and musical release. **BMcR**

Philly Joe Jones

1923-1985

Drums Around the World: Big Band Sounds **Jones** (d); **Lee Morgan**, **Blue Mitchell** (t); **Curtis Fuller** (tb); **Herbie Mann** (f, pic); **Cannonball Adderley** (as); **Benny Golson** (ts); **Sahib Shihab** (bs); **Wynton Kelly** (p); **Sam Jones**, **Jimmy Garrison** (b). Riverside Ⓜ OJCCD 1792-2 (49 minutes). Recorded 1959.

⑧ ❼

Philadelphia-born Joe Jones (who added 'Philly' to his name in order to avoid being confused with veteran drummer Jo Jones) is one of the important links bridging the drums' stylistic shift from the swing era's essentially time-keeping mission to the bebop period's stress on a more rythmically independent approach and an expanded soloistic role. Despite the shift, time-keeping has remained the drummer's basic job, and no one did it better than Jones, who studied with Cozy Cole, one of the masters of steady four-to-the-bar swing. In the forties Jones also came under the sway of Max Roach, the bebop drum pioneer who, along with Kenny Clarke, helped set the stage for modern jazz drumming. Having absorbed both traditions, Jones became a sought-after sideman playing for such diverse stylists as Charlie Parker, Billie Holiday, Lee Konitz and Miles Davis.

Here, in a fascinating 1959 date that helped establish Jones as a leader following his tenure with Davis, Jones pursues a thematic programme based on a tour of international rythms. *Land of the Blue Veils*, for example, evokes the Orient while Jones's unaccompanied *Tribal Message* conjures up the

African tradition. There is also a boppish batch of home cooking in Tadd Dameron's *Philly J.J.* and Benny Golson's *Stablemates*. Along with well-crafted horn charts, there are great solos from Cannonball Adderley, Lee Morgan, Blue Mitchell and, of course, the singular Philly Joe Jones. **CB**

Quincy Jones 1933

This Is How I Feel About Jazz **Quincy Jones** (arr, cond); **Art Farmer**, **Bernie Glow**, **Ernie Royal**, **Joe Wilder** (t); **Urbie Green**, **Jimmy Cleveland**, **Frank Rehak** (tb); **Herbie Mann** (f); **Phil Woods**, **Gene Quill**, **Benny Carter**, **Art Pepper**, **Herb Geller**, **Charlie Mariano** (as); **Lucky Thompson**, **Zoot Sims**, **Buddy Colette**, **Bill Perkins**, **Walter Benton** (ts); **Jack Nimitz** (bs); **Milt Jackson** (vb); **Hank Jones**, **Billy Taylor**, **Lou Levy**, **Carl Perkins** (p); **Paul Chambers**, **Charles Mingus**, **Red Mitchell**, **Leroy Vinnegar** (b); **Charlie Persip**, **Shelly Manne** (d). Impulse! Ⓜ GRP11152 (67 minutes). Recorded 1956-57.

✔ ⑧ ❽

Jones, with his use of woodwind and original voicings, was one of the first to break away from the restrictions of the Fletcher Henderson big band line up. Although his innovations were not as significant as, say, those of Gil Evans, he played a major role in establishing the big band sound from the fifties onwards. His arrangements are most original and here provide wonderful settings for some of the finest soloists of the day, notably Phil Woods (who had a long and close association with Jones), Lucky Thompson and Milt Jackson. An outstanding track amongst the six which make up the 1956 New York session is *Evening In Paris*, scored especially for Zoot Sims and drawing out some of Sims's finest ballad work. An 11-minute *Walkin'* displays the young Art Farmer at his best, to be followed by commanding solos from Lucky Thompson, the three trombones, Phil Woods (on devastating form throughout) and Hank Jones. Every track from the session is a classic.

The six tracks included here from a Jones album originally entitled **Go West Young Man** are variously arranged by Jimmy Giuffre, Lennie Niehaus and Charlie Mariano, and Jones's involvement here is minimal. Nevertheless there is stalwart work from the four alto soloists on one set and from the three tenors on the other, so there is much to enjoy. **SV**

Rickie Lee Jones

Pop Pop **Jones** (v); with a collective personnel of: **Bob Sheppard** (cl); **Joe Henderson** (ts); **Dino Saluzzi** (bandoneon); **Charley Shoemake** (vb); **Robben Ford** (g); **Steve Ford** (vn); **Charlie Haden**, **John Leftwich** (b); **Walfredo Reyes** (d); **David Was**, **April Gay**, **Arnold McCuller** (v). Geffen/MCA Ⓕ GEFD 24426 (50 minutes). Recorded 1991.

④ ❽

Jones has assembled an impeccable backing personnel here (the collective list above is a little misleading, as most tracks have trios or quartets behind her); but the album is less than the sum of its considerable parts. The reason? Rickie Lee Jones, who brings a rather overly idiosyncratic approach to a heterodox bunch of latter-day standards which include *My One and Only Love*, *Up From The Skies* and *Dat Dere*.

On the face of it, Jones should be able to bring something new and fresh to such numbers, but she sounds self-conscious and unable to deliver much more than a pose. She sings in tune and on top of the rhythm, so there is nothing bad happening technically; it is just that there is not much being communicated. The backing musicians all make wholehearted efforts to keep the moveable feast moving. **KS**

Sam Jones 1924

Visitation **Jones** (b); **Terumasa Hino** (c); **Bob Berg** (ts); **Ronnie Mathews** (p); **Al Foster** (d). SteepleChase Ⓕ SCCD-31097 (56 minutes). Recorded 1978.

⑥ ❻

Sam Jones was not a bassist with ambitions to lead from the front, and here, except for a gently-paced theme and solo on Paul Chambers's *Visitation*, he remains where he is most comfortable, generating propulsive bass lines in tandem with a sometimes rather noisy Al Foster. The somewhat thin sound, imported from the original analogue session, perhaps relieves Jones's lines of some resonance, but it does not obscure some very fine bebop playing, in particular by Bob Berg. At this time Berg was at the top of his game in the straight-ahead mode he pursued before joining Miles Davis in the early eighties, and his flawlessly structured solo on the title-track is a model example of the post-Coltrane style, demonstrating his acute melodic sense to perfection. The often overlooked trumpeter Terumasa Hino is similarly incandescent, if a little less coherent, and Ronnie Mathews is not unlike Cedar Walton, another pianist who played often with Sam Jones. SteepleChase strove to make this 1988 CD reissue a special event by adding three alternative takes. One of these was Take One of *Visitation*, and it shows that as far as Bob Berg's solos are concerned, the first issued take was the right one. **MG**

Thad Jones

1923-1986

Début **Jones** (t); **Frank Wess** (f, ts); **Hank Jones, John Dennis** (p); **Charles Mingus** (b); **Kenny Clarke, Max Roach** (d). Debut Ⓜ OJCCD 625-2 (64 minutes). Recorded 1954/55.

⑧ ❻

Many will bracket Jones's name with that of Mel Lewis and remember him as co-leader of a very musicianly big band. They will also recall his compositions and arrangements and, perhaps, his *Pop Goes The Weasel* quotation in his *April In Paris* solo with Basie. But the fact is that Thad was an exceptional player by any standards and Charles Mingus called him "the greatest trumpet player that I've heard in this life." The tracks on this CD were made by Mingus for his own Debut label at a time when Jones was with Basie. The trumpet playing is little short of breath-taking in both conception and delivery. Thad had the exciting qualities of Navarro and Gillespie but a technique which enabled him to hit every note so cleanly that even the semiquavers stood out like the strokes of a bell. *I Can't Get Started* is dramatic as Thad plays his trumpet line against the stark sound of Mingus's bass in the first chorus. In the final analysis, these tracks must figure as some of the finest solo playing Jones ever recorded. The CD benefits from extra takes of *Get Out Of Town* and the exciting blues *One More* from the quartet date with the virtually unknown John Dennis on piano. The remastering is well handled and the quartet tracks are pristine but some of the quintet titles, notably *Sombre Intrusion*, suffer from an inherent muddiness due to the original and rather crude overdubbing of additional trumpet, tenor and flute lines. **AM**

Thad Jones/Mel Lewis **Jones** (flh, arr); **Lewis** (d); **Snooky Young, Jimmy Nottingham, Richard Williams, Danny Moore, Al Porcino, Marvin Stamm** (t); **Eddie Bert, Jimmy Knepper, Benny Powell, Cliff Heather** (tb); **Jerome Richardson, Jerry Dodgion, Eddie Daniels, Joe Farrell, Joe Temperley, Billy Harper, Pepper Adams, Richie Kamuca, Joe Farrell** (reeds); **Roland Hanna** (p); **Barry Galbraith, Sam Brown** (g); **Richard Davis** (b); on one track only, add: **Jimmy Buffington, Earl Chapin, Dick Berg, Julius Watkins** (frh); **Howard Johnson** (tba). LRC Ⓑ CDC9004 (58 minutes). Recorded 1969-70.

⑧ (See below)

Jones's arranging talent remained underexposed during his Basie period, but burst into full flower after he moved into studio work in the mid-sixties. While still using trumpets, trombones and saxes as separate sections (unlike Gil Evans), Jones was able to incorporate the full range of post-bop virtuosity. Fellow New York studio musicians who populated the truly all-star line-up of his and Lewis's band were delighted with his writing and the loose-hinged performance it required, originally meeting just for once-a-week live rehearsals. Later, the approach became more idiosyncratic as the leaders undertook regular touring with younger personnel such as Dick Oatts and Steve Coleman.

The material here consists of two of the early band's best studio albums, **Central Park North** (including *The Groove Merchant*) and part of **Dedication** (*Tiptoe; A Child Is Born*). But the somewhat inferior sound of this reissue is explained by the opening and closing tracks of the second set, where the surface noise and flutter of an LP source are clearly heard—in addition, applause has been added at the end of the first six tracks. Happily EMI, who own the master tapes, have embarked on a reissue programme which in due course should do them justice and the Mosaic set, for those who can afford it, has no such imperfections.. Meanwhile, if you cannot wait, then try your luck here. **BP**

Vince Jones

Trustworthy Little Sweethearts **Jones** (t, v); **Russell Smith** (tb); **Ian Chaplin** (as); **Bruce Sandell** (ts); **Paul Williamson** (ts, bs); **Barney McAll** (p, syn); **Doug deVries** (g); **Lloyd Swanton** (b); **Tony Floyd** (d); **Ray Pereira** (perc). Intuition Ⓕ INT 3046-2 (54 minutes). Recorded 1988.

⑥ ❻

Jones has released seven or eight albums in his native Australia, has toured both Europe and the US with his own band, and is a thoroughly committed jazz singer and trumpeter. His style harks directly back to Mark Murphy and Georgie Fame, and beyond them to King Pleasure and Dave Lambert. He is a capable trumpeter and a good songwriter, though here he sensibly opts for a mix of his own material and a few standards (*I'm a Fool to Want You*, *I Didn't Know What Time it Was*, etc.). His band is well-schooled and a pleasant mix of old and new styles: this is not merely a group which is trying to re-create, down to the last detail, something which has already passed. As such, it is a welcome injection of vitality into a harshly depopulated area, with Harry Connick Jr probably being Jones's nearest neighbour, although they are worlds apart in their approach to their material. Key members of the backing band get to solo: always a good sign on a singer's date. **KS**

Scott Joplin

1868-1917

Treemonisha **Carmen Balthrop** (sop); **Betty Allen** (mez); **Curtis Rayam** (ten); **Willard White** (bass); **Houston Grand Opera Chorus and Orchestra / Gunther Schuller**. Deutsche Grammophon Ⓜ 435 709-2 (two discs: 90 minutes). Recorded 1975.

Treemonisha was Joplin's second opera (the earlier *A Guest of Honour* has been lost) and he spent the last decade of his life desperately trying to get it heard. In 1915 a run-through in a Harlem rehearsal hall—minus orchestra and staging—proved a flop. This was Joplin's last great effort on behalf of his opera, for his mental state, already affected by syphilis, was deteriorating rapidly. Late in 1916 he was committed to an asylum, where he died the following spring.

More than 50 years later, thanks to the revival of interest in Joplin's music *Treemonisha* was rediscovered. In 1972 came a semi-professional performance in Atlanta, with an orchestration by the African-American composer Thomas Jefferson Anderson. Then in 1975 the Houston Grand Opera mounted the first fully professional production, with arrangements and orchestration by Gunther Schuller (a piano-vocal score, published in 1911 by Joplin himself, is all that remains of the original opera). This mid-price two-CD set is a reissue of the 1975 recording by the Houston cast. Brief notes and the libretto (also by Joplin) are included, but DG have not replicated the excellent documentation of the original LP issue.

Schuller conducts a lively performance, with Balthrop and White outstanding among the singers. His orchestration proves credibly idiomatic, opting for light textures and nimble pacing. Both plot and libretto have been criticized as undramatic, but Joplin's homespun moral fable was surely intended less as a realistic story than as a ritual celebration of community, a vision of salvation through education. It has its moments of spectacle—the corn huskers dance the climactic real slow drag—and the music is beguiling. *Treemonisha* is not a ragtime opera. It draws on ragtime as it does on gospel, barbershop quartets, folk dances and the European opera tradition. But in particular it draws on Joplin's extraordinary capacity to blend these influences into a coherent and affecting personal language. **GL**

King of Ragtime Writers Player piano rolls by unidentified period musicians. Biograph Ⓕ BCD 110 (55 minutes). Created 1900/1960.

⑥ ❻

This and its companion albums **The Entertainer** (BCD 101) and **Elite Syncopations** (BCD 102) consist of careful transfers of original piano rolls to new copies, played at corrected speeds and checked for authenticity against the published manuscripts. The whole area of piano roll recordings is a minefield, and not worth entering in great depth here; suffice it to say that these transfers are of good quality, although on this volume none of the very few rolls which Joplin himself made are present (they are on the earlier ones).

The biggest single problem with rolls is a lack of touch and gradations of tone: only the most sophisticated pianola companies tackled this problem (Ampico, etc.), and their results were invariably reserved for the classical celebrities of the day. So things here can get a little wearisome after a time, and I would recommend small doses of this CD, rather than long draughts. The big advantage, however, is that the rhythmic emphasis is authentic. These rolls were made long before jazz, with its concomitant radical modifications to the very nature of syncopation, was properly formulated, so the concept of syncopation present on this CD is pre-jazz, and adheres much more closely to, for example, what non-jazz composers created in their own cakewalk imitations, and to the earliest recorded ragtime and jazz piano players.

If you prefer a modern filter on the music, then 70 minutes of Joshua Rifkin's sensitive and ground-breaking 1970 recordings are available on **Piano Rags** (Elektra/Nonesuch 79159-2).The Dick Hyman RCA set has yet to make it onto CD. **KS**

Clifford Jordan 1931-1993

Glass Bead Games **Jordan** (ts); **Stanley Cowell**, **Cedar Walton** (p); **Bill Lee**, **Sam Jones** (b) **Billy Higgins** (d). Bellaphon/Strata-East Ⓕ 660-51-017 (34 minutes). Recorded 1973.

⑧ ❽

Chicago tenorman Clifford Jordan recorded his début **Blowin' In From Chicago** for Blue Note in 1957. In the sixties he worked with Max Roach and Charles Mingus and also recorded several more albums as leader, notably **These Are My Roots** (a collection of Leadbelly songs) for Atlantic and the excellent **In The World** for Strata-East, the label he co-ran with pianist Stanley Cowell and trumpeter Charles Tolliver. None of the three aforementioned records is currently on CD, but Bellaphon/Strata-East have reissued the highly commendable **Glass Bead Games** on two separate LPs. This CD contains the first volume, which features fine playing by Jordan, three of his strongest compositions (*Powerful Paul Robeson*, *Glass Bead Games*, *Prayer For The People*) and a moving version of *John Coltrane*, the tribute written by bassist Bill Lee (father of film-director Spike).

Jordan's timbre sometimes takes on the dark, twisting grain of Von Freeman while his ballad-playing can recall the legato flow of Wardell Gray. But he is mostly an individualist, with a big, friendly tone and a distinctive deftness to his phrasing. "I don't ever try to play anything exact," he once explained, "… I like to kinda float. Abstractly. Put some brush strokes over the music."

Other Jordan albums of note include the live **Highest Mountain** (Muse), the late-night **Royal Ballads** (Criss Cross) and the big band **Down Through The Years** (Milestone). Why both volumes of **Glass Bead Games** could not be fitted on one CD only Strata-East can tell us. **GL**

Duke Jordan

1922

Trio and Quintet **Jordan** (p); **Percy Heath** (b); **Art Blakey** (d); plus on five tracks: **Eddie Bert** (tb); **Cecil Payne** (bs). Denon/Savoy Ⓜ SV-0149 (45 minutes). Recorded 1955.

⑧ ❻

Duke Jordan will always be remembered for his elegant introductions and solos on Charlie Parker's series of recordings for Dial. In later years he emerged as a composer in his own right, with tunes such as *Jor-Du* (originally called *Minor Escamp*), *Scotch Blues, Flight to Jordan* and *Forecast*. Although he has made many albums in Denmark for the SteepleChase label, this CD, recorded originally for Signal, remains one of his best. Opening with four trio numbers (including *Forecast*), Jordan soon establishes himself as a truly melodic improviser. The focus remains firmly on the piano, for Art Blakey respectfully scales the volume of his playing down for the occasion (although he has a most inventive chorus on *Night In Tunisia*). The fifth track is a solo version of *Summertime* which shows how successfully Jordan can operate on his own. The following five tracks add the warm-toned, flexible trombone playing of the underrated Eddie Bert and the fine bebop baritone playing of Payne (who also demonstrates his emotional ballad approach on *Two Loves*). The transfers to CD are clear but one of Blakey's cymbals obtrudes at times. **AM**

Louis Jordan

1908-1975

Let The Good Times Roll—The Complete Decca Recordings 1938-54 **Jordan** (v, cl, as, bs); **Elks Rendezvous Band** Courtney Williams, [t], Lem Johnson, [cl, ts], Clarence Johnson, [p], Charlie Drayton, [b], Walter Martin, [d]; **Tympany Five** Freddie Webster, Eddie Roane, Aaron Izenhall, Harold Mitchell, Emmett Berry, [t], Oliver Nelson, [as], Stafford Simon, [cl, as], Josh Jackson, Eddie Johnson, [ts], Arnold Thomas, Wild Bill Davis, Bill Doggett, [p], Carl Hogan, Bill Jennings [g], Al Morgan, Jesse Simpkins, Dallas Bartley, Bob Bushnell, [b], Shadow Wilson, Slick Jones, Joe Morris, [d]; **Bing Crosby**, **Louis Armstrong**, **Ella Fitzgerald**, **Martha Davis** (v). Bear Family Ⓕ BCD 15 557 (nine discs: 562 minutes). Recorded 1938-54.

⑧ ❼

For the majority of Louis Jordan's more casual fans, I am sure the highlights disc (below) will suffice. However, this deluxe boxed set is a monumental achievement by Richard Weize's small Bear Family label. Jordan is always paid lip service for steering a popular new route between the increasingly beleaguered jazz fraternity of the war years and the successively detached popular market, which was becoming ever more reliant on vocalists or novelty records. Without Jordan, Basie, Lionel Hampton and Lucky Millinder it is difficult to imagine the r&b/jump scene evolving out of this morass in quite such a positive way. Of course Jordan had his models (I am sure he learned a lot about entertainment from Fats Waller) and his formulas, but he was always a complete professional, and a highly exciting alto saxophonist to boot.

The Jordan formulas tend to wear thin if you attempt too much of this set at once: the inane lyrics and shuffle rhythms become tiresomely monotonous. But a judicious usage of the box will reveal a cornucopia of music which repays the effort of sifting through the candyfloss. American Decca, of course, recorded all of Jordan's biggest hits, and they are all here. Also included are fascinating vocal duets with Bing Crosby, Louis Armstrong and Ella Fitzgerald (the latter take up disc nine, the only disc which runs under 70 minutes: it was not until the initial compilation was manufactured that Bear Family obtained clearance to include the Fitzgerald duets in the package. There is some 20 minutes worth of them).

The accompanying 48-page booklet is lavish by any standards, and includes a complete Jordan Decca discography plus a long essay with copious photographs, in both colour and mono, many of them very rare indeed. This is a labour of love and deserves our admiration. If you buy this you will never need another Jordan record. **KS**

Five Guys Named Moe **Jordan** (as, ts, v); **Eddie Roane**, **Aaron Izenhall**, **Bob Mitchell**, **Harold Mitchell** (t); **Josh Jackson**, **James Wright**, **Eddie Johnson** (ts); **Arnold Thomas**, **Wild Bill Davis**, **Bill Doggett** (p); **Carl Hogan**, **James Jackson** (g); **Dallas Bartley**, **Jesse Simpkins**, **Billy Hadnott** (b); **Walter Martin**, **Shadow Wilson**, **Eddie Byrd**, **Joe Morris** (d). MCA Ⓜ DMCL 1718 (49 minutes). Recorded 1942-49.

✔ ⑧ ❽

Issued in response to the success of the musical *Five Guys Named Moe*, this compilation focuses on well-known numbers such as *Ain't Nobody Here But Us Chickens, Let the Good Times Roll* and *Saturday Night Fish Fry*—songs that find Jordan at his happiest and most characteristic, playing master of ceremonies at euphoric celebrations of black nightlife. His music is sometimes called jump blues, but its connections with the blues idioms of his day are only occasional. Both the musical forms and the language of his songs display a variety and sophistication few blues artists could command. We may discern closer analogies in the music of small Harlem swing groups of the thirties like Lil Armstrong's, but the more we look for a line that leads to Jordan, the more inexorably we are drawn to conclude that he was *sui generis.* The line from Jordan, on the other hand, is clear to see: without him the early white rock & roll of a Bill Haley is barely imaginable.

Another good, if overlapping, selection from Jordan's Decca years is the budget-priced **Jump Jive!** (Music Club MCCD 085), while many of the songs on **Five Guys Named Moe** are reprised in their fifties Mercury versions on the mid-priced **No Moe! The Greatest Hits** (Verve 512 523-2). **TR**

Marlon Jordan 1970

The Undaunted **Jordan** (t); **Tim Warfield** (ts); **Eric Reed** (p); **Tarus Mateen** (b); **Troy Davis** (d). Columbia Ⓕ CK 52409 (60 minutes). Recorded 1992.

Born in New Orleans, Jordan had the difficult task of following the success stories of Wynton Marsalis and Terence Blanchard. These two excellent trumpet sons of his city had tempted scribes to make overly romantic comparisons with the King Oliver, Freddie Keppard and Louis Armstrong lineage. Jordan has not been fazed by such talk; he made his record début at 18 and was a prominent member of the fine 1991 edition of Jazz Futures. Previous recording dates had shown Jordan as comparatively immature, his solos restricted by his obsessive concern for musical accuracy and devoid of what Lester Bowie called "good wrong notes". This CD is well-titled because it does begin to break down that last barrier. His almost earthy look at Coltrane's powerful *Village Blues* and his angry muted attack on *In and Out* put content before the empty virtuosity that blighted some of his earlier work. The showboater does surface on the ugly *Confrontation*, and his growling solo on *Laurie's Mood* comes over as slightly inappropriate, but this is a young man 'on the up' and he is already exhibiting great flexibility, as well as a widening emotional range. Judging by this, his best CD to date, he seems set fair to make his mark. **BMcR**

Sheila Jordan 1928

Portrait of Sheila **Jordan** (v); **Barry Galbraith** (g); **Steve Swallow** (b); **Denzil Best** (d). Blue Note Ⓜ CDP7 89002 2 (39 minutes). Recorded 1962.

✔ ⑨ ❾

A product of the Detroit school, influenced by Charlie Parker, Jordan studied under Lennie Tristano and was married to pianist Duke Jordan, with whom she often worked in the fifties. This CD was Blue Note's first by a woman singer and it presents her at her best. She is a jazz singer who manages to combine respect for the meaning of the lyrics with an improvisational sense that makes every solo an investigative process. She has a horn player's awareness of phrase formation and delivery, and she uses her skill with note displacement as the key to her ability as a swinger. She makes sparing use of melismatic effects and this is best appreciated by listening to a title such as *Am I Blue?* On this, *When The World Was Young, Willow Weep For Me* and the other slow items, Jordan's smooth projection shows how she spurns the overly decorative. She turns her odd pitch aberration to advantage on *Dat Dere* but swings throughout with genuine accuracy. Her diction is impeccable, her feeling for dynamics excellent and she responds best to this type of small group. Jordan at her best, as she is here, is one of the finest of all female jazz singers. **BMcR**

Stanley Jordan 1959

Magic Touch **Jordan** (g); **Onaje Allan Gumbs** (kbds); **Wayne Brathwaite** (elb); **Charnett Moffett** (b); **Peter Erskine**, **Omar Hakim** (d); **Sammy Figueroa**, **Buggsy More** (perc); **Al DiMeola** (cyms). Blue Note Ⓕ CDP7 46092-2 (54 minutes). Recorded 1985.

④ ❻

This was the album that launched Stanley Jordan on an amazed world. The world was amazed because it thought that nothing new could be done with the guitar, and here was young Stanley retuning the thing in fourths and playing melody lines with both hands by 'hammering on', which gave rise to such contrapuntal effects that the record sleeve begged you not think that anything had been overdubbed. Eventually it transpired that however fast and cleverly Jordan could play, what he was playing was actually a bit old-fashioned and cosy. He was a bit like a footballer who could dribble like a star but not actually get the ball in the goal, and after a few sensational years Stanley dropped out of the public eye. But this record shows you what it was all about, back in those innocent days when a jazz guitarist was thought smart if he kicked off a record with a Beatles song like *Eleanor Rigby*. **MK**

Julian Joseph 1966

Reality **Joseph** (p, kbds, v); **Peter King** (as); **Jean Toussaint** (ts); **Charnett Moffett**, **Wayne Batchelor** (b); **Mark Mondesir** (d). East/West Ⓕ 93024-2 (77 minutes). Recorded 1993.

Although he first came to the jazz listening public's attention in the UK when he played piano on Courtney Pine's commercially successful début album, it was Julian Joseph's stint learning his trade in the US—a trip which culminated in his playing with Branford Marsalis—which seems to have matured him into the talent capable of embarking on what promises to be a highly acclaimed recording career. His band here, centred on fellow Pine alumnus Mark Mondesir and expatriate ex-Messenger Jean Toussaint, but also featuring virtuosic US bassist Charnett Moffett and one of the UK's finest alto players, Peter King, negotiates Joseph's tricky themes—packed with false stops, unexpected time-changes and sudden flurries of helter-skelter improvisation—with great aplomb, but it is Joseph himself who shines. Whether gently exploring the possibilities of a familiar chord sequence—like that of *Body and Soul*—or driving his sparky band through his own thoughtful compositions, Joseph, with his unusual ability to produce modern-sounding jazz without either sacrificing a blues feel or unduly submerging his classical education, proves with his second album that he is among the UK's brightest jazz prospects. A new album of decidedly different character, recorded live at London's Wigmore Hall, will apparently be released before the end of the year. **CP**

Kamikaze Ground Crew

Madame Marie's Temple of Knowledge **Doug Weiselman** (ldr, ss, ts, bs, cl, perc); **Gina Leishman** (ldr, as, bcl, pic, acc, p, toy-p, v); **Steven Bernstein** (t, slide-t, c, flh); **Jeff Crossman** (tb); **Ralph Carney** (as, ts, cl, toy-p); **Bob Lipton** (tba); **Danny Frankel** (d, perc, whistle). New World Ⓕ 80138-2 (62 minutes). Recorded 1991/92.

⑥ ❽

This mainly San Francisco-based septet share a musical catholicity that relates to their experience in multi-media spheres such as theatre and circus work. Individual members have played with Robin Holcomb, Wayne Horvitz, Carla Bley and Peter Apfelbaum, who was on the Crew's previous New World album, **The Scenic Route**. Co-leaders Weiselman and Leishman are reed specialists, although Leishman also plays piano and sings on one track, and the five horns are supported most of the time by a relatively conventional drums and tuba rhythm section. They use jazz sounds and techniques while simultaneously inhabiting Mexican border towns, Weimar Berlin and the Middle East; the result is like a mixture of Charles Mingus and Kate Westbrook. The closing arrangement of *You Are My Sunshine*—one to put alongside George Russell's 1962 version (see below)—is the only piece not written by the co-leaders. The lack of a strong solo voice robs the result of a jazz cachet, although trombonist Jeff Crossman (featured only on the long *Blue Lake Dances*) comes close, but the writing and its performance is convincing and entertaining. **BP**

Richie Kamuca

1930-1977

Tenors Head On **Richie Kamuca** (ts); **Bill Perkins** (ts, bcl, fl); **Pete Jolly**, **Hampton Hawes** (p); **Red Mitchell** (b); **Stan Levy**, **Mel Lewis** (d). Pacific Jazz Ⓜ CDP7 97195 2 (63 minutes). Recorded 1956.

⑥ ❻

Kamuca envied Perkins's ability to play ballads with consummate beauty, whilst Perkins felt that he could not match Kamuca's natural and irrepressible swing. The chance offered by this album to make close comparisons shows that any stylistic weaknesses are at most a matter of fine tuning.

Both men were in thrall to the playing of Lester Young to an even greater degree than their eminent predecessors Stan Getz, Zoot Sims and Al Cohn (Perkins was later to become a Rollins disciple, but public demand forced him to return to his original image). Both had also shone brightly in the ranks of the Woody Herman and Stan Kenton orchestras.

If there is a fault in these typically smooth West Coast sessions it lies in the reticence of the two main exponents to go for the jugular. The result is a tight-knit series of improvisations made the more effective by the outstanding rhythm sections. One wonders how much Young himself would have benefited from such stimulating accompaniment. Amongst a preponderance of up-tempo performances, the slow *I Want A Little Girl* and *Sweet And Lovely* stand out for their beauty. The latter has an effective setting of Perkins's bass clarinet against a high register statement of the theme by Kamuca's tenor. **SV**

Shake Keane

1927

Real Keen **Keane** (flh); **Henry Holder** (kbds); **John Kpiaye** (g); **Dennis Bovell** (b, d machine, kbds); **Angus Gaye**, **Jah Bunny** (d); **Geoffrey Scantlebury** (perc). LKJ Ⓕ CD 001 (37 minutes). Recorded 1991.

⑦ ❻

As befits a man whose nickname is derived from a love of poetry and Shakespeare, Keane is an essentially lyrical trumpeter. He came to prominence in England in the mid-fifties, worked with Joe Harriott and Michael Garrick in the sixties and, in the next decade, moved on to Europe, the Kurt Edelhagen Orchestra and the Clarke-Boland Big Band. He has always led a somewhat Bohemian life and was persuaded to remember his Caribbean roots by a postman he met in Somerset. This CD is the outcome and it shows that its sub-heading *Reggae Into Jazz* is not misplaced. Keane uses the instant throb of reggae as a background and overlays it with a sparkling display of swinging flügelhorn playing. He brings a variety of moods to what is ostensibly a limiting form. On *Gorby Gets Them Going* long drawn out notes lend an arhythmic aspect to a form that is basically rigid; *Tiananmen Square* mixes a little rebellion with a lick of resilience, while *Prague 89* is treated with a sad lyricism. *Rift* is the most angry title, but on this form, Keane would be at home in any musical situation. **BMcR**

Geoff Keezer
1970

Here And Now **Geoff Keezer** (p); **Donald Harrison** (as); **Steve Nelson** (vb); **Peter Washington** (b); **Billy Higgins** (d). Blue Note Ⓕ CDP7 96691-2 (61 minutes). Recorded 1990.

⑧ ❽

Pianist Jeff Keezer is one of the young lions to emerge from the eighties. A winner of the International Association of Jazz Educators Young Talent Award in 1987, Keezer, after a brief stint at Boston's Berklee School of Music, was soon on the road with Art Blakey and the Jazz Messengers. In his Blue Note début, Keezer impresses as much by what is not played as by what actually is. In the leisurely revealing of *Leilani's Mirror*, for instance, the comping behind Harrison and Nelson nudges rather than pushes. His solo breathes with similar spatiality, as does his elegant reading of Rodgers and Hart's *It Never Entered My Mind*, where echoes of Art Tatum build subtly for added drive and extra dimensions.

Keezer, though, is a thorough-going modernist. He has formidable technique as well as a forge of disciplined fires. For his boppish side, check out the provocative stroll through *Scandal In Shinjuku*. For out-and-out Sturm und Drang, there are the tumultuous Tynerisms of *There But For The Grace Of ...* by Harold Mabern. Throughout, bassist Washington and drummer Higgins are exemplary in supporting roles.

Keezer's thoughtfulness and dash are reflected not only in his playing but in such striking compositions as *Headed Off At The Pass* and *Turning Point*, as well as *Leilani's Mirror* and *Scandal in Shinjuku*. **CB**

Roger Kellaway
1939

Fifty-Fifty **Kellaway** (p); **Red Mitchell** (b); **Brad Terry** (whistling). Natasha Imports Ⓕ NI-4014 (50 minutes). Recorded 1987.

⑧ ❻

Jazz duos, rare in the fifties, have become quite fashionable these days, and one of the reasons for this, oddly, is the licensing laws. In Britain you can present a duo without going through the bureaucracy necessary for a trio, which explains all those duos at the Pizza Express over the years, and it seems that New York's weird cabaret laws say something of the same sort—at any rate, this duo was formed for an engagement at Bradley's there, and the result is as good as anything you are likely to hear when bass and piano get together. Kellaway is a sparkling, quirky pianist who is not afraid to do something silly like *Take The A Train* at funeral pace (and it works) or invite someone called Brad Terry to come and whistle on *Doxy* in bop style (and it works). Mitchell does not have quite the mobility that this sort of close quarter encounter demands—it would be great to hear Kellaway with Nils Pedersen or Miroslav Vitous—but he is wonderfully solid and does some nice double stopping. *'A' Train* is the best track, but the opening *Gone With The Wind* is very good and the final *St Thomas* never loses momentum, even when Mitchell is tapping rather than plucking his solo. **MK**

Wynton Kelly
1931-1971

Kelly Blue **Kelly** (p); **Nat Adderley** (c); **Bobby Jaspar** (f); **Benny Golson** (ts); **Paul Chambers** (b); **Jimmy Cobb** (d). Riverside Ⓜ OJCCD 033-2 (57 minutes). Recorded 1959.

⑧ ❽

The vitality of Kelly's piano work is under-recognized these days, even though he had a considerable long-term influence through his recordings with, among others, Miles Davis, Hank Mobley and Wes Montgomery. Maybe he is best appreciated by contrast with front-line instrumentalists, hence his high reputation as an accompanist, but the recent reissue of his early **Piano Interpretations** (Blue Note, from 1951) underlines how individual was his particular slant on bebop piano.

This album was made just after he joined Davis, and takes five selections as trio performances. Here Kelly is responsible for setting up his own contrasts between different themes and between theme and improvisation, while his rhythm-section colleagues of the next seven years abet his surging, inventive approach to standards such as *Do Nothin' Til You Hear From Me* (an addition for the CD edition) and *On Green Dolphin Street*. The remaining three tracks (one a new alternate take) add the three horns and feature an intriguing blend of personalities who seldom worked together. The title-number, later covered by Cannonball Adderley, is slight but brilliantly arranged for the forces available, bringing out everyone's best solos. Throughout the 27 minutes by the sextet, Kelly's driving but responsive accompaniments complement his own featured spots. **BP**

Stan Kenton

1911-1979

Retrospective **Kenton** (p, ldr); with a collective personnel including: **Ray Wetzel**, **Chico Alvarez**, **Buddy Childers**, **Shorty Rogers**, **Maynard Ferguson**, **Conte Candoli**, **Stu Williamson**, **Sam Noto**, **Vinnie Tano**, **Jack Sheldon**, **Marvin Stamm**, **Gary Barone**, **Jay Daversa** (t); **Fred Zito**, **Kai Winding**, **Skip Layton**, **Eddie Bert**, **Harry Betts**, **Milt Bernhart**, **Frank Rosolino**, **Bob Fitzpatrick**, **Milt Gold**, **Kent Larsen**, **Carl Fontana**, **Don Sebesky**, **Dee Barton** (tb); **Gene Roland**, **Ray Starling** (mellophonium); **Gene Roland** (ss); **Boots Mussulli**, **George Weidler**, **Art Pepper**, **Bud Shank**, **Lee Konitz**, **Dave Schildkraut**, **Charlie Mariano**, **Lennie Niehaus**, **Gabe Baltazar** (as); **Red Dorris**, **Vido Musso**, **Bob Cooper**, **Richie Kamuca**, **Zoot Sims**, **Bill Perkins**, **Dave Van Kriedt**, **Sam Donahue**, **Don Menza** (ts); **Bob Gioga**, **Don Davidson**, **Marvin Holladay** (bs); **Laurindo Almeida**, **Sal Salvador**, **Ralph Blaze** (g); **Eddie Safranski**, **Don Bagley**, **Pete Chivily** (b); **Bob Varney**, **Shelly Manne**, **Jerry McKenzie** (d); **Anita O'Day**, **June Christy**, **Nat King Cole**, **Chris Connor**, **Ann Richards**, **Jean Turner** (v). Capitol Ⓜ CDP7 97350-2 (four discs: 263 minutes). Recorded 1943-68.

⑩ ❽

This is the most successful and comprehensive selection from the body of work which Stan Kenton recorded over the quarter of a century which commenced in 1943. It illustrates clearly how Kenton was always anxious to provide a platform for young writers and there are some splendid scores here from Shorty Rogers (*Viva Prado*, *Jolly Rogers*, *Art Pepper*, etc.), Bill Holman, Bill Russo, Gene Roland, Bill Mathieu, Dee Barton, Johnny Richards and, of course, Pete Rugolo who was the 'Strayhorn' to Stan's 'Ellington'. From those opening bars of *Artistry In Rhythm* on the first of the four discs this is music which evokes an era and the tireless dedication of a man. Compiler Ted Daryll has not spared us the occasional failure (there is one movement from Bob Graettinger's over-ambitious *City of Glass* suite) but most of the music has its part in a history of orchestral jazz and the wealth of soloists listed above is an indication of the quality of the improvisers Stan employed to add spice to the arrangements. The four-CD set comes in a box with an 88-page booklet which contains full discographical information, details of soloists and arrangers and a selection of historic photos. Strongly recommended to those looking for an accurate picture of Kenton's music. Well mastered and digitally transferred. **AM**

New Concepts of Artistry In Rhythm **Stan Kenton** (p, ldr, narr); **Conte Candoli**, **Buddy Childers**, **Maynard Ferguson**, **Don Dennis**, **Ruben McFall**, **Bob Fitzpatrick**, **Keith Moon**, **Frank Rosolino**, **Bill Russo**, **George Roberts** (t); **Lee Konitz**, **Vinnie Dean**, **Richie Kamuca**, **Bill Holman**, **Bob Gioga**, (reeds); **Sal Salvador** (g); **Don Bagley** (b); **Stan Levey** (d); **Derek Walton** (perc); **Kay Brown** (v). Capitol Ⓜ CDP7 92865-2 (44 minutes). Recorded 1952.

⑦ ❼

Kenton, the Richard Wagner of big band jazz, was an indefatigable champion of musical extremes. Seemingly intent on organizing the largest, loudest and highest jazz group on the planet, Kenton hit the mark with the 43-piece Innovations In Modern Music Orchestra of 1950. Dismissed for its decidedly unjazzy pomposity, Kenton returned to the 1949 'Progressive Jazz' format with a 21-strong group of all-stars for **New Concepts of Artistry in Rhythm**.

It is a mixed, although always provocative, affair. At one extreme is *Prologue (This is an Orchestra!)*, in which Kenton, portraying a paternalistic despot (i.e. himself), orates a self-important brief on his musical aims; there are also condescending intros for the players which have a godlike omniscience comparable to that of Charlton Heston playing Moses. At the other end, exuberant numbers like Bill Holman's *Invention for Guitar and Trumpet* and Gerry Mulligan's *Swing House* prove that, in spite of the critics, Kenton's bands could swing with the best.

Indeed, the downsizing of the Innovation Orchestra's doggedly determined modernistic approach actually helped make Kenton's 21-piece group texturally leaner and rhythmically more supple. It also created greater elbow room for the band's great soloists, namely Konitz, Kamuca, Ferguson, Rosolino and Salvador. Even some of the overtly 'progressive' tracks, like Gene Roland's *Lonesome Train*, simmer nicely—in this case due to Kay Brown's smouldering vocal. **CB**

Stan Kenton In Hi-Fi **Kenton** (p) with: **Maynard Ferguson**, **Pete Candoli**, **Sam Noto**, **Ed Leddy**, **Vinnie Tanno**, **Don Paladino** (t); **Milt Bernhart**, **Carl Fontana**, **Bob Fitzpatrick**, **Kent Larsen**, **Don Kelly** (tb); **Skeets Herfurt**, **Lennie Niehaus** (as); **Spencer Sinatra**, **Bill Perkins**, **Vido Musso** (ts); **Jack Nimitz** (bs); **Ralph Blaze** (g); **Don Bagley** or **Red Mitchell** (b); **Mel Lewis** or **Shelly Manne** (d); **Chico Guerrero** (perc). Capitol Jazz Ⓜ CDP7 98451-2 (60 minutes). Recorded1956-58.

✔ ⑧ ❽

Like it or not, the group of Kenton musicians who started what was known as 'progressive' jazz in the mid-forties spread out to occupy a considerable area of the West Coast jazz scene, and Kenton continued to create a musical commotion until his death. This disc is a pulling together and a re-creation of the music from the first decade of his career. It is enormously successful, and the massed ranks of Kenton's brasses and saxophones have seldom been better served on a single album. The compositions, many of them the work of Pete Rugolo, are among the best and most memorable of the leader's variable career. All the bombast and pretentiousness is here, but so too is the sheer power and discipline of a great band. Once one accepts that there was a dimension missing from Kenton's music it becomes easier to relax and enjoy it, particularly when as here there is the bonus of some excellent solos from Carl Fontana (the trombone was Kenton's favourite instrument) and section work of a quality not often found elsewhere. **Kenton In Hi-Fi** is a warts and all job, with the leader's cloying piano on the pretentiously-titled *Concerto To End All Concertos* retained in all its full horror. But even this is made acceptable when Maynard Ferguson and the band enter to kick the hell out of the piece. These recordings feature men who solo with an authority which was missing from the inferior bands of Kenton's last decade. **SV**

Robin Kenyatta 1942

Blues For Mama Doll **Kenyatta** (ts); **François Coutourier** (p); **Reggie Johnson**, **François Laizeau** (b); **Jean-Pierre Arnaud**, **Jean-Paul Celea** (d). Jazz Dance Ⓕ (54 minutes). Recorded 1987/89.

⑥ ❼

This curious CD—which does not even possess a catalogue number—collates Kenyatta's performances from two separate sessions in Switzerland. It is produced by Kenyatta, with the 1987 tunes coming from a radio studio session and the 1989 efforts from the Cully Jazz Festival. Kenyatta sticks to tenor throughout (which is a little surprising, considering his long history on the alto), and sounds a good deal like Archie Shepp. In fact, his speech-like inflections on *In Your Own Sweet Way* made me double-take, convinced that in fact this really was Shepp after all.

Kenyatta came to the fore rapidly in the late sixties, and took a memorable alto solo on Bill Dixon's only album as a leader in that decade, **Intents & Purposes**, on RCA of all labels. It indicated a unique talent. Subsequent projects under his own name never quite reached those levels again, and the seventies and eighties saw him spending much of his professional life funkin' it up in much the same manner as another alto original, John Handy, did. Both outings on this disc are in the tradition, and Kenyatta plays with commitment and verve. The backing trios are on both occasions sympathetic and professional, with Coutourier being impressive as a soloist in his own right. But the saxophonist unnerves me: if the emcee did not announce Kenyatta to the audience at the beginning of this disc I would put money on it being Shepp on a good day. **KS**

Barney Kessel 1923

Red Hot And Blues **Kessel** (g); **Bobby Hutcherson** (vb); **Kenny Barron** (p); **Rufus Reid** (b); **Ben Riley** (d). Contemporary Ⓜ CCD 14044-2 (61 minutes). Recorded 1988.

Kessel appeared in the legendary *Jammin' The Blues* film, made by Gijon Mili in 1944. He went on to record with the likes of Charlie Parker and Lester Young, played in several big bands and was a stalwart with Jazz at the Philharmonic. In the seventies he was a vital part of the Great Guitars Group and continued to lead small groups devoted to jazz with a bebop flavour and a cosmopolitan aspect. As this CD shows, Kessel is a sympathetic combo member and a natural improviser who builds his solos with careful attention to their overall symmetry. He has occasionally allowed himself to be trapped in empty virtuoso situations as a weaver of pretty patterns, but here, with a forthright and driving rhythm section and with the creative challenge of Hutcherson to stimulate him, he does not coast for a moment. His uncharacteristically convoluted solo on *Barniana*, his intriguing re-balancing of *You've Changed* and his joyful blues playing on the rollicking *Blues For Bird* are three standout performances from a three-day session which maintained consistently high standards. Kessel is a player who responds to positive musical stimulation and he certainly gets it here. **BMcR**

Steve Khan 1947

Crossings **Khan** (g); **Michael Brecker** (ts); **Anthony Jackson** (elb); **Dennis Chambers** (d). Verve Forecast Ⓕ 523 269-2 (69 minutes). Recorded 1993.

⑥ ❽

One of the unanswered questions of recent jazz history concerns Steve Khan's abrupt metamorphosis in 1981 from the hard-rocking fusion player who produced memorably penetrating work on The Brecker Brothers's **Back To Back** and Steely Dan's **Gaucho** into the relatively low-key small group player heard on this and a host of other records over the past 12 years. Nevertheless, although he has scaled down the intensity of his playing, Khan continues to work the fusion seam, using deep chorussing on his guitar and giving all the numbers here—eight standards and two originals—a Latin treatment. The sense of exoticism is enhanced by the stealthy, tastefully understated playing of fellow former Steely Dan sideman and unsung pioneer of the low bass guitar, Anthony Jackson and by percussionist Manolo Badrena.

One of the hazards of Khan's current style is a tendency for the soft, unfocused sound of his guitar to become cloying after a while, but the presence of Michael Brecker's unfailingly incisive tenor on three tracks adds a contrast missing from hornless albums by the band. **MG**

Carol Kidd

Crazy For Gershwin **Kidd** (v); **Mark Bailey** (c); **David Newton** (p); **Nigel Clark**, **Dominic Ashworth** (g); **Fraser Spiers** (hca); **Miles Baster**, **Peter Markham** (vn); **Michael Beeston** (va); **Ronnie Rae** (b); **Tony McClennan** (d). Linn Ⓕ AKD 026 (56 minutes). Recorded 1993.

⑥ ❻

It is hard to come up with a new or refreshing angle on music as frequently performed as the seven Gershwin tracks that form the core of this 14-track album. Carol Kidd succeeds in doing so, at least in part due to the sensitivity of her accompanists, Ray and Newton (who both solo briefly from time to time, Newton also acting as musical director). The album also benefits from the thought and care that have gone into the settings. Using a pair of acoustic guitars and a harmonica in addition to the basic jazz trio creates a light, springy backdrop for the material, treading a careful path between out-and-out jazz interpretation and a style more suited to the musical stage. On a number of tracks the Edinburgh String Quartet blend effortlessly with singer and regular accompanists, giving the same gravitas in this simple setting as a full string section. The recording is clear and clean, devoid of echo and effect, and Ms Kidd sensibly relies on art not artifice to interpret not only Gershwin but equally distinguished songs by McHugh and Fields, Harold Arlen and Henry Mancini. **AS**

Franklin Kiermyer

1956

Solomon's Daughter **Kiermyer** (d); **Pharoah Sanders** (ts); **John Esposito** (p); **Drew Gress** (b). Evidence Ⓕ ECD 22083 (60 minutes). Recorded c. 1994.

⑦ ❽

Born in Canada, Kiermyer got his first set of drums at 12. Adulthood found him as part of the Montreal jazz scene but, after a period of commuting, he settled in New York. Unsure of the future, he was delighted to be recommended to Esposito. Their partnership rapidly fostered their mutual interests; Kiermyer's quick admiration for John Coltrane (and by inference Elvin Jones and Rashied Ali), became a major factor in his career.

This CD endorses that devotion and points to the importance that Kiermyer places in the jazz of the sixties. His well-established rapport with Esposito and Gress offers flexibility, and his choice of Sanders, an extension of the Trane tradition, is both logical and challenging. Kiermyer wrote all of the material and, although he imbues it with his own personality, he captures the spiritual values established by the Coltrane/Sanders partnership. In some ways he favours the Ali path, but he remains the extrovert musical thespian, acting for the benefit of all. Sanders is free to play with unbridled passion and the music is, in places, powerfully hostile. Kiermyer is looking back to the sixties without nostalgia, selling its intensity from a contemporary sales list. **BMcR**

David Kikoski

Dave Kikoski. **Kikoski** (p); **Essiet Essiet** (b); **Al Foster** (d). Sony Epicure Ⓕ EPC 478174 2 (60 minutes) Recorded 1994.

⑥ ❿

Kikoski has been garnering strong press notice for the past half-decade, after his becoming part of the Roy Haynes band (Haynes appeared on his first release on the Freelance label, **Presage**). This new effort, for the jazz wing of the Epic label, offers brilliant recorded sound, greatly sympathetic companions in Essiet and Foster, and some burning piano playing from the leader (notably on Coltrane's *Giant Steps*). It also features a cover design so appallingly conceived that the record company have had to add a sticker to the jewel-box with the pianist's name on it, so as to help potential buyers spot it in the racks.

Kikoski deserves more than this because, although he is another of the unending stream of pianists whose roots lead back to the triumvirate of Hancock, Corea and Evans, he has great natural flair, considerable harmonic dexterity and imagination, and a sense of excitement at the music which he is creating. All of which makes for pleasant and occasionally moving listening. Maybe the next one will see the breakthrough. **KS**

Morgana King

1930

For You, For Me, Forever More **King** (v); with orchestral accompaniment featuring: **Chauncey Welsch** (tb); **Hank Jones** (p); **Al Caiola**, **Mundell Lowe** (g); **Rick Hayman** (arr). EmArcy Ⓜ 514 077-2 (36 minutes). Recorded 1956.

⑥ ❻

In later years Morgana King's voice has dropped in range, and she has developed a very individual delivery. Yet little in her more recent repertoire transcends this early session, cut before her 25th birthday, where her voice is remarkable for its clarity and perfection. She takes few liberties with line or lyric, and when she does, such as on the gravelly phrase "sweet chickadee" on *It's De-Lovely*, she foreshadows her more recent style. This is clear, uncomplicated cabaret singing, with just enough depth in her girlish talcum-powder voice to avoid the bland. The ambitous restructuring she brought to later songs like her 1963 *Taste of Honey* can only be glimpsed in her style here, but this is one of the better EmArcy vocal albums from the mid-fifties, despite its very short playing time. **AS**

Peter King 1940

Brother Bernard **Peter King** (as); **John Horler** (p); **Dave Green** (b); **Tony Levin**, **Martin Drew** (d); **Alan Skidmore** (ts); **Guy Barker** (t). Miles Music Ⓕ MM CD076 (56 minutes). Recorded 1988-89.

⑧ ❽

From the opening of the very first track, an unaccompanied version of *Yesterdays*, this is clearly the work of a superb and mature jazz musician. Peter King's strength as a soloist lies in the rare combination of a faultless technique with a resourceful and often devious imagination. This enables him to pursue ideas in the most unlikely directions and to continue the pursuit beyond the point at which most others would have stopped. There are many examples here, notably in the Latin-style version of Stevie Wonder's *Overjoyed*.

At the same time, King is a master of the slow-to-medium ballad, playing a melody virtually straight with a little judicious decoration. that elegant but well-worn song *For All We Know* emerges pristine and shining from this treatment. The addition of Skidmore and Barker for the title-track is an extra bonus, since it provides brief examples of the work of two more leading British players. **DG**

John Kirby 1908-1952

The John Kirby Sextet **Kirby** (b); **Charlie Shavers** (t); **Buster Bailey** (cl); **Russell Procope** (as); **Billy Kyle** (p); **O'Neil Spencer** (d); **Maxine Sullivan** (v). Columbia Ⓜ 472184 2 (two discs: 129 minutes). Recorded 1939-41.

⑦ ❽

This best-known line-up of the Kirby Sextet was celebrated for its translations into a 'chamber jazz' style of classical themes from Grieg (*Anitra's Dance*), Chopin (*Minute Waltz*), Dvořák (*Humoresque*) and Schubert (*Serenade, Who Is Sylvia?*), as well as of folk melodies like *Little Brown Jug* and *Molly Malone*. The legacy of these polished performances has been a certain critical impatience: like the Modern Jazz Quartet later, the band has been perceived as too genteel for its own good. Its more polite side is most aptly employed in the accompaniments to *St Louis Blues, If I Had a Ribbon Bow* and four other songs by Maxine Sullivan, a limpid and graceful singer. Considerable skill, much of it Shavers's, went into the group's arrangements, and there is much variety of tone colour. Yet some of the band's instrumental pieces seem to exhibit good manners at the expense of good jazz. Shavers, though a greatly gifted player, tended to tiptoe rather than stride or swagger, muted in both senses, while Procope readily lapsed into parsonical bleating. But when the group had done with its bland drawing-room exchanges and settled to the lively jazz discussions of *Effervescent Blues* and *Jumpin' in the Pump Room*, or the exceptionally vivacious *Front and Center* and *Opus 5* (all written or co-written by Shavers), it became a more daring organization altogether. This French Columbia set is complete for its period: an admirable survey. **TR**

Andy Kirk 1898-1993

Mary's Idea Collective personnel on 18 tracks: **Harry Lawson**, **Paul King**, **Earl Thompson**, **Clarence Trice**, **Harold Baker** (t); **Ted Donnelly**, **Henry Wells**, **Fred Robinson** (tb); **John Harrington**, **John Williams**, **Dick Wilson**, **Earl Williams**, **Don Byas**, **Rudy Powell**, **Edward Inge** (reeds); **Mary Lou Williams** (p, arr); **Claude Williams** (vn); **Ted Brinson**, **Floyd Smith** (g); **Booker Collins** (b); **Ben Thigpen** (d, v); **Pha Terrell**, **Harry Mills** (v); on two tracks: **Harold Baker** (t); **Ted Donnelly** (tb); **Edward Inge** (cl); **Dick Wilson** (ts): **Mary Lou Williams** (p, arr); **Booker Collins** (b); **Ed Thigpen** (d). MCA/Decca Ⓜ GRD-622 (59 minutes). Recorded 1936-40.

⑧ ❽

In the first half of the thirties Andy Kirk led a popular band in the Midwest, operating out of Kansas City, but his band became a much better-known proposition thanks to the records he was asked to make from 1936 onwards. This release concentrates on that period; by this time Kirk had the talented Mary Lou Williams in the band, playing fine two-handed piano as well as writing much of the library. She and tenor saxist Dick Wilson were the band's strongest soloists, a fact borne out here, for this CD contains most of Kirk's best recordings. The ensemble sound is light and attractive, swinging gently in an unforced manner. Pha Terrell, Ben Thigpen and Harry Mills (from the Mills Brothers) have a few vocals but it is the keyboard work of Mary Lou and her most attractive arrangements which lift the band to the heights. Miss Williams was always a forward-looking writer and her *Walkin' And Swingin'*, which opens this collection, contains an ensemble phrase which later became known as *Rhythm-A-Ning* (credited to Thelonious Monk) and *Opus Caprice* (Al Haig). *Baby Dear* and *Harmony Blues* are by a septet comprising the band's soloists and rhythm section made originally under Mary Lou's name, for inclusion in Decca's **Kansas City** album. These are fine examples of small band jazz, with outstanding trumpet from Harold Baker. The audio restoration has been achieved using the NoNoise system, giving a clean, sharp sound, although some tracks seem to cut off in peremptory fashion at the end. **AM**

Rahsaan Roland Kirk

1935-1975

Kirk's Work **Kirk** (ts, mzo, str, f, siren); **Jack McDuff** (org); **Joe Benjamin** (b); **Arthur Taylor** (d). Prestige Ⓜ PR 7210 (34 minutes). Recorded 1961.

✔ ⑨ ❽

Blind from the age of two, Kirk began his musical career as a tenor saxophonist in r&b bands. His main claim to fame—playing three instruments at once—came about while he was still a teenager with his own Vibration Society, a band he led for more than 15 years. As this CD shows, his tenor could range from the forthright on *Makin' Whoopee* to the outright romantic on *Too Late Now*. The manzello, a relation of the soprano, was often his story-telling horn in a piece where the tenor had stated the melody, while the alto-like stritch, heard here on *Skater's Waltz*, was used more sparingly. By structural amendments to the tenor, adroit false fingering and sustained drones, he transformed all three into a one-man saxophone section. On *Funk Underneath*, his flute and growling voice-over effect added another dimension to his playing, and it was one that none of his copyists have ever quite matched, possibly because it is a hopeless task to bring the same degree of spirit and verve to the job that Kirk could manage. As a soloist on a single horn, Kirk would not perhaps have attracted so much publicity, but the three-into-one flights were wholly musical, Kirk was not one given to parading gimmicks, and he was, incidentally, one of the most visually exciting of all jazzmen. He would have won his audience regardless of his choice of instrument. **BMcR**

We Free Kings **Kirk** (f, ts, mzo, str, siren); **Richard Wyands, Hank Jones** (p); **Art Davis, Wendell Marshall** (b); **Charlie Persip** (d). Mercury Ⓜ 826 455-2 (43 minutes). Recorded 1961.

✔ ⑧ ❻

Whenever you sat and watched Roland Kirk, before or after he became Rahsaan Roland Kirk, you could not help wondering if people who had never seen him would ever have any idea of the impact in the flesh or, after his death, whether people could hear on record the sounds he made you hear in person. Even now it is hard to know. When you listen to this early Kirk record it all seems to be there—the growling flute, the three-reed interludes, the moaning and groaning—but do you hear it on the record, or does the record merely act as a nudge to the memory?

I think it is actually all there. The opening blues, *Three For The Festival*, is quite electrifying after thirty years, not so much for Kirk's one-man reed section, though that still gets you smiling and feet-tapping, as for the flute work. His unison blowing and humming still manages to get the hairs on the back of the neck doing a dance, and the stop time solo (which, unaccountably, starts in the fifth bar of a twelve bar blues) is just wonderful. The very slow blues on this record, *You Did It, You Did It*, is only two-and-a-half minutes long, but anyone who can play the blues like that does not need more than two-and-a-half minutes. He was to make bigger and splashier records, but I would hate to be without this one. **MK**

"Rahsaan"—The Complete Mercury Recordings **Kirk** (f, ts, str, mzo, siren); **Kirk Quartet** (Richard Wyands, Wynton Kelly, Andrew Hill, Harold Mabern, Tete Montoliu, Horace Parlan, Jaki Byard, [p], Art Davis, Richard Davis, Niels-Henning Ørsted Pederson, [b], Charlie Persip, Roy Haynes, Walter Perkins, J.C. Moses, Elvin Jones, [d], Sonny Boy Williamson, [hca]; **Orchestra** (Virgil Jones, Richard Williams, Joe Newman, Clark Terry, Ernie Royal, [t], Charles Greenlea, Jimmy Cleveland, Kai Winding, Melba Liston, [tb], Don Butterfield, [tba], Julius Watkins, Bob Northern, Willie Ruff, [frh], Phil Woods, Zoot Sims, James Moody, Budd Johnson, Jerome Richardson, reeds, Harold Mabern, Lalo Schifrin, [p], Kenny Burrell, Jim Hall, [g], Richard Davis, Milt Hinton, Art Davis, George Duvivier, [b], Albert Heath, Osie Johnson, Ed Shaughnessy, [d] **/ Benny Golson**, **Quincy Jones** (arr); **All-Stars** (Virgil Jones, [t], Tom McIntosh, [tb], Tubby Hayes, James Moody, [ts], Walter Bishop Jr, Harold Mabern, [p], Sam Jones, Richard Davis, [b], Louis Hayes, Walter Perkins, [d]. Mercury. Ⓜ 846 630-2 (11 discs: 565 minutes). Recorded 1961-65.

⑩ ❽

This is a boxed set fully worthy of its subject. Roland Kirk (the 'Rahsaan' was not added until after he left Mercury/Limelight and went to Atlantic Records) spent five very fruitful years with the label, and it is arguable that he made his very best albums there, although such gems as **Volunteered Slavery** and **The Inflated Tear**, both Atlantic dates, would also have to be taken into consideration in such a list. When he arrived at Mercury in late summer 1961 he was known locally around New York as the guy who tore it up with Mingus for a few months. By the time he left the label he was an internationally established star. This collection includes such classic albums as **We Free Kings**, **Domino, Reeds and Deeds**, **Meets the Benny Golson Orchestra**, **Kirk in Copenhagen** and **Gifts and Messages** on the Mercury label, and **I Talk with the Spirits**, **Rip, Rig & Panic** and **Slightly Latin** from the Mercury jazz subsidiary, Limelight. The extra material here (and we are truly blessed that it isn't just a case of bucketfuls of alternative takes) comes from a Tubby Hayes album on Smash records (a

Mercury subsidiary), an Eddie Baccus Smash date, three Mercurys and one Limelight album by Quincy Jones, plus a couple more Mercury compilations. The record which is most tellingly fleshed out here is the Copenhagen album. Originally just six tracks were released: here there are no less than 16, covering two whole CDs in the set. Kirk, working with a European band which includes Tete Montoliu and NHØP, and on a couple of numbers jamming furiously with no less a guest than Sonny Boy Williamson, gives the listener some inkling of just what a devastating live performer he was.

Also included here is arguably Kirk's greatest single album, **Rip, Rig & Panic** (see below), plus the exquisite and sadly unappreciated all-flute album, **I Talk With The Spirits**, featuring Kirk's old Mingus ally Horace Parlan, and which includes the nearest thing to a hit Kirk ever had: *Serenade to a Cuckoo*. The booklet which comes with this package is well laid out, and carries a full Kirk Mercury discography. The only thing which annoys me about this set (and it is a mistake repeated on the single-issue version reviewed below) is the mis-spelling throughout of the first track on **Rip, Rig & Panic**, *No Tonic Pres*. Lester Young's nickname has somehow acquired an extra "s" to become "Press". Considering the long explanation of the rationale behind the title from Kirk himself in the original LP liner notes, this oversight is, to put it mildly, baffling. **KS**

Rip, Rig & Panic/Now Please Don't Cry, Beautiful Edith Kirk (ts, f, mzo, str, perc, siren); **Jaki Byard**, **Lonnie Liston Smith** (p); **Richard Davis**, **Ronnie Boykins** (b); **Elvin Jones, Grady Tate** (d). Emarcy Ⓜ 832 164-2 (68 minutes). Recorded 1965-67.

✓ ⑩ ❿

Combining two of the multi-instrumentalist's finest recordings, this compilation is a superb showcase for the unique artistry of Roland Kirk, packed with virtuosic idiosyncrasy but based, as always, on his encyclopaedic knowledge of and enthusiasm for the entire jazz tradition from Fats Waller through Lester Young to Charles Mingus and free music. 1965's **Rip, Rig & Panic** features Kirk with probably the most sympathetic rhythm section he ever encountered; Jaki Byard, a fellow Mingus adherent, is a perfect foil for the leader, equally adept in all modes from stride to avant-garde piano; Richard Davis has a tigerish fluency particularly well adapted to Kirk's approach; Elvin Jones is, by turns, superbly aggressive and delicately controlled. On material ranging from the famous Lester Young tribute *No Tonic Pres* through the multi-referential but strangely homogeneous *From Bechet, Byas and Fats* to the archetypal Kirk stormer *Slippery, Hippery, Flippery*, Kirk produces his customarily unpredictable but peerlessly flamboyant virtuosity on instruments ranging from tenor, through stritch (an archaic straight alto) and manzello (a soprano-type saxophone), to flute, sirens and various percussion instruments, including a breaking glass pane. The result is simply one of the finest recorded group performances in the music, one of the few sessions where everything gels perfectly. The 1967 session, originally released on Verve, is a less stellar affair, but like **Rip, Rig & Panic** ranges through an astonishing variety of jazz forms; a blowsy, slow blues, charming ballads, gospel-influenced material and plaintive laments, all filtered through Kirk's irreplaceably original vision. Both sets are available in The Complete Mercury box reviewed above, but if you want just a single CD of the man, this is it **CP**

The Inflated Tear Kirk (ts, cl, f, eng hn, mzo, str, whistle, perc); **Ron Burton** (p); **Steve Novosel** (b); **Jimmy Hopps** (d); **Dick Griffin**, (tb). Rhino/Atlantic Ⓜ 790045-2 (38 minutes). Recorded 1967.

⑧ ❻

Before the Art Ensemble of Chicago declared its intention to encompass music "from the ancient to the future," decades before Wynton Marsalis and his disciples developed a pan-stylistic historicism spanning old New Orleans and modern modal jazz, visionary Rahsaan had his own inclusive music policy. His 5/8 theme *A Handful of Fives* sounds remarkably Brubecky; *Black and Crazy Blues*, employing english horn and tenor sax, is a funeral dirge that turns into a bar-room blues and back again. On the frothy *A Laugh for Rory*, Kirk plays/sings the distinctive flute multiphonics which have been widely imitated by other jazz and rock flautists (such as Jethro Tull's Ian Anderson). He also anticipates the Art Ensemble by making atmospheric use of little percussion instruments on the title track. As on Ellington's *Creole Love Call*, rendered down and dirty, Kirk roughly harmonizes on two saxes at once, a speciality.

The stylistic range and exuberant execution confirm Rahsaan's expansive sensibility; his able backing trio can follow him anywhere. In a way, Kirk's sophistication, playfulness and receptiveness to many styles would come to be his undoing. His later Atlantic recordings became increasingly r&b oriented; this slick and pretty, raw and powerful date is among his last great sessions. **KW**

Does Your House Have Lions? Kirk (ts, bs, bass sax, str, mzo, flexaphone, cl, f, nose f, pic, t, reed t, eng h, black mystery pipes, hca, whistle, harmonium, perc, music box, bird sounds, v); **Charles Mingus**, **Jaki Byard**, **Hilton Ruiz**, **Trudy Pitts**, **Richard Tee**, **Ron Burton**, **Sonelius Smith**, **Hank Jones**, **Lonnie Smith** (p); **Doug Watkins**, **Henry Pearson**, **Bill Salter**, **Vernon Martin**, **Steve Novosel**, **Ron Carter**, **Major Holley**, **Metathias Pearson** (b); **Robert Shy**, **Bernard Purdie**, **Khalil Mhridi**, **Charles Crosby**, **James Madison**, **Jimmy Hopps**, **Sonny Brown**, **Oliver Jackson**, **Harold White** (d); various horns, strings, and percussion on individual tracks. Rhino/Atlantic Jazz Ⓜ R2-71406 (two discs: 138 minutes). Recorded 1961-76.

⑦ ❽

Rahsaan Roland Kirk was a beloved figure to many musicians and listeners alike, because of his great spirit and humour as well as his enormous energy and improvisational skills. Over the course of his unfortunately abbreviated career he recorded for a number of labels, with varying results. Inevitably, however, his strongest dates were the simplest ones; those on which he was able to draw upon a love and deep knowledge of the jazz tradition while extending it with soulful variations and madcap imagination. His connection with Atlantic Records was the final stage of his career and, Stanley Crouch's persuasive liner note argument notwithstanding, not the most musically rewarding. Much is written here about the "complete freedom" Kirk was given in these sessions, and it is unfortunate that the selection of material on these two discs was apparently meant to impress the listener with the breadth of his conceptions rather than the depth of his playing. For Kirk, jazz was a popular music, and he was able to inject tunes ranging from the commercial (*I Say A Little Prayer*) to the spiritual (*Old Rugged Cross*) with unapologetic power and exhilaration. He had no qualms about appropriating melodies from The Beatles or medieval folk tunes, Stevie Wonder or Dvorák, and finding the humour, pain, and dignity in each. Few could match the sheer expressiveness of his tenor saxophone playing. But there were certainly times when his instrumental prowess could not inspire merely competent sidemen, or invigorate bland material and humdrum arrangements, as is too often the case here, where the choice of performances overemphasizes Kirk's multi-instrumentalism, vaudevillian slapstick, and experimental eccentricities rather than his considerable musical abilities. The result is a view of a wildly expressionistic artist at his most colourful instead of his most profound. **AL**

Kenny Kirkland

1955

Kenny Kirkland **Kirkland** (p, kbds); **Roderick Ward** (as); **Branford Marsalis** (ss, ts); **Charnett Moffett**, **Chris McBride**, **Andy Gonzalez**, **Robert Hurst** (b); **Jeff 'Tain' Watts** (d); **Steve Berrios** (d, perc); **Don Alias**, **Jerry Gonzalez** (perc). GRP Ⓕ 96572 (63 minutes). Recorded 1990.

⑥ ❽

The presence of synthesizers on several tracks might suggest typical GRP sweetening of the jazz pill, but by and large this is uncompromised modern jazz from one of the most consistent American inheritors of the Hancock-Tyner-Jarrett legacy. In any case, notwithstanding his long purist gig with Wynton Marsalis in the early eighties, Kirkland has never made any secret of his timbral promiscuity. Thus here the electronically orchestrated samba *Celia* is sandwiched between *Steepian Faith*, which swings with the stealth of Wayne Shorter's *Deluge*, and *Chance*, a bright, swinging waltz of similar stylistic vintage. Elsewhere, Shorter's *Ana Maria* and Kirlkland's own *Revelations* reveal Kirkland's delicate, introspective side and the brisk *Mr J.C.*, while carrying Shorter's compositional imprint, features strong Coltrane-style tenor from Kirkland's long-time associate Branford Marsalis. Perhaps the freshest playing here is in *When Will The Blues Leave?*, which is fired by Roderick Ward's loose-limbed amalgam of Ornette and Coltrane, and in Monk's *Criss Cross*, arranged as a Latin piece complete with tuned percussion. **MG**

John Klemmer

1946

Waterfalls **Klemmer** (ts, ss); **Mike Nock** (p); **Wilton Felder** (b); **Eddie Marshall** (d); **Victor Feldman** (perc); **Diana Lee** (v). Impulse! Ⓜ MCAD-33123 (41 minutes). Recorded 1972.

⑧ ❽

Critics have often damned Chicago-bred saxophonist John Klemmer with faint praise. Thus, while his technical prowess has been noted, his overall work has often been qualified as "uneven" or "derivative." In this seminal 1972 date recorded live at the Ash Grove in Los Angeles, Klemmer is revealed as a moving player of extraordinary talent and vision.

The first thing one notes is his exceptional use of the echoplex. As employed in the two solo *Preludes*, Klemmer's electrified tenor spews sounds that spill and splash, leaving sonic rainbows suspended in the mist. Equally impressive is his poignant balladry on *Waterfall*. Here, he soars with an ethereality reminiscent of Stan Getz. In the aptly titled *Centrifugal Force*, his tenor explodes outward with Trane-like intensity. On soprano, Klemmer's laser lyricism signals *There's Some Light Ahead*.

Supple fusionistic force fields are energized by electric pianist Mike Nock, electric bassist Wilton Felder, drummer Eddie Marshall, percussionist Victor Feldman, and singer Diana Lee whose haunting vocalese on *Utopia* takes us to a lush, exoticized Eden. At the centre of each vortex is the volcanic lyricism of the estimable John Klemmer. **CB**

Earl Klugh

1954

The Earl Klugh Trio, Volume 1 **Klugh** (g); **Ralphe Armstrong** (b); **Gene Dunlap** (d). Warner Bros Ⓕ 926750-2 (51 minutes). Recorded 1991.

⑦ ❽

Klugh has been at the top of his profession for many years, but little of the music he has played in the past 15 years has had much jazz content: if anything, jazz was used as a flavouring, much as Lee Ritenour was using it. Both guitarists, though, have recently come back to jazz, albeit in very different ways.

This album finds Klugh sticking exclusively to acoustic guitar and well-worn standards such as *Bewitched*, *I'll Remember April*, *Insensatez* and *Too Marvellous for Words*. His playing reminds one of a number of players from an older generation, and in that sense it is a backward-looking album which certainly makes no attempt at all to break new ground. That said, the playing is of a very high standard indeed: Klugh's fabled technique enables him to articulate any idea which comes his way, but more than that, he plays very tastefully at all stages: there is no flash and superficiality, and no obvious catering for people who just want to hear the melody and nothing else. Klugh also communicates a great deal of warmth, and clearly cares deeply for these songs. He is expertly supported in every mood and at every tempo by his colleagues. **KS**

Jimmy Knepper 1927

Special Relationship **Knepper** (tb) with, on seven tracks: **Joe Temperley** (ts, bs); **Derek Smith** (p); **Michael Moore** (b); **Billy Hart** (d); on five tracks: **Bobby Wellins** (ts); **Peter Jacobsen** (p); **Dave Green** (b); **Ron Parry** (d). HEP Ⓕ CD2012 (78 minutes). Recorded 1978/80.

⑧ ❽

Although his name is almost inextricably linked with that of Charles Mingus, it would be a gross inaccuracy to assume that Jimmy Knepper has no other claim to fame. He is, quite simply, one of the most individual of all trombone soloists and certainly one of the most experienced with all manner of bands ("the worse the music, the better they pay" he remarks). This long-playing CD contains nearly all the tracks from two Hep LPs, the first jointly made under the leadership of Knepper and Joe Temperley in New York, the second commemorating a short British tour with Bobby Wellins in 1980. The session with Temperley shares the solo honours fairly evenly and Joe responds to the challenges of pure bebop (*Yardbird Suite*) and the writing of Duke Ellington on *Aristocracy Of Jean Lafitte* (from the *New Orleans Suite* and taken in waltz time) and *Sophisticated Lady*. The rhythm section has the crisp 'New York' sound but the British trio is equally excellent, with well-selected and long bass notes from Dave Green and splendid piano from the underrated Pete Jacobsen. Wellins's unique keening sound makes an ideal foil for the warm-toned, agile trombone of Knepper who came up with three distinctive originals for the date including a Parker-like blues *Gnome On The Range*. The stark *'Round Midnight* is a duet featuring Wellins and Jacobsen. **AM**

Franz Koglmann 1947

L'Heure Bleue **Koglmann** (flh, t); **Tony Coe** (ts, cl); **Burkhard Stangl** (g); **Klaus Koch** (b); **Misha Mengelberg** (p). hatART Ⓕ CD6093 (71 minutes). Recorded 1991.

⑨ ❾

Vienna's Franz Koglmann is now established as one of Europe's most original jazz composers, his reputation confirmed by a series of eighties recordings for hatART that includes **About Yesterday's Ezzthetics** and **The Use of Memory**. His music draws on a huge pool of influences; film, painting and poetry; Webern and Berg; plus, in particular, what he has termed a "white line" of jazz improvisers such as Bix Beiderbecke, Lennie Tristano and Paul Desmond. Their "considered design, lucid coolness, detached lyricism" are qualities that inform the music he plays, whether with his jazz chamber-orchestra, the Pipetet, in various small groups or with guest artists who, on record, have included Ran Blake, Bill Dixon and Steve Lacy.

On **L'Heure Bleue**, his most sophisticated recording to date, he transforms his sources into a seamless personal art that sounds both fresh and mature. Although his primary talent is as a composer, Koglmann proves a fluent soloist too, an elegant foil to the dramatic piano abstractions of Misha Mengelberg on their four duos here. The outstanding voice on the quartet tracks is Tony Coe, particularly for his liquid clarinet on *Monoblue*, *L'Heure Bleue* and *For Bix*. But these are essentially group pieces, with Koch's bass and Stangl's versatile guitar shadings equal partners in Koglmann's thoughtful distillations of jazz and Vienna, twilight and dawn. **GL**

Hans Koller 1921

Out On The Rim **Koller** (sns, ss, ts); **Wolfgang Puschnig** (as); **Martin Fuss**, **Warne Marsh** (ts); **Klaus Dickbauer** (ts, bs); **Bernd Konrad** (as, bss). In & Out Ⓕ 7014-2 (69 minutes). Recorded 1984-91.

⑥ ❽

Viennese-born Koller has been a prime mover on the German jazz scene since the early fifties, playing with a string of top German and visiting American instrumentalists. Since the sixties he has been very

involved in saxophone workshops, so the line-up on this, his latest record and first in a decade, should come as no great surprise. Neither should it be suprising that the level of technical ability is very high amongst all the players here, with precision virtually taken for granted on even the most complex passages. The music tends to the ascetic, with lone, bleak tunes emerging from complex passages and helter-skelter solo lines. Two dedications mark the album like bookends, the music starting with *In Memoriam Stan Getz* and finishing with *Warne Marsh (In Memoriam)*, a 1984 duo with the master saxophonist and his only appearance on the disc.

This music is not easy, but nor is it so wild and woolly as to be an assault on the ears. It is complex, and reveals its subtleties slowly. Have patience and you will be rewarded. **KS**

Klaus König

Time Fragments **Mark Feldman** (vn); **Reiner Winterschladen** (t); **Kenny Wheeler** (flh); **Jörg Huke** (tb); **Michel Godard** (tba); **Robert Dick** (f, pic); **Frank Gratkowski** (f, ss, as); **Matthias Schubert** (ob, ts); **Wollie Kaiser** (ss, bcl); **Stefan Bauer** (mba); **Mark Dresser** (b); **Gerry Hemingway** (d); **König** (cond, arr). Enja Ⓕ ENJ 8076-2 (54 minutes). Recorded 1994.

⑦ ❽

König belongs to a forward-looking tradition in jazz which hasn't had a great deal of encouragement outside of Europe since Stan Kenton hung up his spurs and Don Ellis rediscovered common time. Not that König's music, or his orchestra, sounds much like either of those musicians, but there is possibly a similarity of intent, if nothing else. In a sense it is an Apollonian, intellectual approach gone very skewed indeed, with Dionysian elements constantly being ushered in at the joins. The CD booklet which accompanies this music folds out to something like six times its closed size and is crowded with essays and even diagrams of how the music is structured and how and where its themes interlink and disperse. Conventional musical notation is mostly avoided, and the substitutes become something of an art-form in themselves. The subtitle to the project is **Seven Studies in Time and Motion**. Each but the last piece carries a dual dedication, emphasizing the perceived links between classical and jazz musics—Berg/Mingus; Monk/Bartók; Threadgill/Mahler and so on.

The music when actually listened to becomes something of a collage—not so surprising when you consider what has come before—but the accomplished musicians involved give the music a consistent voice which would be impossible to achieve otherwise. This is music to be closely considered first and reacted to later; which is no bad thing. In the long-postponed wedding between European art music and jazz, this is a positive communication between the two families of the bride and groom. **KS**

Lee Konitz

1927

Subconscious-Lee **Konitz** (as); **Warne Marsh** (ts); **Lennie Tristano**, **Sal Mosca** (p); **Billy Bauer** (g); **Arnold Fishkin** (b); **Shelly Manne**, **Denzil Best**, **Jeff Morton** (d). Prestige Ⓜ OJC186-2 (40 minutes). Recorded 1949/50.

✔ ⑩ ❼

Although he had previously recorded as part of the Claude Thornhill Orchestra, this album, consisting of four separate sessions, was Konitz's first under his own name. The timing was serendipitous; the initial date, with Tristano, Bauer, Fishkin and Manne, took place just a few months before Tristano's legendary Capitol recording, and only days before Konitz waxed with the first of Miles Davis's **Birth of the Cool** sessions. More than 40 years later the results remain spectacular, a slice of jazz history. The effortless manner in which Konitz negotiates the labyrinthine contours of *Tautology* and *Progression* is a tonic; the music combines bebop intricacy with different rhythmic accents and fresh harmonies (*Subconscious-Lee*, based on altered chords to *What Is This Thing Called Love?* has proven especially durable over the years). The next four tunes, with alter-ego Warne Marsh, include telepathic counterpoint and a breathtaking unison on Marsh's treacherous roller-coaster *Marshmallow*. In contrast to such dazzling invention, *Rebecca*, a duet with Bauer's lithe guitar, is an unbroken thread of pure, fragile melody. Blending elements from Benny Carter, Johnny Hodges and Lester Young in the face of Bird, Konitz's fluidity, uninhibited spontaneity and vulnerable, nearly transparent tone set him in good stead for a career of consistently inspired, risk-taking improvisation. **AL**

Live At The Half Note **Konitz** (as); **Warne Marsh** (ts); **Bill Evans** (p); **Jimmy Garrison** (b); **Paul Motian** (d). Verve Ⓜ 521 659-2 (two discs: 97 minutes). Recorded 1959.

✔ ⑧ ❽

For most of his career Lee Konitz has been saddled with a reputation for chilly abstraction. This was undeserved but understandable in view of the contrast between his limpid, unemphatic style and the vehemence of hard bop, which was the height of jazz fashion at the time of this live recording. His style had changed hardly at all since the late forties, when he and Warne Marsh were members of the coterie of young players which clustered around that severe guru Lennie Tristano. Konitz and Marsh had been perfecting their unique form of interplay over the same period, and their act never sounded tighter than it does here. The deftness with which the two of them weave and twine their lines, aided by the impeccable match of their tones, is truly phenomenal. A further recommendation is the rhythm section. Instead of the studied blandness or neutrality of the Tristano school, this team, an early version of the Bill Evans Trio, leans quite hard on the beat, creating a superb feeling of momentum. How this remarkable session came to languish unissued between 1959 and 1994 is a mystery. **DG**

Zounds **Konitz** (as, ss, v); **Kenny Werner** (p, syn); **Ron McClure** (b); **Bill Stewart** (d). Soul Note Ⓕ 121219-2 (55 minutes). Recorded 1990.

⑧ ❽

The one consistent factor in Konitz's chequered career has been his unswerving devotion to improvisation. Whether in cool combo, on the concerts stage or in a free music environment, he has always regarded it as a prime duty to be creative. This CD certainly upholds that principle and, in the sense that much of it champions the ideal of spontaneous composition, it is very much nearer to the Lennie Tristano *Intuition* session in the late forties than to any more obvious source. Known tunes such as *Prelude to a Kiss* and *Taking a Chance on Love* are of special interest, being orthodox extemporizations only in that they start with a known theme. The solos (on the former in particular) follow the changes in a quite devious way, although Konitz is happy to return to them when his own personal meanderings are exhausted. The benchmarks by which the album should be judged are the excellent *Zounds* and *Synthesthetics*, where all four players allow themselves the utmost freedom and in the process produce a collection of extended phrases that could, in their own right, be compositions of the future. Not even on his own *Blue Samba* does Konitz ignore the freedom ethic, and with a rhythm section that involves itself to the extent of being very much more than a rhythm section, he has documented his current career with some style. **BMcR**

Diana Krall

Only Trust Your Heart **Krall** (v, p); **Ray Brown**, **Christian McBride** (b); **Lewis Nash** (d); **Stanley Turrentine** (ts). GRP Ⓕ 98102 (47 minutes). Recorded 1994.

⑥ ❽

Krall is a young Canadian (still in her 20s) but is possessed, on the evidence of this, her second album, with a rare maturity of phrasing and expression both as a vocalist and as a pianist. She is a self-professed fan of all the great pianist-singers, from Fats Waller and Nat Cole to Carmen McRae and Roberta Flack. Indeed, McRae's phrasing is the most obvious model for her vocal style, and she enjoys taking a phrase from a song, then moulding it into an entirely different shape, just as McRae so often does. She remains largely faithful to the contours of a song's melody and is evidently in love with the standards of the thirties, forties and fifties. Her rich alto gives her singing a presence naturally denied lighter-toned women, and she swings without resorting to the Showbiz histrionics so beloved of others. Hence the maturity noted at the outset of this review. Turrentine is a warm and able soulmate for the three tracks on which he appears. **KS**

Wayne Krantz

1956

Long To Be Loose **Krantz** (g); **Lincoln Goines** (elb); **Zach Danziger** (d). Enja Ⓕ ENJ 7099 2 (62 minutes). Recorded 1993.

Wayne Krantz made several impressive if stylistically unexceptional showings as a sideman with fellow guitarist Leni Stern in the late eighties, but on his second album as leader he has stumbled on something quite fresh. You have heard everything here somewhere before—in the wry harmonic abstraction of Scofield's late seventies funk, in a thousand and one country licks, in the Strat rattle of Mark Knopfler, in the riffing of Led Zeppelin—but where it might have seemed no further permutations were possible, Krantz has hammered out a new configuration of the old verities. It is fusion, and one which draws on some quite disparate resources, but thanks to Krantz's assured sense of form, pacing and mood, even the most oblique juxtapositions seem to flow together. His goal was to find a new direction for the time-worn guitar-bass-drums format, and in Goines and Danziger he has two players able to interpret his often demanding, heavily through-written charts with skill and sympathy. The result is an often exhilarating, always intriguing hour of trio music, and, coincidentally, a comprehensive exposition of modern guitar playing. **MG**

Karin Krog

1937

Hi-Fly **Krog** (v); **Charles Greenlee** (tb); **Archie Shepp** (ts); **Jon Balke** (p); **Arild Andersen** (b); **Beaver Harris** (d). Meantime Ⓕ MR3(48 minutes). Recorded 1976.

⑦ ❻

Krog, a Norwegian, first made her name outside her native country in the mid-sixties, making both live appearances and records in Europe which showed her to be a gifted technician and original stylist. She toured in the US in the latter part of that decade and the roots of her enduring reputation in that country were formed then. Around the same time she became associated with some of the more adventurous players in European jazz, and her musical relationship with John Surman dates from this time (she makes decisive contributions to Surman's **Such Winters of Memory**).

This CD is a reissue on her own label of an album on Compendium made largely with Archie Shepp and his mid-seventies band. Her cool and pure voice blends to great effect with the gritty and expostulatory Shepp, and she also gives over generous amounts of room to the band for solos which, on the whole, are well sustained. One of the album's weaknesses is a surfeit of slow numbers, but having said that, its most dramatic track is a curiously intimate a cappella duet rendering by Krog and Shepp of *Solitude*. On it, Krog sticks close to what Billie Holiday did with the song in the early fifties, but her wonderful control and steady tone, allied to Shepp's flutters, produces something else entirely.

An album, perhaps, to listen to in small portions rather than all at once, but there is much to marvel at nonetheless. **KS**

Gene Krupa

1909-1973

Drum Boogie **Gene Krupa** (d, ldr) **and His Orchestra**, including **Norman Murphy**, **Torg Halten**, **Rudy Novak**, **Shorty Sherock** (t); **Pat Virgadamo**, **Jay Kelliher**, **Babe Wagner** (tb); **Clint Neagley**, **Musky Ruffo** (as); **Walter Bates** (ts); **Sam Musiker** (cl, ts); **Bob Kitsis** (p); **Ray Biondi** (g); **Buddy Bastien** (b); **Irene Day** (v); **Jimmy Mundy** (arr). Columbia Legacy Ⓜ 473659 2 (50 minutes). Recorded 1940/41.

⑥ ❻

Krupa left Benny Goodman's employ in spring 1938 and quickly pulled a big band together under his own name. The early sides were short on subtlety and long on drums, but the fans got the message and Krupa's popularity was asssured. His records for Brunswick emphasized the killer-diller approach he had got such praise for when with Goodman. Two years down the line, however, with a change of record company, Krupa finally felt the need to jettison an image which had become something of a straightjacket, where each number had to top the last. This collection reflects that increasing moderation, and although the leader's drums are ever-prominent, the musicianship around him is allowed to blossom and dynamics are carefully observed.

For a man whose visual impact was so enormous, it is always surprising to hear just how much of that flair came across intact on his records. Krupa may have been criticized for being somewhat unsubtle, and at times his work with Goodman could be unswinging, but on this selection there is no doubt about his ability alternately to kick his band along or to ride close behind it, keeping things lightly swinging. Strange that some of his hits are boogies, because the band itself isn't very good at playing boogie or shuffle beat (pianist Kitsis is quoted in the notes as saying "God, but I hated boogie-woogie", and it shows). Still, it helped keep his name in front of an adoring public, and Krupa was able to keep his unoriginal but accomplished band successful, just as Chick Webb had with nursery rhymes a couple of years previously. Soon after the last session on this CD was recorded, Roy Eldridge and Anita O'Day were to join the band and give it a completely new lease of life. **KS**

Compact Jazz **Krupa** (d); **Roy Eldridge** (t, v); **Joe Ferrante**, **Nick Travis**, **Dizzy Gillespie**, **Bernie Glow**, **Al De Risi**, **Ernie Royal**, **Doc Severinson**, **Al Stewart**, **Marky Markowitz**, **Charlie Shavers** (t); **J.J. Johnson**, **Kai Winding**, **Jimmy Cleveland**, **Fred Ohms**, **Willie Dennis**, **Urbie Green**, **Frank Rehak**, **Eddie Bert**, **Billy Byers**, **Bill Harris** (tb); **Sam Marowitz**, **Phil Woods**, **Hal McKusick**, **Willie Smith** (as); **Aaron Sachs**, **Eddie Shu**, **Eddie Wasserman**, **Al Cohn**, **Frank Socolow**, **Ben Webster**, **Eddie Davis**, **Illinois Jacquet**, **Flip Phillips** (ts); **Danny Bank** (bs); **Dave McKenna**, **Ronnie Ball**, **Hank Jones**, **Teddy Wilson**, **Bobby Scott**, **Oscar Peterson** (p); **Barry Galbraith**, **Herb Ellis**, **Steve Jordan** (g); **John Drew**, **Jimmy Gannon**, **Israel Crosby**, **Red Callender**, **Wendell Marshall**, **Ray Brown** (b); **Anita O'Day** (v); **Lionel Hampton** (vb). Verve Ⓜ 833 286-2 (59 minutes). Recorded 1953-58.

⑥ ❻

Krupa's slick on-the-beat drumming was an essential part of the Benny Goodman band and the Swing Era in general. Four of these tracks are by studio-assembled orchestras re-creating Gene's past glories with exciting versions of *Drummin' Man* and *Let Me Off Uptown* featuring Anita O'Day and Roy Eldridge. The two Gerry Mulligan arrangements are less successful, due largely to Krupa's inappropriate drum accents, but there are good solos by Phil Woods, Cohn and Wasserman. There are two over-long and tedious tracks with 'killer-diller' drum solos in which Eddie Shu is almost superfluous (but Shu is excellent in a Lester Young-inspired solo on *Hippdeebip*). The rest is very worthwhile small band material with fine solos from Ben Webster, Eddie 'Lockjaw' Davis, Shavers, Bill Harris and Wilson. *Just You Just Me* is a 'Goodman-less' quartet on which Gene is joined by Teddy Wilson and Lionel Hampton for an exciting whiff of nostalgia. The closing *Gene's Blues*, although recorded in a studio, has a Jazz At The Philharmonic type of group and atmosphere with solos from Jacquet, Eldridge, Phillips and Gillespie (in that order; the notes fail to identify soloists), urged on by Gene and the Oscar Peterson Trio. **AM**

Joachim Kühn 1944

Live **Kühn** (p); **J.F. Jenny-Clark** (b); **Daniel Humair** (d). CMP Ⓕ CD43 (57 minutes). Recorded 1989.
⑧ ❽

A classical pianist until he was 17, Kühn later worked in the jazz company of Eje Thelin and Jean-Luc Ponty in Paris and spent some time in the seventies and eighties in New York. His more recent recordings have been in Europe and none better than with the excellent trio heard on this CD. It is a virtuoso performance by three outstanding musicians; it has a power that is electrifying, it sets daunting, creative standards and is performed by three men confident in their own ability. Jenny-Clark, like Kühn, has been involved in music outside the jazz field but he dovetails effortlessly with the ever-flexible Humair, who was actually a Dixielander in his youth. If there is a reservation about the prodigious Kühn, it is that his eclecticism occasionally leaves the listener unsure of his true métier. He is comfortable with bop but there are times when his modal forays take him into an impressionistic maze. Only *Guylène* hints at this on this CD and, for the main part, it is easy to appreciate the audience's enthusiasm for a session that must have thrilled all at the Théâtre de la Ville in Paris. **BMcR**

Steve Kuhn 1938

Oceans In The Sky **Kuhn** (p); **Miroslav Vitous** (b); **Aldo Romano** (d).Owl Ⓕ 056CD 3800562 (57 minutes). Recorded 1989.
⑥ ❽

The impenetrable purple-on-black printing on the back of the CD case would be a poor inducement to investigate any recording, but those with a taste for elegant yet often impassioned piano trio music should not be discouraged; the packaging may be obtuse, but it is no reflection on the clarity and colour of the music it contains. The session's treasures are revealed a few minutes into the opening number, Ivan Lins's *The Island*. Kuhn first came to attention in John Coltrane's quartet (he preceded McCoy Tyner) and he has also enjoyed a long creative friendship with Sheila Jordan. On ths album Kuhn at first plays with a precision and lyricism which reflect his rigorous classical training and his taste for Erik Satie, Bill Evans and the like, but as his beautifully contoured solo gathers pace, he produces muscular, probing, intensely swinging right hand lines in the style of Bud Powell. There is more of the same, but faster, and worrying the piano's highest octave at length, on the following item, Kenny Dorham's *Lotus Blossom*. Several other tracks, hewing a gentler line, are less substantial, and Carlos-Jobim's *Angela* offers more than a glimpse of Kuhn the cocktail pianist. But when he is good, he is compelling, and his pursuit of the perfect swing is hardly hindered by the presence of two deft and sympathetic colleagues. **MG**

Charles Kynard

Reelin' With The Feelin'/Wa-Tu-Wa-Zui **Kynard** (org, elp); **Wilton Felder** (ts); **Joe Pass, Melvin Sparks** (g); **Carol Kaye, Jimmy Lewis** (b); **Paul Humphrey, Idris Muhammed, Bernard Purdie** (d); **Virgil Jones** (t); **Rusty Bryant** (ts). Beat Goes On Ⓜ CDBGPD 055 (74 minutes). Recorded 1969/70.
⑤ ❻

Kynard, along with many others, carved a career for himself playing funky organ at the end of the sixties, usually with some form of backbeat, and with a liberal helping of blues changes. At the time these two albums were recorded jazz was under seige, and most journeymen players like Kynard were attempting to appeal to the younger audience in the hope of achieving financial survival. So their usual riffs and routines were dressed up in quasi-soul or rock forms (a lot of this music is only one step away from King Curtis sessions, or James Brown without the vocals). It was only the improvisations which pushed this music into the jazz arena. Indeed, on the first date, Wilton Felder plays thoroughly contemporary tenor, unafraid to acquaint his listeners with subtle harmonic routes through dead-ordinary changes. Joe Pass, on the other hand, pretty well capitulates to the simplistic approach, and does it half-heartedly, too, only shining when given a bossa beat and the more sophisticated harmonic basis of *Be My Love* to solo over.

The second date is painfully under-rehearsed, with Jones and Bryant often unable to phrase together on the simple song 'heads'. Kynard has, meanwhile, moved closer to out-and-out soul, and much of this date could have been played by Junior Walker and The All-Stars. The use of Melvin Sparks instead of Pass accelerates this process. Of all the players here, predictably only Jones plays with what could be called a jazz inflection and awareness of passing tones. Kynard's electric piano playing robs him of his usual energy and shows his musical thought to be essentially unoriginal. I would imagine that, today, this would be music to dance to in clubs, so things have come full circle. It serves its purpose, and when Felder or Jones solos occasionally surpasses it. **KS**

Dean Laabs

Invisible Maniac **Laabs** (t, evi); **Jeff Song** (elb, kayagum, g); **Matt Turner** (vc, kbds; **Dan Stein** (kbds); **John Mettam** (perc). Asia Improv. Records Ⓕ AIR 0018 (73 minutes). Recorded 1993.

⑤ ❽

The playing of Laabs and Song could be seen as belonging to a less than clearly defined musical genre. Academically trained, experienced in jazz, contemporary improvised music, rock and its many relatives, they are producing music drawing from all of these sources. Laabs served as a composer/artist in residence in his hometown Wisconsin before moving to the Boston area. He has been playing throughout New England since 1988 and his partnership with Song has proved to be very fruitful.

This challenging CD has its slightly pretentious lows in the rock-style prevarications of *Lucy, Lucy Talkin' Twice* and in the static percussion interlude on *Namu*, but these are balanced by some fine trumpet by the joint leader. He has a distinctive tone and is at his best when he allows his lyricism to carry through his harmonically liberated solos. On *Parting With Regret*, he conjures up a mood of plaintive resignation and, although he essays little in the way of overt passion, there is a soulfulness in all he does. The atmospherics of *The Canal* are unconvincing but this is primarily clean-lined free jazz with the emphasis on control. Drummer Mettam's occasional journeys into the frenetic are isolated and irrelevant, but this is New Age music with attitude. **BMcR**

Steve Lacy

1934

The Straight Horn of Steve Lacy **Lacy** (ss); **Charles Davis** (bs); **John Ore** (b); **Roy Haynes** (d). Candid Ⓜ CD 9007 (37 minutes). Recorded 1960.

⑦ ❽

At the time this record was made Steve Lacy was one of the very few soprano players around, and also one of the few players (white or otherwise) to enlist enthusiastically under the colours of Monk and Cecil Taylor, composers of all bar one of the tunes on this CD. What was most extraordinary about this allegiance was that Lacy had come almost directly from the ranks of the Dixielanders in converting to this new music, and it shows in his playing. Not that he has any Dixieland licks in his solos; rather that he has no preconceptions about how to play modern. His somewhat inconsistent front-line partner, the baritone player Charles Davis, has a whole range of bop mannerisms to offer which now sound almost quaintly dated, but nobody had taught Lacy the tricks of the trade, so you get on this record a rather rare sound in jazz; someone working it out for himself how he should sound. The effect is cerebral, but fascinating, as he carves his way into the unknown, almost deliberately choosing the notes en route, using his musical intelligence and not his reflexes. Worth hearing, even at this distance from the event. Roy Haynes's drumming, especially on *Air*, is crisp and attentive. **MK**

School Days **Lacy** (ss); **Roswell Rudd** (tb); **Henry Grimes** (b); **Dennis Charles** (d, perc). hatART Ⓕ CD 6140 (55 minutes). Recorded 1963.

Following his comparative success with synthetic Dixieland, Lacy spent two years studying and playing with avant-garde guru Cecil Taylor. He had, however, always been fascinated by the work of Thelonious Monk and had welcomed the chance to join him in the early sixties. Monk's lessons were delivered on site and for Lacy it became another graduate course. It was perhaps inevitable that the group he led from 1961 to 1964 should mine this rich field of music and the appropriately-titled **School Days**, with its full programme of Monk compositions, documents the changes that were accommodated within Lacy's style.

Themes were approached in a straight manner, but both Lacy and Rudd take more liberties than is usual in readings of Melodious Thunkery. Rudd's bucolic ramblings on *Brilliant Corners* and *Monk's Mood*, the almost folk-like quality of Lacy on *Monk's Dream* and the jaunty gait of both on *Bolivar Ba-Lues-Are* suggests that Dixieland experience attended the range of expression they used. In support Grimes gives a fine exhibition of 'changes' bass playing and Charles keeps time surefootedly. For Lacy it proved to be a natural launching pad for the next stage of his career: his take-off into even freer musical areas. **BMcR**

Futurities **Lacy** (ss); **Steve Potts** (as, ss); **George Lewis** (tb); **Jef Gardner** (p); **Gyde Knebusch** (hp); **Barry Wedgle** (g); **J.J. Avenel** (b); **Oliver Johnson** (d, perc); **Irene Aebi** (v). hatART Ⓕ 6031/32 (46 and 50 minutes: oas). Recorded 1984.

✔

⑩ ❿

As a soprano saxophonist, Lacy is a lone wolf; much of his most striking work has been solo, in edgy duos with Derek Bailey, Maarten Altena, Evan Parker, Waldron, or interactive small groups. For these he has written countless tunes, with chiselled melodies and deceptively simple, cagey structures. But there is a lesser-known, more ambitious side to his composing too, that includes a song cycle on Russian poems (*Rushes*); large ensemble scores (*Itinerary*); and this extended song cycle on poems by the American poet Robert Creeley. The epigrammatic concision, double meanings and veiled mysteries of Creeley's verse are tailor-made for the twists and transformations of Lacy's intricate lines. In an interesting reversal of the usual procedure, the words often set the tone for solos, not vice- versa, with George Lewis's versatile trombone an especially articulate voice. Loaded with irony, seduction and bittersweet emotions, the music and words are fully integrated, sustained from song to song by an indivisible palette of instrumental colours and textures—canny use of the harp, guitar, piano, and percussion. Irene Aebi plays Lotte Lenya to Lacy's Kurt Weill; she interprets his settings with nuance and determination. There's nothing like **Futurities** anywhere else in jazz. **AL**

Remains **Lacy** (ss). hatART Ⓕ CD 6102 (64 minutes). Recorded 1991.

⑨ ❾

Lacy began playing solo in 1972 after hearing Anthony Braxton's **For Alto**, the first-ever album of solo saxophone music. Together with Braxton, Roscoe Mitchell and Evan Parker, he has become one of the outstanding solo saxophone recitalists in contemporary jazz, although unlike the other three he has not developed a specifically 'solo music', preferring to play solo versions of tunes he also performs in other contexts.

Remains is a fine exhibition of his solo skills, its stark beauty traversing a typically varied set of material. *Tao* is Lacy's earliest surviving piece, a six-part suite begun in 1967 and still in the process of "elaboration and realization". Its evolution exemplifies his modus operandum of building improvisations around a structural germ, often a simple sing-song phrase (as on *Bone* here), then reworking the music—adjusting the pulse, reshaping the contours—until all its possibilities have been teased out.

A second long piece, *Remains*, is mostly notated and "explores the nature of decay", its austere poetry showing why Lacy has been called "the Samuel Beckett of the soprano saxophone". *Afterglow*, a bright Kansas City blues, and *Epistrophy* reveal his friendlier aspects, the latter a happy example of his gift for refashioning Monk tunes to often brilliant effect (see too his Soul Note discs **Only Monk** and **More Monk**) **GL**

Guy Lafitte

1927

Joue Charles Trenet **Lafitte** (ts); **Marc Hemmeler, Hank Jones** (p); **Milt Buckner** (org); **Jack Sewing, George Duvivier** (b); **Philippe Combelle, Sam Woodyard, J.C. Heard** (d). Black & Blue Ⓕ 59 190 2 (55 minutes). Recorded 1977-84.

⑥ ❽

Lafitte has never had to rely on music for a living, and he seems to have recorded only when attracted by the musical company or intrigued by the concept. For all that, his work on record does not offer the rewards his abilities promise. Probably his most satisfying album is this programme of songs associated with the much-loved French singer Charles Trenet, not least because the unfamiliarity of the tunes as jazz vehicles allows the listener to concentrate, without the distraction of recognizable procedures, on his sensitive and at times ravishing explorations. His playing recalls Coleman Hawkins yet his approach is drier, more restrained in expression, less rhapsodic. The core 1984 session with Hemmeler, Sewing and Combelle is augmented by three 1977 tracks with Buckner and Woodyard and one from 1978 with Jones, Duvivier and Heard. The seventies readings of *Bonsoir Jolie Madame* and *Que Reste-t-Il de Nos Amours* (which, translated, became *I Wish You Love*) find Lafitte wrapping the notes with Ben Websterish breaths, and they have an air of wistfulness absent from the more trenchant versions of 1984. Apart from the bright *France Dimanche* the prevailing tempo is that of the ballad, and this seems to be where Lafitte is happiest. **TR**

Bireli Lagrene

1966

Standards **Lagrene** (g); **Niels-Henning Ørsted Pedersen, Dominique DiPiazza** (b); **André Ceccarelli** (d). Blue Note Ⓕ CDP7 80251-2 (69 minutes). Recorded 1992.

⑧ ❽

French guitarist Bireli Lagrene is a young master of the neo-bop mainstream. Initially influenced by his guitarist father and grandfather as well as his family's gypsy background, the seven-year-old Bireli came under the sway of the idiosyncratic style of Django Reinhardt. As a teenager, he played with swing legends Benny Goodman, Stephane Grappelli and Benny Carter; at the other end of the stylistic spectrum he also helped stoke the jazz-rock fires of Jaco Pastorius.

Here, in a stunning 1992 session with virtuoso bassist NHØP and dynamic drummer Andre Ceccarelli, Lagrene adds sheen to a set of glistening standards which includes *Softly, As In a Morning Sunrise*, *Stella by Starlight* and *Ornithology*. In contrast to many recent 'standards' projects, Lagrene hews closely to each tune's original melodic and harmonic contours; yet, with his unflagging inventive flow and sensitivity to shadings of timbre, texture and dynamics, the guitarist gives each tune a fresh, 'first-time-through' feel. Lagrene is a virtuoso capable of non-stop torrents of precisely structured tones. At heart, though, he is a romantic whose medium is a music that breathes deeply. He also possesses one of jazzdom's most beautiful guitar sounds, and one which is comparable to the late Jim Hall's. **CB**

Cleo Laine

1928

Blue And Sentimental **Laine** (v); **John Dankworth** (as, ss, cl); **Ray Loeckle** (ts, ss, fl); **Allen Smith** (t); **Dean Hubbard** (tb); **Larry Dunlap** (p, syn); **Mike Renzi** (p); **Mark Whitfield** (g); **Rich Girard**, **Jay Leonhart** (b); **Jim Zimmerman**, **Keith Copeland** (d, perc); string section. Guest soloists: **Gerry Mulligan** (bs); **George Shearing** (p); **Joe Williams** (v). RCA Victor Ⓕ 61419-2 (60 minutes). Recorded 1994.

⑧ ❽

This CD was released almost 40 years after the first album under Cleo Laine's name (**Cleo Sings British**, 1955). In that time she has pursued several parallel careers in jazz, acting, opera, song recitals and stage musicals. She has also made many excellent records, but this is the equal of almost any of them. The programme is typically wide-ranging, from a sentimental waltz by Irving Berlin (*What'll I Do?*) to a piece of late-eighties metropolitan cynicism by Francesca Blumenthal (*The Lies Of Handsome Men*), by way of Ellington (*Creole Love Call*) and Duncan Lamont (*Not You Again*). As always, her interpretation is calculated to convey an exact and minutely-detailed reading of the words, while at the same time keeping the vocal line free and airborne. The arrangements are by John Dankworth and, just like the ones of 40 years before, they are delicate, swinging and clever. Appearances by the guest stars are discreet and appropriate—two each for Mulligan and Shearing and one for Joe Williams. For another aspect of Cleo Laine, more loosely connected with jazz and sometimes hardly at all, I would recommend **Wordsongs** (Philips 830 461-2), which contains, among other things, her Shakespeare songs and poem settings. **DG**

Oliver Lake

1942

Compilation **Lake** (saxes); **Geri Allen, Frank Abel** (p); **Fred Hopkins, Santi De Briano, Billy Grant** (b); **Anthony Peterson, Alphonia Tims** (g); **Pheeroan akLaff, Andrew Cyrille, Gene Lake, Brandon Ross** (d); **Jawara** (perc). Gramavision Ⓕ GV 79458-2 (63 minutes). Recorded 1982-88.

⑨ ❽

Another student from St Louis' Black Artist's Group, Lake is probably best known for his involvement in the seventies loft movement and his pre-eminent role in the World Saxophone Quartet. This CD presents a selection from four previously issued albums and spans a period of six years. *Sun People*, from the 1982 **Jump Up**, shows that a jaunty funk base is not the ideal environment for his carousing free lines. In contrast, *France Dance*, from the 1986 **Gallery**, reassures the listener that there is nothing wrong with jauntiness if that climate is created by Allen, Hopkins and akLaff, and Lake is in a strongly creative mood. The Dolphy-like *Olla's Blues,* from the same date, offers Lake's more laid-back character and, like *Gano Club* from the 1988 **Otherside** date, shows how he makes judicious use of bluesy distortion. *We're in the Moment* is the pick of the 1987 **Impala** release, and it takes him on a chromatic path, one which is populated by more devious harmonic turns. The selection of titles is excellent and judged as a whole this CD accurately introduces newcomers to a man who knows how to balance his playing between a search for melodic freedom and a loyalty to the structural limits of a theme. **BMcR**

Lambert, Hendricks & Ross

Sing A Song Of Basie **Dave Lambert, Jon Hendricks, Annie Ross** (v); **Nat Pierce** (p); **Freddie Green** (g); **Eddie Jones** (b); **Sonny Payne** (d). Impulse! Ⓜ GRP 11122 (31 minutes). Recorded 1957.

⑧ ❽

In 1957 Lambert, Hendricks and Ross undertook a project to sing the instrumental parts of certain Count Basie compositions in the company of ten other singers. In the event the exercise failed, but the three prime movers decided to do the job on their own. This CD shows how, with the aid of multi-tracking, they succeed in following the Eddie Jefferson and King Pleasure tradition of fitting words to horn sounds. The very positive nature of the arrangements used by the Basie orchestra of the period helped enormously and the sheer musicality of the LHR team ensured a successful outcome. The support players used were ideal, with Pierce on piano and the unit completed by Basie's then-current rhythm section. All of the 'lyrics' save for *Everyday* were written by Hendricks, and for their part the singers managed to reproduce the demanding twists of horn techniques with surprising ease. Highlights of their vocalese performances are Hendricks's reading of Wardell Gray's *Little Pony*,

Ross's Buck Clayton trumpet part on *Fiesta in Blue* and Joe Newman's trumpet on *Down For The Count*, but the full ensemble, with their brass 'shakes' and superbly sighing reeds, are handled with equal skill. Were these singers the forerunners of today's rappers? **BMcR**

Byard Lancaster 1942

Worlds **Lancaster** (ss, as, ts, bcl); **Alfie Pollitt** (p); **Jim Dragoni** (g) **Kenny Davis** (b); **Webb Thomas** (d); **Keno Speller** (perc). Gazell Ⓕ GJCD 4005 (49 minutes). Recorded 1992.
⑥ ❻

Lancaster followed a familiar path for those who came to their first maturity in the sixties. After completing music studies in Boston and New York, he embraced the burgeoning New York avant-garde scene, appearing and recording with, among others, Bill Dixon, Sunny Murray and Sun Ra. The seventies saw a considerable retreat across a whole range of radical music activities, the jazz avant-garde being no exception, and Lancaster came to rest for six years in the McCoy Tyner group. This was clearly a formative experience, because the Tyner/Coltrane stylistic axis, leavened with borrowings from the James Brown brigade, Caribbean music and by his own past playing, has remained the core around which his playing revolves.

This is demonstrated here by his opening the CD with a spirited eight-minute version of *My Favourite Things*. However, he goes on to encompass funky blues, funk and bop into the mixture, so by the end we have a pretty clear view as to where Lancaster stands today. There is even a solo soprano piece, *Internal Security*. The musicians on **Worlds** are largely from Lancaster's home town of Philadelphia, and have long been his associates, so there is a high degree of unity in their playing. **KS**

Harold Land 1928

Harold In The Land Of Jazz **Harold Land** (ts); **Rolf Ericson** (t); **Carl Perkins** (p); **Leroy Vinnegar** (b); **Frank Butler** (d). Contemporary Ⓜ OJCCD 162-2 (48 minutes: AAD). Recorded 1958.
⑧ ❻

At this period Harold Land's tone, articulation and turn of phrase were all instantly recognizable—similar in some ways to Hank Mobley but with more edge to the sound. Later, like so many others, he fell under the influence of John Coltrane and his playing lost some of its sly charm. As Dr. Johnson said of Milton, it is better to admire Coltrane than to imitate him.

This disc (a CD transfer from the original LP, with one additional track) catches Land at his best and most characteristic. Among other attributes he had the knack of making interesting shapes out of mid-tempo tunes in minor keys, something which eluded many of his contemporaries. There is a splendid example here in *Grooveyard*. This set also contains one of Land's best slow ballad performances, *You Don't Know What Love Is*, in the course of which he grows positively expansive. The Perkins-Vinnegar-Butler rhythm section, working as a semi-regular team, was one of the best on the West Coast at the time, while Rolf Ericson's bright and nimble trumpet provides a perfect foil for Land. **DG**

Eddie Lang 1904-1933

A Handful Of Riffs **Lang** (g); with a collective personnel of: **King Oliver** (c); **Leo McConville** (t); **Tommy Dorsey** (t, tb); **Bill Rank** (tb); **Jimmy Dorsey** (cl, as); **Izzy Friedman** (cl, ts); **Hoagy Carmichael** (p, cel, perc); **Arthur Schutt, Frank Signorelli, J.C. Johnson** (p); **Lonnie Johnson** (g); **Joe Tarto** (b); **Stan King** (d). ASV Living Era Ⓜ CD AJA 5061 (64 minutes). Recorded 1927-29.
⑧ ❽

Lang is, beyond argument, the first great guitarist in jazz. There is a case for going further and calling him the first great guitarist in American popular music, and most of the exhibits required for putting that case are on this record. The first half is concerned less with the values of improvisation or hot jazz than with material that reveals Lang's technical powers as a guitarist: the masterly shaping of notes, his practically faultless fingering and immense chordal vocabulary. The Rachmaninov *Prelude* and the standard songs *Jeannine* and *There'll Be Some Changes Made* are performances without fireworks yet full of light, space and grace.

Lang's most startling recordings—and they are still that, 65 years later—are the duets with blues guitarist Lonnie Johnson. In *Bullfrog Moan* Lang's low chords evoke froggy plops and croaks, while in the faster title track and *Two-Tone Stomp* the players maintain interdependent lines of some complexity with enormous élan. Their comparative restraint on the quartet sides *Jet Black Blues* and *Blue Blood Blues* tactfully supports the simple, affecting blues cornet of King Oliver.

The selection concludes with five band numbers featuring some of New York's leading jazz professionals at their most trenchant, Tommy Dorsey contributing a remarkably low-down trumpet solo to *Hot Heels*. Lang's rhythm playing is, as always, exemplary. He died before he was thirty, a less resonant and romanticized fate than his contemporary Bix Beiderbecke's, but perhaps not much less of a loss to jazz. **TR**

Don Lanphere

1928

Go Again **Lanphere** (ss, ts); **Jon Pugh** (t); **Jeff Hay** (tb); **Marc Seales** (p, syn); **Chuck Deardorf** (b); **Dean Hodges** (d); **Jay Clayton** (v). Hep Ⓕ HEP2040 (63 minutes). Recorded 1987-88.

⑧ ❽

Lanphere has had two separate careers with the first coming to an abrupt halt in 1951 when he was arrested for heroin addiction. Prior to that he had been active in New York jazz circles and had done two recording sessions with Fats Navarro, the second of which produced the tunes *Stop* and *Go*. After running the family music business he emerged from his native Washington State in 1982 with a fine band of comparative youngsters (heard here) and has made a number of albums for release on the Hep label. *Go Again* harks back to the Navarro session and is a brisk workout on the chords of *The Way You Look Tonight*, with assured solos by everyone. Pugh in particular is in spectacular form throughout, constructing fleet trumpet lines which lift the excitement level on the faster tempos. Jeff Hay was a late arrival and caused Lanphere to enlarge his quintet and add trombone parts to his arrangements. Eight of the 11 tracks are by the sextet and *Darn That Dream* is by just tenor, bass and Jay Clayton, who succeeds in staying perfectly in tune. Lanphere has taken considerable care in producing an album which gets well away from the ordinary, and older jazz enthusiasts will be pleased to know that the occasional hints of Parker and Lester Young show that Don has not forgotten that first career phase.
AM

Ellis Larkins

1923

A Smooth One **Larkins** (p); **George Duvivier** (b); **J.C. Heard** (d). Black & Blue Ⓕ 59 123 2 (52 minutes). Recorded 1977.

⑥ ❻

Larkins has always succeeded in keeping a relatively low profile both at the keyboard and in terms of the availability of his records. He will be remembered by many for the successful LPs he made with Ella Fitzgerald and Ruby Braff on which his impeccable sense of taste and knowledge of correct chords added greatly to the professionalism of the music. This CD dates from one of his rare visits to Europe (he appeared at the Nice Festival with singer Joe Williams) and it is easy to understand why he has been rated so highly as an accompanist to vocalists and as an entertainer on the supper-club circuit. With the strong, warm sound of Duvivier's bass Larkins tends to use the upper half of the keyboard, leaving Heard to keep perfect time, usually with brushes. This is the kind of music which cannot be faulted, but by the same token it seldom raises the temperature above blood heat. One of the most successful tracks is a beautiful solo version of the Benny Carter song *Blues In My Heart*, a comment which also applies to the solo *Day Dream*, one of the two previously unissued titles added to the original LP to make up this compact disc.
AM

Pete LaRoca

Basra **LaRoca** (d); **Joe Henderson** (ts); **Steve Kuhn** (p); **Steve Swallow** (b). Blue Note Ⓜ CDP 832091 2 (41 minutes). Recorded 1965.

⑧ ❼

LaRoca, who like Steve Kuhn had a short stint in the first version of John Coltrane's classic quartet (the bassist was Steve Davis, and Elvin Jones and McCoy Tyner were soon drafted in), has only made one album as a leader, and this is it. It is hardly more than he deserves, for he was at the time of its recording a fiery and forward-looking drummer with an unusually broad musical vision. Born Pete Sims, he adopted his more musicianly professional name in the fifties, and it suits his explosive, Elvin Jones-derived style. He quit the music scene by the end of the sixties, but his small recorded legacy is a worthwhile one.

Basra has never been reissued since its initial release, and has consequently acquired a semi-legendary status. Two tracks from it were included in the Blue Note Henderson retrospective, but the album here is complete. At the time of the recording, the rhythm section was then functioning as three-quarters of the Art Farmer Quartet, and the substitution of Henderson for the lyrical trumpeter/flügelhornist gives the music a wider dynamic range and a more exploratory feel. Kuhn is an unusually resourceful and imaginative pianist with a conception more original than most, and this early stage of his career finds him crammed full of ideas both as a soloist and as an accompanist. He can play with great fire, but his ballad work is outstanding here. All in all, then, **Basra** is an album that was taken for granted on first release, but now sounds like exactly the type of exploratory, urgent album made at the cutting edge of the modern mainstream which is virtually impossible to record any more, because all the discoveries were subsequently claimed and the new musical soil trampled into submission.
KS

Yusef Lateef

1920

The Centaur and the Phoenix **Lateef** (fl, ob, ts, argol); **Clark Terry** (t, flh); **Richard Williams** (t); **Curtis Fuller** (tb); **Tate Houston** (bs); **Josea Taylor** (bn); **Joe Zawinul** (p); **Ben Tucker** (b); **Lex Humphries** (d). Riverside Ⓜ OJCCD 721 (38 minutes). Recorded 1960.

✔ ⑩ ❼

Lateef's long and varied career as a leader is well-covered on records, but at the present moment that legacy is peculiarly ill-served on CD. Of his long-standing relationships with various labels (Savoy, Prestige, Impulse! and Atlantic for starters), only the Prestige material has been reissued in any depth on CD. So this Riverside reissue would be welcome even if it was a lesser achievement than it actually is. This was his first opportunity to write for a larger ensemble than just a five or six-piece, and he manages to seize the opportunity with relish and abundant imagination. Medium-tempo swingers full of flair and unusual progressions lie in close proximity to moody, angular slower pieces, or pastoral sketches such as *Summer Song*. This is a fully-realized album, from the opening power and urgency of *Revelation*, with its stabbing ensemble figures and preaching tenor from Lateef himself, through to the weird tenderness of *Iqbal*, written for Lateef's young daughter.

Lateef has been on the wrong end of a fair amount of criticism; occasionally his albums have justified it, betraying an attitude close to indifference to the end result. Yet there are plenty which point to his passionate and continuing commitment to experiment, expression and beauty, and a few which achieve and sustain a very high level of artistry. Of the handful currently on CD, this stands above the others as a testament to his real musical stature. **KS**

Eastern Sounds **Lateef** (ts, f, ob); **Barry Harris** (p); **Ernie Farrow** (b, rabat); **Lex Humphries** (d). Prestige Ⓜ OJCCD-612-2 (40 minutes). Recorded 1961.

⑥ ❽

The peripatetic wind-player was here recorded for the Prestige Moodsville series. Thus the album contains Alex North's *Love Theme From Spartacus*—Bill Evans the pianist also included it in his **Conversations With Myself** from two years later—but Lateef goes one better by adding Alfred Newman's *Love Theme From 'The Robe'*, played on oboe and flute respectively. Nevertheless, most Moodsvilles consisted of very familiar standards and uniformly slow tempos, so Lateef was in fact countering expectations in a number of ways. Much of the material is original and the only other exception, the tenor ballad *Don't Blame Me*, is played without any obvious reference to the well-known theme. In fact Lateef's tenor work, which was featured with Cannonball Adderley at this period, is prominent here and reveals an individual tone and uncluttered musical thinking.

The vaguely exotic thematic approach, which earlier was acknowledged by Coltrane in his scalar explorations and set the tone for much sixties jazz, is evident in the modal basis of the originals. In the opening and closing tracks Ernie Farrow, the future Alice Coltrane's brother, uses the single-stringed rabat, in the first case alongside Lateef's Chinese clay flute. **BP**

Live at Pep's **Lateef** (ts, f, ob, shenai, argol); **Richard Williams** (t); **Mike Nock** (p); **Ernie Farrow** (b); **James Black** (d). Impulse! Ⓜ GRP 11342 (61 minutes). Recorded 1964.

⑧ ❽

Lateef's career falls into two distinct phases. As Bill Evans he played his own brand of extrovert tenor in the bands of Dizzy Gillespie, Lucky Millinder and Hot Lips Page. In 1950, he returned to his home town Detroit, embraced the Moslem faith, adopted the name of Yusef Lateef and re-evaluated his musical outlook. Initially the Eastern element introduced into his music seemed little more than a veneer, lending an exotic flavour to the improvisational method of a good journeyman be-bopper. This was perhaps true of albums such as **Other Sounds** (New Jazz OJCCD 399-2) from 1957, but by 1964, the effects of Third Stream projects and free-form experimentation were being more widely felt and some of the more modest aspects had entered the fabric of Lateef's playing. The use of the 12-note row recurs on this album, but it is the way that his soulful shenai is Americanized on *Sister Mamie*, his highly vocalized flute deals with *Slippin' and Slidin'* and the way he captures genuine blues feeling with the plaintive sound of the oboe on *See See Rider* that distinguishes this CD. It was not a synthesis of cultures that had any universal effect but Lateef made a statement in the sixties that was unquestionably valid. This CD incorporates three more tracks than the original vinyl release, although all of the music here has been available before. **BMcR**

The African American Epic Suite **Lateef** (ts, f) with **Charles Moore** (flh, perc); **Ralph Jones** (ss, ts, bcl, f)); **Adam Rudolph** (d, gongs, perc); **Federico Ramos** (g); **Cologne Radio Orchestra / David de Villiers.** ACT Ⓕ WDR 892 142 (46 minutes). Recorded 1993.

⑥ ❽

Although his earliest recordings marked Lateef as a good, orthodox tenor saxist his interests in music outside the normal jazz ambit were soon apparent. Some of his first albums caused critics to home in on the trick effects (blowing across the next of soft drink bottles or letting air out of balloons) but the passage of the years has seen the emergence of Lateef as a writer and performer iof considerable merit. This CD, recorded in Cologne, is Yusef's ambitious attempt to set in music the history of his people, from the days of the slave traders to the present day, the kind of thing which motivated Duke Ellington to write his *Black, Brown & Beige*. As a work it must be said that it lacks the impact of Ellington's writing and a lot of it simply cannot be classified as jazz, even using the widest definition of the term. This will probably worry Lateef not at all for he was one of the first musicians to state publicly that he was not just a jazz musician. The writing here is extremely competent, the handling of the string and woodwind sections in particular being well beyond the capabilities of many jazz writers. But the *Suite* could have benefited from compression and editing to give it more momentum in places.

AM

Andy LaVerne

1947

First Tango in New York LaVerne (p); **Joe Lovano** (ss, ts); **Steve LaSpina** (b); **Bill Stewart** (d). Musidisc Ⓕ 500472 (48 minutes). Recorded 1993.

⑧ ❽

It is something of a surprise to find two Andy LaVerne originals apparently tacked on to the end of what is basically a standards album, since the New York pianist is a distinguished composer, having once produced a symphony for his one-time leader Stan Getz. Nevertheless, the mature, finely honed, occasionally quite exquisite sound of the band on these standards, which range from a burly, vigorous *You and the Night and the Music* through a slow-burning, moody *Goodbye* to a fluent but neat *Melancholy Baby*, more than justifies this policy. LaVerne is a supremely cultured pianist, equally adept at sparkling solo improvisational flights, discreetly mellifluous comping and leading a tight, virile rhythm section, but it is saxophonist Joe Lovano who makes perhaps the most memorable contributions. His playing on the album's six standards is uniformly cogent and controlled, his smoky, warm tenor incorporating swing, bop and even occasional avant-garde influences to produce an entirely personal and instantly identifiable sound. His artistry, and his rapport with fellow ex-Herd member LaVerne, raise **First Tango in New York** head and shoulders above the mass of similar standards-oriented ventures.

CP

Hubert Laws

1930

The Laws of Jazz/Flute By Laws Laws (f, pic); **Chick Corea, Rodgers Grant** (p); **Sam Brown** (g); **Jimmy Owens, Marty Banks** (t); **Garnett Brown, Benny Powell, Tommy McIntosh** (tb); **Richard Davis, Chris White, Israel 'Cachao' Lopez** (b); **Bobby Thomas, Jimmy Cobb, Ray Lucas** (d); **Carmelo Garcia, Victor Pantoja, Raymond Orchart, Bill Fitch** (perc). Rhino/Atlantic Jazz Gallery Ⓜ R2 71636 (68 minutes). Recorded 1964.

⑦ ❽

With Herbie Mann already under contract, Atlantic cornered the sixties market in jazz flute with the 1964 signing of Hubert Laws. A virtuoso player with classical training at Juilliard and the chops to cut regular gigs with the New York Philharmonic and the Metropolitan Opera, Laws got his first jazz experience in his hometown of Houston with high school friends who eventually grew up to become the Jazz Crusaders. Here, we catch Laws at the onset of his recording career in his first outings as a leader on Atlantic.

The Laws of Jazz, recorded in 1964 but not issued until 1965, was an impressive debut. With spare yet supple backing by pianist Chick Corea, bassist Richard Davis and drummer Bobby Thomas, Laws proved in *Miss Thing* that he could stroll with a funky strut, à la Mann. Even more telling was his lovely ballad treatment of *All Soul* and the perky piccolo spicings of *Black Eyed Peas and Rice*. His follow-up album, **Flute-By-Laws** (yet another punny title) released in 1966, sets the flautist's quicksilver flights against pungently Latinized horn charts also by Laws. Again, Laws's appealingly low-key virtuosity is ably abetted by Corea's effective and economical comping.

CB

Yank Lawson

1911

Something Old, Something New, Something Borrowed, Something Blue Lawson (t); **George Masso** (tb); **Johnny Mince** (cl); **Lou Stein** (p); **Bucky Pizzarelli** (g); **Bob Haggart** (b); **Nick Fatool** (d). Audiophile Ⓕ APCD 240 (41 minutes). Recorded 1988.

⑥ ❽

A trumpeter with his heart in Dixieland jazz, Lawson's early career included spells with Wingy Manone and Ben Pollack. In 1935 he became a founder member of the Bob Crosby Orchestra, a reluctant big band that always found time for items like *Come Back, Sweet Papa*, *Royal Garden Blues* or others from the Dixieland 'song book'. Often in the company of Haggart, Lawson has continued to play with men associated with this style and he played a major part in the formation, in 1968, of the World's Great Jazz Band (sic). This CD features players associated with the WGJB and effectively showcases the work of the trumpeter. His brassy tone and team leading qualities are evident throughout and his strong blowing style, devoid of histrionics, is an obvious motivating factor in the playing of his sidemen. Not always the hard-hitting front runner, he resorts to old world preaching horn on *What Else Is New*, while on *Come Back, Sweet Papa* he produces a stop time chorus of real class, slightly dragging at the coat tails of the beat and keeping just a little in reserve. A 77-year-old is perhaps justified in protecting his 'chops', but Lawson gives value, even if it is in shorter bursts. **BMcR**

Nguyên Lê

Miracles **Lê** (g, danh tranh, programming); **Art Lande** (p); **Marc Johnson** (b); **Peter Erskine** (d). Musidisc Ⓕ 500102 (57 minutes). Recorded 1989-90.

⑧ ❿

Although much of Nguyên Lê's plangent, spangly-toned solo guitar playing is somewhat reminiscent of John Scofield's in overall sound and approach, his personal strengths - an ability to coax an attractive range of surprising sounds and textures from pleasant but unremarkable themes, and a confident fluency and infectious exuberance as both soloist and leader mark this album out as worthy of sustained attention. Of course, the importance of a rhythm section comprising three of the most experienced practitioners in this area of music, operating in the fertile area bounded by fusion on one side and jazz on the other, is difficult to overestimate: pianist/educator Art Lande draws on experience with everyone from Steve Swallow through Jan Garbarek to Ted Curson; Marc Johnson collaborated most famously with Bill Evans and Stan Getz before producing his seminal **Bass Desires** album with Scofield and Bill Frisell. But it is Peter Erskine who holds the album together, justifying his reputation as one of the world's leading jazz and fusion drummers with a sustained performance of great power and subtlety, notable not only for its felicitous use of a stunning variety of percussive sounds and effects, but also for the delicacy and control of his more straightforward time playing. Drawing as it does on a strikingly original selection of sounds, from electronic, synthesized washes and splashes to the traditional Japanese danh tranh, **Miracles** is a highly enjoyable and accomplished album. **CP**

Barbara Lea

c1930

Lea In Love **Lea** (v); **Johnny Windhurst** (t); **Dick Cary** (ah, p, arr); **Ernie Caceres** (cl, bs); **Garvin Bushell** (ob, bn); **Jimmy Lyon** (p, cel); **Adele Girard** (h); **Al Casamenti, Jimmy Raney** (g); **Al Hall, Beverley Peer** (b); **Osie Johnson** (d). Prestige Ⓜ OJCCD-1742-2 (37 minutes). Recorded 1957.

⑥ ❻

"I believe in jazz and singing but not necessarily in jazz singing" wrote Lea in the notes to this album, one of a handful she made in her brief contract with Prestige. Along with her eponymous sister album (Prestige OJCCD-1713-2) this is a collaboration with trumpeter Johnny Windhurst and multi-instrumentalist Dick Cary. Lea disproves her apparent disenchantment with "jazz singing" by revealing a voice rich in nuance and subtlety, as adept at timing a well-turned lyric as other singers are at wordless scatting.

She had chart success with her gallic *Autumn Leaves* and Cole Porter's *True Love* (somewhat dominated by Adèle Girard's harp) and both are here, but as jazz performances they are outclassed by *We Could Make Such Beautiful Music* and *The Very Thought Of You*, the former dominated by Windhurst's clean Bixian trumpet, the latter by Jimmy Raney's guitar, and both set by Cary to use the unusual instrumental tone colours of double reeds and alto horn to add depth and texture. **AS**

Lee Ann Ledgerwood

You Wish **Ledgerwood** (p, syn); **Jeremy Steig** (f); **Bill Evans** (ts, ss); **Eddie Gomez** (b); **Steve LaSpina** (b); **Danny Gottlieb** (d). Triloka Ⓕ 187-2 (53 minutes). Recorded 1991.

⑦ ❽

The list of pianists who have played at Bradley's Piano Bar in New York is impressive. The superb instrument is perhaps the magnet, but the late Bradley Cunningham saw to it that only musicians worthy of the task enjoyed the privilege. Ledgerwood was one such player and her exposure at Bradley's was important to a career that had begun in kindergarten and embraced classical training. She came through the Berklee Academy of jazz know-how, arrived in New York in 1982, became a familiar face at Bradley's and has since played throughout the City.

This CD is not a recording début but is her first as a leader. It shows her good touch, fine attack and an improvising style unconcerned with musical euphemisms. Melodic ideas are developed on their own merits and, as the title track illustrates, piano solos are designed to accommodate progress reports from bass and drums. *Nardis* establishes her imaginative use of the synthesizer and the reflective *I Want To Talk About You* shows that, even at slow tempo, she has no need to rely on rhythmic support. *Taisho Pond* and *You Wish* mark her out as a fine composer and suggest hers is a writing style that grows from her improvisational method. **BMcR**

Jeanne Lee

1939

You Stepped Out Of A Cloud **Lee** (v); **Ran Blake** (p). Owl Ⓕ 055 CD (58 minutes). Recorded 1989.

⑧ ❽

Lee met Blake while studying dance at Bard College, and in 1961 they made a recording for RCA, **The Newest Sounds Around**, which was hailed by some observers as the most innovative vocal record since the Sarah Vaughans of the forties. Lee has worked with the likes of Gunter Hampel, Archie Shepp, Anthony Braxton and Cecil Taylor but has always kept a spiritual link with Blake. This CD renews that feeling in musical terms and scales similar artistic heights. It emphasizes the rare empathy that exists between these two creative spirits and displays them as painters in sound. They embark on a journey of half-tones and shading as they add their own subtle tints to each shared melodic sound pattern. Lyrics are not robbed of their meaning, but they are felt rather than expressed vehemently. Lee's timing on *Mysterioso Rose* and *I Like Your Style* is distinctly Monkish. *You Go To My Head* takes a more Lee Konitz-like route, most especially in its tone and off-centre note placement. Her rubato is further exploited on her unaccompanied *Newswatch*, a swinging recitation that at one point hints at a drummer's sticks on a hi-hat and leaves no doubt that she is a creatively uncompromising jazz singer of the highest order. **BMcR**

Julia Lee

1902-1958

Ugly Papa Lee (p, v) with various bands including **The Tommy Douglas Orchestra**; **The Bob Dougherty Orchestra**, and groups with **Geechie Smith**, **Ernie Royal** (t); **Vic Dickenson** (tb); **Henry Bridges**, **Dave Cavanagh**, **Gene Carter** (ts); **Nappy Lamare**, **Jack Marshall**, **Jim Daddy Walker**, **James Scott** (g); **Billy Hadnott**, **Harry Babasin**, **Leonard Johnson** (b); **Sam 'Baby' Lovett**, **Bill Nolan**, **Corky Jackson** (d). Jukebox Lil Ⓕ RBD 603 (45 minutes). Recorded 1945-57.

⑥ ❻

Julia Lee spent the formative years of her life in Kansas City, and this fortuitous circumstance governed the style of her music for the vast majority of her career. Although a professional singer and entertainer from the early twenties onwards, she was a latecomer to success, not moving much out of KC and consequently remaining a local rather than national act. She was renowned for the salacious side of her nightclub act, and much of this sauciness filtered onto her recordings when she finally made her studio debut. This came in 1944 (two sides cut in 1923 were never released) when she was already 42 and a throwback to a style of singing fast either updating to r&b or disappearing altogether. Yet she, along with Nellie Lutcher, a singer from Georgia with a not dissimilar style but a singularly different voice, made a special combination of boogie, swing and the then-popular 'jump' style to register serious commercial success in the next five years.

The tracks on this compilation for the most part avoid the crassest end of her sexually audacious lyrics (there's no *My Man Stands Out* or *Don't Come Too Soon* here, although we are treated to *King Size Papa*), most of which were made at the end of the forties when her career began to fade. The vast majority of tracks fall into the 1945-50 period, just three coming after that, with the single 1957 track, *Bop & Rock Lullaby*, featuring a heavy back-beat absent elsewhere, though the sax solo is undiluted mid-forties Arnett Cobb. Good fun and fine, if basic, musicianship all round. **KS**

Peggy Lee

1920

Beauty And The Beat! **Lee** (v); **George Shearing** (p); **Toots Thielemans** (g); **Warren Chaisson** (vb); **James Bond** (b); **Roy Haynes** (d); **Armando Peraza** (cga). Capitol Jazz Ⓜ CDP7 98454-2 (39 minutes). Recorded 1959.

⑧ ❻

It can only be snobbery towards their 'popular' status that nourishes the theory that the likes of Lee and Sinatra are not jazz singers. A singing (and swinging) performance such as this concert recording is more rewarding than many a 'dedicated' jazz album. Miss Lee has the knack of sounding spontaneous but in fact every vocal and visual nuance is premeditated and polished to perfection. With that in mind, the latest version of this album reveals that the 'in concert' announcements were dubbed on the day after the event and that even the photograph on the sleeve was concocted in the studio. No matter; the music of both Lee and Shearing is beyond reproach, reaching its zenith in a previously unissued studio duet version (done the day after the concert) of *Nobody's Heart*, a surprisingly neglected Richard Rodgers ballad. Amongst the good songs are two instrumentals from Shearing, who was just beginning to feel his oats as one of the giants of jazz piano. **SV**

Michel Legrand

1932

Legrand Jazz **Legrand** (arr, cond); **Miles Davis**, **Ernie Royal**, **Art Farmer**, **Donald Byrd**, **Joe Wilder** (t); **Frank Rehak**, **Billy Byers**, **Jimmy Cleveland**, **Eddie Bert** (tb); **James Buffington** (frh);

Herbie Mann (f); **Gene Quill**, **Phil Woods** (as); **Ben Webster**, **John Coltrane**, **Seldon Powell** (ts); **Jerome Richardson** (bs, cl); **Teo Macero** (bs); **Eddie Costa**, **Don Elliot** (vb); **Betty Glamann** (hp); **Bill Evans**, **Nat Pierce**, **Hank Jones** (p); **Paul Chambers**, **George Duvivier**, **Milt Hinton** (b); **Major Holley** (b, tba); **Don Lamond**, **Kenny Dennis**, **Osie Johnson** (d). Philips Ⓜ 830 074-2 (38 minutes). Recorded 1958.

⑧ ❽

This is a good example of an orchestrator moving a collection of soloists out of their usual milieus and stimulating them anew with his writing. When it is borne in mind that this music was created at the time when Quincy Jones was at his peak, it becomes almost (but not quite) understandable that this collection was largely overlooked, despite all the star names.

It works on many levels. The writing is inventive and well voiced. The idea of wedding Miles Davis and John Coltrane to unlikely tunes like Armstrong's *Wild Man Blues* and Waller's *Jitterbug Waltz* was a good one, for this is material which can be handled in any idiom. Davis's response is completely unruffled, and his wistful solos will appeal to anyone who values his work from the period. He has *Django* to himself. Coltrane is intimidating on *Jitterbug* in contrast to Woods, who is his usual outgoing self. Woods and the ill-starred Gene Quill are to be found in full flight on *Night In Tunisia* which also has characteristic fireworks from Jimmy Cleveland and a much-to-be-prized solo from Joe Wilder, along with the other practised trumpeters on the session. Evans appears on the four tracks with Davis and Coltrane and shows his ability in a large group, away from the intimacy of the smaller groups which were to dominate in the rest of his professional life.

Webster gives a towering performance, opening *Blue And Sentimental* in an unaccompanied duet with Rehak. He is at his most voluptuous here, in stark contrast to the driving, tearing solo on *Rosetta*. *Don't Get Around Much Anymore* is given to Mann's flute, but the four trombone chases in the long *Rosetta* have much more of the red meat of jazz. **SV**

Le Jazz Grand **Legrand** (p, comp, arr); with small band: **Jon Faddis** (t); **Phil Woods** (as); **Gerry Mulligan** (bs); **Ron Carter** (b); **Jimmy Madison** (d); **Portinho** (perc); group activities: **Joe Shepley**, **Burt Collins**, **John Gatchell**, **John Clark**, **Albert Richmond**, **Brooks Tillotson**, **Tony Price** (brass); **Bernie Leighton**, **Tom Pierson** (kbds); **Harry Leahey** (g); **Don Elliott** (b); **Grady Tate**, **'Crusher' Bennett** (perc). Castle Communications Ⓑ PACD 027 (46 minutes). Recorded 1978.

⑧ ❽

Legrand has had a phenomenally successful musical career, most especially as a soundtrack composer, but in many other fields besides. He only rarely gets involved in a full-scale jazz project, but when he does it is invariably a worthwhile one. This late-seventies date (originally released on the Gryphon label) is no exception. The major work on it is Legrand's suite, *Southern Routes*. It is quite possible to hear the distant echoes of the Miles Davis/Gil Evans collaboration, **Sketches of Spain**, especially in the brass writing, but then Legrand is dealing with music adapted from a film score dealing with the south of France and Catalonia, so the echoes are not inappropriate. The section writing is clear, colourful and always of interest in its own right: Legrand is a masterful arranger (he trained under Nadia Boulanger) and continually extracts potent instrumental mixes from the charts here.

Of the soloists, Mulligan sits most naturally with the music, easing his way into his section of the suite called *East* and playing consummate baritone on his other feature, *Malagan Stew*. Faddis is somewhat frantic at times, but his enormous technical facility enables him to retain his poise. Phil Woods is his usual passionate, hard-driving self on his featured pieces. This is a very satisfying big-band jazz album where the featured soloists are done proud by the composer/arranger/leader. One can only bemoan the fact that, probably due to the sheer expense of such enterprises, they are all too rarely made these days. **KS**

Peter Lemer

1942

Local Colour **Lemer** (p); **Nisar Ahmed Khan** (ts); **John Surman** (bs, ss); **Tony Reeves** (b); **John Hiseman** (d). ESP-Disk Ⓜ 1057-2 (43 minutes). Recorded 1966.

⑥ ❻

British-born Lemer studied jazz piano with Paul Bley and Jaki Byard, as well as classical piano at the Royal Academy of Music. He has worked with big bands and be-bop combos as well as with fusion musicians. He is also well known for his work with the men who launched the country's free music movement in the sixties. This CD comes from that era and also features the emerging talent of Surman and the eccentric but colourful ramblings of Khan. Even then, Lemer's own piano style was the product of fairly wide experience and he exerts a strong influence on all involved on this recording date. His articulation is clean, he has a distinctive touch as well as an innate ability to swing. Despite superficial similarities, his playing is somewhat divorced from the Cecil Taylor school. His solos are less abstract and their direction, if not actually signposted, is re-affirmed by harmonic hints as the solo progresses. His comping behind the soloists is percussive and (as he shows on *In And Out*) at times startlingly inspirational. The under-recorded Reeves provides a firm musical chassis and, although Hiseman had not yet grasped the full implications of this music, the album shows British free-form jazz at an important early stage of development. **BMcR**

Stan Levey

1925

Quintet Levey (d); **Conte Candoli** (t); **Richie Kamuca** (ts); **Lou Levy** (p); **Monty Budwig** (b). VSOP Ⓕ # 41CD (30 minutes) Recorded 1957.

⑤ ❻

This is the archetypal West Coast session. It proceeds so smoothly it could be on tramlines, and has as much roughage in it as childrens' breakfast cereal. Nobody plays badly, everybody swings, but nobody gets worked up into a sweat either, and few moments of music here stay in the memory past the end of the track. Which is another way of saying that this pleasant but unremarkable record is an audio definition of the word mediocre, although that is perhaps being a little harsh on Kamuca, a good tenor player who has certainly risen to much greater things than he manages here, however pretty his tone may be.

If you like your jazz to go down smoothly without touching the sides, this will be your idea of heaven, though you'd better listen closely, as heaven doesn't last very long. **KS**

Milcho Leviev

1937

Blues for the Fisherman Leviev (p); **Art Pepper** (as); **Tony Dumas** (b); **Carl Burnett** (d). Mole Jazz Ⓜ CD MOLE 1 PLUS (70 minutes). Recorded 1980.

⑧ ❽

Although this is an Art Pepper recording in all but name, Bulgarian pianist Milchio Leviev's unhurried, deeply thoughtful playing, capable both of sustaining a subtly chiming accompanying role under Pepper's extended improvisations and of slowly building unspectacular but deeply-felt soloing, makes an indispensable contribution to the group's overall sound. Recorded at Ronnie Scott's at the height of the alto player's hard-won rehabilitation, **Blues for the Fisherman** documents an archetypal Pepper live set: a mixture of plaintive, slowish blues numbers and affectingly simple heart-on-sleeve ballads, spiced up with brisk boppish material. Pepper's is one of the most intimate saxophone styles in the music, earnest, confiding, almost painfully personal, conveyed through a unique and instantly identifiable combination of breathless flurries interspersed with sustained single notes terminating in a melancholy vibrato effect. The combination of a familiar and highly accomplished rhythm section—Carl Burnett is an old Pepper hand and Tony Dumas has stints with Joe Henderson and Nat Adderley to his credit—and a strongly supportive audience makes for a highly enjoyable, relaxed and informal session of airily accessible music. **CP**

Lou Levy

1928

Lunarcy Levy (p); **Pete Christlieb** (ts); **Eric Von Essen** (b); **Ralph Penland** (d). Verve Gitanes Jazz Ⓕ 514 317-2 (69 minutes). Recorded 1992.

⑥ ❽

Lou Levy is a musicians' musician. Indeed, he is probably best known for his tasteful comping for such jazz divas as Sarah Vaughan, Peggy Lee and Ella Fitzgerald. He has also held down the piano chair for Stan Getz, Benny Goodman and Supersax. When helming his own groups, it is the bop-inflected lexicon of Bud Powell and company which prevails.

For this consistently satisfying 1992 outing, Levy conjures up mesmerizing spells with the assistance of tenor saxophonist Pete Christlieb, bassist Eric Von Essen and drummer Ralph Penland, all important figures on Southern California's acoustic mainstream scene. The repertoire, from Levy's own pell-mell title track to the emotionally charged *I Hadn't Anyone 'Til You*, is similarly first-rate. Johnny Mandel, who a number of years ago Levy called "our greatest living composer," is represented in indelible versions of *The Shadow of Your Smile* and a little known but engaging line called *Zoot*, an homage to tenor great Zoot Sims.

The disc is also a showcase for Christlieb, a robust tenorman who simultaneously invokes the legacies of the lyrical Lester Young and declamatory Coleman Hawkins. Throughout, one gets the impression of fully interactive and involved dialogue laced with good cheer. **CB**

George Lewis

1900-1968

Trios & Bands Lewis (cl); **Louis 'Kid Shots' Madison, Avery 'Kid' Howard** (t); **Jim Robinson** (tb); **Alcide Pavageau, Ricard Alexis, Chester Zardis** (b); **Lawrence Marrero** (bj); **Baby Dodds, Edgar Moseley** (d). American Music Ⓕ AMCD 4 (60 minutes). Recorded 1943-45.

⑦ ❷

When the deterioration of New Orleans's post-war economy encouraged a mass migration of the city's outstanding jazzmen, Lewis remained. During the twenties he worked with the Eureka Brass Band, the Olympia Orchestra and with the likes of Buddy Petit, Red Allen and Kid Rena. He first worked with Bunk Johnson in the thirties but he was the producer's choice to support the trumpeter as the New Orleans style was revived in the forties. It was not the happiest of stylistic weddings and this CD supports the theory that Lewis's best work was done elsewhere. By the standards of contemporaries Dodds, Noone and Simeon, Lewis had a thin sound, but it was a soulful, sweet tone that could wring emotion from almost any material. His introduction to *Over The Waves* does come dangerously near to maudlin sentimentality but moving hymns like *Lead Me Saviour* are more representative. His trio playing throughout is commendable and he successfully overcomes the at-times stiff rhythmic backgrounds. Two of the full band titles are blighted by Madison's fumbling technique and suspect intonation, but Lewis's partnership with Howard on the final three items is far more fruitful. The series of recording dates shows that Lewis's outright dismissal by the technique-conscious moderns is no more justified than is the incontinent praise heaped upon him by the passionate traditionalists. **BMcR**

George Lewis 1952

Homage to Charles Parker **Lewis** (tb, electronics); **Douglas Ewart** (bcl, as, cymbals); **Anthony Davis** (p); **Richard Teitelbaum** (syn). Black Saint Ⓕ 120029-2 (36 minutes). Recorded 1979.

⑧ ❽

Graduating from the AACM in the mid-seventies, Lewis began his career with a brief stint in the Count Basie Orchestra, but has since worked chiefly with leading avant-gardists such as Anthony Braxton, Steve Lacy and John Zorn. Two of his central projects—a long association with reeds virtuoso Douglas Ewart and a pioneering involvement with computer music—are scantily represented on disc, though **Homage to Charles Parker** does afford a glimpse of the former.

Comprising just two tracks, the album shows Lewis building on elements from the tradition to create a new music of great beauty. *Blues*, in his words, "has four basically diatonic 'choruses', each of which uses the essential harmonic sequence of the classic blues as a starting point". The soloists take their turns, each fronting a flux of 'collective orchestration' as Lewis, displaying the structural nous that is an AACM trademark, festoons the pace with smudges and trickles of sound. *Homage to Charles Parker* opens on a mêlée of whispers, sizzles and resonant, gong-like shimmers from synthesizers and electronically modulated cymbals. The music then reverts to "the traditional improvised solo with chordal accompaniment", the latter provided by serene synthesizer over which Ewart blows sweetly elegiac alto and Lewis later adds a mellow trombone. **GL**

John Lewis 1920

Grand Encounter: Two° East, Three° West **Lewis** (p); **Bill Perkins** (ts); **Jim Hall** (g); **Percy Heath** (b); **Chico Hamilton** (d). Pacific Jazz Ⓜ CDP7 46859-2 (35 minutes). Recorded 1956.

⑧ ❺

This album, Lewis's first under his own name, brought his composition *Two Degrees East, Three Degrees West* to the world, and for that alone we ought to be thankful. The disc displays all the usual qualities associated with the pianist/composer: restraint, a high degree of organization, delicacy, perceptive accompaniment of soloists, a relaxed feel. This last quality is amply displayed on his feature *I Can't Get Started*, where he unhurriedly unveils his treatment of the beautiful theme, subtly alters its harmonic accompaniment then builds a leisurely, spare but well-structured solo on top. Perkins is in a decidedly romantic frame of mind on this record, displaying in equal measure his admiration for Lester Young and Stan Getz, while Hall is quite withdrawn, even for him. Hall's solo on *Degrees* is an intriguing exercise in minimalism in a blues context, but he leaves Lewis and Perkins to take the lion's share of solo space.

An album of almost casual beauty, it has a very low emotional temperature, but rewards close study. The recording (mono only) is not great the instrumental balance, being decidedly unhappy—but it is no worse than contemporary albums on Atlantic. **KS**

The Wonderful World Of Jazz **Lewis** (p, ldr); **Jim Hall** (g); **George Duvivier** (b); **Connie Kay** (d); **Herb Pomeroy** (t), **Paul Gonsalves** (ts); **Herb Pomeroy** (t); **Gunther Schuller** (frh); **Eric Dolphy** (as); **Benny Golson** (ts); **Jimmy Giuffre** (bs). Rhino/Atlantic Ⓜ 7 90979-2 (56 minutes). Recorded 1960.

⑩ ❽

John Lewis's presence on record or the concert platform has always brought a sense of dignity. For years he guided the MJQ as the power behind the throne, often allowing Milt Jackson to take the spotlight. This CD version of a long-unavailable LP is especially valuable and contains two previously unissued titles, one by the basic quartet (Tadd Dameron's *If You Could See Me Now*) and Arif Mardin's *The Stranger* by the nonet, which means we hear a new, explosively exciting alto solo from Eric Dolphy. But most of the satisfaction to be obtained from the CD is the careful, often understated piano playing by Lewis, one of the least demonstrative but most effective keyboard players in jazz. Like Basie, he concentrates on the notes that matter, allowing them to stand alone with plenty of space around them. The most memorable track is the longest: *Body And Soul* is over 15 minutes of timeless perfection. Paul Gonsalves spins out a tenor solo of such warmth and invention that it rivals even the classic Coleman Hawkins version, thanks largely to the prodding, sensitive piano backing from Lewis. This is a five-star performance by any standard. The sound is good with just a hint of tape hiss in places; a small price to pay for the retention of the original recording characteristic. Recommended without reservation. **AM**

Meade Lux Lewis

1905-1964

1927-1939/1939-1941 **Lewis** (p, cel); with a collective personnel including **J. C. Higginbotham** (tb); **Albert Arnmons, Pete Johnson** (p); **Teddy Bunn** (g); **Walter Page, Johnny Williams** (b); **Jo Jones, Sid Catlett** (d). Classics Ⓜ 722, 743 (72, 70 minutes). Recorded 1927-41.

✔ ⑧ ❺

Lewis was not the first boogie boogie pianist, but he had one of the earliest successes with the style when his first version of *Honky Tonk Train Blues* was released at the end of the twenties. A Chicagoan, Lewis had spent his youth in Kentucky before returning to his home town and linking up with his friend Albert Ammons. Out of luck and money, by 1927 he was reduced to driving cabs, but the release of *Honk Tonk Train Blues* that year enabled him to attempt music as a career. This met with only partial success and it was not until his appearance at John Hammond's famous Carnegie Hall concert of 1938 that he was able to sustain his career's momentum.

He recorded briefly for a number of companies at the dawn of the thirties, but the intense bout of recording for Blue Note which began in 1939 perhaps stand as his best work, although a 'live' set from a mid-forties Jazz At The Philharmonic concert (doubtless to be dealt with on a subsequent Classics release) is thrillingly immediate and worth seeking out. On these discs we have the complete Blue Note output, mixed with other sides made for Vocalion, Victor and Solo Art. The sound quality is not brilliant (the originals are generally poor), but Lewis's unusually large stylistic range is immediately apparent. While he could keep his left hand rolling around in boogie patterns all night long, he tried many different approaches echoing other players as disparate as Earl Hines and James P. Johnson, moving between stride and blues patterns at will. His work with the Higginbotham group on *Basin Street Blues* shows him to have a strong grasp on jazz piano practice, and he fits smoothly into the rhythm section.

Athough his powerful boogie duets with Ammons and Johnson are rightly enthused over, his most affecting work is done alone. *Far Ago Blues* is a wistful, regretful blues performance which incidentally has an almost complete statement of the melody to *Blue Monk* some decade or so before that famous piece was first brought before the public. It should be noted that on some tracks here Lewis plays the celeste, an instrument for which he retained an affection throughout his career. Lewis is a musician who has more complexity of thought and execution than often given credit for, and these two CDs are an essential purchase for those who wish to comprehend the development of piano in the years between the Jelly Roll Morton Victors and Charlie Parker's first records with the Jay McShann band. **KS**

Mel Lewis

1929-1990

The Definitive Thad Jones **Lewis** (d); **Earl Gardner, Joe Mosello, Glenn Drewes, Jim Powell** (t); **John Mosca, Ed Neumeister, Douglas Purviance, Earl McIntyre** (tb); **Stephanie Fauber** (frh); **Dick Oatts, Ted Nash** (as); **Joe Lovano, Ralph Lalama** (ts); **Gary Smulyan** (bs); **Kenny Werner** (p); **Dennis Irwin** (b). MusicMasters Ⓕ 5024-2-c (52 minutes). Recorded 1988.

⑧ ❻

Thad Jones loved to spread himself when he wrote, but never wasted a note. The band he led with Lewis was one of the greatest in the whole pantheon of jazz; after Jones's death Lewis carried on the tradition using younger musicians. Naturally he kept most of Thad's writing in the book and the five titles here are well-chosen examples. Lewis rightly trusted his audience's attention span. *Three In One* runs for 13 minutes and *Little Pixie,* another variation on *I Got Rhythm,* for more than 15.

The Jones/Lewis band had the pick of the crop of contemporary New York musicians of all styles. Lewis's band had younger men of similar stature, particularly in soloists Dick Oatts and Joe Lovano, but the sections also play with outstanding finesse and this is a worthy tribute to Jones. His writings were far too good to waste, and are ideal for new generations of musicians to cut their teeth on.

All of which makes this sound like a worthy album rather than an enjoyable one. That is unfair: it is filled with fire from the drums up. **SV**

Ramsey Lewis

1935

Live **Lewis** (p); **Eldee Young** (b, vc); **Isaac 'Red' Holt** (d). Stereo Ⓑ JHR 73524 (70 minutes). Recorded 1965.

④ ❻

The first half of this CD was originally released as an album called **The "In" Crowd**, and it sold more than a million copies. The mid-sixties were a good period for Lewis; the soul-jazz movement was firmly in place and the Chicagoan's churchy, rolling style was just right for that climate. He had become fully established, had a consistent personnel and was full of confidence. His large following had begun to demand the same tunes rather too frequently, but he was equipped with a formula that worked. Technically he was a good player, but his improvisational processes were predictable and this repetitive approach became wearing even to the dedicated listener. As his popularity waned in the seventies he tried keyboards and the world of funk. His return to the acoustic instrument in the eighties did not see him return to critical favour, but although he is still a popular performer he remains a figure somewhat on the jazz fringe. Despite the claim on the CD, the final seven titles were recorded at the Lighthouse on Hermosa Beach. **BMcR**

Ivory Pyramid **Lewis** (p); **Mike Logan** (kbds); **Henry Johnson** (g); **Charles Webb** (b); **Steve Cobb** (d, perc). GRP Ⓕ 96882 (48 minutes). Recorded 1992.

⑤ ❽

One man's meat…
Depending on your point of view, this is either a highly successful marriage of contemporary rhythms with the type of melody and chord sequence one would normally find in popular music written 40 years ago, or it is a cliché-ridden sell-out. Lewis has been riding this dichotomy of opinion for the whole of his career and it shows no sign of abating. One thing not at issue is the man's talent: he has a great deal of that, and the technique to match it. He plays acoustic piano exclusively on this disc, allowing his mostly electronically-powered working group to supply backdrops which really only have their parallel in the type of accompaniment once supplied to George Shearing and Nat King Cole. 'Lush' is the word.

Lewis gives tantalizing glimpses of what he is truly capable of as a soloist on track after track, but does not sustain it, preferring to pull back into understatement and well-turned phrases. His ear is very good and he has a developed orchestral sense, but he has chosen to use it for the most part to create sophisticated popular music with a touch of jazz. That is not his fault, but he could do otherwise. I get the feeling this brings us back to the opening dilemma. **KS**

Vic Lewis

1919

Vic Lewis West Coast All Stars Play The Music Of Bill Holman, Volume 1 **Lewis** directing **Conte Candoli, Jack Sheldon** (t); **Rob McConnell** (vtb); **Andy Martin** (tb); **Ron Loofbourrow** (frh); **Bud Shank, Lanny Morgan, Lennie Niehaus** (as); **Bob Cooper** (f, cl, ts); **Bill Perkins** (f, ss, bs, bcl); **Mike Lang, Alan Broadbent, Dudley Moore** (p); **John Clayton** (b); **Jeff Hamilton** (d); **Ruth Price** (v). Candid Ⓕ CCD 79540 (61 minutes) Recorded 1989.

⑧ ❽

Each winter Vic Lewis goes to California and persuades the West Coast 'giants' to record for him for scale (standard union fees). No matter how it is done, we can only be grateful for the results. Holman, for example, is shamefully under-exposed on record, running an artistically successful rehearsal big band for the best part of 20 years during which time it has done little but rehearse.

Holman specializes in an oblique look at familiar melodies. *Yesterdays* and *Easter Parade* are re-composed in this way, both stretched out at length to allow potent series of solos. Candoli is brutally powerful on the Kern tune, which is also distinguished by a maverick and forceful bass-clarinet solo from Perkins and wistful valve trombone from the excellent McConnell. Both tenors grace *Easter Parade*, taking advantage of another aspect of Holman's writing, the opportunity to swing. Holman's originals are splendid, with a particularly attractive slow theme for the multi tempo *As We Speak*. Previously issued on Mole CD 14, this new version of the album has been re-edited and completely re-balanced by Bill Perkins, with a second version of *Oleo* being added. **SV**

David Liebman

1946

If They Only Knew **Liebman** (ts, ss); **Terumasa Hino** (t); **John Scofield** (g); **Ron McClure** (b); **Adam Nussbaum** (d). Timeless Ⓕ CD SJP 151 (45 minutes). Recorded 1980.

⑥ ❽

This, the second of two albums by Liebman's well-regarded late-seventies/early-eighties quintet, presents him in transition from the largely undifferentiated Coltrane-styled tenorist heard with Elvin Jones, Miles Davis and others in the seventies to the distinctive soprano specialist he became during the eighties. In recent years he has espoused an esoteric music much in debt to twentieth-century art music, but at this time he was drawing from a wide range of less elevated influences, including rock, hard bop, samba and jazz ballad—sometimes, it seems, all in one number. His *If Only They Knew*, for example, sounds like a through-composed acoustic jazz-fusion suite, developing from an intimate ballad feel into ferocious modal rock; it also gives a taste of Liebman's chilling, intense and soon-to-be readily identifiable soprano playing. The band are superb, with Terumasa Hino giving several good accounts of his strong amalgam of Davis, Hubbard and others, but one sideman, John Scofield, was essential to the band's character. The individuality and maturity of his soloing on *Move On Some* and McClure's *Reunion*, and of his writing on *Capistrano*, will be an education to those weaned on his much-publicized Blue Note work. **MG**

Kirk Lightsey

1937

Temptation **Lightsey** (p); **Freddie Hubbard** (t); **Santi Debriano** (b); **Eddie Gladden** (d); **Jerry Gonzalez** (perc). Timeless Ⓕ CD SJP 257 (51 minutes). Recorded 1987.

⑦ ❽

His earliest reputation was established as a sensitive accompanist to singers, but Lightsey emerged as a soloist in the mid-sixties with combos led by Sonny Stitt and Chet Baker. In the eighties his career development continued and was furthered by periods spent under the leadership of Dexter Gordon,

Jimmy Raney, Clifford Jordan and with the Leaders Co-operative Group. He also began to record as a leader himself, and this CD finds him in the company of Hubbard as well as three men with whom he works regularly. The programme is made up of three Hubbard originals, one Thelonious Monk classic and two standards. All receive thorough jazz treatment, with themes stated clearly and improvisationed examinations conducted in style by the two principals. The pianist's work is consistently good and shows his dynamic awareness in solos that grow in creative and rhythmic tension as they progress. His handling of *Evidence*, a Monk theme developed without reference to the basic Thelonious piano vocabulary, is typical, but every little phrase speaks of an individuality with which he has not always been credited. Hubbard is in daunting form on this date, but Lightsey is not inhibited by it, in fact producing some of his most imaginative patterns in support of the trumpeter's work. **BMcR**

Abbey Lincoln

1930

Talking to the Sun **Lincoln** (v); **Steve Coleman** (as); **James Weidman** (p); **Billy Johnson** (b); **Mark Johnson** (d); **Jerry Gonzalez** (perc); **Arlene Knox, Bemshee Shirer, Naima Williams** (v). Enja Ⓕ 79635-2 (39 minutes). Recorded 1983.

⑩ ❽

Lincoln's trademark as a singer is her lack of artifice—her way of experiencing a song and expressing to the listener what the words and melody mean to her, in the most direct and honest means possible. After a start as a lounge singer in the fifties, she became a singing spokeswoman for the civil rights movement, participating on her then-husband Max Roach's **We Insist** and **Percussion Bitter Sweet**. In the nineties, relatively late in her career, she has acquired something approaching a mass following on the strength of a trio of albums for Verve which have surrounded her with all-star accompanists. Her most satisfying album though may be this one for Enja, which features her working band of the period. **Talking to the Sun** includes material by Villa-Lobos, Johnny Mandel and Stevie Wonder, as well as *You're My Thrill*, an erotic chant of a song that Lincoln owns, iconic interpretations by Billie Holiday and Chet Baker notwithstanding. What gives this disc its edge, however, are Lincoln's own songs. *People on the Streets* might be the most empathic song ever written about the homeless, but it takes second place to the title song, in which the orb around which the earth revolves is given human qualities and compared to a lover—the implication being that no man under the sun could be as steadfast as the singer desires. As is also true of Betty Carter, Lincoln has been so celebrated as a singer that her gifts as a lyricist have gone overlooked. In their unpretentious way, the lyrics here approach poetry. So does Lincoln's delivery of them. **FD**

Nils Lindberg

1933

Sax Appeal & Trisection **Lindberg** (p, arr) leading **Idrees Sulieman**, **Jan Allan** (t); **Eje Thelin** (tb); **Rolf Billberg** (as); **Harry Backlund** (ts); **Lars Gullin, Erik Nilsson** (b); **Sture Nordin** (d) and others. Dragon Ⓕ DRCD 220 (67 minutes). Recorded 1960-63.

⑧ ❽

Seven of the titles on this album were made at Lindberg's debut session as composer/arranger. The first day in the studio was a disaster and Lindberg had to beg for a further four hours the next day. It was then that the seven included here, all first takes, were recorded. The three giants of the saxophones, Backlund, Billberg and Gullin, sail through the finely written charts with an easy serenity, and *Just A Take*, an improvised track recorded at the end of the session, turns out to be a variation on *Yesterdays* with some well-oiled baritone from Gullin, later joined in some nice interplay by Billberg on alto. The more ordered tracks by an eleven-piece make up the **Trisection** suite and again display Lindberg's bias towards the saxophones in his original writing and in the solo space allocated to them. However *Ars Gratia Artis* features a free solo from one of the two great Scandinavian trombonists, Eje Thelin (Ake Persson was the other). Thelin has a more conventional solo on *Joker* which also has a tough tenor solo from Backlund. There is melodic trumpet from Sulieman and a piano solo from Lindberg which seems to draw its inspiration from Eddie Costa and, as with much of Lindberg's work, Hank Jones. **SV**

Erica Lindsay

1955

Dreamer **Lindsay** (ts); **Howard Johnson** (tba, bs, flh); **Francesca Tanxley** (p); **Anthony Cox** (b); **Newman Baker** (d); **Robin Eubanks** (tb). Candid Ⓕ CCD 79040 (45 minutes). Recorded 1989.

⑥ ❽

Lindsay is a large talent both as a composer and as a player, but this album is not really delivering all that it promises. The leader plays to a high level and comes across as a saxophonist with sufficient of her own voice to be called distinctive, although the ghost of Coltrane hovers nearby. What she brings to the music, however, is a tangible desire to communicate emotionally, however sophisticated her own concepts may be. This communication certainly takes place when she is soloing or stating themes (drummer Baker is also at his best when backing her), and Howard Johnson can never be anything less than 100%. But the rest of the supporting cast sound a little perfunctory occasionally, while at other times somewhat lacking in imagination (surely there isn't just the McCoy Tyner patented method for comping and soloing in 6/8?). The three stars are mostly for Lindsay; let's hope for more consistent things to come. **KS**

Rudy Linka

1960

Czech It Out! Linka (g); **George Mraz** (b); **Marvin 'Smitty' Smith** (d). Enja Ⓕ ENJ-9001-2 (53 minutes). Recorded 1994.

⑦ ❿

Linka came west from Czechoslovakia in 1981, studied under a string of Americans including Red Mitchell and John Abercrombie, settled in America and began recording as a leader as the nineties dawned. This, his fourth date as a leader, shows increasing maturity and the ability to sustain interest in an exposed format, that of the trio. Of course it helps that his fellow-musicians are such powerful identities, able to fill the spaces with intelligent and meaningful note-choices, but the spotlight rightly falls mostly on Linka.

He helps his own cause by showing himself equally adept at playing jazz on both electric and acoustic six-string guitars (a feat suprisingly few guitarists manage convincingly), and while he sticks by and large to an undistorted tone and a linear approach, he constantly exhibits the sort of wide harmonic knowledge and resourcefulness usually associated with the likes of Jim Hall. His ease with the blues also suggests a familiarity with Scofield. Seven of the nine tunes here are Linka originals, and each is designed to showcase a different aspect of his improvisatory skill, while *How Deep Is The Ocean?* and *Love Letters* find him conversant in traditional modern jazz guitar language. Linka has a lot to offer the serious listener. **KS**

Booker Little

1938-1961

Out Front Little (t); **Eric Dolphy** (f, as, bcl); **Julian Priester** (tb); **Don Friedman** (p); **Art Davis, Ron Carter** (b); **Max Roach** (d). Candid Ⓜ CD 9027 (44 minutes). Recorded 1961.

⑩ ❼

Booker Little came to prominence with the Max Roach Quintet (he worked alongside tenor player George Coleman), playing with that group at the 1958 Newport Jazz Festival when he was just 20 years old. By the time of this, his last album as a leader, he had developed at a phenomenal rate, becoming a resourceful composer as well as a uniquely gifted trumpeter. While his style and sound came directly from the late Clifford Brown, he was one of very few to take Brown's legacy and make something new with it.

Out Front is conceived as a display album for Little: all the tracks are his own compositions and the front line of three horns allows the trumpeter to investigate harmonic combinations unusual in jazz, mostly involving dissonance. There is also considerable experimentation with different metres, sometimes within one piece. His beautiful tone and ear for melody, as well as Roach's inspired drumming, keep this from becoming a dry or ugly exercise, and Little solos convincingly throughout. Dolphy is the other principal soloist, with his alto work on *Moods in Free Time* still coming across as some of his fiercest and most free. But Little is the main attraction, and his playing here often has a beauty which is breathtaking. **KS**

Charles Lloyd

1938

Forest Flower/Soundtrack Lloyd (ts, f); **Keith Jarrett** (p); **Cecil McBee, Ron McClure** (b); **Jack DeJohnette** (d). Rhino/Atlantic Ⓜ R2 71746 (77 minutes). Recorded 1966-68.

⑧ ❽

One of the seminal figures of the sixties, Memphis-born Charles Lloyd forged a unique style conjoining the blues of his hometown, the modal forays of John Coltrane and at times an almost folk music-like lyricism. In Los Angeles, Lloyd studied composition at the University of Southern California and came into contact with Eric Dolphy and Ornette Coleman. His star rose through important gigs with Gerald Wilson, Chico Hamilton and Cannonball Adderley, during which Lloyd made a pivotal shift from alto to tenor. Along with Coltrane's influence, the impact of Lloyd's years as an altoist can be heard in his penchant for the tenor's upper register and his gauzy, mystical tone.

In 1966, Lloyd and his newly-formed quartet with Jarrett, McBee (later replaced by McClure) and DeJohnette became a cause célèbre. Appealing to rock as well as jazz audiences, Lloyd's kaleidoscopic soundscapes encompassed bucolic meditations as well as cascading freefalls. It was fresh, even audacious, and bubbling with sounds-of-surprise. Lloyd's top-drawer status was solidified with the landmark **Forest Flower**, recorded at the Monterey Jazz Festival in 1966, but released in 1967. The mesmerizing title track became Lloyd's anthem. In *Sorcery* and *Sombrero Sam*, Lloyd proved himself a compelling flautist in the soaring, open-ended manner of Jeremy Steig. Equally impressive is the quartet's hand-in-glove interplay and Jarrett's sparkling pianistics sans grunts and groans. **CB**

The Call Lloyd (ts); **Bobo Stenson** (p); **Anders Jormin** (b); **Billy Hart** (d). ECM Ⓕ 1522 (517 719-2) (77 minutes). Recorded 1993.

Lloyd begins this, the album before his latest, **All My Relations** (ECM), with a song called *Nocturne*, and immediately the listener is overwhelmed by its affinity with Coltrane's *After The Rain*. Lloyd always did have a passing resemblance to the older man, but here it is spelled out quite deliberately. His tone has never been richer (perhaps it has never been this well recorded before?), and he sings the melody line on his horn.

Not that the saxophonist has not played melodically before; his phenomenal popular success in the mid-sixties, after a useful training in the Chico Hamilton band which also nurtured Gabor Szabo, was based as much on his memorable extended sketches—*Forest Flower*, for example, always sounded as if it were going somewhere, evolving, rather than being used as a stock item for a bunch of guys to jam on—as on the phenomenal talents which made up the original Charles Lloyd Quartet: Lloyd himself, Keith Jarrett, Ron McClure and Jack DeJohnette.

Most of the great Lloyd albums from the sixties, all on Atlantic, are currently unavailable on CD. This new album is deliberately looking back to that time. In a short note to the purchaser, Lloyd refers to an occasion in France in 1966 when "a group of mystics with saxophones initiated me into their society." That group was the Ellington sax section, and certainly this whole album has the ineffable mood of relaxation and peace which Ellington small groups often achieve. Although individual solos or tracks on his classic sixties albums may reach headier heights than anything here, I doubt whether Lloyd has surpassed this album as a sustained effort. The group (his current working band) is, to these ears at least, a more integrated unit than the one which brought Petrucciani to international attention, and Lloyd's own playing is at a new peak. **KS**

Mornington Lockett

Mornington Lockett **Lockett** (ts, p, b); **Jonathan Gee** (p); **Laurence Cottle** (b); **Ian Thomas** (d, b); **Jim Mullen** (g – 2 tracks); **Sarah Jane Morris** (v – 1 track) EFZ Ⓕ EFZ1006 (58 minutes). Recorded 1993.

⑥ ❽

The young Scottish musician celebrated here was for a couple of years the second saxophonist in Ronnie Scott's group. He shows his paces in what is predominantly a quartet context and, like many debut albums, it has something of the sampler about it, with different tracks coming from different directions. The two pieces with Mullen are an altered blues (seemingly with jazz-bar crowd noises dubbed in) and a promising version of *Lush Life*, which loses direction slightly after going into a steady tempo. Apart from an excellent Rollinesque *I Got Rhythm*-type number (*Laphroaig*) with just Cottle and Thomas, the rest has Jonathan Gee and includes two versions of an acoustic duo with Gee called *Demusiado* – wittily subtitiled *Satie Mix* and *Debussy Mix*.

The more funky items are also well carried off and have Lockett wailing expansively in a manner that even the record compares to Mike Brecker. The whole is expertly recorded, if in that rather dry way typical of British studios which robs the music of its impact, but only Sarah Jane Morris's vocal on the Etta Jones speciality *Don't Go To Strangers* seems a waste of space. **BP**

Giuseppi Logan

1935

More Giuseppi Logan **Logan** (fl, as, bcl, p); **Don Pullen** (p); **Reggie Johnson, Eddie Gomez** (b); **Milford Graves** (d). ESP-Disk Ⓜ 1013-2 (39 minutes). Recorded 1964/65.

④ ❹

Logan was a significant theorist and fellow-traveller during the New York avant-garde jazz explosion of the early and mid-sixties. Trained at New England Conservatory, he later went against most of the accepted tenets of instrumental expertise in an attempt to win a new approach to music. His first album for ESP-Disk (simply titled **Giuseppi Logan**) is so laboured in its perverseness that, through no fault of his accompanying musicians, it becomes quite painful to listen to at times. There is a left-over from that date on this disc (*Wretched Saturday*) which gives ample demonstration of the point. However, there was more to Logan than that record suggested, and the first two tracks on this album, recorded live at a concert in New York's Town Hall (the same gig where Ayler's *Bells* was recorded), are quite presentable. Logan restricts himself to some atmospheric flute and bass clarinet arabesques, leaving Pullen, Graves and Johnson to get down to business. They do this very well indeed, and it is a shame that the recording quality on these two tracks is really very poor. That Logan was quite capable of producing memorable music is evident from his role on Roswell Rudd's 1966 album **Everywhere**, where his own composition *Dance of Satan*, so poorly played on the above self-titled album, gets a rousing performance. **KS**

London Jazz Composers Orchestra

1970

Portraits **Barry Guy** (b, dir); **Henry Lowther**, **Jon Corbett** (t); **Marc Charig** (c); **Paul Rutherford**, **Radu Malfatti**, **Alan Tomlinson** (tb); **Steve Wick** (bb); **Howard Riley** (p); **Trevor Watts**, **Evan Parker**, **Simon Picard**, **Peter McPhail**, **Paul Dunmall** (reeds); **Phil Wachsmann** (vn); **Barre Phillips** (b); **Paul Lytton** (d). Intakt Ⓕ CD 035/1994 (two discs: 115 minutes). Recorded 1993.

⑧ ❽

The London Jazz Composers Orchestra is a band that matches improvisation with structured writing in a way that dispenses with the word 'paradox'. Formed in 1970, it has continually sought to provide cohesive direction to solo or small group freedoms under an orchestral banner. Following the band's initial success, an overtly academic route was pursued; pointing the music toward atonality and introducing certain restrictive practices. The period was brief and a degree of constructive mutiny led the band back to more righteous values.

This CD ideally illustrates leader Guy's current performance principles. He is helped by the quality of solos, while group sequences that he uses smooths their path with orchestral textures to suit each situation. Typical is the way that Wick is cossetted on *Study III* and the manner in which almost Ellingtonian calm eases the path for Corbett on *Crackle*. Sheer drama showcases Parker on *Triple*, light counterpoint is the tool in use on *Sunnyman*, while the entire orchestra bellows on *Five Pieces*. The important point is that the solo interludes and combo cameos are organic entities, vital to the musical progress of every work. They ensure that the formal and the free are balanced and explain how the LJCO confronts the concept of 'jazz orchestra'. **BMcR**

Joe Lovano 1952

Tenor Legacy **Lovano** (ts) with **Joshua Redman** (ts); **Mulgrew Miller** (p); **Christian McBride** (b); **Lewis Nash** (d); **Don Alias** (perc). Blue Note Ⓕ CDP 8 27014 2 2 (67 minutes). Recorded 1993.

⑦ ❽

Lovano's story is one of an excellent journeyman becoming a major soloist almost without anyone noticing. He had performed admirably with Herman's Herd in the seventies and with the Mel Lewis Band in the eighties. He toured with Carla Bley in 1983 but has emerged over the last five years as a first-call player and a welcome maverick in all manner of musical environments. His authoritative work has been welcomed by John Scofield, Paul Motian, Charlie Haden and the Smithsonian Repertory Orchestra, as well as just about anyone in need of a boss saxophone soloist.

This CD finds Lovano with an outstanding rhythm section and in the company of a fine young tenor player. In many ways, it represents a logical extension of the progress documented by the 1990 **From The Soul** (CDP7 98636-2) but the challenge here is greater and the response commensurate with it. It outlines his arranging skills on *Introspection*, his ballad acumen on a superbly devleoped *Laura* and the economy of his contrapuntal playing on *Web Of Fire*. Redman's talents are covered elsewhere but this tenor duel is rather special and it confirms that the curve on Lovano's success spiral continues upward. **BMcR**

Frank Lowe 1941

Decision in Paradise **Lowe** (ts); **Don Cherry** (t); **Grachan Moncur III** (tb); **Geri Allen** (p); **Charnett Moffett** (b); **Charles Moffett** (d). Soul Note Ⓕ SN 1082 CD (39 minutes). Recorded 1984.

⑧ ❼

Lowe's first love was the soul music of his home town, Memphis. Later he moved to New York, played with Sun Ra and, inspired by John Coltrane, became associated with the wilder fringes of free jazz. Since the early seventies, however, he has explored many varieties of contemporary music, studied the tradition and worked with artists as diverse as Billy Bang, Eugene Chadbourne and Leo Smith. **Decision in Paradise** is the finest example of this mature versatility. It teams the sixties generation of Lowe, Cherry and Moncur with eighties newcomer Allen and underscores this cross-generation dialogue with a father-and-son rhythm section. The blend works well, with Moncur's vintage radicalism and Allen's bright-eyed stylings being particularly effective.

Lowe's gruff-toned, knotty lines retain a good deal of warmth, not least on *I'll Whistle Your Name*, a solo tenor track delivered with passion. His *Lowe-ology* and *Decision in Paradise* are droll, catchy tunes; a hint of Monk plus a pinch of funk. Moncur's *You Dig!* and Lowe's *Dues and Don'ts* are the long tracks; the former a witty swing through post-sixties bebop, the latter a labyrinthine affair which, declares Lowe, is about "finding one's own way through a musical maze." That all the soloists here manage this with aplomb sums up the spirit of this greatly enjoyable disc. **GL**

Mundell Lowe 1922

The Mundell Lowe Quartet **Lowe** (g); **Dick Hyman** (p, org); **Trigger Alpert** (b); **Ed Shaughnessy** (d). Riverside Ⓜ OJCCD-1773-2 (37 minutes). Recorded 1955.

④ ❻

In the mid-fifties Lowe and Hyman were anchoring the rhythm sections of numerous New York studio bands for radio and TV, and this quartet got together (rather as Bud Shank's groups did on the West Coast) to escape the studio grind and play some jazz. This is an only partially successful escape, and recapture seems imminent throughout, as both men's nonchalant studio technique and chameleon tendencies keep hi-jacking the best jazz moments with displays of stunning superficiality.

When things start cooking, however, the jazz is very good indeed. Low and Hyman pace each other through a series of chase choruses on *All Of You*, while *Yes, Sir, That's My Baby* features the whole group. Shaughnessy's drum accents underpinning the theme and Alpert's accomplished bass work before launching him into a clattery solo on his rims. Lowe's guitar work is on par with Raney or Kessell, and his quote-laden solo on *Cheek To Cheek* is masterly. Hyman sounds better on piano, his organ work owing more to Reginald Dixon than Jimmy Smith. He never gets the volume changes right, sounding too abrupt, and his mock church playing on *Bach Revisited* is too pious for comfort. **AS**

Jimmie Lunceford

1902-47

Rhythm Is Our Business **Lunceford** (ldr, as, v); **Eddie Tomkins, Tommy Stevenson, William Tomlin, Paul Webster, Gerald Wilson, Snooky Young** (t); **Sy Oliver** (t, v); **Henry Wells, Russell Bowles, Elmer Crumbly** (tb); **Eddie Durham** (tb, g); **Trummy Young** (tb, v); **Willie Smith** (as, cl, v); **Dan Grissom, Ted Buckner** (as, cl); **Farl Carruthers** (bs, as, cl); **Laforet Dent, Ed Brown** (as); **Joe Thomas** (ts, cl, v); **Edwin Wilcox** (p); **Al Norris** (g); **Moses Allen** (b); **James Crawford** (d). ASV Living Era Ⓜ CDA JA5091 (71 minutes). Recorded 1933-40.

⑧ ❻

Observers of the day claim that Lunceford's band was the greatest show band working in Harlem during the thirties and that its section work was never less than immaculate. The latter comment is certainly borne out on the two dozen tracks selected for this truly representative collection by compiler Vic Bellerby. With Willie Smith leading the reed section and men such as Sy Oliver and Edwin Wilcox both writing for and playing in the band it was certainly a most musicianly orchestra. Lunceford was obviously concerned with putting on a show at the dance halls, but there was still room for a sizeable jazz content too. Bellerby's selection creams off the best of the latter (the Lunceford discography is certainly not without dross, but none of it is here). This CD contains two of the Duke Ellington numbers which the band used in its earlier days, Willie Smith's arrangement of *Sophisticated Lady* (with Smith playing the theme immaculately on clarinet) and Oliver's score of *Black And Tan Fantasy*, with fine growl trumpet from Sy. The collection also includes two more popular Oliver arrangements in *Margie* and *'Tain't What You Do*, but the peak of jazz involvement is the classic *Uptown Blues* with solos from Smith on alto and trumpeter Snooky Young. The transfer from 78s is good. **AM**

Jan Lundgren

1966

Conclusion **Lundgren** (p); **Jesper Lundgaard** (b); **Alex Riel** (d). Four Leaf Clover Ⓕ FLC CD 136 (61 minutes). Recorded 1994.

⑧ ❽

Lundgren is a Swede but this CD was recorded in Copenhagen, when his trio was completed by two of Denmark's leading musicians. It is a fine example of the maturity now to be found in Scandinavian jazz circles where countries with small populations continue to produce high-quality players in numbers quite out of proportion with the inhabitants. Jan is a player with considerable knowledge of the standard jazz repertoire (I have never heard anyone play the verse to *My Ideal* before) and a fluent approach to improvisation. He has a firm touch and is not one of the army of pianists trying to sound like Bill Evans. Yet there is something of Evans in his harmonic approach and his own tunes (five out of the 11 tracks) have the logical construction of Evans's own works. Lundgren's *Short Life* is an extension of Strayhorn's *Lush Life* and it is good to find someone playing a tune by the neglected Elmo Hope, in this instance *So Nice*. Lundgren is a pianist of considerable expertise playing very attractive music and it would be regrettable if he failed to receive the recognition which is so obviously his due. The work of Lungaard and Riel is beyond reproach. **AM**

Carmen Lundy

Self Portrait **Lundy** (v) with a collective personnel including: **Gary Herbig** (f, ss); **Ernie Watts** (ts); **Cedar Walton** (p); **John Clayton** (b); **Ralph Penland** (d); orchestras arranged and conducted by **Jeremy Lubbock**. JVC Ⓕ JVC-2047-2 (59 minutes). Recorded 1994.

⑥ ❽

Lundy has a superb, richly dark alto voice, great timing and perfect diction. She has chosen a goodly bunch of tunes to work out on here, and her selection of supporting musicians could hardly be bettered. Her approach reminds occasionally of the young Abbey Lincoln, and from time to time the more arch and unappealing side of that singer's work can also be found in Lundy's delivery. It may not be coincidental that her best singing tends to come on her own material, where the collective weight of past interpretations doesn't have to be grappled with. That said, she makes a very fair pass at *My Favorite Things*, rarely associated in jazz with someone interpreting the lyrics; more with swirling saxophone flights. But then, the very fact that Coltrane has so dominated this song's jazz image means that Lundy has a pretty clear run at it. Watts takes a biting Brecker-inspired tenor solo on this track.

There is plenty to recommend: for one thing, the orchestra only crops up from time to time (I'm not entirely convinced she knows what to do with an orchestral accompaniment: she seems a touch unsure of her angle on a song when it oozes around her), and the trio is light and sure. Lundy only needs to deepen her interpretations to move up alongside the best of the current jazz voal crop. **KS**

Nellie Lutcher 1915

Ditto From Me To You **Lutcher** (p); with a collective personnel of **Harry Edison**, **Taft Jordan**, **Sy Oliver** (t); **Marshall Royal** (as); **Fred Williams** (ts); **Ulysses Livingstone**, **Hurley Ramey**, **John Collins** (g); **Billy Hadnott**, **Truck Parham**, **Benny Booker**, **Sandy Block** (b); **Lee Young**, **Alvin Burroughs**, **Earl Hyde** (d); **The Billy May Orchestra**; **The Harold Mooney Orchestra**. Jukebox Lil Ⓕ RBD 1103 (43 minutes). Recorded 1947-55.

⑥ ❼

Nellie Lutcher, sister of r&b saxophonist Joe Lutcher, was born in the hamlet of Lake Charles, Louisiana, and by the late twenties was already sufficiently proficient on the piano to help out Ma Rainey when her regular pianist dipped out of the show one night in Lake Charles. In 1935 Lutcher moved to California and pursued a career as a solo nightclub singer and pianist, filling in with band work for local leaders around Los Angeles when times were hard. A contemporary of such singers as Mildred Bailey, Billie Holiday and Julia Lee, Lutcher had to wait until 1947 before making her first records, but then her success was immediate. Her unique, coy, fun-filled voice, her slightly risqué lyrics and her forthright piano style combined to win her an eager audience. For a period of two years after her 1947 signing to Capitol she could do no wrong in the studio and most of her best work was done at this time. In a sense she took up from where Fats Waller left off, although her piano style was nowhere near as comprehensive as Waller's. However, that infectious sense of fun, of sharing a secret or joke with the listener, is equally strong. As she proved with the hit *Cool Water*, she was also capable of communicating simple, deeply-felt emotions. This compilation, one of a number on the Jukebox Lil label but the only one so far to have been transferred to CD, is not her best work, and the hits on it are in her novelty style - *The Pig-Latin Song* and *Princess Poo-Poo-Ly Has Plenty of Papaya* - but it gives the newcomer some idea at least of her inimitable style. The last two tracks come from an old Epic 10" LP from the mid-fifties. Perhaps EMI/Capitol will someday do us all a favour and hurry on down with the ultimate Lutcher CD collection. Until then, this will have to suffice. **KS**

Bobby Lyle

Best of **Lyle** (elp, syn, p); **Oscar Brashear** (t); **Ernie Watts** (ts); **Bill Rogers**, **Roland Bautista**, **Michael McGloiry**, **L. Marlo Henderson** (g); **Michael Boddicker** (syn progs); **Donnie Beck**, **Nathaniel Phillips**, **Nathaniel Watts** (b); **Steven Guitierrez**, **Harvey Mason**, **Kenneth Rice** (d); **Babtunde**, **Sunship**, **Joe Blocker**, **Paulhino da Costa**, **Bobbye Hall** (perc); **Flo Lyle**, **Marjie Lyle**, **Saundra Alexander** (v). Blue Note Ⓜ CDP 7 89284 2 (44 minutes). Recorded 1977-79.

⑥ ❼

Lyle first came to prominence in the Young-Holt Ltd set-up (Young and Holt being two thirds of the most famous Ramsey Lewis trio). This compilation is from three vinyl Lyle-led discs originally released on the Capitol label. Some of it, such as the first track *Pisces*, has little relationship to jazz of any description, and my old elevator nightmare comes back to haunt me, but there is a good deal of excellent playing elsewhere, not least from Lyle himself, who may not be a wonderfully original stylist but who is a superbly competent player and an imaginative arranger in the Hancockian electric mode. There are good moments, too, from Oscar Brashear, especially on *Night Breeze*, where he carries a melody attractively.

Although 44 minutes may not seem particularly generous, culled as it is from three different albums, space has been found to include three solo acoustic piano run-throughs: *What Is This Thing Called Love?*, *Blues For Scott Joplin* and *I Didn't Know What Time It Was*. Apart from demonstrating that he can play the piano in the mode of Monty Alexander and other technique freaks, and that he has a lively sense of humour à la Jaki Byard, they don't add a great deal of cohesion to this programme. **KS**

Brian Lynch 1956

At The Main Event **Lynch** (t); **Ralph Moore** (ts); **Peter Bernstein** (g); **Melvin Rhyne** (org); **Kenny Washington** (d); **Jose Alexis Diaz** (perc). Criss Cross Ⓕ 1070 CD (58 minutes). Recorded 1991.

⑦ ❽

Brian Lynch's trumpet has graced the small groups of Horace Silver and Charles McPherson; he broadened this experience in the big bands of George Russell, Mel Lewis and Toshiko Akiyoshi and, most significantly, was the last trumpeter in the Jazz Messengers. In the early nineties he gained in reputation by filling the difficult space created by Tom Harrell's departure from the Phil Woods Quintet. The impression given on this CD is of a 'working' band; in his notes, Lynch talks of the jazz of his youth and the clubs that sired it. To endorse it, the orthodox hard bop of the 1986 album **Peer Pressure** (Criss 1029 CD) is replaced by more functional 'club' music.

Rhyne plays an important part, his ensemble backgrounds being assured and his solos well articulated and buoyant. Moore plays with similar authority and Bernstein signals that he is an

emerging talent. This is Lynch's album, however, and he is a confident and versatile player. His tonal quality is highlighted on *Cry Me A River*, his uncompromising attack is a feature of *Blues For Woody* and *Nite 'Vidual*. The extent of his improvisational ability is showcased in imaginative solos on *Ecaroh* and the title track, but throughout, his flair for logical thought and unpredictable delivery complements that for swinging. This is jazz from the nineties that provides a continuous link with the early sixties.
BMcR

Jimmy Lyons
1932-1986

Give It Up **Lyons** (as); **Enrico Rava** (t); **Karen Borca** (bn); **Jay Oliver** (b); **Paul Murphy** (d). Black Saint Ⓕ BSR 0087 CD (45 minutes). Recorded 1985.

⑧ ❼

Jimmy Lyons spent 25 years as loyal collaborator-cum-interpreter to Cecil Taylor, whom he met in 1960 and in whose groups he then played until his death in 1986. During that period Lyons also led his own groups from time to time, though he made only a handful of records under his own name. **Give It Up** is the last and arguably the best of these, although its predecessor **Wee Sneezawee** (not yet on CD) runs it close.

The main appeal of **Give It Up** is that it is such a good 'group' record. Rather than go for extended solos, Lyons sets up a series of animated conversations in which Rava's mercurial trumpet and the grainy cry of Borca's bassoon bob and weave around his propulsive alto in playful call-and-response chases. For all its busy surfaces however, there is a broad seam of lyricism running through the music that is finally openly acknowledged on the closing *Ballada*, a passionate, singing elegy with distant echoes of *Parker's Mood*. Charlie Parker was Lyons's chief influence and it was through Lyons's alto—coursing, sinuous, bluesy—that Parker's metrical assurance was first translated into a freer context. **Give It Up** allows the listener to savour the tough-minded elegance which is Lyons's trademark.
GL

Johny Lytle
1932

The Loop / New And Groovy **Lytle** (vb, ldr); **unknown** (p), (b); probably **'Peppy' Hinnant** (d). BGP Ⓜ CDBGPD 961 (70 minutes). Recorded 1966.

⑥ ❹

Lytle cut his musical teeth in his father's band in Springfield Ohio and as drummer with Ray Charles and Gene Ammons. When he switched to vibes in 1953 he moved inexorably towards dance-hall based soul jazz, backed by organ, bass and drums but occasionally working alongside Johnny Griffin or Frank Wess, and often with star sidemen like bassists Milt Hinton, Bob Cranshaw or Major Holley. He cut the two albums that comprise this CD for Tuba, a minor Detroit-based label, during the unparalleled explosion of small independent soul record companies in the fifties and sixties. The fuzzy sound, the artificial echo, and the dreamy quality of the playing, especially on the medium-paced *Selim*, made the records a cult among jazz-dance enthusiasts, and before this reissue the originals had become expensive collector's items. The legend, cultivated by rarity, is overstated on this evidence, but Lytle has a deft vibraphone style and a sound that is quite unlike Hampton, Jackson or Burton, though at times close to Bobby Hutcherson. This is unpretentious, straight-ahead rhythmic playing, with solos designed to entice the listener onto the dance floor. Standards like *The More I See You* and *Time After Time* are more rewarding than Lytle originals like *The Snapper* and *Possum Grease*. **AS**

Harold Mabern
1936

Straight Street **Mabern** (p); **Ron Carter** (b); **Jack DeJohnette** (d). DIW Ⓕ 608 (58 minutes). Recorded 1989.

⑧ ❽

Harold Mabern has not exactly led a career in the limelight, but he has held down some pretty impressive positions, including the piano chair in the groups of Miles Davis, Roland Kirk, J.J. Johnson, Wes Montgomery and The Jazztet. Instructed—and influenced—by Phineas Newborn, Mabern still has a distinctive identity, a suppleness and flexibility of rhythm unusual in a pianist, and a highly sophisticated harmonic sense. His trio here performs little miracles at every turn, the three musicians knitting together seamlessly.

The programme is a mixture of Mabern originals and cover versions of some quite unusual pieces—the title track, by John Coltrane, Stevie Wonder's *Don't You Worry 'Bout a Thing* and another Coltrane composition, *Crescent*. His approach to these pieces is very creative: he has refused to treat them as museum pieces, yet has preserved the underlying character of both the music and its originators. On his own songs Mabern shows his heart to be inextricably linked to the sixties, but the firm touch and decisive improvising abilities exhibited guarantee that this will not be an exercise in wistful nostalgia. Definitely a piano trio album worth releasing. One certainly cannot say that about all of them.
KS

Cecil McBee

1935

Mutima **McBee** (b); **Tex Allen** (t, flh); **George Adams** (ts); **Allen Braufman** (as); **Art Webb** (f); **Onaje Allen Gumbs** (p, kbds); **Cecil McBee Jr** (elb); **Jimmy Hopps**, **Allen Nelson** (d); **Lawrence Killian** (pc); **Michael Carvin** (p); **Jaboli Billy Hart** (perc); **Dee Dee Bridgewater** (v). Strata East/Bellaphon Ⓕ 660-51-006 (45 minutes). Recorded 1974.

⑦ ❽

Having already made a name for himself in Detroit, McBee moved to new York in 1964. Since that date, a list of the leaders for whom he has worked would read like a who's who of contemporary jazz. Comfortable with bop, modal or free jazz, he has consciously served all with his special brand of bass skill, whether with finger or bow. This CD finds him at the helm of his own ship, playing his own compositions and with the personnel of his choice. Stylistically, the music comes from the New York loft scene of the seventies, committed to strong melodic lines but with soloists essentially free to exploit them as seems appropriate.

Cut in one day, the session was built around *Mutima (forces unseen)*. This title track is a well-structured work by McBee, evoking the spirit and culture of black Africa while allowing the solo roster free reign. Gumbs and the horn men make particularly ferocious progress on *Life Waves*, perhaps the archetypal loft jam number, and transform *Tulsa Black* from a funky languor to the mood of a free rambler with faked all-in passages to match. If proof of McBee's instrumental skills is required, it is to be found in the superb backgrounds of *Life Waves* and in his inspired 'duet' with himself *From Within*.

BMcR

Christian McBride

1972

Gettin' To It **McBride** (b); **Roy Hargrove** (t); **Steve Turré** (tb); **Louis Nash** (d) **Joshua Redman** (ts); **Cyrus Chestnut** (p); **Ray Brown**, **Milt Hinton** (b). Verve Ⓕ CD 523 989 2 (56 minutes). Recorded 1994.

⑧ ❽

The young bassist Mr McBride got to it a long time ago and has had a profound effect on the New York jazz scene. Most of his appearances have been on Blue Note, often with the Bennie Green Trio, but the label has apparently slipped up in not being the one to give him his first album under his own name. It was predictable that such a display of virtuosity should be quite overwhelming, and it is appropriate that McBride should be joined for one track by an earlier 'best in the world', fellow bassist Ray Brown and by the ubiquitous Milt Hinton, 63 years older than he.

Each track is dominated by McBride's huge tone and measured dexterity and it is unusual to find the music from an instrument not usually regarded as a solo voice so riveting. McBride uses a good variety of settings with his basic quintet, which plays hard bop tempered by the prodigious bass lines. Pianist Cyrus Chestnut and drummer Louis Nash, both from the quintet, back McBride on an imaginative version of *Stars Fell On Alabama*, while McBride and Redman evoke shades of the immortal Lucky Thompson/Oscar Pettiford duets in McBride's unusual voicing of *In A Hurry*. It is not until the final track, *Night Train*, that McBride indulges himself in a splendid solo mixture of traditional walking bass and vigorous arco.

SV

Les McCann

1935

Swiss Movement **McCann** (p, v); **Benny Bailey** (t); **Eddie Harris** (ts); **Leroy Vinnegar** (b); **Donald Dean** (d). Atlantic Ⓜ 781365-2 (39 minutes). Recorded 1969.

⑤ ❻

Born in Kentucky, McCann settled in California after leaving the navy and, armed with a Pacific Jazz contract, found that his rolling, bluesy piano style fitted neatly with the soul/jazz movement that was under way in the sixties. **The Truth** and **On Time** were typical albums as his version of the 'baptist rock' became a trademark. By the close of the sixties his popularity had overrun jazz's boundaries, and his new contract with Atlantic reflected that fact. This CD is the re-issue of what was a best-selling album. The line-up is impressive and their collective potential, at one of the biggest jazz Festivals and in front of an enthusiastic audience, was unlimited. In the event, the outcome is disappointing; Bailey injects a little personal spice into *You Got It In Your Soulness* and Harris gambols along in his usual manner on *Cold Duck Time* but the leader's work is somewhat perfunctory. His Fats Domino-type vocal puts across the social message of *Compared To What* but, although his solos on *Cold Duck Time* and *Generation Gap* take him on his canorously churchified route, the listener finds himself looking for more content in a style that lacks variety. For a more complete picture of his real abilities, we will have to wait for some of the better Pacific Jazz or Limelight albums of the early and mid-sixties to be reissued.

BMcR

Ron McClure

1941

McJolt **McClure** (b); **John Abercrombie** (g); **Richie Beirach** (p); **Adam Nussbaum** (d). SteepleChase Ⓕ SCCD 31262 (68 minutes). Recorded 1989.

⑥ ❽

Although McClure, who came to attention in the sixties with Charles Lloyd Quartet, has a wide-ranging and distinguished pedigree as a sideman and freelance with such diverse musicians as Wynton Kelly and the seventies jazz-rock group Fourth Way, he has recently been heard mostly in trio with Richie Beirach and Adam Nussbaum, often supporting a horn, such as David Liebman or Conrad Herwig. It was the unity of that trio that led McClure to choose his colleagues for this date, and it was their habitual role as trio to a horn that led McClure to ask Abercrombie along as a guest. Abercrombie has subsequently been heard regularly in the straight-ahead idiom, but this was one of the earliest indications that he was becoming rehabilitated to bop and the sound of the unmodified electric guitar after several albums of abstracted guitar synth music. Revelling perhaps in the rediscovery, he plays with uncharacteristic fire and abandon, making sparing and effective use of the tremolo arm. The synth is still there, but set to double certain guitar notes rather than obliterate them. Beirach is his usual tart self, subverting the harmonies on *Stella*, and while McClure does not pull rank as far as solo space is concerned, he takes a goodly share, producing a singing tone rich in high frequencies, not unlike that of Eddie Gomez.

MG

Rob McConnell

1935

Our 25th Year **McConnell** (tb); **Arnie Chycoski**, **Steve McDade**, **John MacLeod**, **Guido Basso**, **Dave Woods** (t, flh); **Alistair Kay**, **Bob Livingston**, **Jerry Johnson** (tb); **Ernie Pattison** (btb); **Gary Pattison**, **James McDonald** (frh); **Moe Koffman**, **John Johnson** (f, cl, ss, as); **Eugene Amaro** (f, cl, ts); **Rick Wilkins** (cl, ts); **Bob Leonard** (f, cl, bcl, bs); **Don Thompson** (p); **Ed Bickert** (g); **Steve Wallace** (b); **Terry Clarke** (d); **Brian Leonard** (vb, perc). Concord Ⓕ CCD 4559 (60 minutes). Recorded 1993.

⑥ ❽

When Canadian-born McConnell formed Boss Brass in 1968 it was a group without a reed section. They were added in 1971 and the band has gained in reputation since that date. They made their American debut in the 1981 Monterey Jazz Festival and won a Grammy in 1984 with **All In Good Time**. This CD celebrates their 25th year and is typical of their work. The players are highly professional, the arrangements are mainly good, with *Imagination* the best here, and the solos are always up to an acceptable standard. The best individual efforts on this session come from the leader, imaginatively positive on *4BC* and *TO2*, Bickert, who has original ideas regarding *Broadway*, and Don Thompson, a Bill Evans stylist, who puts his own decorative brand on Evans's *My Bells*. Basso, who basks in the comfort of the *Imagination* chart, is the pick of the trumpets, while Amaro is the best saxophone on view. Over-busy arrangements, such as those on *Nightfall* and *TO2*, are not the rule, but there are moments when the band's ability to swing is restricted. The indefinable elasticity that leads to swing is even missing on *Flying Home*, but with live dates reported as being very different from recorded efforts, it could be that the band does not fully respond to the studio environment.

BMcR

Susannah McCorkle

From Bessie to Brazil **McCorkle** (v); **Randy Sandke** (t, flh); **Robert Trowers** (tb); **Dick Oatts** (as, f); **Ken Peplowski** (ts, c); **Alan Farnham** (p); **Howard Alden** (g); **Kiyoshi Kitagawa** (b); **Chuck Redd** (d). Concord Jazz Ⓕ CCD-4547 (60 minutes). Recorded 1993.

⑧ ❽

McCorkle is a singer whose shining virtues include the insight she brings to lyrics, the wholesome sexuality she projects, and her refusal to take gratuitous liberties with a song in the name of jazz. She first attracted attention for the excellent series of lyricist songbooks for Inner City and Pausa in the early eighties. None of these has yet appeared on CD. Her albums since then have been more eclectic in their range of material, and this has sometimes worked against them. Along with **No More Blues** from 1989, this is the most successful of her efforts for Concord Jazz. The Brazilian numbers are fairly lightweight, but McCorkle turns in winning interpretations of several standards, including Harold Arlen and Johnny Mercer's *Hit the Road to Dreamland*. What is more remarkable, she manages to make Rupert Holmes's *The People That You Never Get To Love* and Paul Simon's *Still Crazy After All These Years* sound like trenchant modern urban blues songs. Best of all, though, is her version of the Bessie Smith-associated *My Sweetie Went Away*, on which she evokes Bessie without resorting to caricature. *Thief in the Night*, which attempts to do the same for Ethel Waters, is less convincing because it is a little too reverential. The accompaniment provided by music director Farnham and the others is overcrowded enough in places to make you wish that Concord would acknowledge McCorkle's relationship to cabaret and record her with just a pianist.

FD

Jack McDuff

1926

Another Real Good'un **McDuff** (org); **Cecil Bridgewater** (t); **Ron Bridgewater** (as, ts); **Houston Person** (ts); **John Hart, Randy Johnston** (g); **Rudy Williams, Cecil Brooks III** (d). Muse Ⓕ MCD 5374 (46 minutes). Recorded 1989/90.

⑥ ❻

McDuff swapped to organ late in the fifties from his first instrument, piano, and vestiges of his pianistic touch remain, especially when he is not playing the blues. However, McDuff has rightly earned the reputation of a grease merchant, and when he is in good shape, he can funk it up with the best of them. On this album, as opposed to the disappointing **The ReEntry**, recorded the year before on Muse, McDuff was definitely in the mood, and is as impressive in his own way as on any of the Prestige dates he made with Willis Jackson in the sixties. He is greatly aided here by willing playing from all the soloists, and driving work from both drummers, sharing alternate tracks. Person stamps his authority on proceedings every time he steps up to solo, getting very basic and rather exciting. Both guitarists have the grit and edge in their tone to make an impact, and McDuff himself, though he doesn't overtax his imagination, gets a very satisfying groove going. Some of the themes are basic to the point of minimalism. **KS**

Malcolm Macfarlane

The Mulford-MacFarlane Group: Jamming Frequency **Malcolm Macfarlane** (g); **Pete Murray** (kbds); **Phil Mulford** (elb); **Mike Bradley** (d). Bridge Ⓕ BRGCD13 (59 minutes). Recorded 1994.

⑧ ❽

If anyone still wonders why good money is spent on jazz education they will find an answer in this musicianly and imaginative British fusion group, which is composed entirely of well-schooled alumni of the National Youth Jazz Orchestra.

The co-principles are both strong soloists, Macfarlane in particular working an attractive seam which ranges from clean, crisp Stratocaster lines to warm distorted tones, but like most fusion groups, the MMG places most emphasis on composition and arrangement. As well as essaying a variety of styles, from the mellifluous Metheny-esque samba of *Bar Italia* to the heavy-duty Scofieldian funk of *Mr T.P.*, the composers are careful to extract a broad range of texture, timbre and dynamic variation from relatively small forces, writing continuously-evolving compositions rather than sketchy preambles to strings of solos. Thus instead of them appearing in dull sequential form over largely unvarying rhythms and textures, solos emerge as organic elements in ingeniously constructed compositions. This may seem an uncool constraint on the hallowed soloist, but for the listener it is a good deal more fun than a thousand unstructured blowing choruses. **MG**

Bobby McFerrin

1950

& Chick Corea: Play **McFerrin** (v); **Corea** (p). Blue Note Ⓕ CDP 795477-2 (50 minutes). Recorded 1990.

⑥ ❻

McFerrin had a deserved hit a few years back with *Don't Worry, Be Happy* from his **Simple Pleasures** album. That was an absorbing and masterful collection, piling up layers of McFerrin voice tracks on such songs as the title track and *The Sunshine of Your Love*, but it had little real connection with jazz, being more a fantasia for voices. This duet album with Corea takes McFerrin back to the type of work he was doing for Elektra Musician—spontaneous compositions, playful improvisations, outrageous invention.

McFerrin has a clean and easy control of a voice with a wide range but not spectacular depth; he can move it around at will and give it sudden crescendi and decrescendi without wavering from pitch or losing his natural voice quality. Some of the material suffers from being a recording of a concert— the spontaneous humour of *Autumn Leaves* certainly gets the audience, but a few listenings take the edge off the tomfoolery. Victor Borge he is not. However, on the plus side, Chick Corea certainly is Chick Corea, and he plays sensationally throughout, giving McFerrin phenomenal support as well as adding beautiful touches of his own. On balance, then, this is certainly worth investigating, and the combination of McFerrin and Corea during Corea's solo on Ornette's *Blues Connotation* really is something special, even if the head is not that accurately sung. The recording balance is sometimes not ideal. **KS**

Bernie McGann

Ugly Beauty **McGann** (as); **Lloyd Swanton** (b); **John Pochee** (d). Spiral Scratch Ⓕ 0010 (54 minutes). Recorded 1991.

⑧ ❼

McGann finally stopped being Australian jazz's best-kept secret when he played briefly in the US during the eighties, alerting the keen-eared there to a talent which, had it been settled closer to New

York, would long ago have been accorded world-wide acclaim. As it is, McGann has been a first-rate altoist playing around the razor's edge of bebop and freer styles since the mid-sixties, and he long ago evolved a personal mode of expression which makes both his sound and his angle of approach instantly recognizable.

This trio date, one of a lamentably few number of records McGann has made under his own name in a long career, gives him plenty of room to expound on the improviser's art and very few places to hide. Playing Monk without a piano, for example, is usually left to the likes of Steve Lacy, but McGann is completely at ease with *Ugly Beauty*. *Without a Song* was memorably covered by Rollins but here McGann fashions a set of personal paraphrases which recast the tune in his own image, while *Daydream*, long synonymous with Johnny Hodges, is approached from such a different angle, both emotionally and architecturally, that McGann pretty much reinvents the environment within which the melody exists. In all this he is helped enormously by Swanton and Pochée, both of whom have long been masters on their instruments. This may not be the easiest CD in the world to find (it will in all likelihood be a special import) but it is worth the bother. **KS**

Howard McGhee

1918-1987

Howard McGhee and Milt Jackson **McGhee** (t); with a collective personnel including **Trummy Young** (tb); **Jimmy Heath** (as, ts); **Billy Smith, unknown** (ts); **Milt Jackson** (vb, v); **Vernon Biddle, Will Davis** (p); **Percy Heath, Victor McMillan** (b); **Joe Harris** (d). Denon/Savoy Ⓜ SV 0167 (31 minutes). Recorded 1947/48.

⑤ ❺

There is considerable confusion as to the precise personnel on both of the sessions which go to make up this album. Denon date them February 1948, and place them in Chicago, but what Denon (and Arista/Savoy before them) give as the personnel often does not tally with what is clearly the case from close listening (Denon seem to have taken their listings direct from Ruppli). There *is* a vocalist—not Eckstine, who probably wasn't even at the session, but Milt Jackson, performing under the pseudonym of The Hammer. The trombonist is an orthodox slide player, not Billy Eckstine on valve trombone, as given by Denon and Ruppli. There are also two saxophones on this same session, which Bruyninckx gives as late 1947, probably Detroit. This is definitely true, because on *Flip Lip* their solos actually overlap for a couple of notes. On *Belle From Bunnycock* they clearly trade fours. A different line-up (with Davis on piano and Heath on bass) made the 1948 sides, which Bruyninckx gives as later in the year than February.

Anyway, what about the music itself? I'm afraid to say that it's rather undistinguished, and not up to the usual quality of work McGhee—easily one of the greatest bop trumpeters—achieves when he leads a studio date. His own playing is excellent, but the songs (apart from *Merry Lee*, which is a direct steal from Monk of *Hackensack*) are pretty dull, and the track lengths indicate a lack of inspiration: they range from just 1 min. 57 secs to 2 min. 59 secs. Jimmy Heath and Milt Jackson hot things up a little when they are featured, but if it is prime early McGhee you're after, then try his live work with JATP or Gene Norman, his date with Parker (Bird's nightmare date, where Maggie plays very well indeed), or his brilliant solos with Coleman Hawkins.

The playing time is ridiculous, especially when two alternative takes, which have been available for years, are overlooked here. **KS**

Maggie's Back in Town! **McGhee** (t); **Phineas Newborn Jr** (p); **Leroy Vinnegar** (b); **Shelly Manne** (d). Contemporary Ⓜ OJCCD 693-2 (43 minutes). Recorded 1961.

⑧ ❽

Trumpeter Howard McGhee is one of the players who figured prominently in the transition from swing to bebop. Though he had studied clarinet, he fell in love with trumpet and started playing in midwest territory bands in the late thirties. Following stints with Lionel Hampton and Andy Kirk, McGhee was ushered into bebop's inner circle by Dizzy Gillespie. A quick learner, he soon found himself playing with Charlie Parker as well as with Charlie Barnet and Coleman Hawkins. In 1949, Down Beat designated him 'Best Trumpeter'. Drug-related problems kept him mostly off the scene during the fifties, but when he returned in 1960, there was if anything a new maturity. His tone was more burnished, and while he could still dazzle with lightning licks, he was also willing to let the music breathe.

Here, on one of his finest dates, McGhee is given hand-in-glove support by the amazingly inventive Phineas Newborn Jr and the supple, steady team of Leroy Vinnegar and Shelly Manne. With his full yet edgy tone and torrid technique ablaze, McGhee relentlessly pursues the blues in *Demon Chase*. He smoulders on the poignant *Willow Weep for Me* and *Summertime*, and flies passionately through fallen trumpeter Clifford Brown's *Brownie Speaks*. **CB**

Jimmy McGriff

1936

The Starting Five McGriff (org); **Rusty Bryant** (as, ts); **David 'Fathead' Newman** (as, ts, f); **Mel Brown, Wayne Boyd** (g); **Bernard Purdie** (d). Milestone Ⓕ MCD-9148 (42 minutes). Recorded 1986.

⑧ ❾

Organist Jimmy McGriff, who describes himself as a 'blues' rather than a 'jazz' player, is—whatever the nomenclature—an exemplar of the power of positive swing. With a toe-tapping, gritty approach falling somewhere between the jazz of Jimmy Smith and the soulful r&b of Booker T and the MGs, McGriff remains one of the last of the 'chicken and chitlins' circuit players whose appearances are guaranteed to make everyone feel good about music, themselves, and life itself. Everyone loves Jimmy McGriff. Whether cruising in the fast lane with a cooker like *BGO* or caressing a ballad such as *You Belong To Me*, McGriff evokes poignantly felt responses that keep bodies, limbs and digits in perpetual motion. Part of McGriff's appeal lies in the economy of his utterances. Though possessing as great a technique as any of his peers on the Hammond B-3, McGriff allows his grooves to unfold leisurely. He's also a superb accompanist, as his sensitive backings for saxmen Rusty Bryant and David 'Fathead' Newman aptly demonstrate. And his bass pedal work? Well, it seems to come from the very bowels of the earth.

Along with the inspired flights of the aforementioned saxmen and McGriff himself, the super-solid, in-the-pocket drumming of Bernard Purdie is yet another wonder. However, it is McGriff who is at the centre. Amen!

CB

Ken McIntyre

1931

Tribute McIntyre (f, as, ob, bn); **Thierry Bruneau** (bcl, as, bn); **Richard Davis** (b); **Severi Pyysalo** (vb); **Jean-Yves Colson** (d). Serene Ⓕ SER 02 (62 minutes). Recorded 1990.

⑦ ❽

In 1961 Ken McIntyre concluded that a teaching career made better sense than trying to survive as a full-time musician. As a result his appearances on disc have been limited. He did record with Eric Dolphy, Bill Dixon and Cecil Taylor in the sixties and made five strong albums for the Steeplechase label in the seventies, but **Tribute** marks his first date as leader for more than a decade. A live set from France's Tourcoing Jazz Festival, it's dedicated to Eric Dolphy, whose gentle spirit presides over the music and whose evolution from bebop to the more tuneful areas of free jazz paralleled McIntyre's own.

McIntyre is still a captivating player, less startling than Dolphy but an eloquent soloist here on alto, flute and plaintive oboe. He is a talented if quirky composer too: *Smile*, latest of his many Caribbean-inspired pieces, is an attractive 53-bar calypso; *Tomorrow? Tonight!* with its dreamy oboe/bass-clarinet unisons, is the set's most haunting tune. But, despite the presence of Richard Davis and a vibist, this is no **Out to Lunch**. **Tribute** is a pleasantly laid-back blowing album, not the radical group interplay of Dolphy's masterpiece. It also ends disappointingly, co-leader Bruneau's 20-minute *The Cry* comprising a series of disjointed a cappella solos.

GL

Dave McKenna

Left Handed Compliment McKenna (p). Concord Ⓕ CCD-4123 (39 minutes). Recorded 1979.

⑥ ❻

Dave McKenna has been rather oversold as a kind of complete pianist who not only plays with both hands and needs no rhythm section, but also knows by heart every song ever written. He is certainly two-fisted, but that is not nearly as unusual as it used to be in the days of left-hand-tied-behind-your-back modernism, and nowadays a lot of young pianists have rediscovered the bottom half of the keyboard. What is unusual about McKenna is not that he has an active left hand, but that he never breaks into stride patterns. At up tempo he generally favours a walking bass; on his more luscious ballads he prefers a kind of fanning chordal pattern in the left hand; and it has to be said that both become more tiresome than they should quicker than they should, and that you sometimes want to jump up and shout: "Stop being so tasteful and elegant! Stop wandering through the storehouse of American song, and start swinging that left hand a bit more!" But he never does.

In his liner notes Nat Hentoff says that the word which comes to mind with McKenna is 'joy', which is a lot shorter than many of the words Hentoff uses in his notes, like 'paradigm', 'manifestly', 'wondrous' and 'pathetic'. It is not joy I hear in these tracks, it is effortlessness, but in the slightly perjorative sense of 'not working up a sweat'. Everything jogs along nicely, but it never gets anywhere. It is a record you want to like a lot, but your attention keeps wandering. Still, I have never heard *Indiana* played so slowly on record; nice to think of it as a ballad for once.

MK

Red McKenzie

1899-1946

1935-1937 McKenzie (v); **Eddie Farley, Bunny Berigan, Dave Wade, Jonah Jones** (t); **Bobby Hackett** (c); **Mike Riley, Al Philburn, Vernon Brown** (tb); **Slats Long, Sid Stoneburn** (cl, ts); **Forest**

Crawford, Paul Ricci, Sid Trucker (cl); **Babe Russin, Dave Harris** (ts); **Adrian Rollini** (bss); **Conrad Lanoue, Frankie Froeba, Frank Signorelli, Raymond Scott, Fulton McGrath** (p); **Eddie Condon, Arie Ens, Carmen Mastren, Dave Barbour, Dick McDonough** (g); **George Yorke, Sid Weiss, Lou Shoubee, George Hnida, Artie Shapiro, Pete Peterson** (b); **Johnny Powell, Vic Engle, Stan King, Johnny Williams** (d); **Al Sidell** (d, vb). Timeless Ⓜ CBC 1-019 (69 minutes). Recorded 1935-37.

⑤ ❻

The early thirties saw the demise of the Mound City Blue Blowers and **1935-1937** presents McKenzie's Rhythm Kings and Orchestra of the middle thirties. On the strength of his singing, it is unlikely that such music would have survived into the CD era. A natural baritone, he delivered the lyrics with punctilious accuracy, his intonation was good and his timing very much of the era. He sang the lyrics as if he meant them and he avoided both euphoria and unreal sadness. He was not, however, a jazz singer; he sang the songs as written and took no liberties with the composer's required cadence.

What makes this a worthwhile issue is the quality of the McKenzie sidemen. His comb/paper playing is not heard here but, in its original form, it was intended to imitate the trumpet part of the ensemble. Because of this, he enjoyed the company of good trumpeters and there is outstanding playing by Berigan on eight titles. Despite restricted space, there is also fine playing by Jones on two, Hackett on four and, the surprise, some lyrical Red Nichols-inspired work by Farley on eight more. The clarinet of Slats Long and piano contributions by Froeba and Signorelli are an added bonus and the spirit of **1935-1937** is perfectly captured. **BMcR**

McKinney's Cotton Pickers

The Band Don Redman Built **John Nesbitt, Langston Curl, Joe Smith, Leonard Davis, Sidney De Paris, George 'Buddy' Lee** (t); **Rex Stewart** (c); **Claude Jones, Ed Cuffee** (tb); **Don Redman, Milton Senior, Jim Dudley, Benny Carter** (cl, as); **George Thomas** (cl, ts, v); **Prince Robinson, Ted McCord** (cl, ts); **Coleman Hawkins** (ts); **Todd Rhodes, Leroy Tibbs** (p); **Fats Waller** (p, cel); **Dave Wilborn** (bj, g); **Ralph Escudero, Billy Taylor** (bb); **Cuba Austin, Kaiser Marshall** (d). RCA/Bluebird Ⓜ ND 90517 (65 minutes). Recorded 1928-30.

✔ ⑧ ❽

With William McKinney as business manager, McKinney's Cotton Pickers came into being in 1926. In trumpeter Nesbitt the band had a fine arranger and he must take credit for the band's original musical personality. In 1927, however, the band took on Redman as musical director, and by the time they began recording one year later they had begun to develop a new identity. As this CD demonstrates, the band responded to Redman's charts with enthusiasm. Stomping performances such as *Crying And Sighing* and *Stop Kidding* were models of their kind, showing that the arranger had freed himself from the restrictions of section harmonies. The soloists were not the band's strongest point but Jones, Nesbitt and Redman do make some worthwhile contributions. While at the Greystone Ballroom in Detroit, their activities overlapped with the Jean Goldkette Orchestra and band members were occasionally interchanged. Redman was attracted to this practice and himself introduced Benny Carter, Coleman Hawkins and Fats Waller for guest spots on sessions that produced outstanding performances like *Miss Hannah* and *Wherever There's A Will.* The band's last recording was in 1931, and by 1933 it had ceased to exist. During its heyday it had been a band to stand comparison with Duke Ellington, and was seen by many as superior to Fletcher Henderson. Bill McKinney did try to keep a band of sorts together, but in 1941 quit the music business altogether. **BMcR**

John McLaughlin 1942

Extrapolation **McLaughlin** (g); **John Surman** (ss, bs); **Brian Odges** (b); **Tony Oxley** (d). Polydor Ⓜ 841598-2 (41 minutes). Recorded 1969.

✔ ⑩ ❽

This, the Yorkshire-born guitarist's first album as leader, not only set the agenda for UK jazz-rock, but also showcased a composing and instrumental talent which would be of crucial importance on the US musical scene in the seventies, illuminating albums by Tony Williams, Miles Davis and Carla Bley and storming the citadels of both critical and commercial success as leader of the Mahavishnu Orchestra. Like the seventies work of UK-based composer-bandleaders Mike Westbrook and Mike Gibbs, *Extrapolation* is a beguiling and satisfying mix of jazz-rock with elements of freer jazz, but it is the truly original blend of McLaughlin's guitar with John Surman's superb baritone saxophone which gives the album its unique sound. The compositions range from relatively straightforward slow-burners, through the haunting 11/8 *Arjen's Bag* to feverish free-for-alls. Throughout, McLaughlin's angular clanging chords and blistering runs and Surman's tenacious virtuosity, twin flames constantly stoked by the perfect rhythm section of Tony Oxley and Brian Odges, mark this as one of the most accomplished and influential debut recordings in jazz history. **CP**

Inner Mounting Flame **McLaughlin** (g); **Jerry Goodman** (vn); **Jan Hammer** (kbds); **Rick Laird** (b); **Billy Cobham** (d). Columbia Ⓕ CK 31067 (46 minutes). Recorded 1970.

✓ ⑩ ❽

This album, officially released as being by the Mahavishnu Orchestra, could only have been McLaughlin's date. It is his vision, his intensity, his urgency and tortured lyricism which gives the music its character, and while drummer Cobham plays so dazzlingly and with such an overwhelming density of sound that he made his reputation overnight from this one disc, he is always following the guitarist's lead. As such, this band has the same rhythmic fulcrum as most of the greatest jazz combos —that between the leader and the drummer.

There is very little music which carries the burning, steely intensity of this first album: utterly humourless and completely relentless, it demands total submission from the listener and is as wildly exciting as an uncontrollable adrenalin rush. On reflection, the joins in the music show a little, and the seeds of the group's eventual demise are present here, including their collective inability to write music which aspires beyond the episodic. But on this first album, these qualities are still part of the good things the group brought to the world, and are used to generate drama and rework the musical vocabulary: even the relative weakness of Goodman as a soloist in this context becomes a release from the power of the other players, and his sweet tone helps the ballads involve the listener.

An album, then, which is very much more than the sum of its parts. **KS**

Electric Guitarist **McLaughlin** (g); **David Sanborn** (as); **Jerry Goodman** (vn); **Patrice Rushen** (p); **Stu Goldberg** (p, org, moog); **Chick Corea** (p, moog); **Tom Coster** (org); **Devadip Carlos Santana** (g); **Fernando Saunders, Neil Jason, Alphonso Johnson, Stanley Clarke, Jack Bruce** (b); **Billy Cobham, Narada Michael Walden, Tony Smith, Jack DeJohnette, Tony Williams** (d); **Alyio Lima, Armando Peraza** (perc). Columbia Ⓜ 467093 2 (40 minutes). Recorded 1970.

⑧ ❽

Made at a crossroads in McLaughlin's career, this was a reaction to three years with his acoustic Shakti finding him reunited with many of his colleagues from the first Mahavishnu Orchestra and Tony Williams' Lifetime. The essence of the disc is power and McLaughlin flexes his muscles to hold his own alongside drummers Cobham, DeJohnette and Williams, let alone bassists Bruce and Clarke. Ironically, the most moving piece on the album is a solo version of *My Foolish Heart*, where McLaughlin's pure sound triumphs over a volley of effects.

McLaughlin doesn't come out of the jazz tradition so much as the English rock preoccupation with urban blues. His hard-edged solo and wah-wah on *Are You The One?* with Bruce and Williams recalls Cream—especially in the opening lick, where Bruce slots into a mesmeric groove as he might have with Clapton and Baker, before Williams blows in with a virtuoso display. Yet as a melodic soloist McLaughlin has the power to stay level pegging with David Sanborn or to dominate entirely a quartet with Corea, Clarke and DeJohnette (whose total technical command even down to the finesse of his cymbal rhythms reveals him as the most masterly drummer present). As a whole, this album is a demonstration of the best in fusion by the man who pointed the way for the Scofield generation. **AS**

Free Spirits Featuring John McLaughlin: Tokyo Live **McLaughlin** (g); **Joey De Francesco** (org, t); **Dennis Chambers** (d). Verve Ⓕ 521 870-2 (75 minutes). Recorded 1993.

⑧ ❽

There seemed to be good reason in the eighties to suspect that the creative force which had long guaranteed McLaughlin's position at the forefront of contemporary music was spent: his intimate trio of readings of Spanish, Asian and other world music, the appearance of a dated and bombastic new edition of the Mahavishnu Orchestra and a disappointing showing on Miles Davis's **You're Under Arrest** all suggested a not entirely graceful slide towards retirement.

Thus this remarkable live date came as a complete surprise: not only was McLaughlin back on top form, but he was also demonstrating a mastery of a harmonic style which might have appeared to be the domain of such younger players as John Scofield and Pat Metheny. The easy harmonic ingenuity and rhythmic mastery of the opening blues demonstrates as much, as well as providing clear notice that McLaughlin's extraordinary plectrum technique is still fully intact. Joey De Francesco's work on Hammond keyboard and pedals keeps things rolling along and Dennis Chambers is typically propulsive. The only reservation one might express concerns McLaughlin's perhaps over-enthusiastic use of the vibrato bar. **MG**

Jackie McLean

1932

Lights Out **McLean** (as); **Donald Byrd** (t); **Elmo Hope** (p); **Doug Watkins** (b); **Art Taylor** (d). Prestige Ⓜ OJCCD-426-2) (46 minutes). Recorded 1956.

⑧ ❽

When this session took place both McLean and Byrd were already playing with the kind of assurance normally associated with older, more experienced players. In fact both were just 23 at the time (and bass player Watkins was only 21), clear evidence that they were destined for greatness. The album title takes its name from the fact that the long eponymous blues was played with the studio lights dimmed in order to provide an increased atmosphere of relaxation. It certainly worked and *Lights Out* is a splendid performance, drenched with the blues feeling that hallmarked so much of Charlie Parker's work. This is living, vital music by determined young men and it still possesses the original urgency more than three decades later. There is little in the way of written, or even pre-planned, arrangements throughout the date, but the strength and quality of the solo playing is the major factor. The themeless *Lorraine* is actually an examination of the chords of *Embraceable You* with a few references to Bird's Dial versions. Watkins, who was to be killed in a tragic motor accident almost exactly six years after this session, shows just how fine a bass player he was and Rudy Van Gelder's engineering captures all the nuances of the music to perfection. The transfer to CD is excellent. **AM**

New Soil McLean (as); **Donald Byrd** (t); **Walter Davis Jr** (p); **Paul Chambers** (b); **Pete LaRoca** (d). Blue Note Ⓜ CDP7 84013-2 (45 minutes). Recorded 1959.

⑧ ❿

The release of this album announced an important comeback for McLean and the start of a long line of strong releases which lasted until the late-sixties, when he began a sabbatical from the recording studios. As well as achieving a previously elusive mastery over his instrument, Jackie had harnessed his uniquely sour tone to consistently expressive purposes. Although the evidence so far was slight, the altoist was beginning to look for ways to adapt (and eventually loosen) bebop's theme/solos/theme structures. He was also reconsidering the need for textural variety, as opposed to "interesting" chord sequences. Thus *Minor Apprehension* (previously recorded with Miles Davis as *Minor March*) had become a charging modal piece on which the great Pete LaRoca, after virtually duetting with the front-line, solos freely in an historic departure from the stated pulse. The title-track, on the other hand, is a long and intense blues in which each alternate chorus forces the players to invent over a Mingus-like pedal-point.

Compared to these two McLean originals, the four by pianist Davis are more conventional, as are his Powell-inspired quote-filled solos, but the shuffle-beat *Greasy* inspires all concerned. In particular Donald Byrd, who could already be so average when the spirit didn't move him, is outstanding throughout and sets the seal on a splendid session. **BP**

Destination Out! McLean (as); **Grachan Moncur lll** (tb); **Bobby Hutcherson** (vb); **Larry Ridley** (b); **Roy Haynes** (d). Blue Note Ⓜ CDP 832087 2 (35 minutes) Recorded 1963.

⑩ ❿

McLean has enjoyed a long and illustrious career, but there is little doubt that his best and most original recordings were made during the time he was contracted to Blue Note. Apart from the outstanding appearances he made from time to time as a sideman on others' dates, there is hardly a duff session from **Jackie's Bag** through to **Demon's Dance**, a period of close to 10 years. Within that time-span is a sequence of ground-breaking titles, starting perhaps with **A Fickle Sonance** (1961) and including **Let Freedom Ring**, **One Step Beyond**, this title, **Right Now!** and **New & Old Gospel** (which had Ornette on trumpet), where McLean was creating music in a new form and free from cliché, either that of the immediate past (bop) or the then-present (the so-called avant-garde). In a sense he was one of the key inheritors of the progressive banner from people like Mingus and John Lewis, using new structures, finding new subject-matter and creating new musical backdrops and textures upon which to improvise.

On this album, as on **One Step Beyond** (released on CD but now deleted), trombonist/composer Grachan Moncur lll is the key collaborator, contributing three of the four compositions, while Bobby Hutcherson, also a hold-over from the previous session, gives the music his uniquely spare, flowing accompaniment. The crucial difference between the two records is the substitution of Haynes for Tony Williams (who had by then joined Miles's band). Williams brought a wildly exhilarating (and occasionally downright astonishing) concept of time-keeping to **One Step Beyond**, and Haynes, for all his accomplishment, simply cannot compete with that level of originality and inspiration. Still, everything else is as before, and although **One Step Beyond** would be the Basic Jazz Library recommendation if it were still available on CD, this is an entirely acceptable substitute. **KS**

Rene McLean 1947

In African Eyes McLean (ss, as, ts, f); **Hugh Masekela**, **Prince Lengoasa** (flh); **Moses Molelekwa**, **Themba Mkhize**, **Rashid Lanie** (p); **Jonny Khumalo**, **Jonny Chancho**, **Prof. Themba Mokoena**, **Bheki Khasa** (g); **Bakhiti Khumalo**, **Fana Zulu**, **Vcitor Masondo** (b); **Sello Montwedi**, **Ian Herman**, **Lulu Gontsana** (d); **Jon Hassan**, **Papa Kouyate**, **Bill Summers**, **Zamo Mbuto** (perc). Triloka Ⓕ 203 195-2 (47 minutes). Recorded 1992.

⑦ ❽

Rene McLean would long ago have established himself as an individualist saxophonist if it were not for the fact that his father, Jackie, is still going strong and making fine music. As it is, Rene perhaps doesn't get the critical attention he deserves. This new album certainly shows that he is a careful musical thinker and listener, drawing as it does deeply from the well of contemporary African instrumental music. McLean recorded the album in Johannesburg, and many of the pieces on the date are from the backing musicians themselves. It is to McLean's credit that he went alone to this assignation and worked entirely with local musicians (Hugh Masekela is the exception, but then he came from there to start with), thereby not approximating the highly inflected jazz feel which African musicians create, but immersing himself within it.

The emphasis is very much on the ensemble rather than the individuals; although there are solos from McLean, his flügelhornists and pianists, they are made very much to fit into the fabric of sound built up around them. There are many felicitous moments to be heard in this long programme, but the most important overall conclusion is that this joining of two different strands of musical culture is a happy success. **KS**

Big Jay McNeely 1927

Road House Boogie McNeely (ts, v); **John Anderson** (t); **Jesse Ewing** (tb); **Bob McNeely** (as, bs); **Jimmie O'Brien** (p); **Prinze 'Candy' Stanzel** (g); **Ted Shirley**, **Cecil Harris**, **Buddy Woodson** (b); **Leonard Hardiman**, **Johnny Walker** (d); **McNile** (cga); **Clifford Blivens** (v). Saxophonograph Ⓕ RBD 505 (45 minutes). Recorded 1949-52.

④ ❼

McNeely grew up in Los Angeles, musically influenced by the Texas Tenor school of Arnett Cobb and Illinois Jacquet. He became a professional musician at a time when men like these, soloing in big-band settings such as the Lionel Hampton orchestra, were inspiring dozens of tenor saxophonists in small groups to outdo them and each other in excesses of feverish blowing at fast tempos. There were matching extravagances of performance: players would bend over backwards, lie down on stage, walk through the audience, even leave the club and go out on the street, playing all the while. In heating r&b to a temperature that anticipated the boiling waters of rock & roll, the tenor honkers of the early fifties dispensed with melodic development and concentrated on simple blues structures, often playing a single note repeatedly for an entire chorus. McNeely was one of the leaders of this unsubtle but galvanic pack. His recordings seldom depart from the formula implied by titles like *Jaysfrantic, Deac's Blowout* or *Just Crazy,* but with such music, records are scarcely the point: live performance is all. Fortunately for admirers of the genre, McNeely is still performing with gusto. **TR**

Jim McNeely 1949

East Coast Blow Out McNeely (p, arr); **John Scofield** (g); **Marc Johnson** (b); **Adam Nussbaum** (d) and the **West Deutschen Rundfunks Big Band**. Lipstick Records Ⓕ LIP 89007 2 (53 minutes). Recorded 1989.

⑧ ❽

Best known as a one time pianist in the Stan Getz Quartet, McNeely is also a music teacher of prodigious experience. His music is broadly in the post Gil Evans-Thad Jones field and, like Mike Gibbs he weaves contemporary ideas into classic big band pieces. His main weapon in doing this is the playing of guitarist John Scofield, a virtuoso with fundamental jazz values, who has also played a similar role to this with Gibbs. Both Scofield and Marc Johnson are somewhat larger than life in that they transcend comparison with other instrumentalists. McNeely's charts are long (three over 11 minutes and the other two over seven) and give Scofield plenty of scope to combine with the band. On this showing McNeely is as gifted at composing and arranging as he is at playing the piano. There is some refined writing for the band in *Skittish*, which features the three major soloists, and the WDR band interprets the scores with great precision and fire. An unaccompanied passage by Scofield, who plays with considerable vigour, culminates in a delicate entry by the band which typifies McNeely's discriminating creation of stimulating settings. **SV**

Jimmy McPartland 1907-1991

That Happy Dixieland Jazz McPartland (c, v); **Charlie Shavers** (t); **Cutty Cutshall** (tb); **Bob Wilber** (cl, ts); **Ernie Caceres** (cl, bs); **Dick Cary** (p, arr); **George Barnes** (g); **Harvey Phillips** (tba); **Joe Burriesce** (b); **George Wettling** (d). RCA Living Stereo Ⓜ 118518-2 (35 minutes). Recorded 1959.

⑧ ❼

McPartland was a cornettist whose style didn't ossify around early (and doomed) attempts to sound and play like Bix Beiderbecke. In this he was different from many contemporary white players, let alone the players who came to the fore on both sides of the Atlantic in the Revivalist phase of the forties and fifties. Indeed, when it comes to Dixieland, as opposed to Trad (original or revivalist), it is Chicago, with its marriage of front-line polyphany and tightly-arranged performances with a rhythmic thrust which is closer to swing than to classic jazz, from whence the major stylistic influence or thrust came.

McPartland shares the lead role here with Charlie Shavers, a self-confessed Armstrong worshipper whose bright tone, easy technique and imaginative variations help keep afloat this ramble through the usual repertoire. Pianist Katz contributed the arrangements, and they hover between recreating the Bix & Tram sound when Adrian Rollini was present and going for a more straightforward mainstream approach. McPartland himself plays cleanly and with a deal of fire, while the spacious stereo recording helps concentrate the listener's attention by giving clarity to the often quite dense lines woven by the group. McPartland's vocals come from somewhere between Jack Teagarden (phrasing) and Jimmy Rushing (range and timbre). **KS**

Marian McPartland
1920

Piano Jazz with Guest Bill Evans **McPartland**, **Bill Evans** (p). Jazz Alliance Ⓕ TJA-12004 (60 minutes). Recorded 1978.

⑨ ❽

Marian McPartland, one of Britain's great gifts to American jazz, is a musicians' musician. Recognised as one of the New York scene's most accomplished and versatile pianists, her tenures at the Embers and Hickory House during the 1950s and 1960s are now the stuff of legend. During the past 15 years, McPartland has been busy establishing yet another facet of her outstanding career as host of the radio programme, 'Piano Jazz'. Whether sitting (and playing) opposite Dave Brubeck, Dizzy Gillespie or Eubie Blake, McPartland has proved an ideal intermediary, coaxing rare insights and performances from a who's-who of jazz stars which continue to illuminate our understanding of jazz from a perceptive insider's position.

Thanks to The Jazz Alliance, a subsidiary of Concord Records, we now have access to a growing catalogue of 'Piano Jazz' programs originally aired in North America on National Public Radio. "What's really nice about the series", McPartland notes, "is that people who've wanted copies of the program can now get them". Indeed, until released on CD, the Bill Evans broadcast of November 6, 1978, was the most coveted of the "Piano Jazz" bootlegs. The program typifies McPartland's congenial and informative talk and play format. In the Evans program, as we learn something of the pianist's ideas on reharmonization, we hear telling examples in spontaneous performances of *In Your Own Sweet Way* (a stirring Evans-McPartland duet) and *Waltz for Debby* (a fascinatingly prolix Evans solos). McPartland's "Piano Jazz" is destined to be one of music's most valued documents, a living history told by those who played and lived it. **CB**

Piano Jazz with Guest Dizzy Gillespie **Gillespie** (t, p); **McPartland** (p). The Jazz Alliance Ⓕ TJA-12005 (57 minutes). Recorded 1985.

✔ ⑩ ❻

The eighteenth volume of McPartland's radio series arrived the day I wrote this; and volume five, with Gillespie talking and playing both trumpet and piano easily remains my favourite to date. Some listeners may prefer more music and less talk, although the real value of these shows is when historical and musical information is exchanged—and no one was more willing to share such knowledge (even with critics) than Dizzy. The deep intelligence and musicality that pervaded his personality and his life shine through here, offering an experience similar to any conversation Gillespie participated in where a piano was at hand. My guess is that the justifiably celebrated fourth volume, with Bill Evans, will receive the most choices; but anyone who has the **Complete Fantasy** Bill Evans boxed set already has that one. **BB**

Willow Creek And Other Ballads **McPartland** (p). Concord Ⓕ CD-4272 (41 minutes). Recorded 1985.

⑧ ❽

From her early years of formal training and her inevitable involvement with the Condon brand of music via her marriage to Jimmy McPartland, Marian has emerged as a major figure. She has shown on her many trio albums that she is at home with fast tempos and hard-hitting tunes, but this quite beautiful solo album is a valuable example of the care that goes into the making of a superior ballad set. The choice of tunes is excellent but listen to the sheer pianistic skill of her playing, weighting all the notes correctly and using space in the right places. *Long Ago And Far Away* takes on an almost French Impressionist feeling without once losing the character of this Jerome Kern song. Billy Strayhorn's moving *Blood Count* is a memorable experience and the CD opens and closes with tunes by two other jazz pianists, Ahmad Jamal's *Without You* and Dave Brubeck's *Summer Song*. She has also utilized an unlikely but eminently suitable song in Stevie Wonder's *All In Love Is Fair*. This is solo piano playing of great class. **AM**

Joe McPhee
1939

Topology **McPhee** (c, ts); **Radu Malfatti** (tb, el); **André Jaume** (ts, bcl); **Daniel Bourquin** (as, bs); **Irène Schweizer** (p); **Raymond Boni** (g); **Michael Overhage** (vc); **François Mechali** (b); **Pierre Favre** (perc); **Tamia** (v). hatART Ⓕ CD 6027 (64 minutes). Recorded 1981.

⑦ ❽

McPhee did not take up the tenor saxophone until after his first recording on trumpet in 1967. From 1969 to 1971 he lectured at the Vassar College for Black Studies on 'The Revolution In Sound' before transferring for some time to Europe. A series of records for the then Hat Hut label documented that part of his career and they highlight his progress on saxophone, with circular breathing, leg-muting and other instrumental devices to show what contact with the likes of Steve Lacy and Evan Parker had inspired. This CD from 1981 is the finished article, with McPhee presenting the full emotional range of his style on brass and reeds. *Age* is his excursion into a form of tenor terror, *Blues for New Chicago* takes his cornet into Roscoe Mitchell's sixties sound experiments, while the whole band's performance of *Pithecanthropus Erectus* perpetuates the Charles Mingus-held belief that every time a piece is played it should develop. McPhee's investigation of this Mingus classic is imbued with a friction-induced luminescence as the individual horns make their own brand of abrasive contact with each other. *Violets for Pia* is story-telling from the old school, while *Topology* is an acknowledgement of his regular trio's work. None is governed by a set series of rules, and they confirm McPhee as one of the most expressive and stylistically versatile of avant-garde musicians. **BMcR**

Charles McPherson 1939

Bebop Revisited! **McPherson** (as); **Carmell Jones** (t); **Barry Harris** (p); **Nelson Boyd** (b); **Al Heath** (d). Prestige Ⓜ OJC 710-2 (46 minutes). Recorded 1964.

⑨ ❽

It is appropriate that this, Charles McPherson's début as a leader, be an album of tunes closely associated with Charlie Parker. Though primarily thought of today as a longtime associate of yet a third Charles (Mingus), who certainly stretched McPherson's harmonic vocabulary beyond bop syntax, the altoist was from his beginning days in Detroit a fervent Ornithologist. His playing here is assured and appealing; an excellent solo on *Variations on a Blues by Bird* and a passionate rendition of *Embraceable You*, the latter based upon Parker's incomparable account, reveal McPherson's response to Bird as highly personal, suggesting his role (along with other individualists like Jackie McLean, John Jenkins and Ernie Henry) as an intermediary between Parker's breakthrough and the extensions of a Jimmy Lyons. Fellow Detroiter Barry Harris's presence here is both a stabilizing factor and an inspirational one; he is faultlessly fluid in the Bud Powell mode, especially on Bud's *Wail* (more Monk would creep into his playing in later years). Carmell Jones displays the prerequisite bop trumpet chops, with focused ideas and a clear vision. Add drummer Tootie Heath (who learned alongside brothers Percy and Jimmy) and bassist Nelson Boyd, himself a frequent Bird sideman, and you have an impeccable bop quintet, offering music of a bite, wit and authenticity that hasn't lessened with time, and which current reboppers can't match. **AL**

Carmen McRae 1922-1994

Here To Stay **McRae** (v); with various personnel including: **Billy Strayhorn, Dick Katz** (p); **Herbie Mann** (f); **Mundell Lowe** (g); **Wendell Marshall** (b); **Kenny Clarke** (d); **Ernie Wilkins Orchestra with Jimmy Maxwell, Richard Williams, Ernie Royal** (t); **Jimmy Cleveland, Billy Byers** (tb); **Phil Woods** (as); **Zoot Sims, Budd Johnson** (ts). MCA/Decca Ⓜ 16102 (53 minutes). Recorded 1955-59.

⑧ ❾

Beginning her career with Benny Carter in 1944, McRae later sang with Count Basie and Mercer Ellington. She had a spell as intermission singer at Minton's Playhouse and made her début as a leader in 1954. This CD includes some of her finest work and finds her dovetailing well with Wilkins's fine big band arrangements, sitting comfortably with her own quartet, and overcoming bizarre instrumentation (flute and accordion included) to make *Yardbird Suite* one of her more memorable performances. As befits a devoted Billie Holiday fan, she is a naturally inventive singer. Her muscular delivery can sometimes have the 'caged animal' intensity found in *It's Love*, but this is contrasted by *Supper Time*, a heartfelt rendition in which her jazz artistry is perfectly balanced with the meaning of the lyrics. Her control at slow tempos is exemplary and her easy vibrato adds warmth to all performances. It is interesting to hear how even the opening theme statements are slightly modified and given different points of emphasis. Her improvisations never become too tortuous, however, and they are certainly free from the rhetorical excesses that confuse the work of some singers. More was to be heard of her clever scat singing later in her career, but by 1959 she was already the finished article, as this CD attests. **BMcR**

The Great American Song Book **McRae** (v, p); **Jimmy Rowles** (p); **Joe Pass** (g); **Chuck Domanico** (b); **Chuck Flores** (d). Atlantic Jazz Ⓜ 7-81323-2 (72 minutes). Recorded 1970.

⑧ ❽

Considering how well she succeeds with her material it is perhaps surprising to note that Miss McRae has neither a big range nor a beautiful voice. Most singers have one or the other or, in the case of the Ellas and Sarahs, both. So Miss McRae on paper is no match for Peggy Lee or Anita O'Day.

Happily she doesn't sing on paper, and her talents for sound and imaginative improvisation are what sells her recordings. Her voice is unbeautiful in a way that Charlie Parker's alto tone was (when compared with Hodges or Jefferson). She made a direct bridge between the singing of Billie Holiday and the harmonic innovations of bebop and this makes her a singer who gets deeply into her material rather than just adding a veneer to it. More than any other vocalist she extemporizes like an instrumentalist and, unlike most 'instrumental' singers, her work is not flawed by artifice or histrionics.

This generous collection puts her in a crucible with the sparest but most accomplished setting any singer could ask for. Rowles is as good an accompanist as any and is also a distinguished improviser.

Those qualities were also present in the work of Joe Pass, whose cushion for the singer on *What Are You Doing For The Rest of Your Life?* is perfectly conceived. It is unlikely that McRae ever recorded a better collection than this one, done live in Los Angeles. She certainly never received better backing. **SV**

Carmen Sings Monk **McRae** (v); **Clifford Jordan**, **Charlie Rouse** (ts); **Eric Gunnison**, **Larry Willis** (p); **George Mraz** (b); **Al Foster** (d). RCA Novus Ⓕ 3086-2 (66 minutes). Recorded 1988.

⑧ ❽

Thelonious Monk's music places a special burden on improvisers; generally interpreters lean toward Monk's angularity and blocky harmonies in order to integrate the written and improvised parts of a performance. McRae goes against the grain, emphasizing the beauty of Monk's melodies. About half the selections are ballads, including *'Round Midnight*, *Ruby, My Dear* and *Ask Me Now*. She makes it work; at age 66, her voice was surprisingly limber, heavier but no less pleasing than in the fifties.

The two pianists do not imitate the composer, taking their stylistic cues from the leader's smooth approach. McRae's effective foils are tenor saxists Charlie Rouse, a Monk sideman for over a decade (he is on two live cuts), and Clifford Jordan, who was playing exceptionally well in the eighties, and whose dramatic use of space and silence suggests how much he learned from Monk. Between Jordan's elliptical improvising and McRae's sensitivity to the composer's melodies, they do Monk justice.

The lyrics, by Jon Hendricks, Abbey Lincoln and others, are not in Monk's league; you don't mind that McRae slurs a few words. But the lyrics are good for one thing. Even Monk fans have trouble remembering which melody goes with which title; this disc enables you to learn the names of 14 of them. **KW**

Jay McShann

1909

Blues From Kansas City On three tracks, **McShann & His Orchestra**: **McShann** (p) **Harold Bruce**, **Bernard Anderson** (t); **Joe Baird** (tb); **Charlie Parker**, **John Jackson** (as); **Bob Mabane**, **Harry Ferguson** (ts); **Gene Ramey** (b); **Gus Johnson** (d); **Walter Brown** (v). On three tracks **Jay McShann Trio: McShann** (p); **Gene Ramey** (b); **Gus Johnson** (d); **Walter Brown** (v). On eight tracks add **Leonard Enois** (g). On seven tracks **Jay McShann Orchestra**: **McShann** (p) with musicians including **Bob Merrill**, **Jesse Jones**, **Willie Cook** (t); **Alonzo Pettiford**, **Alfonso Fook**, **Lawrence Anderson** (tb); **Rudy Jackson**, **Rudolph Dennis** (as); **Paul Quinichette**, **Fred Culliver**, **Bill Goodman** (ts); **Rae Brodely** (bs); **Leonard Enois** (g); **Gene Ramey** (b); **Dan Graves** (d). MCA/Decca Ⓜ GRP 16142 (61 minutes) Recorded 1941/42.

⑦ ❻

The three tracks which the McShann band made while Charlie Parker was with them guaranteed its immortality. They also somewhat distorted the legacy which McShann's aggregation had to offer, for this was indeed a band straight out of the Basie and Kansas City tradition, and Parker at this stage was very much under the spell of Lester Young. What Parker went on to become has made these brilliant examples of Kansas City-style blues and swing into some form of harbinger of bop. They may be, but hindsight is a wonderful thing, and they sound more like backward glances at a tradition which was already fading. Just how conservative McShann was is indicated by the long string of small-group sides which follow *Swingmatism*, *Hootie Blues* and *Dexter Blues*. This is a cross between the Basie quartet sides for Decca and an Albert Ammons or Pete Johnson boogie date, with vocals from Walter Brown to match.

McShann was and is a capable pianist with a fine swing beat in both hands. His band plays straightforward arrangements of simple tunes, almost invariably blues-based and often with a shuffle beat from the drums. The small-group sides could do with another horn to liven things up a little, especially as the ubiquitous Walter Brown was hardly the most inspired of blues vocalists. What the later band represented here desperately needed was what Basie had in abundance: fine soloists. Parker had moved on and McShann would not progress without him. **KS**

At Café Des Copains **McShann** (p). Sackville Ⓕ SKCD2-2024 (58 minutes). Recorded 1983-89.

⑧ ❽

McShann usually enters the history books, if at all, as the Kansas City-based bandleader who emulated Count Basie's group and who had Charlie Parker as the leading light of his saxophone section for a couple of years in the early forties. That band's commercially issued recordings are on McShann's **Blues From Kansas City** (MCA/Decca–see above) and their live work, including a fascinating, recently-discovered broadcast from the Savoy Ballroom, is the subject of **Early Bird** (Spotlite/Stash). But, as with his band, McShann is a player (and sometime vocalist) who covers a number of bases, capable of functioning equally well for dancing or neighbourhood-bar background music.

Fortunately, in comparison with some of his other late recordings, even some of those done for Sackville, here he is on top of his form as solo pianist in three live sets from the eighties. The wealth of his experience includes blues and boogie, suggestions of Earl Hines and Erroll Garner, and a wide repertoire from *Indiana* to Michel Legrand's *Watch What Happens*. He is insufficiently familiar with the latter (perhaps the result of a request?) but makes it work anyway, while elsewhere the authority of his playing is hand in glove with its entertainment aspect. **BP**

Jack McVea

1914

Two Timin' Baby **McVea** (as, ts); **Cappy Oliver, Jesse Perdue, Sammy Yates, Russell Jacquet, Joe 'Red' Kelly** (t); **Melba Liston** (tb); **Marshall Royal** (cl); **Wild Bill Moore** (ts); **Bob Mosley, John Shackleford, Call Cobbs, Tommy Kahn** (p); **Irving Ashby, Gene Phillips** (g); **Frank Clarke** (b); **Rabon Tarrant** (d, v). Jukebox Lil Ⓕ RBD 612 (48 minutes). Recorded 1944-47.

⑥ ❻

McVea was a competent saxophonist, arranger and bandleader who appeared at the first Jazz at the Philharmonic concerts in 1944 and whose early recording career, in the second half of the forties, was shaped by the demands of the Californian record industry. Independent labels with low budgets found him a reliable and craftsmanlike producer of small-group blues, boogies and novelty numbers patterned on more successful contemporaries like Louis Jordan. McVea was sometimes able to commission names like Marshall Royal or Maxwell Davis, who arranged *House Party Boogie,* but most of his work was done with a core of little-known journeyman players like pianist Kahn and drummer Tarrant, the featured blues-singer on about half the tracks here. The general effect is similar to that of local contemporaries like Roy Milton and Joe Liggins. *Bulgin' Eyes,* a brisk if formulaic jump number, scores a few more jazz points than usual. The earlier and slightly better collection **Open the Door Richard** (Jukebox Lil JB-607) has not yet been transferred to CD. At last report, McVea was playing clarinet in a strolling band at Disneyland. **TR**

Kevin Mahogany

Double Rainbow **Kevin Mahogany** (v), **Ralph Moore** (ts); **Kenny Barron** (p); **Ray Drummond** (b); **Lewis Nash** (d). Enja Ⓕ ENJ 7097-2 (67 minutes). Recorded 1993.

⑧ ❽

If you are constitutionally allergic to scat singing you will have to give Kevin Mahogany a miss, but if you can tolerate it at all this CD will charm you. He has a smooth, dark voice, slightly reminiscent of the young Joe Williams, miraculous pitch, and diction that can handle Eddie Jefferson's tongue-twisting words to Parker's *Anthropology* with complete ease. Also, unlike most super-hip vocalists, he sings ballads simply and with understanding. The material adventurously chosen and includes Miles's *All Blues*, John Lewis's *Two Degrees East, Three Degrees West* (with words by Judy Spencer) and an extraordinary Coltrane-like recitative performance of a piece of James Baldwin prose. Add to this the impeccable Ralph Moore on tenor and Stan Getz's favourite rhythm section and you have a most noteworthy debut. **DG**

Mike Mainieri

1938

Wanderlust **Mainieri** (vb, mba); **Michael Brecker** (ts, ss); **Don Grolnick** (kbds); **Steve Khan, Kazumi Watanabe** (elg); **Marcus Miller, Tony Levin** (elb); **Peter Erskine** (d); **Warren Bernhardt** (p); **Jeremy Steig** (f); **Randy Brecker** (t); **Manolo Badrena, Sammy Figueroa, Roger Squitero** (perc). NYC Ⓕ 6002 2 (50 minutes). Recorded 1981.

⑥ ❽

Former Buddy Rich sideman Mike Mainieri became most visible as leader of Steps Ahead, the much-admired 'acoustic fusion' band which brought his spectacular vibraphonic talents before a new generation in the eighties. Some 13 years on from the inception of the band, Mainieri plans to reissue material by Steps Ahead and others through his new label, NYC. This early Mainieri date will appeal to those with a taste for early Steps Ahead, since it features several musicians—and two tunes—closely associated with the group. One of those tunes, and one of the best things here, is *Bullet Train*, an urgent samba driven with enormous flair by Marcus Miller. It prompts excellent Coltrane-inspired soloing from Mainieri, as does *Flying Colours*, another Miller-propelled Latin piece. *Sara's Touch*, the other Steps Ahead anthem here, is a seductive index of Mainieri's often obscured reflective side, and *Crossed Wires*, with its Pastorius-like pedal point and big synthesizer textures, is reminiscent of Weather Report's *Birdland*. This CD adds a track—the Silverish gospel soul of *Pep's*—to the original analogue release, but unfortunately it is transposed in the track listing with *L'Image*, which is suite-like jazz-rock of the Mahavishnu stripe, and thus rather scuppers Mainieri's nostalgic recollections of early sixties Buddy Rich gigs at Pep's in Philadelphia. **MG**

Bob Malach

Mood Swing **Tom Harrell** (t); **Bob Malach** (ts); **Bob Mintzer** (bcl); **Russ Ferrante** (kyb); **Dr John** (p,v); **Robben Ford** (elg); **Eddie Gomez** (b); **Will Lee** (elb); **Vinny Colaiuta**; **Charley Drayton**; **Steve Gadd** (d). Go Jazz R Ⓕ vBr 2045 2 (59 minutes). Recorded 1990.

⑧ ❽

Bob Malach is one of the least exposed of the New York school of white post-Coltrane tenor saxophonists typified by such players as Michael Brecker, Bob Mintzer and Bob Berg. Here his pared-down version of the Brecker style receives a long-deserved airing in a programme which reflects his interest in a wide variety of music, from New Orleans r&b to the semi-swing of Bob Mintzer's *Mr Fone Bone* and Russ Ferrante's *Whistle While You Walk*. His versatility is illustrated by his equal ease with the Latin modalism of *In Your Eyes*, which prompts some skilfully handled polytonal Traneisms, and the unashamed bar-room sentimentality of his duo with Dr John on *I'm True*, where he proves the perfect accompanist, embellishing the vocal with taste and sensitivity. The supporting cast are faultless, though it would have been nice to have heard more from Tom Harrell, who is inexplicably limited to a brief but finely wrought obbligato on *In Your Eyes*. On one level this may appear as easy listening jazz, but the wide range of mood and strong playing give it a seductive appeal.

MG

Radu Malfatti

Ohrkiste **Malfatti** (tb); **Reiner Winterschladen** (t); **Martin Mayes** (flh); **Melvyn Poore** (tba); **John Butcher** (ss, ts); **Wolfgang Fuchs** (bcl); **Peter Van Bergen** (cl, bcl); **Phil Wachsmann** (vn); **Karri Koivukoski** (va); **Alfred Zimmerlin** (vc); **Wolfgang Güttler** (b); **John Russell** (g); **Fred Van Hove** (p). ITM Ⓕ 950013 (74 minutes). Recorded 1992.

⑨ ❽

Note that there is no drummer among the 13-piece ensemble listed above—it is one indication that Radu Malfatti's music is less concerned with controllable tempi or regularity of pulse than with sounds that breathe at irregular intervals. A well-travelled veteran in European and British free music circles (ranging from a trombone/bass duo with the late Harry Miller to participation in Brotherhood of Breath), Malfatti has assembled an impressive body of like-minded improvisers who follow his scores through varied compositional instructions if not strict notation, and their selflessness on behalf of such indeterminate events is convincing and gratifying. The result is music of gradual growth, terse details and silences filled with often unrecognizable colours and forms—everything is a surprise. The two long multisectional works (*Notes* and *Graukanal*) create a marvellously intense, dynamically modulated tension between unpredictable improvisational gestures and compositional direction and unity. More chamber music ensemble than traditional big band, the instrumentation, although sectionalized (reed trio, brass quartet, string quartet, guitar and piano), belies such rigid compartmentalization; the fluid, amorphous sound mass may be closer in character and spirit to music from composers like Ligeti, Xenakis and Varèse than Ellington or even Gil Evans. Comparisons aside, this is difficult but fascinating, frequently magical music.

AL

Russell Malone

Russell Malone **Malone** (g, v); **Donald Brown, Harry Connick Jr** (p); **Robert Leslie Hurst III, Milt Hinton** (b); **Yoron Israel, Shannon Powell** (d). Columbia Ⓕ CK 52825 (60 minutes). Recorded 1991/92.

⑥ ❽

Russell Malone is a young guitarist equally adept on electric and acoustic instruments, as this début album demonstrates. He has come to this session fully prepared, with a pleasant mix of old and new standards (that is, songs from the pre-war and the present eras, from W.C. Handy through to Burt Bacharach), plus a couple of his own pieces. His most immediate stylistic antecedents would be George Benson and Kenny Burrell, with the longer melodies of Wes Montgomery occasionally invoked. But he has an individual touch, mostly in the way he begins and ends his notes within single-line statements (he manages to impart a nicely conversational timing through this technique of avoiding an overly legato approach). Malone has also tried to cover a fair amount of stylistic territory, from the present-day synthesis of post-Coltrane modality to the neo-Django (this last is strikingly evident on *When I Take My Sugar To Tea*, with Milt Hinton accompanying on bass. Just to show that he can take a Johnny Smith approach to life, he strokes his way through a sleepy *It's The Talk of the Town*, but there is a lot more zip in the acoustic work on *St Louis Blues*. If there is an obvious weakness in the album, it is the fact that, for 60 minutes, all you get is Malone. Nobody else really gets a look-in. Even when Harry Connick Jr appears, it is Malone who takes the vocals. Perhaps now the first one is out of the way and the points have been proved, he can relax somewhat and give us a more balanced record which is just a little less of a showcase.

KS

Junior Mance

1928

Junior Mance Trio at the Village Vanguard **Mance** (p); **Larry Gales** (b); **Ben Riley** (d). Riverside Ⓜ OJCCD204-2 (43 minutes). Recorded 1961.

⑦ 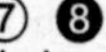

Discounting purely generic players, Junior Mance is about as much of a blues pianist as anyone in jazz (though there was a time when Ray Bryant could have given him a good tussle for the title). Later

albums have illustrated more fully the span of his abilities, but they have seldom if ever captured the effervescence and young man's bullishness of this début appearance at the famous New York club. Though only one tune-title (*Smokey Blues*) admits it, blues form and blues feeling are spread over this record like a mulch, from the rocketing opener *Looptown* through Johnny Griffin's *63rd Street Theme* to the Basie band's *9.20 Special*. Even *Girl Of My Dreams*, a danceband tune from the twenties that Mance picked up from his one-time employer Dizzy Gillespie, rocks to a beat that Louis Jordan might have counted off. Mance's trenchant phrasing, crisp attack and fondness for soulful figures lend this record a precise location in time and style, close to the contemporary work of Horace Silver and cheek-by-jowl with that of Cannonball Adderley, whose first band Mance worked with for almost two years. The 1980 trio session **Smokey Blues** (JSP CD219) can also be recommended for a quieter display of many of the same characteristics.
TR

Joe Maneri 1927

Get Ready To Receive Yourself **Maneri** (reeds); **Mat Maneri** (vn); **John Lockwood** (b); **Randy Peterson** (d). Leo Lab Ⓕ CD 010 (52 minutes). Recorded 1993.

⑦ ❻

Maneri delayed his free jazz recording début until he was in his sixties. Born in New York, he became part of the Schoenberg circle. He made a living at wakes, bar mitzvahs and other ethnic events, but a piano concerto was written for the Boston Symphony in 1960. In 1965 he performed with Gunther Schuller at Carnegie Hall in an Ornette Coleman dedication and he became theory and composition professor at the New England Conservatory in 1970. He has written a book on microtonal studies but, since the mid-eighties, has been increasingly involved in his own specialized brand of jazz.

This CD reflects Maneri's many influences and the quartet speaks specifically in abstract terms. Superficially, there is a serenity about titles such as *One Track Minds*, *Anton* and *Don't Look Now* but they have an ascetic edge; one that, in fact, imbues intriguing tensions. It pressurizes otherwise loose-limbed counterpoints and transforms the uncomplicatedly boppish *Be Hop* into something rather more sinister. More than any other title, *Body And Soul* provides an excellent entrée to his music. It proposes aspects of the piece that previous generations have ignored and converts Green's classic into a musical hologram, showing the multi-dimensional aspects of Maneri's brand of free jazz.
BMcR

Albert Mangelsdorff 1928

Live In Berlin '71 **Mangelsdorff** (tb); **Peter Brotzmann** (ts); **Fred Van Hove** (p); **Han Bennink** (perc). FMP Ⓕ FMPCD 34/35 (two discs: 118 mins). Recorded 1971.

⑧ ❽

Underrated, underrecorded, overlooked, for over 30 years now the German trombonist Albert Mangelsdorff has been one of Europe's most innovative jazz musicians. Playing music as diverse as bebop, free jazz and fusion, and working with musicians as heralded as Barre Phillips, Jaco Pastorius and even Ravi Shankar, it is his staggering technical innovations which have kept him paradoxically in the forefront of European jazz and yet hidden from wider public scrutiny. Just as Evan Parker has developed the use of circular breathing to achieve hitherto unheard (and previously unimaginable) sounds, Mangelsdorff has pioneered and perfected the use of multiphonics. By simultaneously humming or growling and playing the trombone, Mangelsdorff not only produces double stops but, by emphasizing the resulting harmonics, he is able to play three and even four-note chords which make his improvising at times unrecognizable as that of a trombonist. Such technical stuff aside, this two-disc set captures one of free jazz's finest-ever quartets at their most vibrant. Merrily mincing up pieces penned by each of the four, the band make the sort of spontaneous, joyous racket that lesser musicians could only dream of (and arguably not even that). If only punk had looked to this music for a blueprint instead of the MC5 and the Stooges.
SH

Three Originals **Mangelsdorff** (tb); **Palle Danielsson, Jean François Jenny-Clark** (b); **Jaco Pastorius** (elb); **Elvin Jones, Alphonse Mouzon, Ronald Shannon Jackson** (d). MPS Ⓜ 519 213-2 (two discs: 125 minutes). Recorded 1976-80.

⑦ ❽

Mangelsdorff came to prominence in the early fifties as an outstanding J.J. Johnson trombone stylist in Hans Koller's Quintet. After touring Asia in 1964, he became increasingly involved with the free jazz movement and throughout the seventies produced a string of recordings that show his mastery of the style. Despite earlier recorded evidence of Iskra 1903 and Paul Rutherford, Werner Stiefele's CD notes infer that Mangelsdorff's solo concert of 1972 was the world's introduction to trombone and voice polyphony. Not that this matters, because he is a superb player in his own right and his mastery of multiphonics is well in evidence in these three sessions: it is a skill that is deployed to fuel an intense improvisational process. His technical command of the trombone is awesome and he uses his 'voice-covers' and his colossal range to colour and enhance the creative aspects of his solo building. The various rhythm teams on duty on this CD are also variable in quality. The Jones/Danielsson combination is perhaps the most stimulating, with *Up And Down Man* and *Wide Point* most typical. Pastorius and Mouzon are at their most supportive on the inappropriately named *Accidental Meeting*, while the less cohesive Jenny-Clark/Jackson duo do nothing to deter Mangelsdorff from making *Rip Off* a dazzling performance. The German trombonist is a major league player and this CD finds him at the top of his game. **BMcR**

Chuck Mangione

1940

Recuerdo **Mangione** (t); **Joe Romano** (ts, as, f); **Wynton Kelly** (p); **Sam Jones** (b); **Louis Hayes** (d). Jazzland Ⓜ OJCCD 495-2 (50 minutes). Recorded 1962.

⑥ ❽

This CD presents a fine young trumpeter potentially on the brink of a major career in jazz and playing in good company. Mangione had paid his dues in the bands of Woody Herman, Maynard Ferguson and Art Blakey, but instead of taking the pure jazz route, he saw a 'niche in the market' and throughout the seventies switched to flügelhorn and led his own band, playing gentle original tunes and standards to a formula. The softly contoured pieces, often with a Latin flavour, essayed little in the way of improvisation and they took him into sales figures normally associated with pop music. No instrumental concessions were made; Mangione remained a very good musician and it must be conceded that his uncomplicated, sanitized jazz did introduce a whole generation to the real thing. It was just that, in 1962, he was attracting little international attention but was unobtrusively producing albums as good as this one with brother Gap Mangione and with the outstanding rhythmic support of bop masters like Kelly, Jones and Hayes. He had assimilated the hard bop message and was putting his own steel into items such as *Big Foot* and *Blues For Saadar*. Moreover, as alternative masters demonstrate, he was more than capable of making improvisational adjustments from take to take. Perhaps the real Mangione stood up too soon. **BMcR**

Manhattan Transfer

The Best of Manhattan Transfer **Tim Hauser**, **Cheryl Bentyne**, **Alan Paul**, **Janis Siegel**, **Laurel Masse** (v); **Randy Brecker**, **John Faddis**, **Marvin Stamm** (t); **Quentin Jackson**, **Wayne Andre** (tb); **Jerry Dodgion**, **Dave Sanborn** (as); **Mike Brecker**, **Seldon Powell** (ts); **Don Grolnick** (p, elp); **Ira Newborn** (g, mus.dir.); **Andy Muson** (b); **Roy Markowitz** (d). Atlantic Ⓜ 781582-2 (44 minutes). Recorded 1975-81.

⑧ ❽

The dilemma of close harmony groups such as Manhattan Transfer and Singers Unlimited is that they usually fall between two stools. Far too musicianly and hip for the wider audience to appreciate, they are also treated with suspicion by older jazz enthusiasts. But there is so much to enjoy which can only be rated as jazz that those committed enthusiasts who ignore these records are the losers. This 'Best of' collection is the CD equivalent of an LP and, in turn, draws its dozen tracks from five previous albums. It contains the astonishing *Four Brothers*, on which Hauser, Masse, Paul and Siegel (Cheryl Bentyne was a later replacement for Laurel Masse) contrive to sing Jon Hendricks's lyrics to the original instrumental solos by Zoot Sims, Serge Chaloff, Herbie Steward and Stan Getz. *Body And Soul* is a quite marvellous recreation of Coleman Hawkins's classic performance, complete with a careful transcription of Gene Rodgers's piano introduction. But the unforgivably sloppy presentation gives none of this information and restricts itself to a listing of titles and singers' names. Mike Brecker takes the tenor solo on *Operator*, Ira Newborn is the sensitive guitarist on *Java Jive* and the closing *Nightingale Sang In Berkeley Square* is a perfect example of a cappella singing. Recommended. **AM**

Herbie Mann

1930

The Evolution of Mann: The Herbie Mann Anthology **Mann** (f); with a collective personnel of: **Leo Ball**, **Doc Cheatham**, **Jerry Kail**, **Ziggy Schatz**, **Pedro Paulo**, **Clark Terry**, **Marky Markowitz**, **Joe Newman**, **Jimmy Owens**, **Wayne Jackson** (t); **Mark Weinstain**, **Quentin Jackson**, **Sam Burtis**, **Barry Rogers** (tb); **Paulo Moura** (as); **King Curtis**, **Ed Logan**, **Andrew Love**, **David 'Fathead' Newman** (ts); **Pepper Adams**, **James Mitchell** (bs); **Charlie Palmieri**, **Antonio Carlos Jobim**, **Sergio Mendes**, **Bill Evans**, **Chick Corea**, **Jimmy Wisner**, **Bobby Wood**, **Barry Beckett**, **Richard Tee**, **Pat Rebillot** (p); **Bobby Emmons** (org); **Baden Powell**, **Durval Ferreira**, **Mundell Lowe**, **Al Gorgoni**, **Charlie Macey**, **Larry Coryell**, **Sonny Sharrock**, **Reggie Young**, **Eddie Hinton**, **Duane Allman**, **Cornell Dupree**, **Jerry Friedman**, **Jerry Friedman**, **Bob Mann**, **Hugh McCracken**, **Jeff Mironov**, **Hux Brown**, **Rod Bryan**, **Nick Woodland**, **Ricardo Silveira** (g); **Nabil Totah**, **Juan Garcia**, **Ahmad Abdul-Malik**, **Ben Tucker**, **Otavio Bailly, Jr.**, **Chuck Israels**, **Earl May**, **Joe Macko**, **Mike Leech**, **David Hood**, **Richard Davis**, **Reggie Ferguson**, **Chuck Rainey**, **Andy Muson**, **Willie Weeks**,

Al Gorry, Tony Levin, Jackie Jackson, Gary Unwin, Paul Socolow (b); **Rudy Collins, Dom Um Ramau, Paul Motian, Bruno Carr, Mel Lewis, Don McDonald, Reggie Ferguson, Bernard Purdie, Gene Christman, Roger Hawkins, Aynsley Dunbar, Steve Gadd, Rick Marotta, Michael Richard, Martin Harrison, Ricky Sebastian, Buddy Williams** (d); **Johnny Rae, Ray Mantilla, Ray Barretto, Michael Olatunji, Willie Rodriguez, Chief Bey, Carlos 'Patato' Valdes, Warren Smith, Phil Krauss, Ralph MacDonald, Armen Halburian, Rubins Bassini, Elmer Lewis, Tessie Coen, Joe Spector, Cyro Baptista** (perc); **Jose Andreu, Daniel Gonzalez, Joe Silva, Stephane Grappelli** (vn); **Johnny Rae, Hagood Hardy, Dave Pike, Roy Ayers** (vb); **Maya Angelou, Dolores Parker, Rannelle Broxton, Cissy Houston, Eunice Peterson, Sylvia Shemwell, Jerry Rix** (v). Rhino/Atlantic Gallery Ⓜ R2 71634 (two discs: 138 minutes). Recorded 1960-92.

⑥ ❼

Herbie Mann deserves credit for making the flute a full-fledged jazz voice. Indeed, his funky chart-busters, *Comin' Home Baby* (1961) and *Memphis Underground* (1969), helped create a boom in flute sales and lessons. From Mann on, reedmen had to prove themselves on flute as well as sax as fans and musicians alike embraced the instrument. In addition to popularizing various amalgams of rock and jazz, Mann was in the vanguard of American exponents of the bossa nova. Mann, a global traveller responsive to indigenous musics, was one of the first American jazzmen to incorporate African rhythms and Japanese melodies, making him a trail blazer leading to what in the late-eighties would be called world music.

In this two-disc anthology spanning 1960-1992, we catch Mann's varied personas from the Muscle Shoals nitty gritty of the genuinely infectious *Memphis Underground* to the enraptured Brazilian insouciance of *One Note Samba* with composer Jobim wafting the vocal. Mann's most engaging and enduring works float simple melodies atop rhythmically charged undercurrents. On more ambitious fare, such as *I Love You* with the Bill Evans Trio, results are tentative. And though much of the commercialized jazz-rock of Mann's Atlantic career is decidedly dated, it nonetheless provides a revealing snapshot of the musical changes then blowing in the wind. By the end of the sixties, Mann had been esclipsed by a phalanx of new flute stars such as Hubert Laws and Charles Lloyd. Still, Mann's place in jazz history is secure as the chief popularizer of jazz and jazz-pop flute. **CB**

Caminho De Casa **Mann** (f, af); **Eduardo Simon, Mark Soskin** (p); **Romero Lubambo** (g); **Paul Socolow** (b); **Ricky Sebastian** (d); **Café** (perc). Chesky Ⓕ JD40 (54 minutes). Recorded 1990.

⑥ ❿

The English translation of this title, as supplied by Mann on the back cover, is 'pathway home'. It is not his latest release (he also has a couple of CDs on his own label, Kokopelli), but it is still his most recently-recorded album. In the extensive liner notes Mann states that he discovered Brazilian music on a tour to Latin America in 1961, and that this album is his return to a long-term love of his. Of course, with a musician like Mann, the result is hardly undiluted Brazil. He has also had long-term fascinations with a range of musics including Memphis r&b, Near-Eastern popular and classical forms, and Afro-Cuban rhythms. It all comes through on this album. He says "I buy a lot of ethnic music albums, along with classical. I find a lot more surprises in ethnic music nowadays."

Mann's strength has always been his phenomenal ear for new sound and rhythm combinations, his ability to pick the top musicians from any style he works in, and his acute arranging skills in a small-group setting. This album is no exception to that general rule, and its very high recording quality only aids appreciation of such traits. He has never been much more than mediocre as an improviser, but when his other assets are working at peak capacity as they are here, this is not so important. He is convincing on the ballads and secure in the up-tempo numbers. His group blend together marvellously, giving him an inspiring cushion of Latin sound. The blend is always pleasurable and occasionally intoxicating. **KS**

Shelly Manne

1920-1984

The Poll Winners **Manne** (d); **Barney Kessel** (g); **Ray Brown** (b).Contemporary Ⓜ OJCCD 156-2 (41 minutes). Recorded 1957.

⑦ ❽

Initially a saxophonist, Manne switched to drums in his teens and gained experience in various big bands including, most significantly that of Stan Kenton. Almost by coincidence he was present on one of Dizzy Gillespie's early bebop dates, as well as on several free-form sessions with Ornette Coleman. This show of versatility was a central factor in Manne's career; he seemed to be as much at home navigating the occasionally cumbersome Kenton aggregation as he was bringing his guile to the lighter traceries of a trio's music. The Poll Winners worked as a group from 1957 to 1960 and re-appeared in the seventies. This CD shows them at their best, wise in their choice of material, creative in their approach to it and sympathetic to each other's musical needs. Manne was the group's heartbeat, and his rhythmic security and sure technique were that of the complete professional. Titles such as *Jordu* and *On Green Dolphin Street* combine the light touch and the headlong drive and mark him out as a totally musical drummer. Occasionally his willingness to 'follow' the tune confirms his intuitive bent and helps him add melodic grace to items like *Satin Doll* and *Mean To Me*. From 1960 to 1974 he managed Shelly's Manne-Hole, a club in Los

Angeles, then in the seventies he played with the L.A. Four and various other small groups, all of which showed him to be comfortable with the post-Art Blakey hard drive. The Poll Winners date may have concentrated his attention on his brushes, but the gifted Manne was a drummer for all occasions. **BMcR**

Shelly Manne And His Men Live at the Blackhawk, Volumes 1-5 **Manne** (d); **Joe Gordon** (t); **Richie Kamucka** (ts); **Victor Feldman** (p); **Monty Budwig** (b). Contemporary Ⓜ OJC 656/7/8/9/60-2 (five discs: 280 minutes: oas). Recorded 1959.

⑩ ❼

Shelly Manne was by a long way one of the most tasteful musicians in jazz history, and also one of the most open-minded. He led a very high percentage of outstanding albums, of which **2,3,4** on Impulse! (see below) and **Checkmate** on Contemporary (not on CD at present) spring to mind. Yet none of them is more valuable than this then-unprecedented documentation of a band at work in a nightclub. Contemporary released four volumes on LP, and they have been classics since their first appearance. The CD release carries extra material on each volume (usually alternative versions of already-released tracks), plus a whole new volume (Volume Five, of course) of previously unissued material.

The band on this recording just happens to have that perfect balance few groups ever achieve, and even fewer achieve with a microphone nearby. Nobody is out to cut anyone else, everyone is proficient on their instruments and at ease with the material (a mixture of group originals and standards), and the level of inspiration is high. Kamuca is a particularly warm and involving tenor player, with great tonal beauty but none of the enervation often to be found on the West Coast, while Gordon combines audacious ideas with superb execution. Feldman is, of course, little short of a genius.

Everybody should have at least one of these albums on their shelves, not because the music is important, but because it is so damn enjoyable. **KS**

2, 3, 4 **Shelly Manne** (d); **Coleman Hawkins** (ts, p); **Eddie Costa** (p, vb); **Hank Jones** (p); **George Duvivier** (b). Impulse! Ⓜ GRP 11492 (42 minutes). Recorded 1962

⑧ ❽

A combination of inventiveness and eccentricity make this a unique and classic album. The playing is largely of the stream-of-consciousness variety, but that should not deter the faint-hearted, for these men, giants all, communicate with great clarity and skill.

In such a setting Coleman Hawkins would be expected to dominate, but a lot of the time the initiative is taken by Manne. It is important to accept that Manne was the most un-drummer-like drummer in that he used his instruments in a most musical way and was never remotely overbearing. He worked in partnership with those he accompanied and, although a superlative big band player, his forté was the intimate small group. Most of these he found on the West Coast, but these performances were done in New York with the locals.

Hawkins was at his most inspired and plays both tenor and piano in the amazing duet *Me And Some Drums.* Costa, whose piano work is both beyond value and unjustly rare, plays on only two of the seven tracks with his typical muscular locked-hands rumble appearing two minutes into *Lean On Me*. **SV**

Wingy Manone

1900-1982

1927-1934 **Wingy Manone** (c, t, v) with, on four tracks, **Hal Jordy** (cl, as); **Bob Sacks** (ts); **Johnny Miller** (p); **Steve Brou** (g); **Arnold Loycano** (b); **John Ryan** (d); **Earl Warner** (v). Two tracks with **Wade Foster** (cl); **Bud Freeman** (ts); **Jack Gardner** (p); **Gene Krupa** (d). Two tracks with **Frank Teschemacher** (cl); **George Snurpus** (ts); **Art Hodes** (p); **Ray Biondi** (g); **Augie Schellange** (d). Two tracks with **George Walters** (cl); **Joe Dunn** (ts); **Maynard Spencer** (p); **Dash Burkis** (d). Four tracks add to previous personnel **Miff Frink** (tb, bj); **Orville Haynes** (b); **Bob Price**, **Ed Camden** (t). Four tracks with **Matty Matlock** (cl); **Eddie Miller** (ts); **Gil Bowers** (p); **Nappy Lamare** (g, v); **Harry Goodman** (b); **Ray Bauduc** (d). Four tracks with **Dicky Wells** (tb); **Artie Shaw** (cl); **Bud Freeman** (ts); **Jelly Roll Morton**, **Teddy Wilson** (p); **Frank Victor** (g); **John Kirby** (b); **Kaiser Marshall** (d). Classics Ⓜ 774 (67 minutes). Recorded 1927-34.

⑧ ❻

Born in New Orleans, Manone was an exact contemporary of Louis Armstrong and there were many occasions throughout his life when his trumpet and cornet-playing echoed that of Louis. In 1935 he had a massive record hit with *Isle Of Capri* and subsequent recordings often contained elements of burlesque, but this excellent CD groups together seven 'pre-*Capri*' sessions of lasting interest. The first of two Chicago dates finds Wingy in the company of Bud Freeman, Gene Krupa and 'Jumbo' Jack Gardner, although the absence of a bass player tends to overemphasize Gene's drumming. The next date had Art Hodes and Frank Teschemecher (as if to reinforce Wingy's jazz credentials) while a 1930 session produced *Tar Paper Stomp* by Manone, a tune which became better known years later as *In The Mood.* There is an outstanding New York date on which the trumpeter teamed with other white New Orleans musicians in the persons of Eddie Miller, Nappy Lamare and Ray Bauduc and which is hallmarked by the clean ensemble playing. The final session on the CD has one of the most unexpected line-ups in jazz and includes DickyWells, Artie Shaw, Jelly Roll Morton and Bud Freeman, but the music has cohesion and clarity. In fact Manone's solo on *Never Had No Lovin'* from this session is one of his best in the Armstrong vein. Wingy conquered the tragedy of losing an arm in a road accident as a boy and was able to laugh when, years later, Joe Venuti gave him, as a birthday present, one cufflink in a box! **AM**

Michael Mantler

1943

Many Have No Speech **Danish Radio Concert Orchestra**; **Mantler** (t); **Rich Fenn** (g); **Jack Bruce, Marianne Faithfull, Robert Wyatt** (v). WATT Ⓕ 19 (835 580-2) (36 minutes). Recorded 1987.

⑥ ❽

Despite his deep involvement with the Jazz Composer's Orchestra, his work with Steve Lacy and Jazz Realities and his membership of Charlie Haden's Liberation Orchestra, Mantler remains a figure on the jazz fringe. He is a trumpeter of limited improvisational skills, but this CD affords the opportunity to examine his considerable composing and arranging talent. He has written backgrounds for the work of writer/poet Samuel Beckett, Ernst Meister and Philippe Soupault, enlisting along the way the help of Jack Bruce, Marianne Faithfull and Robert Wyatt as presenters. The compositions are imaginative and are underwritten by Mantler's commitment to serialism. The arrangements are well handled by the Dutch Radio Orchestra and they exude a feeling of tortured weariness which fits the majority of Beckett's pieces. There is, however, a somewhat stilted feeling about them, confirming an impression that few strides have been made in merging formal orchestral parts with jazz or folk elements since Eddie Sauter's superb work with Getz in 1961.

The proceedings here come to life most obviously when helped by Fenn's guitar, or by the leader's clear toned trumpet. That is when the strong ties with jazz are patently evident and when the appropriately mournful endorsements by the ensemble meld perfectly with the realities achieved by Faithfull, Bruce and most especially Wyatt. **BMcR**

Steve Marcus

1941

Smile **Marcus** (ss, ts); **John Hicks** (p); **Christian McBride** (b); **Marvin 'Smitty' Smith** (d). Red Baron Ⓜ JK 53751-2 (53 minutes). Recorded 1993.

⑧ ❾

Marcus made his first impact on the jazz scene back in the late sixties, becoming known internationally through his stints with Larry Coryell and Herbie Mann. The latter sojourn brought him his first date as a leader, on Mann's Vortex label, and for a while Marcus was a member of the short-lived jazz-rock boom which quickly foundered between the twin stools of Fusion and Soul. Escaping into the big band ranks, Marcus worked successfully with Woody Herman before settling down for a twelve-year stint with Buddy Rich's outfit, where he also took over much of the arranging work.

This present album, the second and decidedly superior of his latter-day records, has him essaying into the deepest saxophone waters, and generally acquitting himself creditably. The programme here is given over largely to compositions by, or closely associated with, greats such as Parker, Gillespie, Rollins, Coltrane and Dolphy. Marcus is far from overawed by precedent, and is quoted in the liner notes as saying each song chosen has long been a personal favourite, so there is nothing arbitrary here. Marcus has no evident technical weaknesses, his tone and conception is a personal amalgam of Coltrane and Rollins, and he has more than just heat and sound to communicate. The cohesion of his own approach and of the group he has chosen to play with is a definite plus, and although the set could have done with a few less bass solos, the album as a whole gives us much to admire and enjoy. **KS**

Rick Margitza

Work It **Margitza** (ss, ts); **James Williams** (p); **George Mraz** (b); **Billy Hart** (d). SteepleChase Ⓕ SCCD 31358 (59 minutes). Recorded 1994.

⑥ ❽

Margitza came to international attention with a brace of albums on Blue Note, both of which fell into the 'promising' category without managing to suggest how the tenorist would escape from under the Coltrane shadow. This latest effort, on SteepleChase, suggest he's seen the way ahead. He's still using Coltrane's language, but the examples of people such as Joshua Redman and Don Braden in their combination of many different influences and their preference for a softer, rounder tone than most post-Coltrane tenors of the older generation preferred, seem to have helped Margitza to a more personal stance. That said, Margitza's one essay on soprano, Coltrane's *Your Lady*, is still wholly cast in the master's mould.

Having such mature players in the band behind him may have helped focus his mind. Mraz's powerful pulse and judicious note-choices leave Hart free to react dynamically to Margitza, while Williams is a discreet but unending font of ideas. His work on *My Foolish Heart* avoids the obvious, and sidesteps the Bill Evans legacy, but still manages to be both affectingly pretty and quietly supportive. All of which is captured by a pleasingly natural recorded sound typical of SteepleChase's high standards. **KS**

Charlie Mariano

1923

Jyothi **Mariano** (ss, f); **Karnataka College of Percussion**: **R.A. Ramamani** (v, tamboura); **T.A.S. Mani** (mridangam); **R.A. Rajazopal** (ghatam, marsing, konakkal); **T.N. Shashikumar** (kanjira, konakkal). ECM Ⓕ 1256 (811 548-2) (46 minutes). Recorded 1983.

⑧ ❽

Although musical collaborations between West and East frequently result in the strengths of both traditions being diluted to form a bland pap bearing little resemblance to either, *Jyothi* is strong enough in its ambition and overall direction to avoid such a dilution. This success is possibly due to the fact that the necessary accommodation appears to have operated mostly in one direction; Charlie Mariano, with extended musical studies in Japan (while married to Toshiko Akiyoshi), Malaysia and India behind him, is undoubtedly one of the most versatile and open-minded jazz musicians on the planet, and on both flute and soprano here he manages to complement perfectly R.A. Ramamani's pure, silken vocals and the College's almost miraculously empathetic percussion work. As other, less successful experiments in similar fields have shown, mere virtuosity is not enough: the understanding and sympathy that comes only from proximity and study (à la John McLaughlin) is a prime requisite. Deprived of a jazz musician's familiar chord sequence structure upon which to improvise, Mariano demonstrates no unease, simply submerging himself (like the other members of this excellent ensemble) in an organic whole whose overall effect is infinitely greater than the sum of its parts. There are therefore no gratuitous displays of virtuosity, no grandstanding, no star turns here, and the result is that this meditative but intense music is served by the musicians rather than vice versa. **CP**

Dodo Marmarosa

1925

Jug and Dodo **Marmarosa** (p); **Gene Ammons** (ts); **Sam Jones** (b); **Marshall Thompson** (d). Prestige Ⓜ PCD-24021-2 (69 minutes) Recorded 1962 .

⑥ ❽

The innovative and musically exciting sides Marmarosa cut for the Dial label in the mid-forties are the foundation of his reputation, but they await transfer to CD, and considering Spotlite have recently brought their fine Dexter Gordon and Red Norvo Dial sessions out on CD, it is entirely possible that Spotlite's old Marmarosa lp of the Dial material will soon follow suit.

Meanwhile this is all that you can get. It's not at all bad, but the marriage between Marmarosa and Gene Ammons was not made in heaven. Ammons here is intent on showing his 'tough tenor' credentials, and so although he plays winningly stating the melody on ballads such as *Georgia On My Mind* and *Where or When*, his improvisations at times border on the brutal. With medium-tempo swingers it doesn't matter so much, and the band gels more happily, Sam Jones's bass being a standout for tone and rhythm. Marmarosa continually hints at the deeper emotions all through the aforementioned ballads, and though he gets little solo space, his accompaniment is spellbinding in the way Bud Powell's could be. Half the numbers on the disc are actually minus the saxophonist, and here Marmarosa gets a chance to shape the material more thoroughly. His technique is still in excellent shape, his ideas attention-grabbing. It intensifies the loss Marmarosa was to the music when he drifted out of the profession in the fifties. He has not recorded since this isolated date in 1962, which went unreleased at the time. **KS**

Joe Marsala

1907-1978

1936-1942 **Joe Marsala** (cl) with: on two tracks **Pee Wee Erwin** (t); **Frank Signorelli** (p); **Carmen Mastren** (g); **Artie Shapiro** (b); **Stan King** (d). Three tracks with **Marty Marsala** (t); **Ray Biondi** (vn); **Joe Bushkin** (p); **Adèle Girard** (h); **Eddie Condon** (g); **Artie Shapiro** (b); **Danny Alvin** (d). On four tracks **Condon** and **Alvin** out, replaced by **Jack LeMair** (g, v) and **Buddy Rich** (d). Four tracks with **Bill Coleman** (t, v); **Pete Brown** (as); **Carmen Mastren** (g); **Gene Traxler** (b); **Dell St. John** (v). Four tracks with **Marty Marsala** (t); **Ben Glassman** (as); **John Smith** (ts); **Dave Bowman** (p); **Adèle Girard** (h); **Carmen Mastren** (g); **Jack Kelleher** (b); **Shelly Manne** (d). Four tracks with **Max Kaminsky** (t); **George Brunies** (tb); **Dick Cary** (p); **Carmen Mastren** (g); **Haig Stephens** (b); **Zutty Singleton** (d). Classics Ⓜ 763 (65 minutes). Recorded 1936-42.

⑧ ❻

The clarinet playing of Jimmy Noone was an early and continuing influence on Joe who, with his brother Marty, was born in Chicago but found jazz fame in New York. This CD collects together six complete sessions under Joe's name made during the period when he was working clubs, principally the Hickory House, and using the pick of the New York-based jazzmen. His wife Adèle adds an unusual but attractive tone colour with her harp playing on three dates. Marsala's own clarinet playing is lucid, clear-toned and melodic; the varying instrumentations mean that the music is never repetitious and in many ways this music is the very essence of the Golden Age of small band swing. On one date, supervised by Leonard Feather (predictably all four tunes are Feather's own), Marsala shares the front line with two other highly individual players in the persons of Bill Coleman and Pete

Brown. Another date boasts a nine-piece group with proper arrangements for the ensemble and some effortless low register work from Marsala on a delightful *I Know That You Know*. The final session, dating from 1942, leans heavily on the Condon form of 'Nicksieland' jazz and finds Marsala flanked by Max Kaminsky and George Brunies. Two sessions mark the recording début of two important drummers, Buddy Rich and Shelly Manne. **AM**

Branford Marsalis 1960

Scenes in the City **Branford Marsalis** (ss, ts); **John Longo** (t); **Robin Eubanks** (tb); **Mulgrew Miller**, **Kenny Kirkland** (p); **Ron Carter**, **Ray Drummond**, **Charnett Moffett**, **Phil Bowler** (b); **Marvin Smith**, **Jeffrey Watts** (d); **Wendell Pierce** (narr); **Ed Williams** (radio announcer). Columbia Ⓕ CK 38951 (41 minutes). Recorded 1983.

⑨ ❿

Although he had recorded prominently with his brother trumpeter Wynton Marsalis, and with Art Blakey and the Jazz Messengers, saxophonist Branford Marsalis's 1983 début as a leader still stands as a remarkable maiden voyage. Though only 22 at the time of the first of the two sessions comprising the album, Marsalis shows incredible maturity and an uncanny absorption of the lexicons of John Coltrane and Sonny Rollins. Indeed, in the tumultuous *No Backstage Pass,* Branford evokes the Rollins legacy in a furiously dense, motivically constructed solo nudged by Carter's pendulous bass and Smith's swift brushes. Coltrane's sheets-of-sound intensity are refracted in *Solstice*, Branford's 7/4 reworking of Trane's *Equinox*.

The title track, Mingus's *Scenes in the City*, is an aural collage that today might be classified as 'performance art'. A confessional glimpse into the psyche of a black jazz fan of the fifties, it embraces snippets of period radio newscasts, a collection of 'wild' sounds recorded in Greenwich Village, and Branford's stirring sextet. We also get the 'voice' of Mingus' alter ego through the device of a narrator who concludes: "You see, I love jazz music." So, too, does Branford, who in spite of tasting the heady lotus fruit of show-biz fame and fortune—first with Sting, and now as leader of the Tonight Show Band—is still one of the era's most absorbing jazz voices. **CB**

Crazy People Music **Marsalis** (ss, ts); **Kenny Kirkland** (p); **Robert Hurst** (b); **Jeff 'Tain' Watts** (d). Columbia Ⓕ 466870 2 (65 minutes). Recorded 1990.

⑥ ❽

Many disciples of the sixties masters have adapted and refined their sources to their own needs. Not so Branford Marsalis: here he presents a virtually unmodified view of the early-sixties playing of Coltrane, Wayne Shorter and Ornette Coleman. The tunes too are shamelessly modelled on tunes from that period by the big three. The minor blues *Mr Steepee* borrows not only its form but also its opening thematic figure from *Mr. PC*, Keith Jarrett's *Rose Petals* is treated as a dirgeful lament reminiscent of Trane's *Alabama*, the ensemble heaving and rolling in broad, undulating phrase patterns, and *The Ballad of Chet Kincaid* is a modal swinger, paced like *Impressions* but without the half-step modulation. *Spartacus* and *The Dark Knight* have the quality of Wayne Shorter tunes, the latter founded on a bass riff similar to that used in Shorter's *Footprints* and, like *Footprints*, a slow minor blues in waltz time. *Wolverine* has the tipsy, dancing quality associated with Ornette Coleman, and *Random Abstract* is as free as its title suggests. However, absence of originality apart, there is much compelling playing. Marsalis occasionally becomes one-dimensional, but he is always convincing, and Kirkland offers an exciting amalgam of Tyner and Hancock. The ensemble is perfectly integrated. **MG**

Buckshot LeFonque **Marsalis** (ss, as, ts, d prog) with a collective personnel including: **Roy Hargrove**, **Chuck Findley** (t); **Matt Finders** (tb); **Delfeayo Marsalis** (tb, p); **Kenny Kirkland** (p); **Greg Phillinganes** (kbds); **David Barry**, **Kevin Eubanks**, **Ray Fuller**, **Nils Lofgren**, **Albert Collins** (g); **Robert Hurst**, **Darryl Jones**, **Larry Kimpel** (b); **Jeff 'Tain' Watts**, **Chuck Morris** (d); **Mino Cinelu**, **Vicki Randle** (perc); **DJ Premier** (d prog), **Maya Angelou**, **Blackheart**, **Uptown** (v); **Clare Fischer** (string arr). Columbia Ⓕ 476532 2 (two discs: 113 minutes). Recorded 1994.

⑧ ❿

This just might turn out to be the **Bitches Brew** of the current jazz generation. Like Miles's epoch-marking album, it is a sprawling double-disc, full of half-developed and fascinating ideas. Again like Miles's initial electric forays, very little of the elements Marsalis pulls together into this huge musical stew could be described as newly-minted: they've all been around for a number for years

now. But it's the mix which is new and absolutely electrifying. Many musicians have been on the cusp of this sort of thing for a while, and in related fields a number have already been there (Bill Laswell, Eno, Prince et al) but Marsalis is one of the few jazz musicians with sufficient scope, knowledge and interest in the world outside to even want to attempt such a synthesis. What he can effortlessly pull off is a track with a sampled funky drum pattern, over which runs a rap vocal which then seamlessly segues into a fully-fledged and scored sax-section figure which would not disgrace Woody Herman (and which in turn launches more lyrics, then a sax conversation where one of the horns quotes Monk). This all happens on *Breakfast At Denny's (Uptown Version)*. On *Breakfast at Denny's (Live Version)*, rhythm scratches and Hancock-inspired electric piano support some finely-etched, laconic tenor work from the leader. The second disc has various different versions and mixes of the "original" pieces to be found on disc one. So we have no less than four remixes of *No Pain, No Gain*, one with a wicked heavy metal riff guitar supporting a lightning-quick rap from Uptown.

Meanwhile, if you really want to scare yourself to death and you know your Coltrane, try *The Blackwidow Blues*: in the first forty or so seconds there is an object lesson in Marsalis's methods on this album, and Elvin Jones has never before sounded like this.

This is an important album. Even if you hate it, it is an important album. It doesn't matter that Buckshot LeFonque is an old Cannonball Adderley pseudonym: all that proves is that, apart from having a sense of history, Branford's also got a sense of humour. KS

Delfeayo Marsalis

1965

Pontius Pilot's Decision **Delfeayo Marsalis** (tb); **Wynton Marsalis** (t); **Branford Marsalis** (ss); **Mark Gross** (as); **Joshua Redman**, **Mark Turner** (ts); **Kenny Kirkland**, **Victor Atkins** (p); **Jason Marsalis**, **Jeff Watts** (d). RCA Novus Ⓕ 63134-2 (70 minutes). Recorded 1992.

⑥ ❽

Since the export of Marsalises became the most successful New Orleans cottage industry, it is equally easy to under-rate or over-rate members of the family. No doubt Wynton, who guests here on his brother's CD, is the most gifted. There is a jubilant and youthful quality to much of Delfeayo's writing and it seems to stimulate his soloists, who notably include the pianists Atkins and Kirkland. But Wynton, as he shows in an uncredited solo on the title track, is the outstanding player. He is propelled here by his impossibly young brother Jason (14 at the time of the recording). Branford Marsalis has consolidated his position as one of today's leading saxophone players, and here confines himself to soprano, well catered for in Delfeayo's scores. Delfeayo writes well and, with pieces like *Adam's Ecstasy*, shows how well he can evoke a mood. His trombone playing is mature and polished, free from cliché, and his tone recalls that of the long dead Bennie Green. The 'religious' qualities ascribed to the pieces are ersatz and can be ignored. This is just good jazz powerfully blown by a family of youngsters who seem to grow quicker than mushrooms. **SV**

Ellis Marsalis

1934

Piano in E **Marsalis** (p). Rounder Ⓕ CD 2100 (39 minutes). Recorded 1986.

⑥ ❼

Born in New Orleans, Ellis Marsalis is the father of the Marsalis clan as well as being one of his home town's leading educators. This CD was recorded live at his farewell concert to the city when he relocated to Richmond, Virginia, but fortunately for Louisiana he subsequently returned to the town of his roots and currently once again works out of New Orleans. Marsalis is not an easy player to categorize and he uses bebop as he does other styles. It can be a means of expression or equally a colouring agent to be employed as an element in a style born of his background. He is a pianist who comes to terms with his material rather than trying to change its spirit. Here, he retains the quizzical air of John Lewis's dedication to Django and he astutely fits the cool dude's elegant swagger to Fats Waller's charming *Jitterbug Waltz*. In the process, he does not forget that *So In Love* is, in fact, a love song or that *Hallucinations* was intended by Bud Powell as a test piece. He treats his own compositions with equal respect. *Zee Blues* , being a jaunty twelve bar, tempts him to emphasize the 'down-home' quality that has sometimes deflected listeners' attention from the sheer musical proficiency of his playing. A rhythm section is not missed. **BMcR**

Wynton Marsalis

1961

Wynton Marsalis **Marsalis** (t); **Branford Marsalis** (ss, ts); **Kenny Kirkland**, **Herbie Hancock** (p); **Clarence Seay**, **Ron Carter**, **Charles Farnborough** (b); **Jeff 'Tain' Watts**, **Tony Williams** (d). Columbia 468708 2 (42 minutes). Recorded 1981.

⑥ ❽

Prompted by this début album, jazz critics have spent much of Marsalis's career trying to define his original contribution. He has not created a new style (although he has aroused a movement of historical and stylistic awareness, as well as politicizing many of the current critical debates) and his technically perfect, but to many ears rather cold, trumpet has a chameleon quality that would not make him immediately identifiable on first hearing except in the context of his own more recent Sextet compositions. Here he flits from the Milesian (especially when accompanied by the ex-Davis rhythm section of Hancock, Carter and Williams) to the Morganesque. His ballad playing (notably on *Who Can I Turn To?*) is exceptionally mature for his then 20 years. As the album that marked his emergence from Blakey's talent school to the world stage in his own right, this is important, but since Marsalis's playing was still developing (even if its eventual destination is still unclear), the sum of its parts is substantially greater than the whole. **AS**

Hot House Flowers **Marsalis** (t); **Branford Marsalis** (ss, ts); **Kent Jordan** (f) **Kenny Kirkland** (p); **Ron Carter** (b); **Jeff Watts** (d); **Robert Freedman Orchestra**. Columbia Ⓕ CK 39530 (42 minutes). Recorded 1984.

⑧ ❽

Haydn's *Trumpet Concerto* at 14, Jazz Messenger at 19, record date leader at 20 and first musician to win a Grammy for both jazz and classical work, Marsalis could not fail. In fact, he didn't. It is just that his success has been misunderstood to some extent. By 1984 he was suffering from the expectation syndrome. This CD gets ⑧ ❽ because it succeeds in all it sets out to do. Freedman's luxurious textures are not an empty background wash; they are worthy support figures for a trumpeter with something to say about a series of fine tunes and equipped with the technique, tone and imagination to do it well. Unfortunately, critics and lay press alike had discovered Marsalis and were looking for classical perfection of execution. This they get and it would be difficult to imagine a more faultless reading of *Lazy Afternoon*, *Melancholia* and *I'm Confessin'*. What it lacks is the kind of fire in the belly of which Marsalis is eminently capable. *When You Wish Upon A Star* threatens to prove the point as he cuts loose, but these arrangements are not about to allow him space to continue, so brother Branford comes in and the strings re-establish the calm. When this session took place, the composition of superb Ellingtonian-type suites and the best of his breathtaking solo performances had still to come. It does, however, monitor a corner turned. **BMcR**

Citi Movement **Marsalis** (t); **Todd Williams** (ss, ts); **Wes Anderson** (as); **Wycliffe Gordon** (tb); **Eric Reed** (p); **Reginald Veal** (b); **Herlin Riley** (d); plus **Herb Harris** (ts); **Marthaniel Roberts** (p). Columbia Ⓕ CK 53324 (two discs: 123 minutes). Recorded 1992.

✔ ⑩ ❿

Citi Movement is the music written by Wynton Marsalis for Garth Fagan's ballet *Griot New York*. The composer's challenge was, in his own words, "to write a piece that could come close to dignifying their [the dancers'] grace". It is in three parts, all broadly illustrative of the black American experience: *Cityscape*, a musical impression of city life; *Transatlantic Echoes*, an examination of black history; and *Some Present Moments of the Future*, which explores jazz's response to this century, from Buddy Bolden to John Coltrane and beyond. But the bare bones of the piece, thus dispassionately (and somewhat distortingly) laid out, give no impression of the wealth of creative imagination Marsalis has expended on the composition; a short cut to conveying a sense of this would be to compare it, as Stanley Crouch does in his liner notes, with the work of Duke Ellington (for its scale, dignity and grace) and of Charles Mingus (for its superb use of the septet format, the ease and familiarity with which it draws on the whole of jazz and blues for its means of expression, and—crucially—for its exuberance and vitality, expressed through effortlessly negotiated time-signature changes and its plethora of musical references, from spirituals, blues and New Orleans polyphony through swing, to modal, bop and beyond). In **Citi Movement** Marsalis has produced a work of great importance, both in the context of his own career and in the broader context of the music generally, since it unequivocally demonstrates the power, subtlety and complexity of the music when sensitively allied with other art forms. **CP**

In This House, On This Morning **Marsalis** (t); **Wycliffe Gordon** (tb); **Wessell Anderson** (as); **Todd Williams** (ts, ss); **Eric Reed** (p); **Reginald Veal** (b); **Herlin Riley** (d). **Marion Williams** (v on one track). Columbia Ⓕ 474552 2 (two discs: 115 minutes). Recorded 1992-93.

⑧ ❽

The sheer volume and diversity of Wynton Marsalis's recorded output can make the listener a little blasé; equally the confrontation with a two-CD set of his septet playing nearly two hours of a work purporting to present an evocation of a service at an Afro-American church may not cause the pulse rate to quicken. But in fact this is a quite breathtaking display of Wynton's mastery as both instrumentalist and composer. Stanley Crouch's excellent notes should be read in conjunction with the music, but even without them the listener will surely be impressed by Marsalis's uncanny knack of producing the kind of ensemble sounds seldom heard since Duke Ellington's earlier works. The parallel with Ellington is heightened by the playing of trombonist Wycliffe Gordon, who would have been at home sitting alongside Tricky Sam Nanton. The sheer breadth of the ensemble work, the tone colours and the unity of the solo playing will bring to mind such episodic Ducal works as *Black, Brown & Beige*. The actual shapes of some of the written melodies sound fresh simply because Marsalis is using the kind of intervals and hard-to-play octave jumps often avoided by trumpeters. Yet the music is never pretentious; Marsalis is not trying to prove his superiority, but his mastery of both form and technique gives his writing a freshness which is invigorating. **In This House** is worthy of consideration by anyone interested in both the tradition and contemporary direction of jazz. **AM**

Tina Marsh

The Heaven Line **Marsh** (v, ldr); **Martin Banks**, **Dennis Gonzalez**, **Larry Spencer** (t); **Randy Zimmerman**, **James Lakey** (tb); **Jay Rozen** (tba); **Alex Coke** (f, ts); **Greg Wilson** (as, ts); **John Mills** (bs); **Bob Rodriguez** (p); **Ken Filiano** (b); **Billy Mintz** (d). CreOpMuse Ⓔ 002 (74 minutes). Recorded 1992/93.

⑦ ❼

Tina Marsh has led the Texan large ensemble CO2 for the past 15 years and this recording of it comes from a live concert in Austin, Texas. It picks up on a jazz tradition which stuttered and virtually died with the ending of the sixties, only to be re-formulated by brave outfits like Toshiko Akiyoshi's various bands and the Thad Jones-Mel Lewis group. Marsh's band are unafraid to mix a variety of styles and techniques to create long-form acoustic music tailor-made for an imaginative big-band setting. In that sense, they perhaps find echoes in the work of units such as George Grunz's Big Band and the defunct British aggregation, Loose Tubes. These two made very exciting music live, but their recorded legacy generally doesn't quite capture that fire.

Marsh's group uses the killer-diller punch much more sparingly and takes different kinds of musical chances: the use of near-silence in Marsh's own *Cloud on Cloud, Movement ll: Sally's Storm* is a risky thing indeed, but its place in the overall structure of the piece makes it work brilliantly. The scoring, mostly undertaken by Rodriguez, Filiano and Zimmerman, is fresh, at times beautifully transparent, and at no time awkward or bombastic, even when the group is really wailing. The brass writing is especially crisp. For a singer, Marsh is exceedingly backward in coming forward, mostly preferring to use her voice as a wordless lead or part instrument. Her improvisation on Lakey's *Circle* is neither too long nor too exhibitionist, though she certainly gives her voice a workout. This is a record which improves with each listening, and while there are no standout soloists, Marsh's Texans deserve our attention. **KS**

Warne Marsh

1927-1987

Two Days in the Life of... **Marsh** (ts); **Ron Eschete** (g); **Jim Hughart** (b); **Sherman Ferguson** (d). Storyville Ⓔ STCD 4165 (40 minutes). Recorded 1987.

⑧ ❼

A student and disciple of Lennie Tristano, Warne Marsh believed that players should try to reach beyond ego to "purely musical expression." His saxophone idols were Charlie Parker and Lester Young, though Tristano remained his mentor and he shared the pianist's belief in a total dedication to music, vowing "to play only what I want to play". This idealism kept him out of the recording studios and jazz clubs for long periods, especially in the sixties. He recorded more frequently towards the end of his life, and a late album such as *Two Days in the Life of...* shows that his chief stylistic traits—subtle time, oblique phrasing, a sinuous gracefulness—have been refined to the point where he has become a brilliant and highly original improviser.

The album catches him in sparkling form (he far outshines his colleagues). There is an infectious energy to his playing, the tone vibrant as he twists and feints through faster pieces such as *Initially K.C.* and *All God's Chillun Got Rhythm,* while the ballads shimmer with his delicate touch. Marsh understood harmony so well that for him a sequence of chord changes was a launching pad to almost infinite possibility. Listen to *Asterix* (a *These Foolish Things* variant), where he unfolds a line of lyrical invention as beautiful as it is unpredictable—the essence of great improvising. **GL**

Claire Martin

The Waiting Game **Martin** (v); **Jonathan Gee** (p); **Jim Mullen** (g); **Arnie Somogyi** (b); **Clark Tracey** (d). Linn Ⓔ AKD 018 (50 minutes). Recorded 1991.

⑥ ❽

This is a remarkable début album by a British singer. Martin's voice is attractive and she combines considerable range with a clean, bright tone. Her material (including one original, the title track, by herself and pianist Gee) is unhackneyed. Even in settings as varied as Mullen's solo guitar on *If You Could See Me Now* and the full quartet on Thomas Dolby's *The Key To Your Ferrari* she sounds incapable either of putting a foot wrong, singing a tasteless or false note, or failing to swing. She carries such accomplishments across songs by writers as stylistically divergent as Joni Mitchell, Tadd Dameron, Sammy Cahn, Richard Rogers and Betty Carter.

Her accompanists never obtrude, yet their interplay with her is more than background comping; Mullen and Gee weave beautiful gospel-tinged lines round her on Leiber and Stoller's *Some Cats.* It would be hard to disagree with Richard Rodney Bennett's observations in the liner note that her "pitch, musicianship and vocal control are immaculate". A fine balance of musicianship, clean recording quality and a genuine joy in performance. **AS**

Pat Martino 1944

Consciousness **Martino** (g); **Eddie Green** (elp, perc); **Tyrone Brown** (elb); **Sherman Ferguson** (d, perc). Muse Ⓕ MCD 5039-2 (39 minutes). Recorded 1974.

⑥ ❽

Unlike such peers as John McLaughlin and Larry Coryell, Pat Martino remained largely immune to the explosion of the guitar's resources occasioned by rock. He touched on fusion in the mid seventies with his group Joyous Lake, but his chief inspiration remained the unadorned bop combo sound of Wes Montgomery. However, although he adopted Montgomery's general approach, including a dark tone, the mature Martino played faster and denser than did Wes, and rarely used his idol's trademark octave and chord soloing style. Where Wes refined and extended on bebop, Martino was one of the first jazz guitarists to successfully apply Coltrane's modal style to the guitar. Thus his playing is more scalar than chordal, and marked by extensive chromatic embellishment and connection of scale tones. It has its formulas, and his sometimes unrelieved 16th-note phrasing can want rhythmic variety, but, on *Impressions* and the breathless 12-bar *On The Stairs* his chromatic lines generate staggering harmonic and kinetic energy. Martino's career was wrecked in 1980 when undiscriminating fate dealt him a cerebral aneurysm, and he has made tenacious efforts to rekindle the old fire, but on the evidence of recent recordings the formidable form heard here has yet to be recovered. **MG**

Hugh Masekela 1939

Uptownship **Masekela** (t, flh, perc, v); **Mark Ledford** (t, kb, v); **Morris Goldberg** (as, penny wh, v); **Rico Tyler** (kbds); **Tony Cedras** (kbds, acc, v); **Mbongeni Ngema** (org); **John 'Blackie' Selolwane** (g, v); **Emmanuel 'Chulo' Gatewood**, **Bakithi Khumalo** (b); **Damon Duewhite**, **Francis Fuster**, **Sipho Kunene**, **Remi Kabaka** (d, perc, v); **Leleti Khumalo**, **Lindiwe Hlengwa**, **Thandi Zulu**, **Ntomb Khona Dlamini**, **Branice McKenzie**, **Sharon Brooks**, **Jenny Douglas** (v). RCA Novus Ⓕ PD 83070 (62 minutes). Recorded 1988/89.

⑥ ❻

Some of Masekela's earlier albums were a search for the right blend between the raw township jazz of South Africa and the slicker sounds of the US. This album is the ideal balance, made up of a simple formula, as Masekela, Ledford and Goldberg play unison riffs over a rhythm section that carries a variety of world music beats with aplomb. The soul backbeat of Smokey Robinson or the reggae of Bob Marley fuel the riffing horns and Masekela's impassioned behind-the-beat flügelhorn just as effectively as the more overtly South African title track.

Amid the jazz solos, mainly taken by the leader and Morris Goldberg in the most elegant style on alto, there is a wealth of vocal material. Branice McKenzie stands out for her reading of *If You Don't Know Me*, and everyone gets together for the still-timely South African protest song *Just Hold On ('Til Freedom Comes)*. The politicized message here is more overt than elsewhere on the album, but in many ways the mixture of music and the consummate ease with which Masekela brings off the blend of styles is a successful political message in itself. **AS**

Cal Massey 1927-1972

Blues To Coltrane **Massey** (t); **Julius Watkins** (frh); **Hugh Brodie** (ts); **Patti Brown** (p); **Jimmy Garrison** (b); **G.T. Hogan** (d). Candid Ⓜ CD 9029 (41 minutes). Recorded 1961.

⑧ ❻

Massey was a heartbreakingly unlucky musician. His luck was so bad that this, his only album as a leader in a career spanning 30 years, was never released in his lifetime: a victim of the early demise of the original Candid label in 1961, it had to wait until the mid-eighties for its first full release (one track, in edited form, appeared on the Candid sampler LP, **The Jazz Life**). Considering all the blowing sessions thrown onto the market in the late fifties, the failure of this carefully-prepared album to see the light of day is all the sadder. A painfully out-of-tune piano aside, everything slots perfectly into

place and each soloist has something meaningful to say. Each track is a Massey composition: that he was a superior composer and arranger is attested by the many songs and settings of his recorded by the best players of his generation and beyond, from Charlie Parker to John Coltrane to Lee Morgan to Archie Shepp.

His trumpet style is related to the lyricism of Johnny Coles, although he seems not to have had the overall technical security Coles enjoys; yet his vulnerability somehow makes his playing that much more affecting. His companions here are all good, interesting players, with Brodie soloing strongly in the manner of early Coltrane (a pleasant change from the post-**Giant Steps** acolytes) and Julius Watkins, as always, arresting in his ideas. **KS**

Zane Massey

1957

Brass Knuckles **Massey** (ss, ts); **Hideiji Taninaka** (b); **Sadiq M. Abu Shamid**, **William Parker** (d). Delmark Ⓔ DD-464 (47 minutes). Recorded 1992.

⑧ ❽

Were it not for critic/producer Nat Hentoff the jazz world at large may not have been aware of the talents of Cal Massey as a trumpeter and composer (although Archie Shepp did much at the end of the sixties to commit Massey's compositions and arrangements to disc). It was Hentoff who was responsible for Massey's only album, **Blues To Coltrane** (see above). Zane is Cal's son, a young man who grew up in a household where it was not unusual to find men such as Coltrane and Cedar Walton rehearsing with Massey Sr. Tuition from people like Frank Foster and Jimmy Heath, plus the encouragement of his father, has resulted in Zane's emergence as a powerful, confident soloist whose music is thankfully devoid of the filibustering self-indulgence of many post-Coltrane players. Although he has worked and recorded with Sun Ra, Ronald Shannon Jackson and Roy Campbell, this disc is Zane's début as a leader and there have been fewer more impressive beginnings. The eight-tune programme contains two of his father's works, *Message From Trane* and *Assunta* (the latter is the only track on which he plays soprano). The Japanese bass player Taninaka produces a full, rich sound reminiscent of the great Leroy Vinnegar and Wilbur Ware, and the compactness of the trio makes this a unit which has the flexibility to cover a range of expression. **AM**

Ricky May

The Best Of Ricky May May (v); **Bob Barnard**, **John Hoffman**, **Bill Burton**, **Ken Brentnall**, **Paul Panichi** (t); **Bob McIvor**, **Jack Grimsley**, **Bob Johnson**, **James Morrison**, **Arthur Hubbard** (tb); **Errol Buddle**, **Clair Bail**, **Dave Rutledge**, **Col Loughnan**, **John Homan**, **Charlie Munro**, **Paul Williams**, **Steve Giordano** (reeds); **Julian Lee** (p); **Ron Philpott**, **Ike Issacs**, **George Golla** (g); **Clive Harrison**, **Darcy Wright** (b); **Mark Bowden**, **Alan Gilbert**, **Len Barnard** (d); **Kenny Powell** (acc); **String Orchestra**. ABC Jazz Ⓔ 512006-2 (78 minutes). Recorded 1975-85.

⑤ ❼

May was born in New Zealand and he moved to Australia for a night club spot in 1962. It was the start of an illustrious career that took him to Britain, Singapore, Spain, Finland, Italy and the USA. His qualifications as a jazz singer are barely in doubt; his style is somewhere between Matt Munro and Harry Connick Jr and Frank Sinatra would seem to be an obvious inspiration. This CD presents his many virtues even if it does expose the odd weakness. Without being contrived, he shows on titles like *Blueberry Hill* and *Hit That Jive, Jack* that he can bring his own special construction to a tune. When he is at his most relaxed and understated, as on *Now You Has Jazz* and *Christopher Columbus*, he swings well. He is not a natural improviser but spurious word juggling and scatting efforts are used sparingly. He sometimes injects hip lyrics rather than rebuild his line, but this trait is kept within reasonable bounds. He may lack the elasticity that Armstrong brought to *Mack The Knife* and *I'm Confessin'*, but when May died in 1988 the world lost a useful jazz singer. **BMcR**

Tina May

Fun May (v); **David Newton** (p); **Dave Green** (b); **Clark Tracey** (d); **Don Weller** (ts) on 3 tracks; **Gerard Presencer** (t) on 2 tracks. 33 Records Ⓔ 33 Jazz 013 (66 minutes). Recorded 1993.

⑥ ❼

May has now produced three albums under her own leadership, this being the second of those three. More assured than her debut **Never Let Me Go**, more stylistically centred and less disparate than the 1994 **It Ain't Necessarily So**, this one explores for the most part the types of emotions catered for by having the musical equivalent of the title while performing. This seems to best suit May's light and agile voice, one which sounds most comfortable on the medium-tempo swingers which make up the bulk of this set. There seems to have been a discreet intelligence at work also when it comes to arrangements, so that a potentially tricky piece such as Don Weller's *Here To Stay* finds May's vocal line doubled caressingly by the tenorist's supple tenor. Weller also solos affectingly on the three tracks on which he is featured.

Occasionally the type of over-excitement which can sound great live but doesn't exactly endear itself on repeated listening creeps into May's vocalising (*Out of This World* suffers from this in places), but as a rule she shows admirable control and awareness of dynamics, and a desire to impress through deft understatement rather than hyperbole. May clearly has a laudable taste for Strayhorn ballads (there's one on every album so far released), but the strange, overheated, fugitive world created by the composer (so memorably captured by Ellington and Fitzgerald on **Ella At Duke's Place**) largely escapes her here. That may simply leave us with a fun record, but as such it should not be discounted, and can safely be enjoyed for what it comfortably accomplishes.. **KS**

Lyle Mays 1953

Fictionary **Mays** (p); **Mark Johnson** (b); **Jack DeJohnette** (d). Geffen Ⓔ GEFD 24521 (65 minutes). Recorded 1992.

⑨ ❾

Pianist Lyle Mays, though best known for his electronic keyboard work with various editions of guitarist Pat Metheny's popular fusion group, is also an exceptional acoustic pianist. Here, in the good company of Johnson and DeJohnette, Mays may often evoke the Bill Evans lineage, but remains his own man. As is also the case in the pianistics of Richie Beirach, one hears the luminescent colours and subtly washed lines of turn-of-the-century composers such as Scriabin, Ravel and Debussy, especially in the picaresque title tune.

There is also a harder, neo-bop edge in tracks like *Sienna*, where the furious pace seems as driven as that of that fabled city's annual Palio horse race around the Piazza del Campo. Contrastingly, there are lyric meditations such as the poignant *Something Left Unsaid* and the aptly-titled *Bill Evans*. Interactions between Mays, Johnson and DeJohnette are deep, touching on the profound. Considering the status of all three players, that should perhaps be no surprise. However, it is Mays whose seal finally provides the authorial stamp on this sublime exhibition of the art of the modern piano trio. **CB**

Medeski, Martin & Wood

Friday Afternoon In The Universe **John Medeski** (org, p, elp); **Billy Martin** (d, perc); **Chris Wood** (b, hca, wood f). Gramavision Ⓔ GCD 79503 (57 minutes). Recorded 1994.

④ ❽

Although Medeski, Martin and Wood have been acclaimed for their "daring genre smashing" among Manhattan's self-consciously progressive East Village community, this, their second album for Gramavision, seems more a demonstration of the triumph of style over content than a significant musical event. The trio's attitude, presumably one they share with their audience, is routinely post-modernist, a concern simultaneously to demonstrate an awareness of tradition (in this case early seventies Miles, the organ trio, and—shorthand for real jazz roots—the acoustic bass) and a serious embrace of the avant-garde. Nice concept, but in MMW's case the musical substance is slight to say the least, amounting to an agglomeration of somewhat skewed *r&b* riffs and free-ish interludes in which spontaneity and self-expression are favoured over the stuffy and prohibitive old values of form and development. The result is the appearance of jazz—probably quite sufficient for those pretentious enough to subscribe to it. **MG**

Myra Melford

Even The Sounds Shine **Melford** (p); **Dave Douglas** (t); **Marty Ehrlich** (cl, as); **Lindsey Horner** (b); **Reggie Nicholson** (d). hatART Ⓔ CD 6161 (70 minutes). Recorded 1994.

⑤ ❻

Melford, a young pianist/composer who put in her stint at New York's Knitting Factory, has been making records for a few years now, the latest two on hatART. The previous one, **Alive In The House of Saints**, concentrated on her trio. This one adds the two horns and is the better for it. Recorded in Wuppertal during a European stint in summer of 1994, it shows that her resourcefulness as a composer is perhaps not yet matched in her improvisations, where her indebtedness to models such as Cecil Taylor and Don Pullen occasionally pull the music out of shape. This was a more glaring problem on the previous album, where she was carrying most of the improvisatory load, so the presence of other soloists who are interesting in their own right makes for a generally more varied

and satisfying synthesis. Her compositional gift is not inconsiderable and it is not confined to merely coming up with a couple of nice themes - she is able to shape and finish a form through a number of stages which have their own continuity. The band respond positively to this musical stimulation, and Melford herself never sounds anything less than completely engaged in what she plays. Perhaps time itself is all she needs to evolve a more personal improvisatory style: it's there in embryo already. **KS**

Gil Melle

1931

Primitive Modern/Quadrama **Melle** (bs); **Joe Cinderella** (g); **Billy Phillips**, **George Duvivier** (b); **Ed Thigpen**, **Shadow Wilson** (d). Prestige Ⓜ OJC 1712-2 (68 minutes). Recorded 1956-57.

⑥ ❽

During the fifties Melle was identified with the modernist side of jazz. He acknowledged being influenced by contemporary composers like Bartók and Varèse, but outside of the uncommon care he took to structure his pieces there is little overt evidence, and he never lost the desire or ability to swing. Recordings for Blue Note early in the decade found him playing tenor sax with a cool Getzian demeanour, but soon the baritone became his main instrument. This disc generously combines two LPs. Without trombonist Eddie Bert, his front line partner on the Blue Notes, the quartet arrangements take on a more intimate character, with a greater emphasis on interplay between the baritone and guitar. On the first album, **Primitive Modern**, Melle plays with a light, velvety tone and attractive ideas, and guitarist Cinderella offers a flexible harmonic balance, in unison, counterpoint, or as accompanist. By the time of the second date, a year later, Melle's tone had grown a touch more gruff and Mulliganesque with Cinderella adopting a Barney Kesselish twang. In retrospect, outside of some unusual rhythmic accents and a soupçon of dissonance, the music is not all that experimental, and remains easily likeable, whether it is a mellow *In A Sentimental Mood*, the open-textured *Dominica*, or a full-bodied *It Don't Mean A Thing*. **AL**

George Melly

1926

Frankie and Johnny **Melly** (v); **John Chilton** (t); **Ron Rubin** (p); **Eddie Taylor** (d). D Sharp Records Ⓕ DSH CD7001 (49 minutes). Recorded 1992.

⑥ ❽

In the first part of his career Melly confined himself to reworking classic blues (usually the ones sung largely by women) in a macabre manner, becoming in effect a singing version of the cartoonist Charles Addams. When he and his current trumpeter/musical director John Chilton formed their liaison more than two decades ago, the two men set about broadening the range of Melly's material to incorporate Broadway songs and other popular pieces. Melly, with his superbly jigged histrionics, has always provided the most spectacular visual display on the British scene. Over the years he has cultured his voice to move away from the earthy shouting of his early years. This album, his best yet, represents the fruition of his and Chilton's efforts. The material is treated with sophistication and Melly's gallows humour still manifests itself when the opportunity offers.

The backing by John Chilton's Feetwarmers is essential to Melly's success. Chilton is a fine trumpeter and he plays several good solos, displaying also an instinctive feel for obbligato. He and pianist Rubin shepherd the singer through each track. Rubin is a particularly delicate blues player and this is probably the best example of his work on disc. Chilton's arrangements exploit the limited line-up to the full and his composition *Living On My Own* has real poignance, bringing out the best in the singer. Melly's cheerful bawdiness is another element in his repertoire and it is unleashed on a handful of these tracks. **SV**

Vince Mendoza

1960

Sketches **Mendoza** (cond, arr); **Andy Haderer**, **Rob Bruynen**, **Klaus Osterloh**, **Rick Kiefer**, **John Marshall** (t); **Dave Horler**, **Henning Berg**, **Bernt Laukamp**, **Roy Deuvall** (tb); **G. Kedves**, **L. Rasch**, **M. Putnam** (frh); **H. Waldner** (tba); **Dave Liebmann** (ss); **Charlie Mariano**, **Heiner Wiberney**, **Harald Rosenstein** (as); **Olivier Peters**, **Rolf Romer** (ts); **Jens Neufang** (bs); **Frank Chastenier** (p); **Nguyên Lê** (g); **Dieter Ilg** (b); **Peter Erskine** (d). ACT Ⓕ 892 152 (63 minutes). Recorded 1993.

⑥ ❽

Despite a rather uneasy integration of flamenco with big band jazz, Mendoza's previous album **Jazzpaña** was nominated for a Grammy and marked him out as an arranger of originality and power. Raw flamenco has too much strength of its own to be happily contained in a formal band setting, and much of Mendoza's writing sounds contrived, yet it brought him sufficient recognition that this new collaboration with the WDR Big Band is liberally labelled 'The Man From **Jazzpaña**'. This is a far more effective disc in its own right, solving a different compositional problem; how to set almost free improvisation in a formal structure. The Cologne musicians produce a near-perfect example of section discipline and, driven by Erskine's *tour-de-force* drums plus some excellent guest soloists, the results are exhilarating. Some unusual voicings and pairings ebb and flow in the eight-movement suite written for the album, but the whole thing is prefaced by Ravel's *Pavane*: a showcase for Mariano's sumptuous alto and Dave Liebmann's upwardly-mobile soprano. **AS**

Misha Mengelberg

1935

Who's Bridge **Mengelberg** (p); **Brad Jones** (b); **Joey Baron** (d). Avant Ⓕ 038 (60 minutes). Recorded 1994.

⑧ ❽

Never one to travel in a straight line when there are curves to consider, the Russian-born, Dutch-bred Misha Mengelberg is a brilliant composer, arranger and pianist, fluent in a wide variety of twentieth-century musical styles. He has written for classical ensembles, but his work in jazz allows him to bring together his eclectic interests. Like the Dadaists, Mengelberg constantly seeks to erase the boundary between the 'serious' and the 'humorous'. His arrangements for the ICP Orchestra, the Berlin Contemporary Jazz Orchestra and other large ensembles often use elements of collage, slapstick and repetition to confuse and delight listeners. Working in the traditional piano trio, as here, allows him affectionately to parody its conventions—those established by Art Tatum, Bill Evans and Oscar Peterson—distorting but never destroying them completely. Mengelberg flits from style to style within a single tune—sometimes from phrase to phrase, as in *Rumbone*, where he plays funky chords in one hand and atonal clusters in the other, or *Gare Guillemans*, which at first glance could be a fifties Broadway show tune, until his solo gradually deconstructs the theme down into a few stumbling pitches and then smoothly shifts back into the groove. Monk is a major influence, as can be heard in the leaping intervals and theme interruptions of *Romantic Jump Of Hares*, and the lovely unexpected angular chords and lyrical line of *Peer's Counting Song*. This programme is the closest Mengelberg has yet come to the jazz mainstream and the blend of playfulness and precision is always engaging. A pity about the gaffe in the title. **AL**

Helen Merrill

1930

Collaboration **Merrill** (v); **Lew Soloff** (t); **Shunzo Ono** (t, flh); **Jimmy Knepper** (tb); **Dave Taylor** (b tb); **Danny Bank** (f, bcl, bs); **Phil Bodner** (f, alf, ss); **Chris Hunter** (f, cl, ob, ss, as, pic); **Wally Kane** (bcl, bn); **Roger Rosenberg** (b cl); **Gil Goldstein** (p, kbds), **Harry Lookofsky** (vn); **Lamar Alsop** (vn, va); **Harold Colletta**, **Theodore Israel** (va); **Jesse Levy** (vc); **Joe Beck**, **Jay Berliner** (g); **Buster Williams** (b); **Mel Lewis** (d, perc); **Gil Evans** (arr, cond); **Steve Lacy** (ss-2). EmArcy Ⓕ 834 205-2 (45 minutes). Recorded 1987.

✔ ⑩ ❿

A singer whose cool timbre resembles that of Chris Connor or June Christy, but who brings her emotions much closer to the surface, Merrill has surrounded herself with superior musicians throughout her career—her album with Clifford Brown from the fifties compares favourably with Sarah Vaughan's date with him from the same period. We have Merrill to thank for what amounted to Evans's last hurrah as an arranger. **Collaboration** is a remake of **Dream of You**, Merrill's 1956 album with Evans which is said to have inspired **Miles Ahead** and Evans's subsequent albums for Miles Davis. Because failing health prevented Evans from writing new charts for this reunion with Merrill, the two recorded new versions of 11 of the 12 songs from **Dream of You**. If anything, these remakes swim deeper emotional currents than the originals, and they certainly sound more like Evans's work than most of what he recorded with his own wayward big band in the last decade of his life. The heartstopper is *Anyplace I Hang My Hat Is Home*, a prime example of how an Evans arrangement could make a great song even better: with its unlikely combination of boogie-woogie rumble and existential doleur, it sounds like something written by Meade Lux Lewis and Jean Paul Sartre, instead of by Harold Arlen and Johnny Mercer. Steve Lacy's solos on two tracks are an inestimable bonus, but the star soloist is Merrill, a class act who has rarely sounded better than she does here. **FD**

Pat Metheny

1954

Bright Size Life **Metheny** (elg); **Jaco Pastorius** (elb); **Bob Moses** (d). ECM Ⓕ 1073 (827 133-2) (38 minutes). Recorded 1975.

⑥ ❽

Most of Pat Metheny's début as leader stands alone within his catalogue. Only the closing medley of Ornette Coleman's blues, *Round Trip/Broadway Blues*, acquired a later parallel when, in 1985 on the album **Song X**, Metheny once again demonstrated his seemingly unlikely admiration for Coleman's music. But there is little suggestion here of the mellifluous pop-jazz which brought Metheny international acclaim and a respectable degree of commercial success. This trio's work bears more stylistic affinity with the rock and country styles heard in the Pat Metheny Group than with, say, the bebop of Tal Farlow, but it has a complexity, abstraction and cerebralism which makes it less easily assimilable than the music of that group. The tunes are marked by unorthodox and rapid chord changes, the rhythms tend to be disjunct, and the pulse is ever-shifting. However, Metheny's strong lyrical sensibility enables him to unify his unruly material, and despite its frequent angularity, the music has a poetic quality. It's also interesting for presenting the new star of the electric bass in a setting he perhaps would not have sought out himself. **MG**

Travels **Pat Metheny** (g); **Lyle Mays** (p, syn); **Steve Rodby** (b); **Dan Gottlieb** (d); **Nana Vasconcelos** (perc, v). ECM Ⓕ 1252/53(810 622-2) (two discs: 96 minutes). Recorded 1982.

⑧ ❽

Metheny as guitar synthesizer whizz, composer, arranger, restless improviser, ambient soundscape constructor and above all virtuosic lyrical jazz guitar hero: 1982's **Travels** has it all, and all live at that. By this stage, Metheny's partnership with keyboardist and composer Mays was several albums old, and the magic they weave—a magic as successful commercially as artistically—was at its peak. Arguably, as the Pat Metheny Group has developed (and it's notched up a good five or so albums since **Travels**) the lushness of the arrangements and precision of the playing has taken the music further into the instrumental rock category and further away from any sort of jazz base, but no such criticisms could be levelled at the music they were making together on their 1982 world tour. Old favourites dating right back to the group's 1978 eponymous début, and then-recent but now-classic pieces like the achingly lovely ballad *Are You Going With Me?*, as well as material still not recorded elsewhere (most notably the dazzling guitar/synth freak out of *Song For Bilbao*) all get an airing. Of special note are the contributions of the extraordinary Brazilian percussionist and berimbau specialist Vasconcelos, who débuted on the group's Grammy-winning **Offramp**, and who brings a rhythmic vitality and textural earthiness to the group's sound that helps make this album unique in the guitarist's entire canon. **SH**

The Road To You–Live in Europe **Metheny** (g, g-syn); **Lyle Mays** (kbds); **Steve Rodby** (b); **Paul Wertigo** (d); **Armando Marcal** (perc); **Pedro Aznar** (v). Geffen Ⓕ 24601 (74 minutes). Recorded 1992.

⑦ ❽

The Pat Metheny Group has been responsible for some pretty boring albums in recent years, however nice the subtleties may have been. This album, taken from their 1992 European tour, re-establishes some muscle in their playing, touches base with some of their best-known compositions of the past, and conjures echoes of one of their best past efforts, the ECM album **Travels** from ten years ago. Tunes such as *First Circle, Last Train Home* and *Third Wind* get new workouts here, and Metheny himself plays them with a great deal more variety in tone and approach than he did the more standard jazz repertoire on the disappointing 1990 trio album with Dave Holland and Roy Haynes, **Question and Answer**. One still gets the impression that occasionally Metheny finds certain complex fingerboard patterns utterly irresistible, so that phrases come out in the most unlikely places and for no particular musical reason. Yet, on balance, there are a lot more good things going down than poor, and even though the material needs close attention to detail before it will reveal its true character, there is enough spirit in the highly professional playing of all Group members to make the effort rewarding. **KS**

Hendrik Meurkens

Slidin' **Meurkins** (hca); **Dado Moroni, Mark Soskin** (p); **Peter Bernstein** (g); **David Finck, Harvie Swartz** (b); **Tim Horner** (d). Concord Jazz Ⓕ CCD4628 (63 minutes). Recorded 1994.

⑥ ❽

Meurkens was born in Hamburg of Dutch parents, attended Berklee College in Boston and taught himself to play the vibraphone. He plays harmonica here, as he has done on his three previous CDs on the Concord label. Many jazz enthusiasts, including the present writer, have quite serious reservations about the harmonica, preferring to relegate it to film soundtracks or blues bands. However Toots Thielemans, Max Geldray and now Hendrik Meurkens will cause a re-examination of long-held opinions if one adopts the view that these men play music first and foremost. Meurkens seems to have overcome most of the technical problems, although he admits in his notes to the difficulties in playing *legato*. His solos have all the interest of a good improvising saxophonist and he had taken care in his choice of companions, selecting men whose work complements the sound of the harmonica. Peter Bernstein is an excellent guitarist, both pianists (they play on six tracks apiece) are sensitive and inventive players while Horner is simply one of the most tasteful and intelligent of drummers. The music is based on good standards such as *All Of You*, tasteful originals and two timeless jazz standards, Oliver Nelson's *Stolen Moments* and Kenny Barron's *Voyage*. If the listener is prepared to set aside preconceptions and prejudice he will be repaid with some fine music. **AM**

Mezz Mezzrow

1899-1972

The King Jazz Story, Volume 2 **Mezzrow** (cl); **Sidney Bechet** (ss, cl); **Hot Lips Page** (t, v); **Sammy Price, Fitz Weston** (p); **Pops Foster, Wellman Braud** (b); **Sid Catlett, Baby Dodds, Kaiser Marshall** (d); **Pleasant Joe, Coot Grant, Douglas Daniels** (v). Storyville Ⓜ STCD 8213 (77 minutes). Recorded 1945-47.

⑧ ❻

Mezz Mezzrow was a much maligned man who more literally than most lived for jazz. His prime skill was in propagandizing the music and organizing record dates, and his efforts in this direction with regard to Tommy Ladnier and Sidney Bechet should not be underestimated. Although his clarinet technique was limited, he excelled within its boundaries, and his instinctive support and obbligati behind Bechet could not be bettered, with the result that he held the book of jazz open while Bechet wrote some of the greatest words in it.

The King Jazz label was Mezzrow's own, and while the recordings were predominantly of himself with Bechet (the versions of *Where Am I?*, *I'm Speaking My Mind* and *I Want Some* have declamatory Bechet at his most powerful) he gave Sam Price the opportunity to record some of his best solo tracks, and these are scattered throughout this and the other four volumes of King Jazz issues on Storyville. Storyville STCD 8212, 8214 and 8215 are every bit as good as this one, whilst STCD 4104 is at variance only in being the sole CD with a playing time under 70 minutes.

Singers like Pleasant Joe and Coot Grant inhabited the backwaters in jazz, but thanks to Mezzrow they have their day here. Mezzrow's recorded comments on the music pop up between some of the tracks, and while they are an hilarious anachronism, they are heartfelt if misguided. **SV**

Palle Mikkelborg

1941

Aura Mikkelborg (comp, flh); **Miles Davis** (t soloist); **Jesper Thilo**, **Per Carsten**, **Uffe Karskov**, **Bent Jaedig**, **Flemming Madsen**, **Niels Eje** (reeds); **Benny Rosenfeld**, **Palle Bolvig**, **Jens Winther**, **Perry Knudsen**, **Idrees Sulieman** (t); **Vincent Nilsson**, **Jens Engel**, **Ture Larsen**, **Ole Kurt Jensen**, **Axel Windfeld** (tb); **John McLaughlin**, **Bjarne Roupe** (g); **Thomas Clausen** (p); **Ole Koch-Hansen**, **Kenneth Knudsen** (synth); **Niels-Henning Ørsted Pedersen**, **Bo Stief** (b); **Vince Wilburn**, **Lennart Gruvstedt** (d); **Marilyn Mazur**, **Ethan Weisgaard** (perc); **Lillian Tbernquist** (harp); **Eva Thaysen** (v). Columbia Ⓕ 463351-2 (66 minutes). Recorded 1985.

⑧ ❽

Though understandably released under Miles Davis's name, there is a strong case that this astonishing work should be listed under Danish trumpeter/ flügelhornist/composer Palle Mikkelborg. Inspired by the 1984 awarding of Denmark's prestigious Sonning Prize to Davis, an honour usually reserved for art music composers (past honourees include Igor Stravinsky and Leonard Bernstein), Mikkelborg composed his stunning ten-part suite as a personal homage. Recorded a year later with Davis as the principal soloist, Mikkelborg's work was designed as a projection of "an image which reflected Miles's musical aura". As such, Mikkelborg's dazzling time machine spins out reconfigured shards, actual as well as extrapolated, from the trumpeter's multi-dimensional and enigmatic persona.

Combining state-of-the-art electronics, rich yet austere orchestral textures, and the cool but impassioned improvisations of McLaughlin, Pedersen, Stief and Clausen, Mikkelborg's exquisite tapestry spills out over a shimmering hour-long frame upon which Miles brushes exotically coloured webs of musical intrigue. The piece's organizing principle is a ten-tone scale derived from the letters MILES DAVIS which Mikkelborg permutates through various serial techniques. Throughout looms the presence of Gil Evans, with whom Mikkelborg and Davis both worked. This was, in fact, Miles's first recording with an orchestra since his final collaborations with Evans in the mid sixties. In all, it is a galvanizing landmark in the Davis discography and a prime example of Mikkelborg's uniquely compelling compositional vision. **CB**

Glenn Miller

1904-1944

The Essential Glenn Miller Miller (tb, ldr) with a collective personnel including: **Dale McMickle**, **Bob Price**, **Legh Knowles**, **Clyde Hurley** (t); **Glenn Miller**, **Al Mastren**, **Paul Tanner** (tb); **Hal McIntyre**, **Wilbur Schwartz** (cl, as); **Gabe Gelinas** (as, bs); **Al Klink**, **Stanley Aronson** (ts); **Tex Beneke** (ts, v); **Chummy McGregor** (p); **Richard Fisher** (g); **Rowland Bundock** (b) **Maurice Purtill** (d); **Ray Eberle**, **Marion Hutton**, **Jerry Gray**, **Glenn Miller** (v) RCA Bluebird Ⓜ 66520 2 (two discs: 150 minutes). Recorded 1939-42.

⑧ ❽

Listening to *In The Mood* for the millionth time in preparation to write about this compilation, I happened on an entirely banal but useful thought: this really is just *Woodchopper's Ball* with an asymmetrical riff thrown over the verse. Which makes you wonder about the relationship between Woody's original and Wingy Manone's *Tar Paper Stomp*. Which also led me to think about the isolation ward Miller's music is often pushed into by jazz writers. Many critics would dispute the need to have *any* Glenn Miller records in a Guide of this nature – and indeed he is not in some recent ones I've seen – but this would seem more to be pique at his continued popularity than any really objective judgement. Miller, an adroit leader and arranger but a so-so instrumentalist and poor improviser, often recorded songs and ditties with only a tangential link to jazz, but then so did Harry James and Nat King Cole, and nobody denies them their jazz standing.

There are literally hundreds of Miller compilations on the market at present, but I've chosen this one because it has a good playing time, is midprice, has much of the essential jazz-based Miller (*Little*

Brown Jug, Tuxedo Junction, Pennsylvania 6500, In The Mood, A String Of Pearls and *American Patrol*, for example), as well as all the hits and is released by RCA Bluebird, who own the original masters. This is an important point, because the producer of this quite lavish edition, Paul Williams, writes in the CD booklet "we examined every metal part still remaining in our vaults (masters, moulds and stampers) together with some test pressings...After extensive restoration work, we were able to work with the original takes on all but three of the selections". The difference in quality over previous releases is marked, as a quick check against a predecessor such as **The Ultimate Glenn Miller** reveals. The full recording and personnel details are also available in the booklet, along with lots of pictures and a good essay from Colin Escott.

Some of the material included here is well beyond the realms of jazz, and if anyone should want just the instrumentals with clear jazz content, a sister reissue, **Swinging Instrumentals** (Bluebird 66529 2) should suffice. If anyone happens to want the *complete* RCA Glenn Miller, 1938-42, then that is also currently available, on no fewer than 13 CDs and in a deluxe black box (RCA Bluebird ND 90600) containing a 140-page booklet which exhaustively documents the civilian band from 1938-42. You have been warned... **KS**

Glenn Miller's Men In Paris On four tracks **Bernie Privin** (t); **Peanuts Hucko** (cl, as, ts); **Mel Powell** (p); **Django Reinhardt** (g); **Joe Shulman** (b); **Ray McKinley** (d). On 14 tracks same personnel but **Carmen Mastren** (g) for **Reinhardt**. On four tracks **Peanuts Hucko** (cl); **Mel Powell** (p); **Ray McKinley** (d). On four tracks **Mel Powell** (p solos). Starlite Ⓜ STD1 (73 minutes). Recorded 1945.

⑧ ❻

The sextet tracks here have appeared over the years under a variety of band titles. It was the small swing group from the American Band of the AEF but by the time these recordings were made in Paris (in January and May, 1945) Glenn Miller had been reported missing and the unit was under the joint leadership of Ray McKinley and Jerry Gray. Now, for the first time, all of the tunes have been carefully gathered onto one CD, including a previously unissued take of *At Sundown*, by producer Peter Newbrook and remastered by Dave Bennett. Many will have fond memories of these delightful examples of small band swing, with Django Reinhardt taking the place of the regular guitarist Carmen Mastren on the first four tracks and taking some typical solos. It is a joy to have Mel Powell present on all 26 tracks and esepcially so on his four beautifully concise solos, which include tributes to Fats Waller and Debussy. There are four Goodman-like trio tracks on which Ray McKinley's drive is noteworthy while the work of Peanuts Hucko throughout is excellent. Bernie Privin too is inspired and these tracks have great musical value, apart from any obvious historic interest. Many of these tracks have appeared previously on Esquire and French CBS but these must rate as the cleanest transfers. Highly recommended. **AM**

Marcus Miller

1959

Tales **Miller** (v, f, g, p, kbds, bcl, elb, programming); **Michael 'Patches' Stewart** (t); **Kenny Garrett** (as); **Joshua Redman** (ts); **Hiram Bullock**, **Dean Brown** (elg); **Bernard Wright** (syn, org, kyb, marimba); **Poogie Bell**, **Lenny White** (d); **Lalah Hathaway**, **Joe Sample** (v); **Me'Shell NdegeOcello** (v, syn); **Bashiri Johnson** (perc samples); **David Ward** (programming). Dreyfus Ⓕ FDM 36571-2. Recorded 1995.

④ ❽

Miller's mid-eighties début as leader, in which he posed Jacko-like atop a stack of hackneyed disco clichés, sat uncomfortably with his burgeoning reputation as one of the hippest young bassists in New York. Unfortunately, on the evidence of his last two solo records, not a lot has changed, certainly not enough to meet the high expectations attendant on the man who was indispensable to the success of David Sanborn's last all-electric records and conceived and almost single-handedly realized Miles Davis's final studio triumphs.

It is probably a warning sign that Miller has an extra-musical agenda for **Tales**. Its nature is hardly significant but it may explain the record's mystifying musical moribundity. The drum programming, all either slow or mid-tempo, is dense and static, there is little attempt at dynamic variation, the bass, dominant in themes and solos, is slapped and popped in an archaic mid-eighties style, several tunes seem to work the same pedestrian chord sequence and others are largely unmodified readings of seventies soul standards. There is some mild jazz interest from Garrett and Stewart, but one of the most successful pieces is Me'Shell MdegeOcello's *Rush Over*—good soul, but not much to do with jazz. **MG**

Mulgrew Miller

1955

Wingspan **Miller** (p); **Kenny Garrett** (as, f); **Steve Nelson** (vb); **Charnette Moffett** (b); **Tony Reedus** (d); **Rudy Bird** (perc). Landmark Ⓕ 1515-2 (54 minutes). Recorded 1987.

⑧ ❽

The names McCoy and Herbie dog younger pianists; these days, Tyner or Hancock are almost inescapable influences. Miller absorbed a lot of both, Tyner especially, but the Mississippi-born, Memphis-schooled pianist's style has also been shaped by bluesy southern roots and by significant stints with leaders Mercer Ellington, Betty Carter, Woody Shaw, Art Blakey and Tony Williams. Mulgrew's lines are graceful and flowing, sometimes long and intricate, yet tolling middle-register chords keep his flights tethered. **Wingspan**, his first non-trio album, demonstrates that Miller the leader does not follow the example of any former employer too closely. He writes fetching tunes, conspicuously the uptempo romp *Wingspan* and *One's Own Room*, with lovely unisons for flute and vibes floating over a static bassline.

With Garrett's pungent alto up-front (the ballad *You're That Dream* makes effective use of his sour, keening long tones) Miller gets to show off his propulsive comping. Nelson's Hutcherson-like drifting lines contrast sharply with Miller's grounded chords; the two do not snarl each other up. The vibist makes a particularly strong statement on *I Remember You*, the only non-original. But then bringing out the best in sidefolk is a hallmark of any good leader. **KW**

Punch Miller 1894–1971

Punch Miller's New Orleans Band 1957 **Miller** (t, v, ldr); **Eddie Morris** (tb); **Simon Frazier** (p); **Ricard Alexis** (b); **Bill Bagley** (d). 504 Ⓕ CD 34 (57 minutes). Recorded 1957.

⑤ ❷

Miller was a widely acclaimed trumpeter, not best served by some of the recordings he left. He featured in New Orleans with Kid Ory, Jack Carey and Jelly Roll Morton in the twenties and worked New York and Chicago in the thirties and forties. His recording début was in 1925 but it was not until 1941 that he fronted his own studio session. He settled in New Orleans in 1956 and was best known for his playing with George Lewis and for the 1971 film *'Til The Butcher Cut Him Down*.

His earliest influence had been Louis Armstrong and Miller was (then) blessed with a comparable attack. His moments of daring rivalled Jabbo Smith, his solos avoided the easy route and he had the power to carry even the most pedestrian ensemble. Little is available on CD and his latter-day playing is uneven. Restricted by a modest rhythm section and hampered by a fumbling trombone colleague on this CD, he faces an uphill battle. His powerful lead on *You Rascal You*, the swing he generates on *Sheik Of Araby* and *Royal Garden Blues* recall the master of the past, however, and he says enough on *All Of Me* to endorse his reputation as an improviser. **BMcR**

Lucky Millinder 1900-1966

Lucky Millinder 1941-42 **Millinder** (v, dir); **William Scott**, **Archie Johnson**, **Nelson Byrant**, **Freddy Webster**, **Dizzy Gillespie** (t); **George Stevenson**, **Donald Cole**, **Eli Robinson**, **Floyd Brady**, **Edward Morant**, **Sandy Williams**, **Joe Britton** (tb); **Billy Bowen**, **George James**, **Ted Barnett**, **Tab Smith** (as); **Buster Bailey** (cl, as); **Stafford Simon**, **Dave Young** (ts); **Ernest Purce** (bs); **Bill Doggett**, **Clyde Hart** (p); **Sister Rosetta Tharpe** (v, g); **Trevor Bacon**, **Sterling Marlow** (g); **Abe Bolar**, **George Duvivier**, **Nick Fenton** (b); **Panama Francis** (d). Classics Ⓜ 712 (61 minutes). Recorded 1941-42.

⑦ ❻

Millinder was not a musician, but notable sidemen such as Gillespie have spoken of his exceptional talent as a conductor. He first became a band leader in 1931, toured Europe in 1933, and in the following year assumed the leadership of the Mills Blue Rhythm Band. In 1940 he assembled his own band for a spot at the Savoy Ballroom and the tracks on this CD come from that period. It was music for dancers, but there were also jewels for the listener; all editions of the band had good rhythm sections and solos by Simon on *Apollo Jump*, Stevenson on *Slide, Mr Trombone*, Doggett on *Let Me Off Uptown*, Smith on *Little John Special* and Gillespie on *Mason Flyer* and *Little John Special* are highlights. Most of all, there is Tharpe's swinging guitar and stunningly secularized gospel vocals on *That's All, Trouble In Mind, Rock Me* and *Shout, Sister Shout* where she intones that "there ain't no reason why a band can't swing" and, as an endorsement, gives the band a Jimmy Rushing-like lift whenever she is featured. Millender led bands into the fifties and later stayed in touch with the music industry as a disc jockey. However, it was his romping band of the early forties for which he will be best remembered. **BMcR**

Mills Blue Rhythm Band

Rhythm Spasm **Wardell Jones**, **Shelton Hemphill**, **Ed Anderson**, **Eddie Mallory** (t); **Harry White**, **Henry Hicks**, **George Washington** (tb); **Charlie Holmes** (cl, as); **Gene Mikell** (as); **Joe Garland** (cl, ts, bs); **Crawford Wethington** (as, bs); **Edgar Hayes** (p); **Benny James** (bj, g); **Hayes Alvis** (b, bb); **O'Neill Spencer** (d). Hep Ⓜ CD 1015 (73 minutes). Recorded 1932-33.

⑦ ❼

The Mills Blue Rhythm Band has with some justification been identified as a Cab Calloway Orchestra clone. One suspects that Manager Irving Mills's 'control' of the Calloway and Ellington orchestras led to his manipulating the MBRB virtually as an available second choice to bookers. Such a situation was unfortunate, because this was a very good band. They were pushed along by a lively rhythm section and the roster of soloists was impressive. Anderson, an up-dated King Oliver rather than a

Louis Armstrong devotee, shone with both open horn or as a passionate growler. Washington, as fiery as Jimmy Harrison on *Kokey Joe* or as suave as Dorsey as the occasion demanded, was an all-purpose trombonist; Garland excelled on both clarinet and tenor, while Hayes continually proved himself to be amongst the best pianists of his generation. The one drawback was that the MBRB may have been said to lack real personality as a band. It was not instantly recognisable and used a team of arrangers who too often produced charts which sounded like 'stocks', the off-the-shelf arrangements shunned by any band with ambition. White's *White Lightning*, Hayes's *The Growl* or Benny Carter's *Jazz Cocktail* are exceptions, but the band's overall anonymity was due not to what it played but rather to how its sidemen were asked to play it. **BMcR**

Charles Mingus

1922-1979

Pithecanthropus Erectus **Mingus** (b, ldr); **Jackie McLean** (as); **J.R. Monterose** (ts); **Mal Waldron** (p); **Willie Jones** (d). Atlantic Jazz Ⓜ 781456-2 (36 minutes). Recorded 1956.

✓ ⑩ ❼

There are classics and there are the extra-special ones. In terms of fifties and sixties jazz, **Kind of Blue** and **A Love Supreme** are the most oft-quoted examples of the latter group. There is a strong case to be made for adding **Pithecanthropus** to the list, although many would put **Blues & Roots** or **The Clown** before this one if a choice were to be made of Mingus's late-fifties Atlantic material. Sadly, **The Clown**, which includes *Haitian Fight Song* and *Reincarnation of a Love-Bird* (not to mention the extra material from the session released finally on **Tonight At Noon**), is not currently on CD, while **Blues & Roots** is covered below. These facts notwithstanding, it is on this date that Mingus recorded some ground-breaking music and gave a clear indication of where his concerns in small-group music-making would lie for the next decade.

The title track is usually singled out as the most provocative composition here, with its programmatic qualities and its imitations of bestial screams. It certainly re-enacts drama, and its cyclic form allows the story to be told in a cohesive way which avoids the usual jazz pitfall of opening theme-solos-end theme. The onslaught of the sixties has drained away the shock of this music, but the content is still intact. This revolves around the dymanism inherent in the interaction between soloist and arrangement, and here *Pithecanthropus* is largely better off than **The Clown**, with stronger soloists all round (with the sole exception of **The Clown's** Jimmy Knepper). Yet to dwell on *Pithecanthropus* is to unfairly downgrade the sly charms of *A Foggy Day (In San Francisco),* the beautiful and moving ballad *A Profile of Jackie*, with its utterly typical Mingus melody and counterline, and the remarkable *Love Chant*. At 15 minutes, *Chant* is the longest track on the album, but it never once falters, being a simple but ingeniously constructed exercise in extended form which finds the whole group engaged in inspired melodic and rhythmic interplay. **KS**

East Coasting **Mingus** (b, ldr); **Clarence Shaw** (t); **Jimmy Knepper** (tb); **Shafi Hadi** (as, ts); **Bill Evans** (p); **Dannie Richmond** (d). Bethlehem Ⓜ BET 6014-2 (39 minutes). Recorded 1957.

⑧ ❻

Nothing was ever placid in Mingus's life, and the three LPs he made in 1957 with more or less the same group (two for Bethlehem, one for RCA) are remarkable not only from the standpoint of the music itself, but also for the fact that the recordings took place at all. This CD is a literal transferral of the original Bethlehem **East Coasting** LP to the digital format: the other Bethlehem vinyl release, **A Modern Symposium of Music and Poetry**, is available on a separate CD (BET 6015-2). Considering the playing time of this disc, it is conceiveable that both LPs would have fitted onto one CD. Be that as it may, the music is at least available. In retrospect, having Shaw, Knepper, Hadi, Evans and Richmond in his band simultaneously gave Mingus the broadest and most exciting palette to work from; each was an individual both in sound and ideas. Like Ellington, Mingus drew on their individuality to enhance his writing. Without these men this music would sound very different, and the tempestuous atmosphere of the rehearsals and performances must have contributed to the overall success of the music, hard though it may have been for thos eont he receiving end of Mingus's often brutal criticisms. There is a fragile beauty to *Celia* and a hectic, headlong excitement to the *Blues Conversation* in its final choruses, where a round of four-bar exchanges by the front line gets pared down to one bar apiece. This CD is vital in any serious consideration of Mingus's music, for it reveals much about both the leader and his men. **AM**

Mingus Ah Um **Mingus** (b); **John Handy III**, **Shafi Hadi** (as); **Booker Ervin** (ts); **Horace Parlan** (p); **Willie Dennis**, **Jimmy Knepper** (tb); **Dannie Richmond** (d). Columbia Ⓜ 450436-2 (46 minutes). Recorded 1959.

✓ ⑩ ❻

This comes from a magic period when jazz was oozing with self-confidence. Bop had matured into modern jazz. Men like Mulligan, John Lewis and Mingus were using the language of jazz to make bigger statements. College kids felt bereft if they didn't have a few Brubeck, Miles or Mingus LPs in their collection. Rock still meant Elvis, or Buddy Holly. Everything looked good for jazz. Nobody knew that round the corner lay the Beatles, the rock explosion, free jazz and a lot of lean years for jazz musicians.

There is no better record from this era to show how a masterful composer/leader like Charles Mingus could create a series of miniatures which would satisfy anyone looking for either excitement or structure. Mingus could create near-abstract patterns. He could also get close to the heart of gospel and the blues, as in the joyous *Better Get It In Your Soul*. He could play the bass like a demon. And he was, quite unusually for the time, aware of jazz history; at least four of the tracks are tributes to such different musicians as Lester Young, Charlie Parker, Duke and Jelly Roll Morton. This record swings lightly and croons softly; it is very humorous and intensely serious. It is also one of the great jazz records of all time. **MK**

Blues And Roots **Mingus** (b); **Jimmy Knepper**, **Willie Dennis** (tb); **Jackie McLean**, **John Handy** (as); **Booker Ervin** (ts); **Pepper Adams** (bs); **Horace Parlan**, **Mal Waldron** (p); **Dannie Richmond** (d). Atlantic Jazz Ⓜ 781336-2 (38 minutes). Recorded 1960.

✔ ⑧ ❽

Mingus was a gifted leader of men and a composer of substantial power. His pieces are notable for their originality and his interpretations of them for the expression of his deep passion. His self-defined role as a freedom fighter was no doubt aided by his inborn bloody-mindedness.

This album is one of his most passionate and exciting and is the one which first infected the general jazz audience with his message. The band is as good as any he ever led, with Ervin, Knepper and Richmond being the Mingus equivalent of Ben Webster, Tricky Sam Nanton and Sonny Greer. Ellington was Mingus's muse, with Parker also generating strong inspiration. Mingus was of course his own Jimmy Blanton and is one of the exceptions to the rule that bassists should accompany and not solo. His driving, hard plucked solos put the bass on equal terms with the horns.

Opening with *Wednesday Night Prayer Meeting*, this collection has much of the gospel music influence from Mingus's youth. The use of the colours in his small orchestra is extraordinary, benefiting here from the presence of Pepper Adams. Mingus relishes the lower register of the baritone and Adams makes a fine complement to the bassist's prime soloist, Booker Ervin, he of the declamatory ideas, dry tone and gymnastic solos. Knepper was peculiarly good on all the Mingus albums on which he appeared taking all the trombone solos except the one on *Prayer Meeting*, where Dennis, a similarly radical player with an absorbing style, shows that he too was steeped in the Mingus idiom.

The antithesis of Miles Davis's **Kind Of Blue** album and recorded a year later, this ranks with the latter album as an example of the best music of the period. **SV**

Mingus at Antibes **Mingus** (b, p); **Ted Curson** (t); **Eric Dolphy** (as, bcl); **Booker Ervin** (ts); **Dannie Richmond** (d); **Bud Powell** (p). Rhino Atlantic Ⓜ 790532-2 (72 minutes). Recorded 1960.

⑩ ❻

Much as Mingus idolized Ellington, he knew you didn't need a big band to sound like one. The Antibes quintet is the musical equivalent of three movie cowboys who defend a fort by making all the noise of a battalion. On these loose live pieces, one or two horns will function as a section, riffing behind a soloist to egg him on. These classic blues-and-gospel-drenched performances support the contention that Mingus got more impassioned performances from sidemen than they got on their own (Dolphy's own LPs from the period are noticeably more conservative). He and Mingus converse on `talking' bass clarinet and bass. Curson's hard-driving attack and Ervin's blues-soaked timbre and sensibility were also perfect for the band. It frequently achieves a telepathic elegance, as on *Folk Forms No. 1*, a magnificent blues collectively improvised around a rhythmic figure played by Mingus and his alter ego Richmond.

Here and elsewhere, this fluid approach to quintet dynamics looks forward a decade to the Art Ensemble of Chicago. *I'll Remember April*—featuring the great pianist Powell, sounding spry despite his continuing personal problems—demonstrates Mingus's time, plump sound and solid lines, and his ability to push soloists hard without tripping them. This is small group music of uncommon power. **KW**

Charles Mingus Presents Charles Mingus **Mingus** (b); **Ted Curson** (t); **Eric Dolphy** (bcl, as); **Dannie Richmond** (d). Candid Ⓜ CD 9005 (46 minutes). Recorded 1960.

✔ ⑩ ❼

Recorded with the studio lights turned off to simulate the ambience of a nightclub, **Charles Mingus Presents Charles Mingus** captures the spontaneous and intimate fire of live performance. The group, which had been playing with Mingus during his long residency at the Showplace (in Greenwich Village), were familiar with both the material and each other. Their rapport is instantly apparent on **Folk Forms No. 1**, a freewheeling piece built on a brief rhythm pattern. The ensuing mêlée is wildly exciting—dashing ensembles, a cappella flourishes, frenetic altercations—at its centre a magnificent Mingus solo. Similar dialogues of form and freedom run—in and out of tempo—through the other pieces. Mingus and Richmond hold everything together with uncanny empathy, Curson blows with new boldness, Dolphy's volatile alto soars into the outer reaches of tonality.

Two of Mingus's best-known tracks are here: *Original Faubus Fables* (the definitive, uncensored version) is his put-down of the Arkansas governor who opposed integration; *What Love*, famous for its bass/bass-clarinet 'conversation', is a duet based on speech patterns that erupts into a slanging-match. A very humorous piece, it shows Mingus extending the range of instrumental expression just as his experiments with time and form were extending the parameters of group improvisation. Fiercely played, intensely felt, daringly conceived, **Charles Mingus Presents Charles Mingus** is one of his essential albums. **GL**

Oh Yeah **Mingus** (p, v); **Jimmy Knepper** (tb); **Roland Kirk** (ts, mzo, str, f, siren); **Booker Ervin** (ts); **Doug Watkins** (b); **Dannie Richmond** (d). Atlantic Jazz 90667-2 (68 minutes: 46 music; 24 interview). Recorded 1961.

⑧ ❽

If the practice of reissuing of old material in CD format is to earn any respectability, opportunities to correct anomalies connected with previous vinyl issues must be seized with both hands. The extraordinary material from this December 1961 session—particularly valuable because Mingus plays piano rather than bass throughout, and sings the odd blues—was issued on vinyl, split between **Oh Yeah** and one half of **Tonight at Noon**. A CD reissue could have created something approaching a masterpiece, albeit an eccentric and unusually rumbustious one, even by Mingusian standards, simply by collecting together again all the material—conveniently CD length—from that original session and issuing it as recorded. Instead, Atlantic have unearthed a 24-minute conversation between Nesuhi Ertegun and Mingus and included that where *'Old' Blues for Walt's Torin*, *Invisible Lady* and *Peggy's Blue Skylight* should have been. This beef—and it's a big one—aside, what remains is well worth having; wailing, blowsy, wonderfully overblown blues; church music given the unique Mingus treatment; a humorous Fats Waller tribute, all performed by Mingus regulars at the peak of their powers. Roland Kirk is a delight throughout: raw, emotional and totally unpredictable; Booker Ervin is his perfect foil, all contained passion; Jimmy Knepper produces several solos of great warmth and quirky humanity; Mingus himself plays utterly distinctive piano, oddly phrased and percussive, and he sings the occasional blues in an affecting, high smoky whisper. The session as issued here, however, tilts too far towards the humorous; the missing tracks would have restored the balance and created a near-perfect album—as it is, what remains is a highly entertaining novelty. **CP**

The Black Saint And The Sinner Lady **Mingus** (b, p, arr); **Rolf Ericson**, **Richard Williams** (t); **Quentin Jackson** (tb); **Don Butterfield** (tba); **Charlie Mariano** (as); **Dick Hafer** (ts, f); **Jerome Richardson** (ss, bs, f); **Jaki Byard** (p); **Jay Berliner** (g); **Dannie Richmond** (d). Impulse! Ⓜ MCAD-5649 (39 minutes). Recorded 1963.

✔ ⑩ ❿

A classic album standing at the intersection of Mingus's staggeringly individual small-group work and his generally less original writing for big band. Not only for reasons of size, the ensemble manages to combine the loose discipline of the very greatest large units with the controlled freedom associated with Mingus at his best. Although possibly conceived for a larger band (some of the material was originally prepared for use in the abandoned **Epitaph**, where it is titled *Ballad (In Other Words, I Am Three)*, the music was probably tried out and worked over by the unit which recorded it during the weeks preceding the session.

Described by its composer as ballet music, this is a single work in four tracks or six 'movements', linked in a complex manner determined partly by tape-editing and creative use of an overdub by Mariano. Although he is the chief soloist (in what has been described as the performance of a lifetime), there is also excellent work from the two trumpets, Spanish guitarist Berliner and trombonist Jackson, whose Ellington echoes are the other unforgettable sound of the piece. While also echoing other Mingus works, the summation of his concerns here makes this a peak experience. **BP**

Town Hall Concert **Mingus** (b); **Johnny Coles** (t); **Clifford Jordan** (ts); **Eric Dolphy** (as, bcl, f); **Jaki Byard** (p); **Dannie Richmond** (d). Jazz Workshop Ⓜ OJCCD 042-2 (46 minutes). Recorded 1964.

⑧ ❹

Fresh from the critical acclaim afforded **Black Saint**, the mixed response to his solo piano album and the astute use of older material in the composing and re-arranging exercise **Mingus Mingus Mingus**, this CD presented his working band, live in concert in New York's Town Hall. The mood on the night was optimistic: the band were about to embark on a European tour and everyone was playing well. The power of the leader's bass defeats the cloudy recording quality and he and Richmond had long been an unbeatable team. The tempo changes are handled with seamless ease and, as with most concert performances, everyone gets generous solo space. There are only two titles, with the solo accompaniments functional rather than elaborate. Mingus is impressive with bow or fingers, Richmond's main solo almost plays the tune and Byard is his normal, rollicking self. Cole is consistently lyrical on both titles, while Jordan is fiercely bluesy on *So Long Eric* and a touch repetitive on *Praying With Eric* which is, in fact, a re-titled version of *Meditations on Integration*. Dolphy is sinuously inventive and unpredictable on both alto and bass clarinet, but on this occasion he reserves his more heartfelt playing for the flute. The group's collective music does not aspire to the textural layers of earlier Mingus works; it is a concert that shows the leader in his working clothes as opposed to his Sunday best, but in the process it demonstrates that his artistic inclinations make it impossible for him to do anything casually. **BMcR**

Right Now: Live at the Jazz Workshop **Mingus** (b); **John Handy** (as); **Clifford Jordan** (ts); **Jane Getz** (p); **Dannie Richmond** (d). Fantasy Ⓜ OJC CD-237-2 (47 minutes:). Recorded 1964.
⑩ ❽

There is much of Charles Mingus the composer, arranger, virtuoso soloist and ensemble leader on his many classic albums. The galvanic effects of the Mingus/Dannie Richmond rhythmic section is less scrupulously preserved; recording studios simply did not encourage the all-out time bending that the pair generated in person (but hear **Folk Forms No. 1** on **Mingus Presents Mingus**). **Right Now** captures this in a surprisingly bold nightclub set. This was actually a quartet, with former sideman Handy added on *New Fables* (an opened-up *Fables of Faubus*) only. Not the most imposing of personnels, with the little-known Jane Getz and the already-journeyman Clifford Jordan. Those who paid belated attention to Jordan at the end of his career will love this album, where he plays as extravagantly and well as anywhere on record. While the free-to-funky *Fables* is great, the other lengthy piece, *Meditations (for a Pair of Wire Cutters)* puts the larger orchestral versions to shame and reaches a fiery plateau during Jordan's solo that makes it an indispensable part of the Mingus legacy. **BB**

Let My Children Hear Music **Mingus** (b); **Lonnie Hillyer**, **Joe Wilder**, **Snooky Young** (t); **Julius Watkins** (frh); **Jerry Dodgion**, **Charles McPherson** (as); **Bobby Jones** (ts); **Sir Roland Hanna** (p); **Charles McCracken** (vc); **Ron Carter**, **Richard Davis**, **Milt Hinton** (b); **Danny Richmond** (d); **Sy Johnson** (arr); **James Moody** (ts-l). Columbia/Legacy Ⓜ CK 48910 (60 minutes). Recorded 1971.
✓ ⑩ ❽

The incomplete personnel listing is from various other sources in addition to the CD booklet—you'd think that after 20 years CBS would have got it right. The label also should have reprinted in its entirety Mingus's original liner essay, instead of boldfacing selected passages within an admittedly more informative essay by George Kanzler. Packaging aside, however, there's nothing to complain about here. Along with two live albums from France and the publication of his autobiography, *Beneath the Underdog*, **Let My Children Hear Music** announced Mingus's return to activity following a drawn-out bout with clinical depression. This is Mingus with the weight of the world upon his shoulders, but nobody ever brooded with such heroic physical force, or swung harder while so doing. Combining the structural abstraction of Mingus's work from the early fifties with the fulmination and combustibility of his **Pithecanthropus Erectus**, Eric Dolphy, and **Black Saint and the Sinner Lady** periods, this music can be interpreted as Mingus's attempt to sum himself up as he neared the age of 50. Significantly, a few of the pieces are reworkings of earlier ones, with *The Chill of Death* dating all the way back to the composer's adolescence. Although solos generally take second place to compositional layering, there are animated simultaneous improvisations between Hillyer, Jones and McPherson in various combinations—and between Mingus and Moody on a shouting stoptime shuffle called *Hobo Ho* which (according to Kanzler's notes) was pieced together from various takes by producer Teo Macero, but gives the illusion of being a carefree, one-take performance. Given its focus on composition, it is no surprise tha this is the favourite Mingus album of many of the most ambitious composers to emerge from jazz in the last two decades. What tends to draw in the average listener, though, is the dark emotional undercurrent of this music, signified by the low brass on *The Shoes of the Fisherman's Wife* and six arco basses on *Adagio ma non Troppo*. **FD**

Mingus Big Band

Mingus Big Band 93 Collective personnel: **Randy Brecker**, **Ryan Kisor**, **Jack Walrath**, **Lew Soloff**, **Chris Kase** (t); **Art Baron**, **Sam Burtis**, **Dave Taylor**, **Ku-umba Frank Lacy** (tb); **Alex Foster**, **Steve Slagle** (as); **Chris Potter** (as, ts); **John Stubblefield**, **Craig Handy** (ts); **Ronnie Cuber**, **Roger Rosenberg** (bs); **Joe Locke** (vb); **Kenny Drew Jr** (p); **Mike Formanek**, **Andy McKee** (b); **Marvin 'Smitty' Smith**, **Victor Jones** (d); **Ray Mantilla** (cga); **Ronnie Cuber**, **Jack Walrath**, **Sy Johnson**, **Charles Mingus** (arr). Dreyfus Jazz Ⓕ FDM 36559-2 (78 minutes). Recorded 1993.
⑩ ❽

This is such a successful evocation of Charles Mingus's music that it deserves a place in any collection of Mingus records. All too often 'tribute' albums are pale copies of the original, sometimes produced to cash in on the name of a major departed figure, but the Mingus Big Band grew out of a 'workshop' unit which started to perform in September 1991 in New York's Time Cafe. It has the advantage of containing several men who actually played with Mingus, soloists such as Ronnie Cuber, Jack Walrath and arranger Sy Johnson. All ten numbers were composed by Mingus over a fairly long period (the CD contains a version of the 1947-vintage *Mingus Fingers*, for example), and in a number of cases the original Mingus arrangements have been used. But there is a vitality to the music, a raw, flaring passion which demands to be heard. Everyone involved is deeply committed to the Mingus concept, and the newer musicians include a fine wah-wah trombonist in Art Baron, some excellent saxophone soloists and Kenny Drew Jr, continuing the distinguished tradition of his late father at the keyboard. The final stamp of approval is the presence of Mingus's widow, Sue, who produced the album and presumably chose the musicians to be heard here from the pool of approximately 100 who have played at the Time Cafe workshop. **AM**

Bob Mintzer

1953

Departure **Mintzer, Lawrence Feldman, Bob Malach, Roger Rosenberg, Peter Yellin** (saxes, f); **Marvin Stamm, Laurie Frink, Tim Hagens, Bob Millikan, Mike Mossman** (t, flh); **Dave Bargeron, Mike Davis, Keith O'Quinn, Dave Taylor** (tb); **Phil Markowitz, Jim McNeeley** (p); **Michael Formanek** (b); **Lincoln Goines** (elb); **Peter Erskine, Jon Riley** (d); **Sammy Figueroa** (perc). DMP Ⓕ CD-493 (64 minutes). Recorded 1992.

⑧ ❿

Bob Mintzer's avowed aim in making **Departure** was to focus on "counterpoint and elaborate syncopation...to expand on the concept of taking an orchestral approach to improvisation and groove music." Extremely experienced not only in the big-band field—his credits include stints with Buddy Rich, Hubert Laws, Louie Bellson and, most crucially, the Thad Jones-Mel Lewis band—but also in classical music, playing with the New York Philharmonic, the Brooklyn Philharmonic and the American Ballet Theatre, Mintzer brings to his composing and arranging for his own big band an open-minded, eclectic approach which has borne fruit here in a rich, vigorous and fresh-sounding album, packed with ideas and bursting with vitality. The material ranges from the driving opener, *Dialogue*, a musical conversation between Mintzer's tenor and Jon Riley's drums, through a semi-humorous 'production number', *The Big Show*, with its simple, growling riff; the evergreen Victor Feldman classic *Joshua*, to *Horns Alone*, where the rhythm section drops out and allows the horns to exploit Mintzer's extensive experience in and enthusiasm for chamber music, in his own words "particularly Bartók, Stravinsky and early music". In addition to Mintzer's own breadth of experience, the album also draws on New York's street rhythms, Latin, rock—even children's songs—and the result is a thoroughly contemporary-sounding big band romping enjoyably through an original and varied repertoire. **CP**

The Missourians

Cab Calloway & The Missourians, 1929-30 **Calloway** (v); **Roger Quincey Dickerson, Lammar Wright, Reuben Reeves** (t); **De Priest Wheeler, Harry White** (tb); **George Scott, William Thornton Blue** (cl, as); **Andrew Brown** (cl, ts); **Walter Thomas** (cl, ts, bs); **Earres Prince** (p); **Morris White** (bj); **Jimmy Smith** (bb); **Leroy Maxey** (d). JSP Ⓕ JSPCD 328 (74 minutes). Recorded 1929/30.

✔ ⑦ ❻

The Missourians were one of the most animated territory bands. Beginning life in St Louis as Wilson Robinson's Syncopators, adopted as the Cotton Club Orchestra in New York, they became the Missourians at the end of 1927. They were never the most imaginative of bands and, as this CD shows, their attempts at plagiarism are somewhat transparent. They borrow Bennie Moten's *South* to shore up *You'll Cry For Me*, they use distinctly Ellingtonian voicings on *Prohibition Blues* and lift *Stoppin' The Traffic* from McKinney's Cotton Pickers's *Milenberg Joys*. There is more than a hint of the Fletcher Henderson reed section on several titles, yet the band could be electrifyingly exciting. Maxey and Smith are at the heart of a highly propulsive rhythm section and they assist superbly growling trumpet solos by Dickerson, shapely clarinet work by Blue and punchy trombone fundamentals from Wheeler. The take-over by Calloway in 1930 did dilute this dynamic musical cocktail to some extent and eccentric scats on *Viper's Drag* or good jazz vocals like *Happy Feet* hardly compensate. Nevertheless, for a short time the Missourians were a unit that, if only for their vitality, seriously rivalled the contemporary Ellington, Henderson and Luis Russell bands. **BMcR**

Blue Mitchell

1930-1979

Big Six **Mitchell** (t); **Curtis Fuller** (tb); **Johnny Griffin** (ts); **Wynton Kelly** (p); **Wilbur Ware** (b); **Philly Joe Jones** (d). Riverside Ⓜ OJCCD-615-2 (43 minutes). Recorded 1958.

⑧ ❻

Mitchell had a warm, burnished sound and roots in the work of Fats Navarro and, perhaps, Clifford Brown. This was his first album as a leader, a heavywight date which finds him in full control of his playing and not subjugated by the machine-gun style of Philly Joe Jones's drumming nor the powerful tenor work of Johnny Griffin, a man usually capable of cutting any new soloists down to size. The most impressive track is also the longest, Benny Golson's 2/4 time *Blues March* (this was the anthem-to-be's initial recording). But there are no weak tracks in this seven-tune programme, and Blue features himself with just the rhythm section on a slow tempo version of *There Will Never Be Another You*, showing off his tone and a fine vibrato control. The rhythm section is as good as one has a right to expect, but Wilbur Ware's bass lines are unusually subdued, which may be a fault in the original balance. Otherwise there is the bright immediacy associated with hard bop recordings of the period. Shortly after this session Mitchell joined the Horace Silver Quintet, at which point his career took off, but this initial recording remains one of his best. **AM**

Red Mitchell

1927-1992

Red Mitchell-Harold Land Quintet: Hear Ye!!!! Hear Ye!!!! **Mitchell** (b); **Land** (ts); **Carmell Jones** (t); **Frank Strazzeri** (p); **Leon Petties** (d). Atlantic Jazz Ⓜ 781376-2 (39 minutes). Recorded 1961.

⑧ ❻

Red Mitchell became closely associated with the West Coast movement in the fifties, but was originally from New York. His approach to the bass was always more hard-driving and imaginative than most of the Californian set. Like many of his generation he came up through the big bands, playing with both Chubby Jackson and Woody Herman before coming to prominence with the Gerry Mulligan Quartet. A measure of his enquiring musical mind is that he was one of the few to record with Ornette Coleman before the latter's successful move to New York. Mitchell's partner on this record (and in this group), Harold Land, was another player whose approach hardly fitted the West Coast stereotype, being the tenor player in the Clifford Brown-Max Roach Quintet for close to two years, then going on into the sixties and seventies in a creative musical partnership with Bobby Hutcherson which is excellently documented on records.

The quintet these two shared was together only briefly as a working unit, making this one album. It is a classic hard-bop session, combining exceptionally strong compositions from both Land and Mitchell with a fully-formed group sound and exciting soloing from the two principals and the gifted trumpeter Camrell Jones. The opening track, Land's *Triplin' Awhile*, deserves to be much better known and is the type of tune the inner ear simply cannot dislodge for hours afterwards. Other pieces have a similar effect. Land plays with precision and purpose, while Jones has a flair and a sense of excitement rare in the bop trumpet circles of the time, which with rare exceptions (Morgan, Hubbard, Dorham, Mitchell) had already ossified into stylisation and cliché. That excitement is shared by the whole group. Buy a copy and share it with them. **KS**

Roscoe Mitchell

1940

L-R-G, The Maze, S II Examples **Mitchell** (perc, f, ob, cl, ss, as, ts, brs, bss, perc); **Leo Smith** (pic-t, t, flh); **George Lewis** (sousaphone, Wagner-tba, alto-tba, tenor-tba); **Thurman Baker**, **Anthony Braxton**, **Douglas Ewart**, **Malachi Favors**, **Joseph Jarman**, **Don Moye**, **Henry Threadgull** (perc). Chief Records Ⓕ CD4 (75 minutes). Recorded 1978.

⑧ ❽

This disc presents a gripping progress report on Roscoe Mitchell's sonic explorations some dozen years after his groundbreaking 1966 LP, **Sound**. That record, the first to emerge from Chicago's newly-formed AACM, had laid out the guidelines for a new kind of jazz, with its twin focuses on sound as texture and the integral role of space/silence.

On *L-R-G* and *The Maze*, texture is still a primary consideration. The former pitches Mitchell's range of woodwinds, plus a brass spectrum that extends from piccolo-trumpet to sousaphone, into a steady through-composed flow of timbral contrasts and complements. *The Maze*, for eight percussionists, is a flow of textures too, though with the emphasis on groups of sounds—wood timbres, metal timbres, high bells, low bells, household objects etc.

SII Examples, with Mitchell solo on the curved soprano, is, he explains, "from a set of fingerings I've developed ... that allows the individual to play quarter-tones, semi-quarter tones, between notes, the same notes with different timbres.". These examples, set mostly in the lower or middle registers, feature long, breathy tones and tremolos, often barely louder than a metallic sigh. This is sound under the microscope, with Mitchell as analyst, scrupulously eschewing the more populist gestures of his work with the Art Ensemble of Chicago. If their records are the shop window, this one is a glimpse into the laboratory. **GL**

Live At The Knitting Factory **Mitchell** (ss, as); **Hugh Ragin** (t, flh); **A. Spencer Barefield** (g, p); **Jaribu Shahid** (b); **Tani Tabbal** (d, perc). Black Saint Ⓜ 120120-2 (61 minutes) Recorded 1987.

⑧ ❻

If, within the Art Ensemble of Chicago, Joseph Jarman is the dramatist, Roscoe Mitchell is the conceptualist; though Lester Bowie wears the symbolic lab coat, Mitchell has always been the scientist of sound—dissecting, stimulating, and experimenting with form, making microscopic examinations of pitch and intervallic relationships. His 1966 **Sound** (Delmark, not yet on CD), predating the AEC, was a shocking manifesto, with subsequent albums scarcely less valuable,

illuminating possibilities in sound organization. **Live At The Knitting Factory** is a fairly representative sample of his work—minus the nearly clinical investigations of his solo concerts or pieces like *Nonaah*, *L-R-G* or *S-II Examples* (on Nessa). One advantage here is the ensemble; working with such longterm associates (they have been together, off and on, at least since 1980's **Snurdy McGurdy** (Nessa), one of Mitchell's best recordings) is essential in unlocking his compositional designs. Ragin's virtuosity is a tonic—his solo on *The Reverend Frank Wright* has the trumpet imitating a tuba, rather than vice versa—and his concentration and empathy with Mitchell on open-ended structures like *The Stick And The Stone* is stunning. This version of *Nonaah*, the cornerstone of Mitchell's compositional aesthetic, is exquisite, with a reverence that only faith in one's creativity affords, and a section of delicate pointillism that creates its own swing. Discovering other aspects of one's self through intellect and intuition is what Mitchell's music is all about. **AL**

Hank Mobley

1930-1986

Soul Station **Mobley** (ts); **Wynton Kelly** (p); **Paul Chambers** (b); **Art Blakey** (d). Blue Note Ⓜ CDP7 46528-2 (37 minutes). Recorded 1960.

✔ ⑩ ❽

This is Mobley's masterpiece and one of the great jazz records, on a par with Rollins's **Saxophone Colossus**. Hank Mobley has been consistently undervalued because his prime virtues—elegance, rhythmic poise, warmth of tone, subtlety of nuance—fell out of fashion just as he was reaching his maturity.

A former member of the Miles Davis Quintet and the Jazz Messengers, he was as well qualified as it was possible to be, a master of both the chromatic and modal approaches to improvisation. One number here, *This I Dig of You*, demonstrates how he could move between the two with absolute stylistic consistency. The tune alternates eight bars of a single scale with eight bars of chromatic changes, the first winding up the tension and the second releasing it. The sheer agility which he exploits this musical drama would alone be enough to place him in the highest company.

Listen also to his brisk, spare statement of the theme to *Remember,* the clear, measured lines in the stop-time choruses of the blues *Dig Dis*, the calm, knowing exploration of *If I Should Lose You.* This CD conveys better than any other the purity of Mobley's imagination and the vigorous candour of his expression. **DG**

The Modern Jazz Quartet

Odds Against Tomorrow **Milt Jackson** (vb); **John Lewis** (p); **Percy Heath** (b); **Connie Kay** (d). EMI/UA/Blue Note Ⓜ CDP7 93415-2 (33 minutes). Recorded 1959.

✔ ⑩ ❼

If you will excuse the pun, it is odd that two of the MJQ's greatest records are derived from John Lewis film soundtracks; most jazz groups usually provide rather sub-standard fare when it comes to music for films. But this is to reckon without John Lewis, the group's artistic director, and the remarkable creativity of this group. Both this album and the other (**One Never Knows**—Atlantic, not yet transferred to CD) gave the group some of their most challenging material to play. This present album contains the original version of what was to become one of the MJQ's most-requested concert items, *Skating in Central Park*, as well as memorable themes in *A Cold Wind is Blowing* and *Odds Against Tomorrow* itself.

The MJQ were often accused during their first 15 years together of an overly-precious and unswinging approach to their material. This album has a very small dynamic range, and is mostly *piano* or *pianissimo*, but the music is very intense, the improvising inspired (in the case of Jackson, it is certainly some of his best and most authoritative work on records), and the band really *do* swing when the occasion requires it. Lewis's arrangements, dealing as they do with just four instruments, are marvellously imaginative, evoking an unusually full range of images and feelings for the listener. In this case, economy certainly does pack a punch. **KS**

The Comedy **John Lewis** (p); **Milt Jackson** (vb); **Percy Heath** (b); **Connie Kay** (d) **Diahann Carroll** (v). Atlantic Ⓜ 781390-2 (35 minutes). Recorded 1962.

⑧ ❽

A seven-part suite, six of whose individual pieces are named for characters from Italian *commedia dell'arte*, this is probably one of the albums that critics of John Lewis have foremost in mind when they dismiss his entire output for the MJQ as corseted and precious. But this is also an album that demonstrates, perhaps better than any other, the implicit influence of the blues and early jazz on Lewis's music, even at its most seemingly removed from them. Much of **The Comedy** affects a fey, music box shimmer; and this is one instance in which Jackson really does sound as handcuffed as the MJQ's detractors tend to portray him. But Lewis's piano solo on the opening *Spanish Steps* has the controlled abandon of stride or boogie woogie to it, and the flawless *Harlequin* is a scherzo which accumulates its humour through Kay's steady rimshots, as well as a series of musical fits and starts more evocative of a Kansas City barrelhouse than of a Roman piazza. Throughout the suite there are artful and unexpected group crescendos that could serve as reminders of the part played by the MJQ (and Lewis in particular) in furthering the cause of collective improvisation. Despite a bit of hiss, the digital transfer adequately captures the group's interplay. Carroll, a supperclub chanteuse, is quite charming on *La Cantatrice*, sounding more like a brittle Greenwich Village chick of the sixties than like the frustrated stand-in for the leading lady in sixteenth-century Italy. **FD**

Echoes **John Lewis** (p); **Milt Jackson** (vb); **Percy Heath** (b); **Connie Kay** (d). Pablo Ⓜ CD2312.142 (45 minutes). Recorded 1984.

✓ ⑧ ❽

In 1974, after 22 years of playing and recording, the MJQ disbanded, but by 1981 requests for its reformation, particularly from Japanese bookers, had become too insistent to ignore. This CD is a studio-recorded reunion comprising six tracks, with three compositions by John Lewis, two by Milt Jackson and Percy Heath's *The Watergate Blues*, which is a feature for the composer's rich, warm-toned bass. The return of the four men has resulted in music which carries on, seamlessly, from the pre-1974 albums. Lewis is still the controlling factor and the temperature of the music is fairly mild, but the quartet was never designed to allow a free spirit to take off on an unscheduled series of improvised choruses. At the same time Milt Jackson's solos, within the constraints of the MJQ formula, are masterpieces of concision played over a near-perfect backing. On the opening vibes choruses in *Connie's Blues*, for example, Lewis's chords are an object lesson in piano accompaniment, each of them weighted perfectly to achieve the right amount of springiness. Tempo changes, even drum accents, appear to be rehearsed, the quartet always achieving the correct internal balance. If jazz can be said to have its equivalent of chamber music, this might be it. Nat Hentoff has written some good notes but Pablo have seen fit to print them white-on-black and reduce the original LP sleeve to a quarter of its size, so a magnifying glass may be needed. **AM**

Cody Moffett

Evidence **Moffett** (d); **Wallace Roney** (t); **Kenny Garrett** (as); **Antoine Roney**, **Ravi Coltrane** (ts); **Kenny Drew Jr** (p); **Charnett Moffett** (b) Telarc Jazz Ⓕ CD-83343 (57 minutes). Recorded 1993.

⑥ ❽

The young drummer is the son of Charles Moffett who used to play with Ornette Coleman in the sixties, and this debut album features him with varying small groups, all including his more famous brother Charnett on bass. The permutating personnel consists of another pair of siblings (impressive trumpeter Wallace Roney and Shorteresque tenor Antoine Roney), a couple of sons of the famous (Kenny Drew Jr and Ravi Coltrane, who appears to be the tenor player who doubles on soprano and who has also recorded a couple of double-header albums with Antoine Roney), and a rank outsider, the altoist Kenny Garrett.

The programming is a cornucopia of fairly short performances of jazz standards by such as Gillespie, Davis, Rollins, Monk and Coltrane, the latter's *Equinox* being sadly in the wrong key with the wrong bass figure. Even the more recent repertoire consists of minor classics (Freddie Hubbard's *Red Clay* and Cedar Walton's *Bolivia*), with only one old pop-song (*Beautiful Love*) and, more surprisingly, only one original piece by each Moffett. The leader's drumming is reliable rather than recognisable but it will, like the names of his colleagues, be a guarantee of quality on future releases. **BP**

Louis Moholo

1940

Exile **Moholo** (d, v); **Claude Deppa** (t, flh, v); **Sean Bergin** (ts, f, concertina); **Steve Williamson** (ts, as); **Frank Douglas** (elg); **Paul Rogers** (b); **Thebe Lipere** (perc, v). Ogun Ⓕ OGCD 003 (63 minutes). Recorded 1990/91.

⑥ ❽

As a member of Chris McGregor's Blue Notes, Moholo arrived in London in 1965. Initially a bebop band, the Blue Notes had already begun to explore freer musical climes. Moholo's role in this development was important and his powerful style proved itself equally effective at the heart of McGregor's Brotherhood Of Breath big band. Work with diverse figures such as Steve Lacy, Peter Brötzmann, Elton Dean and Keith Tippett chronicles his development during the seventies and eighties but he always retained his South African connection. Its sheer rhythmic strength is evident throughout this CD and with Moholo, Lipere and Rogers at full bore, it is a powerful potion. Moholo's drumming style has been likened to Elvin Jones but, as his 'toppy' driving work on *Dudu Pukwana* and *Plastic Bag* demonstrates, it is a style tempered by high life elements at all times. His compositions are similarly African in their tone and his excellent Viva-La-Black band play them with a rare élan. The ensembles are a trifle untidy in places, the singing on *Kwa Langa Kumandi* amateurish and Douglas's solo style a little incongruous but this is real music with the emphasis on communication and the spirit, one of joy. **BMcR**

Grachan Moncur III

1937

Some Other Stuff **Moncur** (tb); **Wayne Shorter** (ts); **Herbie Hancock** (p); **Cecil McBee** (b); **Tony Williams** (d). Blue Note Ⓜ CDP8 32092 2 (41 minutes) Recorded 1964.

✓ ⑩ ❽

Moncur, son of the swing bassist, first made his mark with the Ray Charles band at the beginning of the sixties. After that, a stint with The Jazztet gave him some much-needed exposure and led to his work with altoist Jackie McLean. This in turn led him to Blue Note, who recorded him both with McLean and -just twice- as a leader. The first album, **Evolution**, has already been and gone as a CD reissue, and the music it had to offer was not far from what McLean's own band of the time (1963) was playing. A glance at the personnel on this album would perhaps lead you to believe that a Miles Davis-minus-Miles date would ensue: after all, Blue Note were by this time specialists at such things. This album, however, truly is some other stuff.

There are just four tracks (two per side of the old vinyl release) and the opener, *Gnostic*, immediately plunges us into the type of music with which, along with Eric Dolphy's **Out To Lunch**, some Andrew Hill albums and the early Bobby Hutcherson dates, suggested that Blue Note really did have an alternative thoery of avant-garde jazz to propose to the world at large. Using a slow, simple melody, it is woven together by the extraordinary patterns Hancock uses and anticipates by close to a decade the type of 'space music' musicians would explore via synthesisers in the seventies and eighties. *Thandiwa* is a more conventional triple-time piece, but again, with *The Twins*, we have a miracle of sustained invention, this time collective, where the reactions between each soloist and the rhythm team, their bending of time and metre, have to be hear to be believed. Listening to the Shorter solo here, with its dense interlocking with Hancock, McBee and Williams, one wonders what worlds the Miles group could have developed into had the leader been amenable. *Nomadic* finishes the album, and it's a setting created for a Williams drum solo. Moncur comments in the notes "I thought it would just be nice to have a relaxed drum solo...that would be soothing." Quite an extraordinary idea, and perhaps the only way to end this completely out-of-the-ordinary album. **KS**

Thelonious Monk

1917-1982

Complete Blue Note Recordings **Monk** (p) with various personnels including **Idrees Sulieman**, **George Tait**, **Kenny Dorham** (t); **Danny Quebec West**, **Sahib Shihab**, **Lou Donaldson** (as); **Lucky Thompson**, **Sonny Rollins**, **John Coltrane** (ts); **Milt Jackson** (vb); **Gene Ramey**, **Bob Paige**, **Al McKibbon**, **Nelson Boyd**, **John Simmons**, **Paul Chambers**, **Ahmed Abdul Malik** (b); **Art Blakey**, **Max Roach**, **Shadow Wilson**, **Roy Haynes** (d); **Kenny Hagood** (v). Blue Note Ⓜ CDP8 30363 2 (four discs: 208 minutes). Recorded 1947–1958.

✓ ⑩ ❽

This major boxed set contains Monk's first recordings as a leader, made between 1947 and 1952, plus a session with Sonny Rollins from 1957 and a recently rediscovered 1958 live recording with John Coltrane from New York's Five Spot Cafe. As well as proving that Monk was one of the handful of truly great jazz composers, on a par with Morton and even, at times, with Ellington, these early pieces bear out an uncomfortable truth—namely that the best jazz records have often been produced under the worst conditions. They were held in a cheap New York studio, with little time and a piano badly in need of tuning, yet the results are superb: spare, cogent and uniquely haunting. The original version of *'Round Midnight*, Monk's most famous composition, illustrates perfectly how original a composer he was. The piece is now established as a minor standard, and because of its slow tempo most people play it as a romantic ballad. But listen to this performance and you will hear it as the composer heard it—sombre and menacing, a thing of flitting shadows and midnight fears. The nervous atmosphere is sustained by having the melody passing unpredictably from one instrument to another, by ghostly piano runs on the whole-tone scale, even by the slightly sour intonation. It reminds us that, after Ellington, Monk is the great impressionist composer of jazz. He never surpassed early works like *'Round Midnight*, *Misterioso* and *Evidence*, although he did equal them later. Their very bareness reveals the great originality of his mind and the completeness of his vision. The alternate takes included here offer added insight into his creative process. The inclusion of the poor-fidelity Five Spot recordings (taken from a private tape made by Coltrane's wife, Naima) is a decidedly questionable decision by the present-day Blue Note powers-that-be, whatever the music's undoubted historical significance. **DG**

The Unique Thelonious Monk **Monk** (p); **Oscar Pettiford** (b); **Art Blakey** (d). Riverside Ⓜ OJCCD-064-2 (38 minutes). Recorded 1956.

✓ ⑩ ❽

With a programme comprising seven standard tunes, this is an ideal introduction to the quirky, unexpected approach that Monk used. The material is familiar, the treatments are certainly not. There is a glancing, oblique quality to the theme statements of songs such as *Tea For Two* and *Honeysuckle Rose,* for example. On the former Pettiford introduces the verse *arco* then Monk moves into the chorus, subtly reharmonizing the song to suit his individual recasting of the melody. It is a little like taking a watch apart to see what makes it work; Monk was always concerned with the insides of tunes and he would often state the melody with such care that it would sound as if he was playing it for the first time. *Memories Of You* (played as an unaccompanied solo) and *You Are Too Beautiful* benefit from the charm of his apparent 'discovery' of these songs as he goes along. The fact of the matter is that his musical vocabulary was immense and his method of improvisation was well rooted in the swing era, where musicians played the tune 'as written' before carefully moving away from it. Art Blakey was always the perfect drummer for Monk, and Pettiford's surging bass lines provide him with the foundation he needed on what is, without doubt, one of his most important trio records. **AM**

Brilliant Corners Monk (p, celeste); **Ernie Henry** (as); **Sonny Rollins** (ts); **Oscar Pettiford** (b); **Max Roach** (d); **Clark Terry** (t); **Paul Chambers** (b). Riverside Ⓜ OJCCD-026-2 (43 minutes). Recorded 1956.

✓ ⑩ ❽

This is one of Monk's most impressive band records, and it followed the trios which, as at Blue Note and Prestige, had opened his account with Riverside the previous year. It includes three then-new and challenging compositions that, contrasting with the deceptive concision of the early Blue Notes, show Monk letting the soloists have their head within his carefully constructed enclosures. These players include the neglected Henry and the masterly Rollins, who had gained considerably in authority in the two years since he had last recorded with Monk, largely as a result of constant work in the group of Max Roach. Roach too is on excellent form here, collaborating with the pianist to vary the textures behind the improvisations, nowhere more than in the title track which is one of the relatively few examples of Monk giving his soloists a specifically rhythmic hurdle to negotiate.

It is a pity the bass is consistently under-recorded and that the piano intro to *Ba-lues Bolivar Blues-are*, missing from earlier reissues, was not restored; equally, the gradual settling of the pitch in the first half-minute of *Pannonica* could be rectified with modern technology. But such reservations are insignificant beside the strength of the music. **BP**

Monk's Music Monk (p); **Ray Copeland** (t); **Gigi Gryce** (as); **Coleman Hawkins, John Coltrane** (ts); **Wilbur Ware** (b); **Art Blakey** (d).Riverside Ⓜ OJCCD 084-2 (48 minutes). Recorded 1957.

✓ ⑧ ❼

The music here is hard to beat, but in historical terms this is a tantalising and frustrating issue. It stands as a huge signpost in what was then regarded as modern jazz in that Coleman Hawkins, who had been Monk's mentor and employer during the 1940s, was present along with John Coltrane, then just beginning to take the music forward in a way which would make him Hawkins' replacement as the main influence on tenor saxophone playing. Incredibly, apart from what is here, Monk recorded only three further tracks with Coltrane, even though the tenorist was part of Monk's quartet for almost a year.

Monk's work is crisp and beautiful and his solos on these splendid themes (all but one are his) are amongst his finest work. A Monk session leaves the soloists uniquely exposed, and even Hawkins has occasional problems, although his interpretation of *Ruby, My Dear* ranks with his wonderful Capitol output of the mid-1940s. Gryce is rather swiped by the backwash, and Copeland operates at a fairly safe and thus unambitious level.

That apart, there is a constant moment to each track which probably indicates that things were going to Monk's liking. When that happened in the quartet wlth Rouse there was a burning and unmissable exhilaration in the music. Here that indicator is replaced by a deep underlying satisfaction which is just as palpable. The commendable recording quality helps to make this album indispensable to a serious collection of Monking. **SV**

The Thelonious Monk Orchestra at Town Hall Monk (p); **Donald Byrd** (t); **Eddie Bert** (tb); **Robert Northern** (frh); **Jay McAllister** (tba); **Phil Woods** (as); **Charlie Rouse** (ts); **Pepper Adams** (bs); **Sam Jones** (b); **Art Taylor** (d). Riverside Ⓜ OJCCD-206-2 (53 minutes). Recorded 1959.

✓ ⑩ ❻

The orchestrations of six Monk tunes that Hall Overton produced in collaboration with the composer remain a marvel, full of the restless energy of Monk's piano and quartet and matched by a brash sound from the tentet that is both tinny and just right. Monk's basic group of the time featured the wide bottom of Sam Jones's and Art Taylor's time-playing, and the head-first logic of tenor saxophonist Charlie Rouse, who had only recently arrived. They power the massive locomotive of the Monk orchestra through haunting versions of *Monk's Mood* and *Crepuscule with Nellie*, hard bop jams of *Off Minor* and *Friday the 13th*, a signature *Thelonious* and pièce de resistance *Little Rootie Tootie* that features an arrangement of Monk's 1952 solo for the full band. One might have wished that Bert, Woods and Adams had a bit more solo space, and Byrd a bit less. Still, this was an exciting occasion that actually worked, and a key event in Monk's ascension to his position of pre-eminence among postwar American artists. The CD reissue supplements the original vinyl release with the complete version of *Thelonious* and second encore take of *Rootie*. **BB**

Big Band and Quartet in Concert Monk (p); **Charlie Rouse** (ts); **Butch Warren** (b); **Frank Dunlop** (d); with an ensemble comprising: **Thad Jones** (c); **Nick Travis** (t); **Steve Lacy** (ss); **Phil Woods** (as, cl); **Gene Allen** (bs, cl, cl); **Eddie Bert** (tb); **Hall Overton** (arr). Columbia/Legacy Ⓜ C2K 57636 (two discs: 108 minutes). Recorded 1963.

⑨ ❽

Monk's landmark December 30, 1963 Philharmonic Hall concert at New York's Lincoln Center came at the height of Monkmania, when the pianist was being lionized by the popular press as well as by jazzophiles. Though calling the ten-piece ensemble a 'big band' was hyperbolic, especially given the horn section's primarily supportive role, the broader palette made possible by Monk's commercial as well as artistic success was greeted by the jazz press with wine and roses. Today, the spartan yet pungent enlargements of classic Monk lines like *Evidence*, *Epistrophy*, *Four in One* and *Misterioso* resonate with a timelessness that like all of Monk's music, simultaneously embracing the past as it points towards the future.

This was Monk's second venture with an expanded ensemble. Like the 1959 Town Hall concert, the task of fleshing out Monk's deliciously quirky lines and 'weird' harmonies fell to the under-appreciated Hall Overton. Indeed, it was Overton's ability to both preserve and magnify Monk's stylistic eccentricities, the angular lines and biting phrases, that is largely responsible for the project's enduring appeal. Monk was obviously inspired. So, too, were the members of his working quartet, especially tenor saxophonist Charlie Rouse. Also praiseworthy is the energized soloing of Phil Woods and the ensemble's overall empathy for this sublimely grand project. It should be noted that the 1964 release was severely edited to accommodate the LP format. For this CD reissue the entire concert, including previously deleted drum solos, has been restored. **CB**

It's Monk's Time **Monk** (p); **Charlie Rouse** (ts); **Butch Warren** (b); **Ben Riley** (d). Columbia Ⓜ 468405-2 (48 minutes). Recorded 1964.

⑩ ❿

It's not only because I am very partial to *Lulu's Back in Town* that I'm going to sing the praises of this album. I happen to believe that it is one of Monk's best, and it is certainly among the best-recorded (I can only think of the follow-up studio album, **Monk**, as having recording quality to match this one). But *Lulu* does get things off to a flying start. Monk begins with an unaccompanied quasi-stride routine, played on a deliberately out-of-tune piano, doing wonderfully mischievous things to the song (such as slipping a semitone down on the last beat of the first measure of the melody proper, thereby rendering the jaunty mood of the song fit only for a bar-room scene) before coming to a pedal point, slowing almost to a stop, then swapping pianos and launching the quartet full tilt into a burning medium-tempo rendition. Under one of Rouse's best-ever solos, Monk is exceptionally busy and authoritative, prodding away at the harmonic base of the ditty. At the close, Thelonious returns to his bar-room relic and gets lugubrious. Beautiful.

The rest of the date keeps on or near this level, with two quite sane solo excursions on old standards (*Memories of You* and *Nice Work If You Can Get It*), plus vital updatings of some relatively untouched early Monk material (*Brake's Sake* and *Shuffle Boil*). Monk sounds very happy. Rouse is also in oustanding form, his sound warmer and more varied in expression than is often the case, his patterns refreshingly free of cliché. Warren and Riley, beautifully recorded, do everything right. **KS**

The London Collection, Volumes 1-3 **Monk** (p); **Al McKibbon** (b); **Art Blakey** (d). Black Lion Ⓜ BLCD 760101/116/142 (three discs, aas: 153 minutes). Recorded 1971.

⑧ ❽

This London session was Monk's last studio date. A decade of illness and neglect awaited him, but there was no hint of the troubles to come on this night of glorious music-making, which included Monk's first trio performances for 15 years, his first recordings with Art Blakey for 14 years and his best solo playing since 1959's **In San Francisco**.

The session, which began with Monk solo and concluded with the trio, lasted for six hours. Volume One of this three-CD series (the discs are also available separately) collects nearly all of the solo masters, Volume Two nearly all of the trio masters. The third disc comprises mostly alternate takes, though it also has the only takes of *The Man I Love*, *Something In Blue* (both solo) and *Introspection* (solo and trio), plus the nine-minute solo improvisation *Chordially*. The latter is actually Monk trying out the piano at the beginning of the evening and, as Brian Priestley remarks in his insert-notes, "what is fascinating is that Monk, being a composer, is unable to carry out this routine task without at the same time experimenting with chord densities and creating potential new melodies."

Even so, the third disc is perhaps best left for completists. Volumes One and Two, however, are near-essential items in the Monk discography and contain some of the liveliest, most engaging playing of his later years. Blakey has often been described as the ideal drummer for Monk: if he sounds a little busy here at times, perhaps that was the spur necessary to keep Monk fully extended. The music is certainly compelling and the rhythm section remain surefooted through both the bright flow of *I Mean You* and more complex feintings of *Evidence*, *Misterioso* and *Criss Cross*. The solo

disc is better still, as Monk rings out the dissonances on *Trinkle Tinkle*, *Jackieing* and *Loverman*, turns reflective for *Darn That Dream*, negotiates the intricacies of *Little Rootie Tootie* and allows himself a little dry humour at the close of *Nice Work If You Can Get It*. This is and you should. **GL**

J.R. Monterose

1927-1933

A Little Pleasure **Monterose** (ss, ts); **Tommy Flanagan** (p). Reservoir Ⓕ RSR CD 109 (46 minutes). Recorded 1981.

⑧ ❽

Monterose, not to be confused with the Los Angeles-based tenor saxist Jack Montrose, was a needlessly neglected player who succeeded in keeping a remarkably low profile in terms of records for years. He is hardly well represented now, and this fascinating release is a CD reissue of an LP. When Monterose cropped up on record in the fifties with his single Blue Note album and on his appearances with Mingus and Kinny Dorham's Jazz Prophets his sound was often hard-edged, but during his eight years in Europe (1967-75) his tone, and his playing, mellowed somewhat. This is the most intimate of settings, with a close microphone set-up giving the listener the impression that he is sitting next to the two musicians. Monterose still had the "Phase One Coltrane" sound, sometimes overlaid with the scooped-out tone of Don Lanphere, but he was a fully rounded soloist with a warm approach to ballads (his *Never Let Me Go* here is a gem) and an easy sense of swing when the tempo increases. Flanagan is the ideal pianist in this context, always harmonically correct and with an enviable gradation of touch. The CD contains what are probably Monterose's only recorded examples of his soprano playing; on the title tune, Coltrane's *Central Park West* and *A Nightingale Sang In Berkeley Square*. He produced a unique and oboe-related sound. Recommended without reservation. **AM**

Marian Montgomery

1934

I Gotta Right To Sing **Montgomery** (v); **Mitch Dalton** (g); **Laurie Holloway** (p); **Lennie Bush** (b); **Allan Ganley** (d). Jazz House Ⓕ JHCD 003 (48 minutes). Recorded 1987.

⑤ ❺

Montgomery was born in the US but in 1965 decided to settle in England. She has continued to be based here while maintaining a successful international career. A regular performer at Ronnie Scott's, she runs through a typical set on this disc, recorded live at the club in early 1987. Standards such as *That Old Black Magic*, *Mean To Me*, *Georgia On My Mind* and *The Lady Is A Tramp* make up the vast majority of the set, and Montgomery utilizes her smooth, elastic method of vocalizing, where she seems to embrace rather than merely sing a note, to pump new life into such material.

This album is not very distinguished, for a number of reasons. The recording quality is not at all good, considering the vintage: the sound is rather muffled and the vocals, through no fault of their own, lack presence. Montgomery quite naturally often seems to be singing to the crowd rather than to the potential CD listener, so there are some moments when things are happening onstage that were probably all part of a good night out, but on repeated listening tend to wear thin. There is also that other plague of 'live' recordings, token solos for the band which are enshrined for all time on tape. On *Mean To Me*, the minutes tick by as the bass solos, the drums and piano trade fours, and everybody lets their hair down in public. For an example of what this group and this singer can do when everything clicks, try the title track. It has got all the intimacy, individuality and expressiveness many of the other tracks are missing. **KS**

Wes Montgomery

1923-1968

The Incredible Jazz Guitar **Montgomery** (g); **Tommy Flanagan** (p); **Percy Heath** (b); **Albert Heath** (d). Riverside Ⓜ OJCCD-036-2 (44 minutes). Recorded 1960.

⑩ ❻

After Charlie Christian there was Wes Montgomery. His impact on jazz critics with the World Pacific LP **Montgomery Brothers And Five Others** was universal. Apart from his undoubted musicianship and improvising abilities, he had perfected a trick of playing phrases in unison octaves (although it should be pointed out that Django Reinhardt had also done this during the thirties). **The Incredible Jazz Guitar** is one of the best albums he ever made and is thankfully free from added strings or an organ to cloud the beautiful tone of his instrument. He attacks the Sonny Rollins tune *Airegin* at a tempo which would leave many lesser players gasping, yet he works all his ideas out to logical conclusions. There are four originals included in this eight-tune programme, and two of them, *Four On Six* and *West Coast Blues,* have gone into the library of lasting jazz standards. Both use unexpected time signatures although the former, which commences in 4/4 against 6/8, reverts to common time for the improvised choruses. The rhythm section is faultless but spatially a little distant in the overall recording balance. This does not detract, however, from Wes's incredible guitar playing. **AM**

Impressions: The Verve Jazz Sides **Montgomery** (elg) with the orchestras of **Johnny Pate, Oliver Nelson** and **Don Sebesky** and small groups featuring **Jimmy Smith** (org); **Wynton Kelly** (p); **Paul Chambers, Ron Carter** (b); **Ray Barretto** (cga); **Grady Tate, Jimmy Cobb** (d). Verve Ⓜ 521 690-2 (two discs: 152 minutes). Recorded 1964-66.

✔ ⑩ ❽

Wes's orchestral work for Creed Taylor is quite reasonably regarded as one of the great jazz betrayals, and certainly things don't get off to a particularly good start in this double-CD collection, with Johnny Pate's arrangements of *West Coast Blues* and *Caravan* sounding like Sunday night at the Palladium. But the compilers have striven for damage-limitation, and things quickly look up with three Oliver Nelson big band arrangements which give Wes a chance to get up a head of steam, plus such Wes and Jimmy Smith classics as the cooking hothouse blues *James And Wes*. But Wes's Verve best—now, finally, available complete—is reserved to last.

As Pat Metheny says in the insert note, **Smokin' At The Half Note** "is the absolute greatest jazz-guitar album ever made", and it is here in total on disc two. Even the stoutest atheist could believe that divine inspiration was in the Half Note that night. On *No Blues*, Wes produces 24 ceaselessly inventive choruses, working perfectly finished bop phrases and imginatively varied blues riffs into a flawless grand design. The Kelly trio is invested with the same muse and the result is 13 of the richest minutes in jazz, worth the price of this CD alone. **MG**

Down Here On The Ground **Montgomery** (g); **Hubert Laws, George Marge, Romeo Penque** (f, ob); **Gene Orloff, Raoul Poliakin** (vn); **Emanuel Vardi** (va); **George Ricci** (vc); **Herbie Hancock** (p); **Mike Mainieri** (vb); **Ron Carter** (b); **Grady Tate** (d); **Ray Barretto, Bobby Rosengarden** (perc). A&M Ⓜ CDA 0802 (32 minutes). Recorded 1967/68.

⑧ ❽

It has become traditional—and almost mandatory—to dismiss or ignore the albums Montgomery made towards the end of his life for Creed Taylor, first at Verve and then at A&M. It is true that some are less than successful, often restricting Montgomery to a single octave melody line in an overcrowded and hopelessly passé arrangement on trite song after trite song. Listen to those albums after a dose of **Live at the Half-Note** (Verve, not on CD) and you will immediately become depressed.

However, by the time Wes made his final two records—both for A&M—the formula had been much refined, the more crass aspects of commercialism eliminated, and the quality of the repertoire substantially improved. This present album, the last he made, is a very good record indeed if you judge it by relevant and not irrelevant criteria. It is not a blowing date, and Montgomery rarely opens up into a full-power solo (though just such a thing occurs on *The Other Man's Grass Is Always Greener*), but he dominates the music, often playing non-stop for the duration of a title. The backing group, used sparingly throughout, is notably without any brass instruments, the strings a mere string quartet, and the rhythm section gives the guitarist first-rate, intelligent support, with the four musicians sounding like a real working band, so unified in thought and deed are they. **KS**

Tete Montoliu

Songs for Love **Montoliu** (p). Enja Ⓕ ENZ-2040 2 (43 minutes). Recorded 1974.

⑧ ❽

An unpretentious record—just one man sitting and playing mostly ballads—but one that grows on you. His version of *Here's That Rainy Day* is utterly convincing. His reworking of John Lewis's *Django* is equally satisfying, though it is hard to go too far wrong with *Django*, which is one of the few modern jazz compositions which really are compositions and have structures which stand up by themselves. The only tune that doesn't work is *Gentofte 4349*, probably because it is the only up-tempo one and therefore the only one on which you really miss the bass and drums. Otherwise this Catalan musician (I am sure he would object to being called Spanish) shows that he is a complete pianist; odd that he is not mentioned more when people draw up their lists of favourites. **MK**

James Moody

1925

Hi Fi Party **Moody** (as, ts); **Dave Burns** (t); **William Shepherd** (tb); **Numa 'Pee Wee' Moore** (bs); **Jimmy Boyd** (p); **John Latham** (b); **Clarence Johnson** (d); **Eddie Jefferson** (v). Prestige Ⓜ OJCCD-1780-2 (47 minutes). Recorded 1955.

⑧ ❽

James Moody, in spite of the implications of his surname, is one of the most ebullient forces in all of jazz. Indeed, while a complete and totally dedicated jazz musician, Moody is also a natural entertainer who can, if the situation warrants, keep dancing feet happy and an audience smiling. Part of that ability was undoubtedly nurtured by Moody's long-standing association with Dizzy Gillespie, with whom he frequently and significantly teamed.

In 1955, when this swinging little-big-band date was waxed, Moody had patterned his alto style largely after Charlie Parker. For tenor, the weather vane was Lester Young, though Moody subsequently incorporated John Coltrane's modernist primer into his unique and energetic approach; flute was also added later. But here Moody impresses mainly with a musically sophisticated attack that also reflects such then-popular r&b performers as Earl Bostic, Bull Moose Jackson and Screamin' Jay Hawkins.

Moody, Burns and Shepherd—who had worked together in Gillespie's big band—handle the bulk of soloing chores with gusto and good cheer. It is a tightly knit ensemble with a loose, relaxed feel and a solid book that includes challenging originals like Benny Golson's *Big Ben* and John Acea's *Little Ricky*. There's a swinging romp through *There Will Never Be Another You* and a vocal, *Disappointed*, from Eddie Jefferson, who primarily served as Moody's road manager. All in all, an upbeat and consistently pleasing date. **CB**

Oscar Moore

1912-1981

Oscar Moore **Moore** (g); **Carl Perkins** (p); **Joe Comfort** (b); **Lee Young** (d); **Mike Pacheco** (perc). VSOP/Tampa Ⓕ VSOP #34/22CD (51 minutes). Recorded 1954.

⑥ ❺

If Oscar Moore is known to a wider public, it is only as the guitarist in the Nat King Cole Trio between 1937 and 1947. He combined the intricacy and instrumental sound of Les Paul with the harmonic attack of Charlie Christian, and was a highly-regarded player during his years with Cole. He left Cole to pursue a solo career but was diverted into his brother Johnny's group, the Three Blazers. It was downhill all the way from there, and within a year of recording this, one of only four albums as a leader from his whole career, he was working as a bricklayer.

He doesn't sound like someone who should be laying bricks. In fact, his humour and complete professionalism make him a likeable musical personality without being the type you would never forget. Pianist Perkins more neatly fits into the latter category, being one who promised much and died young. His playing here is considerably mellowed, and he often seems to be consciously mimicking Cole's piano style. A modest, competent album (in fact, it combines two old vinyl dates, from Tampa and from Skylark) which will help while away the time. **KS**

Ralph Moore

1956

Who It Is You Are **Moore** (ts); **Benny Green** (p); **Peter Washington** (b); **Billy Higgins** (d). Denon/Savoy Ⓕ CY 75778 (70 minutes). Recorded 1993.

⑦ ❽

London-born Moore moved to California at the age of 15. He studied at Berklee in Boston, MA, before moving to New York in 1980. He was a sideman with Horace Silver and the Mingus Dynasty band and also worked with Dizzy Gillespie, Freddie Hubbard and J.J. Johnson. His earliest recordings exhibited more individual personality than some critics were prepared to allow but he was determined to break through as a leader in his own right. This status he realized in the mid-eighties and this CD, like its recent predecessors, finds him in good company. His playing is now very assured and titles like *Skylark* demonstrate the extent to which his breathing patterns accommodate his solo conception and not vice versa. He employs a wide dynamic range and his control of vibrato is emphasized on *But Beautiful*. Despite his original background, *Testifyin'* suggests that he has more than a little gospel in his soul, while *Yeah You* confirms that a spicing of contemporary funk need have no detrimental effect. Moore is also a useful composer, with *Esmeralda* in particular showing the extent to which his solos follow his theme shapes. They proclaim a musician whose improvisations combine the logical with the spontaneously creative. **BMcR**

Airto Moreira

1941

The Other Side Of This **Moreira** (v, perc); **Mickey Hart**, **Zakir Hussain**, **Babatunde Olatunje**, **Kitaro**, **Vikku Vinayakaram** (perc); **Dr. Verna Yater**, **Flora Purim**, **Caryl Ohrbach**, **Rose Solomon**, **Cheryl McEnaney** (v); **Frank Colon**, **Giovanni Hidalgo**, **Diana Moreira**, **Justine Tons**, **Margaret Barkley**, **Leah Martino**, **Amrita Blair**, **K.C. Ross**, **Jana Holmer** (v, perc). Rykodisc Ⓕ RCD10207 (59 minutes). Recorded 1992.

⑧ ❽

Mickey Hart, drummer with legendary San Franciscan psychedelic rockers The Grateful Dead and all-round drumming historian-philosopher-spokesperson, claims that Airto Moreira "literally created the role of percussionist in the West." This is, of course, a little extravagant, but Hart is always deadly serious on the subject of percussion, and there is no doubt that the Brazilian Moreira (commonly recognized as simply 'Airto'), one-time member of Miles Davis's trail blazing seventies-period electric doom-jazz group and founder member of Chick Corea's Return to Forever (just about the other end of the entire fusion spectrum), has been one of the most consistently astonishing and yet satisfying drummers in recent jazz, and never a musician to let his awesome technique get in the way of the music. **The Other Side Of This**, a document of 1992 sessions organized and ultimately produced by Hart, is at first sight far removed from the electric jazz of

Airto's youth. A purely percussion and vocals recording, the album pulls together percussion music and its practitioners from cultures as diverse, musically and geographically, as India, the US and Brazil, and this clearly with pan-global, deeply spiritual intentions. If this sounds a tad New Agey, rest assured; the spontaneity, virtuosity and sheer bravado of the performances make for hugely enjoyable listening. **SH**

Frank Morgan

1933

Listen To The Dawn **Morgan** (as); **Kenny Burrell** (g); **Ron Carter** (b); **Grady Tate** (d). Antilles Ⓕ 518 979-2 (52 minutes). Recorded 1993.

⑧ ❽

This arresting and well put together album is a magnificent cameo by Morgan, who returned to the limelight only relatively recently after years of obscurity. On three compositions he is backed by Burrell alone, giving a soft chordal cushion for Morgan's breathy, delicate but hard-edged alto. Morgan is a player who picks up the threads of Charlie Parker's work and weaves them into an entirely different pattern from the Bird-influenced players of the fifties and sixties, excels in this intimate dialogue, his flurries of notes decorating an essentially ballad style in a completely personal way. When Ron Carter and Grady Tate add their almost telepathic skills to the rhythm section, the result is a light (but far from lightweight) and apparently effortless piece of music making that repays re-listening. Frank Morgan's years away from the public eye were hard and difficult. His playing has a lyric intensity rare in soloists who have no autobiographical pain or beauty to express. **AS**

Lee Morgan

1938-1972

Candy **Morgan** (t); **Sonny Clark** (p); **Doug Watkins** (b); **Art Taylor** (d). Blue Note Ⓜ CDP7 46508-2 (43 minutes). Recorded 1957/58.

⑧ ❿

At the time of this, his only quartet recording, Morgan had just finished his year-and-a-half in the Dizzy Gillespie big band and was shortly to join the Jazz Messengers. Such an impressive reputation had already earned him a considerable number of recording opportunities (this was, after all, boom time for the 12-inch LP format), but none was carried out in quite such accomplished manner as this set, done when he was 19.

Already in evidence was Morgan's individual approach, built on elements of Gillespie and especially Clifford Brown (to the extent of quoting from his *Brownie Eyes* solo on both *C.T.A.* and the title-track). Outlining the tune on each number, he is able—like Brown—to be affectingly melodic and, at the same time enlivening things with his shaded dynamics and bluesy half-valve inflections, harking back to earlier players such as Rex Stewart. The pacing of his phrases is remarkable for one so young, and equally striking is his habit of repeating a humorous off-key figure, as at the start of the *Candy* solo or in *Personality*.

The rhythm section perform excellently, with Taylor frequently on brushes and Clark (unfairly maligned in another recent guide) providing a piquant contrast to the leader. **BP**

The Best of Lee Morgan **Morgan** (t); **Jackie McLean**, **Gigi Gryce** (as); **Hank Mobley**, **Joe Henderson**, **Wayne Shorter**, **Benny Golson** (ts); **Pepper Adams** (bs); **Herbie Hancock**, **Barry Harris**, **Bobby Timmons**, **Harold Mabern**, **Ronnie Mathews**, **Sonny Clark**, **Wynton Kelly** (p); **Paul Chambers**, **Larry Ridley**, **Bob Cranshaw**, **Doug Watkins**, **Victor Sproles**, **Butch Warren** (b); **Billy Higgins**, **Philly Joe Jones**, **Art Taylor**, **Charlie Persip** (d). Blue Note Ⓜ CDP7 91138-2 (73 minutes). Recorded 1957-65.

✔ ⑧ ❽

There is no doubt that hard bop is one of the least pretentious and most trenchant forms of jazz expression. Its ugly name embraces a wealth of fine jazz music and Lee Morgan became one of its greatest practitioners. As far as can be ascertained Morgan never recorded a bad solo. Fortunately his short career was crammed with recording sessions and, since most of them were recorded for Blue Note by Rudy Van Gelder, their quality. is high on all counts.

Morgan matured in Art Blakey's Jazz Messengers and it is notable that, although Blakey is not present on any of these sessions, his high standards and the general aura of good feeling generated by the Messengers permeates these nine tracks. Morgan's earliest influence was Clifford Brown, his near-contemporary, but he was not as agile as Brown and his playing had mainstream qualities in it—his half-valve work could, for instance, have come from listening to Rex Stewart. Some of the pieces here reflect the Blue Note penchant for funky blues—the medium must have made a fortune for the company—but tracks like *The Sidewinder* and *The Rumproller* are nevertheless filled with uncompromising solos of the highest calibre.

Morgan's five-minute work-out on a solo feature, a r&b ballad by Buddy Johnson called *Since I Fell For You*, is a trumpet jazz classic by anyone's standards and would serve as a marvellous introduction to a minor jazz giant. **SV**

The Sidewinder **Morgan** (t); **Joe Henderson** (ts); **Barry Harris** (p); **Bob Cranshaw** (b); **Billy Higgins** (d). Blue Note Ⓜ 821Y 84157 2 (41 minutes) Recorded 1963.

⑧ ❽

This album has been accorded such iconic status in certain circles that it's worth reminding ourselves that most of the music on it doesn't in fact fit the funky jazz scene at all. In that at least it is a typical Blue Note product of its period. The label had been starting Horace Silver and Art Blakey records with funky gospel-tinged hard bop tracks for years, then leaving the musicians free to pursue whatever they wanted for the remainder of the disc. The only difference here is that the LP's side two also kicks off with another funky little number, so you get two for the price of one.

Not that such music doesn't suit Morgan and his band perfectly: after all, the trumpeter himself came up with the tune, so he clearly felt good about it. All that aside, everyone plays well here, whether they are funking it up or hitting a more mainstream groove. Morgan and Henderson mesh very well - well enough for the front line to remain intact when the follow-up, **The Rumproller**, came to be made (the title track of which is on the compilation above), and for Henderson to then be hired by Horace Silver as a replacement for the departing Junior Cook. I was going to make this part of the Basic Jazz Library, but then the compilation album above has the tracks off it everybody talks about, plus a more rounded picture of Morgan's career, so that's maybe a better place to start. Meanwhile, seek out the now-deleted **Search For The New Land**, a very different type of Morgan album from the same period. **KS**

Butch Morris

1940

Dust to Dust **Morrls** (cond); **Vickey Bodner** (ehn); **J.A. Deane** (tb, elect.); **Marty Ehrlich** (cl); **John Purcell** (o); **Janet Grice** (bn); **Myra Melford** (p); **Wayne Horvitz** (kbds, elp); **Brian Carrott** (vb); **Jason Hwang** (vn); **Zeena Parkins** (hp); **Jean-Paul Bourelly** (g); **Andrew Cyrille** (d). New World Ⓕ 80408-2 (61 minutes). Recorded 1990.

⑦ ❽

As a cornettist Morris was prominent on the West Coast before moving to New York and becoming involved with the loft movement of the seventies. He lived and worked in Paris for some time, but once back in America, he has become increasingly involved with 'conduction', his own very special musical form. As this CD shows, the conductor becomes an organic part of the ensemble. He initiates rhythmic, melodic and harmonic changes and actually develops new musical structures while the piece is being performed. It is essentially a collective form, although Bourelly on *Othello B*, Ehrlich on *Long Goodbye* and Purcell on *Othello A* show how solos can be an integral part of an ensemble whole. The degree of Morris's conductive involvement is not always immediately apparent, a quandary complicated by the fact that he wrote all of the originals and that each of them has his distinctive stamp. They range from pastoral restraint to multiphonic turbulence, but there is no descriptive intent. It is an essentially orchestral form, with no theme-and-development system. It certainly accommodates the juxtaposition of musical anger and gentle beauty, and provides jazz with another important performance option. **BMcR**

Joe Morris

1955

Illuminate **Morris** (g); **Rob Brown** (as); **William Parker** (b); **Jackson Krall** (d). Leo Lab Ⓕ CD 008 (54 minutes). Recorded 1993.

⑦ ❽

Morris is a player who believes that loud enough is good enough. He is a highly original guitarist and his musical background takes in fusion, blues and the less extreme sixties horn men. He lives in the Boston area and was involved in the formation of the Boston Improvisers' Group, the Magnetic String Trio, as well as odd units like Racket Club and Sweatshop. This CD is not his first but it finds him in the company of musicians with whom he is conversant. In particular, it serves as a fine introduction to a coherent solo style, strong in content and paced by a naturally legato rhythmic approach.

His free improvisational skills are well displayed on *Results* and *Pivotal*. On both he paints attractively in monochrome, putting emphasis on the picture he actually produces and not on how he decorates it for presentation. He displays a subtlety of expression and assembles his ideas in a controlled yet assertive manner. His musical relationship with the equally creative Brown is intimate; each is aware of the other's musical direction, rhythmic emphasis and dynamic level and their counterpoint on *Illuminate* and *Inklings* indicates the ease with which their different free jazz ways interact. **BMcR**

Thomas Morris

1898–c.1949

When A 'Gator Hollers **Morris** (c); **Rex Stewart**, **Jabbo Smith** (c); **Geechie Fields**, **Charles Irvis**, **Joe Nanton** (tb); **Ernest Elliott**, **Happy Cauldwell**, **Bob Fuller** (reeds); **Mike Jackson** (p, v); **Lee Blair**, **Buddy Christian** (bj, g); **Bill Benford** (bb); **Wellman Braud** (b); **unknown** (d). Frog Ⓕ DGF 1 (79 minutes). Recorded 1926 .

⑥ ❹

A cornettist who made a recording début in 1922, played with Sidney Bechet in Clarence Williams's Blue Five, passed on his know-how with mutes to Bubber Miley and made more than one hundred and fifty recordings, deserves greater recognition. His style was personal if unspectacular and he played a significant part in the early New York scene. His timing lacked the rubato of the Oliver-Ladnier-Armstrong lineage but, like Johnny Dunn and others of the New York school, he coloured his more rigid delivery with muted effects that gave the impression of greater elasticity.

The titles on this CD come some time after his first breakthrough, but with improved recording quality they do show a more polished performer. *King Of The Zulus* suggests that he had listened constructively to the New Orleans avant garde but his powerful lead through the tempo changes of *Blues For The Everglades*, his well-organized solo on *PDQ Blues* and his preaching blues accompaniment on the title track are not the work of a primitive. In the thirties he quit music, working at Grand Central Station before joining a religious order. His contribution to jazz may appear modest but he was a significant figure in a New York scene trying to cope with the New Orleans jazz of the First World War and beyond. **BMcR**

James Morrison

Two The Max **Morrison** (t, tb, flh); **Benny Green** (p); **Ray Brown** (b); **Jeff Hamilton** (d). East/West Ⓕ 77125-2 (58 minutes). Recorded 1991.

⑧ ❽

Of all the current crop of young Australian instrumentalists, Morrison seems to have most successfully flown the coop, as is evidenced by both the music and the musicians on this album as well as by the label he is recording for. Morrison is equally adept on all three of his instruments and certainly lacks nothing in confidence: the opening track here, Jeff Hamilton's *Max*, has a stop-time structure which Morrison exploits wickedly with out-of-tempo half-valve growling. He then seamlessly devolves back into the hard-swinging rhythm section at the appropriate moment. No hesitant seconds there, for trumpeter or rhythm section. Of course, Ray Brown has been doing things like that to perfection all his working life, but this band he and Morrison are guiding breathes like a working unit rather than the studio pick-up outfit it actually is.

Honeysuckle Rose has a delicious duet opening between Brown and a flügelhorning Morrison before the piano and drums saunter in. During Morrison's long and engaging stint in the spotlight on this track hints of a decided liking for Clark Terry became evident. In this he may be unusual amongst trumpeters and flügelhornists, but Terry is an excellent musician to take as any sort of model, and the relatively unexplored territory thus made available gives Morrison a head start on many other players.

His trombone playing equally glances back towards similarly pivotal figures with stylistic feet in both swing and bop camps—players such as Frank Rosolino and Jimmy Knepper—but what is most evident is that Morrison is building on the vocalized tradition of horn playing, whichever instrument he chooses for any given track. Terry's stint with Ellington places him in a similar stream, and both Rosolino and Knepper have a wonderful facility with smears and glissandos used as an adjunct to their melodic developments, so the patterns of Morrison's heritage seem remarkably consistent. As does this nicely-paced and immaculately executed showcase album. **KS**

Jelly Roll Morton

1890-1941

The Pearls **Morton** (p, comp); with various groups including: **George Mitchell**, **Ward Pinkett**, **Ed Anderson**, **Edwin Swayzee**, **Sidney de Paris** (t); **Kid Ory**, **Gerald Reeves**, **Geechy Fields**, **Charlie Irvis**, **Claude Jones** (tb); **Omer Simeon**, **Barney Bigard**, **Darnell Howard**, **Johnny Dodds**, **Russell Procope**, **George Baquet**, **Albert Nicholas** (cl); **Stump Evans**, **Paul Barnes**, **Joe Garland**, **Walter 'Foots' Thomas**, **Sidney Bechet**, **Happy Cauldwell** (saxes); **Johnny St Cyr**, **Bud Scott**, **Lee Blair**, **Lawrence Lucie** (bj); **John Lindsay**, **Wellman Braud** (b); **Andrew Hilaire**, **Baby Dodds**, **Tommy Benford**, **Manzie Johnson**, **Zutty Singleton** (d). Bluebird Ⓜ ND 86588 (73 minutes). Recorded 1926-39.

✔

⑩ ❽

Where do we begin our praises for Jelly Roll Morton's work? We might mention the endless variety which he contrives to draw from the seven instruments of the standard New Orleans dance band, the individual brilliance of the players, even the high quality of the recording, quite remarkable for such an early date. But more important than these is the almost physical sense of vitality and relish for life that fills the air when Morton's music is playing.

Finest of all is the sequence of pieces by Morton's Red Hot Peppers recorded between September and December 1926, beginning with the sublime *Black Bottom Stomp,* the first fully-realized composition in the jazz idiom and still among the finest, meticulously prepared yet sounding free as air. If the composition of European classical music resembles architecture, the composition of jazz is more akin to gardening; the materials have a life of their own and the composer's work is to trim, shape and combine them—which is exactly how these masterpieces were produced.

It would be difficult to compile a better anthology of 23 Morton pieces than this. Along with the complete 1926 sequence it includes, among others, *Shreveport Stomp,* its hideously demanding solo clarinet part faultlessly played by Omer Simeon, the haunting *Deep Creek* and two songs of yearning nostalgia from Morton's last years. The digital restoration does justice to the already excellent mono recording. **DG**

His Complete Victor Recordings **Morton** (p, v, arr); with the following collective personnel: **George Mitchell** (c); **Ward Pinkett, Ed Anderson, Edwin Swayze, David Richards, Boyd 'Red' Rosser, Red Allen, Bubber Miley, Sidney De Paris** (t); **Kid Ory, Gerald Reeves, Geechie Fields, William Cato, Charlie Irvis, J.C. Higginbotham, Wilber De Paris, Claude Jones, Fred Robinson** (tb); **Sidney Bechet** (cl, ss); **Omer Simeon, Ernie Bullock** (cl, bcl); **Barney Bigard, Darnell Howard, Johnny Dodds, George Baquet, Albert Nicholas** (cl); **Russell Procope** (cl, as); **Paul Barnes** (ss); **Walter Thomas** (as, bs); **Stump Evans** (as); **Joe Thomas** (cl, ts); **Joe Garland, Happy Cauldwell** (ts); **Rod Rodriguez** (p); **J. Wright Smith, Clarence Black** (vn); **Johnny St Cyr, Lee Blair, Barney Alexander** (bj); **Will Johnson, Bernard Addison, Howard Hill, Lawrence Lucie** (g); **John Linsday, Pops Foster, Billy Taylor, Wellman Braud** (b); **Quinn Wilson, Bill Benford, William Moore, Harry Prather, Pete Briggs** (tu); **Andrew Hilaire, Baby Dodds, Tommy Benford, Manzie Johnson, William Laws, Paul Barbarin, Zutty Singleton, Cozy Cole, Bill Beason** (d); **Lew LeMar** (v); **Marty Bloom** (sound effects). RCA Bluebird Ⓜ ND82361(2) (five discs: 342 minutes). Recorded 1926-39.

✔ ⑩ ❽

Morton's place in jazz history is assured, for he was its first real composer/arranger. He himself claimed that he had invented jazz itself, and while this is clearly an overstatement, the fact remains that his own organizational methods are still in use today. This is beautifully exemplified on this set of over 100 tracks covering his most important and productive sessions for RCA Victor. There are a number of alternative takes here (all known to Morton experts, incidentally) but most of them simply reinforce the fact that Jelly had the music worked out in advance of the first attempt; there was little room for spontaneous improvisation on a Morton date. The first tracks, cut at a morning session in a Chicago hotel, are classics, with Morton leading a hand-picked band of mainly New Orleans-born musicians through *Black Bottom Stomp*, *Smoke House Blues* and two takes of *The Chant*, the latter written by the young white pianist Mel Stitzel. This was the beginning of Jelly's purple patch, when virtually everything he recorded had something beyond what others could achieve, however hard they tried. In 1927 Morton headed for New York, where the recordings he made still show the class and care of his Chicago dates, for Jelly used nothing but the best available musicians, men who were formally trained as well as being fine jazz soloists.

But the thirties were not kind to Morton, and nine years elapsed in between these and his subsequent Victor dates; yet his 1939 comeback titles are excellent, four of them featuring featuring both Albert Nicholas and Sidney Bechet. The CDs also contain three attractive trio sessions, with the clarinets of Johnny Dodds, Barney Bigard and Omer Simeon featured on various titles.

The importance of the Morton Victors cannot be overstated, and while this five-CD boxed set has a lot to commend, including a 60-page booklet giving complete recording information, the production is flawed. Both *Freakish* and *Original Jelly Roll Blues* are listed as existing on the discs in two takes, but in each case take two is repeated and the first takes are therefore absent. The album title is also misleading; "his complete Victor recordings" actually refers only to those under Morton's own leadership, and a replanning of the masters could surely have given us the eight tracks under Wilton Crawley's name, the two by Lizzie Miles and the four by Billie Young, all of which have Jelly Roll at the keyboard. For such a significant set it would have been worth sweeping aside any commercial considerations and opting for a six-CD compilation. The sound is generally acceptable, but RCA's much vaunted 'NoNOISE' reprocessing system is not a complete success. There are occasional and disturbing increases in volume during ensemble passages and the notes admit that some (unspecified) tracks have been taken from "early (fifties and sixties) tape transfers". These caveats notwithstanding, the set is recommended as a vital and vibrant slice of jazz history. **AM**

The Library Of Congress Recordings **Morton** (p, v, speech). Affinity Ⓜ CD AFS 1010-13 (three discs: 231 minutes). Recorded 1938.

⑧ (see below)

The first recorded jazz 'documentary' resulted from the Depression-era interest in 'folk music'. Alan Lomax had been making field recordings of a wide range of folk artists for several years for the Library of Congress when he discovered the once-successful pianist/bandleader, working in utter obscurity in the nation's capital.

The talking and playing reflects Lomax's unawareness of Morton's personal achievements, concentrating to a large extent on his reminiscences of New Orleans, of otherwise unknown pianists around the country, and the influence of ragtime, folk-song and European music. This is fascinating stuff, enhanced by the fact that it all comes out Mortonized. Fortunately, Jelly was not overmodest and includes around 20 of his own compositions (authorship being sometimes disputed), with interesting variations from the commercial versions and including a couple otherwise unknown. That these recordings were never intended for release is underlined by the perfunctory recording, full of distortion and with the balance between Morton's piano, voice and tapping feet varying wildly from session to session. The remastering on these discs minimizes the listener's problem and, while discs one and three have some speech with piano backing, omits virtually all the passages where Morton merely talks. For the above reasons this set is impossible to compare with the rest of this book, but it remains required listening for the historically minded. **BP**

1939-1940 **Morton** (p, v); add on twelve tracks **Henry 'Red' Allen** (t); **Albert Nicholas** (cl); **Eddie Williams** (as); **Wellman Braud** (b); **Zutty Singleton** (d). On eight of these tracks, add **Joe Britton** or **Claude Jones** (tb). Classics Ⓜ 668 (62 minutes). Recorded 1939-40.

⑧ ❻

This is the final volume in Classics' chronological appraisal of Jelly Roll Morton. It does the collector the great service of making available all but two tracks of the material Morton made for the General Record company, reissued on 78rpm by Commodore and first issued on CD (though subsequently deleted) by the German company, Teldec. This material falls into two groups: piano solos (there are ten such tracks here) and small group sides (of which this disc carries twelve). It becomes clear, through direct comparison, that the most likely source of Classics' transfers are the Teldec CD remasterings (there is little difference, track-by-track, between the two), which is nothing to fear, because these were fundamentally accurate. So much for discographical history: what about the music?

The solo piano sides reveal little about Morton's playing not already known, but show his keyboard abilities to be unimpaired by the hard times he had come through in the 1930s, and his style to be completely untouched by more modern jazz movements. Here was a man at peace with his talent and his music. On the faster numbers he generates tremendous drive, while his slower pieces, often accompanied by his light baritone vocals, are relaxed and heartfelt. His own *Don't You Leave Me Here* is given a definitive and unusually moving performance, as is *Winin' Boy*. The melancholy of past joys simply cannot be held in check, even by the legendary Jelly Roll. The small-group sides find Red Allen in fine fettle though somewhat lost for a role to fill. The ensemble passages are disciplined, but Jelly himself seems uncomfortable in the spotlight, his vocals curiously workmanlike. Perhaps the band is simply under-rehearsed. These are the songs of experience, rather than innocence, and 1926 is now a long way away **KS**

Bob Moses

Time Stood Still **Moses, Bill Martin** (d), **Mike Peipman, Miles Evans** (t); **Rob Scheps, Bob Gay, Ole Mathisen, Rafael Moses, Stan Strickland, Evan Ziporyn** (reeds); **Brian Carrot** (vb); **Duke Levine, Tisziji Munoz** (g); **Jamshied Sharifi** (kbds); **Yossi Fine, Matthew Garrison, Wesley Wirth** (b); **Bill Martin, Ben Wittman, Simone Haggaig** (perc); **Luciana Souza, Alvin Roberts** (v); **Jimmy Slyde** (tap dancer). Gramavision Ⓕ R2 79493 (60 minutes). Recorded 1993-1994.

⑧ ❽

Drummer Bob Moses is a musical mystic, a metaphysical time-traveller whose open-ended forays emcompass and yet transform essences derived from the giants of the realm, "the powerful, ubiquitous spirits of Monk, Trane, Duke, Mingus, Rahsann, etc." Moses comes with solid credentials. Indeed, his charged percussive alchemy has provoked Larry Coryell, Gary Burton, Rahsaan Kirk, Jack DeJohnette, Dave Liebman, Mike Gibbs and Pat Metheny to some of their most ambitious explorations. Here, Moses continues the kind of large-ensemble, multi-cultural probe first initiated in **Bittersweet in the Ozone** (1975).

It's an adventure that traverses time and space. In *Prelude*, using a technique Moses calls "simul-circular loopology", the air is simultaneously still and vibrant. For *Felonious Thunk*, a funky backbeat and aphoristic rap help pay Dadaistic tribute to the aforementioned Thelonious Monk. Wesley Wirth's cosmic bass carries the day in a heartfelt tribute to *Jaco* (Pastorius). The lyric playfulness of *Gregarious Chants* with Brian Carrot's vibes solo conjures up echoes of Moses' days with Burton. Also arresting are the Gil Evans-like orchestral colours of *Elegant Blue Ghosts* with Rob Scheps's plaintive tenor and Miles Evans' jabbing trumpet. Throughout, the members of the Boston Philharmonic prove worthy companions to Moses's grand and compellingly idiosyncratic quests. **CB**

Bennie Moten

1894-1935

Kansas City Orchestra 1923-1927/1930-32 **Moten** (p, ldr); with a collective personnel of **Lammar Wright, Harry Cooper, Ed Lewis, Paul Webster** (c); **Oran 'Hot Lips' Page, Joe Keys, Dee Stewart, Booker Washington** (t); **Thamon Hayes** (tb, v); **Dan Minor** (tb); **Eddie Durhan** (tb, g); **Woody Walder** (cl, ts); **Harlan Leonard** (cl, ss, as); **Eddie Barefield** (cl, as); **La Forest Dent** (as, bs, bj); **Jack Washington** (cl, as, bs); **Ben Webster** (ts); **Ira 'Buster' Moten** (p); **Count Basie** (p, v); **Sam**

Tall, **Leroy Berry** (bj); **Vernon Page** (bb); **Walter Page** (b); **Willie Hall**, **Willie McWashington** (d); **William Little**, **Jimmy Rushing**, **Josephine Garrison**, **Sterling Russell Trio** (v). Classics Ⓜ 518, 519 (two discs: 70, 69 minutes: oas). Recorded 1923-32.

✓ ⑧ ❽

Moten represents yet another stumbling block to the 'jazz up the river from New Orleans' theory. Born in the ragtime heartland of Missouri, he played baritone horn before switching to piano in his teens. In the early twenties he led a quintet, but by the time he made his recording debut in 1923, this had become a sextet. The collective playing on *Elephant Wobble*, from the first CD above, shows how far removed the band's uncompromising ensemble sound was from the accepted Louisiana formula. Admittedly the 1925 band's arrangements used unison cornet breaks in the manner of the King Oliver Creole Jazzband on titles such as *South*, but the similarity ended there. Moten was certainly not helped by Walder's eccentric clarinet style, but the arrival of Leonard in his reed section in 1924 gave him other options. The 1926 nonet did bear a superficial resemblance to Oliver's Savannah Syncopators, but the pulse of the band was altogether different, with the Moten band maintaining its 'rural' identity by retaining a place for the banjo-picker and giving a hint of the chicken-reel. Changes were becoming more obvious, however, and the band was moving ever closer to the even four-beat, rhythmic pattern as more accomplished sidemen joined the band and the outlook became more sophisticated.

The second CD shows that, by 1930, the band had been enriched by the arrival of Lips Page's driving trumpet, Basie's powerful piano, Durham's cultured guitar and forthright trombone, as well as by Rushing's already outstanding jazz singing. The introduction of string bassist Walter Page also transformed his rhythm section from its still slightly rustic verticality into a more flexible unit, one perfectly equipped to deliver the four-beat bass in its natural form. Durham's loose-limbed arrangements were a further asset, and the Luncefordesque mobility of the *Milenberg Joys* chant provides lasting evidence of the band's influence on those that came after. With the new foundation, Lips Page gained in stature and his masterful playing on *Toby*, *Moten Swing* and *Prince of Wails* made him a serious rival to Louis Armstrong as the trumpet king. The Hawkins-inspired Webster strengthened the reed section as well as the band's solo strength, and the young Rushing produced little masterpieces of jazz singing like *New Orleans*. The December 1932 *Two Times* was the band's last recording; Moten died from complications following a tonsillectomy. Fortunately for us, Basie was on hand to carry on the tradition. **BMcR**

Paul Motian

1931

Psalm **Motian** (d); **Billy Drewes** (as, ts); **Joe Lovano** (ts); **Bill Frisell** (g); **Ed Schuller** (b). ECM Ⓕ 1222 (847 330-2) (48 minutes). Recorded 1981.

⑧ ❽

Paul Motian is one of a handful of drummers who have moved decisively beyond the role of a mere accompanist and into the sphere of musical leadership. He not only shapes the styles and directions of his groups, but he also tends to write much of the material recorded by them. His long association with ECM (he has recorded for them since the early seventies) faithfully logged many great moments with an impressive array of bands (1974's **Tribute**, with guitarists Sam Brown and Paul Metzke and the altoist Carlos Ward, was a particular stunner), and the personnel on this present album is on a par with any of them. Bill Frisell, on an early outing, plays with the broad imagination expected of him, and a great deal more fire than of late. It is also refreshing to hear him as one of three main soloists, rather than as the guiding instrument: his colouristic playing becomes all the more valuable for the contexts it suddenly gets thrown into on each track.

The album is more varied than many ECM efforts, with plenty of grit and hard playing emanating from all three major soloists. Lovano here is lively and experimental, and while he is probably a more complete player today, what he does here is fascinating in its own right. Motian himself is an inspiration: he knows how both to understate and overstate to bring the right message from his own music, and to stimulate the front line perceptively. The compositions he has served the band with are memorable in their own right, and contribute mightily to the album's success. **KS**

Reincarnation Of A Love Bird **Chris Potter** (as, ts); **Chris Cheek** (ts); **Kurt Rosenwinkel**, **Wolfgang Muthspiel** (g); **Steve Swallow** (elb); **Paul Motian** (d); **Don Alias** (perc). jmt Ⓕ 514016-2 (54 minutes). Recorded 1994.

Paul Motian was once noted for his abstraction, but like many of his peers he has responded at length to the new awareness of jazz's past. **Reincarnation** is yet another example of his sustained reconciliation with the modern mainstream, one which was already spawned imaginative tributes to Monk, Bill Evans and the Broadway repertoire.

Less resourceful or flexible individuals, discovering or re-discovering bebop, have been happy enough just to do it, but while **Reincarnation** includes such familiar fare as *Half-Nelson*, *Two Bass Hit*, *Ornithology* and *'Round Midnight*, Motian thoroughly reinvents the old standards in a way that Parker, Gillespie, Mingus et al would have been bound to salute. The combination of such non-idiomatic timbres as distorted and chorussed guitar (the resultant legato actually very bebop), post-bop harmonic vocabulary and a joyously sprawling delivery produces music as vibrant and fresh as its inspirations and distinctly non-neoclassical. Indeed, in a world where imitation is too often equated with authenticity, **Reincarnation** is a rare, genuinely creative reading of bebop, easily the most impressive of Motian's recent retrospectives. **MG**

Mound City Blue Blowers

Mound City Blue Blowers **Red McKenzie** (v, comb); **Bunny Berigan**, **Yank Lawson** (t); **Al Philburn** (tb); **Eddie Miller** , **Forrest Crawford** (cl, ts); **Sid Trucker** (cl, as); **Frank Signorelli**, **Gil Bowers** (p); **Nappy Lamare** (g, v); **Dave Barbour** (g); **Bob Haggart**, **Sid Weiss**, **Pete Peterson**, **Mort Stuhlmaker**, **Harry Goodman** (b); **Ray Bauduc**, **Dave Tough**, **Stan King** (d). Timeless Ⓜ CBC 1-018 (73 minutes). Recorded 1935-36.

⑥ ❻

The Blue Blowers centred on McKenzie, a vocalist who made his name by making the paper and comb an acceptable jazz instrument. He was so expert at this that he could lead a band in the trumpet role without any apparent diminution of power. Additionally he was a very good in-tune singer who, although he sounds a bit ripe now, had a big influence on Bing Crosby. His most famous recordings were in 1929 with the Blue Blowers featuring Coleman Hawkins and Pee Wee Russell in profound ground-breaking roles. This third-generation version of the band (the first was a quartet of paper and comb, kazoo, banjo and a suitcase played as drums) finds McKenzie surrounded by the embryonic Bob Crosby band, plus worthy citizens like Berigan and Tough.

The jazz is light and invariably delightful. Berigan and Lawson played great lead and solo and Miller was a typically melodic New Orleans player, albeit better equipped technically than a lot of them. The light rhythm sections provide springy support for the soloists while instrumentals like *High Society* and *Muskrat Ramble* present some very good ensemble playing between the front line of Lawson and Miller. This is a treasure-house of little-known music from the dawn of the swing era. **SV**

Bheki Mseleku

1955

Timelessness **Mseleku** (as, ts, p, v); **Kent Jordan** (f); **Joe Henderson, Pharoah Sanders** (ts); **Rodney Kendrick** (p); **Elvin Jones, Marvin 'Smitty' Smith** (d); **Abbey Lincoln** (v). Verve Ⓕ 521 306-2 (78 minutes). Recorded 1993.

⑧ ❻

South African multi-instrumentalist Bheki Mseleku is a formidably talented musician, and made a considerable splash in the UK a couple of years back when, as a virtual unknown, he was nominated for the inaugural Mercury Prize through the strength of his first recording, **Celebration** (World Circuit). On this début Verve recording he has justified the larger label's faith in him by producing a varied, intense but entertaining collection of nine original compositions. Virtually every track has a guest musician mingling with Mseleku's piano, saxophones or voice. His own playing and singing is often multi-tracked, but also from time to time he produces genuinely simultaneous musicalities, as he has often at live concerts.

The title track is the most accomplished piece: a breakneck hard-boppish feature for tenor saxophonist Joe Henderson, with Mseleku's piano pacing him and then tearing into a magnificent solo. Apart from a guest appearance from Elvin Jones, Marvin 'Smitty' Smith provides some of the most straight-ahead drumming he has recorded for years, ably teamed with bassist Michael Bowie. Mseleku's singing on *Vukani*, with its African overtones, is in complete contrast to Abbey Lincoln's almost world-weary *Through The Years*, the other predominantly vocal track. With additional guests like Pharoah Sanders, Rodney Kendrick and Kent Jordan, this is obviously an album which could in lesser hands disintegrate into its constituent parts, but Mseleku's talent is remarkable enough to pull it together into a cogent whole. He could have made it work without them: with them, it's an embarrassment of riches. **AS**

Jim Mullen

1945

Soundbites **Mullen** (elg); **Dave O'Higgins** (ts); **Lawrence Cottle** (elb); **Ian Thomas** (d). EFZ Ⓕ 1003 (52 minutes). Recorded 1992.

⑥ ❽

Ten years ago, Scots-born stringsman Jim Mullen suffered the usual neglect reserved for domestic prophets. There were a few albums with the late-lamented funk band Morrissey-Mullen, one or two sideman dates and, in 1983, **Thumbs Up**, a début solo album for Coda Records. But since 1990 things have got better. The sideman gigs have increased and Mullen has recorded two albums as leader in as many years. There was 1990's **Into the 90's**, a funk set on the sadly short-lived Six Strings And A Plank Of Wood label, and then in late 1992 came **Soundbites**, a set which registers a return to straight-ahead values while simultaneously retaining the funky, visceral quality which has made Mullen a favourite with local audiences for almost two decades. Although Mullen has consciously tried to curb the effect when preparing the eight strongly-written originals here, John Scofield clearly remains a prominent late influence, and it is a credit to his exceptional musicianship that on several tracks he is able to so faithfully replicate Scofield's melodic curves and chord movement and voicings. However, the guitar solos remain distinctively Mullenian, the singing lines and phlegmy tone inimitable. Fellow EFZ signatory Dave O'Higgins plays the Joe Lovano role superbly but uses Michael Brecker as his solo model, and there is impeccable support from two redoubtable London rhythmatists. **MG**

Gerry Mulligan 1927

Best of Gerry Mulligan with Chet Baker **Mulligan** (bs): **Chet Baker** (t); **Bobby Whitlock, Carson Smith, Henry Grimes** (b); **Chico Hamilton, Larry Bunker, Dave Bailey** (d). Pacific Jazz Ⓜ CDP7 95481-2 (49 minutes). Recorded 1952-57.

✔ ⑧ ❽

The first Gerry Mulligan Quartet had one of the most completely realized sounds in jazz. The roles of the four instruments, the blend of their tones, the balance of solo and ensemble, the choice of tempo and control of the general mood—all these are judged to perfection. Since there is no piano to add harmonic colour, each part stands out sharply, contributing an active and coherent strand to the pattern. Above all, it is an attractive sound—tuneful, good-humoured and welcoming—qualities that remain undimmed to this day.

This is a good selection from the quartet's three ten-inch albums of 1952-53 (plus one track from the 1957 reunion date), a typical half-and-half mixture of standards and originals, with some of the best tunes *(Walking Shoes, Nights at a Turntable*, etc.*)* being Mulligan's own. His baritone playing is at its most agile and debonair, his lines simple but never obvious. Baker, an infant phenomenon of 22, displays a harmonic-melodic flair that is a little short of genius at times. He follows his ear unhesitatingly, occasionally getting into tight corners, from which he extricates himself nimbly. In this he is uncannily like Bix Beiderbecke. He is also a master of the winsome ballad, of which there are several examples here, including the celebrated *My Funny Valentine*.

The original bright mono recording is faithfully transferred to CD. **DG**

What Is There To Say? **Gerry Mulligan** (bs); **Art Farmer** (t); **Bill Crow** (b); **Dave Bailey** (d). Columbia Ⓜ 475699 2 (41 minutes). Recorded 1958-59.

⑧ ❽

Farmer spent less than a year with the Mulligan Quartet; it is unfortunate that his term of service was so short, for the recorded evidence shows that he was an ideal partner. His dry, precise sound and clean articulation, added to a well-schooled musical background, gave his playing a different approach to that of Chet Baker, whose intuitive playing and warm tone had made such a huge impact on jazz of the fifties. This is in every way an excellent album, benefiting from the accuracy of the ensemble playing and the steady, reliable time keeping of Crow and Bailey. There is a freshness to the music which has withstood the passage of the years and even when the quartet turns the clock back to look at a Mulligan 'hit' of six years earlier, the brooding *My Funny Valentine* with Crow's dramatic bass line descending in semi-tones behind the horns, the listener is soon aware of the individuality of Farmer rather than someone trying to sound like Chet Baker. These four men could produce a quite astonishing drive on the up-tempo material and there is just such a feeling on *Festive Minor, As Catch Can* and *Blueport*. The harmonic understanding of Mulligan, Farmer and Crow enables them to imply the sound of rich, full voicings, rendering absurd the blurb on the back of the package which states that "a piano-less small-group sound ... serves as a reminder that Mulligan was interested in chordless jazz well before the innovative Ornette Coleman". **AM**

And The Concert Jazz Band Featuring Zoot Sims **Mulligan** (bs, p); **Don Ferrara, Conte Candoli, Nick Travis** (t); **Bob Brookmeyer** (vtb, p); **Willie Dennis, Alan Ralph** (tb); **Gene Quill, Bob Donovan** (as); **Zoot Sims, Jim Reider** (ts); **Gene Allen** (bs, cl); **Buddy Clark** (b); **Mel Lewis** (d). Europe 1 Ⓕ 710382/83 (two discs: 91 minutes). Recorded 1960.

⑧ ❹

The Concert Jazz Band is one of Mulligan's greatest achievements. It came to deserved fame at the end of what was surely the most magnificent decade in big band jazz, when orchestras led by Quincy Jones, Duke Ellington, Gil Evans and Count Basie amongst others had set new standards in the skilful interpretation of quality arrangements.

Mulligan transferred the idea of the piano-less rhythm section to the big band with sometimes perilous results. Pivoting a 14-piece on bass and drums required caution as well as skill and sometimes the music sounds inhibited as a result. That is the only qualification which can be made about this exhilarating concert recorded in the Paris Olympia for French radio. The concert atmosphere is relaxed compared to a studio date, and the soloists are given their heads—*Piano Blues* runs for 21 minutes, *Moten Swing* for 13 and *Blueport* for 11. Zoot Sims and Bob Brookmeyer are at their wailing best, as is Mulligan when he plays baritone, and they make a small but formidable solo team. On piano Mulligan is long-winded and, given that he is an eccentric pianist who functions simply as a soloist and never as a constructive rhythm section member, has a tendency to self-indulgence. But let us not carp at his genius. This is an enjoyable album reflecting the freshness and excitement which the Concert Jazz Band brought into big band jazz. It served to awe and startle us until the Thad Jones-Mel Lewis Orchestra came along five years later. **SV**

The Age of Steam **Mulligan** (ss, bs, p, arr); **Harry Edison** (t); **Bob Brookmeyer** (vtb); **Jimmy Cleveland, Kenny Schroyer** (tb); **Roger Bobo** (frh); **Bud Shank** (fl, as); **Tom Scott** (ss, ts); **Ernie Watts** (ts); **Roger Kellaway** (p); **Howard Roberts** (g); **Chuck Domanico** (b); **John Guerin, Joe Porcano** (d); **Emil Richards** (perc). A&M Ⓜ CDA 0804 (38 minutes). Recorded 1971.

⑧ ❽

This was Mulligan's first album under his own name in close on eight years when originally released in the summer of 1972, and it was significant that he chose to return as a composer, arranger and performer in front of a sizeable band. In the undoubted attractiveness of many of the themes, and the clarity of the scoring, this album is typical Mulligan fare. In the use of then-contemporary instruments (electric piano) and rhythms (Latin and shuffle beats, amongst others), it isn't quite so typical. The listener is fortunate that Mulligan's great good taste steers him well clear of any obvious pandering to prevalent trends, allowing the music's integrity to reveal itself from within.

Needless to say, all the pieces here are Mulligan originals, and he is generous enough to leave blowing room for people such as Edison, Scott and Brookmeyer from the above line-up. His own soloing belies the 'cool' epithet often used against him—not that he was ever really a member of that school. Although his sound has never had a rough edge, his improvising energy has always been high, his sense of humour puckish rather than laconic, and since the late fifties his preference has been for rhythm sections with a bit of life about them.

Every chart used here is evocative of the title ascribed, and can be dwelt upon at length for greater pleasure. This is an album of lasting value. One small query: the original liner notes mentioned a track called *Dancin' All Day Sunday*. The music was never released. Does it still exist and if so, wouldn't it make a nice CD-only fill-up? One of Mulligan's latest albums, **Lonesome Boulevard** (1990), is also on A&M and worth seeking out. **KS**

Mark Murphy

1932

Bop for Kerouac **Murphy** (v); **Richie Cole** (as, ts); **Bruce Forman** (g); **Bill Mays** (p); **Bob Magnusson, Luther Hughes** (b); **Roy McCurdy, Jeff Hamilton** (d); **Michael Spiro** (perc). Muse Ⓕ MCD-5253 (39 minutes). Recorded 1981.

⑥ ❽

Singer Mark Murphy is perhaps America's last self-consciously hip hipster. And while there is something oddly out-of-time and out-of-place in this 1981 pre-postmodern ode to Beat Generation chronicler Jack Kerouac (and also with Murphy himself), it is an anachronistic blip that is nice to have around, especially for anyone who passed through the roiling cultural currents of the fifties. The biggest stretch in this project is Murphy's reading of an excerpt from Kerouac's *On The Road* as a set-up for *Ballad of the Sad Young Men*, a strangely moving yet pathetic performance of Las Vegas proportions.

The theme is amplified on *Be-Bop Lives (Boplicity)*, a tribute to the giants of the genre that, while often musically lithe and heartfelt, teeters on the brink of parody. Murphy's problem here, and throughout his career, is the carefully cultivated, hipper-than-hip persona, where 'hip' is expressed by the white Murphy largely through an appropriation of black mannerisms that border, albeit unintentionally, on caricature. But regardless of how outrageous his posture may appear, Murphy prevails by dint of his sincerity. We believe that he believes. Murphy is also a singer with whom to reckon. He is a wonderful balladeer in the Tony Bennett-Jack Jones tradition, as demonstrated on *You Better Go Now*, and though his scatting is somewhat laboured, he swings like mad and has great intonation. Here, he benefits from the inspired ebullience of Richie Cole, Bruce Forman, Bill Mays and friends. **CB**

David Murray

1955

Hope Scope **Murray** (ts, bcl); **Hugh Ragin, Rasul Siddik** (t); **Craig Harris** (tb); **James Spaulding** (as, f); **Dave Burrell** (p); **Wilber Morris** (b); **Ralph Peterson Jr.** (d). Black Saint Ⓕ 120 139-2 (44 minutes). Recorded 1987.

✔ ⑩ ❽

Murray has spent the better part of nearly two decades securing a reputation as one of the most vibrant soloists in jazz, with many duo, trio, and quartet dates as evidence. But the octet, first recorded in 1980 and intermittently thereafter, is undoubtedly the best showcase for the full measure of his talents. Each of these recordings contains something of merit; this is the most recent and in some ways the best. Murray's writing for the band has been at a consistently high level, but at this point the ensemble seems tighter, and just as exciting, than any previous edition. The upbeat swagger of *Ben* (for Ben Webster, one of his touchstones on tenor), with wah-wah brass and jolting background figures, could be a contemporary view of the Ellington jump bands (Murray himself suggests that Ragin and Saddik fill the Cat and Cootie roles, respectively). *Lester*, for Lester Young, is a romantic ballad with warm, willowy chromatic tenor cushioned on a bed of brass and flute. The title tune winds through episodes of chattering horns, free polyphony, and a pogo'ed ending. For the first time Murray allows outside contributions, and Harris's *Same Places New Faces* roars congenially. Murray's his own best soloist, but Harris and Spaulding let off sparks when let loose. A powerful sample of one of the best bands of the eighties and nineties.. **AL**

Ming's Samba **Murray** (bcl, ts); **John Hicks** (p); **Ray Drummond** (b); **Ed Blackwell** (d). Portrait Ⓕ PRT 465457 2 (40 minutes). Recorded 1988.

⑨ ❾

Sandwiched between his eighties recordings for Black Saint and his later series of works for DIW, **Ming's Samba** was the result of Murray's brief flirtation with a major US label (Portrait being part of Columbia). Whether by chance or design, it contains some of his most ebullient, accessible music.

Murray's ongoing re-examination of the tenor tradition—moving back through Ayler, Gonsalves, Hawkins—has been filtered through the avant-garde techniques he learned early in his career. On this CD he employs a full range of contemporary vocabulary—tonal distortion, overblowing, huge intervallic leaps—to breathe new life into familiar territory. His tenor swarms over the music with irrepressible bravura, *Ming's Samba*'s latino swing and *Rememberin' Fats*' barrelhouse opened up by rampaging solos and fiery group interaction. The sauntering *Walter's Waltz* has Murray on bass clarinet, recalling Eric Dolphy's arabesque abstractions. Murray is not a great innovator, but **Ming's Samba** should leave no one doubting his phenomenal prowess as a player. **GL**

Spirituals **Murray** (ts, bcl); **Dave Burrell** (p); **Fred Hopkins** (b); **Ralph Peterson** (d). DIW Ⓕ DIW 841 (48 minutes). Recorded 1988.

⑧ ❽

This album is selected because it pitches the familiar Murray Quartet into not-so-familiar musical territory as far as his committed fans go, and music which may allow listeners unfamiliar with his huge body of recorded work a relatively straightforward introduction to his talents. Not that Murray is simply reinterpreting a bunch of airs from the public domain: four of the seven tracks are composed either by himself or by pianist Burrell. Still, the idea is there, and the form the four musicians continually mould and reshape allows the listener a convenient touchstone.

Murray plays superbly throughout. His bass clarinet on *Amazing Grace* may lie deep in Dolphy territory, but then that is hardly a drawback, and Murray uses the Dolphy vocabulary of swoops and vocalized smears, tempered by a legato line descended from Ayler, to his own ends. His tenor is less beholden to anyone in particular, his phrasing more plastic and flexible, his tone more personalized. On this album he tends to stick closer to the theme than he would normally contemplate, and this aids a more immediate comprehension of the overall form of each piece. This does not for one moment mean that his playing here is tame: it has fire aplenty. The fire, however, is directed to an easily perceivable result, and is fully in keeping with the origins and character of the spirituals, original and traditional, recorded here. The quartet, by the way, works beautifully together and deserves much of the credit for the full realization of the task at hand on this album. **KS**

Sunny Murray 1937

Sunny Murray **Murray** (d); **Jacques Coursil** (t); **Jack Graham** (as); **Byard Lancaster** (as); **Alan Silva** (b). ESP-Disk Ⓜ 1032-2 (52 minutes). Recorded 1966.

A surprise guest on a Cecil Taylor session in 1961, Murray played with John Coltrane and later made a vital contribution to Albert Ayler's sessions for ESP in the middle sixties. He lived for some time in Paris, working with most of the American expatriates in the city, but after returning to New York in the seventies he performed in the company of the younger loft movement musicians in a style that had withdrawn from its arhythmic concentration and assumed the more obvious mantle of bop. This CD finds him in his more pioneering days and marks his début as a leader. As with the Ayler sessions, it shows him to be one of the first drummers to pass the pulse-carrying function of the conventional drummer over to the listener. His style's legato flow made few vertical contacts with the music and, in fact, Coursil's trumpet lines do more to calibrate the music than do either Murray of his similarly free partner Silva. As a consequence, the collective passages are sometimes incontinently frenetic, Coursil is on no fixed route and neither saxophonist seems able to embrace free melodic development in the motif-building sense. The colourful sound banks they do produce are sustained by a Murray-inspired rhythmic background, but they do not always seem to respond with the flexibility that the drummer offers them. Most of the themes are rudimentary, though *Giblets* raises a smile.

The star rating is based almost entirely on the strength of Murray's drumming. Recording quality is not good. **BMcR**

Music Revelation Ensemble

Elec. Jazz **David Murray** (ts); **James Blood Ulmer** (g); **Amin Ali** (b); **Cornell Rochester** (d). DIW Ⓕ DIW-839 (50 minutes). Recorded 1990.

⑦ ❽

With James Blood Ulmer's best records—**Tales of Captain Black**; **America—Do You Remember the Love?**—currently unavailable on CD, **Elec. Jazz** provides a more satisfactory sampling of his jazz guitar than his recent DIW recordings as leader, which are very rock-oriented and often rather dull. The Music Revelation Ensemble is essentially Ulmer's group (and all the tunes here are his), with Murray sitting in as a guest co-frontliner.

After working with Big John Patton, Larry Young and Arthur Blythe, Ulmer came to notice in the mid-seventies as a member of Ornette Coleman's Prime Time. For a while he was categorized as a harmolodics player, but basic rock and blues formats continue to play a central role in his music. On **Elec. Jazz**, Coleman's influence is discernible both in the jaunty themes of *Big Top* and *Taps Dance* and in the rhythm section's simultaneous improvising with the soloists—a harmolodic disjunction that, for all the heat generated by the frantic, crabbed phrases and snagged rhythms, seems a less sympathetic setting for Ulmer's guitar (with its echoes of country blues) than the simpler flows of *America—Do You Remember the Love?* Murray's writhing, squealing solos are a bonus, however, and the music is vigorously inventive. **GL**

Vido Musso

1913

Loaded **Musso** (ts) with a collective personnel of **Leonard Hawkins**, **Shorty Rogers** (t); **Kai Winding, Gene Roland** (tb); **Boots Mussuli**, **Lem Davis** (as); **Stan Getz** (ts); **Marty Napoleon, Shorty Allen, Sanford Gold** (p); **Eddie Safranski**, **Iggy Shevak** (b); **Denzil Best**, **Shelly Manne** (d). Denon/Savoy Ⓜ SV 0227 (37 minutes). Recorded 1945/46.

⑥ ❻

Musso made very few dates as a leader (of the sessions on this album, he was only the nominal leader of one), but was a major soloist for both Goodman and Kenton despite not being able to read a music score (usually something of a handicap for a big-band player). His style was moulded in the thirties, long before the advent of bop, so although he is found in the company of the young turks of the day, his own playing is entirely within the Hawkins-inspired swing idiom. He had a large, powerful sound and a strong rhythmic drive, and was not afraid to growl and grimace through his phrases; in that sense he was one of the logical ancestors of the r&b players.

This album finds Musso on eight of the 12 tracks (the other date, recorded by Kai's Krazy Kats in December 1945, features a very young Stan Getz and more comfortably sits within the bebop ambience), and Musso performs consistently throughout, his Herschel Evans-tinged ballad playing on *My Jo-Ann* being a particular delight. Other attractions include a fine feature for bassist Safranski (the nominal leader of the second 1946 date) on *Bassology* and some driving work from both Musso and altoist Lem Davis on *Lem Me Go*. The recording quality is average for the period, but at least it is well-balanced and no-one is lost in the nether wilds of the Savoy studios. **KS**

Amina Claudine Myers

1943

Salutes Bessie Smith **Myers** (p, org, v); **Cecil McBee** (b); **Jimmy Lovelace** (d). Leo Ⓕ CD LR 103 (45 minutes). Recorded 1980.

⑦ ❽

Myers performed with gospel groups while still at school and even today it shows in everything she does. In Chicago she played with many visiting stars before becoming involved with the Association for the Advancement of Creative Musicians. Her involvement in the free form movement of that city continued after her move to New York and, latterly, Europe, and she has recorded with Lester Bowie, Muhal Richard Abrams and Frank Lowe. This CD, made at a time when she was actually touring with a gospel group, reflects her wide interests. She sings Bessie Smith tunes in her own light and soulful, rather than bluesy, way. She treats *It Makes My Love Come Down* to her rolling style of piano playing and takes *The Blues Straight To You* very close to Tamla-Motown soul. The main piece, however, is *African Blues*, with straight-ahead piano but with Myers moaning an 'African' part. It is full of melismatic extravagance all of which takes the performance into a different creative field, equally powerful and possibly more demanding. Myers is a difficult artist to classify, but her gospel roots have made it possible for her to branch out to all jazz-and-blues-related areas. **BMcR**

Simon Nabatov

Tough Customer **Nabatov** (p); **Mark Helias** (b); **Tom Rainey** (d). Enja Ⓕ 7063-2 (74 minutes). Recorded 1992.

⑧ ❽

First things first: don't let the truly dumb cover of this album put you off. This is challenging, exciting, well-worked-through jazz from a trio of players who know and like each other's approach. Nabatov was born in Moscow and left there for New York in 1978. Although he still has a base there, in the eighties he relocated to Europe, where he now centres his operations.

Nabatov's piano playing and compositions show the signs of a classical training, both in his impeccable technique and in his quest for musical structures which balance classical form with jazz freedom. In this he shares similar concerns with the Denny Zeitlin of the sixties, and also Dave Brubeck, both of whom are effective composers as well as comprehensively equipped pianists. Nabatov's touch is firm and precise and he is a sophisticated musical thinker, always able to work through any harmonic sequence he initiates and come up with worthwhile ideas. The record is composed of originals (five by Nabatov, two by Helias), so they are charting their own territory and nobody else's. Good thing, too: we don't need any more Evans or Hancock clones. **KS**

National Youth Jazz Orchestra

In Control **Bill Ashton** (ldr); **Andy Cuss, Jim Lynch, Brad Mason, Olly Preece, Neil Yates** (t); **Malcolm Smith, Jeremy Price, Elliot Mason, Mark Penny, Adrian Hallowell** (tb); **Howard McGill** (as, ss, f, cl); **Lisa Grahame** (as, f). **Jim Tomlinson** (ts, cl); **James Hunt** (ts); **Mick Foster** (bs, bcl); **Simon Carter** (p); **Andy Jones** (g); **Mark Ong** (b); **Chris Dagley** (perc); **Jenny How** (v). Jazz House Ⓕ JHCD 037 (78 minutes). Recorded 1994.

⑥ ❻

Baritone sax player Bill Ashton first formed NYJO in 1965. He has laboured unremittingly ever since to make it the best band he can, in the process giving a start to an incredibly large number of the best young British musicians. The present crop shows every sign of being as productive as the personnels of the earlier bands.

The band here is beautifully rehearsed, although *Hi Speed Gas*, which had no rehearsal whatsoever, sounds every bit as polished as the other tracks. The sections sound as though they had been playing together for years and there is none of the disjointed feel that one sometimes get from inexperienced soloists in youth bands. There is no way that an uninformed listener could tell that this was a youth band; it is also vastly superior to many of the parallel American university bands. Rather than pick out the many individual soloists, it can be said that they are all up to par and the charts that they have to play are well-tailored to them. Jenny Howe sings beautifully on her track and is helped by Jim Tomlinson's tenor playing. Ronnie Ross's *Willow, Green Willow* makes a succulent platform for Mick Foster's baritone. Humphrey Lyttelton wrote a tune called *50,000 Flies Can't Be Wrong* back in the fifties and there is another tune of the same title here which features a good trumpeter, Neil Yates, and the expert pianist Simon Carter.

Ashton's grovelling to his sponsor British Gas (all the song titles of the band's previous album **Cookin' With Gas** were suborned to them and five of the ones here are too) should not be inflicted on someone who pays for the album. **SV**

Fats Navarro

1923-1950

Nostalgia **Fats Navarro** (t); **Charlie Rouse, Dexter Gordon, Eddie 'Lockjaw' Davis** (ts); **Tadd Dameron, Al Haig** (p); **Huey Long** (g); **Nelson Boyd, Gene Ramey** (b); **Art Blakey, Art Mardigan, Denzil Best** (d). Denon/Savoy Ⓜ SV-0123 (34 minutes). Recorded 1946/47.

✔ ⑧ ❻

Although his reputation stands as one of the pioneers of be-bop, Fats Navarro is highly untypical in one respect, and that is the almost complete lack of nervous tension in his playing. The lines roll out, spacious and elegant, with a broad tone and crackling articulation. Be-bop, in its classic late-forties phase, has a clenched, driven, neurotic quality. Short bass notes and the unremitting top cymbal contribute to this effect, and the soloists seem to be hanging on by the skin of their teeth. In contrast to Navarro the three tenor players on these sessions sound quite frantic—even the famously deliberate Dexter Gordon. Not until Clifford Brown came along, some years after Navarro's death, was such assurance and poise heard again.

This is a good (if short) introduction to the work of Fats Navarro. The tunes, all in the theme-solos-theme format, consist mainly of lines constructed on standard changes, including two of Fats's favourites: *Out of Nowhere (Nostalgia)* and *Pennies From Heaven (Bebop Romp)*.

The original recording quality was rather variable, but the remastering has improved this somewhat. The main drawbacks are limited playing time and the lack of decent liner notes. **DG**

Memorial **Navarro** (t); with **Kenny Dorham** (t); **Sonny Stitt, Ernie Henry** (as); **Morris Lane** (ts); **Ed de Verteuil** (bs); **Bud Powell, Tadd Dameron** (p); **Al Hall, Curley Russell** (b); **Kenny Clarke** (d); **Kay Penton** (v). Denon/Savoy Ⓜ SV-0181 (45 minutes). Recorded 1946/47.

⑧ ❻

Until his premature death Navarro was thought of as the practitioner of an alternative style of bop trumpet, more controlled and classically proportioned than Gillespie's. Some commentators (though few musicians) have decided that he was superior to Gillespie, though this is hardly true of his harmonic and rhythmic imagination. However, his tone and articulation provided early inspiration to Clifford Brown and many others.

The availability of his best work is currently a problem, as his Blue Note recordings await re-release as a double CD and his formidable live date with Parker (formerly assembled as **One Night In Birdland**) is once again scattered among a variety of issues of dubious origin. This, along with another Savoy album called **Nostalgia**, is none too well recorded for the period, especially the octet originally released as by 'The Bebop Boys' (which supplements the Gillespie-dominated anthology, **The Bebop Revolution**). In addition, the small print makes clear that, though listed as the leader, Navarro is only present on two-thirds of the tracks; Kenny Clarke is the one constant factor, also appearing in the fine quintet with Dorham and Stitt. In the items with both trumpeters, it should be noted that Navarro is always the first brass soloist. **BP**

The Necks

Acquatic **Chris Abrahams** (p, org); **Lloyd Swanton** (b); **Tony Buck** (d); **Steve Wishart** (hurdy-gurdy). Fish of Milk Ⓔ 0002 (53 minutes) Recorded 1993.

④ ❽

The Necks is a young Australian group who are combining jazz techniques with the type of sampling and recycling of rhythm and fragments that people such as Holger Czukay, Robert Fripp and David Sylvian have perfected over the past decade or so. As such they're on the outer rim of the jazz movement, but what they have to bring to the listener is consistent enough in its stimulation to merit its inclusion. One would wish, however, that they had been a little more savage with their self-editing. Some of this music simply goes on too long before it decides to make the next point.

This would be the perfect soundtrack for a long journey in a car you really enjoyed driving. Maybe in Australia: you can go for long, uninterrupted journeys there. **KS**

Oliver Nelson

1932-1975

Blues and The Abstract Truth **Oliver Nelson** (arr, ts, as); **Eric Dolphy** (as, f); **Freddie Hubbard** (t); **George Borrow** (bars); **Bill Evans** (p); **Paul Chambers** (b); **Roy Haynes** (d). Impulse! Ⓜ MCAD 5659 (47 minutes). Recorded 1961.

✔

⑧ ❽

This was Oliver Nelson's finest hour, when his gifts as a composer and arranger intersected most happily with the jazz spirit of the age. At times there is a slight air of **Kind of Blue** about the music, at others a whiff of Mingus, but the bright, confident simplicity of the writing is archetypal Nelson. Having only four front-line instruments, he uses great ingenuity to extract more tonal variety from them than many arrangers could get out of twice that number. Particularly delightful is his voicing of the melody in *Stolen Moments,* with its plangent semitones at the centre of the chord, and the call-and-response effect utilized in *Hoe-Down*. Both these devices were subsequently done to death by all and sundry, but the original still sounds as fresh as ever.

Nelson's choice of musicians was impeccable: Dolphy had just broken surface and was obviously a major talent, with Hubbard just behind him. Evans was already universally admired by musicians, but then only beginning to become well known to the listening public as a result of his time with Miles Davis. The real surprise, however, turned out to be Nelson's own rumbustious tenor playing, which often upstages the lot of them. **DG**

Sound Pieces **Nelson** (ss, arr); with a big-band personnel on three tracks of **John Audino**, **Ollie Mitchell**, **Conte Candoli**, **Bobby Bryant**, **Al Porcino** (t); **Richard Leith**, **Mike Barone**, **Ernie Tack**, **Dick Noel**, **Bill Byers** (tb); **Gabe Baltazar**, **Bill Green**, **Bill Perkins**, **Plas Johnson**, **Jack Nimitz** (reeds); **Bill Hinshaw**, **Richard Perissi** (frh); **Red Callender** (tba); **Mike Melvoin** (p); **Ray Brown** (b); **Shelly Manne** (d); a quartet personnel on remaining tracks of **Steve Kuhn** (p); **Ron Carter** (b); **Grady Tate** (d). Impulse! Ⓜ GRD-103 (55 minutes). Recorded 1966.

⑧ ❽

In contrast to his most celebrated recorded work, **Blues and the Abstract Truth**, which featured Oliver Nelson on tenor fronting a small ensemble, **Sound Pieces** features the late composer on soprano—then returning to prominence in jazz courtesy of Steve Lacy and John Coltrane—in front of what must rank as some of his finest orchestral writing and, from a different session, with a quartet. There are three orchestral pieces, all rich, vigorous and subtle, and featuring the cream of West Coast studio musicians, including Conte Candoli on trumpet, the late Red Callender on tuba, Ray Brown on bass and Shelly Manne on drums. The title-track is a wonderfully rumbustious affair, written for the Stuttgart Radio dance band and later performed by Stan Kenton's Neophonic Orchestra, and its drama, propulsion and intensity are echoed by the TV theme *The Lady from Girl Talk*, which successfully attempts to mimic the sound of chattering conversation. The third orchestral selection, *Flute Salad*, is more ethereal, accurately described by Nelson himself as "essentially melodic", a try-out for his just-beginning career as a writer of film and TV scores.

The rest of the album is a quartet session featuring the unusual rhythmic clatter of Steve Kuhn on piano and a superb rhythm section, Ron Carter and Grady Tate. Nelson's soprano snakes sinuously above their solid foundation and the two bonus tracks (originally issued on the double-vinyl **Three Dimensions** Nelson compilation), Thelonious Monk's *Straight No Chaser* and Nelson's own *Example 78*, bristle with imaginative energy. By demonstrating just what an accomplished instrumentalist and composer Nelson was, **Sound Pieces** underlines the tragedy of his early death from a heart attack at the age of 43. **CP**

Phineas Newborn Jr. 1931-1990

Harlem Blues **Newborn** (p); **Ray Brown** (b); **Elvin Jones** (d). Contemporary Ⓜ OJCCD662-2 (38 minutes). Recorded 1969.

⑧ ❽

Something of a multi-instrumental prodigy, Newborn finally settled for the piano and established a reputation as a brilliant soloist. He had experience with Lionel Hampton before moving to New York in 1956, where he worked for a time with Charles Mingus. He moved to Los Angeles in 1960, but unfortunately his career took a bad turn on the West Coast as ill health and a hand injury made him less active. He was less able to display his breathtaking technique, but his playing on this CD seems to benefit from the physical restrictions forced upon it. There is no diminution of strength or reduction of fluency evident in the Baptist rock atmosphere of *Harlem Blues* or in the headlong drive of *Cookin' At The Continental*. He handles the strange middle eight of *Sweet And Lovely* with imagination and plays *Tenderly* and *Stella By Starlight* with an emotional depth not always evident in his more flamboyant days. In this he is helped considerably by the challenging yet sympathetic input by Brown and Jones. It is as if the need to be less exhibitionistic forced him to re-examine his goals, to put content before rhetorical embellishment and, as a result, be a better balanced musician. He did not always maintain this standard; although various comebacks were signalled, subsequent records proved less satisfying. **BMcR**

New Departures Quartet

Hot House **Bobby Wellins** (ts); **Stan Tracey** (p); **Jeff Clyne** (b); **Laurie Morgan** (d). HHCD Ⓕ 1010 (44 minutes). Recorded 1964.

⑧ ❻

Stan Tracey's exquisite jazz suite **Under Milk Wood** (reviewed under Tracey's entry, and one of the most outstanding British jazz records) didn't just fall out of an empty sky. For almost two years beforehand the quartet that made it (with the exception of drummer Jackie Dougan) had been appearing regularly with poets Michael Horowitz and Pete Brown in their jazz and poetry venture New Departures. In the summer of 1964 critic Victor Schonfield produced this session, with a texture so similar to the more famous suite that it is rather like a second helping of something particularly delicious. On the original sixties Transatlantic album there were two other tracks, but Hot House producers Pete Fincham and the late Ed Dipple chose instead to replace them with a previously unissued version of *Let Them Crevulate* (a Wellins/Tracey collaboration that they subsequently recorded for a different label). This is vintage Tracey, his asymmetric chords and jagged rhythms offset against Clyne's rock-steady bass lines and acting as a voluptuous cushion for Wellins. These are the definitive versions of Wellins's *McTaggart* and *Culloden Moor*, the composer's tenor investing both themes and variations with a spacious melancholy. **AS**

David 'Fathead' Newman 1933

Back To Basics **Newman** (f, as, ss, ts); **Pat Rebillot**, **George Cables**, **Hilton Ruiz** (kbds); **Jay Graydon**, **George Davis**, **Lee Ritenour** (g); **Abraham Laboriel**, **Wilbur Boscomb** (elb); **Idris Muhammad** (d); **Bill Summers** (perc). Milestone Ⓜ MCD 9188-2 (50 minutes). Recorded 1977.

⑤ ❽

Born in Dallas, a near-contemporary of Ornette Coleman and a man who worked with Buster Smith as well as Coleman, Newman never became involved in the free-form revolution that had its birth in that city. Experience with Lowell Fulson and T-Bone Walker pointed him in the direction of the r&b field, but he had the technique in reserve to enable him to work comfortably with top bop men when the opportunity arose. This CD has him in the company of highly professional sidemen such as Cables, Ruiz, Ritenour and Muhammad and bridging his two worlds with perhaps an eye to the commercial potential of such a release. This aspect is most evident in his alto work on *Knocks Me Off My Feet* or *Clouds*; less obvious when his driving tenor takes on *Blues For Ball*. The more subtle side of his personality is heard on *Save Your Love For Me* on soprano, or on *Keep The Dream Alive*, where his flute just avoids crossing the border into the musically saccharine. His earlier records for Atlantic with the likes of Ray Charles generally show him at his best. **BMcR**

Joe Newman

1922-1992

Jive At Five **Newman** (t); **Frank Wess** (ts); **Tommy Flanagan** (p); **Eddie Jones** (b); **Oliver Jackson** (d). Prestige Swingville Ⓜ OJCCD 419-2 (37 minutes). Recorded 1960.

⑧ ❽

Warm, fat tones seem to abound amongst jazz musicians from New Orleans, and trumpeter Newman's was one of the fattest. Fired by Louis Armstrong, he became one of the major soloists in the second generation Basie band of the fifties and, with Buck Clayton and Ruby Braff, one of the outstanding mainstream voices of the period.

He recorded prolifically and his sessions were divided between the polished and well-scored and the informal 'blowing session' as captured here (Newman had not played with Flanagan or Jackson until the day of this recording). Newman's regular partnership with Basie colleague Wess was highly productive and more refined sessions with Newman muted and Wess on flute produced some unique jazz voicings. Here Wess confines himself to robust tenor. Newman plays fine, cascading solos and takes the only ballad, *More Than You Know*, as a feature.

At the time Eddie Jones was having difficulties in the Basie band with the incumbent drummer Sonny Payne. Jackson is a much lighter player and, in tandem with Flanagan, produces a light sound in the rhythm section which enables the two horns to improvise with easeful eloquence. **SV**

New Orleans Owls

1922–1929

The Owls Hoot **Bill Padron** (c); **Red Bolman** (c, v); **Frank Netto** (tb); **Benjamin 'Benjy' White** (cl, as, dir); **Irvine 'Pinky' Vidacovitch** (cl, as); **Lester Smith** (ts); **Edward 'Mose' Ferrer**, **Sigfre Christansen** (p); **Rene Gilpi** (bj, g); **Nappy Lamare** (g); **Dan LeBlanc** (bb); **Earl Crumb** (ldr); add four tracks by **New Orleans Rhythm Kings** (Paul Maures [c], Santo Pecora [tb], Charles Cordella [cl]); four tracks by **John Hyman's Bayou Stompers** (John Hyman, Johnny Wiggs [c], Charles Hartman [tb], Elery Maser [cl], Monk Hazel [d]). Frog Ⓔ DGF 2 (78 minutes). Recorded 1925-27.

⑤ ❹

The New Orleans Owls are a good example of the white Crescent City bands of the period. They came into being in 1922 and drew the majority of their personnel from the Invincibles String Band. Players certainly made the transition to horn playing with some ease, although it was outsiders Padron and LeBlanc that put the backbone into the musical carcass. Padron in particular was impressive and this CD is littered with muted cornet solos, owing far more to Joe Oliver and Paul Mares than to Nick La Rocca. *Piccadilly* and *Tampeekoe* presents the unit's dance band persona but on obvious jazz standards such as *Eccentric* or *That's A Plenty* Padron and White produce solos of genuine merit and serious improvisational intent. None of the saxophone work is of similar quality, however, and Vidacovitch's naïve alto solo on *Meat On The Table* typifies their lack of jazz know-how. The Owls' final recording session in 1927 finds them saddled with inappropriate arrangements and perhaps unsure of their position in a changing jazz world. They bring some life to *Goose Pimples* but within two years they were to disband. Excluding the unissued *Zero*, all of their known titles are here and the album is completed by a latter-day New Orleans Rhythm Kings band and Hyman's Bayou Stompers. **BMcR**

New Orleans Rhythm Kings

N.O.R.K and Jelly Roll Morton **Paul Mares** (c); **George Brunies** (tb); **Leon Ropollo** (cl); **Jack Pettis** (cms, ts); **Glenn Scoville** (as, ts); **Don Murray** (cl, ts); **Elmer Schoebel**, **Jelly Roll Morton**, **Mel Stitzel**, **Kyle Pierce** (p); **Steve Brown** (b); **Chink Martin** (bb); **Lou Black**, **Bob Gillette** (bj); **Frank Snyder**, **Ben Polack** (d). Milestone Ⓜ MCD 47020-2 (74 minutes). Recorded 1922/23.

✔

⑧ ❻

The New Orleans Rhythm Kings were a very influential group, even if the source of their own inspiration is less clear. Their choice of material and the town of their origin could explain why the Original Dixieland Jazz Band is their oft-quoted role model. The fact remains, however, that they sound nothing like Nick La Rocca's band. Even allowing for the five year time difference, NORK had advanced ODJB's jazz playing techniques by some distance. Mares had always claimed King Oliver as his mentor and, as this CD demonstrates, NORK had more of that band's legato mobility than it dld the upright rigidity of the ODJB. With Pettis dominant, numbers like *Discontented Blues* and *Oriental* are little more than dance items but the majority of the band's output is jazz of a high standard. Mares's fine lead is typified by his work on titles like *Eccentric* and *Sweet Lovin' Man*, while Ropollo is consistently inventive in a style that eschews the empty arpeggio running of many of his contemporaries and, on *Tiger Rag* and *Tin Roof Blues*, displays timing that is surprisingly Doddsian. Brunies, like Miff Mole and Charlie Green, a forgotten man when the birth of jazz trombone is discussed, is a remarkable player, subtle in solo on *Tin Roof Blues* and an emsemble master throughout. Morton's involvement remains something of a mystery and his organising hand is more prominent than his solo piano. His presence is felt rather than asserted but the NORK were a band that needed little outside support. **BMcR**

Sam Newsome

1965

Sam I Am **Newsome** (ts); **Steve Nelson** (vb); **Mulgrew Miller** (p); **James Genus** (b); **Billy Drummond** (d). Criss Cross Ⓕ 1056 (61 minutes). Recorded 1990.

⑦ ❽

Newsome began playing tenor when he was admitted to his school's jazz band at the age of 13. A friend's record collection introduced him to Sonny Rollins, John Coltrane and Ornette Coleman, as well as to earlier figures such as Ben Webster and Lester Young. He then won a Kool Jazz Festival Scholarship that led him to Berklee College and to playing offers in the Boston area. He was with Donald Byrd in 1987 and, at the time of this session, was about to join Terence Blanchard's hard hitting quintet. His suitability for that particular post is made more than evident on this CD, where he matches himself against the most powerful of rhythm sections. His slow-burn treatment of *Vein Of Trane* does full justice to the dedicatee, the rollicking gait of *Indiana* evokes thoughts of Sonny Rollins, while *I Thought About You* takes a laconic mainstream route, treating the ballad to the most relaxed of examinations. Newsome is certainly an accomplished technician but his playing refutes the contention held by some observers that all of today's 'new wave' young men lack emotional involvement and historical perspective. This CD suggests that he has Lester Young's pork-pie hat in his wardrobe, even if it is decked out with a nineties hat-band. **BMcR**

David Newton

1958

Eye Witness **Newton** (p); **Dave Green** (b); **Allan Ganley** (d). Linn Records Ⓕ AKD 015 (48 minutes). Recorded 1990.

⑧ ❽

A clear-toned pianist with an approach whose neatness and delicacy verge on fastidiousness, David Newton's limpid style is particularly well suited to accompanying singers, and he is frequently still to be found in that role, backing label-mates Carol Kidd and Claire Martin, and 33 Records's Tina May. In recent years he has launched himself into a solo career, recording three albums in quick succession for Linn, two with stellar UK rhythm sections, the third, **Return Journey** (1992), a solo effort featuring his own gently romantic compositions. **Eye Witness,** by the shortest of heads, is the pick of the bunch, courtesy of the control Newton exerts upon it of his besetting sin, a slight tendency to gush, and thanks to the balance it contains of slow-burning ballads (a Newton speciality) and more vigorous fare written by Herbie Hancock (*Eye of the Hurricane*) and Newton himself (*Ol' Blues Eyes*, a relaxed walking blues opener, and the attractively jaunty title-track). Thus, although Newton's playing is still chiefly remarkable for the burnished, luminous clarity he brings to such material as *Angel Eyes* and *Stars in My Eyes*, both he and his elegant, utterly dependable rhythm section generate considerable swing on the more up-tempo pieces, and **Eye Witness** is something of a high-water mark in recent UK mainstream jazz. The Eyes have it. **CP**

Frankie Newton

1906-1954

Frankie's Jump **Newton** (t); **Edmond Hall**, **Mezz Mezzrow** (cl); **Pete Brown**, **Russell Procope**, **Gene Johnson**, **Tab Smith**, **Stanley Payne** (as); **Cecil Scott**, **Kenneth Hollon** (ts); **Don Frye**, **James P. Johnson**, **Kenny Kersey** (p); **Richard Fullbright**, **John Kirby**, **Johnny Williams** (b); **Cozy Cole**, **O'Neil Spencer**, **Eddie Dougherty** (d); **Clarence Palmer**, **Slim Gaillard**, **Leon LaFell** (v); **John Smith**, **Frank Rise**, **Al Casey**, **Ulysses Livingstone** (g); **Dickie Wells** (tb). Affinity Ⓜ CDAFS 1014 (64 minutes). Recorded 1937/39.

⑧ ❻

Newton's bands epitomized the very best of the little 'jump' units to be found in pre-war Harlem clubs. Newton played on Bessie Smith's last record session and also worked for some time with Billie Holiday, so his jazz credentials were never in doubt. He was a lyrical player with great taste and a natural sense of what was right in both solos and arrangements. This is an essential compilation, bringing together the products of six beautiful sessions featuring men such as Pete Brown, Ed Hall and Cecil Scott. Also included are Slim Gaillard's very first vocals on record (*There's No Two Ways Bout It* and *'Cause My Baby Says It's So*), which are balanced by the 'crooning' of Leon LaFell on Ralph Rainger's lovely song *Easy Living*. (For collectors of the bizarre, LaFell also inserted himself into a Johnny Hodges session about this time!) The album abounds with highlights, but mention must be made of the 1939 date with Mezzrow, James P. Johnson and Al Casey, from which comes the fine *Rompin'*. The transfers are from 78s using the CEDAR process and while the sound is never less than acceptable (and often very good), the compilers were obviously at the mercy of the source discs. **AM**

James Newton

1953

Axum **Newton** (f, af, bf). ECM Ⓕ 1214 (835 019-2) (43 minutes). Recorded 1981.

⑧ ❾

Though *Axum* is one of James Newton's earlier recordings, it's also one of the few currently available on CD (his two excellent Blue Note albums, **The African Flower** and **Romance and Revolution** appeared on compact disc only to be deleted again almost immediately). The solo **Axum** gives little indication of Newton's skills at extended composition or arranging for large ensemble (where his models are Ellington and Mingus), but it does offer a breathtaking display of technique and invention on flute, his principal inspiration here being Eric Dolphy.

To describe **Axum** as a solo album may be slightly misleading, since Newton over-dubs his flutes on several tracks to extend his tonal palette. On *Choir* he hums while he plays, producing extraordinary harmonic and vocal effects. And on *Axum* itself vocalizing, overdubs and electronics are all used to create an eerily enchanting soundscape. Even the strictly solo tracks are nicely varied; *Susenyos and Werzelya* uses some virtuoso blowing techniques, while the dramatic *Maalak 'Uqabe* and a majestic *Solomon Chief of Wise Men* (on bass flute) reveal a mature musical sensibility at work. **GL**

New York Art Quartet

New York Art Quartet **Roswell Rudd** (tb); **John Tchicai** (as); **Lewis Worrell** (b); **Milford Graves** (d); **LeRoi Jones (Amiri Baraka)** (recitation on one track). ESP-Disk Ⓜ 1004-2 (43 minutes). Recorded 1964.

⑧ ❻

This underrated cooperative band formed in 1964 from the city's burgeoning New Thing scene; Tchicai, Rudd, and later NYAQ bassist Reggie Workman had recorded together on Archie Shepp's **Four For Trane**, and the altoist and trombonist joined Albert Ayler on the **New York Eye And Ear Control** date. But as an ensemble the NYAQ adopted neither Shepp's theatrical nor Ayler's extreme brands of expressionism, developing instead an almost classical sense of compositional design that balanced their focus on freedom. Their unanimity is striking; once beyond the initial theme each composition is based upon spontaneity and instrumental equality. Textures change constantly, from four-part polyphony to unaccompanied solos and all combinations inbetween. Due to the group's rhythmic flexibility, the time expands and contracts, demanding—and receiving—acute responsiveness from each musician. A clue to their cohesive interaction is Rudd's *Rosmosis*, suggesting the music's fluid density and exchange of position within its flow. Tchicai's willowy, lyrical phrasing contrasts with Rudd's exciting expressionism, and together they luxuriate in linear improvising, buoyed by Graves's waves of sound and Worrell's thoughtful foundation. Free music of drama and finely-wrought proportion. **AL**

New York Jazz Quartet

Song Of The Black Knight **Frank Wess** (ts, ss, f); **Roland Hanna** (p); **George Mraz** (b); **Richard Pratt** (d, perc). Sonet Ⓕ SNTCD 753 (40 minutes). Recorded 1977.

⑥ ❽

This quartet, formed in 1971, was the brainchild of Hanna and was not related to the Herbie Mann group operating in the mid-fifties with the same name. The original line-up included flautist Hubert Lewis, bassist Ron Carter and drummer Billy Cobham: the above personnel came together in the mid-seventies. The entire programme of this typical CD is made up of originals by members of the group, and they range from Hanna's elegant ballad *Time For The Dancers* to Wess's romping *Estoril Soul* blues. The style is refined bebop while the group's reputation for detailed rehearsal is reflected in the poise of their music and in their natural ease of execution. The rhythm section pivots around Mraz's immaculate and imaginative bass lines and there are continual harmonic affirmations from Hanna's keyboard. The pianist also solos impressively throughout, showing us his finest in the delicate climate of *Time For The Dancers* or rolling out the blues on *Estorial Soul*. Wess plays well on all of his horns, although his beautiful tenor reading of *After Paris*, his dancing soprano on *Romp In The Woods* and his fine attacking flute on *Terezia* are standouts. The group's demise in the eighties left a considerable gap in the overall portfolio of jazz styles. **BMcR**

New York Unit

Tribute to George Adams **Javon Jackson**, **Dan Faulk**, **George Adams** (ts), **John Hicks** (p), **Richard Davis** (b), **Santi Debriano** (b), **Tatsuya Nakamura** (d). Paddle Wheel Ⓕ KICJ 156 (68 minutes). Recorded 1991/92.

⑦ ❽

Initially comprising Adams, Davis, Hicks and Nakamura, the New York Unit first recorded in 1989, but it was not until the following year that they became a working and touring group. Hicks was a versatile solo voice at the heart of the core rhythm section and was well supported by Davis and Nakamura. However, they have always taken a sensible view of personnel flexibility in the current musical climate, and men such as Hannibal Peterson have featured with them. The first seven titles on this CD were made with Debriano in place of Davis and with Jackson playing on six. The new bassist fitted in well and *Fly Me To The Moon* suggests that the men concerned could do justice to a pure trio recording opportunity. The group is designed for a broader outlook, however, and former Messenger Jackson, a suitably extrovert player and NYU style aspirant, was a highly successful candidate for the horn chair. His solos on *Exodus, A Nightingale Sang* and *Moritat* are certainly the work of a saxophonist who thinks ahead and is able to present his ideas in a lucid and imaginative manner. Faulk contributes two adequate performances but it is Jackson's best work that presents the excellent New York Unit in full flower on this disc **BMcR**

New York Voices

What's Inside **Peter Eldridge**, **Caprice Fox**, **Laurence Kinham**, **Darmon Meader**, **Kim Nazarian** (v); **Claudio Roditi** (t); **Jay Ashby** (tb, perc); **Andy Erin** (p); **Randy Landau** (b); **Tommy Igoe** (d). GRP Ⓕ 97002 (53 minutes). Recorded 1993.

⑦ ❽

Vocal groups have not had an easy time of it in jazz, those enjoying the most successful careers having to usually criss-cross-over between the popular style of the day and straight-ahead jazz styles. This young group is no exception but happily everything it attempts it does with panache and good musical taste. Thus the opening track, *All Blues*, has an excellent and accurate arrangement by Darmon Meader (it even uses an arpeggio'd quotation from the piano accompaniment by Bill Evans of Miles's solo from the original recording) and while the lyrics are not deep or meaningful, they're not a liability either.

Of course other vocal outfits have beaten this path before (just as others have also treated soul classics like *Ain't No Sunshine* to this type of approach), and the most obvious models are LHB and Manhattan Transfer, so what New York Voices do isn't markedly original. The original compositions are the tracks most removed from the above models. But, be it on originals or covers, they blend beautifully, phrase accurately, and generally avoid tasteless elaboration and grandstanding. This alone makes **What's Inside** a highly enjoyable experience, as does the general lack of saccharine sentimentality. The musical accompaniments are highly competent, and everything is attacked with great spirit. The chancy idea of actually using Ella Fitzgerald's 1947 scat vocal for the central section of *Lady Be Good* (logically enough delivered as a tribute to Ella) in fact works very well (the rhythm tracks are—mercifully—perfectly matched, and it means no-one has to imitate Ella.

This is an impressively disciplined and varied album from a group with a jazz future. **KS**

Herbie Nichols

1919-1963

The Art of Herbie Nichols Nichols (p); **Al McKibbon**, **Teddy Kotick** (b); **Art Blakey**, **Max Roach** (d). Blue Note Ⓜ CDP7 99176-2 (65 minutes). Recorded 1955/56.

⑩ ❽

A splendid representation of the archetypal 'musician's musician'. It has 14 original pieces excerpted from the five sessions (available complete on a five-LP Mosaic set) which, his Bethlehem sessions aside, constitute almost his entire legacy; two of the items not issued at the time are included.

Spending his working life as an obscure backing pianist, Nichols created works which, until the eighties, were thought to be irredeemably bound up with his own playing style. This was often compared to his friend and contemporary Thelonious Monk—he was the first person to praise Monk in print—but is gentler and more flowing. He is also similar in being best-known for a ballad, called by the singer who added lyrics (and used the title for her book) *Lady Sings The Blues*. There is also a distant Ellington-Strayhorn influence; despite their diverging development, *Third World* could be a rewrite of *'A' Train*, while *Spinning Song* starts out on *Chelsea Bridge*.

Younger musicians such as Misha Mengelberg, Geri Allen and the annotator of this album Roswell Rudd have perpetuated Nichols's memory, but these recordings, with their highly creative percussion parts, are the equal of Monk's fifties trios with the same drummers. **BP**

Red Nichols

1905-1965

Rhythm of the Day Nichols (c); with a collective personnel including **Charlie Teagarden**, **Manny Klein** (t); **Miff Mole**, **Glenn Miller** (tb); **Jimmy Dorsey**, **Adrian Rollini**, **Benny Goodman**, **Fud Livingston** (reeds); **Arthur Schutt**, **Lennie Hayton** (p); **Eddie Lang**, **Dick McDonough**, **Carl Kress** (g); **Vic Berton** (d); **Joe Venuti** (vn) and others. ASV Living Era Ⓜ CD AJA 5025 (59 minutes). Recorded 1924-32.

It isn't often that jazz historians openly apologize for anything to their readers, but in the second volume of his long-running history of jazz, Gunther Schuller admits that he had many protests over his brusque treatment (in the first volume) of the music of Red Nichols. Schuller says that in the light of this lobbying he has listened again to Nichols's records and now fells he did the man an injustice.

Poor old Red Nichols. He has always suffered. Suffered from not being Bix Beiderbecke, not being black, not being an influence on other jazz players, not drinking himself to death. But what he did do was good enough; he surrounded himself with the best white New York musicians in the late twenties and evolved a brittle theatrical style of jazz which never got within hailing distance of any deep feeling, but did create attractive little miniatures. The number of records he made then and the number of angry letters Schuller got 50 years later shows that Nichols had and has a big fan club. This collection shows the pluses of the Nichols approach—a bright, shallowly-swinging feel, some quirky original arranging and some oddball tunes among the pop stuff. As 1930 approached, the bands got bigger and more cumbersome (it's the Jelly Roll Morton story all over again), but even then, in 1929, there was the unexpected bonus of Jack Teagarden and Glenn Miller running in tandem. All but forgotten ten years later, Red Nichols must have rubbed his eyes at the world-wide popularity of Glenn Miller, his erstwhile employee. **MK**

Lennie Niehaus

1929

The Octet No. 2 **Niehaus** (as); **Stu Williamson** (t); **Bob Enevoldsen** (vtb); **Bill Holman** (ts); **Jimmy Giuffre** (bs); **Pete Jolly** (p); **Monty Budwig** (b); **Shelly Manne** (d). Contemporary Ⓜ OJCCD 1767-2 (40 minutes). Recorded 1955.

⑧ ❽

Niehaus came to attention through his work with Stan Kenton, both as alto soloist and arranger. His move away from the playing side of jazz is a source of regret, although his behind-the-scenes work on the soundtrack music for the Clint Eastwood film **Bird** was valuable. This is actually the third album he did for Lester Koenig's Contemporary label, and it has the classic West Coast sound, with its beautifully-played ensemble passages, tight voicings, and a rhythm section sparked by Manne's highly imaginative drumming. Niehaus's tone is an amalgam of Parker and Benny Carter, warmer than that of Lee Konitz but lacking the emotion of Art Pepper. Lennie's arrangements certainly pack a great deal into a comparatively small space (the longest of the dozen tracks is just four minutes), such as the clever key changes in the last chorus of *Love Is Here To Stay*. There are four originals by Niehaus, and his *Circling The Blues* succeeds in revolving the chords of the blues through 12 keys with Lennie himself modulating from B to E then to A and into D before leading the ensemble into G. Everyone is given a chance to solo, the music retaining the freshness it possessed when it first appeared on LP. **AM**

Judy Niemack

Heart's Desire **Niemack** (v); **Kenny Barron** (p); **Eric Friedlander** (vc). Stash Ⓕ ST-CD-548 (57 minutes:) (57 minutes). Recorded 1991.

⑨ ❽

A tangential Tristano-ite by virtue of having studied with Warne Marsh, this young singer has developed a following among French hard-bop devotees on the strength of two discs she recorded for Freelance in the late eighties. This American release gives a better sense of her wide range. Coming across as a Barbra Streisand without the hysterics (although the influence of Sheila Jordan is also discernible), Niemack gives *Over the Rainbow* what might be its definitive interpretation. Combining the best of both worlds—a cabaret singer's respect for melody as written and a jazz singer's eagerness to have a go at it—she unearths a lyric to Monk's *Well, You Needn't*, takes the twitter out of Joni Mitchell's *All I Want*, and scats the bridge of Richard Rodgers's *The Sweetest Sounds* with genuine élan. Friedlander provides an effective one-man string section on a few tunes, including a lovely reading of Dave Frishberg's title tune. Barron displays the same sensitivity behind Niemack as he displayed behind Stan Getz. This is one of the finest vocal albums of recent years. **FD**

Mike Nock

1940

Dark and Curious **Nock** (p); **Tim Hopkins** (ts, recorder, v); **Cameron Undy** (b); **Andrew Dickeson** (d). veraBra Ⓕ vBr 2074-2 (49 minutes). Recorded 1990.

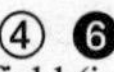

Nock, in many ways, is a down under version of Joe Zawinul. He also came to jazz from far afield (in Nock's case, New Zealand), initially arrived in the US to attend Berklee College, and relocated to the West Coast before founding an even-earlier electric jazz-rock group. The Fourth Way was less successful than Weather Report, though, and Nock soon returned to the piano in acoustic settings. Since 1985, he has been based in Australia, where this set was recorded by his quartet. While more satisfying jazz can be heard on his 1981 trio album **Ondas** (ECM 1220 829 161-2), where he works with Eddie Gomez and Jon Christensen, or on a Tomato quintet date yet to appear on CD, this session represents a broader range of his compositional interests, placing some of the trans-national notions of **The Fourth Way** in an acoustic context (*Dance of the Global Village*, for instance). The playing is workmanlike—one wishes Tim Hopkins would let loose more in his tenor solos. Hopkins also reads an original poem on the title track, while Nock applies clusters in the background. The studied nature of much of this music is indicative, though Nock does have the capacity to transcend the poses. **BB**

Jimmie Noone

1895-1944

Complete Recordings, Volume 1 **Jimmie Noone** (cl) with various personnel including **George Mitchell** (c); **Joe Poston** (as, cl); **Earl Hines, Zinky Cohn** (p); **Bud Scott** (g); **Johnny St Cyr**, **Junnie Cobb**, **Alex Hill** (bj); **Bill Newton** (tba); **Johnny Wells** (d). Affinity Ⓜ CD AFS 1027-3 (three discs: 210 minutes). Recorded 1926-30.

⑧ ❽

Most of the music on the three discs comes from Noone's rather grandly named Apex Club Orchestra. Over the years, this six-piece band has acquired semi-legendary status, largely because it was the first permanent virtuoso jazz group, the kind that other musicians talked about.

Despite his Irish name Jimmie Noone was a New Orleans Creole, part of the great Creole clarinet tradition that included Lorenzo Tio, Sidney Arodin, Barney Bigard and Albert Nicholas. The Creole clarinet style combined classical facility with the glissandi and bent notes of the blues. The famous opening to Gershwin's *Rhapsody In Blue* is a frank reference and tribute to the expressive power of the Creole clarinet, and its importance to jazz can hardly be exaggerated. Noone became the stylistic model of the young Goodman and through him influenced the whole of development of jazz.

The other great presence on the early Apex Club numbers is the piano of Earl Hines, very much an equal musical partner with Noone, as can be heard on this magnificent version of his composition *A Monday Date*. Between them they evolved a band style and a repertoire that is recognizably part of the modern world, based not on the multi-themed ragtime and march pattern but on the repeated 32-bar chorus which remained the staple jazz form through swing, bebop and beyond. But above all it is the sheer exuberance and sparkle of Noone's clarinet that catches the ear and lightens the spirit. **DG**

New Orleans Jazz Giants 1936-40 **Jimmy Noone, Johnny Dodds, Edmond Hall** (cl); **Red Allen, Natty Dominique, Guy Kelly, Charlie Shavers** (t); **Preston Jackson, Benny Morton** (tb); **Pete Brown** (as); **Francis Whitby** (ts); **Lil Armstrong, Richard M. Jones** (p); **Teddy Bunn, Lonnie Johnson** (g); **Israel Crosby, Pops Foster, Johnny Lindsay** (bs); **Baby Dodds, Tubby Hall, Zutty Singleton, O'Neil Spencer** (d). JSP Ⓕ JSPCD 336 (79 minutes). Recorded 1936-40.

✔ ⑧ ❽

It was rare for the clarinettist Jimmy Noone to achieve his potential. Too often his voluptuous and immaculate tone was directed at cloying performances of trivial tunes. Uniquely, ten of the 14 tracks by him on this album have him at his best and the apparently perverse setting of him against emergent young mainstream giants Charlie Shavers and Pete Brown works wonderfully, reaching its ultimate in *Four Or Five Times*, a classic which is graced, as are 14 of these titles, by the eloquent acoustic guitar playing of Teddy Bunn. By this period the veteran Noone was an anachronism, as was Johnny Dodds, but the eight sides under the leadership of the latter contain his only recorded work since the twenties, and although often ragged, they bulge with hot and potent improvisation.

Four tracks featuring the comparative youngster Edmond Hall in a band which doubles under the leadership of Henry Allen and Zutty Singleton are amongst the first to display his waspish tone at its best, and his smooth agility and facile mastery of the registers shows how Noone and Dodds had been left behind. Splendid trumpet from Allen and trombone from the neglected Benny Morton earn these tracks a place with the rest of the classics on an album of remarkable value. Like other JSP issues the body of the sound on the original 78s has been preserved in transfer by the gifted engineer John R.T. Davies. Some of the bigger companies could benefit from his example. **SV**

Red Norvo

1908

Knock On Wood **Norvo** (xyl, mba, vb); **Jimmy Dorsey, Artie Shaw, Johnny Mince** (cl); **Fulton McGrath, Teddy Wilson** (p); **Dick McDonough, Bobby Johnson, George Van Eps** (g); **Artie Bernstein, Hank Wayland, Gene Krupa, Billy Gussak** (d); **Benny Goodman** (bcl); **Jack Jenny** (tb); **Charlie Barnet, Chu Berry** (ts); **Bunny Berigan, Harry James** (t); **John Simmons** (b). Affinity Ⓜ CD AFS 1017 (66 minutes). Recorded 1933-37.

✔ ⑧ ❻

Norvo went on using the xylophone and marimba long after the vibraphone had become a more popular instrument. Even when he switched to vibraphone (which he does on a few titles here) he played it with the motor turned off, giving it a xylophone-like sound. This CD is made up of his earliest pick-up group recordings, plus some 1937 titles under Teddy Wilson's name. They predate his own band, the one with the vocals by his wife Mildred Bailey and the Eddie Sauter arrangements, and some idea of the quality of the music may be judged from the important soloists who appear, men such as Artie Shaw, Bunny Berigan, Jack Jenny, Chu Berry and Jimmy Dorsey. Benny Goodman provides the unusual bass clarinet sound on Beiderbecke's tune *In A Mist* and Norvo's own impressionistic *Dance Of The Octopus*. Norvo's solos have weathered the years well, even his habit of hammering away at the occasional note in the absence of a mechanical way of sustaining the tone. James performs well in this small group setting, and it is worth listening out for John Simmons's musicianly bass lines. The transfers have been generally well done using the CEDAR system. **AM**

The Red Norvo-Charles Mingus-Tal Farlow Trio Volume 2 **Norvo** (vb); **Tal Farlow** (g); **Charles Mingus** (b). Vintage Jazz Classics Ⓜ VJC-1008-2 (78 minutes). Recorded 1943-50.

⑧ ❹

This trio's mixture of lilting melody and bebop improvisation is unique. The music is devoid of crowd-pleasing elements and maintains an unusually high standard of improvisation. From his earliest ventures on vibraphone in the thirties Norvo always showed a subtlety on the instrument which kept him from depending on the raw rhythmic impact of Lionel Hampton. He usually kept to a tighter sound than Hampton's, probably something of a throwback to his earliest days on the xylophone.

The speed and facility of the trio at first frightened both Farlow and Mingus; 'Tal used to quit every night,' Norvo recalled. The setting gives Tal Farlow every opportunity to play and his radiant solos are amongst the best recorded by a guitarist during the bebop period.

There are 30 tracks here by the trio of 1949-50 and three added tracks by a Norvo Septet backing Helen Ward on recordings for V-disc. These last tracks are, however, very poorly recorded and are mostly of interest for some early Flip Phillips tenor. **SV**

Jivin' The Jeep **Norvo** (xyl); **Bill Hyland**, **Stewart Pletcher**, **Louis Mucci**, **George Wendt** (t); **Leo Moran**, **Eddie Sauter** (tb); **Frank Simeone** (as); **Slats Long**, **Hank D'Amico** (cl, as); **Len Goldstein** (as); **Charles Lamphere** (as, ts); **Herbie Haymer** (ts); **Joe Liss**, **Bill Miller** (p); **Dave Barbour**, **Red McGarvey** (g); **Pete Robinson** (b); **Mo Purtill** (d); **Mildred Bailey**, **Lew Hurst** (v). Hep Ⓜ CD 1019 (64 minutes). Recorded 1936/37.

⑧ ❻

Norvo, after a series of unflattering jobs at the end of the twenties, joined the Paul Whiteman Orchestra in 1929 on the recommendation of his sweetheart and subsequent wife, Mildred Bailey. For much of the early thirties he played around New York, and made at least one immortal session in 1933 (not included here) where he coupled his arrangement of Bix's *In A Mist* with his own Ravel-influenced *Dance of the Octopus*. At the beginning of the period covered by this CD, Norvo was married to Bailey and leading his own small orchestra. He had single-handedly wrested the xylophone from the clutches of vaudeville (much as Hawkins had done with the tenor sax a decade previously) and had taken on board as an arranger Eddie Sauter, a singularly gifted musician with a significantly different approach from the predominating swing style of the time.

The music which resulted from all this has a passing resemblance to the Teddy Wilson aggregations, often featuring Billie Holiday, which were being made for Brunswick at this time, but Norvo's was always the more formal band. Bailey, no match for Billie as an extemporizing singer, required a firmer arranging hand and got it from Sauter, delivering some of her happiest and most memorable performances in the process, while Norvo showed just why connoisseurs regard him as one of the great unrecognized improvisers of jazz. His incredible freedom over the regulation swing beat, his limitless technique, and his familiarity with several improvisatory procedures (paraphrase, theme-and-variations, etc.) are all to be savoured. This is not the most obvious music from the swing era, but it is some of the most rewarding for those prepared to break the surface. **KS**

Anita O'Day

1919

Pick Yourself Up **O'Day** (v); **Harry Edison** (t); **Larry Bunker** (vb); **Paul Smith** (p); **Barney Kessel** (g); **Joe Mondragon** (b); **Alvin Stoller** (d); **Buddy Bregman Orchestra**. Verve Ⓜ 517 329-2 (66 minutes). Recorded 1956.

⑧ ❽

Anita O'Day is incapable of singing anything which is not jazz, *vide* her attempt here at making a hit record with the almost unjazzable *Rock 'n' Roll Waltz*. Let us hasten to add that the tune's presence is an aberration and that most of the 21 songs are ideal material for O'Day.

Her long career reached its peak in the fifties and sixties when she recorded for Verve. Her very best session (with the Gary McFarland Orchestra) remains unissued on CD, but her Verve performances which are already on CD are of uniformly high quality.

O'Day takes to herself the freedom of an instrumentalist more than any other of her peers. Impeccable timing and imagination make her improvisations exceptionally fine, and her dexterity with fast numbers is matched by the beautiful poise of her ballad singing. Her voice is mannered with some of the soft rasp of Billie Holiday, but she justifies any of her quirks with the high quality of her beautifully crafted jazz performances. Incidentally, the date's arranger Buddy Bregman has been consistently undervalued, usually by being cast in the shade of Nelson Riddle. His orchestras are always good and his arrangements sometimes rival Riddle's. He uses good soloists sparingly: Bob Cooper makes a lovely entry after the cool brass ensemble on *I Never Had A Chance*. Harry Edison heads the typical Verve small group on five tracks. This band could have been much improved by the substitution of regular pianist Jimmy Rowles for Smith. **SV**

Claus Ogerman 1930

Featuring Michael Brecker **Randy Brecker** (t, flh); **Michael Brecker** (ts); **Robben Ford**, **Dean Parks** (g); **Alan Pasqua** (kbds); **Marcus Miller**, **Abraham Laboriel**, **Eddie Gomez** (b); **Vinnie Colaiuta**, **Steve Gadd** (d); **Paulinho DaCosta** (perc). GRP Ⓕ GRD-9632 (44 minutes). Recorded 1991.

⑧ ❽

As might be expected from an album masterminded by a man equally at home in the classical and jazz worlds, with a string of compositions for the likes of Carlos Jobim, Bill Evans and Oscar Peterson behind him, this is by no means conventional fusion fare, despite its overall sound, its instrumentation and the fact that it features the cream of contemporary jazz fusion musicians. True, Marcus Miller, the master of the ubiquitous percussive bass, and Robben Ford, ditto of the strangled-sounding electric guitar, are strongly featured, as are many other indispensable figures from the genre—Steve Gadd and Randy Brecker prominent among them—but Claus Ogerman has used this highly respected pool of musicians chiefly as providers of a sound palette for five startlingly original compositions. The strength of the album thus derives from the extraordinary variety of textures, ranging from light washes of synthesized sound to muscular, vigorous backdrops enlivened by energetic percussive effects, against which Michael Brecker, one of the world's undisputed masters of contemporary saxophone technique, can perform. As ever, Brecker, his sound perhaps over-familiar these days from having been paid the sincerest form of flattery, performs faultlessly, and his grainy but sophisticated sound is perfectly complemented by his collaborators. It is Ogerman's subtly memorable compositions, however, evocative but with a surprisingly tense and virile core, which make the album so rewarding to sustained and close attention. **CP**

Dave O'Higgins 1963

Beats Working for a Living **O'Higgins** (ss, ts); **Joe Locke** (vb); **Joey Calderazzo** (p); **James Genus** (b); **Adam Nussbaum** (d). EFZ Ⓕ 1009 (53 minutes). Recorded 1994.

⑧ ❽

After a well-received début, **All Good Things**, where he led a UK rhythm section, British saxophonist Dave O'Higgins has sensibly decided to throw himself in at the deep end by fronting a stellar New York band. They play with all the easy virtuosic bustle and commitment associated with such musicians, Joey Calderazzo all scalding, sure-footed runs and his rhythm-team partners fleet, assured and cogent. The presence of Joe Locke, however, lifts the recording out of the ordinary run of such albums; his addition to the front line imparts an attractive buoyancy to the overall band sound, his soloing is always fluent and tasteful (despite his irritating habit of humming tunelessly in support of it) and he is careful not to get in Calderazzo's way during their comping duties. As with O'Higgins's début the material is mostly original, but the album opens with a robustly swinging *Alone Together* and finishes with a fine, slow-burning version of Charles Mingus's *Duke Ellington's Sound of Love*. On the meat of the album, six pithy themes ranging from straightforward blowing vehicles to gently lilting ballads, O'Higgins, as he used to do with his previous bands Roadside Picnic and Gang of Three, shows off a world-class talent, his swirling tenor and plangent soprano by no means overawed by the heavy company he is keeping on this highly enjoyable album. **CP**

Toru 'Tiger' Okoshi 1950

Two Sides To Every Story **Okoshi** (t); **Mike Stern** (g); **Gil Goldstein** (p); **Dave Holland** (b); **Jack DeJohnette** (d). JVC Ⓕ 2039-2 (66 minutes). Recorded 1994.

⑥ ❽

Okoshi made his first recording in homeland Japan in 1971 before moving to America the following year. There he rapidly came to public notice with Gary Burton and made his US recording debut, with guitarist Baird Hersey in 1977. He also led a band of his own, playing strident, hard-hitting trumpet with Miles Davis's group as role model and stylistic guide for his 'Baku' brand of jazz-rock. In fact, his own playing was some distance from Davis. Okoshi delivered clean-cut power, where Davis dealt in implication; Okoshi was outspoken and his approach was patently more vertical.

Although it was a style with its own appeal, this album, with its outstanding rhythm section and basically hard bop policy, suggest that this might be a more productive route for him. His fusion mode translates easily into straight-ahead blowing and his full-frontal trumpet on titles like *Finders Keepers* and *What It Was* illustrate this perfectly. On the debit side, his blues playing on *Monday Blues* remains too verbose, but his more restrained muted work on the waltz, *Yuki No Furu Machi O* and the relaxation he displays on the album's title track point to a direction that could serve him better in future. **BMcR**

Old and New Dreams

A Tribute to Blackwell **Don Cherry** (t); **Dewey Redman** (ts); **Charlie Haden** (b); **Ed Blackwell** (d). Black Saint Ⓕ 120 113-2 (48 minutes). Recorded 1987.

⑧ ❽

Old and New Dreams, formed in 1976 by four former Ornette Coleman alumni, continued up to the recent death of drummer Blackwell to champion the beautiful free jazz that its initiator has now largely abandoned. In the process, the band has continually produced jazz that maintains the high compositional and improvisation standards set by the instigator. Three of the tunes on this CD are Coleman originals and *Dewey's Tune* sounds as if it could have been another. The formula for performance also follows the classic quartet's pattern, allowing reasonably lengthy horn solos on every track. On this occasion it is Redman who is the pick of them; in each solo he draws questions from the parent theme and answers them convincingly. His journeys away from each original motif can become tortuous as he moves from an easily identifiable point of departure to a solo conclusion that is less obvious.

This was not a good period for Cherry, but here he plays well. His plaintively whispy tone is exploited to good effect on *Law Years* and, most especially on *Street Woman*, we have the 'old' Cherry dancing through his solos in a waywardly perverse, yet naturally appealing way. Haden and Blackwell formed the best of all Coleman's excellent rhythm teams and there is no lowering of standards as Old and New Dreams perpetuate the original Coleman ethos. **BMcR**

King Oliver

1885-1938

King Oliver's Jazz Band 1923 **Oliver**, **Louis Armstrong** (c); **Honore Dutrey** (tb); **Johnny Dodds** (cl); **Lil Hardin** (p); **Bud Scott** (bj); **Baby Dodds** (d) on eight tracks, add **Johnny St Cyr** or **Bud Scott** (bj); **Charlie Jackson** (b). Jazz Archives Ⓑ 157 46-2 (44 minutes). Recorded 1923.

✔ ⑩ ❹

Nowhere on the sleeve or in the liner notes of this album are you told as much, but these are all 15 of the famous Oliver band Okeh sides. Why this should be something worth noting has everything to do with the greatly superior sound quality of the Okeh recording process over the contemporaneous Gennett. Oliver recorded his band for both labels in 1923 and although the resultant music is glorious in both instances, the listening pleasure is greatly enhanced on the Okehs for the simple reason that you can hear it so much better. Indeed, this CD seems to be an improvement on the excellent job achieved by World Record Club on their vinyl transfers of the early eighties, so there is an added reason to acquire this disc.

So much for the sound quality (or lack of it—these, after all, are still imperfect acoustic-process recordings); what about the music? Stepping aside from its historical importance for a moment (the Oliver band was the greatest living example of the New Orleans outdoor tradition when it made these Chicago recordings), this music is so full of invention, spirit and wit that it is still a lesson in creativity to anyone who cares to listen. The dual lines worked out for the two cornets by Oliver and Armstrong are fascinating enough, but add the brilliant accompanying figures of Johnny Dodds and the overall cohesion-through-interplay, on a remarkably supple rhythmic base, and you have a heady musical brew. Something else of which Oliver is also a master is drama and contrast (on a personal level he displays this in his various tonal distortions through the use of mutes and growls), and there are countless times (the most famous is probably *Snake Rag*) where this happens. It is worth remembering that Oliver—as opposed to Armstrong—was a songwriter of some significance, and his overall sense of form is reflected in the way his band functions here. **KS**

Volume 1: Great Original Performances 1923-29 **Oliver** (c); **Louis Armstrong**, **Bob Shoffner** (t); **Honore Dutrey**, **Kid Ory** (tb); **Bert Cobb** (bb); **Johnny Dodds**, **Jimmie Noone**, **Buster Bailey** (cl); **Charlie Jackson**, **Albert Nicholas**, **Billy Paige**, **Barney Bigard**, **Stump Evans**, **Darnell Howard** (reeds); **Lil Hardin**, **Jelly Roll Morton**, **Luis Russell** (p); **Bill Johnson**, **Bud Scott**, **Johnny St. Cyr** (bj); **Eddie Lang**, **Lonnie Johnson** (g); **Baby Dodds** (d); **Paul Barbarin** (d, v); **Richard M. Jones**, **Georgia Taylor** (v). (**Tommy Dorsey** (t); **Arthur Schutt** (harmonium); **Eddie Lang** (g); **Jimmy Williams** (b); **Stan King** (d). Robert Parker/CDS Ⓕ RPCD 607 (62 minutes). Recorded 1923-29.

⑧ ❼

Oliver's position is secure as the first great New Orleans bandleader who left substantial aural evidence of his achievements. Freddie Keppard or Mutt Carey, who recorded less and later, may have been considered more important instrumentalists, as indeed were several players who made no records at all such as Buddy Bolden, but Oliver did what mattered when it mattered, and with a microphone near. While it's true that the amazing 1922-23 Creole Jazz Band—heard on the first ten tracks—is now studied for the earliest recorded work of Armstrong and Johnny Dodds, Oliver's bluesy lead has a direct simplicity which is moving in itself (and a clear influence on the mature Armstrong). The collective interplay which is the true joy of classic New Orleans jazz doesn't stifle variety, as may be savoured by comparing *Mabel's Dream*, *Weather Bird* and *Snake Rag*, all at the same tempo and in the same key.

The clarity of Robert Parker's remastering makes these and the Oliver/Jelly Roll Morton duo *King Porter Stomp* eminently listenable, while it merely emphasizes the inferior sound of the seven tracks of Oliver's Henderson-influenced Dixie Syncopators. The last track, included in order to dissuade cloth-eared discographers from hearing Dorsey's trumpet on the preceding Blind Willie Dunn items, merely underlines Oliver's superiority. **BP**

Sugar Foot Strut **Oliver** (c); **Bob Shoffner**, **Tick Gray** (t); **Kid Ory**, **Jimmy Archey** (tb); **Albert Nicholas**, **Barney Bigard**, **Darnell Howard**, **Stump Evans**, **Johnny Dodds**, **Omer Simeon**, **Arville Harris** (reeds); **Luis Russell**, **Clarence Williams**, **Richard M Jones** (p); **Bud Scott**, **Leroy Harris** (bj); **Bert Cobb**, **Cyrus St Clair** (tba); **Paul Barbarin** (d). MCA/Decca Ⓜ GRP 16162 (64 minutes). Recorded 1926-28.

⑧ ❻

This is the band which Oliver formed following the break-up of his Creole Jazz Band. The Creole Jazz Band had played pure New Orleans dance-hall music and its records, in effect, launched jazz on the world. The Dixie Syncopators was an entirely different kind of band, an early form of the standard American dance orchestra, arranged in sections and playing mainly from written parts, with improvised solos interspersed. Even so, it was still a band of New Orleans players capable of producing that loose, rolling beat and those hot, blues-inflected solos which the rest of the world was only just beginning to get the hang of (compare this with the stiffness of the contemporary Fletcher Henderson band).

At their best, in numbers like *Wa Wa Wa* and *Too Bad*, the Syncopators are magnificent and Oliver's bright, clear-toned cornet comes through clearly for the first time, thanks to the new electrical recording process. The only trouble is with the arrangements. The craft of jazz arranging was still at a very crude stage, and there is a great deal of footling around with tricky breaks and novelty effects, not to mention some truly appalling saxophone playing by men who were nearly all superb New Orleans Creole clarinettists. Nevertheless, these are classic recordings in a well-chosen and very effectively transferred selection. **DG**

Oregon

Oregon **Paul McCandless** (ss, ob, f, ehn h, bcl, musette); **Ralph Towner** (kbds, g); **Glen Moore** (b, va, p); **Collin Walcott** (perc, sitar, v). ECM Ⓕ 1258 (811 711-2) (45 minutes). Recorded 1983.

⑧ ❿

Few, if any, ensembles so successfully incorporate such a welter of musical influences as the jazz chamber group Oregon. Formed in 1970 from four former members of the Paul Winter Consort, Oregon assemble their adventurous but utterly distinctive music from astonishingly diverse sources, classical, so-called 'world' music and jazz chief among them. From a bewildering array of available instrumentation—the group members play around 70 instruments between them—and exploiting both the improvisational latitude of jazz and the attention to nuance and dynamic subtlety commonly associated with classical music, Oregon construct closely worked sound-sculptures of great textural variety and harmonic originality. Their material ranges from composed tunes with flowing, sinuous themes set against a wash of synthesized and percussive sound to improvised pieces involving, say, a viola, oboe and hand drums or sitar and Indian-style vocals. The result might be a mite ethereal for some tastes, and titles like *Beside The Brook* and *There Was No Moon That Night* misleadingly locate the group as New Age pioneers, but the skill, commitment and patent sincerity of the musicians shines through everything they do, and on this, their definitive album, made for ECM with its customary flawless Eicher production, their considerable strengths are showcased to perfection. **CP**

Original Dixieland Jazz Band

The 75th Anniversary **Nick LaRocca** (c); **Eddie Edwards** (tb); **Larry Shields** (cl); **Henry Ragas** (p); **Tony Sbarbaro** (d); **Benny Krueger** (as); **J. Russel Robinson** (p); **Frank Signorelli** (p); **Clifford Cairns**, **Eddie King**, **Al Bernard** (v). Bluebird Ⓜ ND 90650 (70 minutes). Recorded 1917-21.

⑦ ❼

It is an over-simplification to see the ODJB, unquestionably the first jazz band to record, as a mere copy of the Negro original. The black origins of jazz are indisputable, but the cross-fertilization of ideas between all ethnic groups, not least the Creoles, complicated the New Orleans situation. This CD shows the ODJB's early work for Victor as a mixture of inspired composition, strategic borrowing and ragged performance. The trumpet-trombone-clarinet line-up and its faintly hick version of the New Orleans ensemble satisfied the purist historians, but the actual performances were frequently untidy. LaRocca's cliché-laden lead was effective, however, and his willingness to leave the decoration to Shields and the punctuation to Edwards worked for the band. Titles such as *Livery Stable Blues*, *At The Jazz Band Ball*, *Tiger Rag* and *Fidgety Feet* became models for nearly all later recordings of these pieces, although the introduction of Krueger in 1920 produced sophistry rather than refinement. It was not until their return from Europe in 1921 that the band, now with the excellent Signorelli on piano, recaptured something of its early spirit. RCA Victor did a series of remakes in the thirties (available on an RCA Jazz Tribune 2-CD set), but these are the genuine article. **BMcR**

Orleysa

Orleysa **Jan Magne Forde** (t, flh); **Tore Brunborg** (ss, ts); **Arve Furseth** (p, syn, kbds, acc); **Rolf Presto** (b); **Terje Isungset** (d, perc); **Berit Pheim**, **Ann Elisabeth Lunde** (v) Odin Ⓕ NJ 4039-2 (39 minutes) Recorded 1991.

⑥ ❽

This is part of the Jazz Out of Norway series on Odin records, a Norwegian label which has the assistance of that country's arts council. For which we must be thankful, because this band is unique in its combination of traditional Norwegian folk music and the jazz idiom. The most obvious place where the Norwegian influence strikes one's ear is the singing of Pheim and Lunde, often in unison or harmony, mostly using Nordic rhythm and simple folkish melodies. The way this sits with jazz syncopation and some occsionally very complex meters is exciting, and it often makes up for some of the trumpet solos, which are routine in what they have to say and how they say it.

The group is least interesting when they use conventional jazz techniques for too long, the music tending to drift too close for comfort to the softer edges of fusion and daytime TV sounds. But when it works (mostly on the arrangements of traditional songs), the effect is well worth a listen. **KS**

Anthony Ortega

1928

New Dance! **Ortega** (as); **Chuck Domanico**, **Bobby West** (b); **Bill Goodwin** (d). hat ART Ⓕ 6065 (70 minutes). Recorded 1966/67.

⑧ ❽

This disc combines **New Dance!** and **Permutations,** two remarkable LPs by this Mexican-American from Los Angeles, a onetime Lionel Hampton sideman then working with Gerald Wilson's big band. These duo (with Domanico) and trio (West and Goodwin) performances parallel contemporary developments—Ornette Coleman's elastic approach to song form, the eerie openness of Albert Ayler's trio—but Ortega sounds like neither saxophonist. His plaintive but muscular sax sound and ensemble dynamic set him apart.

These intimate settings convey a great sense of mood, often stark and melancholy, on both original tunes and lightweight fare like *The Shadow of Your Smile*, a ten-minute free dialogue with Domanico, who is an unusually nimble and full-sounding arco player and a close listener. There is a constant air of discovery about these pieces, meditative as chamber music but full of risk. Every detail sounds revealed to both players and listeners simultaneously.

Exquisite as these recordings are, there is nothing similar among Ortega's rare later albums. Like other West Coast jazzers, thereafter he devoted most of his energies to anonymous studio work. However his (credited) solos waft memorably across the soundtrack to John Cassavetes' 1980 film **Gloria.** **KW**

Kid Ory

1886-1973

Ory's Creole Trombone **Kid Ory** (tb, v); with a collective personnel including **Mutt Carey** (c, t); **King Oliver**, **Bob Shoffner**, **George Mitchell** (c); **Louis Armstrong** (c, v); **Dink Johnson**, **Johnny Dodds**, **Omer Simeon**, **Jimmie Noone** (cl); **Albert Nicholas**, **Billy Paige**, **Darnell Howard**, **Stump Evans** (cl, ss, as); **Barney Bigard** (cl, ss, ts); **Joe Clarke** (as); **Fred Washington**, **Luis Russell**, **Lil Armstrong**, **Jelly Roll Morton**, **Buster Wilson** (p); **Bud Scott** (bj); **Johnny St. Cyr** (bj, g); **Bud Scott** (g); **Bert Cobb** (bb); **Ed Garland**, **John Lindsay** (b); **Ben Borders**, **Paul Barbarin**, **Zutty Singleton**, **Andrew Hilaire** (d). ASV Ⓜ CD AJA5148 (76 minutes). Recorded 1922-44.

⑧ ❻

This CD gathers together some of the finest and most representative examples of Kid Ory's unique tailgate trombone playing from his musically most productive years. The collection opens with *Ory's Creole Trombone* and *Society Blues,* dating from 1922 and generally considered to be the very first recordings by a black New Orleans band. Although probably more of historic than musical interest, the elements of Ory's style are clearly on display. His massive, powerful sound was always producing just the right notes in the ensemble and although many tried to copy him, none succeeded. He plays a vital role with the 'big' band of King Oliver, but some of his finest work will be found on the six tracks by what was in fact the Armstrong Hot Five minus Louis and with Joe Clarke added on alto. George Mitchell's cornet-playing is excellent but obviously not on a par with that of Armstrong, yet Louis's absence seems to give the band a more balanced feeling. The fine recording balance allows us to savour the clarity of the New Orleans Bootblacks. Four tracks under Jelly Roll Morton's name a few months later reunited Ory and Mitchell for more classic music (listen to Kid on *Smokehouse Blues*) but a lack of interest in this kind of music caused Ory to leave the business for a decade. The final five tracks come from the Orson Welles-sponsored Mercury Theatre broadcasts and mark Ory's comeback with a fine band containing Jimmie Noone, who died a matter of days after the last of their titles were recorded. The music is exuberant good fun but Ory was already past his peak in creative terms, although he continued to lead excellent bands right into the sixties. **AM**

Kid Ory's Creole Jazz Band 1954 **Ory** (tb, v); **Alvin Alcorn** (t); **George Probert** (cl); **Don Ewell** (p); **Bill Newman** (g); **Ed Garland** (b); **Minor Hall** (d). Good Time Jazz Ⓜ L 12004 (47 minutes). Recorded 1954.

⑦ ❻

For those suspicious of the Original Dixieland Jazz Band's credentials, it has been suggested that the Ory's Sunshine Orchestra titles of 1922 were the first genuine jazz recordings. What is not in doubt is that Ory led a well-regarded band in New Orleans from 1913 to 1919 and that, after moving to Chicago in 1925, worked for King Oliver as well as making superb records as a sideman with Louis Armstrong, Jelly Roll Morton and the New Orleans Wanderers. He retired from music in 1933, but when he did return, he was on hand to play a prominent part in the New Orleans revival. This CD comes from the middle of his second career, which stretched from 1942 to 1966, and is rather better than albums featuring spectacular trumpeters such as Teddy Buckner or Red Allen, thereby demonstrating how well Ory balanced his own bands. Hardly an inventive soloist himself, he was a master of the tailgate trombone and an adept user of mutes. More significantly, titles like *The Saints, Yellow Dog Blues* and *Clarinet Marmalade* show him as a wise selector of tempos, an adroit exploiter of dynamic levels and a leader able to bring out the best in his soloists. In a revival movement beset by a large number of obvious amateurs, Ory was always a professional. **BMcR**

Mike Osborne 1941

Outback **Osborne** (as); **Harry Beckett** (t); **Chris McGregor** (p); **Harry Miller** (b); **Louis Moholo** (d). Future Music Ⓕ FMR CD07-031994 (44 minutes). Recorded 1970.

⑧ ❽

A Guildhall School Of Music graduate, alto saxophonist Osborne distinguished himself in the big bands of Mike Westbrook and Brotherhood Of Breath. He was part of SOS with John Surman and Alan Skidmore and made up a stunning duo with Stan Tracey. Many listeners were introduced to his music during a five-year residency at London's Peanuts Club, but little more than ten years later his passionate musical voice had been silenced by ill health.

Jackie McLean was an early influence but, wooed by the greater freedoms of Ornette Coleman, Osborne evolved a style that acknowledged both. Little of his work is currently available but this CD shows him to be a distinctive and dynamic player. It marks him out as a saxophonist of creative consistency, natural lyricism and as one blessed with a poignancy of tone that instantly engages the listener. For Osborne, swinging was not something to be achieved; it was something he did instinctively. Rather than disrupt his line, startling intervallic leaps inspired his soloing process and made his entire style unpredictable. His note placements are especially deft and on *So It Is*, in particular, he benefits from a rhythm section as capable of grass-rustling subtlety as they are of gale force challenge. **BMcR**

Greg Osby 1960

3-D Lifestyles **Osby** (as, ss); **Darrell Grant**, **Geri Allen** (p); other instrumentalists unnamed; Bad Newz, RM, Lamar Supreme, Mal-Blak, Mustafo (vl). (**Cassandra Wilson** (vl) -1 track only.). Blue Note Ⓕ CDP 7 98635 2 (53 minutes). Recorded c.1993.

⑥ ❽

Altoist Osby has made a considerable name for himself in the last few years by his association with Steve Coleman and others, and guest appearances for Andrew Hill and Dianne Reeves. As shown in his earliest albums, his playing is potentialty as versatile as Coleman's, despite a similar urge to be at the cutting edge. This is his second collaboration with rappers and more than its predecessor, makes their recitations less stilted through his much-needed live input. The verbal content of the different tracks is a fair old mix-up, ranging from typical self-promotion to brief praise for such as Thelonious Monk the dedicatee of one whole track which alludes to his *Green Chimneys*. The pianists' contributions on three tracks each are decorative rather than organic and, though Osby plays virtually throughout he is frequently subordinated to the rapping and the apparently sampled rhythms. (No credits are given for these, and there is no mention anywhere of a further version of the opening *Mr. Gutterman* as the closing track). Whether or not you accept the comment of black-music expert Taj Mahal that hiphop is now as significant as bebop was, this is an example that deserves to be heard. **BP**

Johnny Otis 1921

The Original Johnny Otis Show **Johnny Otis Big Band**: **Otis** (d, ldr, arr); **Teddy Buckner**, **Billy Jones**, **Loyal Walker**, **Harry Parr** (t); **Henry Coker**, **Eli Robinson**, **John Pettigrew**, **Jap Jones** (tb); **Gene Bloch**, **Bob Harris** (as); **Paul Quinichette**, **James Von Streeter** (ts); **Leon Beck** (bs); **Bill Doggett** (p, arr); **Bernie Cobbs** (g); **Curtis Counce** (b); **Jimmy Rushing** (v) (4 tracks. **Johnny Otis & His Orchestra**: from - **Don Johnson**, **Lee Graves**, **John Anderson** (t); **George Washington** (tb); **Floyd**

Turnham (as); **Lorenzo Holden, James Von Streeter, Big Jay McNeely** (ts); **Walter Henry, Bobby McNeely** (bs); **Devonia Williams** (p, v); **Johnny Otis** (vb, v); **Pete Lewis** (g); **Mario Delgarde** (b); **Leard Bell** (d); **Little Esther, Junior Ryder, Red Lyte, Mel Walker, The Robins, Preacher Lee Graves** (v); **Marilyn Scott** (remaining tracks). Savoy Ⓜ SV-0266 (76 minutes). Recorded 1945/51.

⑦ ❻

Otis has spent the vast majority of his 50-year career in the realms of r&b and soul, but his beginnings were in jazz, and jazz inflected everything he did up to the mid-fifties at least. These sides, made for the Exclusive and Savoy labels and all recorded in L.A., are his first sessions, with the first date comprising three straight-ahead Basie-type jazz outings and the big ballad, *Harlem Nocturne*, a major juke hit at the time. The rest of the music on this CD (which duplicates a mid-seventies double-lp compiled by Bob Porter, but omits the final 6 tracks due to space limitations) veers between straight instrumental r&b and a range of vocal styles which move from blues to protoype fifties harmony groups. As such it has little place in this guide, but there is enough jazz juice for it to be a fascinating parallel odyssey to what else was going on, and a valuable glimpse into the black hinterland between straight blues, chart-type pop and mainstream jazz: a hinterland which was eventually to become the mainstream of popular youth music as the fifties gathered pace. **KS**

Roberto Ottaviano

Items From The Old Earth **Ottaviano** (ss); **Mario Arcari** (ob, eng h, ss); **Sandro Cerino** (cl, bcl, f, bf); **Martin Mayes** (frh); **Roberto Rossi** (tb, shells); **Fiorenzo Gualandris** (tba). Splasc(h) Ⓕ 332-2 (51 minutes). Recorded 1990.

⑧ ❽

As his imaginative solo soprano saxophone album, various quartet dates, and featured sideman role in Franz Koglmann's Pipetet show, Ottaviano is a singular player with a warm lyric flow and almost classical sound. But this fine disc finds him in another format, fronting an ensemble of unusual breadth for jazz. Known as the Six Mobiles, the band's first LP was devoted to Mingus material, a remarkable début that emphasized their links to the jazz tradition. In this CD they expand into original territory, and it is the intricate writing which distinguishes the music. Each member contributes at least one composition and arrangement, no two are alike. The group can sound like a classical wind quintet or a brass band in an Italian piazza, and they swing when it's needed. At times the music threatens to become too genteel, but at that point they are liable to slide into a foot-tapping riff or just as easily dissolve into a prismatic polyphony. Such a democratic approach means that Ottaviano and the phenomenal oboist Mario Arcari must sacrifice solo space; the ensemble's interplay is a marvel, however. **AL**

Oran 'Hot Lips' Page

1908-1954

Hot Lips Page And His Band, 1938-40 **Page** (t, v); with on four tracks: **Ben Smith** (cl, as); **Sam Simmons** (ts); **Jimmy Reynolds** (p); **Connie Wainwright** (g); **Wellman Braud** (b); **Alfred Taylor** (d); on 12 tracks: **Bobby Moore, Eddie Mullens, Dave Page** (t); **George Stevenson, Harry White** (tb); **Ulysses Scott, Ben Williams** (cl, as); **Benny Waters, Ernie Powell** (ts); **Jimmy Reynolds** (p); **Connie Wainwright** (g); **Abe Bolar** (b); **Alfred Taylor** (d); **Delores Payne, Ben Bowers** (v); on six tracks: **Buster Smith** (cl, as); **Jimmy Powell** (as); **Sam Davis** (ts); **Jimmy Reynolds** (p); **Abe Bolar** (b); **Ed McConney** (d); **Romayne Jackson, The Highlanders** (v); on four tracks: **Eddie Barefield** (cl, as): **Don Stovall** (as); **Don Byas** (ts); **Pete Johnson** (p); **John Collins** (g); **Abe Bolar** (b); **A.G. Godley** (d); **Beal Morton** (v). Classics Ⓜ 561 (72 minutes). Recorded 1938-40.

⑥ ❻

Lips Page was a big star with the Bennie Moten and early Basie bands to the point where agent Joe Glaser signed him to an exclusive contract in which he would be featured in front of the Basie band. Unfortunately for Page, Glaser forgot to ask the Count first, so the trumpeter became the leader of his own small bands, notably those featured here on this excellent chronology. Louis apart, no-one could better Lips as a blues singer-cum-trumpeter, and the tracks of the greatest value here are those using the 12-bar formula. The 12 tracks made for Bluebird with a 13-piece band are pleasant and efficiently performed (Page had a knack of discovering lesser-known but fine players such as pianist Jimmy Reynolds and tenor saxist Sam Simmons), but the meat of the collection is the ten tracks made in 1940 for Decca. Six of these have 'Professor' Buster Smith on alto, one of Charlie Parker's early idols. *Lafayette* and *South* are by a specially assembled band and were made for Decca's **Kansas City Jazz** album; there is a lurching increase in tempo in the last chorus of *South*, a remastering fault. That aside, the transfers are excellent. **AM**

Marty Paich

1925

Moanin' **Paich** (p, arr, leader); with a collective personnel of **Conte Candoli, Jack Sheldon, Al Porcino, Frank Beach, Stu Williamson** (t); **Bob Envoldsen, George Roberts** (tb); **Vince DeRosa**

(frh); **Art Pepper** (as); **Bill Perkins** (ts); **Bill Hood, Jimmy Giuffre** (bs); **Russ Freeman** (p); **Victor Feldman** (vb); **Joe Mondragon, Scott LaFaro** (b); **Mel Lewis** (d). Discovery Ⓜ DSCD 962 (71 minutes). Recorded 1959.

⑥ ❼

Paich established his reputation during the fifties through his flexible and imaginative work for a string of top-flight singers, including Peggy Lee, Ella Fitzgerald, Anita O'Day and Mel Tormé At the end of that decade he made a series of fine albums under his own leadership for Warner Brothers, and this CD compiles some of the better moments from those albums. Paich is a thoroughly schooled musician, having obtained a Masters in music from the LA Conservatory, and this schooling stands him in good stead when it comes to arranging the most advantageous mix of line and colour between brass and reeds on such pieces as *Violets for Your Furs* or Ellington's *Warm Valley*. During Pepper's solo on the former his backing is so beautifully sonorous that it becomes a pleasure in its own right. On the latter, Paich's swapping of the melody onto baritone sax is a nicely-judged move.

The second half of the CD comes from Paich's tribute to Broadway, and although the trumpet section is not as brilliant, soloists such as Pepper, Giuffre and Feldman make up for it while LaFaro makes his presence felt. The charts are relaxed, transparent and pleasurable without being in the least challenging. CD sound is commendable. **KS**

Eddie Palmieri

1936

Palmas Palmieri (p); **Brian Lynch** (t); **Conrad Herwig** (tb); **Donald Harrison** (as); **Johnny Torres, Johnny Benitez** (b); **Robbie Ameen** (d); **Richie Flores, Anthony Carrillo, Jose Claussell** (perc). Elektra Nonesuch Ⓕ 61649-2 (52 minutes). Recorded 1993.

⑦ ❿

Palmieri came up in New York surrounded by Cuban music and musicians, and saw Tito Puente as his mentor. He admits that he "hated jazz" when he was young. "All I wanted to hear was Latin." It wasn't until the close of the fifties that he started hearing and understanding jazz pianists like Bud Powell and Thelonious Monk, and began to appreciate what they were doing. By the mid-sixties he was ready to begin incorporating what he liked into his own bands.

This album is an extension of those beginnings, combining what Palmieri calls "the Afro-Caribbean dance form and the instrumental jazz form without losing the individuality of the soloists' voices." This he certainly achieves, with an at times overwhelmingly powerful and complex rhythmic thrust, which is centred on his pianistic patterns, keeping buoyant anything the horns care to try out. There is an engaging vitality about the music and, though it occasionally becomes a little relentless, all one has to do is get up and dance around the room to it to appreciate its felicities all over again. **KS**

Tiny Parham

1900-1943

Tiny Parham and His Musicians Parham (p, vc); **B.T. Wingfield, Claude Alexander, Roy Hopson, Punch Miller** (t); **Charles Lawson, Kid Ory** (tb); **Junie Cobb** (cl, as, ss); **Charles Johnson** (cl, as); **Leroy Pickett, Elliott Washington** (vn); **Charlie Jackson, Mike McKendrick** (bj); **Quinn Wilson** (bb); **Jimmy Bertrand** (d); **Ernie Marrero** (d, wbd). Classics Ⓜ 661 (67 minutes). Recorded 1926-29.

④ ❻

Despite a Kansas City background, Parham is better known for his work in the Chicago area. He was leading a comparatively large band there while still in his early 20s, but despite his reputation and the quality of some of the sidemen recording with him, his records do him less than justice. On this CD, no group is larger than an octet; Parham's own piano is unspectacular and he seems only too willing to afford solo space to pedestrian players such as Hopson, Lawson, Jackson and Wilson. Although Cobb and Johnson are in various bands, the quality of the reed playing is little better and on titles like *Blue Melody Blues* they come over as a pure dance band. Parham's writing is mainly derivative and with arrangements which are naïve even by the standards of the late twenties, it is left to the sidemen to give the music what little distinction it has. The fine blues accompanist Wingfield leads the Pickett-Parham Apollo Syncopators with some fire, Ory's rustic trombone adds backbone to Parham's Forty Five and Miller has fleetingly good moments with the Musicians on titles such as *Stuttering Blues*, *Snake Eyes* and *Jogo Rhythm*. This apart, one cannot help but wonder why the RCA Victor company persevered for nearly three years. **BMcR**

Charlie Parker

1920-1955

The Complete Birth of Bebop Parker (as, ts); with (i) **Efferge Ware** (g) ; **Phil Philips** (d); (ii) various peronnels including: **Dizzy Gillespie, Billy Eckstine** (t); **Goon Gardner** (ts); **Hurley Ramey** (g); **Oscar Pettiford** (b); plus Parker playing over 78 rpm discs of **Hazel Scott, Benny**

Goodman Trio and **Quartet**; (iii) **Dizzy Gillespie's Rebop Six** (Gillespie (t); Parker (as); Milt Jackson (vb); Al Haig (p); Ray Brown (b); Stan Levey (d)). Stash Ⓕ STCD 535 (73 minutes). Recorded 1940-45.

⑥ ❷

When genius appears fully-fledged in all its astounding splendour, part of the afterglow of its effect is to awaken interest in how such perfection came about. In the case of Charlie Parker, as opposed to that of Lester Young, the trail has gradually become illuminated by the indefatigable researches of a legion of Parker historians and fans. While Young's playing prior to his 1936 début on discs remains a matter only of spoken testimony, we now have the unmistakeable sounds of Parker's evolution stretching back to 1940, still four years away from his first mature commercial recordings.

Group i) of the above comes from Kansas City. The first track is from 1940, and presents Bird unaccompanied and in dreadful sound quality. The following four find him with guitarist Efferge Ware. Between the two dates, Parker made his first records with the Jay McShann Orchestra, lived in New York as a freelance, then returned to his hometown. His feet are still firmly in swing soil here, with little of the double-timing or rhythmic displacement of his later playing, but his harmonic sense is already sophisticated. Group ii) finds Bird for the most part on tenor sax, and his oft-remarked derivation from Lester Young is at its most obvious here; he even quotes whole Young phrases in his solos. Yet there is also Herschel Evans and Coleman Hawkins in his increasing exploration of extended chords. Sound quality is bearable most of the time. Group iii) jumps to fully mature Parker and a fabulous session for Jubilee Radio in LA in good mono. Both principals are in exciting form, with Parker fully emerged from the chrysalis he inhabits on the earlier sides.

As a potted history of the birth of Charlie Parker, genius and revolutionary, this will do just nicely. As an essay in recorded sound, worry later. **KS**

Early Bird **Charlie Parker** (as); with the **Jay McShann Orchestra** and various other disputed personnel. Stash Ⓕ ST-CD-542 (73 minutes). Recorded 1940-44.

⑧ ❹

Although everything by Charlie Parker is valuable, this must be counted among his minor works. The most important pieces here are among the very first items in the Parker discography—seven numbers recorded at a radio station in Wichita, Kansas in November 1940 by the Jay McShann Orchestra, of which the 20-year-old Parker was a junior member. His unique, thick-tongued articulation is immediately recognizable and so is his tone and phraseology. This is strange, because he had not yet advanced very far beyond Lester Young from the harmonic point of view, but the way he turns his phrases and their loose relationship with the beat could not be the work of anyone else.

A further McShann session, from the Savoy Ballroom, reveals the band to have grown into a far slicker outfit by 1942, and Parker rather more careful in his short solo. However, a fragment of *Cherokee*, recorded in the same year at Monroe's in Harlem, finds him getting well into his stride. This and some other tracks have not survived the years particularly well, from a physical point of view. It should also be pointed out that eight of the 23 tracks are actually by the McShann band in 1944, without Parker. **DG**

The Immortal Charlie Parker **Parker** (as, ts); **Miles Davis** (t); **John Lewis**, **Bud Powell**, **Dizzy Gillespie**, **Clyde Hart** (p); **Tiny Grimes** (g); **Curley Russell**, **Tommy Potter**, **Nelson Boyd**, **Jimmie Butts** (b); **Max Roach**, **Harold West** (d). Denon/Savoy Ⓜ SV-0102 (54 minutes). Recorded 1944-48.

✔ ⑩ ❻

A somewhat haphazard but nevertheless valuable selection of Parker material culled from his Savoy sessions. For once a sleeve timing is overly modest; the duration is actually some eight minutes longer than stated and the reason is that takes one and two of *Tiny's Tempo* and take one of *Red Cross*, all from the 1944 Tiny Grimes session (Parker's first commercial small group recordings) are complete and not faded as have been previous reissues. Although the interest is clearly Parker, these Grimes titles are excellent small band pieces with fine piano from Clyde Hart and steady time-keeping from West. *Now's The Time* is from the famous *Ko Ko* session (a blues with a theme similar to *The Hucklebuck*) with a faltering 19-year-old Miles Davis partnering Parker for the first time. Davis is present on all the other tracks but his playing on the 1947 and 1948 sessions is far more assured, the tone dry and distinctive. *Chasin' The Bird* has an involved contrapuntal theme (as does *Ah-Leu-Cha*, not included here), possibly an indication of Parker's desire to get away from convention. Four titles find him switching to tenor, slowing down his fast articulation slightly but still sounding light years ahead of the competition. The transfers are variable in quality, but never less than acceptable. A number of second-choice takes and breakdowns are included, but with Parker everything is worthy of study. **AM**

The Charlie Parker Story **Parker** (as); **Miles Davis** (t); **Dizzy Gillespie** (t, p); **Sadik Hakim** aka **Argonne Thornton** (p); **Curly Russell** (b); **Max Roach** (d). Denon/Savoy Ⓜ SV-0105 (35 minutes). Recorded 1945.

✔ ⑩ ❹

Bebop begins here! This disc contains Charlie Parker's first commercial date as leader, on November 26 th 1945. Parker's Savoy recordings, all made in the mid-forties, are one of the main pillars of his oeuvre and have been reissued in many configurations over the years. The label is currently owned by Denon/Nippon Columbia, whose Parker CD reissue programme leaves a lot to be desired—such as, for example, a definitive collection of the original master takes (last available as a two-CD set on Savoy ZDS 8801, but withdrawn on the label's acquisition by Denon).

The Charlie Parker Story is a reissue of an LP that Savoy released in the mid-fifties and comprises that first session in its entirety, complete with false starts, warm-up tracks and alternative takes. Denon have also included the original fifties LP artwork, which is ghastly, and the original liner notes by John Mehegan, who wrongly identifies the musicians on several tracks. By reprinting these errors without a word of correction, Denon have done the jazz public a sloppy disservice. Mehegan assumed that Bud Powell plays piano on the date; in fact, although Powell had been booked to play, he didn't turn up and Dizzy Gillespie is the pianist on all tracks except for the three takes of *Thriving From A Riff* and the first take of *Ko Ko*, where Sadik Hakim (then known as Argonne Thornton) takes over. Mehegan also speculates that Gillespie plays trumpet on a number of tracks, but this happens only on the two takes of *Ko Ko* that closed the session.

The whole event seems to have been somewhat chaotic. Parker has recurring trouble with his saxophone which 'squeaks' throughout; Miles Davis fell asleep on the floor; Hakim, who didn't have a union card, had to exit hurriedly when a union rep arrived. Yet from this shambles emerged undeniably brilliant music; specifically, the master takes of *Billie's Bounce*, *Now's The Time*, *Thriving From A Riff* and *Ko Ko*. The other tracks, some just seconds long, make up a fascinating document of a Parker recording session. However, with one or two exceptions, such as the lovely alto solo on *Meandering*, they will probably be of interest only to collectors.

The four masters are a fair example of Parker's repertoire at the time. *Billie's Bounce* and *Now's The Time* are blues, *Thriving From A Riff* is based on the chords of *I Got Rhythm*, *Ko Ko* on the chords of *Cherokee*, one of Parker's favourite tunes and one on which he had already been improvising for many years. The session's masterpiece, *Ko Ko*, is one of the high points of Parker's entire recording career; his headlong, convoluted lines are an astonishing display of saxophone virtuosity. The bebop revolution is usually seen as an expansion of jazz's harmonic language, but what *Ko Ko* makes clear is Parker's dynamic rhythmic invention—his dramatic entrances, quicksilver lines, daring resolutions. All are played at breakneck speed yet remain fluent, melodic and intrinsically musical. **GL**

Charlie Parker On Dial: The Complete Sessions **Parker** (as); **Dizzy Gillespie**, **Miles Davis**, **Howard McGhee** (t); **J.J. Johnson** (tb); **Lucky Thompson**, **Wardell Gray** (ts); **George Handy**, **Dodo Marmarosa**, **Jimmy Bunn**, **Russ Freeman**, **Erroll Garner**, **Duke Jordan** (p); **Arv Garrison**, **Barney Kessel** (g); **Ray Brown**, **Vic McMillan**, **Bob Kesterson**, **Arnold Fishkind**, **Red Callender**, **Tommy Potter** (b); **Stan Levey**, **Roy Porter**, **Jimmy Pratt**, **Doc West**, **Don Lamond**, **Max Roach** (d); **Earl Coleman** (v). Spotlite/Dial Ⓕ SPJ-CD 4-101 (four discs: 257 minutes). Recorded 1946-47.

✔ ⑩ ❻

The iconic status of Parker's Dials is often bracketed with the Savoys overlapping the same period. On most of these studio sides, from *Diggin' Diz* to *How Deep Is The Ocean*, the altoist is at the peak of his powers—which contrasts starkly with the drowning-not-waving *Lover Man* solo. Material is impressively varied, including such unique Parker originals as *Yardbird Suite* and *Bongo Beep*, and (unlike the Savoys) several more standard ballads.

A further distinction between the Dial and the Savoy material is that all the studio alternative takes (presented here in exact chronological order) are complete performances, apart from two Parker excerpted solos on *Crazeology* and the *Famous Alto Break*, which Bird then re-created on the subsequent versions of *A Night In Tunisia*. Another brief contrast is the so-called 'Chuck Kopely' jam-session (13 minutes on disc one), which is the earliest instance of live work featuring only Parker's solos with the recording apparatus switched off during others' efforts. The studio sidemen, on the other hand, do far more than earn their keep, especially on the 40 tracks by the classic 1947 working group of Roach, Jordan, Potter and Davis (who probably wrote the unusual introduction to *Don't Blame Me*). The sound is somewhat variable, depending on the state of the source material, but is considerably improved over the 20-year-old Spotlite LPs. Parker's invention is so varied that there is no incentive to programme out multiple versions, although Spotlite have done that job for the listener recently by issuing a 2-CD set of just the master takes. This handsome package, its combined notes by original and reissue producers substantially rewritten, does justice to the eternal flame of the music itself. **BP**

Jazz At The Philharmonic, 1946 **Parker** (as); **Dizzy Gillespie**, **Al Killian**, **Howard McGhee**, **Buck Clayton** (t); **Willie Smith** (as); **Charlie Ventura**, **Lester Young**, **Coleman Hawkins** (ts); **Mel Powell**, **Arnold Ross**, **Ken Kersey** (p); **Irving Ashby** (g); **Billy Hadnott** (b); **Lee Young**, **Buddy Rich** (d). Verve Ⓜ 513 756-2 (73 minutes). Recorded 1946.

✔ ⑨ ❻

This CD, containing material never conceived as being under the leadership of the altoist, is anachronistic in that it offers a chance to hear extended solos by men such as Parker at a time when this was not normally possible. It also places Parker amongst the modernists of an earlier era and, in so doing, highlights the vast innovatory strides he had made away from them. The harmonic complexity of his playing is at odds with their swing-era orthodoxy, and this is brought into even sharper relief by his use of rhythmic accentuation that they find almost completely incompatible. The music comes from two concerts, but with the common factor that neither had a rhythm section ideally suited to Parker, Gillespie or McGhee. It is Parker, however, who most effectively shrugs off their retrograde pull. He is at his exacting best on *Lady Be Good*, and is calmly controlled on *After You've Gone* where, after a momentary false start, he takes a melody chorus that is a joy and then tops it with a stunning solo. The second concert finds him reaffirming his blues credentials on *JATP Blues* and swinging alongside the swingers on *I Got Rhythm*, which incidentally has a head-on cutting contest between the then-reigning tenor sax kings, Coleman Hawkins and Lester Young, plus some wonderful Buck Clayton trumpet. It must be said that Young plays gloriously at all tempos in this set, as do Hawkins and Clayton. In company such as this, Parker's roots show clearly. However, along with Gillespie and Monk, he was the way forward. **BMcR**

Bird: The Complete Charlie Parker on Verve **Parker** (as, ldr); with a collective personnel of **Mario Bauzá**, **Buck Clayton**, **Paquito Davilla**, **Kenny Dorham**, **Harry Edison**, **Roy Eldridge**, **Dizzy Gillespie**, **Chris Griffin**, **Benny Harris**, **Al Killian**, **Howard McGhee**, **Jimmy Maxwell**, **Doug Mettome**, **Carl Poole**, **Al Porcino**, **Bernie Privin**, **Red Rodney**, **Charlie Shavers**, **Al Stewart**, **Ray Wetzel**, **Bobby Woodlen** (t); **Hal McKusick**, **John LaPorta** (cl); **Benny Carter**, **Johnny Hodges**, **Gene Johnson**, **Toots Mondello**, **Sonny Salad**, **Freddie Skerritt**, **Willie Smith**, **Harry Terrill**, **Murray Williams** (as); **Coleman Hawkins**, **Jose Madera**, **Pete Mondello**, **Flip Phillips**, **Hank Ross**, **Sol Rabinowitz**, **Ben Webster**, **Lester Young** (ts); **Manny Albam**, **Danny Bank**, **Leslie Johnakins**, **Stan Webb** (bs); **Artie Drelinger** (reeds); **Walter Bishop Jr**, **Al Haig**, **Rene Hernandez**, **Hank Jones**, **Ken Kersey**, **John Lewis**, **Thelonious Monk**, **Oscar Peterson**, **Mel Powell**, **Arnold Ross** (p); **Irving Ashby**, **Billy Bauer**, **Jerome Darr**, **Freddie Green**, **Barney Kessel** (g); **Ray Brown**, **Billy Hadnott**, **Percy Heath**, **Teddy Kotick**, **Charles Mingus**, **Tommy Potter**, **Roberto Rodriguez**, **Curly Russell** (b); **Max Roach**, **Arthur Taylor**, **Lee Young** (d); **Machito**, **Jose Manguel**, **Luis Miranda**, **Umberto Nieto**, **Chano Pozo**, **Carlos Vidal** (perc); **Ella Fitzgerald**, **Dave Lambert Singers** (v). Verve Ⓜ 837 141-2 (ten discs: 624 minutes). Recorded 1946-54.

⑨ ❽

This extraordinary, ten-disc compilation of Charlie Parker's output for Verve provides a revealing longitudinal glimpse of the alto saxophonist. By including every available out-take and false-start, we get a sense of Bird's exceptional powers and also his very human fallibilities. For example, in a 1952 small group setting for the Latin tune, *La Cucaracha*, we hear several fluffs and, interestingly, Parker's less than fluid mesh with a surprisingly staid rhythmic section anchored by Max Roach. We also hear the controversial 1949 and 1950 string sessions which, while being the fulfilment of a Parker dream, sound rather clunky in spite of the saxophonist's spirited flights. More satisfying are big band tracks like *Night and Day*, where Bird soars above a solid rhythm section (Oscar Peterson, Freddie Green, Ray Brown and Don Lamond) and a no-nonsense arrangement by Joe Lipman.

Parker was one of the quintessential figures who redirected jazz from the arranger-determined large ensembles of the swing era to the virtuosic soloist-determined small bebop groups of the forties . It should not be surprising, then, that the set's musical core consists of the combo waxings with fellow bebop giants like Dizzy Gillespie, Red Rodney, Thelonious Monk, Walter Bishop Jr., Charles Mingus, Kenny Clarke and Max Roach. Also of value is the unearthing of Chico O'Farrill's *Afro-Cuban Jazz Suite* and some of the uninhibited jam sessions organized by Verve impresario Norman Granz. A meticulously prepared booklet by producer Phil Schaap, with complete discographic information, a collection of poignant photos and a warm appreciation by Dizzy Gillespie helps contextualize Bird's singular contribution. In sum, a must for Parker completists and those committed to understanding the evolution of modern jazz. **CB**

Charlie Parker Jam Session **Charlie Shavers** (t); **Parker**, **Johnny Hodges**, **Benny Carter** (as); **Flip Phillips**, **Ben Webster** (ts); **Oscar Peterson** (p); **Barney Kessel** (g); **Ray Brown** (b); **J. C. Heard** (d). Verve Ⓜ 833 564-2 (62 minutes). Recorded 1952.

⑧ ❽

This was nearly a classic session. Certainly it was the only occasion on which Parker, Hodges and Carter played together. Had another Norman Granz acolyte, Willie Smith, been present, then this would have been the definitive alto sax summit. Granz specialised in cornucopia-style jam sessions. The result was usually a string of solos by top class musicians, and this is the format here. Parker towers above everybody with his terse and pithy improvisations, and only Flip Phillips comes near to matching him for telling and spontaneous creation. However, *Funky Blues* parades Hodges, Carter and Parker in sequence, and gives the chance for a most interesting comparison of their styles. The Peterson-led rhythm section plays in the idiom favoured by Carter and Hodges, but Parker easily steps over it for the most pungent solo of the three. Hodges is bluesy and sensuous, whilst Carter as usual concerns himself more with the construction of his solo than with any jam session abandon. This was the first of nine such studio jam sessions organised by Granz. The shortest track runs for nearly 14 minutes, and the ballad medley almost 18. Parker aside, some of the best improvising is done on *What Is This Thing Called Love?* where Shavers, Carter and Hodges hit hard in their home idiom. **SV**

The Quintet: Jazz at Massey Hall **Charlie Parker** (as); **Dizzy Gillespie** (t); **Bud Powell** (p); **Charles Mingus** (b); **Max Roach** (d). Debut Ⓜ OJCCD 044-2 (47 minutes). Recorded 1953.

✔ ⑧ ❺

The story behind this album, recorded live at the famous concert in Toronto's Massey Hall, has become a mixture of myth and legend—how the five men dragged themselves through ice and snow to get to Toronto, how Mingus just happened to record the concert on his tape recorder, how the sparse audience realized they were present at a historic occasion, namely the conjunction of the five greatest individuals in bop... No hint of all this on the CD notes, as there are no notes, just ads for other records. Even in the personnel Charlie Parker is listed as 'Charlie Chan' on alto. Surely it is safe for Parker to come out from behind his pseudonym, now that he has been dead 40 years or so? Actually, the audience doesn't sound sparse but quite big and warm, and the recording is not at all bad for an ad hoc live recording, though the prominence of the bass does encourage you to believe those stories about Mingus overdubbing all his bass lines the following day.

The music is pretty damn good, without being quite breathtaking or superb. This is what a top-class bop group sounded like in the mid-fifties; energetic, edgy, swirling, allusive, slightly neurotic and technically beyond anything that had gone before. There are six tunes, of which four are bop standards and two are standards-by-proxy (Kern's *All The Things You Are* and the Ellingtonian *Perdido*), and the concert conditions prompt the participants to try harder than they might in the studio. If it never quite takes off into the empyrean, maybe it's because all five were thinking unconsciously of the heavyweight boxing match they'd just watched on the television in the bar across the street. **MK**

Errol Parker 1930

A Night in Tunisia **Parker** (d); **Philip Harper** (t); **Michael Thomas** (t); **Tyrone Jefferson** (tb); **Doug Harris** (ss); **Donald Harrison** (as); **Bill Saxton** (ts); **Patience Higgins** (bs); **Cary De Nigris** (g); **Reggie Washington** (elb). Sahara Ⓔ 1015 (56 minutes). Recorded 1991.

⑦ ❹

Born Ralph Schecroun in North Africa, Parker recorded with Kenny Clarke under his real name in 1948. For that session he played piano, although he later recorded on organ in the Jimmy Smith manner. In the early sixties he adopted his new name and in 1971 formed Sahara, his own record company. As the decade progressed, he became involved with his own unique brand of jazz and with many of New York's young 'tigers'. To help out with the Parker Experience's studio booking expenses, he at times multi-tracked on both piano and drums, but by the time he formed his Tentet in 1982, he had begun to concentrate mainly on the latter. This CD, with its strange recording balance, putting the drums up front, documents the jazz of the group very well. It shows the full scale of the ensemble arrangements and especially how Parker projects individuals as well as two voice conversations in solo form. These exciting dialogues enrich most titles and dovetail well with Parker's foreground drum parts and Washington's fender, the two instruments which bear the brunt of rhythmic responsibility in the keyboardless unit. The group's stylistic aspirations are best summarized in the contrast of formality and deliberate mayhem in *Ol' Man River*. **BMcR**

Evan Parker 1944

Process and Reality **Parker** (ss). FMP Ⓔ CD37 (67 minutes). Recorded 1991.

⑧ ❽

Evan Parker has given us some of the most extraordinary solo saxophone music of the last two decades, the bulk of it on the LPs he made for Incus between 1975 and 1986. Unfortunately, those albums are not currently available on any format. **Process and Reality**, his most recent solo CD to date, departs radically from his previous work in certain particulars, though whether it signals a new direction or is simply a side-step remains to be seen.

What has not changed here is Parker's singular playing style which, through the use of circular breathing techniques, allows him to produce a constant stream of sound. His superb control in the overtone range and mastery of complex fingering patterns further enable him to create what he calls "the illusion of polyphony", as lines thread and flutter together in mazy counterpoints which are totally improvised.

Where this album differs from its predecessors is in its use of shorter durations—the result of Parker's interest in "trying to improvise a larger form through the use of short pieces"—and, especially, in its use of overdubbing, a surprising move from a player whose preference had always been for 'real time' recording. Three of the CD's 16 tracks feature two saxophones, five feature four, the latter paradoxically including the CD's most lyrical moments with *And I will Sing of This Second Kingdom* and *Diary of a Mnemonist,* as well as its funniest, in *Blindflight*'s rainfall of tiny quacks. **GL**

Leon Parker 1965

Above & Below **Parker** (d, perc, v); **Lisa Parker** (f); **David Sanchez**, **Mark Turner**, **Joshua Redman** (ts); **Jacky Terrasson** (p); **Ugonna Okegwo** (b); **Adam Cruz**, **Natalie Cushman** (perc); **Jay McGovern** (v). Epicure Ⓔ 478198 2 (47 minutes). Recorded 1994.

⑧ ❽

Despite earnest talk among the post-Marsalis generation about extending tradition, only the merest handful have travelled beyond reiteration of fifties and sixties hard bop. The enormously talented

Leon Parker is one of that rare breed, and his intriguing perspective on acoustic jazz is amply evidenced in this striking début.

Parker's vibrant, virtuosic drumming is a joy in itself, but more importantly he is a drummer who genuinely leads from the drums at every level of the music. He does this not merely by being loud, but by realizing that rhythm is the most essential and only sufficient element of music: this allows him to compose and rearrange from the ground up. The five standards here are thus radically transformed, *Bemsha Swing* couched as a fusion of powerful hip-hop and breakneck swing, *You Don't Know What Love Is* reinvented by the application of a simple double-time Latin bass and drum ostinato and *Epistrophy* enlivened by constantly deceptive rhythmic sleights-of-hand as Parker shifts from rock to latin to swing. There are further delights in the originals, among which the title track, a solo recital for percussion, cymbal and voice which perfectly captures the intensity, conviction and invention of Parker's music. **MG**

Maceo Parker

Life on Planet Groove **Parker** (as, v); **Fred Wesley** (tb); **Pee Wee Ellis** (ts); **Larry Goldings** (org); **Rodney Jones** (g); **Kenwood Dennard** (d); **Kym Mazelle** (v); **Candy Dulfer** (as); **Vinvent Henry** (as, b). Minor Music Ⓕ 801023 (76 minutes). Recorded 1992.

⑥ ❽

Parker and some of his sidemen were important members of James Brown's backing group, the JBs, and many of the routines found on this live album can be directly traced back to the James Brown stage show. Consequently, there may be a few eyebrows raised about this being included here. While it is true that the rhythms are associated with funk and soul, the album is predominantly instrumental, and the solos, while basic and relying on well-used blues paths through life, are fiery, exciting and rely on improvisation just as much as any trad jazz revivalist solo does.

Hair-splitting aside, this album packs a tremendous punch and portrays a very tight and super-efficient band delivering a killer-diller set to its fans. The section-work, while hardly intricate, is well-judged and completely compatible with the music. Each horn player has a distinct voice and the rhythm section hits an intoxicating groove. If Lionel Hampton had his time over again, starting now, this is what he would be doing. **KS**

Horace Parlan

Little Esther **Parlan** (p); **Per Goldschmidt** (bs); **Klavs Hovman** (b); **Massimo De Majo** (d). Soul Note Ⓕ 21145-2 (54 minutes). Recorded 1987.

⑥ ❽

A Pittsburgh native, Parlan has worked in the Charles Mingus Workshop, with Lockjaw Davis/Johnny Griffin, Roland Kirk and Michal Urbaniak in a career of considerable variety. He is a second-generation bebop pianist and, as befits a man who includes Ahmad Jamal and Bud Powell amongst his prime influences, is a strongly chordal player. His is not a spare style, however, and, as *Snow Girl* shows, he does not waste time on empty rhetoric. His direction-pointing harmonies are supported by a good story-telling right hand and, as *Something For Silver* demonstrates, he has no reticence in the swing department.

Living away from the US in Denmark could have blunted his cutting edge, but here he is capably assisted by Hovman and De Majo, a Dane and an Italian conversant with the international jazz language. The sole horn is Goldschmidt, another Dane and a man whose relaxed solos show the influence of Gerry Mulligan and Serge Chaloff in about equal parts. Like his own solo playing, Parlan's accompaniment of a saxophonist is equally expert. **BMcR**

Joe Pass

1929

I Remember Charlie Parker **Pass** (g). Pablo Ⓜ OJCCD-602-2 (50 minutes). Recorded 1979.

④ ❽

Having proved himself one of the most formidably well-equipped jazz guitarists ever to riffle through the pages of the American popular songbook, Joe Pass began in the early seventies to record numerous unaccompanied albums for Norman Granz, of which this one—on a nylon strung guitar—is a typical example. It has all the elements of Pass's brimful orchestral approach to the guitar—the florid, lavishly filigreed bebop licks, the chord melodies and the bass line sketches. Yet for all its apparent comprehensiveness, the music is perpetually in danger of seeming like a demonstration of the technical possibilities of the guitar rather than a musical event which is complete, integrated and resourceful on anything other than a mechanical level. It seems that in Pass's pursuit of virtuosity lie the seeds of his downfall: he solves the technical puzzles of *Just Friends*, *Summertime*, *Laura* and the like with exhaustive rigour, but inevitably, since the object of the exercise seems technical, Pass appears as a first-rate craftsman rather than one who has expanded the musical vocabulary at large or added much to the expressive potential of his instrument. Ironically, such players seem to have a special appeal to those with only passing interest in jazz. **MG**

Jaco Pastorius

1951

Jaco Pastorius **Pastorius** (elb); **Randy Brecker**, **Ron Tooley** (t); **Peter Graves** (btb); **Peter Gordon** (frh); **Hubert Laws** (pic); **Wayne Shorter** (ss); **David Sanborn** (as); **Michael Brecker** (ts); **Howard Johnson** (bs); **Herbie Hancock**, **Alex Darqui** (kbds); **Richard Davis**, **Homer Mensch** (b); **Narada Michael Walden**, **Lenny White**, **Bobby Economou** (d); **Don Alias** (perc); **Othello Molineux** (alto steel d); **Leroy Williams** (tenor steel d); **Sam and Dave** (v); **David Nadien**, **Harry Lokofsky**, **Paul Gershman**, **Joe Malin**, **Harry Cykman**, **Harold Kohon**, **Matthew Raimondi**, **Max Pollikoff**, **Arnold Black** (vn); **Selwart Clarke**, **Manny Vardi**, **Julian Barber**, **Al Brown** (va); **Charles McCracken**, **Kermit Moore**, **Beverly Lauridsen**, **Alan Shulman** (vc). Epic Ⓜ CDEPC81453 (43 minutes). Recorded 1975.

✔ ⑧ ❽

Pastorius's introduction of himself to Joe Zawinul as the world's greatest bass player was not perhaps the most modest of opening gambits. However, Pastorius was no stranger either to bravado or egotism, and this extraordinary début showed that on a musical level none of it was insupportable. It declared a revolution in bass playing—apparent here in the exquisite use of harmonics on *Portrait Of Tracy*, the singing, lyrical flights, expressive slurring and gorgeous double and triple stops of *Continuum*, the urgent, funky drive of *Kuru*, and the casual bebop virtuosity of *Donna Lee*—but it also showed that these previously unimagined technical innovations were born of a broad orchestral conception and an innocent eclecticism which could fearlessly juxtapose Charlie Parker with soul singers Sam and Dave. Jaco's orchestral awareness is evident in an obvious way in his string and horn arrangements for *Come On, Come Over* and *Speak Like A Child*, but it is there too on a more extemporary level, in the way the placement of a single harmonic during the steel pan solo on *Opus Pocus* completely shifts the mood of the piece. It seems strange to mention Herbie Hancock's fine work on *Kuru* as an incidental delight, but this was Pastorius's day, and his brilliance here would eclipse greater men. **MG**

John Patitucci

Another World **Patitucci** (b, elb); **Jeff Beal** (t); **Steve Tavaglione** (ss, ts, EWI); **Michael Brecker** (ts); **John Beasley** (p, syn); **Andy Narell** (steel pans); **Armand Sabal-Lecco** (elb, v); **Will Kennedy**, **Dave Weckl** (d); **Alex Acuna**, **Luis Conte**, **Will Kennedy** (perc); various backing vocals. GRP Ⓕ 97252 (52 minutes). Recorded 1993.

⑧ ❽

As titles like *Ivory Coast* and *The Griot* and the presence of African bassist Armand Sabal-Lecco announce, this is Patitucci's African record. Several pieces, most effectively perhaps the darkly grooving title track, have a pronounced African flavour, but Patitucci's long-standing admiration for Weather Report is also frequently in evidence, as is shown by *Ivory Coast Part II* and *I Saw You*, where Tavaglione phrases Shorter-like along with the bass, and by the steel pan quotient of *Soho Steel*. GRP is not a label noted for its substance, but among its fusion signatories John Patitucci is one of the most satisfying. His writing is derivative but effective, and he has always employed and left plenty of space for good jazz soloists, including himself. Like his writing, his post-Coltrane solo vocabulary is now commonplace, but no other electric bassist has a better command of it, and this fluency is allied to an immediately recognisable sound and a strong melodic sensibility. Any collection professing an interest in contemporary bass playing ought to have at least one Patitucci album, and this is as good as any. **MG**

Big John Patton

1935

Let 'Em Roll **Patton** (org); **Grant Green** (g); **Bobby Hutcherson** (vb); **Otis Finch** (d). Blue Note Ⓜ CDP7 89795-2 (40 minutes). Recorded 1965.

⑧ ❽

Patton made a substantial impact on the chitlins circuit in the US during the sixties, when so many organists clung to the coat-tails of Jimmy Smith, as he crossed over with a vengeance. Big John made his impact—and remains a pleasant memory for many listeners—because of his unfailing taste as a player and as a leader. He eschewed the more blatant bump and grind routines of many at that time, and continued to both write and improvise on attractive themes (an example here is *Latona*, which he was later to record more than once). Though his pedal patterns were not of the most varied type, his fresh approach to chording and his finely-attuned ear for the most attractive part of the Hammond B3 range of sounds kept the listener fully involved. By the end of the sixties he was also experimenting with stylistic syntheses undreamed of by any other organist except Larry Young, as the recently reissued **Understanding** (Blue Note) shows.

He is greatly helped here by a typically first-rate set of Blue Note sidemen, and for once the absence of a horn player may well be seen by many as a positive gain: certainly the sterling improvising and accompaniment of Green and Hutcherson keep this set continually on the boil, whether it is on the nicely-paced blues inflections of *Shadow of Your Smile* or the more funked-up groove of Hank Mobley's *The Turnaround.* Green occasionally gets stuck on his own personal clichés during his solos, but his attack and bite are beyond reproach. Hutcherson, a player of great imaginative resources in every musical situation, is oustanding here. **KS**

Les Paul

1915

Les Paul Trio **Paul** (g); **Milt Raskin** (p); **Cal Goodin** (g); **Clint Norquist**, **Bobby Morrow** (b) unidentified (v) on one track. Laserlight Ⓑ 15 741 (43 minutes). Recorded c.1947.

⑧ ❺

The personnel is courtesy of Paul; the disc does not list any, and the recording date might be off by a few years. Once described by *The New Yorker* as "the Thomas Edison of reverb," Paul owes his reputation as a progenitor of rock 'n' roll to his invention of the solid-body electric guitar and to his and Mary Ford's hit records of the early fifties, which more or less introduced the concept of overdubbing (these are available, along with plenty of period curiosities, on **The Legend and The Legacy**, a prohibitively-priced Capitol four-disc boxed set). Short of making a pilgrimage to the Greenwich Village club where Paul's trio has held forth every Monday night since 1984, the way to discover his uncelebrated prowess as a jazz guitarist is to hear his subtle chase sequence with Nat King Cole on the inaugural **Jazz at the Philharmonic** blowout from 1944, or to pick up this budget-priced disc of dubious legality before it is driven off the market. In one sense, Paul is not really an improviser —his solos give evidence of being set pieces, although they're no less beguiling as a result of this. Although the group's sense of itself as an extroverted chamber group seems modelled on the Nat Cole Trio, Paul's playful tremolo and steamroller propulsion also reveal the influence of Django Reinhardt. **FD**

Cecil Payne

1922

Patterns of Jazz **Payne** (bs); **Duke Jordan** (p); **Tommy Potter** (b); **Art Taylor** (d); **Kenny Dorham** (t). Denon/Savoy Ⓜ SV-0135 (44 minutes). Recorded 1956.

⑧ ❻

Payne started out on alto (he had lessons from Pete Brown) and this may account for his fluency on baritone, which he started to play in 1947. He was one of the very first bebop soloists on the larger horn and was featured with the Dizzy Gillespie band to good effect. The opening four titles here form an excellent introduction to his qualities as a major jazz soloist, opening with a jaunty *This Time The Dream's On Me* and including a warm-toned version of *How Deep Is The Ocean*; on ballads he shows off his vibrato control and manifests the breathy tone of Ben Webster on the upper reaches of the baritone. Adding Kenny Dorham on half of the titles does not increase the impact of the music greatly, for Payne is clearly in more confident mood than the trumpeter. The rhythm section is exactly in keeping with Cecil's playing (Jordan and Payne worked together on many occasions, going right back to their days with Roy Eldridge's big band) and the release is recommended as a good example of a fine baritone player who has often been in danger of being overlooked. **AM**

Nicholas Payton

From This Moment **Payton** (t); **Monte Croft** (vb); **Mulgrew Miller** (p); **Mark Whitfield** (g); **Reginald Veal** (b); **Lewis Nash** (d). Verve Ⓕ 527 073-2 (67 minutes). Recorded 1994.

⑦ ❾

We have become used to extreme vituosity and unseasonal maturity in young jazz musicians, but Nicholas Payton (still a teenager when this album was recorded) is truly remarkable. His trumpet style derives from Clifford Brown, although it reminds also of the young Freddie Hubbard from the era of Herbie Hancock's **Empyrean Isles**. His playing is fluent, authoritative and crackles with ideas; on the ballads he has a lovely, lazy vibrato. Payton always seems able to add one more devastating little afterthought when it seems that he has come to the end of a musical sentence. Peter King plays the same trick, and it certainly keeps you paying attention. Payton is accompanied by a very good band, with Mulgrew Miller on piano and the bass-and-drums team of Reginald Veal and Lewis Nash being outstanding. Another benefit is the lack of a saxophonist, for a change. There is not a moment here that you might not have come across on a superior Blue Note session from 30 years ago, but then the jury is still out as to whether that is a good or bad thing.

Meanwhile, it is worth pondering on the thought that, if brilliant young players like Payton can devote themselves to an established idiom such as this, there must be plenty of mileage still left in it. **DG**

Paz

Love In Peace **Phil Todd** (ss); **Ray Warleigh** (f, as); **Dick Crouch** (vb); **Geoff Castle** (kbds); **Phil Lee, Glen Cartledge, Allan Holdsworth** (g); **Ron Mathewson, Paul Carmichael, Laurence Cottle, Henry Thomas, Billie Kristian** (elb); **Matin Drew, Neal Wilkinson, Steve Arguelles, Dave Sheen, Les Cirkel** (d); **Frank Ricotti, Chris Fletcher Bosco, Simon Morton** (perc); **Simon Morton, Dave Sheen** (v). Master Mix Ⓕ checd 00102 (69 minutes). Recorded 1978-86.

⑥ ❻

The Latin-Fusion band Paz has been through various incarnations over the years, and some of those changes are reflected in the shifting personnel above. However, the players have always kept a fierce commitment to expression at the heart of their music and so, even at the height of their popularity, their performances always carried the sort of conviction expected from internationally-established bands such as Steps Ahead. The style of the group always included large dollops of Latin rhythms interwoven with rock and jazz methodologies and instrumentation; hence it always had an attractive lilt to its material and its interpretations, with a pleasing emphasis on melody as well as improvisational heat. This collection, as near to a "best of" as one could reasonably expect, is well-balanced, and shows the band to good advantage. Even the singing is palatably authentic. **KS**

Annette Peacock

I Have No Feelings **Peacock** (v, p, syn); **Roger Turner** (perc). Ironic Records Ⓕ IRONIC 4CD (34 minutes). Recorded 1986.

⑧ ❾

Singer, composer and pioneer of synthesizer music, Annette Peacock has marked out a personal musical territory that draws on elements of jazz and pop while owing few obvious allegiances to either. She first attracted attention in the mid-sixties, writing initially for bassist Gary Peacock, then for pianist Paul Bley. Both men, but especially Bley, have continued to re-interpret on records the compositions she gave them at that time. She toured with Bley, becoming one of the first to play synthesizer in concert and develop a method to process her vocals electronically, as exemplified on her early albums as leader, **Revenge** and **I'm The One**. Settling in England in the mid-seventies, she explored an idiosyncratic jazz-rock fusion on **X-Dreams**, then turned to a more abstract, improvised music for later releases on her own label, Ironic.

I Have No Feelings is a particularly elegant set, its collation of fragmentary melodies carried by Peacock's finely-honed vocals, minimal keyboards and the discreet free percussion of Roger Turner. Her epigrammatic lyrics traverse romantic whimsy, political protest and, on *Not Enough* and *Nothing Ever Was, Anyway*, the wry philosophical detachment that has become her signature. Her singing can be both intimate and ethereal, while her music here comprises mostly fragile, dreamy tunes that seem to float by on a breeze, a perfect expression of her focus on the transitory. **GL**

Gary Peacock

1935

Tales of Another **Peacock** (b); **Keith Jarrett** (p); **Jack DeJohnette** (d). ECM Ⓕ 1101 (827 418-2) (49 minutes). Recorded 1977.

⑧ ❿

Peacock's endless list of credits includes vital work done with Paul Bley, Albert Ayler, Miles Davis and the Bill Evans Trio. The group heard on this CD represents another high point in his illustrious career, being together on and off for nearly ten years. All of the tunes are by Peacock and they are well suited to the musicians involved. Jarrett's notorious scene-stealing never surfaces: as well as he plays, it is never at the expense of his colleagues. Peacock's bass really sings on *Vignette*, his solo a model of adventurous, personal projection and group awareness. He is especially powerful on *Trilogy II* and the superb sonority of his full tone is never better displayed than on the aptly-titled *Tone Field*. He lays down throughout the blueprint of the Peacock method; every solo stays logically on its directional rails, there is never an angular phrase and everything he plays has a buoyancy that could sustain a group of any size. With a trio such as this, there is obviously adequate solo exposure and Peacock puts it to full use. **BMcR**

Duke Pearson

1932-1980

Sweet Honey Bee **Pearson** (p, arr); **Freddie Hubbard** (t); **James Spaulding** (f, as); **Joe Henderson** (ts); **Ron Carter** (b); **Mickey Roker** (d). Blue Note Ⓜ CDP7 89792-2. (40 minutes). Recorded 1966.

⑥ ❻

Pearson was an unusually sensitive small-group arranger and pianist, and his talents also occasionally embraced big-band sessions for Blue Note. It is no surprise that this organized and disciplined man had, by the time of this date, begun helping producer Alfred Lion to prepare Blue Note recording sessions, and would eventually become for a time Blue Note's main producer.

Although Nat Hentoff's liner notes claim this as Pearson's best date for Blue Note, this is unfortunately not the case: his earlier record, **Wahoo**, is a much more cohesive and resourceful session, with consistently inspired solo work from the sidemen (who, incidentally, included both Spaulding and Henderson). **Wahoo** was reissued a number of years ago on CD, but is now once again unavailable. Yet there are some outstanding pieces here, and probably the one to most treasure is the exquisite 6/8 time ballad *After The Rain* (a Pearson original, and not the Coltrane ballad of the same name). Apart from that, and the intriguing voicing and harmonic movement of what sound on first acquaintance like very straightforward compositions (*Gaslight*, for example); probably the most noteworthy music comes from Hubbard, who at this time was playing with great warmth and imagination.

The recorded sound is not Van Gelder's best (there is rather a lot of reverb on the piano sound, in particular), but is is crisp and clean, so it is in the Blue Note tradition. Pearson was too good a musician to be completely overlooked as he is today. This album has sufficient of what made him special to be worth buying. **KS**

Ken Peplowski

1958

The Natural Touch **Peplowski** (cl, ts); **Frank Vignola** (g); **Ben Aronov** (p); **Murray Wall** (b); **Tom Melito** (d). Concord Jazz Ⓕ CCD 4517 (65 minutes). Recorded 1992.

⑧ ❽

Although he has recorded quite prolifically in the nineties (notably a live duet session with guitarist Howard Alden), this remains one of Peplowski's most impressive CDs. It displays both his glittering clarinet technique and his warm tenor saxophone sound to advantage, in the context of the band which he had been leading for the previous couple of years. Peplowski is essentially a latter-day swing player, but he stretches the idiom considerably. One of the 13 tunes here is *Evidence*, one of Thelonious Monk's most elusive and disjointed pieces, which is given a suitably dry, quirkish treatment. At the other extreme comes *Guess I'll Hang My Tears Out To Dry*, to which Peplowski accords the full romantic works. The arrangements follow the Goodman small-band practice of stitching solos neatly together with simple riffs and bridge passages, imparting a sense of completeness to the entire set. **DG**

Art Pepper

1925-1982

The Route **Chet Baker** (t, co-ldr); **Pepper** (as); **Richie Kamuca** (ts); **Peter Jolly** (p); **Leroy Vinnegar** (b); **Stan Levey** (d). Pacific Jazz Ⓜ CDP7 92931 2 (53 minutes). Recorded 1956.

⑧ ❻

It would be hard to think of a more representative album of the best of the West Coast jazz of the fifties. Certainly Pepper has made records which are every bit as good, but this has him set with a group of near-peers. Baker's improvising was at its most energetic, Kamuca, recently in from the east, swung hard in a way that was purportedly alien to the west, and the rhythm section was as good as any which could be found on either coast or in the middle. Jolly is a quite outstanding jazz pianist who, despite his best efforts, has managed to get himself overlooked. Never mind; Pepper, with Vinnegar tucking in behind him, wails with feeling. *The Route*, sprung on Vinnegar's bass, shows everyone at their individual best.

Having noted the disc as a good example of Pepper within a group, two of the most remarkable numbers here, *I Can't Give You Anything But Love* and *The Great Lie*, have him with just bass and drums, while another, *Old Croix*, adds piano to the trio. Here is Pepper at his best, spinning delicate improvisations played with a style and panache which are as tough as steel. **SV**

Art Pepper Meets The Rhythm Section **Pepper** (as); **Red Garland** (p); **Paul Chambers** (b); **Philly Joe Jones** (d). Contemporary Ⓜ OJCCD 5338 (50 minutes). Recorded 1957.

✔ ⑩ ❽

Alto saxophonist Art Pepper, as revealed in his autobiography *Straight Life* (written with wife Laurie Pepper, 1979), more than paid his dues. Indeed, on the morning of this landmark 1957 session, Pepper was not even aware that the date had been scheduled. But like an archetypal fifties jazzer sent to the gig by Hollywood's Central Casting, Pepper—in spite of not having played for several weeks and going through tough times because of narcotics—played like an angel.

So, too, did the stellar rhythm section of pianist Red Garland, bassist Paul Chambers and drummer Philly Joe Jones. And though recorded in Los Angeles, none of the mannerisms of the so-called West Coast school is present. Indeed, there's a focused intensity that is never forced, especially at the medium and slower tempos of *You'd Be So Nice To Come Home To*, *Imagination*, *Star Eyes* and the Pepper-Chambers line called *Waltz Me Blues*. However, when flags start waving, as they do on *Straight Life* (based on the changes of *After You've Gone*), Pepper and friends soar; again, despite the brisk pace, all things flow, albeit with virtuosic élan.

The match of Pepper with the then-current Miles Davis rhythm section of Garland-Chambers-Jones was a stroke of genius. Everything clicks, from the breezy take on Gillespie's *Tin Tin Deo* to the hauntingly poignant *The Man I Love*. There is even a boppishly hip reframing of Tom Delaney's Dixieland classic, *Jazz Me Blues*. Throughout, it is Pepper, one of jazzdom's pre-eminent lyricists, who sails with melodic, indeed, poetic abandon. **CB**

Art Pepper + Eleven: Modern Jazz Classics **Pepper** (as, ts, cl); **Pete Candoli**, **Al Porcino**, **Jack Sheldon** (t); **Dick Nash** (tb); **Bob Enevoldsen** (vtb, ts); **Vince de Rosa** (frh); **Herb Geller**, **Charlie Kennedy**, **Bud Shank** (as); **Richie Kamuca**, **Bill Perkins** (ts); **Med Flory** (bs); **Russ Freeman** (p); **Joe Mondragon** (b); **Mel Lewis** (d); **Marty Paich** (arr). Contemporary Ⓜ OJCCD 341-2 (55 minutes). Recorded 1959.

✔ ⑩ ❽

This album pointedly begins with a cover of Miles Davis's great **Birth of The Cool** vehicle *Move*, by Denzil Best. The Miles nonet's sound and aesthetic heavily influenced Los Angeles jazz in the fifties; arranger Paich was a leading exponent of cool's harmonic and timbral schemes, and had already provided splendid settings for singers Ella Fitzgerald and Mel Tormé.

Pepper, an altoist with a singing, stinging attack, responds beautifully to Paich's sleek expansions of jazz tunes by Monk, Gillespie, Parker, Rollins and others; charts designed to frame Art's solos (Paich's harmonized reed choruses on Dizzy's *Groovin' High* look back to Benny Carter and ahead to sideman Flory's Supersax group of the seventies). California's Pepper was no typical West Coaster; even then his flame burned hot, like Charlie Parker's. He shows an aggressive approach to rhythm, soaring over and slicing through the arrangements, many of which betray an admiration for Basie's band (Paich had written for Basie, too).

Pepper also leads the sax section on either alto or tenor, to which he brings the same burning conception, and displays his skills as an overlooked if cooler clarinettist on Bird's *Anthropology*. On this classic Coastal date Pepper did nothing wrong, and many things right. **KW**

Among Friends **Pepper** (as); **Russ Freeman** (p); **Bob Magnusson** (b); **Frank Butler** (d). Storyville Ⓕ STCD 4167 (50 minutes). Recorded 1978.

⑨ ❽

1975's **Living Legend** was Pepper's first record as leader for 15 years. It heralded one of the great comeback stories in jazz and in *Lost Life* had a masterpiece to set beside his most affecting ballad performances. But better was to come.

Pepper rated **Among Friends** as possibly the most pleasant date he ever played. The music is relaxed, full of vim and suffused with a feeling of joyful group rapport. The session was a reunion of sorts, since both Freeman and Butler had played with Pepper in his first heyday, from 1955-1960. It was also a second 'comeback' for the altoist who, after making **Living Legend**, **The Trip** and **No Limit** in quick succession, had not recorded for a year due to health and drug problems.

The set showcases the main areas of Pepper's talent. The bright mercurial lines of *I'll Remember April* are handled with fleet assurance that reveals his debt to Charlie Parker; a cool, wistful *'Round Midnight* exhibits the rhythmic poise and economy of phrase he brings to ballads; *Besame Mucho* shows how he can lace the most lilting tune with a tart poignancy.

Many of Pepper's late performances attain a genuinely tragic stature. **Among Friends** is refreshingly unassuming; he shows that personal happiness, no less than personal tragedy, can be an effective spur to making great music. This Storyville issue, by the way, includes an alternate take of *Blue Bossa* not on the original Discovery CD. **GL**

The Complete Galaxy Recordings **Pepper** (as, cl); with a collective personnel of **Stanley Cowell**, **Hank Jones**, **Tommy Flanagan**, **George Cables** (p); **Cecil McBee**, **Ron Carter**, **Charlie Haden**, **Tony Dumas**, **Red Mitchell**, **David Williams** (b); **Howard Roberts** (g); **Roy Haynes**, **Al Foster**, **Billy Higgins**, **Carl Burnett** (d); **Kenneth Nash** (perc). Galaxy Ⓕ 1016-2 (16 discs: 1052 minutes). Recorded 1978-82.

⑩ ❽

For all of his early triumphs, there's much to be said for Art Pepper's final recordings, here collected. The last three-and-a-half years of his life were staggeringly prolific, and the level of artistry amazingly high. Of these 137 performances, 63 were unreleased on LP (nine of them were once available in Japan), spread over ten recording sessions (two of them thoroughly documented live dates in Tokyo and Los Angeles clubs). As the only horn, Pepper is almost always in the spotlight, and he never falters. Over the years he remained fiercely competitive, if only with himself, and the inner conflict he felt put him on a quest that drove his music into such emotionally uplifting (and occasionally tortured) states as can be heard here. As such, the songs were merely vehicles; he returns to *Landscape* and *Mombo Koyama* five times each over the course of several sessions, for example, and many tunes receive two or three distinct interpretations. But his obsession would not allow him to repeat himself. His ballads are breathtaking, vulnerable and quizzical, wounded and wary. Uptempo, he is exhilarating. If forced to choose a single favourite session I might take the 1979 date with Haden, Cables and Higgins since it includes three torch songs on unaccompanied alto and two of his plucky clarinet numbers. But I would hate to be without the final, gem-like duos with Cables or *Nature Boy*, a singular masterpiece with Tommy

Flanagan's risky piano, or the increasingly vivid, vigorous live performances. Taken together, they emphasize the fact that few improvisers in jazz have been so ruthlessly open, immediate and rewarding as Art Pepper. **AL**

Danilo Perez

The Journey **Perez** (p); **David Sanchez** (ss, ts); **George Garzone** (ts); **Larry Grenadier**, **Andy Gonzalez** (b); **Ignacio Berroa** (d); **Milton Cardona**, **Kimati Dinizulu**, **Giovanni Hildalgo**, **Guillermo Franco R**. (perc). RCA Novus Ⓕ 163166-2 (59 minutes). Recorded 1994.

⑦ ❽

Perez is a young Panamanian with an excitingly direct style. His self-avowed aim on this record is to tell the story of a journey—that of the African people to the New World. This has been told many times before, but the fresh twist here is that the journey this time is to the Spanish-speaking parts of the new continent, and the second half of this collection of pieces places the Africa-descended peoples in today's rapidly-evolving Central America. There are no lyrics: this is an instrumental odyssey, but no less graphic for that. All the pieces have descriptive titles (*Chains, The Arrival, The Awakening, Flight To Freedom* and so on), and the music faithfully represents those titles. The rhythmic cauldron Perez conjures is heady in its effect, to say the least, and when this impetus coincides with bassist Grenadier (Gonzalez appears as a second player on one track only) and pianist Perez, the momentum is terrific; exhilarating, even. What is more, Perez avoids all the tiresomely familiar tricks of the latin pianist's trade, including the locked-hands octave patterns. The only real let-down is the paucity of imagination shown by saxophonist Sanchez, who does his Coltrane and Sanders impressions and doesn't really aspire to more. Still; he is only one element in a very potent brew, mixing as it does fiercely swinging jazz with head-shakingly exciting latin rhythm. Perez is clearly someone to keep a close eye on (and ear open for) in the very near future. **KS**

Bill Perkins

1924

I Wished On The Moon **Bill Perkins** (f, ss, ts); **Metropole Orchestra / Rob Pronk**. Candid Ⓕ CCD79524 (51 minutes). Recorded 1989/90.

⑧ ❽

After being noted for the smoothness of his Lester Young-derived work during the earlier part of his career, Perkins entered a turbulent middle period which involved him with many contemporary influences, notably that of Sonny Rollins. By the time he made this outstanding album he had returned to a more lyrical groove, largely through a renewed association with Shorty Rogers and Bob Cooper. Perkins has seldom given such a consistent display of his artistry as he does here, both on tenor and on flute. On *Beautiful Love* he displays outstanding grace as a flautist, and amongst this refreshing set of ballads he is able to show both lyrical playing on tenor and, as on *Besame Mucho*, a stern and unsentimental approach to his improvising. On this showing Perkins must rate as one of the most successfully inventive tenor soloists of the day.

Not since the Stan Getz-Eddie Sauter **Focus** album has such stimulating use been made of a string orchestra in jazz, although there are conventional big band sounds in, for example, Frank Strazzeri's *Opals*. The arrangements of Rob Pronk are quite magnificent, and had Perkins not been present, this would still have been an album to wonder at. Pronk's is a remarkable orchestra, and for my money amongst the best of his time. **SV**

Eric Person

1963

Prophecy **Person** (as, ss, key, perc); **Cary De Nigris** (d); **Kenny Davis** (b). Soul Note Ⓕ 121287-2 (57 minutes). Recorded 1992/93.

⑥ ❽

No stranger to big band work, St. Louis-born Person has the tone and arhythmic confidence identifiable with such activity. He has also worked with Kelvynator, Living Colour, Chico Hamilton's Euphoria and the Decoding Society and he happily acknowledges his r&b and soul listening experiences. More recently, he has worked with the World Saxophone Quartet and angled himself again toward jazz. This CD presents many aspects of his music. The likes of *Plummett*, *Next Love* and *Ancient Sun* use electronic aids to give body to the group sound and a fillip to its commercial appeal.

In contrast, *Up Against The Wall*, *Improvisation In Linear B*, *Interstellar Space Suite* and the title track are jazz directed solo performances. They make sparing use of multiphonics and circular breathing and they show Person to have admirable creative standards, an expressive tone and an awareness of dynamics. His whole approach would find sympathy with the M-Base collective; all means directed to the creative process are acceptable and an effort is continually made to relate to other contemporary musical forms. Here he uses tunes by John Coltrane and Wayne Shorter but he also provides eight of his own, even if three are not developed beyond the theme statement. **BMcR**

Houston Person 1934

The Talk of The Town **Person** (ts); **Cecil Bridgewater** (t); **Stan Hope** (p); **Buster Williams** (b); **Grady Tate** (d); **Ralph Dorsey** (perc). Muse Ⓕ MCD 5331 (40 minutes). Recorded 1987.

⑧ ❽

Person has long been identified as king of the tenor-and-organ circuit and the true successor to Arnett Cobb and Gene Ammons as a burning soul-stirrer on the instrument. As with both the aforementioned gentlemen, this description of his talents doesn't really do him justice. It is true that he has spent most of his working life with a tenor-and-organ combo or backing Etta James; but this record reflects not only his ease with a good pianist, but the fact that this pianist was his partner on the road.

As such, it could be claimed that this is not the archetypal Person recording date, and that may be true, but his earliest records under his own name were with army buddy Cedar Walton, and this date carries that tradition forward. Person here is beautifully relaxed, playing neither too much nor too hard, his phrasing light and deft: he is not merely blowing for effect or recycling old clichés, but playing from the meat of each standard in the set. On *Only Trust Your Heart*, his restrained delivery at a medium tempo is a delight and full of little efficacies of phrase and melody, while his caressing of the beautiful theme to *Everything Happens to Me* puts him squarely in the mainstream jazz tradition. His accompanists, especially pianist Hope, are in complete accord with Person, and never distract from the central performance. Tate and Williams breathe time together. Bridgewater is not present on every track, but where he solos he makes concise and tidy points of his own. **KS**

Now's The Time **Person** (ts); **Ron Carter** (b). Muse Ⓕ MCD 5421 (49 minutes). Recorded 1990.

⑥ ❽

Initially a pianist, Person took to the tenor saxophone at 17. He enjoyed working with organists and recorded or toured with Johnny Hammond, Groove Holmes and Charles Earland. His musical partnership with Etta Jones began in 1968 and is still productively in place. Person is a natural small group player, and this partnership is ideal for him. Carter thinks like a horn player, tending to work in parallel with the tenor rather than merely supporting him with guiding lines. Person takes advantage of both the rhythmic and harmonic freedom this gives as their performance is elevated to true counterpoint. The various moods on this album, a sequel to their fine 1989 **Something In Common** (Muse), are immediately obvious. Person treats Monk's *Bemsha Swing* with some circumspection, *Einbahnstrasse* skilfully avoids any implied cul-de-sacs, while *Memories Of You* gets the full romantic treatment. *Quiet Nights* maintains its Latin implications without the aid of elaborate percussion support, while it is left to the title track to parade the loping blues serenader. Person is a tidy improviser who reaps the harvest sowed by swing bopsters such as Don Byas and Lucky Thompson as well as the r&b moguls. As this CD shows, he does it without fuss, in a style that is very much his own. **BMcR**

Hannibal Marvin Peterson 1948

Now's the Time **Peterson** (t, v); **John Hicks** (p); **Richard Davis** (b); **Tatsuya Nakamura** (d). King Ⓕ KICJ 108 (56 minutes). Recorded 1992.

Another talented product of the North Texas State University assembly line, Peterson is one of the most multi-stylistic of trumpeters. For many years with Gil Evans, he is as much at home with free-formers such as Roswell Rudd, Enrico Rava and Pat Patrick as he is with stalwarts like John Hicks, Kenny Barron and Roy Haynes. As this CD shows, he has the confidence and technical facility to take on anything and any style. Here he also has the advantage of being with musicians endowed with similar instrumental gifts. It is just that, with Hicks' forceful, rippling piano, Davis' assured and full toned bass and Nakamura's fine timekeeping, there is less temptation to go outside. The situation does not, however, restrict Peterson's musical range. The pure-toned lyricist is heard on *In A Sentimental Mood*, the blisteringly hot bebopper marauds through *Now's The Time*, while the harmonic investigator makes a detailed interrogation of *Smoke Gets In Your Eyes*. In contrast, the doleful blues man protests through *Turquoise* before donning his clown's hat to jive *The Saints*. Although he brings a gospel fervour to his singing on *Glory, Glory Hallelujah*, he is not the most deeply emotional of trumpeters. It is almost as if he finds it too easy to play. **BMcR**

Oscar Peterson 1925

The Trio Live From Chicago **Peterson** (p); **Ray Brown** (b); **Ed Thigpen** (d). Verve Ⓜ 823 008-2. (47 minutes). Recorded 1961.

⑧ ❻

Although the admirable Norman Granz had not always presented Peterson in the best possible light, his sale of the Verve label to MGM in 1961 did not look likely to improve the situation. New executive director Creed Taylor's normal method of soloist showcasing was some distance from Peterson's concept, but in the event, his methods were not imposed. It was Jim Taylor who produced this session and, to some extent, it was he who directed Peterson on a fresh career path. This Chicago date typifies his approach. Peterson is in ebullient mood and it is one of those sessions where his awesome technical command is subjected to the greater creative needs of improvisational forays such as *Never Been In Love Before*, *Sometimes I'm Happy*, and *Whisper Not*. He makes it all seem easy, with the underlying rhythmic thrust as evident at the meandering pace of *Wee Small Hours Of The Morning* as it is on a medium tempo driver like *Chicago*. Brown gives a magnificent display of both supportive as well as scrupulously accurate bass playing, while Thigpen, who arrived in the trio in 1959, adds the stiffening element not always evident in the previous partnership with guitarist Herb Ellis. This is, in fact, the ideal trio for Peterson and, with the added stimulation of a noisy 'live' audience, all three are inspired to produce their best work. **BMcR**

Night Train **Peterson** (p); **Ray Brown** (b); **Ed Thigpen** (d). Verve Ⓜ 821 724-2 (45 minutes). Recorded 1962.

✔ ⑩ ❽

When Herb Ellis decided to leave Peterson in 1958, Oscar did not think any other guitarist could adequately take Herb's place, so he changed the trio's instrumentation and hired drummer Ed Thigpen. The Peterson-Brown-Thigpen trio remained in being for five years and **Night Train** is arguably the best representative album the group made; it certainly proved to be the most popular in terms of sales figures. The transfer to CD was a logical step and the reproduction is excellent. Setting himself a programme of music closely associated with others was a self-imposed challenge for Oscar, but he knew exactly what he was doing. Four of the 11 tunes are by Duke Ellington (five, if you count *Night Train* which, although credited to Jimmy Forrest, is actually based on a couple of Ducal themes) and two are from the Basie book. Joe Higgins had a hit in the forties with *The Honeydripper* but it never swung as much as Oscar's version here. Peterson has come in for a lot of ill-judged criticism over the years, perhaps because he is so consistently good as a player. He has only infrequently featured as a composer, but this CD has his *Hymn To Freedom*, surely one of his finest pieces of musical architecture, building steadily to a climax before returning gracefully to the opening mood. **AM**

Trio + One: Clark Terry **Peterson** (p); **Clark Terry** (t, flh, v); **Ray Brown** (b); **Ed Thigpen** (d). EmArcy Ⓜ 818 840-2 (41 minutes). Recorded 1964.

⑨ ❼

Peterson has of course been amongst the most gregarious as well as most prolific of recording artists and, as this album attests, there are some solid successes to count among the collaborative efforts. This date was one of his most popular at the time of its initial release, spawning as it did the hit track *Mumbles* and its follow-up, *Incoherent Blues*. Both of those tracks remain enjoyable today, Terry's inspired vocal babblings still able to raise a laugh from even the most curmudgeonly of listeners, but it is the more solid musical virtues of the union between the trio and guest which invite our continued respect and attention and earn this album its classic status. The opening title, Frank Loesser's *Brotherhood of Man*, finds the trio digging in deep behind a wailing Terry, blues-drenched near-vocalizations pouring from his instrument. The same is true of Peterson's *Blues for Smedley*, but then there is also the unadorned way Terry and the band treat the pretty melody of *Roundalay*. By this time, this edition of the Peterson trio had been in place for over half a decade, and it swung like no other. Terry is arresting all through, striking an imaginative musical angle on every track and playing with overwhelming conviction. This is one to keep the home fires burning. **KS**

Exclusively for My Friends **Peterson** (p); **Ray Brown**, **Sam Jones** (b); **Ed Thigpen**, **Bobby Durham**, **Louis Hayes** (d). Verve/MPS Ⓜ 513 830-2 (four discs: 238 minutes). Recorded 1963-68.

⑦ ❽

Peterson tends to get either deified or trashed. I find his proficiency both amazing and limiting, and this mega-survey, originally released on six LPs, makes the point as well as any single collection. Among its strengths are uniformly superb sound on the 36 tracks, recorded over a six-year span in producer Georg Brunner-Schwer's Villingen villa; the informal flow of repertoire and mix of solo and trio performances; and the chance to sample various combinations of the sixties Peterson trios. The piano playing has a technical uniformity about it, though I disagree with the argument advanced by some that Peterson does not swing. He shows what happens to the virtuosity of Art Tatum when tempered by the leaner sensitivities of Nat Cole and surrounded by a strong if ultimately servile rhythm section. The best Peterson unit, with Brown and Thigpen, gets only six of the 26 trio tracks (check Thigpen's long ride cymbal decay as a gauge of the recording quality) and, oddly, the Jones/Hayes combination a measly one. Peterson's trio concept was the norm that Evans, LaFaro and Motian exploded; after this extended exposure, one understands why it needed exploding. But Peterson sure can play, as the performances here, including 10 solo tracks from the end of the project, more than adequately demonstrate. **BB**

Ralph Peterson

1962

Presents the Fo'tet **Peterson** (d); **Don Byron** (cl, bcl); **Bryan Carrott** (vb); **Melissa Slocum** (b); **David Murray** (ts, bcl); **Frank Lacy** (tb, flh). Blue Note Ⓕ CDP7 95475-2 (60 minutes). Recorded 1989.

⑧ ❽

Peterson is a paradox. Live, he is easily one of the loudest drummers in jazz, yet he listens closely to soloists, tailoring his phrasing to answer and propel them, even as he threatens to drown them out. In the studio, he has led several groups, of which the most interesting is the Fo'tet (short for Fourtet), not least because of who is in it: piping clarinettist Byron, who often phrases like a drummer himself; Carrott, arguably the most talented and creative vibist to come along in years; Slocum, whose deep bass sound is partly due to her use of gut strings.

Like Peterson's drumming, the music mostly rollicks. There are exceptions, like Byron's *Homegoing*, a lament for the late Lee Morgan centred around one repeated, incantatory melodic fragment. All of the band's members contribute tunes, but the quartet also plays Sammy Fain's ballad *I Can Dream, Can't I?* and a revved-up arrangement of Strayhorn's riff tune *Johnny Come Lately*, with dramatic rests added to give the drummer room to punch through. Murray and Lacy are welcome guests, but the Fo'tet needs no help to carry the day. This fiery modern acoustic music catches some young lions at close to their very best. **KW**

Michel Petrucciani

1962

Promenade with Duke **Petrucciani** (p). Blue Note Ⓕ CDP7 80590-2 (48 minutes). Recorded 1992.

⑧ ❽

Two traditions come together in this record. One is the process whereby the French seem endlessly capable of producing technically gifted jazz pianists quite happy to sustain solo concerts: before Petrucciani there was Martial Solal, and before him there was the now nearly forgotten Bernard Peiffer.

The other is the tradition of artists recording Ellington compositions. Sometimes, as with Thelonious Monk back in the fifties, it is to get the artist introduced to a wider public. With Petrucciani, one imagines that it was simply because he wanted to (the CD notes tell you nothing about this—indeed, they tell you nothing about anything, not even the date), and it is no short cut to fame and fortune to record a Duke album; it must be a labour of love. That is what it sounds like; a chance to get inside such familiar territory as *Caravan*, *Satin Doll* and *Take The 'A' Train* and explore the hidden corners. *Caravan* starts out as a slow, moody tone poem—the camels sound very tired—until somebody puts something in their water. *Take The 'A' Train* is a swinging, rocking number with Chinese overtones (all those parallel fourths and fifths) while *C Jam Blues* is an inspired bit of fantasy which, alas, stops after a paltry 90 seconds. None of it proves anything, but it is an enthralling and gripping record all the same. A solo recital from the following year on the Dreyfus label, is two CDs of the same thing but with a wider repertoire base. **MK**

Oscar Pettiford

1922-1960

Deep Passion **Pettiford** (b, vc); **Ernie Royal**, **Art Farmer**, **Ray Copeland**, **Kenny Dorham** (t); **Jimmy Cleveland**, **Al Grey** (tb); **Julius Watkins**, **David Amram** (frh); **Gigi Gryce** (as, arr); **Lucky Thompson**, **Benny Golson** (ts, arr); **Jerome Richardson** (ts, f); **Danny Bank**, **David Kurtzer**, **Sahib Shihab** (bs); **Tommy Flanagan**, **Dick Katz** (p); **Whitey Mitchell** (b); **Osie Johnson** (d); **Betty Glamman** (hp) Impulse! Ⓜ GRP 11432 (68 minutes). Recorded 1956/57.

⑥ ❽

The almost big band that Pettiford put together in 1956 was not employed frequently enough to keep a regular personnel, but it did make two LPs (the first in particular is excellent of its kind). It also preserved some of the few large arrangements by Lucky Thompson and some of the first by his replacement, Benny Golson. The forces at their disposal included four saxes, two trumpets, one trombone and two French horns. Watkins and Amram (two of the few constants through the band's six studio sessions, all gathered here) were mainly used in a much more punchy way than Claude Thornhill's ever were, and are given an up-tempo solo feature ensemble on *Two French Fries*. The harpist, spread thinly through nine of the 17 tracks, is only there for colouration but intriguing nonetheless.

Pettiford gets a reasonable amount of space for bass and cello solos, though by no means on every track, and the most affecting soloists are Farmer and Thompson, both on the first album's ten tracks. The second album seems on the whole less ambitious in its choice of material and arranging style, but it does contain a fine *I Remember Clifford* (featuring Kenny Dorham, unidentified in the notes) and Randy Weston's *Little Niles*, both classics of the period. **BP**

Vienna Blues: The Complete Session **Pettiford** (b, vc); **Hans Koller** (ts); **Attila Zoller** (g, b); **Jimmy Pratt** (d). Black Lion Ⓜ BLCD 760104 (50 minutes). Recorded 1959.

⑧ ❻

Pettiford was one of the most important links between Jimmy Blanton and today's bass players. He was a member of the first regular bop group (with Dizzy Gillespie and Don Byas) and worked with the Duke Ellington band for more than two years. He came to Europe with a touring package show in 1958 and never returned to the US. For the first time all nine titles recorded in Vienna with a truly international quartet have been transferred to one disc. (Pettiford, a full-blooded Red Indian, was joined by Austria's Koller, Hungary's Zoller and Jimmy Pratt from California.) There is a superlative version of Pettiford's fine ballad, *The Gentle Art Of Love*, and what is probably the definitive solo bass version of *Stardust*. Oscar started to experiment with the cello in 1950, and uses it here on *All The Things You Are* and the lengthy *Oscar's Blues* (Zoller switches to bass on these two tracks). The fidelity of the recording picks up the occasional finger squeak on the strings, but overall this is bass playing of an exceptionally high level. The CD is also a triumph for Koller, whose Warne Marsh-Zoot Sims style is entirely in sympathy with Pettiford's lines **AM**

Barre Phillips

1934

Mountainscapes **Phillips** (b); **John Surman** (ss, ts, bs, bcl, synth); **Dieter Feichter** (synth); **Stu Martin** (d, synth); **John Abercrombie** (g). ECM Ⓕ 1076 (843 167-2) (38 minutes). Recorded 1976.

⑦ ❽

This was an important album for both Phillips and ECM when it first came out. For one thing, it was the best-recorded and most articulate documentation of the newly-resurgent trio with Surman and Martin; for another, it utilized the at-that-time new sound panoramas generated by the synthesizer. It also kicked off the still-intact recording relationship between Surman and ECM. Lastly, the edge and energy to be found here was paralleled in few other contemporaneous ECM projects (although Benny Maupin's **The Jewel in the Lotus**—not yet on CD—approached it from a rather different path) and gave the label enhanced credibility in the progressive music arena.

Phillips had for most of his career been establishing standards (his **Unaccompanied Barre** from 1968 was the first solo bass recital album in jazz-related music) and on ECM had previously made the delectable **Music for Two Basses**, a series of astonishing duets with Dave Holland. This album, however, was perhaps the most ambitious to date, because even though it had an episodic nature, there was a definite intention to link the movements of *Mountainscape* into a unified entity. Some of the parts are exquisite; others border on the ferocious. The sum of the parts? Still impressive, partly because the sectionalization has allowed the music more drama and more linear development than much of the more sprawling music which was being created at this time, and partly because it still sounds uncompromisingly thought-through. **KS**

Joe 'Flip' Phillips

1915

Flip Wails: The Best Of The Verve Years **Phillips** (ts); with a collective personnel of **Howard McGhee**, **Harry Edison** (t); **Bill Harris** (tb); **Hank Jones**, **Oscar Peterson**, **Mickey Crane** (p); **Herb Ellis**, **Billy Bauer** (g); **Ray Brown** (b); **J.C. Heard**, **Buddy Rich**, **Jo Jones**, **Max Roach**, **Alvin Stoller**, **Louie Bellson** (d). Verve Ⓜ 521 645-2 (74 minutes). Recorded 1947-58.

⑧ ❻

Remarkably Flip Phillips sounded as good at his 80th birthday celebrations as he does on these classic recordings made in his middle life. He moved rapidly from being a clarinet player with Frankie Newton and Pete Brown in Harlem to becoming one of the most adventurous tenor soloists of the forties and was a prime mover in the innovative Woody Herman First Herd. While still with Woody he recorded with Parker and Gillespie and his later experience with Jazz At The Philharmonic (JATP) as stablemate to Lester Young (a particular friend and influence), Coleman Hawkins, Ben Webster and Illinois Jacquet rounded out his experience.

This collection of his work for Norman Granz excludes the JATP sessions. Those concerts were regarded as frantic, but retrospective listening reveals glorious music, often in ballad form, from Phillips and the others. The tracks here have a more compact and rehearsed feel to them. It is little known that Phillips is a good composer and arranger. That is confirmed by his few originals here and by the disciplined and lean music produced by his groups. But above all he is an expansive and eloquent soloist in the grand tenor tradition. He swings as hard as any of the mainstream players and would have been equally at home with Ellington or Basie as he was with Herman. His long-time friendship and musical partnership with Bill Harris is regrettably represented on only four of these 20 tracks, where both men play with typical strength of character. This excellent collection deserves to bring Phillips's music to a much wider and younger audience, which would surely accept such timeless art **SV**

Enrico Pieranunzi

1949

The Dream Before Us **Pieranunzi** (p); **Marc Johnson** (b). Ida Ⓕ CD 028 (57 minutes). Recorded 1990.

Pieranunzi is a fantastic talent: try his version of Cole Porter's *Night and Day* on this disc to discover the freshness of his musical approach. Just when it seemed impossible to squeeze anything new and adventurous out of the Bill Evans-Herbie Hancock tradition of modern jazz piano, this classically-trained Italian, now in his 40s and still under-appreciated outside of his native country, has managed to do so. The method he has used involves the avoidance of any conscious borrowings from Evans or Hancock, and an equal avoidance of indiscipline or self-indulgence in his playing.

His most exciting playing is to be found on his **Space Jazz Trio** albums for Divox (both now deleted), but on this release his sensitivity is to the fore as he and Johnson produce wonderfully intuitive collaborations on a mixture of spontaneous pieces, old standards and originals from both players. It is probably a little unfair to Johnson not to co-credit this album, but Pieranunzi remains the driving force of the music, and his flow of ideas is strong and involving for the duration of the record. Utterly devoid of tricks and self-conscious mannerisms, he plays music with a rare level of commitment and inspiration. **KS**

Billy Pierce

1948

Rolling Monk **Pierce** (ts); **Donald Brown** (p); **Christian McBride** (b); **Billy Drummond** (d). Paddle Wheel Ⓕ KICJ 154 (58 minutes). Recorded 1992.

⑦ ❽

A Berklee graduate, Pierce began his musical career as something of a house saxophonist in Boston soul clubs. In 1980 he took one of the saxophone chairs as Art Blakey assembled a new and exciting edition of the Jazz Messengers and toured extensively with the drummer for two years. He returned to Boston in the eighties, worked with pianist James Williams and taught both privately and at Berklee. As the title of this CD indicates, he has taken on, in Sonny Rollins and Thelonious Monk, two of the music's strongest personalities. It speaks volumes for his melodic selectivity and rhythmic awareness that he emerges unscathed. The basic cadence of his style gives him a natural affinity with Rollins and by ignoring the fine details of the New Yorker's game plan he successfully puts his own trademark on titles like *Old Cowhand* and *Strode Rode*. There is no marauding away from the theme and it is this fact that makes his Monk readings similarly effective. On *Ugly Beauty* and *Epistrophy* in particular he uses the original framework as a guideline to his own improvisational path and it proves to be a considerable creative stimulant. Pierce is fortunate in not being touted as another neo-classical wonderman. He is a mainstream/modern professional with a voice of his own. **BMcR**

Nat Pierce

1925-1992

Easy Swing **Nat Pierce Band** (Pierce [p], Doug Mettome [t], Urbie Green [tb], Med Flory [as], Richie Kamuca [ts], Jack Nimitz [bs], Freddie Green [g], Walter Page [b], Jo Jones [d]); **Mel Powell Band** (Powell [p], John Glasel [t], Jim Buffington [frh], Chuck Russo [cl, as, bs,], Boomie Richman [ts], Mundell Lowe [g], Joe Kay [b], Eddie Phyfe [d]). Vanguard Ⓕ 662 133 (41 minutes). Recorded 1954/55.

⑥ ❻

Pierce was unique in starting his career as a progressively modern pianist in the late forties and later retrenching to the swing idioms of Basie and Ellington. He was notable also for his ten years as straw boss and musical director of the Woody Herman band. Here he uses Basie's original rhythm section and adds his own friends. Pierce's sense of time was so good that it is impossible to detect the seams when he 'does a Basie' (he actually appeared anonymously *as* Basie on some of the Count's records—now there is a problem for discographers!)

The music is feather-light swinging with a powder-puff punch (the classic Basie band rarely hit hard). The image is complemented by Kamuca's Lester Young-inspired tenor and there is a rare chance to hear the solo work of Doug Mettome, one of the finest players of the time. The more ubiquitous Urbie Green is on good solo form, too.

The five tracks by Mel Powell's unit are immaculately arranged and played by the unusual front line and employ a similar light touch. Apart from the piano, the feature for the eccentric french horn on *When Did You Leave Heaven?* is particularly appealing. **SV**

Dominique Pifarely

Oblique **Pifarely** (vn); **Yves Robert** (tb); **Louis Sclavis** (cl); **Francois Coutourier** (p, syn); **Riccardo Del Fra** (b); **Joel Allouche** (d). Ida Ⓕ 034CD (61 minutes) Recorded 1992.

⑤ ❿

Oblique it certainly is. Pifarely has been associated with Sclavis for a number of years, and Sclavis appears here fleetingly. Pifarely has a nervous energy, married to a rhapsodic approach which it is hard to altogether escape on the violin. This gives him a thoroughly modern sound, especially when in the company of musicians who are prepared to stretch metred time to the point of extinction. Yet his ideas don't significantly move his playing away from the Central European tradition of the earlier part of this century. When left to his own devices, he sounds distinctly Bartòkian as did Leroy Jenkins for a number of years early in his career. Perhaps it's a problem endemic to the instrument. Or perhaps not. Stuff Smith and Ray Nance never sounded like warmed-over Bartòk.

The most arresting playing often comes from the pianist Francois Coutourier, who has the energy and technical command to match his ideas. He's also on just over half the CD, so he has time to make his mark, as opposed to the superb Sclavis and trombonist Robert, given two tracks each. He saves *Crepuscule With Nellie* from becoming a re-write of Debussy's violin sonata, and for that alone he deserves our gratitude. **KS**

Dave Pike

1938

Times Out Of Mind **Pike** (v); **Tom Rainier** (as, ts, p, synths); **Ron Eschete**, **Kenny Burrell** (g); **Luther Hughes**, **Harvey Newmark** (b); **Ted Hawke** (d). Muse Ⓕ MCD 5446 (41 minutes). Recorded 1975.

⑥ ❻

Pike has led a varied creative life, playing with Paul Bley in the fifties and then having a six-year stint with flautist Herbie Mann in the early sixties, when Mann established himself as one of the most popular players in jazz. After a period of residence in Europe in the late sixties leading The Dave Pike Set, he returned to California in 1973, and has stayed based there since then. Probably because of his long tenure with Mann, Pike has never garnered a strong critical press, and so his real achievements as a vibraphonist and leader have gone mostly unnoticed. While his style is rooted in Milt Jackson and Cal Tjader, he has a smooth and varied technique, clear improvisational ideas, and a musical taste which leads him away from the crasser aspects of commercial musical life. This present album finds him with a talented small group which allows him plenty of blowing room and which has a strong rhythm section. Tom Rainer is definitely preferable on piano to saxophone, and when he sticks to his keyboards the band gels effortlessly. Burrell doesn't have a great deal to say in his solo spots but, that aside, the musicians all play with spirit. A likeable album of fusion-tinged modern jazz. **KS**

Courtney Pine

1964

To The Eyes of Creation **Pine** (ts, bcl, ss, WX7); **Dennis Rollins** (tb); **Keith Waite** (f, perc); **Julian Joseph** (p, org); **Bheki Mseleku** (p); **Tony Remi**, **Cameron Pierre** (g); **Wayne Batchelor**, **Gary Crosby** (b); **Mark Mondesir**, **Peter Lewinson**, **Brian Abrams** (d); **Frank Tontoh** (d, perc); **Thomas Dyani**, **Mamadi Kamara** (perc); **Cleveland Watkiss**, **Juliet Roberts** (v). Island CID 514044 2 (58 minutes). Recorded 1992.

⑥ ❽

None of Pine's recorded releases has done justice to the man. In person he gives uncompromising jazz performances and competes at the highest level. Unforunately, a look at his overall output suggests that the promise of **Journey To The Urge Within** (Island CID 9846) or the ethnic honesty of **Closer To Home** (Mango 846528) are neither better nor worse than **Realms Of Our Dreams** (Antilles ANCD 8756) which teams him with a top flight American rhythm section. This CD at least tries to cover the full Pine canvas. It has powerful tenor outings on *Country Dance* and *Cleopatra's Needle*, his soprano takes a sensitive look at *Psalm* and *Redemption Song*, while *X-Caliber* is an excellent, if short, soliloquy. In contrast, his simple lines set against a Latin base reduce *The Healing Song* to little more than supermarket music and *Eastern Standard Time* is a pop dance song. The CD closes with *The Holy Grail*, a beautiful piece of music that, perhaps more than any other title, reminds us that Pine is an enigma, a writer with a classic book in him, but still writing paperbacks and, even then, unsure whether they should be romantic fiction or high drama. **BMcR**

Armand J. Piron

1888-1943

Piron's New Orleans Orchestra **Piron** (vn, v, dir.); **Peter Bocage** (t); **John Lindsay** (tb); **Lorenzo Tio Jr** (cl, ts); **Louis Warnecke** (as); **Steve Lewis** (p); **Charles Bocage** (bj, v); **Bob Ysaguirre** (bb); **Louis Cottrell** (d); **Lela Bolden**, **Ida G. Brown**, **Willie Jackson** (v). Azure Ⓕ AZ-CD-13 (78 minutes). Recorded 1923-26.

⑥ ❻

Although he was active at the turn of the century, the story of violinist Piron really begins when he replaced Freddie Keppard as leader of the star-studded Olympia Orchestra in 1912. King Oliver, Sidney Bechet and Zue Robertson were sidemen but extra-curricular publishing activities diverted Piron during the First World War. Fortunately, he continued to lead bands in New Orleans and his 1919 unit provided the nucleus for the twenties orchestra. The sessions that make up this CD came about when Piron accepted a residency in New York and represent a complete contrast to the power of the contemporary King Oliver band.

The basis of Piron's music was ragtime; the delivery was elegant and all of the best traditions of Creole musical etiquette were observed. The ensembles encouraged contrapuntal interplay but arrangements on the likes of *Bouncing Around* and *Mama's Gone, Goodbye* avoid tailgate trombone patterns and rely on the tastefully relaxed lead of Bocage and the flowing clarinet and dancing breaks of Tio. A different balance is achieved on the trombone-less *Red Man Blues*, excellent violin and clarinet counterpoint illuminates *Lou'siana Swing* and the swing generated throughout is genteel. The odd over-arranged item like *Ghost Of The Blues* takes the band to the fringe of jazz, but Piron's entire recorded output is on this CD and it documents an important stage of the ragtime and jazz overlap. **BMcR**

Bucky Pizzarelli 1926

The Complete Guitar Duos **Bucky Pizzarelli**, **John Pizzarelli** (g). Stash Ⓕ ST CD 536 (74 minutes). Recorded 1980/84.

⑥ ❻

The depth of tone and pitch of the seven-string guitar means that even when playing alone, as both father and son do from time to time on this compelling album of chamber jazz, the sound is far richer than on the average guitar solo album. Together, they pace each other perfectly, and bring a gently swinging grace to standards like *In a Mellotone* or *Love for Sale*, as well as less familiar fare such as their arrangement of Beiderbecke's *In a Mist*.

Perhaps it's a genetic peculiarity, but the only other duo who switch so effortlessly from accompaniment to solo, telepathically swapping roles, and challenging each other's ingenuity, are the brothers Boulu and Elios Ferré. Pizzarelli père et fils have this knack, although they apply it best to material different from their European counterparts: Django's *Nuages* is less fulfilling a performance than material drawn from Chick Corea or veteran guitarist Carl Kress. In general, after some kind of vamp introduction, Bucky leads off on the melody or digs straight into a solo. John's solos are less classically elegant, but when they trade fours or eights it fast becomes hard to tell who's who. They excel at medium tempo, never better than on the opener *Love For Sale*. **AS**

John Pizzarelli 1960

Naturally **John Pizzarelli** (v, g); **John Frosk**, **Anthony Kadleck**, **Michael Ponella**, **Jim Hynes** (t); **Clark Terry** (t, flh); **Bob Alexander**, **Mark Patterson**, **Wayne Andre**, **Paul Faulise** (tb); **Walt Levinsky**, **Frank Griffith** (as); **Scott Robinson**, **Frank Wess**, **Harry Allen** (ts); **Jack Stuckey** (bs); **Dominic Cortese** (acc); **Ken Levinsky** (p); **Bucky Pizzarelli** (g); **Martin Pizzarelli** (b); **Joe Cocuzzo**, **Tony Corbiscello** (d). RCA Novus Ⓕ 63151-2 (51 minutes). Recorded 1993.

⑧ ❽

Imagine a distinguished guitarist who is the son of a distinguished guitarist, a young, personable singer with a penchant for early Nat Cole and the courage to tackle Django's *Nuages* with the original French lyrics, and you have John Pizzarelli. Why he is not infinitely more famous than Harry Connick Jnr I cannot understand, unless it is simply a matter of being too hip.

This is Pizzarelli's third album, and his first with a big band. Among its high points are a guitar feature dedicated to Charlie Christian (*Seven On Charlie*), an impeccable unison guitar and scat blues (*Splendid Splinter*) and a Sinatra-style swinging ballad (*You Stepped Out Of A Dream*). The versatility and accomplishment is quite staggering. His follow-up album, **Dear Mr Cole**, has more singing and less guitar, so this slightly earlier one has the preferred balance. **DG**

King Pleasure (Clarence Beeks) 1922-1981

King Pleasure Sings/Annie Ross Sings **Pleasure**, **Betty Carter**, **The Dave Lambert Singers**, **Jon Hendricks**, **The Three Riffs**, **Blossom Dearie**, **Annie Ross** (v); **Ed Lewis**, **Merril Stepter** (t); **J.J. Johnson**, **Kai Winding** (tb); **Lem Davis** (as); **Charlie Ferguson**, **Lucky Thompson**, **Ray Abrams** (ts); **Danny Bank**, **Cecil Payne** (bs); **Ed Swanston**, **John Lewis**, **Jimmy Jones**, **Teacho Wiltshire**, **George Wallington** (p); **Ram Ramirez** (org); **Peck Morrison**, **Percy Heath**, **Paul Chambers**, **Leonard Gaskin** (b); **Herbie Lovelle**, **Kenny Clarke**, **Joe Harris**, **Teddie Lee**, **Art Blakey** (d). Prestige Ⓜ OJCCD 217-2 (47 minutes). Recorded 1952-54.

✔ ⑧ ❻

Yes, King Pleasure has other compact discs all to himself; but 12 of the 16 performances here are his, and one of the two CD bonus tracks is the original recording of *Moody's Mood* (still called *I'm In The Mood for Love* here) with Blossom Dearie singing the second bridge. Initial versions of such other Pleasure vocal trademarks as *Parker's Mood*, *Red Top* (with Betty Carter) and *Jumpin' With Symphony Sid* are also included, not to mention the classics *Twisted* and *Farmer's Market* among the Ross titles. Both singers favoured tenor soloists (Ross likes Wardell Gray, Pleasure prefers Getz, Pres and Moody) and, as the collective personnel suggests, both had an ear for a supporting cast and a functional arrangement, as well as due reverence for the source material. In sum, one for the five-foot vocal shelf. The elusive Pleasure was never as consistent in his later recordings, where his voice shows wear—although **Golden Days** (OJC1722-2) should be consulted for the liner notes, where he declares himself "the saviour of humanity" in the second paragraph and proceeds cosmologically to out-Ra Sun Ra. **BB**

Paul Plimley

Kaleidoscopes **Plimley** (p); **Lisle Ellis** (b). hat ART Ⓟ CD 6117 (58 minutes) Recorded 1992.

⑥ ❽

I wonder if Ornette is feeling his age? Within the space of a few years there have been a number of recorded tributes and reinterpretations of his music. Soon they'll be calling *Ramblin'* a jazz classic. That aside, few pianists have ever attempted to come to grips with Ornette's songs, although Paul Bley has always been partial to them. That's a good reason to welcome this pianist's long and heartfelt look into the interior workings of such witty and entertaining pieces as *Poise*, *Moon Inhabitants* and *Chronology*, as well as the more heart-on-sleeve songs such as *Beauty Is A Rare Thing* and *Peace*. In fact, *Beauty* becomes a direct descendent of Monk in the version here, which is a fascinating tranformation to behold.

Plimley and bassist Ellis have a fine understanding of each other's playing and of Ornette's music. Happily there is no attempt to bend the piano to an approximation of Ornette's intensely human saxophone cry, and this completely alien instrument becomes a continual object of fascination within these songs. Plimley, a great believer in space and the value of proper phrasing, comes across as a fine interpreter of this music and an original thinker. A commendable effort. **KS**

Jimmy Ponder

1946

Come On Down **Ponder** (g); **Houston Person** (ts); **Lonnie Smith** (org); **Winard Harper** (d); **Sammy Figuera** (perc). Muse Ⓟ MCD 5375 (45 minutes). Recorded 1990.

⑥ ❽

Ponder is not exactly a household name, but just a glance at the other major players here will make you covet this album. This is the musical territory carved out by Jimmy Smith and Kenny Burrell in the mid-sixties, and with the addition of tenor player Person, we have a worthy updating of that tradition. Organist Smith (not to be confused with Lonnie Liston Smith) in fact made one of the cult Blue Note organ records in the late sixties and had a long stint with George Benson. His playing here is driving but ever-tasteful (witness his sensitive backing of Ponder on the ballad *Ebb Tide*), and he knows just what effects will work for which instrument he is accompanying. Ponder himself freely admits admiration for Wes Montgomery, though his own playing on this disc has a more liberal helping of rhythm & blues than Wes mostly showed. He has an easy and complete technique, a tone which is not too mellow, and he is also a driving accompanist. Tenorist Person, who produced this session, adds some worthily meaty solos in just the right spirit: sophisticated but with fire to spare.

This is a fine mainstream jazz album masquerading as just another good'n. **KS**

Jean-Luc Ponty

1942

Mystical Adventures **Ponty** (vn, kbds); **Jamie Glaser** (g); **Chris Rhyne** (kbds); **Randy Jackson** (b); **Rayford Griffin** (d); **Paulinho DaCosta** (perc). Atlantic Jazz Ⓜ 781933-2 (41 minutes). Recorded 1981.

⑥ ❽

Although originally trained as a classical violinist and equally adept at all forms of jazz from swing through bop and modal to free music, Jean-Luc Ponty is perhaps most celebrated for having firmly established the violin—with a number of original electronic modifications—in jazz-rock. As a sideman to such eminent composer/leaders as Frank Zappa and John McLaughlin (with whose Mahavishnu Orchestra he played in the mid-seventies), Ponty is a peerless provider of exhilarating violin breaks, as interesting for their textural subtlety and variety as for their sure-footed fleetness. As a composer/leader himself, however, he is less successful, his simple riffs and jaunty rhythms not quite substantial enough to support their somewhat overblown pretensions; the overall effect of **Mystical Adventures** is of a slightly superior version of that plague of the seventies rock scene, the concept album, replete with pseudo-mystical/mythical references to everything from Hobbits to Buddha and lovingly packaged with trippy artwork. This is a shame, because Ponty's virtuosity and originality—especially his use of the retuned five-string violin, vocoders and a battery of fascinating electronic effects—need no such ephemeral gimmicks to recommend them, and the lasting power of the album would have been considerably greater had the music, rather than the mysticism, been its main focus. Nevertheless, Ponty's biting, gutsy sound—even in these slightly pompous settings—is exciting enough to maintain interest through an intriguing if flawed album. **CP**

Odean Pope

1938

Out for a Walk **Pope** (ts, v); **Gerald Veasley** (elb); **Cornell Rochester** (d). Moers Music Ⓟ 02072 (67 minutes). Recorded 1990

In addition to working with Max Roach since 1979, this disciple of the enigmatic Philadelphia pianist Ibn Hassan Ali now leads two bands of his own. Pope's Saxophone Choir (heard to best advantage on **The Ponderer**, Soul Note 121229-2) recalls the legend that Coltrane embraced soprano as the 'top' range he heard but could not reach on tenor. Pope, another Philadelphia tenorist of mystical bent, likewise must have been tracking down secret overtones in convening a band including nine saxes. Perhaps the best way to describe Pope's trio with Rochester polyrhythm-a-ning on drums and Veasley going one step beyond Jamaaladeen Tacuma on six-string electric bass is to ask the unexposed listener to imagine a 'harmolodic' synthesis of jazz and funk as created by Coltrane rather than Ornette Coleman. Not that Pope is especially beholden to either: if anything, he is a Sonny Rollins man, as witnessed here by the the calypso gait of the title track and the deep, athletic subtone that Pope reveals on *Zip, Part 1*. At this point, Pope owes little to any of what one assumes were his formative influences. When he does evoke Coltrane, it is deliberately, as *Philly in 3*, where the resemblance to Coltrane is not superficial; it is a matter of Pope's penetrating cry, rhythmic intensity, and harmonic reach. **FD**

Chris Potter

1970

Pure Potter (f, ss, as, ts, bcl); **Larry Goldings** (p, org); **John Hart** (g); **Larry Grenadier** (b); **Al Foster** (d). Concord ℗ CCD-4637 (61 minutes). Recorded 1994.

⑧ ❿

Potter has come a long way in a short time. After meeting the late Red Rodney at a South Carolina festival when he was just 18, Potter moved to New York to study music and ended up joining Rodney's group. Within a short space of time he was also playing with the Mingus Big Band and Paul Motian's Electric BeBop Band, and making freelance recording appearances. This, his second under his own name (his debut as a leader had an invaluable and memorable contribution from pianist Kenny Werner), shows impressive maturity of thought. Potter has taken the decision to concentrate on the tenor as his main solo horn, and while that may seem like closing down options, it focuses his personality. It also allows him to use his other horns effectively as arranged support, with the bass clarinet particularly colourful in this role. Pianist Goldings plays sensitively, but is not in the Werner league. This is compensated for by Foster, an enlivening presence.

Like many young horn players, Potter's solos sometimes sound like a flashing kaleidoscope of previous masters, but what impresses about him is that he doesn't sound as if he's desperately attempting to run through every idea he's ever borrowed from elsewhere in the course of a solo. He sounds like he enjoys what he plays, and that each solo really expresses something about his own personality. His tone - a fashionably timeless combination of Rollins, Coltrane, Redman (Dewey) and even Ornette - has a great deal of warmth and plasticity, while his harmonic and rhythmic conceptions are an individual fusion of Coltrane and Rollins. But you can safely put all that to one side and listen with unalloyed pleasure to the playing of a man who has a secure identity which is worth communicating. **KS**

Bud Powell

1924-1966

The Bud Powell Trio Plays **Powell** (p); **Curly Russell**, **George Duvivier** (b); **Max Roach**, **Art Taylor** (d). Roulette Ⓜ CDP7 93902-2 (43 minutes). Recorded 1947/53.

⑩ ❽

For sheer fluency and impetus only Charlie Parker could rival Bud Powell at his best. Like Parker, he communicates a kind of intensity bordering at times on desperation, but alongside this there is ebullience, as he frankly revels in his speed of thought and execution.

This collection of 16 numbers includes the whole of Powell's first recording session, generally considered to be the best and most consistent of all. Of special note are the headlong *Indiana* and a beautifully hard-edged version of the Matt Dennis ballad *Everything Happens To Me*. Despite the fact they were recorded so early there is nothing in the least bit dated about these performances, and it is interesting that the same year, 1947, saw Thelonious Monk's equally auspicious début.

The 1953 tracks are almost as good, but Powell was subsequently prevented from keeping up his artistic development by addiction, mental illness and the aftermath of electro-convulsive therapy. So we are left with this blazing start to a sadly blighted career. **DG**

The Complete Blue Note and Roost Recordings **Powell** (p); **Curly Russell**, **Tommy Potter**, **George Duvivier**, **Paul Chambers**, **Sam Jones**, **Pierre Michelot** (b); **Max Roach**, **Roy Haynes**, **Art Taylor**, **Philly Joe Jones**, **Kenny Clarke** (d); **Fats Navarro** (t); **Sonny Rollins** (ts); **Curtis Fuller** tb. Blue Note Ⓜ 8 30083 2 (four discs: 277 minutes). Recorded 1947-63.

✔ ⑩ ❽

Powell's Blue Note years encompass the artistic brilliance, high drama and low comedy that were all part of his art. The early trio classics—among them *Un Poco Loco* and *Parisian Thoroughfare*—show his mastery of the harmonic and rhythmic displacements (and speed) of Charlie Parker, and close voicings indebted to Monk. This is bebop piano at its freshest and purest (the earliest session here is one of two that eventually turned up on Roost).

That spare trio format, broken up by one session for quintet, and one for an odd quartet with trombone, always spotlights piano, not to dismiss the excellent support he gets from a succession of fine rhythm sections. Given Powell's psychological problems in the fifties, there is a tendency to dismiss his later sides as sad and fumbling, although only one encore, recorded in Paris, postdates 1958 in this collection. It is time for re-evaluation. There is a stark and pitiless economy to the dark minor pieces he then favoured, cut with the unexpected lightness of change-ups like his cowboy lope *Buster Rides Again* and chipper children's song *Borderick*. Good notes by Bob Blumenthal and Alfred Lion, marred only by aggressive typesetting design. Sound is quite good; some sides have been speed-corrected from previous issues. **KW**

The Complete Bud Powell on Verve **Powell** (p) with the following collective personnel: **Ray Brown**, **Curly Russell**, **George Duvivier**, **Percy Heath**, **Lloyd Trotman** (b); **Max Roach**, **Buddy Rich**, **Art Taylor**, **Art Blakey**, **Kenny Clarke**, **Osie Johnson** (d). Verve Ⓜ 521 669-2 (five discs: 314 minutes) Recorded 1949-56.

✔ ⑧ ❻

Powell's personal downward curve is a well-documented and immensely sad fact, and it would be vain to pretend that all the music in this set is consistently good or at times even passable. Yet there is little of it which doesn't inform the listener, and the best of it not only excites and overwhelms, but it is at the very centre of modern jazz piano. It is impossible to conceive of jazz history without the impact of such impossibly heroic miniatures such as the 1950 trio version of *Tea For Two* (there are three takes here), taken at a murderously fast tempo at which Powell manages to articulate amazing right-hand leaps of the imagination. These were the textbooks for a generation. Likewise the rich invention and deep feeling of the 1951 piano solos, such as *The Last Time I Saw Paris*, *Dusky 'n' Sandy*, *Hallucinations* and, particularly, *Parisian Thoroughfare*.

As noted above, not everything here is even near this level, and there are times when Powell is clearly not on the same planet as his accompanists: he meanders through well-known songs and forgets the changes, or decides to play at a slightly different tempo, or simply cannot make his fingers do what he wants them to (try *Crazy Rhythm* from 1955, where all of these things happen). Yet the intensity of his vision always hovers (not always the case on the more or less contemporaneous Blue Note sessions), and even when technique deserts him, there are the feelings. A 1954 version of *It Never Entered My Mind* is heartbreakingly sad, Powell's left-hand stabbing out ugly, darkened chord alterations which don't hint at personal pain, they scream it. But not all is doom and misery: much of the more ordinary performances, from 1956 for example, find Powell quite bouncy and almost fleet, audibly enjoying himself. He also gets in a couple of Monk pastiches (*Mediocre*, *Epistrophy*) which combine great eccentricity with occasional wry touches of humour.

This essential jazz set is compiled and documented in exemplary fashion (though Powell's name could have been more prominent on the cover), its essays and interviews giving worthwhile insights into the man and the music. The inside pictures are a treat as well. If you fancy a single disc of the Verve years then **The Genius of Bud Powell** is still available. But when it comes to the overall picture don't hesitate: buy this. **KS**

Jazz At Massey Hall **Powell** (p); **Charles Mingus** (b); **Max Roach** (d). Debut Ⓜ OJCCD 111-2 (35 minutes). Recorded 1953.

⑧ ❻

Recorded primarily in May 1953 by Charles Mingus, the New Jazz Society of Toronto's justly-celebrated Massey Hall concert brought together four of the giants of bebop—Parker, Gillespie, Powell and Roach—along with Mingus. One of the concert's pinnacles was the trio segment featuring Powell, Roach and Mingus. Powell, the most significant of the early bebop pianists, suffered a series of debilitating psychiatric problems from 1945 until his death. Still, his influence was felt through a handful of indelible recordings, including this stunning Massey Hall date. Obviously stirred by being reunited with his erstwhile colleagues, Powell more than rose to the occasion. His trademark fleet-fingered right-hand runs combined with pungent left-hand accompaniment liberally bedeck George Shearing's *Lullaby of Birdland*, while the influence of Art Tatum is apparent in Powell's evocative treatment of *Embraceable You*. Throughout, Powell is buoyed by the supple rhythmic undercurrents supplied by Mingus and Roach. Some tracks on this album are reputed to be from night-club performances lter the same year. **CB**

Blues For Bouffémont **Powell** (p) **Michel Gaudry, Guy Hayat** (b); **Art Taylor**, **Jacques Gervais** (d). Black Lion Ⓜ BLCD 760135 (54 minutes). Recorded 1964.

⑧ ❻

Although Bud Powell's five-year sojourn in Europe probably did much for his peace of mind, the level of his artistic output on record seldom reached that of his New York sessions. This is arguably the best album he made while in Paris, although it is flawed. Despite his early formal training Bud was essentially an 'ear' player and there are many examples on record where he busks his way uncomfortably through the chords of certain tunes. Here, his theme choruses on *Like Someone In Love*, for example, sound like the work of a man who has probably never checked the song copy. Nevertheless there are more moments of greatness than near-failure, and the reunion with Art Taylor (who was on a number of his earlier American dates) was a sound move by producer Alan Bates. The opening *In The Mood For A Classic* is a Powell original in the great tradition both in terms of composition and performance. He is equally at home with bebop classics such as *Relaxin' at Camarillo*, *Moose the Mooche* and, in particular, the fleet *Little Willie Leaps*, while the title tune is unusual in that it is a slow tempo blues played with great feeling and deliberation. The three additional CD-version tracks have their highs and lows and suffer somewhat from the location recording and a poor piano. **AM**

Mel Powell
1923

Mel Powell Trios: Borderline/Thigamagig **Mel Powell** (p); **Ruby Braff** (t) or **Paul Quinichette** (ts); **Bobby Donaldson** (d). Vanguard Ⓕ 662223 (62 minutes). Recorded 1954.

⑧ ❻

The voluntary exit of Mel Powell from playing jazz was an extended torture for his fans which endured from 1954, when he last made a substantial number of recordings, until the mid-sixties when he irrevocably moved his talents to what we must call serious music and taught at music colleges. He revisited our music briefly in 1986 but was then laid low by a muscular disease which has trapped his playing abilities but not his spirit nor his fertile musical mind.

Whenever he recorded, even in the awesome presence of a giant like Goodman, Powell's solos stood out as the precious metal of jazz. His clean, clipped but eloquent playing, derived but yet far removed from Earl Hines and Teddy Wilson, had total authority and it was rare for him not to dominate any session on which he played. Here are two of his best on one CD reissue, with sparse groups which allow his full talent to emerge. Powell, a swing pianist by repute, ventures firmly into his own grounds in these interpretations and spins elegant inventions on pieces like *What's New?* and his own *Bouquet*. Sprinting, stride-like piano also abounds, as on *California Here I Come*.

The young Braff, so appropriate here with his melodic style, and the more experienced Paul Quinichette can but be carried along by the great talent, although neither is intimidated. Braff went on to even greater things, but Quinichette's seven performances must be regarded as his most substantial legacy. This is probably one of the finest piano albums of them all. **SV**

Roy Powell
1965

A Big Sky **Powell** (p, kbds); **Richard Iles** (t, flh); **Rick Taylor** (tb); **Mike Walker** (g); **Iain Dixon** (ts); **Jake Newman** (b); **Steve Gilbert** (d). Totem Ⓕ CD101 (52 minutes). Recorded 1994.

⑧ ❽

This extraordinarily accomplished recording shows that while London was congratulating itself on being the focus of Britain's eighties jazz renaissance, rather greater things were fermenting in the north-west. Improbably, Powell thanks his studies with Harrison Birtwistle at the Royal Northern College of Music and former employers Anthony Braxton and Mike Gibbs for lending inspiration to this record. It turns out that Braxton's input was philosophical rather than stylistic, and that is no surprise given that the basis of Powell's success is a virtuosic command of harmony and orchestration and their application to jazz-rock.

Using every imaginable resource to vary texture and motive, Powell produces an endlessly compelling parade of dynamic and dramatic variation within the idiom, drawing a seemingly impossible degree of detail from the instruments at his disposal. The soloists, among them the monstrously talented Mike Walker and a beautifully poised Iain Dixon, are icing on an already unimaginably rich confection. It would be surprising if a more comprehensively conceived electric jazz record were to be issued this side of the millennium. **MG**

André Previn
1929

Shelly Manne and His Friends: My Fair Lady/André Previn and His Pals: West Side Story **Manne** (d); **Previn** (p); **Leroy Vinnegar**, **Red Mitchell** (b); **Manne** (d). Contemporary/Ace Ⓜ CDCOPD 942 (74 minutes). Recorded 1956/59.

④ ❻

One of the favourite sports of jazz reviewers in the late fifties was (after Brubeck-bashing) the act of Previn-bashing. Brubeck-bashing was more fun, because Brubeck was the bigger star and had a higher profile, but Previn-bashing was also much enjoyed because Previn had committed the sin of being on the LP which sold more than any other in jazz history up to that time. It was **My Fair Lady**. What you did to bash Previn was say he was facile, shallow, fleet, superficial and all those other things that suggest he was not drenched in the blues. You don't need to be drenched in the blues to do a version of *My Fair Lady*, of course, and it is hard to see now why everyone got so steamed up, or indeed why everyone bought this and the follow-up **West Side Story** record. Jazz musicians don't make records of 'the music from the show' any more (classical conductors do that now). Classical conductors don't make swinging (but facile) piano records any more; at least not very often. Jazz records don't sell a million copies. How long ago it all was. But you may care to note that a much better album of the *Fair Lady* tunes was made in the eighties by a duo: Ruby Braff and Dick Hyman. Now, that deserved to sell a million. **MK**

Bobby Previte

Weather Clear, Track Fast **Previte** (d); **Graham Haynes** (c); **Robin Eubanks** (tb); **Marty Ehrlich** (f, cl, bcl, as); **Don Byron** (cl, bs); **Anthony Davis**, **Steve Gaboury** (p); **Anthony Cox** (b). Enja Ⓕ R2 79667 (US no) (55 minutes). Recorded 1991.

✔ ⑧ ❽

Composer/percussionist Previte is especially hard to define by a single album. Individual projects may attain totally singular sounds, like Claude's **Late Morning** (Gramavision 18-88112), where the nonet includes electric and pedal steel guitars, harp and accordion; or looser blowing structures may give way to programmatic specificity, as on Previte's vivid **Music of the Moscow Circus** (Gramavision R2 79466). My preference for this, his most 'straight-ahead' album, can be traced to his exceptional taste in putting the band together and success in drawing his talented partners out with seven pithy compositions. This is Previte's **A Day at the Races**, with a horsetrack reference in each title and a shifting thematic focus that gives each player room to impress. Everyone is at their best—Haynes, the most overlooked of both the M-Basers and the young trumpets (he plays cornet here); Cox, as consistent and flexible as anyone on the creative music scene; Davis, who plays piano on all but one track and should put himself in such open settings more often; and on it goes. Previte the composer employs repetition to spur rather than lull; Previte the drummer moves the music from underneath. One of the best statements from the bright lights of the nineties. **BB**

Sammy Price

1908-1992

And His Texas Blusicians 1929-41 **Price** (p, v, wbd, ldr); with a collective personnel including **Douglas Finnell**, **Joe Brown**, **Eddie Mullens**, **Shad Collins**, **Bill Johnson**, **Chester Boone**, **Emmett Berry** (t); **Bert Johnson**, **Floyd Brady**, **Ray Hogan** (tb); **Lem Johnson** (cl, v); **Fess Williams** (cl, as); **Don Stovall** (as); **Ray Hill**, **Lester Young**, **Skippy Williams** (ts); **Percy Darensburg**, **Duke Jones**, **Bass Hill**, **Billy Taylor** (b); **Wilbert Kirk**, **Doc West**, **Herb Cowens**, **J.C. Heard** (d); **Effie Scott**, **Ruby Smith**, **Jack Meredith** (v). Classics Ⓜ 696 (71 minutes). Recorded 1929-41.

✔ ⑧ ❻

Price never exactly hit the headlines in his long career, but early on he was a gifted and tasteful swing-style pianist and small-group leader in the manner of Earl Hines and Count Basie. At various times after the Second World War he veered first towards out-and-out boogie woogie and later to jump-style r&b (with King Curtis on tenor). This disc contains all his sessions as a leader up to 1942, and it can be argued that this is the cream of his jazz-based work. Certainly the bands are tight, swinging and entertaining, with altoist Don Stovall contributing some fine solos on the 1940 sessions. Price also plays well on the 1941 dates featuring Lester Young, not then long out of the Basie band, and it is fair to say that the four sides featuring Young are consciously apeing the Basie small-group approach of the time. Price is certainly not an original stylist, but his well-tailored music and tidy arrangements make this a consistently entertaining disc. The sound quality is variable but bearable. **KS**

Louis Prima

1911-1978

Let's Swing It **Prima** (t, v, ldr) with **His New Orleans Gang**: collective personnel includes **George Brunies** (tb); **Sidney Arodin**, **Eddie Miller**, **Pee Wee Russell** (cl); **Claude Thornhill**, **Frank Pinero** (p); **George Van Eps**, **Nappy Lamare**, **Gerry McAdams** (g); **Artie Shapiro**, **Jack Ryan** (b); **Stan King**, **Ray Bauduc** (d). Charly Ⓑ CDCD 1160 (65 minutes). Recorded 1934/35.

⑦ ❻

Prima is not these days primarily associated with jazz. His latter-day career in Hollywood and Vegas and on the latin side of the music entertainment business constitute the more lasting memory. But his small groups of the thirties were an adroit mixture of a Dixieland not dissimilar to Bob Crosby's with the enjoyable hamming which was to gradually point the leader on a different career path. His trumpet playing was simple and entirely under the spell of Armstrong, but it was strong and effective when carrying a melody, while his vocals were always engaging, to say the least. Then there is the not inconsiderable achievement of having spawned *Sing, Sing, Sing* in 1936–a song now indissolubly associated with Benny Goodman's dominance of the Swing Era. This chronological collection pulls up 12 months short of Prima's version, but there are plenty of jolly up-tempo rave-ups here to compensate. Of the soloists, the clarinettists tend to impress most, but the real stars are the rhythm section, whose precise and buoyant teamwork make this a very disciplined and swinging outfit. Swing may be something of a misnomer if applied rigorously, because the two-beat rhythm points clearly to the Dixie mentioned above, but the music remains very danceable indeed.

One last point - although the playing-time is good and the price attractive, why did Charly give the purchaser a brief biographical note on Prima but no personnel details? The above listing is from Rust. **KS**

Marcus Printup

Song For The Beautiful Woman **Printup** (t); **Walter Blanding** (ts); **Eric Reed** (p); **Reuben Rogers** (b); **Brian Blade** (d). Blue Note Ⓕ CDP 8 30790 2 (60 minutes). Recorded 1994.

⑥ ❽

Printup is another new arrival from the Wynton Marsalis school of neo-classicism. He is a regular with the Lincoln Centre Jazz Orchestra and has also been in pianist Marcus Roberts's band. This date finds him in the company of Eric Reed, another musician closely associated with Marsalis; he provides the sort of support to the soloists and rhythm section one would expect from the likes of Cedar Walton and Bobby Timmons. Tenorist Walter Blanding is taking the currently fashionable route away from the influence of latter-day Coltrane, combining elements of early Trane, Rollins and people like Hank Mobley to create that amorphous and rather characterless (but highly accomplished) approach which fits so adeptly into recherché exercises such as this.

Printup himself has the bright brassy tone of a Clifford Brown or Freddie Hubbard, immaculate articulation and rhythmic assuredness, and does nothing wrong. He plays *I'll Remember April* like a born-again Lee Morgan, and everything goes along swimmingly. Yet it is hard to escape the conclusion that, for all its undoubted finesse and expertise, this album remains somehow sterile. They could all do with getting their hands dirty; maybe even take a chance and play something crass. Make the heart jump a little. So far the brain might tick, but the ticker doesn't race. **KS**

Clarence Profit

1912-1944

All The Solo And Trio Sides Plus Washboard Tracks **Profit** (p solos) on six tracks; on a further six tracks add **Billy Moore** (g); **Ben Brown** (b). On four tracks **Jimmy Shirley** (g) replaces **Moore**. On two tracks **Profit** (p) with **Harold Randolph** (kazoo); **Teddy Bunn** (g); **Bruce Johnson** (washboard, v); **Gladys Bentley** (v). On two tracks **Profit** (p) with **Taft Jordan**, **Dave Page** (t); **Ben Smith** (cl, as); **Carl Wade** (ts); **Steve Washington** (bj, g); **Ghost Howell** (b); **Jake Fenderson** (washboard, v); **Eddie Foster** (v). Memoir Ⓕ CD MOIR 504 (62 minutes). Recorded 1930-40.

⑧ ❻

Jazz hagiography abounds with tales of unknown talent, many of the stories probably apocryphal, but in the case of Profit we have a genuinely underrated and influential figure who made only a handful of record dates. Memoir have done a considerable service by releasing virtually all of his known work on this CD (it is possible that he plays on other as yet untraced washboard sides) which reinforces the public opinions of men who heard him play. Oscar Peterson has credited Profit with being his main inspiration when he formed his own trio while Teddy Wilson placed Clarence's work immediately after that of Tatum, Waller and Hines. On the evidence of the solo and trio performances he was well ahead of his time both in conception and execution. Some of the runs and cadences are very Tatum-like on the solo titles while George Wallington's admiration for Profit is manifest in the first chorus of George's 1951 version of *I Didn't Know What Time It Was,* for this is virtually a note-for-note transcription of Clarence's solo. Profit is less visible on the four washboard titles but they are extremely good fun. The excellent and very informative notes are by another jazz pianist, Britain's Pat Hawes, making this a highly recommended release made up entirely of fascinating and stimulating keyboard playing. **AM**

Dudu Pukwana

1938-1990

In The Townships **Pukwana** (as, p, perc, v); **Mongezi Feza** (t, perc, v); **Biso Mngqikana** (ts, perc, v); **Harry Miller** (b, elb); **Louis Moholo** (d, perc). Earthworks/Virgin Ⓜ CDEWV5 (36 minutes). Recorded 1973.

✔ ⑧ ❼

Born in Port Elizabeth, Pukwana came to London with Chris McGregor's Blue Notes in 1965. Moving from hard-bop beginnings, he became an important part of the musical revolution of the late sixties. He was never really part of the free music scene but he had a natural affinity with its players; when the circumstances were right, he could desert the melodic and harmonic principles that he had brought from South Africa. This CD is coloured by such contacts, but more significantly it is fiercely African. Pukwana wrote all of the tunes and the rhythm of the Kwela musical heritage is pre-eminent. His jaunty composer's piano has an Abdullah Ibrahim-ish insistence and, when required, fulfils the task of laying good foundations. In the context of this riff-based music, it certainly encourages extrovert solo statements from his colleagues. Pukwana's own saxophone solos have an unmistakably passionate edge and are as much about the townships as they are about Charlie Parker. Every one displays a natural melodic gift as well as a flair for uncomplicated improvisation while still retaining contact with their ethnic origin. The horrors of apartheid are not paraded; Pukwana's brand of music speaks of joyful abandon and not morale-sapping distress. Feza makes his own contribution with the 'angry bee' lyricism of his pocket trumpet and the whole package comes over as African music realized in the manner of American jazz. **BMcR**

Don Pullen

1941-1995

New Beginnings **Pullen** (p); **Gary Peacock** (b); **Tony Williams** (d). Blue Note Ⓕ CDP7 91785-2 (49 minutes). Recorded 1988.

✔ ⑩ ❿

Although Pullen had previously recorded solo albums, as well as duets with the drummer Milford Graves and the tenor saxophonist George Adams, this was his first recording to utilize conventional trio instrumentation. But its instrumentation is the only thing conventional about **New Beginnings**, a disc deserving a place alongside classic trio recordings by Duke Ellington, Art Tatum, Herbie Nichols, Bud Powell, Thelonious Monk and Paul Bley. Pullen's genius lies in incorporating the percussive techniques associated with avant-garde piano into a mainstream setting; he is the after-the-fact transitional figure between Horace Silver and Cecil Taylor. His peripatetic keyboard style ensures variety, not only from track to track, but from phrase to phrase—as on *Once Upon a Time*, for example, where he spins an expansive waltz, then skewers it and gradually smashes it into little pieces. **New Beginnings** also reaffirms Pullen's status as a versatile composer who obviously learned a trick or two during his time with Charles Mingus. Although not billed as such, the infectiously syncopated *Jana's Delight* could pass as a homage to Ahmad Jamal. *Reap the Whirlwind* recalls the agitated, open-ended performances that Pullen recorded with Giuseppi Logan in the sixties, but it is much better focused. In their alert responses to Pullen, Peacock and Williams show a resourcefulness that recalls the bassist's work with Bill Evans and Albert Ayler and the drummer's work with Miles Davis. Not another tedious exercise in eighties classicism—just a classic. (About the playing time: Blue Note's timings add up to just over 37 minutes, although the actual total is as listed above. One of the few instances of a label short-changing itself, rather than the consumer!) **FD**

Flora Purim

1942

Butterfly Dreams **Flora Purim** (v); **Joe Henderson** (f, ts); **George Duke** (p, syn); **David Amaro** (g); **Stanley Clarke** (b); **Airto Moreira** (d, perc); **Ernie Hood** (zither). Milestone Ⓜ OJCCD-315-2 (37 minutes). Recorded 1973.

⑨ ❽

Brazilian vocalist Purim came to prominence in Chick Corea's Return to Forever alongside husband and master percussionist Moreira; **Butterfly Dreams**, her first outing for Milestone as leader, ploughed a similar furrow to her former employer's group: light, Latinesque jazz-rock, with more emphasis on good-time, good-humoured group interplay than on the virtuosic thrashing of the Mahavishnu Orchestra or the introspective tone poems of early Weather Report. Coming from a family of classical musicians, Purim has always been the possessor of an overridingly musical voice. Whether singing in Portuguese or English (both of which she does here) or indulging in her wordless scatting flights, which are often heavily enhanced with special effects, her voice always fits into the group context as just another instrument—no mean feat in jazz rock, not exactly the most vocal-friendly of musics. Of course the rhythm section, whether funking it up on *Dr Jive* or laying down the Latin groove of *Light As A Feather* (something of a latter-day fusion standard), deserves special mention here. Seldom has Clarke's playing integrated better with percussion, and Moreira is as stunning as one would expect. And Joe Henderson, recently a star all over again, blows as cool as this music demands. **SH**

Nick Purnell

Onetwothree **Purnell** (arr, ldr); **Kenny Wheeler**, **Paul Edmonds** (t, flh); **Mike Gibbs** (tb); **Ashley Slater** (btb, tba); **Ken Stubbs**, **Julian Argüelles** (ss, as, ts); **Django Bates** (kbds); **John Taylor** (p); **Mike Walker** (g); **Laurence Cottle** (elb); **Mick Hutton** (b); **Peter Erskine** (d); **Dave Adams** (perc). Ah Um Ⓕ 006 (57 minutes). Recorded 1990.

⑦ ❽

Purnell has gathered an impressive cast and given them material with which to show off their abilities as section men and soloists across a wide range of styles. His writing is not busy (the rhythm section is very active, but I doubt that it is too precisely scored in that fashion: most of the time I would presume directions and patterns rather than notes on paper), but it is full of colour and character, has a big personality and reaches across the gap between the speakers and the listener quite successfully. Of the soloists, Wheeler surprises as usual, and Julian Argüelles continues to impress with his logic and consistency.

The strange thing about this album is that it is so identifiably from Britain: there is a definite humour or feel to the music which one only finds in Britain, and its elements include whimsy, surrealism, self-deprecation and a type of manic high spirits which nonetheless avoids the extremism of some continental European countries' conceptions. There is also an eclecticism which comes of the unusual cultural mix to be found in Britain. All this may sound by-the-by, but it helps explain the richness and boldness of the instrumental writing and soloing. The execution is not always spot-on (there are the occasional sax section wobbles), but it is always done with commendable spirit. A rewarding album. **KS**

Ike Quebec

1918-1963

The Art of Ike Quebec **Quebec** (ts); with a collective personnel of **Bennie Green** (tb); **Stanley Turrentine** (ts); **Sonny Clark** (p); **Freddie Roach**, **Earl Vandyke** (org); **Kenny Burrell**, **Grant Green**, **Willie Jones** (g); **Paul Chambers**, **Milt Hinton**, **Sam Jones**, **Wendell Marshall**, **Butch Warren** (b); **Art Blakey**, **Willie Bobo**, **Al Harewood**, **Billy Higgins**, **Wilbert Hogan**, **Philly Joe Jones** (d); **Garvin Masseaux** (chekere). Blue Note Ⓜ CDP7 99178-2 (64 minutes). Recorded 1961/62.

⑧ ❽

A heavy-toned tenor from the Hawkins/Webster lineage, Ike Quebec made nearly all of his best music in two brief recording stints for Blue Note. The first, from 1944-46, yielded the hit single *Blue Harlem*, but was followed by years of obscurity and drug problems. The second, from 1959 until his death from lung cancer in 1963, flowered into a swansong of remarkable beauty and eloquence. In this period, Quebec recorded more singles, guested on LPs by artists such as Sonny Clark, Grant Green and Jimmy Smith, and made a series of outstanding albums as leader: **Heavy Soul**, **Blue and Sentimental**, **It Might As Well Be Spring**, **Easy Living** and **Soul Samba**, all but one of which were released in his lifetime.

This compilation is drawn almost entirely from those albums. The emphasis is on ballads, which were Quebec's forte, plus a couple of blues. Most are quartet tracks, nearly half of them with organ. A distinctive stylist, Quebec's deep-hewn sound was shaped by a delicacy of phrasing that forbade indulgence or sentimentality. The disc is a treasure-house of delights—the sensuous freight of his tone on *It Might As Well Be Spring*, the sinuous elegance of *I've Got A Crush On You*, the tender fervour he imparts to *Flavela*, but it is still small recompense for not having the original albums on CD, although **Heavy Soul** is now part of Blue Note's Connoisseur series of reissues. **GL**

Alvin Queen

1950

I'm Back **Queen** (d); **Fablo Morgera** (t, flh); **Amadou Diallo** (ts); **James Weldman** (p); **Fred Hunter** (b). Nilva Ⓕ CD NQ 3421 (62 minutes). Recorded 1992.

⑥ ❽

Drummer Alvin Queen ran a record label, Nilva, for most of the eighties, but got caught in between formats when it came to the exodus from vinyl to CD. Previously he had garnered a reputation with Stanley Turrentine before settling permanently in Switzerland and leading his own groups. His albums as a leader have all been on Nilva, but this one is the first to appear on CD. It is a brand-new session, recorded with his current group, and while bassist Fred Hunter is an old friend, newcomers Diallo and Morgera both impress. Diallo is one of the few of his generation not to pay an excess of tribute to Coltrane in his solos: he has a tone and approach quite removed from that of the late giant's, and has ideas of his own. Queen is a model drummer in many ways, laying down appropriate and perfectly-grooved beats on every track. On *Sketch* he inserts a Blakey-type backbeat which instantly recalls the Messengers, while the drum solo *Much Elvin and Max* is exactly what its title would lead you to expect, apart from the fact that it's just a little over two-and-a-half minutes long. An excellently-paced and well-crafted record. **KS**

Boyd Raeburn

1913-1966

Boyd Meets Stravinsky **Raeburn** (ts, bs, ldr); **Ray Linn**, **Dizzy Gillespie**, **Tommy Allison** (t); **Ollie Wilson**, **Trummy Young**, **Johnny Mandel** (tb); **Johnny Bothwell** (as); **Ralph Lee**, **Frankie Socolow** (ts); **Dodo Marmarosa**, **Ike Carpenter** (p); **Harry Babasin**, **Oscar Pettiford** (b); **Shelly Manne**, **Jackie Mills** (d); **Ginny Powell**, **David Allyn** (v). Denon/Savoy Ⓜ SV0185 (36 minutes). Recorded 1945-47.

⑧ ❽

Boyd Raeburn's schizophrenic big band was one of the most innovative of the forties , the darling of critics and musicians, but it never hit it big. Prior to 1940 Raeburn led a dance band of the 'sweet' variety; afterwards, with new arrangers like Budd Johnson from Earl Hines's orchestra and Basie-acolyte Ed Finckel, the music grew hotter. But a trace of sweetness—necessary, perhaps, for commercial considerations—remained, as in the David Allyn-crooned *I Only Have Eyes For You*. Through all of its incarnations the band depended upon a parade of arrangers for its identity. George Handy was undoubtedly the most ambitious and occasionally the wackiest. His witty *Dalvatore Sally* is an example of why the band was branded 'surrealistic'; more so was his version of *Over The Rainbow*, scored as John Zorn might today, with cartoonish collisions of colour (including harp and cor anglais) and mood shifts nearly every four bars. With soloists like Johnny Bothwell and Frankie Socolow, who emulated Johnny Hodges and Ben Webster respectively, the Ellington influence on *Summertime* and *Blue Prelude* is no surprise. This recording of *Interlude*—actually the original version of *Night In Tunisia*, with Dizzy on hand—is quite a surprise. All of Raeburn's recordings for Savoy (reissues from the Jewell label) could have fitted on a single CD; this is less than half, but unless you're a fan this may be all you need. **AL**

Ma Rainey

1886-1939

Ma Rainey Rainey (v); **Joe Smith**, **Shirley Clay** (c); **Louis Armstrong** (t); **Charlie Green**, **Ike Rodgers** (tb); **Buster Bailey** (cl); **Coleman Hawkins** (bs); **Fletcher Henderson**, **Jimmy Blythe**, **'Georgia Tom' Dorsey** (p); **Tampa Red** (g, kz); **Charlie Dixon** (j); **Kaiser Marshall** (d). Milestone Ⓜ MCD-47021-2 (72 minutes). Recorded 1924-28.

⑦ ❻

Evaluating Ma Rainey will never be easy. Early recording processes sapped the strength and weight of her voice, and even this tolerably remastered collection requires the listener to enhance the music with imagination.

Like Bessie Smith, Rainey worked almost entirely at slow or slowish tempos; unlike her, she seldom used anything but the conventional 12-bar blues verse, so her recordings are varied only by their subject-matter and accompaniments. Sombre or violent narratives predominate, as in *Chain Gang Blues*, *Black Eye Blues* and *Sweet Rough Man* ("every night for five years I've got a beatin' from my man ..."), though in *Prove It On Me* she asserts with spirit her right to choose her own sexual identity. Some of these songs so fixed themselves in the minds of their first listeners that whole verses would turn up, years later, in the compositions of other blues-singers.

The earlier tracks employ lineups with two or three horn-players, notably Armstrong (*See See Rider*) and Joe Smith, while the latest put Rainey with the piano and slide guitar of Georgia Tom and Tampa Red—who also accompany her in the Tub Jug Washboard Band, a novelty combination with banjo, jug and kazoo. **Ma Rainey's Black Bottom** (Yazoo 1071) is better remastered but contains only 14 tracks and is full price, giving the Milestone, weighing in at 24 tracks and a few pounds cheaper, the nod for value.

TR

Jimmy Raney

1927-1995

Here's That Raney Day Raney (g); **Hank Jones** (p); **Pierre Michelot** (b); **Jimmy Cobb** (d). Black & Blue Ⓕ 59.756 2 (55 minutes). Recorded 1980.

⑧ ❻

Raney's guitar became a familiar sound on record when he was working during the fifties with the Stan Getz Quintet, his instrument usually voiced a third away from the tenor in the theme statements. A sensitive and highly melodic player, his veiled, cloudy tone became the epitome of 'cool' guitar. After a withdrawal from the centre stage of jazz he returned with a harder attack and this fine CD, recorded in France, is one of the best examples of his more contemporary style. Backed by a superb rhythm section he is inspired to produce long solos, building chorus upon chorus and generating more excitement than he did three decades earlier. This CD contains alternative takes of two numbers and Raney's solos are so different that their inclusion is more than justified. He plays a total of 12 improvised choruses on the two versions of *Indiana*, exhibiting a 'stream of consciousness' which is exhilarating. There are a number of bebop tunes in the programme including *Au Privave*, *Scrapple From The Apple* and *Chasin' The Bird*. On the latter Raney and Jones play the two contrapuntal lines originally taken by Parker and Miles Davis. There is an occasional increase in the volume of the guitar on some tracks.

AM

Enrico Rava

1943

Quatre Rava (t); **Franco D'Andrea** (p); **Miroslav Vitous** (b); **Daniel Humair** (d). Gala Ⓕ 91030 (48 minutes). Recorded 1989.

⑨ ❽

As befits a world-class trumpeter, Rava's impressive career has ranged from a sixties free jazz quartet alongside Steve Lacy to a tango-tinged eighties band with Argentinian bandoneonist Dino Saluzzi, from Lee Konitz to Carla Bley. But few settings have shown off his ravishing powers of invention any better than this spectacular group, which unites four all-stars from three different countries. Their sense of ensemble is pin-point accurate and remarkably flexible, making this the epitome of a listening band the musicians able to respond immediately to each other's playing with imagination and authority. By subtly shifting rhythmic accents into a constantly varied progression of seamless episodes, the music remains continually fresh and engaging. This demands exquisite balance and awareness of spontaneous design, but the four seem to be in telepathic agreement. The way they interact, the harmonic framework and floating rhythm of the compositions, is reminiscent of the Miles Davis band of the mid-sixties; in fact, Rava's burnished tone—alternately dark and lustrous—and his thrilling lyricism could be considered a personal homage to Miles. Combined with Humair's playful and propulsive drumming, D'Andrea's embroidery and Vitous's virtuosity, it accounts for the sublime sounds to be heard here.

AL

Lou Rawls 1935

Stormy Monday Rawls (v); Les McCann (p); Leroy Vinnegar (b); Ron Jefferson (d). Blue Note Ⓜ CDP7 91441-2 (46 minutes). Recorded 1962.

⑥ ❻

Although younger than Joe Williams and Ray Charles, Rawls came to fame at the same period that they did. Rawls is a consistent performer whose style has not changed since this recording was made. He spans the field between soul music and jazz with a more natural ease than either Williams or Charles does and Rawls's 'popular' recordings are of a higher musical quality than those of the other men.

All his CDs will appeal to the eclectic jazz fan, but the one under review concentrates more on jazz material than the others and the backing by Les McCann, whose work elsewhere tends towards the superficial, is ideal, the two men cooking up a spanking funky swing. McCann's solos sound righteous in this appropriate setting for him and he works well with Vinnegar, surely the most gifted bassist for this sort of event, and the admirable Jefferson.

Apart from the classic blues, *See See Rider*, *In The Evening* et al, there is a clutch of appropriate standards, with *Willow Weep For Me* and *God Bless The Child* being well bent to the singer's talents. **SV**

Jason Rebello 1969

Make It Real **Rebello** (p); **Wayne Batchelor** (b); **Jeremy Stacey, Darren Abraham** (d); **Thomas Dyani Akuru** (perc); **Maysa Leak, Maxi Jazz, Joy Rose, Donna Gardner, Cleveland Watkiss** (v). BMG Ⓕ 122408 2 (64 minutes). Recorded 1994.

⑥ ❽

Although he has often shown himself to be one of the most able of the generation of British players spawned by the eighties jazz explosion, since the uncompromised fusion of his début album, Jason Rebello has become a musical fashion victim. His recent removal to a religious retreat, coupled with his departure from BMG, bespeaks a radical reassessment of what he has done so far.

This last BMG album moves in the right direction, featuring him almost exclusively on piano with only a hint of synthesized strings on one track, but the unadulterated jazz does not start to flow until the seventh out of 12 tracks, and even then Rebello seems to be pulling punches. Tracks one to six are dominated by soul or rap vocals, and one has to wonder at the reasoning which sees its inclusion. The jazz does take off on *Beautiful Day* and *Heartless Monster*, but it often fails to attain the intensity Rebello has produced in concert. Furthermore, although *Wait And See* has a light rock pulse, it seems a shame, given this taste for backbeats, that Rebello has not picked up on the radical reassessments of piano jazz being essayed by Ilg/Copland/Hirshfield and Leon Parker on issues reviewed elsewhere in this volume. **MG**

Re-Birth Brass Band

Feel Like Funkin' It Up **Kermit Ruffins** (t, v, perc); **Derrick Shezbie** (t, perc); **Derek Wiley** (t, v, perc); **Keith 'Wolf' Anderson** (tb); **Philip Frazier** (bb, perc); **John Gilbert** (ts, v, perc); **Keith Frazier** (bass d, v, perc); **Kenneth Austin** (snare d, v, perc). Rounder Ⓕ CD 2093 (46 minutes). Recorded 1989.

⑥ ❻

Formed by a group of high school friends in the Treme district of New Orleans in 1984, the Re-Births have followed the lead taken by the Dirty Dozen Brass Band. Like them, the Re-Births have added funkier, more extrovert elements to the tradition previously established for the marching bands of the city. They have introduced the jump blues, tempered with bebop material and more modern phraseology, but most essentially they have still retained the exuberant spirit of the music. There is still little to choose between their various issues, but this CD has an especially streetwise vitality and youthful verve. Both Frazier and Austin form the nucleus of an oft-augmented and highly effective rhythm section, while the horn duties are shared by Ruffins, Gilbert and Anderson. Gilbert, rumbustious on *Do Watcha Wanna* and *Big Fat Woman*, is the pick of the bunch, but their collective musical frailties do tend to be exposed on record. Ruffins's best solo is on *Leave That Pipe Alone* and Anderson scores on *Mexican Special*, but it is the collective good time cacophony of titles like *I'm Walkin'* and *Shake Your Body Down To The Ground* that would be most likely to sell the band and its brand of jazz to an audience out to enjoy itself. **BMcR**

Freddie Redd 1928

Music from *The Connection* **Jackie McLean** (as); **Redd** (p); **Michael Mattos** (b); **Larry Ritchie** (d). Blue Note Ⓜ CDP8 89392 2 1 (39 minutes). Recorded 1960.

✔ ⑩ ❽

The peripatetic Freddie Redd is one of several musicians (including Dexter Gordon, Cecil Payne and Cecil Taylor) to have written and recorded a score for Jack Gelber's notorious off-Broadway chronicle of heroin addicts (including the members of the musical ensemble) waiting for the man. This is the best version of the best score (Redd, under the *nom de disque* I. Ching, re-recorded his seven compositions under Howard McGhee's name for Felsted within the year) and a definitive hard bop programme. McLean's early phase reaches glorious fruition here, with acidic passion and stunning command of the chord changes, while Redd's seven tunes are structurally fresh, melodically indelible and ferociously swinging. They also hang together, similar yet singular, to create as complete an album's-worth of music as any composer/player offered at the time. Also of note is Redd's piano, a good-timey take on Powell and Monk that shares some of Horace Silver's rollicking quality while remaining quite distinctive. The obscurity of the rhythm section in no way reflects upon how hard it swings. **BB**

Dewey Redman

1931

Choices **Redman** (as, ts, musette, v); **Joshua Redman** (ts); **Cameron Brown** (b); **Leon Parker** (d). Enja Ⓕ 7073-2 (55 minutes). Recorded 1992.

Redman became known in the sixties working with Ornette Coleman and bearing a tenor style indebted to Ornette's playful alto (in the seventies, Dewey was in Keith Jarrett's American quartet). On this trio/quartet set, Redman features his own alto on two tracks heavily influenced by Coleman's playing and writing, although Dewey plays with tenor heft and a distinctly darker tone. On tenor for a ten-minute *Everything Happens to Me*, his sound is in the grand Hawkins tradition, and is remarkably straight-ahead. He plays the chord changes straight, something Coleman's band was not known for doing. *O'Besso*, a West African-flavoured vamp tune, is an extended showcase for—and one of his best recorded outings on—Chinese musette, a simple double-reed instrument of short range and precarious intonation.

Son Joshua joins in on the two tracks where his dad plays alto; Joshua and the rhythm duo get *Imagination* to themselves. He is a good balladeer, if not yet a match for his father. Dewey's best album as tenorist, ECM's **The Struggle Continues**, is not yet on CD, and his best work overall has depended on rhythm sections more ferocious than this amiable one. Even so, **Choices** is a strong statement from an uneven but underrated veteran. **KW**

Don Redman

1900-1964

Don Redman And His Orchestra 1931-33 **Redman** (as, v); **Leonard Davis**, **Bill Coleman**, **Henry Allen**, **Shirley Clay**, **Langston Curl**, **Sidney De Paris** (t); **Claude Jones**, **Fred Robinson**, **Benny Morton** (tb); **Edward Inge**, **Rupert Cole** (cl, as); **Robert Carroll** (ts); **Horace Henderson**, **Don Kirkpatrick** (p); **Talcott Reeves** (bj, g); **Bob Yasguirre** (b, bb); **Manzie Johnson** (d); **Louis Deppe**, **Harlan Lattimore**, **Cab Calloway**, **The Mills Brothers** (v); **Bill Robinson** (tap). Classics Ⓜ 543 (70 minutes). Recorded 1931-33.

✔ 

Redman was one of the most important jazz arrangers, a situation perhaps initially helped by the fact that he played nearly all of the instruments associated with jazz. He joined Fletcher Henderson in 1923 and for the next four years provided many of the band's best charts. He became musical director of McKinney's Cotton Pickers and in 1931 formed his own band. Although by no means the only major arranger by this stage, he put an indelible stamp on bands with which he was associated. The music on this CD comes from an influential period. It is imaginative, often descriptive and, although not as accomplished as the works in the latter part of the band's life, had the unmistakable Redman stamp. He produced impressionistic compositions such as his famous *Chant of the Weed*, plus novelty pieces such as *Shakin' The African* as well as rather too many vehicles for his own strangely emasculated vocals. The band's main problem at this time was that, despite a personnel which included such considerable figures as De Paris, Coleman, Allen and Jones, it had continuing intonation troubles. Ironically, by the time this had been eradicated, the band had lost much of its individuality. **BMcR**

Joshua Redman

1969

Moodswing **Redman** (ts); **Brad Mehldau** (p); **Christian McBride** (b); **Brian Blade** (d). Warner Bros Ⓕ 245643-2 (70 minutes). Recorded 1994.

Redman's second for Warners moves him on convincingly from **Wish**, the first. For a start, he's reached the point of confidence where he is recording with a working group of which he is the undisputed centre. That Redman is a good leader, and not just a gifted sideman, can also be judged by the thought that has gone into shaping this latest album. In his admirable and lucid liner notes, he writes of creating each tune to evoke a specific mood or atmosphere, so that the album takes the listener through a set of experiences and feelings and arrives at the end with a sense of having participated in a substantial event, rather than an arbitrary collection of head arrangements or personal favourites. This continuity runs through every aspect of the CD, including the cohesion of a quartet which allows a thought or a feeling to be passed from instrument to instrument when it comes to solo time.

Redman has an unusually individualistic tone on the tenor, his rhythm is easy and unruffled at every tempo and his interest in lyricism means that he rarely comes across as a dry, scale-running post-Coltrane clone. His music has much more to offer than that, and at the heart of it all lies the elusive quality that both Coltrane and his father Dewey could summon at will: soul. I don't mean that they could out-funk James Brown - it's nothing to do with style. All three tenor players have that additional dimension which touches us like no other. Redman may well prove to be more than just the coming man. **KS**

Dizzy Reece

1931

Blues In Trinity Reece (t); **Donald Byrd** (t); **Tubby Hayes** (ts); **Terry Shannon** (p); **Lloyd Thompson** (b); **Art Taylor** (d). Blue Note Ⓜ CDP8 32093-2 (47 minutes). Recorded 1958.

⑥ ❽

Reece was born in Kingston, Jamaica, and among his schoolmates were Joe Harriott and Bogey Gaynair. He came to England in 1948 and worked around the continent before finally getting noticed by expatriate US musicians, who were quick to recognise his talent. An endorsement from Miles Davis went a long way in the fifties, and ultimately led to Reece making this record for Blue Note. It is cast in the prevalent hard bop style of the day, and local British units such as The Jazz Couriers had a bearing on the types of sounds this unit makes. This is not surprising with Hayes, a founder Couriers member, in the band. The larger shadow behind that is, of course, The Jazz Messengers, and the presence of the American Donald Byrd on two tracks helps bring that information through to the listener.

If this had been an American session, it would be perceived as a superior late fifties blowing date. As it is, it is part of the 'might-have-been' story of many talented British players of this time. Reece and Hayes both made major impressions on musicians the other side of the Atlantic, but never excited popular interest. It was left to people like George Shearing and Victor Feldman to do that. Meanwhile, the continuing force of the original impact Reece made allows this album to be reissued close to 40 years after it was made. **KS**

Eric Reed

1970

The Swing and I Reed (p); **Ben Wolfe**, **Rodney Whitaker** (b); **Greg Hutchinson** (d); **Eddie Bailey**, **Denise Morgan**, **Suzanne Williams**, **Beverly Taylor** (v). MoJazz Ⓕ 530 468-2 (68 minutes). Recorded 1994.

⑤ ❼

Reed has occupied the piano chair with both the Art Blakey and Wynton Marsalis groups, and for a man so young he's made an impressive number of albums as a leader, this being the third I've heard in the last three years. It is his most assured to date, and it easily inhabits that area of expression most fully explored by pianists who came to their peak in the late fifties, pianists such as Wynton Kelly, Ahmad Jamal, Oscar Peterson and Erroll Garner. In this at least, Reed has skipped a generation of influences and looked closer to the source than many, and this diligence reaps its own dividends. The one problem I find hard to overcome is his relatively narrow expressive range when compared to the players listed above (compare his version of *Ahmad's Blues* with that of the composer's). There is a modest dynamic range, and while Reed can spin a good ballad and swing convincingly at mid-tempo, there is much to be developed in the way of touch, shadings and suggestions, to make for a more complete personal connection with his audience.

It's probable that this will come in time, and that other types of light and shade will work themselves into his music, but for now, what he does go for he accomplishes with ease. His rhythm section is accurate and responsive, and the singers, on the one track on which they appear, are convincing. **KS**

Dianne Reeves

1956

Quiet After the Storm Reeves (v); **Roy Hargrove**, **Gary Grant** (t); **Ron Blake** (ss, ts); **Everette Harp** (as); **Joshua Redman** (ts); **Hubert Laws** (f); **Dori Caymmi**, **Kevin Eubanks** (g); **George Duke** (kbds); **David Torkanowsky**, **Jacky Terrasson**, **John Beasley** (p); **Chris Severin** (b); **Billy Kilson**, **Terri Lyne Carrington** (d); **Luis Conte**, **Airto Moreira** (perc). Blue Note Ⓕ CDP8 29511 2 (59 minutes). Recorded 1995.

⑧ ❽

Like many of her jazz-singing contemporaries (UK examples include Claire Martin, Tina May, Carol Kidd and Ian Shaw), Dianne Reeves casts her net wider than conventional jazz standards and originals in her search for material suitable for her attractively smoky voice. On this, her fifth EMI recording, she switches between big band jazz, small group torch songs, sophisticated rock and ethnic music with great aplomb, demonstrating a maturity and confidence not always apparent on earlier recordings. The hallmark of this newfound assurance is the restraint with which she approaches all she sings. Her voice's many individual strengths, from its unusual range through its textural variety to its sure dynamic control, are kept firmly in check, held in reserve until the most telling moment for their deployment. Thus, in the moody ballad *Come Love*, she intelligently accentuates the contrasts inherent in the song's lyrics by moving easily and unaffectedly between an attractively informal, insinuating warmth and sudden eruptions of emotion; in *Country Preacher*, a tribute to Cannonball Adderley, she positively smoulders; in Joni Mitchell's *Both Sides Now* she sustains interest through three wordy verses, despite a murderously slow tempo, by the sheer emotional intensity which she invests in the performance. Rounded out by an excursion into Brazilian music (an echo of her early experience with Sergio Mendes) and a song recalling childhood experience, *Nine*, which just steers clear of sentimentality courtesy of Reeves's patent sincerity, and featuring accomplished versions of standards such as *In a Sentimental Mood* and *Detour Ahead*, this is Dianne Reeves's finest album by some distance. **CP**

Django Reinhardt

1910-1953

Chronological Volume 1 **Stephane Grappelli** (vn, p); **Reinhardt**, **Joseph Reinhardt, Roger Chaput** (g); **Arthur Briggs**, **Frank 'Big Boy' Goodie** (t, cl, ts); **Louis Vola** (b). JSP Ⓕ CD 341 (75 minutes). Recorded 1934-35.

✔ ⑧ ❽

The Quintet of the Hot Club of France has been badly served on record. The multitude of their LPs were mostly taken from bad sources, such as poorly centred and badly pressed 78s. Often, later albums were simply careless copies of the first, haphazardly-produced, LPs.

The music on this CD has been restored from the best available 78 copies, which have been carefully checked for pitch by the sound engineer Ted Kendall. His work is so good that it can literally be said that Reinhardt has never been heard with such presence before. The guitarist's fingers can be heard moving across the fingerboard, and there is a new resonance as he plucks each note. Kendall has cleared away audio rubble, using the skills he learned from his mentor John R.T. Davies, and has brought out sounds in the music which haven't been heard since the recordings were made in the studio.

This chronological collection has a handful of rather dated vocals, but every track on which the singers appear is dominated by jazz solos from Reinhardt and Grappelli, and on the out-and-out jazz tracks, the two men showed a combination of swing and virtuoso playing which must have stunned their American contemporaries.

One might expect *Dinah* or *Lady Be Good* to sound hackneyed, but they emerge here as newly refreshed classics. This is Volume One of what is projected to be a major Reinhardt series. There have been five volumes to date, following on chronologically from this one. **SV**

Swing From Paris **Reinhardt** (g); **Stephane Grappelli** (vn) with various personnel, including **Quintet of the Hot Club of France**. Conifer Ⓜ CDHD 165 (58 minutes). Recorded 1937-38.

⑧ ❺

In a recent BBC Radio Three series on Django, Max Harrison made the rather daring and provocative suggestion that Django would have been better off with another violinist, Michel Warlop, who not only was around in Paris but would have provided a more driving partner for Reinhardt than the slightly sweet Grappelli (or Grappelly, as he was known before the war). But as it is, the Django/Stephane partnership is the one we all know and love, and a collection of pre-war recordings like this, before the Germans marched in and separated the two, shows amply that the combination of the gypsy Django and the suave dandy Stephane had its own magic. For all I know, Michel Warlop might be on this CD somewhere, but even my powerful magnifying glass fails to make the tiny print on this record liner very legible. I can just make out that half the personnel details are missing, and that the pianist I can clearly hear on *J'Attendrai* is not listed anywhere, so I suppose it must be Stephane himself. Even when you have got used to the splendid music on this CD, there will be hours of fun trying to sort out who is playing and with whom. **MK**

Swing in Paris, 1939-40 **Reinhardt** (g); with a collective personnel including **Rex Stewart** (c); **Bill Coleman**, **Philippe Brun** (t); **Benny Carter** (t, as); **Dicky Wells** (tb); **Barney Bigard** (cl); **Frank 'Big Boy' Goudie**, **Alix Combelle**, **Bertie King**, **Hubert Rostaing** (cl, ts); **Andre Ekyan** (as); **Coleman Hawkins** (ts); **Stephane Grappelli** (p, vn); **Joseph Reinhardt**, **Pierre Ferret**, **Marcel Bianchi**, **Roger Chaput**, **Eugene Vees** (g); **Eddie South**, **Michel Warlop** (vn); **Louis Vola**, **Eugene d'Hellemes**, **Wilson Myers** (b); **Pierre Fouad** (d); **Freddy Taylor** (v). Affinity Ⓜ CD AFS 1003-5 (five discs: 327 minutes). Recorded 1936-40.

✔ ⑩ ❼

Where to start with Django? With the chord playing that takes a bulldog grip on Coleman Hawkins' *Crazy Rhythm* and *Honeysuckle Rose*, or treads fearlessly alongside an Eddie South, a Bill Coleman or a Dicky Wells in the blues' remembered hills? With the single-string solos, audacious yet never fanciful, that spill out of dozens of performances? Or the combination of both in a masterly reshaping of a standard like *I'll See You In My Dreams*, where Broadway is translated to the Boul' Mich'? Or rather should we begin with that matchless sound, the bitter-sweet zither's ring that spirals from every note, like a waft of Chanel or a whiff of Gauloises?

For most of Reinhardt's admirers the story begins, as this collection does, with his recordings alongside the violinist Stephane Grappelli in the Quintet of the Hot Club of France. This was the first small-group jazz made outside the US that not only rivalled the music's originators in its execution but revealed something to them, and expanded the vocabulary of jazz by the originality of its conception. The only American musicians at all comparable with Grappelli and Reinhardt, namely Joe Venuti and Eddie Lang, never hit upon such twirling arabesques, never achieved that boulevardier's elegance, even at their most extravagantly imaginative.

Reinhardt was the first incontestably great jazz musician from Europe. As the list of musicians above shows, this is a conclusion several excellent American players had already arrived at in the thirties, and the sessions with Hawkins and Benny Carter or with Rex Stewart and Barney Bigard are collaborations of the highest quality. Stretched by the presence or the recollection of these visitors, the other European musicians, Combelle and Ekyan, Brun and Rostaing and their peers, play with fresh vigour without losing their essentially European character. This superb collection embraces Reinhardt's recordings in his own name, with the QHCF, and as an accompanist or sideman, for the HMV and Swing labels. **TR**

The Great Blue Star Sessions 1947–53 **Reinhardt** (g); with a collective personnel of **Joseph Reinhardt, Jean-Claude Forenbach, Eugene Vees** (g); **Michel de Villers** (as); **Eddie Bernard, Maurice Vandair** (p); **Willy Lockwood, Ladislas Czabanyck, Emmanuel Soudieux, Pierre Michelot** (b); **Al Craig, André Jourdan, Ted Curry, Jean-Louis Viale** (d); **Vincent Casino, Louis Menardi, Jo Boyer** (t); **André Lafosse, Guy Paquinet** (tb); **Michel de Villers** (cl, as); **Gerard Levecque** (arr); **Hubert Rostaing** (cl, as); **Rex Stewart** (c). Verve Ⓜ 835418-2 (two discs: 97 minutes). Recorded 1947-53.

⑥ ❻

Reinhardt went to America at the end of 1946 to undertake a not wholly successful tour with the Duke Ellington orchestra. He formed a quintet with Hubert Rostaing on his return and 25 of these 33 titles were made for the French Blue Star (later Barclay) record label in 1947. With clarinet in place of violin, the group sometimes takes on the quality of a sub-Benny Goodman unit, but there is no mistaking Django, even when he occasionally fights against the low-tech amplification that he elected to use at this time. But nothing can hide his unique genius and there is some magnificent blues playing to be heard on *Django's Blues* and its alternative take labelled *Love's Mood.* Bebop was beginning to impinge on Reinhardt's sensibility at the time and the fast *Moppin' The Bride* has all the hallmarks of a European jazzman's attempts to come to terms with a new development. The two titles with Rex Stewart added on cornet are pleasant but unmomentous, lacking the magic of the 1939 Feetwarmers session, but the final 1953 date is a complete success due to the superior rhythm section, recording quality and Django's mastery of the amplification problems. These eight titles have often received less than critical acclaim but *Blues For Ike, Manoir Des Mes Reves* and *September Song* are particular joys, while this 1953 version of *Nuages* is perhaps the best of all. **AM**

Emily Remler 1957-1991

Transitions **Remler** (g); **John D'Earth** (t); **Eddie Gomez** (b); **Bob Moses** (d). Concord Ⓕ CCD-4236 (37 minutes). Recorded 1983.

✔ ⑧ ❽

The breadth and range of Emily Remler's talent—**Transitions**' title track alone moves easily between 4/4, 7/4 and 3/4 and incorporates Latin rhythms as naturally as its closing track uses African ones—is faultlessly displayed on this thoughtful, well-balanced album. The New York-born guitarist was a regular in Astrud Gilberto's band in the early eighties (**Transitions**' opening track, *Nunca Mais*, is a tribute to her fellow band members) and her front line collaborator, trumpeter John D'Earth, featured in a number of Latin bands in the same period. This experience explains the intelligent and uncontrived use of Latin and African sounds and rhythms on the album's Remler originals which marks the recording out from many contemporary efforts, where a characterless pastiche too often results from a similar process. Furthermore, Remler's unostentatious versatility and D'Earth's flaring but tasteful tone are perfectly complemented both by Eddie Gomez's sensitivity in accompanying roles and quiet assertiveness in solos and by Bob Moses's richly sympathetic drumming, so that although Remler clearly sets the agenda for the album, it is nevertheless very much a group effort. It is therefore as a leader eminently capable of thus drawing a variety of unusual sounds into the jazz mainstream—here represented by Sam Jones's *Del Sasser*—and for her ability to grant sympathetic collaborators the space everywhere evident on **Transitions**, that she will be most sorely missed. **CP**

Don Rendell 1926

If I Should Lose You **Rendell** (cl, ss, ts, f); **Martin Shaw** (t, flh); **Richard Edwards** (tb); **Brian Dee, John Burch** (p); **Peter Morgan, Mario Castronari** (b); **Robin Jones, Bobby Worth** (d). Spotlite Ⓕ SPJCD 546 (60 minutes). Recorded 1990/91.

⑥ ❻

Rendell came up at the same time as Sims and Getz and similarly absorbed Lester Young's influence but, unlike the other two, Rendell also modified his style to acknowledge the innovations of Coltrane and Rollins. His tenor playing is good enough to make one wonder why he has not received the acclaim of, say, a Tubby Hayes, yet over the years his work with far better groups than the ones here has gone similarly unnoticed, so perhaps it is a case of counting your blessings. Rendell uses the soprano sax with purpose and an individual sound, which is refreshing after the routine struggling with which many tenorists approach the horn. As well as tenor, *All Too Soon* features sparse, somewhat shrill 'saxophone player's clarinet' but Rendell's work on both saxes is well displayed on *Calas Vinas,* which also has a rare solo from Richard Edwards, a name to watch amongst British trombonists. **SV**

Return to Forever

Hymn Of The Seventh Galaxy **Chick Corea** (p, elp, org, h, gongs); **Stanley Clarke** (elb, perc); **Bill Connors** (g); **Lenny White** (d, perc). Polydor Ⓜ 825 336-2 (43 minutes). Recorded 1973.

⑥ ❽

By 1973, Chick Corea's list of musical involvements might have invited charges of stylistic opportunism: hard bop with Blue Mitchell in 1964, middle-of-the-road sambas with Stan Getz in 1967, McCoy Tyner-influenced trio jazz in 1968, proto-fusion with Miles Davis in 1969, free atonality with Anthony Braxton and Barry Altschul in 1970-71, fey Latin fantasies with the first incarnation of RTF in 1972, and 12 months later the brow-beating jazz-rock of **Hymn Of The Seventh Galaxy**. However, musical chameleon or not, Corea has made a constant out of exemplary musicianship. The second edition of RTF began as an attempt to emulate the suite-like jazz-rock of the Mahavishnu Orchestra, but the technical superiority of Corea's players enabled it to bring extra finesse and form to the style. It also introduced novel elements; Corea's proclivity for Hispanic flavours is apparent in several places, and so is the funk of Sly Stone and Stevie Wonder and the fuzz bass of Stanley Clarke. But the jazz is still there too: Corea's ecstatic solo on *Theme To The Mothership*, melding the hot new sound of an overdriven Rhodes with searching modal jazz improvisation, seems a perfect response to the period's appetite for new sonic combinations. **MG**

Vladimir Rezitsky

Hot Sounds From The Arctic **Rezitsky** (as, ts, v, hca, kbds, cond); **Georg Graf** (f); **Tim Hodgkinson** (reeds); **Sainkho Namchylak**, **Konstantin Sedovin**, **Valentina Ponomareva** (v); **Nikolai Klishin** (b, v); **Roberto Bellatalla** (b); **Vladimir Turov** (syn); **Oleg Yudanov** (d); **Ken Hyder** (d, v); **Nikolai Yudanov** (perc); **Albert Kuvezin** (p, v); **Alexey Saaya** (morin khuur); **Vladimir Tarasov** (d, pc). Leo Ⓕ CD LR 218 (65 minutes). Recorded 1991-94.

⑥ ❺

Rezitsky was invited to occupy the third chair in the Ganelin Trio before Vladimir Chekasin joined in 1971. At the time he was living in Arkhangelsk, a town on the Arctic Circle; since then he has been, amongst other things, leading the Jazz Group Arkhangelsk and promoting jazz in the freezing conditions that prevail there. He is primarily a saxophonist but this CD gives a comprehensive look at his many talents.

Full Stop, Full Stop, Coma finds him fully exposed in a duet, with his alto showing how confidently he can create an abstract fine weave, using space as a component part of his solo. On *Voices*, Namchylak's poignant vocal wrings full emotional capital from the piece without making meaningful creative progress. It is Rezitsky's voice that moves into the improvisational hinterland using Namchylak as a contrapuntal straight woman. The devious route of Rezitsky's tenor contrasts with the oddly 'African' chanting on *Zolotitsa*, while it is his keyboard work that provides the ensemble body on *Shut Out The Devil*. Finally, *Planet Rezitsky* finds him conducting the JGA, the Ensemble Kamerata and the String Quartet Arkhangelsk and building to the sound crescendo that typifies the excitement of such jazz. **BMcR**

Melvyn Rhyne

1936

Boss Organ **Rhyne** (org); **Joshua Redman** (ts); **Peter Bernstein** (g); **Kenny Washington** (d). Criss Cross Ⓕ 1080 CD (62 minutes). Recorded 1993.

⑩ ❽

After getting over the shock of seeing who is making up the tenor part of the tenor 'n' organ set-up here, you may have bigger problems coping with the first track. It's a long, long blues, slow and blissful, midnight-cool, no-one straining, no-one grandstanding, everyone pulling their weight. Things haven't been like this for some time down funk city way. Blue Note gave up making records like this 30 years ago, and it comes as a sad commentary on the current Stateside scene that while this CD may have been recorded in New York, it was at the behest of a Dutch record label. Still, I don't care who makes albums this good, as long as someone does. There is such refinement here (it's not a mere blowing session on the first blues head arrangement anybody could think of) along with a real sense of continuity and understanding between the participants. People fit into the area they've been allotted, and with Rhyne keeping such good time with his feet, Washington sounds especially happy. Rhyne also eschews the more blatant stops on his instrument, keeping the groove mellow, the swing deep, letting the rhythm work for him rather than blasting everyone within reach.

His comping for Redman is wonderfully supple, and he and guitarist Bernstein have a great understanding about the best ways to balance their support roles. Redman himself plays with controlled freedom and imagination, at all times sounding completely at home. This is a fine album in the t 'n' o tradition. **KS**

Buddy Rich

1917-1987

Gene Krupa and Buddy Rich **Rich**, **Gene Krupa**, (d); **Roy Eldridge**, **Dizzy Gillespie** (t); **Flip Phillips**, **Illinois Jacquet** (ts); **Oscar Peterson** (p); **Herb Ellis** (g); **Ray Brown** (b) Verve Ⓜ 835 314-2 (55 minutes). Recorded 1955-62.

④ ❽

One is reminded of the man in hell who, when he asked when the everlasting banjo solo was going to end, was told 'You do know, don't you, that the drum solo comes next?' Questions must be asked about the listener who can sustain a whole CD-full of drum solos.

Rich, who had the killer instinct, laces Krupa who did not. In fact it might be regarded as reckless of Krupa to put his head in the lion's mouth in this way, for Rich was unsurpassable within his idiom, which was also Krupa's (it is only when Max Roach is brought into the equation that Rich's playing becomes approachable).

If one must have a display of pure dexterity, then this is as good as any, and we must be grateful for the relief in heated and expressive solos from the likes of trombonists Frank Rehak and Jimmy Cleveland, Flip Phillips, Roy Eldridge, Gillespie and other stalwarts of Jazz At The Philharmonic in circus mood. **SV**

Dannie Richmond

1935-1988

Three Or Four Shades **Richmond** (d); **Jack Walrath** (t); **Kenny Garrett** (as); **Bob Neloms** (p); **Cameron Brown** (b). Tutu Ⓕ CD888 120 (71 minutes). Recorded 1981.

Richmond began his musical career as an r&b saxophonist, but apart from a period in the early seventies when he flirted with rock, his career was inextricably bound up with Charles Mingus, the man and his music. In the early years the bassist was his leader, friend, inspiration and teacher, but Richmond's style of loose-jointed drumming matured quickly. He had a total grasp of suspended rhythms and his work in the fifties opened stylistic doors for drummers such as Andrew Cyrille and Sunny Murray. After Mingus's death he played with Mingus Dynasty and, up to the time of his own premature demise, with the superb George Adams/Don Pullen Quartet. This CD provides an excellent overview of his style. It demonstrates clear melodic expressiveness and shows how he was able to reconcile lyricism with an exciting cut-and-thrust which stimulated fellow band members. Walrath has played with greater authority elsewhere, and the 1981 Garrett was comparatively inexperienced, but the rhythmically assertive Neloms and the propulsive Brown were his natural bedfellows. Students of Richmond's drumming will want to return to the Mingus classics and the Adams/Pullen band, but this release gives an insight into the way in which he led from the drum stool. **BMcR**

Howard Riley

1943

Procession **Riley** (p). Wondrous Ⓕ WM 0101 (50 minutes). Recorded 1990.

A product of David Baker's Indiana School of Excellence, Riley established himself as a leading figure on the European free music scene in the seventies and eighties. He worked with the London Jazz Composer's Orchestra as well as in duos with fellow pianists Jaki Byard and Keith Tippett. He also gained a reputation as a composer in his own right and wrote all of the selections on this solo CD. They present an extremely varied range of moods and encourage solo responses that complement them. They also take the pianist into a series of fine, spontaneous improvisations and exploit his solo status. The absence of a bass line allows him greater rhythmic freedom and encourages him to take liberties wtih his own built-in metronome. He is certainly not an empty eclectic, but there are performances here that call to mind figures of the recent and distant past. The rolling insistence of Cripple Clarence Lofton attends *April Again*, *Procession* has an almost Ellingtonian dignity, while *Inseparable* is as one imagines Bud Powell would have played had he been born in another generation. *Striding* appropriately reminds us of Willie 'The Lion' Smith and there is a fractured, Thelonious Monk-like air to *Tell Me*. The distinctive Riley personality overlays them all and it shows how well the pianist balances his creative impetus with his impressive technical facility. **BMcR**

Lee Ritenour

1952

Wes Bound **Ritenour** (g, perc); **Alan Broadbent** (p, arr); **Bob James** (p, kbds); **John Beasley** (kbds); **Dave Witham**, **Ronnie Foster** (B-3 organ); **Melvin Davis** (elb); **John Patitucci** (b); **Gary Novak**,

Harvey Mason, Steve Gadd (d); **Cassio Duarte, Harvey Mason** (perc); **Maxi Priest, Phil Perry, Kate Markowitz, Carmen Twillie** (v); **Jerry Hey** (arr). GRP Ⓕ 97052 (54 minutes). Recorded 1992.

⑥ ❽

Encouraged perhaps by jazz's new cultural correctness, Lee Ritenour hastened along with a multitude of other errant jazzers in the late eighties to protest his long-standing fealty to the jazz mainstream. The first gesture in this direction was 1990's efficient **Stolen Moments**, featuring Rit's Gibson L-5 in a straightahead quartet. A couple of years on, feeling perhaps that he had seen jazz all right, Ritenour relaxed his jazzman's rigour and re-embraced funkier values on **Wes Bound**. Of course there could be no better model for compromised jazz than Wes Montgomery, and even when he was playing jazz rather than Creed Taylor's arrangements, Wes was funky. Five of the 11 tunes here are Montgomery's, and three of those are from his string-bound Verve period; of the other two, *4 On 6* is the most representative of hard-bopping Wes, and Ritenour rises to the occasion with penetrating jazz guitar, nudged along by Jerry Hey's superbly judged horn prompts. The six non-Wes tunes tend towards Earl Klugh's and George Benson's diluted readings of the Montgomery style, and bottom-out with Maxi Priest singing Bob Marley's maudlin love long *Waiting In Vain*. Purists might prefer **Stolen Moments**, but for all its shortcomings, **Wes Bound** has a warmth missing from the earlier session; it also offers a fuller picture of Ritenour's blend of bop, blues and funk. **MG**

Sam Rivers

1930

Waves **Rivers** (f, ss, ts, p); **Joe Daly** (tba, brh); **Dave Holland** (b, vc); **Thurman Barker** (d, perc). Tomato Ⓕ 269649-2 (44 minutes). Recorded 1978.

⑧ ❽

Sam Rivers has not been well served by the advent of compact disc. Many of his best recordings have yet to appear on CD, including such outstanding items as 1965's **Fuchsia Swing Song** on Blue Note and the 1979 **Contrasts** on ECM. His early interests ranged across gospel, blues, bebop and classical music but the sixties saw him forging a personal jazz style via stints with Miles Davis, Andrew Hill and Cecil Taylor. In the seventies he recorded for Impulse!, became a leading light of New York's avant-garde loft scene and began a long association with Dave Holland that is heard to good advantage on **Waves**.

Rivers has likened this recording to the motion of waves, changing currents, changing flow; apt analogies for music that is in a constant state of flux, each track a series of fleeting exchanges, tempos and moods. Daley's tuba propels the beat, allowing Holland to wax melodic, while Barker is sensitive yet forceful. Rivers himself plays superbly; his tenor fiercely expressive on *Surge* and *Shockwave*, his flute slipping gently through *Torch*. Best of all is *Pulse* which begins with a lively tuba/bass duet, then settles into a rhythmic groove over which Rivers snakes hypnotic soprano. Abstract, funky, intense; *Waves* covers the spectrum in scintillating style. **GL**

Max Roach

1924

Deeds, Not Words **Roach** (d); **Booker Little** (t); **Ray Draper** (tba); **George Coleman** (ts); **Art Davis** (b). Riverside Ⓜ OJCCD 304-2 (44 minutes). Recorded 1958.

⑧ ❼

This group played the 1958 Newport Jazz Festival and stayed intact for close on two years; it was not the first piano-less band Roach had tried, but it was the first one to receive widespread recognition. Roach had formed the group with the clear intention of establishing a very young band with a new direction, and he certainly hit the jackpot with Little and Coleman. By the time of this record's first release, Little was already being talked of as the most significant arrival on trumpet since the death of Roach's friend and erstwhile partner, Clifford Brown, while George Coleman, a fine technician with a beautiful melodic turn, would go on to perform brilliantly with Miles Davis, amongst others. Ray Draper has not made such a large mark on the music, but his arranging and compositional talents were considerable, and were vital in defining the character of this Roach group.

Back in 1958, piano-less modern jazz small groups were still unusual (Mulligan's 1952 band had remained very much the exception to the rule), so this was an important step forward. Listened to today, the lack of a harmony instrument certainly allows the overall contours of the music to emerge more clearly and the soloists to form their phrasing without undue harmonic interference. But it would perhaps have been interesting to hear the occasional harmonic interjection from the non-soloists, supplying different colours as the numbers progressed, rather than using them solely in the theme statements at the beginning and end of each piece. The CD carries an extra track, a duet between Oscar Pettiford and Max Roach made during Sonny Rollins's **Freedom Suite** sessions. One wonders then why it wasn't added to *that* album's reissue? **KS**

We Insist!—Freedom Now Suite **Roach** (d, arr); **Booker Little** (t); **Julian Priester** (tb); **Walter Benton, Coleman Hawkins** (ts); **James Schenck** (b); **Michael Olatunji, Ray Mantilla, Thomas Duvail** (perc); **Abbey Lincoln** (v). Candid Ⓜ CCD 9002 (37 minutes). Recorded 1960.

✔ ⑧ ❽

Many critics and fans were upset by the espousal of the civil rights movement by musicians—if musicians were espoused by the movement, fans and critics didn't mind so much—but the critics and fans, being white, could afford to condemn the politicization of art. This was in any case not new, as black jazzmen had been privately outspoken since at least the thirties (note the contribution of Coleman Hawkins to the present album), but the explicit connection dates from the late-fifties influence on jazz of gospel music in addition to blues.

By 1960, it was possible for Roach to emulate his colleague Charles Mingus and attempt a musical depiction of the condition of blacks in the US and in Central and South Africa. Very different in tone from his quintet co-led by Clifford Brown, this group was descended from his 1958 album **Deeds Not Words** (and presaged the also-excellent **Percussion Bitter-Sweet**, recently reissued on CD), and has telling contributions from Little and Priester added to considerable rhythmic interest, with its opening and closing tracks in 5/4. But the most affecting voice is Lincoln's, heard on all five numbers; sometimes using the lyrics of Oscar Brown Jr, she also duets wordlessly with Roach on the powerful *Triptych*. **BP**

To The Max **Roach** (d, perc); **Cecil Bridgewater** (t); **Odean Pope** (ts); **George Cables** (p); **Ronnell Bey** (v); **Uptown String Quartet** (Diane Monroe, Lesa Terry [vn]; Maxine Roach [va]; Eileen Folson, [vc]); **M'Boom** (Roy Brooks, Joe Chambers, Omar Clay, Eli Fountain, Fred King, Ray Mantilla, Francisco Mora, Warren Smith [perc]); **John Motley Singers**. Enja Ⓕ ENJ 7021 22 (two discs: 100 minutes). Recorded 1990/91.

⑧ ❽

"If you're a creative artist, you have to have new ideas." In 1985 the man who had played bebop with Charlie Parker was following his credo by playing hip-hop with Fab Five Freddie. It was just the latest venture from the 40-plus years of tireless experimenting that have seen Max Roach develop into the most complete percussionist in jazz history. As well as continuing to lead his fine post-bop quartet, his projects in the seventies and eighties included working with gospel choirs and string quartets, co-founding the percussion ensemble M'Boom, writing extended compositions and recording excellent improvised duos with avant-gardists Anthony Braxton and Cecil Taylor.

To the Max celebrates Roach's multi-faceted creativity and offers a splendid introduction to some of his current interests. The opening 30-minute suite *Ghost Dance* features his vocal writing; *A Little Booker* blends jazz and string quartets to dramatic effect; two exquisite solo pieces let his drums sing out with scintillating artistry. His regular group contributes four tracks of fierce, passionate bop, while M'Boom add enchanting percussion sonorities, *Street Dance* a carnival shuffle, *A Quiet Place* all chiming liquidity. Roach's trap drumming, meanwhile, remains superbly lean and crisp, his rapid-fire cymbal lines setting the pace throughout this hugely impressive and enjoyable set. **GL**

Charles Luckyeth 'Luckey' Roberts 1887-1968

Luckey and The Lion: Harlem Piano **Roberts**, **Willie 'The Lion' Smith** (p). Good Time Jazz Ⓜ GTJCD 10035-2 (44 minutes). Recorded 1958.

⑧ ❻

The usual definition of Harlem 'stride' piano focuses on the superimposition of formulaic right-hand patterns over a rhythmic 'oompah' bass played by the left in a more swinging version of ragtime. This is, however, simplistic. On this disc the boundaries of the genre are tested by two very different exponents. Roberts is a bravura stylist, his rapid-fire flourishes and flurries undimmed on this relatively late recording by the effects of a traffic accident and a stroke. His *Spanish Fandango* brings the Hispanic elements of East Harlem to bear on some of the formulas of stride, while his *Railroad Blues* is as effective a piece of onomatopoeic programme music as the more familiar efforts of the boogie-woogie players. *Complainin'* is the most unusual—but the most subtle—of Roberts's pieces, his mumbling interruptions of complaint breaking the flow of a forward-moving piece of conventional stride, much in the manner of James P. Johnson's *Riffs*. Smith's pretty ragtime-based pieces like *Morning Air* and *Relaxin'* break the mould in another way. The Lion favoured left-hand ostinatos, repeated chords and suspensions in preference to 'striding'. When he eventually unleashed the full power of his left hand, the effect was genuinely dramatic. **AS**

Howard Roberts 1929-1992

The Real Howard Roberts **Roberts** (g); **Ross Tompkins** (p); **Ray Brown** (b); **Jimmie Smith** (d). Concord Jazz Ⓕ CCD-4053 (47 minutes). Recorded 1977.

⑥ ❽

The title has at least two interpretations. It could refer to Roberts's delivery from the Californian studios after the best part of 20 years; or it could announce his return to the post-Christian mainstream after such early seventies forays into jazz-rock psychedelia as **Antelope Freeway** and **Equinox Elevator Express**. Either way, this typically well-behaved Concord date is how Roberts is most likely to be remembered. Despite occasional rock and blues inflections and 'modern' colourations with phase shift and swell pedal, he is captured here in his natural habitat, playing politely daring jazz guitar in the Kessel-Burrell mould.

Inevitably, a good deal of single string soloing ensues. This is serviceable enough but, unsurprisingly in a man used to providing guitar soundbites, the solos are somewhat short on grand design and dramatic contour. For Roberts at his most completely satisfying it is perhaps best to turn to the swaggering comping with which he propelled the Bobby Troup band in the mid-fifties (audible on the recently-issued **Bobby Troup: The Feeling Of Jazz**, on Starline SLCD-9009). **MG**

Marcus Roberts

1963

Alone With Three Giants **Roberts** (p). Novus Ⓕ PD 83109 (64 minutes). Recorded 1990.

⑦ ❽

If only by association, Roberts is seen as part of the neoclassical jazz school in America. He has, however, done a great deal more than investigate the roots of bebop and the work of the pioneers in that movement. In building a personal style he has taken his field of research far beyond that area. This CD has him Robertizing the work of three great pianist/composers from past jazz history. The choice is superficially obvious, but the way in which he confronts each challenge is edifying. He has to contain Jelly Roll Morton's suspended rhythms, he must successfully temper Duke Ellington's dangerously deceptive romanticism and harness Thelonious Monk's idosyncratic approach to harmony for his own ends. Each victory is different, as he masters Morton's Spanish tinge on *New Orleans Blues* and *The Crave*, contrasts Ellington's reverential *Prelude To A Kiss* and *Mood Indigo* with the stride master's *Shout 'Em Aunt Tillie*, and then captures Monk's arrogant stride on *Trinkle,Tinkle* and the slower *Pannonica*. Yes, it is an act of revivalism, but Roberts has shown great sympathy for each of his subjects. To present a coherent study of jazz using the multi-strained ragtime compositional form, the James P. Johnson and Fats Waller stride lineage, and music from the once-exclusive bebop club, is to register oneself as an important young player. **BMcR**

Dick Robertson

1903

And His Orchestra, 1937-1939 **Robertson** (v); with a collective personnel of **Bobby Hackett** (c); **Johnny McGhee**, **Ralph Muzzillo**, **Johnny Carlson** (t); **Al Philburn**, **Buddy Morrow**, **Jack Teagarden** (tb); **Paul Ricci**, **Sid Trucker**, **Don Watt**, **Tony Zimmers** (cl); **Frank Froeba**, **Frank Signorelli** (p, cel); **Frank Victor**, **Dave Barbour** (g); **Haig Stephens** (b); **Sammy Weiss**, **Stan King** (d). Timeless Ⓜ CBC 1-008 (70 minutes). Recorded 1937-39.

⑥ ❻

Robertson wasn't much more than a mediocre singer with a modicum of jazz style, his light baritone most accurately described as 'pleasing', but he deserves to be remembered, if only for the fine Dixieland-style small groups he invariably assembled behind him for his recording sessions. His career in the studios lasted just seven years, but in that time he was prolific, cutting many more sides than could be contained on a single CD. This compilation was selected by Chris Ellis and re-mastered by John R.T. Davies, so you're getting pretty much the best from what is available.

It is the presence of Bobby Hackett which enlivens the first clutch of performances, his sound getting the the listener's heart to race just a little when he enters. Other notable characteristics are a steady, stomping beat of the type favoured by Bob Crosby, slashing trombone work and dexterous clarinet fills. A January 1938 date finds Jack Teagarden's trombone combining elegantly with trumpeters McGhee and Muzzillo, while pianist Froeba, present on 15 of the 24 tracks, starts the vast majority of those with the same descending piano arabesque. If it was a private joke, it must have been wearing thin after a year or so. **KS**

Jim Robinson

1892-1976

Classic New Orleans Jazz, Volume 2 **Robinson** (tb); **Kid Thomas**, **Ernest Cagnolatti**, **Tony Fougerat** (t); **Capt. John Handy** (as); **Sammy Rimington**, **Albert Burbank**, **Orange Kellin** (cl); **Bill Sinclair** (p); **Dick Griffith**, **George Guesnon**, **Father Al Lewis** (bj); **Dick McCarthy**, **'Slow Drag' Pavageau**, **James Prevost** (b); **Sammy Penn**, **'Cie' Frazier**, **Louis Barbarin** (d). Biograph Ⓕ BCD 128 (57 minutes). Recorded 1964-74.

⑤ ❹

Returning from military service in 1919, trombonist Robinson spent more than ten years in Sam Morgan's excellent band in New Orleans. His playing with the band and later with Lee Collins and Kid Howard called for a modified version of the tailgate tradition. It was the New Orleans revival of the late forties and the need to assume his place in the bands of Bunk Johnson, then George Lewis, that forced Robinson to return to the purer aspects of the style.

As this CD with his own bands shows, he was highly successful. He provided the forthright punctuation and ensemble linkage that was required, putting greater emphasis on glissando effects and, on *Shake That Thing* and *Gasket Street Blues* in particular, showing the fine balance he could achieve. His solo work was less impressive and *Lady Be Good* and *Washington And Lee Swing* are

typical of his rudimentary approach. The melody is lightly paraphrased, points of emphasis are adjusted but no real attempt is made to improvise. The simplified approach served his collective playing well, however, and although he may not have deciphered the somewhat cluttered ensemble patterns of the first six titles here, the remainder provide a yardstick by which New Orleans's revivalist trombone is judged.
BMcR

Orphy Robinson

1960

When Tomorrow Comes **Robinson** (vb, mba, perc); **Rowland Sutherland** (f, af, pic); **Tunde Jegede** (kora, vc); **Joe Bashorun** (p, kbds); **Dudley Phillips** (b); **Winston Clifford** (d, perc). Blue Note Ⓕ CDP7 98581-2 (59 minutes). Recorded 1991.

⑥ ❽

Although Orphy Robinson has been a regular feature on the UK scene for some time, both collaborating with Andy Sheppard and fronting his own bands, this was his début main-label recording as a leader. He shares the composing credits with keyboard player Joe Bashorun, but the album's wide-ranging musical reference points, covering the whole spectrum from acoustic traditional music to urban funk, are very much Robinson's own. He himself plays not only African music's staple marimba but also jazz vibes, and his collaborators similarly veer between continents and musical styles. The results are distinctly variable. In general, Bashorun's compositions are better vehicles for good improvisation, being more immediately accessible and tuneful than Robinson's (unsurprising, given the keyboard player's session and tour experience with the Womacks and his stints with electric bands like Desperately Seeking Fusion), but the album as a whole suffers from a shortage of sustained improvisational interest to flesh out the occasionally ponderous, over-fussy compositions. Too often an intriguing rhythm is set up, a strikingly unusual instrumental mix assembled, and then the piece's potential remains unrealized for lack of a biting soloist. The album thus leaves an overall impression of simply being too long for the number of musical ideas it contains, which is a shame, because those that are there are usually original and striking. Still, it remains better than the follow-up, **The Vibes Decides**.
CP

Perry Robinson

1938

Call To The Stars **Robinson** (cl); **Simon Nabatov** (p); **Ed Schuller** (b); **Ernst Bier** (d). West Wind Ⓕ 2052 (64 minutes:). Recorded 1990.

⑧ ❽

Although that rarest of breeds, the modern jazz clarinettist, Robinson has never quite received the attention he deserves. From the time of his first, early-sixties LP for Savoy he has straddled the populist folk and experimental traditions à la Jimmy Giuffre, adding an Eastern slant in the seventies by recording with percussionists Badal Roy and Nana Vasconcelos. He brings all of these influences to bear on **Call To The Stars**. *Farmer Alfalfa*, a Henry Grimes tune from the Savoy days, shows how subtly his style has changed, from a 'cool' Lesterian chromaticism to a harder Coltrane swing. He has always liked to contrast low swoops with high squeals, and there are more slurs, bent pitches, and unorthodox effects today, equal parts mid-eastern reed technique and Pee Wee Russell. Robinson's chalumeau *sotto voce* entry on bassist Schuller's *Shu Bass Blues* is pure Pee Wee, as are his curious note choices, changes of direction and harmonic curves. Similarly, *Henry's Dance* shows off his circuitous logic to good advantage. Nabatov's Tyneresque heft is an excellent foil and grounding force to Robinson's freer tendencies; he turns Darius Brubeck's *Sindaram Song* from a raga with eastern european modes to a soulful romp. Like Pee Wee, Sandy Brown, and Ed Chace, Robinson's unconventional playing is still denied acceptance in certain quarters. A pity.
AL

Reginald R. Robinson

1973

Sounds In Silhouette **Robinson** (p). Delmark Ⓕ DE 670 (61 minutes). Recorded 1994.

⑧ ❽

As the dates above reveal, Reginald Robinson was 21 years old when he made this, his second CD. Jazz musicians nowadays are making their débuts younger every year, so this would not normally be a matter for comment. But Reginald Robinson is not exactly a jazz musician: he is a ragtime pianist and composer. The 19 tracks here are all his compositions, except for one, which is his medley of three pieces by Charles L. Johnson, a contemporary of Joplin. They include rags, cakewalks and one charming tango, *Dream Natasha*, and all have that dignified but jaunty air which is unique to ragtime. Both composition and playing sound meticulously authentic. How an African-American child growing up in Chicago in the eighties came to be obsessed with ragtime, to the extent of setting out to teach himself the piano with the aid of library books and eventually going on to study at the American Conservatory, is one of those mysteries which occur from time to time. They bring with them the cheering message that there is no such thing as a completely dead musical language, that youth and fashion do not necessarily go together, and that everybody is not the same as everybody else.
DG

Spike Robinson

1930

Henry B. Meets Alvin G. / Once In A Wild **Robinson**, **Al Cohn** (ts); **Richard Wyands** (p); **Steve LaSpina** (b); **Akira Tana** (d). Capri ℗ 1061787 (67 minutes). Recorded 1987.

⑦ ❻

Like Buck Hill, another 'recent' tenor saxophone discovery, Robinson worked full-time at another career and only turned to music as a vocation in 1985 when he retired as an engineer. He's been written about in some circles as an extension of the 'cool' West Coast fifties sound, but this album is quite a heated affair. All he really shares with a number of the 'cool' saxists is an affinity for Lester Young—witness his relaxed phrasing on the laidback *Sweets Blues* as well as his breathy, elaborate ballad playing on a favourite of Pres', *These Foolish Things*. Rhythmically, both he and Cohn inhabit that grey area between swing and bop, leaning towards the former. More complementary than combative, they mesh well together on Bob Brookmeyer's bouncy *Rustic Hop* and the evergreen *Once in a While*, taken at a slightly brighter tempo than usual. But they are capable of high-spirited blowing too, primarily on *Sippin' At Bells*, and they put an old warhorse like *Bye Bye Blues* through some lively paces, concluding with a contrapuntal chorus sans rhythm section. Wyands is an underrated journeyman accompanist with a light touch: he introduces *Sweets' Blues* with a casual insouciance worthy of Count Basie. LaSpina and Tana combine as a solid, unobtrusive rhythm team (audio note: the slightly lower rating for the digital sound was due to a tad too much echo on the horns, though it's still quite easy to distinguish Robinson's burnished tone from Cohn's bristling tenor). **AL**

Claudio Roditi

1946

Two Of Swords **Roditi** (t, flh); **Jay Ashby** (tb); **Edward Simon**, **Danilo Perez** (p); **Nilson Matta** (b); **David Finck** (b); **Duduka Forseca, Akira Tana** (d). Candid ℗ CCD 79504 (73 minutes). Recorded 1990.

⑥ ❽

Born in Brazil, Roditi was introduced to jazz by records, firstly of Louis Armstrong, then, in his teens, Dizzy Gillespie and Miles Davis. He came to the US in 1970 to study at the Berklee School in Boston, and after moving to New York in 1976 helped establish a Brazilian jazz scene at the remarkably seedy Jazzmania loft. By then established in the New York scene, he was to become a member of Gillespie's United Nations Orchestra and is ever-present on the world festival circuit. As yet, he has not been consistently captured on record in a way that does him justice. He is a gifted and flamboyant trumpeter, but this CD, like several others, projects his technical skill rather more than the content of his work. He is heard in two groups; the first enhanced by the confident Curtis Fuller-ish trombone of Ashby and the second with a rhythm section superior by virtue of the presence of Perez and Finck. Roditi's best work is on *Secret Love*, with a dramatic solo that shows his ability to develop a theme, and *Blues For H.Q.*, a tidy 12-bar that shows something of the warmth communicated consistently in his live work. **BMcR**

Red Rodney

1927-1994

Then And Now **Rodney** (flh); **Chris Potter** (as, ts); **Garry Dial** (p); **Jay Anderson** (b); **Jimmy Madison** (d); **Bob Belden** (arr). Chesky ℗ JD79 (75 minutes). Recorded 1992.

⑧ ❽

A great deal of care and preparation went into the making of this album and the title says it all. Here are nearly a dozen bebop tunes played with equal ackowledgement of the time of their original creation and of contemporary 1992 music. Rodney and arranger Bob Belden have made adjustments, updating the pieces without losing the character of the compositions. Tadd Dameron's *The Scene Is Clean*, for example, is played as a waltz (and very attractively too) and an adjustment has been made to the middle-eight of *Confirmation*. But none of these changes is likely to upset even the most ardent bebop enthusiast, for the music must be judged in its totality and this is a very successful album, far better than yet another attempt to produce note-for-note versions of music first recorded over four decades ago. Rodney is fluent on flügelhorn and Potter fits in well on both saxes (although he is not at heart a bopper). The rhythm section plays with a smooth, efficient continuity and does not attempt to emulate the often harsh and jagged backings of a 1947-vintage team. The final ten minutes of playing time is devoted to an interesting interview with Rodney, although it is not the kind of thing one would want to hear as frequently as the music itself. **AM**

Shorty Rogers

1924-1994

The Big Shorty Rogers Express **Rogers** (t, arr) with a collective personnel of **Conrad Gozzo**, **Maynard Ferguson, Pete Candoli, John Howell, Conte Candoli, Harry Edison** (t); **Milt Bernhart**, **John Halliburton, Harry Betts, Frank Rosolino** (tb); **Bob Enevoldsen** (vtb); **John Graas** (frh); **George Roberts** (btb); **Gene Englund, Paul Sarmento** (tba); **Charlie Mariano** (as); **Art Pepper** (as, ts, bs); **Bud Shank** (as, bs); **Bill Holman, Jack Montrose** (ts); **Jimmy Giuffre** (cl,ts, bs); **Bob Cooper** (ts, bs); **Marty Paich, Lou Levy** (p); **Curtis Counce, Ralph Pena** (b); **Shelly Manne, Stan Levey** (d). RCA Living Stereo Ⓜ 18519 2 (43 minutes). Recorded 1953/56.

⑩ ❽

This was where West Coast Jazz began. Rogers had been using his small group, The Giants, on club dates and featured it in front of what was virtually the Stan Kenton orchestra on those first eight big band tracks made for RCA. Issued originally as a ten-inch LP called **Cool And Crazy**, four additional tracks were recorded in 1956 to make it into a 12-inch with a new title, **The Big Shorty Rogers Express** and this CD is the exact equivalent of that LP complete with the picture of Shorty sitting on the front of the Sante Fé engine. All the big and important West Coast names are here, Pepper, Shank, Cooper, Giuffre, Manne, Paich, the Candolis, etc., and the music still packs that tremendous punch, like an even more powerful Basie band using the same kind of contrast between the incredible brass passages (with Ferguson doubling Gozzo's lead an octave higher) and the economic piano work from 'Count' Paich and 'Count' Levy. In this context Rogers's own somewhat limited powers as an improvising soloist are masked by the aptness and sheer unbridled excitement of the ensemble work. Pepper and Cooper sound marvellous, Manne is perfect and the dynamics on *Infinity Promenade*, logically building to a splendid climax in just over three minutes, is still a thing to wonder at. The playing time is short because this is an obvious facsimile of an LP; in fact RCA could easily have added the eight titles by Shorty's Giants which they recorded a couple of months before the **Cool And Crazy** album. Despite this shortcoming the CD is highly recommended, because of the lasting quality of this superb big band's music. **AM**

Sonny Rollins 1930

The Complete Prestige Recordings Rollins (ts); with a collective personnel of **Miles Davis, Kenny Dorham, Art Farmer, Clifford Brown** (t); **J. J. Johnson, Bennie Green** (tb); **Julius Watkins** (frh); **Jackie McLean** (as); **Charlie Parker, John Coltrane** (ts); **John Lewis, Miles Davis, Walter Bishop Jr, Kenny Drew, Thelonious Monk, Horace Silver, Elmo Hope, Ray Bryant, Tommy Flanagan, Richie Powell, Red Garland, Wade Legge** (p); **Milt Jackson** (vb); **Leonard Gaskin, Percy Heath, Tommy Potter, George Morrow, Paul Chambers, Doug Watkins** (b); **Max Roach, Roy Haynes, Art Blakey, Philly Joe Jones, Willie Jones, Kenny Clarke, Art Taylor** (d); **Earl Coleman** (v). Prestige Ⓕ 7PCD-4407-2 (seven discs: 496 minutes). Recorded 1949-56.

⑨ ❽

Rollins grew up as an artist while he was under contract to Prestige. His first session as a leader occurred in 1951: previous to that, from 1949 onwards he had been a sideman on J.J. Johnson and Miles Davis dates for Prestige (and a Johnson date for Savoy), and had also recorded for Bud Powell over at Blue Note.

There are efficacious things amongst the earlier tracks, but life gets serious in late 1953 with the Rollins/Milt Jackson session, followed one month later by the four tracks with Monk. By this time, Rollins had made great stylistic strides and was an instantly recognizable player, both for the sound he created and for the personal way he negotiated the harmonic structures of the repertoire being recorded. Yet within a year the tenor player had taken himself off the scene, unhappy with both himself and his playing. A 12-month silence was broken by the spectacular success of the quartet album **Worktime**, contained on disc four here, recorded in December 1955. Its mastery was only overshadowed by the towering achievements, just six months later, on **Saxophone Colossus** (which takes up the first half of disc six). By the end of 1956 Rollins was moving on to other record companies and other ideas, but one wonders whether anything he did later was *better* than what he did in that annus mirabilis, or whether it was simply *different*. Different peaks, different troughs. All equally fascinating.

This boxed set is a superb presentation, and neatly encapsulates early Rollins in a way the similar Prestige box of early Coltrane (1955-58), with its sprawling 16 CDs and multitude of sideman dates for the saxophonist, cannot hope to. The 48-page booklet contains an erudite commentary by Bob Blumenthal, a full Prestige Rollins discography and plenty of first-class photographs. The playing times are exemplary. Prestige got this one right. **KS**

Saxophone Colossus Sonny Rollins (ts); **Tommy Flanagan** (p); **Doug Watkins** (b); **Max Roach** (d). Prestige Ⓜ OJCCD 291-2 (40 minutes). Recorded 1956.

✔ ⑩ ❽

Saxophone Colossus is one of the undisputed masterpieces of jazz. In form it is very simple—tenor saxophone and rhythm section playing a set of five tunes; two standards, an original, a West Indian folk song and a blues. Like all great works, it operates at many levels. It is swinging, optimistic and entirely understandable music; the balance of the instruments and the subtlety of their interplay represent perfection in the post-bop idiom; Rollins's sound is massive yet flexible and intimate, with none of the slightly hectoring tone which it later assumed.

At a deeper level, Rollins builds his improvisations with a cogency that is little short of miraculous. Gunther Schuller produced a famous thematic analysis of one of the album's pieces, *Blue Seven*, demonstrating that Rollins's entire long solo is constructed from motifs based on the intervals of the third and flattened fifth. Just as remarkable is his rhythmic freedom within the gridlines of the beat and the chord sequence, creating endless patterns of tension and release. In short, **Saxophone Colossus** is a record with which you can happily spend a lifetime. **DG**

Way Out West **Rollins** (ts); **Ray Brown** (b); **Shelly Manne** (d). Contemporary Ⓜ OJCCD 337-2 (71 minutes). Recorded 1957.

⑧ ❽

Way Out West was recorded during Rollins's first visit to the West Coast. His sense of humour was evident in the famous cover-photo of him with stetson, holster and horn and immediately confirmed by the opening *I'm An Old Cow Hand*, with its tongue-in-cheek clip-clop beat ("I want that cat out on the range all the way", Rollins told drummer Manne) and droll tenor dissections of the tune.

Such comic guying was a gift Rollins had honed in his stint with Thelonious Monk, and this album also shows him following Monk's advice to "use the melody" (not just the chord changes) when improvising. He had, moreover, been keen to try working without piano; **Way Out West** was his first trio record and he revels in the extra space. He ranges all over his horn, from high peals to gruff interjections, and rhythmically is both buoyant and assured. He devours the uptempo *Come, Gone* (to the initial discomfiture of Manne) and elsewhere rides the beat with authority as he delivers his jaunty dabs and flourishes, turning to smoother lines and a more imploring tone for the ballads *Solitude* and *There Is No Greater Love*. It all makes for an exhilarating display of saxophone virtuosity.

The CD contains three alternate (longer) takes that were not on the original **Way Out West** LP, but which did appear on Contemporary's **Alternate Takes** LP. **GL**

A Night at the Village Vanguard, Volumes 1 & 2 **Rollins** (ts); **Wilbur Ware** (b); **Elvin Jones** (d); **Donald Bailey** (b); **Pete LaRoca** (d), Vol. 2. Blue Note Ⓜ CDP46517/18-2 (58 and 69 minutes, oas). Recorded 1957.

✔ ⑩ ❻

In 1957, Sonny Rollins began a decade of superior recordings bracketed by **Way Out West** and 1966's **East Broadway Rundown**. The absence of piano on many of them gave Rollins freedom to ignore or transcend the disciplines of harmony and time-keeping the instrument imposed and linked him implicitly with piano-averse Ornette Coleman.

The Vanguard sessions were recorded at afternoon and evening shows one Sunday. Sonny's harsh tone complements his booting rhythmic energy and embodies Monk's concept of 'ugly beauty'. A flood of ideas pours from his tenor, as on *Striver's Row* (vol. two). *Old Devil Moon* (vol. one) demonstrates how much his celebrated penchant for thematic improvisation involves careful attention to the melody (in that sense, this modernist is decidedly conservative). He brings radical rhythmic displacements to *Get Happy* (two), and tosses in typically outlandish quotes, tagging *Woody 'n' You* (one) with *March of the Siamese Children*.

Elvin's loose accents goad Rollins on; the harmonic simplicity of Ware's plump, propulsive bass further liberates rather than restricts him. The less-noted Bailey and LaRoca, heard at the matinée, are similarly progressive, never a hindrance. These separately-available volumes are evenly matched; the first features both rhythm sections, the second contains perhaps a few more peaks. A good collection deserves both. **KW**

Freedom Suite **Rollins** (ts); **Oscar Pettiford** (b); **Max Roach** (d). Riverside Ⓜ OJCCD 067-2 (41 minutes). Recorded 1958.

⑧ ❽

Commonly regarded as the link between Charlie Parker and John Coltrane—although Dexter Gordon, an early influence on Rollins, also deserves mention—Rollins has been one of jazz's most productive innovators. Noted for his thematically-based improvisations, his unique permutations of the pulse where he alternatively lags behind and then rushes past the centre of the beat, and his barrel-chested yet plaintive sound, Rollins continues to be one of the medium's most influential voices.

In 1958, when Rollins was fresh from galvanizing associations with the Clifford Brown-Max Roach and Miles Davis quintets and was in the process of establishing his own credentials as the leader of a working group, he was also in the midst of creating a set of landmark recordings for both Riverside and Blue Note. With the Riverside release of **Freedom Suite**, however, Rollins both consolidated and expanded his visionary style. First was his use of a piano-less trio, here with the superlative bassist Oscar Pettiford and drummer Max Roach, a format he had initiated in 1957 for the still fascinating **Way Out West** (see above). Second was his employment of an extended compositional form, the kaleidoscopic, multi-metred, 20-minute long *Freedom Suite*, which had additional significance in its anticipation of the racial politiciation of jazz in the sixties. Third was his continued exploration of waltz-time in *Someday I'll Find You* and *Shadow Waltz*, which was also a further affirmation of his good-humoured devotion to show tunes. **CB**

The Bridge **Rollins** (ts); **Jim Hall** (g); **Bob Cranshaw** (b); **Ben Riley** (d). RCA Bluebird Ⓑ ND 90633 (41 minutes). Recorded 1962.

✔ ⑧ ❽

It seemed strange that the passionate and urgent series of improvisations Rollins recorded for Prestige should come forth from such a reticent and modest man. Hindsight tells us that this was a time of great turbulence in Rollins's life. At the beginning of the sixties, he chose to drop from the public eye to re-evaluate his musical resources. Famously he was heard practicing on his tenor at night on New York's Williamsburg Bridge, and when, in late 1961, he returned to the jazz scene, a legend had built up around the incident and considerable hype resulted in the music press about what was to all intents a non-event. On his return Rollins was found to be dispensing the potent mixture much as before and this, his first post-Williamsburg Bridge album, found his dry and pithy embellishments not radically different. What did make a difference was the presence of Jim Hall on guitar instead of a pianist. Hall's chording gave Rollins much more freedom - this was a variation on the pianoless quartet theory operated by Gerry Mulligan and the guitarist proved to be a match for Rollins in his creative soloing. The long and impressive improvisation on *John S.* has a free atmosphere about it and has pre-echoes of the later and much longer *East Broadway Rundown*. The title track consists of two choruses, one alternating 6/8 with 4/4 whilst the other chorus is straight fours. In contrast to the overall idea that Rollins was a 'hard' player, *Where Are You?* and *God Bless The Child* are ballad performances of great sensitivity and again Hall's chording is vital. Typically of Rollins' work, the music has not dated at all, and indeed the comparatively concise nature of the playing makes this one more attractive than many of his later albums. **SV**

What's New? **Rollins** (ts); **Jim Hall** (g); **Bob Cranshaw** (b); **Ben Riley** (d); with, on various tracks, **Candido Camero** (cga); **Willie Rodriguez**, **Dennis Charles**, **Frank Charles** (perc); unidentified. vocal group, **Jimmy Jones** (arr) RCA Bluebird Ⓑ 352572 2 (44 minutes). Recorded 1962.

⑥ ❽

The quartet which successfully marked Rollins's return to playing with **The Bridge** (see above) was back to the studio within weeks to cut this album. Whether or not word had already leaked out that bossa nova was to be the next 'big thing' in popular music, the finished album was certainly marketed as Sonny's answer to the new rhythm. Nevertheless, there is only a single suggestion of that style in one track, *The Night Has a Thousand Eyes*, while the other quartet number *If Ever I Would Leave You* is treated as a much more urgent samba. Rollins is clearly himself and a million miles from Getz, and indeed he gets quite abstract on two tracks with just Cranshaw and Candido. Sonny's favourite calypso rhythm surfaces on the entertaining *Brown Skin Girl* with the quartet, percussion section and vocal group combining gleefully. In fact, the similar if less interesting *Don't Stop The Carnival* (which replaced *If Ever I Would Leave You* on the original UK and French issues and has never been released on CD) ought to be here as well, especially when the playing time is considered. But, as one of the many and various faces presented by Rollins, this album is worthy of attention. **BP**

On The Outside **Rollins** (ts); **Don Cherry** (t); **Bob Cranshaw** (b); **Henry Grimes** (b); **Billy Higgins** (d). Bluebird Ⓜ ND 82496 (62 minutes). Recorded 1962/63.

✔ ⑧ ❽

The two sessions that comprise this CD were made one year apart after Rollins had returned from his second sabbatical. Inexplicably, the unassailable leader in jazz had been plagued with self-doubts and had retired to ponder the musical directions being taken by his friends John Coltrane and Ornette Coleman. Rollins and Coleman actually practised together during the lay-off, and those sessions are strongly reflected in the jazz played on this CD. As implied by the personnel, the Coleman free-form mantle is draped over the proceedings, with Rollins adapting enthusiastically to the new circumstances. In the event, he never allows himself harmonic abdication, preferring to toy with the chord sequences instead. *Doxy* is typical of the way in which he ignores the exact details of the passing harmonic structure while relating his solo to its overall form. The relationship between Rollins and Cherry varies; a degree of compatibility exists on *Dearly Beloved* but on *Oleo* they seem total strangers. The three studio-recorded titles completing the programme are not as strong. On *I Could Write A Book*, Rollins's two short statements are more radical than the single one by Cherry. This release represents a brief period in Rollins's career, and one which he seems not to have directly built upon, but at the same time he never returned to his pre-sabbatical approach, so it had the desired effect. And the music is magnificent. **BMcR**

Alfie **Rollins** (ts); **Jimmy Cleveland**, **J.J. Johnson** (tb); **Phil Woods** (as); **Bob Ashton** (ts); **Danny Bank** (bs); **Roger Kellaway** (p); **Kenny Burrell** (g); **Walter Booker** (b); **Frankie Dunlop** (d); **Oliver Nelson** (arr, cond). Impulse! Ⓜ MCAD-39107 (33 minutes). Recorded 1966.

✔ ⑩ ❽

Although this is advertised as containing "original music from the score" of Lewis Gilbert's 1966 film starring Michael Caine as the eponymous cockney Casanova, that is not quite true. The themes are those written by Rollins for the movie, where he plays them with just a rhythm section. On disc, those themes are re-recorded, with orchestrations by Nelson. *Alfie's Theme*, the jukeing Rollins blues heard under the titles, expanded to ten glorious minutes here, has latterly become a rival to *St. Thomas* as Rollins's signature tune. Meant to signal the title character's raffishness, the tune also signals the saxophonist's. It features a solo that, if transcribed, might appear to be one by any hucklebucking r&b saxophonist of the fifties or sixties. What identifies it as Rollins on actual hearing is his elliptical note placement and the sardonic vehemence of his honks and growls. The other five tracks, all of which have something going for them, include a lovely waltz in *On Impulse* and one of Rollins's most affecting ballad performances on *He's Younger Than You Are*. Burrell and Kellway spell Rollins nicely, and although Nelson falls short of being Sonny's Gil Evans, his arrangements are serviceable: he does not blunt the rough edges, as he later would Pee Wee Russell's and Thelonious Monk's. This is from a period when Rollins, although working steadily and placing high in polls, was somewhat taken for granted in some quarters because his music lacked the political and spiritual connotations of Coltrane's. The evidence here, and on the RCA albums which preceded his Impulse! deal, suggests that he was then at the top of his game, regardless of whether or not he was still in fashion. **FD**

Sonny Rollins In Japan **Rollins** (ts); **Yoshiaki Masuo** (g); **Bob Cranshaw** (el b); **David Lee** (d); James Mtume (cga). JVC Ⓜ VICJ-23001 (47 minutes). Recorded 1973.

⑦ ❻

For Rollins, the seventies, on record at least, was hardly a memorable decade. Many of his albums were disappointing displays of self-indulgent filibustering, bolstered by an overdose of electronics and occasional forays on the soprano saxophone. This CD stands out from many surrounding it and sounds like a return to the days of the Impulse!, even the Prestige, sessions. Recorded at a Tokyo concert, it opens with a lengthy work-out on one of those Rollins compositions based on a repeated, and largely rhythmic, figure which, when spread over 18 minutes, becomes hypnotic. *Powaii* has comparatively short solo passages by the leader, but Sonny's massive presence is felt throughout and Masuo plays with logic and conviction. The other three tracks will appeal immediately to long-term Rollins enthusiasts for they comprise welcome reworkings of *St. Thomas, Alfie's Theme* and *Moritat*, all of which receive careful examination from Sonny and are not merely thrown into the programme to satisfy the groundlings. After his initial impact on the Prestige, Riverside, Blue Note and RCA labels, Rollins appeared often to be in danger of losing his artistic direction, but this Tokyo concert shows that, in 1973, he was still playing living, vital music when the occasion demanded it. **AM**

G-Man **Rollins** (ts); **Clifton Anderson** (tb); **Mark Soskin** (p); **Bob Cranshaw** (b); **Marvin 'Smitty' Smith** (d). Milestone Ⓕ MCD-9150-2 (44 minutes). Recorded 1986.

⑧ ❻

One could assemble a magnificent CD with the best tracks from Sonny Rollins's 18 Milestone albums. Finding a great single album is another matter. **G-Man**, recorded at an outdoor concert (and documented in the Robert Mugge film Saxophone Colossus), gets my vote for three reasons. The audience inspires Rollins to more intense playing than he usually delivers in the recording studio. Smitty Smith's presence elevates the overall work of the rhythm section. Finally, on the title track, Rollins gives us his greatest single recorded performance of the last quarter-century. *G-Man*, which like other titles in his canon (*Ee-ah, Blessing in Disguise*) is more a favourite lick from his Harlem youth than an actual tune, manifests every accolade regarding invention, continuity, drive and sheer magnetism that the critical fraternity can muster. Rollins hurtles phrases off the hoary riff in ever-lengthening episodes, illustrating the twin secrets of his genius—his continued reliance on material at the heart of the jazz tradition and his willingness to see how far these bluesy, mercilessly swinging verities can be stretched in the hands of a brilliant improviser. Three other tunes, including the CD bonus *Tenor Madness*, are good but inevitably anticlimactic. **BB**

Aldo Romano

1941

Ten Tales **Romano** (d); **Joe Lovano** (ts). Owl Ⓕ 053CD (47 minutes). Recorded 1989.

⑧ ❽

Putting two musicians in a studio and expecting an album to emerge from their creative interplay could be a somewhat risky strategy, but the odds are considerably shortened if the musicians in question have track records like Romano's and Lovano's. The drummer, after learning his trade in Paris backing locals like Barney Wilen and Michel Portal and visiting Americans like Jackie McLean, became immersed in free jazz in the mid-sixties, collaborating with Steve Lacy, Don Cherry and Joachim Kühn in the medium before becoming a leader in the late seventies. Joe Lovano was sitting in with his father's rhythm section when he was 13, studying at Berklee at 20 and recording with Lonnie Smith at 22. Since then he has become one of the most prodigious and sought-after talents on the scene, collaborating tellingly with guitarists Bill Frisell and John Scofield, but he is equally at home playing free music. **Ten Tales** he himself describes as "completely free, but an attempt to put together the harmony and rhythm I felt within that free form to create structure and form without playing a re-creation of it." A particular pitfall in wait for unwary players of such music is repetition, throwing off stock phrases by rote, but both participants combine to mould a rewarding, varied and imaginative set, impeccably performed. **Ten Tales** is, as one of its track titles suggests, a *Monologue For Two*, an object lesson in intense, sustained duo improvisation. **CP**

Dom Um Romao

1925

Dom Um Romao **Romao** (d, perc); **William Campbell** (t); **Jimmy Bossey** (tb); **Lloyd McNeil** (f); **Jerry Dodgion** (as, f); **Mauricio Smith** (ss, ts, f); **Sivuca** (org, p, g); **Dom Salvador** (p); **Richard**

Kimball (syn); **Amauri Tristao** (g); **Stanley Clarke**, **Frank Tusa** (b); **Eric Gravatt**, **Portintio** (perc). Muse Ⓕ MCD-6012 (64 Minutes). Recorded 1973.

⑧ ❽

Brazilian drummer/percussionist Dom Um Romao first came to prominence in Rio de Janeiro with Sergio Mendes' Bossa Rio. Moving to the US in the mid-sixties, he worked with Oscar Brown Jr and with Mendes' Brazil 66 and Antonio Carlos Jobim. In 1971, he took over the percussion chair with Weather Report from former student Airto Moreira. In the sixties, Brazil had become associated with the breezy and wistful bossa nova. While Romao benefited from its popularity, his first love was the street music of the people, particularly the working black underclass, rather than the Spanish and Portuguese gentry. That commitment is reflected in these uniquely appealing sessions from 1973, recorded in the midst of Romao's highly successful tenure with Weather Report. Indeed, on tracks like *Shake* (*Ginga Gingou*) we catch the spirit of the samba de rua or street samba. And though the mood and density are lighter in lines like *Highway*, where Lloyd McNeil's quicksilver flute dances freely, even in these there is a gritty edge.

Throughout, Romao's infectious rhythmic currents seethe and swirl. In sum, these are well-produced and well-rehearsed sessions where the Afro-Brazilian impulse is paraded with brio and carnivalesque high spirits.

CB

Antoine Roney

1963

The Traveler Roney (ts); **Wallace Roney** (t); **James Spaulding** (ss, as, f); **Jacky Terrasson** (p); **Dwayne Burno** (b); **Louis Hayes** (d). Muse Ⓕ F MCD 5469 (52 minutes). Recorded 1992.

⑦ ❽

Antoine Roney, Wallace's younger brother by 3 years, has taken a little longer to come to his first recording session than his brother. A thinker, he has done much reappraisal of his music as an ongoing commitment and this has probably slowed his journey into the spotlight. Judging by the fact that he bought a copy of Wayne Shorter's **The All-Seeing Eye** at the age of just eight, it may not be too surprising to find that the music on this record often sounds like the more imaginative and progressive efforts to come out of the Blue Note stable between, say, 1963 and 1966 (James Spaulding, present on four tracks here, was actually on some of those records).

Roney has chosen a very capable rhythm section, with Louis Hayes being a truly great -and greatly undervalued- drummer who once formed a vital part of one of the classic modern jazz rhythm sections - Timmons, Jones and himself with Cannonball. Jacky Terrasson has gone on to make his own record as a leader, and here shows hundreds of felicitous touches, both behind others and in solos of his own. Which leaves the two Roneys. Wallace here is concise, fiery and controlled, while Antoine sounds more diffuse, as if searching for the optimum way of expressing his musical thoughts. In a sense, Antoine, certainly the less consistently successful improviser and still clearly indebted to Shorter, is the more exciting, precisely because of that sense of the unknown, being on the edge of possibility. The date is nicely paced and the compositions thoughtful. A good start for a promising career.

KS

Wallace Roney

1960

Obsession Wallace Roney (t); **Gary Thomas** (ts, f); **Donald Brown** (p); **Christian McBride** (b); **Cindy Blackman** (d). Muse Ⓕ MCD 5423 (43 minutes). Recorded 1991.

✔ ⑧ ❽

Wallace Roney is without a doubt the finest of the remarkable crop of young trumpet players who sprung up during the eighties. Technique is taken as read these days, and even imagination; what Roney has is poise, stillness, a sense of ease. It is true that he does sound uncannily like Miles Davis when playing through a harmon mute; this is because everybody playing through a harmon sounds a bit like Miles and partly because Roney's articulation is very similar. The likeness largely disappears when the mute comes out, but it has come in handy for him when playing in various Miles Davis Tribute bands.

It is entirely possible that this CD will come to be regarded as a classic of its time.

DG

Mistérios Roney (t, arr) with: **Antoine Roney**, **Ravi Coltrane** (ts); **Geri Allen** (p, arr); **Gil Goldstein** (kbds, arr); **Clarence Seay** (b); **Eric Allen** (d); **Steve Barrios**, **Steve Thornton**, **Valtinho Anastacio** (perc); and string/woodwind orchestra cond. by **Gil Goldstein** (**Geri Allen**, 1 track). Warner Bros .Ⓕ 245641-2 (59 minutes). Recorded 1993.

⑧ ❿

The tradition which this album continues is clear, from Dizzy to Clifford Brown to Miles to Hubbard to Marsalis and on up to now. A solo trumpeter supported by orchestra and rhythm section. Roney has possessed the technical chops for such a venture for a number of years now, but this album shows that the timing was pretty much right: Roney is neither cowed by the situation into playing falsely, nor is he merely exhibitionistic. He uses the skilful arrangements as a carefully designed cushion for his melodic statements, and uses the rhythm section as an alert and colourful partner in his controlled and concise improvisational flights. It seems to me that the arrangements are the best I've heard in a context such as this since the Gil Evans/Miles days, and that's not because they imitate those classic sessions, because they don't. This is more like Legrand at his peak.

But Roney is the soloist under the spotlight, and he deserves to be there, playing with poise and intelligence, not going for flash, but winning the listener through his warmth and sincerity. Neither does he play down to the situation: his solos bristle with his usual arsenal of inversions, chromaticisms and rhythmic displacements. Thus the album can be listened to on two levels - as mood music or as something much more substantial. It works well either way. **KS**

Michele Rosewoman

Harvest **Rosewoman** (p, v, perc); **Steve Wilson** (ss, as); **Gary Thomas** (ts, f); **Kenny Davis** (b, elb); **Gene Jackson** (d); **Eddie Bobe** (cgas, cajon, quinto, palitos, v). Enja Ⓕ 7069-2 (71 minutes). Recorded 1993.

⑧ ❽

Rosewoman first arrived in New York in 1978, and by 1983 she had impressed observers sufficiently to begin winning critics' polls. A key reason for that quick respect is that she is gifted both as a pianist and as a composer, and has originality to offer in both areas. She is also able to realize her compositions powerfully through the deployment of imaginative arrangements. In all this she at times evokes the angularity and intellectual challenge of Andrew Hill: she shares his clear, firm touch and his liking for fragmented rhythms across a steady tempo; they also both enjoy the investigation of long series of dissonant inversions.

Her choice of support on this album is sound, with Steve Wilson in particular having the agility and angularity to play with the structures Rosewoman sets up for each soloist. But she herself remains at the centre of the music throughout, and contributes mightily to the success of the final track, *Warriors*, which sees her unite with Yoruba musician Eddie Bobe for 15 minutes of sustained interaction between two related musical cultures.

Harvest is a challenging and fully mature album which nonetheless is immensely approachable for the uninitiated. If you doubt me, then try the heartfelt treatment of Billy Strayhorn's lament on mortality, *Blood Count*. **KS**

Renée Rosnes

1962

Without Words **Rosnes** (p); **Buster Williams** (b); **Billy Drummond** (d); **String Orchestra / Gene Orloff**. Blue Note Ⓕ CDP7 98168-2 (46 minutes). Recorded 1992.

⑦ ❽

Rosnes made three albums for Blue Note (although they all stem from the production house of Somethin' Else), and for the third disc this erstwhile Joe Henderson sideperson came up with a strong, if rather recherché, idea. The programme is a set of very familiar ballads (*You and The Night and The Music*, *I've Got You Under My Skin*, *Dear Old Stockholm*, etc.), played in fifties style by the trio with a decidedly fifties-style set of string arrangements to help it all along. On paper, there is little that could sound worse. In practice, though, it comes off handsomely. Rosnes knows just when to pull back and let the melodies speak for themselves, and when to push out into some spirited solo work. The strings never intrude to the point of distraction, but their presence gives weight to the romanticism of the idea and also help recall the times when great singers of the past put the words to these songs. Her trio partners, Williams and Drummond, give truly inspired support.

A clever idea by an enterprising musician, and I am glad to report that it works. At least, it does this time. **KS**

Frank Rosolino

1926-1978

Free For All **Rosolino** (tb); **Harold Land** (ts); **Victor Feldman** (p); **Leroy Vinnegar** (b); **Stan Levey** (d). Speciality Ⓜ OJCCD1763-2 (58 minutes). Recorded 1958.

⑥ ❽

Rosolino had all the right credentials for a major jazz soloist; he was a master of the trombone and had years of experience with the big bands of Gene Krupa and Stan Kenton. He enlivened many a West Coast recording date and it is difficult to say why this album lacks the spark of, say, the two he did for Capitol (not yet transferred to CD). All the right ingredients are here, including a fine rhythm section made up of men who played together often. Harold Land is a most dependable tenor player but somehow the music just lacks the spark which would have pushed it over the dividing line between good and very good. Perhaps the arrangements are over-fussy at times and the inclusion of three alternative takes does little to improve the quality of the record. Although made in 1958, the music was not issued in any form until 1986, a fact which may be its own quality assessment; perhaps the parent company waited until they felt the field was less competitive than at the time of the original session. **AM**

Ronnie Ross

1933-1991

Messages From Munich Ross (bs) with the following collective personnel: **Rick Kiefer** (t); **Rudy Friesen** (tb); **Rudi Risavy** (f); **Dick Spencer** (f, as); **Olaf Kubler** (ss, ts); **Don Menza** (as, ts); **Hans Koller, Rudi Fierl** (ts); **Pepsi Auer, Joe Haider, Bill Le Sage** (p); **Peter Trunk, Hans Rätenbacher, Jiri Mraz** (b); **Cees See, Meinrad Geppert, Pierre Favre** (d). Hot House Ⓕ HHCD 1017 (57 minutes) Recorded 1963-67

⑥ ❽

No less a jazz authority than John Lewis recognized Ross's importance and individuality as a baritone soloist as far back as 1958 when he employed him as the featured voice on **European Windows** (RCA LP, nla). The following year Ronnie toured the UK with the Modern Jazz Quartet. This CD comprises previously unissued material recorded in Munich studios, and although the multi-national groups included Americans Don Menza, Rick Kiefer and Dick Spencer, Ronnie's is the most commanding solo voice. Virtually all of the music was composed by Ross and is played by varying combinations, most of which produce the tight, clean ensemble sound associated with West Coast jazz. *Since Yesterday* has a relaxed, Basie-like feeling while *Sub-Basement Blues*, done at the same session, is arguably one of Ronnie's finest solos on record, a beautiful performance by just baritone, bass and drums. The 1963 date has some splendid playing by an all-saxophone front line while the 1967 session has the youthful Jiri Mraz on bass (soloing on two tracks). At the time of these sessions most of the musicians were working in the German studios, an almost exact parallel with the circumstances which gave rise to West Coast jazz in the previous decade. The result is musicianship of the highest order sparked by fine solo playing by Spencer, Koller, Menza and especially Ross.

AM

Charlie Rouse

1924-1988

Takin' Care Of Business Rouse (ts); **Blue Mitchell** (t); **Walter Bishop** (p); **Earl May** (b); **Art Taylor** (d). Jazzland Ⓜ OJCCD491 (38 minutes). Recorded 1960.

⑥ ❻

Charlie Rouse is usually remembered as the tenor saxophonist in Thelonious Monk's quartet. It is true that he spent more than a decade with Monk, but he was nobody's sidekick. Prior to Monk, for example, he co-led with Julius Watkins a most imaginative small group, Les Jazz Modes. Rouse's playing provides perfect evidence for the proposition that it is quite possible for an artist to exercise individuality while remaining entirely within a convention. Stylistically he was a hard-bopper of the Hank Mobley/Junior Cook school, but you could never mistake him for anyone else. His tone is thick and furry and his phrasing has an energetic, perky gait. The effect is amiable and never strident.

This album is in the convention of its time—a blowing session for two horns and rhythm. Nobody could call it revolutionary, mind-searing, mould-breaking etc., but you can have too much of that sort of thing. All goes smoothly and everybody plays well. Rouse, in particular, shines in this relaxed setting: fast-thinking and eloquent.

DG

Jimmy Rowles

1918

The Peacocks Rowles (p); **Stan Getz** (ts); **Buster Williams** (b); **Elvin Jones** (d). Columbia Ⓜ CK 52975 (59 minutes). Recorded 1975.

⑧ ❽

This album was intended to be made by Rowles, both solo and accompanied by rhythm. It was the idea of Stan Getz, who had agreed to record 'commercial' albums for CBS provided they let him produce more committed albums featuring artists of his own choice. This was to be his first. But the producer was so carried away by the music that he went home for his tenor sax and joined in.

The result is a jazz classic. Rowles is a superb all-round player who, as Getz knew, has made ridiculously few albums under his own name. Since this one he has made more. A modest man, he easily fell into the accompanying role that he played so well and yet he ranks with Hank Jones, Mel Powell and Oscar Peterson in terms of musical stature. Like Powell he swings hard without ever being heavy-handed. He sings on several of these tracks and has a gentle, world-weary voice, ideal for the kind of music he plays. *I'll Never Be The Same* and *My Buddy* have particularly appealing combinations of voice and piano and solo tenor. It is one of those sets where new delights come tumbling out at each hearing.

SV

Plays Duke Ellington and Billy Strayhorn Rowles (p). Columbia Ⓜ 467691-2 (48 minutes). Recorded 1981.

⑧ ❽

For many years, Rowles has enjoyed the highest of reputations as an accompanist to vocalists (he also sings himself) so it might have been excusable to overlook his talents as a solo or trio player. He fell in love with the music of Duke Ellington around 1938, a love affair which has lasted all his working life. Pianist/producer Henri Renaud, a fervent admirer of Rowles and his music, has been responsible for several excellent albums by Jimmy but this one is the best. Few other pianists understand the Duke's music better than Rowles, who has a quirky, individual approach which is ideally suited to getting inside the ten Ellington and Billy Strayhorn tunes played here. His superb sense of touch enables him to build to climaxes and release the tension at just the right time—even *Take The 'A' Train* receives unhackneyed treatment, while the moving *Blood Count* is masterly. As a bonus, the CD is completed by a short track where Jimmy talks about the Duke. Strongly recommended. **AM**

Gonzalo Rubalcaba

1963

Suite 4 y 20 **Rubalcaba** (p); **Reynaldo Melian** (t); **Charlie Haden** (b); **Felipe Cabrera** (elb); **Julio Barreto** (d). Blue Note Ⓕ CDP7 80054-2 (69 minutes:). Recorded 1992.

⑥ ❽

Cuban-born Rubalcaba's earlier Blue Note albums contained some performances on which his technique seemed to take the upper hand. On this very attractive release, recorded in Madrid, he plays with such poise, such careful attention to detail, that there are times when it might almost be a different pianist. As on his previous Blue Notes, Charlie Haden is present on bass (although this time on only five of the 13 tracks), while Melian plays trumpet on nine, occasionally multi-tracking his efforts. The most impressive titles are those on which the thematic material is strongest; songs such as the Lennon/McCartney ballad *Here, There and Everywhere*, *Love Letters* and *Perfidia*. The delicacy of Gonzalo's playing is at its most marked here, for his style is based on the careful delineation of melody. Some of the tracks are too self-indulgent for repeated listening, as when the quartet hits relentlessly on a repeated phrase of no great importance. But overall Rubalcaba is a most interesting performer who has successfully united the musics of North and Central America without relying simply on what has gone before. **AM**

Vanessa Rubin

I'm Glad There Is You **Rubin** (v) with: **Cecil Bridgewater** (t); **Grover Washington Jr** (ss, ts); **Antonio Hart** (as); **Frank Foster** (ts); **Aaron Graves**, **Carlos McKinney**, **Monty Alexander** (p); **Kenny Burrell** (g); **Charles Fambrough** (b); **Yoron Israel** (d); **Michael Rubin** (perc); and string section led by **Akua Dixon**. RCA Novus Ⓕ 163170 2 (57 minutes). Recorded 1993.

⑤ ❽

Rubin is a young American singer whose admiration for Carmen McRae has led her to dedicate this album to the older musician. Rubin's homage to McRae extends to the treatment she gives her material as well as the edge she projects into her voice. At this stage of her career she seems more inclined to concentrate on musicality and swing than on interpretation, and it would be mistaken of a listener to approach this disc with too much hope of an emotional experience. On the technical side, she is promising but has much to develop. Her intonation, generally accurate, can go worryingly wrong at times, especially on sustained notes, while her rhythm can be leaden (the even notes of *Midnight Sun*'s chromatic theme defeat her to the point where the listener is longing for the melody to end, so as to escape the four-square singing). Yet her personality comes across quite pleasantly, the arrangements are serviceable, and the vocal colour is attractive. Let us hope for subsequent recorded development. **KS**

Roswell Rudd

1935

Regeneration **Rudd** (tb); **Steve Lacy** (ss); **Misha Mengelberg** (p); **Kent Carter** (b); **Han Bennink** (d). Soul Note Ⓕ 121054-2 (41 minutes). Recorded 1982.

⑧ ❽

Though this is actually a co-operative group with roots that separate and intertwine back some 20 years, the neglected trombonist/arranger Roswell Rudd gets pride of place due to his fervency behind this project, his closeness to and advocacy of Herbie Nichols, and his invigorating presence in the proceedings. And it is an important disc, for the first time fleshing out with horns Nichols' at-one-time impenetrable piano pieces, proving that they were possible to play and reminding musicians weaned on freedom that Monk continues to be a source of strength and stimulation. Lacy's own experience with Monk, and his previous collaboration with Rudd in a sixties quartet that played nothing but Monk, assures integrity and illumination. Monk's influence on Mengelberg is reflected in his splashes of Dada wit and frequent harmonic curves. The Nichols tunes, meanwhile, are loaded with irony, whether the ricky-tick rhythm (goaded by Rudd's juicy slides) of *Twelve Bars* or the humorous, deceptively simple (even Monk-like) *2300 Skidoo*, where Lacy's logic is simultaneously formal and elusive, Rudd bursts with almost scatological humour and Mengelberg accents with aplomb. Throughout, Bennink reminds us of his ability to swing a small band eloquently. By suggesting that the jazz repertory could be expanded, both faithfully and creatively, this disc was a breakthrough. **AL**

Hilton Ruiz

1952

A Moment's Notice **Ruiz** (p); **Kenny Garrett** (as); **George Coleman** (ts); **Dave Valentin** (f); **Andy Gonzales**, **Joe Santiago** (b); **Steve Berrios** (d); **Daniel Ponce**, **Endel Dweno** (perc). RCA Novus Ⓕ 83123-2 (54 minutes). Recorded 1991.

⑦ ❽

Pianist Hilton Ruiz is an outstanding young player with roots in both Latin and mainstream jazz. His credits include Frank Foster, Freddie Hubbard, Joe Henderson, Rahsaan Roland Kirk and a host of Latin bands. In his own groups the emphasis, though Latin tinged, has been on achieving a synergetic balance between the two stylistic tendencies. Instead of setting (and leaving) the fire at the boiling point as most Latin bands tend to do, Ruiz keeps varying the temperature through frequent shifts in texture and dynamics. Typically, as in *Cuchi Chuchi* and *Mambo Inn*, the flame smoulders rather than sears. Things bubble over here and there, but even in these instances there's a breeze that suddenly appears to provide contrast and perspective.

Ruiz's decision to use acoustic rather than electric piano also helps in constantly re-invoking the bop-based mainstream. So, too, does his choice of standards like Coltrane's *Moment's Notice* and *Naima*, and Van Heusen's *Like Someone in Love*. With soloists the calibre of saxophonist George Coleman and flutist Dave Valentin, it is clear that Ruiz is a jazzman, through and through. He is a spare but effective pianist; classically trained and influenced by the bop piano heritage of Bud Powell, his effectively understated solos—and compositions—are compellingly taut and structurally sound. But then, seeing him live is another matter altogether. **CB**

Howard Rumsey

1917

Sunday Jazz à la Lighthouse **Rumsey** (b); **Shorty Rogers**, **Maynard Ferguson** (t); **Milt Berhart** (tb); **Jimmy Giuffre**, **Bob Cooper** (ts); **Frank Patchen**, **Hampton Hawes** (p); **Shelly Manne** (d); **Carlos Vidal** (cga). Contemporary Ⓜ OJCCD-151-2 (50 minutes). Recorded 1953.

⑧ ❻

There was always a strong Stan Kenton connection with the Lighthouse Club at California's Hermosa Beach. Rumsey, the ex-Kenton bass player, formed the jazz policy there in 1949 and it was, in many ways, the birthplace of West Coast jazz. The album here was actually recorded at the club by the resident band which featured many of the principal figures in the movement, including Rogers, Giuffre and Manne. With the brittle, driving piano of Hampton Hawes on two tracks, including the superb Hawes-Rogers duet version of *All The Things You Are*, this is a CD of both musical and historic importance. Later Rumsey-led groups presented a variety of tone colours including the most attractive chamber jazz set featuring the flute and oboe of Bud Shank and Bob Cooper. The music is exquisite and some tracks have a timeless quality which not even Rumsey's sometimes leaden bass can destroy. Essential West Coast history for even the most casual listener. **AM**

Jimmy Rushing

1902-1972

The You and Me That Used to Be **Rushing** (v); **Ray Nance** (c, vn); **Budd Johnson** (ss); **Al Cohn**, **Zoot Sims** (ts); **Dave Frishberg** (p, arr); **Milt Hinton** (b); **Mel Lewis** (d). RCA Novus Ⓜ 6460-2 (44 minutes). Recorded 1971.

✔ ⑩ ❻

This was deleted almost immediately after its initial LP release, despite being voted album of the year in a Down Beat critics' poll. Its reissue on CD in 1988 was cause for jubilation, even though its muffled transfer left something to be desired. Rushing died little more than a year after these sessions. Nicknamed Mister Five by Five, he was revered for the impudent cheer he brought to his blues performances with Count Basie in the thirties and forties, and to a series of classic albums produced by John Hammond for Vanguard and Columbia in the fifties. It was sometimes forgotten, though, that the blues was not all that Rushing could sing. His swan song turned out to be the finest album he ever recorded, thanks in large part to its uncharacteristic material—torch songs such as *I Surrender, Dear* and lightly swinging vintage pop tunes such as *Bei Mir Bist Du Schoen* and *When I Grow Too Old To Dream*, with nary a blues among them except for *Fine and Mellow*. All four of the featured horn soloists shine here, as do Frishberg's piano accompaniments and captivating small group arrangements. **FD**

George Russell

1923

Ezz-Thetics **Russell** (p); **Don Ellis** (t); **Dave Baker** (tb); **Eric Dolphy** (as, bcl); **Steve Swallow** (b); **Joe Hunt** (d). Riverside Ⓜ OJCCD-070-2 (43 minutes). Recorded 1961.

✔ ⑨ ❽

In the early fifties Russell developed his Lydian Concept of Tonal Organization. A theory based on the ancient Lydian mode, it transformed chords into scales and took his music into the field of pantonality. In practice, the music was still accessible to laymen: it shunned the discipline of bebop and its adherence to the chord sequence and introduced scalar relationships that were uniquely his. In a manner far removed from that of Ornette Coleman, it proffered melodic expression and left it in the hands of his band members,

This CD is particularly blessed in this direction. Three startlingly different horn stylists accept the Russell brief and present their own excellent reactions to it. To the facile Baker, triple tonguing is no empty gimmick and the bombast of his *Ezz-Thetics* reading is in contrast to his more studied manipulations of tempo changes on *Thoughts*. Ellis combines lyrical delivery with attacking conviction and he excels on *Ezz-Thetics* and *Lydiot*. Dolphy is outstanding throughout, but very special indeed on Monk's *'Round Midnight*; spare during his theme statement, he grows richly rhetorical during a solo that makes this title the climax of a session with an important place in jazz history. **BMcR**

The Outer View **Russell** (p, arr); **Don Ellis** (t); **Garnett Brown** (tb); **Paul Plummer** (ts); **Steve Swallow** (b); **Pete LaRoca** (d); **Sheila Jordan**. Riverside Ⓜ OJCCD 616-2 (51 minutes). Recorded 1962.

✔ ⑧ ❼

For such an important creative and theoretical force in the music, Russell is woefully under-represented on recordings, and of those recordings, dotted over a 50-year career, only a handful are presently on CD (this handful was recently reduced by the deletion of his 1956 album for RCA, **Jazz Workshop**). Thankfully, two of his brilliant small-group Riverside dates are still with us. This, the second of them (see above for **Ezz-Thetics**), is the less celebrated, perhaps due to the absence of the galvanic Dolphy. However, it contains piquant and highly original arrangements of material originally written by, among others, Charlie Parker, Carla Bley and Russell himself. The group interplay is even more developed than on the 1961 album, Ellis in particular distinguishing himself with a series of finely-wrought solos, bringing an intensely personal vision and expressive range to the material. Ellis also adds mightily to the character of the ensemble sections.

The standout track here—and the abum's perennial talking point since its original release—is the old thirties hit *You Are My Sunshine*. Russell's treatment is radical but observant of the song's core meaning, allowing the melody to rise untrammelled from his new setting. Sheila Jordan contributes an arresting delivery of the lyrics. **KS**

The London Concert Volumes 1 & 2 **Russell** (comp, arr); **Stuart Brooks, Ian Carr, Mark Chandler** (t); **Pete Beachill, Ashley Slater** (tb); **Andy Sheppard, Chris Bisco, Pete Hurt** (reeds); **Brad Hatfield, Steve Lodder** (kbds); **David Fiuczynski** (g); **Bill Urmson** (elb); **Steve Johns** (d). Stash Ⓕ ST-CD 560/61 (two discs, oas: 51 and 37 minutes). Recorded 1989.

⑧ ❼

In the second half of the sixties Russell, like so many other American jazzmen, became an exile in Europe. During a five-year stay he began an important series of recordings, eventually released or re-released by Soul Note, which are slowly appearing on CD. It was also then that he laid the groundwork for the output of his mature period, although this has not always been palatable to listeners who admire his earlier production. In this also he is again like some other writers, notably Gil Evans, but unlike the later Evans he performs almost all original material and plots his performances more rigorously.

In his first issued recording since two Blue Note albums from a 1983 concert, **The African Game** and **So What**, the great composer and theoretician adds eight London-based horn-players and Lodder to his American rhythm-section, artfully combining heavy ensembles, rock-influenced backings and adventurous solos that sometimes incorporate collective improvisation. The repertoire is mostly new, except for a new performance of part of the 1969 *Electronic Sonata For Souls Loved By Nature* and the closing *So What*, where he uses not the theme but Miles Davis's original solo, contained on **Kind of Blue**, the album which first popularized Russell's theories. **BP**

Hal Russell

1926-1992

The Hal Russell Story **Russell** (t, ss, ts, vb, d, v); **Mars Williams** (as, ts, bss, f, bells, perc, v); **Brian Sandstrom** (b, t, g, perc, v); **Kent Kessler** (b, tb, perc, v); **Steve Hunt** (d, vb, perc, v). ECM . Ⓕ 1498 (517 364-2) (67 minutes). Recorded 1992.

⑧ ❽

Hal Russell, for over two decades the paterfamilias and Puck of Chicago's free jazz scene, was a remarkable man and musician. Originally a drummer, his career in the forties and fifties was typical of the times—swinging big bands or ones offering saccharin charts, theatre pit bands, vaudeville and burlesque house bands, and those occasional magical gigs where he would back a visiting Miles or Billie, Rollins or Sarah. Come the sixties, he was a member of possibly Chicago's first "free" trio, simultaneous with Ornette, and shortly thereafter, inspired by Albert Ayler, learning the saxophone at age 50 and picking up the trumpet again after 30 years, and starting the polystylistic NRG Ensemble. He cut a fistful of freer, more volatile recordings than this one, but **The Hal Russell Story**, recorded just a few weeks before his untimely death, is not only a celebratory, hallucinogenic overview of his career, but a cornucopia of delights—from the priceless spoken/poetic interludes between tunes to Russell's own striking multi-instrumentalism and the versatility and devotion of the supporting NRG cast. The music essays mock fanfares, pseudo-swing, hard-edge blowing, and free fantasies, each reflecting the humour which was so much a part of Russell's vision. Flowing together as a near-cinematic suite, the 21 pieces include all-but-unrecognizable, tongue-in-cheek reconstitutions of standards like *You're Blasé*, *My Little Grass Shack*, and a haunting *Gloomy Sunday*; pun-filled transformations of fondly-remembered tunes like *Air Mail Special* (*Hair Mail*); *Woodchopper's Ball* (*Wood Chips*), and *Rockin' Chair* (*Mildred*); and his own volcanic, post-Ayler conflagrations. **AL**

Luis Russell

1902-1963

Luis Russell 1929-30 **Russell** (p, arr); **Louis Metcalf**, **Henry Allen**, **Bill Coleman**, **Otis Johnson** (t); **J.C. Higginbotham**, **Henry Hicks** (tb); **Charlie Holmes**, **Albert Nicholas** (cl, ss, as); **Teddy Hill**, **Charlie Grimes, Greely Walton** (ts); **Will Johnson** (bj, g); **William 'Bass' Moore** (tba); **Paul Barbarin** (d, vb); **Elmer Snowden** (bj); **Henry Edwards** (tba, perc); **Pops Foster** (b); **Walter Pichon, Jesse Cryor, Andy Razaf** (v); aslo on two tracks **J.C.Higginbotham And His Six Hicks** (Henry Allen (t); Higginbotham (tb); Charlie Holmes (as); Will Johnson (g); Pops Foster (b); Paul Barbarin (d)). JSP Ⓕ CD 308 (71 minutes). Recorded 1929/30.

⑧ ❽

This CD catches the Russell band at the peak of its powers. Some of the undoubted elation may be due to the fact that, during late 1929 and early 1930, Louis Armstrong used the band for both public and record appearances (in fact Louis plays and sings on *Song of The Islands* from the January 1930 session, a fact which the inlay card fails to mention). From the performances here it is easy to understand why the Russell band was such a sensation; it had a fine sax team, an outstanding trombone soloist in J.C. Higginbotham and, of course, Red Allen taking most of the trumpet solos. But the lightness of the ensemble was due in large part to Pops Foster who came into the band to play string bass in place of Henry Edwards and his tuba. The music still sounds fresh, notably tunes such as *New Call of the Freaks, Jersey Lightning* and the two takes of *Louisiana Swing* with Foster playing *arco* rhythm bass. The two tracks under Higginbotham's name are by a 'band-within-a-band' featuring soloists including the underrated Charlie Holmes on alto. The remastering has been done to perfection by John R.T. Davies, who allows us to hear Foster's bass notes in their correct spatial relationship to the ensemble. **AM**

Pee Wee Russell

1906-1969

Jack Teagarden's Big Eight/Pee Wee Russell's Rhythmakers **Russell** (cl); with **Max Kaminsky** (t); **Dicky Wells** (tb); **Al Gold** (ts); **James P. Johnson**, **Billy Kyle** (p); **Freddie Green** (g); **Wellman Braud**, **Billy Taylor** (b); **Zutty Singleton** (d, v); **Teagarden** (tb, v) with **Rex Stewart** (c); **Barney Bigard** (cl); **Ben Webster** (ts); **Brick Fleagle** (g); **Dave Tough** (d). Riverside Ⓜ OJCCD-1708-2 (32 minutes). Recorded 1938/1940.

⑧ ❻

Pee Wee Russell was unique, even in the company of the individuals who have made up the jazz world. His strangulated tone, glottal effects and unpredictable turns of phrase are well represented on these six tracks made by a strange grouping of players (Wells and Green from the Basie band, Johnson from the Harlem stride school and Singleton from Sidney Bechet's group). But there is homogeneity here thanks to the powerful lead playing of Kaminsky and the all-pervading swing of the rhythm section. Russell always finds a place for himself in the ensembles and comes into his own as a soloist on *I've Found A New Baby* and *Everybody Loves My Baby,* the two trio numbers. A special mention must be made of Dicky Wells whose blues playing both solo and in obbligato to the vocal on *Zutty's Hootie Blues* is in the same class as the records he made in Paris with Django Reinhardt a year before. The Teagarden tracks feature three fugitives from the Duke Ellington band and another good rhythm section. All ten titles come from the old HRS catalogue (Hot Record Society) and have been dubbed from, we assume, the best available 78s. The sound is not perfect but is certainly superior to the original Riverside LP. **AM**

We're In The Money **Russell** (cl); **Doc Cheatham** (t); **Wild Bill Davison** (c); **Vic Dickenson** (tb); **George Wein** (p); **John Field, Stan Wheeler** (b); **Buzzy Drootin** (d); **Al Bandini** (v). Black Lion Ⓜ 760909 (49 minutes). Recorded 1953/54.

⑨ ❼

Pee Wee was so much more than an eccentric sideman amongst the rowdy Condon crew. His maverick approach epitomized the jazz ethic—true immediacy of purpose and self-expression—and he was, with Monk, the most unpredictable and exhilarating of improvisers. Although this disc, combining two separate sessions, is not his best recording (and who could pick a best anyway? I'd recommend hearing anything Russell ever played on), it is representative of his work in this period. He was the most amazing colourist of the clarinet, able to shade each surprising note choice with a different hue, and his tonal options included a piping chirp, asthmatic growl, or husky chalumeau. His irreverently spontaneous phrasing was usually on the brink of a disaster—he would interrupt a straightforward melody to insert a brief flurry of unrelated notes, a worried blue note, or shift registers (as on *Sugar*) —rescued by unorthodox interval leaps (*Lulu's Back In Town*). He could be wistfully romantic (*Missy*), irascible as a grizzly bear (*Sweet Georgia Brown*), or whisper a sotto voce plea with the sincerity of a supplicant (*The Lady's In Love With You*). Of the others' contributions, Dick Cary's arrangements of the first six tunes involve modulations and ensemble dynamics that spice up the familiar repertory, and there is a rare view of Doc Cheatham prior to his septuagenarian rediscovery. In the second group, Wild Bill is a more incendiary character, and the music's temperature rises accordingly; he is positively ferocious on *She's Funny That Way*. Wein is mild-mannered throughout, and Drootin is no George Wettling but keeps things moving. *If I Had You* elicits a howl of delight from one of the musicians, and it is hard to argue with him. **AL**

Jazz Reunion **Russell** (cl); **Emmett Berry** (t); **Bob Brookmeyer** (tb); **Coleman Hawkins** (ts); **Nat Pierce** (p); **Milt Hinton** (b); **Jo Jones** (d). Candid Ⓜ CCD 79020 (46 minutes). Recorded 1961.

✔

⑨ ❼

"For 30 years I've been listening to him play those funny notes," Coleman Hawkins remarked at the end of this session. "He's always been way out, but they didn't have a word for it then." By the early sixties Pee Wee Russell's wheezy, waif-like tone, his slurs and flutters of notes, had been given a context by newer forms of jazz that helped people to appreciate his eccentricity as 'way out' rather than simply wayward. Encounters with modernists such as Jimmy Giuffre and Thelonious Monk left him unfazed, though it was more the forward-looking of his various mainstream dates on which he seemed to thrive best. A 1960 Prestige date with Tommy Flanagan and Buck Clayton found him in fine form, as did this **Jazz Reunion** with the ever-versatile Hawkins.

Russell and Hawkins had last played together in the Mound City Blue Blowers in 1929, when they made a famous recording of James P. Johnson's *If I Could Be With You One Hour Tonight*. **Jazz Reunion** opens with a new version of the tune, Russell's diffident, skewed lines a riveting contrast to Hawkins's forceful bustle. The dichotomy is maintained throughout this enjoyable set, which also boasts two Ellington tunes, a slinky *Tin Tin Deo* and Russell's own *Mariooch*, a ballad feature that calls forth a marvellous display of breathy, sidling, squeaky poetry from his singular clarinet. **GL**

Paul Rutherford

1940

1989—and All That **Rutherford** (tb); **George Haslam** (bs). Slam Ⓕ CD 301 (77 minutes). Recorded 1989.

⑧ ❼

A founder member of the Spontaneous Music Ensemble, Rutherford is a major voice in Europe's free music scene. He was comfortable performing in the more orthodox atmosphere of the Mike Westbrook Concert Band, but in 1970 he formed Iskra 1903 with guitarist Derek Bailey and bassist Barry Guy. This challenging group's commitment to free improvisation was total and Rutherford emerged as an extremely influential figure, inspiring fellow European trombonists with the possibilities of his horn and voice overlay. With solo albums **Gentle Harm Of The Bourgeoisie** and **Old Moer's Almanac** unavailable, this CD with the admirable Haslam represents the best opportunity to hear Rutherford's superbly rustic free playing. The session includes duets but it is the solos that best display his talents. His *Sigma* solo makes use of his daunting range while the outstanding *Orion*, with its mixture of throaty growls and declamatory statements, acknowledges his links with the music's past. It introduces breaks with the alacrity of the Dixielander and delivers his glissandi with the delicious slur of the tailgate primitives. As with the trio he led in the eighties, this CD has him setting himself high creative standards but it still leaves one of jazz's most daringly inventive players struggling for work because 'free improvisation', his chosen method of self expression, is not 'nice'. **BMCR**

Ali Ryerson

Portraits In Silver **Ryerson** (f, af); **Kenny Werner** (p); **Dennis Irwin** (b); **Danny Gottlieb** (d). Concord Ⓕ CCD-4638 (59 minutes). Recorded 1994.

⑥ ❿

Ryserson has been around for a while now, and this is by no means her first album as a leader, but it is far and away her best. The most immediately noticeable thing about this date is the beautifully natural recording, which captures Ryerson's full tone to great advantage (I've heard other records of hers where too much breath has been hitting the microphone, greatly distorting her sound). Almost as quickly the quality of the supporting trio makes itself felt, and with Kenny Werner at the piano Ryerson would have to be a poor musician indeed not to respond. That she gives her most consistent performances to date, should not surprise. It helps as well that the material selected includes such gems as Chick Corea's *Windows* and J.J. Johnson's *Lament*: this pushes Ryserson to avoid the usual flute platitudes and patterns (something she hasn't always done) and to get into some meaty soloing. Of course in the end a whole CD of flute out front may be too much for some people, but those with a taste for the purity of sound and lightness of mood it can create will have much to savour here. **KS**

Terje Rypdal

1947

EOS **Rypdal** (g, Casio MT-30); **David Darling** (vc). ECM Ⓔ 1263 (815 333-2) (46 minutes). Recorded 1983.

⑧ ❿

Norwegian guitarist/composer Rypdal joined the ECM stable early on, along with his partner from George Russell days, Jan Garbarek. His early albums helped define the ECM sound, where broad washes of music could hang in space for minutes on end (his partly-orchestral album **Whenever I Seem To Be Far Away** is an apt illustration of this side to his work). Yet his subsequent career on records has shown him to be greatly more diversified a talent than this, and he has made trio albums with Vitous and DeJohnette, quasi-heavy metal albums with his own band, and fascinating collaborations such as this disc with cellist David Darling. His latest album on ECM, **QED**, returns to orchestral realizations of some of his most recent compositions.

EOS has a lot going for it in the sheer diversity of the music to be found therein. The first track, a solo venture by Rypdal, verges on an all-out heavy metal power-chord assault worthy of AC/DC, but subverts it in the way Rypdal distorts the textures and contexts he plays the chords within. The sombre tones of the cello dominate the album's eponymous longest track, but Rypdal also contributes an impassioned solo which again is unthinkable without the absorbed legacy of rock and fusion guitarists such as Hendrix, Beck and McLaughlin. The rest of the album is taken up with smaller-scale realizations of different sonic combinations.

On this album, Rypdal gets the balance between passion and beauty just right. **KS**

Sakhile

African Echoes **Kyaya Mahlangu** (ts, ss); **Jabu Nkosi** (kbds); **Sipho Gumede** (elb, b); **Menyatso Mathole** (g); **Bheki Kunene** (d); **Mabe Thobejane** (perc). Kaz Ⓜ CD 17 (43 minutes). Recorded 1989.

④ ❻

Since their formation, Sakhile have lived in the hope of presenting their music in its unadulterated form. At times they have been locked into a (albeit successful) disco music groove, and this CD represents their conscious push towards their African cultural heritage. It is unlikely that their route toward that ideal would have been quite as clearly defined had it not been for South Africans such as Dudu Pukwana, Abdullah Ibrahim or Louis Moholo, who found their own way to African expression made easier by passing their own experience through the jazz spectrum. On this CD, titles like *Maluti, Song For Bra Zakes* and *Tears Of Joy,* with their mildly improvised saxophone work by Mahlangu, will be of most interest to jazz followers. The main rhythmic thrust is a trifle heavy-handed, but ancillary decoration gives it a lighter overall feeling and although vocals are applied sparingly, they have more to do with chart aspirations than African heritage. This is very much music on the fringe of jazz. It satisfies its own demands with professional competence but such music has often been passed off to the uninitiated as the genuine article. **BMcR**

Sergio Salvatore

1981

Tune Up **Salvatore** (p); **Randy Brecker** (t); **Michael Brecker** (ts); **Gary Burton** (vb); **Chick Corea** (p); **Jay Leonhardt**, **Jay Anderson**, **Jimmy Haslip** (b); **William Kennedy**, **Danny Gottlieb** (d). GRP Ⓔ 97632 (59 minutes). Recorded 1994.

⑧ ❿

This is Sergio Salvatore's second album; his first came out in 1993. As is now the practice with second albums, it features a number of star guests. Each collaboration shows the young pianist's talent in a slightly different light; the Breckers, Burton and Corea play sensitively and well, and nobody tries to upstage anyone. It is astonishing enough that Salvatore was still aged only 13 when this CD was recorded, but the really remarkable point is that he does not sound in the least like a child. He has the kinds of qualities, like grace and restraint, that supposedly come only with maturity. Five of the 11 tunes here are his own compositions, and he already shows signs of developing a distinctive style in this department, too. **DG**

Joe Sample

1939

Did You Feel That? **Sample** (p, kbds); **Oscar Brashear** (t); **Joel Peskin** (ts); **Arthur Adams**, **Michael Landau** (g); **Freddie Washington** (b); **Steve Gadd** (d); **Lenny Castro** (perc). Warner Bros Ⓔ 2 45729-2 (54 minutes). Recorded 1993.

⑧ ❽

Some of Sample's late eighties work veered towards the anodyne, with the odd exception like *Ship of Fools* from **Roles** (1988). By contrast, this collection, recorded with a band branded the 'Soul Committee', is very strong and muscular. It is built round an acoustic rather than a synthesized sound, and Sample's long-term associates Castro and Landau are joined by the effortless drumming of Gadd and the sure touch of Adams and Washington in a rock-steady rhythm section. As a backdrop for Sample's piano, but particularly for the soloing and riffing teamwork of Brashear and Peskin, they barely put a foot wrong, and the repetitive, infectious beat is consistently lively, even if in a comfortably samey groove from one end of the album to the other. This is a vital and successful album, within the self-imposed disciplines and aims of the Soul Committee—to be laid back to an angle of about 89 degrees. **AS**

David Sanborn

1945

Close Up **Sanborn** (as, v); **Hiram Bullock, Nile Rodgers, G.E. Smith, Paul Jackson Jr** (g); **Jeff Mironov** (g); **Richard Tee** (p); **Ricky Peterson** (elp, kbds); **Marcus Miller** (elb, kbds, p, perc, g, v); **Steve Jordan, Andy Newmark, Vinnie Colaiuta, William Ju Ju House** (d); **Paulinho da Costa** (perc); **Vocal Chorus**. Reprise Ⓜ 925715-2 (51 minutes). Recorded 1988.

✔ ⑧ ❽

Not withstanding the interest excited among the arts pages by **Another Hand**, David Sanborn's 1991 excursion into post-modernism, there is little doubt that history will remember Sanborn for the work he least intended for serious consumption—the polished but impassioned funk which reached a hi-tech peak on **Close Up**. Although the session has its slack moments—the rock routines of *J.T. and Lesley Ann* and the maudlin sentiment of *You Are Everything* can be safely passed over—the more muscular funk tracks—*Slam*, *Pyramid*, and, in particular, *Tough*—have a steely, combative quality which is infectiously exciting. Much of the credit for this is due to Marcus Miller's ingenious arrangements, but anyone still puzzled by Gil Evan's glowing endorsement of Sanborn's 'cry' should examine the extraordinary note with which Sanborn leaves the bridge of *Pyramid*. His vocabulary may lack harmonic depth, but this searing, penetrating sound, and the simple but urgent variations which constitute his solo on *Touch*, have been enough to make him one of the most imitated altoists of his generation. He has regretted any part he may have played in inspiring 'a certain blandness' in instrumental pop music, but at moments like these, he plays as if his life depended on it. **MG**

Another Hand **Sanborn** (as); **Lenny Pickett** (ts, cl); **Art Baron** (tb); **Bill Frisell, Marc Ribot, Al Anderson, Dave Tranzo** (g); **Terry Adams, Mulgrew Miller** (p); **Leon Pendarvis** (org); **Charlie Haden, Greg Cohen, Marcus Miller** (b); **Joey Baron, Steve Jordan, Jack DeJohnette** (d); **Don Alias** (perc); **Syd Straw** (v). Elektra Musician Ⓕ 961088-2 (58 minutes). Recorded 1991.

⑧ ❽

Despite David Sanborn's almost unmatched celebrity as a rock and fusion alto saxophonist, the Velvet Underground's rather gloomy *Jesus* is the only indication of this predilection on **Another Hand**, and it is arguably the album's weakest track, the tune simply too repetitive to spark interesting improvisation. Otherwise, Sanborn's interpretations, both of his band-members' originals (Bill Frisell, Charlie Haden, Terry Adams and Marcus Miller all provide compositions), and of an ambitious medley composed of familiar themes, are consistently arresting. Sanborn's strengths—a no-nonsense ability to home in on a tune's essence and exploit it, a fine straightforward rhythmic sense and great technical facility—are considerable, and his work with Frisell—always a superb collaborator with saxophonists—is particularly sensitive, their combined sound an affecting, plaintive melancholy. Like his most identifiable influence, Jackie McLean, however, Sanborn is at something of a disadvantage when interpreting ballad material, handicapped by the astringent harshness of his sound, so on the title-track—the most jazz-based on the album—he is not as convincing as he is on, say, *Adams' Hobbies*, a jaunty medium-paced tune with a pronounced backbeat. In general, though, this is a well-programmed, considered album, Sanborn's plangent saxophone superbly complemented by a peerless selection of New York's finest. **CP**

David Sanchez

1969

Sketches of Dreams **Sanchez** (as, ts); **Roy Hargrove** (t); **Danilo Perez, David Kikoski** (p); **Larry Grenadier** (b); **Adam Cruz** (d); **Milton Cardona, Jerry Gonzalez, Leon Parker** (perc). Columbia Ⓕ 480326 2 (60 minutes) Recorded 1994.

⑦ ❿

Sanchez is a young Puerto Rican who concentrates on tenor but also has a fine way with the alto saxophone. He first made an impact in the early eighties when he came to the attention of Dizzy Gillespie and subsequently appeared with him. Other early mentors included Paquito D'Rivera. His sound touches base with players such as Eddie 'Lockjaw' Davis, Johnny Griffin and Gene Ammons among others, and his conception is a deep fusion of jazz and Latin musics. He can play *Falling In Love With Love* dead straight, with a rinky-tink rhythm behind him, or he can wail with the fieriest of the Latin brigade. He can also use the calmer side of his Latin connection to stroke a ballad softly, such as in *Tu Y Mi Cancion* (which to my ears has borrowed a good deal of the *Misty* changes).

This is Sanchez's second album for Columbia, and he still takes the spotlight for most of the time. Where he gets a solo, Hargrove impresses with his increased maturity, while pianist Perez confirms the immense promise of his debut album on Novus, **The Journey**. **KS**

Pharoah Sanders

1940

Thembi **Sanders** (ts, as, ss, perc, koto, etc); **Michael White** (vn, perc); **Lonnie Liston Smith** (p, elp, bailophone, perc); **Cecil McBee** (b, perc); **Clifford Jarvis, Roy Haynes** (d); **James Jordan, Chief Bey, Majid Shabazz, Anthony Wiles, Nat Betis** (perc). Impulse! Ⓜ MCAD-5860 (42 minutes). Recorded 1970-71.

⑥ ❽

Although Archie Shepp made some appearances as an added starter with the Coltrane quartet (including the last chord of the **A Love Supreme** album), it was Sanders who became a regular member of Trane's group from the second half of 1965 onwards.

Coltrane's addition of African percussion and other more exotic instruments during his last period fed Sanders's late-sixties recordings, some of which (especially **Karma**) sold faster than his mentor's ever had. Pharoah's southern origin may have encouraged his development of a tenor style simpler than either Trane and Ayler, which was very easy for Gato Barbieri to reduce to its essentials. Later in the seventies pianist Lonnie Liston Smith, who also worked for Barbieri, took the formula into definitive blandness.

The saxophonist is the chief soloist here, at the expense of Smith and violinist White (who also enjoyed some popularity at the time), but bassist McBee has an unaccompanied bowed bass solo on *Love*, which functions as an introduction to *Morning Prayer/Bailophone Song*, on which Pharoah plays the Japanese koto in emulation of Alice Coltrane's harp, then swaps to flute and sax over a distinctly African rhythmic base. Sanders's music of this period, though rather bitty and dated, is more vital and significant than his recycling of Coltrane in the late eighties. **BP**

Journey To The One **Sanders** (ts); **Eddie Henderson** (flh); **John Hicks, Joe Bonner** (p); **Mark Isham** (synth); **Carl Lockett, Chris Hayes** (g); **Ray Drummond** (b); **Idris Muhammad** (d); **Yoko Ito Gates** (koto); **James Pomerantz** (sitar); **Bedria Sanders, Paul Arslanian** (harmonium); **Vicki Randle, Ngoh Spencer, Bobby McFerrin, Donna Dickerson** (v). Evidence Ⓕ ECD 22016-2 (73 minutes). Recorded 1980.

⑦ ❽

Now more than a decade old, this album still accurately reflects the type of music Sanders is playing today. It was recorded for the now-defunct Theresa label, its first issue on CD by Evidence. This was originally a gatefold double-album vinyl release, and the transfer to CD sees no dropping of tracks.

Sanders has travelled a long way since his brain-scorching solos in the last John Coltrane group. He has developed a larger, more majestic tone than of old, has picked up a handy line in ballad interpretation, and has revisited many of Coltrane's compositions. This date has the beautiful *After The Rain*, and Sanders does his reputation no harm at all with a reverential interpretation. Elsewhere, the album is clearly set up to show the tenor player to his best advantage in a variety of musical groupings. He plays good lean tenor solos on a string of quartet and quintet tracks, all but *Easy To Remember* being Sanders originals. On what was originally side two of the first vinyl disc, his sole accompanists on the majority of the side are koto, sitar and harmonium players, and the music is very peaceful. Elsewhere, as on the street-cred *You've Got To Have Freedom*, there is a small group of backing vocalists urging the group on.

Taken in tandem with 1981's **Rejoice** (Evidence 22020-2: another single-CD reissue of a double-vinyl set), which details his continuing involvement in African rhythms and melodies and also features a ravishing version of *Central Park West*, this shows conclusively where Sanders now rests his case. **KS**

Randy Sandke

Get Happy **Sandke** (t); **Ken Peplowski** (ts, cl); **Robert Trowers** (tb); **Kenny Barron** (p); **John Goldsby** (b); **Terry Clarke** (d). Concord Ⓕ CCD-4598 (64 minutes). Recorded 1993.

⑥ ❽

Buck Clayton used to speak of his protégé 'my young Randy' in the days when the younger trumpeter was just a name to us. Sandke has since become known in the Dixieland idiom for his recreations of Beiderbecke, but in fact he is further on than that and was not bested in a recent series of duets he played with the trumpeter's yardstick, Joe Wilder. His playing has rapidly developed character to go with his great facility and imagination. Although not quite in the same class he is in this a parallel in brass to Ken Peplowski, the outstanding reed virtuoso of the day.

Sandke shows how wide his vistas now are with music from bebop, Monk and beyond, displaying deep talents as both composer and adapter: Fauré's *Sicilienne* is tastefully transformed into a refreshing jazz piece, to follow Sandke's similar work with Bach's *Goldberg Variations*. His *Tuscaloosa* turns out to be an imaginative and stomping variant on *I'm Coming, Virginia*.

Peplowski moves with ease from the accelerated tenor of Monk's *Humph* to Noone-like clarinet on an evocative version of Ellington's *Black Beauty.* Kenny Barron, another great jazz chameleon, accompanies and solos on every track. **SV**

Arturo Sandoval

1949

I Remember Clifford **Sandoval** (t, flh); **Ernie Watts** (ts); **David Sanchez**, **Ed Calle** (ts); **Kenny Kirkland** (p); **Felix Gomez** (kbds); **Charnett Moffett** (b); **Kenny Washington** (d). GRP Ⓕ GRP 96682 (62 minutes). Recorded 1991.

⑧ ❽

In the early seventies Sandoval became a founder member of Cubana De Musica Moderna. The name later became Irakere and the trumpeter remained with them until 1981. Initially he was influenced by Dizzy Gillespie but he was not happy with life in his homeland and he emigrated to the US in the late eighties. He was already a virtuoso trumpeter, bebop was his language and he was delighted to add his own prodigious fire power to Gillespie's last United Nations Big Band. Sandoval's records have tended to favour a Latin-based rhythm section but this CD uses a straight ahead hard bop unit. It also uses multi-tracking to allow a trumpet choir of four Sandovals to play Clifford Brown's original solos, as well as some of the ensemble parts. Not that Sandoval's own solos are carbon copies; their style and cadence belongs to the dedicatee but they take an altogether different path. The exception is *Jordu* but the contrast is especially evident on titles like *Joy Spring* and *Cherokee*, where four Sandovals play Brownie alongside a newly conceived Sandoval improvisation. A superb set of arrangements are the icing on the cake; Brown's solos are used imaginately as the main theme of *Cherokee* and *I Get A Kick Out Of You* and, because it is more appropriate, part solo is used as the theme statement of *Caravan*. **BMcR**

Mongo Santamaria

1920

Mongo Explodes/Watermelon Man **Santamaria** (cgas, bgs); with: **Marty Sheller** (t); **Nat Adderley** (c); **Bobby Capers** (f, as); **Mauricio Smith** (f); **Hubert Laws** (f, pic, ts); **Rodgers Grant** (p); **Victor Venegas** (b); **Ray Lucas**, **Jimmy Cobb** (d); **Frank Hernandez** (d, perc); **Carmelo Garcia**, **Joseph Gorgas**, **Osvaldo Marinez**, **'Kako'**, **Wito Kortwright** (perc); **Chihuahua Martinez** (perc, v). Ace/Fantasy Ⓜ CDBGPD 062 (78 minutes). Recorded 1962-64.

⑦ ❻

Cuban-born Santamaria moved to America in his late twenties. He paid his dues in the commercial bands of Tito Puente and Perez Prado, then in 1957 was confronted with jazz when he joined Cal Tjader. In the years since he has played an important part in spreading the Cuban/jazz doctrine. In 1958 he began his own recording career as a leader and his band, rich in rhythmic complexity, was populated by timbales, guiro, cow bells and sundry noise-creating equipment. By 1962 he had become increasingly committed to jazz, with men such as Paul Serano, Pat Patrick, Chick Corea and Al McKibbon appearing in his ranks. He had also begun to work in New York jazz nighteries, and the first half of this CD was recorded live at the Village Gate. The basis of his music remained Cuban, but jazz solos became an increasingly important part of his music, as if he was aware of spicing up a Latin dance band. Adderley's three guest spots at the Gate offer very little, but Sheller, his regular trumpeter, shows himself as a more than capable alternative. Since the palmy days of the sixties, Santamaria has to some extent fallen from commercial grace, but recordings for Concord and jazz tour performances have maintained the public's awareness of him. **BMcR**

Akio Sasajima

1952

Humpty Dumpty **Sasajima** (g); **Joe Henderson** (ts); **Renée Rosnes** (p); **Kelly Sill** (b); **Joel Spencer** (d). Enja Ⓕ ENJ 8032 2 (47 minutes). Recorded 1988.

⑦ ❽

You may wonder what a guitarist with a Japanese name is doing in this book. Well—he happens to be a fine musician in the Wes Montgomery tradition, and someone who has a superb group with him on this album playing the heck out of a selection of originals and what can safely be called 'jazz standards'; that is, songs which jazzmen other than the composers often play. Sasajima came to the US from his native Japan in 1977 and quickly made himself known to local musicians in the Chicago area. By the mid-eighties he had formed a particularly close musical understanding with Joe Henderson—this is, in fact, their second album together under Sasajima's name—and the fruits of that friendship can be heard here. Henderson himself is in burning form on this disc, playing with the type of élan and occasional abandon which has rarely surfaced since his early Blue Note records. This may be to do with the impressively energetic rhythm section where Rosnes and Spencer, in particular, shine (Rosnes also takes some fine solos). Sasajima himself has a burnished tone, an individual way of phrasing and a natural sense of play. He sounds happy in the music and it is a thoroughly enjoyable modern jazz date, the type of which Blue Note used to make about three a month in its sixties heyday. **KS**

Lalo Schifrin

1932

More Jazz Meets the Symphony **Schifrin** (p); **James Morrison** (flh); **Paquito D'Rivera** (as, cl); **Ray Brown** (b); **Grady Tate** (d); **Jon Faddis** (t); **The London Philharmonic**. Atlantic Ⓔ 82653-2 (61 minutes). Recorded 1993.

⑧ ❾

Argentinian pianist/composer Lalo Schifrin came to jazz prominence with Dizzy Gillespie in the early sixties. From 1962 on Schifrin has focused his energies on establishing a successful career in Los Angeles as one of Hollywood's most resourceful and respected composers of film and television scores. Here, we meet both sides of the Schifrin persona, the master painter of vividly coloured soundscapes and the encyclopaedic jazz aficionado whose musical passions range from Satchmo to Miles as well as to Tin Pan Alley.

The first of the set pieces, *Sketches of Miles*, is an artful melding of eight Davis-associated lines including *All Blues*, *So What* and *Four*. Buoyed by the lush strings of the London Philharmonic and the boppish flights of Faddis, Morrison, De'Rivera and the strong rhythmic currents let loose by the leader's piano, bassist Brown and drummer Tate, Schifrin's iridescent chart sparkles. So, too, does his evocative *Portrait of Louis Armstrong*, a Gershwinized pastiche seamlessly stitching together such Armstrong classics as *Nobody Knows the Trouble I've Seen*, *When It's Sleepytime Down South* and *Struttin' with Some Barbeque*. In these lovingly-crafted Hollywood Bowl-esque tributes as well as in the poignant takes on standards such as *Begin the Beguine* and *Django*, Schifrin offers an engaging and musically substantive jazz-pops stroll with broad appeal.

CB

Rolf Schimmermann

Suru **Schimmermann** (kbds, p); **Stuart Brookes** (t); **Tony Roberts** (ss, ts, f); **Ray Russell** (g, g-syn); **Dill Katz, Fredy Studer** (d); **Miriam Stockley** (v). B&W Ⓔ 009 (49 minutes). Recorded 1991.

⑥ ❽

Schimmermann and company deliver a lovingly-constructed and finely recorded set of originals which, by and large, re-investigate territory originally mapped out by various members of Weather Report, and by Miles in his last decade. Nothing wrong with that—not all bands have to deliver something new to make it good. In fact, there is much tasteful playing, especially from Russell and Brookes, and the group by and large manage to avoid the sort of pomp-fusion which tends to send the jazz end of the instrumental electric audience screaming from the room. Most of the material consists of vamps upon which to lay suggestive harmonic inversions through which a solo will snake in a generally satisfying fashion. Schimmermann opens the album with a solo piano piece which is atypical of the rest of the album, so do not be put off by it. The vocals are of a piece with the instruments, and mostly there to add atmosphere, apart from on the penultimate track, *Endless Longing*, where Stockley sings some lyrics, and her voice shows itself to be lacking in individuality but still a pleasant experience. This is the modern-day electric equivalent of fifties West Coast.

KS

Rob Schneiderman

1957

Radio Waves **Schneiderman** (p); **Brian Lynch** (t); **Ralph Moore** (ts); **Gary Smulyan** (bs); **Todd Coolman** (b); **Jeff Hirschfield** (d). Reservoir Ⓔ RSR CD 120 (71 minutes). Recorded 1991.

⑥ ❾

Born in Boston, raised in San Diego, Schneiderman had a mother who was a piano teacher, yet it was not until he heard jazz at high school that he took advantage of that fact. Nevertheless, by the time he was 16, he was already playing semi-professionally. He moved to New York in 1982, has since worked with Art Farmer, Eddie Harris and Slide Hampton and has already made three albums as a leader. This CD presents Schneiderman the writer as well as pianist. Seven of the nine titles are by him and none are mere outlines for a mainstream hard bop, blowing session. Themes like the blues waltz *The Juggler* and the dance-inspired *Slapdance-Tapstick* demonstrate the range of his composing brief, and all boast arrangements that are similarly imaginative. With quality horn men like Lynch and Moore it would have been easy to take the soft option, but the leader ensures that soloists are correctly framed and that textural depths are cleverly regulated. The listener becomes increasingly aware that Schneiderman has provided a serious up-dating of the late-fifties message and has done so in a very colourful way. As a pianist, he shines because his impressive technique is put to real work and not just paraded. He works the full length of the keyboard and there is conviction in all he plays.

BMcR

Lauren Schoenberg

Time Waits For No One **Laurie Frink, John Eckert, Dick Sudhalter, Burt Collins** (t); **Matt Finders, Eddie Bert, Bobby Pring** (tb); **Chuck Wilson** (as, f, cl); **Jack Stuckey** (as, cl, ss);

Schoenberg, **Doug Lawrence** (ts); **Ken Peplowski** (ts, cl); **Danny Bank** (bs, bcl); **Dick Katz** (p); **Chris Flory** (g); **Phil Flanigan** (b); **Mel Lewis** (d). MusicMasters Ⓕ 5032-2 (54 minutes). Recorded 1987.

⑥ ❻

Time did wait for Schoenberg, a highly gifted musicologist and musician whose association with Buck Clayton and some of the veteran jazz musicians has given him a sharp ear for period music. The range of his recreations spreads from Henderson's *Queer Notions* to Gil Evans's *Buster's Last Stand*, by way of charts from Benny Carter, Buck Clayton, Ellington, Rugolo, Brookmeyer and McFarland. The soloists are imaginative and sympathetic and the drumming of Mel Lewis, appearing on one of his last recordings, is responsible for a most successful rhythm section. Every track is invigorating—the brass ensembles on Buck Clayton's *Smoothie*, the transcription of Artie Shaw's solo on *Lady Day* for an ensemble of clarinets, and a similar job on Duke's *Harmony In Harlem* succeed completely. Schoenberg must be congratulated on his ability to rehouse these classics of the past in a way which preserves their qualities without making his band sound old fashioned or arch. **SV**

Louis Sclavis

Ellington On The Air **Sclavis** (cl, bcl, ss); **Yves Robert** (tb); **Dominique Pifarely** (vn); **François Raulin** (p, kbds, melodica); **Bruno Chevillon** (b); **Francis Lassus** (d, fedounon, keles). Ida Ⓕ 032 CD (68 minutes). Recorded 1991-92.

✔ ⑧ ❿

This is certainly one of the most unusual Ellington invocations on record. Sclavis has, of course, established himself as a man with strong ties to both the regional French music he still plays and to jazz. Here he moulds the two traditions together in a most extraordinary way. For the most part, Ellington themes appear either as a prologue or an epilogue to what is probably best described as a fantasy on that theme or its harmonic structure, composed by one of the band members. The use of clarinet, harmonium and violin adds to the distancing of the familiar melodies from their normal environment, and increases the excitement of discovery, both in the sense of what can be found in Ellington and what these men can reveal about themselves and their own talents, brought into sharp relief by the Duke. As Sclavis writes in the liner notes, "Duke Ellington is the link between the American jazz tradition and its contemporary European expression...Duke Ellington is the origin, the point of reference and the inspiration. He is...in the air."

At times, these musicians wander very far from that source, but the way they always dovetail their explorations back into Ellington territory is fascinating. The trombone of Robert, wah-wah mutes and all, very clearly evokes the Ducal spirit: his solo in *Harlem Pancake/A Tone Parallel to Harlem/West Indian Pancake* is one to treasure, as are the steel drums. A masterful and wide-ranging album which confirms Sclavis's increasing importance in contemporary music. **KS**

John Scofield

1951

Still Warm **Scofield** (g); **Don Grolnick** (kbds); **Darryl Jones** (elb); **Omar Hakim** (d, perc). Gramavision Ⓕ 18-8508-2 (43 minutes). Recorded 1985.

✔ ⑧ ❽

Still Warm is perhaps one of the records critics have in mind when they put forward the risible suggestion that Scofield's playing acquired a new impetus under the tutelage of Miles Davis. Miles was no doubt happy to give the impression of hiring Scofield for his potential, but when Miles discovered him, Scofield was already one of the most distinctive, dues-paid guitar stylists of his generation, and the arrival of **Still Warm**, his most dynamic funk record, was the culmination of a development which had begun in the mid-seventies. There are references to the past—*Rule Of Thumb*, for example, operates rather like Scofield's 1981 recording *Holidays*—but two tracks—*Techno* and, in particular, *Protocol*—suggest a quite new perspective. Both are brisk funk stomps, based, unremarkably, on two-bar bass pockets. However, in *Protocol*'s quasi-atonal riff and the wide intervallic leaps of both themes (*Protocol*'s arching hysterically from end to end of a diminished arpeggio), Scofield contrived a new, darker angle on the funky verities. Unsurprisingly, the discovery prompted solos of fearsome intensity. Other tracks are less unusual, some previewing the spongy bluesy vamps of later albums in the Gramavision series, but on the pieces mentioned, fusion was jolted into a new dimension. **MG**

Hand Jive **Scofield** (g); **Eddie Harris** (ts); **Larry Goldberg** (p, org); **Dennis Irwin** (b); **Bill Stewart** (d); **Don Alias** (perc). Blue Note Ⓕ CDP827327 2 (64 minutes). Recorded 1993.

⑧ ❿

Scofield has always displayed deep blues roots, even at his most reserved and discreet. It's there in his phrasing, in his approach to the placement of a bent tone, in his conversationalism. No matter how extended the harmonic sequence may be, that blues power is one of the prime sources of his momentum. On **Hand Jive** he makes no bones about it. After a sequence of fine but rather subdued albums featuring tenorist Joe Lovano, he has dirtied up his tone again, gone for a more biting angularity, and brought in one of the founders of funky tenor playing, Eddie Harris. The saxophonist's role seems in part to be a staff of formal stylistic identification around which Scofield can strut his more unorthodox patterns. If so, the juxtaposition works a keen magic, giving Harris a reflected lustre not always present on his own albums. however sophisticated his playing occasionally became.

The presence of pianist Goldings also releases Scofield from the dilemma of being the eternal harmonic provider to all and sundry, so he can go along with the flow in his own chosen way rather than have to steer the vessel of each tune. Harris is not present on every track, although variations of the funky beats most closely associated with him are. But Scofield rightly commands our closest attention, and on a piece like *Do Like Eddie*, where Harris is present, Scofield takes a quite extraordinary solo over a single pedal note, twisting and turning, sliding and diving around the tonic, using distantly related scales which suddenly dovetail back into the simple riff, taking chances at every turn. It's a benchmark solo and one worth returning to repeatedly. As is the album. **KS**

Jimmy Scott

Lost & Found **Jimmy Scott** (v); **Frank Wess** (ts); **David 'Fathead' Newman** (ts, fl); **Ray Bryant**, **Junior Mance** (p); **David Spinoza**, **Eric Gale**, **Billy Butler** (g); **Richard Davis**, **Ron Carter** (b); **Billy Cobham**, **Bruno Carr** (d); strings arranged and conducted by **Eumir Deodate**, **Gene Orloff**, **Selwart Clarke**, **William Fischer, Arif Mardin**. Sequel Ⓜ RSACD 804 (49 minutes). Recorded 1969/72.

② ❻

Jimmy Scott could have been one of the great oddball voices of popular music, like Johnnie Ray or Eartha Kitt. His sound, as producer Joel Dorn observes in the notes to this release, 'defines androgyny'. It is high, almost falsetto, with a little sobbing catch in it, and projected with quite alarming force. He often takes songs at tempos so slow that you could, as the saying goes, eat lunch between the beats. Ray Charles loved Scott's style, and so did Atlantic Records boss Nesuhi Ertegun, but their efforts to help him came to little because he was tied hand and foot by a youthful contract with Savoy. This CD consists partly of material recorded by Ertegun in 1969 but not issued until now. The 1972 tracks came out that year on an Atlantic album entitled **The Source**. A glance at the personnels above suggests that Ertegun was quite sincere in his admiration and ensured that the very best players and arrangers were hired to accompany Jimmy Scott. I can only say that, after puzzling long and hard, I cannot for the life of me understand his enthusiasm. **DG**

Ronnie Scott

1927

Never Pat A Burning Dog **Ronnie Scott**, **Mornington Lockett** (ts); **Dick Pearce** (t); **John Critchinson** (p); **Ron Mathewson** (b); **Martin Drew** (d). Jazz House Ⓔ JHCD 012 (74 minutes). Recorded 1990.

⑩ ❿

Given his long career and the admiration which his playing has always attracted, Ronnie Scott has recorded remarkably little. When this CD was issued in 1991 it arrived after a gap of almost 14 years, during which time the Ronnie Scott Quintet had been working regularly, both at his own club and around the world. It is perhaps the best he has ever made, displaying his formidable musicianship and grasp of the jazz idiom.

Whether it is a modal piece such as McCoy Tyner's *Contemplation* or a ballad like *This Love Of Mine*, Scott's playing has that effortlessly authoritative feel to it which is a mark of rare distinction. He also possesses a beautiful tone, warm and fibrous, with a delightful, lazy vibrato creeping in at slow tempi. This is much more readily appreciated on record than in person, because modern amplification tends to drain the individuality out of saxophone sound.

Recording also reveals what a superb band the quintet is, with its supple rhythm section and mellow front-line blend. Dick Pearce is a world-class trumpeter who has been sadly undervalued by the critics. On one track Pearce is replaced by the tenor saxophone of Mornington Lockett.

The CD title is the punchline of a Ronnie Scott joke, the full import of which can be adequately conveyed only by its creator in person. **DG**

Shirley Scott

1934

Queen Of The Organ Scott (org); **Stanley Turrentine** (ts); **Bob Cranshaw** (b), **Otis 'Candy' Finch** (d). Impulse! Ⓜ GRP 11232 (72 minutes). Recorded 1964.

⑧ ❽

Initially a pianist and trumpeter, Scott was encouraged to switch to the organ by hearing Jimmy Smith. She was in a trio with John Coltrane in 1955 but came to prominence in the tenor and organ trios of the fifties and sixties. In this field her finest work was with Lockjaw Davis and one-time husband Turrentine, although into the eighties she worked with Jimmy Forrest and Dexter Gordon. This CD presents the Turrentine partnership and confirms her status as one of the finest of all jazz organists. Her streetwise bebop is delivered with a stinging attack, her solo lines are well marshalled and titles like *Cute*, *Rapid Shave* and *That's For Me* demonstrate her skill at solo conjugation. Her latent power on *Like Blue* and *Mean, Angry, Nasty And Lowdown* is a reminder of the organ's role in blues since Fred Longshaw. Turrentine plays well and Cranshaw and Finch show that they know how to accept the special responsibilities of a rhythm team in an organ group. When the roles are reversed, however, it is the sparse and superbly buoyant backgrounds that Scott supplies that confirm she is also a master of understatement. These complete the package and totally justify the album's title. **BMcR**

Tom Scott

1948

Born Again Scott (ts, as, ss, ww); **Randy Brecker** (t, flh); **George Bohanon** (tb); **Pete Christlieb** (ts); **Kenny Kirkland** (p); **John Patitucci** (b); **William Kennedy** (d); **Mike Fisher** (perc). GRP Ⓕ 96752 (46 minutes). Recorded 1992.

⑥ ❽

While still a teenager, Scott had worked with Don Ellis and Oliver Nelson. He later studied Indian music under Ravi Shankar, but his reputation was really made in the studios, backing singers like Joni Mitchell and Carole King and with his main interest centred on the commercial end of jazz-rock fusion. On this CD he goes back to his alleged roots and in his liner notes he claims that he wanted to record something more mainstream. In the event he has had a fair stab at it. The three-man rhythm section, with Kirkland assertively at its head, conjures up just the right box of tricks while Scott's own solos, most particularly on *Back Burner* and *Song No. 1*, have a degree more content than his output over the last 15 years has led us to expect. He has wisely included Brecker on four tracks and the two men work well together, but it is the loose-jointed quartets like *Close View* and *Silhouettes* that will come as a shock to listeners who have come to regard Scott's work as the most perfect sleeping draft yet devised. Patitucci and Kennedy certainly stir up the rhythmic activity on the former, but it is the alto of the leader that captures the interest on the latter. **BMcR**

Tony Scott

1921

Dedications Scott (cl, bs, p, g); **Juan Sastre** (g); **Shinichi Yuize** (koto); **Bill Evans, Horst Jankowski** (p); **Scott LaFaro, Peter Witte** (b); **Paul Motian, Hermann Mutschler** (d). Core Records (Germany) Ⓕ COCD 9 00803 0 (54 minutes). Recorded 1957-60.

⑧ ❻

Clarinettist Tony Scott was a major jazz star in the fifties but, dismayed by the deaths of friends such as Charlie Parker and Billie Holiday, he left America at the end of that decade and spent several years travelling through Europe and the Far East. Before departing, however, he recorded an LP of tributes to many of his idols; this remained unreleased until 1986, when it appeared under the title of **Sung Heroes** on the American Sunnyside label. Sunnyside have since made it available on CD, but this CD version, **Dedications**, released by the German company Core, carries an additional three tracks; a hard-blowing *Blues for Charlie Parker,* recorded live in Yugoslavia in 1957 with the Horst Jankowski Trio, plus two 1960 duos from Japan on which Scott improvises with koto player Yuize.

The **Sung Heroes** tracks are quiet, reflective and imbued with blues feeling. Scott plays clarinet (superbly) on most pieces, but switches to piano for *Remembrance of Art Tatum* while *Memory of My Father* is a brief, affecting guitar solo. *Portrait of Anne Frank* is an overdubbed duo for clarinet and baritone saxophone, a novel idea for its time. These 1959 sessions also marked the first meeting of Evans, LaFaro and Motian, soon to become the most famous of the many Bill Evans Trio line-ups. Their delicate support on *Misery (to Lady Day)* and *Requiem for 'Hot Lips' Page* brings an extra touch of poignancy to Scott's heartfelt salutations. **GL**

Gil Scott-Heron

1949

Winter in America **Scott-Heron, Brian Jackson** (p, v); **Danny Bowens** (b); **Bob Adams** (d). Strata East/Bellaphon Ⓕ 660 51 015 (45 minutes). Recorded 1973.

⑤ ❻

By the time he was 21 Gil Scott-Heron had published two novels and a book of poems. Turning to music in the early seventies, his half-sung, half-spoken vocals looked back to African griots and forward to eighties rappers, while his barbed social commentaries introduced aspects of "the black experience" (his phrase) into mainstream pop. He scored hits with *The Bottle*, *Johannesburg* and *B-Movie* and several of his songs were covered by other artists, notably *Labelle* (*The Revolution Will Not Be Televised*) and Esther Phillips (*Home Is Where The Hatred Is*).

Winter in America is among his earlier, more jazz-oriented albums (the jazz deriving chiefly from Brian Jackson's electric piano accompaniments). It includes two of his best-known songs in *The Bottle* and *H_2O Gate Blues* but is otherwise negligible. Scott-Heron is a fine rapper but a poor singer, his vocals here sounding extremely mannered. Several of the songs are little more than sentimental clichés and even *H_2O* Gate Blues now seems laboured and self-conscious. Only *The Bottle* has retained its sharpness, its biting attack on alcoholism wrapped in an infectious dance groove with propulsive bass and brilliant (uncredited) flute. It also points to the fact that Scott-Heron's best work was done in a soul context, his jazz-inflected pieces rarely proving as successful. **GL**

Al Sears

1910-1990

Sear-iously Sears (ts); **Harold Baker, Lester Collins, Taft Jordan** (t); **Tyree Glenn, Lawrence Brown** (tb); **Eddie Barefield, Budd Johnson, Rudy Powell, Sam 'The Man' Taylor, Haywood Henry** (saxes); **Milt Jackson** (mba); **John Acea, Ernest Hayes** (p); **Mickey Baker** (g); **Joe Benjamin, Lloyd Trotman** (b); **Sonny Greer, Joe Marshall, Panama Francis** (d). Bear Family Ⓕ BCD 15668 (71 minutes). Recorded 1949-56.

⑦ ❻

Al Sears had the misfortune to be hired by Duke Ellington to take Ben Webster's place in his greatest-ever line-up. The critics never forgave Sears, an honest, swinging tenor player who was one of Webster's greatest fans. His finest moments with Ellington usually came on the mid-tempo jump-type swingers where he could get his energized lope into gear and drive the whole band by the power of his soloing. After his departure from Ellington in 1949 he had a small group under his own name, then joined Hodges in 1951 when the altoist took his own sabbatical from Duke. The resultant *Castle Rock*, with Sears's supercharged but simple solo, made Hodges a draw by himself and immortalized the tenor player.

This album is made up of the 78rpm sides Sears made under his own name for Coral, RCA and Herald either side of *Castle Rock*, and shows that he was capable of such exciting playing at the drop of a hat. This is probably not his best album (the 1960 **Swing's The Thing**, recorded for the Prestige offshoot label Swingville, holds that distinction), but it presents him unfailingly in jazz guise (he also made some rather mediocre r&b tracks in the mid-fifties) and shows this instantly-recognizable saxophonist to be a player of consistent taste and drive in the great jump-band tradition, harbouring also a significant degree of subtlety on ballads. **KS**

Shakti

Shakti With John McLaughlin **John McLaughlin** (g); **L. Shankar** (v); **R. Raghavan, T.S. Vinayakaram, Zakir Hussain** (perc). Columbia Ⓜ CK46868 (52 minutes). Recorded 1976.

⑧ ❽

A record that effectively launched two jazz careers and took a third, already established, in an altogether unexpected direction, Shakti remains one of the most delightful statements of art-as-culture-clash, a truly genuine, unembarrassed missive from the global village. By 1975 McLaughlin had blown his brains out for several years, transporting his blistering, take-no-prisoners guitar playing from Tony Williams' Lifetime to Miles's seminal **Bitches' Brew** band and on to his own personal jazz rock apocalypse with the Mahavishnu Orchestra. Shakti brought McLaughlin together with an otherwise all-Indian group: violin prodigy L. Shankar (nephew of the famed sitarist Ravi and now a star of sessions with artists as diverse as Jan Garbarek, Peter Gabriel and Frank Zappa, not to mention the creator of a series of highly acclaimed albums for ECM), percussionists Vikayakaram and Raghavan, and tabla master Zakir Hussain, recently reunited with McLaughlin for two or three sold-out world tours and a live album. The music on this, the first of three albums by the group, is primarily raga-based, and its resulting modal nature allows the guitarist more space for extended improvising than practically anywhere else in his oeuvre, and amply demonstrates that many critics' dismissal of this intensely lyrical musician's playing as purely that of a technique fetishist is hugely unfair. **SH**

Bud Shank

1926

The Doctor Is In Shank (as); **Mike Wofford** (p); **Bob Magnusson** (b); **Sherman Ferguson** (d). Candid Ⓕ CCD79520 (63 minutes). Recorded 1991.

⑧ ❽

Shank's work with the big bands of Charlie Barnet and Stan Kenton, plus his many years as a busy session musician in Los Angeles, point to his consistency and reliability. Yet none of this has prevented him from playing jazz with great commitment and understanding. One of the first post-war jazzmen to use the flute, he tends to concentrate on alto nowadays, as he does on this excellent CD. He is capable of producing driving, slashing solos at fast tempo but his ballad work is equally impressive. He turns in a fine version of *I Can't Get Started*, spinning his phrases out in duet over Magnusson's long bass notes, and his approach to *Over The Rainbow* owes nothing to the Art Pepper version. One of Shank's earlier problems was ridding himself of comparisons with Pepper (the two had sat alongside each other in the Kenton band and often worked together in the Hollywood studios). But Shank has no need to worry; CDs such as this show that he is very much his own man and the way he works with this closely-knit rhythm section is faultless. The recording catches all the finest nuances of the music. **AM**

Kendra Shank

Afterglow **Shank** (v, g); **Larry Willis** (p); **Steve Novosel** (b); **Steve Williams, Paul Murphy** (d); **Steve Berrios** (d, perc); **Gary Bartz** (as on 2 tracks). Mapleshade Ⓕ 02132 (49 minutes). Recorded 1992.

⑥ ❽

Shank is a young singer from California who has spent a number of years in Paris and so has a slowly burgeoning reputation on both sides of the Atlantic. Her full-toned, vibrato-less singing recalls Helen Merrill and Shirley Horn at their early peak, and while she tends to go for the slow tempos once favoured by another influence, Billie Holiday, the material is varied enough in style to stave off listener ennui. She also has the priceless advantage of having Larry Willis at the piano to support her every musical move (although the Holiday dedication here, *Left Alone*, is a stark and convincing duet between voice and bass).

Shank has some way to go before she matches the expressive levels of her models, but she has made an impressive start here, and her honesty and sincerity is evident in every performance. Her approach eschews the glitz which often substitutes for real feeling in this type of singing, and the album is an enjoyable experience for the listener from beginning to end. Bartz appears on two tracks and plays sensitively, but the main focus lies elsewhere. There is a decided bossa cast to a number of the tracks, and within this style Shank is entirely at home. **KS**

L. Shankar

1950

Vision **Shankar** (dbl vn, perc); **Palle Mikkelborg** (t, flh); **Jan Garbarek** (ss, ts, bss, perc). ECM Ⓕ 1261 (811 969-2) (45 minutes). Recorded 1983.

⑥ ❽

Shankar (or to give him his formal name, Lakshminarayana Shankar) first came to international attention as one of the more vital components in John McLaughlin's Shakti, the generally rather misunderstood group McLaughlin formed after the dissolution of the Mahavishnu Orchestra. Shankar came to ECM therefore with solid credentials in both Indian classical music and modern Western styles. Both avenues have been explored on the label: this record is the most rewarding from a more orthodox jazz point of view, although it is by no means a trip down swingsville lane, or even a *Blues March*.

This album benefits greatly from the energy and cutting edge Garbarek brings to the ensemble passages and his own solos: his work carries great conviction and generates a lot of power. Shankar, left to his own devices, can get worryingly disparate at times, losing all sense of forward movement, but his two colleagues help him generate momentum again. This is not to deny the considerable grace and beauty of his playing and of the compositions he has presented here: they all have their moments, and flesh-and-blood emotions always finally win through. Worth sticking with to the end. Excellent sound quality. **KS**

Sonny Sharrock

1940

Ask the Ages **Sharrock** (g); **Pharoah Sanders** (ts); **Charnett Moffett** (b); **Elvin Jones** (d). Axiom Ⓕ 848 957-2 (45 minutes). Recorded c. 1991.

✔ ⑩ ❿

Sharrock's small cult following probably includes more metalheads (cerebral metalheads, to be sure) than hard boppers, who tend either to shrink in horror from him or to ignore him altogether. Like most on-edge black guitarists, regardless of genre, he's often stereotyped as Jimi Hendrix's progeny, but some of us are old enough to remember him playing more or less the way he does now as early as 1966, a full year before Hendrix's *Are You Experienced?* was released in the US. **Ask the Ages**, which reunites Sharrock with Sanders, with whom he made his recording debut on **Tauhid** in 1967, burns from beginning to end in a way that conjures up a sixties 'chitlin circuit combo', despite deliberate echoes of the same decade's jazz avant-garde. Elvin Jones's thunderous rolls lend authenticity as well as urgency to *As We Used To Sing*, a see-saw modal waltz à la Coltrane (Sharrock's chief influence, rather than any jazz or blues guitarist). He doesn't comp behind Sanders, but their unison heads and overlapping freakouts illustrate that their rapport is as complete now as it was 25 years ago, with one important difference—Sharrock no longer sounds at a disadvantage for only phrasing like a horn, not actually playing one. **FD**

Artie Shaw

1910

Begin the Beguine **Artie Shaw** (cl); with big band including: **Billy Butterfield** (t); **Al Hendrickson** (g); **Johnny Guarnieri** (h); **Jud DeNaut** (b); **Nick Fatool** (d). RCA Bluebird Ⓜ ND 86274 (67 minutes). Recorded 1938-41.

✔ ⑧ ❽

Essentially, this is a '20 Greatest Hits' compilation and some of the pieces, including the title tune, feature no full-blown jazz at all. Yet in any consideration of the swing era Artie Shaw is a large and unignorable fact, and this CD represents his work very adequately.

The sound of Shaw's clarinet, in tone and especially in articulation, is quite different from Goodman's. Whereas Goodman cultivated a limpid, legato flow, Shaw fired out staccato volleys of sharp-edged notes. He made much of the extreme top of the clarinet's range and in the middle register had a most remarkable and unorthodox sound—dark, woody and fibrous. You hear this quality to perfection in the opening theme statement to *Begin The Beguine* (set in the key of D in order to exploit it) and in *Frenesi*. At its best, Shaw's playing is full of character and it can sound marvellously exciting, riding high above the band in full cry on a number like *Traffic Jam*.

Apart from a couple of tunes by the Gramercy Five, there are no notable solos by anyone else, but there is one vocal by Billie Holiday (*Any Old Time*) and several by Helen Forrest. **DG**

The Complete Gramercy Five Sessions Shaw (cl); **Billy Butterfield**, **Roy Eldridge** (t); **Johnny Guarnieri** (h); **Al Hendrickson**, **Barney Kessel** (g); **Jud DeNaut**, **Morris Rayman** (b); **Dodo Marmarosa** (p); **Lou Fromm**, **Nick Fatool** (d). RCA Bluebird Ⓜ ND 87637 (46 minutes). Recorded 1940-45.

⑧ ❽

The Gramercy Five held a very special place in Shaw's on-off love affair with music. It came about in 1940 after one of his anti-music sabbaticals, and was far from being the first band-within-a-band. Duke Ellington, Benny Goodman, Bob Crosby and Tommy Dorsey had already ploughed that field, but Shaw sowed it in his own inimitable way. For some, the use of the harpsichord in the 1940 unit was seen as a gimmick, but Guarnieri was an articulate soloist and it is difficult to imagine his famous *Summit Ridge Drive* solo on piano. Butterfield's well-designed solos, with their adroit use of mutes, gave the group genuine impetus but it was Shaw's suave, cleverly improvised solos that gave the Five its urbane appeal. In terms of technique, the 1945 was the better of the two units. In Eldridge and Kessel it had superior soloists and, together with Marmarosa, they helped the clarinettist stay abreast of the bebop revolution. Shaw's solos were never actually conceived in the Minton language but, as his excellent excursions on *The Sad Sack* and *Scuttlebutt* show, Shaw's timeless artistry could be accommodated by groups of any size and of most stylistic persuasions. The Gramercy Five gave notice of being neoteric in aspirations but had, in fact, only dressed an excellent establishment style in new clothes. **BMcR**

The Last Recordings: Rare and Unreleased Shaw (cl); **Hank Jones** (p); **Tal Farlow**, **Joe Puma** (g); **Tommy Potter** (b); **Irv Kluger** (d); **Joe Roland** (vb). MusicMasters Ⓕ 65071-2 (two discs: 114 minutes). Recorded 1954.

⑥ ❻

These quintet/sextet sessions were the last of the Gramercy Five and Shaw's last as clarinettist. But little identifies this small-group swing as a product of the mid-fifties, despite modernists Jones and Potter in the rhythm section. *Pied Piper Theme* and *Lyric*, for the sextet with vibes and featuring Farlow, sound rooted in Charlie Christian and the Goodman sextet of 1939 and 1940. In fact the Gramercy Five's takes of Shaw's *Misterioso* are darker, more garish and effective than the 1945 version—as if Tristano had replaced Ellington as a key inspiration.

Shaw's instrumental control, legato phrasing and cool lyricism are intact; witness a slow *My Funny Valentine*, and a *Besame Mucho* where his solo ends with very modern, scalar 'sheets of sound'. Contemporary touches notwithstanding, the harmonic and rhythmic landscape had changed so radically in the previous decade that Shaw sounds old-fashioned, and he knew it: he was a pre-bopper in a post-bop world. Where an unclassifiable soloist like Pee Wee Russell might settle for any setting, Shaw felt the burden of leadership, and had no real postwar plan, nor the inclination to follow jazz where it went. Retirement was a radical way for a 44-year-old to deal with the problem, but an honourable one. **KW**

Ian Shaw

Taking It To Hart Shaw with a collective personnel including **Guy Barker** (t); **Mornington Lockett**, **Iain Ballamy** (ts); **Matthew Barley** (vc); **Adrian York** (arr, p); **Tim Wells** (b); **Mark Fletcher** (d); **Mari Wilson**, **Carol Grimes** (v). Ronnie Scott's Jazz House Ⓕ JHCD036 (53 minutes).

⑥ ❻

Shaw's second CD for Jazz House concentrates on the lyrics of Lorenz Hart (which means the music of Richard Rodgers). From the listener's point of view the self-imposed discipline of quality show songs is an advantage and I found this to be an unexpectedly attractive release. Some of the pleasure stems from the variety of backings, commencing with a big band sound on *I Wish I Were In Love Again* (fine Guy Barker trumpet) down to *Blue Moon* in which there are no instruments at all, just the voices of Shaw and Carol Grimes, multi-taped to provide a choral backing. On one track Shaw and Mari Wilson pull off a favourite Mel Tormé trick by combining two quite different songs which happen to share the same chord progression, *My Romance* and the first Rodgers and Hart joint venture ever published, *Any Old Place With You*. In fact the whole album is a praiseworthy piece of home-grown artistry. **AM**

Woody Shaw

1944-1989

Cassandra Night **Shaw** (t); **Joe Henderson** (ts); **Harold Vick** (f, ts); **Garnett Brown** (tb); **Larry Young, Herbie Hancock** (p); **George Cables** (elp); **Ron Carter, Paul Chambers, Cecil McBee** (b); **Joe Chambers** (d). Muse Ⓔ MCD 6007 (43 minutes). Recorded 1965-71.

✓ ⑧ ❻

Woody Herman Shaw got used to critics mistaking him for Freddie Hubbard, but the obscure quintet recordings which form five-sixths of this CD show that his own voice was already clearly defined by 1965. Although Shaw shared similarities of tone, phrasing and attack with Hubbard, his harmonic concept, derived from Coltrane and Tyner, was strikingly different; in fact, until Wynton Marsalis came along, Shaw was the only trumpeter significantly to investigate such an approach. The theme of his briskly swinging title track, composed almost entirely of perfect fourths, major and minor seconds and pentatonic scale runs, offers a slow-motion enumeration of his approach to improvisation. Joe Henderson is outstanding, supplying the slyly altered blues *Tetragon* and unfailingly lucid solos, like that on Larry Young's *Obsequious*, which begins with a compellingly elliptical orbit around a simple tremelo figure before flying off into outer space. Larry Young (here on piano) and Herbie Hancock also flirt deliciously at the edges of harmonic propriety. Shaw's mid-seventies prime was eclipsed by the media obsession with fusion, and when bebop came around again in the mid-eighties he was overlooked once more, too old to qualify as a neo-bopping young lion. Such was the lot of one of the most distinctive of modern trumpet stylists. **MG**

George Shearing

1919

More Grand Piano **Shearing** (p). Concord Ⓔ CCD 4318 (49 minutes). Recorded 1986.

⑥ ❽

George Shearing is that infuriating artist, a man capable of producing jazz of breathtaking brilliance, but too often content to satisfy his MOR following with pretty piano and improvisation that allow the comfort of accessibility to the layman. With the 'Shearing Sound' firmly behind him, his classical excursions and his triumphs as Bill Basie's replacement safely in the pocket, he made a series of recordings for Concord throughout the eighties, with this CD a typical, although superior, example. It displays his unforced charm and comes over as a session where he simply 'turned up to play'. His approach to *Ramona* is faintly soporific, while on *Change Partners* he sounds like a piano salesman demonstrating the tonal beauty of the instrument. The real Shearing stands up to be counted when he injects a hint of stride into his playing or when he takes a wry Tatumesque look at a title like *You Don't Know What Love Is*. He also impresses when he gets under the skin of good compositions and produces far from transparent re-workings of tunes like *People* and *East Of The Sun*. Throughout the date he turns the absence of a rhythm section to his advantage, taking liberties with his timing and adding an extra spice to a gently simmering main course. **BMcR**

I Hear a Rhapsody **Shearing** (p); **Neil Swainson** (b); **Grady Tate** (d). Telarc Jazz Ⓔ CD 83310 (71 minutes). Recorded 1992.

⑧ ❽

Shearing has had to live down success beyond the wildest dreams of most jazz and jazz-associated musicians. For long stretches of his career he played a type of small-group music which at best could only be described as a sort of jazz, and during his peak years as a popular attraction he was making records with banks of strings, voices and the like which were about as jazz-inflected as Eddy Duchin.

However, at either end of his career he has played strong, imaginative piano. At the present moment his early years, when he first moved to the US from London, are poorly served on CD, so the above is an example of his current form. The most immediately obvious thing is that for this date Shearing abandoned the piano-vibes-guitar unison statements which dominated his sound 30 years ago, and allows his own playing to carry the major load (although a more recent album re-convenes his classic 'sound' instrumentally). This can only be a good thing as far as jazz is concerned, because Shearing is uncommonly gifted when it comes to the inner voicing of chords, paraphrasing melodies, and extracting a beautiful sound from the instrument he is playing. His area of greatest weakness, his rhythm, is occasionally exposed, but this is not such a problem in the overall scheme of things, and his suppleness is extraordinary, bearing in mind his age. Check out Brubeck's *The Duke* on this disc to hear Shearing's current capabilities. **KS**

Jack Sheldon

1931

On My Own **Sheldon** (t, v); **Ross Tompkins** (p). Concord Ⓔ CCD-4529 (62 minutes). Recorded 1991.

⑧ ❽

Sheldon, one of the most gifted soloists to emerge from the West Coast era of the fifties, has since gone from strength to strength. His playing and singing is now better than ever, due to his continuing studies with eminent trumpet and voice teachers in Los Angeles.

While the singing is often a lugubrious send-up of itself (Sheldon's humour is both brilliant and irrepressible), his trumpet playing has the sincerity and feeling of a Hackett or a Berigan and there are few more effective jazz soloists playing today.

The trumpeter easily handles the exposed setting of the simple piano accompaniment, and it is obvious that Tompkins and he have worked together regularly, for there is a close affinity between Sheldon and the younger man. Ballad improvsations like that on the Ellington/Strayhorn *Day Dream* and Sondheim's *Losing My Mind* have always been Sheldon's forte and his brisk recycling of *Opus One* produces a crackling string of trumpet fireworks. Delightful surprises come tumbling from every track, and at a time when jazz is often po-faced, this is a radiant lesson that humour and easy virtuosity can still complement each other in the great Armstrong tradition. **SV**

Archie Shepp

1937

Fire Music **Shepp** (ts); **Ted Curson** (t); **Joseph Orange** (tb); **Marion Brown** (as); **Reggie Johnson** (b); **Joe Chambers, J.C. Moses** (d); **David Izenson** (b). Impulse! Ⓜ GRP 39121 (40 minutes). Recorded 1965.

⑧ ❼

Fire Music may not be the most strikingly beautiful or convincing of Archie Shepp's early, severely underrated Impulse discs—my vote would go to **Four For Trane** (released on CD in Japan only)—but, motivated by his deeply-felt political and social concerns, it is a meaningful one, with an emotional urgency barely under control. Shepp, a poet and playwright in this period as well, pushed the music towards a dramatic, near-theatrical, immediacy; for example, the background riffs behind the soloists on *Hambone* contain strong echoes of r&b, but seem inescapably claustrophobic, like life in a ghetto. Similarly, the episode of rootless tonality in the middle of *Los Olivados* seems to reflect the homeless, the hopeless, the politically disenfranchised. The pop idealization of *The Girl From Ipanema* must be bitterly ironic to a ghetto black. The necessity for beauty is revealed in the reharmonization of *Prelude to a Kiss*, an act of homage to both the master, Ellington, and the saxophonists most inspirational to Shepp's own expressionistic style, Webster and Gonsalves. This is the true basis for David Murray's tenor style a decade later; likewise, the voicings of Shepp's sextet—the open, often gleefully dissonant, clashing harmonies, the way solos emerge or erupt from the jostling interaction of instruments, the dramatic multisectional charts—are undoubtedly an outgrowth of Mingus's mid-sized groups, and a direct precedent for Murray's eighties octet. **AL**

On This Night **Shepp** (ts, p, v); **Bobby Hutcherson** (vb); **David Izenzon, Henry Grimes** (b); **Rashied Ali, J.C. Moses, Joe Chambers** (d, perc); **Ed Blackwell** (rhythm logs); **Christine Spencer** (v). Impulse! Ⓜ GRP 11252 (72 minutes). Recorded 1965.

⑧ ❽

Archie Shepp has always talked a good fight—he describes **On This Night** as "the essence of a people fighting for emancipation"—but his actual performances are frequently a touch disappointing. This CD reissue sensibly replaces the original album's live-at-Newport *Gingerbread, Gingerbread Boy* (now to be found, along with the rest of the Newport set, on **New Thing At Newport** with hitherto scattered material from a trio session with Izenzon and Moses designed to fill **Fire Music**, plus an alternative take of *The Mac Man*. This new material, however impressive, cannot quite rescue the two sessions' music from Shepp's besetting sins: an over-reliance on unusual tonal effects and a lack of overall cogency in his soloing. Thus the title track tellingly features Christine Spencer's soprano voice against an interestingly-textured backdrop of vibes, bass, drums and timpani, augmented by Shepp's piano, but never sufficiently coheres to fulfil its considerable promise. *The Mac Man* highlights Shepp's trademark bleary tenor, replete with growls, smears and honks, and Bobby Hutcherson's fluent vibes, but the restless shifts between tempos dissipate rather than concentrate the music's impact. The trio sides feature superbly expressive free playing from Izenzon and Moses—especially on *The Chased* (take 3)—but Shepp often plays on past the point of inspiration. Nevertheless, **On This Night** remains an exhilarating and important recording, both as an early peak in Shepp's career, and as an archetypal example of mid-sixties radicalism, musical and social. **CP**

Goin' Home **Shepp** (ts, ss); **Horace Parlan** (p). SteepleChase Ⓕ SCCD 31079 (51 minutes). Recorded 1977.

✔ ⑨ ❾

Although traditional elements had long played a part in Archie Shepp's music, it was his experiences as an educator that convinced him of the need to play what he termed "re-creative music". "If I say 'who's Sidney Bechet?', nobody knows," he reported of his students. In response, his own music has since the mid-seventies been largely devoted to upholding and celebrating the black music tradition up to and including John Coltrane.

Goin' Home, a collection of spirituals, was among the first of Shepp's 're-creative' projects and remains his most striking success. Horace Parlan (his partner on many of these later recordings) provides sensitive accompaniments that ground the performance in respect for the music's fundamental dignity. Shepp's contemporary argot of cracked tones and jagged phrasing is used sparingly, edging the material with a declamatory passion that illuminates but never overwhelms its deeper spirituality. The results have a stark grandeur, the tenor a taut, rasping preacher against the piano's calm. On four tracks Shepp turns to his more poignant soprano, notably for a tender, intense version of Ellington's *Come Sunday* that was not included on the original LP. **GL**

Attica Blues Big Band **Shepp** (ss, ts, p, ldr); **Kamal Alim, Roy Burrowes, Charles McGhee, Eddie Preston, Malachi Thompson** (t); **Charles Greenlee, Dick Griffin, Ray Harris, Charles Stephens, Steve Turré** (tb); **Marion Brown, John Purcell** (as); **Patience Higgins, Marvin Blackman** (ts); **James Ware** (bs); **Art Matthews** (p); **Clyde Crimer** (synths); **Brandon Ross** (g); **Hakim Jami** (b, tba); **Avery Sharpe** (b); **Clifford Jarvis** (d); **Kevin Jones** (perc); with **Candice Greene, Terry Jenoure, Carl Extor, Akua Dixon** (vn); **Irene Datcher, Akua Dixon, Terry Jenoure, Joe Lee Wilson** (v); **Ray Copeland** (arr, cond). Blue Marge/FD Music Ⓕ 151982 (2 discs: 96 minutes). Recorded 1979.

⑦ ❼

Shepp has often worked with larger units during his career, but the key recordings featuring augmented ensembles, such as **For Losers** and **Kwanza**, have yet to make it to CD (come on, Impulse!). Meanwhile, this is a worthy 'live' substitute, recorded in concert at the Palais de Glaces in Paris. The band is disciplined and decently rehearsed, the charts are for the most part imaginative, with even the singing controlled and for the most part to-the-point. Most importantly, Shepp himself sounds involved. Whether he is on soprano or tenor, his attack is arresting, his tone full and his intonation accurate. He also largely eschews the improvising prolixity which has occasionally bedeviled some otherwise excellent performances, and his exhortations behind the various vocalists are not only apt but often exciting.

Listening to the arrangement of Dave Burrell's oft-recorded *Crucificado*, for example, one once again gets a glimpse of the divine, heady wedges of sound which Shepp can conjure from a large ensemble when at his best, a gift he shares with Charles Mingus and precious few others in jazz. This is music with a real cutting edge of excitement, and you can feel the frisson within the band as they work out on the arrangements. Shepp's concept is large enough to sustain the amplification it receives from a big band setting. The concert preserved for us here embraces a wide repertoire of styles and ideas, touching on Shepp's musical concerns from gospel to African to the modified boogaloo of **Attica Blues**. In fact, the live version of *Attica Blues* contained here is comfortably superior to the original Impulse studio workout and sets the tone nicely for the whole event. **KS**

Soul Song **Shepp** (ts, ss, v); **Kenny Werner** (p); **Santi DeBriano** (b); **Marvin 'Smitty' Smith** (d). Enja Ⓕ 4050 2 (46 minutes). Recorded 1982.

⑦ ❽

Although recorded when Shepp was firmly on his retreat from a musical freedom policy, this CD does not fit comfortably into his potted history of the tenor saxophone. He does not set himself up in the didactic driving seat and makes no attempt to remind the jazz world of Coleman Hawkins, Don Byas and Paul Gonsalves through the bell of his own horn. For a start, he has chosen a rhythm section that chops up the rhythmic flow, thereby stopping titles like *Mama Rose*, where he plays soprano in any case, from taking an easy mainstream gait. This is a John Coltrane quartet-type contest with horn forced, at least partially, to free itself from the busy background turmoil cooked up by Werner, De Briano and Smith. The title track follows the *Mama Rose* pattern despite Werner's ostinato piano, while *Geechee*, an excellent tenor foray, keeps Shepp in his investigative rather than educational role and produces a lengthy solo that reminds the listener of nobody save Shepp himself. Only on *My Romance*, which concludes this powerful session, is the listener treated to a rhapsodic, Ben Webster-ish piece of story-telling, but even this performance, built up on roughened terrain, is not prepared to surrender to the excesses of romanticism. **BMcR**

Andy Sheppard 1957

Rhythm Method **Sheppard** (ss, ts); **Claude Deppa** (t); **Kevin Robinson** (t, flh); **Gary Valente** (tb); **Steve Lodder** (kbds); **Sylvan Richardson** (b); **Dave Adams** (d); add on one track only: **Ashley Slater** (tb); **Jerry Underwood** (ts); **Julian Argüelles** (bs). Blue Note Ⓕ CD BLP 1007 (62 minutes). Recorded 1993.

⑧ ❽

Sheppard's first new album for Blue Note found him in the main sticking to the group of players with which he had grown comfortable, In Co-Motion, with additional players (Gary Valente, Kevin Robinson) appearing to make effective contributions to a couple of the longer and more ambitious tracks. The added depth this brings to even the slightest compositional ideas here certainly justifies their inclusion, and also nicely offsets the quintet line-up of the majority of the album. Sheppard himself plays with great poise and assurance, and his tone on either of the two saxes is full and pleasing: his essential good manners and equable temperament as a soloist preclude him from ever outstaying his welcome. Some of the tracks are very long, and occasionally lapse into shapelessness when one too many player bags some solo space, but then there are pieces such as the opener, *Sofa Safari* and the remarkable slow burn of *So...*, which exhibit all the signs of careful organization and maximum usage of minimum resources. On *So...* Sheppard has clearly listened to the work of other fusion players (as well as used the ideas of band members), but then has taken some core ideas—such as encouraging group interplay at all stages, rather than allowing one solo voice to dominate—and expanded them into a musical raison d'être. It works beautifully; similarly, parts of *Well Kept Secret* cohere in this fashion, although overall it is a more diffuse construction.

Other pieces fit more comfortably into large-group styles which Sheppard has mined successfully in the past, and are therefore a continuation of his musical processes, but there is sufficient which is new and good to merit a recommendation for this as his most completely realised disc yet. Sadly, this and its partner, **Delivery Suite**, are the only product of Sheppard's short period at Blue Note, as he and the label have since parted company. **KS**

Derrick Shezbie

1974

Spodie's Back **Shezbie** (t); **Corey Henry** (tb); **Mark Turner**, **Branford Marsalis**, **Mark Gross** (ts); **Victor 'Red' Atkins**, **Kenny Kirkland**, **Ellis Marsalis** (p); **Greg Williams**, **Robert Hurst** (b); **Kirk Joseph** (tba); **Martin Butler**, **Herlin Riley**, **Jeff 'Tain' Watts** (d). QWest/Reprise Ⓕ 245299-2 (54 minutes). Recorded 1993.

⑤ ❽

A brief glance at the names of the supporting cast here gives you pretty clear indication of where this album is coming from. Cover versions of *Royal Garden Blues*, *Dusk on the Delta*, *St James Infirmary* and *Back O'Town Blues* fill in most of the blanks. The liner notes, by producer Delfeayo Marsalis, omit to mention that he has played with the Rebirth Jazz Band, the New Orleans brass ensemble which is always a hit on the festival circuit, but they do paint 19-year-old Shezbie as a sincere, dues-paying young jazz musician, part of "a generation of trumpeters who firmly believe that innovation must not preclude preservation." End of sermon, you might think: what about the music? It's o.k. Shezbie is technically secure within the limits he's set himself here, but has little voice of his own, and sounds ruinously intimidated by the studio atmosphere. Only the old stagers really get going and move outwards from the rather bashful respectfulness of the leader to spontaneity and jauntiness. So: as a snapshot of what's bubbling under down in the Big Easy, it's quite a useful venture. As some sort of state-of-the-art statement, it's got a lot of maturing to do yet. **KS**

Sahib Shihab

1925-1989

Jazz Sahib **Shihab** (bs); **Phil Woods** (as); **Benny Golson** (ts); **Hank Jones**, **Bill Evans** (p); **Paul Chambers**, **Oscar Pettiford** (b); **Art Taylor** (d). Denon/Savoy Ⓜ SV-0141 (45 minutes). Recorded 1957.

⑥ ❻

Shihab (as Edmund Gregory) played alto with Roy Eldridge's big band in the late forties before becoming identified with the boppers, notably the groups of Art Blakey, Thelonious Monk and Tadd Dameron. He switched to baritone and worked with Dizzy Gillespie's small group in 1953, remaining with the larger horn in subsequent years. All the writing on this CD was done by Melba Liston and Shihab; both of them make expert use of the three-sax front line, although the addition of a brass instrument would have made for more varied tone colours. All three saxophonists take good solos but it is Phil Woods who invariably makes the most lasting impression. He erupts from the ensemble on *Jamila* with startling results. The leader's baritone playing is warm-toned, as is that of tenor saxist Golson. For the reissue on CD Denon/Savoy have added *Ba-Dut-Du-Dat,* which was not on the original LP, but they have not included *Sugar Dugar,* made at the session with Hank Jones and Chambers and which was released as part of a sampler LP. Logic, anyone? **AM**

Matthew Shipp

1961

Points **Shipp** (p); **Rob Brown** (as); **William Parker** (b); **Whit Dickey** (d). Silkhead Ⓕ SHCD 129(71 minutes). Recorded 1990.

⑦ ❼

Although one of a younger generation which has drawn upon the jazz past for inspiration, Matthew Shipp does not accept the current orthodox of the neo-conservative gospel. He has instead sought an alternative direction and cites, along with Ellington, Scriabin and Debussy, quixotic artists Andrew Hill and Hasaan Ibn Ali as piano influences. Thus it is easy to see why Shipp's attention to melody proceeds not in a straight line, but is quick to curve, to stop and start in ellipses, to piece together asymmetrical phrases in mosaic fashion or to cluster in percussive gestures. Saxophonist Rob Brown is also quite comfortable with sustaining a melodic line around angular intervals (often punctuated with a spirited alto cry, both reminiscent of the late Jimmy Lyons); considering that Whit Dickey is a light, lyrical drummer and William Parker sharpened his ability to unify discursive counterpoint during a long tenure with Cecil Taylor, it is apparent that this is a quartet capable of transforming emotion into articulate musical detail. The two long versions of *Points* highlight the group's methods of construction. As composer, Shipp's graphic design provides an open architectural shape, allowing solo, duo and trio combinations, continuously shifting textures and dynamics, creating peaks and valleys of intensity.

Chameleonic in nature, the two interpretations are vastly different in mood and detail. *Piano Pyramid* uses the checks and balances of the piano trio format unchanged from that of, say, the classic Bill Evans Trio, but by working outside of the song form they construct a radically shaped new edifice with unexpected edges and angles that reflect light and shadow in fascinating ways. **AL**

Wayne Shorter

1933

Speak No Evil **Shorter** (ts); **Freddie Hubbard** (t); **Herbie Hancock** (p); **Ron Carter** (b); **Elvin Jones** (d). Blue Note Ⓜ CDP7 46509-2 (42 minutes). Recorded 1964.

⑧ ❿

The saxophonist who became most widely known for his work with Weather Report in the seventies was in an interesting period of transition here. He had been signed to Blue Note as a solo artist earlier in 1964, when it was becoming obvious that he might end his five-year stint with Art Blakey and give in to the blandishments of Miles Davis.

With Davis a matter of months away by the time of this Christmas Eve session, Shorter's two previous albums **Night Dreamer** and **Juju** had created much memorable material and a couple of pieces which are still played around the world, while four out of the six tracks on the present album have since become standards. The 14-bar A-section of the title-track and the melodically-related *Witch Hunt* are both disguised blues, while an insinuating *Fe-Fi-Fo-Fum* and the ballad *Infant Eyes* stray just far enough from the Shorter-directed Jazz Messengers to presage his later work for Miles.

Meanwhile, Shorter's astonishing tenor tone and his dramatic use of dynamics are captured in an ostensibly relaxed atmosphere which conceals enormous expertise. While Hancock and Hubbard sound typically excellent for the period, Jones and Carter are understatedly at the service of the compositions. **BP**

The All Seeing Eye **Shorter** (ts); **Freddie Hubbard** (t, flh); **Alan Shorter** (flh); **Grachan Moncur lll** (tb); **James Spaulding** (as); **Herbie Hancock** (p); **Ron Carter** (b); **Joe Chambers** (d). Blue Note Ⓜ CDP 829100 2 (44 minutes). Recorded 1965.

⑧ ❽

Shorter's earliest albums as a leader coincided with his long stint as soloist, songwriter and arranger with Art Blakey's Jazz Messengers, and many of them reflect in large part the style and values of that aggregation. By the time his association with Blue Note got under way, Shorter was moving on from the hard-bop format, aiming at more elusive goals, re-ordering seemingly familiar musical building-blocks, and generally taking an increasingly oblique approach to music-making. This process accelerated once he joined the Miles Davis Quintet in 1965, and **The All Seeing Eye** certainly marks a peak in his early career as a writer and arranger. Utterly distinctive, his angular lines sit jaggedly over constantly shifting tempos, the rests and unexpected cadences being as integral to the composition as the notes themselves. Shorter has also given much thought to the pacing of a piece: nothing here merely starts with a theme run-through, moves on to a string of identikit solos and wraps it up on the theme again. Each piece is a construction through which each soloist must negotiate his own ideas of its meaning. With players of the calibre of Hubbard (at this time going through a patch of extraordinary creativity), Moncur and Spaulding this makes for exceptionally thought-provoking, image-laden music, especially as the overall theme -God and his creation of the Universe- has a ready-made bank of images to conjure. But the key musician here is Hancock. His interpretative abilities and his razor-sharp musical mind keep the texture, speed and shape of each composition in a continual state of evolution. His sense of drama is uncanny, his accompaniment often miraculous in what it adds to what the soloist is doing. He did this on numerous Blue Note dates around this time (Grachan Moncur lll's **Some Other Stuff**, recently reissued, is a spell-binding case in point) and every example is worth searching out. This one's a good enough place to start. **KS**

Native Dancer **Shorter** (ss); **Herbie Hancock** (kbds); **Airto Moreira** (perc); **Milton Nascimento** (v); **Dave McDaniel**, **Roberto Silva**, **Wagner Tiso**, **Jay Graydon**, **Dave Amaro** (unk inst). CBS Ⓜ 467095 2 (44 minutes). Recorded 1974.

⑥ ❽

It's hard to imagine that Shorter could ever transcend the extraordinary originality of his writing for Blue Note in the mid-sixties, and although **Native Dancer** essays some novel fusions, its tone and content are both significantly lighter and markedly less sophisticated than anything else Shorter had produced heretofore. In large part this derives from the dominance of Milton Nascimento who, except when creating a pleasingly mystical melancholy on such tracks as *Tarde*, pursues a decidedly individualistic vocal and songwriting style which often leaves Shorter with nothing more to do than embellish and perhaps solo briefly.

Better results emerge from Shorter's own compositions, although, unusually, there have been far more subtle readings of *Beauty And The Beast*'s vamping middle section. Shorter's lush, rolling tone poem *Diana* lacks the focus and direction which distinguish his best writing, and it is only perhaps his strong melody on *Ana Maria* which fully resists the scrutiny of hindsight; this track also seems to escape the rather thin production which does little to help an album which could benefit from rather more ballast to counterbalance Nascimento's fey vocalizing. **MG**

Ben Sidran

1943

Have You Met...Barcelona? Sidran (p, v); **Johnny Griffin** (ts); **Jimmy Woode** (b); **Ben Riley** (d); **Clementine** (v). Orange Blue Ⓕ OB 002 CD (57 minutes). Recorded 1987.

⑤ ❽

It feels like Sidran has been around for a lot longer than in fact is the case: he certainly has a style that has been around a long time. If there was a stylistic slot to fill midway between the countrified urbanities of Mose Allison and the witticisms of Dave Frishberg, then Sidran would do that job quite comfortably. His piano playing is adequate for the task, his voice is not particularly strong and he has not been trained to the point where he will sustain a note, but none of those aspects of his performance really touches the core of what he is on about. What he really seems to enjoy is twisting the meanings of lyrics, whether they are his or someone else's, to the point where they are a wry smile and a shared aside. The supporting band is sympathetic and in good spirits throughout, but nothing surprising happens here. Griffin interjects some tasty expostulations, but sensibly stays well below boiling point: it is not his album, after all. The title, by the way, is explained by the fact that, yes, *Have You Met Miss Jones?* is given a tryout, and that tryout, along with the rest of the music, was made in Barcelona. **KS**

Alan Silva

1939

Alan Silva Silva (vn, p, vc); **Becky Friend** (f); **Karl Berger** (vb); **Mike Ephron** (p, org); **Dave Burrell** (p); **Barry Altschul** (perc); **Lawrence Cooke** (d, perc). ESP-Disk Ⓜ 1091-2 (38 minutes). Recorded 1968.

⑤ ❺

Initially trained on piano, violin and trumpet, Silva took up the bass in 1962. He was a prominent figure in the late sixties free movement, playing with Cecil Taylor, Sun Ra, Albert Ayler and Archie Shepp. On this rather strange album nothing is heard of his first choice instrument; his composer's piano and Ornette Coleman-like violin are heard on *Skilfulness* and *Solestrial Communications Number One*, but only his cello gives any real satisfaction. Silva delivers his solos with a sawing intensity, full of jangling dissonance and with strangely macabre overtones. Little effort is made to improvise, either in free mode or traditionally, and much of what he plays is mood-provoking rather than musically enquiring. Friend contributes thin-toned flute solos and, together with Berger's hollow-sounding vibes, produces some interesting ensembles. In the main, freedom overtakes them and the music becomes vaguely static. Only Burrell's genuinely exciting piano seems to have any real purpose and the temptation is to see this as a fashion-following session of the time. **BMcR**

Horace Silver

1928

Horace Silver and the Jazz Messengers Silver (p); **Kenny Dorham** (t); **Hank Mobley** (ts); **Doug Watkins** (b); **Art Blakey** (d). Blue Note Ⓜ CDP7 46140-2. Recorded 1954/55.

✔ ⑩ ❽

The funk starts here, as far as modern jazz is concerned; and the passage of nearly 40 years has only enhanced the gritty invention of these eight tracks, originally released on two ten-inch LPs. The Jazz Messengers was a co-operative quintet at the time, and wisely chose to focus on Silver's compositions in their initial studio recordings. The results gave instant popularity to the earthy, percussion-driven brand of bop that had also been forming on contemporary Miles Davis sessions (several of which included Silver and/or Blakey). The busy, brittle comping of both piano and drums gain importance in this music, allowing the horn players to slow down and attend more to phrasing and sound. Dorham and Mobley are masters at this approach, incorporating the heat of Blakey and Silver into their improvisations. The pianist blends bop and church in both his playing and writing, and introduces his fundamental yet elegant approach to harmonizing trumpet and tenor sax. While *The Preacher* and *Doodlin'* were major hits, *Room 608*, *Creepin' In* and the other titles (including Mobley's *Hankerin'*) are also inspired frames for blowing. Everything that Silver would create subsequently stems from these classic performances. **BB**

Song For My Father Silver (p); **Carmell Jones, Blue Mitchell** (t); **Joe Henderson, Junior Cook** (ts); **Teddy Smith, Gene Taylor** (b); **Roger Humphries, Roy Brooks** (d). Blue Note Ⓜ CDP7 84185-2 (61 minutes). Recorded 1963/64.

✔ ⑧ ❽

Undoubtedly Silver's most famous album, **Song For My Father** marks a turning-point for the specialist jazz record market, since both this and Lee Morgan's **The Sidewinder** were unexpected hits in the popular field. Alfred Lion, who produced them, had (as Michael Cuscuna wrote) "inadvertently proved that you do not have to bury jazz in gimmicks and sweetening to sell records," but Silver's subsequent output was less affected by thoughts of fame and riches than some others'.

Horace had, after all, been creating catchy Latin-jazz material for a decade already, and the title-track is matched for modal moodiness by *Que Pasa* (now also included on this CD in a trio version from a year before). The new line-up heard on these and two up-tempo blues brings attacking solos by Henderson and, to a lesser extent, Jones. Whatever affected the earlier Mitchell/Cook band, it is significant that their tracks (two on the original LP, six on CD) have Silver as the only soloist.

It goes unnoticed by most people that tape stretching has caused some wow, especially on the title-tune. If anyone has that unlikely object, an unplayed LP copy, Blue Note ought to use it for further remastering. **BP**

The Cape Verdean Blues **Silver** (p); **Woody Shaw** (t); **Joe Henderson** (ts); **J. J. Johnson** (tb); **Bob Cranshaw** (b); **Roger Humphries** (d). Blue Note Ⓜ CDP 7 84220 2 (44 minutes). Recorded 1965.

⑧ ❽

Coming from the same mid-sixties period that produced the watershed **Song for My Father** (see above), this edition of Horace Silver's cookin' unit featured a galvanizing front line with rising stars Henderson on tenor and trumpeter Shaw, plus (on half the tracks—one side of the old LP) veteran trombonist Johnson. Anchored by bassist Cranshaw and drummer Humphries, Silver's sextet was a sizzling exemplar of the pianist-composer's patented hard-bop approach where elements of gospel and r&b fused with a no-nonsense boppish attack.

Silver's most compelling accomplishment has been the ability to combine catchy melodies and intriguing harmonies with simple yet insinuating rhythmic grooves that swing with understated power and panâche. On the sextet tracks the recipe is given spicy up-tempo expression in the bubbling, burbling *Nutville*. In contrast, the exotic *Bonita* sways with a mysterious, drums-in-the-distant-jungle pulse set in motion by Humphries mallets.

The title track is a jaunty, calypso-propelled outing with exuberant forays by Silver and Henderson. Here, as in the bulk of Silver's work, we glimpse a music of immediate and mesmerizing appeal, whose subtle complexities percolate beneath seductive surfaces that engage body, soul and brain. Also notable are Silver's spartan pianistics. Indeed, Silver might be thought of as the Basie of Bop, a stylist of unusual economy whose every note (and rest) counts. **CB**

Sonny Simmons

1933

Staying on the Watch **Simmons** (as); **Barbara Donald** (t); **John Hicks** (p); **Teddy Smith** (b); **Marvin Pattilo** (d). ESP-Disk Ⓜ 1030-2 (44 minutes). Recorded 1966.

⑧ ❻

Simmons had the bad luck to be a sixties avant-gardist based in California. He and Prince Lasha more or less held the fort after Ornette jumped ship in 1959, heading for New York and fame. It was only in the late sixties that Simmons made the move to the East Coast, but there he was an isolated figure, and his talent was consequently overlooked. Judging by this disc and others made under his name, this is a real pity. He plays in a style which has grown out of Coleman's, but is freer than that of his model's. The tremendous fire and energy he develops is not dissipated in typical mid-sixties screechings and brawlings for minutes on end, and it is clear from the care he has shown with his compositions here that he did not regard a performance simply as an event where you stand up, play a minimal theme as an excuse to get started, then blow until you drop. Each track here has a clear structure, often with different solos receiving completely separate tempi and instrumental backing. Much of the album is in metre, with free-tempo sections. Pianist Hicks is a complete player even at this early stage, while Barbara Donald is one of a tiny handful of trumpeters to make sense out of the sixties without ignoring them. A very good album indeed. Simmons has in the last year made his major label début with.**Ancient Ritual** on Q West/Reprise, but **Staying On The Watch** remains his most significant statement. **KS**

Nina Simone

1933

Feeling Good: The Very Best **Simone** (p, v) with various unidentified aggregations, including trio, strings, brass sections. Verve Ⓜ 522 669-2 (73 minutes). Recorded 1957-71.

⑦ ❼

Simone albums with similar titles are not exactly hard to find, but this is the only one of them to come within a half-mile of the truth. Of course, long ago the pop charts claimed Simone as one of their own, so every latter-day compilation tends to keep not one but two eyes firmly fixed on that side of her recording activity. With such matters in mind, if you want to concentrate on her more jazz-based output, you'll have to seek out either CD reissues of the original Bethlehem and RCA albums, or the original vinyl efforts on Colpix, RCA and Philips themselves. In terms of jazz ouput, the current CD unavailability of most of the Colpix material and the RCA effort **Nina And Piano!** is the greatest loss, and on this disc only *Don't Smoke In Bed, Strange Fruit, Don't Explain, The Other Woman* and *I Loves You, Porgy* show Simone at her most unadorned and burningly intense. Indeed *Don't Smoke In Bed* is a terrifyingly powerful evocation of loss and regret.

Still, if you want the more insouciant side of Simone, then *My Baby Just Cares For Me* is here, as is *Here Comes The Sun, Work Song* and *To Love Somebody*. But there isn't a single Simone treatment of Kurt Weill here - one of her greatest strengths - and the powerful **Wild Is The Wind** album, recorded with just a trio, is not represented at all. Nor, strangely, are a couple other of her RCA hits, *Mr Bojangles* and *I Shall Be Released*, though the dreadful *Mississippi Goddam* crops up yet again. There's still that half-mile to go... **KS**

At The Village Gate **Simone** (v, p); **Al Shackman** (g); **Chris White** (b); **Rob Hamilton** (d). Roulette Ⓜ CDP7 95058-2 (46 minutes). Recorded 1961.

⑥ ❻

The informal atmosphere of the Village Gate is the perfect setting for Simone, who is always at her best with just her own piano and rhythm section for support. She proves on *Bye Bye Blackbird* that she is a remarkable pianist—a neo-classical introduction giving way to a funky, swinging piano version with no vocal. When she does sing, her highly individual approach to pitch and timing, coupled with her inimitable low timbre, raises the hairs on the back of the neck. Her anguished entry to *Just in Time*, with its repeated piano phrases, transmutes into a swinging vocal over White's walking bass line, proving that Simone can outswing most vocalists who concentrate on a narrower stylistic range than her own.

The CD version of this album, which was first released on the Colpix label (both Colpix and Roulette are now owned by EMI), has no extra music, but the sound is much crisper than on the original vinyl. **AS**

Zoot Sims

1925-1985

Zoot! **Zoot Sims** (ts, as); **Nick Travis** (t); **George Handy** (p); **Wilbur Ware** (b); **Osie Johnson** (d). Riverside Ⓜ OJCCD 228-2 (40 minutes). Recorded 1956.

⑧ ❻

Zoot Sims's playing began to blossom as he entered his 30s. The warm, slightly furry tone and spacious phrasing that made him one of the great jazz voices are both immediately recognizable here. Like his contemporaries (Stan Getz, Al Cohn, etc.) Zoot had been strongly influenced by bebop in his early days and gradually moved away from it as his mature style developed. This session is particularly fascinating because lingering traces of bebop can be heard quite clearly in what is otherwise quintessential Zoot. His masterly exposition of the theme of *Fools Rush In*, for instance, contains several linking phrases which are pure Parker.

Superb though it is, this CD falls short of being one of the really great Zoot Sims records for two reasons; firstly because he plays a couple of numbers on alto saxophone, which simply was not his instrument, and secondly because he shares solo space with Nick Travis. There is nothing wrong with Travis's playing, but the interest inevitably flags when he takes over. On the other hand, if you have a particular liking for Zoot and the 'Brothers', this long-unavailable session offers many delights. **DG**

Al Cohn and Zoot Sims: Body And Soul **Sims** (ts, ss); **Cohn** (ts); **Jaki Byard** (p); **George Duvivier** (b); **Mel Lewis** (d). Muse Ⓕ MCD 5356 (47 minutes). Recorded 1973.

⑧ ❽

Both Sims and Cohn based their styles on that of Lester Young, and both came to prominence in Woody Herman's Second Herd of 1947-49. Singly they were powerful and inventive swingers, and when they played together the effect was compounded—theirs was easily the best of any of the fashionable two-tenor teams. The tandem recorded with many different rhythm sections, but few gave them better support than this one, and the ever-happy Sims responds with some of his best work, including a notable feature on *Recado Bossa Nova*.

Sims had an unstable relationship with the soprano saxophone, which he played very well (he nicknamed his horn Leprosy). His delicate work on another feature, *Jean*, shows him at his best on the instrument. But once Sims and Cohn had locked horns it was not practical to separate their performances for appraisal. This is one of the best of the recordings by that most cheerful of bands and no more needs to be said. **SV**

Zoot Sims Meets Jimmy Rowles **Sims** (ts); **Rowles** (p); **George Mraz** (b); **Mousie Alexander** (d). Pablo Ⓜ OJCCD-683-2 (46 minutes). Recorded 1977.

⑥ ❻

An extremely welcome reissue of the kind of session which smoothes away the cares of the world and makes you think life is all right after all. This is the kind of effect you can also get out of a good bottle of wine, and they both have the same sorts of qualities; the co-leaders on the record are vintage musicians who have mature styles which are still highly potent, and their repertoire comes from the vintage years of American song. One odd result of the reissue of this kind of LP on CD is that the original sleeve notes also resurface (why waste money getting new ones written?), and here we have Benny Green's notes from 15 years ago, so verbose that on a CD liner they have to be printed so small that only a magnifying glass will unlock Green's vintage learnedness. So anxious is he to create a good impression of his references that he manages to mention Oscar Wilde, George Moore, James Whistler, Rossetti and Walter Pater before he gets round to Zoot Sims. I wonder if Zoot Sims ever read these notes? Or understood them? **MK**

Frank Sinatra
1915

Come Dance With Me! **Sinatra** (v) **Orchestra / Billy May** (arr). Capitol Ⓜ CDP7 48470-2 (42 minutes). Recorded 1958.

✔ ⑩ ❽

There seems little point in arguing that Sinatra, as the greatest popular male singer of his age, does not deserve inclusion in a guide to the best in jazz recordings. Not only did he first come to international attention as a featured singer with the swing bands of Tommy Dorsey and Harry James, but his whole approach to rhythm, phrasing and intonation comes from listening to jazz instrumentalists and to singers who could use their voices almost in the manner of a solo instrument. Certainly his contemporary jazz audiences appreciated him. He not only won *down beat* polls with monotonous regularity, but he also appeared one year at the Newport Jazz Festival when it was still in Newport, Rhode Island.

His jazz heritage has rarely been more evident than on this superb 1958 session, when his voice was still wholly intact and his interpretative artistry had reached its mature peak. The album starts with the title track, and in the second verse Sinatra makes no secret of his intentions when he alters the lyrics to "hey there cutes/put on your Basie boots/come dance with me." Billy May, for years used as the forceful, swinging big-band accompanist for so many of Capitol's jazz-inflected singing stars, continually pushes Sinatra towards some of the most relaxed and open music he ever made. The singer, clearly inspired by the waves of sound behind him and the infectious Basie-type groove of the rhythm section, on *Something's Gotta Give* actually interrupts his closing chorus to shout to the band "c'mon, let's tear it up!" And tear it up they do.

The album is not just a collection of Maynard Ferguson-like scorchers, however. Sinatra shows he has lost none of his patented romantic approach on titles such as *Just In Time* or *The Last Dance*, while the transformation of *I Could Have Danced All Night* from frothy Broadway show-stopper to carefree swinger is little short of miraculous. The CD version adds four extra tracks to the original vinyl, three from the same March 1958 session (including two duets with Keely Smith), plus a previously-unissued *It All Depends On You* from September of the same year. **KS**

Alan Skidmore
1942

Tribute To Trane **Skidmore** (ts); **Jason Rebello** (p); **Dave Green** (b); **Stephen Keogh** (d). Miles Music Ⓕ MMCD 075 (46 minutes). Recorded 1988.

⑦ ❽

Son of tenor saxophonist Jimmy, Skidmore has worked with big names on both sides of the Atlantic. He once declined a Berkley scholarship but was a member of the widely influential SOS group with Mike Osborne and John Surman. He worked for some time with the George Gruntz Concert Band, the European Jazz Quintet, SOH and Tenor Tonic. On this CD he literally takes on his mentor, John Coltrane, in a programme of the great man's music seen very much through Skidmore's eyes. The Englishman has deliberately chosen powerful Trane themes and has homogenized them in his own image. The raw passion has been replaced by a caring involvement and, on *Resolution* and *Crescent* in particular, he has taken his own improvisational routes. The spirit of the original recording is most retained on *Lonnie's Lament* and *Naima*, where Skidmore shows his emotional commitment as well as his instrumental facility. The rhythm section, built around Rebello's buoyant piano and Green's steadfast bass, provide just the right support. No attempt is made to pressurize the leader and the expressive reins remain with him throughout a recital that could introduce the newcomer to the music of Coltrane without a hint of compromise on Skidmore's part. **BMcR**

Slickaphonics

Wow Bag **Ray Anderson** (tb, perc, v); **Steve Elson** (ts, kbds, perc, v); **Allan Jaffe** (g, v); **Mark Helias** (b, v); **Jim Payne** (d, perc, v). Enja Ⓕ GEMA 4024 (42 minutes). Recorded 1982.

⑤ ❻

This pioneering rock-jazz collective formed in 1980 was the toast of New York clubland when its brand of highly vocal jazz-funk first hit the streets. The horns have a particular tonality, being tenor and trombone, and their riffs and tightly-structured solos are deftly worked into the pulsing texture of the band's predominantly vocal pieces. The first track here, *You Can Do What You Want*, typifies their approach: a repeated vocal line over a mesmeric funk beat, with the horns adding richness after a chorus or two. But ultimately the band suffers from the qualities suggested in its very name. It is too slick by half, and lacks the excitement and experiment of, say, Steve Coleman and the Five Elements, who also avoid Slickaphonics's tendency toward the bland. **AS**

Bessie Smith

1925-33 **Smith** (v); **Louis Armstrong, Joe Smith, Ed Allen** (c); **Tommy Ladnier, Demas Dean, Frankie Newton** (t); **Charlie Green, Jimmy Harrison, Jack Teagarden** (tb); **Buster Bailey, Benny Goodman** (cl); **Garvin Bushell** (as); **Chu Berry, Coleman Hawkins, Greely Walton** (ts); **Fletcher Henderson, Clarence Williams, James P. Johnson, Porter Grainger, Fred Longshaw, Buck Washington** (p); **Eddie Lang, Bobby Johnson, Lincoln Conaway** (g); **Charlie Dixon** (bj); **Billy Taylor** (b); **June Cole, Cyrus St Clair** (bb). Hermes Ⓜ HRM 6003 (64 minutes). Recorded 1925-33.

✔ ⑩ ❽

If history had denied us the opportunity to hear any blues-singer but Bessie Smith, we should still think the blues a rich and subtle music. Knowing what we do, we realize that she also conferred on it a quality that most of her peers did not attempt or were unable to attain: a monumental grandeur.

It appears in almost all her work, from the marmoreal *Dyin' by the Hour* to the feisty *Lock and Key*; it is not confined to her weightier subjects or slower tempos, but rises equally from the resignation of *Nobody Knows You When You're Down and Out* and the hedonism of *Gimme a Pigfoot*. The weight and texture of her voice have something to do with it, but its essence is an authority derived from personal experience and an extraordinary command of the musical means of expressing it.

This selection is not quite perfect—although it includes the songs mentioned, it lacks *St Louis Blues* and *Young Woman's Blues*—but it admirably conveys her different moods and manners. It also couples her with her aptest associates: Armstrong, her own favourite Joe Smith, and also Tommy Ladnier and James P. Johnson. The transfers, made not from 78s but from new vinyl pressings from the original metal parts, are outstandingly clear. **TR**

Jimmy Smith

1925

Open House **Smith** (org); **Blue Mitchell** (t); **Jackie McLean** (as); **Ike Quebec** (ts); **Quentin Warren** (g); **Donald Bailey** (d). Blue Note Ⓜ CDP7 84269-2 (77 minutes). Recorded 1960.

✔ ⑧ ❿

Not until Smith arrived on the Blue Note record lists did the organ have a genuine jazz identity. Claims had been made on behalf of Fats Waller, Count Basie and Wild Bill Davis, but there was no traceable jazz language. Smith's switch from piano to organ in the mid-fifties changed that and in the process shored up a slightly ailing record label. His bebop on the organ reached New York in 1956 and he was an instant success. Here was a one-man combo; his feet were the bass line, his left hand the pianist's feeds and the right the solo horn improvisations. He used a greater variety of stops than his predecessors and made telling use of the instrumental devices unique to the organ. Initially he worked with a guitar and drum trio, but the advantage of added horns became obvious and this CD has him in fast company. Needless to say, he matches it blow for blow. He is found caressing the gentle curves of *Old Folks*, driving remorselessly on *Plain Talk* and providing an improvisational investigation of *My One And Only Love* that cannot be bettered, even by the impressive horn soloists present here. Smith had made the breakthrough; by the time of this session he had a legion of copyists and, some time later, Verve records would give him big band recording projects which would make him a worldwide household name by the mid-sixties. **BMcR**

Trio Salle Pleyel, May 28, 1965 **Smith** (org); **Quentin Warren** (g); **Bily Hart** (d). Europe 1 Ⓕ 710379-380 (two discs: 112 minutes). Recorded 1965.

⑧ ❼

After this, nobody can say they can't get enough of Jimmy Smith. The great organ revolutionary had two golden periods, the first with Blue Note, the second (immediately after) with Verve. The Blue Note period documented his rise from obscurity to international jazz star. The Verve period saw him become an international celebrity and *the* influence on a million Hammond organ freaks, no matter what music they played or where they played it. At present, the Blue Note years are reasonably well represented on CD, but the Verve years are poorly served, with one or two reasonable compilations, but of the original albums only **The Cat** and the second of the two Wes Montgomery summit meetings available to keep the faithful happy. That's what makes this such a good release: vintage Smith from his years of peak popularity, and what is more, it's 'live'. Verve didn't get round to recording Smith 'live' for another couple of years after this.

The organ grinder gets through some of his best-known pieces, including *The Sermon*, *Who's Afraid of Virginia Woolf?*, *Walk on the Wild Side* and *Organ Grinder's Swing*, and even opens the show with the title song from his great album with Kenny Burrell, **Blue Bash**. You won't want for excitement or thrills at this concert, and while it is not the most subtle date Smith has ever played, it's smack dab in the middle of the pocket. Recorded in mono. **KS**

Further Adventures of Jimmy and Wes **Smith** (org); **Wes Montgomery** (g); **Grady Tate** (d); **Ray Barretto** (perc); also 14-piece big band arranged and conducted by **Oliver Nelson**. Verve Ⓜ 519 802-2 (40 minutes). Recorded 1966.

⑥ ❽

'Further' because it was originally a follow-up to their successful album **Dynamic Duo**, currently unavailable. **Adventures**, however, is pitching it a bit strong. The atmosphere of the whole session is serene and laid-back, with Jimmy Smith revealing a lightness of touch and a feeling for subdued tone colours which must have come as a surprise to those who knew him only from his skirling, funky-bebop records. Montgomery's guitar is at its mellowest and, wrapped around with dark, woody organ tones, it imparts a wan, ethereal beauty even to a jaunty little tune like Roger Miller's *King Of the Road*. Everything is so tastefully and lovingly done that it hardly seems to matter that little is actually going on. There is nothing wrong with tunes like *Call Me* and *Maybe September*, but they do seem to induce a kind of languor in the participants. The producer, Creed Taylor, made a speciality of turning out records of the highest technical quality by the very best players, which were nevertheless intended not to be listened to too closely. This is a typical Creed Taylor product—not exactly background music, but not foreground music either—and as such it is not really typical of either Smith or Montgomery. On the other hand, only musicians of their calibre could have made it. **DG**

Johnny 'Hammond' Smith

1933

That Good Feelin'/Talk That Talk **Smith** (org); **Thornel Schwartz** (g); **George Tucker** (b); **Leo Stevens**, **Art Taylor** (d); **Oliver Nelson** (ts); **Ray Barretto** (perc). Prestige New Jazz/Beat Goes On Ⓜ CDBGPD 061 (70 minutes). Recorded 1959/60.

⑤ ❽

Smith has become—at least in England—something of a cult figure in recent years, largely as a result of his funkin' it up in the late sixties and early seventies. The vinyl changes hands for silly money. However, there is precious little of his material available on CD, and of that selection, this very generous coupling represents his most jazz-oriented approach to the best advantage. It reveals him to be, at the opening of the sixties, a player still greatly in debt to Wild Bill Davis, Milt Buckner and others, and still in the throes of plumbing the radical new Hammond Organ territory then being opened up by another fellow by the name of Smith. The 1959 session really is pretty turgid stuff, but *Talk That Talk* has a lot more going for it, not least the presence of that superior musician Oliver Nelson. Apart from this, Smith himself has moved up a gear and manages to swing quite convincingly, introducing the Jimmy Smith-patented blue phrases at every meaningful moment. For this reason it is enjoyable, unpretentious stuff, and certainly will not upset a quiet evening at home with the partner of your choice. **KS**

Keely Smith

1932

Spotlight on Keely Smith **Smith** (v); with orchestras arranged and conducted by **Nelson Riddle**, **Billy May**. Capitol Ⓜ CDP 7 80327 2 (61 minutes). Recorded 1957/58.

⑧ ❽

Keely Smith (born Dorothy Keely; her name was changed by her first major employer and future husband, Louis Prima) had only the merest of professional experience when at the age of sixteen she joined Prima's band in 1948. By the mid-fifties Prima and Smith were both professionally and personally a duo and opening in Las Vegas. Within a short space of time they were the toast of the town and under contract to Capitol. We must be grateful to Prima that his good musical taste and professional ethics allowed his wife to record not only the best songs available, but songs she actually wanted to sing.

The results are evident in this fine collection. If the arrangements more than hint at the Ella Song Books and the classic Sinatra albums then being recorded, this is no coincidence: Smith admired both singers, and they all shared the talents of Nelson Riddle and Billy May. That Smith has her own style and makes these versions of such standards as *You Go To My Head*, *I Can't Get Started*, *Someone To Watch Over Me* and *Stormy Weather* as distinctive as any others of her era is a tribute not only to her professionalism and talent, but to her integrity as an artist. Her clear, ringing voice, perfect intonation and graceful phrasing is perfectly joined with her expressive ability. This is an acute selection from her best period and a complete delight **KS**

Leo Smith

1941

Process Of The Great Ancestry **Smith** (t, flh, kalimba, v); **John Powell** (ts); **Bobby Naughton** (vb); **Louis Myers** (g); **Joe Fonda** (b, elb); **Mchaka Uba** (b). Chief Ⓕ CD6 (48 minutes). Recorded 1983.

✔ ⑧ ❽

A member of the Association For The Advancement of Creative Musicians, Smith formed the Creative Construction Company with Leroy Jenkins and Anthony Braxton in 1967. In the seventies he worked with an impressive list of free formers in his own New Dalta Ahkri. He played at London's Company event and occupies a very special role in free music; a trumpeter committed to self-expression at the possible expense of all other jazz virtues. As this CD demonstrates, he is also one of the most poignant of all musicians; he expresses himself with any sound that can be extracted from his horn, yet at times plays with a ringing clarity that calls to mind Miles Davis. The title-track here gives notice of his group awareness; there is a superb interaction between all involved but it is 'space' that comes over as the most potent ingredient. The tragedy of *The Third World* is captured in the highly distinctive timbre of his tone, while on *Celestial Sparks In The Sanctuary Of Redemption* emotional anguish is matched by the near-strangulated pain of note production as 'means' and 'result' come together. Naughton and Fonda have a good grip on the spatial needs of the group, but this remains an area of music off-limits to listeners expecting sequential logic in their jazz. **BMcR**

Lonnie Smith

1943

Drives **Smith** (org); **Dave Hubbard** (ts); **Ronnie Cuber** (bs); **Larry McGhee** (g); **Joe Dukes** (d) Blue Note Ⓜ CDP 828266 2 (36 minutes) Recorded 1970.

⑤ ❽

Smith - not to be confused with the keyboardist Lonnie Liston Smith who played with Pharoah Sanders and then went on to considerable fame in the crossover end of fusion - came to attention first with Lee Morgan, in whose group he played, and who appeared on his first Blue Note album, **Think!** (reissued on CD but now deleted). **Drives** comes from two years later and is unequivocally trailing its r&b and soul credentials across a set of instrumentals which includes a tough version of Blood, Sweat & Tears' big hit, *Spinning Wheel*. However, all is not groove, and there is a racy outing on Victor Feldman's *Seven Steps To Heaven* which demonstrates not only that Lonnie could pedal the bass line at horse-race tempo, but could also come up with some tasty improvising at the same time. Cuber and Dave Hubbard eat up the pulse in their solos, and a nice halving of the tempo through a vamp tag gives a bluesy outro, the band strutting off into the wings à la James Brown.

Smith is no mere touter of other people's clichés, although he has had no hesitation in using the popular modes of the day. He is still playing professionally, being a member of Lou Donaldson's band, and he recently surfaced on records playing as strongly as ever. An album on Mike Manieri's NYC label celebrating the Blue Note years called **Chartbusters** finds Smith also rubbing keyboards with John Scofield, Craig Handy and Lennie White. On the recent **Secret Agent Men** he was coupled with Rufus Reid, among others. **KS**

Louis Smith

1931

Strike Up The Band **Smith** (t, flh); **Vincent Herring** (as); **Junior Cook** (ts); **Kevin Hays** (p); **Steve LaSpina** (b); **Leroy Williams** (d). SteepleChase Ⓕ SCCD 31294 (70 minutes). Recorded 1991.

⑥ ❽

When he first recorded for Blue Note in the fifties, Louis Smith led bands including Tommy Flanagan, Cannonball Adderley and Duke Jordan, but he left a promising career with Horace Silver in the late fifties to become a schoolteacher, returning to recording only some 20 years later. Smith is a highly competent trumpeter with a pleasing enough sound, but who sometimes lacks sparkle and fire. Here, given material which includes too many over-familiar tunes unremarkably treated, the result is a competent but unspectacular session. The medium up-tempo tunes—including the only Smith original, an identikit hard-bop vehicle—are notable as much for their sidemen, the unflappable Junior Cook and ebullient young lion Vincent Herring, as for the leader, and indeed the contrasting styles of the two saxophonists—the elder all sly sophistication, the younger almost naïvely enthusiastic—provide much of what tension there is in the album. Left to himself on the ballad feature *Don't Misunderstand* Smith's relaxation verges on lugubriousness, and worthy as the music overall is, it never really catches fire. **CP**

Mike Smith

Unit 7 **Smith** (as); **Ron Friedman** (t, flh); **Sid Jacobs** (g); **Jodie Christian** (p); **John Whitfield** (b); **Robert Shy** (d); **Alejo Provedo** (perc). Delmark Ⓕ DD-444 (51 minutes). Recorded 1989.

⑧ ❽

Like his later album **On a Cool Night**, **Unit 7** showcases an alto style which owes a great deal—especially in its agility and power, its blues roots—to Cannonball Adderley. Here, this debt is made overt, the album dedicated to the late alto player and containing material with which he was associated. It is a tribute to Mike Smith's artistic integrity that he has managed to retain his individuality in this process. As Nat Adderley comments in his liner notes, Smith has managed to emulate without slavishly copying his chief influence on a selection of tunes ranging from the Sam Jones title-track through Randy Weston's *Hi Fly* to Adderley classics like *Work Song* and Bobby Timmons's celebrated *Dat Dere*. The overall group sound is less harsh and frenetic than Adderley's, particularly when the wonderfully laid-back and mellow-sounding Ron Friedman is compared with Nat Adderley, but the spirit and freshness of the original group imbues Smith's entire album with infectious vitality, enabling it to avoid completely the air of bloodless contrivance that often permeates such projects. Smith and his augmented rhythm section will win no prizes for adventurous innovation, but for gutsy, tight, well-arranged small-group jazz, they are hard to beat. **CP**

Stuff Smith

1909-1967

Stuff Smith-Dizzy Gillespie-Oscar Peterson Smith (vn); with, on eleven tracks: **Carl Perkins** (p); **Red Callender**, **Curtis Counce** (b); **Oscar Bradley**, **Frank Butler** (d); on nine tracks: **Oscar Peterson** (p); **Barney Kessel** (g); **Ray Brown** (b); **Alvin Stoller** (d); on five tracks: **Dizzy Gillespie** (t); **Wynton Kelly** (p); **Paul West** (b); **J.C. Heard** (d); **The Gordon Family** (v, one track). Verve Ⓜ 521 676-2 (two discs: 154 minutes). Recorded 1957.

⑦ ❽

Smith was born in Portsmouth, Ohio, and was already playing professionally in 1924. By the early thirties, after spending half a decade with the Alfonso Trent band, he was ready to set up his own small sextet, a band which played in and around Buffalo, New York. With Jonah Jones on trumpet, this band landed a spot at the Onyx Club and thereafer Smith's reputation was assured, making his first recordings in 1936, one of which, *I'se a-Muggin'*, was a hit. Like many swing stars, by the early fifties Smith had hit hard times, and this string of dates for Norman Granz was an oasis indeed for a somewhat forgotten man.

The first disc starts off with the Carl Perkins session. For a West Coast rhythm team these men accompany the hard-swinging Smith with crisp fire, and Perkins takes a number of typically neat, varied solos. The spotlight is kept firmly on Smith, who responds with the type of playing which made his reputation. His tone is thin and gritty, but this he uses to his advantage, manipulating it to give him attack and great rhythmic drive. It also enables him to avoid the tendency to saccharine or lugubrious expression which jazz violinists find hard to escape. Smith clips his notes and phrases more than, say, Grappelli, giving more forward momentum; he also allows pauses and rests to give pacing and variety to his playing. This all helps keep his solos consistently interesting, and he always swings. The tracks with Gillespie are all quite long, and are considerably more exotic than the rest of the programme, Gillespie quite clearly lending his big-band exprience to throw together some head arrangements (*Rio Pakistan, Purple Sounds*) which are unusually provocative for the time. The two main soloists work particularly well together while the Peterson trio in support do nothing wrong. One anomaly to point out: on the Peterson session without Gillespie (from which there are three previously unissued tracks, including a long but engaging *Body and Soul*), there is clearly a guitarist present (Barney Kessel, according to Ruppli) who is nowhere credited in the CD personnel listing, though he is mentioned in the liner notes. He takes a fetching blues-drenched solo on *In A Mellotone*. The Gordon Family add a vocal-harmony treatment of *Oh Lady, Be Good!* in a style which may have sounded fine in the forties, but was fast growing a cornfield by 1957. **KS**

Tab Smith

1909-1971

Jump Time Smith (ss, as, ts, v); **Sonny Cohn** (t); **Leon Washington** (ts); **Lavern Dillon**, **Teddy Brandon** (p); **Wilfred Middlebrooks** (b); **Walter Johnson** (d); **Louis Blackwell** (v). Delmark Ⓕ DD 447 (59 minutes). Recorded 1951/52.

⑥ ❻

Tab Smith is not exactly a name to conjure with these days, but he was a fine altoist who graced both the Count Basie and Lucky Millinder bands in the early forties, and a player who never deserted his original inspirations. On this, the first of a projected series of Delmark CDs covering Smith's 92 sides recorded for the United label from 1951 to 1957, the altoist's indebtedness to Hodges comes across loud and clear on the ballads (*Because of You*, his big hit, is virtual daylight robbery of Hodge's style), but his medium-tempo 'jump' playing is more cosmopolitan in its influences. Smith was someone playing jump music from a strictly jazz background, for there are no hysterics, no grandstanding and little hyperbole on these sides. Smith either sings a melody with a great deal of soul and panàche, or he swings a number against the drummer's back-beat as if he is still sitting in the Basie or Millinder sax sections. This is not front-rank music, but it is tasteful and eminently enjoyable for what it is. **KS**

Tommy Smith

1967

Misty Morning And No Time Smith (ts, ss); **Julian Argüelles** (as, ss); **Guy Barker** (t, monette); **Steve Hamilton** (p); **Terje Gewelt** (b); **Ian Froman** (d). Linn Records Ⓕ AKD 040 (70 minutes). Recorded 1994.

⑧ ❽

Amidst the windy rhetoric of the time, the horn-splitting, Coltrane-inspired tenor of the 17-year-old Tommy Smith on the 1984 **The Berklee Tapes** (Hep 2026) was one of the real revelations of the eighties jazz boom. Oddly, its intensity was in inverse proportion to the sponginess of Smith's subsequent first dates for Blue Note, but happily **Standards** (1991) indicated renewed focus, and **Paris** (1992) restated the old virtuosity and announced a striking writing talent.

That new strength of purpose is sustained and advanced in this outstanding second album for the Scottish label Linn. While referring often enough to the post-bop touchstones (Miles, Coltrane, Hancock, Tyner) which informed **Paris**, Smith also explores more esoteric, sometimes classical ideas, as on the stark, perhaps serialist, *Rag & Bone* and the bleak, Garbarek-ésque soprano duet *Two Friends*. Above all, as on **Paris**, welcome attention is paid to the totality of the music. Composition seems to be the watchword at every level, whether Smith is considering the programme sequence or the merest detail of voicing and instrumentation. There is generous space for the superb soloists, but improvisation is part of the means rather than an end in itself, and by sidestepping the blowing session mentality and heeding various non-jazz influences, Smith has considerably freshened the jazz sound palette. **MG**

Willie Smith

1910

Snooty Fruity **Harry James** (t); **Willie Smith** (as); **Corky Corcoran** (ts); **Ed Rosa** (cl); **Ziggy Elmer**, **Juan Tizol** (tb); **Arnold Ross**, **Stan Wrightsman**, **Bruce MacDonald** (p); **Ed Mihelich**, **Artie Bernstein** (b); **NickFatool**, **Jackie Mills** (d). CBS Ⓜ 4663643 2 (76 minutes). Recorded 1944-55.

✔ ⑨ ❼

Much of James's recorded output was compromised by 'commercial' music - although he came near to committing violence if *Sleepy Lagoon* or *Carnival In Venice* were so described. But there are no such problems with this, probably the most sterling collection of his music ever assembled. Because he kept his musicians for such long periods (Willie Smith for 18 years and Corky Corcoran for about ten) his band had a stable and characteristic sound. During the late forties he seems to have placed an emphasis on good jazz arrangements, and those are what is to be found here . Additionally every track features an alto solo from Willie Smith. Smith was a most potent alto player for whom the word 'wail' might have been invented. He, Benny Carter and Johnny Hodges dominated the field of the jazz alto saxophone in the post and pre-war period. Each of the three excelled apart from their solo abilities - in Smith's case it is arguable that, as well as being one of those soloists one always relished in anticipation, he was perhaps the finest big band lead alto player of all time. Smith was also a good arranger, but James professed, despite Smith's long tenure in his band, not to have known of Smith's gifts in this direction until after the alto player's death. James's own solos have weight and great power, and here he suborns the florid side of his work to concentrate on a meaty, attacking style that often reminds of Buck Clayton and Harry Edison. Corky Corcoran is an outstanding soloist out of the Hawkins school and both Ed Rosa and Ziggy Elmer, homely rather than glamorous, are most effective. Elmer lurches gratifyingly into Bill Harris country on East Coast Blues. Some of the longer tracks - notably a six and a half minute *Tuxedo Junction*,are especially attractive and the excellent section work on *Cottontail* bears testimony to the fact that a band which stays together plays together with admirable unity. James became rich with the 'commercial' numbers and it is much to his credit that he persisted at the same time with consummate jazz performances like these. The generous playing time is not wasted, and some of the tracks pack the wallop of a Basie or Herman group. **SV**

Willie 'The Lion' Smith

1897-1973

Willie 'The Lion' Smith and His Cubs **Smith** (p, v) with: on 12 titles **Ed Allen** (c); **Cecil Scott** (as, ts); **Willie Williams** (wbd); on four titles **Dave Nelson** (t); **Buster Bailey** (cl); **Robert Carroll** (ts); **Jimmy McLin** (g); **Ellsworth Reynolds** (b); **Eric Henry** (d); on eight titles **Frankie Newton** (t); **Buster Bailey** (cl); **Pete Brown** (as); **Jimmy McLin** (g); **John Kirby** (b); **O'Neil Spencer** (d, v). Timeless Ⓜ CBC 1-012 (69 minutes). Recorded 1935-37.

✔ ⑧ ❻

The Lion was one of the great Harlem stride pianists, a close friend of keyboard men such as Duke Ellington, Fats Waller and James P. Johnson. This chronologically programmed CD, containing four alternative takes from the two 1935 sessions with cornettist Ed Allen, brings together the products of five sessions. The ones with Allen are driven along in fine fashion by a two-man rhythm section comprising just The Lion (listen to that left hand!) and the impeccable washboard playing of Williams. The music is joyful and effervescent, just the kind of thing to keep the patrons happy at the Harlem speakeasys and after-hours clubs. One interesting discographical point; pianist Pat Hawes has pointed to the fact that there are two piano players on *Breeze (Blow My Baby To Me)* and suggests that it is Clarence Williams sharing the keyboard with Smith. The 1937 sessions have a different musical character and feature such excellent swing musicians as Frankie Newton, Pete Brown and Buster Bailey, but the strength of Smith's playing remains the important pivot. The clarity of the sound has been achieved by John R.T. Davies who was responsible for the remastering. **AM**

Gary Smulyan

Saxophone Mosaic **Billy Drewes**, **Ralph Lalama** (fl, cl, ts); **Dick Oatts** (fl, ss, as); **Scott Robinson** (bcl, bs); **Richie Perry** (ts); **Smulyan** (bs); **Mike LeDonne** (p); **Dennis Irwin** (b); **Kenny Washington** (d); **Bob Belden** (arr, cond). Criss Cross Ⓕ 1092 CD (55 minutes). Recorded 1993.

⑧ ❽

Pepper Adams lives, to judge by the playing of Gary Smulyan, who followed Adams into the Mel Lewis Jazz Orchestra. On this, as on his previous two Criss Cross sessions, he puts himself in an environment recalling his model. Jimmy Knepper and Tommy Flanagan were on the earlier volumes, while here the reed section of the Lewis/Vanguard Jazz Orchestra surround Smulyan's featured horn, which still sports a sure attack and honest feeling and comes out a bit from under Adams's shadow. The programme is choice, with a heavy emphasis on neglected jazz tunes from the fifties (Horace Silver's *Speculation*, Russ Freeman's *The Wind* and Quincy Jones's *Stockholm Sweetnin'* among them), placing the session more in the hard bop orbit the rhythm section has favoured on LeDonne's Criss Cross recordings than the late-middle Coltrane proclivities usually preferred by the saxophonists involved. Belden's arrangements are brisk and well-executed, succeeding in their intent to showcase the leader. The above-referenced LeDonne albums, two of which feature Smulyan and Tom Harrell, are also highly recommended. **BB**

Jim Snidero

Blue Afternoon **Brian Lynch** (t); **Jim Snidero** (as); **Benny Green** (p); **Peter Washington** (b); **Marvin 'Smitty' Smith** (d). Criss Cross Ⓕ 1072 CD (59 minutes). Recorded 1989.

⑥ ❽

Snidero's decade as the main alto soloist in Toshiko Akiyoshi's big band has tumed him into a robust and eloquent player whose heart is steeped in the Blakey tradition. This was the last of his three recording sessions with trumpeter Lynch (Snidero now works with the equally imposing Tom Harrell) and the power and range of the partnership gives this wide-ranging session its appeal. The opening fast tempo variation on *Speak Low*, which Snidero calls *Enforcement,* has him at his flag-waving best with a fast and ideas-packed solo, matched by a fiery one from the trumpeter. The ballad treatments of Mal Waldron's *Soul Eyes* and Shorter's *Infant Eyes* show Snidero's maturity and these are both outstanding performances. The Blakey feel is heightened by the drumming of Smith who, while not emulating Art in any way, keeps a similar control of the band by replacing Blakey's thunder with a busier precision which places more emphasis on the top of the drum kit. The piano role of Benny Green is restrained when it needs to be and very buoyant elsewhere, with the expected worthy solos. **SV**

Soft Machine

The Collection **Allan Holdsworth**, **John Etheridge** (g, elg); **Rick Sanders** (vn); **Alan Wakeman** (ts, ss); **Karl Jenkins** (p, elp, pianette, syn, ob, ss); **Mike Ratledge** (org, elp, syn); **Roy Babbington**, **Steve Cook** (elb); **John Marshall** (d, perc). Castle Communications Ⓜ CCSCD 281 (78 minutes). Recorded 1975-78.

⑥ ❽

By the mid-seventies, Soft Machine had largely abandoned the abstraction and free improvisation which had drawn critical acclaim for such early albums as **Third** (1970) in favour of the more formally constrained jazz-rock heard on this compilation of tracks from **Bundles** (1975), **Soft** (1977) and **Alive And Well in Paris** (1978). However, one of the group's chief distinguishing characteristics—a fascination with soloing over mesmeric pentatonic and blues vamps in such asymmetric time signatures as 7/8, 5/4 and 11/4—remained. This finally becomes wearying, but the **Bundles** tracks do feature Allan Holdsworth, still inchoate but with many elements of his style (and much of his renowned technique) about to crystallize. On the later two albums it often seems that John Etheridge is trying to step into Holdsworth's stylistic shoes, although, as *Camden Tandem* shows, he also sports a staccato McLaughlin-like attack. For all its edifying moments, the disc ends with Jenkins's *Soft Space,* Giorgio Moroder-styled electro-pop which sounds like a paraphrase of Donna Summer's *I Feel Love*. However, since Jenkins and Ratledge have spent the post-Softs years producing TV jingles, it seems a logical enough link in a career progression from experiment to orthodoxy. **MG**

Martial Solal

1927

Live 1959-85: The Best Solal (p); **Roger Guerin** (t); **Lee Konitz** (as); **Stephane Grappelli** (vn); **Paul Rovere**, **Gilbert Rovere**, **Niels-Henning Ørsted Pedersen** (b); **Daniel Humair**, **Charles Bellonzi** (d). Flat & Sharp Ⓕ 239963 (61 minutes). Recorded 1959-85.

⑧ ❻

Few pianists of any persuasion can boast of virtuosity the equal of Martial Solal. He is also a fascinating composer, having written piano concertos, chamber music, big band scores, extended suites, and solo pieces. Yet outside of France, where he is revered, he is probably better known as a sideman to the likes of Django Reinhardt, Sidney Bechet, Lucky Thompson, Stephane Grappelli or Lee Konitz. Considering the large number of recordings he has made, Solal's unique talents are under-represented on CD, so this potpourri of scattered performances from concerts and festivals is a good place to start, despite the uneven sound. NHØP, Konitz and Grappelli appear on only one track each, illustrating Solal's quick reflexes in parrying with the altoist on *Just Friends*, and providing solid support for the fiddler's brilliance on *Fascinating Rhythm*. His roots in Art Tatum and Bud Powell can be heard in his solo fantasias on *Sophisticated Lady* and *Night In Tunisia*—the latter especially becomes a patchwork quilt of quotes, counter-themes, and wildly chromatic episodes. His technique can be dazzling, but not always put to the best use; for example, his *Blue Danube* becomes a frothy Gershwinesque divertissement. For a fuller view of this remarkable artist, though, do try to hear one of his trio recordings and adventurous big band discs. **AL**

Improvisie pour France Musique **Solal** (p). JMS Ⓕ 18638-2 (2 discs: 125 minutes). Recorded 1993-94.

⑧ ❽

Solal is a prodigiously gifted musician who achieved the notoriously difficult feat of establishing his jazz credentials on both sides of the Atlantic during the fifties, a time when virtually all European musicians were seen as poor imitations of the original. Time has not dimmed his abilities, as this two-CD set of solo performances culled from over 40 recitals made for French radio amply demonstrates. Most often found in trio format, he has the technical and imaginative facility to surmount with ease any inherent difficulties to be found in a solo recital, and these two discs contain an avalanche of challenging and freshly-conceived thoughts on a well-chosen but unexceptional set of jazz standards. Solal has a completely personal style which amalgamates pieces of Tatum, Powell, Garner and Ellington with his own insights: time and again the listener is taken by surprise on material as well-worn as *Just You, Just Me* and *Tea For Two*. Solal is able to take such songs and completely re-cast their harmony, or just concentrate on a small fragment of the overall design and amplify that piece into a new and coherent whole, thus giving his audience a spellbinding lesson in spontaneous creation.

For those who want to explore this man's music further there is a five-CD box on the Erato label, the **Martial Solal Edition**, which contains not only a solo set and duet albums with Toots Thielemans and Michel Portal, but two CDs of his orchestral music, one dedicated to film music, the other to his piano concertos. Released only in France, it may be available on import in specialist stores. **KS**

Lew Soloff

1944

Little Wing **Soloff** (t); **Ray Anderson** (tb); **Gil Goldstein** (p, syn, acc); **Pete Levin** (org, syn, vocoder); **Mark Egan** (elb); **Kenwood Dennard** (b); **Manolo Badrena** (perc). Sweet Basil/Bellaphon Ⓕ 660 55 015 (65 minutes). Recorded 1991.

⑥ ❽

In recent years, Lew Soloff has been most visible as a dynamic hard bop trumpeter on several Nippon-generated straightahead dates. However, his experiences in the New York studios through the seventies and in Blood, Sweat & Tears and the later Gil Evans Orchestras also left him well-equipped for the funkier line of work heard here. Soloff has a first-class technique, but he does not fit the studio archetype, all chops and no taste; his virtuosity is married to an impeccable aesthetic sense and a strikingly wide range of expression. Thus he is able to deliver the tightly-phrased theme of Kenwood Dennard's *La Toalla* with absolute precision, and follow it with a loose-knit solo rich in perfectly controlled vocal effects. His versatility is also apparent on *Coral Canyon*, where he affects a muted sound reminiscent of Miles Davis before shifting to a rounded flügel-like tone. Trombonist Ray Anderson might have a less formidable technique, but in sharing an interest in the vocal potential of his horn he makes the ideal front-line partner for Soloff. There are also fine solos from Gil Goldstein on Orlando Lopez's *Para Los Papinos* (wrongly credited to Don Alias) and Mark Egan on *Little Wing*, a theme that was virtually a signature tune for the later Gil Evans Orchestra. **MG**

Eddie South

1904-62

Eddie South 1923-37 **South** (vn, v); **Walter Wright**, **Stephane Grappelli**, **Michel Warlop** (vn); **Jimmy Wade** (c); **William Dover** (tb); **Arnett Nelson** (cl, as); **Vernon Roulette** (cl, ts); **Clifford King** (cl, bl, as); **Sterling Conway**, **Django Reinhardt**, **Roger Chaput**, **Mike McKendrick** (g); **Everett Barksdale** (bj, g, v); **Teddy Weatherford**, **Antonia Spaulding** (p); **Louis 'Buddy' Gross** (bb); **Milt Hinton**, **Wilson Myers**, **Paul Cordonnier** (b); **Edwin Jackson** (d); **Jerome Burke** (d, v); **Jimmy Bertrand** (d, perc); **Nino** (v). Classics Ⓜ 707 (72 minutes). Recorded 1923-37.

✔ ⑧ ❻

A child prodigy on violin, South studied under Charles Elgar and at the age of 20 became musical director of Jimmy Wade's Syncopators in his adopted town. As the 1923 *Someday, Sweetheart* shows, he was already a mature soloist, his phrase shapes capturing something of the Armstrong magic and his solos built with genuine musical logic. In 1928 he led his own band to Europe and introduced another continent to his superb brand of jazz violin. The driving solo on *Doin' The Raccoon* is typical, but on his return to America in the early thirties he did not always fully grasp his recording opportunities. Items like *La Rosita* answered Depression-hit America's call for compensatory schmaltz, even if the jazz hand was kept in shape with the impressive *Nagasaki* and *Gotta Go*. This CD also documents his 1937 European visit and the superb partnership he forged with Reinhardt, especially on *Sweet Georgia Brown* and *Somebody Loves Me*, which are models of creative construction. His throbbing *Eddie's Blues* is proof that his ability to hit the crown of a note was no barrier to emotional projection or the ability to swing. He remains, along with Joe Venuti, Stuff Smith, Leroy Jenkins and Billy Bang, one of the five giants of jazz violin. **BMcR**

Jeri Southern 1926-91

Southern Breeze **Southern** (v); **Frank Beach**, **Don Fagerquist** (t); **Bob Enevoldsen** (tb); **Vince DeRosa** (frh); **John Kitzmiller** (tba); **Herb Geller** (as); **Georgie Auld** (ts); **Jack Dulong** (bs); **Bill Pitman** (g); **Bud Clark** (b); **Mel Lewis** (d); **Marty Paich** (arr). Fresh Sounds Ⓕ FSR-CD104 (39 minutes). Recorded c. 1959.

⑧ ❽

Miles Davis is supposed to have scouted this stage-shy singer's albums for tunes no less vigilantly than he did Sinatra's and Ahmad Jamal's, and she tied with Annie Ross as a new star in Down Beat's first critics' poll, in 1953. Yet her electronic cameo (singing *Ev'ry Time We Say Goodbye*) on Charlie Haden's **Haunted Heart** in 1992 was probably the first that most contemporary jazz fans had ever heard of her. Southern's lack of jazz recognition has much to do with her withdrawal from performance in the early sixties, but even more to do with the widening of the gap between jazz and pop in the last three decades. Southern was more a pop singer than a jazz singer, which is to say she in no way improvised or riffed on a song. But if there is such a thing as jazz *feeling*, and if it is mostly a question of phrasing, she had it in abundance. She rivalled Davis, Sinatra, and Chet Baker in setting a mood with a ballad. Even her slight lisp worked in her favour, adding to the virginal shiver she could bring to a love song. The ideal introduction to Southern would be **You Better Go Now**, a reissue of her first LP (named after her first and biggest hit), last in print on Official, a label from Denmark. Although lacking the intimacy of those performances on which Southern accompanied herself on piano and seemed to be singing as much to herself as to the listener, this date with what amounts to a choir of brass and woodwinds is an agreeable substitute. **FD**

Muggsy Spanier 1906-1967

The 'Ragtime Band' Sessions **Spanier** (c); **George Brunies** (tb); **Rod Cless** (cl); **Ray McKinstry**, **Bernie Billings**, **Nick Calazza** (ts); **George Zack**, **Joe Bushkin** (p); **Bob Casey** (g, b); **Pat Pattison** (b); **Marty Greenberg**, **Don Carter**, **Al Sidell** (d). RCA Bluebird Ⓜ 366550 2 (67 minutes). Recorded 1939.

✔ ⑧ ❽

Alun Morgan has observed that music contained on this collection "has served as the best introduction to real jazz for several generations of collectors," and it is indeed a pleasure to acknowledge its late arrival on the shelves, just in time to beat the publishing deadline. Reissue producer Orrin Keepnews claims this to be "the first American compilation to include all existing alternative takes. It may even be the first anywhere...I do know that there is no evidence of metal parts having been requested from the vaults in this country, so this is in any case the first all-original-parts CD." Certainly the sound quality has benefited greatly from having the metal parts to work from. The combination of the CEDAR system of noise suppression and superior originals means that little presence or sparkle has been removed from the upper tonal characteristics. The 24 tracks here make up the complete sessions which created 'the great 16' of 1939, the two sessions of eight tracks apiece which pleased contemporary fans so much.

Of course, the music on this disc bears little resemblance to Ragtime. This is New Orleans courtesy of Chicago, no frills, plenty of drive and melody, and none the worse for it. Spanier sticks mostly to the theme, leaving the tricky bits in between mostly to his reeds and piano, but this only helps the flow and variety of these short, powerful swingers. For those unaccustomed to the type of music Spanier played, it is unassuming but driving thirties small-group jazz of the very best kind. **KS**

James Spaulding 1937

Gotta Be A Better Way **Spaulding** (as, f, pic); **Monte Croft** (vb); **Mulgrew Miller** (p); **Ron Carter** (b); **Ralph Peterson** (d); **Ray Mantilla** (perc). Muse Ⓕ MCD 5413 (55 minutes). Recorded 1988.

⑦ ❽

Following early experiences with Sun Ra, Spaulding moved to New York in 1962. Since then he has been something of a perpetual sideman. He has worked with Freddie Hubbard, Art Blakey, Horace Silver and Bobby Hutcherson and has only rarely fronted a recording date. This CD has him leading an impressive line-up and taking full advantage of a fine Miller-led rhythm section, with its Peterson power base. The arrangements are a trifle perfunctory, but Spaulding's fiercely propulsive alto bites hard into *Bold Steps*, *Little Niles* and the title track. His shrill flute lines dance their way through *Ginger Flower Song* and flatter the languid *Remember There's Hope*, while his attacking piccolo adds its spark to *In Flight Out*. Whatever the horn, the language is hard bop and Spaulding ensures that full weight is given to the adjective as well as the noun. His solos do not have gentle contours but they are all well-constructed and there is an excitement about nearly everything he does. The little-known Croft impresses in all of his solo opportunities but it is Spaulding, allowed the driving seat for once, who puts his own brand on a useful showcase for his often undervalued talents. **BMcR**

Sphere

Pumpkins Delight **Charlie Rouse** (ts); **Kenny Barron** (p); **Buster Williams** (b); **Ben Riley** (d). Red Ⓕ 123207-2 (55 minutes). Recorded 1986.

⑦ ❽

This group was formed in 1982 by the four musicians involved here. It was dedicated to the memory of Thelonious Sphere Monk and the choice of title was a mere formality. Rouse and Riley had been stalwarts of Monk groups for many years, but Barron and Williams's commitment to the project was equally steadfast. As this CD shows, no attempt is made merely to play Monk's themes or to simulate the sound of a Monk quartet. Barron is particularly careful to avoid the minefield that has led to the downfall of countless would-be Monks. He plays pure Barron quite brilliantly and is at the heart of a very accomplished quartet. Williams's beautiful tone lights up every track, Riley bristles to order and Rouse shoulders a good share of the solo responsibilities. The tenor saxophonist's strangely stifled tone is well on show and titles like *Tokudo* and *Christina* in their different ways both suggest that there is something of the latter-day Coleman Hawkins in a style reputed to belong to Monk bebop. In the early days of their association, certain critics thought the partnership inappropriate. In practice, however, Rouse's near swing-era-style phrasing and strangulated sound seemed to fit the deliberately sour temper of Thelonious's music ideally. Sphere kept that tradition intact. **BMcR**

Spontaneous Music Ensemble

Karyobin **Kenny Wheeler** (t, flh); **Evan Parker** (ts); **Derek Bailey** (g); **Dave Holland** (b); **John Stevens** (d). Chronoscope Ⓕ CPE 2001 2 (50 minutes). Recorded 1968.

✔ ⑧ ❼

Formed in 1965, the SME proved to be an important training ground for British modernists of the day. Initially it reflected the then-flourishing New York-style avant-garde movement, but it was not long before Karyobin documented a turning point in the group's policy. As they struck out along their own very distinctive path, they sought a more total commitment to freedom. Stevens was nominal leader and he had an important part to play. He made no attempt to calibrate the music in a vertical manner, and it was his control of rhythmic displacement which fuelled its linear progression. Wheeler's flashing runs and Don Cherry-like flurries maintained earlier traditions while Parker had already begun to extend his free developments well beyond the melodic intent of American freeformers. Holland's full tone and rhythmic elasticity served all well and Bailey was giving notice of a new guitar language that was to stamp him as one of the most important improvisors of his generation. The Ensemble and its brother group Amalgam (with Trevor Watts) remained active through the seventies and still re-assembles for concerts today. Although all five musicians were to become better players this initial foray was still an excellent recording in its own right, indicating the extent of the influence this group had in Europe and the UK during its existence. **BMcR**

Jo Stafford

1920

Jo Plus Jazz **Stafford**(v) with the following collective personnel: **Ray Nance**, **Don Fagerquist**, **Conte Candoli** (t); **Lawrence Brown** (tb); **Johnny Hodges** (as); **Ben Webster** (ts); **Harry Carney** (bs); **Russ Freeman** (cel); **Jimmy Rowles** (p); **Bob Gibbons** (g); **Joe Mondragon** (b); **Mel Lewis** (d); **Johnny Mandel** (arr). Corinthian Ⓕ COR 108 CD (42 minutes). Recorded 1960.

⑥ ❻

Jo Stafford was one of the Pied Pipers with Tommy Dorsey before moving on to become a solo artist and recording under her own name for Capitol and Columbia. She appears to have perfect pitch and her intonation is one of the remarkable aspects of her work, along with her clear diction and keen rhythmic understanding. She is not, in the narrowest sense, a jazz singer but is very content to allow jazz to happen around her, playing her part as the academically correct singer of the lyrics. This is her very successful involvement with high-flying jazzmen, four of them (Nance, Hodges, Brown and Carney) from the Duke Ellington orchestra plus that noted ex-Ellingtonian Ben Webster. It is Ben who gets most of the instrumental solo space here, closely followed by the individual trumpet work of Don Fagerquist. Johnny Hodges takes beautiful solos on *Just Squeeze Me* and, of course, *Day Dream* where his creamy sound adds a truly Ducal atmosphere. Jo's singing is perfect in this context, helped by Rowles's expert accompaniment (and occasionally Russ Freeman's celeste) and a very obvious love for the chosen songs, which include gems such as *Midnight Sun*, *Imagination* and Ellington's neglected *I Didn't Know About You.* Issued originally on Columbia and Philips, this has now reappeared on Stafford's own label. **AM**

Marvin Stamm

1939

Mystery Man **Stamm** (t, flh) **Bob Mintzer** (ts); **Bob Malach** (ss, ts); **Bill Charlap** (p); **Mike Richmond** (b); **Terry Clarke** (d). MusicMasters Jazz Ⓕ 65085-2 (66 minutes). Recorded 1992.

⑧ ❽

Stamm's playing will be familiar to followers of the Stan Kenton, Woody Herman, Duke Pearson, Oliver Nelson, Thad Jones-Mel Lewis big bands and countless other studio-formed units. This is the best showcase to date of his talents as small-band leader, trumpeter and flügelhorn soloist. "This is a 'live-in-the-studio' recording, no overdubbing," Stamm writes in the notes and there is certainly a lot to be said for the immediacy of performances which actually took place as we hear them on record. Marvin is not only a most fluent soloist but is also the possessor of a lovely sound on ballads. He additionally knows how to pick suitable tunes; four of the ten tracks are by European-based writers, two apiece by Kenny Wheeler and Sweden's Lars Jansson. A sextet is present on three tracks (the accompanying notes identify the two tenors where necessary) with various groupings on the remaining titles. This is contemporary music which retains strong links with what has gone before; Jansson's thoughtful *Marionette* produces exceptional trumpet and piano playing from Stamm and Bill Charlap. Strongly recommended. **AM**

Marc Steckar

Steckar Tubapack–Tubakoustic **Steckar**, **Christian Jous** (euph); **Philippe Legris**, **Daniel Landreat** (tba); **Didier Havet** (sousaphone); **Franck Steckar** (p, perc); **Ramon Lopez** (d, perc). Ida Ⓕ 024 CD (48 minutes). Recorded 1989.

⑦ ❽

Tuba choirs are in short supply, so we ought to be grateful for the perseverance of Marc Steckar's group, whose third album and first CD release this is. We should be doubly grateful that this is a carefully-prepared session as well, with many originals from the Steckars, plus fetching arrangements of a couple of Ellington's better known pieces (*In a Sentimental Mood* and *Caravan*). The inclusion of a piano and drums helps immeasurably in pinning the whole thing together and giving the date proper forward momentum, freeing the arrangements up no end. There is a glorious euphony (no pun intended) in the combined sounds of euphoniums and tubas together and these men certainly know how to exploit that sound. In addition, nothing is awkward; everything flows, whether in solos or ensembles. No pink elephants here. **KS**

Jeremy Steig

1942

Outlaws **Steig** (f); **Eddie Gomez** (b). Enja Ⓕ 2098 2 (39 minutes). Recorded 1976.

⑥ ❻

Skilful and committed as Jeremy Steig and Eddie Gomez are, this recording of a German duo concert never completely commands the attention. This fatal lack of bite may be partly due to the inescapably ethereal nature of the flute itself in any hands other than Roland Kirk's, although Steig does manage to produce unusually gutsy and rhythmic sounds from it, particularly in Miles Davis's *Nardis*, with which the album concludes. But most probably its lack of grip on the listener can be attributed to the somewhat rambling, unfocused nature of the material. Both the informal improvised duo pieces and the two solo features pale in comparison with *Nardis*, which explores textural variety through the use of electronics and elicits punchy performances from both men. Gomez's taut, sinuous growl perfectly complements Steig's breathless harmonic and rhythmic daring, but it is too little, too late in the context of the album as a whole. The echoey sound quality, too, does the album no favours, serving only to emphasize the effete, over-diffuse nature of the music. **CP**

Steps Ahead

Yin-Yang **Mike Mainieri** (vb, synth, perc); **Steve Khan**, **Jimi Tunnell**, **Chuck Loeb**, **Dean Brown**, **Wayne Krantz** (g); **Bendik**, **Rick Margitza** (ts); **Rachel Z.** (p, synth); **George Whitty** (synth); **Bruce Martin** (synth, perc); **Jeff Andrews** (b, elb); **Victor Bailey** (elb); **Steve Smith** (d). NYC Ⓕ 6001 2 (62 minutes). Recorded 1991

⑥ ❽

In the beginning, around 1980, Steps Ahead music was referred to as 'acoustic fusion', but within five years, almost all the band had plugged in and it had started producing brassy, synth-dominated electric funk. Although this album has its banging backbeats, the busy and rather superficial hi-tech sound which dominated such albums as the 1986 **Magnetic** has given way to a more considered approach and a more eclectic repertoire, as if the new Steps Ahead, which Mainieri announced in the late eighties, has finally settled into its stride. Its broad stylistic compass sweeps from the stealthily altered funk blues of *Nite Owl* to two driving small-group bop tracks, one of which, *Gory Details*, is redolent of something Bobby Hutcherson might produce. With the exception of Mainieri, who is consistently strong, the latest edition of the band lacks soloists of the calibre of such earlier incumbents as Michael Brecker and Eddie Gomez, but Rick Margitza is a good Brecker-styled soloist, and the Scandinavian saxophonist Bendik is effective too, blending a haunting Garbarekian lyricism with something of Brecker's funk. The set has its routine moments, but on balance it presents a comprehensive picture of the styles essayed by Steps Ahead over the years. **MG**

Leni Stern

Secrets Stern (g); **Bob Berg** (ts); **Wayne Krantz** (g); **Dave Tronzo** (slide g); **Lincoln Goines** (elb); **Harvie Swartz** (b); **Dennis Chambers** (d); **Don Alias** (perc). Enja Ⓕ CD 5093-2 (48 minutes). Recorded 1988.

⑦ ❽

Stern plays a Fender Strat with great skill and imagination and is one of very few jazz guitarists to favour this instrument over the Gibsons and Gretschs of this world. She uses the earthy, shallow sound it produces naturally to great effect, generating a tone which is both flexible and highly vocalized without being too derivative of the legions of rock heroes who made the Strat their own. All but one of the tracks on the album are written by her, and she exhibits a flair for melodic composition which makes the album very easy to listen to repeatedly. Like most of the latter-day guitarists, she is not afraid to bend a note (an approach which largely seemed to disappear from jazz guitar for about two decades), so her improvisations over blues or minor chord sequences are especially piquant. Bob Berg's muscular saxophone adds a pleasing contrast to Stern's approach and gives the album a balance which Stern was clearly looking for. An accomplished and spirited record. **KS**

Mike Stern

1953

Standards (And Other Songs) Stern (g); **Bob Berg** (ts); **Randy Brecker** (t); **Gil Goldstein** (kbds); **Jay Anderson, Larry Grenadier** (b); **Al Foster, Ben Perowsky** (d). Atlantic Ⓕ 782419-2 (62 minutes). Recorded 1992.

③ ❽

This is one for those who heard nothing but rock 'n' roll in Mike Stern's early eighties playing with Miles Davis. Even in those highly amplified environs it was apparent that Stern knew more than the Jimi Hendrix licks Miles had commissioned from him. The other element in his playing—there for anyone who cared to listen beyond the rock dynamic and sonority—was bebop. Stern has cited among his favourites Jim Hall and Wes Montgomery, and in the late eighties, while he was producing high-octane fusion albums for Atlantic, he also ran a weekly trio gig at 55 Christopher Street in lower Manhattan, playing standards. He is heard in a similar setting here, flexing his bebop chops to a length they cannot always stand. The effect is initially convincing, but a few moments into the first solo it becomes apparent that although Stern has a command of the mannerisms and gestures of bebop, his playing could benefit from more rhythmic and melodic variety and a stronger sense of dramatic structure. His solo on *Nardis* is perhaps the best example of what can happen when those elements come into play. However, the session never lacks warmth or passion, and that quality is augmented on some tracks by top New York horn men. **MG**

John Stevens

1940

Re-Touch & Quartet Stevens (d); **Trevor Watts** (ss); **Jeff Young** (p); **Allan Holdsworth** (g); **Barry Guy, Ron Mathewson, Ron Herman** (b); **Julie Tippetts** (v, g). Konnex Ⓕ KCD 5027 (66 minutes). Recorded 1971-77.

⑧ ❼

Stevens is a important figure in European jazz, not only for his leadership of the Spontaneous Music Ensemble and other bands, but also for the inspiration he gave to a generation of European drummers. Originally inspired by Max Roach, Phil Seaman and Elvin Jones, he fashioned a style of free drumming very much his own. He was a founder member of the SME in 1965 and this CD presents two contrasting versions of the group. The 1971 edition has subtle rhythmic accents from Herman and Stevens scurrying behind Tippetts's anguished voice and Watts's fluent soprano. Stevens was keen on using the human voice at this time and *One, Two, Albert Ayler* was one of Tippetts's most expressive contributions. *No Fear* offers one of Stevens's gentle brushes with post-Miles Davis electronics, with Young and Guy imaginative as the play-makers, and Holdsworth's superbly fleet improvisations making their own special mark. It was a session with the occasional gentle moment which also shows that Stevens never surrendered to the throb of rock drums. Whatever the emotional temper of the music, he remained the dynamo around which all of his groups revolved, even in the calmest moments. **BMcR**

Rex Stewart

1907-73

Rex Stewart and The Ellingtonians **Stewart** (c); **Joe Thomas** (t); **Lawrence Brown** (tb); **Barney Bigard** (cl); **Otto Hardwick** (as); **Harry Carney** (bs); **Billy Kyle**, **Jimmy Jones** (p); **Brick Fleagle** (g); **Wellman Braud**, **John Levy**, **Billy Taylor** (b); **Dave Tough**, **Cozy Cole**, **Shelly Manne** (d). Riverside Ⓜ OJCCD 1710-2 (35 minutes). Recorded 1940-46.

⑧ ❻

It has been noted under entries for Duke Ellington that Stewart was an under-rated composer. He had a knack for atmospheric and original blues mood pieces—the genre is here represented by *Solid Rock*, so beautifully graced by vivid solos from the leader, Billy Kyle, Barney Bigard and Lawrence Brown, and the wistful *Blues Kicked The Bucket*. Bigard and Stewart always seem to have recorded well together—the clarinettist achieved peaks with Stewart that are otherwise only to be found in his work with Ellington. His voluptuous solos on the four tracks here by Stewart's Big Seven are amongst his best.

A session of four tracks by Stewart's Big Four is not as well recorded as the others. Two tracks by Jimmy Jones's Big Eight (without Stewart) have been included as makeweight to the LP which in CD form is short on playing time. One, a beautiful ballad called *A Woman's Got A Right To Change Her Mind*, is notable for a barrel-chested solo from Harry Carney in one of his rare appearances away from the Ellington band. The other track is interesting for early bop-tinged drumming from Shelly Manne and another rummaging solo from Carney. **SV**

Slam Stewart

1914-87

Two Big Mice **Stewart** (b, v); **Major Holley** (b, v); **Hank Jones**, **Gerry Wiggins** (p); **George Duvivier** (b); **Oliver Jackson** (d). Black & Blue Ⓕ 59 124 2 (59 minutes). Recorded 1977.

⑥ ❻

Stewart is usually credited with the popularizing of the singing and playing style of bass work, anathema to many dedicated jazz enthusiasts but undoubtedly a great crowd pleaser. Six of the tracks here have Stewart with another bowing-singing bassist, Major Holley, plus George Duvivier to keep time (he also takes the occasional solo). With such a plethora of 'novelty' bass playing it is best to sit back and enjoy it, for it is all very musical and extremely good fun. Slam sings an octave above the notes he bows, Major in unison (for he has a deeper voice); both men have very good intonation and are adept at inserting amusing quotations into their solos. Added to that there are the occasional, and quite beautiful, solos from Hank Jones. On five tracks Stewart drops out and Wiggins takes over at the keyboard. There is less bowing-singing here; in fact the tender *Lush Life* is virtually a feature for Wiggins, who treats the tune with considerable respect. On both sessions the recording engineer has captured the depth and resonance of the basses with clarity. **AM**

Sonny Stitt

1924-1982

Prestige First Sessions **Stitt** (as, ts, bs) with various personnel including **Bill Massey** (t); **Eph Greenlea**, **Al Outcalt**, **Matthew Gee** (tb); **Gene Ammons** (ts, bs); **Kenny Drew**, **Duke Jordan**, **Junior Mance**, **Charles Bateman**, **Clarence Anderson** (p); **Tommy Potter**, **Gene Wright**, **Earl May** (b); **Art Blakey**, **Jo Jones**, **Teddy Stewart** (d); **Teddy Williams**, **Larry Townsend** (v). Prestige Ⓜ PCD 24115-2 (69 minutes). Recorded 1950-51.

⑦ ❻

Stitt's closeness of conception to Charlie Parker, and the comment it provoked, got to him so severely that for a number of years around the end of the forties and beginning of the fifties he rarely ventured forth on the alto, so intent was he on showing daylight between himself and Parker. That this plan was only partially successful can be judged by the fact that everyone still comments on how close Stitt's playing on alto was to Bird. C'est la vie. I happen to prefer his tenor playing, so the feast of Stitt tenor on this disc sits well with me. For one thing, it stresses his allegiance to Parker's avowed model, Lester Young. The ballad-playing on this album such as *Mean to Me* and *Stairway to the Stars* (all initially released as 78s, of course), has even taken over the slightly lost, hesitant quality Young acquired later in his career, as his confidence and health began to fail. On faster tempos Stitt carves out a more individual niche, his muscular and harmonically-sophisticated style in clear focus, his solos bristling with ideas which are an individual amalgam of all his initial influences. The extra weight of the tenor gives him more forward thrust and offers the listener more visceral thrills than his alto playing, so this early set of performances, still wholly within the original bebop framework, becomes a record to be listened to for pleasure as well as for being a valuable piece of bop history. **KS**

Sits In With The Oscar Peterson Trio **Stitt** (as, ts); **Oscar Peterson** (p); **Ray Brown** (b); **Ed Thigpen**, **Stan Levey** (d); **Herb Ellis** (g). Verve Ⓜ 849 396-2 (51 minutes). Recorded 1957-59.

⑧ ❽

On the basis of his considerable volume of work on record, Sonny Stitt was seldom, if ever, off form, with the performance level heightened by the quality of the rhythm section available, but Sonny could drag even a weak team along with him. Needless to say he is immaculately served here by two different Peterson Trios (with drummer Levey added to the 1957 edition), and it is fascinating to observe the slight changes in style when he switches from alto to tenor. On the smaller saxophone he subdivides the beat like Charlie Parker and takes off like a rocket on the faster tempos. He plays tenor on three tracks from the 1959 date and immediately drops slightly behind the beat, like Lester Young. His tenor playing on a blues and the Trummy Young tune *Easy Does It* are highlights on this recommended album, but all the saxophone playing is exemplary. The original LP has been fleshed out with three previously-unissued titles, which might have been limbering up exercises for the **Only The Blues** date (with Roy Eldridge added) which took place a few hours later. Peterson and his cohorts provide faultless and very helpful support throughout, and the remastering gives the music an immediacy which is exhilarating. **AM**

Billy Strayhorn

1915-1967

...And His Mother Called Him Bill **Strayhorn** (arr); **Cat Anderson**, **Herbie Jones**, **Mercer Ellington**, **Cootie Williams** (t); **Clark Terry** (flh); **Lawrence Brown**; **Chuck Connors**, **Buster Cooper** (tb); **John Sanders** (vtb); **Johnny Hodges** (as); **Russell Procope** (as, cl); **Jimmy Hamilton** (ts, cl); **Paul Gonsalves** (ts); **Harry Carney** (bs); **Duke Ellington** (p, arr); **Aaron Bell**, **Jeff Castleman** (b); **Steve Little**, **Sam Woodyard** (d). RCA Bluebird Ⓜ ND 86287 (61 minutes). Recorded 1967.

⑦ ❻

No conventional X-plays-Y tribute for, although performed by and issued as the Ellington orchestra of the day, this was the organization for which Strayhorn's compositions were first conceived. To enhance the symbiosis, for one session each Duke added Clark Terry and the valve-trombone of Sanders, sounds unavailable since their departure from the band in 1959.

Robert Palmer's notes have useful pointers to Strayhorn's elusive musical identity and this is an impressive collection of his shorter pieces. Some of the innovations include the concealment of 32-bar song-forms on *Raincheck* (from 1941) and *Midriff* (1945)—both heard in uncut versions—and the orchestrating of piano stab-chords for trombones in *Rock-Skippin' At The Blue Note* (1951, some years before Gil Evans popularized the idea). In addition there are some wonderful solos, including Carney's on *Lotus Blossom*—originally rejected in favour of Duke's informal solo, which is also included—and several vehicles for Hodges, who turns *Blood Count* into a passionate lament for the late composer.

Very close miking and/or inexpert mixing on some tracks compares unfavourably to the 'natural' blend of the *Far East Suite*, done mere months before. Nevertheless, the warts-and-all immediacy is part of the album's unique aura. **BP**

String Trio of New York

Time Never Lies **James Emery** (g); **Charles Burnham** (vn); **John Lindberg** (b). Stash Ⓕ 544 (69 minutes). Recorded 1991.

✔ ⑩ ❽

The String Trio of New York's initial reputation was based on extended improvisation and an open compositional format that integrated elements of freedom. They recorded only original material on their first five albums. But in 1986 Charles Burnham replaced violinist Billy Bang, which seemed to provoke a reconsideration of their repertoire. **Time Never Lies** is their second disc to incorporate refreshing takes on jazz standards, exotic (including Asian and Middle Eastern effects) originals, and seldom-encountered items by the likes of Bud Powell and Charles Mingus. Though they may have sacrificed some of the exploratory verve of their early days, they've consolidated their many and varied influences into a satisfying, tunefully accessible identity. The juxtaposition, for example, of the southwestern swing of Ornette Coleman's *Ramblin'* (which reflects the STNY's roots in the small string bands, black and white, of the twenties and thirties, like the Tennessee Chocolate Drops and the Hackberry Ramblers) with the 'sophistication' of W.C. Handy's *St. Louis Blues* (performed both bluesily and 'jazzed up') is striking, energized by Burnham's expressive technique and Emery's bent notes and slides. Their links to the Reinhardt/Grappelli Hot Club tradition are displayed on *Honeysuckle Rose*, and bebop is recast in prickly timbres on Bud Powell's *Celia*. A nearly flawless disc. **AL**

John Stubblefield

1946

Countin' On The Blues **Stubblefield** (ts, ss); **Hamiet Bluiett** (bs); **Mulgrew Miller** (p); **Charnett Moffett** (b); **Victor Lewis** (d). Enja Ⓕ 5051 (46 minutes). Recorded 1987.

⑧ ❽

In the early part of his career Stubblefield was something of a chameleon, as much at home in support of the Drifters as he was in the Jones/Lewis reed section. He worked with Charles Mingus and Miles Davis but in neither set-ups did the real Stubblefield surface. This CD is probably his best. It is pitched in the 'consolidation of free' field, using some of the vernacular of sixties free jazz but tempering it with a large amount of hard bop know-how. Although capable of playing lines usually associated with high-note trumpeters, he makes sparing use of multiphonics. He teams well with Bluiett and lets the excellent rhythm section get on with its work. The quality of his solos on both horns is impressive. His tenor puts the backbone into a ballad like *Those Who Didn't Know*, hints at the romantic on *My Ideal*, but forges real steel in the blues duel on the title track. *Remembrance* has his soprano dancing elegantly over Miller's brawny chordal calibrations, while on *Montauk* he sets out his own structural patterns. The reason for his successful involvement with the World Saxophone Quartet, George Russell and the under-rated McCoy Tyner big band becomes obvious as the listener becomes increasingly aware of his improvisational conviction, his genuine emotional commitment and his relaxed rhythmic authority. **BMcR**

Ira Sullivan

1932

Nicky's Tune **Sullivan** (t); **Nicky Hill** (ts); **Jodie Christian** (p); **Victor Sproles** (b); **Wilbur Campbell** (d). Delmark Ⓕ DD-422 (44 minutes). Recorded 1958.

⑥ ❹

Sullivan was an elusive multi-instrumental marvel on Chicago's modern scene in the fifties, then he became even more elusive by moving to the Miami area in the early sixties. Only when he rejoined an early associate, Red Rodney, in 1980 did Sullivan receive some of the attention he deserved. This session, one of the very few under his name, is indicative of the muscular hard-bop slant of several Chicago regulars, many of whom suffered the same familiar problems that formerly kept Sullivan off the scene and all of whom were competitive with more frequently recorded New York peers. Hill's presence keeps the leader confined to trumpet, however. Too bad Delmark has not made its other Sullivan session of similar vintage, most recently available on LP as **Blue Stroll** (DL-402), available on disc. It includes Johnny Griffin with the same rhythm section and features a spirited jam on which the latter plays alto, tenor and baritone saxes while Sullivan is heard on trumpet, peck horn, alto and baritone. **BB**

Maxine Sullivan

1911-1987

Swingin' Sweet **Sullivan** (v); **Scott Hamilton** (ts); **Chris Flory** (g); **John Bunch** (p); **Phil Flanagan** (b); **Chuck Riggs** (d). Concord Ⓕ CCD 4351 (50 minutes). Recorded 1986.

✔ ⑧ ❽

It may seem perverse to recommend the last recording of a 75-year-old singer, but Maxine Sullivan was a most remarkable woman. In 1937 her record of *Loch Lomond* made her as popular as Ella Fitzgerald was later to become. Her speciality was gentle swinging versions of folk songs and old ballads like *Nellie Gray*, charming but very lightweight. From those early records it is obvious that she was capable of much more. Being a supremely level-headed and well-adjusted person, she gave up show business when it stopped being either profitable or enjoyable and trained as a school health counsellor.

When she finally returned to full-time performing she was approaching her 60s and it was this second career that brought out the real artistry in Maxine Sullivan. Changing musical fashion had completely passed her by and she simply took up where she had left off. She was born four years before Billie Holiday, but far from deteriorating with age her voice had matured and warmed, and her natural sense of swing responded wonderfully to the relaxed rhythms of modern mainstream jazz.

Her accompanists on this 1986 concert recording, made in Japan, are the Scott Hamilton Quintet, and she sings with a relaxed grace that has rarely been heard since the swing era. The vital link between jazz and American song was rarely more conclusively or delightfully demonstrated. **DG**

Stan Sulzmann

1948

Feudal Rabbits **Sulzmann** (ss, as, ts, f); **Mick Hutton** (b); **Patrick Bettison** (elb); **Steve Argüelles** (d). Ah Um Ⓕ 011 (54 minutes). Recorded 1990.

⑥ ❻

Almost half of this album by one of Britain's most consistent and inventive reed players is taken up by Sulzmann's suite *Owen's Field*. All but two of the remaining five tracks are also by Sulzmann. The rather unusual instrumentation of drums, double bass and electric bass also means that, tonally and melodically, Sulzmann has to carry the bulk of the performances here, so this is very much his album. Both bassists and Arguelles acquit themselves admirably, but further variety would enrich an already impressive album, and perhaps in the process provide an even better showcase for Sulzmann's talents. His work over the years with NYJO and the London Jazz Orchestra suggest that he is a soloist who excels against the tonal backdrop of a large band, and although he is both exposed and energetic here, this is just one aspect of a player whose talents cover a broader field. **AS**

Sun Ra

1914-1993

Jazz in Silhouette **Sun Ra** (p); **Hobart Dotson** (t); **Julian Priester** (tb); **Marshall Allen**, **James Spaulding** (as, f); **John Gilmore** (ts); **Pat Patrick** (bs, f); **Charles Davis** (bs); **Ronnie Boykins** (b); **William Cochran** (d). Evidence Ⓔ ECD 22012-2 (45 minutes). Recorded 1958.

⑨ ❽

In 1992 Evidence reissued 13 early Sun Ra recordings, first released on his own Saturn label, that had been virtually impossible to find for almost 30 years. Beautifully repackaged and with the original sound quality much improved, these albums confirmed Sun Ra's reputation as the most brilliant big band leader of the post-bebop era. The batch of 13 LPs (accommodated on ten CDs) included 1963's weirdly wonderful **Cosmic Tones For Mental Therapy** and 1961's **Interstellar Low Ways**, arguably the first masterpieces of Ra's embryonic space-age jazz. The real surprise, however, was **Jazz In Silhouette**, which showed just how adept Ra could be in more traditional areas, though already enhancing the music with his distinctive touches and colours.

His swing roots are evident (*Hours After*), as is his assimilation of bebop (*Saturn*, *Horoscope*), but more fascinating is his ability to create the uncategorizable frisson of, say, *Enlightenment*, with its sumptuous baritone sax lines, brass/reed counterpoints and darting excursion into Latin bop. Another captivating hybrid is *Ancient Aiethiopia*, which does point to the future with its percussive polyrhythms and free passages, though no less striking is the elegant trumpet solo by the underrated Hobart Dotson. There are strong solos too by John Gilmore (*Saturn*, *Blues At Midnight*) but the emphasis, characteristic of Ra, is on a highly-disciplined group-playing to match those early big bands which, like the Ancient Egyptian civilization to which his music so often makes reference, represented for him a pinnacle of black achievement. **GL**

The Heliocentric Worlds Of Sun Ra, Volumes 1 and 2 **Sun Ra** (p, cel, clavioline, bass mba, timp, perc); **Chris Capers**, **Walter Miller** (t); **Teddy Nance**, **Bernard Pettaway** (tb); **Marshall Allen** (pic, f, as, perc); **Danny Davis** (f, as); **John Gilmore** (ts, perc); **Pat Patrick** (bs, perc); **Robert Cummings** (bcl, perc); **Ronnie Boykins** (b); **Jimhmi Johnson**, **Roger Blank** (d, perc). ESP-Disk Ⓜ 1014/17-2 (35 and 37 minutes, oas). Recorded 1965.

✔ ⑩ ❼

These two discs, although recorded seven months apart, fit together like the halves of a Chinese painted screen, and the picture we see when they are combined is a view of the future. Although he had broken with song form to explore new organizations of sound a year or two earlier (on-hard-to find Saturn LPs **Cosmic Tones For Mental Therapy** and **Other Planes Of There**, now reissued on Evidence), these ESP discs reveal him experimenting with a new approach to arranging based on disciplined freedom. The shorter performances on Volume One plot a drastic change in the relation between instruments, distinct from recognizable jazz interaction. These are tone poems with a chamber music approach to dynamics, colours and textures, the material organized by spontaneous cues. The search for new sonorities led him to a particularly mysterious, dark sound (with bass marimba, bass clarinet, bass trombone, timpani and acoustic bass prominent—Ronnie Boykins is the unsung hero here). The result is largely arhythmic, with atonal lines, harmonic clusters and starkly dramatic contrasts of timbres. On volume two Ra puts this concept into the framework of the full band, extending the music longer (with the exception of *Other Planes Of There*) than he had ever previously recorded. On *The Sun Myth* and *Cosmic Chaos* the full band plays fractured rhythms; their individual lines do not coalesce but intersect in free polyphony. This seems the precedent not only for larger ensembles like Globe Unity, but also the spontaneous 'conduction' of Butch Morris. (The personnel listed above is compiled from both discs; actual personnel differs slightly, but not significantly, between the two. The refurbished sound quality is quite good, considering the originals.) **AL**

Sunrise in Different Dimensions **Sun Ra** (p); **Michael Ray** (t); **Marshall Allen** (as, ob, f); **Noel Scott** (as, bs, f); **John Gilmore** (ts, cl, f); **Kenneth Williams** (ts, bs, f); **Danny Thompson** (bs, f); **Chris Henderson**, **Eric Walker** (d). hatART Ⓔ 6099 (71 minutes). Recorded 1980.

⑧ ❻

In the seventies, Sun Ra added something new to his Arkestra's psychedelic mix of antic spectacle and free jazz: a brace of thirties swing tunes—five from Fletcher Henderson's book here, two from Ellington's—which fit right in, being pitched on the same riotous energy level. Sun Ra, like Ellington and other smart leaders, let key soloists set much of the band's style. Standouts include trumpeter Ray, a solid lead player with an arsenal of special effects at his command, and glissando-master Allen, whose note-bending skills unite his abrasive tea-kettle squeals and affectionate recreations of Johnny Hodges's soothing blues.

The raucous swing and bop covers illuminate the leader's piano style, with its hot flashes of early jazz devices and Hinesian chaos. Despite his deft stride and penchant for close-interval dissonances, on '*Round Midnight* he owes little to composer Monk.

This concert recording is atypical in two ways. The touring band is roughly half the size of the full Arkestra, although with five saxes it can summon appropriate bluster. More critically, in reducing two LPs to one CD, hatART regrettably dropped the chant *On Jupiter*, featuring vocalist June Tyson, one of the Arkestra's signature stylists. There was room for it. **KW**

Live At The Hackney Empire **Sun Ra** (p, kbds, v); **Michael Ray** (t, v); **Jothan Callins** (t); **Tyrone Hill** (tb); **Marshall Allen** (as, f, pic, ob); **Noel Scott** (as, bcl); **John Gilmore** (ts, cl perc, v); **Charles Davis** (bs); **James Jackson** (bn, perc); **India Cooke** (vn); **Kash Killion** (vc); **John Ore** (b); **Earl 'Buster' Smith**, **Clifford Barbaro** (d); **Talvin Singh** (tab, v); **Elson Nascimento** (perc); **June Tyson** (v). Leo Double CD Ⓕ LR 214/15 (two discs: 149 minutes). Recorded 1990.

⑦ ❻

Too much of Sun Ra's discography is taken up by indifferent live concert recordings in the Arkestra's final years. There was suspicion of pirate label activities in certain cases and some issues were inferior both in terms of musical performance and sound quality. This CD is found wanting on neither count and presents the Year 2000 Myth Science Arkestra playing near to the top of its game.

The leader's piano is prominent throughout, producing his own unique brand of stride and, on *Blue Lou*, actually sounding like Basie. His arrangements offer an 'over-view', ranging from the blues band sound of *Skimming And Loping* to the exotic and almost Ellingtonian *Sunset On The Nile*. Riffs are used judiciously on *Planet Earth Day* and *Frisco Fog*, a string trio plus tabla suggest a contemporary spasm band on *Astro Black* and *String Singhs*, while the rattling percussion and permutation of vocal chants make their customary appearance. The trumpet division apart, the quality of the solos is high. The strings of Cooke and Killion are used sensitively and, although the extrovert sax parts are left mainly to Allen, all of the reeds play well. Cognizance is taken of individual needs and despite failing health, Sun Ra ensures that each musician is showcased appropriately. **BMcR**

Supersax

Plays Bird **Med Flory** (as, ldr); **Conte Candoli**, **Ray Triscari**, **Larry McGuire**, **Ralph Osborne** (t); **Charley Lopez**, **Mike Barone**, **Ernie Tack** (tb); **Joe Lopes** (as); **Warne Marsh**, **Jay Migliori** (ts); **Jack Nimitz** (bs); **Nonnell Bright** (p); **Buddy Clarke** (b); **Jake Hanna** (d). Capitol Jazz Ⓜ CDP7 96264-2 (37 minutes). Recorded 1972.

⑥ ❻

Maybe only a collection of studio musicians would ever think of scoring Charlie Parker's alto solos for a full sax section, then building a book of arrangements and a band around them. Maybe only someone with the dedication of leader Med Flory and bassist/transcriber Buddy Clarke could find the time to do it.

This material works best if you don't know that it is transcribed from solos. It is a set of fiendishly difficult charts, supremely well executed, with the long loping saxophone lines having an internal logic and an architectural integrity which sounds composed not spontaneous. Sometimes the scoring makes Bird's improvisational genius sound ponderous—*Hot House* lumbers, rather than flashing with inspiration. But Parker's blues genius comes over well, Parker's *Mood* having a far bluer sound to its phrases than a similarly transcribed Gillespie or Davis solo might. This band is at its best with the full brass section (Candoli alone does the brass duties for all but three tracks). On *Just Friends* the warm-toned brass is cunningly scored to wrap round the harsher, more angular reed lines to produce a genuinely original piece of jazz. **AS**

John Surman

1944

Such Winters of Memory **Surman** (ss, bs, bcl, rec, p, synth, v); **Karin Krog** (v); **Pierre Favre** (d). ECM Ⓕ 1254 810 621-2 (46 minutes). Recorded 1983.

✔ ⑩ ❿

Odd that this, one of Surman's most complete efforts, has taken the longest to appear on CD from his back-catalogue, arriving only in the summer of 1993, almost ten years after its recording date. It may be that the tack Surman takes on each of his fascinating albums for ECM determines one's reaction to them and that, independent of subjective viewpoints, they are all as good as each other. However, I hold a torch for this one. Surman seems to have been in outstanding solo form and also seems to be happy to give us plenty of himself as a soloist, which is not invariably the case on his own albums. His compositions are perhaps better described as frameworks, but they are uncommonly evocative frameworks at that, and set him enough problems and points of stimulus for the listener to be grateful that his compositional mind works in that way. He has a sure gift for memorable and oddly dignified melody, often built on whole-tone steps much in the way that Coltrane's were, and it seems therefore appropriate that there is a compelling solo piano rendering of the initial theme of Coltrane's tune *Expression*.

Surman has pursued a mostly solitary creative path for the last couple of decades, and one that has taken him away from Britain a great deal, but he is quite probably Britain's greatest post-Coltrane musician working in an avowedly modern idiom, and it is a triumph for everyone concerned that this album could never in a million listenings be mistaken for New Age music, regardless of instrumentation or the number of synthesizer patterns set up. As Ira Gitler said in a very different context, "This is jazz, Jim." **KS**

The Brass Project **Surman** (acl, bcl, ss, bs, p); **Henry Lowther**, **Steve Waterman**, **Stuart Brooks** (t); **Malcolm Griffiths**, **Chris Pyne** (tb); **David Stewart**, **Richard Edwards**, **Andrew Waddicor** (btb); **Chris Laurence** (b); **John Marshall** (d, perc); **John Warren** (cond). ECM Ⓕ 1478 (517 362-2) (62 minutes). Recorded 1992.

⑨ ❾

Surman formed the Brass Project with John Warren in 1981. With the trio of Surman, Laurence and Marshall acting as a focal point, the plan was for Warren to cue in the brass section "when the trio's improvisations needed it". This notion proved unworkable in practice so the tracks here, on the group's début CD, are more carefully arranged. In the event, Warren has deployed his forces with great skill, whether blending them into bright, sumptuous textures or pitting them against each other in thrilling two and three-part rhythmic counterpoint.

One of the chief pleasures of the record is to hear Surman rekindle the excitement of his youthful glory days in the Mike Westbrook big band. He is superb blowing against a large ensemble, his baritone riding the punchy groove of *Wider Vision*, the soprano darting above the racing brass lines of *Tantrum Clangley*. His fondness for pastoral moods reemerges on *Coastline*, but there is an unexpected dabble in more abstract areas on *Spacial Motive* and the multi-tracked *All for a Shadow*. The brass sound magnificent, with notable solo contributions from Henry Lowther and Stephen Waterman. A bold contrast to the private reflections of his solo records, **The Brass Project** stands among Surman's most ambitious and original works to date. **GL**

Ralph Sutton

1922

Last Of The Whorehouse Piano Players (The Original Sessions) **Sutton**, **Jay McShann** (p); **Milt Hinton** (b); **Gus Johnson** (d). Chiaroscuro Ⓕ CR(D) 206 (71 minutes). Recorded 1979.

✔ ⑧ ❽

As to the question of its fitness to be in a Basic Jazz Library, "it's a resounding yes," as Philip Larkin might have said. It is difficult to imagine that this is not what the jazz deity who invented the music had in mind when he first thought it up. The combination of melody, good extemporization and perfect, swinging rhythm is completely irresistible. Ignore the sensationalist title, demeaning to both the sensitive and shy Ralph Sutton and to his guest McShann. The music is happy piano which rolls from stride to boogie and deep blues. More importantly, it is as good as you will get in any of these idioms, *pace* James P. Johnson and Fats Waller. *Little Rock Getaway* is only one of several tours de force, the two men distilling beautiful melody in a slow section before racing away in the best Sullivan manner. Sutton came along a little later than Willie The Lion, Fats and James P., but even though he emerged after Jess Stacy, Joe Bushkin and Mel Powell his devotion is to the earlier ticklers and he is a throwback of the most welcome kind.

McShann must not be downgraded in all this, for he matches Sutton in every bar, and probably has not made a better recording. Apart from his fine blues and boogie he also gets a chance to sing (as does Sutton). A perfect jazz partnership in action here, with veterans Hinton and Johnson suitably inspired by the occasion. **SV**

Steve Swallow

1940

Real Book **Swallow** (b); **Tom Harrell** (t, flh); **Joe Lovano** (ts); **Mulgrew Miller** (p); **Jack DeJohnette** (d). Watt Ⓕ XTRAWATT 7 (521 637-2) (50 minutes). Recorded 1993.

⑧ ❿

Steve Swallow himself describes this album as an attempt to capture the feeling he associates with the original *Real Book*, "of friends meetings to leaf through the book and work out a few tunes to see where they lead." That there were no rehearsals, and few takes needed, is a tribute both to the professionalism of the band assembled and to the limpid clarity of the tunes—all by Swallow—they were asked to play. They range from bustling themes with bright horn arrangements through to bluesy or Latin-tinged informal readings from Swallow's state-of-the-art studio band. The front-line soloists are in particularly good form; Joe Lovano plays with his customary cultured approach, all bustling querulousness laced with occasional moments of fluting tenderness; Tom Harrell is almost unrivalled in contemporary jazz for purity of tone, precision of intonation and sheer flair and sure-footedness. The rhythm section with Swallow and Mulgrew Miller discreetly alternates between crisp comping and fluent, sparkling solos with unruffled aplomb. Jack DeJohnette is constantly active, alive to every rhythmic nuance. A first-class album by a supremely accomplished band. **CP**

Lew Tabackin

1940

What A Little Moonlight Can Do **Tabackin** (ts, f, af); **Benny Green** (p); **Peter Washington** (b); **Lewis Nash** (d). Concord Ⓕ CCD 4617 (58 minutes). Recorded 1994.

⑧ ❽

Lew Tabackin is a man with considerable big band and studio experience but his tenor and flute are equally at home in the jazz combo. An inmate of various orchestras over the years, he has in more recent times worked with smaller units. An early influence was Sonny Rollins but (as this CD demonstrates) he now has a style of his own. *Love Letters* and the title track admit to the inspiration but show that Tabackin is creatively driven at any tempo. *Easy Living* squeezes choice tenor saxophone oratory between a challenging cadenza and a dashing coda to confirm his sense of formal presentation, while on *Poinciana* he transforms a straight theme statement into pure jazz with only a modicum of phrase re-emphasis and contour adjustment. *The Dream's On Me* gently simmers with a trace of Ben Websterish romance, whereas *Dig*, cooked from an old style bebop receipe, shows how effortlessly he lends fluency to an angular line. The high standard of his writing is confirmed by *Broken Dreams* and he endorses that theme's inherent quality by developing its melody line into an equally coherent solo. He fully merits the excellent rhythmic support he enjoys here and he remains a player with few rivals in his chosen area of jazz. **BMcR**

Jamaaladeen Tacuma

1956

Live In Köln **Tacuma** (b); **Walter Wierbos** (tb); **Paul Van Kemenade** (as); **Jan Kuiper** (g); **Cornell Rochester** (d). Timeless Ⓕ CD SJP 421 (70 minutes). Recorded 1993.

⑤ ❽

Tacuma fits comfortably into absolutely no stylistic homestead. He sang doo-wop in his youth, played with organ trios and happily embraced soul bands. In 1975, he went harmolodic with Ornette Coleman and his own first album reflected that influence. His relationship with Coleman's Prime Time was an on-off affair but he looked in a similar musical direction with the likes of Blood Ulmer. He is probably most at home in a heavy funk environment but he can be relied upon to confuse the issue by taking propulsive and inventive solos.

On this CD he is joined by Podium 3 and Rochester, a drummer who infallibly makes rock verticalities swing. As *Mo's Mood* emphasizes, the Dutch three are essentially jazzmen but they do know the harmolodic route and, with Tacuma to drive them along, there is a potent alchemy. The funk element puts the power into the other titles but jazz is never neglected and the bassist shows his own solo agility most especially on *Mr. Monk*. He does not once spurn his rhythm section responsibilities, however, and it is doubtful if Podium 3 has ever been more rhythmically focused. Tacuma dance band dates have always remained important to him but, for every one of them, there is probably a more challenging one such as this. **BMcR**

Aki Takase

Shima Shoka **Takase** (p). Enja Ⓕ 6062-2 (60 minutes). Recorded 1990.

⑦ ❽

Aki Takase has recorded a handful of discs in intimate settings—including with string quartet, duos with vocalist Maria João and saxophonist David Murray. Yet the best showcase for her impressive talents is solo, where she exhibits a bright, percussive touch and fluid ideas. She also has good taste in repertoire (Ellington, Mingus, Rollins, Coltrane and Carla Bley) to which she brings surprisingly fresh viewpoints. For example, her harmonic approach to Duke's *Rockin' In Rhythm*, a lively stride romp, may be that of a Modernist, but even the staunchest trad fan would have to admire her strong left hand. Elsewhere she attaches an elegiac prelude to *Goodbye Porkpie Hat* and turns *Giant Steps* into an episodic tour de force. Most expressive is her interpretation of Carla Bley's rhapsodic homage to actress and film director *Ida Lupino*, where Takase first plants a thicket of moody, noirish chords, then proceeds on a long chromatic journey, drifting in and out of relation to the theme. Her own compositions have not quite the same bite or substance, and none of them blossoms with the delicacy of detail and adept handling of transparent themes she brings to husband Alex von Schlippenbach's *Point*. Takase's thoughtfulness and willingness to take a risk place her among a select few. **AL**

Horace Tapscott

1934

The Dark Tree, Volumes 1 and 2 **Tapscott** (p); **John Carter** (cl); **Cecil McBee** (b); **Andrew Cyrille** (d). hatART CD Ⓕ 6053/83 (60 and 68 minutes, oas). Recorded 1989.

⑧ ❽

A pianist, composer, arranger, educator and leader of the Pan-Afrikan People's Arkestra, Horace Tapscott has been a major force on the Los Angeles music scene for the last 30 years. His decision to work within the local community has resulted in his neglect by the mainstream record business, although his rare sixties LP **The Giant is Awakened** was reissued by Novus in 1991 as one half of their **West Coast Hot** CD. In the last decade Tapscott has recorded more prolifically, making several fine solo albums for the tiny Nimbus label, but to date little of this music has made the transition to compact disc.

The Dark Tree is his most recent release. The two discs (available separately) come from a series of live concerts and feature some of Tapscott's best-known compositions, titles such as *Lino's Pad, Sketches of Drunken Mary* and *A Dress For Renée* underlining his claim that his music's concern is with the everyday struggles and dreams of black people in America. Tapscott has cited his mother (a stride pianist), Art Tatum, Andrew Hill and Vladimir Horowitz as his chief keyboard influences. From these sources he has forged a richly personal style that is terse, dramatic and lyrical by turn; brittle, haunting tunes skewed over brooding ostinatos. His solo albums best reveal the filigree charms of this style but on *The Dark Tree*, spurred by a strong rhythm section and John Carter's wailing clarinet, Tapscott is at his most compelling, the piano dancing through fierce riffs, cascading phrases, sinuous runs. **GL**

Buddy Tate

1915

The Ballad Artistry of Buddy Tate **Tate** (ts, cl); **Ed Bickert** (g); **Don Thompson** (b); **Terry Clarke** (d). Sackville Ⓕ CD 2-3034 (70 minutes). Recorded 1981.

⑦ ❽

An extrovert tenor saxophonist in the territory bands of Terrence Holder, Andy Kirk and Nat Towles, Tate gained International recognition when he replaced Herschel Evans in the Count Basie Orchestra in 1939. Since then he has carried the mainstream banner through the world and recorded with a large number of the music's major league players. This CD presents him doing what he perhaps does best. On *A Foggy Day* he is the swaggering jam session cavalier, but for most of the remainder he shows his way with a ballad. His style is untouched by the bebop revolution and his respect for the details of original melodic lines denies him access to the outer limits of improvisational extravagance. He literally nurtures titles such as *Isfahan* and *Laura* and his Ben Websterish assignation with *Darn That Dream* shows how he makes a breathy, softly contoured examination of a pretty tune into a serious piece of jazz workmanship. He is helped in mood setting by an excellent Canadian trio, Bickert an articulate guitarist, Thompson a fleet fingered bassist and Clarke an unobtrusive wielder of the brushes. In the eighties a growing army of neo-swingers emerged but Tate remains the genuine article and newcomers need only listen to the simple art of melody inversion found on *Kiss To Build A Dream On* to hear a minor master parading his skills. **BMcR**

Art Tatum

1909-1956

Classic Early Solos (1934-37) **Tatum** (p). MCA/Decca Ⓜ GRP 16072 (58 minutes). Recorded 1934-37.

⑧ ❻

When Tatum was heard by travelling musicians in his native Ohio, and when he arrived in New York backing Adelaide Hall, he seemed too good to be true. His concentration on musical sound focused by his extremely restricted vision, he had the kind of technical command of an instrument that was unheard of until Parker and Coltrane, both of whom listened to him avidly.

In addition, he had seemingly absorbed everything he needed from the showy stride piano of Johnson and Waller and the rhythmic independance of Hines, as these 1934 tracks demonstrate (only the last four are from 1937). Less noticed immediately except by other musicians, a harmonic sophistication equal to Ellington's was lurking in the background, and what contemporaries made of touches such as the coda to the first *After You've Gone* or the whole-tone passages in the second *Liza* is anyone's guess.

Remastering uses the NoNOISE system, now largely abandoned in favour of CEDAR, and while the piano sound is reasonably consistent, it is quite thin. In addition, several items (not just the few alternate takes) have continuous surface sound, from which the piano is a fortunate distraction. **BP**

1935-43 Transcriptions: The Standard Sessions **Tatum** (p). Music & Arts Ⓕ CD 673 (two discs: 149 minutes). Recorded 1935-43.

It really is very difficult to point at a series of Tatum recordings and say "these are sub-par", because Tatum simply didn't make sub-par records. There were times when what he did was run-of-the-mill for him, according to his own high standards, or when he was saddled with less than congenial helpmates and turned out distracted, insular work, but these are relatively few in what is a substantial legacy.

These recordings come from radio transcriptions which were never intended for commercial release. They cover the years when Tatum first came to the attention of the wider public and so impressed his audience and peers that he even managed a bit part in a Hollywood movie (playing night-club piano in The Dorsey Brothers Story). Much of this double set contains numbers also recorded by Tatum for the American Brunswick and Decca labels at around the same time, and comparisons between the two reveal that Tatum often had set arrangements of songs from which he deviated only slightly on any given performance. This does not lessen the worth of any particular track; it just means that Tatum worked very hard at his material to arrange it according to his own needs and taste. What he evolved were performances no other pianist could come near, couched in a quasi-orchestral conception that no other pianist in jazz, Earl Hines included, had begun to dream of.

The sound quality often leaves something to be desired, due to the poor condition of the originals. **KS**

The Complete Capitol Recordings, Volumes 1 and 2 **Tatum** (p); **Everett Barksdale** (g); **Slam Stewart** (b). Capitol Ⓜ CDP7 92866/67-2 (two discs: 84 minutes). Recorded 1949-52.

✔ ⑩ ❹

Art Tatum signed for Capitol Records in 1949 and from then until 1952 produced the titles to be heard on these two CDs. All were recorded for 78 rpm issues and as a result were restricted to little more than three minutes. Despite this, Tatum played at his brilliant best, treating each parent melody to a breathtaking improvisational face-lift. He imbued the rather trite *Dardanella* with stature, turned Rubinstein's *Melody In F* into a swing classic and made any other piano treatment of *Someone To Watch Over Me* seem like a travesty. Every aspect of the jazz piano art is on view: there is the ineluctable power of his striding left hand, the brilliantly-articulated treble runs and, above all else, the architectural perfection of his re-designs. His command of the instrument is awesome and the listener becomes increasingly aware of a harmonic sophistication matched by an unpredictable rhythmic audacity. Despite the time constraints and the complexity of improvisations, many of these Capitol versions became blueprints for all subsequent Tatum performances of these tunes. **BMcR**

The Complete Pablo Solo Masterpieces **Tatum** (p). Pablo Ⓜ 7PACD 4404-2 (seven discs: 503 minutes). Recorded 1953-56.

✔ ⑩ ❻

Thanks to impresario Norman Granz, Art Tatum recorded more music in the last three years of his life than in the previous 21. The solo titles, which appeared originally as 13 LPs, are the product of four marathon record sessions at which Art was given complete freedom in terms of choice of material, tempos, lengths of performances, etc. It was Granz's idea to place as much of Tatum's artistry on record before it was too late. This package comprises 119 of the 121 tracks previously issued on the LPs, omitting *Blues In My Heart* and *I Gotta Right To Sing The Blues* but adding the four solo performances from Art's Hollywood Bowl appearance less than three months before his death. (Note: this applies to the copy under review, but a later edition of the **Solo Masterpieces**, with the same catalogue number, contains all 121 solos and the four Hollywood Bowl titles. The reader is advised to check carefully before buying.) It goes without saying that this is an important body of recorded work in which Tatum worked his way through established material such as *Elegie, Tea For Two, Sweet Lorraine* etc. but the set also includes no less than 20 songs which Art never recorded at any other time, tunes such as *The Way You Look Tonight, You're Blasé, I've Got A Crush On You* and *There's A Small Hotel.* Unhampered by other musicians, Art is allowed to change key, tempo and the direction of his extemporizations at will, for it was as a solo performer that he really excelled. The sheer volume of his output here may have a daunting effect on listeners who have not immersed themselves in this man's genius, but the advice is to persevere; you will not hear a finer, more complete and wholly talented jazz pianist than Art Tatum. The remastering, by Danny Kopelson, has resulted in the best sound yet; the Pablo LPs were disappointing and not as good as the old British Columbia Clef albums. There is occasional tape hiss, but the full resonance of the instrument has been preserved. **AM**

The Tatum Group Masterpieces **Tatum** (p); **Benny Carter** (as); **Louie Bellson** (d). Pablo Ⓜ PACD 2405-424-2 (71 minutes). Recorded 1954.

⑧ ❽

These elegant takes of Tatum's pianistic genius came just two years before his death. And although part of the 'Group Masterpiece' series produced by impresario Norman Granz, which also included teamings of Tatum with trumpeters Roy Eldridge and Harry 'Sweets' Edison, tenor saxophonist Ben Webster, clarinettist Buddy De Franco, vibraphonist Lionel Hampton, bassists Red Callender and Larry Simmons, and drummers Alvin Stoller, Buddy Rich, Jo Jones and Bill Douglass (available in the eight-CD box set, **The Complete Pablo Group Masterpieces**), the juxtaposition of Tatum with alto saxophonist Benny Carter and drummer Louie Bellson is arguably the most compatible of the 'group' couplings.

Here, one senses a level of emphatic interplay where everyone listens—and responds. Yes, Tatum the nonpareil virtuoso is front and centre with his fabled feather touch, unerring sense of swing and dazzling right-hand runs all on display. But also on hand is Tatum the supportive accompanist, a far less appreciated aspect of his overall musical persona. Indeed, whether comping for the up-tempo *S'Wonderful* or languorous *Street of Dreams*, Tatum's backdrops have just the right weight and texture, a somewhat surprising revelation given his prodigious technique. Also of note is the sublime Benny Carter, whose alto saxophone is the quintessence of swing era sophistication, and the self-effacing Louie Bellson, whose subtle rhythmic webs shade and tone with élan. **CB**

Arthur Taylor

1929-1995

Wailin' At The Vanguard **Taylor** (d); **Abraham Burton** (as); **Willie Williams** (ts); **Jacky Terrasson** (p); **Tyler Mitchell** (b). Verve Ⓕ 519 677-2 (63 minutes). Recorded 1992.

⑧ ❽

During the fifties and early sixties Taylor seemed to be on every other jazz record made in New York, appearing with such men as Monk, Bud Powell, Donald Byrd, John Coltrane, Miles Davis, George Wallington and Buddy De Franco. He lived in Europe from 1963 to 1981 (publishing a book of interviews while there) and on his return to New York he had assembled an exciting, vital band of young musicians who were obviously inspired by his great rhythmic drive and musicianship. This CD starts with the sounds of walking from the street into the Village Vanguard club, where Taylor's band is already playing. Art's style of drumming changed little over the years; his alert and explosive approach stems from Blakey but he never overpowered his soloists, and soloed rarely himself.

In Abraham Burton he had a very fluent and exciting player who continues the Parker tradition without sounding like a copyist. Four of the tunes were written by fellow drummer Walter Bolden, *Dear Old Stockholm* is incorrectly credited to Stan Getz, and there is a good Ellington medley, with Burton making full and expert use of the alto's range on Strayhorn's *Chelsea Bridge*. Terrasson plays Bud Powell's *So Sorry Please* with great understanding of the bop piano idiom and it is clear that Taylor had an exceptional band here. **AM**

Billy Taylor

1921

My Fair Lady Loves Jazz **Taylor** (p); **Earl May** (b); **Ed Thigpen** (d); **Ernie Royal** (t); **Don Elliott** (t, mph); **Jimmy Cleveland** (tb); **Jimmy Buffington** (frh); **Don Butterfield**, **Jay McAllister** (bb); **Anthony Artega** (as, ts); **Charles Fowlkes**, **Gerry Mulligan** (bs). Impulse! Ⓜ GRP 11412 (34 minutes). Recorded 1957.

⑥ ❽

For some years house-pianist at Birdland, Taylor was something of a musical chameleon. He was able to sound convincing with swing era men and boppers alike and he became a player of immense experience. The trio is perhaps his happiest hunting ground but this CD shows that, with the aid of arranger Quincy Jones, he could expand the scope of the three-man unit. This is not a trio with 'bolt-on' horn parts; Jones has integrated them into arrangements that have them as both rhythm section and as a unit within the band. Taylor's cultured piano, with the occasional nod toward George Shearing, is well displayed. His ideas on *Show Me* and *Street Where You Live* are delivered with studied care; the emphasis is on paraphrasing rather than tune dismantling and he does all with a light, easy swing. His strength as a bandsman is shown by his orthodox support for the soloist on most titles but almost more by his adroit linking parts of *Church On Time*. His style has changed little since these 1957 sides. He is now an eminent educator but there is something about his somewhat sanitized style that is as valid today as it was in the cool era. **BMcR**

Cecil Taylor

1929

Jazz Advance **Taylor** (p); **Buell Neidlinger** (b); **Dennis Charles** (d); **Steve Lacy** (ss) on one track. Blue Note Ⓜ CDP7 84462-2 (53 minutes). Recorded 1956.

⑩ ❼

It's staggering to look at the date of recording and realize that this, Taylor's début, was done just a year after Bird died, a year before Monk recorded with Coltrane, five years before Wynton Marsalis was born. The music's shock remains vibrant, its methodology mystifying. *Bemsha Swing* and *Sweet And Lovely* were inspired introductory choices, registering Taylor's intention to push beyond Monk's own boundaries at a time when Monk himself was still considered radical in many corners. In retrospect it's possible to hear later Taylor breakthroughs in preliminary stages—the percussive hammering on *Rick Kick Shaw*, plunging through the dense harmonic terrain of *Charge 'Em Blues*, the drastic gap between piano and rhythm section in *Sweet And Lovely*. Yet what Taylor needed at this point were precisely the conventions he was destroying; without the 12-bar phrases of *Charge 'Em Blues*, the familiarity of *You'd Be So Nice To Come Home To*, the regularity of the rhythm section, his variations of rhythm and harmony would have had no context, no contrast, no perspective. Eventually he would liberate himself from such conventions, but here he's still in a formative stage, so the traces of Stravinsky, Bartók, even Ellington's clunky chording in *Azure*, are clues to future developments. Stunning music then, and now. **AL**

Jumpin' Punkins **Taylor** (p); **Clark Terry** (t); **Roswell Rudd** (tb); **Archie Shepp** (ts); **Steve Lacy** (ss); **Charles Davis** (bs); **Buell Neidinger** (b); **Billy Higgins** (d); **Dennis Charles** (d). Candid Ⓜ CD 9013 (34 minutes). Recorded 1961.

✔ ⑧ ❼

The lack of recording opportunities was the bane of Taylor's early musical life (he would make up for it later). Between the time of his first recording in 1955 and the mini series he made for Candid in

1960, he fronted only three studio dates. The well-known Contemporary session **Looking Ahead** introduced Taylor to the international jazz world, but the 'nuts and bolts' of his style are clearer on this CD. *O.P.* shows him trading in pure improvisation, his roaring tone clusters pouring over the urgent punctuation of his left hand while totally ignoring the syntactical rules of earlier jazz forms. The remaining three titles are less iconoclastic and, by their very nature, approach the music in a different manner. The trio, joined by Shepp on *I Forgot*, takes a similarly free route but the reflective mood allows ideas to breathe, illustrating Taylor's structural line of musical thought. The principle is further developed on the Ellington themes as his irreverent piano interjections transform the strengths of the originals into a Taylor-controlled world which is so close as to be an extension of the Thelonious Monk music ethic. **BMcR**

Unit Structures **Taylor** (p); **Eddie Gale Stevens** (t); **Jimmy Lyons** (as); **Ken McIntyre** (as, ob, bcl); **Henry Grimes**, **Alan Silva** (b); **Andrew Cyrille** (d). Blue Note Ⓜ CDP 784237-2 (57 minutes). Recorded 1966.

✓ ⑩ ❽

For the first 20 years of his professional life, Taylor was a sparsely-recorded artist. This album and its Blue Note stablemate **Conquistador!** (see below) fall roughly in the middle of that period, and for many years it was possible to see them as the culmination of his art. Today, close on 30 years further down the line, the perspective has shifted, and **Unit Structures**, in particular, seems both a summation of all that has gone before in Taylor's career and the first definitive statement of a stylistic position which the pianist/composer has never completely abandoned since.

There are four compositions here, played by a band made up mostly of old sweats, with Stevens and McIntyre being the relative newcomers. *Steps* is a type of work to be found on many a Taylor album, a short opening statement which sets the rhythmic and harmonic patterns to be explored, then every man for himself. *Enter, Evening* is something quite different, and harks back to some of the more formally laid-out compositions Taylor recorded in 1961 on **Into The Hot**. It moves through several phases and at points arrives at a hushed poignancy all the more moving for being so rare in the pianist's music. Bassist Silva is paticularly impressive. **Unit Structures** combines elements of both procedures, having a firm episodic structure which helps to maintain the impression of forward movement in the work and the solos. The final track, *Tales (8 whisps)*, is almost entirely a solo piano piece (the basses and drums enter for a couple of the whisps), and in some ways is the most remarkable performance on the record. Clearly much of it is composed, with Taylor moving between written sections and improvisation at will, but the music is so tightly-knit, the themes so cleverly developed and transformed, and the whole performance conceived on such a dense and cryptic level that it repays intense study as well as an immediate emotional reaction. Taylor has often approached but never attained such pregnant concision again. **KS**

Conquistador! **Taylor** (p); **Bill Dixon** (t); **Jimmy Lyons** (as); **Henry Grimes**, **Alan Silva** (b); **Andrew Cyrille** (d). Blue Note Ⓜ CDP 784260 2 (55 minutes). Recorded 1966.

✓ ⑩ ❽

Featuring three extended performances—the stirring *Conquistador!* and two takes (one a CD bonus track) of the slower and more fitful *With (Exit)*—this followed **Unit Structures** and was a transitional album for Taylor, who hindsight suggests was as much influenced by the free jazz of this period as he was influential upon it. The pianist is cracking his containers here; there is little of the mathematical calculation one senses even in his seemingly open-ended Cafe Montmartre recordings with Lyons and Sunny Murray. At the same time, Taylor's performances hadn't yet taken on the air of ritual, or become endurance contests between him and his audiences. One senses him looking for, and finding, organic form in these three performances, and the line between composition and improvisation is bracingly thin on all of them. *Conquistador!*, in particular, with its late-emerging and mordant central theme, pinpoints an irony central to Taylor's music of this period. Although thought of as being the antithesis of hard bop, this music furthers one of hard bop's pet causes in granting the rhythm section parity with the horns. Although there are horn 'solos' here, most of these play out more dialogues, due to Taylor's strategy of testing Dixon and Lyons rather than 'accompanying' them in the conventional sense. Many bands of this period experimented with the use of two bassists, and not always successfully. In the case of Grimes and Silva, the concept works because each adheres to his well-defined role: Silva is the floater and Grimes the one who digs in and probes the chords (or the absence of them). Lyons is as penetrating as always and Cyrille again shows that he has few equals in supplying an insistent pulse without shifting into predictable metre. But the man who makes the biggest difference here is Dixon. An important if insufficiently recognized figure in his own right, he takes his time and refuses to be rushed, even with Taylor eddying around him. His lyricism wounds, as does Taylor's. **FD**

For Olim **Taylor** (p). Soul Note Ⓕ SN 121150-2 (45 minutes). Recorded 1986.

⑩ ❾

Cecil Taylor's solo piano work did not appear on record until the mid-seventies. Since then, however, solo albums have been released at regular intervals, with **Indent, Silent Tongues, Garden and Erzulie Maketh Scent** among the recitals that explore this particular facet of his art.

Listeners deterred by the intensity and textural density of Taylor's group performances may find his solo music less daunting, although the phenomenal technique can seem even more awesome heard in its naked glory. In fact the speed, power and relentless energy of Taylor's playing long disguised his music's formal principles. These were analysed, however, in an important 1988 essay by Ekkehard Jost, *Instant Composing as Body Language*. Jost identifies both recurring elements in Taylor's solo music— staccato runs, clusters, brief bass figures, parallel chords—and its main structural procedures, such as call-and-response, layering and motivic development. He also makes the point that for all its torrential attack, Taylor's music is always precisely articulated and often shows great delicacy of touch.

All of these qualities are evident on **For Olim**, recorded live at Berlin's annual Free Music Workshop and probably the most diverse of Taylor's solo recordings. Its atypical mixture of one long track and several short pieces means there is a rich variety of moods, textures, forms. *Mirror and Water Gazing* and *The Question* are darkly ruminative; *Glossalalia—part four* rocks like a train; *For the Rabbit* is a collage of spectacular right-hand runs and crashing bass clusters. The long *Olim*—"an Aztec hieroglyph meaning movement, motion, earthquake" exemplifies the breadth of Taylor's resources. **GL**

Remembrance **Taylor** (p); **Louis Moholo** (d). FMP Ⓕ CD4 (64 minutes). Recorded 1988.

⑥ ❻

This is one of ten CDs drawn from Taylor's 1988 **Improvised Music** project in Berlin, and within that series, it is part of a subset of duo albums that show many aspects of Taylor's uncompromising approach to improvisation. There are three pieces from Moholo and Taylor's concert here—a grand 40-minute piece *Remembrance*, *The Great Bear* at half that length, plus the briefest of encore fragments. Taylor retains the ability to impose stucture and form on his extended pieces, but with even more daring now than in his work of the previous three decades. He is shadowed (complemented rather than competed with) by Moholo in a wholly sympathetic and almost telepathic way.

Remembrance reverts to solo piano at various stages roughly a third and then halfway through. Between, it is an exercise in building tension and momentum, Moholo only dominating shortly before the halfway mark when his restless shifting rhythms are joined by a loud clicking sound that threatens the safety of the speaker cones. The start of *Great Bear* is almost Taylor self-parody—a relentless barrage of sound in a maelstrom of piano flurries and thunderous drums, Moholo sensing a set of abrupt chordal punctuations that bring in a quieter more reflective phase. If Taylor is a taste already acquired, this album will heighten it as a landmark in improvisational co-operation. **AS**

John Taylor 1942

Ambleside Days **Taylor** (p); **John Surman** (ss, bs, cl, bcl). Ah Um Ⓕ 013 (46 minutes). Recorded 1992.

⑧ ❽

Like John Surman's highly successful **Road To St Ives** and Ian Carr's **Old Heartland**, John Taylor's **Ambleside Days** is a selection of connected pieces inspired by countryside familiar from childhood. All Taylor's pianistic and compositional strengths are represented; an ability to sustain vigorously rhythmic tempos without sacrificing either fluency or lyricism; a sensitivity and delicacy of touch, never lapsing into sentimentality; an imaginative improvisational skill which enables him to sustain ideas without contrivance over lines of unusual length. Surman is the perfect partner; not only does he have a special rapport with Taylor, having played with him for nearly three decades—since the 1964 Surman octet—but he has also amassed considerable experience playing this sort of intensely personal, impressionistic music on his series of ECM solo albums. Unsurprisingly, given these ingredients, **Ambleside Days** is a memorable album, gentle and beguiling, airy, tuneful and hauntingly atmospheric. Taylor's virtuosity and Surman's robustness—and the range of sound available from his selection of reeds—militate entirely successfully against any suggestion that the music could be merely a pretty soundtrack to Lake District scenery, and the recording confirms both men's position in the very front rank of UK jazz players. **CP**

Martin Taylor 1956

Don't Fret **Taylor** (g); **David Newton** (p, syn); **Dave Green** (b); **Allan Ganley** (d). Linn Ⓕ AKD 014 (48 minutes). Recorded 1990.

⑧ ❽

Equally effective as a solo performer or fronting a small group, and celebrated for his regular collaborations with Stephane Grappelli, Martin Taylor is the UK's most accomplished mainstream guitarist. **Don't Fret** is the perfect showcase for his many gifts; a peerless, pure tone, producing a mellow, warm but always penetrative sound; an apparently unquenchable flow of improvisational ideas, which imparts a relaxed informality (not unlike Grappelli's) to everything he plays; a discreetly propulsive power which imbues all his music with a gentle but powerful swing. All these gifts are set off here by the Rolls-Royce of UK rhythm sections; bassist Dave Green is justly ubiquitous on the British jazz scene, demonstrating his assured technical prowess with everyone from Stan Tracey to Humphrey Lyttelton; Allan Ganley is his drumming equivalent, winner of mainstream awards year after year. David Newton too is an excellent foil, luminous yet cogent. Indeed, if **Don't Fret** has a fault, it is in the undemanding nature of its standard material; the two originals on the album, especially Taylor's own title-track, stretch the participants more than the warhorses by the likes of Cole Porter and Oscar Pettiford, and are high points of an excellent mainstream album. **CP**

John Tchicai

1936

Timo's Message **Tchicai** (as, ts); **Thomas Dürst**, **Christian Kuntner** (b); **Timo Fleig** (d, perc). Black Saint Ⓕ 20094-2 (42 minutes). Recorded 1984.

⑦ ❽

Born in Copenhagen to a Danish mother and a Congolese father, John Tchicai moved to the US and became a leading figure in the avant-garde jazz of the mid-sixties. He recorded with both the New York Contemporary Five and the New York Art Quartet and also played on John Coltrane's **Ascension**. On returning to Europe, Tchicai was less in the limelight but continued to record through the seventies and eighties, notably with Johnny Dyani and Pierre Dørge. **Timo's Message** is the only album he made with a young Swiss group whose drummer, Timo Fleig, died before the record was released.

Timo's Message also marks Tchicai's switch from alto to tenor saxophone. He plays the latter on the disc's six quartet tracks but retains his alto for three brief solo improvisations (inspired by the surrealist painter Yves Tanguy) that are heavily indebted to AACM saxophonists such as Anthony Braxton and Roscoe Mitchell. The quartet tracks are more striking, with the tenor's gravitas lending new authority and interest to Tchicai's agile phrasing. The wide range of material includes Marilyn Mazur's funky *Frisk Baglaens*, the tersely lyrical *Stella by Starlight* and a dark, grieving tribute to Albert Ayler on *Mothers*. **GL**

Jack Teagarden

1905-1964

The Indispensable Jack Teagarden **Teagarden** (tb,v); featuring: **Leonard Davis**, **Charlie Teagarden**, **Max Kaminsky**, **Billy Butterfield** (t); **Benny Goodman**, **Peanuts Hucko** (cl); **Happy Caldwell**, **Bud Freeman** (ts); **Joe Sullivan**, **Roy Bargy**, **Gene Schroeder** (p); **Ramona Davies** (p,v); **Nappy Lamare** (g,v); **Eddie Lang** (g); **Eddie Condon** (bj); **Joe Venuti** (vn); **Art Miller** (b); **George Stafford**, **Ray Bauduc**, **George Wettling** (d); **Red McKenzie** (comb); **Gene Austin**, **Red McKenzie**, **Johnny Mercer**, **Ben Pollack**, **Charles Roberts** (v). RCA Jazz Tribune Ⓜ 89613-2 (two discs: 105 minutes). Recorded 1928-57.

⑥ ❻

Born not far from the Red River, raised in Texas and Oklahoma, Jack Teagarden is often called the first great white jazzman—a claim usually accompanied by testimony to his authentic trombone blues, which stem from early exposure to black music. But Teagarden brought his own roots to jazz, conspicuously in his singing; he never lost the offhand manner or lazy drawl of a cowpoke. Singing *I Cover the Waterfront* he sounds like he is sitting by the campfire. It is one of three late pieces here from 1957, but there are cowboy echoes even on a 1935 *Ain't Misbehavin'*. In jazz, where biography often has a mythological cast, Teagarden the singer and legato trombonist updated an American stock figure: the slow-drawling cowpuncher who nonchalantly does virtuoso rope tricks. Teagarden was among the first to show by example that jazz could cross-pollinate with most any strain of ethnic music.

There are several blues in this anthology, culled from RCA's vaults, which mostly finds Teagarden as sideman—with early employers Ben Pollack, Paul Whiteman and the Mound City Blue Blowers, and various permutations of the Condon/Freeman Chicagoans which sometimes include Jack's brother Charlie. The set's desultory nature matches the haphazard spirit of Teagarden's career; like some other great soloists, he was an indifferent leader. **KW**

A Hundred Years from Today **Jack Teagarden** (tb, v); **Charlie Teagarden**, **Sterling Bose**, **Manny Klein**, **Shirley Clay** (t); **Benny Goodman**, **Pee Wee Russell**, **Rod Cless** (cl); **Frank Trumbauer** (cms); **Jimmy Dorsey** (as); **Bud Freeman**, **Art Karle**, (ts); **Adrian Rollini** (bss); **Joe Venuti** (v); **Casper Reardon** (hp); **Fats Waller** (p, v); **Joe Sullivan**, **Charlie LaVere**, **Terry Shand**, **Frank Froeba** (p); **Nappy Lamare**, **Dick McDonough** (g); **Artie Bernstein** (b); **Gene Krupa**, **Stan King** (d). Conifer Ⓜ CDHD 153 (74 minutes). Recorded 1931-34.

⑧ ❽

These classic tracks have Teagarden and his friends playing with the fire and spirit of comparative youth. They show clearly what a daunting example the Texan's playing must have been to younger trombonists of the period. Within the limited range of material he chose Teagarden's melodic sense and timing were superb and his vocals and solos in this generous collection are as good as any that could have been collected.

The riotous collaborations with Fats Waller on *You Rascal You* and *That's What I Like About You* rank amongst the most infectiously cheerful jazz records on CD and there is always the chance that Bose, Charlie Teagarden or Goodman will pop up with a good solo when Jack is not holding the floor.

Tucked away amongst this well-chosen accumulation of Teagarden's best tracks is the charming *Junk Man*, an unusual feature for the harp of Casper Reardon, which also has good solos from the two

Teagardens and Goodman. If, as seems likely, these recordings were originally intended for the mass market, then it says much for the state of 'pop' music of the day. As so often the crisp and clear transfers are the work of engineer John R.T. Davies.. **SV**

Big T's Dixieland Band/Gotham Jazz Scene **Teagarden** (tb, v); **Dick Oakley** (t); **Jerry Fuller** (cl); **Don Ewell** (p); **Stan Puls** (b); **Ronnie Greb** (d). **Bobby Hackett And His Jazz Band** on 11 tracks; **Hackett** (c); **Dick Cary** (frh); **Ernie Caceres** (cl, bs); **Tom Gwaltney** (vb, cl); **Mickey Crane** (p); **John Dengler** (tba); **Al Hall, Mit Hinton** (b); **Nat Ray** (d). Dormouse Ⓕ DMI CDX03 (74 minutes). Recorded 1957/58.

⑥ ❽

For the last decade of his life Teagarden fronted small bands of his own (occasionally disbanding to tour Europe with Earl Hines or reunite with Ben Pollack), and the 11 titles on this CD are by a very musicianly and successful sextet. Oakley was a more interesting and individual player than his replacement, Don Goldie, and Fuller a smooth, Goodmanesque clarinettist who knew all the tunes that Teagarden wanted to play. But in Don Ewell the sextet had an exceptional pianist, heard here to advantage on his own tune *Walleritis.* The music is smooth and polished but Teagarden's own playing—and singing—hew close to the manner of expression he used so successfully with the Armstrong All Stars. There is a particularly fine version of *Casanova's Lament* and an authoritative *Someday You'll Be Sorry.* The CD is, in fact, the precise equivalent of two Capitol LPs and although Teagarden does not play on the Hackett tracks, there is a close affinity between the music produced by both bands. **AM**

Joe Temperley

1929

Concerto For Joe **Temperley** (bs); **Steve Sidwell, Gerard Presencer** (t); **Eddie Severn** (t, flh); **Gordon Campbell, Nichol Thomson** (tb); **Peter King** (as); **Duncan Lamont** (ts); **Brian Lemon, Brian Kellock** (p); **Alec Dankworth, Dave Green** (b); **Martin Drew, Jack Parnell** (d). Hep Ⓕ CD 2062 (70 minutes). Recorded 1993/94.

⑥ ❽

Born in Scotland, Temperley was playing with top-flight British leaders by the age of 20. He joined Humphrey Lyttelton's first mainstream band in 1958 and, on leaving it in 1965, settled in New York. There he established a reputation with Woody Herman, Buddy Rich and actually took Harry Carney's place in the Duke Ellington Orchestra.

Latterly he has been something of a festival traveller and this CD, recorded in Britain, offers two sides of the Temperley persona. The first a programme of jazz standards with a well-knit, professional trio behind him; the second, as ensemble backbone, soloist and dedicatee in a suite played by an 11 piece. On the combo dates he shows that his baritone line flows as comfortably over Monk's angularities on *Hackensack*, Ellington's soft contours on *Snibor* or over a driving blues of his own. His ensemble presence is pronounced on *Concerto For Joe* and, although his improvisational skills have less room to flourish, his attention seems more focused and solos on *Slow For Joe* and *Sixes And Sevens* have much to say. The nineties Temperley is a consummate artist at home in the baritone chair of a big band or swinging lightly with his own combo. **BMcR**

Tempo King

1936/1937 **King** (v); **Marty Marsala** (t); **Joe Marsala** (cl); **Queenie Ada Rubin** (p); **Eddie Condon** (g); **Mort Stuhlmaker, George Yorke** (b); **Stan King** (d). Timeless Ⓜ CBC 1-002 (68 minutes) Recorded 1936/37.

⑦ ❻

First things first: nobody seems to know or remember much about Tempo King. Such basic biographical facts as his real name seem to have eluded even the record company he made these old 78s for. Someone with a long memory recollects him as a thirties bandleader down in Florida, and-well, that's about it. So much for personal profiles. Whoever he was, he had enough clout to assemble an excellent studio band to make these sides, and a casual dip into any of the 23 titles on this collection will reveal his intentions. He is a Fats Waller imitator (even down to the vocal interjections), which is another strange twist, because Tempo King's entire output was made for RCA Victor's Bluebird label at a time when Waller himself was constantly in the studios for RCA Victor. Why have an imitation (who doesn't even play the piano and isn't particularly witty) when you've got the real thing? The clue is the the personnel playing with him: they're all white, and it's just conceiveable that RCA wanted to create a white version of Waller.

Whatever their intentions, the true interest in these sides today is not Tempo King but the well-recorded group supporting him. They have a fierce and natural swing (the equally obscure Queenie Ada Rubin is a very acceptable Waller substitute on piano and Condon, of course, is impeccable), with the two Marsala brothers playing biting section work and solos. It is fine small-group music, and if Lee Wiley or Mildred Bailey had been the vocalist, these would long ago have been pronounced classics of the genre. As it is, Tempo King landed on his feet when he fell in with this tidy group. **KS**

Ten Part Invention

Ten Part Invention **John Pochée** (d, ldr); **Michael Bukovsky, Warwick Adler** (t, flh); **James Greening** (tb); **Bernie McGann** (as); **Bob Bertles** (f, as, bs); **Ken James** (ss, ts); **Dale Barlow** (f, ts); **Roger Frampton** (p, snino s); **Steve Elphick** (b). ABC Jazz Ⓔ 846 729-2 (61 minutes). Recorded 1987.

⑦ ❼

This band is made up of a large chunk of the best players Australian jazz has come up with in the past quarter-century, and it is fitting that the outfit is led by drummer John Pochee, for many years the living incarnation of what to do right when you are trying to get a band of any size to swing loose and easy.

The programme is entirely made up of originals by writers from within the band, and while some of the charts smack of Oliver Nelson somewhat short of 100% inspiration, the playing is uniformly sharp, disciplined and powerful. The soloists—often the weak link in larger ensembles—are here always at least interesting, although Roger Frampton, a superb pianist, takes a long sopranino sax solo on *So It Goes* which is not entirely convincing (Ken James, soloing on conventional soprano on *Plain Talk*, has a surer touch). A more complete—and more varied—success is *And Zen Monk*, which uses a typically Monkish melodic construction, with wide intervals and deliberately odd rhythmic displacements, and which has a more imaginative chart.

The sound this band makes is a generation behind that of Loose Tubes, but what is here possesses sufficient verve and spirit that this bare fact does not become a handicap to listening pleasure. **KS**

Jacky Terrasson

Jacky Terrasson **Terrasson** (p); **Ugonna Okegwo** (b); **Leon Parker** (d). Blue Note Ⓔ CDP 8 29351 2 (56 minutes). Recorded 1994.

⑦ ❽

'Discovered' by Cindy Blackman, Jesse Davis and Art Taylor, Terrasson's is a genuinely new and innovative keyboard talent well displayed in this eponymous début album. He is spare and verging on the minimalist in his linear playing, but nimble, dextrous and powerful enough to have plenty of heavy artillery to call on when needed. He is daring as well in his approach to standards, *Bye Bye Blackbird* undergoing not merely a change in tempo but a progressive acceleration, before being reined in for the out-choruses. On *Just A Blues*, Okegwo and Parker settle into a slow groove allowing Terrasson to tease away at the familiar sequence. For much of the time just his spare, probing, right hand is in evidence, but two-handed flurries and locked chord sequences interrupt the evenness of his exploration and he applies a similar method to other ballads with great effect, notably a six-minute *Time After Time*. What comes across most on this album is a sense of committed and thoroughly enjoyable music making. When the rhythm section pitch into a high life groove on the closing *Cumba's Dance*, Terrasson throws himself after them with abandon, his jagged chords summoning up images of African street bands and a powerful sense of well-being. An impressive first album. **AS**

Clark Terry

1920

Color Changes **Terry** (t, flh); **Jimmy Knepper** (tb); **Julius Watkins** (frh); **Yusef Lateef** (ts, fl, ehn, ob); **Seldon Powell** (ts, fl); **Tommy Flanagan, Budd Johnson** (p); **Joe Benjamin** (b); **Ed Shaughnessy** (d). Candid Ⓜ CD 9009 (43 minutes). Recorded 1960.

⑧ ❽

At the time of this recording, Terry was regarded as a virtuoso trumpet player on the strength of his work with Duke Ellington. His earliest recordings under his own name, the best of which included sessions with Thelonious Monk and Johnny Griffin, tended to concentrate on athletic displays of bebop improvisation. As well as using a powerful and versatile array of soloists, this album is notable for the six finely-crafted arrangements by Bob Wilber, Yusef Lateef, Al Cohn and Budd Johnson. The result is an album in which the arrangers are given the upper hand. The depth and originality of the writing gives the set an unusual strength of character and guides the soloists into channels where they are able to solo with a freshness and enthusiasm absent from the less organized 'blowing sessions' so popular at the time.

Flutin' And Fluglin' has an early example of Terry duetting with himself on trumpet and flügelhorn and, although some of the musicians are prompted to play above themselves, the outstanding trombonist Jimmy Knepper has a field day, and is heard at his best on Cohn's delicate arrangement of Terry's *La Rive Gauche*. The subtle use of flute and oboe in the ensembles recalls some of the best of Rod Levitt's writing for his octet. **SV**

Frank Teschemacher

1906-1932

Muggsy, Tesch And The Chicagoans **Teschemacher** (cl, as); **Muggsy Spanier, Jimmy McPartland, Dick Fiege, Charley Altier, Red Nichols** (c); **Jack Reid, Miff Mole** (tb); **Charles**

Pierce (as); **Bud Freeman**, **Ralph Rudder** (ts); **Maurie Bercov** (cl, as); **Mezz Mezzrow** (ts, cl); **Rod Cless** (as); **Joe Sullivan**, **Dan Lipscomb** (p); **Jim Lanigan** (b, bb); **Johnny Mueller** (b); **Stuart Branch** (bj); **Eddie Condon** (bj, v); **Gene Krupa**, **Paul Kettler** (d); **Red McKenzie** (v). Village Ⓕ VILCD 001-2 (60 minutes). Recorded 1927/28.

✔ ⑦ ❹

A member of the Austin High School gang in Chicago, Teschemacher played tenor, alto, violin and banjo as well as his beloved clarinet. He worked with the bands of Charlie Straight and Floyd Towne but came to the notice of jazz followers world-wide due to his involvement in the 1927 McKenzie/Condon Chicagoan recordings found on this CD. Teschemacher was an enigmatic figure; his ensemble playing often encroached on the trumpet's part, although the presence of a good tailgate trombonist like Mole returns him to a more orthodox role on *Windy City Stomp*. He was essentially an inspirational musician, capable of the stunning melodic inventiveness that made his fluent *Darktown Stutters Ball* solo a virtual test piece for subsequent performances. There were, however, also moments of pedestrian mediocrity and *Baby Won't You Please Come Home* has him at his most stiff and unyielding. Titles such as *Jazz Me Blues*, *I've Found A New Baby* and *Nobody's Sweetheart* display a mobility of purpose that runs in parallel with the uniquely agitated aspect of his playing. His consciously sour tone is ideal for his style and his use of dissonance adds colour to items such as *There'll Be Some Changes Made*. Although dead at 26, Teschemacher was a strong influence on early white clarinettists. **BMcR**

Toots Thielemans 1922

Do Not Leave Me **Thielemans** (hca, g); **Fred Hersch** (p); **Marc Johnson** (b); **Joey Baron** (d). Stash Ⓕ ST CD 12 (48 minutes). Recorded 1986.

④ ❻

Thielemans is the best-ever harmonica player in jazz, which does not mean much as he is one of a small band, although it enables him to win the miscellaneous section in jazz polls with comparative ease. He is good enough to have shared a stage with soloists like Dizzy Gillespie and held his own, but here he is content to delight his home crowd in Brussels with an engaging promenade through standards like *Autumn Leaves*, a Jacques Brel song which gives the album its name and a lengthy blues foray after (some way after) Miles Davis. Thielemans has poise, a nice tone, nice inflections, and charm...but the harmonica is a slightly uncomfortable instrument to play in jazz, like the accordion or balalaika. On *Bluesette*, his catchy three-time number which was a hit for him in the sixties, Toots whistles the theme and gets the audience to whistle along with him more or less in time and tune, which must be some kind of world record. **MK**

Gary Thomas 1961

By Any Means Necessary **Thomas** (ts, f, syn); **Greg Osby** (as, syn); **Tim Murphy**, **Geri Allen** (p, syn); **John Scofield**, **Mick Goodrick** (g); **Anthony Cox** (b); **Dennis Chambers** (d); **Nana Vasconcelos** (perc). JMT Ⓕ 834 432-2 (55 minutes). Recorded 1989.

✔ ⑧ ❽

Gary Thomas made clear his distaste for funk licks in 1987, when he quit the Miles Davis band rather than play "pentatonic scales and big loud blues-scale things over funk grooves." Nevertheless, this record, presenting his band Seventh Quadrant at its peak, might be thought pretty funky: most tracks are punched along by the thundering backbeats of former Funkadelic juggernaut Dennis Chambers, most feature synthesizers, and John Scofield's *You're Under Arrest*, here more fully realized than on its first appearance on the Miles Davis album of the same name, boasts an unequivocally funky bass line. However, funky or not, Thomas's music with menaces is a million miles from Davis' candied readings of *The Perfect Way*, *Human Nature* and the like. As Davis became more diatonic, Thomas became more diabolical, using remorselessly atonal harmony, a complex rhythmic conception and Gothic synthesiser textures to create a chilling, apocalyptic soundscape. He rejects suggestions that his austere harmonic vocabulary is modelled on Coltrane, but it may be, indirectly through his major influence Woody Shaw. There are excellent guest spots by Scofield and Goodrick, two guitarists much in sympathy with their host's stylistic objectives. **MG**

René Thomas 1927-1975

Guitar Genius **Thomas** (g); **Jacques Pelzer** (f); **Robert Jeanne** (ts); **Leo Flechet**, **Rein de Graaff** (p); **Henk Haverhoek**, **Benoit Quersin**, **Jean Lerusse** (b); **Eric Ineke**, **Jacques Thollot**, **Felix Simtaine** (d). Prestige Record Co Ltd Ⓜ 009 (69 minutes). Recorded 1964-74.

⑧ ❹

The title overstates the case, but Thomas was one fine guitarist. A Belgian who spent significant periods working in Paris, Montréal and New York, and who recorded with Chet Baker, Stan Getz and others, Thomas plays peek-a-boo with his ethnic roots on these seven tracks, drawn from four live gigs with various small bands. Thomas's basic approach is post-Charlie Christian linear swing, but every so often (as on *All the Things You Are* and *Just Friends*) he will end a thought with stinging, vibrato-laden flurries or chords that echo his countryman and early idol Django Reinhardt. Perhaps due to Django's influence, Thomas's tone has more edge and bite than that of the many jazz guitarists who keep their treble controls turned down low.

Thomas is not the only soloist, but it is his show; the sidemen—like Pelzer, whose thin-sounding flute dominates *Deep Purple*—are not always up to his level. An exception is drummer Ineke, who swings *All the Things You Are* with a minimum of effort, sometimes cantering quietly on rims.

Also noteworthy is Thomas's 1960 New York date **Guitar Groove** (on the American Prestige OJC label, no relation to this English one). But **Guitar Genius** offers more generous helpings of his smartly swinging guitar. **KW**

Barbara Thompson 1944

Breathless **Thompson** (ss, as, af); **Malcolm Macfarlane** (g, g-syn); **Peter Lemer** (kbds); **Phil Mulford** (b); **Jon Hiseman** (d); **Noel Langley** (t); **Ashley Slater** (tb); **Hossam Ramzy**, **Frank Holder** (perc). veraBra Ⓕ CDM 13-2 (62 minutes). Recorded 1990/91.

⑧ ❿

Along with Ian Carr's Nucleus, Barbara Thompson's various versions of her band Paraphernalia can arguably lay claim to having established jazz-rock in the UK. Her music is always highly accessible yet surprisingly subtle, full of delicate embellishments and dynamic contrast, propelled and ornamented by her husband Jon Hiseman's excellent drumming. **Breathless** is a sound collage of the moods engendered by city life, embracing the self-explanatory *Jaunty, Cheeky, Squiffy* and *Gracey* through the dark, faintly sinister *Bad Blues* with its breathy flute, to the abrasive *You Must Be Joking* and the extrovert back slapping beat of *Sax Rap*, featuring Thompson's conversational saxophone—usually vocal—rapper's part. Like a number of her previous albums, particularly the excellent live set **A Cry From The Heart**, **Breathless** is anthemic without being ponderous, infectiously perky without sliding into cuteness or banality, and impeccably and enthusiastically performed. It is also faultlessly produced and cleverly presented, with three of its most commercial tracks thoughtfully edited and added at the end for the convenience of radio plays. **CP**

Sir Charles Thompson 1918

Takin' Off **Thompson** (p, ldr); with, on four tracks: **Buck Clayton** (t); **Charlie Parker** (as); **Dexter Gordon** (ts); **Danny Barker** (g); **Jimmy Butts** (b); **J.C. Heard** (d); on four tracks: **Joe Newman** (t); **Bob Dorsey** (ts); **Leo Parker** (bs); **Freddy Green** (g); **John Simmons** (b); **Shadow Wilson** (d); on eight tracks: **Joe Newman**, **Taft Jordan** (t); **H.B. Mitchell** (tb); **Bob Dorsey** (ts); **Pete Brown** (as); **Tate Houston** (bs); **Hank Morton** (g); **John Simmons** (b); **Shadow Wilson** (d). Delmark Apollo Series Ⓕ DD-450 (50 minutes) Recorded 1945-47.

⑧ ❼

Thompson, given his nickname 'Sir Charles' by Lester Young, was from Springfield, Ohio, and initially learned violin before making the switch to piano. By the early forties he was working in small groups up and down New York's 52nd Street, including that led by Young and his drummer brother, Lee. By the end of that decade he had worked with Charlie Barnet and also toured overseas as a solo, gradually reaching th epoint where he was consistently making albums as a leader. That he has always had a gift for leadership can be heard on this collation of mid-forties performances, and those on the Vanguard reissue below. The four tracks with Parker and Gordon are not the usual mid-forties frantic jams: they have written arrangements and a proper order of performance. Unsurprisingly, then, they hang together very well indeed, in a sort of late blooming of the swing style. Even *The Street Beat*, a typically brisk bop line although it was written by Thompson, has humorous -and identifying- breaks and pauses in it. All three soloists repsond with hard-hitting work, with Clayton clearly pointing the way for Howard McGhee's later style.

Thompson, of course, wrote *Robbins' Nest*, a hit in the forties with a number of bands. Naturally he wrote a number of medium-tempo swingers along the same lines, and one of the more distinguished of these is *Strange Hours*, recorded in the summer of 1947, which has a varied arrangement and fetching work from Joe Newman and Bob Dorsey. In a sense, this music points to a direction Basie could have taken up, had he wanted to update at this time. The final session, from the winter of the same year, has an expanded ensemble and seven previously unissued alternative takes. Pete Brown in this context is an interesting choice, and although the arrangements hue a little closer to the Basie-cum-Hampton model, the playing is disciplined and the sound quality good. **KS**

His Personal Vanguard Recordings **Thompson** (p); with, on four tracks **Joe Newman** (t); **Benny Powell** (tb); **Pete Brown** (as); **Gene Ramey** (b); **Osie Johnson** (d); on four tracks **Freddie Green** (g); **Walter Page** (b); **Jo Jones** (d); on five tracks **Emmett Berry** (t); **Benny Morton** (tb);

Earl Warren (as); **Coleman Hawkins** (ts); **Steve Jordan** (g); **Aaron Bell** (b); **Osie Johnson** (d); on six tracks **Skeeter Best** (g); **Aaron Bell** (b). Vanguard (Fr) Ⓕ 662143 (two discs: 99 minutes). Recorded 1953-55.

⑩ ❽

John Hammond conceived the idea of recording the near-forgotten middle period jazz soloists under optimum studio conditions and this fine release comprises reissues of the original four ten-inch Vanguard LPs under Thompson's name, complete with readable reprints of the original sleeve-notes by Hammond. Sir Charles was a key figure on many of those important mainstream recording dates from the fifties, including some of the Buck Clayton Jam Sessions and the Vic Dickenson Septets on Vanguard. Possessed of a light touch and an ability to swing at any tempo, the value of his work can be judged from the second session here, the one on which he took Basie's place with the 'All American Rhythm Section' (Green, Page, Jones). He retains the springiness and economy of notes associated with the Count and turns in four deft performances of tunes such as *Honeysuckle Rose.* The first date pairs a couple of Basie men with the quirky, piping alto sound of Pete Brown to produce splendid swing-cum-bebop. But the jewel in the crown is the third date and particularly the magnificent solo features for Coleman Hawkins, the majestic *Talk of the Town* and Thompson's own *Sweetheart Tree.* Berry and Morton are also superb and having Jordan on rhythm guitar is an asset. The sound is the best yet for these sessions and the two CDs are housed in an ingenious 'gate-fold' case.
AM

Lucky Thompson 1924

Tricotism **Thompson** (ts); **Jimmy Cleveland** (tb); **Hank Jones, Don Abney** (p); **Skeeter Best** (g); **Oscar Pettiford** (b); **Osie Johnson** (d). Impulse! Ⓜ GRP 11352 (66 minutes). Recorded 1956.

⑧ ❽

The alarmingly high rate of attrition among leading jazz musicians has usually been the result of self-abuse or mental illness, with sometimes little separation between the two. But there have been a considerable number of performers who, from dissatisfaction and disillusionment, have merely given up playing. For example the querulous Lawrence Brown, leaving the Ellington band in his early 60s, vowed never to touch his instrument again and Lucky Thompson, still living in Seattle, has done likewise since he turned 50. The promise he displayed on his 1946 sessions with Gillespie and especially Parker flowered briefly and spectacularly in the mid-1950s, when these sessions (as well as work with Miles Davis, Milt Jackson and Quincy Jones) found his Byas-derived sinuosity at its most ingratiating. The combined contents of two LPs include seven quintet tracks featuring Cleveland, here more creative than on many occasions, but the jewels are the nine drum-less trios with Pettiford as the other main soloist. *Deep Passion* takes off explicitly from Hawkins's *BodyAnd Soul* and is not disgraced by the comparison, while *Dancing Sunbeam*'s chord-sequence (*I Remember You*) should be an injunction to every reader not to overlook Thompson.
BP

Lucky Strikes **Thompson** (ts, ss); **Hank Jones** (p); **Richard Davis** (b); **Connie Kay** (d). Prestige Ⓜ OJCCD 194-2 (40 minutes). Recorded 1964.

⑨ ❼

A very underrated saxophonist, Lucky Thompson is a superbly inventive and melodic player. Although his early style bore a resemblance to Don Byas, he absorbed the harmonic and rhythmic subtleties of Charlie Parker and Lester Young, then continued to evolve, his playing becoming simultaneously more forceful yet more sensitive. Much of his best work has still to appear on CD. *Just One More Chance* (one of the great tenor solos of the forties) is on the now deleted Bluebird compilation **Esquire's All American Hot Jazz Sessions**, but his exquisite mid-fifties work with Oscar Pettiford and most of his fine 1956 Paris recordings await a CD release.

Lucky Strikes is an elegant, example of his sixties music for Prestige. Thompson himself is in disarming form and the rhythm section complement him with the discretion of true class. Thompson features soprano saxophone on several tracks, his sleek phrasing and pure tone very different from either Coltrane or Steve Lacy (the other leading straight horn players at the time). He is an able composer too, his charts here encompassing the spry *Prey-Loot*, the lightly swinging *Reminiscent* and the intimate balladry of *I Forgot To Remember*. Top honours, however, go to Duke Ellington's *In A Sentimental Mood*, fashioned by Lucky into a wafted soprano reverie.
GL

Malachi Thompson 1941

The Jaz Life **Thompson** (t); **Joe Ford** (ss, as); **Carter Jefferson** (ts); **Kirk Brown** (p); **Harrison Bankhead** (b); **Nasir Abadey** (d); **Richard Lawrence** (cga). Delmark Ⓕ DD 453 (48 minutes). Recorded 1991.

⑤ ❻

'Jaz', in Thompson's attenuated spelling, represents a return to gritty improvised music, played on acoustic instruments, with none of the repetitive monotony of the 'designer jazz' of the eighties.

Thompson, who composed some of the tracks here for a show of the same title, aims at "creative self-expression that stimulates the intellect." Partly because of the obvious emotional depth of his own playing, which marks a return to his horn after a year battling off a rare form of cancer, the album succeeds. The playing is powerfully direct and Thompson displays the aggressive style that marked him out when a member of Lester Bowie's Brass Fantasy.

The extended trumpet solo on Rodgers and Hart's *My Romance* has the odd split note, but it brings passion to the old standard, while Thompson's gifts as arranger emerge on the old Ray Charles hit *Drown In My Own Tears*, where the wailing saxophones bring a chill to the spine over the soul-inflected beat. The rest of the band pick up the mood well, especially on Thompson's tribute to Miles and Trane, where the fiery alto of Joe Ford stands out. **AS**

Claude Thornhill

1909-1965

Best Of The Big Bands **Thornhill** (ldr, p, arr) with the following collective personnel; **Rusty Dedrick**, **Conrad Gozzo**, **Bob Spretall**, **Randy Brooks**, **Steve Steck**, **Jake Koven**, **Louis Mucci**, **Clarence Willard**, **Emil Terry**, **Ed Zandy**, **Red Rodney** (t); **Tasso Harris**, **Bob Jenney**, **Bud Smith**, **Ray Schmidt**, **Jerry Rosa**, **Tak Takvorian**, **Allan Langstaff** (tb); **John Graas**, **Vincent Jacobs**, **Mike Glas**, **Fred Schmidt**, **Sandy Siegelstein**, **Al Antoucci** (frh); **Harold Wekel**, **Bill Barber** (tba); **Irving Fazola**, **Dale Brown**, **George Paulson**, **John Nelson**, **Hammond Russum**, **Ted Goddard**, **Buddy Dean**, **Conn Humphries**, **Carl Swift**, **Chet Pardee**, **Joe Aglora**, **Jack Dulong**, **James Gemus**, **Vic Harris**, **Bob Glover**, **Ed Stang**, **Mickey Folus**, **Mario Rolo**, **Bill Bushey**, **Les Clark**, **Lee Konitz** (reeds); **Chuck Robinson**, **Barry Galbraith**, **Zeb Julian** (g); **Harvey Cell**, **Marty Blitz**, **Barnet Spieler**, **Iggy Shevack**, **Joe Shulman** (b); **Gene Leman**, **Irv Cottler**, **Billy Exiner** (d); **Gil Evans**, **Bill Borden**, **Charles Naylor** (arr); **Fran Warren**, **Buddy Hughes**, **Snow Flakes** (v). Columbia Ⓜ CK 46152 (62 minutes). Recorded 1941-47.

⑧ ❻

Miles Davis's 1948-vintage Birth Of The Cool band and its subsequent Capitol recordings (reviewed above) focused attention, retrospectively, on the Claude Thornhill orchestra. Miles, Gerry Mulligan and the rest never denied the influence of the band on their work and while Thornhill's recordings have been dusted off by the critics to illustrate the earlier work of Gil Evans, Lee Konitz, Red Rodney, etc., it must not be forgotten that Thornhill's orchestra had a highly individual personality of its own. Although this release contains the expected Evans scores such as *Robbin's Nest*, *Yardbird Suite* and *Anthropology,* it also presents some of Claude's own quite masterly work both at the keyboard and the composer's desk. Thornhill flourished (the term is entirely relative) during the big dance band era when orchestras invariably comprised six or seven brass, four or five saxes and a rhythm section. Claude changed that; some of his writing called for six clarinets and two French horns (and this was before Gil Evans joined his staff). The ensemble sound of Thornhill's band "hung like a cloud", as someone once remarked. This is a well-compiled CD opening with Thornhill's signature-tune, the lovely *Snowfall*, and containing Fran Warren's features *Sunday Kind Of Love* and *Early Autumn* (not the Ralph Burns composition). Both are arranged by Charles Naylor and each is a minor classic in the vocalist-with-band division. Although now deleted it is worth trawling through the second-hand catalogues for Thornhill's **Tapestries** (Affinity CD CHARLY 82), which contains ten of the tracks on the present CD plus 13 more from the same period. **AM**

Henry Threadgill

1944

Carry The Day **Threadgill** (as, f); **Mark Taylor** (flh); **Brandon Ross**, **Masujaa** (g); **Edwin Rodriguez**, **Marcus Rojas** (tba); **Gene Lake** (d). **Wu Man** (pipa); **Jason Hwang** (vn); **Tony Cedras** (acc); add, on two tracks **Johnny Rudas**, **Miguel Urbina** (perc, v); **Sentienla Toy**, **Mossa Bildner** (v). Columbia Ⓕ CK 66995 (37 minutes). Recorded 1994

⑧ ❽

It is difficult, if not impossible, to rate this music: by what standards? under what category? Threadgill would no doubt be pleased at such indecision; after all, throughout his impressively varied career he has made a point of frustrating expectations and erasing stylistic boundaries. It is a shame that none of his excellent Sextett records from the eighties are currently available on CD—they at least build upon more explicit jazz references. Threadgill's most recent work, exhibited on the brief and at times bewildering **Carry The Day**, incorporates so many of his compositional interests that his septet Very Very Circus resembles no other 'jazz' band of my acquaintance. The opening piece alone, *Come Carry The Day*, mixes Tex-Mex accordion, African Highlife, Latin/Caribbean percussion, a Spanish vocal chant and the unconventional instrumentation of the core band into a dense, swirling, multicultural stew. The guests bring additional spice, and the simultaneous layers of activity do approximate the colourful near-chaos of a three-ring circus. But even on those selections where the unadulterated Circus performs—like the patchwork quilt of tubas, guitars and flute on *Growing A Big Banana* and the spikier *Jenkins Boys Again, Wish Somebody Die, It's Hot*—Threadgill's off-kilter rhythmic accents, labyrinthine harmonic progressions and polyphonic interplay can be as dazzlingly enigmatic as his song titles. **AL**

Bobby Timmons

1935-1974

This Here is **Timmons** (p); **Sam Jones** (b); **Jimmy Cobb** (d). Riverside Ⓜ OJCCD 104-2 (38 minutes). Recorded 1960.

⑦ ❻

It is important to remember that Timmons was an outstanding songwriter as well as a fine pianist. It was his compositions, more than anyone else's (Horace Silver included), which really got the soul-jazz craze out of the clubs and beyond the clutches of the hipsters and established groups like the Jazz Messengers and Cannonball Adderley's quintet on a popular basis which went beyond the usual jazz audience. This was his first album as a leader, and it is somewhat schizophrenic, containing trio versions of his three big hits, *This Here*, *Moanin'* and *Dat Dere*, but also having its fair share of evergreens and jazz standards (*Lush Life*, *My Funny Valentine,* etc.) which are given a pretty much straightforward interpretation and are certainly not souled-out. Timmons was a considerable and sophisticated talent at the keyboard, not given to ostentation or the trotting out of clichés, and this is why his own albums always deliver a lot more than they promise on the cover. Like many others, he became trapped by the public's demands for him just to stick to the hits, but it is to his credit that he always went beyond just doing that. **KS**

Keith Tippett

1947

The Dartington Concert Tippett (p). Editions EG /Virgin Ⓕ 2106-2 (48 minutes). Recorded 1990.

⑧ ❽

Keith Tippett made his mark at the helm of a number of fine varied groups ranging from the intimate (duos with Stan Tracey or Louis Moholo) to the gargantuan (the 22-piece Ark and the 50-piece Centepede). None of these are yet on CD, which forces us to focus on his underrated talents as a solo pianist. With great stamina, dexterity, and an expansive technique he can draw on a near-orchestral spectrum of sonorities, as this remarkable recital shows. The piano once belonged to Paderewski; Tippett incorporates its clear, crisp responsiveness and bell-like tone into the development of this single extended improvisation. The dedication to Dudu Pukwana provides an emotional frame for the music, beginning with a dark left hand motif stalking the fleet right hand theme and eventually exploring the lower and upper registers by way of contrasting timbres and attacks. Often energized by fervent trills, notes drizzle from Tippett's hands--one section approaches Conlon Nancarrow in its intensity--growing into an outpouring of melody. As in certain Middle-Eastern musics, Tippett seeks an ecstatic state of inspiration; his alternating power and delicacy sustains the music through to its haunting, elegaic conclusion. **AL**

Claude Tissendier

Saxomania Starring Phil Woods **Tissendier**, **Woods**, **Philippe Portejoie** (as); **Nicholas Montier**, **Claude Braud** (ts); **Jean Eteve** (bs); **Stan Leferriere** (p); **Pierre Maingourd** (b); **François Laudet** (d). Ida Ⓕ 031 CD (51 minutes). Recorded 1991.

⑦ ❽

Tissendier has now made three such albums, the one prior to this guest-starring Benny Carter, so perhaps we can expect Dave Sanborn guesting on the next one? Be that as it may, this energetic and committed band swings like the American ones of the sixties used to, with genuinely colourful arrangements of material such as *Bloomdido*, *Star Eyes*, *Quill* and *Yardbird Suite*. Woods's urgent voice gives a pleasing cutting edge to both the ensembles and the solos, pushing the other players to out-do their previous efforts. The section work is very clean, perfectly in tune, and has plenty of gusto. This is the sort of date Oliver Nelson could turn out by rote when he was at the top of his game, so the standards are very high. Recommended to those who like their jazz to swing like crazy. **KS**

Cal Tjader

1925-1982

Cal Tjader-Stan Getz Sextet **Tjader** (vb); **Getz** (ts); **Vince Guaraldi** (p); **Eddie Duran** (g); **Scott LaFaro** (b); **Billy Higgins** (d). Fantasy Ⓜ OJCCD 275-2 (43 minutes). Recorded 1958.

⑧ ❼

Tjader first came to the wider jazz audience in the George Shearing Quintet which patented the Shearing Sound—the unison piano-vibes-guitar theme statements and the touch of Latin rhythm. Some of this clearly rubbed off on Tjader, who continually looked to Latin music of all kinds to recharge his creative batteries when they were running low. It worked for him in the same way as it did for Shearing, and for a number of years Tjader was very big commercial news indeed.

This date, made when Tjader was rapidly coming to the attention of the record-buying public, uses Latin elements but is mostly a straight forward blowing session, albeit with consummate blowers. The rhythm section of Guaraldi, Duran, LaFaro and Higgins is very strong indeed, having an admirable combination of imagination and drive. At this time, both LaFaro and Higgins were West Coast unknowns, but both make big contributions here. Tjader and Getz fit together beautifully, and while the saxophonist has the emotional depth to tear you to pieces on *I've Grown Accustomed to Her Face*, Tjader always plays with great sensitivity and economy. His straight jazz style is inextricably bound up in Milt Jackson's, but then there wasn't a post-war vibes player who escaped Bags's groove until the following decade.

As a rather bizarre footnote, the CD sleeve and booklet both claim that this record was made in 1963, while the liner notes mention 1958. The later date is of course a nonsense, as LaFaro died in 1961. **KS**

Charles Tolliver

1942

Grand Max **Tolliver** (t, flh); **John Hicks** (p); **Reggie Workman** (b); **Alvin Queen** (d). Black Lion Ⓜ BLCD 760145 (67 minutes). Recorded 1972.

⑦ ❻

In November 1993, Tolliver opened to enthusiastic audiences at a New York residency, and the critical reaction to his playing centred around his ability to respond to and manipulate the mood of an audience. Twenty-one years before, he demonstrated just how much this has always been an essential part of his art in this tight performance, recorded at Loosdrecht in Holland, by his Music Inc. quartet. The title track is dedicated to Tolliver's former mentor, Max Roach, but the most impressive playing here is on the central performance of *Prayer For Peace* which swells from a gentle bass and drums duo to an impassioned piece of preaching trumpet. Tolliver's hallmark is long, flowing solos that turn ideas inside out and upside down over many choruses, and his co-operative quartets of the early seventies were an ideal vehicle for him to do this within. The Loosdrecht concert was clearly a happy affair for all concerned, and the Dutch radio engineers who recorded it caught much of the live atmosphere, especially in the rousing encore based on Neal Hefti's *Repetition*. **AS**

Mel Tormé

1925

In Hollywood **Tormé** (v, p); **Al Pellegrini** (cl, p); **James Dupre** (b); **Dick Shanahan** (d). MCA/Decca Ⓜ GRO16172 (59 minutes). Recorded 1954.

⑧ ❻

Over the years Tormé has succeeded in balancing a number of careers simultaneously: singer, songwriter, screen actor, pianist, drummer and author. But it is as a most musical and jazz-influenced singer that he is probably best known, and this album, recorded live at Hollywood's Crescendo club, proved to be a turning point in an already established career. It contains the version of *Mountain Greenery* which became a considerable hit in Britain (and the subsequent success led to his albums with the Marty Paich Dekette). The CD version of the original LP is especially valuable as it contains seven previously unissued titles, including another Tormé original, *Stranger In Town*. His voice is high and light, the pitching and diction clear and accurate. The songs are excellent (four by Rodgers and Hart, two by Arlen plus others by Gershwin, Porter, Van Heusen etc.) and there is a scat version of *Bernie's Tune*. Tormé's own episodic and extended *Country Fair* is a highlight in a consistently excellent programme. Tormé and Al Pellegrini share the piano stool, allowing a variation in tone colour when Pellegrini plays Goodman-style clarinet. The only irritation is the repeated "thank you, thank you very much" to the audience after nearly every song. Gratitude like that can get wearing. **AM**

The Duke Ellington & Count Basie Songbooks **Tormé** (v); **Jack Sheldon** (t); **Stu Williamson** (v-tb); **Frank Rosolino** (tb); **Joe Maini** (as); **Teddy Edwards** (ts); **Bill Perkins** (ts, bs); **Jimmy Rowles** (p); **Al Hendrickson** (g); **Joe Mondragon** (b); **Shelly Manne** (d); **Johnny Mandel** (arr, cond). Verve 823 248-2 (37 minutes). Recorded 1961.

⑧ ❽

It is difficult to understand the rejection some jazz fans feel towards Mel Tormé. He is probably the most technically gifted male singer of all and this combined with his good taste, well-controlled histrionics and fundamental knowledge of jazz, give him the standing of one of the better horn players. He works most often with consummate bands of West Coast musicians and his music is subtle as well as dexterous. He is unique in the potential of his appeal to both popular and jazz audiences. Latterly his recordings with George Shearing have been his most rewarding, but it would be hard to improve on the combination on this disc. The material is the best, Mandel's arrangements are perfect and the soloists in the band, with Rosolino, Sheldon, Edwards and Maini outstanding, all on good form. The choice of obscure material like Ellington's *Reminiscing In Tempo* (lyrics by Tormé) and *I Like The Sunrise* was inspired, and Mandel's orchestrations, particularly of the latter, are very fulfilling. Switch straight from those to *In The Evening* and you find Tormé treading Joe Williams/Joe Turner country in his own most effective way. Jimmy Rowles's piano is most effective here, as it is throughout the album. The 'mountain jack' climax is powerful and Torme's held high note beautifully judged. **SV**

David Torn

Tripping Over God **Torn** (g, v, loops, perc, miscellaneous instrs); **Elijah Torn** (b, noise, on *Rollin' & Tumblin'* only) CMP Ⓕ CD1007 (63 minutes) Recorded 1994.

⑧ ❼

Some would seriously doubt the legitimacy of this album's place in a jazz guide, but I don't think it could be denied its presence here on the grounds of style: after all, Garbarek, Frisell and many others have been making music like this for many years, but on (or along with) instruments more closely associated with the jazz tradition. Torn plays an electric guitar at white heat (although there are glimpses of acoustic from time to time), using disortion, effects and all sorts of noise-enhancement techniques. He uses sounds often associated with rock and its siblings, but the contexts are unerringly closer to the jazz mainstream than anything else. Leaving aside the question of there being just the one player multitracked to infinity playing a vast array of instruments (a direct descendent of Lennie Tristano's and Bill Evans's, let alone Les Paul's, experiments with multi-tracking), Torn here is creating a series of highly varied and often emotionally charged environments as backdrops for some truly impressive improvisation, most of which is terse, direct and uncompromising in its intellectual and emotional messages. In this, a true forerunner may be Gil Evans and his fantastic mood pictures of the mid-sixties.
KS

Jean Toussaint 1957

What Goes Around **Toussaint** (ts); **Jason Rebello, Bheki Mseleku, Julian Joseph** (p); **Tony Remy** (g); **Alec Dankworth, Wayne Batchelor** (b); **Mark Mondesir, Clifford Jarvis** (d); **Cleveland Watkiss** (v). World Circuit Ⓕ WCD 029 (63 minutes). Recorded 1991.

⑦ ❼

Toussaint came to international attention with Art Blakey, being a member of his Jazz Messengers between 1982 and 1986, at which point he decided to uproot from America and move to London. The affection and respect he felt for the drummer is reflected by this album's dedication to him. The tenor player made an immediate mark on the London scene, not least because he was not just another Coltrane clone but a tenor player with wide and deep roots in a whole range of styles, and a man who had successfully synthesized what he has heard into a coherent and interesting style of his own. This, his first album under his own name, shows that his music is varied and broad enough to sustain the listener's attention over what is quite a long programme. The decision to use a number of different pianists has helped achieve this variety, because the 'feel' definitely shifts from track to track as the hands at the keyboard change. The album has a carefully measured programme which nevertheless catches fire at the right times. Toussaint's arrangement of *Ruby, My Dear* is stunning, by the way.
KS

Ralph Towner 1940

Solstice **Towner** (g, p); **Jan Garbarek** (ss, ts, f); **Eberhard Weber** (vc, b); **Jon Christensen** (d, perc). ECM Ⓕ 1060 (825 458-2) (41 minutes). Recorded 1974.

✔ 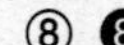

Unsurprisingly, given Ralph Towner's membership of folk/jazz/classical fusionists Oregon, **Solstice** occupies territory abutting on all three genres, but leans most closely towards jazz, courtesy of his distinguished sidemen. The music itself incorporates both free and more structured material, ranging from contemplative, impressionistic sound-collages with titles like *Drifting Petals* and *Nimbus* (featuring Jan Garbarek on flute) to hectic, swirling guitar-saxophone duels set against Eberhard Weber's supple, sonorous bass and Jon Christensen's vigorous but sensitive drumming and percussion work. The following year, Garbarek and Christensen were to collaborate unforgettably with Keith Jarrett on the masterpiece **Belonging**, and Weber was to set out on tour as—unusually for a bassist—featured soloist with Gary Burton, so **Solstice** catches these sidemen at a pivotal period in their careers, all poised to capture world attention. Towner himself employs his much-praised 'pianistic' acoustic guitar style to great effect throughout, although the slightly unfocused, loose nature of the material militates against the album as a whole reaching the summit of four-way improvised interaction achieved by Jarrett's **Belonging**. Nevertheless, **Solstice** neatly epitomizes the seventies ECM sound, one which has maintained its appeal over the intervening years a great deal better than some of the electronic fusion then being played in contemporary US studios.
CP

Blue Sun **Towner** (g, p, synth, frh, c, perc). ECM Ⓕ 1250 (829 162-2) (45 minutes). Recorded 1982.

Towner is best known for his work in the widely acclaimed group Oregon (see above); but he has made a distinctive series of records under his own name on the ECM label, some of them solo, some of them with small groupings of people. **Blue Sun** is a perfect example of his work as a solo artist. Towner was trained as both pianist and guitarist, so there is no drop in quality when he turns from plucked to hammered strings. His musical thinking is clearly orchestral and he arranges the different instruments here so astutely that one always has the sense that a tight-knit group of like-minded souls are recording the music 'live' in the studio. Considering that it is all just multi-tracked Towner, the spark and presence which comes across is no mean feat in itself.

The different tracks here cover a considerable emotional range, although they are stylistically homogeneous. Towner uses his synthesizer tracks as discreet and beautifully-voiced backdrops for the melodies of his improvisations and compositions. On *The Prince and The Sage* they glow, they are so luminescent behind the solo classical guitar. On other tracks, such as *C.T. Kangaroo*, there is a great deal more bounce, humour and rhythmic lift. Like Gil Evans, Towner has the ability to create exciting as well as beautiful and languid things. **KS**

Stan Tracey

1926

Under Milk Wood **Bobby Wellins** (ts); **Tracey** (p); **Jeff Clyne** (b); **Jackie Dougan** (d). Blue Note CDP Ⓜ 7 89449 2 (41 minutes). Recorded 1965.

⑧ ❻

The mixture of spoken poetry and jazz is unique in its ability to induce uncontrollable squirming in the listener. The jazz is usually alright, but the poetry end is invariably a karaoke-like ego trip and should be most diligently avoided. Conversely it would be hard to find a more satisfying poetry-based instrumental composition than Tracey's Dylan Thomas-inspired suite. Tracey's hump-backed piano mirrored the vivid colours of Thomas's words. Nearly three decades on, this great classic makes a belated but most welcome reappearance. Tracey has gone on to many and varied other things, but this album remains unique in his discography, largely because of the perfect way in which four outstanding musicians combined so well to play such outstanding material. The musical contrasts and challenges are well met by Wellins, here showing his full stature for the first time. Tracey tests him continuously, putting him into situations which call forth trenchant and delicate improvisations - the sparse *Starless And Bible Black* is a good example. Clyne and Dougan are perfect. Dougan, at that time regarded as our best big band drummer, shows his versatility in this most demanding role. The solid and substantial music which results is an unusual achievement for such a small group, and places Tracey on a par with Gerry Mulligan. **SV**

Portraits Plus **Tracey** (p); **Guy Barker** (t); **Malcolm Griffiths** (tb); **Peter King** (as); **Don Weller** (ts); **Art Themen** (ss, ts); **Dave Green** (b); **Clark Tracey** (d). Blue Note Ⓕ CDP 780696 2 (59 minutes). Recorded 1992.

⑥ ❻

Quite a mellow Stan Tracey on this recent Blue Note issue, which note-writer John Fordham says is (at the age of 65) his first appearance on a major international label. A faintly nostalgic feel about it too, as Tracey sketches some portraits of musicians who have meant a lot to him in the past—Rollins, Monk, Gil Evans, Duke—although frankly the portraits are rough sketches rather than recognizable likenesses. The scoring is fluid but not startling, and everyone solos in their accustomed manner. Hard to find anything bad about this session, or anything very outstanding either, although it does occur to me listening to Malcolm Griffiths's roaring trombone that he was doing things with the instrument in Britain 20 years ago for which Gary Valente and Ray Anderson got a lot of credit a lot later. **MK**

Lennie Tristano

1919-1978

Lennie Tristano/The New Tristano **Tristano** (p); **Lee Konitz** (as); **Peter Ind**, **Gene Ramey** (b); **Jeff Morton**, **Art Taylor** (d). Rhino/Atlantic Ⓜ 271595-2 (78 minutes). Recorded 1955-62.

✔ ⑧ ❼

Tristano didn't make that many records, and what there are never stays in catalogue that long because he's not an easy listen and people shy away from the effort needed. Fair enough, but when the pianist/theorist/teacher is functioning at peak power, as on much of this generous doubling of two classic Atlantic LPs on one disc, then the music becomes compelling, because the theories are delivered in such an exciting way that what can often sound meretricious suddenly becomes revelatory.

The influence of Tristano on one whole stream of jazz musicians is well documented, and his anticipations of many later developments in jazz have also been widely commented on, but his influence on the mainstream is largely unexplored. A striking example is neatly encapsulated on the first four tracks here, recorded privately by Tristano and using multi-tracking techniques at that time mostly used for novelty records. *Requiem*, a solo blues for Charlie Parker, is a clear antecedent for Bill Evans's *NYC's No Lark*, his lament for Sonny Clark. Tristano here provides a jazz framework within which he uses musical thinking derived from 20th-Century classical music, and thus points the way for the personal synthesis Evans was soon to make. That synthesis remains to this day the basis of the modern jazz piano mainstream. The second album here, **The New Tristano**, finds the pianist for the most part utilizing walking bass figures which root him in an earlier jazz tradition, while his right-hand figures rarely wander far from swing and Tatumesque rhythmic concepts, no matter where the harmony goes. **KS**

Gianluigi Trovesi

1944

From G To G **Trovesi** (as, cl, bcl); **Pina Minafra** (tp, flh, didgeridu, v); **Rodolfo Migliardi** (tb, tba); **Marco Remondini** (vc); **Roberto Bonati, Marco Micheli** (b); **Vittorio Marinoni** (d); **Fulvio Maras** (perc). Soul Note Ⓕ 121 231-2 (59 minutes). Recorded 1992.

⑧ ❽

Trovesi is an excellent example of the European jazz musician who is not content to merely solo over the traditional song forms of American jazz; instead, he finds aspects of his native music which can support improvisational manoeuvres and are compatible with jazz inflections and arrangements. Trovesi goes a step or two beyond most Europeans, however, in his familiarity with Mediterranean dance rhythms plus Italian mediaeval and renaissance music. He recorded an LP in 1978 which featured his improvisations on a thirteenth century saltarello as well as a 12-tone series. Later trio albums reinforced his connections with folk and dance musics; the recent **From G To G** is no exception, but places Trovesi's ideas in a larger ensemble. The results are very attractive, thanks in part due to the unusual instrumentation—two drummers, two bassists, and a cellist among the eight players—and the unexpected ways Trovesi uses them. He makes ingenious use of the two basses, alternating between rhythmic ostinati and contrapuntal lines, and the drummers not only keep time but add splashes of percussive colour. He is also able to integrate his influences into the eclectic, memorable compositions, from the loose-limbed Ornette Coleman flavour of *Herbop* to the twenties two-beat, slap bass parodies (along with 'mumbled' vocals in the manner of Clark Terry) of *Now I Can* and *Hercab*, the Australian didgeridu (reminiscent of the drone of Sardinian reed instruments) and pungent bite of Pina Minafra's trumpet in *Dedalo* to the title tune, in the style of a classical chaconne, with solo variations of a melody of touching simplicity over an unchanging bass line. As **From G To G** shows, Trovesi is one of Europe's best talents, and deserves wider recognition. **AL**

Robert Trowers

Point of View **Trowers** (tb); **Richard Wyands** (p); **Marcus McLaurine** (b); **Gene Jackson** (d); **Al Grey, Slide Hampton, Fred Wesley** (tb) two tracks each. Concord Ⓕ CCD-4656 (61 minutes). Recorded 1994.

⑤ ❿

Trowers is a young veteran of the Illinois Jacquet, Lionel Hampton and Count Basie orchestras, and his style is what membership of those organizations would suggest. He demonstrates his repsect for Johnson, Fuller, Harris and Rosolino among others on every track here, and his choice of trombone guests indicates a thorough familiarity with the modern jazz mainstream. His tone is full and with enough of an edge to keep it for the most part clear of soporific tendencies. His technique is admirably complete, and although his improvisations don't hang together in the way J.J. Johnson's does, then he sustains forward movement and tends to avoid obvious phrases and slide trombone clichés.

His supporting trio is self-effacing and efficient, and his guests (especially Al Grey) add a dimension of grit and smear which Trowers himself tends to avoid. Trowers is an impressively capable player with a sophisticated musical approach, but he could afford to take a few more emotional risks with his listener. **KS**

Gust William Tsilis

Sequestered Days **Gust William Tsilis** (vb, mba); **Joe Lovano** (ts, f); **Peter Madsen** (p); **Anthony Cox** (b); **Billy Hart** (d). Enja Ⓕ 6094-2 (70 minutes). Recorded 1991.

⑧ ❽

Tsilis's jazz philosophy leads him to tight, coherent writing from which long solos develop naturally. His band, obviously used to playing together regularly, is endowed with superior soloists who, while asserting their individuality, all play with the group sound in mind. The leader, who to judge by the skills shown here should be better known, plays eloquent and original vibes in the territory which lies between Milt Jackson and Gary Burton.

Joe Lovano's tenor playing is happily derivative of the great men of the forties—Ammons and Byas come to mind—and, as he has shown elsewhere, he plays with great passion and technique. He is one of the more rewarding saxophone players of the day, who has burgeoned through the Woody Herman, Thad Jones-Mel Lewis and Charlie Haden orchestras and is now a vital component in guitarist John Scofield's quartet, Lovano is able to concoct a direct mixture of traditional and modern elements which give him a unique sound in the jazz of the day. He is perhaps less palpably influenced by John Coltrane than is the fashion and, oddly for such an outstanding player, little has been written about him in the reference books.

Peter Madsen is one of the crop of inventive young pianists who have arrived in the last few years, and as ever Billy Hart franks the character of the session with his crisp and intelligent drumming. The quintet swings with great fire and it would be nice to think that jazz will follow the directions suggested here by Tsilis and Lovano. **SV**

Joe Turner

1907-1990

Sweet and Lovely **Turner** (p). Vogue Ⓜ 111507-2 (42 minutes). Recorded 1952.

⑦ ❻

There is a moment, in the opening statement of the first take of *Sweet and Lovely*, when the figure of Thelonious Monk looms suddenly over this music. Turner has used such an odd harmonization, bottom-heavy and lurching toward the off-beat, that the only parallels which make sense are either the Kurt Weill of *Surabaya Johnny* or of solo Monk. Later in the same performance the harmonic course of the song is normalized, but then Turner breaks up his usually metronomic left-hand patterns to interpolate a whole swathe of rhythms usually associated exclusively with Erroll Garner. All this is the more remarkable when the recording date is taken into account: Garner may have been a popular figure, but Monk was still on the road to Damascus as far as the jazz public was concerned, and was nearing the lowest point of his career. As if admonished from the control room, Turner delivers a second take suitably toned-down from the first, but with small vestiges of the daring which overcame him the previous time round.

This is an important moment on an otherwise typical Turner stride-dominated date, because during it you can glimpse the true range of this great but neglected figure. His roots may well be in the soil of Jelly Roll Morton-inspired ragtime, as transmuted by the next generation of New York stride players such as Waller and Johnson (this is clearly signalled on *Between The Devil and the Deep Blue Sea*), but he continued to listen to each new wave of pianists, and certainly absorbed a great deal of Tatum. This last point is evidenced by his approach to the arrangement of *I Cover The Waterfront* (out-of-tempo intro, delicate stride for the theme and variations; end with a dinky little chord progression).

As with all the best solo pianists, Turner demands close listening while simultaneously evincing a cast-iron *joie de vivre* which would make him the life and soul of any party he played at. Stick to close listening in front of your speakers and you will be amply rewarded. **KS**

'Big' Joe Turner

1911-1985

The Boss Of The Blues **Turner** (v); **Joe Newman, Jimmy Nottingham** (t); **Lawrence Brown** (tb); **Pete Brown** (as); **Frank Wess, Seldon Powell** (ts); **Pete Johnson** (p); **Freddie Green** (g); **Walter Page** (b); **Cliff Leeman** (d); **Ernie Wilkins** (arr). Atlantic Ⓜ 781459-2 (45 minutes). Recorded 1959.

✔ ⑧ ❽

At his best Turner was an unequalled handler of band blues in the Kansas City idiom; a big man with a big, wide-open-space voice, plain in his delivery, little given to ornamentation, but with a wonderful rhythmic insistence. As Whitney Balliert remarked, "it is as if he were driving his voice into your mind". He kept a good part of his voice until near the end of a long life, and consequently was much recorded. Too much, and sometimes in wretchedly inappropriate company, as on the 1960s tracks on **Every Day in the Week** (MCA/Decca). But that album is not to be ignored; most of it dates from two decades earlier, and it includes the stately small-group recordings with pianists Freddie Slack (*Rocks In My Bed*) and Pete Johnson (*Rebecca*).

It has been generally agreed for more than 30 years that Turner's finest studio hours were spent making **The Boss Of The Blues**. The album was subtitled *Joe Turner Sings Kansas City Jazz* and the local connections of several of the musicians need no spelling out. Possibly no finer band was ever assembled for such a purpose, and the producers were rewarded with a programme of majestic, authoritative, yet fluid and mutually responsive blues singing and playing. Many of the songs were or would become the singer's personal standards - *Cherry Red, I Want A Little Girl, Wee Baby Blues, Morning Glories* - but these recordings had an integrity of conception and rightness of execution that were seldom matched. **TR**

Steve Turré

1948

Right There **Turré** (tb, shells); **John Blake** (vn); **Akua Dixon Turré** (vc, v); **Benny Green, Willie Rodriguez** (p); **Buster Williams, Andy Gonzalez** (b); **Billy Higgins** (d); **Wynton Marsalis** (t); **Benny Golson** (ts); **Dave Valentin** (f); **George Delgado, Manny Oquendo** (perc); **Herman Olivera** (v, perc). Antilles Ⓕ 510 040-2 (58 minutes). Recorded 1991.

⑦ ❽

A graduate of North Texas State University and a former Jazz Messenger, Turré and his trombone skills are at home in most musical situations. He is as comfortable in the big bands of Thad Jones/Mel Lewis or Dizzy Gillespie's United Nations Orchestra as he is in a hard bop combo or in a jazz environment such as that found on this CD. Here the basic line-up teams trombone, violin and cello to provide a pleasing, yet unusual, textural base and he is joined on three titles by Wynton Marsalis, with one further piece featuring Benny Golson. Most of the arrangements are by Turré, but it is as a soloist that he stands out. The up-tempo *Ginseng People* tests his prodigious technique, the changing time signatures of *Sanyas* check out his assured sense of timing, while his outstanding plunger mute playing on *Echoes Of Harlem* and *Duke's Mountain* confirms his emotional commitment. His adroit conch shell blowing is no mere novelty effect and, with the aid of Manny Oquendo's rhythm section, he treats *Descarga De Turré* to a full two-shell attack. As this release demonstrates, Turré occupies the middle ground between the occasionally incontinent outpourings of the European trombones and the didactic insistence of J.J. Johnson and his many disciples. **BMcR**

Stanley Turrentine 1934

Up At Minton's, Volumes 1 & 2 **Turrentine** (ts); **Horace Parlan** (p); **Grant Green** (g); **George Tucker** (b); **Al Harewood** (d). Blue Note Ⓜ CDP8 28885 2 (90 minutes). Recorded 1961.

⑦ ❻

In the fifties and sixties, when jazz commentary was very much concerned with the linear progress of jazz styles, Pittsburgh-born Turrentine was perceived as something of a throwback. His tone, articulation and harmonic language stems for the most part from Illinois Jacquet, Gene Ammons and Don Byas, and his early professional career saw him working as much with r&b bands as with jazz (he replaced John Coltrane in Earl Bostic's unit).

This recent reissue of a well-known 'live' session finds Turrentine in preaching mood, playing with a finely-integrated rhythm section (not surprising when you consider it was borrowed from Lou Donaldson's working band of the day). Minton's house piano never was much good (a Barry Harris record made there suffers from the same problem), but the atmosphere is easy, the playing relaxed and focused, the crowd attentive. Turrentine responds with fluent and convincing solos, as well as his special caressing of song melodies, regardless of the speed at which they are being played. Turrentine is one of a number of tenor players who have a stock of personal phrases which they tend to re-arrange in a new order for each solo (Webster and Ammons were both experts at this), but the persuasive confidence with which he plays saves this from becoming a drawback. Guitarist Green plays very little behind the leader, but solos tastefully. Parlan displays his vast musicality in any number of ways. The album, then, is a handy snapshot of a mainstream 'soul jazz' unit at work in front of an appreciative audience, just as the sixties were getting under way. **KS**

Never Let Me Go **Turrentine** (ts); **Shirley Scott** (org); **Major Holley**, **Sam Jones** (b); **Al Harewood**, **Clarence Johnston** (d); **Ray Barretto** (perc). Blue Note Ⓜ CDP7 84129-2 (46 minutes). Recorded 1963.

⑥ ❽

Turrentine, like Gene Ammons before him, occupies the borderland between r&b and jazz, with early experience alongside Ray Charles and Max Roach defining and refining his strengths. And, although some of his later albums sold extremely well, it would be a mistake to dismiss him as a mere popularizer.

Whereas many earnest tenor players of a later generation convey less than they aim for, Turrentine's work appears undemanding and unambitious while frequently achieving considerable depth. Strolling through this straight-ahead 1963 session with his then wife Shirley Scott on the Hammond B-3 organ, the saxophonist makes nuances count and simple ideas speak volumes.

The best of his Blue Notes being unavailable, **Never Let Me Go** is an honourable if unexceptional replacement. The title-track (not the film-song written by Jay Livingston and Ray Evans revived by Keith Jarrett and others) is a rather straight ballad, but *They Can't Take That Away* is a useful addition to the original programme. The inclusion of two standards heard a year earlier on Sonny Rollins's **The Bridge** (*God Bless The Child* and *Without A Song*) may be a coincidence, but it could be an example of the beneficial interchange between high art and middlebrow mellowness. **BP**

Alvin 'Red' Tyler 1925

Graciously **Tyler** (ts); **Clyde Kerr Jr** (t, flh, perc); **David Torkanowsky** (p); **Steve Masakowski** (g); **James Singleton** (b); **Johnny Vidacovich** (d). Rounder Ⓕ 2061 (45 minutes). Recorded 1986.

⑧ ❻

New Orleans, like other American cities, has its share of musicians who prefer the rootedness of home to the hot house of New York. Tyler, veteran of numerous Fats Domino sessions and the Crescent City's sixties hard-bop scene, was still a hometown fixture when he made two albums for Rounder in the mid-eighties.

Tyler at this stage had a dark, pleasing tone, highlighted by varied, nimble phrasing. Decidedly a swinger, he tends to lean into the beat rather than lagging behind. A medium-grooving *Here's That Rainy Day*, for quartet with guitar, shows off his deft balladry, alert and relaxed at once. Elsewhere, Kerr's tart, hot trumpet nicely offsets Tyler's smoke-laced tenor.

The compatible rhythm players are among the city's most sought after, but explicit regionalisms are seldom apparent. Vidacovich lets parade beats emerge, closing Tyler's fetching jazz waltz *Greystoke*, and *My Shoes Hold Out* mambos in good second-line fashion. But usually the local accent comes out more subtly. The way tunes and improvisers drift between 2/4 and 4/4 (*Cutie Pie*), or duple and triple metre (*Greystoke*, *Count 'Em*) reflects a musical environment where Afro-Latin polyrhythms are second nature. **KW**

Charles Tyler

1941-1992

Charles Tyler Ensemble **Tyler** (as); **Joel Friedman** (vc); **Henry Grimes** (b); **Ronald Jackson** (d); **Charles Moffett** (d). ESP-Disk Ⓕ 1029-2 (44 minutes). Recorded 1966.

⑥ ❺

Tyler made two albums for ESP-Disk, the second called **Eastern Man Alone**. This first album is the more coherent. Tyler came to prominence when he joined Albert Ayler's ensemble in the mid-sixties for a brief time, and recorded on the tenor player's epochal **Bells** (also on ESP-Disk). Tyler clearly learned a lot from Ayler (they had known each other back in Cleveland, before either had any general reputation), mimicking his tone and delivery on the higher-pitched alto, and using many of the noise-effects from fierce overblowing of the instrument that Ayler was then specializing in. It is quite possible that Tyler also borrowed the idea of playing with cello and bass, but then it could just as easily have been the other way around. Whatever the true story, Tyler plays with great passion and commitment on every track, and although his music is a little limited in range, it is very effectively delivered here, with each instrument very clear on its role within the music (quite a rarity on ESP Disks in general at this time). We even come across common time on more than one occasion. Ayler's pioneering approach may have ultimately produced a series of dead-ends as far as development goes, but Tyler here suggests that there were other ways out which perhaps were not followed all the way by those following on behind. **KS**

McCoy Tyner

1938

Inception/ Nights Of Ballads and Blues **Tyner** (p); **Art Davis, Steve Davis** (b); **Elvin Jones, Lex Humphries** (d). Impulse! Ⓜ MCAD-42000 (72 minutes). Recorded 1962/63.

⑧ ❻

This 1988 reissue responsibly combines two LPs, Tyner's first and third recordings as leader. It makes an intelligent pairing, since the two albums illustrate contrasting facets of Tyner's art. The first allowed his distinctive harmonic style to be heard unobscured by the tumult of the Coltrane quartet; the later date exposed an aspect of his style hardly ever called upon by that group. The first is the more dynamic, invigorated perhaps by the choice of material and by the presence of Elvin Jones and Art Davis. Half of its tunes—*Inception*, *Blues For Gwen* and *Effendi*—are strongly redolent of Tyner's work with Coltrane, all of them for their use of the quartal harmonies with which Tyner is so strongly identified, and *Effendi* also for its two-chord modalism. Perhaps because of their rich harmonies, these three tunes have an intensity not found in the other pieces, and they excite some sparkling interplay among the trio, Tyner and Davis becoming particularly exercised on *Blues For Gwen*. The only evidence of Tyner's tart 'Coltrane' style on **Nights Of Ballads and Blues** comes in his own 3/4 blues *Groove Waltz*. Otherwise the session is as elegant as the title suggests, with plenty of opportunities for Tyner to flourish his rhapsodic, Tatumish skills in the manner typified by *We'll Be Together Again* and *'Round Midnight*. **MG**

The Turning Point **Tyner** (p, arr); **Kamau Adilifu, Earl Gardner, Virgil Jones** (t); **Steve Turré, Frank Lacy** (tb); **John Clark** (frh); **Howard Johnson** (tba); **Doug Harris** (ss, f); **Joe Ford** (as); **John Stubblefield, Junior Cook** (ts); **Avery Sharpe** (b); **Aaron Scott** (d); **Jerry Gonzales** (perc); **Dennis Mackrel, Turré, Johnson, Slide Hampton** (arr); **Bob Belden, Hampton** (cond). Birdology Ⓕ 513 163-2 (55 minutes). Recorded 1991.

⑧ ❽

Tyner has been extremely prolific on record during the last few years, producing trios and quartets, several solo albums and a couple of big band sessions. Although initially McCoy's piano style might seem just too dense to do other than compete with a large ensemble, some of his seventies Milestone recordings showed the assumption to be too simplistic and this album in particular vindicates the format completely.

At times the section writing doubles the piano theme-statements, but by and large they bounce off each other to great effect, thanks to the work of the five arrangers. And what a band it is! Recorded with just a sufficient halo of reverberation, the brass pack a terrific punch and the soloists (mostly uncredited, unlike the writers) include all the saxes, Clark and one of the trumpeters.

The remakes of *Passion Dance* (originally a quartet track featuring Joe Henderson) and *Fly With The Wind* come up brand new, while Tyner's *Update* (an *I Got Rhythm* variant) and the Monk-dedicated *High Priest* create straight-ahead contrasts. Of the ballads, *Angel Eyes* is a Hampton score influenced by early Gil Evans that would be too lush without Tyner's pianistics, while *In A Sentimental Mood* is his unaccompanied coda. **BP**

Manhattan Moods **Tyner** (p); **Bobby Hutcherson** (vb, mba). Blue Note Ⓕ CDP 828423 2 (58 minutes). Recorded 1993.

✔

⑧ ❿

Hutcherson is actually given co-billing on the album cover, but Tyner's name is first and it is his piano playing which shapes and mostly defines the music which emerges. His is the proactive, Hutcherson's the responsive creative musical force on this particular record. It has ever been thus for Tyner since he left Coltrane in late 1966. He is one of a handful of modern pianists who can effortlessly play the role of a rhythm section single-handedly (an entirely different matter to playing solo piano), and it is fascinating to hear him echo some of his elders' efforts in this area, with the shadow of Oscar Peterson looming in particular over the pianist's comping work on *Blue Monk*. An often underplayed aspect of Tyner's work is his delicacy and lightness of rhythm when it is called for. This is expecially apparent here on faster numbers when Hutcherson is soloing: Tyner never overwhelms him with sound, his chord voicings astutely avoiding the sonic areas Hutcherson is exploring, giving the duets especial clarity.

For his part, Hutcherson revels in the space he receives here. This is not the first time he and Tyner have recorded together, though it is their first as a duet. Like Milt Jackson with John Lewis, he uses the occasion to spring into long and intricate single lines which pulsate with vitality. His bright tone and his concentration on the higher registers of the instrument give him a beautiful, crystalline aura which clearly defines his personality as distinct from that of the piano's. One of the disc's highlights is the moving *I Loves You, Porgy*, which both men treat with quiet, intense dignity, while Mal Waldron's *Soul Eyes*, recorded famously by the classic Coltrane quartet, receives a rhapsodic, almost Tatumesque treatment, Tyner weaving lyrical garlands around Hutcherson's theme statements. **KS**

Michal Urbaniak 1943

Songbird Urbaniak (vn); **Kenny Barron** (p); **Peter Washington** (b); **Kenny Washington** (d). SteepleChase Ⓕ SCCD 31278 (64 minutes). Recorded 1990.

⑦ ❽

A versatile man, Urbaniak began his musical career in Poland as a Dixielander. He progressed firstly to bop and then came under the musical spell of John Coltrane. While still playing saxophone, he worked as a classical violinist before switching to that instrument as his first choice in both musical codes. His imaginative electronic group of the seventies featured his vocalist wife Ursula Dudziak, while in the eighties he worked with Larry Coryell and Archie Shepp. During that time, his playing deliberately retreated from the idea of either fusion or experimentation and he increasingly coloured his music with idiosyncratic Polish elements. This CD nails his colours to the mast most effectively. He has chosen one of jazz's best rhythm sections, the commitment is to his own brand of refined violin jazz and he has written excellent themes to accommodate both contingencies. The quizzical *Doubts*, the impelling *Deadline* and the jaunty *Aladdin's Lamp* stand out, but all are good vehicles for improvisation. Urbaniak's solos in 1990 have returned him to the harmonic approach; no attempt is made to desert the parent structure and it is perhaps significant that his most ingenious solos are on *Beautiful Love* and *Songbird*, the two tunes he did not write. **BMcR**

René Urtreger 1934

Jazzman **Urtreger** (p). Carlyne Music Ⓕ CAR C10 CD (53 minutes). Recorded 1985.

⑧ ❽

Urtreger has been a major part of the French jazz scene since the late fifties (he recorded with Miles Davis on the famous *Elevator to the Scaffold* soundtrack for Louis Malle), but like saxophonist Barney Wilen he had a long period away from the music. His return to jazz in the late seventies found him just as complete a player as before, but one with more confidence in his own abilities. This album has the authoritative ease in execution which only comes through complete mastery, and the opening track, *Budomania*, is a reworking of Bud Powell's *Parisian Thoroughfare* which is the best recording of the piece since the composer's own in 1951. Urtreger, a classically trained player (he studied with Marguerite Long, thereby becoming one of that very rare breed of jazz pianists, those whose training involved a direct link with Debussy, Ravel and Poulenc), never wanders greatly from his bop roots, but at the same time he is not limited by them into regurgitating familiar licks. He takes the harmonic and rhythmic disciplines of the music on board and forges fresh, inspiring music from them. Most of the compositions are his own, although J.J. Johnson's *Lament* and Monk's *Ruby, My Dear* and *'Round Midnight* are revealed in new and enticing ways here. **KS**

Jesus 'Chucho' Valdes

Solo Piano **Valdes** (p); on two tracks, add **Dave Green** (b); **Enrique Pla** (d); **Miguel 'Angar' Diaz** (perc). Blue Note Ⓕ CDP7 80597-2 (63 minutes). Recorded 1991.

⑧ ❽

Valdes hails from a village near Havana and received a formal musical education. In 1967 the Cuban band Irakere was formed, with Valdes as its leader, pianist and principal composer/arranger. Since 1985 Irakere has been a popular attraction at Ronnie Scott's in London with its annual appearances there. This CD was recorded at the club after the night's audience had left. Away from Irakere, Valdes is revealed as a most astonishing soloist with infallible technique and a great understanding of jazz. The note production alone is remarkable, but this is not technique for its own sake. Like Art Tatum,

Chucho clearly has no other way of playing, but remains always the master of his enormous instrumental command, never the other way around. Eight of the tracks are Valdes compositions, and one, *Bill (Evans)*, is a sincere tribute to one of his idols. Although some of the tunes hark back to a Cuban background, most of the music is firmly implanted in North American jazz (a fact reinforced by the final *Blues (Untitled)*, with bass and drums added). Although sub-titled **The Music of Cuba**, this is very definitely an outstanding example of pure jazz piano. **AM**

Jasper Van't Hof

1947

Face To Face **Van't Hof** (p); **Ernie Watts** (ts); **Bo Stief** (b); **Aldo Romano** (d). veraBra Ⓕ vBr 2063-2 (53 minutes). Recorded 1994.

⑥ ❽

Dutch pianist Van't Hof's wide-ranging involvements have stretched from work with Archie Shepp to his commercially successful 1984 world music album **Pili-Pili**, in which he employed African percussion and computer. **Face To Face** represents a largely uncompromising return to first principles. The spirit of Coltrane looms large throughout the date, the lead role played with admirable conviction and virtuosity by Ernie Watts, a player who in recent years has done more than enough to shake off the reputation he garnered in the seventies as a West Coast studio smoothie. Unsurprisingly, Van't Hof sounds not unlike McCoy Tyner and (when essaying later Trane styles) Alice Coltrane.

However, while the quartet adheres firmly to Trane's approach in several respects (most notably in the rolling, elegiac hymn *Il Piacere* and the unreconstructed hard bop of *As Well*) it follows the principle rather than the letter of Trane's pioneering world music explorations, drawing its 'world' influences from such diverse contemporary sources as African High-Life music (*Zaire*) and what sounds like Bulgarian gipsy music (*Three Doors*). **MG**

Tom Varner

The Mystery Of Compassion **Varner** (frh, arr); **Ed Jackson** (as); **Rich Rothenberg** (ts); **Mike Richmond** (b); **Tom Rainey** (d). (**Mark Feldman** (vln) -1 track only; **Matt Derriau** (as); **Ellery Eskelin** (ts); **Jim Hartog** (bs) -1 track only; **Steve Swell** (tb); **Dave Taylor** (btb) - 2 tracks only.). Soul Note 121217-2 (75 minutes). Recorded 1992.

⑥ ❽

Varner is a well-travelled if little-known french-horn player who works with such different leaders as John Zorn avant-garde 'composer' LaMonte Young and big-band specialist George Gruntz. He benefits from a ripe tone and an adventurous ear, and has made several previous albums on Soul Note. Half of the ten tracks here find him leading a quintet including Ed Jackson and Rich Rothenberg of the 29th Street Saxophone Quartet, and he sounds as mobile and forthright as most trombonists. This set, produced by drummer Joey Baron, is impressive for Varner's composition and organisation skills. Some of the items have a subliminal Mingus feel in their mixture of written and improvised material in which the horn playing is more catalytic than cataclysmic. Featuring himself on three short tracks without rhythm, he has elsewhere stimulated some excellent collective playing, with the added attractions of the five extra brassmen on *Death At The Right Time*. The long *The Well*, on the other hand, features violinist Mark Feldman (who has played with Tim Beme and Anthony Davis) on an episodic piece that nods to both Philip Glass and 12-tone composition, while retaining an improvised content. **BP**

Nana Vasconcelos

1944

Saludades **Vasconcelos** (perc, v); **Egberto Gismonti** (g, arr); **Stuttgart Radio Symphony Orchestra**. ECM Ⓕ 1147 (829 380-2) (44 minutes). Recorded 1979.

⑧ ❾

Brazilian drummer Vasconcelos is a percussive painter of exotically shimmering colours derived from South American, African and Asian sources. Having gained prominence in the mid-sixties with countryman Milton Nascimento, he migrated to the US as a member of Argentinian saxophonist Gato Barbieri's group in 1971. In Europe he worked extensively with Brazilian guitarist Egberto Gismonti, and in 1978 co-founded the exploratory trio Codena with Don Cherry and Collin Walcott. Vasconcelos also had a prominent tenure with guitarist Pat Metheny's high-profile fusion group in the early eighties.

On **Saludades**, Vasconcelos conjures up intense percussion-based soundscapes whose *tramontane* other-world ambience is transmitted through Gismonti's ethereal string arrangements and Vasconcelos's inspired percussion and vocal gestures. His use of the berimbau, a bowed single-string affair connected to a resonating gourd, provides a distinctly melodic as well as percussive voice in the extended O Berimbau and elsewhere. Similarly impressive is Gismonti's *Cego Aderaldo* which also features Vasconcelos's long-standing colleague on eight-string guitar. A key element in the project's success is the sublime string playing of the Stuttgart aggregation. **CB**

Sarah Vaughan

1924-1990

Sarah Vaughan With Clifford Brown **Vaughan** (v); **Brown** (t); **Herbie Mann** (f); **Paul Quinichette** (ts); **Jimmy Jones** (p); **Joe Benjamin** (b); **Roy Haynes** (d); **Ernie Wilkins** (arr, cond). EmArcy Ⓜ 814 641-2 (50 minutes). Recorded 1954.

✓ ⑨ ❼

Although she began as a bebopper, trading choruses with Charlie Parker and Dizzy Gillespie, it took Sarah Vaughan nearly ten years to escape the pop market long enough to record her first classic set of jazz vocals. The occasion was her meeting with the young Clifford Brown, already on the verge of greatness, who contributes a handful of excellent solos. Quinichette and Mann add pleasant obbligatos, but they are really just icing on the cake. The two leaders apart, the musical honours go to the rhythm trio, Vaughan's regular group at the time, who accompany with peerless tact.

The session was a relaxed affair, the musicians filling out the arrangements in the studio and leaving plenty of room for improvisation. Vaughan seizes the chance gleefully, scatting duets with the horns on *Lullaby Of Birdland*, skating around the melody of *Embraceable You*, signing-off *You're Not The Kind* with a surprise cascade of notes. Blessed with an extraordinary voice (her range was four octaves), she uses it, with great finesse, like an instrument, letting the long notes shimmer (*September Song*), swooping down to lean on a syllable (*Jim*), or darkening the timbre for a rueful *April In Paris*.

With her sensuous sound wedded to her impeccable timing (honed too on the whetstone of bebop), **With Clifford Brown** offers glorious Vaughan—hence glorious jazz—singing throughout. **GL**

Swingin' Easy **Vaughan** (v); **John Malachi**, **Jimmy Jones** (p); **Joe Benjamin**, **Richard Davis** (b); **Roy Haynes** (d). EmArcy Ⓜ 514 072-2 (37 minutes). Recorded 1954-57.

✓ ⑩ ❽

This CD would be worth buying for the version it contains of Ellington's *Prelude To A Kiss* alone—just one simple delicate, unerring chorus. It is a very un-songlike song, with intervals that might have been specially devised as traps for a singer with an insecure sense of pitch, which is exactly the kind of song that Sarah Vaughan relished. She had a miraculous ear and the vocal equipment to follow it wherever it led, a combination of which she was justly proud. Much of the enjoyment of listening to the young Sarah comes from the delight she takes in making tunes turn somersaults and jump through hoops. She seems, quite frankly, to take little interest in the words at this stage. The last piece here, a breakneck two choruses of *Linger Awhile*, would have been quite outrageous coming from anyone else, but who can object to a bit of showing off when the result is as spectacular as this? It puts one in mind of the completely unjustified but breathtaking swoop of almost an octave in the middle of her famous *Just Friends*—she just could not resist it. These two sessions were recorded when Sarah was aged 30 and 33 respectively, right at the end of her first flush of youthful exuberance, and they are magnificent. Well worth having, despite the short playing time. **DG**

Crazy and Mixed Up **Vaughan** (v); **Roland Hanna** (p); **Joe Pass** (g); **Andy Simpkins** (b); **Harold Jones** (d). Pablo Ⓜ PACD 2312 137-2 (33 minutes). Recorded 1982.

✓ ⑨ ❾

This is simply one of the finest jazz vocal albums ever produced. Sarah Vaughan, at the height of her extraordinary powers in 1982, swings with a god-like combination of authority and abandon. Indeed, if anyone ever sounded like she was born to be a jazz singer, Sarah Vaughan, at least here, is it. The ballads are impeccable. And when she limns *That's All* or *Love Dance*, that dark rich voice cannot help but envelop all in its powerfully seductive wake. Then, when she jumps from a musical cliff as she does on the free-fall flight of *Autumn Leaves*, one is left simply breathless. Vaughan's trademark vibrato quavers in the rubato intro of *The Island* before shifting gears into a hauntingly languid bossa nova. And though pronunciations are typically diffuse, she somehow makes the lyrics lucid and alive.

What makes this album a special case, even for Sarah Vaughan, is the singer's overall control of herself and the project. Pablo chief Norman Granz gave the production reins to Vaughan, who selected the repertoire as well as the musicians. And what a supporting cast! Pianist Hanna, guitarist Pass, bassist Simpkins and drummer Jones weave magic carpets on which Vaughan soars, sails and dips with delight. This was an obvious labour of love in which Vaughan's concentration was totally focused and inspired. **CB**

Joe Venuti

1903-1978

Violin Jazz **Venuti** (vn); **Jimmy Dorsey** (t, cl, as, bs); **Benny Goodman** (cl); **Don Murray** (cl, bs); **Frankie Trumbauer** (c-mels); **Adrian Rollini** (bss, gfs, vb, p); **Arthur Schutt**, **Frank Signorelli**, **Phil Wall**, **Rube Bloom** (p); **Eddie Lang**, **Dick McDonough** (g). Yazoo Ⓕ 1062 (43 minutes). Recorded 1927-34.

✓ ⑧ ❽

Venuti's "blend of solid musicianship and hokum", as the notes observe, "remains exhilarating to this day...confound(ing) conventional distinctions between highbrow and lowbrow art". The hokum character stems in part from the use of novelty instruments like Adrian Rollini's goofus and hot fountain pen, though some listeners may apply the description to the unremitting gaiety of the material, which preserves in a tangy aspic the Charleston-and-cocktail euphoria of its time. To be sure, there is no darkness in this music, and next to nothing of the blues, but to dismiss it as lightweight not only maligns the stupendous virtuosity of the principals Venuit and Lang but proscribes an optimism that is a legitimate part of the expressive vocabulary of jazz.

Louis Armstrong had revealed in his Hot Five and Seven recordings a few years earlier the dominant role a soloist could claim, yet these small-group performances, although nominally led by a forceful musical personality, are essentially collaborative. Instrumental roles constantly alter as the basic musical material is cut up and re-stitched into independent themes or elaborations. The product is not, as sometimes with Armstrong, monologue but the shifting textures of an animated and clever conversation. **TR**

Billy Ver Planck 1930

Jazz For Playgirls Ver Planck (tb, arr); **Clyde Reasinger**, **Joe Wilder, Bernie Glow**, **Phil Sunkel** (t); **Bill Harris** (tb); **Phil Woods** (cl, as); **Seldon Powell** (ts); **Gene Allen, Sol Schlinger** (bs); **Eddie Costa** (p, vb); **George Duvivier, Wendell Marshall** (b); **Bobby Donaldson, Gus Johnson** (d). Denon/Savoy Ⓜ SV 0209 (37 minutes). Recorded 1957.

⑧ ❻

This is a fine mainstream album which might be in danger of being overlooked by collectors unfamiliar with Ver Planck's name and credentials. He is a splendid writer whose scores have enlivened the books of dance bands such as those of Claude Thornhill, Jimmy Dorsey and Ralph Marterie. Savoy gave him a free hand on three or four albums in the fifties and this is a supreme example of his skills at combining orchestral efficiency with deep-rooted jazz feeling. Bill Harris, surely one of the most individual of all jazz trombonists, is one of the main soloists; he is clearly one of Ver Planck's idols. This is shown in another way on *Du-Udah-Udah*, where Ver Planck takes the trombone solo himself, only to reveal a style deeply indebted to Harris. Another heavily-featured soloist is Phil Woods (he has *Aw C'mon Sugah!* to himself), caught here at his most joyfully uninhibited. Rudy Van Gelder's engineering (in mono) captures the music with a sense of immediacy that is most attractive. An additional asset on this rather brief reissue is the playing of the late Eddie Costa on both piano and vibraphone. Recommended. **AM**

Marlene Ver Planck

Live In London Ver Planck (v) with **Andy Vinter** (p); **Roy Babbington** (b); **Mike Smith** (d). Audiophile Ⓕ ACD-280 (53 minutes). Recorded 1993.

⑥ ❼

Marlene is the wife of arranger Billy Ver Planck and is one of that handful of singers - including Peggy Lee and Rosemary Clooney - who benefit from being in jazz company without actually being jazz singers per se. She has all the attributes necessary to a real singer, clear diction, very accurate pitching and a completely musical approach to hundreds of songs. Perhaps understandably she is in great demand in the studios, where she has worked on countless jingles and the like, but when she emerges to work the club circuit she immediately reveals her talents as a marvellous singer. She is also something of a musical archeologist with a knack of discovering and dusting off near forgotten songs; on this album, recorded at two locations in London, she presents a lovely, lesser-known Jerome Kern gem, *Let's Begin* from the stage version of **Roberta** but dropped for the film adaptation. The album bristles with class and Marlene is efficiently served by the rhythm section from the BBC Big Band. **AM**

Edward Vesala 1945

Ode To The Death Of Jazz Vesala (d); **Matti Riikonen** (t); **Jorma Tapio** (as, bcl, f); **Jouni Kannisto** (ts, f); **Pepa Paivinen** (ss, ts, bs, f, cl, bcl); **Tim Ferchen** (mba, bells); **Taito Vainio** (accordion); **Iro Haarla** (p, hp, syn); **Jimi Sumen** (g); **Uffe Krokfors** (b). ECM 1413 (843 196-2) (56 minutes). Recorded 1989.

✓ ⑩ ❽

Vesala's vision is among the most unsettling, exotic, and unique in all of jazz—if you call what he does jazz. Given the (tongue-in-cheek?) title of this magnificent programme, I am not sure he does. Architect of several previous albums of atmospheric design, Vesala composes for contrast and mood rather than cohesiveness. As a percussionist, he has brought knowledge of ethnic musics, rock and a determined rejection of glib virtuosity and convention to bear on a highly personal style, and the same could be said for his scoring. These are magically evocative pieces, manipulating instrumental colour and texture and energy to evoke fascinating soundscapes of light and dark, water and ice, shadow and substance. *Sylvan Swizzle* (suggesting a tour through other-worldly caverns), the hauntingly spare *Time To Think*, and the shimmering *Watching For The Signal* are carefully-constructed ensemble works, full of unexpected details and emotional curves. But there are surprises everywhere—the forceful blend of folkish melody, industrial noise and machine-gun drumming of *Winds Of Sahara,* the wispy, disembodied electronics behind the tribal percussion and horn eruptions of *Infinite Express* and the incongruous tango *A Glimmer Of Sepal*. Absolutely original music, totally engaging. **AL**

Andrea Vicari

1966

Suburban Gorillas **Vicari** (p, kbds, perc): **Simon Da Silva** (t, flh); **Malcolm Earle Smith** (tb); **Martin Dunsdon** (f); **Leigh Etherington** (f, ss, ts); **Mornington Lockett** (ts, perc); **Hilary Cameron** (kbds, v); **Mark Ridout** (g); **Dorian Lockett** (b, elb); **Simon Pearson** (d, perc); **Rony Barrak** (tabla). 33 Records Ⓕ 33Jazz 016 (78 minutes). Recorded 1994.

⑥ ❽

Vicari, born in Florida but based in Birmingham since 1972, studied at Cardiff University, with a postgrad course at the Guildhall to round out her musical background, before beginning a professional career in London in the early nineties. She appeared with David Jean Baptiste, both live and on CD, during the course of 1993, and formed Suburban Gorillas, her own big-band, when the opportunity for a UK tour came about. That tour brought about this record, her début as a leader. As with many débuts it tends occasionally to be over-ambitious in scope, but there is nothing wrong with that, and there is nothing truly bad on this album, although some of the infrequent lyrics come close on occasion.

The playing, from a band of notable talents, is sharp enough without being soulless, and although the improvisations occasionally veer too close to competent rather than inspired or individualistic, the writing is unfussy, melodic and consistently upbeat. Vicari takes the Duke Ellington approach to leading this band, rather than the Cecil Taylor: her presence is discerned through the directions the band takes rather than her own piano work suborning all else to its needs. A good example of this is *Southern Comfort*, which opens with a three-minute unaccompanied piano solo, but then vamps into a piece for the whole ensemble to unfold. Ellington's method in a nutshell, even if the style is unrelated. An enjoyable album which suggests more and better things to come. **KS**

Vienna Art Orchestra

The Minimalism Of Erik Satie **Lauren Newton** (v); **Karl 'Bumi' Fian** (t, flh); **Hannes Kottek** (t, flh); **Christian Radovan** (tb); **John Sass** (bb); **Harry Sokal** (ss, ts, f); **Wolfgang Puschnig** (as, bcl, f, sps); **Roman Schwaller** (ts, cl); **Woody Schabata** (vb); **Wolfgang Reisinger** (perc); **Mathias Rüegg** (ldr, cond, arr); **Ima** (tamboura). hat Art Ⓕ CD 6024 (76 minutes). Recorded 1983/84.

⑥ ❽

Formed by pianist and arranger Mathias Rüegg in 1977, the Vienna Art Orchestra has enjoyed a colourful career. It has worked the jazz festival circuit and has not been deterred from drawing musical inspiration from sources as wide as Scott Joplin, Lennie Tristano and Anthony Braxton. This lengthy CD dedicates itself to the spirit of Erik Satie and introduces the listener to the surrealistic music of the enigmatic Frenchman. It is significant that only one Satie composition is played, but his *Gnossiennes* from 1890 was an important avant-garde work. It was Satie's first experimentation with barless notation, it had no key signature and it dispensed with normal thematic construction. This mood of perambulating free melodic interaction is well-captured by Rüegg in his own arrangements. Throughout the whole album he successfully interprets the spirit of Satie's music in modern guise. He has used the vocal (jazz) talents of Lauren Newton, the present-day vibraphone figures of Woody Schabata and the saxophone playing of Harry Sokal and Roman Schwaller in a way that fits effortlessly into the contemporary jazz world but continues to champion the Satie dictum of "music without sauerkraut". **BMcR**

Leroy Vinnegar

1928

Leroy Walks! **Vinnegar** (b); **Gerald Wilson** (t); **Teddy Edwards** (ts); **Carl Perkins** (p); **Victor Feldman** (vb); **Tony Bazley** (d). Contemporary Ⓜ OJCCD-160-2 (42 minutes). Recorded 1957.

⑧ ❽

From the time of his arrival in Los Angeles in 1954 Vinnegar has been the rock on which many outstanding rhythm sections have been founded. Perhaps 'reliable' does not sound an over-complimentary term, but it is the highest praise for Leroy, whose faultless time-keeping, full tone and ability to mark the passage of time through the most stimulating choice of notes from the chords make him still one of the most in-demand of all West Coast bass players. He has always 'walked' (i.e. played a steady four-in-a-bar) behind others as well as in his own solos and choosing a programme of seven tunes, six of which had the word 'walk' in their titles, was an inevitable A&R man's ploy. Wilson (muted throughout) and Edwards both solo to good effect, but the chief interest lies in the work of the rhythm section and Feldman (the horns are absent on *Would You Like To Take a Walk* and *I'll Walk Alone,* probably the most impressive tracks). Perkins and Vinnegar were actually at school together and the way their work interlocks is masterly, but then so too are the solos of London-born Feldman. This remains Vinnegar's best album as a leader. **KS**

Miroslav Vitous

1947

Journey's End **Vitous** (b); **John Surman** (ss, bs, bcl); **John Taylor** (p); **Jon Christensen** (d). ECM Ⓔ 1242 (843 171-2) (41 minutes). Recorded 1982.

⑧ ❿

Vitous came bursting onto the New York jazz scene from his native Prague in the late sixties, then garnered even greater fame as a charter member of Weather Report. His tenure there was brief, however, and for most the seventies he pursued other interests away from the bass. At the close of the decade, he came back to the instrument and began teaching, finally becoming head of the Jazz Department at New England Conservatory in the early eighties. His return to the recording studio found his faculties unimpaired: he still had one of the most beautiful tones and fecund melodic imaginations in the music, as well as stupendous technique, whether plucking or bowing.

This album illustrates more than just his instrumental facility, however. Two of the album's more evocative songs are his, and the way he has structured the group to play them means that there is nothing conventional or dull in the way they are performed. Surman is generally in an assertive mood on this date, though his two compositions are both marked by a bittersweet tenderness. Vitous grabs the attention at every turn either with his arresting ideas or, more subtly, by the beautiful support he gives the group. Like Mingus, he is a real leader from the bass, and the music is all the stronger for it. **KS**

Alexander Von Schlippenbach

1938

Berlin Contemporary Jazz Orchestra **Von Schlippenbach** (cond, arr); **Benny Bailey**, **Thomas Heberer**, **Henry Lowther** (t); **Kenny Wheeler** (t, flh); **Paul Van Kemenade**, **Felix Wahnschaffe** (as); **Gerd Dudek** (ss, ts, cl, fl); **Walter Gauchel** (ts); **E.L. Petrowsky** (bs); **Willem Breuker** (bs, bcl); **Henning Berg**, **Herman Breuer**, **Hubert Katzenbeier** (tb); **Utz Zimmermann** (btb); **Aki Takase** (p); **Gunter Lenz** (b); **Ed Thigpen** (d); **Misha Mengelberg** (p). ECM Ⓔ 1409 (841 777-2) (50 minutes). Recorded 1989.

⑧ ❽

This band, founded by Von Schlippenbach in 1988, is the chart-playing equivalent of his explosively free unit, Globe Unity. No attempt is made to match that orchestra's unbridled fire, although the BCJO is not without its own slow burn. It fits its soloists into arranged pieces without inhibiting them and it achieves a genuine depth of ensemble sound commensurate with the size of the line-up. Significantly, its three man rhythm team answers every question asked of them and when the need is for attack they show themselves well able to generate the old-style 'American' drive. Von Schlippenbach has recruited many players from outside the city of Berlin and the quality of the solos on this CD is impressive. The score for Wheeler's *Ana* presents an almost stately face, yet it also boasts a string of formidable solos. Mengelberg's compositions *Salz* and *Reef Und Kneebus*, a suite in three parts, have a constrastingly zany quality and perhaps tax the orchestra in a somewhat different manner. In one sense they accommodate Thigpen's rhythmic aspirations rather more but the former still elicits strong individual contributions. The album's best counterpoint is heard in the minuet movement of *Reef Und Kneebus*, but the whole is such a good group effort that it seems invidious to select isolated high spots from a performance that must establish the BCJO as one of the most outstanding big bands in the world. **BMcR**

Vox Office

Boppin' In French **Dominique Hemard**, **Florence Grimal**, **Marc Antony**, **Marc Brochet** (v) with **Jean-Jacques Taib** (saxes); **Laurent de Wilde** (p); **Jean-Luc Arramy** (b); **Jean-Marc La Judie** (d); **Gilles Perrin** (perc). Ida Ⓔ 030 CD (43 minutes). Recorded 1991.

⑦ ❽

Since the demise of the great vocal groups of the late fifties and early sixties (Lambert-Hendrick-Ross, The Double-Six, etc.); there has been a nostalgia for this type of music, and for the times it was borne by. Will big bands ever come back? Will vocal groups ever come back? The Manhattan Transfer showed that such things were possible, even if most of their repertoire veered more towards Broadway and Hollywood than to 52nd Street. So it takes the French to launch an authentic revivalist outfit of suitably youthful singers, and it is no coincidence that they are under the artistic direction of Double-Six leading light, Mimi Perrin. The ensemble work is clean, the voices fresh, the enthusiasm very much in evidence, and the repertoire just as challenging as anything L-H-R ever tackled (try *The Duke* if you are in doubt). The biggest stumbling block for the non-French speaker is that it is all in French, and the booklet, although it carries full French lyrics, has no English translations. Still—if you can shut your eyes and forget about the meaning, the music is quite seductive on its own. **KS**

V.S.O.P.

Live Under The Sky Freddie Hubbard (t, flh); **Wayne Shorter** (ts, ss); **Herbie Hancock** (p); **Ron Carter** (b); **Tony Williams** (d). Columbia Ⓜ COL 471063-2 (77 minutes). Recorded 1979.

⑦ ❼

Formed in 1976, V.S.O.P. were hailed as representing a retreat from fusion excesses. In fact, all five musicians had made their mark on jazz long before the arrival of Miles Davis's **In A Silent Way**, and in most cases had continued with fusion music while still working V.S.O.P. As this CD shows, there was no problem with their return to Jazz Messenger territory. As is perhaps inevitable in a unit boasting five virtuoso musicians, the collective effect is never quite as good as the individual contributions. They were a semi-permanent band, but there were times when a jam session mood prevailed.

The most co-ordinated pieces are *Teardrop* and *Para Orients*, but Hubbard is at his best when the jousting gets serious. Shorter's tenor blossoms on titles such as *Pee Wee*, where he can journey over the consciously uneven terrain laid by a rhythm section roughed up by Williams's brilliant drumming. Carter is wonderfully coherent in all he does and Hancock leaves the listener wondering why he did not always play in the V.S.O.P. way. **BMcR**

Chad Wackerman

1960

Forty Reasons Wackerman (d, ldr); **Allan Holdsworth** (g); **Jim Cox** (kbds, org); **Jimmy Johnson** (b). CMP Ⓕ CD 48 (45 minutes). Recorded 1991.

⑥ ❽

The very aptly-named Chad Wackerman is perhaps best known as a drummer with Frank Zappa but, like bassist Jimmy Johnson, he has also served for several years in Allan Holdsworth's Californian bands. Holdsworth—the album's star attraction—here becomes the sideman, and the role reversal exposes often submerged aspects of his style. His own hi-tech fusion records have frequently foundered under a welter of complexity, but the modal settings, airy textures and regular pulses heard here provide an uncluttered platform for his virtuoso flights. Wackerman, bravura fusion drummer that he is, could easily have dominated the session, but this is very much an ensemble effort. The composed pieces, mostly his, demonstrate a surprising lyricism and restraint, and almost half the tracks appear to be freely improvised. As far as the present writer knows, Holdsworth has not been publicly involved in free collective improvisation since the days of John Stevens's group Plough, and these short pieces, by adding a wide range of natural and electronic tone colours to Plough's fairly orthodox range of instrumental and stylistic resources, add a fresh idiom to the Holdsworth catalogue. **MG**

Collin Walcott

1945-1984

Cloud Dance Walcott (sitar, tabla); **John Abercrombie** (g); **Dave Holland** (b); **Jack DeJohnette** (d). ECM Ⓕ 1062 (825 469-2) (39 minutes). Recorded 1975.

⑧ ❾

Collin Walcott was a true internationalist in terms of philosophy and choice of instruments. After graduating as a percussion major at Indiana University, Walcott studied sitar with Ravi Shankar and tabla with Alla Rakha. In the late sixties he worked with clarinettist Tony Scott, a pioneer in the serious investigation of melding modern jazz with Eastern music. In 1970, Walcott joined Paul Winter's Consort and explored various combinations of ethnic music and jazz. Out of Winter's group came Oregon (with Ralph Towner, Paul McCandless and Glen Moore). Before his tragic death in an auto accident in East Germany, Walcott worked with Codona, the co-operative trio with Don Cherry and Nana Vasconcelos.

Here, in an exceptional date from 1975, Walcott engages guitarist Abercrombie, bassist Holland and drummer DeJohnette in eight varied settings that, in toto, constitute a virtual suite. There are duos such as *Prancing* for tablas and bass, and trios such as *Vedanas* for sitar, bass and guitar, whereas the concluding *Cloud Dance* involves all four musicians. The sonic textures, given the prominence of Walcott's tablas and sitar, ripple with exotic colours and swirling rhythmic currents, but often there is also a driving pulse. Due to the vision of Walcott and his estimable colleagues, this singular meeting of Eastern and Western musics continues to refresh and inspire as it also opens doors. **CB**

Mal Waldron

1926

The Quest Waldron (p); **Eric Dolphy** (as, cl); **Booker Ervin** (ts); **Ron Carter** (vc); **Joe Benjamin** (b); **Charles Persip** (d). New Jazz Ⓜ OJC 082-2 (42 minutes). Recorded 1961.

⑩ ❽

Previous LP reissues of this music under Dolphy's more marketable name did Mal Waldron a disservice, as it was his date and all the compositions his own. As a composer Waldron has been given short shrift; he not only contributed many more or less memorable blowing vehicles to countless Prestige sessions, but also penned a few standards and more formal successes. The seven tunes here are wonderful, ranging from the soulful r&b of *Warp And Woof* to the buoyant *Fire Waltz*, which Waldron and Dolphy would revisit in a celebrated live date a mere three weeks later, in the company of another Booker, Little. Carter's cello is a curious touch, although reminiscent of the chamber music textures of Chico Hamilton's group and Mingus's early experiments. Despite occasionally questionable intonation, he brings a plaintive quality to the melody of *Duquility*, and a secure pizzicato to the haunting *Warm Canto*—the latter with Dolphy especially sensitive on clarinet, Persip's exquisite brushwork on cymbals, and Waldron's motivic insistence that would soon be his trademark. Elsewhere, Booker Ervin's barnstorming tenor seems frequently inspired by Dolphy's careening chromaticism, in solos that are concise and still exciting. All told, a marvellous, fully realized programme. **AL**

My Dear Family **Waldron** (p); **Eddie Henderson** (t); **Grover Washington Jr** (ss); **Reggie Workman** (b); **Pheeron akLaff** (d). Alfa Jazz Ⓕ ALCB5001 (54 minutes). Recorded 1993.

⑦ ❽

Waldron has been a consistent (and consistently inventive) stylist since the mid-fifties. In a long and eventful career, Waldron could be accused of making too many records, although it may be fairer to say that he's made too many indifferent albums, considering the talents displayed on his best efforts. An early peak is detailed above, but the nineties have found him returning to form, eschewing some of the minimal and overly-stretched musical palettes he's occasionally indulged in in between times. Waldron is an instantly recognisable pianist—how many can that truly be said of?—and a stirring accompanist whose artistry has been appreciated by galaxy of singing and solo talent over the decades.

This session, from autumn in New York 1993, is a typical mix of Waldron originals (there's another version of *Left Alone*, Waldron's homage to a previous employer, Billie Holiday), and quality songs from Wayne Shorter, Miles Davis and Jimmy van Heusen, among others. Washington is present on just three tracks, two of which are ballads, while Henderson is absent from just two of eight tracks. Some of his best moments come in the minor-key duet with Waldron, *Red Shoes*, written by Ujo Noguchi. He avoids his Milesian mannerisms and gets a brooding intensity which is very much his own. Waldron's spare style and liking for the piano's middle registers gives the date a sepia hue more finely honed than melancholy, and in this he is superbly assisted by Workman and akLaff. **KS**

Bennie Wallace

1946

The Fourteen Bar Blues **Wallace** (ts); **Eddie Gomez** (b); **Eddie Moore** (d). Enja Ⓕ 3029-2. Recorded 1978. (47 minutes).

⑧ ❽

The last few years have seen Bennie Wallace find success scoring films, often ones with a Southern atmosphere, and celebrating his Tennessee roadhouse roots with the likes of Dr John and the late Stevie Ray Vaughan. It would have been hard to anticipate his current direction from this smashing début album. The hard-edged, volatile improvising found here pushed the limits of song form and jazz convention, rather than indulging in the entertaining avenues of popular culture. It is obvious that the early Wallace had listened hard to Sonny Rollins; although the wild chromaticism owes a debt to Dolphy, his intense thematic construction, long unaccompanied cadenza on *Flamingo*, and the neo-calypso *Green and Yellow* are all Sonny's terrain. At this stage Wallace is feeling out various approaches—Hawkins's finesse and relentless drive, Bird's rhythmic impetus, even a near-parody of Ayler's huge vibrato (on *Vicissitudes*), and breathy Ben Websterism (*Chelsea Bridge*). All stops out, the rhythm section creates eddys of counter-currents, and Gomez is an especially fine foil. His own horn-like lines parry Wallace's, and they exchange roles and later chase each other's tails on the title tune. As soon as Wallace's album with the equally incandescent Jimmy Knepper, **...Plays Monk**, is released on CD, it is unreservedly recommended. In the meantime, this one sizzles. **AL**

Fats Waller

1904-1943

Low Down Papa **Waller, James P. Johnson** (p rolls). Biograph Ⓕ BCD 114 (49 minutes). Recorded 1923-31.

⑥ ❽

Waller disappointed a family that had wanted him to follow a religious calling and, by the age of 15, he was playing the organ at the Lincoln Theater in New York. A student of the great James P. Johnson, Waller became a master of the stride piano. His easy use of broken octaves at all tempos and the rapidly repeated arpeggios on four or five notes of the dominant chord became his trade marks. He first recorded in 1922, but shortly after began making piano rolls for the QRS label. This CD features some of his most colourful, with all the advantages of rolls transposed by modern recording techniques. The disadvantage is that, despite the power of his delivery, Waller was a player of great rhythmic subtlety and, by the very nature of peddling a roll, much of this is lost. The timing becomes very vertical and this is emphasized by clumsy moves into double time as on titles like *Your Time Now*. The persistent choice of medium tempo throughout is a cop-out rather than a policy decision. It might suit the gentle bounce of items such as *Papa Better Watch Your Step* or *Low Down Papa*, but is certainly not appropriate to *Jail House Blues*. This is an important document, but listening to it is like reading about the wonders of the Taj Mahal. It does not replace the real thing. **BMcR**

Fats And His Buddies **Waller** (p); with, on two tracks **Charlie Gaines** (t); **Charlie Irvis** (tb); **Arville Harris** (reeds); **Eddie Condon** (bj); on two tracks **Red Allen** (t); **Jack Teagarden** (tb, vb) ; **Albert Nicholas**, **Otto Hardwick** (as); **Larry Binyon** (ts); **Eddie Condon** (bj); **Al Morgan** (b); **Gene Krupa** (d); **Four Wanderers** (v); on four tracks **Red Allen**, **Leonard Davis** (t); **Jack Teagarden**, **J.C. Higginbotham** (tb); **Albert Nicholas**, **Charlie Holmes** (cl, as); **Larry Binyon** (ts); **Will Johnson** (bj); **Pops Foster** (b); **Kaiser Marshall** (d); **Orlando Robertson** (v); on six tracks **Waller** (org); **Jabbo Smith** (c); **Garvin Bushell** (cl, as); **James P Johnson** (p); on three tracks **Waller** (p, org); **Tom Morris** (c); **Charlie Irvis** (tb); **Eddie King** (d); on four tracks **Waller** (p, org); **Tom Morris** (c); **Jimmy Archey** (tb); **Bobbie Leecan** (g); **Eddie King** (d). RCA Bluebird Ⓜ ND90649 (65 minutes). Recorded 1927-29.

⑧ ❻

These tracks date from the late twenties, before Waller's international success with his small band. The opening *Minor Drag* and *Harlem Fuss* have been written about since Eddie Condon told the story of the session in his autobiography. They are good small band sides in which the massive power of Waller's left hand makes it clear why no bass player or drummer were necessary. The six tracks by a bigger band are noteworthy for the solo work of Red Allen, Jack Teagarden (he is the trombone soloist on *Ridin' But Walkin'*), Albert Nicholas and Charlie Holmes as well as Fats. There is just one Waller vocal on the 21 tracks which comprise this CD, but he does play organ on the six titles by the Louisiana Sugar Babies and the seven by Thomas Waller With Morris's Hot Babies. On the former, the organ tends to get in the way and things only improve when Waller keeps quiet, allowing Johnson to add his support to the wonderful muted trumpet playing of Jabbo Smith. The titles with cornettist Tom Morris come off better, with Fats occasionally switching smoothly from organ to piano. There is merely a hint of the jollity which was to come later with the formation of Fats Waller And His Rhythm in the thirties. The transfers have been achieved using the CEDAR system and are generally successful. **AM**

Turn On The Heat **Waller** (p); with, on two tracks **Benny Payne** (p). Bluebird Ⓜ ND82482 (2) (two discs: 122 minutes). Recorded 1927-41.

⑧ ❻

This is the Waller who was the star pupil of James P. Johnson, rather than the 'family favourite' who savaged fifth-rate songs and turned some of them into standards despite himself. Although the later persona largely buried the dynamic stride player, the humour implicit in the piano style was the basis of his whole approach to entertaining the public.

The 1929 material which takes up more than half of this set contains a few contemporary pops such as the title track and *Love Me Or Leave Me*, as well as Waller's current production including *Ain't Misbehavin'* and the influential chord-sequence of *I've Got A Feeling I'm Falling*. But the meat of this part of the programme, casually tossed off at the same period as his 'Buddies' sessions, consists of his take-on of the Johnson tradition with such as *Handful Of Keys* and *Valentine Stomp*.

A key 1934 date, when the 'Rhythm' series was just taking off, has more sophisticated originals in *Viper's Drag* and *Clothes Line Ballet*, while the remaining numbers are revisited standards. Two are his own, three Hoagy Carmichael's and all receive thoughtful, varied interpretations, while the set comes full circle with two versions of Johnson's *Carolina Shout*. **BP**

The Joint Is Jumpin' **Fats Waller** (p, v); with various personnel including: **Charlie Gaines**, **Herman Autrey** (t); **Rudy Powell**, **Gene Cedric** (ts, cl); **Charlie Irvis** (tb); **Eddie Condon** (bj); **Al Casey** (g); **Cedric Wallace**, **Slam Stewart** (b); **Slick Jones**, **Zutty Singleton** (d). RCA Bluebird Ⓜ ND 86288 (69 minutes). Recorded 1929-43.

✔ ⑧ ❽

A well-chosen one-volume selection of Fats Waller's work, including many of his most celebrated piano solos (*Alligator Crawl, Viper's Drag*, etc.) and several famous small band numbers (*Crazy 'Bout My Baby, Your Feet's Too Big*). This disc does excellent justice to Fats's reputation as perhaps the greatest of all stride pianists, but somewhat less to his genius as an entertainer and bandleader.

The band known as Fats Waller and His Rhythm was one of the finest combos of the swing era—versatile, flexible and infinitely responsive. It acted as an extension of his musical personality and could switch from teashop gentility to gin-mill anarchy in the blink of an eye. One catches glimpses of this here but not the full range. Admittedly this would be difficult to contain on a single CD, since the Rhythm recorded so much, but a double-CD anthology of its output might make a reasonable attempt. Nevertheless this is a hugely enjoyable programme and the best available introduction to the work of a vastly talented artist. For a more extended taste of much of the classic Fats and His Rhythm material, **The Middle Years (Parts One and Two)** are two 3-CD sets on Blue bird which cover copious gems from the years 1936-1940. **DG**

The Last Years (1940-43) **Fats Waller and His Rhythm** **Waller** (p, org, v); **June 'Bugs' Hamilton**, **Herman Autrey**, **Bob Williams**, **Joe Thomas**, **Nat Williams** (t); **Eugene 'Honeybear' Sedric**, **Bob Carroll** (ts); **John Smith**, **Al Casey** (g); **Sedric Wallace** (b); **Slick Jones**, **Arthur**

Trappier (d); **Kathryn Perry** (v); **Fats Waller, His Rhythm and His Orchestra**: **George Wilson, Ray Hogan, Bugs Hamilton, Herb Flemming** (tb); **Jimmy Powell, Dave McRae, George Jones, Lawrence Fields** (as). RCA Bluebird Ⓜ ND 90411 (three discs: 194 minutes). Recorded 1940-43.

✔ ⑧ ❼

RCA's reissue programme played around with Waller on CD for a few years, making tentative stabs at what is an enormous archive (over 400 sides). In the last 12 months or so, there have been signs that their nerve has been steadying. First this three-CD set appeared, and more recently there have been two three-CD volumes of **The Middle Years (1936-40)** launched onto the market. While there are more hits on the thirties collections, many of them turn up on single CD releases, and it is the forties collection which contains the CD rarities and the pleasant surprises. The reason for their rarity has nothing to do with poor playing; it is much more humdrum than that. As reissue overseer Orrin Keepnews explains in his notes to the box, most large reissue programmes falter and fold before they reach the end (RCA France in the vinyl era excepted), and so the early Waller, being the logical place to start, has been oft-revisited, while the later work has remained undisturbed (he didn't point out that the later matrial had until 1993 also still lain in copyright so no-one but RCA could mount a legitimate reissue of it).

This collection contains the original studio versions of *Little Curly Hair in a High Chair*, *Everybody Loves My Baby*, *Mamacita*, *Shortnin' Bread*, *Rump Steak Serenade*, *Buck Jumpin'* (a vehicle for guitarist Casey), *Fat and Greasy* and the beautiful *Jitterbug Waltz*. Waller's humorous asides are not so apparent here as in the late thirties, although he certainly has not dispensed with them, and there is a more mellow atmosphere across the three sides. One wonders whether the approach of middle age was giving him a new light on his material. If so, it did not lead to any shifts in style or content. Waller's career is remarkable for the lack of any real stylistic change once early maturity had been reached at the dawn of the thirties. Yet it seems unlikely that *Jitterbug Waltz* would have been countenanced six years before, and although all speculation is futile, I cannot help wondering where Waller would have placed himself in the post-war entertainment world, had he survived that long. **KS**

Per Henrik Wallin

1946

Dolphins, Dolphins, Dolphins **Wallin** (p); **Mats Gustafsson** (ss, ts, bs); **Kjell Nordeson** (d). Dragon Ⓕ DRCD 215 (64 minutes). Recorded 1991.

⑦ ❽

Although an important, if idiosyncratic, figure on the Swedish jazz scene for over two decades, Wallin has yet to make a deep mark internationally. It may be that his music is an acquired taste, difficult to grasp on first hearing. A pianist of great facility, his lines seem to follow a personal logic; occasionally he will strip a theme down to its essence—or to silence—then ornament it with staggered phrasing or a florid abundance of notes. For example, the pensive solo *J. W.* dedicated to a painter friend, alternates rhapsodic cascades of melody with stark Monkish chords that threaten to turn violent. Even when explosions erupt, Wallin avoids sounding like Cecil Taylor or any other contemporary pianist for that matter. In fact, one wonders if **Dolphins, Dolphins, Dolphins** may not be an unacknowledged homage to Monk; he picks apart *I Should Care*, a standard to which Monk also turned his scalpel, to end the programme, and at various points injects elliptical hints or echoes of Monk lines or a bit of offbeat stride. The younger saxist Gustafsson is an especially good foil for Wallin, chewing up and spitting out notes or relaxing into a loose, limber phrasing to match the pianist's demeanour. Nordeson is an aggressive drummer. The three fit together like pieces of a puzzle, but the music will not behave, there is always an unexpected jolt of emotion, rhythm or colour eager to break into the consensus. At all times, Wallin's peculiar impulses of nonchalance and bravado give the music its contradictory tension—and its curious charm. **AL**

George Wallington

1924-1993

The George Wallington Trios **Wallington** (p); with, on four tracks: **Charles Mingus** (b); **Max Roach** (d); and on one track **Chuck Wayne** (mandola); on four tracks: **Oscar Pettiford** (b); **Max Roach** (d); on eight tracks: **Curley Russell** (b); **Max Roach** (d). Prestige Ⓜ OJCCD 1754 (42 minutes). Recorded 1952-53.

⑧ ❻

Wallington was the pianist in the first bebop group to play on 52nd Street in 1944, the one co-led by Dizzy Gillespie and Oscar Pettiford with Max Roach on drums. He was probably the first white musician to work in the bop idiom, cropping up on many record dates as a sideman. But it was as a trio leader and soloist that Wallington opened many eyes, for his keyboard technique was phenomenal. He was also an important composer, best known for his tunes *Godchild* and *Lemon Drop*. Of the 15 titles here, ten are Wallington compositions, one of them a multi-tempoed reworking of his earlier *Polka Dot*. He moves accurately all over the keyboard on the fast tempos (*Escalating*, for example, is a furious attack on the chords of *Cherokee)* and the comparison with Bud Powell must be made, but Wallington's actual extemporizations were always more melodic, almost as if he was writing fresh tunes along the way. His command of harmony gave his ballad work a richness seldom found in any other pianist of the period. He is superbly served by Max Roach on all tracks, and the three bassists would sound more impressive if the balance did not result in occasional muddiness. These dates were never well reproduced as ten-inch or 12-inch LPs and it sounds as if the remastering has been done from discs rather than original masters or tapes, so not much improvement there. **AM**

Jack Walrath

1946

Out Of The Tradition **Walrath** (t); **Larry Coryell** (g); **Benny Green** (p); **Anthony Cox** (b); **Ronnie Burrage** (d). Muse Ⓕ MCD 5403 (59 minutes). Recorded 1990.

⑧ ❾

Walrath began playing the trumpet at nine years of age, later doing his stint at the Berklee College. While there he played with minor r&b groups before moving to California. In the seventies he did sterling service with Ray Charles and Charles Mingus, more recently leading his own groups worldwide. Produced by fellow trumpeter, Don Sickler, this CD is a fine example of his current work. The cover art suggests a routine trumpet quintet performance and there is certainly ample evidence of Walrath's exciting solo playing. There is, however, very much more; the arrangements consistently bring all five players into play and each has moments of front line action. The language of bebop is enlarged to embrace a plethora of serviceable textures and surprises abound. *Come Sunday* gets an unexpected up-tempo grilling, while *Star Dust* is treated to one of the wildest 'all-ins' that ever disrupted Carmichael's gentle ballad. In contrast, Walrath's own contribution to *Brother, Can You Spare A Dime?* could be the work of a player untouched by bop. Like so much that the trumpeter has done, this session is truly multi-stylistic. **BMcR**

Cedar Walton

1939

Among Friends **Walton** (p); **Buster Williams** (b); **Billy Higgins** (d); **Bobby Hutcherson** (vb). Evidence Ⓕ ECD 22023-2 (62 minutes). Recorded 1992.

⑦ ❽

For more than three years Walton was a member of one of the finest of all Jazz Messengers line-ups. He was also house pianist for Prestige for a similar period, and he chanced his arm with fusion in his Soundscapes unit in the seventies. This CD returns him to what he does best, re-uniting a trio that enjoyed a short residency at San Francisco's Keystone Korner in 1982. The superbly inventive Hutcherson makes a guest appearance on *My Foolish Heart* but the remaining titles, with Buster in the place of Dave Williams from Walton's eighties trio, produce hard, driving bop in the pianist's distinctive manner. His treble investigations on *Midnight Waltz* show his skill as a 'single note' improviser, but like most band pianists, Walton thinks orchestrally. He is equally happy to inhabit the centre of the keyboard and his chord patterns on *For All We Know* and *Off Minor* are powerful and coercive. It is perhaps this assertiveness that makes it easy for the trio to come over as an integrated unit and not as three individuals. Unfortunately, too little is heard here of Walton the writer, but his one composition, *Midnight Waltz*, is up to his own highest standards. **BMcR**

Carlos Ward

1940

Lito **Ward** (as, f); **Woody Shaw** (t); **Walter Schmocker** (b); **Alex Deutsch** (d). Leo Ⓕ 166 (59 minutes). Recorded 1988.

⑥ ❻

The Panama-born altoist's singing, searing lead-alto sound and turbulent improvising have served him well in contexts both tuneful (Abdullah Ibrahim, Carla Bley) and outward-bound (Cecil Taylor, Edward Blackwell). This Dutch concert showcases both sides of his personality. Ward's tunes, notably *Pettiford Bridge*, can be quite catchy, but the blowing is open-ended and adventurous. *Lito* should be of special interest to Shaw fans, as the trumpeter was rarely captured in so loose a context. His bugling tone here is perfect for the setting. Shaw's inflections make you hear Ward's *Lee* as a blues although it is not in standard blues form.

Ward has a knack for writing basslines that stand up on their own. Two movements of the three-part *Lito* suite are anchored to simple, propulsive bass figures—one of them a descending broken chord—which linger in the ear, but do not inhibit soloists. In this open frame, Deutsch provides colour as well as drive.

The leader plays a little leafy flute on *Lito*, but mostly concentrates on emphatic, biting alto, played with a big, broad, distinctive sound. Even so, he does not dominate these stretched-out jams; the set has a real band feel. **KW**

David S. Ware

1949

Third Ear Recitation **Ware** (ts); **Matthew Shipp** (p); **William Parker** (b); **Whit Dickey** (d). DIW Ⓕ DIW-870 (60 minutes). Recorded 1992.

A Berklee graduate, Ware has always been associated with his own uncompromising brand of free jazz. In the seventies he worked with Andrew Cyrille and Cecil Taylor but was not widely recorded. One good solo album and a couple of tenor and percussion duels gave notice of his talent, but not until the eighties was there more available evidence. This CD is a good representative example as he takes his own multi phonic route to detailed and frequently dense improvisational conclusions. He is not without a flexibility of approach, however, and *Autumn Leaves* shows the way in which he can loosely relate his free flights to Shipp's clearly defined structures. *Angel Eyes* is somewhat more orthodox, with convoluted runs used to bridge the space between theme affirmations, while *Mystic* takes on an Albert Ayler-like march quality. His respectful approach to *East Broadway Run Down* is faster than the Sonny Rollins original, *Free Flow* is a more open-ended piece and *Sentient Compassion* displays the degree of intensity he can bring to a dirge. The presence of a pianist means that there are harmonic frames available but, with Parker and Dickey more contrapuntally inclined and deliberately non-supportive in the normal sense, Ware remains loyal to his free form principles. **BMcR**

Washboard Rhythm Kings

Washboard Rhythm Kings Collection, Volume 1: 1931 **Jake Fenderson**, **Buck Franklin**, **The Melody Four** (v); **Dave Page**, **Dave Riddick** (t); **Ben Smith** (as); **Jimmy Shine** (as, v); **Carl Wade** (ts); **Eddie Miles** (p, v); **Teddy Bunn** (g); **Steve Washington** (bj); **Jimmy Spencer** (d, wbd, v). Collector's Classics Ⓜ COCD 17 (73 minutes). Recorded 1931-32.

⑤ ❻

For many observers, it is rather difficult to give credence to the art of rubbing metal thimbles on the ridges of a washboard. Yet, since before the turn of the century, spasm bands were using the likes of kazoos, jugs and, most especially, washboards as part of the 'orchestral' armoury. Men like Washboard Sam ratified its use in the blues world and recordings by washboard bands found a limited market well into the thirties.

The Washboard Rhythm Kings were stalwarts of the style; they had an ever changing line-up and this CD presents all aspects of their music. They were least appealing in comedy numbers with Fenderson's maudlin singing, but more impressive on blues such as *Crooked World* or when their reasonably proficient horns had their say. Early titles were blighted by 'period' alto and, in 1931, Bunn was some way short of his peak. The Kings last recorded in 1933 but the final two sessions here offer what is a fine example of their work. Titles like *Shoot 'Em*, *Pepper Steak* and *Wake 'Em Up* are driven by Spencer's genuinely flexible and swinging washboard patterns and, with Riddick's Armstrong-inspired lead, they make good music. It was not for the academic but in 1931 the Kings were for fun. **BMcR**

Dinah Washington

1924-1962

Mellow Mama **Washington** (v); **Karl George** (t); **Lucky Thompson** (ts); **Jewel Grant** (as); **Gene Thompson** (as, cl); **Milt Jackson** (vb); **Wilbert Baranco** (p); **Charles Mingus** (b); **Lee Young** (d). Delmark Ⓕ DD 451 (34 minutes). Recorded 1945.

⑧ ❽

Dinah Washington, the name given to 18-year-old Ruth Jones by Lionel Hampton when he discovered the young washroom girl at Chicago's Regal Theatre and put her on the road to stardom with his band, was a natural. Nurtured in the rich gospel tradition of the southern Baptist Church, Washington was gifted with an overall vibrancy marked by pinpoint intonation, precise articulation and a penetratingly melismatic bluesiness which she successfully adapted to a variety of settings, including her pop classic, *What a Diff'rence a Day Makes* (1959).

Here, at the threshold of her solo career in 1945, we catch the saucy 21-year-old belting out a repertoire of blues-based lines including *Rich Man's Blues*, *Blues for a Day* and *Wise Woman Blues*. While lacking the wrenching poignancy of a Billie Holiday, Washington displays a compelling bravado not unlike that displayed by such silver screen heroines as Bette Davis and Barbara Stanwyck. Another of the date's great attractions is the sinewy and smooth tenor saxophone of the under-valued Lucky Thompson. Milt Jackson's bluesy vibes are also featured, and the rhythm tandem of pianist Wilbert Baranco, bassist Charles Mingus and drummer Lee Young is perfect in its supporting role. The CEDAR restoration process brings the music to life. **CB**

The Complete Dinah Washington on Mercury, Volume 3 (1952-54) **Washington** (v); featuring **Clark Terry**, **Clifford Brown**, **Maynard Ferguson** (t); **Russell Procope** (as, cl); **Herb Geller** (as); **Paul Gonsalves**, **Paul Quinichette**, **Eddie Chamblee**, **Eddie 'Lockjaw' Davis**, **Harold Land** (ts); **Junior Mance**, **Richie Powell** (p); **Jackie Davis** (org); **Keeter Betts**, **George Morrow** (b); **Jimmy Cobb, Ed Thigpen**, **Max Roach** (d). Mercury Ⓜ 834 675-2 (three discs:198 minutes). Recorded 1942-54.

⑧ ❽

Like Fats Waller, Washington could sing anything, so producers often made her do just that. These 53 selections include such things as Hank Williams' hit *Half as Much*; double-entendre songs (like the wonderful *TV Is the Thing This Year*, with washing-machine organ); Ellington evergreens; forgettable tearjerkers; doo-wop; a homeless woman's calypso; hardcore blues (her *Gambler's Blues* features Procope's Hodges-like alto obbligati); blues with leaden lyrics and melodies the band riffs through unperturbed; even *Silent Night*. She is also heard in two studio jams, one with Terry and Lockjaw, where she sings *A Foggy Day* with the introductory verse, the other (with demonstrative audience) powered by Max Roach. That one produced a hard-bop mambo on *I've Got You Under My Skin*, recorded at the dawn of hard bop, and a *You Go to My Head* where her phrases swing hard even as she sings the pitches as written.

Few singers have ever sounded so comfortable on such disparate material but Dinah was not really a cross-over artist. For her, a song was a song; a heart-render from Nashville got the same treatment as one from Broadway. Her wine-rich voice always had a maturity beyond her years. When the last of these sides was cut, she was two weeks shy of 30. **KW**

For Those In Love **Washington** (v); **Clark Terry** (t); **Jimmy Cleveland** (tb); **Paul Quinichette** (ts); **Cecil Payne** (bs); **Wynton Kelly** (p); **Barry Galbraith** (g); **Keeter Betts** (b); **Jimmy Cobb** (d); **Quincy Jones** (arr). EmArcy Ⓜ 514 073-2 (49 minutes). Recorded 1955.

✔ ⑧ ❽

The jazz establishment has always been grudging about Washington's status as a jazz vocalist. And yet it seems she was incapable of singing anything but good jazz, and many of her 'pop' recordings for EmArcy and Mercury are redolent with fine jazz singing.

This is a much better session for Washington than the sloppy jam sessions which Mercury recorded using her with some of the same musicians who play here. Washington's own form varied little; she is easily able to handle unlikely material like *Blue Gardenia* and *You Don't Know What Love Is* and she imposes her climactic blues feelings into numbers like *This Can't Be Love*, *I Could Write A Book* and *Make The Man Love Me*.

Jones's arrangements are ideal and leave plenty of solo space. The band includes a host of underrated musicians who were or are exceptional jazz soloists—Jimmy Cleveland, Paul Quinichette, Cecil Payne, Wynton Kelly and Barry Galbraith. They all respond tastefully to the opportunities given them by Jones. Terry's effervescent personality comes through in his fine solos, but he is a disciplined and expert contributor to the scored ensembles.

This album shows what could have been. But then what actually was must have made a lot more money. **SV**

Kazumi Watanabe

Dogatana **Kazumi Watanabe** (g); with various personnels including: **Mike Mainieri** (vb); **B.J. Yamagishi**, **David Liebman** (f); **Warren Bernhardt** (p); **Nobuyoshi Ino** (b); **Hideo Yamahi** (d). Denon Ⓕ CY72374 (42 minutes). Recorded 1981.

⑥ ❽

Essentially a guitarist's guitarist, for over ten years Japanese fusioneer Watanabe has been turning in the sort of virtuosic jazz rock that has hoards of impressionable young men at music trade fairs gasping in delight and envy. Drawing as it does on most non-jazz aspects of American pop music—country, funk, r&b—Watanabe's electric playing often over-resembles the jack-of-all-trades approach of seasoned session musicians, a feeling obviously helped by a tendency to use improvised solos as a forum for technical display. But back in 1981, despite an already highly-developed technical facility, Watanabe turned in an all-acoustic (or very nearly so) album that has sufficient grace to convince even the most sceptical jazz-rockophobe. A series of duets and trios with some of his own, equally gifted, if largely unknown, countrymen and with a series of American stars, **Dogatana** is a delight. With the exception of Wayne Shorter's pretty ballad *Diana*, all the pieces are Watanabe's own, and all provide ample room for his cohorts' contributions. Steps Ahead leader Mike Mainieri's vibes solo on the opening *Nuevo Espresso*, a laid-back affair to be sure, sets the affable tone of the set, and a later duet with fusion guitar progenitor Coryell shows the Japanese at ease in such celebrated company. **SH**

Sadao Watanabe

1933

Bird of Paradise **Watanabe** (as); **The Great Jazz Trio** (Hank Jones, p, Ron Carter, b, Tony Williams, d). JVC Ⓕ VIJC 23021 (38 minutes). Recorded 1977.

⑦ ❾

Watanabe has become known outside of his native Japan mostly through his fusion and soul efforts, but he is a much more complete musician than those records would have us believe. This album, dedicated to Charlie Parker and full of tunes closely identified with him, is a handy illustration of what Watanabe can do when he picks up some momentum in bebop territory. Watanabe has been playing bop and its descendents since the fifties, when he took over Toshiko Akiyoshi's Tokyo group after the pianist's departure for New York, and he has also spent a great deal of his time as a teacher, taking up a post of director at the Yamaha Institute of Popular Music.

This record is one of over 50 Watanabe has made during his career, and comes right in the middle of a swathe of fusion albums recorded in New York for the same label. On this disc, Watanabe's style and tone is not far removed from that of Phil Woods, and he is not at a loss for ideas at any point on the date. Having said that, it would be a poor player who got into difficulties in this repertoire with the backing group provided here. The Great Jazz Trio (something of a fixture on JVC at this time) provides both thoughtful (Jones), swinging (Carter) and immensely stimulating (Williams) support to the main soloist, and help greatly to lift this release out of the mundane and into the worth-looking-out-for category. **KS**

Benny Waters

1902

From Paradise (Small's) To Shangri-La **Waters** (as, ts, cl, v); **Don Coates** (p); **Earl May** (b); **Ronnie Cole** (d). Muse Ⓕ MCD 5340 (51 minutes). Recorded 1987.

⑥ ❻

Traditionally, pianists last the longest in jazz. They sit down to play and they do not have to strain their lungs. For a long time Eubie Blake was the oldest survivor in jazz (when Peter Boizot rang up New York to inquire about Eubie Blake's availability next year at his Pizza Express, Mrs Blake said "Honey, we ain't planning that far ahead!"). But now that he has gone, Benny Waters seems to be the oldest and one of the toughest men in jazz. Born in 1902, he gigged happily round New York for many years until he decided to settle in Paris, where he became the senior member of the American jazz community. There is an ageless enthusiasm about Waters's presence and about his music which comes over best in his presence but which is well captured on this record, made in America with an American rhythm section which clicks along together very nicely. I am told that Benny Waters has gone back to the USA now he is over 90. Lucky old USA. **MK**

Ethel Waters

1896-1977

Ethel Waters 1929-39 **Waters** (v); with, amongst others: **Manny Klein**, **Arthur Whetsol**, **Cootie Williams**, **Freddy Jenkins**, **Sterling Bose**, **Bunny Berigan**, **Charlie Teagarden**, **Shirley Clay**, **Taft Jordan** (t); **Tommy Dorsey**, **Joe Nanton**, **Lawrence Brown**, **Jack Teagarden**, **Sandy Williams** (tb); **Tyree Glenn** (tb, vb); **Jimmy Dorsey** (cl, as); **Benny Goodman** (cl); **Johnny Hodges** (as, ss); **Harry Carney** (bs); **Edgar Sampson** (as, vn); **Benny Carter** (as); **Frank Signorelli**, **Duke Ellington** (p); **John Trueheart**, **Danny Barker** (g); **Joe Venuti** (vn); **Joe Tarto**, **Wellman Braud**, **Artie Bernstein**, **John Kirby** (b); **Stan King**, **Sonny Greer**, **Gene Krupa** (d). Timeless Ⓜ CBC 1-007 (70 minutes). Recorded 1929-39.

✔ ⑦ ❽

First recorded in 1921, Waters was hardly a jazz singer. She was, however, highly successful with popular tunes and was often supported by jazz musicians of real quality. She was disliked by classic blues singers like Ma Rainey and Bessie Smith for being, one suspects, too beautiful and too 'white' sounding as a singer. Certainly there was very little of the blues in her style and, although she did swing at times, she was usually governed by the material she used. In that sense only, this CD does give a slightly false impression. *Shoo Shoo Boogie Boo* and *You Can't Stop Me From Loving Me* are just a couple of duds in a programme that otherwise provides her with consistently good tunes. She is least successful when she tries to be a jazz singer as on *Please Don't Talk About Me* and at her best when she merely 'puts over' the likes of *Am I Blue?*, *Black And Blue* or *Stormy Weather*. The backings are excellent but they are designed purely to showcase Waters and only rarely do the soloists get to make a contribution. For the last 15 years of her performing career she sang with evangelist Billy Graham but she remains an important figure in the world of films, vaudeville and popular song. **BMcR**

Bill Watrous

1939

In London **Watrous** (tb); **Brian Dee** (p); **Len Skeat** (b); **Martin Drew** (d). Mole Ⓕ CD MOLE 7 (79 minutes). Recorded 1982.

⑥ ❻

On the evidence of this CD alone Watrous must be the most technically gifted trombonist jazz has ever seen. There seems to be no limit to his range, the semi-quavers he can produce at the fastest tempos and the swaggering sense of swing. With such qualities apparently on tap (there is no hint of a missed note or even a semi-tentative approach to a phrase) it is hardly surprising that Watrous has worked with a number of prestigious big bands as well as serving as a studio musician for a time. If his playing has a fault it is that sometimes his solos lack light and shade, although his slow ballad version of *When Your Lover Has Gone* is a clear indication that he can scale down his massive technique and attack when required. The opening of *Straight, No Chaser* is the kind of thing that must cause acute depression amongst other trombone players; for over three minutes he produces a breathtaking cadenza which almost becomes a composition in itself. Recorded at London's Pizza Express, the sound of the trombone is occasionally foggy, probably due to Watrous shifting his position relative to his microphone. Trombonists can safely add one more star to the rating and the Brian Dee-led rhythm section deserves a special mention. **AM**

Bobby Watson

1953

Midwest Shuffle **Watson** (as); **Terell Stafford** (t); **Edward Simon** (p); **Essiet Essiet** (b); **Victor Lewis** (d). Columbia Ⓕ 475925 2 (67 minutes). Recorded 1993.

⑥ ❽

This album is the latest in the career of Kansas-born altoist Watson who left the Jazz Messengers in the early eighties. Watson has led a string of albums (two of which, **Jewel** and **Horizon Quintet**, resurfaced recently on the Evidence label) but rarely has his in-person presence translated fully to disc. The energetic but communicative mixture he serves up here comes across clearly in excerpts from a three-week 1993 tour by the then-current edition of Horizon, with Terell Stafford (trumpet), Edward Simon (piano), Essiet Essiet (bass) and co-leader Victor Lewis who contributes two tunes.. Certainly the live recording helps, and the maturing of Watson's friendly sound makes this far more successful than earlier dates, where a confusion of purpose often dulled the music's edge. One gets the feeling that Watson has yet to construct a set of performances which will sit as easily in the studio as they do in front of an enthusiastic audience. Blakey had the secret: now it's his acolyte's turn. A pity that this album, which comes closer than any other so far, was his last for Columbia, for the contract has not been renewed. BP

Eric Watson

The Memory of Water **Watson** (p); **John Lindberg** (b). Label Bleu Ⓕ LBLC 6535 (52 minutes.). Recorded 1990.

✔ ⑧ ❽

Watson is a pianist who works primarily in Europe. He has recorded frequently, on his own in solo and group formats and with Lindberg on several occasions as well as John Carter, Steve Lacy and Linda Sharrock, although little of his work has reached the US and his reputation is consequently limited in his native country. A thoroughly schooled musician with an impressive technique, Watson has acquired notice as an interpreter of Charles Ives as well as for his improvisational efforts. This fairly recent example of his longstanding partnership with String Trio of New York bassist Lindberg gives one of the better samplings of Watson's writing (seven of the ten compositions are his), as well as the gently brooding perspective he brings to most musical situations. More recent Soul Note volumes under Lindberg's name, where the pair are joined by trombonist Albert Mangelsdorff, present the more rhythmically intense side of the pianist's playing; but the focus here is more directly on him, and the session builds a stealthy tension that Watson and Lindberg manage to sustain throughout. **BB**

Lu Watters

1911-1989

The Complete Good Time Jazz Recordings **Watters**, **Bob Scobey**, **Benny Strickler** (c, t); **Turk Murphy**, **Bill Bardin** (tb); **Ellis Horne**, **Bob Helm** (cl); **Wally Rose**, **Burt Bales** (p); **Clancy Hayes**, **Russ Bennett**, **Harry Mordecai** (bj); **Squire Girsback**, **Dick Lammi** (bb); **Bill Dart** (d). Good Time Jazz Ⓜ 4GTJCD 4409-2 (four discs: 290 minutes). Recorded 1941-47.

⑥ ❽

Originally a big-band leader, Watters became a leading figure in the New Orleans revival. In 1940, he formed a band using some of his former sidemen and specialized in the music of the Crescent City—most especially, King Oliver. The band was distinguished by a rather leaden-footed rhythmic movement. It had a tuba and heavy banjo emphasis but the front line, with Scobey, Murphy and latterly Helm, produced a righteous noise and no little drive. The Yerba Buena Jazz Band kept solo comment to a minimum and relied strongly on its well-crafted trumpet unisons.

As this four-CD set demonstrates, the band was most comfortable with the strutting medium tempo of tunes like *Georgia Camp Meeting*, *Milenberg Joys* and *Ostrich Walk*. The subtleties required by compositions like *New Orleans Blues* or *Creole Belles* seemed to elude them but, when the band did get up a full head of steam on items like *That's A Plenty* and *Chattanooga Stomp*, the horns seemed able to detach themselves from the restrictive practices of Lammi's lugubrious tuba and Mordecai's jangling banjo. The demise of the Yerba Buenas came in 1951, but as leaders in their own right Scobey and Murphy kept the tradition alive for some years. **BMcR**

Ernie Watts

1945

Unity **Watts** (ts); **Geri Allen** (p); **Eddie Gomez**, **Steve Swallow** (b); **Jack DeJohnette** (d). JVC Ⓕ JVC-2046-2 (65 minutes). Recorded 1994.

✔ ⑨ ❾

In recent years, Ernie Watts, saxophonist extraordinaire, has garnered great and deserved plaudits for his contributions to Charlie Haden's Quartet West (also featuring the superb Alan Broadbent on piano and drummer Larance Marable). Here, under his own name, Watts's jazz credentials are further enhanced in an all-out, no-nonsense date with firm yet supple rhythmic support forged by pianist Allen, bassists

Gomez and Swallow and drummer DeJohnette. It is a heartening session, especially since Watts has too often been encumbered with mono-dimensional fusion settings. Here, we get the unexpurgated Wattsian jazz persona in all its variegated glories.

For starters, there is the exuberant title track where Watts's muscular Trane-tinged tenor lights up the sky in tandem with Allen's pianistics. For Watts's funky side, the strutting *Some Kind A Blue* lopes with a jaunty gait à la Stanley Turrentine. Also impressive is the hand-in-glove rendering of Oscar Pettiford's *Tricotism* where Watts and bassist Gomez shadow and spar with aplomb. In addition there is *Lonely Hearts*, where Watts's plaintive laments distil the emotive and atmospheric essence of Hollywood's indelible *film noir* tradition. Throughout, the simpatico support of Allen, Gomez, Swallow and DeJohnette solidify Watts's date as a landmark. **CB**

Marzette Watts

Marzette Watts **Watts** (ss, ts, bcl); **Clifford Thornton** (c, tb); **Byard Lancaster** (fl, as, bcl); **Karl Berger** (vb); **Sonny Sharrock** (g); **Henry Grimes**, **Juney Booth** (b); **J.C. Moses** (d). ESP-Disk Ⓕ 1044-2 (37 minutes). Recorded 1966.

③ ❹

This is a pretty horrible album, but then it is not as horrible as the record for Savoy Watts made two years later, with Bill Dixon joining in on trumpet. At least all the musicians are in tune on this one. The date suffers from that quandary which bedevilled most mid-sixties free jazz blow-outs: how do you give coherence and meaning to music which arrives by the happenstance of a band arriving in a studio, setting up their instruments and more or less blowing chaotically until they stop? The answer is not to be found here. Despite the impressive line-up of names, no-one grabs the album by the scruff of the neck and makes it work through the sheer force of his personality, and the leader is too busy approximating the free jazz licks he has picked up from other, better players to apply himself in that direction. The wasted opportunity is all the more a shame considering the lack of recording chances sent Byard Lancaster's way and the remarkable work he came up with when presented with a musical equation which worked (the Bill Dixon RCA LP of the same period, for example). **KS**

Chuck Wayne

1923-1993

Jazz Guitarist **Wayne** (g); **Zoot Sims**, **Brew Moore** (ts); **Harvey Leonard**, **John Mehegan** (p); **George Duvivier**, **Vinne Burke** (b); **Ed Shaughnessy**, **Joe Morello** (d). Denon/Savoy Ⓜ SV-0189 (35 minutes). Recorded 1951-53.

⑧ ❽

The post-bop white musician may now seem lacking in emotion to some but, as these tracks show, many of them were highly skilled musicians who swung hard, even if they did not shout about it. Wayne made the transition from being a swing musician via a strong influence from Charlie Christian, and at the end of it he emerged in the period under consideration as an eloquent craftsman much in the manner of Jimmy Raney, Billy Bauer and Tal Farlow. He chose his musicians well, and the presence of Sims and Moore guarantees the impact of both the ballads and the swingers.

Interestingly four of the dozen tracks were actually recorded under the leadership of pianist Mehegan, then the progressive leader of a whole school of students and a man who we can now see as having been a prophet with considerable foresight. The interplay between his piano and Wayne's guitar on *Stella By Starlight* makes one wonder if Wayne was indeed one of his students.

Sidewalks Of Cuba is a number Wayne played with Herman, and here his handful of a Herd spikes it with some fine tenor from both men. While Mehegan's music is the more rewarding long-term, *Sidewalks* was certainly the biggest swinger within the album's desperately short number of minutes. **SV**

Weather Report

I Sing The Body Electric **Wayne Shorter** (reeds); **Josef Zawinul** (p, kbds); **Miroslav Vitous** (b); **Eric Gravatt** (d); **Dom Um Romao** (p); **Andrew White** (Engh); **Hubert Laws Jr** (f); **Wilmer Wise** (pic); **Yolande Bavan**, **Joshie Armstrong**, **Chapman Roberts** (v); **Ralph Towner** (g). Columbia Ⓜ 468207 2 (47 minutes). Recorded 1971/72.

✔ ⑨ ❽

Formed in 1971, Weather Report was the finest of all the fusion bands. This CD acts as a progress report in that it documents the integration of two newcomers. Gravatt and Romao had replaced the powerful Alphonze Mouzon and Airto Moreiro team just months before the band embarked on a Far Eastern tour. This release allows the listener to compare the rather disorganized *The Moors,* made in a studio with guest Towner, to the cohesion of the ferocious *Directions,* made live in Tokyo. Weather Report had needed to re-muster after these important changes and had done so with aplomb. The core design of the band had not changed, however, and was still built around the instrumental and compositional talents of Zawinul and Shorter. Zawinul's pyramid of keyboards distilled an internationally musical brew and provided the entire unit with its inner direction. Shorter remained the jazzer, his intricate lines on tenor and soprano always chastising the odd, vertically slanted, rhythmic passage with a linear reprimand. More than any of his colleagues, it was Shorter who put the creativity of the jazz ideal highest on Weather Report's list of priorities; no mean distinction. **BMcR**

Heavy Weather **Wayne Shorter** (ts, ss); **Joe Zawinul** (p, elp, syn, mel, v, g, perc); **Jaco Pastorius** (elb, mandocello, v, perc); **Alex Acuna** (d, perc); **Manolo Badrena** (perc). Columbia Ⓜ 468209 2 (38 minutes). Recorded 1976.

✔ ⑧ ❽

Like other groups spawned by the late-sixties Miles Davis band, Weather Report began life by investigating abstraction and collective improvisation. But like Chick Corea and Herbie Hancock, its co-founder Joe Zawinul was soon drawn to more visceral delights, and the culmination was **Heavy Weather**, the group's best-selling album. Inevitably, its marketability provoked critical grumbles, but it announced one of the most creative and influential phases in the band's career. By this time, the collective improvisations had virtually disappeared, but the ensemble principle remained, transmuted into such tightly-structured arrangements as *Birdland*, a brilliantly orchestrated series of riffs later tainted by an unfortunate association with aerobics classes. The group also expanded the collection of exotica begun on the early albums there are radical and fruitful re-appraisals of Latin rhythms on several items here, and *The Juggler*, complete with synthesized pipes, expresses Zawinul's imaginings of a mythical pastoral idyll. However, the spectacular synthesis of technique and expression wrought on the bass guitar by the group's most recent recruit—Jaco Pastorius—seemed without precedent anywhere in jazz. Rather like the unbelievably amateurish way in which this major record company persists in presenting its insert notes. Has it no pride in its heritage? **MG**

Chick Webb

1909-1939

Rhythm Man **Webb** (d, ldr): with on three tracks: **Shelton Hemphill**, **Louis Hunt**, **Louis Bacon** (t); **Jimmy Harrison** (tb); **Benny Carter**, **Hilton Jefferson** (as); **Elmer Williams** (ts); **Don Kirkpatrick** (p); **John Truehart** (bj); **Elmer James** (tba); **Louis Bacon** (v); on 20 tracks: **Mario Bauzá**, **Reunald Jones**, **Bobby Stark**, **Taft Jordan** (t); **Sandy Williams**, **Fernando Arbello**, **Claude Jones** (tb); **Pete Clark**, **Edgar Sampson** (as); **Elmer Williams** (ts); **Wayman Carver** (ts, f); **Joe Steele** (p); **John Truehart** (g); **Elmer James**, **Delevan Thomas**, **John Kirby** (b, tba); **Taft Jordan**, **Chuck Richards**, **Charles Linton** (v). Hep Ⓜ HEPCD 1023 (70 minutes) Recorded 1931-34

✔ ⑧ ❽

Despite his physical handicap (an early attack of tuberculosis resulted in a height of only four feet), Chick Webb formed and led what was probably the best of all the pre-war Harlem swing bands. During his long residencies at the Savoy he invariably won band 'battles' with all competitors; on the strength of this essential CD it is not difficult to understand why. Although Webb takes no solos, the thrust and power of his drumming makes itself felt throughout the 23 tracks, underpinning the soloists and cueing in the ensemble figures. No less than 17 of the tracks were arranged by Chick's alto soloist Edgar Sampson, while another alto man present on the earlier tracks, Benny Carter, contributed four more. Taft Jordan, who went on to play with Duke Ellington, is the principal trumpet soloist and vocalist, modelling himself on the playing and singing style of Louis Armstrong. Jimmy Harrison takes his last solos on the tracks from 1933 (he died soon afterwards) while Sandy and Elmer Williams are well featured on the 1933-34 titles. The performances are programmed in chronological order and the sound has never been better. John R. T. Davies is responsible for the magnificent remastering from best-available 78s and the result is an object lesson in the business of jazz reissues. **AM**

Eberhard Weber

1940

The Colours of Chloë **Weber** (b, vc, ocarina); **Ack Van Rooyen** (flh); **Rainer Brüninghaus** (p, syn); **Peter Giger** (d, perc); **Ralf Hübner** (d); **Cellos of the Stuttgart Südfunk Orchestra**. ECM Ⓕ 1042 (833 331-2) (40 minutes). Recorded 1973.

✔ ⑦ ❽

German-born Weber switched from cello to bass in his teens. He met Wolfgang Dauner in the early sixties and they worked together for almost ten years. This CD from the emerging ECM label was his first as a leader and it ideally fitted that company's musical policy. It employs the cellos of the Stuttgart Südfunk Symphony but makes no attempt at a synthesis of 'classical' and jazz forms. The concept is nearer to musique concrète with the background strata set to contrast with the foreground rather than to interact with it. The cello section does all that is asked of it but, apart from the leader, the jazz soloists are not strong enough to make this a totally successful project. The exception is Weber, whose work on the title-track is especially strong, as well as challengingly inventive. All of the themes are by him and they are both varied and stimulating. The arrangements are less convincing, the human voice additions add very little but the whole does have a certain charm. The original release received international acclaim and several European awards but must finally be considered a superior piece of music making which is more concerned with effect than content. **BMcR**

Pendulum **Weber** (b). ECM Ⓕ 1518 (519 707-2) (54 minutes). Recorded 1993.

⑨ ❿

This solo album is an extraordinary achievement. Presaged somewhat by a previous album, **Orchestra**, (ECM 1374) it takes the basic idea of that set—the use of echo machines and various delay and sampling equipment—one step further by using studio edits of Weber's performances. Previously, the bassist had not allowed himself the luxury of such techniques, preferring to release only those tracks made entirely at one time, in one take.

This new freedom enables Weber to be much more structured in his approach, and to build each piece in a more deliberate way. None of the freshness is lost because he is still using musical material derived from spontaneous creation, but some of the longueurs of an unedited performance are avoided. The result is a compelling sequence of tracks, none of them short, yet none of them of any great length (the average is around five minutes), and each very much containing its own character. Weber's resourcefulness on his instrument is awesome, while his addiction to the sheer beauty of the sound he creates and also his basically lyrical approach makes this a delightful aural experience. There are so many layers, and such a texture, created—often by melodies and patterns over deep ostinatos—that one is constantly tempted to luxuriate in its richness. The stunning sound quality here (this is some of the best-recorded music I have ever come across) enhances every such sensation. **KS**

Ben Webster

1909-1973

King of the Tenors **Webster** (ts) with: **Oscar Peterson** (p); **Barney Kessel** or **Herb Ellis** (g); **Ray Brown** (b); **J.C. Heard** or **Alvin Stoller**(d); on six tracks add **Harry Edison** (t); **Benny Carter** (as). Verve Ⓜ 519 806-2 (39 minutes). Recorded 1953.

⑧ ❼

The years Webster spent with Norman Granz's Verve label saw the production of some of his best American-made recordings. He was united in the studios with men of near-equal stature who provided him with the competition which was often lacking in the recordings he was to make in Europe later. This CD comprises his first two sessions for Verve and includes a previously unissued *Poutin'* (a Webster blues in minor key), plus two takes of *That's All* and *Bounce Blues*. The quality and reliability of the support from the Oscar Peterson Trio (plus drums) makes one appreciate what a fine unit this was and how fortunate Granz was to be able to call on it to accompany so many outstanding artistes. There are some gorgeous ballads here, including a superb *Tenderly* and a fine *That's All*, with the notes dying away, leaving just an expressive vibrating column of air. As was usually the case with Webster there are reminders of Ellington, this time in the form of *Cottontail* and *Don't Get Around Much Anymore*. Tom Ruff's remastering remains faithful to what was a good set of mono recordings and the only complaint centres around the miserly playing time. **AM**

Soulville **Ben Webster** (ts, p); **Oscar Peterson** (p); **Herb Ellis** (g); **Ray Brown** (b); **Stan Levy** (d). Verve Ⓜ 833551-2 (49 minutes). Recorded 1957.

✔ ⑩ ❽

The two sides of Ben Webster—the urgent, gritty side and the blowsy, sentimental one—were never captured better than on this album. It was a curious juxtaposition, but Webster expressed himself with such candid simplicity that what emerged was a portrait of himself, a man of complicated and unquiet personality.

Where Are You? is the archetypal Webster ballad, silky and insinuating, with a great deal of breath around the notes and an almost desperately pleading air. This is achieved partly by pitching the piece in the almost unheard-of jazz key of E major, which causes the melody to climb repeatedly to a high, keening B natural. In a matter such as this Webster was the most meticulous of artists.

For mid-tempo swing it would be hard to find a better example than *Makin' Whoopee* (key of A flat, right in the middle of the range), with the impeccable Ray Brown laying down one of his vintage bass lines and Peterson proving yet again what a magnificent accompanist he could be.

This CD reissue contains a further attraction in the shape of hitherto-unknown Ben Webster piano solos. Ben began his musical career as a pianist, playing for silent movies and the patrons of sundry bars and dives, and was always ready to sit down and rattle off a tune. On this evidence he posed no threat to Fats Waller or Willie The Lion. **DG**

Ben Webster Meets Oscar Peterson **Webster** (ts); **Peterson** (p); **Ray Brown** (b); **Ed Thigpen** (d). Verve Ⓜ 829 167-2 (37 minutes). Recorded 1959.

✔ ⑩ ❽

Webster is the obvious exception to the rule that says that no Ellington sideman ever continued to progress after leaving Ellington. His innovative riffing and chord busting on the orchestra's 1941 recording of *Cottontail* notwithstanding, he turned in the work for which he is now most remembered almost two decades later, by which time he had ripened into one of the most economical and seductive slow-and-medium-tempo players jazz has ever known. This date with Peterson catches Webster at a peak, playing what it is tempting to describe as Irish tenor. The prolix Peterson, although more compatible with Webster than he was with Lester Young, tends to approach every number as a medium-tempo bounce, even *In the Wee Small Hours of the Morning* and *When Your Lover Has Gone*. But this hardly deters Webster, who was no less mindful than Young was of a song's lyric, and who succeeds in transforming the seven numbers here into melted tallow and low-burning wick; early-morning recollections of amorous nights. **FD**

The Jeep Is Jumping **Webster** (ts); **Arnved Meyer** (t); **John Darville** (tb); **Niels Jorgen Steen** (p); **Henrik Hartmann** or **Hugo Rasmussen** (b); **Hans Nymand** (d). Black Lion Ⓜ 760147 (44 minutes). Recorded 1965.

⑧ ❽

Recorded not long after he relocated to Europe, this disc is representative of Webster's work during the final period of his life; the sidemen differ but the plot stays basically the same. In light of his increasing reliance on ballads, however, this one sports three up-tempo capers and a few blues, and the accompanying quintet approximates the flavour of an Ellington small band. The setting certainly put Ben at his ease, and he responds warmly. Surprisingly, none of the Ducal tunes were ones identified with Webster. On the title tune he treads on Hodges's turf but sounds quite at home; here, on *Stompy Jones* and the romping *Duke's In Bed* his growl choruses sound like he has Brillo pads on his sax. No one could play a blues with the tone and temperament of Webster, and *Blue Light* and *Brother John's Blues* highlight his impeccable timing—a thing of beauty in itself. Who also could fail to respond to that curious blend of vulnerability and bluster? The most seductive of balladeers, his *Nancy* is likely to sigh rather than laugh, and he paints *The Days Of Wine And Roses* like a Picasso, tonal distortions never obscuring the romantic line. The sidemen provide riffs when required and solo idiomatically, though without the panache of their models, but after all, Webster's the whole show, and he was one of a kind. **AL**

See You At The Fair **Webster** (ts); **Hank Jones** (p); **Roger Kellaway** (p, h); **Richard Davis** (b); **Osie Johnson**, **Grady Tate** (d); **Thad Jones** (t); **Phil Woods** (as); **Phil Bodner** (ts, eng-h); **Pepper Adams** (bs); **Oliver Nelson** (arr, cond) on two tracks only. Impulse! Ⓜ GRP 11212 (49 minutes). Recorded 1964.

⑧ ❿

After his return from California in the early sixties and the ending of his Verve contract, Webster's appearances on disc were few. An unlikely album shared with Joe Zawinul was followed by the above quartet-based set and a few guest shots for Impulse! (including two tracks appended here from Oliver Nelson's **More Blues And The Abstract Truth**). The splendid quartet sessions certainly made a fitting conclusion to Webster's American career, with an appropriate exhibition of his various strengths. Nothing exceeds a bouncing fast-medium tempo, at which speed the title-track is outstanding for its simplicity and vitality, while medium-medium tempos such as *In A Mellow Tone* allow the leader to play fewer notes and express more by mere nuance. But, partly thanks to sensitive accompaniment by either Jones or Kellaway, Ben really shines on the ballads, of which Ellington's *Single Petal Of A Rose* (originally a piano solo) was previously only available on a compilation LP while Dmitri Tiomkin's *Fall Of Love* reflects the jazz vogue for film themes initiated by Eddie Harris's *Exodus*.

The two added octet tracks necessarily diffuse the effect somewhat but, on Hefti's *Midnight Blue*, Webster is featured in a slow blues from **The Atomic Mr Basie**. **BP**

Susan Weinert

1965

Crunch Time **Susan Weinert** (elg, gsyn); **Martin Weinert** (elb); **Hardy Fischotter** (d); **Oliver Heuss** (kbds). veraBra Ⓕ vBr 2144 2 (47 minutes). Recorded 1994.

⑧ ❽

Despite talk of equality, the number of prominent female jazz guitarists—Mary Osborne, Emily Remler, Leni Stern—can almost be counted on the fully functioning fingers of Django Reinhardt's crippled hand. At a time when jazz prodigies are spilling from the music schools, the advent of the extraordinarily capable Susan Weinert is a double phenomenon—such comprehensively virtuosic guitar-playing and writing is a rarity in either sex.

Less can be said about the originality of Weinert's style. Her début album, **Mysterious Stories** (vBr 2111 2), inclined towards John Scofield's lyrical, country-inflected early Gramavision approach. Her second, **Crunch Time**, adopts a heavier attitude, fusing funky, harmonically hip mid-eighties Scofield (cf. **Still Warm**) and Scott Henderson (cf. **Spears**). By half-time, the unrelenting heavy metal guitar textures and the stylistically unvarying writing cloy somewhat, but all reservations evaporate in the heat of such moments as the superbly controlled stop-time interlude of *Don't Try That Again, M.F.*, the beautifully developed solo which follows, the clever metric metamorphosis of *Hopeless Case* and the incisively funky guitar riffing which opens *Don't You Guys Know Any Nice Songs?*. **MG**

Bobby Wellins

1926

Nomad **Wellins** (ts); **Jonathan Gee** (p); **Thad Kelly** (b); **Spike Wells** (d); on 3 tracks **Claire Martin** (v). Hot House Ⓕ HHCD 1008 (65 minutes). Recorded 1992.

⑥ ❼

Wellins, born in the same year as John Coltrane, has been an admirable fixture on the British jazz scene since the early fifties. He served an apprenticeship in the big bands of the time, and also had fruitful stints with creative talents such as Stan Tracey and Tubby Hayes. Of the albums recorded under his own name, this is certainly the most recent, and seems to be the only one currently available on CD. However, this is nothing to worry about unduly, because what is to be found here is excellently crafted and satisfying jazz of the variety spawned by various saxophone giants of the post-war years, including Sonny Rollins, Al Cohn and Wardell Gray. By this stage in his career, however, Wellins is his own man and utterly at home both on his instrument and in his style. He plays with a relaxed power here which is engaging, and he also generously gives a great deal of solo space to the members of his quartet. In fact, I would suggest that he has been a little too generous with space for others and occasionally a trifle mean in the time he has allotted for himself. That said, it is always a pleasure to hear him negotiate effortless lines through such terrain as *Little Rootie Tootie* or *Love For Sale* (which segues seamlessly into an impressive *Willow Weep For Me*).

Claire Martin appears on three Wellins originals, and her usual impeccable control and good taste are well in evidence. To sum up, a highly enjoyable album by one of Britain's unsung greats. **KS**

Dicky Wells

1907-85

Swingin' In Paris **Wells** (tb); **Bill Coleman**, **Bill Dillard**, **Shad Collins** (t); **Howard Johnson** (as); **Django Reinhardt** (g); **Sam Allen** (p); **Dick Fullbright** (b); **Bill Beason** (d). **Charly LeJazz** Ⓑ CD 20 (59 minutes). Recorded 1937/38

✔

⑩ ❽

The two 1937 Paris sessions by sidemen of the visiting Teddy Hill Orchestra, under the leadership of Dicky Wells, produced some of the finest swing chamber music ever recorded. All 12 numbers are included here, plus a further eight by Bill Coleman from around the same period.

Wells, who was shortly to become a star soloist with Count Basie, was just reaching his musical maturity in 1937. His style, a combination of lyrical melancholy and a kind of grave jocularity, which marked him out as one of the great individual voices of jazz, is in full bloom here. In the three blues pieces he plays with the simple eloquence that only a master could achieve, while *Lady Be Good* makes a worthy companion-piece to Lester Young's version of the previous year. Perhaps the most exciting passage of all, though, is the first chorus of *Between The Devil And The Deep Blue Sea*, in which the trombone skips and prances around the melody before launching into an inspired paraphrase of the middle-eight strain. The presence of Django Reinhardt on five of these pieces is a further reason for recommending this fine reissue. **DG**

Alex Welsh

1929-1982

Classic Concert **Welsh** (t, v); **Roy Williams** (tb, v); **Johnny Barnes** (cl, as, bs, fl, v); **Fred Hunt** (p); **Jim Douglas** (g, bj); **Harvey Weston** (bs, bg); **Lennie Hastings** (d). Black Lion Ⓜ BLCD 760503 (75 minutes). Recorded 1971.

⑥ ❻

"To their many admirers Alex Welsh and his band made up the best and best-loved jazz ensemble in Britain, or perhaps anywhere," says Digby Fairweather in his notes, with typical over-statement. (Better than Duke? Better-loved than Louis?) Elsewhere he calls the group "probably Britain's greatest-ever Dixieland band," which again is odd, as there was a lot about the Welsh unit which was not Dixieland at all. Roy Williams's duets with guitar, or his unaccompanied choruses; Barnes's baritone and flute solos—nothing very Dixieland there. In fact Williams's trombone playing—the single finest thing in the group—is pretty modern in its sweep; he is just as nimble and liberated as J.J. Johnson in his prime, and a lot warmer.

Yet when you listen to a concert like this, recorded in East Germany in Dresden's intriguingly named Hygiene-Halle, you can see, and remember, what Digby means. He first heard the band in 1969. I first heard it in 1959. Over the years Welsh, with his American visitors, has given me more pleasure than any other British band, and on this date he was giving a lot of Germans a great deal of pleasure too. You know when the Germans are enjoying it: because their clapping slowly coagulates into a gigantic unison clapping, quite often at the right tempo, so that Welsh can go straight into a reprise...

The good numbers—*Oh! Baby*, *9.20 Special*, *Dippermouth Blues*—are terrific. The not-so-good numbers are usually the flashy features for Fred Hunt, or the ones with vocals. British trad/Dixieland players have a fatal urge to open their mouths and sing the words to such dreary songs as *If I Had A Talking Picture Of You*, *Little Girl*, and *Dapper Dan* as if a) they were any good, and b) they could remember them. I did realize until I heard this record just how bad the words to *Tangerine* were. How can a man like Roy Williams sing so shoddily and play so beautifully on the same number? **MK**

Kenny Werner

Gu-Ru **Werner** (p); **Tim Hagens** (t); **Billy Drews** (ts); **Ratzo Harris** (b); **Tom Rainey** (d); **Jamie Haddad** (perc). TCB Ⓕ 94502 (75 minutes). Recorded 1993.

It might once have seemed that Corea, Jarrett and others had exhausted the possibilities suggested by Bill Evans, but such a conclusion would have reckoned without Kenny Werner. His development of Evans's aesthetic is most readily gauged against the familiar frame of reference provided by the two standards here: The refiguring of *Miss Jones* as a shambling calypso with swing middle-eight is intriguing enough, but *Dolphin Dance*, with its long, winding introduction, impressionist tag section, convoluted phrase lengths and constant dynamic and metrical shifts, leaves no doubt of Werner's individualism. That settled, even greater delights are to be had from such originals as *Little Blue Man*, where the trio negotiate treacherous rhythmic chicanes with daring, sensitivity and virtuosity.

This is a genuine trio affair: the arrangements involve the whole ensemble, and Harris and Rainey are fully in sympathy with Werner's idiosyncratic vision of piano jazz. The trio is augmented on the Jarrettish meditations of *Gu-Ru* and *Shivaya*, by Hagens and Drews, who produce luminous horn textures reminiscent of those on Peter Erskine's *Sweet Soul*. **MG**

Fred Wesley

Swing and Be Funky **Wesley** (tb, v); **Hugh Ragin** (t, flh, v); **Karl Denson** (ts, v); **Peter Madsen** (p, v); **Dwayne Dolphin** (b, v); **Bruce Cox** (d, v). Minor Music Ⓕ MM 801027. Recorded 1992 (77 minutes).

⑥ ❽

Fred Wesley has played in the backing bands for countless funk and soul stars, and has also stacked up useful jazz credentials. This album stresses the jazz side but does not entirely abandon backbeats and the odd spot of funk (Maceo Parker's *Just Like That* is something The Crusaders would have had fun with). The opening track, written by Prince, is called *For The Elders* and is a graceful tribute to the jazz players who have now gone on before. Each solo horn gets plenty of room and the track runs for over 14 minutes. Even longer is a Latinized version of *On Green Dolphin Street*, which finally exhausts itself at 21 minutes. The music, recorded live in Germany, is generally cast in a happy frame and is relatively conservative in style. Each player acquits himself handsomely, and the band sounds commendably relaxed—in fact, the lengths of the tracks (the shortest is over eight minutes) tends to suggest that they occasionally get too relaxed—so, if it is fun you are looking for, you won't go wrong here. **KS**

Frank Wess

1922

Entre Nous **Wess** (ts, f); **Snooky Young**; **Ron Tooley** (t); **Pete Minger** (t, flh); **Joe Newman** (t, v); **Art Baron**; **Grover MItchell**; **Dennis WIlson**; **Doug Purviance** (tb); **Curtis Peagler**; **Bill Ramsey** (as); **Billy Mitchell** (ts); **Arthur 'Babe' Clarke** (bs); **Ted Dunbar** (g); **Tee Carson** (p); **Eddie Jones** (b); **Dennis Mackrell** (d). Concord Ⓕ CCD 4456. Recorded 1990. (57 minutes?).

⑦ ❿

Wess worked in the big bands of Blanche Calloway, Eddie Heywood and Lucky Millinder, but it was his spell with Count Basie from 1953 to 1964 that brought him international attention. This CD features him on tenor and flute and, on *Order In The Court*, *Lover* and *Shiny Stockings* in particular, shows him as an accomplished arranger. This Basie-style, 17-piece orchestra is a good one, if lacking a fraction of the model band's rhythmic elasticity. The reeds flow pleasingly and there is real bite in the brass section. The leader gives *Entre Nous* some delicately creative flute treatment, while his tenor on *Rink Rat* is smoothly assertive. There are also polished solos from Young, Baron, Minger, Dunbar and Carson to give further substance. In the eighties Wess worked with Dameronia and New York Jazz Quartet, as well as in a quintet with former Basie colleague, Frank Foster. He is perhaps most at home, as here, with 17 men swinging. **BMcR**

Kate Westbrook

1939

Goodbye Peter Lorre **Westbrook** (v); **John Alley**, **Mike Westbrook** (p); **Fine Trash** (vocal group). Femme Ⓕ FECD 9.01060 0 (63 minutes). Recorded 1991.

⑧ ❽

Since emerging as a musician and singer with husband Mike Westbrook's Brass Band in 1974, Kate Westbrook has consistently combined a fine literary sensibility with great emotional subtlety to produce startlingly fresh reinterpretations of familiar songs and cogently personal originals. Both these facets of her art are successfully displayed on **Goodbye Peter Lorre**: the centrepiece, Brecht/Eisler's *Hollywood Elegies*, vindicates her reputation for bringing a new perspective to the German's works—a skill also apparent here on Brecht/Weil's *The Sailor's Tango* and the achingly lovely *Surabaya Johnny*—and the opening and closing Westbrook compositions provide a framework by exploring the album's central theme, the tension resulting from the recognition of the gap between appearances and reality, the ideal and the pragmatic. Peter Lorre is a perfect focus for the project, of course, because he links the expatriate Hollywood world of Brecht and company with this theme through his tragic personification of the dichotomy between public persona and true inner character, and the album's title-track is a superb exploration of the emotional conflict thus engendered. Like her work with the trio A Little Westbrook Music and within larger, orchestral Westbrook projects, to which Kate Westbrook gives purpose and direction by selecting the European language texts upon which they comment and around which they revolve, **Goodbye Peter Lorre** not only hums with imaginative life, but helps to place jazz in a somewhat unaccustomed position, at the heart of European culture. **CP**

Mike Westbrook

1936

Bright as Fire—The Westbrook Blake **Westbrook** (p, v); **Kate Westbrook** (h, perc, v); **Phil Minton** (t, v); **Mike Davies**, **Dave Hancock**, **Henry Lowther** (t); **Malcolm Griffiths** (tb); **Alan Sinclair**, **Nick Patrick** (tba) **Alan Wakeman** (ss, ts, f); **Chris Biscoe** (ss, as, cl); **Georgie Born** (vc); **Chris Laurence** (b); **Dave Barry** (d, perc); **Gospel Oak Primary School Children's Choir** (v). Impetus Ⓔ IMP CD 18013 (43 minutes). Recorded 1980.

The UK's premier jazz composer, Mike Westbrook is known both for his ambitious big-band projects and for his links with poetry, cabaret and theatre, pursued chiefly through various small groups such as his Brass Band and his trio, A Little Westbrook Music. His most successful large-scale piece to date is **The Cortège**, a sprawling three-album tour de force that recently appeared on CD on the Enja label. **Bright As Fire**, although smaller in scale, matches it for quality: passionate, incisive settings of seven William Blake poems that Westbrook first composed in 1971 (for Adrian Mitchell's play *Tyger*), performed here by an augmented Brass Band line-up.

Although he makes full use of his two striking vocalists and coaxes a rare fervour from the saxophonists, it is Westbrook's brilliant writing that ultimately illuminates Blake's verse. He finds music to match the ecstatic vision of *I See Thy Form* and the bleakness of *London Song,* turns *A Poison Tree* into a macabre tango and extends *Holy Thursday* into a searing howl of protest. The finale—Minton singing *Let the Slave,* Westbrook himself declaiming *The Price of Experience*—makes a magnificent anthem of Blake's paeans to freedom and compassion. **Bright as Fire** may not offer the most comprehensive view of Westbrook's manifold talents but its power and stark intensity have yet to be surpassed. **GL**

Randy Weston

1926

Monterey '66 **Weston** (p); **Ray Copeland** (t, flh); **Booker Ervin** (ts); **Cecil Payne** (bs); **Bill Wood** (b); **Lenny McBrowne** (d); **Big Black** (perc). Verve Ⓕ 519 698-2 (74 minutes). Recorded 1966.

⑧ ❽

There are many reasons for this album (made from a private tape in Randy Weston's possession) being both historically significant and intrinsically worthwhile. It catches a lively and innovative working band at a peak of creativity, having been together three years and shortly to disband; it documents the live sound of one of the music's most underrated saxophonists, Booker Ervin, just four years before his death; it demonstrates the depth and strength of Weston's commitment to the dissemination of African culture years before such concerns became widespread in the popular-musical world. The music itself—rousing, loosely informal and spontaneous yet tightly organized where necessary—bears all the hallmarks of longstanding intimate association between group members; Weston himself refers to it simply as "the best band I've ever had". In a lengthy set made up entirely of Weston compositions, his septet provide a heady mix of uninhibited front-line blowing over hypnotic, rumbustious percussion and more restrained, contemplative moments, such as Ervin's affecting contribution to *Portrait of Vivian*, dedicated to Weston's mother. What lingers in the mind, however, are the two long, heavily percussive pieces, *Afro Black* and *African Cookbook*, which form the musical and philosophical heart of an unusually fine live recording. **CP**

The Spirit Of Our Ancestors **Weston** (p); **Idrees Sulieman** (t); **Benny Powell** (tb); **Talib Kibwe** (f, as); **Billy Harper**, **Pharoah Sanders**, **Dewey Redman** (ts); **Alex Blake**, **Jamil Nasser** (b); **Idris Muhammad** (d); **Big Black**, **Azzedin Weston** (perc); add on one track each: **Yassir Chadly** (v, genbri, karkaba), **Dizzy Gillespie** (t). Antilles Ⓕ 511 896-2 (two discs, oas: 44 and 62 minutes). Recorded 1991.

✔ ⑩ ❽

There are many memorable recordings from various high points in the career of Randy Weston—solo piano sessions emphasizing his unique link to the blues tradition or acknowledging influences Ellington and Monk; quintet dates with partners like tenor legend Coleman Hawkins or young firebrand Billy Harper; colourful orchestral arrangements, usually by the talented Melba Liston, of Weston's exotic, expansive tunes. Over the years he has been an exciting and consistent performer with

a dark, haunting piano tone, percussive touch, and a wealth of rhythms from Caribbean, American jazz and North African sources. **The Spirits of Our Ancestors** combines these sources brilliantly. Liston's charts on tunes like *African Cookbook*, *The Call* and *Blue Moses* sing with unconventional voicings and subtle use of polyrhythms and polytonalities. Fine contributions from trombonist Powell and saxists Sanders and Harper add spice, and Dizzy Gillespie is special guest soloist on the extended *African Sunrise*, composed by Weston for him and Machito's orchestra. The drummers deserve special mention for providing the intense rhythmic impetus, from the riffing refrains of *African Village Bedford-Stuyvesant* to the evocative Arabic modal *The Healers*. But Weston's superb piano is the glue that holds it all together.
AL

Kenny Wheeler

1930

Music for Large and Small Ensembles **Wheeler** (t, flh); **Derek Watkins**, **Henry Lowther**, **Alan Downey**, **Ian Hamer** (t); **Dave Horler**, **Chris Pyne**, **Paul Rutherford**, **Hugh Fraser** (tb); **Ray Warleigh**, **Duncan Lamont**, **Evan Parker**, **Stan Sulzmann**, **Julian Argüelles** (reeds); **John Abercrombie** (g); **John Taylor** (p); **Dave Holland** (b); **Peter Erskine** (d); **Norma Winstone** (v). ECM Ⓕ 1415/16 (843 152-2) (two discs: 105 minutes). Recorded 1990.

⑧ ❽

Although famously diffident, Canadian trumpeter Kenny Wheeler has long been recognized as a world-class instrumentalist and composer. Based in the UK since 1952, he has participated in many varieties of modern jazz, a valued contributor to groups as diverse as Azimuth and the Globe Unity Orchestra. His earlier ECM recordings present him in a selection of small-group settings but on **Music for Large and Small Ensembles** the emphasis is on his writing for a large big band of the kind he's been leading, albeit on a very occasional basis, for some 25 years.

The eight-part *Sweet Time Suite* takes up the first of the two discs. Its deft timbral shadings and well-framed solos (all excellent) affirm Wheeler's arranging skills, while *Freddy C*'s jaunty swing and the desolate balladry of *Consolation* point to his range as composer. His tunes are often pastoral in mood, their frequent tinges of melancholia offset by a rich harmonic world that is given extra colouring here by Norma Winstone's wordless vocals. The second CD mixes tracks for big band and small groups, the latter including duos, trios and a sparkling quintet version of *By Myself*. If the three further orchestra works substantiate Wheeler's claim that "I'm always trying to write a beautiful tune," his two trio tracks (with Holland and Erskine) demonstrate that his melodic gift can also flourish in the context of free improvisation.
GL

Michael White

1954

New Year's At The Village Vanguard **White** (cl); **Wendell Brunious** (t, v); **Wynton Marsalis** (t); **Freddie Lonzo** (tb); **Steve Pistorious** (p); **Don Vappie** (bj); **Richard Paine** (b); **Louis Cottrell Jr.** (d). Antilles Ⓕ 512 168-2 (65 minutes). Recorded 1992.

⑦ ❽

Born into a family which included Papa John and Kaiser Joseph, White had early experience with Doc Paulin and the Young Tuxedo Brass Band. Work with Wynton Marsalis confirmed his pan-stylistic musical attitudes, but his heart has always been in the music of his birthplace, New Orleans. His faith in the music has not been misplaced and he has become something of a central figure in what has become yet another New Orleans Jazz revival. This CD is a fine example of his work; all of the players involved are from a New Orleans background, if not always totally involved in the city's traditional style. The rhythm section has lightness of touch that shames many of its contemporary rivals, and on the three tracks that include him, Marsalis fits in well. Brunious's lead is assured throughout, and although Lonzo's tailgate playing is sometimes too busy, White's thorough grasp of the clarinet's role in this music ensures a well-integrated ensemble. White's solos are also the best on the album; beautifully articulated, imaginatively improvised and full of feeling. He may lack a little of the fluency associated with Jimmy Noone or Omer Simeon, but as with most of his recordings, he becomes the music's focal point.
BMcR

Paul Whiteman

1890-67

When Day Is Done **Whiteman** (dir); with various personnel, including **George Gershwin** (p); **Henry Busse** (t); **Bix Beiderbecke** (c); **Red Nichols** (t); **Charles Margulis** (t); **Charlie Teagarden** (t); **Tommy Dorsey** (tb); **Bill Rank** (tb); **Jack Teagarden** (tb); **Charles Strickfaden** (as, bs); **Jimmy Dorsey** (cl, as); **Izzy Friedman** (cl, as); **Frankie Trumbauer** (cms); **Roy Bargy** (p); **Art Miller** (b); **Steve Brown** (b); **Casper Reardon** (hp); **Min Leibrook** (bb); **Harold McDonald** (d, vb); **Bing Crosby** (v); **Hoagy Carmichael** (v, p) and others. Conifer Ⓜ CDHD 171 (63 minutes). Recorded 1924-34.

⑥ ❼

From the time Whiteman formed a dance band in 1918 until his retirement, he made more than 600 recordings. It was Whiteman who commissioned Gershwin to write *Rhapsody in Blue* and

thereby realize the potential of 'symphonic jazz'. In the process, he became known as the 'King of Jazz' and, with an orchestra that often included jazz musicians of stature, conducted concert tours to spread his message. As this CD aptly shows, it was a strange and highly personal musical religion. The formula included sham classical music, popular tunes of the day, plus a smattering of trivial novelty numbers. The standard of musicianship was high, and in men like Bill Challis and Tommy Satterfield he had arrangers who knew what was required. Unfortunately, much of the standard arranging was pretentious, and although some imagination is shown in titles such as *Soliloquy,* the outcome was often too laboured. The Beiderbecke contribution is covered elsewhere, but on this disc there are often fine offerings from Trumbauer's solo C-melody sax and from Chariie Teagarden's fine lead trumpet. These were isolated moments of pure jazz, however, and, for most of the time, The King of Jazz produced music that was denied the vital ingredient to make it just that.
BMcR

Mark Whitfield

1966

True Blue **Whitfield** (g); **Nicholas Payton** (t); **Branford Marsalis** (s); **Kenny Kirkland** (p); **Rodney Whitaker** (b); **Jeff 'Tain' Watts** (d). Verve Ⓕ 523 591-2 (75 minutes). Recorded 1994.

④ ❽

It is a sad indictment of a music once prized for its ability to innovate that jazz, like classical music interpretation, now so often makes do with historical authenticity. Mark Whitfield, a routinely able player in the Burrell-Montgomery-Benson line, is a symptom of the lazy, nostalgic present, and a million miles from the New York Times's ill-considered description of him as 'the best young guitarist on the scene today'. His lines on this set of four-to-the-bar blues, ballads and dark modal swingers are fluent and fleet enough, but they lack even a suggestion of the rhythmic and harmonic variety which is surely *de rigueur* in these post-Scofield days. Like the baldly contrived imaging on the case—big-bodied Gibson archtop, folksy back-porch photography circa 1959 and vintage Kay amplifier (Whitfield actually plays state-of-the-art Mesa Boogie amps), his playing is transparently derivative. The same goes for the tired repertoire. The distinguished band are not to be faulted, but they labour in vain to breathe life into this deeply dated conception.
MG

Putte Wickman

1924

Bewitched **Putte Wickman** (cl); **Claes Crona** (p); **Mads Vinding**, **Ove Stenberg** (b); **Bjarne Rostvold**, **Nils-Erik Slorner** (d). Bluebell Ⓕ ABCD 051 (67 minutes). Recorded 1980-82.

⑧ ❽

Like his contemporary and fellow-countryman the late Stan Hasselgard, the Swedish clarinettist Putte Wickman grew up under the overwhelming influence of Benny Goodman but succeeded in developing a personal style quite early in his career. Bop and cool jazz have left distinct marks on his playing, and he has also has also shown a natural affinity for the bossa nova. This collection of 18 short, exquisitely-turned versions of standard tunes shows off his delicate tone and fluid phrasing to perfection. Pianist Claes Crona deserves to be far more widely appreciated; as an accompanist he has the firm lightness of a Hank Jones or a Tommy Flanagan. The recording, by engineers of Swedish Radio, is first rate.
DG

Gerald Wiggins

1922

Reminiscin' With Wig **Wiggins** (p); **Eugene Wright** (b); **Bill Douglass** (d). Fresh Sounds Ⓕ FSR CD 47 (32 minutes). Recorded 1957.

Wiggins has spent most of his long career as an accompanist to a range of first-rate singers, including Lena Horne, Kay Starr and Helen Humes. Occasionally someone who ran a small label would get the idea of making a record featuring the the accompanist, and an album such as the present one would result. Wiggins, influenced by piano stylists as diverse as Art Tatum, George Shearing and Erroll Garner, would always put together a good programme and provide tasteful and inventive music which rarely raised the emotional temperature much above tepid, but which certainly employed a high degree of artistry in the low-key interpretations. Wiggins was particularly under the spell of Garner when he made this date back in 1957, using his tempos, his left-hand figures, and Garner's patented high-treble melody work. It is an enjoyable low-key affair. although the piano is out of tune in some of its registers. Meanwhile, the record still only runs for 32 minutes even though the CD includes an extra track. At full price and for an album now 38 years old, something has got to be wrong somewhere.
KS

Bob Wilber

1928

Summit Reunion **Wilber** (ss); **Kenny Davern** (cl); **Dick Hyman** (p); **Bucky Pizzarelli** (g); **Milt Hinton** (b); **Bobby Rosengarden** (d). Chiaroscuro Ⓕ CR(D) 311 (68 minutes). Recorded 1990.

⑧ ❽

Soprano saxophonist/clarinettist Bob Wilber is one of the true champions of traditional jazz, studying for several years as a teenager with no less a legend than Sidney Bechet. As a prime mover in the traditional jazz revival centred in New York during the late forties and fifties, he worked with Bobby Hackett, Benny Goodman and Jack Teagarden. In 1969, he helped found the World's Greatest Jazz Band, and in 1974 he and fellow reedman Keny Davern organized Soprano Summit. It was a wonderful group that during its five-year run seamlessly fused prime elements from the New Orleans, Chicago and Swing Era heritages, with Wilber and Davern, both virtuoso players, melding their warmly rendered countermelodies with precision and dash. When the group disbanded in 1979, Wilber took on such varied projects as the score for Francis Coppola's film *The Cotton Club* (for which he received a 1986 Grammy) and the directorship of the Smithsonian Jazz Repertory Ensemble.

Here, the 1990 recording reunion of Wilbur and Davern finds Wilber on soprano and Davern on clarinet. It is an upbeat and musically immaculate affair where chestnuts like *Lover Come Back to Me*, *Black and Blue* and *Limehouse Blues* are toasted to perfection. In-the-pocket support by the original rhythm section cements the good feelings and music. There is also an 11-minute dialogue where Wilber and Davern reminisce and opine. **CB**

Joe Wilder

1922

Wilder 'N' Wilder **Wilder** (t); **Hank Jones** (p); **Wendell Marshall** (b); **Kenny Clarke** (d). Denon/Savoy Ⓜ SV 0131 (38 minutes). Recorded 1956.

⑧ ❽

One of the most reliable trumpet sidemen, Wilder worked with Les Hite, Lionel Hampton, Dizzy Gillespie, Jimmie Lunceford and Lucky Millinder in the forties. He worked for six months with Count Basie in 1953, but in 1957 began a career on the musical staff of ABC. It has been contended with some justification that the comfort of studio work somewhat blunted the cutting edge of his jazz performances. The virtuoso trumpeter did not challenge himself enough or bother to put himself into motivating situations. This excellent CD is one of only two recordings issued under his leadership during the 16 years he spent in the studio but it reveals a very fine jazz musician. His masterful interpretations of the testing *Cherokee* or *Darn That Dream* confirm his inherent improvisational skill but throughout he displays his fluency, his unique tone and his highly personal manner of phrasing. On *Six Bit Blues* he adds a little surface grit by growling through a waltzing blues theme ideally suited to this style of treatment. Not all of his output has been of this quality but it does seem that with Jones, Marshall and Clarke to provide the stimulation, Wilder was in the mood to respond. **BMcR**

Barney Wilen

1937

Wild Dogs Of The Ruwenzori **Wilen** (ss, as, ts); **Alain Jean-Marie** (p); **Riccardo del Fra** (b); **Sangoma Everett** (d); **Henri Guedon** (perc). IDA Ⓕ 020 CD (71 minutes). Recorded 1988.

⑤ ❻

Barney Wilen flashed into the jazz consciousness in the late fifties as a young man when he was picked to play with Miles Davis on the sound track for the film *Lift To The Scaffold*, and as far as the British public is concerned has not been heard much of since. Judging by this CD he has developed into a capable, warm swinging tenor player, not much touched by the Coltrane, free or fusion eras. The record is pleasant and quite varied, but... There is no explanation for the title provided, neither what the Ruwenzori is nor why there are wild dogs there, although there is a reproduction of a painting of that name, under which it says (in French) "It is easier to leave no trace behind than to walk without touching the ground." Deep, these French. **MK**

Lee Wiley

1915-1975

Night In Manhattan **Wiley** (v); **Bobby Hackett** (c); **Joe Bushkin**, **Stan Freeman**, **Cy Walter** (p); **unknown** (b, d); strings. Columbia Ⓜ SRS 75010 (38 minutes). Recorded 1950.

✔ ⑧ ❽

One has to search nowadays for Lee Wiley's records, of which this is a quite delectable example. It features her breathy-cool voice against the accompaniment of Hackett's cornet, a rhythm section led by Bushkin and the subtlest and most minimal of string backgrounds. She was one of the very first white jazz singers, along with Connee Boswell and Mildred Bailey, and by 1950 had evolved a style of ethereal, but at the same time worldly, charm. This ambivalence lies at the heart of her singing persona and is inherent in the stylistic means which she employs. There is, for instance, a quite deliberate, girlish breathiness about her higher notes, yet at the same time no one ever handled the trembling downward glissando (indicative of barely controlled passion) to greater effect. But, these devices aside, Lee Wiley's most captivating quality is her ability to make notes and words swing together, which is—or should be—the definition of a good jazz singer. She produces small miracles in this line here, in songs such as *Manhattan* (a strong rival to Ella's version), *Oh! Look At Me Now* and *Sugar*. On four of the 12 titles the accompaniment changes to the piano-duo of Freeman and Walter, with which she does the best she can. But it is worth buying this disc for the remaining eight. It is also worth searching out the Japanese issue of this album, released on CD in the original mono sound. **DG**

Lee Wiley-Ellis Larkins Duologue **Wiley** (v); **Ruby Braff** (t); **Jimmy Jones** (p); **Bill Pemberton** (b); **Jo Jones** (d); on 4 tracks, **Ellis Larkins** (p). Black Lion Ⓜ BLCD 760911 (36 minutes). Recorded 1954.

⑧ ❻

Four out of the dozen tracks are piano solos by Larkins which are very compatible with the tasteful and imaginative performances from Wiley and her group. This CD is a straight transfer of an old 12-inch LP which was cobbled together from an old Storyville ten-inch Wiley LP with the Larkins tracks thrown in to make up the new format's playing-time. Nothing has been added, however, to make up the CD format's rather miserly playing-time.

Wiley is a jazz singer to class with Billie Holiday, Mildred Bailey and Peggy Lee. Listening to her warm and delicately phrased singing, it is difficult to reconcile her with Wild Bill Davison's description of a fist fight in a bar in which she was involved with another musician's wife. According to Davison, Wiley and the other woman, a lady called Sea Biscuit, slugged it out toe to toe like men. Despite her most feminine mien Wiley was often able to physically intimidate her male colleagues.

Regrettably most of Wiley's recordings were marred by oppressive commercial backing or, when she was with jazz small groups, poor recording quality. This makes the album under review doubly valuable for, while George Wein's Storyville recordings hardly count as hi-fi, they are comparatively superior. The backing, with young Braff ideally suited to the singer, is as good as any she ever had and recalls her session with Muggsy Spanier and Jess Stacy of many years earlier. Wiley's choice of material was unerringly good and songs like *My Romance*, *It Never Entered My Mind*, and *My Heart Stood Still* are perfect for her. Larkins's unaccompanied tracks are similarly tasteful and his accomplished solos are the next best thing to four more songs from Wiley. **SV**

Ernie Wilkins

1922

Suite For Jazz Band **Wilkins** (ldr, arr); with **Danish Radio Big Band** (Benny Rosenfeld, Palle Bolvig, Henrik Bolberg, Lars Togeby, Perry Knudsen [t], Vincent Nilsson, Ture Larsen, Steen Hansen, Jens Engels [tb], Axel Windfeld [btb], Jan Zum Vohrde, Michael Hove [as], Tomas Franck, Uffe Marcussen [ts], Flemming Madsen [bs], Nikolaj Bentzon [p], Anders Lindvall [g], Jesper Lundgaard [b], Jonas Johansen [d], Peter Reim [perc]). Hep Ⓕ HEP CD 2051 (68 minutes). Recorded 1991.

⑥ ❻

Wilkins became one of the most prolific writers for big bands, starting his career with the Count Basie Orchestra, which he joined as a saxophonist in 1952. He came to live in Denmark in 1980 and, at the time of writing, the fine LPs by his 'Almost Big Band' made in that country have not been transferred to the compact disc format. On this well-recorded concert transcription he heads the Danish Radio Big Band on one of its annual tours of Britain (the CD was taped at a Croydon concert). Half of the playing time is devoted to music composed and arranged, with typical efficiency, by Ernie. The major work is his *Suite For Jazz Band,* divided into three sections and lasting for 24 minutes. It is an impressive piece of writing and the band is well up to interpreting it with accuracy and verve. The suite reminds us that Wilkins wrote an extended *From Coast To Coast* for Basie in 1956 which the Count seldom performed, presumably preferring more orthodox Wilkins pieces such as *Peace Pipe* and *The Midgets.* Pianist Bentzon and tenor saxist Marcussen are two outstanding soloists in the Radio Big Band and alto saxist Jan Zum Vohrde takes the featured role on Phil Woods's arrangement of *This Is All I Ask* with considerable skill and flair. **AM**

Baby Face Willette

1933

Stop and Listen **Willette** (org); **Grant Green** (g); **Ben Dixon** (d). Blue Note Ⓜ CDP8 28998 2 (50 minutes). Recorded 1961.

⑤ ❽

Willette - nobody seems to have recorded his given first name - made his recording debut on Blue Note with **Face To Face**, an album made in the same year and also featuring Grant Green. Currently unavailable, its bonus was the robust tenor of Fred Jackson. Here Baby Face has to lead the line himself, and while he's a capable player who eschews the grosser combinations of sounds of which a Hammond B3 is capable, he struggles to keep the listener's undivided attention for 50 minutes. Perhaps in a Harlem bar in 1961 this would have been ideal, and there is no doubting that his pedal work is nicely grooved with drummer Ben Dixon, but his right hand is sparing in its use of the unexpected. So it is to Green that we must look for that type of aural stimulation, and he obliges on more tracks than not, even if it is merely in the fine art of rhythmic displacement.

The rating indicates that this is a good album, and it is. Within its given genre it is successful, and if organ jazz is your meat, you will not be disappointed here. For those wishing to dip their toes for the first time, there are better places to start. **KS**

Buster Williams 1942

Something More **Williams** (b, pic b); **Shunzo Ohno** (t); **Wayne Shorter** (ts, ss); **Herbie Hancock** (p, key); **Al Foster** (d). In & Out Ⓕ 7004-2 (59 minutes). Recorded 1989.

⑧ ❽

At home with the bop of Jimmy Heath and Sonny Stitt as well as in the company of singers such as Betty Carter or Sarah Vaughan, Williams moved with the times and worked with Miles Davis and Hancock in the sixties and early seventies. More recently found in the comparatively conservative atmosphere of The Timeless All Stars and Sphere, he remains one of music's finest bassists. This CD is, in fact, just what such a player's session should be like. Williams is at the heart of the ensemble, his full tone and faultless intonation a vital factor in the band's overall sound. Apart from a rather bland piccolo bass outing on *Sophisticated Lady*, his solos are richly inventive and are delivered with an ideally dark-brown resonance. Williams has also written five impressive tunes, with two waltzes, *Air Dancing* and *Something More*, being genuinely memorable. He has also provided the listener the perfect guarantee by picking a lineup at the top of their game. Shorter, close to the theme on *Christina* and *Something More* and raw-edged on *Fortune Dance*, responds splendidly. Ohno excels on *Deception*, while Williams, Hancock and Foster sound as if they have been together for years. The album reflects great credit on its leader. **BMcR**

Clarence Williams 1898-65

1927-34 **Williams** (p, jug, v); **Ed Allen, Louis Metcalf** (c); **Red Allen** (t); **Charlie Irvis** (tb); **Cecil Scott** (cl); **Buster Bailey** (cl, as); **Arville Harris** (cl, as, ts); **Herman Chittison**, **Willie 'The Lion' Smith**, **James P. Johnson** (p); **Leroy Harris, Ikey Robinson** (b); **Cyrus St Clair** (bb); **Floyd Casey** (wbd); **Eva Taylor** (v). CDS Ⓕ RPCD 633 (69 minutes). Recorded 1927-34.

⑦ ❽

Williams was one of the first black musicians to make a success of a multifarious career in the music industry, working as publisher, booker, retailer and record producer. In the mid-twenties he organized sessions by his Blue Five with Louis Armstrong and Sidney Bechet which yielded such classics of their period as *Coal Cart Blues* and *Mandy, Make Up Your Mind.* These are being systematically reissued on Hot 'n' Sweet. The CDS compilation is devoted to his later small groups, which he employed largely on cheerful novelty songs, typically with washboard rather than drums and featuring himself or his wife Eva Taylor as singer. Numbers like *Chizzlin' Sam* and *He Wouldn't Stop Doin' It* are essentially party-blues material in the manner of groups like the Hokum Boys, given musical settings a step or two ahead of the jazzier jugbands but several short of Fats Waller. Scattered amid these effusions are more sober performances like *Log Cabin Blues,* nicely paced by St Clair's brass bass (an important voice in Williams's ensembles), *Trouble* and *Chocolate Avenue,* to which Ed Allen and Cecil Scott supply eloquent blues solos. Williams's track record as a producer enabled him to call on excellent sidemen, and even his more ephemeral pieces have inventive touches, as well as an élan that Robert Parker's transfers reproduce in scrupulous detail. **TR**

James Williams 1951

Talkin' Trash **Williams** (p, org); **Clark Terry** (t, flh, v); **Billy Pierce** (ss, ts); **Steve Nelson** (vb); **Christian McBride** (b); **Tony Reddus** (d). DIW Ⓕ 887 (65 minutes). Recorded 1993.

⑦ ❽

Memphis-born , gospel-inspired and r&b trained, Williams met jazz along with his further education at Memphis State University. He later moved to Boston, taught at Berklee and became a prominent figure on the Massachusetts scene. In the seventies, four productive years with the Jazz Messengers honed up his playing and writing talents so that throughout the eighties he worked as a leader and as an in-demand sideman in New York.

This CD parades his skills effectively. The storefront gospel of *The Orator* is a reminder that he had played church organ in Memphis for six years. In contrast, *Chuckles* offers a pianist with a finely graded touch, flawless execution and a creative bent that makes musical story-telling sound easy. Three choruses of blues piano on *SKJ* show how much he can say with little effort, while *Lotus Blossom* is a gem indicating that he can decorate a thematic line as well as construct a new one. His solos are ever full of confidence, matched only by the support he gives his ebullient colleagues, Terry and Pierce. Even the difficult piano-vibraphone balance is navigated with ease and this is a worthy progress report on a highly professional jazzman. **BMcR**

Jessica Williams

1948

The Next Step **Williams** (p). Hep Ⓕ HEPCD 2054 (75 minutes). Recorded 1993.

⑩ ❽

Jessica Williams has been described as the "best unknown pianist in jazz", and her lack of acceptance as one of the greatest keyboard artistes can only be due to her lack of exposure on record labels with international distribution. She has produced several albums on her own Quanta label, and now has CDs on Timeless and Concord, but her first album for the British Hep label is arguably the very finest showcase for her talents. Not only is she a remarkable pianist, she is also a true composer, not simply a writer of riffs or flimsy lines sketched on top of someone else's chord sequences. There are four of her tunes here, nestling amongst interpretations of works by Mingus, Ellington, Ron Carter and the best Broadway composers. There is also a quite beautiful song by Dave Brubeck, *I Didn't Know Until You Told Me*, which Jessica has taken from the **Real Ambassadors** album which Brubeck made with Louis Armstrong. Her constantly enquiring mind, her knowledge of jazz tradition and her love for the musical philosophy of Thelonious Monk, allied to her ability to extract a beautiful and personal sound from the piano results in music above and beyond the level normally found in a jazz keyboard artist. Her own *Stonewall Blues* is a masterpiece, and sounds like a look back at Leadbelly while simultaneously viewing the future. But there is not a weak track here: this is an essential album of contemporary jazz piano. **AM**

Joe Williams

1918

Every Day: The Best of The Verve Years **Williams** (v); with various ensembles, including **The Count Basie Orchestra:** [Wendell Culley, Renauld Jones, Thad Jones, Joe Newman (t); Henry Coker, Bill Hughes, Benny Powell (tb); Marshall Royal (cl, as); Bill Graham (as); Frank Foster (fl, ts, arr); Charlie Fowlkes (bs); Basie (p); Freddie Green (g); Eddie Jones (b); Sonny Payne (d); Buddy Bregman, Edgar Sampson, Ernie Wilkins (arr)]; and small groups featuring **Clark Terry**, **Joe Wilder** (t); **Al Grey** (tb); **Bobby Watson** (as, arr); **Frank Wess** (ts); **Seldon Powell** (bs); **Norman Simmons** (p, arr); **Shirley Horn** (p, v); **Henry Johnson**, **Kenny Burrell** (g); **Bob Badgley**, **Bob Cranshaw**, **Charles Ables** (b); **Gerryck King**, **Dennis Mackrel**, **Steve Williams** (d); **Marlena Shaw** (v); **Johnny Pate** (arr). Verve Ⓜ 519 813-2 (2 discs: 127 minutes). Recorded 1955-90.

⑥ ❻

Williams has so much going for him as a vocalist - great voice, fine diction, admirably seamless phrasing - it seems odd that for so much of his career he's been perceived as something of an anomaly on the jazz scene. Perhaps the nub of the conundrum lies in that boring and endless argument - what is a jazz singer? It seems to me that if we simply discount Williams as a jazz singer per se, then most of the problems evaporate. One of Williams's favourite latter-day albums of his own (it's featured on this compilation and is reviewed below) is **Ballad and Blues Master**, and this seems a more apt decription of his ambit. If you listen to the powerful impact he makes on the Basie band with his big hit numbers, it's through bringing r&b and popular music techniques to blues structures which have been arranged in a jazz style. Williams skilfully combines traits he's picked up from a multiplicity of artists, including Eckstine, Wynonie Harris, Charles Brown, Memphis Slim, Ella Fitzgerald and even Louis Armstrong, and projects them through his big, gorgeous voice-box to create a sensual and exciting mix. The fact that, with Basie, he invariably sounds like he's smiling, whatever the lyrics are telling us, not only let us know he's having a good time, but that he's not the greatest interpreter we've ever heard, and that, at times, he's closer to showbiz than to jazz. This aspect of his art is much less evident on the latter-day performances, where tenderness, hurt and sorrowful wisdom can also be successfully projected.

Depending on what you're looking for from a singer, Williams can give you either raw excitement a-plenty (with the Basie material) or an all-round musical display (on CD number two, with his own quartet mainly as backing). The only question-mark I would place over this collection as a perfect summing-up of Williams's career is that the second recording of *Every Day*, with the Basie Band and Ella joining in, is missing. **KS**

Ballad And Blues Master **Williams** (v); **Norman Simmons** (p, arr); **Henry Johnson** (g); **Bob Badgley** (b); **Gerryck King** (d). Verve Ⓕ 511 354-2 (51 minutes). Recorded 1987.

⑥ ❽

The impact of Joe Williams and the Count Basie band together created one of the most memorable concert experiences of the late fifties. Williams changed the whole aspect of big-band singing with a narrow programme of blues and blues-based ballads. The surging power of the Basie band and Williams's ability to ride it was most exciting and they had one of the last 78rpm hit records with the double-sided *Every Day I Have The Blues*.

Williams left Basie to follow a solo career in which he used a much wider range of material. A subsequent album with the Thad Jones-Mel Lewis jazz orchestra confirmed that he was at his most potent when pitted against a big band. His flexible bass-baritone had no problems with the songs he sang, but his jazz improvising was suspect, particularly when he indulged in scat singing (as here in *You Can Depend On Me*).

He is still at his best with the blues or blues ballads like Ellington's *I Ain't Got Nothin' But The Blues*. His blowsy approach to the latter and the over-the-top coda is typical and in the blues medley, for example, one sometimes feels that he is parodying himself. But he uses good material well as he shows on *A Hundred Years From Today* and *Tomorrow Night*. His musical director Norman Simmons is probably responsible for filtering out dross from the singer's repertoire. Simmons is a major jazz soloist and accompanist who is in the Hank Jones league and should be starring in his own right. He is possibly the key to Williams's contemporary success. **SV**

Mary Lou Williams

1907-1981

The Chronological Mary Lou Williams, 1927-40 **Williams** (p, arr); **Henry McCord**, **Earl Thompson**, **Harold Baker** (t); **Bradley Bullett**, **Ted Donnelly** (tb); **Edward Inge** (cl) **John Williams** (as, bs); **Earl Miller** (as, cl); **Dick Wilson** (ts); **Ted Robinson, Floyd Smith** (g); **Joe Williams** (bj); **Booker Collins** (b); **Robert Price**, **Ben Thigpen** (d). Classics Ⓜ 630 (73 minutes). Recorded 1927-40.

⑧ ❻

Williams has the distinction of being the most important woman musician of early jazz, and in addition her encouragement was significant for several later generations of players. Consistent with the latter is her contribution to the art of big-band arranging, particularly during her years with the Andy Kirk band, whereas her piano work heard here is more often overlooked these days.

The first six tracks, tolerably reproduced but the least well recorded, find her in the sextet of husband John who later was first to join Kirk, and they afford little scope except for brief, ebullient stride outbursts. The saxophonist is not present on the last six septets led by Mary Lou herself (although Baker, who became her second husband, is on two), where her mature style is matched by the neglected Dick Wilson.

The remaining 13 items, three solo and the rest with the Kirk rhythm secion, are the core of the album. Two 1930 tracks (*Night Life* and *Drag 'Em*) show the stride mixed with a muted Hines influence, while the remainder have a linear approach which is bluesier and meatier than contemporary Teddy Wilson and must have had a considerable effect on the young Nat Cole. **BP**

Tony Williams

1945

Emergency! **Williams** (d); **John McLaughlin** (g); **Larry Young** (org). Polydor Ⓜ 849 068-2 (71 minutes). Recorded 1969.

⑧ ❺

This flawed, wildly exciting, pretentious, groundbreaking album was the real start of the marriage between rock and the cutting edge of jazz which would ultimately deliver up such bands as Weather Report, The Mahavishnu Orchestra and Return to Forever, not to mention Miles Davis's continuing explorations. Although people like Gary Burton and Larry Coryell had attempted an earlier and more measured joining together, Williams's group Lifetime were leaders, not followers. Their music utilized the volume, instrumentation and soundscapes of rock, but applied jazz techniques and attitudes to the material being played. Unfortunately, Williams also made the occasional foray into 'singing', sounding like a lobotomized Mose Allison at the end of a hard day (the painfully self-conscious lyrics didn't help much). If you are willing to overlook these, however, you will discover music with an energy level and exhilaration factor matched at that time only by Jimi Hendrix. It is my guess that Hendrix would have been quite at home jamming with this band (he had already jammed with Young).

The sound quality on the original double-vinyl release was truly appalling. The CD reissue is a considerable improvement against insuperable odds: the reissue engineer notes in the CD disclaimer that there was "distortion in all eight channels" the worst being in Williams's bass drum mike. The original studio recording machine was also completely out of phase with itself. That the sound is now passable is something of a miracle in itself. **KS**

The Story of Neptune **Williams** (d); **Wallace Roney** (t); **Bill Pierce** (ts, ss); **Mulgrew Miller** (p); **Ira Coleman** (b). Blue Note Ⓕ CDP7 98169 2 (45 minutes). Recorded 1991.

⑥ ❽

Williams started his recording career on Blue Note, appearing with Jackie McLean prior to joining Miles Davis in 1963. His first two records as a leader, **Life Time** and **Spring**, have both been transferred to CD and subsequently deleted, so at the present moment his early career as a leader prior to the fusion years is somewhat under-documented. Since leaving Miles Davis in 1969 Williams has led an erratic variety of groups culminating in this one, which has now had a pretty consistent personnel since 1985 and has evolved its own distinct character. Older drummer/leaders Art Blakey and Max Roach were strong influences on Williams, and like theirs, his bands tend to be dominated by his percussion rather than by the horns. Williams is also an arranger of some distinction, and his three-part *Neptune Suite* is a refreshingly robust invention well taken advantage of by Roney, Pierce and Miller, all three of whom are outstandingly gifted soloists as well as worthy leaders in their own right. The third part of the suite, *Creatures of Conscience*, has a brisk display of drumming both in solo and in conversation with the horns. There is also an unusual interpretation of Paul McCartney's *Blackbird* wherein Pierce displays his mastery of the soprano sax, using a much more gentle and melodic approach than is customary in post-bop jazz. Roney is at his most Davis-like in a melancholy ten-minute version of *Poinciana*, but the group returns to prototype hard bop with a searing version of Freddie Hubbard's *Birdlike*. **SV**

Willie Williams

WW3 **Williams** (ts); **Scott Colley** (b); **Harold Summey Jr.** (d). Enja Ⓕ ENJ-8060 2. Recorded 1993 (57 minutes)

⑥ ❻

The album title signifies several layers of meaning: Williams's third album, his own trio and a central apocalyptic composition of the same title. To carry off almost an hour's music in this chordless setting and avoid repetition, deviation and hesitation generally requires a talent of the level of a Sonny Rollins. It would be no exaggeration to say that this album shows Williams moving firmly towards that level, and his tenor playing clearly owes a lot to Rollins, particularly on the opening piece, Odean Pope's *Out For A Walk*, where the saxophone conjures up a Caribbean carnival atmosphere. His soprano playing is less authoritative, but this is not necessarily a disadvantage, and on Summey's excellent composition *You Can If You Try*, Williams injects his playing with delicacy and humour. The title track runs to 12 minutes and ends with the politically-charged *Babylon Falls*. Summey plays consistently well on his début album, while Williams and Colley demonstrate that their work together with T.S. Monk and the early faith placed in Williams by Bobby Watson and Art Taylor has paid dividends. **AS**

Steve Williamson

Journey To Truth **Williamson** (ss, as, ts, p, kbds, v, programming); **Dennis Rollins** (tb); **Anthony Tidd** (p, org); **Jason Rebelllo** (elp); **Henri Jelani Defoe** (g); **Marc Cyril**, **Michael Mondesir**, **Leonard Hubbard** (b); **Ahmir Khalib Thompson**, **Pete Lewinson** (d); **Sola Akingbola** (perc); **Jhelisa Anderson**, **Pamela Anderson**, **Tario Trotter**, **Noel McKoy** (v). Verve Forecast Ⓕ 526 425-2 (71 minutes) Recorded 1994.

④ ❽

Williamson's previous album as a leader showed a deal of promise and individuality, as does this one. A glance at the personnel (that's if you can read the appalling typeface on the insert) will suggest that Williamson attempts various different paths during the course of this new record (most of the individual players don't appear together - all the singers, for example, occupy different cuts, with Noel McKoy being a rapper rather than a singer). The album as a whole hovers between M-Base and Coltrane. At times it picks itself up and delivers a well-focused and exciting musical thought, but too often Williams is echoing the recent past of other players, especially Steve Coleman. That he is an immensely skilled player is unquestionable (a close listen to *Affirmation* will dispel all doubts), but it is not yet clear that he has refined his vision to a point where all coalesces into a powerfully unified entity. He takes the well-known Coltrane quotation about being aware of the 'force for unity' and prints it quite prominently in the CD booklet. A dangerous thing to do, especially with an artist so clearly in flux.

Occasionally, the groove and the instruments synthesise into a sum greater than the parts, such as on *Celestial Blues*, where Williams plays tough tenor against Jhelisa Anderson's words and an in-the-pocket back beat. The spoken and rap tracks are some of the most successful, being able as they are to avoid the dilemnas of fitting a solo instrument successfully into the supporting mix of instruments giving the voice its momentum, but they only point up the partial answers to questions posed elsewhere. Interesting, then. Maybe next time? **KS**

Larry Willis

1940

Just In Time **Willis** (p); **Bob Cranshaw** (b); **Kenny Washington** (d). SteepleChase Ⓕ SCCD 31251 (67 minutes). Recorded 1989.

⑧ ❿

Considering the length and distinction of his ongoing career, Larry Willis is seriously under-appreciated, both as a composer and as a pianist. As long ago as 1965 he was making records as a sideman with Jackie McLean (some of which remained unissued for more than a decade) and contributing absorbing and occasionally dazzling compositions to them in addition to his own playing. The seventies saw him briefly with Cannonball Adderley before he joined Blood, Sweat & Tears for eight years. Between then and now he made a couple of Fusion-based albums, then gradually moved back into an acoustic jazz orbit. His début as a leader in this milieu escaped him until the end of that decde.

Thankfully his recent career has been amply documented by SteepleChase, and from an ongoing array of trio and solo albums on that label I've chosen this 1989 session as one which encapsulates many of his best qualities. If the thought of yet another piano trio record is daunting, then try the extraordinary right-hand figure with which he begins his solo on the self-penned *T's Bag Blues* (dedicated to Monk) as an example of what is on offer here. Or listen to the verve and confidence in his solo on the oft-heard Miles tune, *Solar*. Finally, an interesting contrast is pointed up on Willis's version of Herbie Hancock's *One Finger Snap*, where Willis constantly darts between the Hancockian rhythmic and melodic approach and that of his own. In all this he gets fine support from the stalwart Bob Cranshaw and a very tasteful Kenny Washington. Fine stuff, beautifully recorded. **KS**

Cassandra Wilson 1955

Blue Light 'Til Dawn **Wilson** (v); with, amongst others: **Olu Dara** (c); **Don Byron** (cl); **Charlie Burnham** (vn, mandocello); **Brandon Ross**, **Gib Wharton**, **Chris Whitley** (g); **Kenny Davis** (b); **Lonnie Plaxico** (b); **Tony Cedras** (acn); **Lance Carter**, **Kevin Johnson** (d, perc); **Vinx**, **Bill McCellan**, **Jeff Haynes**, **Cyro Baptista** (perc). Blue Note Ⓔ CDP7 81357 2 (57 minutes). Recorded 1993.

⑦ ❽

Wilson emerged in the eighties as a member of the M-Base movement of New York musicians and she made an immediate impact. Her own compositions complemented her singing style, if they did not always do much to enhance it. There were times when melismatic excess and the desire to surprise led her into improvisational cul-de-sacs. She became too elaborate, a touch overdramatic and seemingly oblivious to the overall meaning of the lyrics. Maturity has seen her address these failings. The 1988 **Blue Skies** (JMT 834419 CD) and the 1991 **After The Beginning Again** (JMT 514001-2) documented the elimination of certain extreme characteristics, but this CD completes the process, matching the quality of her contemporary live performances. *You Don't Know What Love Is* and *Tupelo Honey* demonstrate a balance between lyric projection, rhythmic variety and melodic adjustment that is ideal. The rap influence remains a factor in *Black Crow* and *Children Of The Night*, but it has become an aid to her timing rather than modus operandum. Her daring stab at material by blues legend Robert Johnson is a success but the significant fact is that she applies the same moaning emotionalism to *Can't Stand The Rain* with no loss of credibility. Her jazz standing can never have been higher. **BMcR**

Gerald Wilson 1918

Portraits **Wilson** (arr, ldr); with the following collective personnel: **Al Porcino**, **Ray Triscari**, **Carmell Jones**, **Nathaniel Meeks**, **Freddie Hill**, **Julius Chaikin** (t); **Bob Edmondson**, **John Ewing**, **Don Switzer**, **Lester Robinson**, **Lew McCreary** (tb); **Bud Shank** (f); **Joe Maini**, **Jimmy Woods** (as); **Teddy Edwards**, **Harold Land** (ts); **Jack Nimitz** (bs); **Jack Wilson** (p); **Joe Pass** (g); **Leroy Vinnegar**, **Dave Dyson** (b); **Chuck Carter** (d); **Modesto Duran** (bongos). Pacific Jazz Ⓜ CDP7 93414 2 (38 minutes). Recorded 1963.

⑧ ❻

Gerald Wilson replaced Sy Oliver in the Jimmie Lunceford trumpet section and also contributed compositions and arrangements to the Lunceford library. In later years he wrote for Basie, Gillespie's big band, Duke Ellington, etc. and also retired temporarily from the music business. This is probably the best of the albums he recorded under his own name for Pacific Jazz. The seven tracks are dedications to various people as diverse as a Spanish bull fighter, the Armenian composer Khachaturian and the late Eric Dolphy. Wilson is a master of ensemble writing and achieving section perfection (something he probably learned in his days with Lunceford). A glance at the personnel reveals the presence of some outstanding Hollywood section men, including trumpeters Al Porcino and Ray Triscari. Solos are taken by Carmell Jones, Jack Wilson, Jimmy Woods, Harold Land and Teddy Edwards, but the most impressive performance is by Joe Pass's acoustic guitar on Wilson's brooding arrangement of *'Round Midnight*. The CD is the exact equivalent of the original LP, hence the meagre playing time. It would have been possible to present all three LPs Wilson did for Pacific Jazz as two CDs without any loss of original LP tracks. **AM**

Glenn Wilson

Bittersweet **Wilson** (bs, bcl, f); **Rory Stuart** (g). Sunnyside Ⓔ SSC 1057D (69 minutes). Recorded 1990.

⑧ ❽

Both ex-Cadence recording artists who have been part of the Cadence All-Stars, Glenn Wilson and Rory Stuart developed the repertoire for this album on a duo tour of the Midwest in 1986. Like their thoughtful, careful playing, their taste is impeccable, encompassing tunes by Oliver Nelson, Sam Jones, Duke Pearson, Ron Carter and Wayne Shorter, leavened with a trio of Stuart originals and a couple of reworked standards. The album's chief appeal lies in the way the pair negotiate their way through the problems inherent in the duo format, intuitively swapping leading and accompanying roles and occasionally attaining what Stuart himself refers to as "a sort of loose but energetic two-part counterpoint." Particularly skilful is the way Wilson comps on baritone, functioning (as he points out) "at various times as a pianist, bassist, drummer and horn section." Overdubbing occasionally allows the music to avail itself of a brass-chorale effect, but otherwise the attractive textural contrast between the two instruments, baritone saxophone and guitar—reminiscent of the Surman-McLaughlin masterpiece **Extrapolation**—makes this a consistently enjoyable, if unusual, album. **CP**

Jack Wilson

1936

In New York **Wilson** (p); **James Chirillo** (g); **Leon Maleson** (b); **Jimmy Cobb** (d). DIW Ⓕ DIW-615 (53 minutes) Recorded 1993.

⑥ ❾

Wilson has been moving in heavyweight circles since the early fifties, when he was a member of James Moody's group. Since then he has been a consistent supporter of other people's causes, only occasionally turning up at a recording session which he himself led. This is his latest foray as a leader, and it neatly encapsulates his style. Wilson has the tidiness and elegance of Teddy Wilson or George Shearing, and occasionally sounds a little like Shearing in his blocked-hands approach, but his heart is deeply in a post-bop piano style perhaps most poignantly perfected by Hank Jones. To that he also adds an occasional spice of sanctification, Horace Silver or Oscar Peterson style.

The set of tunes negotiated here are all standards, and the most relaxed approach imaginable is taken to gently swinging each number. That is not to say that the session is somnambulent: Wilson contantly catches the attention with his ear for harmonic detail and his willingness to spin a line further than usual, or land it in an uncommon place. But most of all he has great time, and could easily sustain a solo recital. For openers, try the perfectly-paced version of *Moon Mist*. **KS**

Nancy Wilson

1937

The Swingin's Mutual **Wilson** (v); on seven tracks with **George Shearing** (p); **Warren Chaisson** (vb); **Dick Garcia** (g); **Ralph Peña** (b); **Vernell Fournier** (d); **Armando Peraza** (perc). Capitol Ⓜ CDP 799190 2 (42 minutes). Recorded 1960/61.

⑥ ❽

Critic Harvey Pekar once wrote that Nancy Wilson "falls somewhere between Sarah Vaughan and Dinah Washington; not as blues-tinged as the latter nor as polished and harmonically sophisticated as the former." This is certainly an accurate description of her work on this CD; she has an affinity with jazz, possesses clear diction and knows how to interpret a good song but she is not really a jazz singer. Teaming her with the George Shearing Quintet was an obvious ploy in commercial terms as both were Capitol artistes at the time, but the quintet is perhaps too 'polite' for Miss Wilson's often hard-edged delivery. Another Capitol record of a similar vintage has her teamed with her mentor, Cannonball Adderley, and the general temperature is a ittle higher there. The CD contains five previously unissued titles, extra to the original LP, but only one of them, *My Gentleman Friend,* has a vocal. Two of the new tracks are tunes by Benny Golson, *I Remember Clifford* and *Whisper Not,* which the Shearing unit interprets with care and understanding. This was a particularly fine quintet as it contained the imaginative bass playing of the late Ralph Pena and the tasteful drumming of Chicago's Vernell Fournier. **AM**

Steve Wilson

1961

Step Lively **Wilson** (ss, as); **Cyrus Chestnut** (p); **Freddie Bryant** (g); **Dennis Irwin** (b); **Gregory Hutchinson** (d); **Daniel Sadownick** (perc) Criss Cross Ⓕ 1096 CD (62 minutes) Recorded 1993.

⑥ ❽

Wilson has been making his way in the jazz world since the mid-eighties and this new Criss Cross CD is his third as a leader for the label. Gerry Teekens must be congratulated for moving the altoist along in sympathetic surroundings and surrounded by genuine talent: his previous release, **Blues For Marcus**, had Steve Nelson along to help, while here we can enjoy the entirely simpatico piano of Cyrus Chestnut (listen to his comping on *For Stan* to demonstrate this quality) as well as the rawer edge of Freddie Bryant's guitar. Wilson's style sits nicely in the modern mainstream approach, and his tone is bright, full and bell-like. He has great rhythmic dexterity and a quick musical imagination. His soprano work is a little more derivative than his alto, but both horns sustain the listener's interest. This is good, honest music from the middle of the modern jazz road, well played and excellently recorded. If that attracts you, then purchase with confidence. **KS**

Teddy Wilson

1912-1986

The Complete Piano Solos, 1934-41 **Wilson** (p). Columbia Ⓜ 467690-2 (two discs: 133 minutes). Recorded 1934-41.

⑧ ❺

Wilson's importance as a piano stylist is often obscured by the role he played in the careers of people such as Benny Goodman (as a sideman) and Billie Holiday (as a session organizer and leader). Yet he led a variety of excellent bands from the mid-thirties on, both in the studios and in person, and was also prolific as a solo pianist, as this collection attests.

Wilson's style combines the relative freedom given to the right hand by Earl Hines in the years immediately preceding these sessions with the metronome-like precision of the stride left hand as practised by all the best New York jazz pianists, from James P. Johnson to Fats Waller. What Wilson brought to this synthesis was a very high order of technical accuracy, a neat and logical turn of improvisatory phrase, and (unlike Tatum) a very correct interpretation of each tune's harmonic path. He also (again unlike Tatum) generally avoided rubato, preferring to keep things moving along at a steady clip. Wilson was a musical conservative, and was sometimes severely restricted in the emotional range he brought to his performances. Yet he had a flawless technique, as these sides attest, and a sufficiently orchestral conception of solo piano work to vary his interpretations of each piece and keep a performance alive.

This set, rather indigestible at one sitting (Wilson never intended these solos to be played end-to-end), is very rewarding taken in small doses. **KS**

Teddy Wilson and His Orchestra 1939-41 **Teddy Wilson** (p); with various personnel, including: **Bill Coleman**, **Doc Cheatham**, **Harold Baker**, **Emmett Berry** (t); **Floyd Brady**, **Benny Morton** (tb); **Jimmy Hamilton** (cl); **Rudy Powell** (as, cl); **Ben Webster**, **George Irish** (ts); **George James** (bs); **Al Casey**, **Eddie Gibbs** (g); **Al Hall**, **Johnny Williams** (b); **J.C. Heard**, **Yank Porter** (d, v) **Jean Eldridge**, **Helen Ward**, **Lena Horne** (v). Classics Ⓜ 620 (70 minutes). Recorded 1939-41.

✔ ⑧ ❽

Starting with the short-lived big band led by Teddy Wilson in 1939-40, this excellent compilation of 23 numbers follows his recording career for almost two years. In doing so, it illustrates in microcosm all the musical settings in which he shone. After the big band pieces (including, incidentally, a fascinating alternative arrangement to the then-current Glenn Miller hit *In The Mood)* we come to the chamber music of swing, that delightful genre of which Teddy Wilson was the undoubted master. It involved three or four front-line instruments and rhythm section, often with a vocalist, playing simple head arrangements of standard tunes with short solos all round. The most famous of these are, of course, the sessions built around Billie Holiday, but here the featured vocalists are the young Lena Horne, Benny Goodman's vocalist Helen Ward and the now forgotten Jean Eldridge.

The rest of the disc is taken up with piano solos, both with and without rhythm section, demonstrating yet again what a faultless swing pianist Wilson was. It is astounding to realize that music of this quality was regarded as almost run-of-the-mill stuff at the time, because the general level was so high. **DG**

Cole Porter Classics **Wilson** (p). Black Lion Ⓜ BLCD 760166 (40 minutes). Recorded 1977.

⑧ ❻

Wilson's reputation as a nonpareil accompanist was based on his keyboard sensitivity and his extensive knowledge of songs. Yet in his later years he tended to rely more and more on the expected songs, tunes which had become associated with him since his days with Benny Goodman. Producer Alan Bates tried a different approach for his Black Lion sessions in London at the end of 1977; he gave Wilson lists of songs by Gershwin, Berlin and Cole Porter and asked him to pick enough tunes by each for three albums. The Porter set is so good that one can only regret the non-appearance of the Berlin and Gershwin albums (which were certainly recorded). Cole Porter was a writer of real class, ideally suited as a composer for Wilson's attentions. There are very superior versions here of songs such as *I Love You, Why Shouldn't I?* and *Easy To Love*, each one of which has a freshness which interminable versions of *Airmail Special* and *Stompin' At The Savoy* lack. There is clarity both of touch and conception in Wilson's work which marks him as one of the great jazz pianists of all time and his original, *Too Darn Blue* (a tribute to Porter), sits well with the other ten songs.. **AM**

Kai Winding

1922-1983

Giant 'Bones 80 **Winding**, **Curtis Fuller** (tb); **Horace Parlan** (p); **Mads Vinding** (b); **Ed Thigpen** (d). Sonet Ⓕ SNTCD-834 (39 minutes). Recorded 1979.

⑥ ❻

Winding came to prominence with the Stan Kenton orchestra during the forties, then during the late forties and early fifties he was very active on the New York jazz club scene in a number of small groups. In 1954 he almost accidentally teamed up with Jay Jay Johnson on a two-trombone record date for the Savoy label and Jay and Kai became an attractive and successful group. When the unit broke up after a few years, Winding added more trombones to form a 'choir' of four and even more on record). After some years as MD of the 'Playboy' club circuit he moved to Spain, using it as a base for his new partnership with Curtis Fuller. This is probably the best example of them working together (with a two-thirds American rhythm section) and the two achieve a smooth, seamless blend in the ensembles before taking often elegant, trouble-free solos. The routines are, of course, strongly redolent of Jay and Kai, and the only criticism is that the music lacks almost any element of surprise.

'Professionalism' is an over-used term, often bandied about meaninglessly, but what Fuller and Winding do here is the acme of professionalism. Throughout his playing career Winding was something of a paradox, for he played bebop lines with a swing-style (at times almost Dixieland) sound. The playing time is meagre because this is a straightforward conversion of LP to CD. **AM**

Louis Winsberg

Appassionata **Winsberg** (g, bouzouki); **Jean Rene Dalerci** (b); **Tony Rabeson** (d). Kid Records Ⓕ KR 002-2 (44 minutes). Recorded 1989.

⑦ ❻

Winsberg has played in the French fusion group Nexus and has over the years branched out to make some interesting albums on his own. He is a guitarist with bags of technique and imagination, but more importantly, he is blessed with 'feel'. He is a natural, able to caress, bludgeon, stroke and force his guitar into divulging the essential information about each selection he plays. In this he is perhaps closer to Bireli Lagrene than to John McLaughlin, but he has elements of both players within him. For one thing, he is as completely at home on acoustic as on electric guitars, and again he is utterly at ease both on a blues and a non-blues original. His electric tone has the burnt-ochre timbre of the latter-day John Scofield, but his style owes little to the American. The backing bass and drums are discreet and sympathetic, but this is very much Winsberg's album. It is worth a close listen. **KS**

Norma Winstone

1941

Somewhere Called Home **Winstone** (v); **Tony Coe** (cl, ts); **John Taylor** (p). ECM Ⓕ 1337 (831 107-2) (49 minutes). Recorded 1986.

⑧ ❾

Inspired by Miles Davis and John Coltrane—"I wanted to incorporate that instrumental freedom in a vocal way"—Norma Winstone first made her mark in 1968, singing wordless vocals in the Michael Garrick groups. She later worked with many leading UK musicians (notably Joe Harriott and Mike Westbrook) and in 1972 released her own **Edge Of Time** LP. In the seventies she co-founded the trio Azimuth (husband John Taylor on piano, Kenny Wheeler on trumpet), where she honed her art of wordless improvisation, her 'choirboy's voice' blending with the other instruments to create beautiful, ethereal textures.

Somewhere Called Home, only her second recording as leader, reminds us that she is also a magnificent interpreter of lyrics. Her intimate vocal style owes little to declamatory musics like blues but relies on subtle phrasing and a faultless sense of time. The songs here are taken at a gentle pace, their lyrics tending to a rueful romanticism underscored by Tony Coe's reeds. Winstone has the gift of turning unlikely material in great art here she turns *Hi Lili, Hi Lo* into a meditation on love, then strips the jauntiness from *Tea For Two*, making it a forlorn reverie. Such gripping transformations show why she is Europe's premier jazz vocalist. **GL**

Paul Winter

1939

Anthems **Winter** (as); **Eugene Friesen**, **David Darling** (vc); **Rhonda Larson** (f); **Nancy Rumbel** (eh); **John Clark** (frh); **Oscar Castro-Neves**, **Jim Scott**, **Dan Carillo**, **Kenny Mazur** (g); **Paul Halley**, **Denny Zeitlin** (p, syn); **Russ Landau** (b); **Paul Wertico**, **Ted Moore**, **Glen Valesz**, **Paul Rossi**, **Lui Rocher**, **Marcio Ferreira**, **Guilherme Franco**, **Kimati Dinizulu**, **Neil Clark** (perc); **The Pokrovsky Singers**, **Susan Osborn** (v); various sounds of nature. Living Music Ⓕ LD0023 (72 minutes). Recorded 1980-91.

⑧ ❾

Saxophonist Paul Winter was catapulted to international prominence in the early sixties when his bop-based sextet won the Intercollegiate Jazz Festival and a recording contract with Columbia Records. In 1962, a US State Department tour to South America led to Winter's increasing interest in the world's folk musics. Later, the sounds of whales led to a growing concern with the environment and with the safe passage of 'Spaceship Earth', to cite Buckminster's metaphor, into the future.

With the establishment of his Living Music label in 1980, Winter took control of his own destiny, unfettered by the industry's big labels, who by then didn't know what to make of his work. Subsequently, his music—which has been variously called "acoustic fusion", "classical folk" and "ecological jazz"—has attracted a growing audience, and one which includes environmental groups such as Greenpeace.

In this provocative sampler from the Paul Winter Consort, we are treated to what Winter now calls "earth music", embracing the use of unorthodox instruments, the "speech" of wolves and whales, and natural acoustic spaces like the Grand Canyon. While not jazz in the traditional four-to-the-bar sense, Winter's centreing of improvisation in his celebrations of the planet's cultures and creatures makes his music a friendly witness to jazz's open and pliant nature. **CB**

Jimmy Witherspoon 1923

Rockin' With Spoon **Witherspoon** (v); **Roy Eldridge** (t); **Urbie Green** (tb); **Woody Herman** (cl); **Ben Webster**, **Coleman Hawkins** (ts); **Gerry Mulligan** (bs); **Earl Hines**, **Jimmy Rowles** (p); **Vernon Alley**, **Leroy Vinnegar** (b); **Mel Lewis** (d). Charly Ⓑ CD BM 25 (62 minutes). Recorded 1959.

✔ ⑧ ❽

Witherspoon is conventionally grouped with Joe Turner and Walter Brown under the description of 'blues shouters'. While some of his early work with Jay McShann (collected on Black Lion BLCD 760173) does find him exuberantly riding big-band blues riffs, he is more telling at medium and slow tempos, where he can display his handsome voice and superb sense of pace and dynamics. This collection catches him on two days in late 1959. A set at the Renaissance Club in Los Angeles boasts the odd but satisfying combination of Webster's furry, loquacious tenor and Mulligan's dry, pithy baritone on a programme of blues standards like *How Long* and *Outskirts Of Town*. The remaining tracks are from the Monterey Jazz Festival, where the all-star lineup is self-effacingly discreet, allowing 'Spoon to give a performance he has never surpassed. It is all blues, pleading, caressing, sensuous but unsentimental, and on *Ain't Nobody's Business* Webster joins in with a solo of such feeling that the world seems to stand still until he has completed it.

The Monterey and Renaissance sessions have always been highly thought of as LPs; gathered on a single inexpensive CD they make a programme of astonishing value. **TR**

Rickey Woodard 1956

Yazoo **Woodard** (as, ts); **Ray Brown** (t); **Cedar Walton** (p); **Jeff Littleton** (b); **Ralph Penland** (d). Concord Ⓕ CCD 4629 (61 minutes). Recorded 1994.

⑧ ❽

It is a pleasure to discover the music of Rickey Woodard, for he is a comparatively new saxophonist who is not trying to sound like John Coltrane. His playing is devoid of the aggressive stance adopted by many younger players who seem to have gone out of their way to cultivate unpleasant tones. Woodard has a beautifully clean sound (he plays alto on three tracks, tenor on the remaining seven) and actually seems to be enjoying himself. Although this approach may be anachronistic today, when it is allied to a superb rhythm section piloted by Cedar Walton and with a fluent trumpeter (Ray Brown is not, of course, the bass player of that name), what emerges is an outstanding example of mainstream jazz. Listening to Woodard it is easy to understand his stated preference for the work of departed giants Ben Webster, Gene Ammons and Coleman Hawkins. The tunes selected by Rickey include Dexter Gordon's *Fried Bananas*, Dameron's *Tadd's Delight* and Cedar Walton's memorable *Holy Land*. *Portrait Of Jennie* and *September In The Rain* are tenor-plus-rhythm performances. **AM**

Phil Woods 1931

Flash **Woods** (as, cl); **Tom Harrell** (t, flh); **Hal Crook** (tb); **Hal Galper** (p); **Steve Gilmore** (b); **Bill Goodwin** (d). Concord Ⓕ CCD 4408 (63 minutes). Recorded 1989.

⑧ ❾

Initially better known for his work in the big bands of Dizzy Gillespie, Buddy Rich and Quincy Jones, Woods established his combo skills in the quintet Phil And Quill with Gene Quill. He lived for some time in Europe but one of his finest groups is the American one heard on this CD. It came into being in its present form when Harrell joined in 1983, and this was the trumpeter's final date with the group. Between those dates, the Woods/Harrell team played some very impressive music. Woods, for all his previous triumphs, relished the group interaction and his enthusiasm is projected into all of his solos here. He has always tended to allow his phrases to be somewhat disconnected from the pulse and, particularly at the blistering pace of *Flash,* he relies for success on the linear qualities of his note choices rather than on the ideas they carry. Very different in concept is Harrell, a lucid musical thinker who brings grace to his solos without emasculating them. The contrast works well and, although the presence of a trombonist makes the classic Woods ensemble more Messengers-like, this remains one of the best of a fine series of albums made by an otherwise consistently unchanged personnel. **BMcR**

World Saxophone Quartet

Revue **Hamiet Bluiett** (cl, bs); **Julius Hemphill** (f, ss, as); **Oliver Lake** (f, ss, as, ts); **David Murray** (bcl, ts). Black Saint Ⓕ 120056-2 (45 minutes). Recorded 1980.

⑧ ❽

The WSQ came together for a concert in New Orleans in 1976 and later developed into one of the benchmark groups of the eighties. Their showmanship, instrumental bravura and comprehensive grasp of the jazz tradition fitted in well with the decade's ethos of smartly-dressed conservatism. But—especially on their earlier albums—there was also a thrilling sense of discovery, a willingness to push back limits. Whether drawing on Ellington big band charts or the new solo language developed by the AACM, the WSQ created a group feeling that transcended the sum of its parts (even though all four members continued to pursue parallel careers as leaders).

Revue was their fourth record and remains one of the best: the first time perhaps that the different elements the WSQ were juggling (especially the core dialogue between solo and ensemble) were held in balance. It is also the album that affirmed Hemphill as the group's most original composer. His four tunes spark a variety of ensemble interplays, from the disparate flute and clarinet ribbons that wind through *Affairs of the Heart* to the stabbing unison lines of *Slide.* Other tracks turn the spotlight more on individual players. Bluiett's *I Heard That* sets a melismatic alto solo (by Hemphill) amidst a pack of coursing r&b riffs, while both Lake's *Hymn For The Old Year* and Murray's *Ming* begin with a cappella solos that are later cradled in a web of harmonies. The playing is fierce, tender, impeccable. **GL**

Reggie Workman

1937

Altered Spaces **Workman** (b); **Don Byron** (cl); **Jason Hwang** (vn); **Marilyn Crispell** (p); **Gerry Hemingway** (d); **Jeanne Lee** (v). Leo Ⓕ CD LR 183 (78 minutes). Recorded 1992.

⑦ ❼

Workman came to prominence in the sixties working with John Coltrane, the Jazz Messengers and Thelonious Monk. In the seventies he taught at several US colleges but continued to work with the likes of Max Roach, Art Farmer and Archie Shepp. In the next decade he recorded with David Murray and his involvement in the freer end of the jazz spectrum increased. This CD is an uncompromising example; all the music is his and he has encouraged a committed team to breathe their own life into it. Superficially, titles such as *Apart* present solos, but none of the individual statements are solos in the traditional sense; each is an organic part of the bassist's 'total music' concept. One musician progresses the work up to his/her 'hand-over' point and, in doing so, sets the mood for the successor. Lee's vocal cadenza on *Altered Spaces*, Crispell's courageous exposition on *Apart*, the arco and pizzicato of Hwang's *Ballad For The Silf* contribution and Byron's emotionally charged clarinet on *Ten* are all high points. It may be a long way from Workman's supple hard bop bass world and from the way he played with Coltrane, but this is where he stood in 1992, a composer and bass player in one and the same breath. **BMcR**

Yosuke Yamashita

1942

Crescendo: Live At Sweet Basil **Yamashita** (p); **Cecil McBee** (b); **Pheeroan akLaff** (d). Kitty H32U 20011 (53 minutes). Recorded 1988.

⑧ ❽

When he was playing an extraordinarily intense brand of 'free' jazz in the seventies, Yosuke Yamashita was often compared to Cecil Taylor due to his strength, stamina and concentration. As he has evolved into interpreting standards and more traditionally structured material, the results are not so easily stereotyped. There is a reminiscence of Don Pullen in the percussive chording and slashing leaps of register, often followed by the florid melodic invention of a Tete Montoliu or Martial Solal. So *Take The 'A' Train* becomes a roller-coaster of arpeggios and *Autumn Leaves* is reharmonized and recontextualized into *Autumn Changes.* Nor does this trio fall into the established piano trio guidelines. McBee is an anchor, especially when Yamashita threatens to explode out of the confines of bar lines. AkLaff is the wild card; his individual approach, less timekeeper than rhythmic instigator, opens up the arrangements ever more. *First Bridge* shows how together they stretch song form to the breaking point, creating enormous tension between freer phrasing impulses and the artificial restrictions that song form imposes. When Yamashita's exhilarating Enja recordings with Akira Sakata are issued on CD they are highly recommended; in the meantime **Crescendo** should prove exciting and ear-opening for mainstream and more adventurous listeners alike. **AL**

Jimmy Yancey

1898-51

Barrelhouse Boogie **Yancey** (p, v); **Albert Ammons**, **Pete Johnson**, **Meade Lux Lewis** (p). RCA Bluebird Ⓜ ND88334 (58 minutes). Recorded 1939-40.

⑦ ❽

Yancey's ten performances here are probably the best-recorded, and certainly among the best, of all his work. Despite the album's title, approaching Yancey as a boogie-woogie pianist is to come at him from the wrong direction (it is suggestive that the word 'Boogie' almost never occurs in his tunes' titles). Although older than Albert Ammons, Pete Johnson and Meade Lux Lewis he was active about the same time and admired by the same sort of people, but the character of his music was very different. Not for him their driving abandon, relentlessly hammering left hands and capering tempos; Yancey's style was all sparseness, an affair of considered inflections and suble timing, Monk rather than Hines. Yet it is not technically inferior playing; the interplay of left and right-hand lines is the more gripping for being less obvious, less (one might almost say) mechanical.

Given all that, Yancey's music inevitably seems more introspective and melancholic than, say, Pete Johnson's. There is no denying these properties in the sober and moving vocal numbers *Crying In My Sleep* and *Death Letter Blues*, but *Yancey Stomp* and *Tell 'Em About Me*, on the other hand, jauntily evoke Chicago ambiences of street and bar. The rest of the CD contains nine duets by Johnson and Ammons and two items by Lewis: a very fine compilation. **TR**

Yellowjackets

Collection **Bob Mintzer** (ss, as, ts, bcl); **Russell Ferrante** (kbds); **Jimmy Haslip** (b); **William Kennedy** (d) with **Steve Croes**, **Judd Miller** (syn); **Paulinho Da Costa**, **Alex Acuna**, **Nana Vasconcelos** (perc); **Bill Gable**, **Michael Franks**, **Brenda Russell**, **Marylin Scott** (v). GRP Ⓕ 98092 (63 minutes). Recorded 1988-92.

⑥ ❿

Yellowjackets albums tend to meander in and out of the jazz framework, so this sampler is the ideal way for jazz-minded interested bodies to get a whiff of what they're on about, because the vast majority of this disc exhibits healthy jazz tendencies. One of the most pleasing aspects of their albums is the exact synthesis of the four players into the overall musical balance and landscape. No one instrument dominates, although some play more than others. No-one sticks out like a sore thumb, and it is an unusual and pleasant experience to hear in Mintzer a saxophonist who not only blends seamlessly with his cohorts, but avoids the normal warmed-over stylistic trappings of a post-Tom Scott/ post-David Sanborn clone. He can both carry a melody and improvise dexterously. He also has a tone which blends with the electrics and electronics alongside him.

The rhythm section is uniformly hot and precise, with Jimmy Haslip's fluid bass patterns a particular plus. The compositions on this compilation avoid pomp and posture and are sufficiently open for the players to really come to grips with the underlying structures. There is plenty of soloing. But one of the most surprising and satisfying aspects of this disc is the production and the instrumental balance, or 'mix'. The instruments have been superbly recorded across a number of dates and years, each sounding true and full. Everything can be heard but nothing pushes too far to the fore. A special cheer, then, for the engineer on all these sessions, Mick Guzauski. **KS**

Nora York

To Dream The World **York** (v); **Rich Perry** (ts); **Mark Feldman** (vn); **Rob Schwimmer** (org); **Richie Bierach** (p); **Jack Wilkins** (g); **Michael Formanek** (b); **Terry Clarke** (d). TCOB Ⓕ 94602 (68 minutes). Recorded 1992.

European Nora York has been singing on the New York scene for a while (and, as this album demonstrates, has got to know some interesting accompanying musicians); this first album represents her both as a singer and as an songwriter/arranger. Like may young musicians today, she exhibits an eclectic taste, with her own songs covering stylistic ground which includes old-fashioned mainstream swing and what for lack of a better phrase could be called sub-New Age. Her cover versions include pieces by Cole Porter, The Beatles and Jimi Hendrix.

I get the feeling that her musicality often exceeds her small voice's natural limits. Her range is not great; neither is it greatly expressive. But the musical settings often are evocative and the playing quite engaging. Lennon/McCartney's *If I Fell* is a perfect example of this dichotomy. Always one of their better early ballads, this Beatles song is given a very slow tempo and a steamy, emotive setting which, with the right voice, would provide revelatory listening. But York has yet to learn how to work her delivery to give the listener the full emotional load. Still, an interesting effort. **KS**

Hajime Yoshizawa

1963

Hajime **Yoshizawa** (p); **Bob Mintzer** (ts); **John Abercrombie** (g); **Marc Johnson** (b); **Peter Erskine** (d). Ah Um 008 Ⓕ (65 minutes). Recorded 1990.

⑥ ❻

This is a promising and absorbing début album by a Japanese pianist who has worked with a variety of musicians in jazz and theatre. Above all, it is introspective, even the bravura moments at the keyboard being somehow understated. In *Beyond Twilight*, for instance, the piano is strangely detached, lacking the immediacy of his contemporaries Michel Petrucciani and Benny Green. This works to Hajime's advantage, especially on ballads like *Stardust*, where he seems to dissect the music from inside in a compelling way. It also makes him a more than usually sensitive accompanist, and he plays a willing and perfect second fiddle to Abercrombie on *Bless Me With Your Breath*, the extended opener that was written in tribute to Yoshizawa's father.

Tropic of Cancer is a platform for Mintzer and Erskine, while Marc Johnson opens *Voyage* with a deeply felt solo. Overall, an album of reflection and poetic self-absorption, yet with generous space allotted to his fellow musicians. **AS**

John Young

1922

Serenata **Young** (p); **Victor Sproles** (b); **Phil Thomas** (d). Delmark Ⓕ DD-403 (42 minutes). Recorded 1959.

⑧ ❽

When it comes to rhythm—where musicians place the beat to achieve maximum swing—Chicago has more in common with laid-back Kansas City than hyperactive New York. That mid-continent sense of relaxation is a hallmark of Chicago's John Young, a pianist of uncommon charm. On *I Don't Wanna Be Kissed*, he combines an infectious fingerpop groove with a light touch at the keyboard. In the mid-sixties, Young cited Memphis pianist Phineas Newborn as a favourite. You can hear Newborn's influence in the dancing locked-octaves John plays with his right hand, exploring the piano's brighter sonorities (Young was born in Little Rock, not far from Memphis). There is a subtle Latin influence here too, something many Chicagoans are sensitive to; Windy City bluesmen love to mambo.

Young's rhythm section makes a crucial contribution. Drummer Thomas often plays strong backbeats surrounded by generous amounts of space, letting the music breathe. He eases the trio into hypnotic grooves not unlike what Sun Ra's Chicago band of that time might play (Sproles, who has enviably springy time, had recorded with Ra). Thomas's pet tactics do threaten to wear themselves out, but 41 minutes worth is about right. **KW**

Larry Young

1940-1978

The Art of Larry Young **Young** (org); **Grant Green** (g); **Sam Rivers**, **Joe Henderson**, **Herbert Morgan** (ts); **James Spaulding** (as); **Woody Shaw**, **Eddie Gale**, **Lee Morgan** (t); **Elvin Jones**, **Wilson Moorman III**, **Jerry Thomas**, **Eddie Gladen** (d). Blue Note Ⓜ 7 99177 2 7 (55 minutes). Recorded 1964-69.

⑧ ❽

Organist Larry Young was an original. Although incorporating the Hammond B-3's gospel, rock and soul traditions, this native of Newark, New Jersey, took the instrument into new territory by adapting harmonic and rhythmic concepts associated with John Coltrane. Although primarily known for his contributions to the fusion of Tony Williams's Lifetime and Miles Davis's **Bitches Brew** bands, Young's best work for Blue Note most effectively encapsulates the organist's cutting-edge jazz approach.

The anthology's intimate duo and trio tracks are especially compelling. Indeed, the combination of Young, guitarist Grant Green and drummer Elvis Jones (momentarily on leave from Coltrane) is a dream team whose interplay on the organist's *Talkin' about J.C.* pushes neo-bop assumptions to the mainstream's margins. Young's bluesy jazz waltz, the poignant *Tyrone* with Sam Rivers's probing tenor, juxtaposes modal lines against a gospel groove simmering with a barely muted volatility that was the quintessence of Blue Note 'hip'. Also definitive is the Young-Jones analysis of the provocative yet happily inscrutable *Monk's Dream*.

The hydro-plane ride across *Seven Steps to Heaven* most clearly reflects the influence of Coltrane's mid-sixties free-jazz experiments. Here, waters are set roiling by the combined drums of Wilson Moorman III and Jerry Thomas, Eddie Gale's outré trumpet and the saxes of James Spaulding and Herbert Morgan. **CB**

Lester Young

1909-1959

A Lester Young Story **Lester Young** (ts, cl) with various bands including **Jones-Smith Incorporated**, **Count Basie Orchestra**, **Kansas City Six** and **Seven**, **Teddy Wilson**, **Billie Holiday**. Jazz Archives Ⓑ 157342 (67 minutes). Recorded 1936-40.

✔ ⑩ ❹

As a single-volume anthology of Lester Young's best period this would be hard to beat. Opening with the twin masterpieces that marked his recording début in 1936 (*Shoe Shine Boy* and *Lady Be Good*), the selection includes 11 numbers by the Count Basie Band, featuring celebrated Lester Young solos (*Every Tub*, *Taxi War Dance*, *Tickle Toe*, etc.), a few pieces from the Billie Holiday sessions (*Me, Myself and I*, *If Dreams Come True*, etc.), two by the Kansas City Six (*Way Down Yonder* and *Countless Blues*) and two by the K.C. Seven (*Dickie's Dream* and *Lester Leaps In*). All these contain the most superb playing, by both Lester and his contemporaries, such as Buck Clayton, Dickie Wells, Herschel Evans and Benny Morton—not to mention Billie Holiday.

For this reason I place this CD in the 'essential' category, but it is as well to realize that most of these 22 pieces also appear on 'essential' CDs by Basie and Billie. The sound quality is also slightly odd at times, although nothing like as odd as some of the earlier vinyl editions. A few pieces seem to have been cleaned up rather zealously, with added 'presence', while others retain a generous measure of 78rpm surface noise. Nevertheless if you want an uninterrupted hour of the choicest Lester, this is the edition for you. **DG**

Lester–Amadeus! **Young** (ts, cl); with, on two tracks: **Carl 'Tatti' Smith** (t); **Count Basie** (p); **Walter Page** (b); **Jo Jones** (d); on ten tracks with the **Count Basie Orchestra** with the following collective personnel: **Buck Clayton**, **Ed Lewis**, **Bobby Moore**, **Harry Edison** (t); **George Hunt**, **Dan Minor**, **Dickie Wells**, **Benny Morton** (tb); **Earl Warren** (as, bs); **Hershel Evans** (ts); **Jack**

Washington (bs); **Count Basie** (p); **Freddie Green** (g); **Walter Page** (b); **Jo Jones** (d); **Jimmy Rushing** (v); on eight tracks with the following collective personnel: **Buck Clayton** (t); **Count Basie** (p); **Freddie Green, Eddie Durham** (g); **Walter Page** (b); **Jo Jones** (d); **Helen Humes** (v). Phontastic Ⓜ CD 7639 (65 minutes). Recorded 1936-38.

✓ ⑩ ❻

Some of the finest Lester Young solos will be found on this attractive CD of Swedish origin. Opening with the classic *Lady Be Good* and *Shoe Shine Boy,* from the first record date on which Young was heard solo, the mood is set for music of quite remarkable quality. Nine titles featuring Young come from a June 1937 radio braodcast from Harlem's Savoy Ballroom with the Basie band in exceptional form. The drive from the rhythm section can almost be felt as shock waves from the speakers, and through it all sails the clear-toned beauty of Lester. A further Basie title, *John's Idea,* dates from 1938 and the Famous Door; this time Young shares the solo choruses with Harry Edison. In between are eight tracks from two small group dates, the first in a studio (but later given added applause to simulate a 'Spirituals To Swing' concert held in Carnegie Hall) and the final two, never previously released until the appearance of this CD, from the actual Carnegie Hall concert of December, 1938. The magic, to say nothing of the rarity value, of these tracks brushes aside any quibbles about recording quality (it must be pointed out there is some distortion from Durham's electric guitar on the Carnegie Hall tracks), and Gert Palmcrantz deserves credit for his work on transferring the music from, in some cases, badly worn acetates. **AM**

The Complete Lester Young **Young** (ts); **Buck Clayton** (t); **Dicky Wells** (tb); **Johnny Guarneri, Count Basie** (p); **Freddie Green** (g); **Slam Stewart, Rodney Richardson** (b); **Sid Catlett, Jo Jones** (d). Mercury Ⓜ 830 920-2 (55 minutes). Recorded 1943-44.

✓ ⑨ ❽

These landmark sessions, originally produced by Harry Lim for the Keynote label, conclusively demonstrate why Young became one of jazzdom's most influential stylists. First was his then-unique sound which, in comparison to his stylistic opposite Coleman Hawkins was lighter in weight, at times almost transparent; he also used far less vibrato than Hawkins. Second was his gift for creating long lyrical lines whose logic and natural swingingness were the envy of his peers. In 1944, catapulted by intermittent tenures with Count Basie and by his own recordings, Young took top honours in the tenor category of Down Beat's Readers Poll, the first of many such honours.

The initial 1943 session in this superb reissue puts Lester together with a exceptionally compatible rhythm section, Johnny Guarneri, Slam Stewart and Big Sid Catlett. It's a simpatico-plus date as Lester employs relaxed yet inspired poignancy on standards such as *Just You, Just Me* and *Sometimes I'm Happy*. The 1944 tracks find Young at a bright, happy get-together with the cream of the Basie band heating up such riff-based lines as *Lester Leaps Again* and *Destination K.C.* Working under the title of the Kansas City Seven, with Basie appearing under the pseudonym of Prince Charming, it's a loose, swinging date with a lithe Lester only months away from his traumatic incarceration in the US Army. Here, though, all is sunshine and smiles. **CB**

Blue Lester/The Immortal Lester Young **Young** (ts) with a collective personnel of: **Billy Butterfield, Jesse Drakes** (t); **Jerry Elliott** (tb); **Hank D'Amico** (cl); **Johnny Guarnieri, Count Basie, Junior Mance** (p); **Dexter Hall, Freddie Green** (g); **Billy Taylor, Rodney Richardson, Leroy Jackson** (b); **Cozy Cole, Shadow Wilson, Roy Haynes** (d); on three tracks only: **Earl Warren and his Orchestra**, including **Harry Edison** (t); **Dickie Wells** (tb); **Clyde Hart** (p). Denon/Savoy Ⓜ SV-0112 (45 minutes). Recorded 1944-49.

⑥ ❻

Before these 1944 recordings, Young's post-Basie style had undergone a sea-change, possibly reflecting his initial lack of success as a free-lance. His tone became darker and the phrasing, especially at slower tempos not favoured by Basie, began to hint at the tragic depths beneath the casual exterior.

The four tracks each led by Guarnieri and with a moonlighting Count on piano reveal the incipient transformation, particularly on the ballads *Ghost Of A Chance* and *These Foolish Things* (not to be confused with the superior 1945 version). But the distinction is subtle, like Lester's entire approach, and on the slow-medium *Blue Lester* and *Salute To Fats* the graceful lines disguise the undertow. Four items by his 1949 bop-oriented sextet with Mance and Haynes seem more laboured, presaging his fifties output.

Although all described as 'Take 1', these are not necessarily the first recorded or first issued versions. Unusually for Denon's Savoy reissues, three tracks are appended from a mid-seventies LP with Warren fronting the full Basie band (no personnel given) in material not otherwise recorded for commercial release. Though not as notable as the currently unavailable Commodore or the Keynote sides of the period, the tracks named should be heard. **BP**

Lester Young Trio **Young** (ts); **Nat Cole** (p); **Buddy Rich** (d); on four tracks, the following personnel only: **Dexter Gordon** (ts). **Harry Edison** (t); **Nat Cole** (p); probably **Red Callender** or **Johnny Miller** (b); **Clifford 'Juicy' Owens** (d). Verve Ⓜ 521 650-2 (61 minutes). Recorded 1943-46.

✓ ⑧ ❽

The records Young made as a member of the Basie orchestra had more sway on saxophone players than any body of music since the profound Coleman Hawkins influence which had guided tenor players after 1929. Young's method was the opposite of Hawk's. Whereas Hawk bustled and played with a rich romanticism, Young managed, while playing with fleet dexterity, to sound poised and dry. Even though he was capable of playing as fast as any other saxophonist, his mind moved so quickly that his solos always sounded considered and phrased like the building of Rome. His lightness of touch began to evaporate at the beginning of the forties and his work here is from the second phase of his career. His punch was not quite so feathery and world-weariness had already begun to replace the gaiety of his earlier solos.

Despite a step off the pinnacle of his earlier greatness, most of his work from 1944 to 1947, including the magnificent tracks here, was classic in every respect. The work of the trio with Cole and Rich is exquisite and in particular Young's exploration of ballads offered new signposts to players brought up under the Hawkins spell. The CD is worth acquiring for the delicious piano of Nat Cole alone, to say nothing of the lesson to be learned from Rich's restrained drumming. Every track is good and the stomping *I Want To Be Happy* shows Young to be every bit as effective on an up-tempo as on a ballad.

The addition of four tracks by Young's disciple Gordon is an apparent irrelevance in the face of Young's magnificence. But, even given a particularly on-form Gordon, Nat Cole's piano playing is so good that he steals the limelight. **SV**

The President Plays with The Oscar Peterson Trio **Young** (ts, v); **Oscar Peterson** (p); **Barney Kessel** (g); **Ray Brown** (b); **J.C. Heard** (d). Verve Ⓜ 831 670-2 (63 minutes). Recorded 1952.

✔ ⑩ ❽

Young has by now been the subject of so much mythologizing that sometimes the actual music he created gets buried in the rush to articulate a response to the image rather than the substance. His career has been analyzed from every conceivable angle and virtually every judgement has been turned on its head. Perhaps there is no overall career trajectory to follow, and we should just take every date as it comes.

That said, this 1952 session finds Mr Young in high spirits and playing with unusual clarity and firmness for the period. That he is fully engaged is evident from the first number, *Ad Lib Blues*, where he is not merely joining up his own personal clichés into a string until the solo ends, but fashioning a complete musical statement. On *Tea For Two* his sly humour surfaces in the way he reduces the already bare theme to complete nakedness, then bursts in with a powerful solo at what can confidently be called a fast tempo. On the previously-unissued *These Foolish Things* he avoids comparisons with his mid-forties masterpiece for Aladdin and fashions a hauntingly simple statement where he stays close to the melody most of the way. On *I Can't Get Started* he is even better, toying with the combination of nonchalance and pain inherent in the song's lyrics. By the time the CD gets to *Stardust* the listener could be forgiven for thinking they have made it to heaven, because what Young does here is heavenly. In all this, the Peterson group do everything absolutely right.

The CD reissue contains four previously unreleased tracks, including a Young vocal on two takes of *Two to Tango*. Contrary to the rather hysterical assertions in the liner notes, the latter are a good jape, but nothing more. Pearl Bailey certainly didn't have to worry about the competition. **KS**

Pres and Teddy **Young** (ts); **Teddy Wilson** (p); **Gene Ramey** (b); **Jo Jones** (d). Verve Ⓜ 831 270-2 (43 minutes). Recorded 1956.

⑨ ❽

1956 was arguably the last year that Lester Young made consistently good records. There were still outstanding moments to come, but little to match the quality of his performances on the live **In Washington** albums or the two studio sessions he recorded on consecutive days in January, **Jazz Giants** and **Pres and Teddy**. The former LP reunited him with several old friends—Roy Eldridge, Vic Dickenson and Freddie Green as well as Wilson, Ramey and Jones—and producer Norman Granz was so delighted by Young's playing he decided to record him again the following day in a quartet setting. It was a more testing format but one which Lester Young liked, and with Wilson in vibrant form and Jones showing his customary sensitivity, the results are a joy.

There is no doubt that Young's health deteriorated in the fifties, but the changes in his playing are as much due to his stated desire to 'play modern'. There is a harsher edge to his tone here, the phrasing can seem brusque, but the ideas are still fluent, the timing good. Listen to his attacking flair on *All Of Me*, the delicacy with which he caresses the tune on *Prisoner Of Love*, the surprise twists of his solo on *Taking A Chance On Love*. These are the hallmarks of a man who is not only in control of his art but still seeking to develop it. **GL**

Aziza Mustafa Zadeh

1970

Always **Zadeh** (p, v); **John Patitucci** (b); **Dave Weckl** (d). Columbia Ⓕ 473885-2 (64 minutes). Recorded 1992.

⑥ ❽

Before anyone gets the wrong idea, this is not a conventional piano-and-vocals record. Zadeh is a young Azerbaijani who comes from a family of jazz musicians and who packs a significant level of intensity into her piano playing. She also tends to perform original material. Her singing, mostly a vocalese of considerable dexterity, most clearly signals the folk roots of her own country, with its long, swooping lines and use of Middle-Eastern scales. But the singing is not the centrepiece here: the piano playing is. Zadeh has a formidable technique. She hits the keyboard very hard indeed, and she is not afraid of taking the listener on extended musical flights. Her influences occasionally float very close to the surface, be they classical, folk or jazz, and in this there is the hint of a parallel with Dave Brubeck, who also wrested an original rhythmic and harmonic approach from such a combination, although the specific elements may have differed considerably.

This is her second album (the first was a solo effort, the third a rather curious collaboration with Al Di Meola, Stanley Clarke and Bill Evans, among others) and it is currently the most fully-realised expression of her talents. She could do with finding more subtlety and contrast in her attack (her rhythmic patterns are often complex but oddly static through excessive repetition) and perhaps a more varied harmonic development (there's a few too many Tyneresque vamps for my liking here), but there is no doubting her talent. She has already made a significant impact in Germany, and there is little reason why this success should not be repeated elsewhere. **KS**

Joe Zawinul 1932

Zawinul **Zawinul** (kbds); **Woody Shaw**, **Jimmy Owens** (t); **George Davis**, **Hubert Laws** (f); **Earl Turbington**, **Wayne Shorter** (ss); **Herbie Hancock** (p); **Miroslav Vitous**, **Walter Booker** (b); **Joe Chambers**, **Billy Hart**, **David Lee**, **Jack DeJohnelte** (d, perc). Atlantic Ⓜ 781579-2 (37 minutes). Recorded 1970.

✓ ⑧ ❽

Austrian pianist Joe Zawinul, who studied at the Viennese Conservatory, brought a highly developed technique and classical background to his varied jazz endeavours. When he emigrated to the US in 1959, stints with Maynard Ferguson and Dinah Washington led to an important nine-year association with Cannonball Adderley, for whom he composed such hits as *Mercy, Mercy, Mercy*. He also participated in Miles Davis's move from straightahead to fusion.

In this evocative 1970 "music for two electric pianos, jazz flute, trumpet, soprano saxophone, two contrabasses and percussion," we catch a glimpse of the acoustic-electronic blends and rock rhythms that, while reflecting the experiments with Davis, would also become central to the stylistics of Weather Report, the explosive fusion unit formed by Zawinul and Wayne Shorter in the same year. Prominent among the tracks is a haunting version of the title track Zawinul penned for Davis's pivotal jazz-rock breakthrough, **In a Silent Way** (1969). There is also the stirring yet contemplative *Doctor Honoris Causa*, dedicated to Hancock on the occasion of the awarding of an honorary doctorate from Grinnell University, Hancock's alma mater. The autobiographical dimension emerges as well in *Arrival in New York*, a brief, pithy sound collage resonant with the sounds of gulls, steamship whistles and clattering subway trains. **CB**

Lost Tribes **Zawinul** (p, kbds, acc, v, vocoder, perc, g, kba); **Randy Bernsen** (g, elg); **Gerald Veasley** (elb, v); **Mike Baker** (d, v); **Bobby Thomas Jr** (perc, f, v, didgeridu); **Bill Summers** (perc); **Ron Kunen**, **Abner Mariri**, **Ambition Sandemela**, **Lebo M**, **Carol Perry**, **Darlene Perry**, **Lori Perry**, **Sharon Perry** (v). Columbia Ⓕ 468900 2 (52 minutes). Recorded 1991.

⑥ ❽

Although Weather Report was notionally a co-operative, the extent to which it was dominated by Joe Zawinul became fully apparent when the group's principals formed their own bands in the mid-eighties. While Wayne Shorter produced a series of densely scored hi-tech fusion records, Zawinul's Syndicate took up the option on the global carnival initiated by Weather Report in the seventies. Zawinul's preoccupation with exotica, inspired perhaps by his own emigré status, underscores all of the Syndicate's recordings, and it's variously expressed here in the sound of didgeridu, oriental gong, Red Indian whooping, hysterically ovating crowds, bass ostinatos, clamorous Latin, African and flamenco dance rhythms, babbling, quasi-Asian vocalizing and chanting African choruses. As in post-1973 Weather Report, a sense of spontaneous collective improvisation is conveyed, and beyond Zawinul's Korg Pepe sax-synth bursts—imitating the terse melodic fragments Shorter played in Weather Report—there are no solos as such. This is a pity, since without a soloist of the calibre of Scott Henderson, whose perky, chromatic contributions distinguished the Syndicate's earlier albums, **Lost Tribes** is interchangeable with much other Zawinul work. **MG**

Denny Zeitlin

Time Remembers One Time Once **Zeitlin** (p); **Charlie Haden** (b). ECM Ⓕ 1239 (837 020-2) (54 minutes). Recorded 1981.

⑧ ❽

Zeitlin is something of a stylistic halfway house between Bill Evans and Paul Bley. More adventurous in virtually every way than Evans, he nonetheless has a considerable amount of the clarity and corresponding angularity of the avant-garde pianist without sacrificing his natural warmth and expressivity. Since his first recordings in the early sixties, Zeitlin has pursued an independent course, and although he has combined his musical career with another career in psychiatry, he has never fallen below a very high level of performing excellence.

This album is his only one for ECM and benefits from the towering presence of bassist Haden, who contributes two eloquent compositions to the proceedings as well as his persuasive bass playing. For a great deal of the time, Zeitlin is happy to provide a backdrop for Haden to strike out strongly over, and it is one of the great pleasures of this album to hear Haden be so much to the fore on a date. The obvious comparison is with Haden's duets with Hampton Hawes, and there is a version of *As Long As There's Music* here which provides a fascinating contrast to the earlier one with Hawes. This is an absorbing and beautiful album from two highly intelligent and talented musicians. **KS**

Attila Zoller

1927

Overcome **Zoller** (g); **Kirk Lightsey** (p); **Michael Formanek** (b); **Daniel Humair** (d). Enja Ⓕ 5053 2 (45 minutes). Recorded 1986.

⑥ ❻

Zoller, a Hungarian guitarist who has been in the vanguard of the European scene since the fifties (he played with Jutta Hipp, for example, before she went off to New York), has spent the last decade making records for the German label, Enja. This is the only one to make it onto CD so far, so although it is arguable that this is not his best Enja album, it is the only one we can hear on the smaller format.

The album was recorded live at the Leverkusen Jazz Festival, and that fact points to its deficiencies as well as to its strengths. The recorded sound, for one thing, is rather hollow and lacking in presence, which does not help Zoller to cut through in the comfort of your living room. The tracks are without exception over ten minutes long, so there are the occasional boring bits to practice one's stoicism in. All that aside, Zoller and Lightsey were very much in touch musically on this occasion, and careful listening will bring much of interest and pleasure to your ear. Zoller manages to combine both European and American guitar traditions in his approach, thereby avoiding falling into the stereotyped phrases many guitarists find impossible to refrain from. Drummer Humair is his usual strong, flexible self. **KS**

John Zorn

1953

Cobra **Zorn** (prompter); **Jim Staley**, **J.A. Deane** (tb); **Anthony Coleman**, **Wayne Horvitz**, **David Weinstein** (kbds); **Guy Klucevsek** (acc); **Carol Emanuel**, **Zeena Parkins** (hp); **Bill Frisell** (g); **Arto Lindsay** (g, v); **Elliott Sharp** (g, b, v); **Bob James** (tapes); **Christian Marclay** (turntables); **Bobby Previte** (perc). hatART Ⓕ 2-6040 (two discs: 113 minutes). Recorded 1985/86.

⑧ ❽

Zorn has said he is more interested in how things work than how they sound. His composition *Cobra* makes the point. It is a non-competitive 'game' for improvisers, the object of which is to create a piece of music, using rules which encourage abrupt and frequent change—the deliberate discontinuity of the forties cartoon music he loves. There is no score, but a set of instructions. *Cobra* is designed so each musician periodically directs the flow of the entire unit, using various 'calls' to determine who plays when, or the tactics improvisers might use: for instance, one call requires the music to change but the players to stay the same; another demands the opposite. Players use hand signals to communicate their desires to a prompter, who uses cue cards to direct the band. Typically, change is instant and abrupt—most calls make a clean break with what went before.

These live and studio versions are pretty good, achieving their own choppy flow. But *Cobra* is a spectator sport as well as a musical event; the visual element makes it easier to follow. Since January 1992 there have been monthly performances at New York's Knitting Factory, making *Cobra* the first piece of music from New York's downtown scene to become genuinely shared repertoire. **KW**

News For Lulu **Zorn** (as); **George Lewis** (tb); **Bill Frisell** (g). hatART Ⓕ CD 6005 (74 minutes). Recorded 1987.

⑦ ❽

Of John Zorn's importance to contemporary music there can be little doubt, but there is also little doubt that a lot of his best work lies outside the jazz arena. This project, however, is very much part of the tradition, being an attempt to reinterpret the compositions of Kenny Dorham, Hank Mobley, Sonny Clark and Freddie Redd. Now, before jumping to the conclusion that this is a Blue Note revivalist band, just glance at the instrumentation. This is a collective effort at every stage, and the above attribution of this album to Zorn alone flies in the face of the CD's own titles, where all three musicians are given equal billing. They certainly work very closely together to bring such pieces as Sonny Clark's title-track, Mobley's *This I Dig of You* and Dorham's *Lotus Blossom* to new life. While Zorn and Lewis tend to lead the way here with the melodic statements and embellishments, in many ways guitarist Frisell makes the most telling contributions, being the musical glue which holds the whole thing together. A follow-up album, **More News For Lulu** (hatArt CD 6055), comes from a 1989 performance by the same trio. **KS**

Spy vs. Spy **Zorn**, **Tim Berne** (as); **Mark Dresser** (b); **Joey Baron**, **Michael Vatchér** (d).
Elektra/Musician ℗ 960844-2 (41 minutes). Recorded 1988.

✓ ⑩ ❽

The cover of this disc says the musicians listed above "play the music of Ornette Coleman." Do they? They attack 17 of his themes, in versions ranging in length from barely a minute to nearly five, subjected to a rhythmic context unrecognizable to that of the composer's. There are audible debts to Ornette: the instrumental configuration is a kind of double trio balancing on the fulcrum of Dresser's heroic bass (a reference to **Free Jazz** and classic **Prime Time**?); Berne and Zorn's sparring benefits from the lessons of Coleman and Cherry; there are echoes of Ornette's wail everywhere. Ultimately, the warmth, wit and passion of the originals are replaced by the regimen of hardcore rock speed, wbrevity, intensity, noise. Although not an intentional distortion (they are faithful to the themes), the rearrangements are drastic.—But they are arranged; you can hear it in the consistent theme/simultaneous solos/theme format; the alto's careful articulation; how the drums phrase within the themes of *Enfant* and *Peace Warrior*; how the altos hold the theme of *Space Church* in strict tempo while the background explodes; the fragments of *Blues Connotation* within the solos. It is sometimes painful, and other times exhilarating, to hear the buoyant, basically optimistic themes fight to retain their character within such a barrage. Yet what Zorn does is not all that far, conceptually at least, from bebop's break with swing, or Ornette's break with bebop. **AL**

Various Artists/Collections

The following CDs are but a tiny selection from what is currently available in this genre of release. What is here has been chosen on merit, and has been included according to two sets of criteria: when a particular title is a convenient and valuable example of areas of music and their representative musicians which are not available in other forms; and when a particular all-star grouping is involved in a performance of outstanding musical or historic value. The listing is alphabetical from the CD title.

A Piano Anthology Artists include: **Jelly Roll Morton, Fats Waller, James P. Johnson, Duke Ellington, Frank Melrose, Mary Lou Williams, Meade Lux Lewis, Joe Sullivan, Jess Stacy, Count Basie, Willie 'The Lion' Smith, Art Tatum, Billy Kyle, Clarence Profit, Earl Hines, Nat Cole, Jay McShann, Ralph Sutton, Dodo Marmarosa, Bill Evans**. MCA/Decca Ⓜ GRP 16392 (62 minutes) Recorded 1926-58.

✔ ⑧ ❻

Of course, what this doesn't give you is anything from the past near-40 years, which is a longer time-span than the one on the record. That slightly disturbing point aside, this is a sensible anthology of material over which MCA have control, so although a few rather big names from the period covered may be missing—Teddy Wilson, Bud Powell, Horace Silver, Wynton Kelly and Erroll Garner, just to mention the first few which came to mind—what you get is good quality nonetheless. The Jelly Roll solo piano version of *The Pearls* is not that well-known, compared with his other recordings of it, so it's a pleasure to have it back in circulation, while the Waller/Johnson carve-up with Johnny Dunn's band is fun. But it makes you wonder when MCA here muster one Clarence Profit title, but the English label, Memoir, can summon the courage to do a whole CD's worth (see above). Most of the samples are well-chosen, though towards the end the waning of interest in jazz by American Decca shows a little, with Dodo Marmarosa illustrated only by a track with Charlie Barnet (*The Moose*), rather than one a solo contract may have produced. Bill Evans appears courtesy of another fine pianist, Eddie Costa, whose group he joins for a number while Costa plays vibes for a change. **KS**

A Tribute To John Coltrane: Blues For Coltrane **Pharoah Sanders, David Murray** (ts); **McCoy Tyner** (p); **Cecil McBee** (b); **Roy Haynes** (d). Impulse! Ⓕ MCAD 42122 (53 minutes). Recorded 1987.

⑧ ❽

It is inevitable that a tribute to John Coltrane should concentrate on the saxophonists who are offering it. The choice here is challenging in that Sanders was a former 'student' who went on to play his own part in the great man's later work. He now has a strong personal voice and his style is a faithful development of the original. It is perhaps inevitable that he should move back into his mentor's spirit on Naima but he makes no attempt to reproduce Coltrane's solos. Murray is a player who, perhaps aware of Coltrane's huge musical presence, chose a different route, taking his inspiration from Sonny Rollins (and latterly Albert Ayler) and coming up alongside Sanders in a discernable parallel. He similarly avoids replication, certainly of Trane's monumental 1963 versions of *I Want To Talk About You*, but his reading has the same emotional power and inexorable conclusion. His may be a proxy vote but, as he shows on *Trane*, he is Sanders' peer in perpetuating the memory of the dedicatee. The pair of them are assisted by a rhythm section that does a perfect job: no-one grasped the ineluctable quality of Trane's music better than Tyner - he leads this power unit with an assurance that is daunting, yet it is the drum coda on *Bluesin' For John C*, running on like the pre-ignition of a switched-off car, that shows how difficult it is to close down moods set by the pianist when in this sort of mood. **BMcR**

Avant Garde **Roland Kirk Quintet; Charles Mingus Quartet; Ornette Coleman Quartet; John Coltrane/Don Cherry Quartet; John Coltrane Quartet; Art Ensemble of Chicago** with amongst others **Ted Curson, Lester Bowie** (t); **Eric Dolphy, Roscoe Mitchell** (as); **Joseph Jarman** (as, ts); **Booker Ervin** (ts); **Tommy Flanagan, Ron Burton, Muhal Richard Abrams** (p); **Charlie Haden, Paul Chambers, Malachi Favors** (b); **Dannie Richmond, Billy Higgins, Ed Blackwell, Art Taylor** (d); **Don Moye** (d, perc). Atlantic Ⓜ 781 709-2 (46 minutes). Recorded 1959-72.

⑨ ❽

Avant Garde is not an altogether satisfactory title for this musical anthology. Kirk was never in the vanguard of a musical movement; the magnificent Mingus was more of a John the Baptist, a man whose superb music shaped attitudes and pointed jazz toward greater freedom. Only the position of Coleman, Cherry and Coltrane, as the avant-garde voices of the late fifties/early sixties, is indisputable and, to complicate matters further, the Art Ensemble of Chicago represent a totally different and later movement. This point made, the jazz itself is uniformly outstanding. Mingus's *Wednesday Night Prayer Meeting* may lack the smouldering fire of the Atlantic studio version but it is distinguished by Curson's lyrical trumpet and by the brilliant alto of Dolphy. Both Coleman tracks come from the legendary **Shape Of Jazz To Come** album, *Eventually* being a model free form exercise and *Lonely Woman* a structured reading of a beautiful tune, with Haden outstanding. Cherry makes his sleight-of-hand pocket trumpet statements with Coleman and Coltrane, while Coltrane's virtuosic *Countdown* is an outstanding sample from his almighty **Giant**

Steps. Kirk's musical insight and creative skill illuminate the moving *Inflated Tear* and the album closes with the swirling *Noonah*, a fine example of the Art Ensemble's contrapuntal mastery and compositional skill. **BMcR**

Better Boot That Thing: Great Women Blues Singers Of The Twenties **Spivey**, **Alberta Hunter**, **Ida May Mack**, **Bessie Tucker** (v); Henry **'Red' Allen** (t); **J.C. Higginbotham** (tb); **Charlie Holmes** (ss); **Teddy Hill** (ts); **Luis Russell** (p); **Will Johnson** (g); **Pops Foster** (b). RCA Bluebird Ⓜ 66065 2 (63 minutes). Recorded 1929-30.

⑦ ❽

The sales of her 1926 début recording *Black Snake Blues* put Victoria Spivey among the more bankable blues artists; her predilection for songs about disease, reptiles, nightmares and the supernatural made her one of the oddest. Her voice is small and without obvious charms, but her air of almost prurient glee and the excellent musicians she worked with produced records that were always distinctive and occasionally outstandiing.

Four of her five numbers on this album come from a notable (and well-recorded) 1929 session with a group from the Luis Russell orchestra. Characteristic themes—*Dirty T.B. Blues*, the violent crime of *Blood Hound Blues*—are narrated with gusto, but the high point of the date is the magnificent bragging of *Moaning The Blues*. *Showered With The Blues*, from 1930, just has piano and guitar.

This absorbing collection also includes five tracks each by the sweeter-voiced Alberta Hunter and the rugged Texas singers Bessie Tucker and Ida May Mack. Most of these are accompanied on piano, the Texans by K.D. Johnson, but Hunter offers captivating versions of *Sugar* and *Beale Street Blues* with Fats Waller on organ. **TR**

Blue Boogie **Albert Ammons**, **Pete Johnson** with (Ulysses Livingston [b], Abe Bolar [d]); **Meade Lux Lewis**, **James P Johnson**, **Sammy Benskin** (with Billy Taylor [b], Specs Powell [d]); **Art Hodes** (with Max Kaminsky [t], Sandy Williams ([tb], Jimmy Shirley (g], Israel Crosby (b], Fred Moore (d]); **Earl Hines**, **Art Tatum** (p). Blue Note Ⓜ CDP 799099-2 (74 minutes). Recorded 1939-45.

⑧ ❺

Blue Note may be latterly defined as the sixties progenitor of all which is hip on the dancefloors of acid-jazz discos, but it didn't start life that way. Alfred Lion's first sessions in 1939 were with Albert Ammons and Meade Lux Lewis, and before the year was out he had recorded the third of the great boogie triumvirate, Pete Johnson. These have remained some of the most celebrated of all boogie-woogie recordings, and that reputation is well justified. This sampler can only just hint at what Blue Note recorded at this time, but the selections don't commit any obvious blunders, and we are blessed with boogie basics like *Honky Tonk Train*, *Boogie Woogie Stomp* and *Bass Goin' Crazy*. The album is sub-titled *Boogie woogie, stride and the piano blues*, so that explains the presence of James P. Johnson, Hines and Tatum, none of whom could ever be described as boogie pianists. All perform well, and the heat generated on this disc is tremendous - these people weren't fooling around, no matter what style they espoused. The only caveat on an excellent set of material is the generally sub-standard sound quality (obviously, the fledgling label could hardly afford the best studios of the day), and this point is underlined when the Tatum track appears at the end, superb Capitol sound and all. The other annoying thing doesn't affect the music at all, but puts you off a bit: there are simply no personnel details (past the bare fact of which pianist is playing) in the booklet. All the above sidemen have been supplied courtesy of my Blue Note Ruppli. **KS**

Boogie Woogie: Great Original Performances 1928–1941 One track each from the following artistes; **Tommy Dorsey And His Orchestra**, **Count Basie Quartet**, **Meade Lux Lewis**, **Albert Ammons**, **Jimmy Yancey**, **Bob Crosby And His Orchestra**, **Speckled Red Trio**, **Woody Herman And His Orchestra**, **Meade Lux Lewis**, **Albert Ammons**, **Pete Johnson**, **Will Bradley Trio**, **Woody Herman's Four Chips**, **Maurice Rocco**, **Slim Gaillard And His Flat-Foot-Floogie Boys**, **Pete Johnson**, **Albert Ammons**, **Freddie Slack And His Eight Beats**, **Count Basie And His Orchestra**. Two tracks apiece from the following; **Clarence 'Pinetop' Smith**, **Harry James And His Boogie Woogie Trio**. CDS Records Ⓜ RPCD 601 (61 minutes). Recorded 1928-41.

⑧ ❻

"A joyous manifestation of the blues, (boogie woogie) has enjoyed periods of mass popularity, the last being the late 1930s and early 1940s". The insert card sets the scene for a comprehensive survey of this unique style of keyboard jazz and the CD contains all the expected names plus a few lesser-known players, such as Maurice Rocco who pre-dated Jerry Lee Lewis by playing his slightly spurious boogie standing up. Compiler Robert Parker has included the rare 'B' master of Clarence Smith's *Pinetop's Blues* as well as enjoyable gems such as Will Bradley's *Down The Road Apiece* with its Ray McKinley 'vocal', plus the propulsive sound of the three masters Lewis, Ammons and Johnson charging through *Boogie Woogie Prayer* for nearly five minutes. There are four big-band boogie numbers from the orchestras of Dorsey, Crosby (featuring fine Bob Zurke at the keyboard), Herman and Basie plus the Count's rhythm section version of *Boogie Woogie* and Woody Herman's quartet with the forgotten Tommy Linehan at the piano. Harry James, with Pete Johnson and Albert Ammons alternating at the keyboard, plays hot and muted; his *Boo Woo* sounds like the inspiration for Humphrey Lyttelton's *Bad Penny Blues*. Most of the pianists are skilled in their craft but the notes fail to warn us that Speckled Red (Rufus Perryman) had difficulty in counting; some of his choruses are only eleven bars duration. Parker's transfers give a crisp, clean sound. **AM**

The British Traditional Jazz Collection Volume 1 **Two tracks each by the following ten bands; Mr. Acker Bilk And His Paramount Jazz Band** (Bilk [cl], Colin Smith [t], John Mortimer [tb], Stan Greig [p], Roy James [bj], Ernie Price [b], Ron McKay [d]); **Al Fairweather & Sandy Brown's All Stars** (Fairweather [t], Tony Milliner [tb], Brown [cl], Colin Purbrook [p], Tim Mahn [b], Stan Greig, [d]); **Mike Daniels Delta Jazz Band** (Daniels [t], Gordon Blundy [tb], John Barnes [cl], Des Bacon [p, cl] Geoff Over [bj], Don Smith [b, sou], Arthur Fryatt [d]); **Chris Barber/Monty Sunshine** (Pat Halcox [t], Barber [tb], Sunshine, Ian Wheeler [cl], Eddie Smith [bj], Dick Smith [b], Graham Burbidge [d]); **Ken Colyer's Jazzmen** (Colyer [t], Graham Stewart [tb], Ian Wheeler, Sammy Rimington [cl], Ray Foxley [p], Johnny Bastable [bj], Ron Ward [b], Colin Bowden [d]); **Sims-Wheeler Vintage Jazz Band (**Ken Sims [c], Mac Duncan [tb], Ian Wheeler [cl], Wayne Chandler [bj], Geoff King [b], Jimmy Garforth [d]); **Humphrey Lyttelton And His Band (**Lyttelton [t], John Picard [tb], Tony Coe [cl], Jimmy Skidmore [ts], Ian Armit [p], Brian Brocklehurst, Pete Blannin [b], Eddie Taylor [d]); **Alan Elsdon And His Band** (Elsdon [t], Phil Rhodes [tb], John Barnes [cl], Arthur Wood [p], Johnny Barton [bj], Mick Gilligan [b], Keith Webb [d]); **Alex Welsh And His Band** (Welsh [t], Roy Crimmins [tb], Archie Semple [cl], Danny Moss [ts], Fred Hunt [p], Tony Pitt [bj, g], Bill Reid [b], Lennie Hastings [d]); **Terry Lightfoot's New Orleans Jazzmen** (Dickie Hawdon, Alan Elsdon [t], Phil Rhodes [tb], Lightfoot [cl], Colin Bates [p], Paddy Lightfoot, Wayne Chandler [bj], Vic Barton [b], Johnny Richardson [d]). Philips Ⓜ 830 787-2 (69 minutes). Recorded 1957-62.

⑧ ❽

'Trad' evokes memories of vaudeville-style jazz groups wearing funny hats and playing music for non-specialized audiences. The title of this CD is misleading (a fact which is admitted in the notes by Gerard Bielderman) and a great deal of the music here falls into the mainstream or Condon categories. Even the so-called Trad bands produce music which has weathered the years quite comfortably. All the clarinettists, without exception, are fine jazz soloists and even the dedicated New Orleans-fanatic Ken Colyer comes up with a jaunty version of Irving Berlin's *Cheek To Cheek*. Predictably the Lyttelton and Welsh tracks hew close to the mainstream while the two Fairweather-Brown titles have that unique sound which makes the departure of the two men such a loss; *Big Bill* is, quite simply, one of the best British jazz performances on record. Five of the 20 tracks were unissued until this collection first appeared in 1989 in LP form. They include a fine blues by Terry Lightfoot with great Armstrong-inspired trumpet from Dickie Hawdon. It is unfortunate that so many of the banjos are beautifully recorded, as their relentless plunking sometimes gives rhythm sections a stodgy sound, but if you can ignore them you will find much to enjoy here. **AM**

California Cool Blue **Mark Murphy, Billy May, Gerry Mulligan, Shelly Manne, Chico Hamilton, Chet Baker, Jimmy Giuffre, Hampton Hawes, Lee Konitz, Gloria Wood, Pete Candoli, Art Pepper, Shorty Rogers, Jack Sheldon, Teddy Edwards, Les McCann, Bobby Troup, Bob Gordon, Jack Montrose, Bud Shank, June Christy, Peggy Lee, George Shearing, Curtis Amy, Dupree Bolton, Serge Chaloff, Sonny Criss**. Blue Note Ⓜ CDP7 80707 2 (75 minutes). Recorded 1953-63.

✔ ⑧ ❽

For this issue Blue Note dug into the library of Pacific Jazz, which is now part of the group. A track each from the little heard baritone players Bob Gordon and Serge Chaloff give some idea of the sterling worth of this disc to the collector new to jazz. Both men should be in any collection, to say nothing of the many West Coast tracks included here and not available anywhere else. Chaloff's *A Handful Of Stars* is an outstanding performance, as are Pepper's *Mambo De La Pinta* with Jack Sheldon and Russ Freeman and his feature with Shorty Rogers, *Diablo's Dance*. Sheldon is also on good form on Giuffre's minimalist *Ironic*, a delicate piece which immediately preceded Giuffre's celebrated trio. Mulligan, Konitz and Shank are all well represented, and the vocals by Murphy, Christy, Woods and Lee, each so different from its fellows, are all vigorous jazz performances. **SV**

Classic Jazz Piano **Jelly Roll Morton, Earl Hines, Jimmy Yancey, Meade Lux Lewis, James P. Johnson, Fats Waller, Willie 'The Lion' Smith, Art Tatum, Teddy Wilson, Jess Stacy, Duke Ellington, Billy Strayhorn, Count Basie, Mary Lou Williams, Erroll Garner, Oscar Peterson, Lennie Tristano, Bud Powell, Bill Evans** (p). RCA Bluebird Ⓜ 6754-2-RB (65 minutes) Recorded 1927-56.

✔ ⑧ ❽

The names are a palpable guarantee and it only remains to check this glorious celebration of the heartland of jazz for sound quality and the selection of the tracks. Since the latter has been done by the normally reliable Orrin Keepnews, there are no problems. Bluebird's transfers from 78s to CD have been highly suspect in the past, so it is a relief to find few sonic flaws in this collection. The core of the music is in the work of the stride players; Fats, James P., The Lion and of course Tatum were each capable of playing like a full orchestra. Yancey is the only primitive, *State Street Special* being typical of his confined but powerfully emotional work. There are several other horns involved, Morton with Dodds, the Goodman trio for Wilson, James P. with Frankie Newton's band and with his Louisiana Sugar Babes and George Russell's Sextet to display the emerging talents of Bill Evans. Jess Stacy is backed by an unidentified orchestra on the 1945 *Day Break Serenade*. Some previous transfers of Basie's 1947 material for Victor have been horrendous, but *Shine On Harvest Moon* with Freddie Green, Walter Page and Jo Jones is excellently done. Ellington's mastery as a soloist is confirmed by the 1941 *Solitude* and he and Billy Strayhorn run riot on one piano with *Tonk*. **SV**

Roy Eldridge and the Swing Trumpets Featuring the groups of **Roy Eldridge**, **Charlie Shavers**, **Emmett Berry**, **Jonah Jones**, **Buck Clayton**, **Joe Thomas** (t). Mercury Ⓜ 830 923-2 (two discs: 138 Minutes). Recorded 1944-46.

⑧ ❽

These bright sessions from 1944-1946 capture six of the great swing era trumpeters, Roy Eldridge, Charlie Shavers, Emmett Berry, Jonah Jones, Buck Clayton and Joe Thomas, at the height of their respective powers. Produced by Harry Lim for the independent Keystone label, we hear players whose warm tones and rhythmically supple phrasings hew close to each tune's melodic and harmonic contours. Also included, where available, are the sessions' alternate takes and informative notes by Dan Morgenstern.

In 1944, the bebop revolution had yet to explode. swing was still king, and its reigning trumpet sovereign was Roy Eldridge. In the most notable date, we catch Roy (originally designated as Little Jazz for contractual reasons) mixing it up with Thomas and Berry in the first of Lim's provocative pairings of well-known exponents of the same instrument. On sparkling takes of *Don't be that Way*, *I Want to be Happy* and *St. Louis Blues* the three brassmen are backed beautifully by pianist Johnny Guarnieri, bassist Israel Crosby and drummer Cozy Cole. On Shavers's spirited set we also hear Tab Smith, Earl Hines, Al Lucas and Jo Jones. Sessions with Jonah Jones and Buck Clayton are equally satisfying. From start to finish, regardless of who's soloing, the music is a compelling proof of the unique powers of positive swing. **CB**

Giants of Small-Band Swing, Volumes 1 and 2 Featuring: **Billy Kyle's Big Eight** (Kyle [p], Dick Vance [t], Trummy Young [tb], Buster Bailey [cl],Lem Davis [as],John Hardee [ts], John Simmons [b], Buddy Rich [d]): **Russell Procope's Big Six** (Procope [as], Harold Baker [t], John Hardee [ts], Billy Kyle [p], John Simmons [b], Denzil Best [d]): **Sandy Williams' Big Eight** (Williams [tb], Pee Wee Irwin [t], Tab Smith [as], Cecil Scott [ts,bs], Jimmy Jones [p], Brick Fleagle [g], Sid Weiss [b], Denzil Best [d]): **Dicky Wells' Big Seven** (Wells [tb]; George Treadwell [t]; Budd Johnson [ts]; Cecil Scott [bs], Jimmy Jones [p], Al McKibbon [b], Jimmy Crawford [d]): **Jimmy Jones' Big Four** (Jones [p], Budd Johnson [ts], Al Hall [b], Denzil Best [d]); **Joe Thomas' Big Six** (Thomas [t]; Lem Davis [as]; Ted Nash [ts]; Jimmy Jones [p]; Billy Taylor b]; Denzil Best [d]): Sandy Williams' Big Eight (diff. group to above–Williams (tb], Joe Thomas [t], Johnny Hodges [as], Harry Carney [bs], Jimmy Jones [p], Brick Fleagle [g], Sid Weiss [b], Shelly Manne [d)): **J.C. Higginbotham's Big Eight** [Higginbotham [tb], Sidney De Paris [t], Tab Smith [as], Cecil Scott [ts], Jimmy Jones [p], Brick Fleagle [g], Billy Taylor [b], Dave Tough [d]). Riverside Ⓜ OJCCD-1723/24-2 (two discs, oas: 36 and 35 minutes). Recorded 1945/46.

⑦ ❺

These HRS (Hot Record Society) recording sessions capture the music of 52nd Street as World War Two came to a close. It reflects, obliquely, the effects of bebop, but most of the music is played by men who came up in the Swing Era and were either free-lancing or working with bands under the leadership of men such as J.C.Heard, Ed Hall, John Kirby and Red Allen. A significant difference was that a handful (Hodges, Carney, Baker, Procope, Sandy Williams) were, or had been, working with Duke Ellington. Although the music is seldom less than good it lacks the magic of the dates made for Keynote at the same time, largely because the sessions generally lack the leadership of giants such as Coleman Hawkins, Earl Hines, Benny Carter, Lester Young etc., all of whom fronted bands for the Keynote label. With the exception of the four outstanding titles by Sandy Williams' Big Eight in Volume Two by what is, in effect, an Ellington splinter group, the soloists are merely competent and Jimmy Jones's chordal style of solo playing becomes rather tedious after a time.

The playing times are hardly acceptable (these are unaltered transfers of LPs to CD, and could have fitted onto one disc), especially in the light of the fact that at least nine more titles exist from these same HRS sessions which should have been included, two apiece by Sandy Williams, Joe Thomas, Billy Kyle and Jimmy Jones plus Dicky Wells's *We're Through* , with a vocal by Sarah Vaughan. The original HRS 78s were never very good in terms of surface noise, but I think the remastering for CD might have been done better than that encountered on the occasionally distortion-affected Volume One. **AM**

Harlem Lullaby Featuring: **The Dorsey Brothers, Mildred Bailey, Ethel Waters, Bing Crosby, Lee Wiley, Mae West**. On all tracks **Tommy Dorsey** (tb); **Jimmy Dorsey** (cl, as) with the following collective personnel; **Manny Klein**, **Sterling Bose**, **Bunny Berigan** (t); **Larry Binyon** (cl, as, ts); **Joe Venuti**, **Harry Hoffman**, **Walter Edelstein**, **Lou Kosloff** (vn); **Fulton McGrath**, possibly **Joe Meresco** (p); **Dick McDonough** (g); **Artie Bernstein** (b); **Stan King**, **Larry Gomar**, **Chauncey Morehouse** (d); **Mae West**, **Lee Wiley**, **Bing Crosby**, **Mildred Bailey**, **Ethel Waters** (v). Hep Ⓜ HEPCD 100 (59 minutes). Recorded 1933.

⑥ ❻

In the early thirties, Jimmy and Tommy Dorsey did a lot of studio work, thereby providing musical support for a heterogeneous collection of singers. All 20 tracks here were made in the first half of 1933 and while the jazz content is often small, the solo and obbligato work of the co-leaders and, in particular, the splendid trumpet playing of Bunny Berigan on several tracks makes this more than just a socio-musicological documentary of the period. Mildred Bailey and Lee Wiley sound like real jazz singers while Bing Crosby and even Mae West obviously enjoyed working in a jazz environment. Ethel Waters occasionally becomes slightly histrionic, reminding us that she was primarily a cabaret artiste and actress.

The backings to the singers are uncluttered and have weathered the years remarkably well. Some of the songs are of the 'revival' kind but the eight titles by Mildred Bailey are amongst some of the best she recorded from the period and include a couple of Hoagy Carmichael songs, plus a fine version of Harry Revel's film tune *Doin' The Uptown Lowdown*, with 'hot' solos from the Dorsey brothers. **AM**

The Johnny Hodges All-Stars with The Duke Ellington All-Stars and The Billy Strayhorn All-Stars Collective Personnel: i) **Hodges** [as] with: Taft Jordan, Harold Baker [t], Lawrence Brown [tb], Al Sears [ts], Billy Strayhorn [p], Oscar Pettiford [b], Sonny Greer, Wilbur de Paris [d]; ii) **Strayhorn** [p) with: Cat Anderson, Juan Tizol [vtb], Quentin Jackson, Britt Woodman [tb], Willie Smith [as], Paul Gonsalves [ts], Wendell Marshall [b], Louie Bellson [d]; iii) **Ellington** [p) with: Juan Tizol [vtb], Willie Smith [as], Jimmy Hamilton [cl, ts], Billy Strayhorn [org], Wendell Marshall [b], Louie Bellson [d). Prestige Ⓜ PCD-24103-2 (67 minutes). Recorded 1947-51.

⑨ ❺

These Ellington small-group sessions pick up where the Bluebird CD leaves off. The quite blatant drop in recording quality has everything to do with moving from a large and profitable company to the fledgling Sunrise records, a label which lasted about as long as it takes to say the name. Still; this doesn't affect the quality of the musicianship, which is blissfully high. Hodges' rendering of Strayhorn's *A Flower is a Lovesome Thing* is compelling, and the jump tunes he so loved playing get frisky treatment throughout. *Lotus Blossom* is almost indecently lush and romantic, while *Searsy's Blues* (they must have thought long and hard about that title) gives tenorist Sears one chorus only and allows Hodges to wail most of the way.

The rest of the CD is taken up with various small-group sessions for the better-distributed but equally unsuccessful Mercer catalogue, set up in 1950 as a little label for Duke and his pals to relax on. By this time, Hodges had gone out on his own, being replaced by Willie Smith. He it is who is featured on a stunning version of *Caravan* which has Duke ripping it up on piano and Strayhorn playing Phantom of the Opera organ. On the slow, menacing *Cat Walk*, on which Cat Anderson prowls with menace, Duke plays some of the most radical piano accompaniment of his career. And so it goes on. Not essential Ellingtonia, but I wouldn't part with it for the world. **KS**

Honkers & Bar Walkers, Volumes 1 & 2 Volume 1: **Jimmy Forrest**, **Teddy Brannon**, **Cozy Eggleston**, **Tab Smith**, **Jimmy Coe**, **Doc Sausage**, **Fred Jackson**, **Chris Woods**, **Fats Noel**, **Paul Bascomb**. Volume 2: **Willis Jackson**, **Morris Lane & His Orchestra**, **Panama Francis**, **Bill Harvey & His Orchestra**, **Charlie Ferguson & His Orchestra**, **Bobby Smith**, **King Curtis**. Delmark Ⓜ DD 438/452 (60 minutes).Recorded: (Volume 1): 1949-1958; (Volume 2): 1952-56. (Volume 1): 62 minutes; (Volume 2).

⑥ ❻

With these two CDs Delmark continues the documentation of the Apollo label, wandering into musical styles not usually allowed into the jazz corral. While it is true that, by the mid-to-late-fifties, the remaining honkers and screechers were quickly assimilating themselves into rock & roll bands all over America or moving completely out of the genre and towards sax-and-organ soul-jazz combos, at the time these sides were cut, these players were still able to trace their styles directly to Louis Jordan, Illinois Jacquet, Gene Ammons and Arnett Cobb, all saxophonists with impeccable jazz credentials. Many of these players have vanished into the mists of time or stuck with the day jobs, but the music lives on, and it is surprisingly diverse in nature, from the roughhouse tenor of Jimmy Forrest on *Night Train* (Forrest was a much more sophisticated player than this track may indicate) to the Hodges-inspired Tab Smith on *Because of You*. Nobody on these two discs gets as frenetic or as crude as Big Jay McNeely did in his heyday, and there is plenty of swinging improvising which wouldn't have disgraced the Basie band of the time. If you find that hard to believe, then check out these two discs for yourself. Maybe King Curtis, from 1956, has taken the step into rock and its associated licks, but then he is confined to the last two tracks, after all. **KS**

Introspection One track by each the following: **Hubert Laws** (Laws [f], Chick Corea [p], Gary Burton [vb], Ron Carter [b], Bernard Purdie(d], Mongo Santamaria [cga], Airto Moreira, Warren Smith, Joe Chambers [perc]); **Chick Corea** (Corea [p], Steve Swallow [b], Joe Chambers [d]); **Charles Lloyd** (Lloyd [ts], Keith Jarrett [p], Cecil McBee [b], Jack DeJohnette [d]); **Joe Zawinul** (Zawinul, Herbie Hancock [elp], Woody Shaw [t], George Davis [f], Earl Turbinton [ss], Miroslav Vitous, Walter Booker [b], Billy Hart, David Lee [perc]); **Keith Jarrett** (Jarrett [p,cga], Charlie Haden [b], Paul Motian [d]); **Gary Burton** (Burton[vb]); **Gary Burton-Keith Jarrett** (Burton [vb], Jarrett [p], Steve Swallow [b], Bill Goodwin [d]). Atlantic Jazz Ⓜ 781710-2 (41 minutes). Recorded 1966-72.

⑧ ❻

Within the limitations of the Atlantic and Vortex catalogues, this sets out to illustrate the fusion which took place between jazz and other contemporary music in the late sixties and early seventies. It must be said that only Hubert Laws's *Yoruba*, with its heavy Latin-American influence and Zawinul's *In A Silent Way*, recorded a year after the Miles Davis version, deviate any distance from what might be termed orthodox jazz. Even Charles Lloyd's *Forest Flower–Sunrise*, taped at the Monterey Jazz Festival, sounds like a rather cosy version of the Coltrane Quartet. The strengths of the CD lie in the outstanding work of Corea, nodding his head in the direction of Bill Evans on his own *Tones For Joan's Bones* and Keith Jarrett, who is as always so melodic in concept and such a master of the orthodox keyboard. His trio version of *Standing Outside* makes it obligatory to locate **Mourning Of A Star** (Atlantic 1596), the LP from which this track has been taken. Jarrett is equally impressive in his two solos on *Fortune Smiles* with Gary Burton, while Burton himself shows he is the master of four mallets on the solo vibraphone track *No More Blues*. A significant number of musicians on these seven tracks worked, at some time or another, with Miles Davis, whose own fusion work was less ephemeral than much of what is here. **AM**

Jazz Café-After Hours Artists include **Sonny Rollins**, **Paul Desmond**, **Chet Baker**, **Don Byas**, **Phineas Newborn**, **Lee Konitz**, **Dizzy Gillespie**, **Bob Mintzer**, **Django Reinhardt**, **Coleman Hawkins**, **Gigi Gryce**, **Duke Ellington**, **Red Norvo**, **Lucky Thompson**, **Art Blakey**, **Charles Mingus**, **José Feliciano**, **Gary Burton**, **Zoot Sims**. RCA Ⓑ 121447 2 (78 minutes) No recording dates given.

⑥ ❻

This is one release in a series carrying the generic title Jazz Café, with the sub-title changing each time —**Summertime**, **Swingtime**, **The Blues**, **Piano**, **For Lovers** and so on. More will be coming out every few months so check your local store for them. No personnel details or dates are given; just the leaders are named. The time-span is approximately 1939 to 1981. Most of the material is familiar to say the least, with the majority stemming from the RCA Victor and Bluebird archives, topped up by the Vogue label here and there. The music is mostly of a high standard, some of it in the classic category, and the whole slant is towards the casual listener, although there is nothing particularly compromised about the way the music is played. The only anomaly on this sample title I selected more or less at random is the presence of José Feliciano, playing *Yesterday* (no, not *Yesterdays*) on his guitar with strings, maracas, piano and Peruvian flute accompaniment. Now, I'd be quite interested to know just what *his* angle on jazz is... **KS**

Jazz Concert West Coast, Volumes 1, 2 & 3 Collective Personnel: **Howard McGhee**, **Al Killian** (t); **Trummy Young** (tb); **Sonny Criss** (as); **Wardell Gray**, **Dexter Gordon**, **Wild Bill Moore**, **Gene Montogmery** (ts); **Hampton Hawes**, **Russ Freeman** (p); **Barney Kessel** (g); **Harry Babasin**, **Red Callender**, **Leroy Gray** (b); **Connie Kay**, **Ken Kennedy** (d). Denon/Savoy Ⓜ SV-0164/0165/0166 (Three discs, oas: 39, 43, 52 minutes). Recorded 1947.

⑦ ❺

This set of three separately-available CDs proves conclusively that, by 1947, there was a thriving bebop community in L.A. Recorded at the Elks Auditorium in July of that year, it featured some thrilling duets from two close friends who were intensely competitive players onstage together, Wardell Gray and Dexter Gordon. No track on the two albums which feature them together is shorter than 18 minutes long, so everyone gets plenty of space to play in and the temperature steadily mounts. Although the rather vague sond quality (this is an early location recording, done on a portable tape deck) keeps the rhythm section mostly well in the background, the soloists are well captured, and this is a rare opportunity to hear these players really stretch themselves. Also well worth a listen is the electrifying playing of Howard McGhee, then at the very top of his early form, plus the fleet, Parker-based work of altoist Sonny Criss, a player who vanished for much of the fifties but came back into favour with a series of albums for Prestige in the sixties.

Volume Three of this series features different groupings from the first two, although it is from the same concert. The first two numbers are played by Wild Bill Moore's group and feature Gene Montgomery and Russ Freeman, while the final imaginatively titled *Blow Blow Blow*, has Al Killian fronting a band featuring Sonny Criss, Wardell Gray and Barney Kessel. The personnel details listed on the back of these cds, and even the date of the recording, are either wrong or confused. Considering the easy availability of this information, it is incredible that Denon/Savoy should make such gaffes. Denon even claim that Volume Three is previously unissued. That must be news for the people who bought it on the original 78s and, later, on the lp issues of the same material. **KS**

Jazz In Britain: Pioneers With the following bands: **Jack Hylton's Rhythmagicians**; **Fred Elizade And His 'Hot' Music**; **Lew Stone And His Band**; **The Darktown Strutters**; **Billy Cotton And His Cotton Pickers**; **The New Lyres**; **Danny Polo And His Swing Stars**. CDS Records Ⓕ RPCD 606 (59 minutes). Recorded 1927-38.

⑧ ❻

Jazz made a somewhat stealthy entry into Britain after the barrier-breaking arrival of the ODJB at the Hammersmtih Palais in 1919. Several British band leaders were actually in favour of the music 'ut it was often concealed behind titles in which the word 'jazz' did not appear. This Robert Parker compilation focuses on the 'white' influence; the earlier tracks have the precise and almost deliberate sound of American players such as Beiderbecke, Frank Teschemaker and others, and indeed some of the units actually contain notable American soloists: Fred Elizade's little band had no less than three key men from the California Ramblers in Chelsea Quealey, Bobby Davis and Adrian Rollini while Bill Cotton and his band had the excellent New Jersey-born trombonist Ellis Jackson. By the time the Chicago clarinettist Danny Polo came to London, many local musicians had picked up the jazz language and spoke it fluently. The four Polo Swing Stars tracks are excellent in every way, with splendid solos from Tommy McQuater and George Chisholm, the music taking on a distinct Chicago sound. Other locals who took to jazz naturally were trumpeters Jack Jackson and Teddy Foster, both heard taking noteworthy solos. The remastering has been done with Parker's usual technical competence and the issue benefits from presenting complete recording sessions, rather than single examples from many different dates. **AM**

The Jazz Scene Individual tracks by: **Duke Ellington** with **Harry Carney** (bs); **Billy Strayhorn** (p); **Fred Guy** (g); **Oscar Pettiford** (b); **Sonny Greer** (d); **Neal Hefti Orchestra** featuring **Charlie Parker** (as); **Lester Young Trio** with **Young** (ts); **Nat Cole** (p); **Buddy Rich** (d); **Coleman Hawkins** (ts); **Ralph Burns Orchestra** with **Bill Harris** (tb); **Herbie Steward**, **Lucky Thompson** (ts); **Dodo Marmarosa** (p); **George Handy Orchestra**; **Charlie Parker** (as) with **Hank Jones** (p); **Ray Brown** (b); **Shelly Manne** (d); **Willie Smith** (as) with **Dodo Marmarosa** (p); **Barney Kessel** (g); **Red Callender** (b); **Jo Jones** (d); **Machito and His Orchestra**; **Bud Powell** (p); with **Curly Russell** (b); **Max Roach** (d); **Billy Strayhorn** (p); **Coleman Hawkins Trio**; **Flip Phillips** (ts) with **John D'Agostino**, **Buddy Morrow**, **Tommy Turk**, **Kai Winding** (tb); **Sonny Criss** (as); **Mickey Crane** (p); **Ray Brown** (b); **Shelly Manne** (d). Verve Ⓕ 521 661-2 (two discs: 144 minutes) Recorded 1946-48.

⑧ ❻

A labour of love on two occasions. Firstly, Norman Granz conceived of this incredible array of talent and persuaded the principals to participate. Secondly the people at Polygram Jazz New York found a CD's worth of unissued material, then re-created Granz's original packaging, even down to the ring-binders holding the brown cardboard the CDs are packed in, plus the fascimile of the title page where Granz was announcing his limited edition (as well as fetching black and white photographs on every other page). Is the music, then, worthy of such care? Largely, yes. Granz couldn't persuade those artists tied into other exclusive contracts to record for him, so there is no Armstrong, Goodman, Fitzgerald, Gillespie or Holiday here, just for starters, but the array of talent is awesome, and it was generous of Ellington to give over his sessions to that most ubiquitous of Ellington heroes, Harry Carney. Most of the material on the first CD has been available at one time or another on CD, and all of it on LP, but the whole of the second disc makes its debut on CD, with much of it never being heard since the day of its recording. This includes three piano solos by Billy Strayhorn, some varied material with Hawkins, and some sterling Willie Smith workouts.

This release will either appeal to you immensely or leave you utterly cold. It's of historical significance, and it is also a beautiful artefact. You pays your money... **KS**

Kansas City **Joe Turner** (v); **Buck Clayton**, **Jimmy Nottingham**, **Joe Newman** (t); **Lawrence Brown**, **Vic Dickenson** (tb); **Herbie Hall** (cl); **Buster Smith**, **Pete Brown** (as); **Buddy Tate**, **Coleman Hawkins**, **Paul Quinichette**, **Hal Singer**, **Seldon Powell** (ts); **Jay McShann** (p, v); **Pete Johnson**, **Al Williams** (p); **T-Bone Walker** (g, v); **Freddie Green**, **John Scofield**, **Danny Barker**, **Jim Hall** (g); **Milt Hinton**, **Gene Ramey**, **Walter Page**, **Doug Watkins** (b); **Cliff Leeman**, **Jackie Williams**, **Charlie Persip** (d). Atlantic 781701-2 (51 minutes). Recorded 1956-77.

⑧ ❽

This vibrant collection of Kansas City jazz has some great moments, but one is reluctant to recommend it as a substitute for the complete albums from which these tracks are drawn. Joe Turner's **Boss of The Blues** album, for instance, from whence come *You're Driving Me Crazy* and *Piney Brown Blues,* is an ultimate classic which has recently been reissued on CD. Ignoring that, *The Lamp Is Low* by Vic Dickenson contains one of Buck Clayton's best trumpet solos, to say nothing of shaggy dog trombone from the leader and good piano from the obscure Al Williams. Buster Smith is a most interesting curiosity. Charlie Parker cited Smith as his first influence during his youth in Kansas City, and indeed one can hear pre-echoes of Parker in Smith's playing in Smith's recordings done in the thirties. They persist on the two tracks of his from 1959, both simple riff tunes. McShann is in good form, although the electric piano which he plays here didn't suit him, but it did complement the early plangent blues guitar of a very young John Scofield. Joe Turner and Pete Johnson may perhaps be regarded as the soul of Kansas City, and great singing and piano abounds in the closing *Piney Brown Blues*, supported by a rocking ensemble scored by Ernie Wilkins. Good solos from Frank Wess, Pete Brown and Lawrence Brown complete a mighty extract from a mighty session. **SV**

Mucho Calor **Conte Candoli** (t); **Art Pepper** (as); **Bill Perkins** (ts); **Russ Freeman** (p); **Ben Tucker** (b); **Chuck Flores** (d); **Jack Costanza**, **Mike Pacheco** (perc). V.S.O.P. Ⓕ #47CD (45 minutes). Recorded 1958.

⑥ ❻

On the face of it this album could have been a great one. A glance at the personnel shows some of the finest individual voices in West Coast jazz. Add the fact that most of the arrangements are by Bill Holman and others are from Benny Carter, Johnny Mandel, Candoli and Pepper and the omens are good. The problem is in the obligation to latin rhythms. Gillespie created the fashion and in the fifties it almost became an obsession. Ironically, perhaps the sophistication of Holman's writing is partly to blame – Shorty Rogers's more rugged way was far more successful with matters south of the border. Some of Holman's originals are brilliant, notably *Vaya Hombre Vaya*, where the horns and piano triumph over bongos and the bass and drums come through. The voicing of themes like Porter's *I Love You* is typically silky. Mandel has written the bongos out of his *Pernod*, and everybody sounds the better for it.

Pepper's alto fizzes and broils as ever, and Candoli is powerful and incisive, but both are often swamped by clattering. The great individuality of Russ Freeman manages to triumph over his section chores, but it is rarely possible to detect that Chuck Flores is one of the greatest drummers from the Coast. On the other hand, in the unlikely event that the listener prefers bongo rhythms to fine jazz solos, then this is for him. **SV**

Music Of George And Ira Gershwin Featuring: **Billy May, Bud Shank, Bob Cooper, Chet Baker, Frank Rosolino, Julie London, Thelonious Monk, Bill Evans and Bob Brookmeyer, Hank Jones, Bill Potts, Louis Smith, Lee Morgan, Nat King Cole, Coleman Hawkins, John Lewis, Nancy Wilson, Ike Quebec, Art Pepper**. Blue Note Ⓜ 7 80706 (71 minutes). Recorded 1945-69.

✔ ⑧ ❾

It would be hard to go wrong with Gershwin's music and, apart from a frivolous pastiche of *Rhapsody In Blue* by Billy May, this selection by Blue Note from various labels is of the highest standard. Contrasts abound with some piquant rareities like *I Got Rhythm* played as a piano duet between Bill Evans and Bob Brookmeyer (piano was Brookmeyer's first instrument and his prodigious talents on the instrument have been overlooked in favour of his valve trombone work). Bob Cooper's Octet contribute a vital *Strike Up The Band* which, like so many of these tracks, makes one yearn for the original session in its entirety. Tracks by Rosolino, Pepper and Quebec are good representations of their various talents and the three 'pop' vocals by London, Cole and Wilson are welcome examples of their craft. This is a most useful collection for the jazz tyro with the five tracks of West Coast jazz being balanced by some sterling work from the East, including such delights as the clarion trumpet of Lee Morgan sitting on a mattress of organ from Jimmy Smith on *'S Wonderful* and a mouth watering taste of the Bill Potts band playing *I Got Plenty of Nuttin'*. **SV**

The New New Orleans Music: Jump Jazz **Ed Frank Quintet**: Frank (p); Wendell Brunious (t); Fred Kemp (ts); Erving Charles (b); Joseph 'Smokey' Johnson (d). **Ramsey McLean & the Survivors**: McLean (b, elb, p, perc, v); Charles Neville (ss, as, perc, v); Reggie Houston (ts, perc, v); Steve Masakowski (g, keytor, syn); Herlin Riley (d, perc, v); Charmaine Neville (v, perc). Rounder Ⓕ CD 2065 (43 minutes). Recorded 1985-6.

⑤ ❻

The music on this CD is not the New Orleans-style jazz provided for tourists. This is the jazz of the mid-eighties, as found in bona fide jazz clubs in the city and answerable to nobody in terms of style. The Frank Quintet is a hard bop unit with a generous input of local idiosyncrasies. Brunious wears his bebop hat with pride and there are compatible solos by Kemp and the leader. A little of the area's blues flavour permeates *A Corn For Crip* where boppish solos coalesce with the juke joint rhythm's of Fats Domino's drummer Johnson without a trace of incongruity. The McLean sextet are not a typical New Orleans funk band; they team Wynton Marsalis drummer Riley with one of the Neville Brothers and thus ensure that they are impossible to categorise. *Rock Number Nine* raps out like Crescent City Sun Ra, *Drink Jax Beer* takes the listener back to the fifties world of jump blues, while *Up Up Up* has a taste of the Caribbean. *Still (There's a Mingus Among Us)* mixes gentle bop, earthy blues and torch singing and *Tall Order* rounds out a programme with a good-natured but freer excursion. All of it is music for the people, and it doesn't await critical accolades. **BMcR**

New Orleans **The Eureka Brass Band** and the bands of **Paul Barbarin, George Lewis, Jim Robinson, Wilbur de Paris, Turk Murphy, Punch Miller, De De Pierce** with, among others, **Ernie Cagnolatti, Sidney De Paris, John Brunious** (t); **Louis Cottrell Jr., Willie Humphrey, Omer Simeon** (cl). Atlantic Ⓜ 781700-2 (51 minutes). Recorded 1951-71.

⑥ ❻

This CD looks at the Atlantic label's vision of the New Orleans Revival. Only Murphy's mechanical *Maple Leaf Rag* was not produced by Ahmet or Nesuhi Ertegun, and it is the poorest item on show. For the remainder, Atlantic takes jazz from the consummate musicianship of the Wilbur De Paris band to the honest toil of De De Pierce. Acceptable musical standards are expected and delivered. Cagnoletti and Cottrell bring coherence to the primitive Jim Robinson band, Lewis makes his mark with the poignant *Burgundy Street Blues* clarinet solo and the Eurekas joyfully capture the marching gait of their home city. Despite the dreadful vocal by wife Billie, De De Pierce produces an unambitious but well controlled ensemble performance of *Shake It And Break It*. Trumpeter Miller shows his in-depth instrumental skill on *Tiger Rag* and the Paul Barbarin band uses its fine rhythm section and the articulate solos of Brunious and Humphrey to illuminate the likes of *Sing On*. Simeon, magnificent on Wilbur De Paris' *Shreveport Stomp*, and Sidney De Paris are the undoubted stars in a band which helps Atlantic prove that authenticity does not mean incompetence. **BMcR**

New Thing At Newport **John Coltrane Quartet**: **Coltrane** (ts, ss); **McCoy Tyner** (p); **Jimmy Garrison** (b); **Elvin Jones** (d). **Archie Shepp Quartet**: **Shepp** (ts, v); **Bobby Hutcherson** (vb); **Barre Phillips** (b); **Joe Chambers** (d). Impulse! Ⓜ GRP 11052 (60 minutes). Recorded 1965.

✔ ⑦ ❼

Anything dubbed 'New Thing' will, by its very nature, rapidly become the old thing. In 1965 the second generation of free form players were emerging and Coltrane was taking an earnest change of direction. He was introducing elements of post-Ornette Coleman tonality and solo construction into a musical structure that, for all its emotional intensity, was governed by somewhat different rules. His work with Pharoah Sanders was still in the future, but on *One Down, One Up*, Coltrane gives evidence that the change had begun. *My Favorite Things* even anticipates the rift between himself and Jones, as the drummer seems intent on eliciting a now unlooked-for response from Coltrane. By comparison, the Shepp performance is more integrated. *Skag* , a poem of Shepp's read by the author, is dispensible for aesthetic rather than racial reasons, but for the remainder Shepp pursues his more usual concert goals. *Gingerbread Boy* has him at his swaggeringly authoritative best while *Call Me By My Rightful Name* transports him from almost Johnny Hodges-like lyricism to agonised cries de coeur. *Le Matin Des Noires* draws from him the concert's most adventurously free solo as well as the most successful interface between Hutcherson and Phillips. The conclusion must be that, if only at this stage, Shepp was more comfortable with the new order being suggested by the 'New Thing'. **BMcR**

New York Horns, 1924-1928 **Texas Blues Destroyers**, **Kansas City Five**, **Six Black Diamonds**, **Blue Rhythm Orchestra**, **Gulf Coast Seven**, **Five Musical Blackbirds**, **Te Roy Williams & His Orchestra** featuring among others **Bubber Miley**, **Thomas Morris**, **Louis Metcalf**, **June Clark** (t); **Rex Stewart** (c); **Jimmy Harrison** (tb). Hot 'n' Sweet Ⓜ 151022 (73 minutes). Recorded 1924-28.

✔ ⑧ ❻

In a jazz world which had become dominated by New Orleans players, the musicians featured on this CD had tended to take a back seat. As these performances show, there was no need for such self-effacement, and in fact some of them were about to embark on new careers. Miley is an already mature player on the Destroyers' sides, muted on one version of *Down In The Mouth Blues* and open on the other. Both show the preaching element, as well as the rubato that was to distinguish his later work with Ellington. Metcalf is the broad-toned blues master, whose solos speak of warm-toned authority rather than in-depth improvisation. Not much is heard from Clark the soloist, but his fierce tone and fine ensemble leads are prominent on *Hold 'Er Deacon* and *Keep Your Temper*. Thomas is another fine leader, although in his case, short solo statements on *Hot Coffee* and *Black Horse Stomp* offer greater promise in the way of melody paraphrasing. Ed Allen was originally thought to be Te Roy Williams' cornettist, but it is Stewart in excellent form and producing superb muted work on *Lindbergh Hop* who makes his mark. The immaculate Harrison carries the day on trombone. Showing impressive coherence and invention for 1925, he fashions his first *Santa Claus Blues* theme statement into a solo on the second take, and produces solos of real quality on both editions of *Keep Your Temper*. **BMcR**

The Red Norvo Sessions On Dial: All Existing Takes **Norvo** (vb); **Dizzy Gillespie** (t); **Charlie Parker** (as); **Flip Phillips** (ts); **Teddy Wilson** (p); **Slam Stewart** (b); **Specs Powell**, **J.C. Heard** (d). Spotlite Ⓜ SPJ-(CD) 127 (44 minutes). Recorded 1945.

⑩ ❼

This is the session that gives the lie to the stipulation that good jazz comes from careful planning and rehearsal. Norvo, Wilson and Stewart were with Goodman at this time, Flip Phillips was briefly in New York with Woody Herman while Dizzy Gillespie and Charlie Parker were co-leaders of the first bop group at the *Three Deuces* and had been playing there until 4 a.m. The recording date commenced five hours later with no rehearsal, a most unusual situation for Norvo, one of the most professional and experienced of men. Yet it was a success in the sense that the mixing of styles actually brought out the very best in everyone. A large measure of the credit must go to Norvo, who chose the personnel and signalled his willingness to come to terms with the wild music being produced by Parker and Gillespie. The CD is made up of all the surviving takes, including two breakdowns on the final *Congo Blues*; Parker is in magnificent form, especially so on *Slam Slam Blues* where his improvised choruses showed just what could be achieved with the basic tonic, subdominant and dominant chords underpinning the 12 bars. Here is a clear indication of the way forward, throwing open wide the doors of perception. But all the players are superb not just in their own solos but in the manner in which they come to terms with each other's styles. If ever there was one recording date which marked the turning point between swing and bebop, this is it. Highly recommended. **AM**

Charlie Parker & The Stars Of Modern Jazz At Carnegie Hall, Christmas 1949 **Miles Davis**, **Red Rodney** (t); **Charlie Parker**, **Lee Konitz**, **Sonny Stitt** (as); **Kai Winding**, **Benny Green** (tb); **Stan Getz**, **Warne Marsh** (ts); **Serge Chaloff** (bs); **Bud Powell**, **Al Haig**, **Lennie Tristano**, **Jimmy Jones** (p); **Curley Russell**, **Tommy Potter** (b); **Max Roach**, **Roy Haynes** (d); **Sarah Vaughan** (v). Jass Records Ⓕ J-CD-16 (75 minutes). Recorded 1949.

⑧ ❽

This album collects together some of the greatest be-bop musicians at the height of their often brief careers. Concert recordings which survive from this period were usually badly recorded and often deteriorated in subsequent years. This album is unique in that its component parts, drawn from various sources, are better than average and that someone has subsequently done a good job in restoring the sound. Parker's quintet closes the concert with a 25 minute set which has the giant on top form, with Al Haig nicely recorded in support.

Getz and Winding used Parker's rhythm section for their two numbers, one of which is a fast version of Getz's *Long Island Sound* variation on *Zing! Went The Strings Of My Heart*. Bud Powell opens the concert with a turbulent *All God's Children Got Rhythm*. His trio then backs Davis, Stitt, Green and Chaloff in a jam session. At this stage of his career Davis was playing with great power and making more use of the upper register than he was to do later. His work here sounds fresh and urgent.

After a couple of poised ballads from Vaughan, the Tristano Sextet, similar to the group which had recorded for Capitol, applied the pianist's method to an austere *You Go To My Head*. On *Sax Of A Kind* Konitz and Marsh took solos which were as good as any in the concert. The uncredited guitar here would probably have been Billy Bauer. **SV**

Post Bop Featuring: **George Russell Smalltet**: Art Farmer [t]; Don Butterfield][ba]; Gigi Gryce [as]; J.R.Monterose [ts]; George Barrow [bs]; Mal Waldron [p]; Jimmy Raney [g]; Teddy Kotick [b]; Joe Harris [d]; **Russell** [arr]); **Lee Konitz-Warne Marsh** (Konitz [as], Marsh [ts], Billy Bauer [g], Oscar Pettiford [b], Kenny Clarke [d]) ; **Sonny Rollins With The MJQ** (Rollins [ts], John Lewis [p], Milt Jackson [vib], Percy Heath [b], Connie Kay [d]); **The Jazz Modes** (Julius Watkins [frh], Charlie Rouse [ts], Sahib Shihab [bs], Gildo Mahones [p], Martin Rivera [b], Jimmy Wormworth [d]; **John Coltrane Quartet** (Coltrane [ts], Tommy Flanagan [p], Paul Chambers [b], Art Taylor [d]); **Slide Hampton Octet** (Hampton [tb, arr], Freddie Hubbard, Bob Zottola, Richard Williams [t], Bernard McKinney (euph], Bill Barber [tba], George Coleman [ts], Jay Cameron [bs], Nabil Totah [b], Pete LaRoca [d]); **Von Freeman Quartet** (Freeman [ts], John Young [p], Sam Jones [b], Jimmy Cobb [d]); **Freddie Hubbard Quintet** (Hubbard [t], Lew Tabackin [ts], Joanne Brackeen [p], Eddie Gomez [b], Roy Haynes [d], Hector Andrade [perc]); **Gil Evans Orchestra** (Evans [p, arr] and big band featuring Howard Johnson [tba], Ted Dunbar [g], Herb Buschler [b]). Atlantic Jazz Ⓜ 781 705-2 (51 minutes). Recorded 1955-83.

⑧ ❽

Atlantic have cast their net wide under the generic heading of 'Post Bop'. The earliest track here, the beautiful Konitz-Marsh duet version of *I Can't Get Started*, was recorded just three months after the death of Charlie Parker in 1955, while the feature for Freddie Hubbard's flügelhorn on the tune *Misty* dates from 1983, and is cast in a very similar vein. The most adventurous track is the opening *Lydian M-1*, a George Russell composition and arrangement using his Lydian Chromatic Concept of Tonal Organization, which encourages improvisers to convert chord symbols into scales and to use those scales to imply the sound of the chords. Teddy Charles, Jimmy Raney and Monterose cope adequately with Russell's wishes. Sonny Rollins's muscular tenor adds fire to the MJQ in a live performance of *Bags' Groove*, while the Slide Hampton Octet is crisp and brassy on the leader's *Sister Salvation*. Coltrane roams freely up and down the cyclic chord progression of *Giant Steps*, arguably the most significant piece of music making here, while Gil Evans handles his rich-sounding ensemble with skill and warmth on *Thoroughbred*, taken from the important Atlantic album **Svengali**. By comparison Von Freeman's *White Sand* is pedestrian, but the Jazz Modes feature an unusual blend of instruments on their blues track. **AM**

Prestige First Sessions, Vol 1. Featuring: **Fats Navarro** (t); **Don Lanphere** (ts); **Leo Parker** (bs); **Al Haig**, **Duke Jordan** (p); **Tommy Potter**, **Oscar Pettiford**, **Tubby Phillips** (b); **Max Roach**, **Roy Haynes**, **Jack 'The Bear' Parker**, **Roy Hall** (d). Prestige Ⓜ PCD-24114-2 (70 minutes). Recorded 1949-50.

✔ ⑧ ❽

These Prestige recordings abound with good creative playing, notably from Navarro, Lanphere and Haig, and must be regarded as an adjunct to the 1949 Davis sessions in the move away from the basic Gillespie-Parker bebop era. Within a few months of his recordings with Don Lanphere's Quintet, Fats Navarro was dead at 27. Fortunately he recorded often, although a third of his legacy is in radio broadcasts, often poorly recorded. The nine studio tracks included here are amongst his best, and his fluent, Parker-inspired trumpet offèrs an alternative voice to Gillespie's. In Lanphere's company he displays both his hurtling mode and his gentle ballad style. Navarro was gentler and more thoughtful than the flamboyant Gillespie, while Lanphere was (and is) a quite outstanding tenor player to be classed with Getz, Sims and Cohn, although he was probably more inventive than any of the others at this time. The presence of Al Haig makes this a jazz super group. One of the finest of all jazz pianists, Haig is present on 19 of the 21 tracks including four with his fine trio, and this album holds some of his best ever playing. On the face of it, Leo Parker, often a vulgarian, would be a misfit here, but although not up to the company, he plays better than usual by his own terms. Good digital renovation of the sound allows some fine bass playing, notably from Tommy Potter, to surge through. **SV**

Prestige First Sessions, Vol 3 Featuring: **Eddie 'Lockjaw' Davis**; **Dizzy Gillespie Sextet**; **Red Rodney Quintet**; **Bennie Green & His Band**. Prestige Ⓜ PCD 24116-2 (52 minutes). Recorded 1950-51.

⑥ ❻

All of these artists appear elsewhere in the guide under their own names (and **First Sessions, Vol 2** is wholly dedicated to Sonny Stitt), but this collection encapsulates a period quite neatly, and shows a new light on the players themselves. The four sides featuring Lockjaw Davis are with a small group boasting the talents of Wynton Kelly and Al Casey, but Lockjaw dominates, and plays some pretty rude, crude and fiery 'jump' tenor which is dangerously close to r&b honking and hints little at the accomplished player he was to become. The Gillespie tracks, equivalent to two 78rpm singles, have him fronting an interesting small group (Jimmy Heath on alto, Milt Jackson on vibes) and he plays well, but the material, apart from *Nice Work if You Can Get it*, is rather basic, and not to be taken too seriously. Red Rodney has a much more sober approach, and his band here turns in some quintessential bop performances, with the dual shadows of Miles Davis and Fats Navarro looming long over the music. Finally, there is a return to the jump style favoured at the outset by Lockjaw, and he crops up as one of two tenors on these two 78 sides. The other tenor player is the legendary Big Nick Nicholas, who solos solidly, while on Te*nor Sax Shuffle* those doyens of bop small groups, Tommy Potter and Art Blakey, contribute the primitive shuffle back-beat. Nothing improves on the other track, *Sugar Syrup*. **KS**

Small Group Swing Two tracks each by the following: **Chick Webb & His Little Chicks; Louis Jordan & His Tympany Five; The Spencer Trio; Artie Shaw & His Gramercy Five; Stuff Smith & His Onyx Club Boys; Bunny Berigan & His Blue Boys; Bud Freeman Trio; Joe Venuti's Blue Four; Adrian Rollini Quintet; Kansas City Six; Harry James & The Boogie Woogie Trio; Art Tatum & His Swingsters; Cleo Brown; Fats Waller & His Buddies; New Orleans Rhythm Kings; Johnny Dodds & His Chicago Boys; Benny Goodman Trio; Tommy Dorsey & His Clambake Seven.** Past Perfect Ⓜ PPCD 78102 (65 minutes). Recorded 1929-40.

⑧ ❽

This CD creams off some of the most enjoyable tracks by mostly pre-war small groups, some drawn from the ranks of the big bands (Chick Webb, Artie Shaw, Dorsey), others put together in the studios just for one session (Bunny Berigan, the New Orleans Rhythm Kings, Kansas City Six, etc.). But the overall results are the same; unforgettable invention, swing and sheer unbridled joy all achieved within a playing time of three minutes. The selection contains some pleasant surprises such as the two titles by the Spencer Trio (actually a small group drawn from another small group, in this case the John Kirby band) and the Rollini title with its fine Bobby Hackett solo. Wayman Carver takes some of the earliest jazz flute solos on the Chick Webb tracks and, in the same vein, Johnny Guarnieri adds a fresh sound to the Gramercy Five titles with his harpsichord playing. In fact variety is the name of the game here and the unexpected is never far away. Johnny Dodds makes one of his last appearances on record with *29th And Dearborn* sensitively supported by the trumpet of Charlie Shavers. Using the CEDAR system with considerable intelligence and expertise Past Perfect have come up with a very clean set of transfers which will have the widest appeal to all but those who want the original surface noises, clicks and pops. **AM**

Soul Featuring: **Shirley Scott** (org) with **Stanley Turrentine, Eric Gale, Specs Powell; Johnny Griffin** (ts) with **John Patton** (org); **Aaron Bell** (b); **Art Taylor** (d); **Ray Charles** (as, p) with **Milt Jackson** (vb, p); **Billy Mitchell** (ts); **Skeeter Best** (g); **Oscar Pettiford** (b); **Connie Kay** (d); **Herbie Mann** (f) with **Hagood Hardy** (vb); **Ahmad Abdul-Malik, Ben Hardy** (b); **Rudy Collins** (d); **Ray Mantilla, Chief Bey** (perc); **Yusef Lateef** (ts) with **Thad Jones, Jimmy Owens, Snooky Young** (t); **Hugh Lawson** (p); **Eric Gale** (g); **Cecil McBee** (b); **Chuck Rainey** (elb); **Bernard Purdie** (d); **Eddie Harris** (ts); **Jodie Christian** (p); **Melvin Jackson** (b); **Richard Smith** (d); **Les McCann** (v, p) with **Leroy Vinnegar** (b); **Donald Dean** (d) and string section; **Les McCann** (v, p) with **Eddie Harris** (ts); **Benny Bailey** (t); **Leroy Vinnegar** (b); **Donald Dean** (d); **Hank Crawford** (as) with **Richard Tee** (p, elp); **Eric Gale, Cornell Dupree** (g); **Chuck Rainey, Ron Carter** (elb); **Bernard Purdie** (d); **Nat Adderley** with **Ernie Royal** (t); **Seldon Powell** (ts); **Joe Zawinul** (p); **Sam Jones** (b); **Bruno Carr** (d); **Joe Zawinul** with **Clifford Jordan** (ts); **Bob Cranshaw** (b); **Roy McCurdy** (d). Atlantic Jazz Ⓜ 781708-2 (73 minutes). Recorded 1957-70.

⑧ ❻

As one-label collections go, this would be hard to beat in defining soul jazz. Of course, there's no Jimmy Smith, Horace Silver, Three Sounds or Willis Jackson, but then they never recorded for Atlantic. What is here, though, is an excellent cross section, from the Ray Charles/Milt Jackson selection which perhaps comes closer to blues than soul, on up to seminal pieces such as Herbie Mann's hugely popular but subsequently ignored *Comin' Home Baby*, Nat Adderley's *Jive Samba* (not the original, but a goodie anyway) and Zawinul's *Money In The Pocket* (Zawinul was crucial to the Adderley's continuing commercial success in the late sixties). There is not a poor track here, and a glance at the producers' credits tells you why: both Ed Michel and Bob Porter know this territory like the backs of their hands. So—a message to all those hipsters out there: forget Blue Note for just one moment, and take a long drink at this new bottle with some vintage wine inside. **KS**

Very Saxy . **Eddie 'Lockjaw' Davis, Coleman Hawkins, Arnett Cobb, Buddy Tate** (ts); **Shirley Scott** (org); **George Duvivier** (b); **Arthur Edgehill** (d). Prestige Ⓜ OJCCD 458-2 (39 minutes). Recorded 1959.

⑦ ❼

What an outrageous idea! Four roaring tenor saxophones, any one of whom would normally be enough to bring the house down, and all of whom would never shy away from a musical scrap. The resultant playing pulls no punches. On the opener, *Very Saxy* (a re-worked *Sweet Georgia Brown*), each tenorist doesn't wait to groove himself—they're straight in with a rasp and a flurry as if to announce their arrival. Surprisingly, Cobb takes the longest to begin the low-flying approach to sax playing, pacing himself with light, skilful phrases for the first verse before plunging in with a few choice wails.

The format doesn't change a great deal, and the style is very much the old (ie pre-Ornette) idea of mainstream—which means a minimum of bop inflections. This makes it an album which is not wildly fashionable at present, but to overlook this disc is to miss out on some truly exciting and enjoyable jousting between four true greats of the tenor sax. There is only one shuffle-rhythm track (for which we should probably be grateful), so the style is some distance away from r&b (their *Lester Leaps In* is more JATP than Big Jay McNeely), but the pace rarely slackens, and the playing is never less than committed. Those who listen closely will also find a truly impressive range of improvisational facilities being exercised by these four greats. The backing group is adequate for the task and keeps it all moving along nicely. **KS**

Voices of Cool, Vols 1 and 2 Singers including **Bobby Darin**, **Chris Connor**, **Bobby Scott**, **Lurlean Hunter**, **Diahann Carroll**, **Ann Richards**, **Mel Tormé**, **Nancy Harrow**, **Betty Carter**, **Mose Allison**, **Carmen McRae**, **Austin Cromer**, **Aretha Franklin**, **Jimmy Scott**, **The Manhattan Transfer**, **Bobby McFerrin**, **Jane Harvey**, **Maxine Sullivan**, **Sarah Vaughan**, **Ginnie Powell**, **Earl Coleman**, **Ruth Brown**, **Roy Kral-Jakie Cain**, **Sylvia Syms**, **Bobby Short**, **Mabel Mercer**, **Betty Bennett**, **Al Hibbler**, **Joe Turner**, **Ray Charles**, **Jimmy Witherspoon**, **Joe Mooney**, **Carol Stevens**, **Frances Wayne**, **Jackie Paris**, **LaVern Baker** and **Helen Merrill** accompanied by various small groups and big bands. Rhino/Atlantic Ⓜ 271748/784-2 (two discs, oas: 60, 63 minutes). Recorded 1947-85.

⑧ ❼

If you are just starting out on the jazz trail and want investigate just what was going on in jazz vocals in the twenty years after the end of the war, then these two discswill certainly put you on the right track, with a couple of rather large caveats. The biggest is the absence of Ella Fitzgerald, Billie Holiday and Louis Armstrong, probably the three greatest jazz singers of this period. The second problem is that a lot of the singers here are only featured artists with other bands, or are not at their best on the selections here. But that is the way with one-label compilations: there are bound to be rather alarming gaps. However, what is included is very much worth having, and the presence of Maxine Sullivan, Mabel Mercer, Chris Connor and Frances Wayne in particular is useful, considering the relative dearth of their work on CDs, and the total absence of their complete Atlantic albums from CD. Two good cross-sections, then, and very sensibly annotated as well. **KS**

Weird Nightmare - Meditations on Mingus Collective Personnel: **Art Baron** (tb, tba, wood f, bass recorder, didgeridu); **Bob Stewart** (tba); **Henry Threadgill** (f); **Don Byron** (cl); **Geri Allen** (p); **Bill Frisell**, **Gary Lucas**, **Vernon Reid** (g); **Barry Mitterhoff** (g, mand); **Kenny Kosek** (vn); **Howard Levy** (hca); **Marc Ribot**, **Tony Trischka** (bj); **Greg Cohen**, (b); **Michael Blair** (d, perc); **Don Alias**, **Sue Evans**, **Bobby Previte** (perc); **Elvis Costello**, **Robbie Robertson**, **Henry Rollins**, **Hubert Selby Jnr**, **Diamanda Galas**, **Ray Davies**, **Dr John**, **Chuck D**, **Bernard Fowler** (v) On all but two tracks add the following on various Harry Partch-originated instruments: **Michael Blair**, **Francis Thumm**, **Bill Frisell**, **Art Baron**, **Don Alias**, **Greg Cohen**, **Vernon Reid**, **Geri Allen**, **Marc Ribot**. On two tracks add: **The Uptown Horns** (t, saxes); **Charlie Watts** (d). On one track add: **Bobby Keyes** (ts); **Chuck Leavell** (p); **Keith Richards** (g, v); **Michael Blair**, **Henry Threadgill**, **Greg Cohen**, **Vernon Reid**, **Bill Frisell**, **The Uptown Horns**, **Bobby Previte** (arr); Project overseen by **Hal Willner**. Columbia Ⓕ 472467-2 (74 minutes). Recorded 1992.

⑧ ❽

Re-interpreting Mingus has become almost as obligatory for an artist in recent years as adding a Monk composition to the latest album. But the successful attempts to do something new and exciting and musically successful with Mingus's compositions which Mingus himself hadn't already done can be counted on one hand, and then there would still be a few fingers left over.

Mercifully, this album uses up another finger in that count. Willner has a track record for this sort of thing, having put together all-star interdisciplinary casts for tributes to past greats as stylistically wide apart as Thelonious Monk and Walt Disney musicals. The miracle of this album is that the inquiring and revolutionary spirit of Mingus is evoked without the need for any sort of slavish stylistic adherence. These musicians really do breathe new life into the concepts behind Mingus's compositional notes. So weird things happen constantly, and the use of Harry Partch's custom-made glass instruments aid and abett such weirdness. Readings from Mingus texts and vocalisations of Mingus lyrics are always to the point and help develop the wider picture. The oblique approach taken here means that no-one is in any musical sense standing in dead mens' shoes. No-one is attempting to duplicate that incomparable rhythm team of Mingus and Richmond; no-one precisely evokes the unique sounds of Dolphy, McLean, Knepper or Shafi Hadi in the classic Mingus groups. Each track goes to the core of meaning which each Mingus title contains, and casts entirely new light upon it. For example, when was the last time one heard a guitar and clarinet at the core of an intense and moving interpretation of, say, *Reincarnation of a Lovebird?* For reasons such as that, this is a stimulating and important release which should be heard by anyone worried about the ability of jazz to keep adapting and evolving afresh in each new decade. **KS**

West Coast One track by each of the following: **Eddie Safranski's Poll Cats**: Safranski [b], Ray Wetzel [t], Eddie Bert [tb], Art Pepper [as], Bob Cooper [ts], Pete Rugolo [p], Shelly Manne [d]); **Jack Montrose Quintet**: Montrose [ts], Bob Gordon [bs], Paul Moer [p], Red Mitchell [b], Shelly Manne [d]); **West Coast Wailers**: Conte Candoli [t], Bill Holman [ts], Lou Levy [p], Leroy Vinnegar [b], Lawrence Marable [d]); **Red Mitchell-Harold Land Quintet**: Mitchell [b], Land [ts], Carmell Jones [t], Frank Strazzeri [p], Leon Petties [d]); **Shelly Manne And His Men**: Manne [d], Conte Candoli [t], Frank Strozier [as], Russ Freeman [p], Monte Budwig [b]); **Jimmy Giuffre Trio**: Giuffre [ts], Ralph Peña [b], Jim Hall [g]); **Jimmy Giuffre Trio**: Giuffre [cl], Bob Brookmeyer [vtb], Jim Hall [g]); 2 tracks by **Shorty Rogers And His Giants**: Rogers [t], Jimmy Giuffre [ts], Pete Jolly [p], Curtis Counce [b], Shelly Manne [d]). Atlantic Jazz Ⓜ 781703-2 (56 minutes). Recorded 1947-1966.

⑧ ❽

The New York-based Atlantic label came to West Coast jazz comparatively late, although the first title here, made in 1947 right at the beginning of Atlantic's history, happens by coincidence to feature three significant West Coast figures in the persons of Art Pepper, Shelly Manne and Bob Cooper. All seven men on *Sa-Frantic* were with the Stan Kenton band at the time and the corny Leonard Feather tune has the white, 'reboppy' sound of the day. The meat of the collection here is the two excellent titles by Shorty Rogers' Giants, the splendid *Paradox* on which Jack Montrose and the late Bob Gordon make entrancing music and the virile quintets headed by Manne, Mitchell-Land and the so-called West Coast Wailers. The two pieces by two different Jimmy Guiffre Trios are excellent but are hardly West Coast (one of the tracks was actually made in New York). Yet Giuffre himself made important contributions to Californian jazz in the early fifties (apart from Boots Brown), and his unique clarinet sound is intriguing on both *Topsy* (with his own trio) and the surprisingly Basie-like *Martians Go Home* by Rogers, a track which has some beautifully recorded and musical drumming by Manne. Carmell Jones adds a flavour of Clifford Brown on the Mitchell-Land *Triplin' Awhile* and the CD is blessed with some memorable piano work from Jolly, Levy, Strazzeri and Freeman. A useful introduction to a most interesting phase of jazz development. **AM**

West Coast Jive **Wynonie Harris with Illinois Jacquet All-Stars; Jack McVea All-Stars; Johnnie Alston and His All-Stars; Duke Henderson with Lucky Thompson All-Stars; Shelly Henry's All-Stars; Cee Pee Johnson & His Band; Al 'Stomp' Russell Trio; Frank Haywood with Monroe Tucker & His All-Stars**. Delmark Ⓕ DD-657 (53 minutes). Recorded 1945-46.

⑦ ❼

This Delmark reissue of top West Coast vocalists with various backing bands is all culled from the archives of the Apollo record company, which ceased recording in 1962 but, like Savoy on the East Coast, kept a substantial gospel catalogue in circulation after that date. The purpose of this CD is to demonstrate just how blurred the lines between different sub-genres were in the mid-forties. While the blues and their associated changes are at the root of every track here, the treatment varies considerably from track to track and from band to band. Hence one can have a r&b vocal from Cee Pee Johnson while the backing band, which includes Teddy Buckner and Buddy Banks, plays bop changes on the blues and evidences sophisticated arrangements. Even more straddled on the divide is Duke Henderson, who is a blues belter in the country tradition of Robert Johnson but whose backing band is the Lucky Thompson All-Stars, featuring both the leader's excellent tenor and the forward-looking piano of Wilbert Baranco. The bassist with this band is rumoured to be Charles Mingus, but his presence is confirmed on the track with Wynonie Harris which features Illinois Jacquet's band. A lively cocktail indeed from L.A. **KS**

Information

Manufacturers and distributors

Entries are listed as follows: **Manufacturer** or **Label** – UK Distributor

33 Records New Note
A&M PolyGram Record Operations
Ace Complete Record Company
ACT New Note
Affinity Charly
Ahum New Note
Amadeo PolyGram Record Operations
Antilles PolyGram Record Operations
Arabesque New Note
ASV Koch
Atlantic Warner Music
Avant Harmonia Mundi
B&W New Note
Babel Harmonia Mundi
Bellaphon New Note
Biograph Direct
Black & Blue Koch
Black Lion Koch
Black Saint Harmonia Mundi
Blue Moon New Note
Blue Note EMI
Bluebell Direct
Bluebird BMG
Calligraph New Note
Candid Koch
Capitol EMI
Caprice Complete Record Company
Castle BMG
CBS Sony Music Operations
CBS (France) Discovery Records
Channel Classics Select
Charly Charly
Chesky Complete Record Company
Chess New Note
Chief Cadillac
Chronoscope Harmonia Mundi
Classics Discovery
Claves Complete Record Company
CMP BMG
Columbia Sony Music Operations
Concord New Note
Conifer Conifer
Contemporary Complete Record Company
Cream New Note
Criss Cross Harmonia Mundi
CTI Sony Music Operations
Delmark Cadillac
Delos Conifer
Denon Conifer
DGG PolyGram Record Operations
Discovery Warner Music
DIW Harmonia Mundi
Dormouse BMG
Dreyfus New Note
DRG New Note
East West Warner Music
ECM New Note
Elektra Warner Music
EmArcy PolyGram Record Operations
EMI EMI
Enja New Note
Epic Sony Music Operations
Epicure Sony Music Operations
ESP ZYX
Europe 1 Koch
Evidence Harmonia Mundi
Fantasy Complete Record Company
Flapper Pinnacle
FMP Cadillac
Four Leaf Clover Cadillac
Freelance Harmonia Mundi
Fresh Sounds Charly
Fret New Note
Future Music Harmonia Mundi
Geffen BMG
Go Jazz New Note
Good Time Jazz Chris Wellard
Gramavision Vital
GRP New Note
HatART Harmonia Mundi
Hep New Note
Hot House Harmonia Mundi
Impulse! New Note
In & Out Vital
Intuition New Note
ITM Koch
Jass Direct
Jazz City New Note
Jazz House New Note
JMS New Note
JMT PolyGram Record Operations
JSP Chris Wellard
Jukebox Lil Chris Wellard
Justice Koch
Justin Time Harmonia Mundi
JVC New Note
King Koch
Konnex New Note
Label Bleu New Note
Landmark New Note
Largo Complete Record Company
Laserlight Target
leJazz Charly
Leo Impetus
Limelight PolyGram Record Operations
Linn PolyGram Record Operations
Living Era Koch
Living Music New Note
LRC New Note
Mastermix New Note
MCA BMG
Memoir Target
Mercury PolyGram Record Operations
Messidor Koch
Milan BMG
Milestone Complete Record Company
Minor Music Charly
Mode Harmonia Mundi
MoJazz PolyGram Record Operations
Mole Jazz Harmonia Mundi
MRC PolyGram Record Operations
Muse New Note
Music & Arts Harmonia Mundi
Musidisc Harmonia Mundi

Natasha Direct
New World Harmonia Mundi
Novus BMG
OJC Complete Record Company
Pablo Complete Record Company
Pacific EMI
Paddlewheel New Note
Philips PolyGram
Phontastic Chris Wellard
Polydor PolyGram Record Operations
PolyGram PolyGram Record Operations
Prestige Complete Record Company
QWest Warner Music
RCA BMG
Red Harmonia Mundi
Reservoir Cadillac
Riverside Complete Record Company
Roulette EMI
Rounder Direct
Rykodisc Vital
Sackville Cadillac
Savoy Conifer
Sonet PolyGram Record Operations
Soul Note Harmonia Mundi
Status Harmonia Mundi
Steeplechase Impetus
Strata East New Note
Sunnyside Pinnacle
Tall Poppies Complete Record Company
TCB New Note
Telarc Jazz Conifer
Three Line Whip New Note
Timeless New Note
Totem New Note
Triloka New Note
Vanguard Charly
VeraBra New Note
Verve PolyGram Record Operations
Virgin EMI
Vogue Pinnacle
Warners Warner Music
Watt New Note
World Circuit New Note
World Pacific EMI
Yazoo Koch

For additional information on Manufacturers and distributors, refer to the Label distribution directory published in *Gramophone*.

UK distributors' names and addresses

BMG UK
Lyng Lane, West Bromwich, West Midlands B70 7ST.
Telephone 0121-500 5545 **Fax** 0121-553 6880

Cadillac Distribution
61-71 Collier Street, London N1 9DF.
Telephone 0171-278 7391 **Fax** 0171-278 7394

Charly Records
156-166 Ilderton Road, London SE15 1NT.
Telephone 0171-639 8603 **Fax** 0171-639 2532

The Complete Record Company
12 Pepys Court, 84 The Chase, London SW4 0NF.
Telephone 0171-498 9666 **Fax** 0171- 498 1828

Conifer Records, Horton Road
West Drayton, Middlesex UB7 8JL.
Telephone 01895 447707 **Fax** 01895 420713

Direct Distribution
50 Stroud Green Road, London N4 3EF
Telephone 0171-281 3465 **Fax** 0171-281 5671

Discovery Records
The Old Church Mission Room, King's Corner, Pewsey, Wiltshire SN9 5BS.
Telephone 01672 63931 **Fax** 01672 63934

EMI Sales and Distribution Centre
Hermes Close, Tachbrook Park, Leamington Spa, Warwickshire CV34 6RP.
Telephone 01926 888888 **Fax** 0181-479 5992

Harmonia Mundi
19-21 Nile Street, London N1 7LL.
Telephone 0171-253 0863 **Fax** 0171-253 3237

Impetus Distribution
PO Box 1324, London W5 2ZU.
Telephone/Fax 0181-998 6411

Koch International
24 Concord Road, London W3 0TH.
Telephone 0181-992 7177 **Fax** 0181-896 0817

New Note
Unit 2, Orpington Trading Estate, Sevenoaks Way, St Mary Cray, Orpington Kent BR5 3SR.
Telephone 01689 877884 **Fax** 01689 877891

Pinnacle Records
Electron House, Cray Avenue, St Mary Cray, Orpington, Kent BR5 3RJ.
Telephone 016898 70622 **Fax** 016898 78269

PolyGram Record Operations
PO Box 36, Clyde Works, Grove Road, Romford, Essex RM6 4QR.
Telephone 0181-590 6044 **Fax** 0181-597 1011

Select Music and Video Distribution
34a Holmethorpe Avenue, Holmethorpe Estate, Redhill, Surrey RH1 2NN **Telephone** 01737 760020 **Fax** 01737 766316

Sony Music Operations
Rabans Lane, Aylesbury, Buckinghamshire HP19 3RT. **Telephone** 01296 395151 **Fax** 01296 81009

Target Records
23 Gardner Industrial Estate, Kent House Lane, Beckenham Lane, Kent BR3 1QZ.
Telephone 0181-778 4040 **Fax** 0181-676 9949

Vital Distribution
Portland House, 22-24 Portland Square, Bristol, Avon BS2 8RZ. **Telephone** 0117-944 6777 **Fax** 0117-944 6888

Warner Music (UK) Distribution
PO Box 59, Alperton Lane, Alperton, Middlesex HA0 1FJ. **Telephone** 0181-998 8844 **Fax** 0181-998 3429

Chris Wellard, Independent Record Sales
110 Eltham Hill, London SE9 5EF.
Telephone 0181-850 3161 **Fax** 0181-294 2129

ZYX Records UK
Trinity House, Heather Park Drive, Wembley, Middlesex HA0 1SX.
Telephone 0181-902 6398 **Fax** 0181-902 5896

Recommended specialist dealers

London

Les Aldrich Music Shop
98 Fortis Green Road, Muswell Hill, London N10 3BH. **Telephone** 0181-883 5631

Arcade Music
13-14 Grand Arcade, Tally-Ho Corner, Finchley, London N12 0EH. **Telephone** 0181-445 6369

James Asman
23a New Row, St Martins Lane, London WC2N 4LA. **Telephone** 0171-240 1380

Caruso & Co
10 Charlotte Place, London W1P 1AP. **Telephone** 0171-636 6622

The CD Shop
206 Field End Road, Eastcote, Pinner, Middlesex HA5 1RD. **Telephone** 0181-866 0017

Dillons the Bookstore
82 Gower Street, London WC1E 6EQ. **Telephone** 0171-636 1577

Farringdons Records
64-72 Leadenhall Market, London EC3V 1LT. **Telephone** 0171-623 9605

Farringdons Records
Royal Festival Hall, South Bank Centre, London SE1 8XX. **Telephone** 0171-620 0198

Grahams Hi-Fi
Canonbury Yard, 190a New North Road, Islington, London N1 7BS. **Telephone** 0171-226 5500

Harrods Sound and Vision
Harrods, Brompton Road, Knightsbridge, London SW1X 7XL. **Telephone** 0171-730 1234 ext. 2185

HMV
Unit Y11A, Brent Cross Shopping Centre, Brent Cross, London, NW4 3FG. **Telephone** 0181-201 5430

HMV
2 Waterglade Centre, Ealing Broadway, London W5 2ND. **Telephone** 0181-566 2590

HMV
150 Oxford Street, London W1N 0DJ. **Telephone** 0171-631 3423

HMV
363 Oxford Street, London W1R 2BJ. **Telephone** 0171-629 1240

HMV
70 George Street, Richmond, Surrey TW9 1HE. **Telephone** 0181-940 9880

HMV
Trocadero, 18 Coventry Street, London WC1V 7FD. **Telephone** 0171-439 0447

Honest Jon's Records
278 Portobello Road, London, W10 5TE. **Telephone** 0181-969 9822

Jazzwise Publications
2b Gleneagle Mews, London SW16 6AE. **Telephone** 0181- 769 7725

Mole Jazz
311 Grays Inn Road, London, WC1X 8PX. **Telephone** 0171-278 8623

Mr Bongo
Latin Record Centre, 9 Berwick Street, London W1. **Telephone** 0171-287 1887

Music and Video Club
344-348 Station Road, Harrow, Middlesex HA1 2DR. **Telephone** 0181-861 5344

Music and Video Club
119-121 Brent Street, Hendon, London NW4 2HH. **Telephone** 0181-203 9888

MDC Classic Music
1 Creed Lane, St Pauls, London EC4V 5BR. **Telephone** 0171-489 8077, Mail order 0171-236 0060

Rays Jazz Shop Ltd
180 Shaftesbury Avenue, London WC2. **Telephone** 0171-240 3969

WH Smith Ltd
Brent Cross Shopping Centre, Brent Cross, London NW4 3FB. **Telephone** 0181-202 4226

Templar Records
Leicester Square Bookstore Ltd, 9A Irving Street, London WC2H 7AT. **Telephone** 0171-930 3579

Tower Records
62-64 Kensington High Street, Kensington, London W8 4PL. **Telephone** 0171-938 3511

Tower Records
1 Piccadilly Circus, London W1R 8TR. **Telephone** 0171-439 2500

Tower Records
Unit 001B Whiteleys of Bayswater, Queensway, London W2 4YR. **Telephone** 0171-229 4550

Virgin Megastore
527 Oxford Street, London W1R 1DD. **Telephone** 0171-491 8582

Virgin Megastore
14-16 Oxford Street, London W1R 7DD. **Telephone** 0171-580 5822/0171-631 1234

South East

Abbey Music Store
7 Church Street, Romsey, Hampshire SO51 8BT. **Telephone** 01794 513149

Andys Records
53-54 High Street, Chelmsford, Essex CM1 1DH. **Telephone** 01245 344800

Andys Records
4 Longwyre Street, Colchester, Essex CO1 1LH. **Telephone** 01206 44334

Bastow's Classics
50a North Street, Chichester, West Sussex PO19 1MQ. **Telephone** 01243 533264

Blumlein's
9a Dragon Street, Petersfield, Hampshire GU31 4JN. **Telephone** 01730 266605

Brentwood Hi Fidelity Ltd
2 Ingrave Road, Brentwood, Essex CM15 8AT. **Telephone** 01277 221210

Camden Classics
5 Grosvenor Road, Tunbridge Wells, Kent TN1 2AH. **Telephone** 01892 515705

Camulo's Classics
49 Crouch Street, Colchester, Essex CO3 3EN. **Telephone** 01206 369310

Chew & Osborne
70 South Street, Bishop's Stortford, Hertfordshire CM23 3AZ. **Telephone** 01279 656401

Chew & Osborne
148 High Street, Epping, Essex CM16 4AG. **Telephone** 01992 574242

Chew & Osborne
26 King Street, Saffron Walden, Essex CB10 1ES. **Telephone** 01799 523728

Classical Longplayer
31 Duke Street, Brighton, East Sussex BN1 1AG. Telephone 01273 329534

H & R Cloake Ltd
29 High Street, Croydon, Surrey CR0 1QB. Telephone 0181-681 3965 (Classical) / 0181-686 1336 (Pop/Jazz)

Collectors Items
121 Hersham Road, Walton on Thames, Surrey KT12 3BX. Telephone 01932 242862

The Compact Discount Centre
5 Headgate Buildings, Sir Isaacs Walk, Colchester, Essex CO1 1JJ. Telephone 01206 762422

Crazy Jazz
5 Prospect Road, Cheshunt, Hertfordshire EN8 9QX. Telephone 01992 625 436

James Dace & Son Ltd
33 Moulsham Street, Chelmsford, Essex CM2 0HX. Telephone 01245 352133

Dillons the Bookstore
Unit 59 Bentalls Centre,Kingston-upon-Thames, Surrey KT1 1TR. Telephone 0181-974 6811

Disques
64 High Street, Heathfield, East Sussex TN21 8JB. Telephone 01435 866920

Grammar School Records
The Old Grammar School, High Street, Rye, East Sussex TM31 7JF. Telephone 01797 222752

HMV
61-62 Western Road, Brighton, East Sussex BN1 2HA. Telephone 01273 747221

HMV
90-92 High Street, Bromley, Kent BR1 1EY. Telephone 0181-313 0727

HMV
137 North End, Croydon, Surrey CR0 1TN. Telephone 0181-686 5557

HMV
Units 11/12, 1st Floor, Bentalls Centre, Kingston-upon-Thames, Surrey KT1 1TR. Telephone 0181-974 8037

HMV Megastore
56-58 Above Bar, Southampton, Hampshire, SO14 7DS. Telephone 01703 338398

Just Classics
Unit 8, Royal Star Arcade, Maidstone, Kent ME14 1JL. Telephone 01622 693670

Michael's Classical Record Shop
183 Montague Street, Worthing, East Sussex BN11 3DA. Telephone 01903 207478

Music & Video Club
8 Air Street, Brighton, East Sussex, BN1 3FB. Telephone 01273 727414

Music and Video Club
31-32 South Street, Chichester, West Sussex PO19 1EL. Telephone 01243 539137

Music and Video Club
42-46 Crouch Street, Colchester, Essex CO3 3HN. Telephone 01206 577407

Music and Video Club
Unit 2, 4 Worthing Road, Horsham, West Sussex RH12 1SQ. Telephone 01403 275080

Music and Video Club
24-25 High Street, Maidstone, Kent, ME14 1JF. Telephone 01622 683747

Music and Video Club
309 High Street, Orpington, Kent BR6 0NN. Telephone 01689 891720

Music and Video Club
42-44 London Road, Southend, Essex, SS1 1NT. Telephone 01702 431130

The Music Centre
Grove Hill Road, Tunbridge Wells, Kent TN1 1RZ. Telephone 01892 526659

Octave Recorded Music Specialist
18 High Street, Lewes, East Sussex BN7 2LN. Telephone 01273 473611

Orpheus
27 Marmion Road, Southsea, Hampshire PO5 2AT. Telephone 01705 812397

Record Corner
Pound Lane, Godalming, Surrey GU7 1BX. Telephone 01483 422006

Record House
84 Sycamore Road, Amersham, Buckinghamshire HP6 5DR. Telephone 01494 433311

Seaford Music
24 Pevensey Road, Eastbourne, East Sussex BN21 3HP. Telephone 01323 732553

Second Spin
14 Sackville Road, Bexhill-on-Sea, East Sussex TN34 3JL. Telephone 01424 210894

Showells
94 High Street, West Wickham, Kent BR4 0NF. Telephone 0181-777 5255

WH Smith Ltd
The Bentalls Centre, Kingston-upon-Thames, Surrey KT1 1TR. Telephone 0181-549 7631

WH Smith Ltd
54 The Harlequin, Watford, Hertfordshire WD1 2TF. Telephone 01923 211388

Sound Barrier
24 Tunsgate, Guildford, Surrey GU1 3QS. Telephone 01483 300947

C W A Ticehurst Ltd
39 High Street, Heathfield, East Sussex TN21 8HU. Telephone 01435 862222

Tower Records
17 Fife Road, Kingston-upon-Thames, Surrey KT1 1SB. Telephone 0181-541 2500

Trax
82 Station Road, Birchington-on-Sea, Kent CT7 9RA. Telephone 01843 848494

Trumps
257 High Road, Loughton, Essex IG10 1AD. Telephone 0181-508 4565

The Turntable
1 Corner House Parade, Ewell, Surrey KT17 1NX. Telephone 0181-393 1881

Virgin Retail
157-161 Western Road, Brighton, East Sussex BN1 2BB. Telephone 01273 323216

Virgin Retail
Unit 18-22 Drummond Centre, Croydon, Surrey CR0 1TQ. Telephone 0181-686 8386

Virgin Megastore
93-105 Clarence Street, Kingston-upon-Thames, Surrey KT1 2QN. Telephone 0181-549 9977

Virgin Megastore
228-230 Commercial Road, Portsmouth, Hampshire, PO1 1HG. Telephone 01705 838833

Virgin Megastore
Unit 2, Odeon Development, 67b Above Bar, Southampton, Hampshire, SO14 7DZ. Telephone 01703 330380

Whitwams Ltd
70 High Street, Winchester, Hampshire SO23 9DE.
Telephone 01962 865253

The Woods
12 The Arcade, Bognor Regis, West Sussex
PO21 1LH. **Telephone** 01243 827712

South West

Acorn Music
PO Box 17, Sidmouth, Devon EX10 9EH.
Telephone 01395-578 145

Amadeus Classical Records
7 Frankfort Gate, Plymouth, Devon PL1 1QA.
Telephone 01752 671992

The Collectors Room
Suttons Music Centre, 3 Endless Street, Salisbury,
Wiltshire SP1 1DL. **Telephone** 01722 326153

Compact Records & Tapes
31 High Street, Falmouth, Cornwall TR11 2AD.
Telephone 01326 311936

The Dorset Music House
22 Cheap Street, Sherborne, Dorset DT9 3PX.
Telephone 01935 816332

Duck, Son & Pinker
59 Bridge Street, Swindon, Wiltshire SN1 1BT.
Telephone 01793 522220

Duck, Son & Pinker
51 Oxford Street, Weston-Super-Mare, Avon
BS23 1TL. **Telephone** 01934 621174

Gillian Greig Music
44 Kingston Road, Taunton, Somerset TA2 7SG.
Telephone 01823 333317

HMV
13-15 Stall Street, Bath, Avon BA1 1QE.
Telephone 01225 466681

HMV
138-141 Friar Street, Reading, Berkshire RG1 1EY.
Telephone 01734 560086

HMV
16-17 Regents Street, Swindon, Wiltshire SN1 1JQ.
Telephone 01793 420963

C Milsom and Son
12 Northgate, Bath, Avon BA1 5AS.
Telephone 01225 465975 ext 136

Music and Video Club
1 Sevendials, 43 Monmouth Street, Bath, Avon
BA1 1EW. **Telephone** 01225 311206

Music and Video Club
31-32 Westover Road, Bournemouth, Dorset
BH1 2BL. **Telephone** 01202 311044

Music & Video Club
40-44 Kings Walk, Gloucester, Gloucestershire,
GL1 1PX. **Telephone** 01452 500788

Opus Music
21 Pydar Street, Truro, Cornwall TR1 2AY.
Telephone 01872 223327

The Record Shop
99 High Street, Crediton, Devon EX17 3LF.
Telephone 01363 774299

Solo Music Ltd
22a Market Arcade, Guildhall Shopping Centre,
Exeter, Devon EX4 3HW. **Telephone** 01392 496564

Sounds Good
26 Clarence Street, Cheltenham, Gloucestershire
GL50 3NU. **Telephone** 01242 234604

Square Records
14 High Street, Wimborne, Dorset BH21 1HU.
Telephone 01202 883203

Trax Music
59 High Street, Christchurch, Dorset BH23 1AS.
Telephone 01202 499629

Virgin Retail
The Galleries, Union Gallery, Broadmead, Bristol,
Avon BS1 3XD. **Telephone** 01179 297798

Virgin Retail
140 Armada Way, Plymouth, Devon PL1 1JB.
Telephone 01752 254400

Virgin Retail
1-5 Oxford Road, Reading, Berkshire RG1 7QG.
Telephone 01734 575222

Channel Islands

Seedee Jons
4 Colomberie, St Helier, Jersey, Channel Islands
JE2 4QA. **Telephone** 01534 67858

Teleskill Ltd
3-4 Market Street, St Peter Port, Guernsey, Channel
Islands. **Telephone** 01481 722323

East Anglia

Amberstone Bookshop
49 Upper Orwell Street, Ipswich, Suffolk IP4 1HP.
Telephone 01473 250675

Andys Records
90 St Johns Street, Bury St Edmonds, Suffolk
IP33 1TZ. **Telephone** 01284 767502

Andys Records
31-33 Fitzroy Street, Cambridge, Cambridgeshire
B1 1ER. **Telephone** 01223 61038

Andys Records
8 Buttermarket Centre, St Stephen's Lane, Ipswich,
Suffolk IP1 1DT. **Telephone** 01473 258933

Andys Records
14-16 Lower Goat Lane, Norwich, Norfolk
NR2 1EL. **Telephone** 01603 617047

CMS Records
1A All Saints' Passage, Cambridge, Cambridgeshire
CB2 3LT. **Telephone** 01223 460818

Compact Music
17 North Street, Sudbury, Suffolk CO10 6RB.
Telephone 01787 881160

Garon Records
70 King Street, Cambridge, Cambridgeshire CB1 1LN.
Telephone 01223 62086

Heffers Sound
19 Trinity Street, Cambridge, Cambridgeshire
CB2 3NG. **Telephone** 01223 568562

HMV
23 Market Street, Cambridge, Cambridgeshire
CB2 3NZ. **Telephone** 01223 322521

Virgin Retail
Castle Mall, Castle Meadow, Norwich, Norfolk
NR1 8DD. **Telephone** 01603 767376

Wells
14 Queen Street, Southwold, Suffolk IP18 6EQ.
Telephone 01502 723906

Midlands

Russell Acott
124 High Street, Oxford, Oxfordshire OX1 4DE.
Telephone 01865 241195

Andys Records
37 Bridge Street, Peterborough, Cambridgeshire
PE1 1HA. **Telephone** 01733 345252

Andys Records Ltd
Unit 38, Waterside Centre, High Street, Lincoln,
Lincolnshire LN2 1AP. **Telephone** 01522 568476

James Beattie plc
71-80 Victoria Street, Wolverhampton, West Midlands WV1 3PQ. Telephone 01902 22311

Berry's Music
23 Bridge Place, Worksop, Nottinghamshire S80 1DT. Telephone 01909 473532

Blackwells Music Shop
38 Holywell Street, Oxford, Oxfordshire OX1 3SW. Telephone 01865 792792

Chappell of Bond Street
21 Silbury Arcade, Central Milton Keynes, Buckinghamshire MK9 3AG. Telephone 01908 663366

Classic Music
7 Lime Street, Bedford, Bedfordshire MK40 1LD. Telephone 01234 357221

Classic Tracks
21 East Bond Street, Leicester, Leicestershire LE1 4SX. Telephone 01162 537700

Collectors Record Centre
6 Duckworth Square, Derby, Derbyshire DE1 1JZ. Telephone 01332 345957

Complete Discery
Wallace House, Oat Street, Evesham, Worcestershire WR11 4PJ. Telephone 01386 442899

I M E Counterpoint
1a Clarburgh House, 32 Church Street, Malvern, Worcestershire. Telephone 01684 561860

David's Music
12 Eastcheap, Letchworth, Hertfordshire SG6 3DE. Telephone 01462 483459

Decoy Records
30 Deansgate, Manchester, Lancashire M3 1RH. Telephone 0161-832 0183

Dillons the Bookstore
128 New Street, Birmingham, West Midlands B4 7SL. Telephone 0121-643 0177

Durrant Records
84 Wyle Cop, Shrewsbury, Shropshire SY1 1UT. Telephone 01743 351008

Easy Listening Ltd
1135 Warwick Road, Acocks Green, Birmingham B27 6RA. Telephone 0121-707 1620

GoodPrice Jazz
1 St James Close, Littleworth, Norton, Worcester, Worcestershire WR5 2QF. Telephone 01905-619649

HMV
38 High Street, Birmingham, West Midlands B4 7SL. Telephone 0121-643 0177

HMV
2 Albion Street, Derby, Derbyshire, DE1 2AL. Telephone 01332 210902

HMV
212 The Potteries Shopping Centre, Market Square, Hanley, Staffordshire ST1 1PS. Telephone 01782 283232

HMV
9-17 High Street, Leicester, Leicestershire LE1 4FP. Telephone 01162 539638

HMV
44-46 Cornmarket Street, Oxford, Oxfordshire OX1 3HA. Telephone 01865 728190

Mainly Big Bands
21b Kings Road, Sutton Coldfield, West Midlands B73 5AB. Telephone 0121-355 0426

Montpellier Records
7 The Courtyard, Montpellier Street, Cheltenham, Gloucestershire. Telephone 01242 222009

Music and Video Club
34-38 Midland Road, Bedford, Bedfordshire MK40 1PW. Telephone 01234 211488

Music and Video Club
6 Mardol, Shrewsbury, Shropshire SY1 1PY. Telephone 01743 343247

Music Box
5 Kings Walk, Guildhall Street, Grantham, Lincolnshire NG31 6NL. Telephone 01476 72151

Music Room
Paddock Lane, Ablewell Street, Walsall, West Midlands WS1 2EG. Telephone 0121-556 2434

Not Just Books
The Music Room, 1 Crown Walk, High Street, Oakham, Rutland LE15 6BZ. Telephone 01572 770320

The Outback
19a Church Street, Hereford, Herefordshire HR1 2LR. Telephone 01432 275063

Presto Music
23 Portland Street, Leamington Spa, Warwickshire CV32 5EZ. Telephone 01926 334834

The Record Centre
45-46 Loveday Street, Birmingham, West Midlands, B4 6NR. Telephone 0121-359 7399

Record House
36 High Street, Aylesbury, Buckinghamshire HP20 1SF. Telephone 01296 20770

WH Smith Ltd
29 Union Street, Birmingham, West Midlands B2 4LR. Telephone 0121-631 3303

WH Smith Ltd
14-16 Listergate, Nottingham, Nottinghamshire NG1 7DD. Telephone 01159 582919

Sounds Expensive
12 Regent Street, Rugby, Warwickshire, CV21 2QF. Telephone 01788 540772

Spinadisc Records
83-87 Lower Precinct, Coventry, West Midlands CV1 1DS. Telephone 01203 632004/5

Spinadisc Records
75a Abington Street, Northampton, Northamptonshire NN1 2BH. Telephone 01604 31144

Stamford Music Shop
11 St Mary's Hill, Stamford, Lincolnshire PE9 2DP. Telephone 01780 51275

St Martins Records
23 Hotel Street, Leicester, Leicestershire LE1 5AW. Telephone 01162 539292

Tower Sounds
9 Market Place, Cirencester, Gloucestershire GL7 2NX. Telephone 01285 654283

Virgin Retail
98 Corporation Street, Birmingham, West Midlands B4 6SX. Telephone 0121-236 2523

Virgin Retail
40-44 The Precinct, Coventry, West Midlands CV1 1DE. Telephone 01203 634346

Virgin Megastore
10 Albion Street, Derby, Derbyshire DE1 2PR. Telephone 01332 297197

Virgin Megastore
8 Churchgate, Leicester, Leicestershire LE13 0DR. Telephone 01162 425969

Virgin Retail
6-8 Wheelergate, Nottingham, Nottinghamshire NG1 2NB. Telephone 01159 476126

North East

Adagio Classical Records
Westminster Arcade, Harrogate, North Yorkshire HG1 2RN. **Telephone** 01423 506507

Banks & Son (Music) Ltd
18 Lendal, York, North Yorkshire YO1 2AU. **Telephone** 01904 658836

Calm & Classical
144 West Street, Sheffield, South Yorkshire S1 4ES. **Telephone** 01142 755795

Bernard Dean
10-12 St Thomas Street, Scarborough, North Yorkshire YO11 1DR. **Telephone** 01723 372573

HMV
1 Victoria Walk, Schofields Centre, Leeds, West Yorkshire LS1 6JD. **Telephone** 0113-244 2992

HMV
46-48 Northumberland Street, Newcastle-upon-Tyne, Tyne & Wear NE1 7TT. **Telephone** 0191-232 7470

HMV
10a Coney Street, York, North Yorkshire YO1 1NA. **Telephone** 01904 640218

Playback
122-124 Linthorpe Road, Middlesborough, Cleveland TS1 2JR. **Telephone** 01642 250060

RAD Jazz
Unit 3d, New Exchange Buildings, Queen's Square, Middlesborough, Cleveland TS2 1AA. **Telephone** 01642-231352

Record Collector
233-235 Fulwood Road, Broomhill, Sheffield, South Yorkshire S10 3BA. **Telephone** 01142 668493

Virgin Retail
94-96 The Briggate, Leeds, West Yorkshire LS1 6BR. **Telephone** 0113-244 3681

Virgin Retail
Monument Mall, 15-21 Northumberland Street, Newcastle-upon-Tyne, Tyne & Wear NE1 7AE. **Telephone** 0191-230 5959

Virgin Retail
Orchard Square, Fargate, Sheffield, South Yorkshire S1 2HD. **Telephone** 01142 731175

Robert Wilkie
25 Salisbury Place, South Shields, Tyne and Wear, NE33 2NF. **Telephone** 0191-456 0923

J G Windows Ltd
1-7 Central Arcade, Newcastle-upon-Tyne, Tyne & Wear NE1 5BP. **Telephone** 0191-232 1356

J Wood & Sons Ltd
38 Manningham Lane, Bradford, West Yorkshire BD1 3AE. **Telephone** 01274 307636

J Wood & Sons Ltd
11-15 Market Street, Huddersfield, West Yorkshire **Telephone** HD1 2BH. 01484 427455

North West

Action Replay
24 Lake Road, Bowness-on-Windermere, Cumbria LA23 3AP. **Telephone** 015394 45089

Andys Records
27-29 Victoria Square, Bolton, Lancashire BL1 1RJ. **Telephone** 01204 373388

Andys Records
2 Marble Place, Southport, Merseyside PR8 1DF. **Telephone** 01704 549222

Bookcase
17 Castle Street, Carlisle, Cumbria CA3 8TP. **Telephone** 01228 44560

Chester Compact Disc Centre
18 Paddock Row, Grosvenor Precinct, Chester, Cheshire CH1 1ED. **Telephone** 01244 311991

Circle Records
74a Bold Street, Liverpool, Merseyside L1 4HU. **Telephone** 0151-708 5656

Forsyth Brothers Limited
126 Deansgate, Manchester, Greater Manchester M3 2GR. **Telephone** 0161-834 3281

Kenneth Gardner Ltd
28 New Street, Lancaster, Lancashire LA1 1EG. **Telephone** 01524 841398

HMV
48-50 Foregate Street, Chester, Cheshire CH1 1HA. **Telephone** 01244 310307

HMV
22-36 Church Street, Liverpool, Merseyside L1 3AW. **Telephone** 0151-709 1088

HMV
90-100 Market Street, Manchester, Greater Manchester M1 1PD. **Telephone** 0161-834 8550

HMV
51-53 Merseyway, Stockport, Cheshire SK1 1PW. **Telephone** 0161-460 0548

New Kelly's Music Shop
101 Church Street, Barrow-in-Furness, Cumbria LA14 2HW. **Telephone** 01229 822973

Ken Palk Ltd
Shopping Centre, Bramhall, Stockport, Cheshire SK7 1AW. **Telephone** 0161 439 8479

Rare Records
13 Bank Square, Wilmslow, Cheshire SK9 1AN. **Telephone** 01625 522017

Reidy's Home of Music
9-13 Penny Street, Blackburn, Lancashire BB1 6HJ. **Telephone** 01254 265303

WH Smith Ltd
5-7 Foregate Street, Chester, Cheshire CH1 1HH. **Telephone** 01244 321106

WH Smith Ltd
10-16 Church Street, Liverpool, Merseyside L1 3EG. **Telephone** 0151-709 1435

Smiths of Wigan
41 Mesnes Street, Wigan, Lancashire WN1 1QY. **Telephone** 01942 42810/46270

Smyth's Records
123-125 Highgate, Kendal, Cumbria LA9 4EN. **Telephone** 01539 729595

Virgin Retail
32-36 Foregate Street, Chester, Cheshire CH1 1HA. **Telephone** 01244 322212

Virgin Megastore
Units 8-9 Tops Plaza, Clayton Square Shopping Centre, Liverpool, Merseyside L1 1QR. **Telephone** 0151-708 6708

Virgin Retail
52-56 Market Street, Manchester, Greater Manchester M1 1QA. **Telephone** 0161-833 1111/2

Isle of Man

Island Compact Disc Centre
80 Parliament Street, Ramsey, Isle of Man. **Telephone** 01624 815521

Scotland

Bauermeister Booksellers
15-16 George IV Bridge, Edinburgh EH1 1EH. **Telephone** 0131-226 5561

Casa Cassettes Ltd
325 Sauchiehall Street, Glasgow G2 3HW.
Telephone 0141-332 1127

Concorde
15 Scott Street, Perth PH1 5EJ.
Telephone 01738 21818

HMV
247-251 Union Street, Aberdeen, Grampian AB1 2BQ.
Telephone 01224 575323

HMV
129 Princes Street, Edinburgh, EH2 4AH.
Telephone 0131-226 3466

HMV
Unit 6, Lewis's Centre, Argyle Street, Glasgow G2 8AD. **Telephone** 0141-204 4787

HMV
154-160 Sauchiehall Street, Glasgow G2 3DH.
Telephone 0141-332 6631

McAlister Matheson Music Ltd
1 Grindlay Street, Edinburgh EH3 9AT.
Telephone 0131-228 3827

The Musicmongers
151 South Street, St Andrews, Fife KY16 9UN.
Telephone 01334 478625

Tower Records
217-221 Argyle Street, Glasgow G2 8DL.
Telephone 0141-204 2500

Virgin Retail
133 Union Street, Aberdeen, Grampian AB1 2BH.
Telephone 01224 213050

Virgin Retail
Unit G Level 1, The Wellgate Centre, Dundee, Tayside DD1 2DB. 01382 200755

Virgin Retail
125 Princes Street, Edinburgh EH2 4AH.
Telephone 0131-220 2230

Virgin Retail
28-32 Union Street, Glasgow G1 3QX.
Telephone 0141-221 0103

Virgin Retail
Unit 4, Lewis' Building, Argyle Street, Glasgow G1 2AQ. **Telephone** 0141-221 2606

Wales

Abergavenny Music
23 Cross Street, Abergavenny, Gwent NP7 5EW.
Telephone 01873 853394

City Radio
27a Morgan Arcade, Cardiff, South Glamorgan CF1 2AF. **Telephone** 01222 228169

HMV
51 Queen Street, Cardiff, South Glamorgan CF1 4AS.
Telephone 01222 227147

Jazz Music
Glenview, Moylegrove, Cardigan, Dyfed SA43 3BW.
Telephone 01239 881278

Jelly Roll Records
Pentwyn House, South View, Blackwood, Gwent NP2 1HW. **Telephone** 01495 225530

The Muse
43 Holyhead Road, Bangor, Gwynedd LL57 2UE.
Telephone 01248 362072

The Music & Video Club
29 The Hayes, Cardiff, South Glamorgan, CF1 2DU.
Telephone 01222 394650

Naughty Cat Records
at J P Williams-Jones Booksellers, Eldon Square, Dolgellau, Gwynedd LL40 1PS. **Telephone** 01341 422173

Red Lick Records
PO Box 3, Porthmadog, Gwynedd LL48 6AQ.
Telephone 01766-770990

Spiller's Records
36 The Hayes, Cardiff, South Glamorgan CF1 2AJ.
Telephone 01222-224905

Swales Music Centre Ltd
2-6 High Street, Haverfordwest, Pembrokeshire SA61 2DJ. **Telephone** 01437 762059/763261

Virgin Retail
Units 7-9, Capitol Arcade, The Capitol, Queen Street, Cardiff, South Glamorgan CF1 4HQ.
Telephone 01222 388273

Northern Ireland

Koinonia
6 Pottinger's Entry, High Street, Belfast BT1 2JZ.
Telephone 01232 247873

Virgin Retail
Unit 1C, Castlecourt, Royal Avenue, Belfast BT1 1DD. **Telephone** 01232 236623

Mail order

City Radio
24 Charles Street, Newport, Gwent NP9 1JT.
Telephone 01633 840728

Mole Jazz
311 Grays Inn Road, London, WC1X 8PX.
Telephone 0171-278 8623

Hale CDs
405 Hale Road, Hale Bans, Altrincham, Cheshire WA15 8XX. **Telephone** 0161-980 7093

Music Established Ltd
2 Dukes Court, Princess Way, Prudhoe, Northumberland NE42 6DA. **Telephone** 01661 830600

The Music Group
West Haddon, Northamptonshire NN6 7AA.
Telephone 0788 510693

The Music Store
P O Box 123, Brentford, Middlesex TW8 0BR.
Telephone 01345 123123

Opus 1 Music
19 Brunswick Road, Bangor, County Down BT20 3DY. **Telephone** 01247 457775

Silver Service CD
24 Touch Wards, Dunfermline, Fife KY12 7TG.
Telephone 01383 738159

Wings of Whyteleafe
Eastwood House, Church End, Potterspury, Northamptonshire NN12 7PX.
Telephone 01908 543055

Second hand specialists

Ben's Collectors Records
101 West Street, Farnham, Surrey GU9 7NS.
Telephone 01252 734409

Mole Jazz
311 Grays Inn Road, London, WC1X 8PX.
Telephone 0171-278 8623

Blake Head Record Shop
89 Micklegate, York, North Yorkshire YO1 1NA.
Telephone 01904 625482

Garon Records
65-66 The Covered Market, Oxford, Oxfordshire OX1 3DX. **Telephone** 01865 246887

The 78 Record Exchange
9 Lower Hillgate, Stockport, Cheshire SK1 1JQ.

Index

The Illustrated Lives of the Great Composers

A series of biographies of great composers which presents the subjects against the social background of their times. Each book draws on personal letters and recollections, engravings, paintings, and - where they exist - photographs, to build up a complete picture of the composer's life.

Bach
Tim Dowley
144pp, softcover
ISBN 0.7119.0262.3
OP 42480
$14.95

Bartók
Hamish Milne
122pp, softcover
ISBN 0.7119.0260.7
OP 42464
$14.95

Beethoven
Ates Orga
176pp, softcover
ISBN 0.7119.0251.8
OP 42373
$14.95

Berlioz
Robert Clarson-Leach
128pp, softcover
ISBN 0.7119.0829.X
OP 43744
$14.95

Brahms
Paul Holmes
168pp, softcover
ISBN 0.7119.0826.
OP 43710
$14.95

Chopin
Ates Orga
144pp, softcover
ISBN 0.7119.0247.X
OP 42332
$14.95

Debussy
Paul Holmes
133pp, softcover
ISBN 0.7119.1752.3
OP 45244
$14.95

Dvorák
Neil Butterworth
136pp, softcover
ISBN 0.7119.0256.9
OP 42423
$14.95

Elgar
Simon Mundy
138pp, softcover
ISBN 0.7119.0263.1
OP 42498
$14.95

Gilbert & Sullivan
Andrew Codd
softcover
ISBN 0.7119.1753.
OP 45251
$14.95

Handel
Wendy Thompson
144pp, softcover
ISBN 0.7119.2997.1
OP 46796
$14.95

Haydn
Neil Butterworth
144pp, softcover
ISBN 0.7119.0249.6
OP 42357
$14.95

Liszt
Bryce Morrison
112pp, softcover
ISBN 0.7119.1682.9
OP 44999
$14.95

Mahler
Edward Seckerson
150pp, softcover
ISBN 0.7119.0259.3
OP 42456
$14.95

Mendelssohn
Mozelle Moshan
144pp, softcover
ISBN 0.7119.0252.
OP 42381
$14.95

lozart
00th Anniversary Ed.
'eggy Woodford
44pp, softcover
iBN 0.7119.0248.8
'P 42340 **$14.95**

Offenbach
Peter Gammond
166p, softcover
ISBN 0.7119.0257.7
OP 42431
$14.95

Paganini
John Sugden
168pp, softcover
ISBN 0.7119.0264.X
OP 42506
$14.95

Prokofiev
David Gutman
144pp, softcover
ISBN 0.7119.2083.4
OP 45681
$14.95

Rachmaninoff
Robert Walker
144pp, softcover
ISBN 0.7119.0253.4
OP 42399
$14.95

Ravel
)avid Burnett-
ames
44pp, softcover
iBN 0.7119.0987.3
'P 44015
14.95

Rossini
Nicholas Till
144pp, softcover
ISBN 0.7119.0988.1
OP 44023
$14.95

Schubert
Peggy Woodford
160pp, softcover
ISBN 0.7119.0255.0
OP 42415
$14.95

Schumann
Tim Dowley
144pp, softcover
ISBN 0.7119.0261.5
OP 42472
$14.95

Shostakovich
Eric Roseberry
192pp, softcover
ISBN 0.7119.0258.5
OP 42449
$14.95

ibelius
)avid Burnett-
ames
28pp, softcover
iBN 0.7119.1688.7
'P 45004
14.95

Richard Strauss
David Nice
160pp, softcover
ISBN 0.7119.1686.1
OP 45038
$14.95

The Strauss Family
Peter Kemp
272pp, softcover
ISBN 0.7119.1726.4
OP 45194
$14.95

Verdi
Peter Southwell-Sander
160pp, softcover
ISBN 0.7119.0250.X
OP 42365
$14.95

Villa-Lobos
Lisa Peppercorn
144pp, softcover
ISBN 0.7119.1688.8
OP 45061
$14.95

/ivaldi
ohn Booth
28pp, softcover
iBN 0.7119.1727.2
'P 45202
14.95

Wagner
Howard Gray
144pp, softcover
ISBN 0.7119.1687.X
OP 44817
$14.95

Weber
Anthony Friese-Greene
144pp, softcover
ISBN 0.7119.2081.8
OP 45665
$14.95

Available at all good recordstores and bookstores. For more information contact your local dealer or Music Sales directly.

EUROPE

Music Sales Limited
8-9 Frith Street
London W1V 5TZ
England
Tel: 0171-434-0066

Distribution Center
Newmarket Road
Bury St. Edmunds
Suffolk IP33 3YB
Tel: 01284-702600

USA

Music Sales Corporation
257 Park Avenue South
New York, NY 10010
Tel: 212-254-2100

Distribution Center
5 Bellvale Road
Chester, NY 10918
Tel: 914-469-2271
or 800-431-7187

Gramophone Publications Limited
177-179 Kenton Road, Harrow,
Middlesex HA3 0HA, Great Britain.
Telephone +44 (0)181-907 4476
Fax +44 (0)181 907 0073